Dynamic PE ASAP

The yearly plan lists 36 weeks of lesson plans for three distinct grade levels: K-2, 3-4, and 5-8. The majority of activities for younger children (K-2) are individual in nature and center on learning movement concepts and cooperative activities. Lessons for 3-4 are focused on helping youngsters refine fundamental skills and learn visual-tactile skills. Emphasis is placed on giving students the opportunity to explore, experiment, and create activities without fear. Students in grades 5-8 begin a shift toward learning specialized skills and sport activities. Students learn team play through cooperative sport lead-up activities. Adequate time is set aside for the rhythmic program, body management skills, and gymnastics-type activities.

Grades K-2 ▾

Lesson Plan Name	Introductory	Fitness Development	Lesson Focus	Closing
[K-2] Week 1 + Save to Your Plans	Move and Freeze on Signals	Fitness Challenges	Orientation and Class Management	Toe to Toe; Whistle Mixer
[K-2] Week 2 + Save to Your Plans	Following Activity	Four Corners Movement	Manipulative Skills Using Hoops	Animal Tag; Pigs Fly
[K-2] Week 3 + Save to Your Plans	Group Over and Around	Astronaut Exercises	Throwing Skills - Individual Activities	Aviator; Sneak Attack
[K-2] Week 4 + Save to Your Plans	Bend, Stretch, & Shake	Fitness Games & Challenges	Manipulative Skills Using Beanbags	Midnight
[K-2] Week 5 + Save to Your Plans	Combination Movements	Fitness Challenges	Manipulative Skills using Playground Balls	Teacher Ball; Scarecrow and the Crows

Six types of assessment instruments used throughout Dynamic PE ASAP:

Over 130 different assessment instruments that cover ASAP lesson plans.

1. **Teacher Questioning** is an excellent strategy to probe student understanding and provide time for student reflection.

2. **Teacher Checklists** are designed to help teachers efficiently observe students' performance.

3. **Self-Assessments** are great formative assessment tools that give students the chance to take ownership of their learning.

4. **Peer Assessments** let students showcase their learning in multiple ways.

5. **Written Exit Slips** are designed for efficiency and reflection.

6. **Bike Rack** assessments are an efficient strategy for assessing students' understanding.

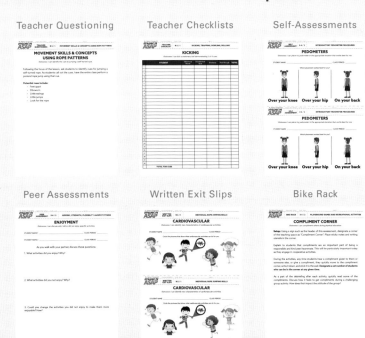

CONTENTS

Creating lesson plans has never been easier!

Browse Lessons

Step 1: Easily filter and browse lessons based on your specific interests! Choose from hundreds of options for grades K-6 that include Introductory Activities, Fitness Development, Lesson Focuses, and Closing Activities.

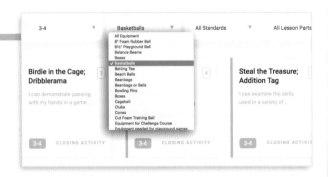

Add the Lessons You Like

Step 2: Once you've found the activities that meet your needs for each class, build your complete lesson by simply dragging and dropping the four components of a complete lesson plan to the designated fields.

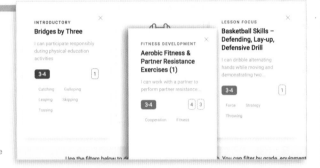

 Introductory Activity
Instant activities that physiologically prepare students for activity and the upcoming lesson.

 Fitness Development
Familiarize students with physical fitness principles and fitness-related activities.

 Lesson Focus
Teach physical skills and movements that are aligned with SHAPE standards and specific instructional objectives.

 Closing Activity
Games or cooperative activities that help students apply skills learned during the Lesson Focus.

Save Lessons

Step 3: Once you have your completed lesson plan, save it and name it! Whether you build just one, or plan your entire year, your lesson plans will be saved and stored for you to use as desired.

> Also available to you is the Dynamic PE Yearly Plan, which has 36 weeks of preconfigured lesson plans for each of three levels: K-2, 3-4, 5-8. There are enough plans to last you the entire year!

Download, Print, and Go

Step 4: Quickly download and print (or just download to use electronically) your lesson plan, and you're ready to go!
It's that easy!

What's in a Lesson Plan?

A yearly curriculum offers a roadmap to success. Without adequate planning it is difficult to know your ultimate goals (SHAPE standards) and your student expectations (DPE outcomes). In addition to standards and outcomes, DPE ASAP lessons are organized by grade level with equipment and keywords listed. These are important, but the real core of instruction is the activities. Instructional activities are listed in order of difficulty to help teachers meet the developmental needs of all students. Teaching hints explain how to organize your lesson and are based on the advice of experienced and successful teachers.

Each lesson falls into one of four lesson parts:
- Introductory Activity
- Fitness Development
- Lesson Focus
- Closing Activity

DPE ASAP outcomes list specific behaviors you should expect your students to learn.

Each lesson contains enough activities for a week of instruction.

It is not expected that all activities will be taught. It is best to teach a few activities well rather than many activities in a cursory manner.

Activities and skills are presented in progression of less to more challenging.

Teaching hints help you teach a quality lesson. They will help you organize your class and equipment. Teaching cues and points of emphasis will focus your verbal feedback to students.

There are many ways to view lessons. They can be printed on 8.5" x 11" paper or 5" x 8" cards. If desired, they can be uploaded to your mobile phone or iPad as a PDF file.

Three distinct sets of lesson plans by grade level are offered.

The amount and type of equipment, music, and instructional signs needed for the lesson are listed.

SHAPE national standards are listed for each lesson.

Movement Skills and Concepts - Walking, Body Part Identification, and Personal Space

LESSON FOCUS

Add to Lesson Plan

Print Lesson

Print on Index Cards

View Assessment

Grade Level: K-2

Equipment: One balloon or beach ball for each student

Standards: 1 2

Keywords:
Spacing   Striking
Volleying   Walking

Outcomes:

I can walk in a straight line demonstrating 2 of 4 cues.
I can walk in various patterns demonstrating 3 of 4 cues.
I can perform various skills demonstrating appropriate personal space.

Instructions:

Fundamental Skill: Walking
1. Walk in different directions, changing direction on signal (90 degrees).
2. While walking, bring up the knees and slap with the hands on each step.
3. Walk on heels, toes, side of the foot, Charlie Chaplin fashion (toes pointed way out).
4. Gradually lower the body while walking; gradually raise the body.
5. Walk with a smooth gliding step.
6. Walk with a wide base on tiptoes; rock from side to side.
7. Clap hands alternately front and back. Clap hands under the thighs (slow walk).
8. Walk slowly. Accelerate. Decelerate.
9. Take long strides. Tiny steps.
10. Change levels on signal.
11. Walk quickly and quietly. Slowly and heavily. Quickly and heavily, etc.
12. Change direction on signal while facing the same way.
13. Walk angrily, then happily; add others.

Teaching Hints:

Select a few activities from each of the categories so students receive a variety of skills to practice. When possible, integrate the manipulative skills activities with fundamental skill activities.

Examples of cues for walking include: Head up; eyes forward. Swing the arms while walking. Keep the shoulders back and the tummy flat."

Keep the balloons in control by tapping them rather than striking them. When first learning the balloon skills, keep the feet in one place rather than moving. As children master the skills, try performing some of the balloon skills while moving throughout the area.

Teach students that most people have a personal space they don't want violated. Encourage youngsters to stay out of other's personal spaces.

Video

Video Training

Dr. Pangrazi walks us through using the Dynamic PE ASAP website. He also shares helpful tips for implementing the lessons into your program.

Activity Videos

The Dynamic PE ASAP digital curriculum now features more than 100 free lesson plan videos. Learn how to teach curriculum lessons from trained PE professionals.

NINETEENTH EDITION

DYNAMIC PHYSICAL EDUCATION FOR ELEMENTARY SCHOOL CHILDREN

ROBERT P. PANGRAZI

ARIZONA STATE UNIVERSITY

AARON BEIGHLE

UNIVERSITY OF KENTUCKY

HUMAN KINETICS

Library of Congress Cataloging-in-Publication Data

Names: Pangrazi, Robert P., author. | Beighle, Aaron, 1972- author.
Title: Dynamic physical education for elementary school children / Robert P.
    Pangrazi, Arizona State University, Aaron Beighle, University of Kentucky.
Description: Nineteenth Edition, Revised Edition. | Champaign, Illinois :
    Human Kinetics, [2020] | "This book is a revised edition of Dynamic
    Physical Education for Elementary School Children, Eighteenth Edition,
    published in 2016 by Pearson Education, Inc."--T.p.verso. | Includes
    bibliographical references and index.
Identifiers: LCCN 2019021069 (print) | LCCN 2019021901 (ebook) | ISBN
    9781492590286 (epub) | ISBN 9781492590279 (PDF) |
    ISBN 9781492590262 (paperback) | ISBN 9781492592280 (loose-leaf)
Subjects: LCSH: Physical education and training--Curricula--United States. |
    Physical education and training--Study and teaching (Elementary)--United
    States. | Physical education and training--Curricula--Canada. | Physical
    education and training--Study and teaching (Elementary)--Canada.
Classification: LCC GV365 (ebook) | LCC GV365 .P36 2020 (print) | DDC
    372.86--dc23
LC record available at https://lccn.loc.gov/2019021069

ISBN: 978-1-4925-9026-2 (paperback)
ISBN: 978-1-4925-9228-0 (loose-leaf)

This book is a revised edition of *Dynamic Physical Education for Elementary School Children, Eighteenth Edition,* published in 2016 by Pearson Education, Inc.

The web addresses cited in this text were current as of July 2019, unless otherwise noted.

Acquisitions Editor: Scott Wikgren; **Developmental Editor:** Jacqueline Eaton Blakley; **Managing Editor:** Anna Lan Seaman; **Copyeditor:** Bob Replinger; **Indexers:** Rebecca McCorkle and Karla Walsh; **Permissions Manager:** Dalene Reeder; **Graphic Designer:** Sean Roosevelt; **Cover Designer:** Keri Evans; **Cover Design Associate:** Susan Rothermel Allen; **Photograph (cover):** SolStock/Getty Images; **Photographs (interior):** © Human Kinetics, unless otherwise noted; **Photo Asset Manager:** Laura Fitch; **Photo Production Manager:** Jason Allen; **Senior Art Manager:** Kelly Hendren; **Illustrations:** © Human Kinetics, unless otherwise noted; **Printer:** Walsworth

Printed in the United States of America   10 9 8 7 6 5 4 3 2 1

The paper in this book was manufactured using responsible forestry methods.

Human Kinetics
P.O. Box 5076
Champaign, IL 61825-5076
Website: **www.HumanKinetics.com**

In the United States, email info@hkusa.com or call 800-747-4457.
In Canada, email info@hkcanada.com.
In the United Kingdom/Europe, email hk@hkeurope.com.

For information about Human Kinetics' coverage in other areas of the world,
please visit our website: www.HumanKinetics.com

Tell us what you think!
Human Kinetics would love to hear what we
can do to improve the customer experience.
Use this QR code to take our brief survey.

E7789 (paperback) / E7861 (loose-leaf)

To my wife, Deb, whom I love and respect. She is not only a valued professional colleague but also a special friend and companion who has enriched my life. I regard Deb as a silent author who has contributed much to this textbook.

To our son and daughter, Charles and Connie, and their wonderful families. I appreciate the joy and love they deliver on a regular basis.

To Dr. Victor P. Dauer, my late coauthor, who taught and mentored me throughout my career and continues to guide my thinking and writing efforts.

Robert P. Pangrazi

To my girls, Heather, Faith, Libby, Hope, and Emily. Your unwavering love, caring heart, humor, spunkiness, and zest for life make me better.

To my parents, Ted and Sheila Beighle. Their love and devotion to family is truly inspirational. I am fortunate to call them Mom and Dad.

Aaron Beighle

PART V   LIFETIME ACTIVITIES AND SPORTS SKILLS

PREFACE

For more than 50 years *Dynamic Physical Education for Elementary School Children (DPE)* has been equipping physical education specialists and classroom teachers with the knowledge and skills to teach physical education to elementary students. A textbook with the storied longevity of *DPE* requires steadfast leadership. A strength of this book has been the ability of its two leaders, Doctors Vic Dauer and Robert Pangrazi, to hold true to quality physical education by advancing the field and pushing future physical educators to a higher level of excellence. This edition of the book marks a change in leadership for this textbook. Dr. Aaron Beighle has previously worked on several editions of this book as a coauthor and a contributing author, and he now has taken the helm as the lead author. As lead author, he will continue to hold to the principles that have solidified *DPE* yet also continue to move the textbook, future physical educators, and the field into the future. Readers can rest assured the textbook will continue to be a book that stretches their thinking, provides contemporary perspectives, examines pertinent literature, includes teacher-tested activities, and exudes a passion for physical education.

Teachers who have learned from this text have gone on to help students acquire the skills, knowledge, and attitudes necessary for an active and healthy life. That's because *DPE* emphasizes the skill development, activity promotion, and physical fitness behaviors that are the foundation of physical literacy. In addition, *DPE* advocates instructional practices designed to create a learning environment where students are free to experiment, learn, and experience physical activity in a positive climate. Going beyond a focus on physical skills, *DPE* equips the new generation of physical educators to promote physical activity before, during, and after school and advocate for student health as leaders within the comprehensive school health program. For years, *DPE* has stood out for its inclusion of a vast array of instructional activities that help teachers in training see theory in practice. No text on the market offers preservice and in-service teachers a greater variety of evidence-based activities and strategies designed to help them develop curriculum that meets the SHAPE America standards defining quality physical education. To make this text even more practical and useful, *DPE* has previously included the free text *Dynamic Physical Education Curriculum Guide: Lesson Plans for Implementation*, which organized the DPE activities into a curriculum guide with lesson plans for the academic year. Together, *DPE* and the curriculum guide have long presented an unbeatable package for equipping effective physical educators.

With the 19th edition, *DPE* is better than ever. Everything that has made it great is still here, but content and features have been updated and revised to reflect current research and best practices. The most exciting update is the development of the Dynamic PE ASAP website (www.DynamicPEASAP.com), which replaces the curriculum guide. Dynamic PE ASAP gives you instant access to the book's activities and allows you to organize them into lesson plans with assessments. You can search activities by developmental level, fitness concept, topic, or a number of other criteria, allowing you to build a curriculum tailored to your needs.

Some of the more significant updates and changes to the text include the following:

- *Chapter realignment:* For the 19th edition, the chapters have been realigned slightly to add space for a new chapter (chapter 3, Youth Physical Activity and Schools). This allows us to house content related to the importance of physical activity in one location as opposed to in several chapters as in previous editions. Brain development, physical activity guidelines, physical activity and academic performance, physical activity and public health, and Comprehensive School Physical Activity Programs are included. The order of the chapters on curriculum development (chapter 4) and lesson planning (chapter 5) was reversed to better reflect the process of first developing a curriculum and then lesson plans.

- *Brain development:* Information on the impact of physical activity on brain development has been added to this edition to highlight this relationship for future physical educators. Information related to the stages of cognitive development are presented. Finally, content pertaining to physical activity and academic performance has been updated to include cutting-edge findings.

- *Health content:* More and more physical educators are being asked to integrate health education into their programs. We have therefore updated the sections related to health concepts to provide activities and learning experiences designed to infuse health-related concepts into physical education lessons. Special care has been taken to ensure the activities retain physical education objectives.

- *Technology:* Throughout the textbook, when appropriate, strategies for using technology to enhance the content are highlighted in the Tech Tip feature. For example, in chapter 8, Assessment, there are tips for using technology to assist and improve assessments. Adding these discussions of technology at key points throughout the book, rather than placing them in a chapter devoted to technology, was deemed more useful for the reader.

General Organization of the Text

Dynamic Physical Education for Elementary School Children is written for both physical education teachers and classroom teachers. The material includes many examples that make it easy to understand. All activities in the text are listed in progression from the easiest activity to the most difficult. This enables teachers to plan a lesson that incorporates proper sequencing of skills.

Part I (Physical Education, Physical Activity, and Youth) includes chapters 1 through 3. Chapter 1 offers a brief history of the profession and sets the framework for the entire text by explaining the SHAPE America standards for physical education and exploring the key concept of physical literacy. Chapter 2 helps teachers understand children's growth and development and their needs in a physical education setting. Physical activity is a pillar of physical education, so chapter 3 provides foundational knowledge to build your teaching practice, including an overview of physical activity for youth, a discussion of the benefits of physical activity, and a look at Comprehensive School Physical Activity Programs.

Part II (Instruction and Administration) includes chapters 4 through 12, which focus on developing the curriculum, planning a quality lesson, and teaching effectively. Class management and discipline often dictate which teachers will succeed or fail, and chapter 7 offers practical information for successfully teaching youngsters in an activity setting. Chapter 8 provides strategies for assessing student performance and provides many practical examples. Chapter 9 shows how to adapt and modify activities to ensure inclusion and purpose for all students. Chapters 10 through 12 focus on successful implementation of a physical education program, including such topics as equipment and facilities, safety issues, and the integration of health-related concepts into physical education activities.

Part III (Foundational Skills) includes chapters 13 through 17 and brings together methods and activities for teaching foundational skills during lessons. Many introductory activities designed to start your lesson off with movement and management are provided in chapter 13. Chapter 14 presents strategies and activities to teach fitness concepts. Movement concepts, locomotor skills, nonlocomotor skills, and manipulative skills are discussed in the next three chapters. Preservice and in-service teachers can identify activities and strategies that will improve student competencies in this important skill area.

Part IV (Specialized Skills) includes chapters 18 through 22 and is designed to improve specialized motor skills among students of diverse backgrounds. Chapters on body management skills, rhythmic movement skills, gymnastics skills, cooperative skills, and game skills offer in-depth coverage for the development of a personalized set of specialized skills.

Part V (Lifetime Activities and Sports Skills) includes chapters 23 through 30. This section focuses on developing the skills that will help children participate in physical activity throughout their life span. These chapters contain many drills and lead-up activities. They use the paradigm of teaching the skill properly, practicing it in a drill, and applying the skill in a lead-up activity.

Instructor Resources

The 19th edition of *Dynamic Physical Education for Elementary School Children* includes access to an integrated and comprehensive set of instructional tools. The instructor guide provides a chapter summary, a list of desired student outcomes, a discussion of the main concepts of the chapter, ideas for presenting the content, discussion topics, suggestions for written assignments, and a cooperative learning project. The test package offers true-false, multiple-choice, and short-answer questions for every chapter. Using the questions supplied in the test bank, instructors can create tests, edit questions, and add their own material. The presentation package offers PowerPoint lecture outlines for each chapter, including key figures and tables from the book, chapter takeaways, and discussion questions.

The need for quality physical education is more critical in the United States than ever. In physical education, elementary kids have the opportunity to develop the skills and knowledge and love for physical activity that will set them on a path to lifelong health. We are proud to continue our tradition of preparing teachers for this crucial task.

ACKNOWLEDGMENTS

Useful textbooks are the result of cohesive efforts between the publisher and authors. We appreciate the professional group at Human Kinetics for their significant contributions to this edition. We thank Scott Wikgren, who has supported and guided us through the transition to Human Kinetics. We also appreciate the attention to detail and great editing given to this text by Jackie Blakley. To the many other individuals at Human Kinetics who go unnamed, we offer a hearty thank you.

Dr. Seth Eckler of the University of Louisville was a valuable asset to this edition, creating supplementary materials: a presentation package, instructor guide, and test bank.

A tradition that continues in this edition is to ensure that all activities have been field-tested with children. We continue to teach elementary school children and evaluate new activities based in part on student reception and instructional effectiveness. A number of experts have been involved in ensuring the content is accurate and on the cutting edge. The authors are indebted to Deb Pangrazi, supervisor of elementary school physical education and more than 80 physical education specialists in Mesa, Arizona, who have field-tested the activities and offered numerous suggestions and ideas for improvement. Bill Jones and the physical education staff at University School in Cleveland, Ohio, have provided feedback on a variety of topics. Don Hicks of St. Francis Episcopal Day School in Houston has offered continuing evaluation of activities on a regular basis.

We would also like to thank Billy and Monica Noble and other physical education teachers in Fayette County Public Schools (Lexington, Kentucky) for their willingness to test new activities and offer suggestions for the textbook and lesson plans. All these individuals have unselfishly contributed their energies and insights to ensure that quality activities and teaching strategies are part of this textbook. The result of this continued field-testing is a book filled with activities, strategies, and techniques that work.

Finally, we are forever grateful for the pioneering work and spirit of Dr. Victor Dauer. His vision to train elementary school physical education teachers and write a textbook that included fitness, skill development, and inclusive games paved the way to quality physical education programs. Now, more than 50 years later, over 1 million future physical educators have experienced that vision through this book. Thank you, Vic!

Elementary School Physical Education

Physical education programs are a crucial element of the school curriculum. If the paradigm of *healthy mind, healthy body* is the path to each child's total growth and development, then physical education must be included to assure that healthy body outcomes are reached. Systematic and properly taught physical education can help achieve major content standards, including attaining movement competence, maintaining physical fitness, learning personal health and wellness skills, applying movement concepts and skill mechanics, developing lifetime activity skills, and demonstrating positive social skills. Cultural and educational factors have influenced modern physical education programs with a common theme being the need for physical activity. Physical educators now see the importance of focusing physical education on physical activity promotion. This entails maintaining quality standard-based physical education programs (i.e., quality instruction and quality curriculum) coupled with efforts to promote physical activity beyond the gymnasium.

Learning Objectives

▶ Justify the need for a quality physical education program in elementary schools based on the health benefits it can offer children.

▶ Discuss the role of the SHAPE America national standards for physical education.

▶ List program objectives and recognize the distinctive contributions of physical education.

▶ Describe the educational reasons for including physical education as part of the elementary school curriculum.

▶ Define physical education and other key terms and their role in the elementary school experience.

▶ Explain how various pedagogical influences have changed the course of elementary school physical education programs.

▶ Identify essential components of a quality physical education program.

▶ Describe how various societal influences and federal mandates have influenced elementary school physical education.

What Is Physical Education?

If you were to ask 20 people on the street what physical education is, you are likely to get 20 different answers. Physical education professionals often describe it as essential subject matter providing students with the skills, knowledge, and attitudes necessary to remain active, healthy, and productive throughout the lifespan. Some equate physical education with athletics or competitive sports, whereas others see it as recess or free-time play. Still others equate physical education and physical activity, believing that any time students move during a school day is considered physical education. Another common belief is that physical education means students exercising to be fit. More recently much confusion has developed as educators equate physical education and physical literacy. The Key Terms sidebar provides some definitions to key terms for physical educators. In short, some people view physical education as worthwhile component of school curriculum, whereas others see it as an unnecessary use of educational time.

Physical education is part of the total educational program that contributes, primarily through physical activity, to the total growth and development of all children. In most instructional programs it is the only component that addresses all learning domains: psycho-motor, cognitive, and affective. Further, no other area of the curriculum is designed to help children learn how to maintain an active lifestyle. It is insufficient to educate children in content areas like science, math, reading, and social studies only; they must also graduate from school with wellness skills that will serve them throughout life. If students, particularly the inactive and unskilled, receive low-quality instruction in physical education, they most likely will mature into inactive adults. For many children, physical education may be the only part of the school curriculum that offers an opportunity to learn active skills they will use for a lifetime. Thus, a strong physical education program emphasizes helping all children succeed—regardless of ability or skill level.

Physical education teachers must do more than teach skills and physical fitness. They must also keep in mind the public health implications of quality physical education. With the current state of public health, the importance of healthy eating habits, stress reduction, substance abuse, sun safety, weight management, and active lifestyles are outcomes that need to be taught to today's students. No longer is it acceptable for physical educators to be viewed as close cousins of sport coaches. No longer can they isolate themselves in the gymnasium and be satisfied teaching exclusively skills, fitness, and sports. If the profession is to thrive, modern physical

KEY TERMS

- *Athletics.* Competitive sports engaged in by players who have trained or practiced for the specific sport. It is typically thought of as interscholastic sports or organized sports based in community-based organizations.

- *Exercise.* Leisure time physical activity used to develop or maintain physical fitness.

- *Fitness.* A state of attributes that people have or achieve in relation to their ability to perform physical activity.

- *Physical activity.* A bodily movement created by skeletal muscles that expends energy. It is usually thought of as health-enhancing movement.

- *Physical education.* Physical education is part of the total educational program that contributes, primarily through physical activity, to the total growth and development of all children. It is provided with instructional best practices using a developmentally appropriate standards-based curriculum with a purpose of providing youth with the skills, knowledge, and attitudes to be active for a lifetime.

- *Physical literacy.* The disposition that enables an individual to be active as a way of life (Whitehead, 2001). It is a disposition, or nature, or outlook, that opens the doors to engaging in movement experiences, and it evolves as people move through the lifespan.

- *Recess.* Scheduled outside class time that allows students to engage in physical and social activities of their choice (ALR, 2012).

educators must be an integral and important part of the total school environment. They must immerse themselves in school-wide initiatives and be viewed by other teachers as teammates and contributors to academic goals.

Essential Components of a Quality Physical Education Program

Physical education teachers must make sure that students receive a quality physical education experience that results in student learning. To do this, programs must be guided by current research, thinking, and philosophy. One of the unique characteristics of physical education is that it is informed by many other disciplines. The information and curriculum provided in this book are deeply grounded in research from exercise physiology, psychology, motor control, and pedagogy and teaching. All these disciplines, and others, are interwoven to provide students with a quality physical education experience designed to teach students skills, provide them knowledge, and develop positive attitudes toward all physical activity. Again, a strength of physical education is that it applies the evidence from a variety of areas to provide evidence-based

practice. This is a complex and difficult task that physical educators must implement for the benefit of youth.

Based on this large body of evidence from many areas, quality physical education programs must address several essential components that interlock to form a program that will be valued by parents, teachers, and students. Each component is described briefly here, whereas in-depth coverage is provided in the chapters referenced under each point. Figure 1.1 summarizes the eight essential components of a quality physical education program.

1. *Quality physical education programs are organized around content standards that offer direction and continuity to instruction and evaluation.* A quality program is driven by a set of content standards. These standards are defined by various competencies that children are expected to accomplish. Standards are measurable so that both teachers and students know when progress has been made. Comprehensive physical education content standards are presented later in this chapter. (Chapter 8 offers some strategies for teachers who evaluate whether they and their students are meeting the standards.)

FIGURE 1.1 Essential components of a quality physical education program.

2. *Quality programs are student-centered and based on the developmental urges, characteristics, and interests of students.* Children learn best when the skills and activities they must learn match their physical and emotional development. Including activities in the program because they match the teacher's competencies—but not the students' needs—is unacceptable. Teachers must teach new activities outside their comfort zone to present a comprehensive program. (Chapter 4 discusses the urges, characteristics, and interests of children and the way that they affect the creation of a quality physical education program. Chapter 6 offers many ideas for understanding and teaching to the personal needs of students.) A quality program focuses on the successes of students so that they are motivated to continue. Developing positive behaviors toward physical activity is a key goal of physical education. (Chapter 6 also discusses essential elements of teaching and ways to give children positive reinforcement in learning situations.)

3. *Quality physical education programs make physical activity, physical fitness, and motor-skills development the core of the program.* Physical education is the only place in the entire school curriculum where students learn motor skills. Therefore, the physical education program must focus on students' skill development and quality physical activity. As part of the physical activity umbrella, students learn the knowledge and skills needed to achieve and maintain a health-enhancing level of physical fitness. (Chapters 2 and 3 explain the importance of physical activity and fitness for children's optimal growth and development.)

4. *Quality physical education programs teach management skills and self-discipline.* Physical education teachers are often evaluated based on how students behave in their classes rather than on how much their students know about physical education. Administrators and parents look to see whether students are on task and receiving competent instruction. When a class is well managed and students work with self-discipline, the experience compares aligns with classroom instruction, bringing credibility to the program. (Chapter 7 suggests many methods for managing a classroom and promoting self-discipline.)

5. *Quality programs include all students.* Instruction is designed for students who need help the most—namely, less-skilled students and children with disabilities. Students who are skilled and blessed with innate ability have many opportunities to learn during private lessons, clubs, and programs. Unskilled students or children with disabilities lack confidence and often cannot help themselves. Physical education may be the last opportunity these children will have to learn skills in a caring, positive environment. Instruction designed to include and encourage the less-skilled and less-motivated children will ensure a positive and successful experience. Students who are not naturally gifted must perceive themselves as successful if they are to enjoy and value physical activity. (Chapter 9 focuses on dealing with children who have disabilities and modifying activities so that all children can succeed.)

6. *Quality physical education programs focus instruction on the process of learning skills rather than on the product or outcome of performing the skill.* When students are learning new motor skills, they should learn proper techniques first and then focus on the product of performing the skill. Put another way, it is more important to teach children to catch a beanbag properly than it is to worry about how many they catch or miss. (Chapter 5 suggests strategies for optimizing skill learning. Chapter 8 examines when to focus on the process or product evaluation of motor skills.)

7. *Quality physical education programs teach lifetime activities that students can use to improve their health and personal wellness.* Children are prepared to participate in activities they can continue to engage in when they become adults. The most popular activities for adults are outdoor activities, individual sports, and fitness activities and not as many team sports as one might think (Physical Activity Council, 2013). Specifically, activities such as stretching exercises, bicycling, strength development exercises, jogging, swimming, and aerobics are popular with adults. By far, walking is the activity most often reported in adulthood. Quality physical education looks to the future and offers activities that children can enjoy and use as adults. (Chapter 3 emphasizes the importance of teaching lifetime physical activity skills and describes ways to teach wellness and develop a healthy lifestyle.)

8. *Quality programs teach social and personal responsibility, including addressing social and emotional learning, gender, and diversity issues.* Physical education is an effective laboratory for students to learn and apply social skills such as cooperation and communication. In addition, it lends itself to teaching skills associated with relationship building and conflict resolution. (Chapter 6 offers strategies for dealing with gender and diversity issues. Chapter 19 includes activities exploring diverse cultures through dance.)

Current Status of Physical Education in the United States

Physical education has changed its instructional focus so often that teachers, parents, and students wonder what a quality program should deliver to students. The changes usually last 5 to 7 years and then, when interest wanes, are replaced by a new trend. For example, a fitness push has occurred three times in the last 50 years. When this effort to justify physical education was not found effective, programs disappeared and the focus switched to the next topic that could potentially justify the existence of physical education. Physical education's focus has changed so often that many people are unsure what physical education represents. When you say you are a physical education teacher, most people ask, "What sport do you coach?" Colleges and universities have compounded the problem by renaming their physical education departments kinesiology, exercise science, sport studies, movement education, and so on. Despite these barriers, we believe that promoting physical activity and healthy eating are outcomes that really matter for our inactive, overweight society. To this end, physical education can have a strong impact on the public health of our society. The profession needs to stop being a moving target and start to encourage others to see the value of a quality physical education program

that improves the health and welfare of students and ultimately mature citizens.

On the other hand, we must acknowledge that outside influences affect what we do in physical education. In recent years, legislation emphasizing the use of standardized testing to measure student academic achievement and thus school effectiveness has influenced physical education. Responding to a perceived decline in academic performance, many school curricula focus heavily, if not entirely, on teaching students math and reading. To increase academic time in these areas, less time is allocated to special areas, including physical education. The demand for uninterrupted academic time often makes it difficult to schedule physical education time for children beyond one, or maybe two, days per week. In some regions, "back to basic" schools have eliminated all curricular content not focused on math and reading.

According to the SHPPS 2014 (USDHHS, 2014), only 20.9%, 21.8%, and 46.6% of elementary, middle, and high schools, respectively, require physical education. Only 38% of states set minimum time expectations for elementary school physical education (SHAPE America, 2016). Regardless of the time, most districts have limited expectations for the quality of the time spent in these programs; only 26% set student–teacher ratios, and just 21% require teachers to use a curriculum (USDHHS, 2016). That is, schools are within their rights to "double up" physical education classes. Teachers

 CASE STUDY

Physical Activity and Physical Education

"Who are we?" asked Thea, a second-year teacher. In her two years of teaching and undergraduate work, she had read and learned about several approaches to physical education.

"What do you mean? I sense some frustration," replied Jim, her teaching partner, who had 25 years of physical education teaching experience.

"Should we focus on skills? If so, which ones: sports skills or fundamental skills? Should we focus on fitness? Are fit kids sign of good P.E.? What about the gymnastics skills they used to teach when P.E. started? Should I integrate math content in my lessons? I read all of this stuff as I've been teaching, and I just can't figure it out."

Jim listened and then calmly replied, "Listen, I've been doing this as long as you have been alive. And I have seen lots of approaches come, and go, and come, and go. Throughout your career you are going to see this same phenomenon. One thing I've learned is that regardless of the approach, the common thread is always physical activity. From the German-Swedish influence you learned about in your coursework, to the new physical literacy push, the bottom line is that we need to get kids to *want* to be active. So, in my opinion, your approach to teaching, the model you use, and the teaching style you use, should all focus on what will get children to enjoy moving. Don't worry about the next hot topic. Keep up to date on them and integrate them in your program, but don't get consumed and worry so much. I probably sound like your dad, but you're a hard worker, and you are going to be an outstanding teacher. You want kids to love to move. Don't forget that. This renewed focus on physical activity leaders in schools is perfect for you. Again, physical activity has always really been what we are about, and this role lets us take physical activity promotion beyond lessons in the gym and show the school community that we care about kids' health and want everyone to get and stay active."

may have 50 to 60 or more students in one class. When physical education is provided at these grade levels, a "specialist" often teaches it—though many people with this title lack valid credentials. As one might expect, these lowered expectations and lack of policy supporting physical education, has led some programs, although not all, to provide low-quality physical education programs.

In most schools, children receive about 25 hours of overall instruction weekly. Physical education may be scheduled for 30 to 60 minutes a week in a school that cares about physical education, meaning that only 2 to 4% of the total instructional time is devoted to the health and wellness of students. How can we expect children to value physical activity if physical education does not receive adequate time for instruction? Instruction may be carried out by a classroom teacher or paraprofessional with little concern for the quality of the experience. Often, up to four classrooms are sent to physical education at one time, so the student–teacher ratio is 120 to 1 (sometimes one or two paraprofessionals are available to help). When class sizes are large, more time is spent on management and discipline, making the experience less than satisfactory. Often, for young children, *how* they are taught is more important than *what* they are taught. Physical education teachers deserve the same respect and class sizes as classroom teachers. Although these facts seem to paint a dim picture of physical education, we believe the future of physical education is bright and that these barriers can be overcome to allow physical education to prosper.

Need for Physical Education Programs

In the past several decades, interest in the benefits of an active lifestyle has spawned a wide assortment of health clubs and exercise and fitness books and magazines, a weekly smorgasbord of distance runs and triathlons, streamlined exercise equipment, and apparel for virtually any type of physical activity. Unfortunately, most of this interest and lifestyle change has occurred among middle- and upper-class Americans. Little change in activity patterns has occurred in lower-middle- and lower-class families.

A 2015 report found that teens spend as much as nine hours a day using media, 8-to 12-year-olds approximately six hours a day, and 5- to 8-year-olds nearly three hours a day (Common Sense Media, 2015, 2017). Further, excessive screen time in youth has been associated with numerous cardiovascular risk factors in youth adulthood. Early research in this area found that children who watched four or more hours of television per day had significantly higher body mass index (BMI) than children who watched less than two hours per day (Anderson et al., 1998).

Health goals for the nation for the year 2020 (USDHHS, 2010) are based on increasing daily levels of physical activity. Many of the goals directly target schools or programs that can take place within the school setting. These goals emphasize reducing inactivity and increasing light to moderate physical activity. How, then, can implementing a quality physical education program teach students how to live an active and healthy lifestyle?

1. The prevalence of obesity among children 6 to 11 years of age has increased from 7% in 1980 to 17.2% in 2014 (Ogden, Carroll, Fryar, & Flegal, 2015). Increased obesity is a function of children consuming more calories through their diet than they are expending through physical activity. The school environment typically discourages physical activity. Everywhere they go, students are ordered to move slowly, sit still, and walk rather than run, resulting in decreased energy expenditure. A 30-minute physical education class can offer 1,200 to 2,000 steps of moderate to vigorous physical activity to counteract the effects of an inactive day (Beighle & Pangrazi, 2000; Morgan, Pangrazi, & Beighle, 2003). Thus, for a student who averages 8,000 steps a day, a quality physical education class could increase the total number of steps by 25% and the accumulated steps to 10,000—a substantial increase in physical activity.

2. Positive experiences in physical education can affect physical activity choices in adulthood (Ladwig, Vazou, & Ekkekakis, 2018). Adults in this study reported their best memories of physical education included interaction with peers, time to be active, and enjoying class activities. Their worst memories included embarrassment and injuries. Other surveys have found that simply having physical education and having physical education more frequently is an avenue for physical activity in adulthood (Physical Activity Council, 2013).

3. Obese youth are more likely than youth of normal weight to become overweight or obese adults and therefore are more at risk for associated adult health problems, including heart disease, type 2 diabetes, stroke, several types of cancer, and osteoarthritis (Dixon, 2010). Thus, we must address obesity in elementary school—before the problem becomes more difficult to rectify.

4. A quality physical education program educates students physically and can contribute to academic learning. It has long been argued that spending time on physical education and recess lowers the academic performance of students because they have less time to study and learn. A review of research examining the relationship between physical activity in school and academic performance found that increasing time during the school day for physical activity does not negatively affect school performance and in fact can improve student academic performance (CDC, 2016).

5. Physical education gives students the skills they need to be active as adults. Adults rarely learn new physical activities because they are too busy and are unwilling to start as beginners. Instead, they often practice and use skills they learned in childhood. Since many adults like to participate in activities having a requisite skill level (e.g., golf, tennis, and racquetball), learning such skills during their school years makes them more likely to feel competent enough to participate in these activities later in life.

6. It has been thought for quite some time that physical activity gives children immediate and long-term health benefits (Bar-Or, 1995). For obese children, increased physical activity reduces the percentage of body fat. For high health-risk children, increased activity reduces blood pressure and improves their blood lipid profiles. Finally, it has long been known that weight-bearing activities performed during the school years offer bone mineral density benefits (i.e., the prevention of osteoporosis) that carry over into adulthood (Bailey, Faulkner, & McKay, 1995).

7. Active children are more likely to become active adults. In initial work examining this relationship, Telama, Yang, Laakso, & Viikari (1997) looked at retrospective and longitudinal tracking studies and concluded that the results "indicate that physical activity and sport participation in childhood and adolescence represent a significant prediction for physical activity in adulthood." This type of research has persisted over time, and the most current research maintains that physical activity levels across the lifespan are steady (Telama et al., 2014). That finding means that students who are active tend to be active adults.

Physical Educators Promoting Physical Activity

Despite the many acknowledged benefits of physical education and a national call for more physical education (Institute of Medicine, 2012), the field continues to be marginalized. To combat this trend, physical education programs must demonstrate that they are instructional, of high quality, and contribute uniquely to the school curriculum and environment. For more than a decade, many national programs and organizations have charged physical educators and schools to take on a larger role in physical education (Pate et al., 2006; NASPE, 2008; National Physical Activity Plan for the United States, 2018). Some have questioned this approach as abandoning the basis of physical education and see it as a threat to the field of physical education. We believe that this approach is essential. First, all the approaches used throughout the history of physical education continue to have one common denominator—physical activity. Although trends come and go, at the root of these approaches is the provision of physical activity for youth. Second, to maintain the profession's existence, the field of physical education must evolve to meet the desires and needs of society. Taking on a focus of physical education allows us to address what we know is a major public health concern—physical inactivity. This position does not suggest that physical educators discard current curricular models and approaches to teaching, nor does it suggest that skills, fitness, and knowledge no longer be taught. We must continue to incorporate quality instruction in physical education. But we must place more focus and emphasis on the public health concern of physical activity promotion.

To meet this goal of establishing physical education as a tool for improving public health, physical educators must take on a larger, more prominent role in schools. Serving as school-based physical activity champions allows physical educators to maintain relevance and position themselves as an essential part of their schools. What might this role look like for a physical educator?

Schools can serve as a cost-effective resource for battling poor health and physical inactivity of Americans. Unfortunately, schools and teachers do not deem that as a priority and are not trained or equipped to carry out such a task. The physical educator in the school is the most appropriate and qualified person to lead this charge. Potential responsibilities of the physical activity leader include organizing staff wellness programs, providing nutrition education, coordinating with food service directors, and helping teachers integrate physical activity and health in the classroom. For the physical activity leader to work most effectively, a shift in job responsibility must occur. Aside from planning and other duties as assigned (e.g., bus duty), most physical educators teach 100% of their time in the schools. Within this "shift," schools need to allocate time for collaboration with others in the school and in the community to advocate for healthier behaviors for the entire school community.

The physical activity leader spearheads environmental change, thus positively influencing the physical environment of the school by working with staff to post bulletin boards as well as point-of-decision prompts promoting physical activity and healthy behavior. These serve as reminders to make good food selections at lunch, wash hands in the restroom, and invite a friend to participate in a recess game. The physical activity leader can promote these behaviors by addressing them during physical education lessons.

The notion of a fitness room or health club is another possibility for promoting healthy behavior with students and teachers. Providing physical activity DVDs, resistance bands, stability balls, and other equipment in a classroom or unused stage creates a place for staff to be active after school, and the teachers can use that space as a reward for student effort in academic work during the school day.

To make favorable changes to the social environment of the school, classroom teachers can be trained to provide activity breaks for their students throughout the day. Another classroom policy that can be endorsed is to limit the amount of "sit time" teachers allow their students. For example, teachers should be encouraged to get their students up and moving at least once every hour, which may be prompted by a school-wide announcement or signal over the intercom. The physical activity leader may present stress relief breaks for staff during faculty meetings or provide informational health-related sessions during lunchtime in the faculty lounge.

Content of Physical Education

Following agreed-upon guidelines or standards that have been proven to ensure that children obtain a quality education are just as important for physical education as they are for traditional academic classes. Content standards are the framework of any program because they determine the focus and direction of instruction. Standards specify broadly what students should know and be able to do before advancing to the next developmental level. Established standards can significantly contribute to the overall goal of school and U.S. society—namely,

to develop well-rounded people capable of contributing to society. Quality programs are driven by standards that motivate children toward high-level achievement.

Physical education content standards are taught nowhere else in the school curriculum. If these standards are not achieved in physical education classes, children leave school without a well-developed set of physical skills. SHAPE America (2014), which stands for the Society for Health and Physical Education, is the national physical education organization in the United States. It has identified five major content standards for physical education. This document (www.humankinetics.com/ products/all-products/national-standards-grade-level-outcomes-for-k-12-physical-education) also provides grade-level outcomes for each of the standards.

To conform to the concepts of standards-based education, this text and the accompanying website (www.DynamicPEASAP.com) present learning experiences that lead students toward meeting fundamental content standards that must be accomplished in physical education. The standards are further broken down into outcomes so that teachers and schools can be held accountable for helping students reach a predetermined level of achievement. Though accountability is important, abuse can occur when teachers are rewarded based solely on student achievement levels. Some teachers may turn to memorization, drill, and rote learning and may encourage practice solely in areas where students will be tested. In physical education, this method often means teaching only fitness test activities so that students score well on a mandated physical fitness test. This approach can result in a program that satisfies the school's accountability concerns but does little to give students a well-rounded physical education.

SHAPE America National Standards for Physical Literacy

This section reviews each of the five SHAPE America national standards and refers to the chapters that offer instructional activities and strategies designed to reach these standards. The 2014 SHAPE America standards include the term "physically literate individuals." As defined earlier in this chapter, physical literacy refers to the disposition that enables an individual to be active as a way of life (Whitehead, 2001). A physically literate individual is one who is motivated to be active and has the ability to engage in physical activity throughout life. Unfortunately, this change in terminology has resulted in some confusion. That is, some equate physical literacy and physical education. In fact, physical literacy is used to represent far-reaching efforts to promote active living by many institutions, government agencies, and organizations, as well as education. For instance, youth sports, scout programs, and parks and recreation programs all provide programming designed to promote lifelong movement and assist students on their physical literacy journey. In essence, physical literacy does not change the focus of physical education, which is to provide students with the skills, knowledge, and attitude to be active for a lifetime. This term works to bring all efforts to promote physical activity, including physical education, under one umbrella.

Standard 1

> The physically literate individual demonstrates competency in a variety of motor skills and movement patterns.

Standard 1 focuses on skill competency. All people want to be skilled and competent performers. The elementary school years are an excellent time to teach motor skills because children have the time and predisposition to learn them. The range of skills presented in physical education should be unlimited; children need to encounter and learn as many different physical skills as possible. Because children vary in genetic endowment and interest, they should have the opportunity to learn about their personal abilities in many types of skills and settings.

Movement Concepts Skills

The classification of movement concepts (chapter 15) includes body and space awareness, qualities of movement, and relationships. Learning the skills is insufficient; children need to explore them in a variety of settings, too. This standard ensures that children will be taught how movement concepts are classified and is designed to give children increased awareness and understanding of the body as a vehicle for movement while acquiring a personal vocabulary of movement skills.

Fundamental Motor Skills

Fundamental skills enhance the quality of life. They are the basis for all physical activities. These skills are sometimes referred to as "basic" or "functional" skills. These are the skills children need to function fully in the environment. Fundamental skills are categorized as locomotor, nonlocomotor, and manipulative skills.

Locomotor Skills

Locomotor skills (chapter 16) are used to move the body from one place to another or to project the body upward, as in jumping and hopping. These skills include walking, running, skipping, leaping, sliding, and galloping.

Nonlocomotor Skills

Nonlocomotor skills (chapter 16) are done in place, with little spatial movement. These skills, which are not as well defined as locomotor skills, include bending and stretching, pushing and pulling, balancing, rolling, curling, twisting, turning, and bouncing.

Manipulative Skills

Manipulative skills (chapter 17) are developed by handling some type of object. Most of these skills involve

Developing manipulative skills.

the hands and feet, but other parts of the body also are used. The manipulation of objects leads to better eye–hand and eye–foot coordination, which are particularly important for tracking items in space. Manipulative skills are basic to many games. Propelling (throwing, striking, striking with an implement, kicking) and receiving (catching) objects are important skills that can be taught by using beanbags and various balls. Rebounding or redirecting an object in flight (e.g., a volleyball) and continuous control of an object, such as a wand or a hoop, are also manipulative activities.

Specialized Motor Skills

Specialized skills are used in various sports and other areas of physical education, including apparatus activities, tumbling, dance, and specific games. Specialized skills receive increased emphasis beginning with Developmental Level II activities. In developing specialized skills, progression is attained through planned instruction and drills. Many of these skills depend on specific techniques, so teaching emphasizes correct form and procedures.

Body Management Skills

Efficient movement of the body (chapter 18) requires the integration of various physical traits, including agility, balance, flexibility, and coordination. Students also need to learn how to control their bodies while on large apparatus such as beams, benches, and jumping boxes.

Rhythmic Movement Skills

Rhythmic movement (chapter 19) involves moving in a regular, predictable pattern. The ability to move rhythmically is basic to the performance of skills in all areas. A rhythmic program that includes dance, rope jumping, and rhythmic gymnastics offers a variety of activities to help students attain this objective. Early experiences center on functional and creative movement forms. Instruction begins with and capitalizes on locomotor skills that children already have—walking, running, hopping, and jumping. Rhythmic activities are a vehicle for expressive movement.

Gymnastics Skills

Gymnastics activities (chapter 20) contribute significantly to children's overall physical education experience in elementary schools. Gymnastics activities develop body management skills without the need for equipment and apparatus. Flexibility, agility, balance, strength, and body control are enhanced by participating in gymnastics. Students learn basic gymnastics skills, such as rolling, balancing, inverted balancing, and tumbling, in a safe and gradual way.

Cooperative Skills

Cooperative activities (chapter 21) teach students to work together for their group's common good. By participating in these activities, students can learn the skills of listening, discussing, thinking as a group, group decision making, and sacrificing individual wants to further group success. Cooperative skills utilize fundamental skills and problem solving. They are active yet demand problem solving and team play.

Game Skills

Games (chapter 22) provide children with the opportunity to apply newly learned skills in a meaningful way. Many games develop large muscle groups and enhance the ability to run, dodge, start, and stop under control while sharing space with others. Through games, children experience success and accomplishment. Social objectives that can be achieved through games include developing interpersonal skills, conflict resolution, accepting rule parameters, and increasing self-knowledge in a competitive and cooperative situation.

Sport Skills

Students learn basic sport skills (chapters 23 through 30) and then practice them in various drills. After learning and practicing the skills, students apply them in lead-up activities. Lead-up activities reduce the number of skills children must use to succeed, thus leading to more successful participation. Sport skills require proper techniques, so cognitive learning is also important.

Standard 2

> The physically literate individual applies knowledge of concepts, principles, strategies, and tactics related to movement and performance.

The school years are a time to experience and learn many different types of physical activities and skills. Standard 2 gives students the opportunity to learn the basic concepts of movement (chapter 15), which can help them understand what, where, and how the body can move. Again, the emphasis is on experiencing the diversity of human movement. By learning the correct mechanics of skill performance, students leave school knowing about stability, force, leverage, and other factors related to efficient movement.

Instruction is focused on teaching students to be self-directed learners who can evaluate their performance and self-correct their skill technique. To become competent performers, they must understand that they learn motor skills only through repetition and refinement (two of the three Rs of physical education). Because many adult activities are done alone, students need to learn how to warm up before an activity and cool down when finished. Simple principles of motor learning such as practice, arousal, and skill refinement can be applied to future experiences.

Standard 3

> The physically literate individual demonstrates the knowledge and skills to achieve and maintain a health-enhancing level of physical activity and fitness.

The physically literate individual demonstrates the knowledge and skills to achieve and maintain a health-enhancing level of physical activity and fitness. Although physical activity and physical fitness are combined here, these two concepts are vastly different. Thus, for the purpose of explanation, although in one standard, they will be discussed separately.

The conceptual basis of including physical activity as a standard is that active children mature into active adults (Telama et al., 2014). Specifically, learning how to monitor personal activity levels, plan meaningful activity programs, and make informed decisions about physical activity are important outcomes. Children need to learn where they can participate within their community and how they can join clubs, YMCAs, and sports programs.

Sallis (1994) first classified the factors that influence people to be active as psychological, social, physical environmental, and biological. A major role of physical education is to foster the *determinants of active living*. Psychological determinants are among the most powerful. For example, students must enjoy physical activity if they are expected to participate as adults. Enjoyment increases when an adequate level of proficiency is attained in a favored activity. Because most adults do not participate in activities unless they feel competent, learning skills becomes a priority in childhood. Another psychological factor is the need for challenge. Physical educators must provide an appropriate balance of challenge for students to experience success and maintain interest. It is important to be intentional in discussing the role of challenge in physical activity choices.

Social factors that influence lifetime activity patterns include the presence of family and peer role models, encouragement from a significant other, and opportunities to participate in activities with others in one's social group. Physical environmental factors include adequate programs and facilities, adequate equipment and supplies, safe outdoor environments, and available opportunities near home and at school. These factors include adequate school opportunities, such as recess, physical education classes, intramural games, recreation programs, and organized sports. Finally, biological factors include age, gender, and ethnic or socioeconomic status. For more details about the determinants of physical activity, refer to Sallis (1994) and Uijtdewilligen et al. (2011).

The 2018 Physical Activity Guidelines for Americans explains why children need daily physical activity and delineates a recommendation that youth accumulate 60 or more minutes of physical activity per day. The importance of participating in different types of physical activity, including lifestyle activity, active aerobics, active sports and recreation, flexibility, and muscle fitness exercises is also discussed. The guidelines offer support and direction for teachers who need to justify increasing their students' daily physical activity.

Children need daily physical activity.

Josie Gealer/Photodisc/Getty Images

Physical fitness instruction (chapter 3) for elementary school children concentrates on their participation in daily physical activity rather than the products of fitness (i.e., how many repetitions, how fast, or how far). Giving students an opportunity to offer input about their fitness program and make personal activity choices prepares them for a lifetime of activity. When students accept responsibility for participating in regular activity, fitness becomes an authentic learning experience that may last a lifetime. Positive experiences in physical activity are a must. Meeting this standard means helping students develop positive attitudes that carry over into adulthood. Little is gained if students develop high levels of physical fitness in elementary school but leave school with a strong dislike of physical activity.

Part of each physical education period should be devoted to teaching children about fitness. Learning the basic facts of fitness, though, is not enough; elementary school children must also participate in fitness. Many people know the facts of fitness but do not stay active because they have not learned the activity habit. The best way for students to learn the amount of effort necessary to maintain personal fitness is to experience it. Too often, fitness is seen solely as an aerobic experience. Aerobics are important, but maintaining strength and flexibility is equally vital. Fitness routines that incorporate interval training (i.e., alternating aerobic activities with strength and flexibility activities) show students that the best lifetime fitness routine is a balanced one.

To meet standard 3, students must understand the basic facts of fitness. Concepts such as overload can be taught in short question-and-answer periods. Because everyone has unique needs, and because programs must be developed according to those needs, an understanding of people's genetic diversity (i.e., differences in muscle type, cardiorespiratory endurance, and motor coordination) is required for helping students understand their physical capabilities. Understanding how to exercise properly, how much activity is enough, and how to participate safely in an activity helps give children a positive mindset. Finally, students learn to evaluate their own fitness levels in a semiprivate setting. By doing self-testing on health-related fitness and charting their physical activity, students can monitor their own progress.

Standard 4

The physically literate individual exhibits responsible personal and social behavior that respects self and others.

Physical education classes offer a unique environment for learning effective social skills. Children have the opportunity to internalize and practice the merits of participation, cooperation, competition, and tolerance. The desired social atmosphere is one of good *citizenship* and *fair play*. Through listening, empathy, and guidance, children learn to differentiate between acceptable and unacceptable ways of expressing feelings. Students must become aware of how they interact with others and how their behavior influences others' responses to them.

Responsible behavior (chapter 7) , the very heart of standard 4, means behaving in ways that do not negatively affect others. According to Hellison (2010) and others, responsible behavior must be taught through experiences where such behavior is continuously reinforced. Accepting consequences for one's behavior is learned and needs to be valued and reinforced by responsible adults. Responsible behavior occurs in a hierarchy of behavior that ranges from being irresponsible to caring and behaving responsibly. Physical education classes are an excellent setting for teaching responsibility because most behavior is highly visible there. Children in a competitive setting may react in an openly irresponsible way, thus providing instructors with a "teachable moment" to discuss types of acceptable and unacceptable behavior. Students must also learn to win and lose in an acceptable way and assume responsibility for their performances. Accepting the consequences of one's behavior is a lesson that arises regularly in a cooperative or competitive environment.

Conflicts must be resolved nonviolently (chapter 7) so that all parties can maintain self-esteem and dignity. Physical education offers an excellent opportunity to apply conflict resolution skills, thus teaching students to resolve conflicts and disagreements in a peaceful and nonthreatening manner. Many diversity and gender issues (chapter 6) arise in activity settings, and insightful and caring instruction can help destroy negative stereotypes. Learning about the similarities and differences among cultures and the way that most people share common values and beliefs is an important outcome.

The lesson plan, the activities presented, the teachers' views of less successful students, and the treatment of children with disabilities send implied messages to students (the hidden curriculum). When teachers and parents respond to children in a caring way, the children learn they are loved, capable, and contributing people. If children believe they belong, are loved and respected, and their successes outweigh their failures, then they are on the road to developing a desirable self-concept.

Cooperation must be taught in elementary school physical education. Competitive games require cooperation, fair play, and respect for teammates; without these elements, the joy of participation is lost. Cooperative games teach children that all teammates are needed to reach group goals.

Standard 5

> The physically literate individual recognizes the value of physical activity for health, enjoyment, challenge, self-expression, and/or social interaction.

Standard 5 focuses on how much the student values physical activity and whether the student has the knowledge needed to make thoughtful decisions affecting his or her health and wellness. Meeting this standard does not have to turn physical education into a sedentary fact-learning experience. Instead, simple principles about nutrition, stress, substance abuse, and safety can be woven into daily activity and skill development sessions to give children an opportunity to learn about healthy lifestyles.

Wellness implies developing a lifestyle that is balanced in all phases, with *moderation* the keyword. Wellness is based on developing a clear understanding of choices and alternatives that lead to making wise decisions. Students cannot make meaningful choices for wellness if they do not understand the consequences of their decisions. Wellness instruction involves studying the wisdom of past generations and integrating it into the lifestyles of current and future generations. In elementary school, basic wellness instruction covers how the skeletal, muscular, and cardiorespiratory systems function. Students also study lifestyle alternatives that affect wellness, including basic facts about nutrition, weight control, stress and relaxation, substance abuse, and safety.

Evolution of Elementary School Physical Education

The previously discussed content in this chapter has evolved throughout the history of physical education. In this time, various educational policies, public health concerns, historical events, and pedagogical influences have significantly affected elementary school physical education programs. Often these programs are created or modified as a reaction to events publicized by the press and other interested parties. Certainly, professionals and curriculum must evolve and in fact, an evolving field is advocated. However, as you read about the following influences, keep in mind that evolutionary changes can be both positive and negative. They are positive if they result in long-term change that offers positive identity to the profession. They are negative if they are emphasized for a few years and then discarded in favor of a focus on the next popular topic. Too often, many of the influences listed in this section have been implemented without adequate research, thought, and planning. Instead, they are selected in an attempt to validate the profession. Years after implementation, research has shown that the program changes had little or no positive effect on student outcomes. Another negative aspect of implementing ineffective trends is that it leaves the public (parents and students alike) wondering what physical education is and what is to be learned in a physical education class. Consider that most program trends last only five to seven years. Nonprofessionals, therefore, find it difficult to understand what constitutes a quality physical education program. In sum, constant changing is an attempt to validate the profession, but more often it serves to marginalize the profession, confuses others about our purpose, and leaves the public wondering, "What is physical education?"

Learning to cooperate to achieve group goals.

German and Swedish Influence

During the 19th century German and Swedish immigrants to the United States introduced physical education that focused on body development. The German system favored a gymnastics approach, which required a lot of equipment and special teachers. The Swedish system incorporated an exercise program into activity presentations. The physical education program in many of the schools that adopted these approaches consisted of a series of structured exercises that children could perform in the classroom. The need for equipment and gymnasiums posed problems for the schools that followed these systems, and many economy-minded citizens questioned the programs. Because of these concerns, a combination of games and calisthenics evolved and became the first scheduled physical education activity offered in some U.S. schools.

Emphasis on Games and Sports

When about one-third of the American men drafted in World War I were rejected as physically unfit for military service, a new demand emerged for physical education and fitness in the schools. (Little improvement in health status has occurred, however, since that time; in 2009, more than 35% of American men were rejected by the military for physical health reasons.) In many states, laws requiring minimum weekly physical activity time resulted in physical education becoming part of the school curriculum. The laws were strictly quantitative, however, and paid little attention to program quality.

Training programs designed for soldiers during World War I emphasized games and sports and proved more effective than calisthenics alone. Therefore, school programs using games and sports for physical development soon followed. John Dewey, professor of philosophy at Columbia University, profoundly influenced educational theory in the mid-20th century. Interestingly, two of Dewey's cardinal aims of education stressed physical activities and gave impetus to the teaching of games and sports in schools. With the influence of Dewey and military training, games and sports were valued and became part of the school curriculum.

Programs stressing sports and games started in secondary schools and filtered down to elementary physical education. Physical education was often described by answering the question, "What game are we going to play today?" During the Great Depression, when equipment was difficult to obtain and physical education teachers were almost nonexistent, physical education was relegated to a minor role, and many schools eliminated it.

National Concern About Physical Fitness

A renewed emphasis on fitness occurred in the 1950s, after the publication of comparative studies (based on the Kraus-Weber tests) of fitness levels of U.S. and European children. Kraus and Hirschland (1954) compared the strength and flexibility of 4,000 New York–area school children with a comparable sample of Central European children. The press publicized the comparative weakness of U.S. children, which led to the birth of the fitness movement. The President's Council on Physical Fitness and Sports was established to promote physical fitness among school children and citizens of all ages. Currently, the council (now known as the President's Council on Fitness, Sports and Nutrition) is increasing the emphasis placed on children's physical activity and nutrition. These changes are a result of research revealing an ever-increasing number of overweight and obese children and adults. In turn, this concern fueled a renewed focus on fitness and physical activity in physical education.

Pedagogical Influences

Teachers and professionals who identify a need for different instructional methods and physical education programs are often motivated by dissatisfaction with the status quo and a desire to make physical education a more necessary part of the school curriculum. The following are some approaches that have influenced the course of elementary school physical education.

Movement Education

Movement education originated in England and was incorporated into U.S. programs in the late 1960s. To some degree, it was a revolt against structured fitness programs, which included calisthenics done in a formal, regimented, military style. The demanding fitness standards advocated by the President's Council led some teachers to teach for fitness outcomes rather than presenting a balanced physical education program that included skills and concepts. This practice created a backlash among some physical educators, who thought that creativity, exploration, and cognition should also be focal points of teaching.

Movement education methodology featured problem solving and exploration, thus shifting some of the responsibility for learning to the children. Adopting movement education led to the rejection of physical-fitness-oriented activities, especially calisthenics, which were labelled *training* and not education. Controversy arose over applying movement principles to the teaching of specific skills, particularly athletic skills. Schools tended to apply the exploration methodology to all phases of instruction without examining its effectiveness. Nevertheless, movement education resulted in better teaching methodologies and increased emphasis on instruction focused on the individual. Movement education also offered an opportunity for diversity of movement through creative instructional methods and allowed students of all ability levels to succeed.

Perceptual–Motor Programs

The focus of perceptual–motor programs were to remedy learning difficulties attributed to a breakdown in perceptual–motor development. Theorists held that children progressed in an orderly way through growth and developmental stages from head to foot (cephalocaudally) and from the center of the body outward (proximodistally). When disruptions, lags, or omissions occurred in this process, certain underlying perceptual–motor bases failed to develop fully and impaired the child's ability to function correctly in both physical and academic settings.

Perceptual–motor programs flourished because of concern for *slow* (or *delayed*) academic learners. Some children, who were identified as academically challenged, demonstrated motor problems involving coordination, balance and postural control, and relationships involving time and space. Perceptual–motor programs attempted to remediate these shortcomings and gave physical education teachers hope that their profession would be viewed as integral to a child's academic success. When researchers examined the effectiveness of such programs, however, they discovered that perceptual–motor activities did *not* improve academic achievement. Today, few perceptual–motor-based physical education programs still exist, but they continue to contribute to today's programs with the integration of perceptual–motor principles into skill-learning sequences, such as using both sides of the body, practicing balance skills, and so forth.

Conceptual Learning

Conceptual understanding (i.e., applying abstract ideas drawn from experience) plays an important part in physical education. In the process of movement, children learn to distinguish between near and far, strong and weak, light and heavy, and high and low. Physical education gives children the opportunity to understand and experiment with such movement concepts.

The *Fitness for Life* program (Corbin & Lindsey, 2007) takes a conceptual approach to physical education. Students receive information associated with physical activity and health in a lecture and then use the infor-

mation on themselves or on peers in a laboratory (i.e., physical education) setting. This program emphasizes information, appraisal procedures, and program planning. Students are expected to understand the "how, what, and why" of physical activity and exercise. They learn to use diagnostic tests in areas such as cardiovascular endurance, muscular strength and endurance, flexibility, body composition, and motor ability.

Fitness for Life is one approach that works to link academic content and physical education. Some teachers believe that taking an academic approach focused solely on knowledge and cognitive growth instead of physical skills, physical activity, and attitudes toward physical activity will place physical education on par with other academic disciplines. Others believe that increasing student knowledge changes students' attitudes and behavior, thus encouraging them to incorporate physical activity into their lifestyles. Research, however, supports neither of these beliefs. Increasing a person's knowledge does not ensure a change in behavior. Most individuals who smoke know that smoking is detrimental to their health, yet they still smoke. Students must experience and learn physical skills and understand their conceptual components. Because it is the only place in the curriculum where physical skills are taught and learned, physical activity is—and must remain—the core component of physical education.

Technology and Physical Education

Technology is everywhere you look. With the insurgence of technology in society comes the uptick of technology in education, which has opened the door to many possibilities. It makes sense that physical educators would begin looking into the use of technology in physical education. Tablets, projectors, and social media are all being used to help teachers plan, teach, and continue their education. Technology is like other tools in a teacher's toolkit; it is useful only when it can improve the learning experience, and it should never be used just for the sake of using technology. Throughout this book Tech Tips will be provided to share ideas for new teachers to incorporate technology in their physical education programs.

Federal Mandates

Occasionally, legislation is passed that affects physical education curriculum and instruction. The following legislative mandates in particular continue to influence physical education programs throughout the United States.

Title IX: Equal Opportunity for the Sexes

Title IX of the Educational Amendments Act of 1972 has significantly affected most secondary school physical education programs. This federal law has less effect on elementary school physical education because most programs at this level have long been coeducational. Title IX rules out separation of the sexes and requires all offerings to be coeducational. The law is based on the principle that school activities and programs are of equal value for both sexes and that students should not be denied access to participation based on gender. The legal ramifications of Title IX have forced schools to provide equal access to physical education activities for boys and girls. Organizing separate competitions for the sexes is permissible, provided that mixed participation in an activity would be hazardous. In principle, the law also dictates that the most qualified teacher—regardless of gender—provides instruction.

Title IX also tries to eliminate sexism and sex-role typing. Human needs and opportunities must prevail over traditional sexual stereotypes of masculinity and femininity. Segregating children by sex in elementary school physical education classes is indefensible because it eliminates the opportunity for children to learn at an early age that gender differences are negligible when it comes to the desire to perform well athletically.

PL 94-142: Equal Rights for Students With Disabilities

Public Law 94-142 mandates that all children have the right to a free and public education and that they must be educated in the least restrictive educational environment possible. No longer can the 3.5 to 4 million U.S. children with disabilities be assigned to segregated classes or schools unless a separate environment is determined by due process to be in the child's best interest. A 1990 amendment, Public Law 101-476 (also known as IDEA—Individuals with Disabilities Education Act), continues with the objective of providing handicapped individuals with the least restrictive environment in the school setting.

Inclusion (mainstreaming) is the term used for the practice of placing children with unique needs into regular classroom settings. These laws have allowed many children with unique needs (special needs) to participate in regular physical education classes. PL 101-476 often necessitates changing the school's structure and educational procedures as well as the viewpoints and attitudes of its personnel. Many teachers lack the educational background, experience, or inclination to handle children with disabilities. The answer is not to ignore the problem but to provide teachers with the knowledge and constructive approaches that allow them to teach children with all levels of ability successfully.

Besides the inclusion of students with unique needs into regular education classes, PL 101-476 also mandates that each such student receive a specific learning program, called an *individualized educational program* (IEP). Establishing the child's due process committee, developing the IEP, and monitoring the program to ensure that it is in the student's best interest is a considerable challenge. IEPs, which help make education more personal and individual, can be used for able children as well.

TECH TIP

Mary Sinjo is a young, energized physical education teacher who loves technology. Her colleague, Jimmy Conn, is a veteran teacher who is well respected in the school and district and is seen as a leader. During a kindergarten throwing lesson Ms. Sinjo used a projector to place moving targets on the wall for students to throw at. After the lesson, Mr. Conn asked, "Why did you use the projector?" Ms. Sinjo responded, "I think it's kind of fun for kids to have a moving target to throw at." Mr. Conn then asked, "So was the goal to hit the targets or to throw with mature pattern. I heard all of the excellent cues you gave them and thought the students caught on pretty well." Ms. Sinjo thought for a minute and said, "You know, I guess they did do well when I was teaching but when throwing at the targets that all went away. Do you think that was because of the targets?" "It could be. I like that you want to integrate technology, but that activity might work best for older kids once they have learned to throw a bit better," Jimmy replied. The point here is that using technology because it can add enjoyment and fun is great, but that cannot be the only reason. In fact, if we are not careful, technology can work against us and undermine great teaching.

Child Nutrition and WIC Reauthorization Act of 2004

Nationally, widespread concern exists about the health status of Americans, particularly physical activity and nutrition. At the time of this legislation in 2004 more than 65% of Americans are overweight or obese (National Center for Health Statistics, 2004). Much of this increase is attributed to a decrease in physical activity and an increase in the number of calories consumed.

Physical education programs must focus on improving students' health status, particularly their eating habits and physical activity. The Child Nutrition and WIC (Women, Infants, and Children) Reauthorization Act of 2004 required that all school districts with a federally funded school meal program must develop and implement wellness policies addressing nutrition and physical activity. This act offered physical educators an excellent opportunity to provide physical activity and eating behavior programs in their classes. In doing so, they had an opportunity to change the entire school environment rather than merely implement a minor curriculum change. Changing the school environment requires the efforts of the entire school community—namely, parents, classroom teachers, administrators, and students. Some hope existed that, if implemented correctly, this mandate could have elevated physical education programs and physical educators to a prominent role in the total school curriculum and school environment. The Healthy, Hunger-Free Act of 2010 reauthorized this act, but in the new language the focus is on nutrition and meal programs with no mention of physical activity.

Every Student Succeeds Act (ESSA)

The Every Student Succeeds Act (ESSA) was signed into law in 2015. This law reauthorized the Elementary and Secondary Education Act (ESEA), which has been a law for more than 50 years, and replaced the No Child Left Behind (NCLB) Act, which was enacted in 2002. The ESEA is the nation's education law and ensures equal opportunity for all students. The ESSA is seen as a positive for physical educators because it marks a change in the focus to a well-rounded education for all students. Physical education, for the first time in federal legislation, was included as part of a "well-rounded education." Therefore, federal funding is now available for physical education. The full implementation of this law has not been realized, but it holds great potential for the future of physical education.

Contemporary Social Influences

Society also influences education. Given that education takes place in the middle of our society, it should be no shock that social influences weigh heavy on educational decisions. Physical education is no different.

Nationwide Concern for Health and Physical Activity

Every decade, the United States sets goals and objectives with 10-year targets designed to guide national health promotion and disease prevention to improve the health of Americans.

The most recent document *Healthy People 2020* (USDHHS, 2010) emphasizes a commitment that all people live long and healthy lives. Four major goals are listed in this document: (1) attain high-quality, longer lives free of preventable disease, disability, injury, and premature death; (2) achieve health equity, eliminate disparities, and improve the health of all groups; (3) create social and physical environments that promote good health for all; and (4) promote quality of life, healthy development, and healthy behaviors across all life stages. The massive *Healthy People* document includes many topics of particular relevance to health and physical educators. Some topics of interest include adolescent health, early and middle childhood health, nutrition and weight control, physical activity, and social determinants of health. This document can be an excellent resource for teachers who want to design a program that will help meet the 2020 goals.

The problem of weight control merits special attention in elementary school. Unless their lifestyle changes at an early age, obese children usually become obese adults. Activity levels track into adulthood—active children become active adults, whereas inactive children become inactive adults (Telama et al., 2014).

Human wellness for children is most effectively enhanced when classroom teachers, physical education specialists, parents, administrators, and the entire community work together. Identifying wellness as a common goal for all school children makes physical education an integral part of the total school curriculum. Wellness instruction teaches concepts that help students develop and maintain an active lifestyle. Although knowledge and concepts are not the only pieces of the puzzle to ensuring lifelong activity, understanding the benefits of physical activity certainly assist youth, and later adults, in their behavior choices.

The Surgeon General's report on *Physical Activity and Health* (U.S. Department of Health and Human Services

(USDHHS, 1996) was the first national-level report to outline the health and wellness benefits of physical activity for all ages. This report was instrumental in spearheading more than 20 years of efforts to promote physical activity among all segments of the population.

Today's educators are increasingly focused on integrating physical activity into a healthful lifestyle. This focus is pushing physical educators to develop programs that teach more than fitness, skill activities, and games.

LEARNING AIDS

HOW AND WHY

1. Identify how various trends and policies have influenced physical education programs.
2. How does physical education fit into a school's curriculum?
3. How can the nationwide focus on health, wellness, and physical activity influence children's lives?
4. How do the SHAPE America national standards help teachers?
5. Why is it important to understand the essential components of physical education?

CONTENT REVIEW

1. Are physical education programs and physical education teachers necessary? Defend your answer and be sure to address key terms in the field.
2. Why is physical education a unique component of the total school curriculum?
3. Describe the evolution of physical education from the 19th century to today. Discuss the role of physical literacy in recent years.
4. What contributions have different pedagogical approaches made to the evolution of physical education?
5. How have federal mandates influenced physical education?
6. What are the content standards, and what role do they play in physical education?
7. What are the essential components of a quality physical education program, and what is the significance of each?

WEBSITES

Centers for Disease Control and Prevention, www.cdc.gov
President's Challenge Activities, www.presidentschallenge.org/challenge/activities.shtml
Public Law 94-142, www2.ed.gov/about/offices/list/osers/idea35/history/index_pg10.html
SHAPE America, www. shapeamerica.org

SUGGESTED READINGS

2018 Physical Activity Guidelines Advisory Committee. (2018). *2018 Physical Activity Guidelines Advisory Committee Scientific Report*. Washington, DC: U.S. Department of Health and Human Services.

Centers for Disease Control and Prevention. (2016). *Results from the School Health and Policies and Practices Study*. Atlanta, GA: Author.

Sallis, J.F., & Mckenzie, T.L. (1991). Physical education's role in public health. *Research Quarterly for Exercise and Sport, 62,* 124–137.

Sallis, J.F., Mckenzie, T.L., Beets, M.W., Beighle, A., Erwin, H., & Lee. S. (2012). Physical education's role in public health: Steps forward and backward over 20 years and HOPE for the future. *Research Quarterly for Sport and Exercise and Sport, 83*(2), 125–135.

Sallis, J.F., Mckenzie, T.L, Kolody, B., Lewis, M., Marshall, S., & Rosengard, P. (1999). Effects of health-related physical education on academic achievement: Project SPARK. *Research Quarterly for Exercise and Sport, 70,* 127–134.

Sporting Goods Manufacturers Association. (2000). *Fitness and sports newsletter.*

U.S. Department of Health and Human Services. (2010). *The association between school-based physical activity, including physical education, and academic performance.* Atlanta, GA: U.S. Department of Health and Human Services, Centers for Disease Control and Prevention, National Center for Chronic Disease Prevention and Health Promotion.

REFERENCES

Active Living Research. (2012). *Increasing physical activity through recess. A research brief.* San Diego, CA: Robert Wood Johnson – Active Living Research.

Anderson, R.E., Crespo, C.J., Bartlett, S.J., Cheskin, S.J., & Pratt, M. (1998). Relationship of physical activity and television watching with body weight and level of fatness among children: Results from the Third National Health and Nutrition Examination Survey. *Journal of the American Medical Association, 279,* 938–942.

Bailey, D.A., Faulkner, R.A., & McKay, H.A. (1995). Growth, physical activity, and bone mineral acquisition. *Exercise and Sport Science Reviews, 24,* 233–266.

Bar-Or, O. (1995). Health benefits of physical activity during childhood and adolescence. *Physical Activity and Fitness Research Digest, 2*(4), 1–6.

Beighle, A., & Pangrazi, R.P. (2000). *The validity of six pedometers for measuring the physical activity of children.* Unpublished manuscript.

Common Sense Media. (2017). *The Common Sense Census: Media use by kids age zero to eight.* San Francisco, CA: Author.

Common Sense Media. (2015). *The Common Sense Census: Media use by tweens and teens.* San Francisco, CA: Author.

Corbin, C., & Lindsey, R. (2007) *Fitness for life* (5th ed.). Champaign, IL: Human Kinetics.

Dale, D., Corbin, C.B., & Cuddihy, T.F. (1998). Can conceptual physical education promote physically active life styles? *Pediatric Exercise Science, 10,* 97–109.

Dixon, J.B. (2010). The effect of obesity on health outcomes. *Molecular and Cellular Endocrinology, 316*(2), 104-108.

Hellison, D. (2010). *Teaching responsibility through physical activity* (3rd ed.). Champaign, IL: Human Kinetics.

Institute of Medicine. (2013). *Education the student body: Taking physical activity and physical education to school.* Washington, DC: Author.

Kraus, H., & Hirschland, R.P. (1954). Minimum muscular fitness tests in school children. *Research Quarterly, 25,* 178–187.

Ladwig, M.A., Vazou, S., & Ekkekakis, P. (2018). My memory is when I was done with it: PE memories are associated with adult sedentary behavior. *Translational Journal of ACSM.* doi:10.1249/TJX.0000000000067

Morgan, C.F., Pangrazi, R.P., &.Beighle, A. (2003). Using pedometers to promote physical activity in physical education. *Journal of Physical Education, Recreation & Dance, 74*(7), 33–38.

National Association for Sport and Physical Education. (2008). *Comprehensive school physical activity programs* [Position statement]. Reston, VA: Author.

National Center for Health Statistics. (2004). *Health, United States, 2004 with chartbook on trends in the health of Americans.* Hyattsville, MD: Centers for Disease Control and Prevention.

National Physical Activity Plan Alliance. (2018). *The 2018 United States Report Card on Physical Activity for Children and Youth.* Washington, DC: National Physical Activity Plan Alliance.

Ogden, C.L., Carrol, M.D., Fryar, C.D., & Flegal, K.M. (2015). Prevalence of obesity among adults and youth: United States, 2011-2014. *NCHS Data Brief, Nov,* 1-8.

Physical Activity Council. (2013). *2013 participation report: The Physical Activity Council's annual study tracking sports, fitness and recreation participation in the USA.* Washington, DC: Author.

Pate, R.R., Davis, M.G., Robinson, T.N., Stone, E.J., Mckenzie, T.L. & Young, J.C. (2006). Promoting physical activity in children and youth: A leadership role for schools: A scientific statement from the American Heart Association Council on Nutrition, Physical Activity, and Metabolism (Physical Activity Committee) in collaboration with the Councils on Cardiovascular Disease in the Young and Cardiovascular Nursing. *Circulation, 114* (11), 1214-1224.

Sallis, J.F. (1994). Influences on physical activity of children, adolescents, and adults or determinants of active living. *Physical Activity and Fitness Research Digest, 1*(7), 1–8.

SHAPE America. (2014). *National standards for K-12 physical education.* Reston, VA: Author.

SHAPE America. (2016). *2016 shape of the nation: Status of physical education in the USA.* Reston, VA: Author.

Telama, R., Yang, X., Laakso, L., & Viikari, J. (1997). Physical activity in childhood and adolescence as predictors of physical activity in young adulthood. *American Journal of Preventative Medicine, 13,* 317–323.

Telama, R., Yang, X., Leskinen, E., Kankaanpaa, A., Hirvensalo, M., Tammelin, T., Viikari, J., & Raitakari, O. (2014). *Medicine and Science in Sports and Exercise, 46*(5), 955–962.

Trudeau, F., Laurencelle, L., Tremblay, J., Rajic, M., & Shephard. R.J. (1998). A long-term follow-up of participants in the Trois-Rivieres semi-longitudinal study of growth and development. *Pediatric Exercise Science, 10,* 366–377.

Uijtdewilligen, L., Nauta, J., Singh, A.S., van Mechelen, W., Twisk, J.W.R., van der Horst, K., & Chinapaw, M.J.M. (2011). Determinants of physical activity and sedentary behaviour in young people: A review and quality synthesis of prospective studies. *British Journal of Sports Medicine, 45*(11), 896–905. doi:10.1136/bjsports-2011-090197

U.S. Department of Health and Human Services. (1996). *Physical activity and health: A report of the surgeon general.* Atlanta, GA: U.S. Department of Health and Human Services, Centers for Disease Control and Prevention, National Center for Chronic Disease Prevention and Health Promotion.

U.S. Department of Health and Human Services. (2010). *Healthy people 2020: National health promotion and disease objectives.* Washington, DC: U.S. Government Printing Office.

U.S. Department of Health and Human Services. (2014). *School health policies and practices study 2014.* Centers for Disease Control and Prevention, National Center for Health Statistics. Washington, DC.

U.S. Department of Health and Human Services. (2016). *School health policies and practices study 2016.* Centers for Disease Control and Prevention, National Center for Health Statistics. Washington, DC.

Whitehead, M. (2001). The concept of physical literacy. *European Journal of Physical Education, 6*(2), 127–138. doi:10.1080/1740898010060205

Growth and Development

A primary goal of physical education is to promote physical activity and good health for youth throughout their life span. Physical activity positively affects children's growth and development, including the brain; in fact, research supports the value of an active lifestyle for optimum growth and development. The incidence of certain health disorders, such as heart disease, is linked to a sedentary lifestyle. Lifetime involvement in physical activity often depends on early participation and the gratification gained from such participation. Developing motor skills at an early age provides the tools needed to be physically active throughout life. Guidelines for safely participating in physical activity, including resistance training, running, being active in heat, and fitness testing, are presented. This chapter provides the rationale and guidelines for safely implementing physical activity and promoting physical education.

Learning Objectives

▶ Describe the need for physical activities.
▶ Cite the stages of growth in children.
▶ Understand the relationship between physical activity and the development of muscular strength, endurance, and skeletal growth.
▶ Define aerobic capacity and discuss its relationship to health and physical activity.
▶ Discuss the role that organized youth sports should play in children's proper growth and development.
▶ Identify the guidelines necessary for children to exercise safely.
▶ Describe the proper approach to distance running and weight training for preadolescent children.

The growth and development of children is a fascinating topic and important for teachers to understand. Often learning experiences are created for youth without considering their development and growth. During their time in elementary schools, children grow physically and mentally at an extremely fast rate. With this come many changes that teachers must consider to provide a safe and appropriate environment for successful learning.

Physical Growth and Development

The growth patterns of children are generally controlled by their genetic makeup. Although an unhealthy environment can negatively affect proper growth and development, this section examines maturation patterns common to most children. Although all children follow a similar general growth pattern, each child's timing is unique. Some children are advanced physically for their chronological age, whereas others mature more slowly. Parents often ask how their child compares with other children who are the same age. Only when aberration from the norm is excessive is there cause for concern. This chapter will help you better understand children and their growth patterns. Teaching is easier if your techniques and expectations are aligned with the needs, interests, and developmental level of your students. If you have a concern about discipline, learning, or skill performance, come back to this chapter and refresh your understanding about the growth and development of the youth you are teaching.

Growth Patterns

Teachers and parents regularly monitor their children to see if they are maturing normally. One way to examine growth patterns is to look at a velocity curve (figure 2.1), which shows how much a child can be expected to grow from year to year. Children go through a rapid growth period from birth to age five. From age six to the onset of adolescence, growth slows. When physical growth is rapid, the ability to learn new motor skills generally decreases. Because the growth rate slows during the elementary school years, this time is an excellent window for children to learn motor skills.

During adolescence, children grow rapidly until they reach adulthood. In elementary school, boys are generally taller and heavier. Girls reach the adolescent growth spurt first, growing taller and heavier during sixth and seventh grade. This growth spurt is likely occurs because girls reach puberty earlier. In recent years, the average age when girls reach puberty has decreased. Research

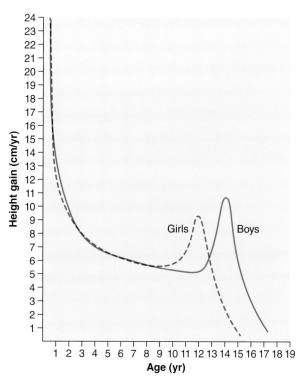

FIGURE 2.1 Growth velocity curve for height.

From J.M. Tanner et al. "Standards from Birth to Maturity for Height, Weight, Height Velocity, and Weight Velocity: British Children," 1965. *Archives of Disease in Childhood* Vol. 41: 454-471.

suggests that, in part, the increased rate of childhood obesity, specifically in girls, may lead to the earlier onset of puberty in girls (Wenyan, Qin, Deng, Chen, Liu, & Story, 2017). Boys quickly catch up and grow larger and stronger after puberty. The National Center for Health Statistics has developed growth charts based on a large sample of children (figures 2.2 and 2.3). These tables identify both stature (height) and weight percentiles for children ages 2 through 20. The tables make it possible to compare individual children to a large sample population.

Children are not little adults. Their proportions are dramatically different from those of adults. Young children have relatively short legs for their overall height. The trunk is longer in relation to the legs during early childhood. The ratio of leg length (standing height) to trunk length (sitting height) is similar for boys and girls through age 11. The head makes up one-fourth of the child's total length at birth but only about one-sixth at age 6. Figure 2.4 shows how body proportions change with growth. Because K–2 students have short legs in relation to their upper bodies, they are top heavy and fall more easily than adults do. For the same reason,

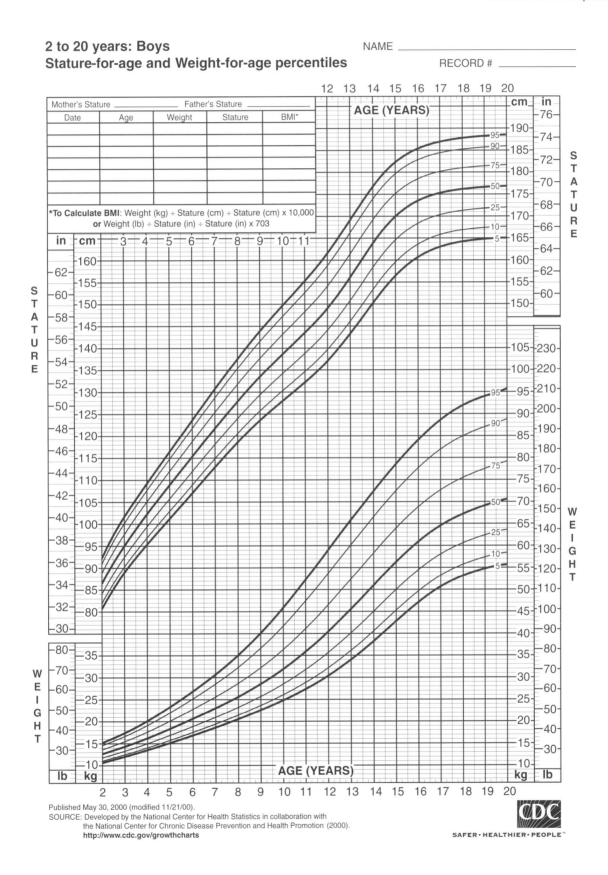

FIGURE 2.2 2 to 20 years: boys' stature-for-age and weight-for-age percentiles.

Developed by the National Center for Health Statistics in collaboration with the National Center for Chronic Disease Prevention and Health Promotion (2000).

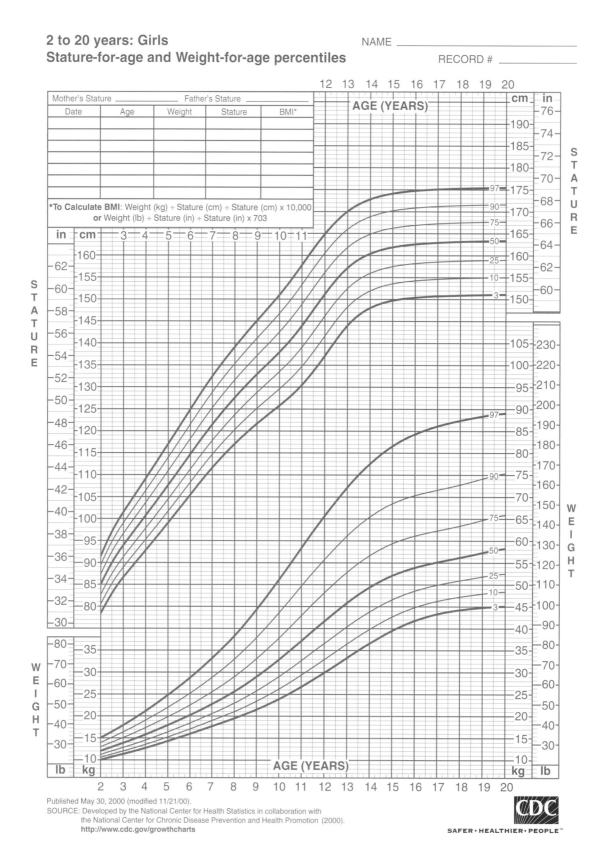

2 to 20 years: Girls
Stature-for-age and Weight-for-age percentiles

NAME _____

RECORD # _____

Published May 30, 2000 (modified 11/21/00).
SOURCE: Developed by the National Center for Health Statistics in collaboration with
the National Center for Chronic Disease Prevention and Health Promotion (2000).
http://www.cdc.gov/growthcharts

FIGURE 2.3 2 to 20 years: girls' stature-for-age and weight-for-age percentiles.

Developed by the National Center for Health Statistics in collaboration with the National Center for Chronic Disease Prevention and Health Promotion (2000).

they also struggle with activities such as push-ups and sit-ups. Their high center of gravity gradually lowers, giving children increased stability and balance.

Body Physique

A child's physique (somatotype) affects motor performance quality. Sheldon, Dupertuis, and McDermott (1954) developed the original scheme for somatotyping that is still used today. This scheme identifies three major physiques: *mesomorph*, *ectomorph*, and *endomorph*. Rating is assessed from standardized photographs on a seven-point scale, with one the least expression and seven the most expression of the specific component. Rating each component gives a total score that identifies an individual's somatotype. A similar system of classification for children (Petersen, 1967) is available for teachers interested in understanding children's physiques.

In general, children with a mesomorphic body type perform best in activities requiring strength, speed, and agility, such as most team sports. A *mesomorph* has a predominance of muscle and bone and is often labeled "muscled." An *ectomorph* is extremely thin, with a minimum of muscle development, and is characterized as "skinny." Ectomorphic children may be less proficient in activities requiring strength and power but are able to perform well in aerobic endurance activities such as jogging, cross country running, and track and field. An *endomorph* is soft and round, with an excessively protruding abdomen. Endomorphic children may perform poorly in many areas, including aerobic and anaerobic skill-oriented activities. Overweight children are generally at a disadvantage in all phases of physical performance. The point of thinking about somatotypes is to be more sensitive about how body type affects physical performance. Somatotype classification illustrates how dramatically children differ in physique and how physical education instruction must be modified to accommodate these inequities.

Skeletal Maturity

Physical maturity greatly affects a student's performance in physical education. *Maturity* is usually measured by comparing chronological age (i.e., age in days, months,

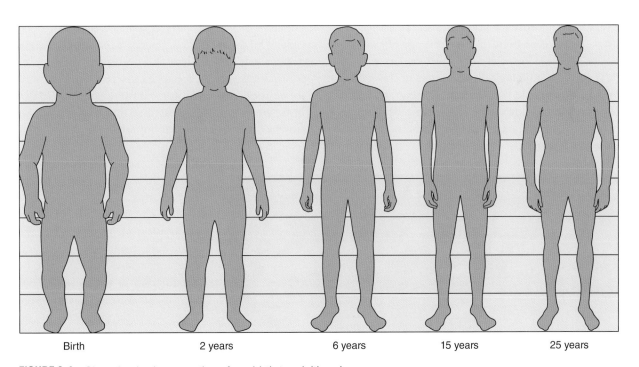

FIGURE 2.4 Changing body proportions from birth to adulthood.

Birth   2 years   6 years   15 years   25 years

TEACHING TIP

Offering instructional equity to meet the needs of all students takes effort. Should it be taught at a level where gifted students are challenged or at a level where less able students find success? If a choice must be made, the level should be adjusted to the needs of the less able students because this opportunity may be the only one they have to learn new skills. Keep in mind that gifted students have many opportunities to practice their skills outside of physical education, such as recreation leagues, youth sport teams, and private clubs. But few opportunities are available for student who lacks competency and confidence. Athletic programs are for elite performers. Equity for all students dictates that you make compromises in your instruction so that it integrates less talented students and helps them discover the joy of an active lifestyle.

and years) with skeletal age. Ossification (hardening) of the bones occurs in the centers of the bone shafts and at the ends of the long bones (growth plates). The rate of ossification accurately indicates a child's skeletal age. Skeletal age is a true measure of maturity that is identified by x-raying the wrist bones and comparing the development of the subject's bones with a set of standardized x-rays (Malina, Bouchard, & Bar-Or, 2004). A child whose chronological age exceeds her skeletal age is said to be a late (or slow) maturer. If a child's skeletal age exceeds her chronological age, on the other hand, she is labelled an early (or fast) maturer.

In a typical classroom, the skeletal age of students can vary greatly. Thus, a class of third graders who are all 8 years old chronologically can range in skeletal age from 5 to 11 years old (Krahenbuhl & Pangrazi, 1983). Therefore, some children who are 5-year-olds skeletally are trying to engage in activities with others who are as mature as 11-year-olds. This circumstance is reason for

concern when students engage in competitive activities because the more mature student may have a distinct advantage and the wide range of physical abilities may raise safety issues. Effective programs offer activities that are developmentally appropriate and matched to the maturity level of all students in the class.

Children of both sexes who mature early are generally heavier and taller for their age than average- or late-maturing students. Overweight children (endomorphs) are often more mature for their age than normal-weight children and carry more muscle and bone tissue. Overweight children, however, also carry a greater percentage of body weight as fat tissue (Malina, Bouchard, & Bar-Or, 2004), making them less efficient and decreasing their motor performance. Skeletal age appears to have limited influence on fundamental motor skills (Freitas et al., 2015). These two findings suggest that motor development follows a different course for boys than for girls (Gidley Larson et al., 2007). Furthermore, Malina (1978) found that late maturation is commonly associated with exceptional motor performance.

Physical education teachers often ask students to learn at the same rate, regardless of maturation level. This practice may be detrimental to the development of students who are maturing at a faster or slower rate. Students do not mature at the same rate and are not at similar levels of readiness to learn. Offering a wide spectrum of developmentally appropriate activities helps ensure that children will succeed regardless of their maturity.

Children the same age vary in size and maturity.

©Robert Pangrazi or Aaron Beighle

Muscular Development and Strength

In the elementary school years, muscular strength increases linearly with chronological age until adolescence, when a rapid increase in strength occurs (Malina, Bouchard, & Bar-Or, 2004). When differences in strength between the sexes are adjusted for height, there is no difference in lower-body strength from ages 7 through 17. When the same adjustment between the sexes is made for upper-body strength, however, boys have more strength in the upper extremities and trunk (Malina, Bouchard, & Bar-Or, 2004). Boys and girls can participate on somewhat even terms in activities demanding leg strength, particularly if their size and mass are similar. But in activities demanding arm or trunk strength, boys have an advantage, even if they are similar to the girls in height and mass. When pairing children for activities, do not partner students with those considerably taller and heavier (or more mature) and thus stronger.

Humans have a genetically determined number of muscle fibers. Muscles become larger when the size of each muscle fiber increases—that is, the size of the muscles is determined first by the number of fibers and second by their size. Musculature, therefore, is somewhat limited by genetics.

Skeletal muscle tissue contains both fast-contracting fibers (fast twitch—FT) and slow-contracting fibers (slow twitch—ST) (Saltin, 1973). The percentage of fast- versus slow-contracting fibers varies from muscle to muscle and among individuals. The percentage of each type of muscle fiber is determined during the first weeks of postnatal life (Dubowitz, 1970). Most people possess a 50–50 split; that is, half of the muscle fibers are FT and half are ST. A small percentage of people have a ratio of 60 to 40 (in either direction), and researchers have ver-

SPORTS AND SPECIALIZATION

As part of a quality physical education program, all students need to experience success. Research suggests that individuals who have a positive experience with physical activity as children will likely engage in physical activity for a lifetime, but no similar findings have been reported on the relationship between beginning participation in a sport at an early age and long-term ability as an all-star athlete. Specializing in one structured, competitive sport as a young child is a debatable topic. Participation in a variety of physical activities, including sports, results in several benefits physically, socially, and emotionally. A number of potential hazards, however, have been documented when a child is exposed to overtraining and devoting excessive time to one specific activity, particularly when the child is not allowed to make the decisions to partake in these activities. General well-being and sleep quality tend to decline if a young athlete is overtrained. These outcomes can be tracked in children using a variety of rating scales (i.e., Recovery-Stress Questionnaire for Athletes or Ratings of Perceived Exertion Scale) with the hope that adjustments can be made for young athletes before overtraining becomes an issue. Parents who devote excessive amounts of time and money toward one sport for their child tend to place much of their worth on the number of resources they invest in the sport. This outlook, in turn, may detract from the child's diversity of physical activities and relationship experiences.

With regard to physical development, overuse injuries often occur with repetitive movements for young children, which may lead to tendon or ligament damage, injuries to joints, and injuries to the spine, among others. Physical development and, ultimately, success in sports are enhanced by participation in a variety of sports teams and programs intermittently throughout the year. Youth who are exposed to a variety of informal games and activities are less prone to drop out of organized sports than those who specialize in one sport from an early age. Emotionally, burnout is likely to occur if a child feels he or she cannot meet the increasingly challenging expectations of the sport in which he or she is participating. Self-esteem, self-efficacy, and self-confidence are enhanced when youth are involved in multiple physical activities and sports.

The role of the physical educator in this matter is to provide a variety of developmentally appropriate physical activities and skill-based lessons for youngsters during physical education, to encourage coaches and parents to allow their children to try a number of different out-of-school sports and lessons, to promote adequate breaks for the children between practices and seasons, and to focus on the positive physical, social, and emotional outcomes children experience from engaging in a diverse array of physical activities.

ified that some people have an even more extreme ratio.

What is the significance of the variation in the ratio of muscle fiber type? ST fibers have a rich supply of blood and related energy mechanisms. These slow-contracting, fatigue-resistant muscle fibers are well suited to endurance (aerobic) activities (e.g., the mile run). In contrast, FT fibers are capable of bursts of intense activity but are subject to rapid fatigue. These fibers are well suited to activities demanding short-term speed and power (e.g., pull-ups, standing long jump, and shuttle run).

Surprisingly, elementary-age children who do best in activities requiring FT fibers also do best in distance running (Krahenbuhl & Pangrazi, 1983). Muscle fiber metabolic specialization does not occur until adolescence, when testosterone increases at the onset of puberty. This finding provides a strong argument for keeping all children involved in a variety of physical activities throughout the elementary years. Children who do poorly in elementary school may do quite well during and after adolescence when a higher percentage of ST fibers will aid in aerobic activities or a higher percentage of FT fibers will help them in team sports that demand quickness and strength. Designing a program that incorporates activities using a range of physical attributes (i.e., endurance, balance, and flexibility) is essential.

Relative Strength and Motor Performance

Strength is an important factor in performing motor skills. Specifically, strength in relation to body size is an important factor. Higher levels of strength in relation to body size are thought predict which students are most capable of performing motor skills. Thus, higher levels of excess body fat are likely to affect skill performance, making overweight children less proficient at performing motor skills. Deadweight negatively affects motor performance because it reduces relative strength. Okley, Booth, and Chey (2004) suggested a significant relationship between weight status and performance on locomotor skills. Overweight children may be stronger than normal-weight children in absolute terms but are less strong when strength is adjusted for body weight. This lack of strength in relationship to body size causes overweight children to find a strength-related task (such as a push-up or pull-up) much more difficult than the task would seem to normal-weight children. The need for varied and personalized workloads is important to ensure that all children find success in strength-related activities. Strength is an important part of a balanced fitness program and offers students a better opportunity for success in various motor development activities.

Aerobic Capacity: Children Are Not Little Adults

Maximal aerobic power is a person's maximum ability to use oxygen in the body for metabolic purposes. Oxygen uptake, all other factors being equal, determines the quality of endurance-oriented performance. Maximal aerobic power is closely related to lean body mass, which helps explain the differences in performance between boys and girls. When maximum oxygen uptake is adjusted per kilogram of body weight, it shows little change for boys (no increase) and a gradual decrease for girls (Rowland, 2005) as they reach maturity. The decrease in females is due to an increase in body fat and a decrease in lean body mass. When maximal oxygen uptake is not adjusted for body weight, it increases in similar amounts on a yearly basis for both boys and girls through age 12, although boys have higher values as early as age 5.

Four out of five adults interested in increasing their endurance-based athletic performance will improve in response to physical training (Timmons, 2011). Will similar training increase children's aerobic performance? A meta-analysis by Payne and Morrow (1993) analyzed 28 studies dealing with the effect of exercise on aerobic performance in children. The results showed that training caused little, if any, increase in aerobic power in prepubescent children. A slight improvement sometimes occurs in running performance, and Rowland (2005) postulates that it may occur because they become more

TEACHING TIP

Children who excel in physical activities in elementary school are often small, lean, and have high strength in relationship to their body size. The chance is good that these youngsters may not excel as they age, but they often receive more attention than students who are larger in stature and weight. These larger students have a good possibility of maturing into excellent athletes. But without reinforcement and encouragement when young, they may become discouraged and drop out of sport and recreational activities. The moral of the story is to encourage all students and share the praise.

efficient mechanically or their anaerobic metabolism improves. Another theory is that young children may be active enough that training effects are negligible (Corbin & Pangrazi, 1992; Rowland, 2005).

Even though children demonstrate a relatively high oxygen uptake, they do not perform up to this level because they run and walk inefficiently. An 8-year-old running at 180 meters per minute is operating at 90% of maximal aerobic power, whereas a 16-year-old running at the same rate is operating at only 75% of maximum. For that reason, young children are less capable than adolescents and adults at competing over long distances, although they can maintain a slow speed for long distances (Rowland, 2005).

Children demonstrate a rapid recovery rate after strenuous exercise. Teachers should use a child's rapid recovery rate to full advantage. Exercise bouts of about 30 seconds should be interspersed with recovery periods of stretching and nonlocomotor movements. Interval training is particularly effective because it allows children to exercise aerobically and then recover. Furthermore, research suggests that intermittent activity provided by interval training releases the optimal amount of growth hormone (Bailey et al., 1995).

Overweight Children and Physical Performance

Overweight children seldom perform physical activities on par with leaner children, in part because of the greater metabolic cost of the overweight child's exercise. Overweight children require higher oxygen uptake to perform a given task. That is, an overweight student needs more energy and oxygen to jog or walk at the same speed as a leaner peer. Overweight children must perform at a higher percentage of their maximal oxygen uptake. Usually, their maximal uptake values are lower than those of lean children. Therefore, overweight children have less reserve capacity and require greater exertion to complete a task as compared with normal-weight youth.

These reactions contribute to the common perception among teachers that overweight children do not like to run. Teachers must understand that asking overweight children to run as far and as fast as normal-weight children is unrealistic. Overweight children need adjusted workloads. Evidence suggests that children's perceptions of their intensity levels are often accurate (Utter, Robertson, Nieman, & Kang, 2002), so if a student perceives an activity to be difficult, it is likely difficult for him or her.

Base student workloads on *time* rather than *distance*. Lean and efficient runners can be expected to move

TEACHING TIP

Most children dislike long endurance activities. Watch students at play during recess and you will see few, if any, long endurance activities. Instead, many students will be running and chasing each other. They chase and flee for about 30 seconds and then stop and argue about whether they were tagged or not. As soon as they recover, the argument is over and they take off on the run again. Take advantage of this intermittent activity when delivering fitness activities to your students.

farther than overweight students during a stipulated period. Children should not all be required to do the same workload. Expecting overweight children to perform workloads similar to those of lean, ectomorphic children is unreasonable. Exercise programs for overweight children should be designed to increase caloric expenditure rather than to improve cardiovascular fitness. The intensity of the activity should be secondary to the amount of time the student is performing some type of moderate activity.

Cognitive Growth and Development

Growth and development of children is not isolated to bones and muscles. Growth and development also occur in the brain. During this time the brain changes tremendously. With these changes in the brain structure come great development cognitively.

Brain Growth

The human brain is an amazing organ. Did you know the brain weighs about three pounds and is 60% fat? Or that the brain gets 20% of the blood and oxygen produced by your body? Or that the brain is made up of 100 billion neurons? Or the reason you cannot tickle yourself is that the brain can distinguish between your own touch and the touch of others? All these fun facts, and many more, are a product of the growth and development of a healthy brain.

The brain begins to grow and develop as soon as the third week of pregnancy and continues growing after the child is born. At the age of 6, the brain is approximately 90% of the 6 pounds (2.7 kg) it will be during adulthood. But during childhood and adolescence the brain changes structurally, which affects the function of the brain. During this time the brain forms and refines a network of connections that are usually biologically driven but enhanced by a child's experiences. As the brain matures it becomes more interconnected with networks that are critical in the development of memories and the ability to connect new learning to previous learning. During the late elementary years (9 to 12 years) the brain continues to mature and change with the long-term memory being formed. This change allows much of what is learned to be stored in one place.

Stages of Cognitive Development

A French psychologist named Jean Piaget first provided a theory that children develop cognitively in four stages: sensorimotor, preoperational, concrete operational, and formal operational. These stages typically coincide with spurts in brain growth.

- *Sensorimotor stage (birth to 2 years).* As the name suggests, during this stage children learn primarily through their senses and manipulating objects. Parents are encouraged to talk to, make faces at, smile at, and interact with their babies often to maximize brain development during this stage. In addition, babies are encouraged to hold objects, play with their feet, and manipulate items hanging from a crib to allow the development of sensory and motor skills.

- *Preoperational stage (2 to 7 years).* This stage is characterized by the development of memory and imagination. During this stage students enter kindergarten, and the stage ends around the second grade. Typically, education experiences during this time emphasize the development of memory and imagination. Think of early kindergarten experiences of learning letters, colors, and simple classroom procedures, and imagining what a book character might look like or do. Many students at this age are eager to learn and find joy in pretend play. During this stage children also develop the ability to understand symbolism and relative time such as past and future.

- *Concrete operational stage (7 to 11 years).* This period is a productive time for development as children begin noticing external events and become aware of the feelings of others. Students begin to understand empathy and the reason that experiences are happening. Up until this time, they are primarily aware only of their own feelings. With this stage they also begin to com-

prehend that not everyone has the same ideas, thoughts, beliefs, and feelings. This circumstance may result in conflict and an opportunity to teach students how to respect others and compromise. Said another way, they begin to understand that the world is not just about them.

- *Formal operational stage (11 years and older).* Children begin to be logical thinkers and problem solvers during this stage. These late elementary years open the doors for teachers to integrate higher level thinking to learn material and understand concepts better. They also begin see the world and can begin planning for the future rather than living in the moment. For educators, students can begin to understand how their behavior now may affect them or others in the future, which can be a potentially powerful time in the educational experience.

Educators need to understand these developmental stages as they consider the learning experiences they create for students. Of particular importance is ensuring that the expectations of teachers are consistent with the developmental stages. For instance, asking a kindergarten class to solve a problem using a cooperative activity in physical education may prove to be more than the class can handle given their current developmental stage. The result may be student behavior issues and teacher frustration.

Helping Children Find Success in Physical Activity

Most children participate in some type of physical activity from dance to youth sports to hiking. Often youth programs are led by people who have limited knowledge about the physical and psychological development of children. Therefore, teachers need to step forward and share their knowledge and serve as experts when needed. Much of this knowledge will be put into use when teachers create lessons and put into action when they teach lessons.

Optimize Skill Learning

Helping students effectively learn motor skills requires knowledge of basic principles of motor learning. Teaching motor skills is not a difficult task when teachers understand the basic tenets of proper performance techniques.

Understand Developmental Patterns

The learning and development of motor skills varies widely among children of similar chronological age. The *sequence* of skill development in children is similar, however, and progresses in an orderly way. Three development patterns typify the growth of primary-grade children:

1. *Development generally proceeds from head to foot (cephalocaudal).* That is, coordination and the management of body parts occur in the upper body before being observed in the lower body. For example, children develop throwing skills before kicking competency.

2. *Development occurs, moreover, from inside to outside (proximodistal).* That is, children control their arms before controlling their hands. They can reach for objects before they can grasp them. Because the fingers direct much of the finer points of throwing and catching, most children are unable to perform these skills with accuracy until they are 10 or 11 years old.

3. *Development proceeds, finally, from general to specific.* That is, gross motor movements are learned before fine motor coordination and refined movement patterns. As children learn motor skills, nonproductive movement is gradually eliminated. When learners begin to eliminate wasteful, tense movements and can reproduce a smooth, consistent performance, motor learning is occurring. Instruction for young children therefore emphasizes large-muscle movements such as skipping and hopping. Likewise, children who are learning motor skills should be allowed to do so without worrying about accuracy or making mistakes.

Motivating Youth

Motivation is a component of youth physical activity and physical education that is often overlooked, so a fundamental understanding of motivation is important for physical education teachers and others working with youth. The motivational research consists of many theories and much has been written to apply those theories to physical education for youth (Alderman, Beighle, & Pangrazi, 2006; Kilpatrick, Hebert, & Jacobsen, 2002). To simplify these multiple perspectives and assist teachers in applying the many dimensions of motivation in physical activity settings, the acronym PRAISE was created (Pangrazi, Beighle, & Sidman, 2007). Figure 2.5

TEACHING TIP

Scrutinize activities you feel uncomfortable teaching to ensure that all safety procedures have been implemented. If in doubt, discuss the activities with experienced teachers and administrators. Ask for tips that will assure a successful experience for you and the students.

details the components of PRAISE. This acronym and table are not exhaustive representations of all motivational concepts for physical educators, but these concepts will assist teachers in promoting intrinsic motivation during physical education and for physical activity outside the gymnasium. This list can be an easy reference for anyone working with youth to analyze whether they are appropriately motivating youth. Research is clear that intrinsically motivated students are more likely to perceive their physical activity experiences positively (Weiss, 2000), which in turn increases the likelihood that these students will be physically active for a lifetime. In summary, by applying the dimensions of PRAISE, teachers are motivating children during physical education and laying the foundation for motivating youth for a lifetime of physical activity through an effective physical education learning environment.

Understand Motivation and Competition

Pressure to perform can positively or negatively affect motor performance. This external motivation to learn is also called *arousal* in motor learning terminology (Schmidt & Wrisberg, 2008). In an elementary school setting, arousal might be termed "getting kids too worked up." They get so excited that they fail to think about how to perform the skills because everything is so exciting and new. The key to proper motivation is to find the amount of encouragement that is just right. With too little motivation, children are not interested in learning. With too much, they may feel stress and anxiety, resulting in a decrease in motor performance. The more complex a skill is, the more likely excessive stimulation is to disrupt learning. If a skill is simple, on the other hand, such as skipping or running, children can tolerate a greater amount of prompting without showing a reduction in skill performance. Optimally, children should be stimulated to a level at which they are excited yet confident about participating.

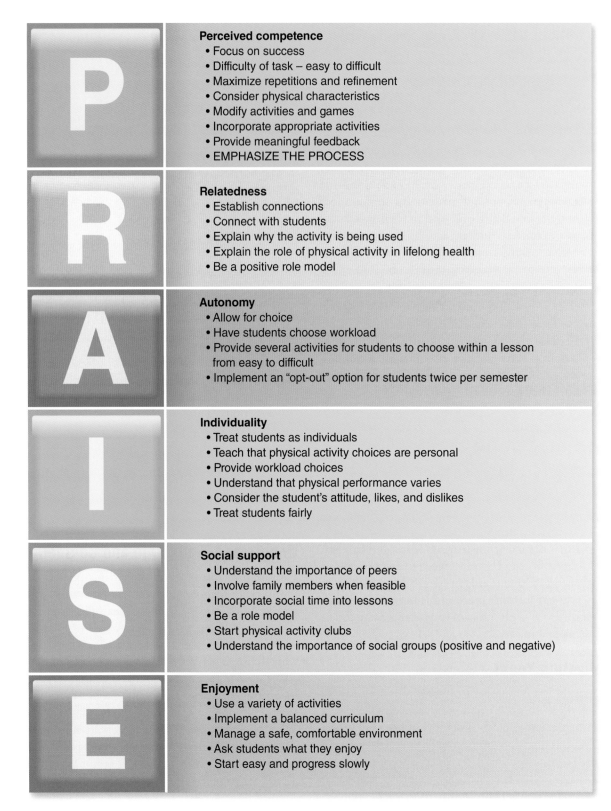

Perceived competence
- Focus on success
- Difficulty of task – easy to difficult
- Maximize repetitions and refinement
- Consider physical characteristics
- Modify activities and games
- Incorporate appropriate activities
- Provide meaningful feedback
- EMPHASIZE THE PROCESS

Relatedness
- Establish connections
- Connect with students
- Explain why the activity is being used
- Explain the role of physical activity in lifelong health
- Be a positive role model

Autonomy
- Allow for choice
- Have students choose workload
- Provide several activities for students to choose within a lesson from easy to difficult
- Implement an "opt-out" option for students twice per semester

Individuality
- Treat students as individuals
- Teach that physical activity choices are personal
- Provide workload choices
- Understand that physical performance varies
- Consider the student's attitude, likes, and dislikes
- Treat students fairly

Social support
- Understand the importance of peers
- Involve family members when feasible
- Incorporate social time into lessons
- Be a role model
- Start physical activity clubs
- Understand the importance of social groups (positive and negative)

Enjoyment
- Use a variety of activities
- Implement a balanced curriculum
- Manage a safe, comfortable environment
- Ask students what they enjoy
- Start easy and progress slowly

FIGURE 2.5   PRAISE.

Adapted by permission from R.P. Pangrazi, A. Beighle, and C.L. Sidman, *Pedometer Power: Using Pedometers in School and Community,* 2nd ed. (Champaign, IL: Human Kinetics, 2007), 54.

Competition affects children's arousal level. When competition is introduced in the early stages of skill learning, stress and anxiety reduce a child's ability to learn. If competition is introduced after a skill has been overlearned, on the other hand, it can improve performance. Because most elementary school children have not overlearned skills, teachers should avoid highly competitive situations when teaching skills. Suppose, for example, that the objective is to practice basketball dribbling. The teacher places students in squads for a relay that requires them to dribble to the opposite end of the gym and return. The first squad finished is the winner. The result is that instead of concentrating on their dribbling technique, students are more concerned about winning the relay. Thinking only about winning overstimulates them, so they run as quickly as possible. They dribble poorly (if at all), the balls fly out of control, and the teacher is dismayed by the result. Unfortunately, their excessive desire to win destroyed the learning experience because they had not yet overlearned dribbling.

Offer Meaningful Skill Feedback

Feedback is important in the teaching process because it affects what is to be learned, what should be avoided, and how the performance can be modified. Skill feedback is any information related to a movement performance. Skill feedback can be intrinsic or extrinsic. *Intrinsic feedback* is internal, inherent in the performance of a skill, and travels through the senses, such as vision, hearing, touch, and smell. *Extrinsic feedback* is external and comes from an outside source, such as a teacher, video, stopwatch, and so on. Most elementary school students use extrinsic feedback (usually verbal) received from a teacher, peer, or parent. Skill feedback should be encouraging (or constructive), given frequently, delivered publicly so that all students benefit, and based on performance or (preferably) effort.

In physical education, most of the feedback given to students should be about how the skill was performed (proper technique) rather than the outcome of the skill. This concept is referred to as knowledge of performance. When using process-focused feedback, how the learner performs the skill is the point of emphasis. For example, a teacher can say, "I like the way you kept your chin tucked," or "That's the way to step toward the target with your left foot." This type of feedback emphasizes the process of performing the skill. In the preceding example, "chin tucked" is a teaching cue. By using an instructional cue, the teacher gives the child feedback on a technical point of the skill. The skill outcome is of little concern.

Instructionally, performance cues provide information about how to improve. Typically, students can succeed in performing at least one part of the skill (e.g., stepping in opposition), which leads to a greater feeling of success and enjoyment. Cues should be short, content-filled, and concise. They should tell the child specifically what was correct or incorrect (e.g., "That was excellent body rotation"). Concentrate on cue at a time to avoid confusing the child. Imagine a young student who is told, "Step with the left foot, rotate the trunk, lead with the elbow, and snap the wrist on your next throw!" Excessive feedback confuses anyone trying to learn a new skill. If corrective feedback is needed, start by saying something positive about the performance to get the child's attention. For example, the teacher might say, "Andre, you sure are working hard today. Next time, try stepping with the other foot and see how that works."

With young children, focus feedback on learning the skill rather than on the skill outcome. A child who makes a basket (outcome measure) might believe that it doesn't matter how the ball is shot as long as it goes in. This approach is how bad habits become ingrained. Incorrect practice results in skills learned incorrectly. More emphasis is placed on skill outcomes as students enter the competitive world of athletics.

TECH TIP

"Don't believe everything you read on the Internet." —Abraham Lincoln

This quote is a great one when considering the use of social media and the Internet for any reason but especially research topics associated with physical education, growth and development, fitness, and youth. The Internet is full of great information and false information. Content presented online must be resourced, validated, and researched to determine its accuracy and utility. Care must be taken to ensure that what you read is truthful. Ask yourself questions such as these: Is the author credible and qualified? Can I contact the author to ask questions? Does the content make sense? Is it too good to be true? Do other sources say the same thing? Can I contact others to determine the credibility of the information? By answering these relatively simple questions, teachers can determine the reliability of the source.

Finally, allow students time to internalize instructional cues and practice without direct observation. Teachers often tell a child something and at the same time ask him or her to "try it again." The child will likely make the same mistake because he or she did not have time to concentrate on the feedback. Offer specific and positive instructional cues and then move to another child. Follow up on your feedback later so that the child has a chance to think, internalize the feedback, and modify future practice attempts.

Design Effective Practice Sessions

Practice is a key part of learning motor skills. Students, however, must receive more than the opportunity to practice; they must practice while focusing on quality of movement (practicing correctly). This section explains how to design practice sessions that optimize motor skill learning.

Practice Rather Than Perfect

Emphasis in practice sessions should be on correct skill performance rather than the skill outcome. Students who think that the teacher is interested only in the skill outcome will be less willing to concentrate on proper skill technique. When teaching skills to elementary school children, emphasize proper technique and encourage experimentation. Placing emphasis on making the most attempts decreases a student's willingness to take risks and try new ways of performing a skill. In most cases, elementary school children should focus on technique because they are learning new motor patterns. If evaluating a skill outcome is necessary, tell students why the outcome is important and say, "We will practice doing our best today."

Decide on Whole Versus Part Practice

Skills can be taught by the whole or part method. The whole method involves learning the entire skill or activity in one dose. The part method breaks down a skill into a series of parts and then combines the parts into the whole skill. For example, in a rhythmic activity, each section of a dance is taught and then the parts are put together. Deciding whether to use the whole or part method depends on the complexity and organization of the skills to be learned. *Complexity* refers to the number of serial skills or components in a task. *Organization* defines how the parts are related to each other. *High organization* means the parts of the skill are closely related to each other, making separation difficult. An example of a highly organized and complex skill is throwing, which is difficult to practice without going through the complete motion. A low-organized skill is a basic locomotor movement in which footwork and arm movements can be rehearsed separately. Generally, if the skills are high in complexity but low in organization, they can be taught in parts. If complexity is low but organization high, on the other hand, the skills must be taught as a whole. A final consideration is the duration of the skill. If the skill is of short duration, such as throwing, batting, or kicking, trying to teach the skill in parts is probably counterproductive. Imagine trying to slow down kicking and teach it part by part. The performer would never develop proper pattern and timing.

Determine the Length and Distribution of Practice Sessions

Short practice sessions usually produce more efficient learning than do longer sessions, which may cause both physical and mental fatigue (boredom). The challenge is to offer as many repetitions as possible within short practice sessions. Keep motivation high by varying approaches, challenges, and activities to develop the same skill. For example, using different variations of beanbag activities helps maintain motivation but still focuses on tossing and catching skills.

Another way to determine the length of practice sessions is to examine the tasks being practiced. If a skill causes physical fatigue, demands intense concentration, or has the potential to become tedious, keep practice sessions short and frequent and provide adequate rest between intervals. Stop practice when students become bored or tired, and play a game until they are ready to learn again.

Practice sessions that are spread out over many days are usually more effective than sessions crowded into a short time. The combination of practice and review is effective for children because activities can be taught in a short unit and practiced in review sessions throughout the year. In the initial stages of skill learning, scheduling practice sessions in this way is particularly important. Later, when success in skill performance increases motivational levels, teachers can lengthen individual practice sessions.

Use Random Practice Techniques

The two ways to organize the practice and learning of activities are blocked practice and random practice. In *blocked practice*, students complete all the trials of one task before moving on to the next task. Blocked practice is effective during the early stages of skill practice because learners are practicing the same skill repeatedly, in which case they improve rapidly. This rapid improvement leads to motivated learners. A drawback to blocked practice is that it makes learners believe they are more skilled than they actually are. When students try the skill in a natural setting, performance levels may decrease, thus discouraging some children.

In *random practice*, the order of learning tasks is mixed, and the same task is *not* practiced twice in succession. Goode and Magill (1986) were the first to demonstrate that random practice was the most effective approach to use when learning skills. Blocked practice gave the best results during the acquisition phase of skill learning, but students who learned a skill using random practice demonstrated much higher retention. Random practice results in better retention because students are mentally generating solutions. When they practice the same task repeatedly, children stop thinking about how to solve the problem. In contrast, students using random practice forget the motor program used and must consciously recreate the solution to be successful, thus minimizing boredom.

Offer Variable Practice Experiences

Motor tasks are usually grouped into classes of tasks. For example, throwing involves a collection or class of movements. Throwing a ball in a sport can be done in many different ways; the ball can travel at different speeds, different trajectories, and varying distances. Even though throwing tasks are all different, the variations have basic similarities. Movements in a class usually involve the same body parts and have similar rhythms but can be performed with many variations. These differences create the need for variable practice in a variable setting.

Practice sessions for motor skills should include a variety of skills in a movement class, with a variety of situations and parameters in which the skill is performed, so that students can respond to various novel situations. If a skill to be learned involves one fixed way of performing it (i.e., a "closed" skill), such as placekicking a football or striking a ball off a batting tee, variability is much less important. Most skills are "open," however, and responses are somewhat unpredictable, which makes variability in practice the usual mode of operation (e.g., catching or batting a ball moving at different speeds and from different angles).

Teach Skills in Proper Progression

Skill progression involves moving the learning process through ordered steps from the least challenging to the most challenging facets of an activity. Most motor skills can be ordered in an approximate hierarchy from simple to complex. Instructional progression includes reviewing previously learned steps before proceeding to new material and learning prerequisite skills before trying more difficult activities.

Allow Students to Learn All Skills and Play All Positions

If the best athletes are always assigned to positions that require the most skill, the gifted will excel at the other children's expense. Because all children deserve an equal opportunity to learn sports skills, teachers must ensure that all children play all positions and receive similar amounts of practice time. The amount of positive feedback needs to be similar for all children, regardless of their current skill level. Children participate in activities that offer them fun and reinforcement; they can easily become discouraged if they receive little encouragement and praise while trying to learn new skills and positions.

Helping children learn all skills and play all positions at an early age gives them equal opportunity to be successful. Is the student a pitcher or a right fielder, a lineman or a quarterback? Often, these questions are answered for students when teachers make judgments and force them to play (or exclude them from playing) a certain position. Many times, such judgments are based on the student's maturity rather than his or her actual skill level. In a classic study by Hale (1956), skeletally mature athletes were found playing in the skilled positions in the Little League World Series. Chronologically, all players were 11, with a skeletal age range similar to that described earlier. The most mature were pitchers and catchers, and the least mature played at less skilled positions. The skeletally mature children received more opportunities to throw at an early age (through pitching and catching in games and in practice), so these children had many more opportunities to become better throwers. In contrast, children who are immature are often assigned to play right field and receive limited throwing or catching opportunities. Because these less mature children receive much less throwing practice, they are unlikely ever to close the skill gap and develop adequate skill competency.

Ensure Success for All Students

The willingness to try new experiences and participate in activities is driven by how people feel about their ability level—their *perceived competence*. Perceived competence becomes more specific as students mature. Young students (ages four to seven years) think they are competent at everything. As they become older (i.e., third or fourth grade), they realize that other students are better in some areas. Less able students receive less feedback, and expectations of them remain low. If these students are not given the chance to succeed in class, then they develop low perceived competence about their ability to perform physical skills. This "learned helplessness" (Harter, 1978) eventually leads students to dislike and drop out of physical education and future sport and recreational activities. They are quite likely to leave school with negative feelings about continuing with an active lifestyle. Dropping out of physical education commonly occurs in middle school and high school, when students are able to make a choice. The process of feeling incompetent, however, likely began in elementary school.

Assume That All Students Have the Ability to Achieve

Even though teachers and parents make early judgments about children's potential, identifying outstanding athletes in the elementary school years is difficult. In a study by Clarke (1968), athletes identified as outstanding in elementary school were seldom outstanding in middle school, and predictions based on elementary school performance were correct only 25% of the time. The wise choice would be to treat all children as if they have the potential to succeed. The goal of a physical education program is not to develop athletes but to help all students develop their physical skills within the limits of their potential. The program must not allow the athletically gifted to excel at the expense of less talented children.

Starting Young Does Not Ensure Excellence

There is no evidence that having a child participate in sports at a young age will make him or her an outstanding athlete. In fact, many professional athletes did not play their sport of excellence until they were in high school. Many parents and coaches push to have children start competing in a sport at an early age. Participating children seem gifted compared with nonparticipants because they have been practicing the necessary skills for four or five years. As a result, "early starters" look advanced compared with children who have not been in an organized program. In most cases, however, a child who is genetically gifted quickly catches up to and surpasses the "early superstar" in one to three years. As Shephard (1984) states, "Any advantage that is gained from very prolonged training probably lies in the area of skill perfection rather than in a fuller realization of physical potential."

Children who participate in documented and competitive programs for many years may burn out at an early age. A documented program is one that offers extrinsic rewards (e.g., trophies, published league standings, ribbons, and excessive parental involvement). Evidence shows that extrinsic motivation (competition to win) may ultimately decrease intrinsic motivation, particularly in children aged seven and older. Researchers (Whitehead & Corbin, 1991) found that younger children (age five) perceived a reward as a bonus, thus adding to the joy of performing a throwing motor task. This effect decreased with age; by age nine, children saw the reward as a bribe and intrinsic motivation was undermined. There is no substitute for allowing young

Treat all children as if they have the potential to succeed.

FatCamera/E+/Getty Ima

children to participate in physical activity for the sheer enjoyment and excitement involved in moving and interacting with peers.

If starting children early can create early burnout, why do parents feel pressured to force their child into a sport program? Some parents constantly compare their children to other children. They see other children participating and practicing sport skills in an organized setting. They worry that their children will be unable to catch up if they are not involved in a similar program immediately. Although this is untrue, parents need reassurance, and they need facts. Physical educators can help parents find programs that minimize pressure and focus on developing skills. A key is to find programs that allow the child to participate regardless of ability—and to have fun while playing. Children consider having fun and improving their skills to be much more important than winning. In fact, numerous surveys of young participants reveal that having fun tops the list while winning is much lower on the rating list. Unfortunately, some programs become elitist and start eliminating and "cutting" less gifted players. This approach is difficult to justify at the elementary or middle school level. All children should have the opportunity to participate if they choose to.

Another reason that parents start children at a young age is that children have free time. Parents have little time to teach new skills, so they want their children to have abundant free time for practice. Unfortunately, if the child shows promise, parents want to increase practice time "so all this talent is not lost." Parents need to be reminded that life includes more than athletic development and that many children have been maimed by stressing sports at the expense of their intellectual and social development. Participation in an activity should be self-selected and student driven rather than externally motivated. Similarly, withdrawal from an activity should be child controlled rather than externally controlled. Participants should not be forced out of the program because of cost, limitation of participants, or injury.

Safety Guidelines for Physical Activity

Moderation is the key to ensuring that children are safe and grow up enjoying physical activity. Two areas of concern for physical educators are (1) to avoid physical injury or harm and (2) to develop and maintain positive attitudes and feelings about movement. Moderate exercise, coupled with opportunities to participate in recreational activity, develops a lasting desire to move. Children can withstand a gradual increase in workload

TEACHING TIP

During an outdoor lesson in the heat, build time into your lesson plan for students to take small-group trips to a water fountain, or provide jugs of water and cups to keep students hydrated.

and are capable of workloads comparable to those of adults when the load is adjusted for height and size. Furthermore, the child's circulatory system is proportionally similar to an adult's and, thus, is not at a disadvantage during exercise. A final reminder is that although high-intensity activity does not physically hurt a student, it is not always appropriate. Remember that activity of any intensity or duration is worthwhile. Recent evidence shows that moderate-intensity activity offers the same benefits as high-intensity activity in terms of weight management and blood chemistry.

Exercise and Heat Stress

For years, research and medical policies have been based on the premise that children were not able to regulate their body temperature as well as adults in hot weather. Recently, a new policy statement was published by the American Academy of Pediatrics (2011) on climatic heat stress and exercising children and adolescents. This policy, based on a number of research studies, refutes previous thinking and advocates that children and adolescents are similar to adults in how they respond to heat stress. Recent studies compared adults and children exposed to equal relative intensity exercise workloads and environmental conditions while minimizing dehydration. This research indicated that youth do not have less effective thermoregulatory ability, insufficient cardiovascular capacity, or lower physical exertion tolerance compared with adults.

Factors that impact performance and exertional heat-illness risk in youth during physical activities are undue physical exertion, insufficient recovery between repeated exercise bouts, and inappropriate clothing and uniforms that retain heat. These findings place a responsibility on teachers to prepare students properly for activity (hydration and proper dress), modify the intensity of the activity, and offer students regular rest and hydration breaks. Another important point is that teachers must learn how to monitor their students closely for heat stress symptoms.

Even though children are more capable of exercising in hot weather than once thought, the following guidelines can help prevent problems in physical education classes.

- The intensity of activities that last 30 minutes or more should be reduced whenever relative humidity and air temperature are above critical levels. Figure 2.6 provides a heat index chart that can be used as a guideline when deciding whether humidity and heat levels are unsafe. As the chart suggests, in general the heat begins to feel uncomfortable for students at around 90 degrees Fahrenheit (32 degrees Celsius). Erring on the side of caution is always best when determining whether conditions are comfortable for outdoor play.

- When beginning an exercise program in warm weather, the intensity and duration of exercise should be restrained initially and then increased gradually over a period of 10 to 14 days to accomplish acclimation to the effects of heat.

- Before prolonged physical activity, participants should be fully hydrated. During the activity, time for periodic drinking (e.g., 10 to 15 ounces [300 to 450 ml] of water every 20 minutes) should be offered.

- Clothing should be lightweight and limited to one layer of absorbent material to facilitate evaporation of sweat and to expose as much skin as possible. Sweat-saturated garments should be replaced by dry ones. Rubberized sweat suits should never be used to produce weight loss.

- The following conditions place some students at a potentially high risk for heat stress: excessive weight, feverish state, cystic fibrosis, gastrointestinal infection, diabetes, type 2 diabetes, chronic heart failure, caloric malnutrition, anorexia nervosa, sweating insufficiency syndrome, and mental retardation.

One other issue related to participation in the heat is sun safety. Outdoor physical education classes present the risk of skin damage caused by the sun. In the United States, one in five people will develop skin cancer. Students are of particular concern because overexposure to the sun at a young age increases the risk of skin cancer throughout life. About 80% of a person's sun exposure occurs before age 18 (Stern, Weinstein, & Baker, 1986). Blistering sunburns during the school years significantly increase the risk of developing skin cancer later in life (American Academy of Pediatrics, 1999). Children should know the risks associated with sun exposure and learn how they can protect themselves. Schools should encourage or require students to wear long-sleeved clothes, hats, and sunglasses (these prevent cataracts from forming later in life) when physical education is scheduled outdoors during the hours 10:00 a.m. and 4:00 p.m.

Distance Running

How much and how far should children be allowed to run, particularly in a competitive or training setting? The answer is difficult to agree on because parents, teachers, and coaches seldom see the long-term effects of excessive running. Although the research is inconclusive so far

		Relative humidity (%)											
		40	45	50	55	60	65	70	75	80	85	90	95	100
Temperature (F)	80	80	80	81	82	82	82	83	84	84	85	86	86	87
	84	83	84	85	86	88	89	90	92	94	96	98	100	103
	90	91	93	95	97	100	103	106	109	113	117	122	127	132
	94	97	100	102	103	110	114	119	124	129	135			
	100	109	114	118	124	129	136							
	104	119	124	131	137									
	110	136												

☐ Comfortable for outdoor play   ☐ Caution   ☐ Danger

FIGURE 2.6 Heat index chart.

From Child Care Weather Watch, Iowa Department Public Health, Healthy Child Care Iowa. Produced through federal grant (mcj19t029 & mcj19kcc7) funds from The US Department of Health & Human Services, Health Resources & Services Administration, Maternal & Child Health Bureau. Heat index information if from the National Weather Service.

on acute running injuries resulting from training, the American Academy of Pediatrics (2009) recommends that any competitive running program involving young athletes should be supervised by a qualified adult. This supervisor should be trained in developing proper training schedules and qualified to educate runners and parents on issues related to running, including the effects of weather and hydration. Most important, as with any physical activity, the child must enjoy running, be free of injury, and have no fear of parental or peer pressure.

The International Athletics Association Federation (IAAF) Medical Committee states in part,

> The danger certainly exists that with over-intensive training, separation of the growth plates may occur in the pelvic region, the knee, or the ankle. While this could heal with rest, nevertheless definitive information is lacking whether in years to come harmful effects may result.

Because of these concerns, the committee asserts that training and competition for long-distance track and road-running events should be discouraged. Up to the age of 12, children should run no more than half a mile (800 m) in competition. Increases in this distance should be introduced gradually; 14-year-olds, for example, should run a maximum of nearly 2 miles (3,000 m) in competition.

Fitness Testing Considerations

Teachers often test children at the start of the school year in the 1-mile (1,500 m) run–walk or some other high-effort aerobic test. This practice should be discouraged because many children may not have the necessary conditioning to participate safely in these activities. In many regions, moreover, the start of the school year is hot and humid, adding to the stress placed on the cardiovascular system. A better approach is to test only at the end of the school year, after students have had the opportunity to be conditioned. If this is not possible, give students at least four to six weeks to condition themselves. Rowland (2005) recommends starting with a 1/8-mile (200 m) run–walk and gradually building to a 1-mile (1,500 m) run–walk over a four-week period. Or you could start with a 2-minute walk–jog and build up to a 10-minute time. A better alternative is to eliminate the mile run and substitute the PACER aerobic fitness test (part of FitnessGram). The PACER can be administered indoors and does not require running to exhaustion. As a cardiovascular fitness measure, the PACER is as accurate

as the mile run and produces much less emotional stress for participants.

Resistance Training

For many years, it was thought that resistance training for children was unsafe and not useful for making strength gains. Evidence contradicting these viewpoints continues to build (Lloyd et al., 2014). This paper provides numerous studies suggesting that prepubescent students can increase strength through resistance training, although prepubescent children gain strength differently from adolescents and adults. In preadolescent children, strength gains seem to occur from motor learning rather than muscle hypertrophy. Children develop more efficient motor patterns and recruit more muscle fibers (i.e., they learn the psychomotor movement pattern and thus become more efficient) but show no increase in muscle size (Malina, Bouchard, & Bar-Or, 2004).

Resistance training is used here to denote the use of barbells, dumbbells, rubber bands, medicine balls, body weight, or machines as resistance. This meaning is in sharp contrast to *weightlifting* and *power lifting*, which are competitive sports for determining maximum lifting ability. Many experts agree that resistance training is acceptable for children, but power lifting is highly undesirable and may be harmful. The American Academy of Pediatrics (AAP) (2008) recommends that preadolescents and adolescents avoid competitive weightlifting, power lifting, bodybuilding, and maximal lifts until they reach skeletal maturity. Roberts, Ciapponi, and Lytle (2008) give an excellent review of research and guidelines for resistance training in physical education classes for children and adolescents. A review of literature (Malina, 2006) found that resistance training has no effect on growth and height.

Safety and the prevention of injury are paramount considerations for those interested in weight training for children. When injuries are reported in a school setting, most have occurred because of inadequate supervision, lack of proper technique, or competitive lifting. The majority of weightlifting injuries occur on home equipment in unsupervised settings (AAP, 2008). A resistance-training program is only one component of a comprehensive fitness program for youth. To ensure an effective, safe program, teachers whose knowledge and expertise are limited should not conduct weightlifting programs for children.

Some experts worry about highly organized training programs that emphasize relative gains in strength. A better approach is to make the resistance-training program one component of a comprehensive fitness program for children. The National Strength and Conditioning Association (Faigenbaum et al., 2009) recommends that prepubescent athletes' training include a variety of activities, such as agility exercises (basketball, volleyball, tennis, and tumbling) and endurance training (distance running, bicycling, and swimming), with resistance training being one, relatively small component of the training program.

When children participate in a variety of physical activities (including resistance training) in elementary school physical education, they have little need for weightlifting. Children's strength can be enhanced in many ways besides using weights, thus circumventing any safety issues (see Roberts et al., 2008). Resistance training is acceptable on an individual basis, though, with parental approval in a club setting. If a resistance-training program for children is developed, it should be well researched and structured. Focus on the correct lifting technique, not the amount of weight lifted. Proper supervision and technique are key ingredients in a successful program. The following instructional guidelines are adapted from the National Strength and Conditioning Association position statement paper (Faigenbaum et al., 2009):

- All workouts should be closely supervised by qualified adults, and the exercise environment should be safe and free of hazards. Most experts believe that a ratio of 1 instructor per 10 students is necessary to assure proper supervision. The exercise area should be large enough so the exercises can be performed correctly.

- Each child should be ready to follow instructions and adhere to training guidelines. Encourage students to ask questions and praise them for participating.

- Students should warm up for 5 to 10 minutes before strength training.

- Students should start with one light set of 10 to 15 repetitions on several upper- and lower-body exercises. Starting with a light weight allows for appropriate adjustments. Starting weights will vary, depending on age, experience, and fitness level. Have students focus on learning the correct form and technique for each exercise.

- When students can perform the desired number of repetitions, increase the weight gradually (by about 1 to 3 pounds [.5 to 1.5 kg]) and perform fewer repetitions.

- Progression may also be achieved by gradually increasing the number of sets, exercises, and training sessions per week. Depending on individual needs and goals, one to three sets of 6 to 15 repetitions performed on two to three nonconsecutive days per week are recommended. Whatever type of training equipment children use, remember that sound teaching methodologies and competent supervision are critical to the safety, effectiveness, and enjoyment of the youth weight-training program.

- Students enjoy activities that are fun, so make them feel good about themselves.

CASE STUDY

Push-Ups and Sit-Ups: Create a Successful Experience

You are a first-year teacher excited to start the school year. You want to be enthusiastic and have your students respond in similar fashion. Your district mandates fitness testing, and you want your students to do well on the fitness test. The first class to arrive at your teaching area is a fifth grade. You take them through an introductory activity, and the class is excited and on task. The next component of your lesson is fitness development. You instruct your class to do push-ups and then sit-ups. They complain loudly. This reaction upsets you because you want them to enjoy fitness and these two exercises are on the fitness test. You wonder, "Will my administrator think I have failed if my students don't score well on these test items?" You move on to the next class thinking it will be much different. Unfortunately, they don't like any upper-body and abdominal exercises either. Now you are really discouraged. Think about the reaction and attitudes of these students. Discuss the following with your peers:

- What do you suppose has happened to make them feel so negative? Are these kids uniform in their reactions, or do some students actually like push-ups and sit-ups? Why do they like them? Are there some similar traits among students who dislike them?

- Do any developmental characteristics affect the success or failure of young children trying to do strength-related items? Should you expect all the children in your class to perform the same number of push-ups and sit-ups?

- How could you modify the exercises for students who are not capable of performing actual push-ups and sit-ups?

LEARNING AIDS

HOW AND WHY

1. How have your views of what is appropriate for children changed after reading this chapter?
2. Why is it important for physical education teachers to understand the growing child?
3. How might physical education be different for an overweight child as compared with a leaner peer?
4. Should children under nine years old be allowed to play youth sports?
5. Is fitness testing in elementary physical education appropriate? Defend your answer.

CONTENT REVIEW

1. What effect do growth patterns, physique, and skeletal maturity have on skill acquisition and performance?
2. What is the importance of physical activity for children?
3. What are the influences of muscular development and strength on physical activity for children?
4. Is training designed to improve aerobic capacity appropriate for children? Explain.
5. What can be done to maximize the youth sport experience for all children?
6. What is the relationship between physical activity and intelligence?
7. How do adults and children differ when it comes to exercising in the heat? Discuss guidelines for exercising students in the heat.

WEBSITES

Child development, www.cdc.gov/childdevelopment/
Childhood obesity, www.cdc.gov/obesity/childhood/index.html
Motivation, www.selfdeterminationtheory.org
Meaningful physical education, www.meaningfulpe.wordpress.com

SUGGESTED READINGS

Beni, C., Fletcher, T., & Ní Chróinín, D. (2017). Meaningful experiences in physical education and youth sport: A review of the literature. *Quest, 69*(3), 291–312.

Clarke, H.H. (1971). *Physical motor tests in the Medford boys' growth study*. Englewood Cliffs, NJ: Prentice-Hall.

Lee, J.M., Appugliese, D., Kaciroti, Corwyn, R.F., Bradley, R.H., & Lumeng, J.C. (2007). Weight status in young girls and the onset of puberty. *Pediatrics* 119, 624–630.

Ní Chróinín, D., Fletcher, T., & Griffin, C.A. (2018). Exploring pedagogies that promote meaningful participation in primary physical education. *Physical Education Matters, 13*(2), 70–73.

Rarick, L.G., & Dobbins, D.A. (1975). Basic components in the motor performances of children six to nine years of age. *Medicine and Science in Sports, 7*(2), 105–110.

Stiles, J., & Jernigan, T.L. (2010). The basics of brain development. *Neuropsychology Review, 20*(4), 327–348.

REFERENCES

Alderman, B., Beighle, A., & Pangrazi, R.P. (2006). Enhancing physical activity motivation in a quality physical education program. *Journal of Physical Education Recreation and Dance, 77*(2), 41–45, 51.

American Academy of Pediatrics. (2009). Clinical report: Overuse injuries, overtraining, and burnout in child and adolescent athletes. *Pediatrics, 119*(6), 1242–1245.

American Academy of Pediatrics. (2011). Policy statement: Climatic heat stress and the exercising child and adolescent. *Pediatrics, 128*(3), 741–747.

American Academy of Pediatrics. (2008). Policy statement: Strength training by children and adolescents. *Pediatrics, 121*(4), 835–840.

American Academy of Pediatrics. (1999). Ultraviolet light: A hazard to children. *Pediatrics, 104*, 328–333.

Bailey, R.C., Olson, J., Pepper, S.L., Porszasz, J., Barstow, T.J., & Cooper, D.M. (1995). The level and tempo of children's physical activities: An observational study. *Medicine and Science in Sport and Exercise, 27*(7). 1033–1041.

Clarke, H.H. (1968). Characteristics of the young athlete: A longitudinal look. *Kinesiology Review, 3*: 33–42.

Corbin, C.B., & Pangrazi, R.P. (1992). Are American children and youth fit? *Research Quarterly for Exercise and Sport, 63*(2), 96–106.

Dubowitz, V. (1970). Differentiation of fiber types in skeletal muscle. *Physiology and biochemistry of muscle as a food* (Vol. 2), ed. E.J. Briskey et al. Madison, WI: University of Wisconsin Press.

Faigenbaum, A.D., Kraemer, W.J., Blimkie, C.J., Jeffreys, I., Micheli, L.J., Nitka, M., & Rowland, T.W. (2009). Youth resistance training: Updated position statement from the National Strength and Conditioning Association. *Journal of Strength and Conditioning Research, 23*(5), S60–79.

Freitas, D.L., Lausen, B., Maia, J.A., Lefevre, J., Gouveia, E.R., Thomis, M., Antunes, A.M., Claessens, A.L., Beunen, G., & Malina, R.M. (2015). Skeletal maturation, fundamental motor skills and motor coordination in children 7–10 years. *Journal of Sport Sciences, 33*(9), 924–934.

Gidley Larson, J.C., Mostofsky, S.H., Goldberg, M.C., Cutting, L.E., Denckla, M.B., & Mahone, E.M. (2007). Effects of gender and age on motor exam in typically developing children. *Developmental Neuropsychology, 32*(1), 543–562.

Goode, S., & Magill, R.A. (1986). Contextual interference effects in learning three badminton serves. *Research Quarterly for Exercise and Sport, 57*(4), 308–314.

Hale, C. (1956). Physiological maturity of Little League baseball players. *Research Quarterly, 27*, 276–284.

Harter, S. (1978). Effectance motivation revisited. *Child Development*, 21, 34–64.

Kilpatrick, M., Hebert, E., & Jacobsen, D. (2002). Physical activity motivation: A practitioner's guide to self-determination theory. *Journal of Physical Education, Recreation, & Dance, 73*(4), 36–41.

Krahenbuhl, G.S., & Pangrazi, R.P. (1983). Characteristics associated with running performance in young boys. *Medicine and Science in Sports, 15*(6), 486–490.

Lloyd, R.S., Faigenbaum, A., Stone, M.H., Oliver, J.L., Jeffreys, L., Moody, J.A., . . . & Myer, G.D. (2014). Positions statement on youth resistance training: The 2014 international consensus. *British Journal of Sports Medicine, 48*, 498–505.

Malina, R.M. (1978) Physical growth and maturity characteristics of young athletes. *Children and youth in sport: A contemporary anthology*, ed. R.A. Magill et al. Champaign, IL: Human Kinetics.

Malina, R.M, Bouchard, C., & Bar-Or, O. (2004). *Growth, maturation, and physical activity* (2nd ed.). Champaign, IL: Human Kinetics.

Malina, R.M. (2006). Weight training in youth-growth, maturation, and safety: An evidence-based review. *Clinical Journal of Sports Medicine, 16*(6), 478–487.

Okley, A.D., Booth, M.L, & Chey, T. (2004). Relationships between body composition and fundamental movement skills among children and adolescents. *Research Quarterly for Exercise and Sport, 75*(3), 238–247.

Pangrazi, R.P., Beighle, A., & Sidman, C. (2007). *Pedometer power* (2nd ed.). Champaign, IL: Human Kinetics.

Payne, V.G., & Morrow Jr., J.R. (1993). Exercise and $\dot{V}O_2$ max in children: A meta-analysis. *Research Quarterly for Exercise and Sport, 64*(3), 305–313.

Petersen, G. (1967). *Atlas for somatotyping children.* Netherlands: Royal Vangorcum Ltd.

Roberts, S.O., Ciapponi, T., & Lytle, R. (2008). *Strength training for children and adolescents.* Reston, VA: National Association for Sport and Physical Education.

Rowland, T.W. (2005). *Children's exercise physiology.* Champaign, IL: Human Kinetics.

Saltin, B. (1973). Metabolic fundamentals of exercise. *Medicine and Science in Sports, 5*, 137–146.

Schmidt, R.A., & Wrisberg, C.A. (2008). Motor learning and performance: A situation-based learning approach (4th ed.). Champaign, IL: Human Kinetics.

Sheldon, W.H., Dupertuis, C.W., & McDermott, E. (1954). *Atlas of men: A guide for somatotyping the adult male at all ages.* New York, NY: Harper & Row.

Shephard, R.J. (1984). Physical activity and child health. *Sports Medicine, 1*, 205–233.

Utter, A.C., Robertson, R.J., Nieman, D.C., & Kang, J. (2002). Children's OMNI scale of perceived exertion: Walking/running evaluation. *Medicine and Science in Sports and Exercise, 34*(1), 139–144.

Stern, R.S., Weinstein, M.C., & Baker, S.G. (1986). Risk reduction for nonmelanoma skin cancer with childhood sunscreen use. *Archives Dermatology, 122*(5), 537–545.

Timmons, T. (2011). Variability in training-induced skeletal muscle adaptation. *Journal of Applied Physiology, 110*, 846–853.

Weiss, M. (2000). Motivation kids in physical activity. *President's Council on Physical Fitness and Sports Research Digest, 3*(11).

Wenyan, L., Qin, L., Deng, X., Chen, Y., Liu, S., & Story, M. (2017). Association between obesity and puberty timing. A systematic review and meta-analysis. *International Journal of Environmental Research in Public Health, 14*(10), 1266.

Whitehead, J.R., & Corbin, C.B. (1991). Effects of fitness test type, teacher, and gender on exercise intrinsic motivation and physical self-worth. *Journal of School Health, 61*, 11–16.

Youth Physical Activity and Schools

3

Physical education provides students the skills, knowledge, and attitude to be physically activity for a lifetime. We know that many benefits are associated with regular physical activity, and we know that youth are not physically active enough. Therefore, it makes sense that the field of physical education looks to associate itself with physical activity promotion. But getting youth active is not the only goal of physical education; as we have seen in previous chapters, physical education has standards and grade-level outcomes to address. Note that all SHAPE America standards and outcomes are specifically developed with an eye toward preparing youth for an active lifestyle. This chapter provides an introduction to the many benefits associated with regular engagement in physical activity for both adults and youth. Further, the effect that physical activity has on brain development, student learning, and ultimately academic performance is discussed. Current physical activity guidelines and data associated with youth physical activity levels as compared with these guidelines are presented. These data serve as a justification for efforts such as physical education designed to increase youth physical activity. An explanation of the difference between physical activity and physical education are provided. Finally, an in-depth look at a whole school approach called Comprehensive School Physical Activity Programs is provided.

Learning Objectives

▶ Discuss the health benefits of physical activity for adults and youth.

▶ Explain the role of physical activity on brain development, student learning, and academic performance.

▶ Argue for the need for physical activity promotion for youth based on current physical activity levels and United States guidelines for physical activity.

▶ Describe the relationship between physical education and physical activity as a public health outcome.

▶ Discuss each of the components of a Comprehensive School Physical Activity Program.

▶ Explain how you would go about starting a Comprehensive School Physical Activity Program at a school.

In 1996 the historic report from the Surgeon General of the United States on Physical Activity and Health (USDHHS, 1996) was released. Since that time, an incredible amount of research has accumulated demonstrating the vast array of benefits associated with regular physical activity. These benefits range from the most obvious physiological, to mental, to social, and cognitive. In fact, physical activity has been identified as a leading health indicator. This finding suggests that physical activity levels have a tremendous effect on a person's health status and quality of life.

Typically, when discussions of concerns around physical activity and health of our nation's youth occur, they are focused on physical fitness testing. The discussion often concludes that children are unfit, we need to test them, and then we must remedy the situation by getting them fit. This approach hasn't worked; the fitness of American youth hasn't improved in the last 60 years. Fitness is an important goal for all who choose to pursue it (and rarely does this group include elementary school children), so it is probably best saved for the late middle and high school years. A better goal for all people is to focus on physical activity and place emphasis on graduating students who are active throughout their lifespan. Many benefits result from participating regularly in physical activity, so pushing students toward an intense and demanding level of fitness is not necessary. All the benefits of high-intensity fitness activity also occur from less demanding, moderate physical activity. Bottom line: More students will be interested if physical activity is not too demanding and they can experience success and competence in a variety of activities such as walking, hiking, individual sports, and even moderate resistance training.

Benefits of Physical Activity

In adults, regular physical activity contributes to good health, prevents chronic illnesses, and improves quality of life. The 2018 Physical Activity Guidelines Advisory Committee Scientific Report (2018) provides a detailed summary of the many benefits of regular physical activity. Physical activity decreases the risk of many diseases and conditions. Increased physical activity can minimize weight gain or help adults maintain a healthy weight. Regular physical activity reduces the risk of many types of cancer, including bladder, breast, colon, kidney, lung, and stomach. Maintaining an active lifestyle can also help decrease the risk of developing chronic diseases such as hypertension, arthritis, and type 2 diabetes. If an individual already has one of these conditions, physical activity can decrease the risk of the condition worsening and help improve the person's quality of life.

Regular physical activity can also help improve an individual's quality of life and health by improving the quality of sleep, the length of time required to fall asleep, the ability to stay asleep, and the length of time slept. Possibly related to better sleep, even short bouts of physical activity can help a person's brain begin to process daily tasks and plan. Further, regular physical activity can improve a person's cognition, ability to learn, memory, mental processing, and attention. Decreased risk of depression and anxiety are also associated with regular physical activity. Lastly, physical activity increases an individual's energy, quality of life, and ability to engage in life with a positive attitude.

Although this list of benefits of physical activity is impressive for adults, what about physical activity benefits for youth? Ideally, active youth will become active adults and realize the health benefits described earlier. In fact, we know that physical activity tracks from youth into adulthood. Telama et al. (2014) found that a physically active lifestyle develops early in life and remains stable into adulthood. This finding supports the movement to promote physical activity early in life. But do youth gain health benefits from physical activity that they experience at a young age as well? Strong evidence indicates that regular physical activity is associated with healthy weight and bone health in youth (2018 Physical Activity Guidelines Advisory Committee, 2018). This finding is of particular importance given the known high levels of youth obesity; the most recent data suggest that 19% of youth are obese (CDC, 2016). Regular physical activity for youth is also associated with decreased risk of cardiometabolic diseases, such as type 2 diabetes, which are a leading cause of preventable death around the world (2018 Physical Activity Guidelines Advisory Committee, 2018). In sum, physical activity has many benefits for adults, physical activity tracks from youth into adulthood, and physical activity has health benefits for youth.

Physical Activity and the Brain

Another health benefit of physical activity is its effect on the brain's health and development. Like most parts of your body, the brain needs blood to provide the nourishment it needs to grow cells. Physical activity that increases your heart rate results in more blood with oxygen going to the brain. That blood also helps release hormones which, like oxygen, provide the brain with what it needs for good health. Physical activity also helps the brain's plasticity. Plasticity is the brain's ability to change throughout life. To ensure plasticity, cell connections are needed throughout the brain. Physical activity stimulates the release of growth factors or chemicals that affect the health of cells, supports the growth of new blood vessels to allow for more blood flow, and helps new brain cells survive after they are created. Regular physical activity can also result in growth in the hippocampus, the part of the brain responsible for emotion, memory, breathing, heartbeat, and digestion. It is also believed that physically active people have more volume in the prefrontal and medial temporal cortexes, the parts of the brain that control thinking and memory. A more in-depth examination of the relationship between physical activity and the brain can be found in Ratey's book *Spark: The Revolutionary New Science of Exercise and the Brain* (2008).

Physical Activity and Academic Performance

Because physical activity affects the health and development of the brain, it would make sense that physical activity also helps with the brain's function, particularly cognition. Cognition is the mental process of gaining knowledge through thinking, experiencing, and sensing. As you might expect, cognition is of particular importance for youth in schools. Further, Basch (2010) identified several causal pathways to student learning that are tied to physical activity. Specifically, student attentiveness and on-task behavior are positively associated with student physical activity (Mahar et al., 2006; Pellegrini, Huberty, & Jones, 1995; CDC, 2010). These studies suggest that students who engage in physical activity during the school day are better able to focus, are less fidgety, and demonstrate fewer off-task behaviors. If you talk to most teachers, they will say that lack of focus and off-task behaviors are major barriers to student learning.

Before further discussion on academic performance and physical activity, it is important to discuss some literature examining physical fitness and academic performance. Many of these studies are correlative studies that examine the relationship between these variables. They are not cause-and-effect studies, so we cannot profess to others that fitness guarantees an improvement in academic achievement. But these relationship studies do offer an indication that those who are more active, fit, or involved in physical education perform better academically. The point to remember is that relationship studies work in both directions. For example, are students who excel academically highly fit, or are students who are highly fit great students? Such questions cannot be answered with correlation studies, but this type of research evidence does lend credence to the theory that

both domains are important. "Healthy mind, healthy body" is right on the mark.

The Centers for Disease Control and Prevention (2010) published an excellent synopsis of 50 relationship studies that were reported in 43 articles. The studies resulted in a total of 251 associations between physical activity and academic performance. Included in the measures of academic performance were academic achievement, academic behavior, and cognitive skills and attitudes. The associations were classified as positive, not significant, or negative. More than half (51.5%) of the associations were positive, 48% were not significant, and only 1.5% were negative. Fourteen of the studies related to increasing the amount time students spent in physical education. Eleven of the 14 studies found one or more positive associations between physical education and indicators of academic achievement. The other 3 studies did not find significant associations. The relationship between extracurricular physical activity and academic achievement was also examined in 19 studies. These activities were organized through the school but conducted outside the regular school day. All of the studies found one or more positive associations between extracurricular activity and academic performance. This offers evidence that physical activity can enhance academic achievement including grades and standardized test scores. As discussed earlier, increased activity results in increased energy, better concentration, and even improved classroom behavior. In fact, given this strong evidence, one could argue that physical activity is a leading learning indicator for youth.

A more recent publication by the Centers for Disease Control and Prevention (2014) titled *Health and Academic Achievement* contains a synopsis of over 60 studies. The following points of evidence were listed.

- Students who are physically active have better grades, cognitive performance, and classroom behaviors.

- Higher physical activity and physical fitness levels are associated with improved cognitive performance.

- More participation in physical education is associated with better grades.

- The document offers a listing of the studies as well as talking points that can used to share with administrators, teachers, and parents.

One of the concerns of teachers and administrators is that increased time for physical education takes away time from learning, which lowers academic performance. A study that tackled this concern was the Trois Rivieres regional experiment (Shephard, 1984). The study provides a well-conceived design for increased physical education programming. Even though students received more time for physical education (and less for academics), their academic performance did not decrease. Additionally, a follow-up study of participants in the Trois Rivieres study 20 years later suggested that students who had more physical education time in school were more likely to be active later in life (Trudeau, Laurencelle, Trembley, Rajic, & Shephard, 1998). Administrators need to be informed about this study, particularly today, when many schools have a back-to-basics emphasis. This emphasis usually means "back to the classroom," without physical education, recess, or the arts. A lack of concern for the body, our "home to the brain," is detrimental to total development of students. No priority in life is higher than physical well-being.

A final word is that physical education makes unique contributions to the total school curriculum: motor skill development, understanding and maintaining physical fitness, and learning how to live an active lifestyle. Considering that these outcomes for the physical well-being of youth cannot be developed elsewhere in the school curriculum, physical educators should work hard to sell their program on these merits. Physical educators can justify inclusion of the program on the basis of its unique contributions. The public has shown support for a physical education program if it aids, nurtures, and shows concern for the physical development of all students.

Current Physical Activity Recommendations

Any behavior that provides the multitude of benefits that physical activity does is obviously a behavior we want youth to engage in. But how much? Just how much physical activity do students need to experience these benefits. Do they need to run for an hour? Have recess daily? Participate in sports? Or just get outside and play?

Since 1996, several organizations have developed a variety of guidelines all aimed at providing youth with a target for physical activity each day. The most recent set, referred to as the Youth Physical Activity Recommendations (2018 Physical Activity Guidelines Advisory Committee, 2018), recommends the following:

- It is important to provide young people opportunities and encouragement to participate in physical activities that are appropriate for their age, that are enjoyable, and that offer variety.
- Children and adolescents ages 6 through 17 years should do 60 minutes (1 hour) or more of moderate to vigorous physical activity (MVPA) daily:

  » **Aerobic:** Most of the 60 minutes or more per day should be either moderate- or vigorous-intensity aerobic physical activity and should include vigorous-intensity physical activity on at least 3 days a week.

  » **Muscle-strengthening:** As part of their 60 minutes or more of daily physical activity, children and adolescents should include muscle-strengthening physical activity on at least 3 days a week.

  » **Bone-strengthening:** As part of their 60 minutes or more of daily physical activity, children and adolescents should include bone-strengthening physical activity on at least 3 days a week. Examples of these types of activities include walking, running, jumping, and hiking.

These guidelines suggest that youth should engage in a variety of physical activities that they enjoy. These activities are typically age appropriate and developmentally appropriate. Note that the guidelines are not intended to have every child reach a specific goal every day. They are exactly what they say they are—guidelines. Schools, parents, teachers, and caregivers can use them as a guideline for how much activity children need to get the health benefits. Some days may be less active than others, but in general, 60 minutes or more of age-appropriate, enjoyable physical activity is a good guideline. The guidelines can also be used in advocacy efforts to support youth getting more opportunities for physical activity, especially if they are in sedentary environment (e.g., sitting all day at school with no recess, classroom physical activity, or physical education).

The Physical Activity Pyramid (figure 3.1) is a model designed to help students understand the physical activity guidelines. This prescription model for good health helps students understand how much and what type of activity they need. The activity pyramid, a visual approach to activity prescription, is useful because people are sometimes confused by scientific reports about the amount of physical activity needed for health and fitness benefits. The Physical Activity Pyramid helps students understand the different types of activity that are required for good health and total body fitness. The pyramid is divided into six categories and four levels that illustrate the benefits of each activity type. Activities with broad general health and wellness benefits for many people are at the base of the pyramid.

A secondary basis for the location of activities in the pyramid is their frequency. As the level increases, the frequency of participation decreases. Activities at level 1 should be performed daily; those at levels 2 and 3 can be performed fewer days per week; and inactivity (level 4) should be limited on all days of the week with the exception of rest.

The Physical Activity Pyramid is an excellent teaching tool. Place a poster version of the pyramid in the teaching area and refer to it during lessons. For example, while students do flexibility exercises, point to that section on the pyramid and remind them what level 3 activities are and how often they should be done. Use the pyramid (placed by the exit door) as a quick review before students leave class. When students are familiar with the pyramid, quiz them verbally on the levels of various activities or ask them to do an activity from a specific level. For example, during the fitness part of the lesson, ask students to do a level 3 activity. Quickly scan the room to check that all students are doing a level 3 activity.

Level 1: Lifestyle Physical Activities

Lifestyle activity is at the base of the pyramid because scientific evidence indicates that inactive people who begin regular exercise have the most to gain. Furthermore, those who are only occasionally active can

TEACHING TIP

Don't say it once! Say it over and over! Physical educators often feel marginalized because their subject matter isn't appreciated. Appreciating an area outside academics is difficult for those who don't know much about it. Be a strong advocate for quality physical education. You are responsible for telling teachers and administrators all the benefits they receive from a quality physical education program. Although you may be reluctant to "blow your own horn," how else will others learn about your program? Tell your staff on a regular basis about the benefits of quality physical education. Public relations is everything!

benefit by meeting the standards for lifestyle activity suggested in level 1 of the pyramid. Benefits at this level are wide ranging and include a reduced risk of diseases, such as heart disease, diabetes, and cancer. The extra calories expended in doing these activities are also useful in controlling body fat and reducing the risk of

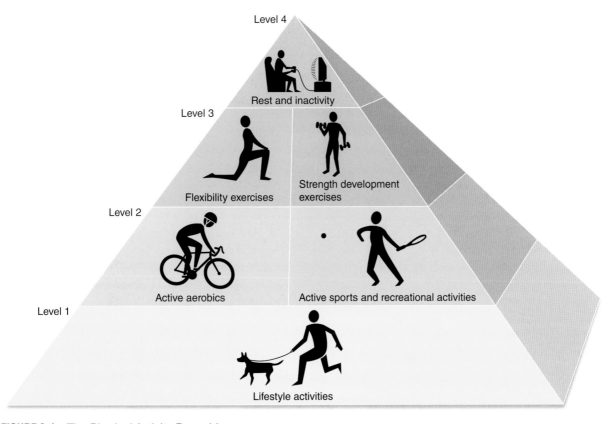

FIGURE 3.1 The Physical Activity Pyramid.

obesity. Wellness benefits include increased functional capacity and improved quality of life. Physical inactivity accounts for roughly 8.7% of U.S. health care expenditures, or approximately $117 billion per year. Adults who are physically active spend nearly $1,500 less per year on health care than inactive adults do (Carlson et al., 2015).

Typically, the greatest portion of accumulated minutes of physical activity for elementary school children comes from lifestyle activities. Lifestyle activities for this age include active play and games involving the large muscles. Climbing, tumbling, and other activities that require lifting the body or relocating the body in space are desirable activities when they can be done safely. Activities are typically intermittent rather than continuous. These activities normally involve few rules and little formal organization. Lifestyle activities such as walking to school and helping with chores at home are also appropriate.

Level 2: Active Aerobics, Sports, and Recreational Activity

Level 2 of the pyramid includes active aerobics, sports, and recreational activities, which implies that these are MVPA in nature and should be done for 60 minutes daily. Active aerobics are performed at a pace at which the body can supply enough oxygen to meet the demands of the activity. Examples of popular MVPA activities are jogging, brisk walking, moderate to vigorous swimming, and biking. Participation in some aerobic activities is appropriate as long as children are not expected to participate in them continuously for a long time. More appropriate are intermittent aerobic activities like recreational swimming, family walking, or aerobic activities in the lifestyle activity category (i.e., walking or bicycling to school or in the neighborhood).

Active sports and recreational activities are also included at level 2 of the Physical Activity Pyramid. Some examples of active sports are basketball, tennis, soccer, and hiking. Like active aerobics, this type of activity is typically more vigorous than lifestyle physical activity. Sports often involve vigorous bursts of activity with brief rest periods. Though they are often not truly aerobic, they can have many of the same benefits as aerobic activities if they are done without long rest periods.

When young children choose to be involved, sports must be modified to suit their developmental level. In general, children at Developmental Levels I and II should not spend an excessive amount of time in organized sports. Their focus should be on learning basic skills used in sports and other recreational activities, such as catching, throwing, walking, jumping, running, and striking objects.

Developmental Level III students are often involved in active and organized sports, so physical education teachers can devote more class time to such activities. Lead-up games and skill development are necessary to make the activities suitable for this age. Emphasizing sports conditioning is unnecessary for this age group; most of the time spent in this type of activity is dedicated to skill learning and playing games rather than conditioning. Encourage age-appropriate recreational activities with a lifetime emphasis or those that can be done with family and friends.

Level 3: Flexibility and Strength Development Exercises

Flexibility and strength development exercises are included at level 3 of the pyramid. Flexibility is the ability to use joints through a full range of motion as a result of having long muscles and elastic connective tissues. Flexibility activities should be done as part of the 60 minutes or more of activity three days a week. There are, no doubt, some activities from levels 1 and 2 of the pyramid that help build flexibility to some extent. Still, developing this part of fitness requires doing special flexibility exercises that involve stretching the muscles and using the joints through their full range of normal motion.

Teaching stretching exercises is important for illustrating the value of flexibility. Active play activities, such as tumbling and climbing, are encouraged for flexibility development. Children at Developmental Level III should spend more time learning and performing structured flexibility exercises. Children have more flexibility than adults, so the goal is to learn exercises they can use to maintain this trait throughout life even though they are currently flexible. What teachers teach, students will value, and maintaining flexibility is important.

Pyramid level 3 also includes exercises and physical activities performed specifically to increase strength (the amount of weight a person can lift) and muscular endurance (the ability to persist in muscular effort). Activities at lower levels of the pyramid may help develop these parts of muscle fitness, but even active people need to build and maintain strength and muscular endurance. Participation in strength exercises as part of a physical education class or a regular family fitness program is appropriate for students. Modified fitness activities are an excellent way to help children learn exercises in a positive and successful manner. Formal resistance training is usually not recommended, particularly in a group setting.

Upper-grade students should participate in strength development activities that require them to move and lift their body weight. Active play and games that require muscle overload are desirable for these students. Exercises using body weight are appropriate when teachers offer alternative exercises, so that all children can succeed. Place emphasis on strength development activities that allow them to do their best but do not require them to compare themselves with peers. The goal of all fitness activities taught in elementary school should be to offer a positive experience that makes students want to be fit for a lifetime. Failure or comparison to others seldom serves as a motivator to become fit as an adult. Children of this age can develop modest gains in strength and muscular endurance using resistance training. Because of safety concerns, however, other activities are generally better suited the physical education setting.

Level 4: Rest and Inactivity

At the top of the pyramid are rest and inactivity. Adequate sleep is absolutely necessary for good health because it allows the body to regenerate. The real issue is inactivity less is more. Sedentary behavior causes an increase in hypokinetic diseases such as heart disease and diabetes. Children need some private time to be involved in play of types other than group activities using the large muscles. Sedentary activities such as classroom learning also have benefits. Even so, the Physical Activity Pyramid is designed to provide information about the benefits of regular physical activity. Sedentary living is not typical of healthy children and should be discouraged as a lifestyle. Long periods of inactivity during the day should be limited in the school setting by incorporating activity breaks and recess. Youth who sit all day in the classroom and then go home and watch television or play video games are not getting the activity they need for good health.

Current Youth Physical Activity

We know the health benefits of physical activity and we know how much physical activity is recommended to garner these benefits. But how physically active are youth? Specifically, how physically active are elementary age children? If we want children to be active and we want to help them get more active, it would be nice to know just how active they are right now. That knowledge

TEACHING TIP

Help students understand that balance and moderation should guide their lifestyle physical activity. Too often, teachers choose only to teach fitness activities in which they excel. A teacher who is a distance runner may believe that everybody should run long distances. If weightlifting is the teacher's thing, she or he may want students to focus on strength. Lifestyle physical activity should have a balance to it, and the Physical Activity Pyramid shows how many types of activities can be beneficial, such as aerobics, recreation, and strength training. The "no pain, no gain" philosophy is not useful for lifestyle activity. All activity is beneficial regardless of intensity, and the experience doesn't have to be painful. For most people, moderate to vigorous activity is the foundation of lifelong activity. Balance and moderation help prevent boredom and burnout.

allows us to know if we are making improvements or if we need to change what we are doing.

Troiano and colleagues (2008) used a sample of 309 boys and 288 girls from across the United States to conduct the most recent national study on the physical activity levels of children. They found that 49.0% of the boys and 34.7% of the girls (42% combined) attained enough physical activity to meet the physical activity recommendation of 60 or more minutes per day. Therefore, more than half of the boys in the study and 65% of the girls are not getting enough physical activity. Another study examined children's compliance with getting 60 or more minutes of physical activity per day with children from 12 countries. Children from China, India, and the United States had the fewest number of students meeting the guidelines. Finland, the United Kingdom, and Colombia had the most students meeting the guidelines. Similarly, another study suggests that students in the United States are far less active than their peers in Australia and Finland (Vincent, Pangrazi, Raustorp, Tomson, & Cuddihy, 2003). The finding that youth in the United States are not meeting physical activity guidelines and are far less active than their peers in other countries not only documents an alarming trend but also sounds a rallying cry for efforts to promote health-enhancing, age-appropriate physical activity for all youth.

Moderate to Vigorous Physical Activity (MVPA)

Experts roughly agree on what constitutes light, moderate, and vigorous physical activity. Metabolic equivalent of tasks (METs) (resting metabolic rate) are used to quantify activity. One MET equals calories expended at rest (resting metabolism). Two METs indicates activity that is twice as intense. Three METs requires three times as much energy and so on. Activities of three METs or less are considered light activities. Examples are strolling (slow walking), slow stationary cycling, stretching, golfing with a motorized cart, fishing (sitting), bowling, vacuuming, and riding a mower (Ainsworth et al., 2011). Activity that expends four to six times the energy expended at rest (four to six METs) is considered moderate in nature. Examples of activity at this level include brisk walking, racquet sports, and lawn mowing with a power mower.

The activity guidelines do not discourage or downplay the value of vigorous activity; in fact, it is encouraged. Activities done at seven METs or higher are considered vigorous in nature. They include very brisk walking, walking uphill, jogging, relatively fast cycling, active involvement in many sports, lawn mowing with a hand mower, and doing exercise routines such as aerobic dance.

For years, people believed that aerobic activity must be performed in one long continuous bout to be beneficial. More recent evidence shows that activity can be beneficial even if accumulated in several shorter bouts throughout the day. For example, 15 minutes of walking and 15 minutes of aerobic dance done at different times of the day, or three 10-minute intervals of continuous cycling done throughout the day, meet the physical activity prescription. Expending calories in activities that equal 60 minutes of moderate to vigorous effort (walking briskly) each day (1,000 to 2,000 kcal per week) achieves health benefits similar to performance-related fitness training. The lifestyle activity prescription for children (table 3.1) covers a broad range of moderate to vigorous activities, including those that students can do as part of work or normal daily routines as well as during free time. Lifestyle activity recommendations are measured in frequency, intensity, and time, but they are not a physical fitness prescription, which requires high-intensity activity (training-zone heart rates). Although they do not require intense physical activity, lifestyle activities have health benefits. Many people remain sedentary or stop exercising because they believe that only vigorous, high-intensity exercise is beneficial. The new recommendations make it easier for less active students to see the value in participating in moderate activity. Teach students that all activity counts the more the better.

Physical Education and Physical Activity Promotion

With a focus on physical activity promotion, physical education is linked to public health. The field of public health includes many professionals working to improve and protect the health of people and the communities

 TECH TIP

We are learning new information about youth physical activity and have new data related to youth physical activity levels available daily. Online learning through webinars, videos, and podcasts is also an excellent source of professional development and way for teachers to garner new information. Webinars are typically lecture-style sessions offered online on a specific date and time. They are usually accessible after that time as well through a website. The advantage to live attendance is the opportunity to interact with the presenter through a question and answer session following the presentation. Various organizations provide webinars that cover a variety of topics and are usually free or relatively inexpensive. Webinars offer flexibility for teachers and allow them to select webinars that interest them. Some websites and organizations offer conferences online. For physical educators this is a bit of a change because we are used to traveling to a conference and engaging in physical activity sessions just as our students do in physical education. Online conferences, however, allow teachers to obtain a considerable amount of professional development in a short time all while never leaving their home or office. Like a typical conference, online conferences provide a variety of sessions during one or several days. Participants log in and select the session, and the rest is similar to a webinar. When the conference is live, attendees can interact with the presenter, ask questions, and hear or read the questions of others. Many organizations make these sessions available after the conference as well for those who can't attend.

TABLE 3.1 Lifestyle Activity Prescription for Children

Frequency	Daily, with frequent activity sessions (three or more) per day
Intensity	Moderate to vigorous activity: Alternating bouts of vigorous activity with rest periods as needed, or moderate continuous activity such as walking or riding a bike to school. Examples of activity include walking, playing running games, doing chores at home, and climbing stairs.
Time	Duration of activity necessary to expend more than 6 to 8 kcal/kg/day. Equal to calories expended in 60 minutes or more of active play or moderate sustained activity, which may be distributed over three or more activity sessions.

where they live. With all the health benefits of physical activity described earlier, one of the charges of public health is physical activity promotion. Therefore, a public health perspective for physical education is warranted. Education and public health working together to promote physical activity makes sense. In fact, some physical educators have been pushing for a public health approach to physical education for nearly 30 (Sallis & McKenzie, 1991). In this perspective, physical education has two goals: (1) preparing students for lifelong physical activity and (2) maximizing physical activity during physical education lessons. This second goal has led to the recommendation that students engage in physical activity for at least 50% of lesson time. That is, if children are in physical education for 30 minutes, they should at least be moving for 15 minutes. Although attaining this goal seems easy, research suggests most youth are active for only 38% of physical education lessons (Fairclough & Stratton, 2006). This finding suggests the progress toward the second goal of a public health approach to physical education is lacking.

Although the implementation of this approach has been slow, the field is making progress toward realizing this focus (Sallis et al., 2012). For instance, many public health groups and organizations such as the Institutes of Medicine and the Centers for Disease Control and Prevention advocate for physical education and include physical education in their recommendations for increasing youth physical activity. Research examining the effect of physical education on youth physical activity levels has increased. Federal and state level grants are now offered to support the implementation and enhancement of physical education programs. Physical education is now recognized as part of a well-rounded education as a part of the Every Student Succeeds Act discussed in chapter 1. Some of the resistance has been a fear that physical education would work solely to get students active during physical education, such as by making students run for the entire class to get them more activity. Although activity promotion during physical education lessons is advocated, it is not the sole focus of quality lessons.

TEACHING TIP

Getting students to learn to move at an MVPA pace is a good idea. MVPA is typically the minimum intensity level needed to maximize health benefits. Teach students how many steps per minute they need to take to attain MVPA. Because the pyramid equates an MVPA walk to a brisk walk, have students walk with swinging arms and an increased pace for one minute while counting their steps. In most cases, the number will range from 80 to 150 steps per minute, depending on the size and condition of the student. A reminder: Walking as fast as possible is not the goal; MVPA activity can be done for long periods without having to stop for aerobic recovery. After students find how many steps per minute equates to a brisk walk, they can monitor themselves.

Cornerstones of Our Profession

In most educations systems, the vast majority of financial and personnel resources are directed toward academic outcomes. Certainly, that focus is to be expected, and we cannot argue the importance of the academic side of education. But ponder what happens if students are well-educated but not healthy. Without health, students are obviously not able to learn, and today there is increased concern about creating an academic setting that is active and healthy. The physical educator is the only teacher in the building who is focused on promoting activity and good health for all students. A quality physical education program offers many benefits to students and teachers with the intent of assuring that the healthy mind and healthy body premise is met.

Physical education is defined in many ways, but the three cornerstones of the profession are always (1) physical activity, (2) physical fitness, and (3) skill development (figure 3.2). They are not listed in any particular order here, although we might argue that physical activity is the most important because a large majority of adults make walking their exercise of choice. A look at how these three parts work together to create a quality physical education program that graduates physically literate students is in order.

Students arrive at school with different needs and personal goals. In the primary grades, most students want to enjoy moderate to vigorous activity and don't even consider the need for personal fitness. With maturity, students recognize that some are more skilled or more fit than others. Skill performance and fitness are influenced by genetics, and even the untrained eye can readily see that some students are more gifted than others. To meet the needs of all students, students will learn to be active, understand and practice fitness, and learn a wide variety of motor skills. This text presents physical activity, skill development, and physical fitness in separate chapters even though the threads of each component are integrated into a quality program.

Physical activity is defined as any bodily movement produced by skeletal muscles that requires energy expenditure. Physical activity is an umbrella term that looks at the process of moving in various ways such as exercise, play, and lifestyle activity. This chapter focuses on MVPA that people of all ages and abilities can perform throughout life. Physical activity is a process-oriented outcome that is done every day with the ultimate goal being an active lifestyle that benefits health. Physical activity doesn't require any specialized skills and is often defined by walking, biking, and working in the yard. MVPA can be done for long periods without undue fatigue and can be done with a minimum of equipment. For the sake of health care containment, great emphasis

is being placed on getting people of all ages active for 30 to 60 minutes a day. A quality physical education program should graduate students who leave school with the habit of being active and knowing how to track their daily activity. Students who leave school with an innate joy for moving should be an outcome that is important for the program and students.

Physical fitness is a product-oriented outcome that emphasizes reaching or maintaining a higher state of physical performance. Physical fitness has a strong genetic component that enhances or limits the level of fitness a person can achieve. For over 60 years, fitness testing has been conducted in schools with the hope that it will encourage all students to strive for an acceptable level of fitness. For many reasons, most adults choose not to pursue a high level of physical fitness but are more interested in living an active lifestyle and maintaining health-related fitness. Similarly, many students are not interested in achieving a high level of fitness but are open to learning to enjoy their bodies through lifetime physical activities. Realistically, being physically active is a goal for the masses, whereas achieving a high level of fitness is pursued by a small, motivated population.

The focus of physical fitness experiences in physical education should be on developing positive feelings about exercises and aerobic activity. Most students will feel positive about fitness if they participate in an environment where all students receive positive feedback, not just the gifted. In addition, the goal should be to teach all students to reach their potential regardless of genetic limitations. Perceived competence is important in the fitness arena. Students need to learn they can achieve and become more fit through effort and grit. When students are praised for their effort rather than their genetic ability, they tend to stay much more positive about the everyday routine of working out for their health. Teach students that fitness is an ongoing part of life, and that how their performance compares with that of others doesn't matter. All students count when it comes to quality fitness experiences.

Skill development is the third component of a quality PE program. Here again, the genetic component is strongly tied to high-level performers. A quality program, however, is designed to help all students learn the basics of specialized skills like throwing, catching, kicking, and striking. For many adults and teenagers, skills are the tools they use to stay active and participate with friends. Everyone wants to be skilled, and one of the best ways to do that in elementary school is to focus on the process of performing (technique) the skills rather

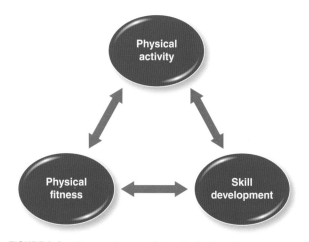

FIGURE 3.2 Cornerstones of physical education.

than the skill outcome. In other words, teach students how to shoot a basketball properly and don't worry about whether it goes in the basket. Success will occur as students mature if the skill technique is learned properly.

School-Based Physical Activity Promotion

Imagine it's 7:00 a.m. on a cold Wednesday morning. School does not start until 8:00 a.m., but already the gym has 15 students jumping rope and playing basketball while a third-grade teacher supervises. At 7:45 a.m., students in the "walking to school" program start arriving at school, led by a parent. As students arrive, they report to the gymnasium where the "Morning Jam" is going on led by two fifth-grade students. During the day, the classroom teachers take a quick activity break every hour. Today, the physical education teacher is teaching students about how what they learn in physical education can be used outside school to be active. Several other classroom teachers are teaching students phonics through movement. Immediately after school, several parents, the physical education teacher, and a county health agent meet in the physical education office to discuss an upcoming physical activity festival. Right outside the door, children enrolled in the after-school program are learning to estimate their steps using pedometers. At 6:30 p.m. that night, the physical education teacher starts the second of four physical education demonstration nights held during the year. This one is for first graders, who get to show off what they are learning in physical education. The event ends at 7:30 p.m., and so does another day at an active and healthy elementary school.

"It takes a village to raise a child" is an old proverb that simply means children must be surrounded by a supportive team of significant adults and community. It could also be said that "it takes a village to raise an active child." The school described earlier would be a part of such a village. It's not a traditional elementary school; it is a part of a community that includes teachers and parents. The Centers for Disease Control Prevention uses the Whole School, Whole Community, Whole Child (WSCC) model to address the notion that it takes a school and community to raise healthy, active students. As seen in figure 3.3 this model focuses on 10 components, including physical education, health education, school health, and health services, to provide a collaborative approach to improve student health in schools.

FIGURE 3.3 The Whole School, Whole Community, Whole Child Model.

Reprinted from ASCD, *Whole School, Whole Community, Whole Child: A Collaborative Approach to Learning and Health*, 2014.

One specific component of WSCC model is physical education and physical activity. This component focuses on school-based efforts to promote physical activity for youth. The Comprehensive School Physical Activity Program (CSPAP) does just that. CSPAPs are multifaceted school-based efforts to promote physical activity in school, out of school, and in the community. The approach includes physical education, physical activity during school, physical activity before and after school, staff involvement, and family and community engagement. Figure 3.4 illustrates the components of a CSPAP.

Quality Physical Education

A quality physical education program is the foundation of a CSPAP. Physical education is the primary place where physical activity is marketed and promoted to students. Therefore, maintaining and increasing student involvement in a CSPAP is important. If students do not enjoy physical education, they are unlikely to want to

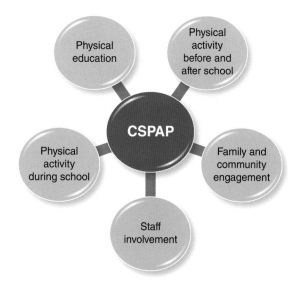

FIGURE 3.4 Comprehensive School Physical Activity Program.

Reprinted by permission from SHAPE America, *CSPAP Comprehensive School Physical Activity Program* (Reston, VA: SHAPER America).

participate in other CSPAP activities. For example, if a typical physical education lesson consists of calisthenics and sitting on the sidelines while half the class plays soccer, not many students will want to join an after-school program supervised by the physical education teacher. Children might be thinking, "You want me to stay after school for more of the same?" This entire book is dedicated to helping physical education teachers establish a quality physical education program to make it the solid foundation of a CSPAP.

Physical Activity During the School Day

Physical activity during the school day typically happens during three times: physical education, in the classroom, and at recess. The preceding section addressed physical education. This section will address physical activity in the classroom and a recess. The Active and Healthy School Program (www.gophersport.com/resources/active-healthy-schools) offers useful materials for implementing this component of a CSPAP.

Physical Activity in the Classroom

Elementary classrooms are full of students who learn by doing or experiencing. Besides, as mentioned earlier, studies show that physical activity is related to the learning process (Donnelly et al., 2009; Donnelly & Lambourne, 2011). With these ideas in mind, it follows that, when possible, teaching through movement is beneficial in the classroom. Not every classroom lesson, or even most of the lessons, has to be movement based, but when possible, integrating movement into instruc-

tion can offer students another medium for learning and increase their activity levels. To implement this plan, schools must overcome two major barriers: Some classroom teachers do not feel comfortable teaching students in an active setting, and they do not know how to integrate movement into their lessons.

Physical education teachers have the luxury of using a large, open space for movement but when designing activities for classroom teachers to implement, they must consider the issues of space and noise. First, how much space is available? In most classrooms, space is at a premium. Strategies for addressing this issue include (1) having students (in upper grades) move their desks to the perimeter of the room and (2) using activities that students can perform without moving desks. Second, the teacher must consider what is happening in the class next door. Children can be reminded to keep their voices down, but a classroom full of students making a reasonable amount of noise while being active can irritate nearby teachers and their students. Teaching students to participate under control and avoiding highly active games can solve the problem. Scheduling when classes are away at music or PE may be an alternative.

In designing effective activities for classroom teachers, the physical educator first must develop an understanding of the standards, objectives, or concepts that the classroom teachers are teaching. In an era of accountability, most teachers will not implement an activity unless it is aligned with a specific state standard. Next, ask how the concept is being taught. If a classroom teacher is using a particular strategy, his or her students may be confused by an activity that uses another strategy. Finally, learn each classroom teacher's comfort zone. Would the teacher be willing to do a dance with students? Is the teacher an outdoors person? Does the teacher like team sports? With this information, physical educators can work with classroom teachers to create effective and active classroom-based learning experiences for students.

Short activity breaks in the classroom allow students to accumulate physical activity in small bouts throughout the day. Typically, a minibreak lasts three to five minutes and may or may not involve leaving the classroom. Pellegrini, Huberty, and Jones (1995) found that offering activity breaks every hour decreased behavior issues and problems with inattentive students. Other research has found that activity breaks, along with journaling activity from the previous day, are effective in increasing daily physical activity levels of children, particularly girls (Ernst & Pangrazi, 1999; Pangrazi, Beighle, Vehige, & Vack, 2003). Unlike activity and lunch breaks, which occur once per day, minibreaks can be offered much more frequently (up to six times per day). These short breaks provide a great source of physical activity and minimize long disruptions to classroom activities. With practice, students are soon quick and efficient at starting minibreaks and immediately resuming class work afterward.

Developing activities from scratch can be difficult, especially because physical educators have their own lessons to develop. Fortunately, many teachers and curriculum developers have created and marketed programs designed for classroom teachers to integrate physical activity into lessons that are aligned with standards. *Promoting Physical Activity and Health in the Classroom* has been written to do just that (Pangrazi, Beighle, & Pangrazi, 2009). The cards included with this text are evidence based and allow classroom teachers to integrate physical activity seamlessly into the school day (Erwin, Abel, Beighle, & Beets, 2011). Many of these programs can be found online, and they include materials such as sample videos, lesson plans, equipment needed, and teaching strategies. When choosing a program and discussing options with classroom teachers, physical educators must be sure that these teachers understand that activity in the classroom is not a physical education program. Rather, the goal is to offer classroom-based strategies for teaching some academic concepts through movement.

Recess

In addition to classroom-based physical activity, recess is another time during the school day in which students have the opportunity to move. Students need at least two 15-minute recesses per day. These breaks have an educational purpose (to promote activity) rather than being a recess from learning. During this time, teachers should encourage students to be active. Providing equipment, activity zones, and organized games supervised by the playground attendant has been shown to increase physical activity during recess (Huberty et al. 2011; Jago & Baranowski, 2004). When using pedometers, students take between 900 and 1,500 steps during a 15-minute recess (Tudor-Locke et al., 2006). Thus, in just 15 minutes children can accumulate approximately 10% of the daily physical activity award threshold for the President's Active Lifestyle Award (PCPFS, 2018). But efforts must be made to maximize recess activity time with the physical educator taking the lead.

Physical educators can also facilitate the use of activity zones, which has shown to be an effective strategy (Ridgers, Stratton, Fairclough, & Twisk, 2007). Activity zones are simply marked-off areas, either with paint or cones, that designate an area for a specific activity. For example, zones at recess might be set up for soccer, dancing, Double Dutch, modified basketball, a walking trail, and

TEACHING TIP

The physical education teacher can also play a role in the physical activity levels during recess. At the beginning of the school year, recess activities can be taught during physical education lessons. For example, Ultimate or modified soccer with four balls rather than one are great recess activities that foster movement. These activities hold much potential for increasing physical activity (Beighle, Morgan, Le Masurier, & Pangrazi, 2006).

disc golf. If the physical education teacher does not have the time to set up these zones, recess aides or responsible older students can assist with setup and cleanup.

Lunchtime recess also offers an excellent opportunity for physical activity. This time differs from recess because children use the allotted time for both eating and activity. Tudor-Locke and colleagues (2006) found that during a 40-minute lunch break, boys averaged 2,521 steps and girls 1,913 steps each day. No data are available regarding how much time students spent eating and how much time they spent playing, but the study clearly indicates that children also use lunchtime to be active. Just as with recess, teachers need to encourage students to be active during the lunch break. Nutritionists recommend that students be active first and then eat lunch, so that they do not eat quickly to have more time for play. Some evidence also indicates that children who eat after being active waste less food. This approach is controversial, however, because it lengthens the lunch hour (decreasing the physical education teacher's time to use the multipurpose room for classes). Also, some schools question whether having less playtime and eating more food is the direction we want children to pursue.

Point-of-decision prompts are simply signs placed in areas around the school where students and faculty will be making choices regarding healthy behaviors. This strategy has been proved effective for increasing physical activity behavior in communities (Heath, 2003). A classic example is placing a sign directly above the "up" button on an elevator in an office building. The sign informs the elevator rider about the health benefits of taking the nearby stairs rather than taking the elevator. Elementary schools can post signs on the playground to encourage students to be active. Signs can simply say, "Be Active," or they can suggest games for students to play during activity breaks (figure 3.5). Making signs

Be Active

Tag
Soccer
Four square
Tetherball
Football
Swing
Five passes
Jump rope
Walk and talk
Invent a game

FIGURE 3.5 Example of a point-of-decision prompt sign for the playground.

that remind students to be active can be a classroom project or an art project, and classes can post their work throughout the school.

Physical Activity Before and After School

Because of the sedentary nature of the school day, it is no surprise that students receive most of their physical activity outside school hours (Morgan, Pangrazi, & Beighle, 2003; Tudor-Locke, Lee, Morgan, Beighle, & Pangrazi, 2006). In many schools, the YMCA or local recreation department uses the gymnasium for after-school programs. These programs are usually activity based; students play in the gym, on the playground, or in a grassy space. After-school programs offer an excellent opportunity to teach students about healthy foods and other healthy behaviors (Beets, Beighle, Erwin, & Huberty, 2009; Beets, Huberty, & Beighle, 2012; Beets, Tilley, Weaver, et al., 2013). Specifically, when a positive environment is created and developmentally appropriate practices such as those taught in physical education are used, after-school programs have great potential for offering children a significant amount of physical activity (Beighle et al., 2010). They also can provide tutoring for students needing extra assistance. Before-school hours present another opportunity for students to be active. Opening the school grounds and offering activities for students who arrive before school

has great promise. At many schools, parents trying to get to work on time often drop off students early. Without before-school programs, these students often just sit and wait outside the school.

Implementing effective extracurricular activities often requires overcoming barriers. The most prevalent barrier is cost. With the emphasis on standardized testing and childhood obesity, funding for programs that offer tutoring for physical activity and nutrition education is often available if teachers just ask. Other sources include private businesses, the PTA, and external grants. Most districts have resources to assist teachers who are seeking grants. Another barrier is transportation. Often the success of a program, particularly an after-school program, is strongly influenced by the availability of student transportation (Jago & Baranowski, 2004). Attendance in such programs can be limited because students who are bused to school have to leave immediately after school. If the additional transportation is a burden for parents, they may not allow their child to participate. Ideas for clearing this hurdle vary from school to school. Some school districts provide transportation in the form of an after-school bus for students participating in district-sponsored after-school activities. Lastly, liability is sometimes a barrier to after-school activities. Districts are often reluctant to allow students in the gym outside of school hours because of increased insurance costs. Many schools are developing community–school programs in which parks are built next to schools so that the two institutions can work together to provide maximum use of both public facilities. Regardless of the roadblocks, they must be overcome for the good of all students.

Staff Involvement

Encouraging faculty to improve their own health through school-based activities is another strategy to consider when developing a CSPAP. Students see teachers as models. If they see their teachers being active during activity breaks, these seemingly small acts can have tremendous potential impact. For example, simply walking with students during recess is great modeling and allows teachers to talk to students outside the seemingly pressure-filled classroom. Physical educators can coordinate walking clubs, after-school aerobics, brief nutrition education presentations at faculty meetings, or even a friendly steps competition among teachers. In fact, steps competitions are an effective way to introduce pedometers, particularly if a school has only a few pedometers. Seeing a few teachers wearing pedometers and discussing their steps often interests other teachers, who then want pedometers. Students also begin asking about pedometers and become intrigued. Some companies sell pedometers at a discount for schools to resell for profit. Schools can then purchase class sets of pedometers for use during physical education. Selling pedometers is a much healthier fund-raising activity than selling candies, cookie dough, and the like.

Family and Community Engagement

For elementary students, parents or guardians are the most significant adults in their lives. Parents substantially affect their child's attitude toward physical activity and their physical activity level (Welk, Wood, & Morss, 2003). Programs that involve parents and encourage them to be active with their children can help promote physical activity for an entire family. Here are some ideas that can be included in a CSPAP to help foster parental involvement.

Activity Calendars

An activity calendar can challenge children and their families to participate in activities listed by day (figure 3.6). When families reach a certain goal (e.g., active 75% of the days), put their name on the Active Family Wall

of Fame posted in the gym.

PE Nights and Demonstration Nights

On PE nights, students and parents participate in physical education activities together. Parents see what their children are learning in physical education, and they discover activities they can do at home with their children. Demonstration nights involve parents watching their children participate in physical education activities. Typically, the grand finale involves parents and students participating in activities together. In a larger school, these events will need to be held for specific grade levels to prevent overcrowding and allow safe activity. Most parents leave these programs thinking, "I wish PE was like that when I was younger," or "PE sure has changed."

Fun Days

Sometimes called field days or play days, these events are generally planned as a year-end celebration. They can also be held in September to kick off the school year. On field days, teachers set up several stations, and classes move from station to station to participate in the activities. Stations can offer the usual physical education activities

February

Sunday	Monday	Tuesday	Wednesday	Thursday	Friday	Saturday
1 Active families stay healthy.	**2**	**3** Play football with a friend.	**4**	**5** Play basketball for 10 minutes.	**6**	**7**
8	**9** Make a snowman.	**10** How many times can you jump rope without stopping?	**11**	**12** Create a dance and practice it for 20 minutes.	**13** NO SCHOOL! BE ACTIVE ALL DAY!	**14** Be kind to your heart... be active.
15 Children should be active at least 60 minutes per day.	**16** Teach someone your favorite stretch.	**17** Teach a family member a PE game.	**18** Do extra chores as a favor to your parents.	**19** Jump rope for a total of 10 minutes.	**20** Invent a new exercise.	**21** Shovel snow.
22	**23** Do your favorite fitness challenge.	**24** Play a new game at recess.	**25**	**26**	**27** Start a game of tag in your neighborhood.	**28**

If you want to do an activity other than the one on the calendar, great! Write the new activity on your calendar. Mrs. Panko may even put your activity on the calendar as an activity next month.

How many minutes of activity should you do a day? _____
What types of activities are cardiovascular activities? _____
Name three lifetime activities. _____
What is locomotor skill? _____

FIGURE 3.6   Example of a family physical activity calendar.

as well as novel activities that are simply safe and fun. Parents are great resources to serve as station attendants and as planning committee members to help coordinate the event. For primary-age student activities, upper-level elementary students can also serve on the planning committee, help set up the event, and supervise the stations.

Charity Events

Charity events give families opportunities to be active together. Events can vary from a walk–run race, a walk-athon, or chores for change to a physical activity festival whose proceeds go to a charity. The charity can be an outside organization or a local family, or support for the physical education program. Like any program, charity events require extensive planning and coordination. Collaborating with the school's parent organization or other school-based organizations may help divide the labor needed for planning.

Every community is full of valuable resources for a CSPAP. These resources may include people experienced in planning events, working with other community organizations, collaborating with schools, or simply generating program funding. Physical educators should constantly seek collaborative, creative involvement from the community. Organizations unable to donate money may have a program that encourages employees to volunteer in the community or some other useful resource. Also, members of the CSPAP committee should be open to volunteering for events held by other community organizations. Building such relationships can have considerable long-term benefit.

Early in the process of developing a CSPAP, potential community resources must be identified. The following organizations may be interested in partnering with physical education teachers. Consider inviting personnel from these organizations to participate in the CSPAP.

- *YMCAs, recreation centers, Boys and Girls Clubs.* These organizations are all interested in physical activity and youth. Furthermore, they are all involved in before-school, after-school, and even during-school programs. One strategy is for the physical education teacher to offer training for their program staff. This approach allows the physical education teacher to teach the staff what is happening during physical education.
- *County health agencies.* Many county health departments and agents are already involved with health-related programs in the schools, so they are an excellent resource and potential collaboration partner in developing a CSPAP. County health

agents may provide sun safety, nutrition education, tobacco education, and other lessons. Some departments, along with the physical education teacher, also can work with classroom teachers in efforts to increase classroom physical activity.

- *Businesses.* Most businesses—particularly health-related businesses such as hospitals, insurance companies, bicycle shops, fitness centers, and doctor clinics—near a school or within a school district have a vested interest in contributing to the lives of youth in their community. Businesses may also be willing to donate funds to purchase physical education equipment in exchange for posting a banner in the gym or having their logo on physical education newsletters. Lastly, many businesses seek ways to engage employees in the community by allowing time to volunteer. Volunteers from corporations can get involved in recess by serving as a recess aide or recess buddy in an activity zone.
- *Youth sports.* Youth sports offer an excellent opportunity for students to be active. To maximize this experience, be sure that parents and coaches receive training, so that all parties involved agree on what is good for the children. Physical educators are the experts at teaching skills and motivating youth in a fun environment. Why not share that knowledge with coaches? One Saturday morning per season could be set aside so that parents and coaches can come together to learn how to teach skills and gain an understanding of how all adults must work together for the good of the children.

Walking-to-school (active commuting) programs are increasingly popular. Local, state, and national events are held throughout the country. Even more important, these programs offer a safe, active, and enjoyable source of physical activity for students. Schools can develop a walking-to-school program by using the procedure outlined here. For more information about this topic, see the Centers for Disease Control and Prevention website or the National Safe Routes to School website (www.saferoutesinfo.org).

1. *Generate interest.* Newsletters, conversations with parents, parent surveys, and discussions with local agencies such as the fire department, police department, or health department will attract interest and provide helpful feedback during the initial planning phase of the program.
2. *Organize.* During this phase of the program,

recruit volunteers and hold meetings to work out program details and logistics. Ask important personnel such as the principal, crossing guards, key district administrators, parent volunteers, and representatives from the police department to serve on the planning committee. Topics to be covered include the following:

a. Safe, practical routes for students to walk to school

b. Traffic management

c. Collecting contact information and addresses of families who are interested in participating as well as obtaining parental consent

d. Location and scheduling of personnel during the event

e. Timeline of the event

f. Media contacts and marketing of the event

3. *Implement and reflect.*

a. After carrying out the plan and holding a walking-to-school event, calling a planning committee meeting is important.

b. At the meeting, members can talk openly about what they found successful and what they think needs to be modified for the next event.

c. If members cannot be present, encourage them to present their ideas in writing.

CSPAP Leader

If schools are to take the lead in promoting physical activity, each school must appoint a leader. In schools seeking to implement a physical activity program as part of the wellness policy, the first choice for a school physical activity leader, or champion, should be the physical education teacher (Castelli & Beighle, 2007). For increased participation, as well as a quality physical education program, a physical activity coordinator is the basis of a CSPAP. In most cases, physical education teachers should serve as the physical activity coordinators in a school, specifically in a CSPAP. Although they may not actively participate in an event or strategy, these teachers probably will have input into virtually every physical-activity-based strategy in a CSPAP. For example, a physical education teacher may organize and teach an after-school aerobics class for teachers. He also may coordinate a group of teachers who supervise a before-school physical activity club for students. Physical education teachers are essential to a CSPAP's success; without them, physical activity is highly unlikely to be an integral part of the school day.

In most cases, physical education teachers should serve as the physical activity coordinators in a school, specifically in a CSPAP. Although they may not actively participate in an event or strategy, these teachers probably will have input into virtually every physical-activity-based strategy in a CSPAP. In fact, delegating CSPAP duties is advised to prevent overworking one person. For example, a physical education teacher may organize and teach an after-school aerobics class for teachers. He also may coordinate a group

 CASE STUDY

Leading a CSPAP

Mr. Will Noble has been teaching for 13 years at the same elementary school. In an effort to challenge himself professionally, 4 years ago he decided to start a school physical activity program. His initial vision was to start an after-school program, work with classroom teachers to get students active in the classroom, and organize employees from a local business to serve as recess activity buddies. He thought that these programs would work best at his school. After the first three months of school he realized that managing this many activities was not feasible for one person. The after-school program required much more paperwork and employee supervision than he expected. Only two classroom teachers liked the idea of getting students active and training the volunteers for recess was more time consuming than expected. Although Mr. Noble was frustrated, he did not quit. He realized he needed to step back and start slow. He formed a small committee, including the two classroom teachers who wanted more activity for students, to help generate ideas and then prioritize the list based on what was most feasible. Based on the committee recommendations, he chose to work on garnering more support and action for classroom-based physical activity. The classroom teachers on the committee thought that if Mr. Noble led a few activities in a faculty meeting, with their assistance, more teachers would buy in. Although the committee has many other ideas for future school-based physical activity efforts, this small step will help solidify more support from teachers and ultimately allow for a strong start for Mr. Noble's vision of teachers who supervise a before-school physical activity club for students. Physical education teachers are essential to CSPAP success; without them, physical activity is highly unlikely to be an integral part of the school day.

One note here is that if the physical educator chooses not to be involved in the CSPAP, another person (e.g., a classroom teacher or other specialist) must be identified to assume the responsibility. The point is that someone must take the lead in ensuring that the school promotes active and healthy behaviors. In the model school program created in the Mesa, Arizona, public schools, the physical education teacher is released a half day a week to carry out CSPAP program administrative duties. As with most effective programs, positive things happen when quality people direct them.

Getting Started

When initiating any project, one of the toughest tasks is getting started. Great ideas may get lost because physical educators do not know where to begin and end up discarding them. Because people often see projects as a huge task that cannot be accomplished, many great ideas remain on the shelf. The key to starting any project, whether it is a paper for school or the organization of a CSPAP, is to develop a series of manageable tasks. Remember that implementing and sustaining a CSPAP program requires knowledge about physical activity promotion, advocacy, public relations, and marketing (McKenzie, 2007). The following suggestions can help make creating and maintaining a CSPAP a series of steps that can be accomplished systematically.

Form a CSPAP Committee

The physical educator should take on the role of the CSPAP coordinator. Without support from others, however, a CSPAP is difficult to achieve. When forming the committee, consider key personnel in the program. Teachers, school administrators, district administrators, parents, students, university faculty, fire department representatives, local business owners, community leaders, and community organizations are just a few potential partners. Invite all these people to a kickoff meeting. At the meeting, be sure to encourage members of the CSPAP committee to invite other people who might be important resources. The Tips for Recruiting a CSPAP Committee sidebar lists some ideas for recruiting potential CSPAP committee members and collaborators. CSPAP coordinators have this opportunity to use their public relations skills.

Develop an Implementation Plan

The CSPAP committee's first task is to develop a plan. As the coordinator, the physical education teacher should provide the committee with some background information, the components of a CSPAP, and a larger vision for the

TIPS FOR RECRUITING A CSPAP COMMITTEE

- *Network.* Talk to other teachers, administrators, parents, friends, and family. One person cannot have all the appropriate contacts. People who are not able to provide what is needed may be able to give you names of those who can.

- *Introduce yourself.* Be sure to introduce yourself to as many people in the school community as possible. When meeting people for the first time, take the time to get to know them if time permits. The first meeting is generally not an appropriate time to seek resources. Let the individual know about the CSPAP.

- *Get involved.* Parent organizations, youth sports, and local youth clubs are always looking for volunteers. Offer to help or ask someone on the CSPAP committee to help out at an event held by these organizations. The best way to get others to help you is to help them.

- *Be persistent.* During the process of starting an CSPAP and seeking resources, you will hear "No" or "Not right now" regularly. Keep moving forward, knowing that what you are working toward is what is best for kids.

- *Ask others to help.* When one person agrees to get involved, ask him or her for names of anyone else who may be interested in helping. Find out the person's background. He or she may have excellent suggestions for getting others involved or may have great contacts.

school. After brainstorming for ideas, the committee needs to prioritize them and develop short- and long-term objectives. Lastly, to prevent overwhelming teachers, students, and communities, the CSPAP should start small. The first CSPAP activity might be to give a short presentation about the program at the school's open house. Also, at the open house, they can set up a booth at the front door to provide fliers and survey parents. After surveying parents, CSPAP members can develop the next steps. Another school might begin by sending fliers home and handing them out during school drop-off and pickup hours, while the physical education teacher begins using pedometers in his or her lessons. The key is to keep the tasks manageable and aligned with the goals. Over time, the CSPAP will evolve into various activities with subcommittees having their own set of objectives related to the program's original purpose.

Reflect, Evaluate, and Progress

The CSPAP should be viewed as an evolving program that will continue to progress and become more effective. Committee members must meet, examine where

SCHOOL WALKING PROGRAMS

School walking programs can be a great way to increase activity for students, teachers, and family. When initiating a during-school walking program, instruct students to walk where they are all within the teacher's view. For most people, walking around a track or field gets boring. With the administration's approval, teachers can design walking courses around the school neighborhood so that students can try many different paths and learn the time required to walk them. Before allowing students to use a path, however, teachers need to drive along it, write directions, and map the mileage. Set up safety guidelines that are integrated into each path. The following are some safety guidelines to consider:

- Make sure that students always use the sidewalk. If there is no sidewalk, have students walk on the left side of the roadway facing traffic.

- Stipulate that students must walk with another person or in a small group. If someone is injured or needs help, one member of the group can return to the school for help.

- Because running from aggressive dogs only makes the problem worse, teach students to stop, face the dog, and give it a stern, "No!"

- Have students sign out and specify the path they will walk. If students are missing, tracking them will be much easier.

- Make sure that the school nurse clears students who have serious health problems. These students must wear "medical tags" in case of an accident requiring emergency care.

- Encourage parents to get their children walking or running shoes with reflective tape built into them. Students wearing these shoes are more visible to automobile drivers.

- Have students warm up before the walk, and teach them to cool down afterward. After they walk a short distance, have them stop and stretch their arms, legs, and back (see chapter 14 for suggested stretches). When they have finished the walk, have them stretch again.

- Make sure that students drink plenty of water, whether it is cold or hot. They should drink 8 ounces (240 ml) of water 15 minutes before the walk. If it is hot and dry, have them drink 5 ounces (150 ml) every 15 to 20 minutes during the walk. At the end of the walk, have them drink another 8 to 16 ounces (240 to 480 ml) of water. Waiting for the thirst signal as a reminder to drink may be too late. Thirstiness usually occurs after the body needs water.

- In cold weather, teach students about layering clothing so that they can remove a layer if they get too hot. Layers of lighter clothing are much more useful than one heavy layer. Students should wear a hat, gloves, and scarf if necessary. In hot weather, have them wear loose, light-colored clothing, a hat, and sunglasses. Emphasize that to avoid skin damage because of ultraviolet light from the sun, students must apply sunscreen when they will be outside for more than a few minutes—in any weather.

they have been and where they are going, and adjust the program. For instance, some events may have low attendance. Was it because the event was not attractive to children and families? Was the event marketed well? Was the event on the same day as Little League opening day? Without thoughtful reflection and honest evaluation, a CSPAP runs the risk of becoming stale, dormant, and, possibly, nonexistent. With quality reflection, programs can continue evolving to meet school and community needs. Information gathered through evaluation also helps when seeking funding from outside organizations.

When evaluating a program, avoid getting bogged down in thinking that evaluation has to include a lot of data or take a lot of time. In the example, the data were the number of people in attendance. In other instances, data could be pictures used to market future events or used in a presentation to garner more support. Think of the evaluation process as getting numbers, stories, and pictures (CDC, 2013).

Meet With Other Schools

Another strategy in developing and maintaining a quality CSPAP is to meet with other schools with similar pro-

grams. "No sense reinventing the wheel" applies here. Your committee can benefit by learning what other schools have found successful. Remember that school demographics may affect the success of some activities; an activity that was not effective at Franklin Elementary may succeed at Monroe Elementary, and vice versa. While working with other schools, keep an open mind, collect as much information as possible, and allow the committee to discuss future directions based on the experiences of other schools.

When all is said and done, a CSPAP demands a whole approach to the school environment. Schools, families, and communities must cooperate to create a setting that educates children physically as well as academically. Again, the proverb "It takes a village to raise a child" could not be truer. No longer can we afford to believe that making children sit in class for long periods will improve their academic performance. Most adults know only too well that even they can sit and concentrate for only a finite amount of time. After that, the process becomes nonproductive. Let's make sure that our schools excel in promoting activity and academic performance. The old saying "A healthy mind lives in a healthy body" must drive the environment of today's schools.

LEARNING AIDS

HOW AND WHY

1. Why is physical inactivity a major health concern?
2. How can teachers use an understanding of brain development to help their teaching?
3. How can a teacher start a Comprehensive School Physical Activity Program?
4. What can be done to encourage students' physical activity outside of school?

CONTENT REVIEW

1. What is the effect of adding at least 60 minutes of daily physical activity to your lifestyle?
2. What are the levels of the Physical Activity Pyramid? How much time should be spent on the components each week?
3. What level in the Physical Activity Pyramid forms the foundation for good health? How can students be taught to change their activity habits to meet the minimum activity requirements?
4. What is the effect of physical activity on academic performance?
5. What are the physical activity guidelines for youth in the United States?

WEBSITES

Youth physical activity promotion, www.health.gov/paguidelines/resources/
Comprehensive School Physical Activity Program, www.shapeamerica.org/cspap/what.aspx
Physical activity and young people, www.who.int/dietphysicalactivity/factsheet_young_people/en/

SUGGESTED READINGS

Bouchard, C. (2012). Genomic predictors of trainability. *Experimental Physiology, 97*(3), 347–352.

Cooper Institute. (2017). FITNESSGRAM/ACTIVITYGRAM test administration manual (5th edition with web resource). Champaign, IL: Human Kinetics.

Fairclough, S., & Stratton, G. (2005). Physical education makes you fit and healthy. Physical education's contribution to young people's physical activity levels. *Health Education Research, 20*(1), 14–23.

Johnson, T.G., & Turner, L. (2016). The physical activity movement and the definition of physical education. *Journal of Physical Education Recreation and Dance, 87*(4), 11–17.

Kohl, H.W., & Murray, T.D. (2012). *Foundations of public health.* Champaign, IL: Human Kinetics.

Hillman, C.H., Pontifex, M.B., Raine, L.B., Castelli, D.M., Hall, E.E., & Kramer, A F. (2009). The effect of acute treadmill walking on cognitive control and academic achievement in preadolescent children. *Neuroscience, 159*(3), 1044–1054.

Pangrazi, R.P., Beighle, A., & Sidman, C.L. (2007). *Pedometer power: Using pedometers in school and community* (2nd ed.). Champaign, IL: Human Kinetics.

Smith, A.L., & Biddle, S.J.H. (Eds.) (2008). *Youth physical activity and sedentary behavior.* Champaign, IL: Human Kinetics.

Strong, W.B., Malina, R.M., Blimkie, C.J.R., Daniels, S.R., Dishman, R.K., Gutin, B., . . . & Trudeau, F., (2005). Evidence based physical activity for school-age youth. *Journal of Pediatrics, 146*(6), 732–737.Trost S. (2007). *Active education: Physical education, physical activity and academic performance.* San Diego, CA: Active Living Research.

Trost, S.G., Pate, R.R., Freedson, P.S., Sallis, J.F., & Taylor, W.C. (2000). Using objective physical activity measures with youth: How many days of monitoring are needed? *Medicine & Science in Sports & Exercise, 32*(2), 426–431.

REFERENCES

2018 Physical Activity Guidelines Advisory Committee. (2018). *2018 Physical Activity Guidelines Advisory Committee scientific report.* Washington, DC: U.S. Department of Health and Human Services.

Ainsworth, B.E., Haskell, W.L., Herrmann, S.D., Meckes, N., Bassett Jr., D.R., Tudor-Locke, C., Greer, J.L., Vezina, J., Whitt-Glover, M.C., & Leon, A.S. (2011). Compendium of physical activities: A second update of codes and MET values. *Medicine & Science in Sports & Exercise, 43*(8), 1575–1581.

Basch C.E. (2010). *Healthier students are better learners: A missing link in school reforms to close the achievement gap.* Report commissioned by the Campaign for Educational Equity. New York: Teachers College, Columbia University. pp. 1–106.

Beets, M.W., Huberty, J., & Beighle, A. (2012). Pedometer-determined physical activity of children attending afterschool programs: Research- & practice-based implications. *American Journal of Preventive Medicine, 42(2)*, 180–184.

Beets, M.W., Beighle, A., Erwin, H.E., & Hubert, J. (2009). Impact of after-school programs to increase physical activity and fitness A meta-analysis. *American Journal of Preventive Medicine, 36*(6), 527–537.

Beets, M.W., Tilley, F., Weaver, R.G., Turner-McGrievy, G., Moore, J.B., & Webster, C. (2013). From policy to practice: Addressing snack quality, consumption, and price in afterschool programs. *Journal of Nutrition Education & Behavior, 46*(5), 384–389.

Beighle, A., Beets, M. W., Erwin, H. E., Huberty, J., Moore, J. B., & Stellino, M. (2010). Physical activity promotion in afterschool programs. *After School Matters, 11,* 24-32.

Beighle, A., Morgan, C.F., Le Masurier, G., & Pangrazi, R. P (2006). Children's physical activity during recess and outside of school. *Journal of School Health, 76*(10), 516-520.

Carlson, S.A., Fulton J.E., Pratt, M., Yang, Z., & Adams, E.K. (2015). Inadequate physical activity and health care expenditures in the United States. *Progress in Cardiovascular Diseases, 57*(4), 315–323. 2014.08.002. Retrieved from www.ncbi.nlm.nih.gov/pmc/articles/PMC4604440/

Castelli, D.M., & Beighle, A. (2007). The physical education teacher as school activity director. *Journal of Physical Education, Recreation, and Dance, 78*(5), 25–28.

Centers for Disease Control and Prevention. (2010). *The association between school-based physical activity, including physical education, and academic performance.* Atlanta, GA: U.S. Department of Health and Human Services.

Centers for Disease Control and Prevention. (2013). *Comprehensive School Physical Activity Programs: A guide for schools.* Atlanta, GA: U.S. Department of Health and Human Services.

Centers for Disease Control and Prevention. (2014). *Health and academic achievement.* Atlanta, GA: U.S. Department of Health and Human Services.

Centers for Disease Control and Prevention. (2016). *National Health and Nutrition Examination Survey* Atlanta, GA: U.S. Department of Health and Human Services.

Donnelly, J.E., Greene, J.L., Gibson, C.A., Smith, B.K., Washburn, R.A., Sullivan, D.K., . . . Williams, S.L. (2009). Physical Activity Across the Curriculum (PAAC): A randomized controlled trial to promote physical activity and diminish overweight and obesity in elementary children. *Preventive Medicine, 49*(4), 336–341.

Donnelly, J.E., & Lambourne, K. (2011). Classroom-based physical activity, cognition, and academic achievement. *Preventive Medicine, 52*(S1), S36-S42.

Ernst, M.P., & Pangrazi, R.P. (1999). Effects of a physical activity program on children's activity levels and attraction to physical activity. *Pediatric Exercise Science, 11*, 393–405.

Erwin, H.E., Abel, M., Beighle, A., & Beets, M. (2011). Effects of integrating physical activity with mathematics on activity levels, *Health Promotion Practice, 12*(2), 244–251.

Fairclough, S.J., & Stratton, G. (2006). A review of physical activity levels during elementary school physical education. *Journal of Teaching in Physical Education, 25*(2), 239–257.

Heath, G.W. (2003). Increasing physical activity in communities: What really works? *President's Council on Physical Fitness and Sports Research Digest, 4*(4), 1–8.

Huberty, J.L., Siahpush, M., Beighle, A., Fuhrmeister, E., Silva, P., & Welk, G. (2011). Ready for Recess: A pilot study to increase physical activity in elementary school children. *Journal of School Health, 81*(5) 251–257.

Jago, R., & Baranowski, T. (2004). Non-curricular approaches for increasing physical activity in youth: A review. *Preventive Medicine, 39*(1), 157–163.

Mahar, M.T., Murphy, S.K., Rowe, D.A., Golden, J., Shields, A.T., & Raedeke, T.D. (2006). Effects of a classroom-based program on physical activity and on-task behavior. *Medicine & Science in Sports & Exercise, 38*, 2086–2094.

McKenzie, T.L., Catellier, D.J., Conway, T., Lytle, L.A., Grieser, M., & Webber, L.A., et al. (2006). Girls' activity levels and lesson contexts in middle school PE: TAAG baseline. *Medicine & Science in Sports & Exercise, 38*(7), 1229–1235.

Morgan, C.F., Pangrazi, R.P, & Beighle, A. (2003). Using pedometers to promote physical activity in physical education. *Journal of Physical Education, Recreation, and Dance, 74*(7), 33–38.

Pangrazi, R.P., Beighle, A., & Pangrazi, D. (2009) *Promoting physical activity and health in the classroom.* San Francisco, CA: Benjamin Cummings.

Pangrazi, R.P., Beighle, A., Vehige, T., & Vack, C. (2003). Evaluating the effectiveness of the state of Arizona's promoting lifestyle activity for youth program. *Journal of School Health, 73*(8), 317–321.

Pellegrini, A.D., Huberty, P.D., & Jones, I. (1995). The effects of recess timing on children's playground and classroom behaviors. *American Educational Research Journal, 32*(4), 845–864.

President's Council on Sports, Fitness and Nutrition. (2018). Retrieved from HHS, the President's Council on Sports, Fitness, and Nutrition website: www.hhs.gov/fitness/index.html

Ratey, John J. (2008). *Spark: The revolutionary new science of exercise and the brain.* London, United Kingdom: Little, Brown.

Ridgers, N.D., Stratton, G., Fairclough, S.J., & Twisk, J.W.R. (2007). Children's physical activity levels during school recess: A quasi-experimental intervention study. *International Journal of Behavioral Nutrition and Physical Activity, 4*(19), 1–9.

Sallis, J.F., & McKenzie, T.L. (1991). Physical education's role in public health. *Research Quarterly for Exercise and Sport, 62*, 124–137.

Sallis, J.F., McKenzie, T.L., Beets, M.W., Beighle, A., Erwin, H., & Lee, S. (2012). Physical education's role in public health: Steps forward and backward over 20 years and HOPE for the future. *Research Quarterly for Sport and Exercise and Sport, 83*(2), 125–135.

Shephard, R.J. (1984). Physical activity and child health. *Sports Medicine, 1*, 205–233.

Telama, R., Yang, X., Leskinen, E., Kankaanpaa, A, Hirvensalo, M., Tammelin, T., Viikari, J.S., & Raitakari, O.T. (2014). Tracking of physical activity from early childhood through youth into adulthood. *Medicine & Science in Sports & Exercise, 46*(5), 955–962.

Troiano, R.P., Berrigan, D., Dodd, K.W., Masse, L.C, Tilert, T., & McDowell, M. (2008). Physical activity in the United States measured by accelerometer. *Medicine & Science in Sports & Exercise, 40*, 181–188.

Trudeau, F., Laurencelle, L., Tremblay, J., Rajic, M., & Shephard, R.J. (1998). A long-term follow-up of participants in the Trois-Rivieres semi-longitudinal study of growth and development. *Pediatric Exercise Science, 10*, 366–377.

Tudor-Locke, C., Lee, S, Morgan, C.F., Beighle, A., & Pangrazi, R.P. (2006). Children's pedometer-determined physical activity patterns during the segmented school day. *Medicine & Science in Sports & Exercise, 38*(10), 1732–1738.

U.S. Department of Health and Human Services. (1996). Physical activity and health: A report of the Surgeon General. Atlanta, GA: U.S. Department of Health and Human Services, Public Health Service, CDC, National Center for Chronic Disease Prevention and Health Promotion.

Vincent, S.D., Pangrazi, R.P., Raustorp, A., Tomson, L.M., Cuddihy, T.F. (2003). Activity levels of body mass index of children in the United States, Sweden, and Australia. *Medicine & Science in Sports, 35*(8), 1367–1373.

Welk, G., Wood, K., & Morss, G. (2003). Parental influences on physical activity in children: An exploration of the potential mechanisms. *Pediatric Exercise Science, 15*(1), 19–33.

Curriculum Development

4

A written curriculum guides any instructional program. A lesson plan guides an individual lesson. This chapter offers a systematic approach for developing curriculum. The steps for planning, designing, and implementing a comprehensive curriculum are described. The concepts of scope, sequence, and balance help ensure that the curriculum meets the needs of all students.

Learning Objectives

▶ Define scope, sequence, and balance as they relate to curriculum development.

▶ List common elements of a quality curriculum.

▶ Explain your philosophy of physical education for children.

▶ List environmental factors that affect curriculum development.

▶ Specify the seven steps in developing a quality curriculum.

▶ Specify the needs, characteristics, and interests of children, and explain how age and maturity factors affect program development.

▶ Cite the three learning domains and discuss characteristics of each.

Curriculum is a framework of learning experiences in physical education that promote physical activity, skill development, and physical fitness. A curriculum is a written plan for content delivery that gives sequence and direction to the physical education program. A quality curriculum is driven by a written philosophy and characterized by a conceptual framework. It contains child-centered, standards-based activities organized in a manner that optimizes appropriate delivery. Assessments are an essential component of a quality physical education curriculum and are used to guide curricular changes. Embedded within a curriculum are beliefs and goals influenced by value orientations. Value orientation is a set of personal and professional beliefs used in determining curricular decisions. For example, one teacher may value individual activities for lifelong physical activity, while another values team sports. Most often, physical educators have several value orientations, so the curriculum choices and instructional model for their physical education program reflect a blend of values. Metzler (2011) compares an instructional model for teachers to a blueprint for a builder.

In elementary physical education, several instructional models can be used to teach standards-driven content. This text uses a broad-based multiactivity model that focuses on promoting physical activity, developing physical skills, and building positive attitudes about physical activity. This is all implemented using standards-based best practices throughout lessons. The multiactivity model uses units of physical activity as the core curriculum. Units vary in length from one to three weeks, depending on program philosophy, frequency of physical education lessons, and student developmental level. The units are typically arranged with a balance of activities from categories such as lifetime activities, team sports, rhythmic activities, personal fitness activities, recreational activities, and low-organized games. This model allows diversity and flexibility in meeting the changing interests and desires of today's students. In fact, Cleland, Dwyer, and Venn (2011) suggest that exposure to a variety of physical activity experiences in childhood is a warranted approach for predicting adult physical activity. Thus, if one of the primary roles of physical education is to affect adult physical activity levels, a curriculum featuring a variety of activities makes sense.

As noted, there are other curriculum models. The sport education model centers on giving students a positive, "authentic" sport experience. The movement education model usually consists of educational dance, educational gymnastics, and educational games that teach movement concepts. Hellison's (2011) model uses physical activity and the physical education environment to teach children skills that promote personal and social responsibility. Teaching games for understanding (TGFU), also called the tactical games model, uses games as the context to teach the skills and knowledge needed to become physically competent. Other curriculum models include outdoor education, adventure education, health-related physical education, and conceptual physical education (see Kulinna, 2008, for descriptions of these models). Bear in mind that no model is the "right" model and that no model fits all needs. In practice, most physical education programs combine several models to teach desired outcomes.

When developing or revising a curriculum, the physical education staff must consider its value orientation toward the existing curriculum and the proposed changes. This process focuses on three major components: the subject matter to be learned, the students for whom the curriculum is being developed, and the community that has established the schools. Curriculums vary depending on the value orientations of the physical educators involved in the planning. Physical educators who place highest priority on mastering subject matter emphasize sports, dance, outdoor adventure activities, physical fitness activities, and aquatic activities. This orientation focuses on helping students learn skills and gain knowledge so that they can actively participate throughout their lives. In contrast, instructors who favor a student-centered approach prize activities that develop the individual student. They emphasize helping students find personally meaningful activities. Other physical educators see student autonomy and self-direction as the most important goals. They focus instruction and curricula on lifetime sport skills and nontraditional activities, such as cooperative games and group activities, to foster problem-solving and interpersonal skills.

These examples illustrate only a few of the different value orientations of physical educators. Usually, most curricula are put together by committee and reflect several value orientations. Finding common ground among value orientations makes it easier for a staff to present lessons that teach common goals and objectives. For this reason, early in the curriculum development process, time allocated to determine common value orientations for the group will enhance the efficiency of the process.

Before accepting a new teaching position, ask yourself the following questions about the school's curriculum. (If you answer no to most of them, working in such a setting may be difficult because it conflicts with your value orientation.)

- Will the curriculum express a viewpoint about subject matter that is consistent with mine?
- Does the curriculum express a viewpoint about student learning that I believe?
- Does the curriculum express a viewpoint about the school's role in accomplishing social–cultural goals that is similar to my beliefs?
- Can I implement the instructional strategies I value within this model?

Designing a Quality Curriculum

Figure 4.1 outlines the steps to constructing a meaningful, well-planned curriculum. The first four steps focus on designing a framework for selecting curriculum activities. These steps are often ignored because the focus is on activities that are easily implemented, even though they may not contribute to content standards. Designing a curriculum without a framework is like building a house without blueprints. Note that this process is ongoing. The "modify" component of step 7 requires revisiting any or all of the previous steps. For example, a teacher

might teach a lesson focusing on catching, specifically catching a ball thrown by a partner. During the lesson teaching behaviors and student performance in catching are evaluated. It may be determined that students are not meeting catching objectives not because they cannot catch but because of poor throws from their partner. Thus, students need more throwing practice before catching a thrown ball is implemented or evaluated. In this case, steps 5 and 6 would be revisited and modified to include more throwing practice before this lesson.

Step 1: Develop a Guiding Philosophy

The first step in curriculum design is to write a philosophy of physical education that reflects the educators' beliefs about how physical education fits into the total school curriculum and what it will accomplish for each student. Here is an example of a philosophical platform for physical education.

Physical education is the part of a child's overall education that teaches and involves movement. Physical education must be largely an instructional program if

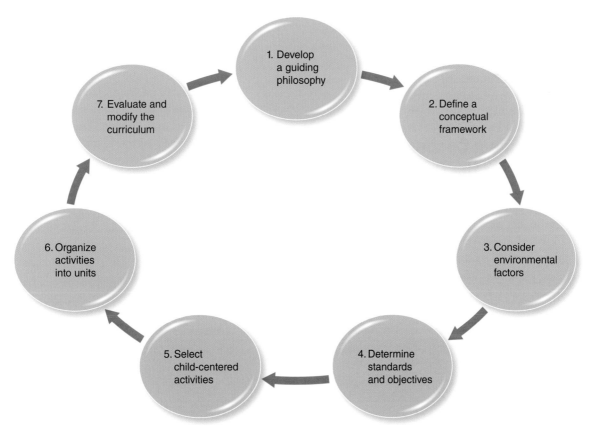

FIGURE 4.1 Steps for designing a quality curriculum.

it is to be a full partner in the child's overall education. Only high-quality programs based on developmental goals with demonstrable, accountable outcomes achieve this respect. The overriding goal of U.S. education—to develop an individual who can live effectively in a democracy—guides the development of this program. Although physical education stresses psychomotor goals, it also contributes to cognitive and affective learning domains. Three major and unique contributions of physical education to the total school curriculum are the following:

1. *To develop personal activity and health habits.* The program teaches children the conceptual framework under which personal fitness and lifetime health habits are developed. This implies teaching the concept of human wellness (i.e., teaching students how to maintain a vibrant and functional lifestyle throughout adulthood).

2. *To develop and enhance movement competency and motor skills.* Movement competency is rooted in developing a broad base of body management skills. The focus is on developing motor skills in a positive and nurturing environment. Personal competency in a wide variety of skills is an overriding theme of instruction.

3. *To gain a conceptual understanding of movement principles.* Moving efficiently requires learning basic concepts of movement and understanding anatomical and mechanical principles. Physical education instruction integrates knowledge and skill performance to teach students how to move.

Step 2: Define a Conceptual Framework for the Curriculum

A conceptual framework is a series of statements characterizing the desired curriculum. These concepts establish criteria for selecting activities and experiences included in the curriculum. The framework directs the selection of activities and reflects beliefs about education and the learner. These statements help define a child-centered, developmental curriculum:

- Curriculum goals and objectives are appropriate for all children. As a result, the curriculum must be balanced—it must cover fundamental skills, sport skills, games, rhythms and dance, gymnastics, and individual and dual activities. It must focus on developing a broad foundation of motor skills for all students.

- Curriculum activities are chosen for their potential to help students reach national and local content standards. The elementary school years are a time of experimentation, practice, and decision making through all movement possibilities. Activities are included in the curriculum not because teachers or students prefer them, but because they help students achieve national content standards.

- The curriculum helps children develop lifelong physical activity habits and understand personal health concepts. Regardless of the curriculum philosophy, it should be designed so that children leave school knowing how to live an active and healthy lifestyle. A meaningful curriculum offers varied, positive, and educational activities students can use throughout life.

- The curriculum includes activities that enhance cognitive and affective learning. Children are whole beings who need to learn more than just how to perform physical skills. They must understand skill performance principles and develop cognitive learning related to physical activity and wellness. Affective development—the learning of cooperative and social skills—can be fostered through group activities, and these skills are just as important as physical skills.

- The curriculum provides experiences that help all children succeed and feel satisfaction. Quality programs minimize failure and emphasize success. Activities that emphasize self-improvement, participation, and cooperation encourage the development of perceived competence. Physical education instruction focuses on learning, without labeling students as winners or losers.

- The curriculum is planned and based on an educational environment that is consistent with other academic areas in the school. Like teachers in other disciplines, physical education teachers need good working conditions. They need class sizes similar to those of classroom teachers (20 to 35 students) and an assigned teaching area (a gym or multipurpose room). They need enough equipment for maximum activity and participation—meaning one piece of individual equipment for each youngster and ample apparatus to limit long lines and waiting for a turn. A daily program gives students maximum opportunity for learning and retention.

- Activities in the curriculum are presented in an educationally sound sequence. Progression is the soul of learning, and the curriculum should reflect progression vertically (between developmental levels) and horizontally (within each level and within each activity).
- The curriculum includes an appropriate means of assessing student progress. Student assessment includes physical activity assessment, healthy eating behaviors, cognitive learning, and attitude development toward physical activity. Any assessment program should benefit students by enhancing curriculum effectiveness, helping teachers individualize instruction, communicating with parents, and identifying students with special needs.

Step 3: Consider Environmental Factors

Environmental factors are conditions in the community and school district that limit or extend the scope of the curriculum. These factors include the amount and type of equipment, the size of the budget, and the cultural makeup of the community. Other factors, such as the support of school administrators, can affect the scheduling or amount of required physical education in the school. Communities may value specific types of activities or experiences for their children. Environmental factors need to be examined carefully, but they should not restrict curriculum scope and sequence. Rather, they should give direction to the curriculum development process.

The following environmental factors can sometimes be limiting, but they can be handled creatively to ensure that the curriculum is effectively implemented. Think big; seek to expand and develop the curriculum beyond these limiting factors.

School Administrators

The support of school administrators significantly affects the curriculum, so informing them about program goals is important. Like the public, administrators may have misconceptions about physical education and its contribution to the overall education of students. Most administrators will support physical education programs built on sound educational principles that are documented and evaluated.

Children's physical activity is strongly influenced by their parents and their geographical location.

Ariel Skelley/DigitalVision/Getty Images

The Community: People and Climate

Occupations, religions, educational levels, cultural values, and physical activity habits in the community can all affect curriculum development. Parents have a strong influence on their children's activity interests and habits. The area's geographical location and climate are important factors, too.

Facilities and Equipment

Facilities dictate the instructional activities that can be offered. Facilities include on-campus as well as off-campus areas in the neighboring community. Off-campus facilities might be a community swimming pool or park. Equipment must be available in quality and quantity. To learn at an optimum rate, each child needs a piece of equipment. Equipment can be purchased with school funds or with special funds raised through student performance programs.

Laws and Requirements

Laws, regulations, and requirements at the national, state, and local levels may restrict or direct a curriculum. Programs must conform to these laws. Examples of two national laws affecting physical education programs are Title IX of the Educational Amendments Act of 1972 and Public Law 94-142. Title IX enforces equal opportunities for both sexes, and PL 94-142 mandates equal access to educational services for students with disabilities (see chapter 9). Individual states also may have laws that affect physical education programming.

Scheduling

The schedule or organizational pattern of the school affects curriculum development. How many times per week classes meet, how long class periods last, and who teaches the classes are factors to consider. Many scheduling alternatives exist: daily, two or three times per week, every other week, and so on. Regardless of the various parameters, most elementary schools have a scheduling committee.

Consider several factors when developing schedules. Physical education classes typically are scheduled for 30 minutes, but duration may vary. Some teachers prefer 45 minutes for upper grades, but this is a long period for primary-grade children. Classes can also be too short. Some schools try to compress primary-grade classes to 20 minutes. A short class makes it difficult to present a balanced and complete lesson. Another important issue is how many periods a physical education teacher should teach per day. Teaching physical education is demanding, and expecting physical education specialists to teach all day without relief is unfair. An acceptable workload is eight or nine 30-minute periods per day with at least 5 minutes of passing time between classes so that teachers can rearrange equipment, talk to students, and take care of personal matters. Passing time also eliminates the situation in which the next class has to wait for the current class to end.

Another important consideration is scheduling classes by developmental levels. Because physical education is equipment and planning intensive, scheduling by developmental level helps reduce the time and energy needed for class area preparation.

Budget and Funding

The funding allocated for purchasing new equipment and replacing old supplies affects curriculum quality. Physical educators deserve parity in funding with other school programs. Students are not expected to learn to read and write without materials and supplies. Likewise,

they cannot learn physical skills without the necessary equipment and facilities.

Step 4: Determine Content Standards

Content standards, which can be dictated or desired by the state, district, or individual school, determine the direction of the program. Such standards are fixed goals for learning. Student progress is dictated by how students compare with the fixed standards rather than how they compare with other students. Content standards determine the criteria for selecting instructional activities for the curriculum. SHAPE America (2013) has identified five national standards that guide the content of this textbook (see chapter 1 for an in-depth discussion of each standard).

Write Student-Centered Outcomes

After defining content standards, physical education teachers must develop outcomes for each developmental level. These outcomes dictate the specific content that students will be learning throughout the school year and throughout the physical education program. They are statements that indicate critical learning and define what students will be able to demonstrate because of physical education. They are more specific statements than standards but are aligned with content-specific standards. Outcomes are written for all three learning domains—psychomotor, cognitive, and affective. A description of each domain follows:

1. *Psychomotor domain.* This domain (Corbin, 1976) is typically the primary focus of instruction for physical educators. The seven levels in psychomotor domain taxonomy are movement vocabulary, movement of body parts, locomotor movements, moving implements and objects, patterns of movement, moving with others, and movement problem solving. Students progress through these levels based on their own developmental level. They learn the vocabulary of movement before proceeding to simple body part movements. More complex movements are taught so that children can participate in activities with others and solve personal movement dilemmas.

2. *Cognitive domain.* The cognitive domain was defined by (Bloom, 1956) and includes six major

areas: knowledge, comprehension, application, analysis, synthesis, and evaluation. The cognitive domain for physical education focuses on knowing rules, health information, safety procedures, and so on, and being able to understand and apply that knowledge. As students mature, they learn to analyze different activities, develop personalized exercise routines (synthesis), and evaluate their fitness levels.

3. *Affective domain.* The affective domain (Krathwohl, Bloom, & Masia, 1964) deals with feelings, attitudes, and values. Major categories of learning in this area are receiving, responding, valuing, organizing, and characterizing. The affective domain changes more slowly than do the psychomotor and cognitive domains. How teachers treat students and the feelings that students develop toward physical education and ultimately physical activity are ultimately more important than the knowledge and skill developed in physical education programs. For this reason, teachers are encouraged to examine their influence on the affective domain often.

Outcomes can be time consuming to write. Some teachers become bogged down and discouraged because the number of outcomes needed can be overwhelming. Fortunately, the website (www.DynamicPEASAP.com) that accompanies this book has lesson plans, all with already written lesson-specific outcomes for teachers.

Step 5: Select Child-Centered Activities

Selecting activities for a child-centered curriculum requires a clear understanding of children's urges, characteristics, and interests. Gathering activities for instruction makes little sense if they are not developmentally appropriate or do not appeal to children. The major criterion to follow when selecting activities for the curriculum is whether the activities contribute to content standards and student-centered outcomes. This approach contrasts with selecting activities because they are fun or because you enjoy them. Some teachers fail to include activities in the curriculum if they lack confidence or feel incompetent to teach them. This approach results in a curriculum designed for the teacher's benefit rather than the students'. If an activity contributes to content standards, teachers need to

develop the requisite instructional competency. Imagine a math teacher choosing not to teach fractions or multiplication tables because he or she lacks confidence or feels incompetent. Teachers have a responsibility to learn how to teach a wide range of activities so that students experience and learn the requisite physical skills. This directive does not suggest that teachers must be experts in all content in the curriculum. It simply means teachers must have the instructional skills requisite to teach the content. Expecting teachers to be proficient in all physical education activities in order to teach those skills is unrealistic. Expecting teachers to be proficient often works in reverse and narrows the breadth of activities offered because teachers feel inept and avoid teaching those activities in which they feel subpar.

In the planning stage, gather as many activities as possible that contribute to content standards. The greater the number of activities considered, the more varied and imaginative the final program will be. In this step, emphasize brainstorming, creating, and innovating without restriction. The finished curriculum will be deficient if it is limited at this step. Later steps offer an opportunity to delete inappropriate activities.

Know the Basic Urges of Children

A basic urge is a desire to do or accomplish something. All children have similar urges, which are hereditary or environmentally influenced. Basic urges are linked closely to societal influences and are affected by teachers, parents, and peers. Usually, basic urges are similar among children of all ages and are unaffected by developmental maturity. These urges provide direction for creating child-centered experiences.

Urge for Movement

Children have an insatiable appetite for moving, performing, and being active. To observe this simply watch youngsters move from one area to another. Unless told by adults to "walk" or "slow down," they skip, run, or walk quickly. They run for the sheer joy of running. For them, activity is the essence of living. Design a physical education program that takes advantage of this craving for movement.

Urge for Success and Approval

Children like to achieve and have their achievements recognized. Ask any group of kindergartners to toss and catch a beanbag. Instantly, you'll hear, "Watch me, look what I can do," throughout the teaching area. Youngsters love to have the teacher watch them perform. Conversely, they wilt under criticism and disapproval. Thus, teachers need to provide encouragement and friendly support to promote growth and development. Failure can lead to frustration, lack of interest, and inefficient learning. Successes should far outweigh failures, and students should achieve some success during each class period. Organize and present curriculum activities to ensure that students will feel successful.

Urge for Peer Acceptance and Social Competence

Peer acceptance is a basic human need. Children want others to accept, respect, and like them. Teach and encourage peer acceptance in physical education and the overall school environment. Learning social skills such as accepting others regardless of skill level is an important outcome of the program for students.

Urge to Cooperate and Compete

Children want to work and play with other children. Learning to cooperate and be a contributing team member are essential programmatic outcomes. Cooperation needs to be taught before competitive experiences because competition is impossible when people choose not to cooperate or follow the rules. Often, the joy of being part of a group far outweighs the gains from peer competition.

Urge for Physical Fitness and Attractiveness

Related to peer acceptance, boys and girls are eager to be fit, active, and attractive. Students who do not fit in can suffer much humiliation. The opportunity to improve personal skills often helps students overcome subpar strength, lack of physical skill, inadequate physical fitness, and obesity.

Urge for Adventure

The drive to participate in something different or adventurous impels children to try new activities. For this reason, among others, physical education units in elementary schools should be limited to two to three weeks in length.

Urge for Creative Satisfaction

Children like to try different ways of doing things. Finding new ways to express themselves physically satisfies the urge for creative action and exploration.

Urge for Rhythmic Expression

Children's physical education should offer a variety of rhythmic activities that they can learn well enough to achieve satisfaction. Emphasize the natural rhythm involved in all physical activity, whether it is walking, running, skipping, or other activities.

Urge to Know

Young people are naturally curious. They are interested in what they are doing and why they are doing it. Knowing "why" is a great motivator. Sharing with a class why they are performing an activity and how it contributes to their physical development takes little time or effort.

Understand the Characteristics and Interests of Children

The urges of children represent broad traits that are typical of children regardless of age, sex, or race. In contrast, characteristics and interests are age- and maturity-specific attributes that influence learning objectives. Table 4.1 lists the characteristics and interests of children, as well as the corresponding program guidelines. This information, which influences the appropriate selection and sequencing of curriculum activities, is analyzed according to the three learning domains—psychomotor, cognitive, and affective—and is grouped by developmental levels (which are discussed in the next section).

Step 6: Organize Selected Activities Into Instructional Units

After selecting appropriate activities that contribute to content standards, design a delivery system that ensures that all activities are taught. Activities are most often grouped by grade or developmental level. To allow for greater variation of skill development among students, this textbook groups activities and units of instruction by developmental level. Even though this developmental skill continuum is common to all students, children exhibit significant variation. This organization offers activities that are appropriate for the maturity and developmental levels of all students. Occasionally, moving to a higher or lower developmental level may be necessary to accommodate students. Table 4.2 shows how developmental levels roughly equate with grades and ages. The following list describes learners at each level and identifies skills and competencies typical of children at those levels.

TABLE 4.1 Characteristics and Interests of Children

Characteristics and interests	Program guidelines
Developmental Level I	
Psychomotor domain	
Noisy, constantly active, egocentric, exhibitionistic; imitative and imaginative; want attention.	Include vigorous games and stunts, games with individual roles (dramatic activities, story plays), and a few team games or relays.
Large muscles more developed; game skills not developed.	Challenge with varied movement. Develop specialized skills of throwing, catching, and bouncing balls.
Naturally rhythmic.	Use music and rhythm with skills. Provide creative rhythms, folk dances, and singing movement songs.
May suddenly become tired but soon recover.	Use activities of brief duration. Provide short rest periods or intersperse physically demanding activities with less vigorous ones.
Eye–hand coordination developing.	Provide opportunity to handle and explore different objects such as balls, beanbags, and hoops.
Perceptual abilities maturing.	Give practice in balance—unilateral, bilateral, and cross-lateral movements.
Pelvic tilt can be pronounced.	Give attention to posture problems. Provide abdominal strengthening activities.
Cognitive domain	
Short attention span.	Change activity often. Give short explanations.
Interested in what the body can do; curious.	Provide movement experiences. Pay attention to educational movement.
Want to know; often ask why about movement.	Explain reasons for various activities and the basis of movement.
Express individual views and ideas.	Allow children time to be creative. Expect problems when children must line up and perform the same task.
Begin to understand the idea of teamwork.	Plan situations that require group cooperation. Discuss the importance of working together.
Sense of humor expands.	Insert some humor (e.g., jokes, funny stories) into the teaching process.
Highly creative.	Allow students to try new and different ways of performing activities; sharing ideas with friends encourages creativity. Promote equipment exploration.
Affective domain	
No gender differences in interests.	Set up same activities for boys and girls.
Sensitive and individualistic; self-concept very important.	Teach taking turns, sharing, and learning to win, lose, or be caught gracefully.
Accept defeat poorly; like small-group activities.	Use entire class group sparingly. Break into smaller groups.
Sensitive to feelings of adults; like to please teacher.	Give frequent praise and encouragement.
Can be reckless.	Stress safe approaches.
Enjoy rough-and-tumble activity.	Include rolling, dropping to the floor, and so on. Stress simple stunts and tumbling.
Seek personal attention.	Recognize individuals through both verbal and nonverbal means. See that all have a chance to be the center of attention.
Love to climb and explore play environments.	Provide play materials, games, and apparatus for strengthening large muscles (e.g., climbing towers, climbing ropes, jump ropes, miniature challenge courses, and turning bars).

(continued)

73

TABLE 4.1 *(continued)*

Characteristics and interests	Program guidelines
Developmental Level II	
Psychomotor domain	
Capable of rhythmic movement.	Continue creative rhythms, singing movement songs, and folk dancing.
Improved eye–hand and perceptual–motor coordination.	Provide opportunity for manipulating hand apparatus. Offer movement experience and practice in perceptual–motor skills (right–left, unilateral, bilateral, and cross-lateral movements).
More interest in competitive activities.	Begin introductory competitive activities, sport and related skills, and simple lead-up activities.
Skill patterns mature in some cases.	Emphasize practice skills through simple games, stunts, and rhythmic patterns.
Developing interest in fitness.	Introduce some of the specialized fitness activities to third grade.
Reaction time is slow.	Avoid highly organized ball games that require and place a premium on quickness and accuracy.
Cognitive domain	
Still active but attention span longer; more interest in group play.	Include active big-muscle programs and more group activities. Begin team concept in activities.
Curious to see what they can do; love to be challenged and will try a variety of activities; some become daring.	Offer challenges involving movement problems and more demanding activities. Emphasize safety and good judgment.
Interest in group activities; ability to plan with others developing.	Offer group activities and simple dances involving cooperation with a partner or a team.
Affective domain	
Like physical contact and belligerent games.	Include dodging games and other active games, as well as rolling stunts.
Developing more interest in skills; want to excel.	Organize practice in a variety of throwing, catching, and moving skills to foster success.
Becoming more conscious socially.	Teach need to abide by rules and play fairly. Teach social customs and courtesy in rhythmic areas.
Like to perform well and be admired for accomplishments.	Begin to stress quality. Provide opportunity to achieve.
Essentially honest and truthful.	Accept children's word. Provide opportunity for trust in game and relay situations.
Do not lose willingly.	Provide opportunity for children to learn to accept defeat gracefully and win with humility.
Gender difference still of minimal importance.	Avoid separation of genders in any activity.
Developmental Level III	
Psychomotor domain	
Steady growth; girls often grow more rapidly than boys.	Continue vigorous program to enhance physical development.
Muscular coordination and skills improving, unless during a growth spurt, during which they may regress; interested in learning detailed techniques.	Continue emphasis on teaching skills through drills, lead-up games, and free practice periods. Emphasize correct form and feedback on process to maximize success.
Differences in physical capacity and skill development.	Offer flexible standards so that all find success. In team activities, match teams evenly so that individual skill levels are less apparent.
Posture problems may appear.	Include posture correction and special posture instruction; emphasize effect of body carriage on self-concept.

Characteristics and interests	Program guidelines
Developmental Level III	
Sixth-grade girls may show signs of maturity; may not wish to participate in all activities.	Have consideration for their concerns. Encourage participation on a limited basis, if necessary.
Sixth-grade boys are rougher and stronger.	Keep genders together for skill development but separate for competition in certain rougher activities. Emphasize controlled movement for efficiency and safety.
Cognitive domain	
Want to know rules of games.	Include instruction on rules, regulations, and traditions.
Knowledgeable about and interested in sport and game strategy.	Emphasize strategy, as opposed to merely performing a skill without concern for context.
Question the relevance and importance of various activities.	Explain regularly the reasons for performing activities and learning various skills.
Desire information about the importance of physical fitness and health-related topics.	Include in lesson plans brief explanations of how various activities enhance growth and development.
Affective domain	
Enjoy team and group activity; competitive urge strong.	Include team games and other competitive activities like combatives.
Much interest in sports and sport-related activities.	Offer a variety of sports in season, with emphasis on lead-up games.
Little interest in the opposite gender; some antagonism may arise.	Offer coeducational activities emphasizing individual differences of all participants, regardless of gender.
Acceptance of self-responsibility; strong increase in drive toward independence.	Provide leadership and followership opportunities on a regular basis. Involve students in evaluation procedures.
Intensive desire to excel both in skill and in physical capacity.	Stress physical fitness. Include fitness and skill surveys to motivate and to check progress.
Respect for teammates a concern for both teachers and students.	Establish and enforce fair rules. With enforcement, include an explanation of the need for rules and cooperation if games are to exist.
Peer group important; want to be part of the gang.	Stress group cooperation in play and among teams. Rotate team positions as well as squad makeup.

TABLE 4.2 Equating Developmental Levels to Grades and Ages

Developmental Level	Grades	Ages
I	K–2	5–7
II	3–4	8–9
III	5–6	10–11

- *Developmental Level I.* For most children, activities used in Developmental Level I are appropriate for kindergarten through second grade. Most activities for younger children are individual in nature and center on learning movement concepts through theme development. Children learn about movement principles, and educational movement themes are used to teach body identification and body management skills. By stressing the joy and personal benefits of physical activity, teachers can help students develop positive behaviors that last a lifetime.

- *Developmental Level II.* Developmental Level II activities are usually appropriate for most third- and fourth-grade children. In Developmental Level II activities, students refine fundamental skills and begin to develop the ability to perform specialized skills. Practicing manipulative skills enhances visual–tactile coordination. At this level, children explore and create activities without fear. Although these activities do not stress conformity, children learn the how and why of activity patterns. Cooperation with peers receives more emphasis through group and team play. Initial instruction in sport skills begins in Developmental Level II, and a number of lead-up activities allow students to apply newly learned skills in a small-group setting.

- *Developmental Level III.* Developmental Level III activities place more emphasis on specialized skills and sport activities. Most fifth- and sixth-grade students can perform activities at this level. Football, basketball, softball, track and field, volleyball, and hockey are added to sport offerings. Students learn and improve sport skills while participating in cooperative sport lead-up games. Less emphasis is placed on movement concept activities, and more of the instructional time is devoted to manipulative activity. Adequate time is set aside for the rhythmic program and for activities involving apparatus, stunts, and tumbling.

After assigning activities to developmental levels, organize the activities in each instructional unit in order of difficulty, starting with the easiest to master and finishing with the most difficult. Organizing activities in progression (1) helps children be successful because the easiest activities are taught first, (2) ensures that safety and liability factors are met since the activities are presented in proper sequence, and (3) aids teachers in finding a starting point for their instructional presentation.

Another element to include in the instructional unit is a list of teaching hints that address safety, teaching for quality, dispersing equipment properly, and providing instructional cues to enhance motor skill development. The Dynamic Physical Education website incorporates activities in this textbook and places them into lesson plans by developmental level. The lesson plans contain activity progressions, teaching hints, and learning objectives that help minimize the demands of planning. Besides the weekly lesson plans, a yearlong curriculum is offered for each of the three developmental levels. This will be discussed in depth later in this chapter.

Figure 4.2 provides an example of a yearlong curriculum for Developmental Level II. The four parts of the lesson—introductory activity, fitness development activity, lesson focus activity, and game activity—are listed in parallel for weeks 1 through 36. This plan ensures that students learn many ways of warming up for activity and approximately 15 different types of fitness activities. In addition, they are exposed to 20 to 25 lesson activities that focus on skill development and 60 to 80 low-organized game activities.

Weekly Units

Organizing the curriculum into weekly activity units, in which instruction focuses on the same activity over an entire week, has three major advantages. First, one comprehensive lesson plan will suffice for the week, which keeps planning duties manageable. The objective is to move children along the path of learning at an optimal

TECH TIP

Teachers want to follow a curriculum that is meaningful to them and their students. Most curriculums are written as hardcopy and appear to be overwhelming and inflexible. For example, changing a couple of units may affect the rest of the curriculum, so you have to reorganize it. This task is time consuming for teachers who are busy preparing for their first lesson of the day. In other words, creating an effective, thoughtful, standards-based curriculum takes time. To help teachers solve the complexity of curriculum, the authors have written *Dynamic Physical Education Curriculum and Lesson Plans* (2016) available online and free of charge. By going to the Dynamic Physical Education website, you can use the Dynamic Physical Education yearlong curriculum for all three developmental levels. In addition, the curriculum can be easily modified to meet the needs of different teachers and school districts. All the lessons can be printed out and used immediately for instruction. The curriculum is evidenced-based and supported by teachers for over 45 years.

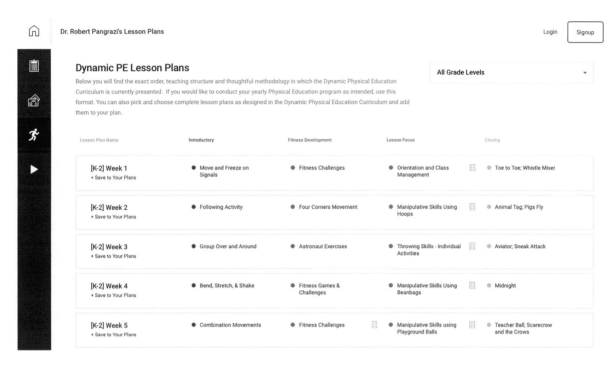

FIGURE 4.2 An example of a yearly plan: Developmental Level II from the Dynamic Physical Education website.
Reprinted by permission from R.P. Pangrazi, *Dynamic PE ASAP* (Owatonna, MN: Gopher Sport).

rate. What cannot be covered one day is taught in the next lesson. That is, not all the content in each lesson plan has to be covered in one lesson. Second, less orientation instruction is needed after the first day. Safety factors, teaching hints, and key points need only a brief review each day; and equipment needs are similar from day to day. Third, progression and learning sequences are evident; both teacher and children can see improvement.

Activities in the "Lesson Focus" section of the lesson plans begin with skills in which all students can experience success and progress to a point where further instruction and skill practice are necessary because students are challenged. Starting each lesson with basic activities ensures that all students begin with success. This outcome is critical for developing positive attitudes toward new activities. If the first thing children experience is failure, the rest of the unit will be a tough sell. Build instructional sequences for each day based on the preceding lesson. Limit the instructional units to one or two weeks so that students do not become bored or discouraged. Long units force children who are unskilled or who dislike the activity to live with failure for a long time. If more time is needed for a specific unit, add another week or two later in the year. Use a game activity for a change of pace when the motivational level of the

class (and of the teacher) seems to be waning.

Another approach to yearly planning is to use the movement theme approach. This approach takes a set of skills or movements and offers an array of activities for instruction related to the same skill. A wide variety of equipment is needed because the same skills are taught using different activities and equipment.

Check the Scope, Sequence, and Balance of the Curriculum

An important step in creating a quality program is to review and monitor the scope, sequence, and balance of the curriculum. These concepts are important for ensuring that the curriculum is comprehensive and varied. Scope is the yearly content of the curriculum. Scope is also referred to as the horizontal articulation of the curriculum. Monitoring the scope of the curriculum ensures that the entire content of the program is covered in a systematic, accountable way. In elementary school physical education, the scope of the curriculum is broad. Student interest wanes if units are too long, so many activities are presented rather than just a few activities in depth. In addition, elementary school physical education should help students learn about all the available types of physical activity, not just a few.

Sequence, or vertical articulation, of the curriculum defines the skills and activities to be covered from year to year. Sequence ensures that students receive different instruction and activities at each developmental level. Of particular importance is the articulation of program material throughout elementary, middle, and high school programs.

Balance ensures that all objectives in the program receive adequate coverage. When reviewing curriculum scope and sequence, adhering to balance avoids a slant toward one particular area. To ensure balance, determine major areas of emphasis based on program objectives. These areas can be allotted a percentage of program time based on students' characteristics and interests. This determination reveals to administrators, teachers, and parents the direction and emphasis of the program. All areas have a proportionate share of instructional time that reflects the needs and characteristics of that area.

Another phase of balance is alternating units based on the type of student interaction required—that is, individual, dual (partner), and small-group or large-group activities. Team sports require organization in a large group, whereas a movement concepts lesson is individual in nature. Learning to catch is a partner activity, whereas a lead-up game requires small groups. The yearly plans offered at www.DynamicPEASAP .com are balanced in this regard. Individual units are followed by small or large-group activities, and

PHYSICAL EDUCATION CURRICULUM ANALYSIS TOOL (PECAT)

The Physical Education Curriculum Analysis Tool (PECAT) is an assessment instrument developed by the Centers for Disease Control and Prevention to help school personnel analyze their physical education curricula. Because student physical activity can be enhanced through a high-quality physical education program, a well-written curriculum provides a solid foundation for maximizing school physical activity opportunities through skill-based and fitness-based instruction, cognitive concepts, and multiple opportunities for improving social and emotional skills.

A high-quality physical education program consists of (1) an effectively written physical education curriculum; (2) policies regarding adequate instructional time, qualified physical education specialists, and appropriate class sizes, equipment, and facilities; (3) instructional strategies that include all students, ample opportunities for physical activity, and out-of-school assignments that support learning but never use physical activity as punishment; and (4) regular student assessment that consists of appropriate use of physical activity and fitness assessments, ongoing opportunities for students to self-assess their physical activity, communication with parents and students about assessments, and a student grading rubric. The physical education teacher of the school can play a huge role in making sure that a quality physical education curriculum exists for the school or district, and one way to do this is to convene a PECAT committee.

Five steps are required for utilizing the PECAT. The first step involves selecting a PECAT coordinator, forming a PECAT committee, and identifying the roles and responsibilities of each member. Next, the team reviews curriculum materials, the PECAT, and any existing state or local standards. Then the committee completes the curriculum description form and the preliminary curriculum considerations (e.g., accuracy, acceptability, feasibility, and affordability). The Content and Student Assessment Analysis is completed next. This determines whether the curriculum content and protocols align with national physical education standards. Finally, the team develops a curriculum improvement plan, which involves interpreting and evaluating PECAT scores and then completing and implementing the improvement plan. From here the team continues to evaluate and modify the curriculum as needed.

For more information about the PECAT and how to get training for the PECAT, visit www.cdc.gov/ healthyyouth/pecat/index.htm.

so on. Balance ensures that children do not have to stay with one type of activity too long, so they can experience the types of physical activity they enjoy on a regular basis.

Step 7: Evaluate and Modify the Curriculum

Evaluating and modifying the curriculum are essential for maintaining the appropriate scope, sequence, and balance. Evaluative data are available from pupils, teachers, consultants, parents, and administrators. The type of data desired can vary. Achievement test scores can supply hard data to compare preassessments and postassessments with those of other programs. Skill assessments include evaluating student performance based on instructional cues, or process evaluation. Subjective assessments might include likes and dislikes, value judgments, problem areas, and needed adjustments. The evaluation schedule can select a limited area for assessment, or assessment can be broadened to cover the entire program. Although assessments do not have to be evident in every lesson, evaluation data are an essential for making curricular modifications.

The Centers for Disease Control and Prevention (2019) developed an instrument for evaluating physical education programs, the Physical Education Curriculum Analysis Tool (PECAT). The PECAT assists schools in conducting a systematic, standards-based evaluation of the content of the curriculum and assessments that are integrated in the curriculum. The PECAT offers tools for evaluating and developing a curriculum improvement plan for the program. Figure 4.3 is an example of the curriculum analysis form for SHAPE America standard 1, grades K–2. As with any process, simply having the data to suggest an area of curriculum deficiency is not enough; instead, an action plan is needed. This action or improvement plan is based on the deficiencies and strengths of the curriculum offerings and assessments. The PECAT is comprehensive and time consuming, so it may be best to use it in small steps—that is, one

4

CASE STUDY

A Common Curriculum Leads to a Strong Program

In recent years, the Pence County School administrators have called on the directors of math and reading to develop or adopt a common curriculum to be used district-wide in their area. The director of physical education in the Pence County, Mr. Ralph Endicott, saw this as a sign of events to come in the near future. He realized that soon administrators would be calling on physical education to have a common curriculum as well. He also understood that if physical educators did not create the curriculum, one would be developed by nonphysical educators and its implementation mandated. To this end, Mr. Endicott created a committee of administrators, physical education teachers, local university professors, and parents to synthesize what is currently being used in physical education in the district and ultimately create a quality physical education curriculum.

In addition to foreseen district mandate, Ralph provided the committee with several other reasons for developing a district curriculum. The curriculum would allow physical educators in the district to use similar language when discussing content. Currently, students who change schools during the school year miss some physical education content because different teachers teach different content at different times in the school year. A common curriculum also allows more useful monthly physical education meetings, or professional development. With all teachers teaching from the same curriculum, during the end of October meeting, content in the curriculum for November can be covered and immediately implemented by teachers. Lastly, this curriculum will foster the creation of a professional learning community within physical education to allow networking among teachers.

Initial barriers to the adoption of a common curriculum identified by the committee included teacher resistance. Based on previous efforts, teachers believed that a common curriculum was confining and eliminated teacher creativity. Mr. Endicott recognized this concern and felt similarly during his time as a physical educator. But as the process moved forward and the curriculum was developed, teachers realized that the curriculum did not tell them how they had to teach the content, but only prescribed when the content was taught. Although acknowledging that the common curriculum took away some of their control, they believed that it provided program and teacher accountability, and demonstrated professional competence within the district.

(K–Grade 5) Standard 1—Demonstrates competency in a variety of motor skills and movement patterns.

STANDARD 1	KINDERGARTEN			GRADE 1			GRADE 2		
	Outcomes	Content	Assessment	Outcomes	Content	Assessment	Outcomes	Content	Assessment
S1.E1 Locomotor: hopping, galloping, running, sliding, skipping, leaping	❏	❏	❏	❏	❏	❏	❏	❏	❏
S1.E2 Locomotor: jogging, running	N/A	N/A	N/A	N/A	N/A	N/A	❏	❏	❏
S1.E3 Locomotor: jumping and landing, horizontal plane	❏	❏	❏	❏	❏	❏	❏	❏	❏
S1.E4 Locomotor: jumping and landing, vertical plane	❏	❏	❏	❏	❏	❏	❏	❏	❏
S1.E5 Locomotor: dance	❏	❏	❏	❏	❏	❏	❏	❏	❏
S1.E6 Locomotor: combinations	N/A	N/A	N/A	N/A	N/A	N/A	N/A	N/A	N/A
S1.E7 Nonlocomotor (stability): balance	❏	❏	❏	❏	❏	❏	❏	❏	❏
S1.E8 Nonlocomotor (stability): weight transfer	N/A	N/A	N/A	❏	❏	❏	❏	❏	❏
S1.E9 Nonlocomotor (stability): weight transfer, rolling	❏	❏	❏	❏	❏	❏	❏	❏	❏
S1.E10 Nonlocomotor (stability): curling and stretching, twisting and bending	❏	❏	❏	❏	❏	❏	❏	❏	❏
S1.E11 Nonlocomotor (stability): combinations	N/A	N/A	N/A	N/A	N/A	N/A	❏	❏	❏
S1.E12 Nonlocomotor (stability): balance and weight transfers	N/A	N/A	N/A	N/A	N/A	N/A	N/A	N/A	N/A
S1.E13 Manipulative: throwing underhand	❏	❏	❏	❏	❏	❏	❏	❏	❏
S1.E14 Manipulative: throwing overhand	N/A	N/A	N/A	N/A	N/A	N/A	❏	❏	❏

(K–Grade 5) Standard 1—Demonstrates competency in a variety of motor skills and movement patterns.

STANDARD 1	KINDERGARTEN			GRADE 1			GRADE 2		
	Outcomes	Content	Assessment	Outcomes	Content	Assessment	Outcomes	Content	Assessment
S1.E15 Manipulative: passing with hands	N/A	N/A	N/A	N/A	N/A	N/A	N/A	N/A	N/A
S1.E16 Manipulative: catching	❏	❏	❏	❏	❏	❏	❏	❏	❏
S1.E17 Manipulative: dribbling or ball control with hands	❏	❏	❏	❏	❏	❏	❏	❏	❏
S1.E18 Manipulative: dribbling or ball control with feet	❏	❏	❏	❏	❏	❏	❏	❏	❏
S1.E19 Manipulative: passing and receiving with feet	N/A	N/A	N/A	N/A	N/A	N/A	N/A	N/A	N/A
S1.E20 Manipulative: dribbling in combination	N/A	N/A	N/A	N/A	N/A	N/A	N/A	N/A	N/A
S1.E21 Manipulative: kicking	❏	❏	❏	❏	❏	❏	❏	❏	❏
S1.E22 Manipulative: volleying underhand	❏	❏	❏	❏	❏	❏	❏	❏	❏
S1.E23 Manipulative: volleying overhead	N/A	N/A	N/A	N/A	N/A	N/A	N/A	N/A	N/A
S1.E24 Manipulative: striking, short implement	❏	❏	❏	❏	❏	❏	❏	❏	❏
S1.E25 Manipulative: striking, long implement	N/A	N/A	N/A	N/A	N/A	N/A	❏	❏	❏
S1.E26 Manipulative: in combination with locomotor	N/A	N/A	N/A	N/A	N/A	N/A	N/A	N/A	N/A
S1.E27 Manipulative: jumping rope	❏	❏	❏	❏	❏	❏	❏	❏	❏
Total number of boxes checked in each column									
Total possible number of boxes checked in each column	15	15	15	16	16	16	7	7	7

FIGURE 4.3 An example of a curriculum analysis form used in the PECAT.

Reprinted from Center for Disease Control and Prevention. www.cdc.gov/healthschools/pecat/index.htm.

standard or grade level at a time. The entire PECAT is available online at www.cdc.gov/healthyyouth/pecat/.

Collecting information is only the first step; the information must be translated into action. The modi-fication of possible program deficiencies must be based on sound educational philosophy. If the program has weak spots, it is important to identify the weaknesses and determine their causes.

LEARNING AIDS

HOW AND WHY

1. What is your value orientation for physical education? How will this influence your teaching?
2. Why have a curriculum?
3. Who should be involved in the curriculum development?
4. What issues must be considered by curriculum designers?
5. How are the needs, interests, and characteristics of elementary students today the same as, and different from, what they were 30 years ago?

CONTENT REVIEW

1. List and discuss the seven steps for designing a quality physical education curriculum.
2. What environmental factors can affect a curriculum? Discuss your answers.
3. Define and discuss the importance of standards, grade-level outcomes, and lesson outcomes.
4. Explain the role of the scope, sequence, and balance of a curriculum.
5. Discuss the three learning domains. Explain each domain.
6. List the common components of quality physical education curricula.

WEBSITES

Dynamic Physical Education curriculum and lesson plans, www.DynamicPEASAP.com
Teaching styles, www.spectrumofteachingstyles.org

SUGGESTED READINGS

Graham, G., Holt/Hale, S.A., & Parker, M. (2013) *Children moving: A reflective approach to teaching physical education* (9th ed.). Boston, MA: McGraw-Hill.

Griffin, L.L., & Butler, J.I. (2005). *Teaching games for understanding: Theory, research, and practice.* Champaign, IL: Human Kinetics.

Mager, R.F. (1997). *Preparing instructional objectives.* Atlanta, GA: Center for Effective Performance.

Pangrazi, R.P. (2016). *Dynamic physical education curriculum guide: Lesson plans for implementation.* New York, NY: Pearson.

Prouty, D., Panicucci, J.P., & Collison, R. (2007). *Adventure education: Theory and applications.* Champaign, IL: Human Kinetics.

Rink, J.E. (2009). *Designing the physical education curriculum: Promoting active lifestyles.* Boston, MA: McGraw-Hill.

Rink, J.E. (2014). *Teaching physical education for learning* (7th ed.). Boston, MA: McGraw-Hill.

Siedentop, D., Hastie, P.A., & van der Mars, H. (2011). *Complete guide to sport education.* Champaign, IL: Human Kinetics.

REFERENCES

Bloom, B.S. (Ed.). (1956). *Taxonomy of educational objectives, the classification of educational goals, handbook I: The cognitive domain.* New York, NY: David McKay.

Centers for Disease Control and Prevention. (2019). *Physical Education Curriculum Analysis Tool.* Atlanta, GA: Centers for Disease Control and Prevention.

Cleland, V., Dwyer, T., & Venn, A. (2012). Which domains of childhood physical activity predict physical activity in adulthood? A 20-year prospective tracking study. *British Journal of Sports Medicine, 46*(8), 595–602.

Corbin, C.B. (1976). *Becoming physically educated in the elementary school.* Philadelphia, PA: Lea & Febiger.

Hellison, D. (2011). *Teaching personal and social responsibility through physical activity* (3rd ed.). Champaign, IL: Human Kinetics.

Krathwohl, D.R., Bloom, B.S., & Masia, B.B. (1964). *Taxonomy of educational objectives, Handbook II: Affective domain.* New York, NY: David McKay.

Kulinna, P.H. (2008). Models for curriculum and pedagogy in elementary school physical education. *Elementary School Journal, 108*(3), 219–227.

Metzler, M.W. (2011). *Instructional models in physical education* (3rd ed.). Scottsdale, AZ: Holcomb Hathaway.

SHAPE America. (2013). *National standards & grade-level outcomes for K–12 physical education.* Reston, VA: Author.

Lesson Planning

5

This chapter focuses on planning strategies for creating lesson plans based on a well-developed physical education curriculum. Before instructing, the teacher must make many decisions that will drive the learning experiences. Lesson-planning steps are designed to ensure that many of these decisions are made before the lesson. Among these decisions is the development and inclusion of measurable outcomes. A structured, consistent lesson is important to ensure quality instruction. Many considerations for teachers are provided in this chapter. Issues such as available equipment, teaching space, and lesson formations should be thought through before teaching. Finally, reflection is an essential component of lesson planning as a means of improving future lessons.

Learning Objectives

▶ Describe the role of planning in preparing for quality instruction.
▶ Discuss the steps to developing a physical education lesson.
▶ Identify preinstruction decisions that teachers must make before teaching a lesson.
▶ Describe effective ways to use equipment, space, time, and formations to enhance instruction.
▶ Discuss the rationale for a four-part lesson and describe each component.
▶ Explain how to improve the quality of a lesson plan using reflection.

Lesson planning is a critical part of the teaching process. As you have seen in chapter 4, the curriculum development process is time consuming and requires extensive planning. Now we will examine planning for specific lessons. Curriculum development provides you with the structure or bones of your curriculum, and the lesson-planning process provides the muscle that allows you to implement the curriculum. The lessons designed and implemented need to be flexible and offer meaningful content for students. On an average day, teachers make many unexpected decisions. Their job is much easier when they make as many decisions as possible before presenting the actual lesson. Preinstructional decisions are as important as the lesson content. Failing to plan the lesson carefully can diminish its effect.

Steps to Developing a Lesson Plan

Writing effective lesson planning takes time and experience. Here several steps will be provided to help guide this process. As you will see, many considerations and variables must be addressed when creating lesson plans. Note that the content of the lessons created are driven by the curriculum. During this phase, teachers take the general content and put it into action with specific activities, skills, and games.

Step 1: Determine Lesson Outcomes

During the curriculum development process the scope and sequence was created. This ensures that your curriculum is balanced in that it covers all standards, addresses content in an appropriate sequence, and presents the content appropriately from year to year in the curriculum. During lesson planning, lesson outcomes are written. Some refer to lesson outcomes as learning targets. For this textbook, they will be referred to simply as outcomes. Outcomes are lesson specific, precise, and measurable because they will drive the creation of assessments. Table 5.1 provides examples of outcomes used in the Dynamic Physical Education website.

These outcomes are made up of four parts that can be thought of as ABCD (Mager, 1997). First is the **A**ctor. In physical education, the actor is the student. Depending on the district, some write this as "the student" and other may use "I" for a student-centered approach. In the examples provided in table 5.1, "I can . . ." statements are used. Next is the **B**ehavior. The behavior must be observable such as demonstrate, list, or explain. For many outcomes, especially those when performing a psychomotor skill, a set **C**ondition is provided. For example, skipping *in a zigzag pathway*. The condition would be a zigzag pathway. Finally, the **D**egree determines the criteria for performing the task

TABLE 5.1 Examples of Outcomes for Each Standard

Standard	Outcome
1	I can skip in a zigzag pathway demonstrating two of four cues (Developmental Level I).
	I can kick a rolling ball demonstrating three of four cues (Developmental Level II).
	I can combine locomotor and manipulative skills in a game setting (Developmental Level III).
2	I can demonstrate locomotor skills at different speeds (Developmental Level I).
	I can demonstrate fleeing and chasing in a game (Developmental Level II).
	I can explain the role of different skills during activities (Developmental Level III).
3	I can list three ways to be active outside school (Developmental Level I).
	I can demonstrate three activities that help to enhance flexibility (Developmental Level II).
	I can set appropriate PE physical activity goals based on my own data (Developmental Level III).
4	I can work as a member of a group or team (Developmental Level I).
	I can listen to and use feedback from the teacher (Developmental Level II).
	I can analyze and critique safety procedures during PE (Developmental Level III).
5	I can explain that some activities are challenging for me (Developmental Level I).
	I can describe the positive feelings I have about physical activity (Developmental Level II).
	I can explain the health benefits of regular physical activity (Developmental Level III).

well. Again, this applies mainly for psychomotor skills and is written relative to the cues that the teacher provides. For example, the teacher may teach students to kick a ball on the ground using the cues "Foot beside, favorite foot back, middle of the ball, and kick through the ball." The degree might be to demonstrate two of the four cues because this skill may be new to a student.

We recommend using four to six outcomes per lesson, or roughly one outcome per lesson part (lesson parts will be discussed later). The outcomes are important because they will drive the specific content of the lesson and the assessment. Some content of the lesson may not be directly tied to the outcome, but a majority of the activities in the lesson will be developed to address the outcomes created in this step.

Step 2: Generate an Assessment Tool

With four to six outcomes selected based on the scope and sequence, an assessment can be generated. Given limited time in physical education, doing more than one assessment per lesson is not feasible; thus, of the selected outcomes, one will be selected to emphasize during the lesson. With the selection of one targeted outcome, teachers can create an assessment to evaluate student progress toward that outcome. Without this assessment, teachers will have no way of knowing if in fact students are learning. By writing the outcome using the ABCD strategy, the assessment can be made. Chapter 8 discusses assessments, types of assessments, and ways to use assessments in depth. Assessment creation is the second step in the lesson-planning process because the assessment, and the outcomes, will drive much of the content of your lessons.

Step 3: Select Specific Activities

This step involves selecting specific activities to use during the lesson that will help students reach the desired outcome. During the curriculum development process, general activities were selected. Now, the specific activities are selected, and the items that the teacher will emphasize during the activity are determined. For example, the activity in the scope and sequence might be "Fleece Ball Fun." In this simple activity, students explore different safe and appropriate ways to use a fleece ball. In the lesson-planning process, the teacher has selected an outcome such as "Moves in safe space while working individually." Thus, in the lesson plan, the teacher would include activities and content to teach students how to engage in "Fleece Ball Fun" while being safe.

Step 4: Organizing a Lesson Plan

A standardized lesson plan allows teachers and substitute teachers to exchange plans within a school district. Include the following basic information in your lesson plan:

1. *Outcomes.* List the outcomes developed in step 1.
2. *Equipment required.* Based on the activities selected and how they will be taught, identify the amounts of materials and supplies required and the way in which the equipment will be distributed.
3. *Instructional activities.* List the actual movements and skills to be taught. These were determined in step 3 above. Place the activities in the proper developmental sequence. You do not need to describe activities in detail, but give enough description so that they can be easily recalled.
4. *Teaching hints.* Record organizational tips and important learning cues, including equipment setup, student grouping, and teaching cues. If needed, list text and video references.

A common format is the four-part lesson plan. Figure 5.1 is an actual lesson plan taken from the Dynamic Physical Education website. Each lesson in this curriculum includes an introductory or warm-up activity, fitness activities, lesson focus, and a closing activity. Using four parts prepares students for the activity, ensures moderate to vigorous activity, teaches skills, and implements skills in a game setting. This structure also allows much flexibility for teachers wishing to use a variety of teaching models. The following sections will describe each part of the lesson in detail.

Introductory (Warm-Up) Activity

The introductory (warm-up) activity lasts 2 to 3 minutes (for a 30-minute lesson) and sets the tone for the rest of the lesson. If you can shape a class into a well-behaved group during the introductory activity, such cooperative behavior is easier to maintain for the rest of the lesson.

Starting a lesson is a difficult phase of teaching that can be made easier by practicing management skills, such as stopping on signal, running under control, and so on. An effective rule of thumb is to move and freeze your class three times. If all students are with you after three freezes, begin teaching an introductory activity (chapter 13). But if students are not well managed at that point, skip the introductory activity and practice management skills. Remember that management skills

[3-4] Week 12

Equipment Needed for Lesson Plan:

None

Beanbag or baton
Cones for walking activities

Beanbag or baton
Cones for walking activities (New engineer)
One spot for each student (Quiet cooperation)

1. INTRODUCTORY

4

Fastest Tag in the West

Outcomes:

I can move safely and in good spacing while playing tag.

Instructions:

All students are it. On signal, they try to tag each other. If they are tagged, they must freeze, but they are eligible to tag other students who pass near them. If two or more players tag each other simultaneously, they are both/all "frozen."

Teaching hints:

The focus of this game is activity. Don't overemphasize rules. When about half of the class is frozen, start the game over.

FIGURE 5.1   Lesson plan from the Dynamic Physical Education website.

Reprinted by permission from R.P. Pangrazi, *Dynamic PE ASAP* (Owatonna, MN: Gopher Sport).

---

need to take priority over physical development skills. You cannot teach children who are not paying attention to you. Learning to respect others takes top billing in all educational settings.

Introductory activities serve the following purposes in the lesson format:

- Students engage in immediate activity upon entering the activity area. Children want to move right away rather than have to sit down, be quiet, and listen to instructions. Offer vigorous activity first; then give instructions or discuss learning objectives while they recover from vigorous activity.

- Introductory activities serve as a physiological warm-up, preparing students for physical activity.

- This part of the lesson can be used for anticipatory set (chapter 6) or to review previously learned skills. Anticipatory set previews the skill and cognitive objectives of the lesson.

Physical Fitness and Activity

The second part of the lesson is designed to enhance health-related fitness and promote lifetime physical activity. Include a variety of exercises so that students experience the wide range of options available for maintaining an active lifestyle. This part of the lesson also teaches students the type and amount of activity necessary to maintain a healthy lifestyle. Discussing the importance of a healthy lifestyle is insufficient; it must be experienced. Teach students how to determine their personal workloads, with an implied expectation that they will do their best. Forcing all students to do the same amount of activity fails to consider the genetic and personality differences inherent in a class of students. (More about physical fitness is discussed in detail in chapter 14.)

Lesson Focus

Many adults use their physical skills as tools for participating in a physically active lifestyle. The lesson focus is designed to teach physical skills. It contains learning experiences to help students meet program content standards. The repetition and refinement of physical skills in a sequential and success-oriented setting characterize the lesson focus. This part of the lesson (15 to 25 minutes) emphasizes the process of performing skills correctly. It teaches students the skills required to function comfortably in a physically active lifestyle. (Chapters 15 through 30 are filled with many instructional units presented in the lesson focus.)

Closing Activity

The closing activity ends the lesson with an evaluation of the day's accomplishments—stressing and reinforcing the skills learned, revisiting performance techniques, and checking cognitive concepts. The closing activity may be a game using skills developed in the lesson focus or simply a low-organized game or activity children enjoy (see chapter 22 for a variety of games). If a lesson is demanding or spirited, focus closing activities on relaxing and winding down so that students can return to the classroom in a calmer state of mind. Taking a few minutes to relax may calm teachers and students and create goodwill between classroom teachers and physical education specialists.

The closing activity may be minimized or deleted entirely. If a game or activity is the lesson focus, you may need more time for instruction. Whether a game is played or not, avoid disciplining a class by suggesting, "We will not have a game if you don't quiet down." Closing activities are a useful part of the lesson and should not be used to bribe students to behave. Doing so may cause students to leave physical education classes with negative feelings.

Other Considerations When Planning Lessons

Lesson planning takes time. Teachers are encouraged to write them when you have ample time to plan and reflect. Lesson plans give direction to the day's lesson and may include many more activities than you can teach in a typical period. For quick reference, many teachers use a 4-by-6-inch (10 by 15 cm) card briefly describing the actual activities they are teaching.

Teaching Skills in Proper Progression

A considerable amount of time during lessons will be spent teaching psychomotor skills. For this reason, as teachers plan they need to consider how the lesson will progress with respect to skills taught. Skill progression involves moving the learning process through ordered steps from the least challenging to the most challenging facets of an activity. Most motor skills can be ordered in an approximate hierarchy from simple to complex. Instructional progression includes reviewing previously learned steps before proceeding to new material and learning prerequisite skills before trying more difficult activities.

Children learn skills in a natural progression but not at the same rate. Encourage students to progress at a rate that is best suited for them. This routine usually means that all children will be learning a similar class of skills (throwing or striking, for instance) but will

 TECH TIP

Social media such as Twitter, Facebook, and Instagram can be a useful tool during the planning phase. Social media provides teachers with access to thousands of colleagues around the globe, many who are experiencing similar issues or working on similar projects. By using social media to create a professional learning network, teachers can discuss ideas, ask questions, and share resources. The key with social media is that physical educators no longer have to go it alone and reinvent the wheel. In many cases the wheel has already been invented.

progress at different rates and practice different skills within the category. This premise forms the basis for presenting a developmentally appropriate physical education program.

Placing activities into developmental levels makes it easier to present activities appropriate to students' maturity and abilities. Understand that placing activities in levels serves as a general guideline for instruction. Some students may be gifted or in need of special instruction. In those cases, present activities that best suit the individual regardless of the recommended level. Schools group children by chronological age and grade rather than by developmental level; table 4.2 shows how developmental levels roughly equate with grades and ages. To help plan lessons in which skills are presented in proper sequence, the activities in chapters 15 through 30 have been placed in order of difficulty, from beginning skills to the most advanced. For instructional and lesson-planning purposes, the Dynamic Physical Education website organizes the activities by developmental level.

Developmental Level I activities (used most often with kindergarten through grade 2) are the least difficult and form the foundation of more complex skills. Most of these skills are performed individually or with a partner to increase the success of primary-grade children. Examples are tossing and catching, striking a stationary object, and playing games that simply incorporate fundamental locomotor movements. The number of complex decisions to make while performing the skill is minimized so that students can concentrate on the skill at hand. As students mature and progress into Developmental Level II (usually grades 3 through 4), the tasks become more difficult; many are performed individually or in small groups. Environmental factors, such as different speeds of objects, different sizes of objects, and games requiring locomotor movements and specialized skills (e.g., throwing, catching, and so on), are introduced at this level. In Developmental Level III (grades 5 through 6), students use skills in various sport and game situations. Simple skills previously learned are sequenced into more complex motor patterns. Cognitive decisions about when to use a skill and how to incorporate strategy into the game are integrated into the learning experiences at this level. See table 5.2 for a quick comparison of typical activities for the three developmental levels. The placement of activities into developmental levels is a general rule of thumb. There will always be exceptions. Expect to make exceptions to meet the developmental needs of your students.

Considering Environmental Factors

The environment where students experience physical education can influence the effectiveness of instruction and learning. Factors such as space, equipment, and safety are important in planning a quality experience. Unlike student response and interest, environmental factors can be managed entirely by the teacher. Teachers have little excuse for not considering and planning for these variables.

Predetermine Your Space Needs

A common error is to take a class to a large practice area, give students a task, and fail to define or limit the space where they are to perform it. In such a large area, communicating with and managing students is difficult,

TABLE 5.2 Characteristics of Activities for Developmental Levels I, II, and III

Level	Typical grades	Level of difficulty	Individual or group?	Examples and characteristics
I	K–2	Least difficult; foundation for more complex skills; much concentration required to perform skills	Mostly individual; sometimes with a partner	Tossing and catching; striking a stationary object; games incorporating basic locomotor skills
II	3–4	More difficult; skills are performed more consistently; less concentration required	Often individual or in small groups; groups and teams introduced	Specialized skills and variation in environmental factors (e.g., speeds and sizes of objects)
III	5–6	Advanced individual and specialized skills and activities; skills often performed automatically without thinking; students able to perform well in group activities	Stress placed on playing with others and using skills in cooperative and competitive settings	Sport and game situations; involves cognitive decisions and strategies; more emphasis on manipulative activity, less on movement concept activities

and many cannot see or hear what is being demonstrated. The skills being practiced and the teacher's management of the class should dictate the size of the space. As students become more responsive, the area can be enlarged. Regardless of its size, delineate the practice area. One easy way to do this is to set up cones around the perimeter (a cone in each corner is satisfactory). Chalk lines, evenly spaced equipment, or natural boundaries can also serve as restraining lines.

The size of the practice area is also affected by the amount of instruction needed. When students are learning a closed skill and need constant feedback and redirection, they must stay near the instructor. Establish a smaller area where students can move in closer for instruction and then return to the larger area for practice.

Dividing your available space into smaller areas to maximize student participation is often effective. An example is a volleyball game in which only 10 students can play on one available court. A more effective approach may be to divide the area into two courts so that more students can play at once. A related consideration when dividing space is safety. If the playing areas are too close together, players from one area might run into those in the other area.

Use Equipment Efficiently

Equipment can be a limiting factor. Before beginning the lesson, determine how much equipment is on hand because availability affects the lesson structure. For example, if only 16 paddles and balls are available for a class of 30, some type of sharing or station work will have to be organized. Know exactly what equipment is available and how much is in working condition. Rolling out a cart of playground balls only to find that half of them are not inflated is frustrating and counterproductive.

How much equipment is enough? When using individual-use equipment, such as rackets, bats, and balls, each student should have one piece of equipment. For group-oriented equipment such as benches or balance beams, no more than four students should be waiting in line. Some teachers settle for less equipment because they teach as they have been taught. A common example is teaching volleyball with plenty of available equipment: Rather than having students work individually (each with a volleyball) against the wall or with a partner, the teacher divides the class into two long lines using one or two balls. Most of the equipment sits on the sidelines while students spend more time waiting in line than practicing skills.

TEACHING TIP

Teachers need to be professional observers. They need to survey the performance of their students regularly to ensure that they are working on developmentally appropriate activities. Because you are a trained professional, you will occasionally need to make a decision to offer activities from a different developmental level. Make a professional decision that best serves your students' needs.

If equipment is limited, adapt the instruction for the time being but try not to accept the situation in the long run without voicing dissatisfaction. Some administrators characterize physical educators as good people who are always willing to make do. Communicate in a professional manner with administrators regularly and explain that instruction is much more effective when equipment is available. Speak with parent–teacher groups about having fund-raisers to buy needed equipment. Math teachers are not expected to teach math without books for each student, so physical educators should not be expected to teach without adequate equipment. If you settle for less, you will get less.

What are temporary alternatives when equipment is lacking? One solution is to teach using the task style—that is, to divide students into small groups so that each group has enough equipment. Another approach is to divide the class in half and have one group work on one activity while another works on an unrelated activity. If paddles and balls are in short supply, half of the class can practice racket skills while the other half plays half-court basketball. This approach is less educationally sound and increases management issues. Another solution is the peer review—that is, one student practices an activity, while a peer offers feedback and evaluation. They share equipment and take turns practicing and evaluating. A final solution is the most common—namely, design drills that involve standing in line and waiting for a turn. This method, however, is unacceptable from an educational standpoint.

Effectively distributing equipment is a key component of a quality lesson; it reduces the time spent on tasks not related to learning. Distribute individual equipment by placing it around the perimeter of the area. Some

TEACHING TIP

Teach students to respect the instructional space by setting out four cones on the corners of the areas. When the class arrives, have them do a locomotor movement throughout the area within the cones. Remind students who go outside that area to return. Soon your classes will always stay within the area you select. You can easily decrease or increase this space during class to suit your needs. As with most management skills, this protocol will become second nature to students if you practice and maintain high expectations.

setup time before the lesson is required, but students can take a piece of equipment without confusion. If a variety of equipment is distributed in the area, young students will need to be reminded to use only the equipment they are instructed to touch. Arrange large apparatus in the safest possible formation, so that all pieces are visible from all angles.

Effective setup of the equipment depends on the lesson. Examples include lowering the basket to focus on correct shooting form, lowering the volleyball net to allow for more successful play, and placing nets at different heights to allow different types of practice. Equipment and apparatus should always be modified to best suit the students' needs. Nothing is sacred about a 10-foot (3.05 m) basket or a regulation-sized ball, and in fact, they are likely developmentally inappropriate. If modifying the equipment improves the quality of skill learning, then do it.

Ensure a Safe Environment

Do not underestimate the importance of a safe environment. Injuries are inevitable in physical education classes, but if they are due to poor planning and preparation, you may have a liability issue (see chapter 11). Teachers are expected to foresee hazardous situations that might result in student injury. Rules dictating safe and sensible behavior need to be taught and practiced.

Another component of a safe environment is a written curriculum for presenting lessons. A written curriculum offers evidence to a safety committee or court of law that instruction and activities were properly sequenced. An appropriate progression of activities also gives students confidence because they develop the skills needed to perform safely before moving on to the next level of difficulty.

Conduct safety inspections at regular intervals. If apparatus has not been used for some time, inspect it

beforehand to avoid having to stop a lesson and fix it. Keep tumbling mats, beanbags, and benches clean to prevent the spread of disease.

Despite taking the foregoing precautions, accidents can happen. All physical education activities have a certain degree of risk because students are moving. An important outcome of a physical education program is to offer students an opportunity to take calculated risks and overcome personal fear. When students believe that adequate safety precautions are in place, they are more likely to try new activities that involve risk.

Choose an Instructional Formation

Appropriate formations facilitate learning experiences. Different formations are needed for activities done in place (nonlocomotor), for activities in which children move (locomotor), and for activities in which balls, beanbags, or other objects are thrown, kicked, caught, or otherwise received (manipulative). Figure 5.2 shows the variety of formations that are possible in physical education. Select a formation based on ensuring maximum activity for all students. To minimize the amount of time that students spend standing and waiting for a turn, limit squads to four students or fewer. In addition, consider the age of students when selecting a formation. Formations that require considerable time to get into may need to be reconsidered and the activity modified to enhance efficiency.

Reflective Teaching

Teaching is a full-time job. Teachers who excel and influence the lives of their students put a great deal of time and energy into their teaching. All who teach physical

Mass or scattered

The class scatters throughout the area so each student has a personal space. This formation is useful for in-place activities and when individuals need to move in every direction. Emphasize not bumping into, colliding with, or interfering with classmates. Scattered formation is basic to such activities as wands, hoops, individual rope jumping, and individual ball skills.

Squad

In squad formation, members stand about three feet apart in a column. In extended squad formation, the squad column is maintained with more distance (10 to 15 ft) between members. (L = leader)

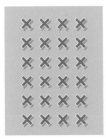

Partner

Partner formation is useful for reciprocal teaching, where partners help each other learn new skills. Keep the pairs aligned if space is limited or objects are being caught and thrown.

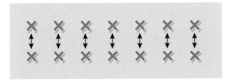

Lane or file

The lane, or file, formation is commonly used with locomotor activity. Students at the front of the lane move as directed and take their place at the rear of the lane.

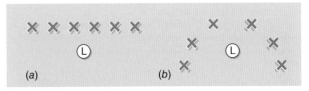

Line and leader

(a) Line-and-leader formation is often used for throwing and catching skills. The leader passes back and forth to each line player in turn. Place students in a (b) semicircle-and-leader formation so they are all the same distance from the leader.

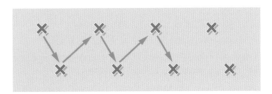

Double line

The double-line formation is used for passing and kicking. This example shows a zigzag formation in which the ball is passed from one line to the next.

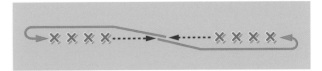

Regular shuttle

Try the regular shuttle formation for practicing passing and dribbling skills on the move. It is often used for hockey, soccer, basketball, and football skills. The player at the head of one line dribbles toward, or passes to, the player at the head of the other line. Each player keeps moving forward and takes a place at the end of the other half of the shuttle.

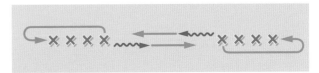

Shuttle turn-back

Shuttle turn-back formation is used for passing, kicking, and volleying for distance. The player at the head of one shuttle line passes to the player at the head of the other. After passing, players go to the back of their line.

FIGURE 5.2 Possible formations in physical education.

(continued)

5

Simultaneous class movement

Some activities require the entire class to move simultaneously. Without some structure and organization, this situation can become chaotic. For such activities, the following formations can be useful.

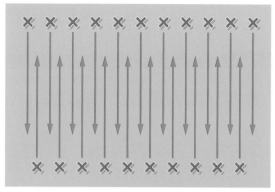

Children can start on opposite sides of the gym and exchange positions. On signal, they cross to the opposite side of the area, passing through the opposite line without contact.

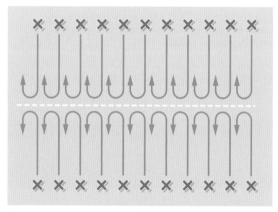

Children can also start on opposite sides of the gym, move toward the center, and then go back. Form a dividing line with ropes, wands, or cones to mark the center.

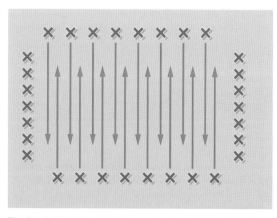

Finally, children can start on each of four sides of the play area and alternately exchange sides. The children on one pair of opposite sides exchange first and then the others exchange. This formation is useful for class demonstrations—that is, half of the class demonstrates, while the other half observes and evaluates.

FIGURE 5.2 *(continued)*

ENCOURAGING PHYSICAL ACTIVITY BEYOND THE SCHOOL DAY

Physical education can substantially contribute to a child's daily physical activity; in fact, low-active kids can accumulate up to 20% of their total physical activity in a quality 30-minute physical education lesson. For youth, however, most of their physical activity takes place outside school during the unstructured time after school and on weekends. For this reason, teachers need to tie what is learned during physical education to activity opportunities outside school or even at recess.

One approach is to assign physical activity homework calendars. These daily, weekly, or monthly calendars can be sent home with students to encourage them to be active alone, with friends, or with family. Each day offers a few suggested activities for the students to choose from. The activities should be conducive for engagement in a home or neighborhood setting and require little to no equipment to accommodate everyone. Early in the year, physical education lessons can teach students activities they can engage in at recess. When more skills and activities are taught that can be used at recess, remind students that what they are learning can be applied outside physical education lessons.

Teachers can also provide students with information about places in their community where they can engage in the activities. Remind students where local parks are. Tell them where nearby tennis courts are during a tennis lesson. Show students on a city map where disc golf courses are. Of course, emphasize safety and teach students to go only with parents or trusted adults. During a walking unit, provide fliers for students that advertise upcoming charity walks or races. Regardless of the lesson, students should always be encouraged to apply what they learn outside physical education.

5

education work hard to reach physical education outcomes. But identifying a truly outstanding teacher who seems to get students to perform at a high level is easy. One element apparent in all great teachers is the level of caring and thought they give to their profession. They spend a great deal of time thinking about the lessons they have presented and looking for new and better ways to get students to respond. This process is often referred to as reflection—sitting back and asking, "How could I have done better so students would have learned more?"

Many things make teaching difficult—the weather, teaching outside, having a limited amount of equipment, not knowing how some children will respond to your discipline techniques, and so on. There are no simple answers; what works one time may not work the next. For these reasons, successful teachers change their lessons often. So rather than teach the same lessons from year to year, their lessons evolve throughout their teaching

careers. Quality teachers find time to reflect on all factors related to their lessons. Most teachers admit that their first lesson of the week is not as polished and effective as those near the end of the week. That first lesson does not include all the finer points learned through trial and error. Instruction improves when teachers reflect on why some things worked and others did not. Leave time at the end of the day to reflect and note ways to improve the lesson. Try keeping a journal in which you record some of the inspiration and insight you uncover during the reflection process. Write down personal growth indicators and situations that show you are growing professionally. Continue to reflect; it is a dynamic, ongoing process. The Questions That Aid the Reflection Process sidebar provides a list of potential questions. Feel free to add other questions that are specific and related to your professional growth.

QUESTIONS THAT AID THE REFLECTION PROCESS

Planning

- Did I prepare ahead of time? Mental preparation ensures flow and continuity in a lesson.

- Did I understand the "whys" of my lesson? Knowing why you are teaching something enables you to present it with greater strength.

- Did I plan the lesson so that students can participate safely? Check that they have safe, open areas for running; no slippery spots, broken glass, or objects to run into; adequate room for striking activities; and so on.

Equipment

- Was my equipment arranged before class? Proper equipment placement reduces management time and allows more time for instruction and practice.

- Did I use enough equipment to keep all students involved and assured of maximum practice opportunities?

- Did I notify the principal about equipment that needs to be repaired or replaced? On a regular basis, do I record areas where equipment is lacking or insufficient in quantity?

- Did I select equipment appropriate for the students' developmental level (i.e., proper size and types of balls, basketball hoop height, hand implements)?

Methodology

- Did I constantly move and reposition myself during the lesson? Moving allows you to be close to more students so that you can reinforce and help them. Proximity usually reduces behavior problems.

- Did I teach with enthusiasm and energy? Energy and zest rub off on students.

- Did I try to show just as much energy for the last class of the day as I did for the first class of the day?

- Did I work just as hard on Friday as I did at the start of the week?

- Did I keep students moving during lesson transitions?

- Did I plan my transitions carefully so that I did not need much time to go to the next part of the lesson?

Instruction

- Was I alert for children who were having trouble performing the activities and needed some personal help? Children want to receive relevant but subtle help.

- Did I praise students who made an effort or those who improved? Saying something positive to children increases their desire to perform at a higher level.

- Did I give enough attention to each student's personalization and creativity? Everybody feels unique and wants to deal with learning tasks in a personal way.

- Did I teach for quality of movement, or just offer many activities in attempting to keep students on task? Repetition is a necessary part of learning new skills.

Discipline and Management

- Did I teach students to be responsible for their learning and personal behavior? Students need to learn responsibility and self-direction skills.

- Did I evaluate how I handled discipline and management problems? Did I preserve my students' self-esteem when correcting behavior? How could I have handled situations better?

- Did I make positive calls home to reinforce students who are really trying and working hard?

Assessment

- Did I bring closure to my lesson? This method gives feedback about the effectiveness of instruction. It also allows students to reflect on what they have learned.

- Did I ask for answers in a way that lets me quickly check that all students understand?

- Did I evaluate the usefulness of activities I presented? Did I make changes as quickly as possible to ensure that my lessons were improving and better meeting students' needs?

- Did I communicate with teachers and the principal about things that need to be improved or better understood? For example, did I say something about classes arriving late, teachers arriving late to pick up their classes, schedule problems that cause excessive work, and so on?

LEARNING AIDS

HOW AND WHY

1. Why is the outcome selected important when designing a lesson?
2. Why are lesson plans important? How are they developed?
3. How does reflection affect lesson planning?
4. How did your physical education learning environment differ from that described in this chapter?
5. Why is it important to follow steps when creating a lesson plan?

CONTENT REVIEW

1. What are the steps to developing a physical education lesson plan?
2. Discuss the importance of the outcomes and assessment in lesson planning.
3. Describe four instructional formations. How can these formations be used?
4. Identify the four parts of a lesson. Discuss the characteristics and significance of each part.
5. What are several issues that physical education teachers must address when preparing to teach?

WEBSITES

Dynamic Physical Education curriculum and lesson plans, www.DynamicPEASAP.com
Teaching styles, www.spectrumofteachingstyles.org

5

 CASE STUDY

Think You Need a Lesson Plan?

Teachers often look at lesson planning as a less important task than instructing students. Experienced teachers believe that they do not need to plan because, they say, "I have taught this unit many times, and I know what I am doing." Other teachers suggest that a lesson plan prevents them from taking advantage of the teachable moment. Then some teachers just say that it takes too much time to write down what they already have planned in their head. So, the question is raised: Is it really necessary to write lesson plans?

Let's ponder some scenarios that might help you see the need for planning your lesson:

- You arrive at school on Monday morning only to find that the principal has called an emergency meeting. You haven't planned your lesson, aren't sure what equipment you need, and then find that another teacher has your equipment. You aren't sure what and how to teach, so you decide that you'll just let them play kickball. Do you think that this approach is professional?

- You come down ill on Sunday afternoon and have to call in sick. Monday morning your substitute arrives and looks for your lesson plans so that she knows what to teach. Unfortunately, none is available, so the substitute decides to roll out a few balls and let students play. When the substitute teacher is finished, she goes to the principal and complains about the lack of lesson plans and uncooperative students. What kind of impression did you make with the principal?

- You are teaching a lesson without plans. Unfortunately, a student is badly hurt. The student is in the hospital, and a number of weeks pass before a lawyer for the student's parents arrives on campus to investigate the accident. The lawyer wants to know the skills you taught and in what order they were taught. The lawyer wants to examine your lesson plan to see exactly what the student was doing when the injury occurred. A number of weeks have passed since the injury, and you are finding it difficult to remember exactly what you were teaching and how the student was injured. When the lawyer asks you to show evidence that these activities were appropriate for your students, what do you say? When the lawyer asks if the activities were taught in proper progression, what proof do you offer? Do you think a written lesson plan would have helped your defense?

SUGGESTED READINGS

Graham, G., Holt/Hale, S.A, & Parker, M. (2013) *Children moving: A reflective approach to teaching physical education* (9th ed.). Boston, MA: McGraw-Hill.

Griffin, L.L., & Butler, J.I. (2005). *Teaching games for understanding: Theory, research, and practice.* Champaign, IL: Human Kinetics.

Hellison, D. (2011). *Teaching personal and social responsibility through physical activity* (3rd ed.). Champaign, IL: Human Kinetics.

Krathwohl, D.R., Bloom, B.S., & Masia, B.B. (1964). *Taxonomy of educational objectives, handbook II: Affective domain.* New York, NY: David McKay.

Metzler, M.W. (2011). *Instructional models in physical education* (3rd ed.). Scottsdale, AZ: Holcomb Hathaway.

Prouty, D., Panicucci, J.P., & Collison, R. (2007). *Adventure education: Theory and applications.* Champaign, IL: Human Kinetics.

SHAPE America. (2013). *National standards & grade-level outcomes for K–12 physical education.* Reston, VA: Author.

Siedentop, D., Hastie, P.A., & van der Mars, H. (2011). *Complete guide to sport education.* Champaign, IL: Human Kinetics.

REFERENCES

Mager, R.F. (1997). *Preparing instructional objectives.* Atlanta, GA: Center for Effective Performance.

Improving Instructional Effectiveness

Effective instruction is the foundation of a quality physical education lesson. Successful teachers use a variety of instructional strategies to create an environment conducive to learning. Instructional cues, demonstration, modeling, and feedback are all examples of sound instructional practice. Students clearly understand better when you offer one or two key points and then demonstrate the desired behavior. Listening skills are as important as speaking skills in establishing meaningful relationships with students. Instructional cues—words or phrases—serve as quick, effective communication about proper technique in performing a particular skill or movement. Teachers can give students feedback in various ways—positive, negative, and corrective. Over time, positive feedback is the most effective way to develop positive attitudes toward activity. Instruction is best when it is personalized and offers something of value to each individual. Diversity and gender particularly affect instruction in physical education. This chapter outlines some strategies for enhancing diversity and reducing gender stereotyping.

Learning Objectives

▶ Learn how to teach in ways that promote diversity in physical education classes.

▶ Understand how gender stereotypes can be minimized.

▶ Identify various ways to communicate with children effectively in a physical education learning environment.

▶ Understand the procedures needed to develop effective instructional cues.

▶ Cite various ways to enhance communication between the teacher and the learner.

▶ Identify essential elements of instruction and discuss how each element relates to the learning environment.

▶ Describe the value of nonverbal behavior in the physical education setting.

▶ Describe various demonstration and modeling skills that help make an environment conducive to learning.

▶ Understand how instructional cues can be used to increase student performance.

▶ Learn how to give students meaningful feedback about their performance.

▶ Describe various ways to personalize instruction in the physical education setting.

▶ Discuss instructional strategies designed to motivate youth to be physically active.

▶ Identify methods for the instructional analysis of teacher behavior.

Quality instructors create a positive atmosphere for learning. They may not know more about skills and activities than less capable teachers do, but they can apply a set of effective instructional skills. That is, successful teachers are not necessarily those with the most physical skills but rather the best teaching skills. This chapter deals with instructional techniques that all teachers can master. These skills serve to improve the efficiency and effectiveness of physical education lessons and greatly affect the physical education experience for students.

Characteristics of a Quality Lesson

An effective learning environment offers a set of instructional behaviors that occur regularly. These behaviors do not describe a specific method or teaching style but allow for individual approaches to teaching content. The focus is less on what the teacher does and more on what the students do. Any teaching style that produces high rates of student-engaged time and positive attitudes toward the subject matter is considered an effective teaching style. Evidence from teacher effectiveness research indicates that, regardless of the teacher's instructional style, an educational environment is most effective when the following elements (figure 6.1) are present. The common thread that runs through these characteristics is a high level of physical activity through well-planned, efficient lessons.

1. Students are engaged in appropriate learning activities for a large percentage of class time. Students should be engaged in physical activity for at least 50% of the lesson time. As a result, effective teachers use class time wisely. They plan carefully and insist on appropriate learning activities that deal with the subject matter while maintaining high levels of physical activity. Students need time to learn; effective teachers ensure that students use class time to receive information and practice skills. They accomplish this goal by selecting learning activities that are matched to students' abilities and contribute to overall class objectives.

2. The learning atmosphere is success oriented and has a positive, caring climate. Teachers who develop a supportive atmosphere foster learning and positive student attitudes toward school. Appropriate social and organizational behavior needs to be supported by teachers. Students and teachers must feel positive about working and learning in the physical education environment.

3. Students are given clear objectives and receive high rates of feedback from the teacher and the environment. Students need to know what they are going to be held accountable for in class. Class activities are arranged so students spend large amounts of time engaged in physical activity and learning the required objectives. Instructional activities are clearly tied to class objectives. Positive and corrective feedback is offered regularly, and students receive feedback on learning attempts even if the teacher is unavailable.

4. Student progress is monitored regularly, and students are accountable for learning in physical education. Instructional strategies and activities are selected to ensure that students progress toward meeting lesson objectives. Youngsters know exactly what is expected of them and how the expectations are tied to the accountability system. The reward system focuses on making small, progressive steps toward a larger goal.

5. Low rates of management time and efficient transitions from one activity to another characterize the environment. Effective teachers manage students well. Students move smoothly from one learning activity to another and spend little time waiting during instructional activities. Equipment is organized to facilitate smooth transitions. Instructional procedures are all well planned and tightly organized with little wasted time.

6. Students spend a limited amount of time waiting in line or in other unproductive behaviors. In effective instructional environments, students are engaged in subject matter most of the time. For physical education, this means high rates of time spent practicing, drilling, and playing. Physical education is activity based, and students learn best when practice and learning times are maximized.

7. Teachers plan their lessons and set high but realistic expectations for student achievement. Effective planning implies that teachers have selected developmentally appropriate learning activities for students. Activities must not be too easy or too difficult. Students need success and challenge from learning activities, and a balance of both is critical to quality teaching. Expect students to learn and hold them accountable for their progress.

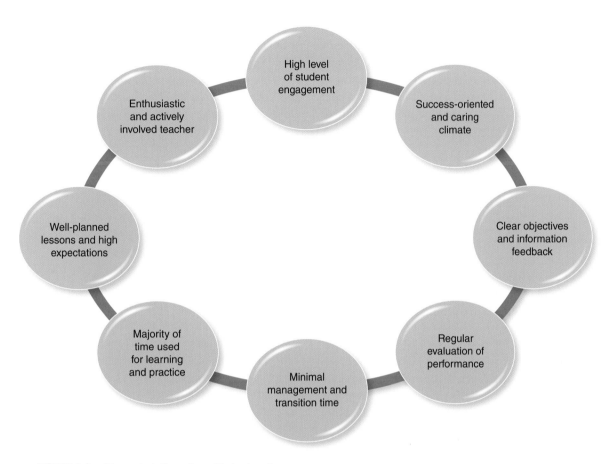

FIGURE 6.1 Characteristics of quality instruction.

8. Teachers are enthusiastic about what they are doing and are actively involved in the instructional process. Students need an enthusiastic model—someone who incorporates physical activity into his or her lifestyle. Active involvement means active supervision, enthusiasm, and high interaction rates with students. These characteristics enhance learning regardless of the teaching style used; they are important for ensuring student achievement and positive attitudes.

Incorporate Essential Elements of Instruction

Learning occurs when a well-planned curriculum is presented using sound instructional practices. Education is effective when a quality curriculum and able instruction are smoothly meshed. The curriculum is a vital component of the educational process, but a poorly taught curriculum limits students' progress.

Write Measurable Outcomes

As discussed in chapter 5, writing lesson outcomes is a foundational step in writing lesson plans. Educational outcomes give a lesson direction and meaning. When clearly stated, outcomes let learners know what they are expected to accomplish. Learning is enhanced when students help select and set personal and group outcomes. Discussions and teaching aids, such as movies, videos, posters, and speakers, can help teachers and students work toward outcomes. Learning outcomes are characterized as follows:

- Outcomes must define observable behavior. Teachers and students must know when an outcome is reached. Thus, the outcome must be observable and measurable. Attainment in physical education is easier than in some other areas because most activities are overt and easy to observe. Outcomes with terms such as "list," "demonstrate," and "identify" as the verb indicate measurability.

- Outcomes must identify, clearly and specifically, the content to be learned. Teachers and students are most comfortable when both parties clearly understand what is expected. Problems arise when students have to guess what the teacher wants them to learn. Students have a right to know what is expected and how they can reach the stated outcome. If outcomes are ambiguous or nonexistent, students have no way of knowing if they have improved or learned anything. Chapter 5 offers detailed strategies for writing measurable lesson outcomes.

Develop outcomes for the three learning domains—psychomotor, cognitive, and affective. Psychomotor outcomes are defined most commonly in physical education and cover areas such as learning physical skills and developing health-related physical fitness. Cognitive outcomes for physical education involve knowledge and comprehension of skill performance principles related to fitness and activity. Affective outcomes focus on attitudes and behaviors, such as learning to cooperate with peers on a team or behaving responsibly. Examples of measurable student outcomes include the following:

Psychomotor

- "The student will demonstrate four ways to perform a forward roll."
- "Using a jump rope, the student will perform three consecutive forward crossover moves."

Cognitive

- "The student will explain when a corner kick is awarded."
- "The student will diagram a sample floor routine for balls."

Affective

- "After participating in physical activity, the students will express their personal satisfaction in their accomplishments."
- "The students will share how they feel about participating in physical activities with friends."

Determine the Instructional Entry Level

To determine the proper entry level for teaching, ask yourself, "At what skill level do I begin instructing my class?" Instruction in a new activity should begin with a successful experience, or students may be turned off and view the rest of the unit negatively. Selecting the skill level for instruction is challenging because of the wide variation in students' abilities and maturities.

One way to determine the proper entry level is to move through a series of activities (easy to advanced) until you notice several students having difficulty. This method accomplishes two things: It allows students to review the skills they have learned (and thus feel successful), and it gives you a general idea of the students' ability levels. Alternatively, let students choose the entry level they think is best suited for them. For example, use task charts listing skills that students are to perform on the balance beam. Students can select activities they feel competent in performing and move at their own rate through the tasks.

Use Anticipatory Set

Anticipatory set is a technique designed to focus students on an upcoming instructional concept and segue to the next portion of the lesson. Use anticipatory set to warm up a class mentally. Anticipatory sets are most effective when they tie into students' past learning experiences. In a beanbag unit, asking students to identify why they had trouble catching in a previous lesson encourages them to think about technique. Instructional focus might be to keep their eyes on the beanbag or make a lower toss. Anticipatory set also reveals the students' knowledge level. For example, asking students, "What are three things we have to remember when tossing and catching?" reveals whether they know the basic catching skills. Identifying what students know is necessary for designing an effective lesson.

Another use for anticipatory set is to tell students the desired outcome. Explain what they are going to learn and why it is important. Few people care about learning if they do not know the outcome or think it is unimportant. The more convinced students are about the importance of learning something, the more motivated they will be to participate.

At times an anticipatory set is unnecessary but have a reason for omitting it. If students already know the necessary information, taking time for an anticipatory set has little value. On the other hand, at the beginning of a lesson, after an interruption, or when choosing to move to a new objective, teachers will find anticipatory sets useful. Examples of anticipatory sets include the following:

- "On Monday we practiced the skills of passing, dribbling, and shooting layups. Take a few moments to think about the problems you had with dribbling or passing skills. (Briefly allow time for thought and discussion.) Today we are going to use some drills that will help you improve in these areas."

- "Think of activities that require body strength and be ready to name some when called upon. (Briefly allow time for thinking and discussion.) This week we are going to learn some activities that will help you become stronger."

- "What is it called when we move quickly in different directions? Identify as many activities as you can that require agility, and be ready to share with the class. (Briefly allow time for thinking and discussion.) This week we are going to learn how to do Tinikling. This rhythmic activity will improve your agility level."

Deliver Meaningful Skill Instruction

Effective instruction is the cornerstone of learning; it is how teachers share information with students. Such information can include defining the skill, describing the elements of the skill, and explaining when, why, and how to use the skill. The following are some suggestions for effective instruction:

1. Limit instruction to one or two key points. Remembering a series of instructions is difficult. Giving students several points related to skill performance leaves them unsure and frustrated; most learners remember only the first and the last points. Emphasizing one or two key points makes it easier for students to focus their concentration.

2. Use the 30-second rule and refrain from lengthy skill descriptions. When instructions last longer than 30 seconds, students become listless because they cannot comprehend and remember all the input. Develop a pattern of short, concise presentations alternated with practice sessions. Short practice sessions allow students to refocus on key points of a skill many times. If you need to instruct for longer than 30 seconds, break the presentation into smaller segments. Allow students to apply your instructions after each segment.

3. Present information in its most basic, easily understood form. If a class does not understand the presentation, you—not your students—have failed. Check to see whether students understand the material (discussed further in the next section).

4. Separate management and instructional episodes. Consider the following instructions, given while presenting a new game: "In this game, we will make groups of five. Each group will get a ball and form a small circle. On the command 'Go,' the game will start. Here is how you play the game . . ." (a long discussion of game rules and conduct follows). Because the instructions are long, students forget what they were asked to do earlier. Or, they think about the group they want to be in rather than the game rules. Instead, move the class into groups of five in circles (management) and then discuss the activity to be learned (instruction). This approach reduces the length of the instruction, and it makes it easier to learn how the game is played.

These strategies for delivering skill instruction offer two benefits: (1) brief bouts of instruction will decrease the likelihood that students engage in off-task behavior, and (2) piecing together instructions between bouts of physical activity increases overall physical activity levels during the physical education lesson and is consistent with the intermittent physical activity levels of children (described in chapter 2).

Actively Monitor Student Performance

Active monitoring ensures that students stay on task and practice activities correctly. Move and make eye contact with all students. Students generally stay on task when they know someone is watching them. Try to be unpredictable when moving around the teaching area. If students always know where you position yourself, some of them will move away from you; others will stay nearby. Random positioning ensures contact and proximity with all students in the class.

TEACHING TIP

Asking, "Does everybody understand?" rarely lets you know if students completely understand safety instructions. Instead, ask questions that can be answered by a thumbs-up or by a raised hand if they think that a demonstration is correct. Also, use peer-checking methods.

Teachers commonly assume they must move to the same area when giving instructions. Students who choose to exhibit deviant or off-task behaviors usually move as far from the instructor as possible. If you always instruct from the same place, some students will find a position that is hard to observe. Furthermore, by staying in one place, you will not be near students who need or want attention. To prevent having your back to students, deliver instruction from the perimeter of the area and vary your location regularly.

Teacher movement, coupled with effective observation, keeps students on task. Positioning yourself to observe skill performance enhances your ability to improve student learning. If you are observing kicking, stand to the side rather than behind the student. When observing students, avoid staying too long with a single group of students, which may cause the rest of the class to begin to move off task. Give a student one or two focus points and then move to another student. If needed, after moving to another area, look back to ensure that the student grasped the feedback.

Because teacher movement affects instructional effectiveness, it needs to be purposeful. To facilitate coverage, divide the instructional area into four (or more) equal areas and deliberately move into the far corner of each area a certain number of times. Try to give instructions and reinforcement from all four quadrants of the area. If you are interested in reaching a personal goal, have a lesson videotaped and analyze or track your movements. (See figure 6.9 for a chart for recording different teacher behaviors.)

TEACHING TIP

Teacher movement can improve teaching effectiveness in a hurry. Students believe you care about them because you interact with more of them. Students who lack confidence will feel better because you made it a point to visit them as well. Teaching is a relationship, and the more that students believe you care about them, the harder they try. At the end of the lesson, take a few minutes and look at your list of students. Check off the students you interacted with on a one-to-one basis. Make a note to speak to those who didn't hear from you during the next class.

Use Instructional Cues

Instructional cues are keywords that quickly and efficiently communicate proper technique and the performance of skills and movement tasks. Children require a clear understanding of critical skill points because they develop motor learning and cognitive understandings at the same time. When using instructional cues, consider the following points.

Develop Precise Cues

Make cues short, descriptive phrases that call attention to key points of the skill technique. Cues must be precise and accurate. They should guide learners and enhance the quality of learning. Cues make it easier for learners to remember a sequence of new motor patterns. Study an activity and design cues that focus student learning on correct skill technique.

All teachers occasionally must teach activities they know little about. Developing cues in areas of less expertise requires some research. Many textbooks and media aids outline key points of skills. For example, Fronske (2012) offers teaching cues for a wide variety of physical activities. Other resources are teachers who have strengths in different activities. Video an activity and analyze points of performance where students are having the most difficulty.

Use Short, Action-Oriented Cues

Effective cues are short and to the point. To avoid confusing and overwhelming the learner, present only one or two cues during each lesson. A general rule of thumb is to have two to four cues per skill. Design cues that contain keywords and are short. When possible, using terms that are child-friendly and catchy will help students remember the cue. Meaningful cues encourage the learner to focus on one phase of a skill during practice. If a student is learning to throw, offer a cue such as, "Begin with your throwing arm farthest from the target." This cue reminds the student not to face the target, which precludes rotation of the trunk in later phases of the throw. Other examples of throwing cues are the following:

- "Step toward the target."
- "Keep your eye on the target."
- "Shift your weight from the rear to the front foot."

To examine the effectiveness of cues, see if they communicate the skill as a whole. Have all the critical points of throwing been covered, or is the skill incorrect in certain phases? Most skills can be broken down into three parts: preparation, action, and recovery. Focus on only one phase of a skill because most people can best concentrate on one thing at a time. Action-oriented words are effective with children, particularly if the words sound exciting, for example, "Pop up at the end of the forward roll," or "Twist the body during the throw." In other situations, let the voice influence the effectiveness of the cue. For example, if a skill is to be done smoothly and softly, speak softly and ask students to "let the movement floooow" or to "move smooooothly across the balance beam." The most effective cues use voice inflections, body language, and action words to signal the desired behavior.

Integrate Cues

Integrating cues involves putting the parts of a skill together so that learners can focus on the skill as a whole. Integrated cues are based on prior cues and assume that the student has learned the parts of the skill. The following are some examples of integrated cues:

- "Step, rotate, and throw."
- "Kneel, tuck chin, and forward roll."
- "Stride, swing, and follow through."

The first cue reminds students to sequence parts of the skill. The second cue helps young children remember a sequence of movement activities. Integrated cues help learners remember the proper sequencing of skills and form mental images of the performance.

Enhance Instruction by Demonstrating Skills

A fast, effective way to present a physical activity is to demonstrate it. Effective demonstration accentuates critical points of performance. While demonstrating, simultaneously call out key focal points so that students know what to observe.

Demonstrating all physical activities is impossible. Even skilled teachers need an alternative plan for teaching activities they cannot perform. By reading, studying, and analyzing movement, you can develop an understanding of how to present activities. If performing an activity is impossible, know what key points of the activity to emphasize. Use visual aids and media to enhance instruction.

When possible, slow down the demonstration and present it step by step. Many skills can be videoed and played back in slow motion. Stop the replay at criti-

cal places so that students can emulate a position or technique. For example, in a throwing unit, freeze at a point that illustrates the arm position. Have students imitate moving the arm into proper position based on the stop-action pose.

Use Students to Demonstrate Skills

If you cannot demonstrate a skill, find a student who can help. Use a student who wants to demonstrate the desired skill, so that he or she will not be embarrassed in front of the class. You can usually find a capable student by asking the class to perform the desired skill. Identify a student who is correctly performing the skill during the practice session, and ask if he or she is willing to demonstrate. Most students will not volunteer to demonstrate unless they feel able. While the student demonstrates the skill, identify key points of the action. Students are in partners spread out about 20 yards (meters) apart; one partner has a football.

- "When kicking the football, take a short step with your kicking foot, a long step with the other foot,

Effective teachers demonstrate skill techniques.

6

and kick (demonstrate). Again, short step, long step, kick (teaching cue)."

- "Listen to the first verse of this schottische music. I'll do the part of the Schottische Step we just learned starting with the second verse (demonstrate). Ready, step, step, step, hop (teaching cue). When I hit the tambourine, begin doing the step."

- "Today we are going to work on developing fitness by moving through the challenge course. Move through the course as quickly as you can, but do your best at each challenge; quality is more important than speed. Travel through the course like this (demonstrate). Move under the bar, swing on the rope, and so forth (teaching cue). When I say go, start at the obstacle nearest you."

Student demonstrations bring original ideas into the lesson sequence and help build children's self-esteem. At opportune times, stop the class and let children volunteer to show what they have done. Make positive comments

Many students enjoy the opportunity to demonstrate skills.

about demonstrations. If you are unsure about a student's ability to demonstrate, ask her to try the activity while all other students are engaged. If successful, have her demonstrate. If not, let her know you will let her try another skill later. Go on to another child without comment or reprimand, saying only, "Thank you, Janet. Let's see what Carl can do." Ensure that all students who want to be selected are given an opportunity at one time or another.

Check for Understanding

To monitor student progress, check to see if they comprehend the content of the instruction. Students may act as if they understand even when they do not. Some teachers have a common (but poor) habit of asking periodically, "Does everybody understand?" or "Any questions?" They appear to be checking for understanding, but this seldom is the case. Such teachers often do not even wait for a response, and in any case, only a brave and confident student will admit in front of the entire class that he or she does not understand. To avoid embarrassing students in front of their classmates or receiving questions not pertinent to instruction, teachers need a quick, easy way to check for understanding. Some suggestions follow:

1. Use hand signals. Examples might be the following: "Thumbs-up if you understand," or "If you think this demonstration is correct, balance on one foot," or "Raise the number of fingers to signal whether you think student 1, 2, or 3 did a correct forward roll." If the teacher then moves on quickly and without comment, students will learn to signal without embarrassment. If the situation is touchy or embarrassing, students can signal with their heads down and eyes closed.

2. Ask questions that can be answered in choral response. Some students may mouth an answer even though they do not know the correct response. A strong response by the class indicates that most students understand.

3. Direct a forthcoming check to the entire class rather than to a specified student. For example, "Be ready to demonstrate the grapevine step." This encourages all members of the class to focus on the activity, knowing they may be called on to demonstrate. This approach does not ensure that everyone understands, but it motivates students to think about the skill check.

4. Use peer-checking methods. Have students pair up and evaluate each other's performance using

a checklist. To ensure the validity of scoring, students can be evaluated by one or more students.

5. Use tests and written feedback to monitor cognitive concepts. For example, use written feedback to see if students understand what muscles are being used during an exercise. Asking students to list safety precautions for an activity ensures student understanding. Use some restraint when administering written feedback—too much can take time away from skill practice. Use these instruments when the information cannot be gathered more efficiently with other methods.

Bring Closure

Closure is a time to review learning that has taken place during the lesson. Closure helps increase retention because students have to think about what they have learned. Focus closure discussions on what students have learned rather than on just naming activities practiced. Closure is not simply a recall of completed activities, but a discussion of the skills and knowledge learned through practice.

Closure can be an opportunity to show similarities between movement patterns in different skills. Students may not realize that a new movement pattern is parallel to one learned earlier. Closure is a time to remind children to tell their parents and others what they have learned. Some prompts for closure discussions follow:

- "Describe two or three key components of skill performance to your partner."
- "Demonstrate the proper skill when I (or a peer) give you a verbal cue."
- "Create a closing activity that uses the skills learned today."
- "Describe and demonstrate a key point for a new skill learned in the lesson."

A caution about closure is in order here. Often, before conducting closure, teachers line up students in preparation for returning to the classroom. Unfortunately, this configuration leaves students standing close to each other, giving them an opportunity to disrupt the class by talking and bothering others. Keep the class spread out in the teaching area during closure discussions.

Provide Instructional Feedback

Delivering student feedback is an important part of instruction. Used properly, feedback enhances a stu-

dent's self-concept, improves the focus of performance, increases the rate of on-task behavior, and improves student understanding.

Types of Feedback

Much of the feedback teachers deliver is corrective, focusing on rectifying or improving student performance. Avoid negative feedback, which is not constructive and can be destructive. An example of negative feedback might be, "That was a poor throw; let's try a little harder." Students expect some corrective feedback, but a concern of overusing corrective feedback is that it creates a climate where students worry about making errors for fear the instructor will embarrass or belittle them. Furthermore, many children surmise that no matter what they do correctly, their efforts are seldom recognized.

As much as possible, focus feedback on positive student performance. A positive atmosphere motivates students to accept a challenge and risk errors or failure. Positive feedback also helps teachers feel upbeat about students because it focuses on their strengths. There is general agreement that a four-to-one ratio of positive to corrective feedback enhances learning and maintains motivation. Teachers commonly teach as they were taught. If your physical education teacher overused corrective feedback, you may do the same. Most teachers need to increase positive feedback and decrease negative feedback.

Use Meaningful Feedback Statements

Teachers often develop positive yet habitual patterns of interaction. They overuse statements such as, "Nice job," "Way to hustle," "Much better," "Right on," and "Great move." After hearing them repeatedly, students tune out these repetitious comments and fail to feel their positive effect. General comments also offer little specific information or value, thus allowing misinterpretation. Suppose that after a student does a forward roll, you say, "Nice job." You are pleased with the performance because the student tucked his or her head, but the student thinks you are pleased because his or her legs were bent. Nonspecific feedback can easily reinforce an incorrect behavior.

Adding specific information or value to feedback improves desired student behavior. The value content of a feedback statement tells students why they need to perform a skill in a certain way. Students clearly understand why their performance was positive and can build on the reinforced behavior. Examples of specific positive feedback with value content are the following:

- "Good throw. When you look at your target, you are much more accurate."
- "Excellent catch. You bent your elbows while catching, which created a soft home for the ball."
- "That's the way to stop. When you bend your knees, you always stop under control."

Some examples of feedback with specific content follow:

- "I like the way you kept your eyes on the ball."
- "Wow! Everybody was dribbling the ball with their heads up."
- "I'm impressed with the way you kept your arms straight."

Distribute Feedback Evenly

Feedback should be evenly distributed to all students by moving systematically from student to student, assuming that no major discipline problems are occurring. This approach fosters contact with students several times during the lesson. It also keeps students on task because they know that the teacher is moving and "eyeballing"

everybody regularly. If skills are complex and refinement is a goal, take more time with individual students. This task involves watching a student long enough to offer specific and information-loaded feedback. The result is high-quality feedback to fewer students.

After delivering instructional feedback to a student, move on and let the student practice without you observing. Most students become tense if you tell them how to do something and then wait to see if they do it exactly as you instructed. Changing skill performance takes time, and students often repeat the same mistake before learning the desired technique. Observe carefully, offer feedback, move on to another student, and recheck progress later.

Effective Feedback: Positive, Focused, and Immediate

Often feedback is group oriented; that is, the entire class receives it. This method is efficient, but it leaves the most room for misinterpretation. Some students may not understand the feedback; others may not listen because it does not seem relevant. When giving individual feedback, do so privately. Avoid humiliating a student by directing negative or corrective feedback quietly.

TECH TIP

A versatile tool for teachers to use while teaching is a projector, which can be used to project videos, pictures, or other materials for the entire class. Most schools have a projector, but if you have to order one, you will want one that is easily transported and offers 2,500 to 3,000 lumens. Such a device will allow a clear display even in a well-lit gym or activity center. Projectors can be used in many ways. First, teachers can project videos of a specific skills being performed. These videos are readily available online, but teachers are encouraged to consider creating their own either with themselves performing the skills, or better yet, with students performing the skills. Such videos allow students to connect with the performer. Note that this approach is not intended to replace the teacher. Typically, the teacher performs the skill and provides some cues for students to remember. Then, as the teacher circulates to provide student specific feedback, the video is playing. This method allows students to reference the skill visually in a self-directed manner as needed. Essentially, the skill is being modeled continually while the teacher is moving around the space. Teachers are encouraged to make their own videos to foster some connection. Appearing in the videos could even be part of a reward system or something special for a student who needs some extra attention.

Projectors can also be used to project other prompts. For instance, teacher questioning and prompting is a way to get students thinking about the activity. A prompt might be, "As we work on rhythmic movements today, think about what activities make you smile." Then leave the prompt on the screen for teachers to refer to and to remind students. At the end of the lesson, an assessment could be about the activities that made students smile with a peer. This approach also allows students to see key words that are often unseen in physical education. Although this method can be done with printed signs, the size of the screen and the ease of creating prompts on a screen put technology to good use. An activity discussed in chapter 10 is Emotional Movement. In this activity students are given an emotion and asked to move in a way that demonstrates that emotion. Teachers can use words or emojis that represent an emotion. Students then move, showing how to move with that emotion. To add some fun, the teacher can try to guess the emotion on the screen (without looking) based on the movements of students.

Focus feedback on the desired refinement of a task. For example, if you want students to "give" while catching a ball thrown by a partner, avoid giving feedback about the quality of the throw. If catching is the focus, feedback should be on catching, as in, "Rachel is reaching out and giving with her hands to make a soft home for the ball." Although students in Developmental Levels I and II enjoy being praised in front of others, older students usually dislike being singled out. In this case, make feedback personal.

Offer feedback to students as soon as possible after a correct performance. If the class is almost over, limit your feedback and write down points of emphasis you want to teach at the next class meeting. Little is gained if students are told how to improve but have no chance to practice before leaving class.

Nonverbal Feedback

Nonverbal feedback is effective because students usually interpret it easily and often view it as meaning more than words. Beginning teachers may have a difficult time coordinating their feelings and words with body language. They may be pleased with student performance, yet display a less-than-pleased response (e.g., by frowning and putting their hands on their hips). They may want to be assertive but take a submissive stance. For instance, when undesirable behavior occurs, an unsure teacher might place his hands in his pockets, slouch, and back away from the class. These nonverbal behaviors signal anything but assertiveness and send students a mixed message.

Many types of nonverbal feedback can be used to encourage a class, such as thrusting a finger into the air to signify "You're number 1," thumbs-up, high fives, shaking hands, and so on.

When using nonverbal feedback, find out how the customs and mores of different cultures affect children's response to different types of gestures. For example, only parents and close relatives may touch Hmong and Laotian children on the head. A teacher who pats the child on the head for approval is interfering with the child's spiritual nature. The OK sign, touching thumb and forefinger, indicates approval in the United States. In several Asian cultures, however, it is a "zero," indicating that the child is not performing properly. In many South American countries, the OK sign has a derogatory sexual meaning. Ask for advice when using nonverbal gestures with children from other cultures.

6

Use positive and encouraging nonverbal feedback with students.

Mark Gail/The Washington Post via Getty Images

To make nonverbal feedback more convincing, practice it by displaying various emotions in front of a mirror. Alternatively, try displaying different emotions to someone who does not know you well. If they can identify the emotions and see them as convincing, you are an effective nonverbal communicator. Video recorders are effective tools for self-analysis. Analyze how you look when under stress, when disciplining a student, when praising, and so on. You may find that you exhibit distracting or unassertive nonverbal behaviors, such as playing with the whistle, slumping, putting your hands in your pockets, or shuffling your feet. Just as verbal feedback must be practiced and critiqued, so must nonverbal behavior.

Consider the Personal Needs of Students

If teaching involved only presenting physical activities to students, it would be a much easier endeavor. The uniqueness of each student in a large class is a factor that makes teaching complex and challenging. This section focuses on ways to make instruction meaningful and personal. Teachers who can make each student feel important will influence those children's lives. Understanding the diversity of classes, encouraging student creativity, and allowing students to make educational decisions are some ways to make a lesson feel as if it were specifically designed for each student.

Teach for Diversity and Equity

Multicultural education allows all students to reach their potential regardless of the diversity among learners. Four major variables of diversity influence how teachers and students think and learn: race or ethnicity, gender, social class, and ability. Multicultural education creates an educational environment in which students from varying backgrounds and experience come together to experience educational equality (Manning & Baruth, 2009). Multicultural education assumes that children come from different backgrounds and helps them make sense of their everyday lives. It emphasizes the contributions of various groups that make up our country and focuses on how rather than what to learn.

Current population trends in the United States are changing our classrooms. Children previously excluded from classes because of language, race, economics, and abilities are now learning together. Teaching now

MAXIMIZING PHYSICAL ACTIVITY

The U.S. Department of Health and Human Services suggests that students engage in physical activity for at least 50% of a physical education lesson. Although doing this sounds simple enough, all the intricacies of a physical educator's responsibilities (i.e., providing content knowledge, transitioning students through different activities, actively involving all students, and assessing student learning) make it challenging to achieve. A number of strategies can be used to maximize the amount of physical activity that students accrue during a lesson, such as implementing efficient transitions, minimizing instruction time, using efficient grouping methods, and providing active instruction time.

Transitions include starting and stopping students, grouping students, and retrieving and distributing equipment. To minimize the time, it takes to start and stop activity, the physical educator should establish regular signals. For instance, a key word, such as the name of the school mascot, may be used to signal students to begin an activity. A whistle, a key word (e.g., "Stop!"), or music stopping might be an indicator for students to stop their activity and get into a predetermined position such as hands on knees. The teacher needs to practice these strategies on a daily basis with students so that they know what to expect. Grouping strategies, such as the toe-to-toe method (for partners) or the Whistle Mixer (for groups), can decrease management time, which will lead to more physical activity time for students. Retrieving and distributing equipment can be made more efficient (leaving more time for activity) if the physical educator tells students what to do with the equipment as they retrieve it. If equipment is distributed evenly around the teaching area, as opposed to being centralized in one bucket in the middle of the gym, students can more easily and quickly obtain what they need because they can find their equipment simultaneously and not wait in a line or fight to get theirs first.

requires a pluralistic mindset and the ability to communicate across cultures. Educators have a responsibility to teach children to live comfortably and to prosper in this diverse and changing world. Students must celebrate their own culture while learning to appreciate the world's diversity. For most students, classroom interaction between teachers and students is the major part of the multicultural education they will receive. Teachers can do several things to teach and value diversity:

1. Help students learn about the similarities and differences among cultures.

2. Encourage students to understand that people from similar cultures share common values, customs, and beliefs.

3. Make children aware of acts of discrimination and teach them ways to deal with inequity and prejudice.

4. Help children develop pride in their family's culture.

5. Teach children ways to communicate effectively with other cultures, races, and genders.

6. Instill respect for all people regardless of race or ethnicity, gender, social class, or ability.

7. Integrate multicultural activities into the curriculum (Pangrazi, Beighle, & Pangrazi, 2009).

How teachers perceive students strongly affects their performance. Teachers who effectively teach for diversity hold high expectations for all students, including ethnic minority children and youth. Studies show that teachers often tend to have lower expectations for ethnic minority youth. These low expectations are seen in interpersonal interactions and in the opportunities that students receive for enrichment and personal growth. At-risk youth need a rich curriculum that provides the necessary support for success.

Teachers who lack knowledge about other cultures must educate themselves so that they better understand the needs of all students. Diversity implies differences within and between cultures. Learning about other cultures increases the teacher's understanding of each student's early experiences and worldview. The focus should be on understanding the cultures as well as the individuals. This approach contrasts with learning about a culture and then stereotyping its members as all the same. When working with a different group or culture, the following answers to the following questions will go a long ways in helping you better understand your students:

1. What is their history? Few teachers can become experts in the history and cultures of all the students they teach, but they can recognize and be familiar with major events and important names within the cultures.

2. What are their important cultural values? Different cultures interact and discipline students in different ways. Ask parents and students how they work with children and what values are particularly important in their households.

3. Who are influential individuals in their group? Students will identify with local individuals who are held in high esteem in their community. Knowing the role models whom their students admire will give teachers insight into those students.

4. What are their major religious beliefs? Many groups belong to similar religions that drive many of their beliefs. These beliefs also influence the values of children in a community.

5. What are their important political beliefs? Important political issues are often discussed at home. By making an effort to learn about these issues, teachers show they are interested in how their students live in their community.

6. What political, religious, and social days do they celebrate? Students will discuss these important days and expect teachers to understand why they celebrate them. Talking about these days with students creates goodwill and makes students feel like their culture is valued.

By addressing these questions, teachers can educate themselves on the many cultures represented in their classes. Consistently seeking information about students and their cultures helps to ensure an effective learning environment and the use of acceptable instructional strategies to meet the needs of students.

Increasing instructional focus on cooperative learning is strongly recommended. This method offers students the opportunity to work together toward common goals and feel positive about each group member's different contributions. Diversity can be increased through discussion sessions. The more participants there are, the better the chances for diverse viewpoints. When students are involved in discussions, they are usually attentive and participating in the learning process.

The following are some teaching tips that can help increase instructional effectiveness in a diverse setting:

6

- At the start of the school year (and at regular intervals thereafter), talk to students about the importance of encouraging and respecting diversity.

- For group activities, insist that groups be diverse in race, gender, and nationality.

- Be aware of how you speak about different groups of students. Do you refer to all students in the same way? Do you address boys and girls differently? Develop a consistent style for addressing all students regardless of their differences.

- Encourage all students to participate in discussions. Avoid allowing some students from certain groups to dominate the interaction. Call on students randomly so that everyone has an equal chance of contributing.

- Treat all students with respect and expect them to treat each other with dignity. Intervene if a student or group of students is dominating.

- When a difficult situation arises over an issue with undertones of diversity, take a time-out and ask students to evaluate their thoughts and ideas. Give all parties time to collect their thoughts and plan a response.

- Make sure evaluations and grades are written in gender-neutral or gender-inclusive terms.

- Encourage students to work with a different partner every day. By getting to know each other, children can learn to appreciate their differences.

- Invite to class guest speakers who represent diversity in gender, race or ethnicity, even if they are not speaking about multicultural or diverse issues.

- When students make sexist or racist comments, ask them to restate the ideas in a way that does not offend others. Teach students to express their opinions, but not in an inflammatory way.

- Rotate the leaders when using groups. Give all students the opportunity to learn leadership skills.

Gender Differences

Teachers greatly influence how children learn to behave. Adults model gender-specific behaviors for children and youngsters, who in turn copy the behavior. For example, teachers often pay more attention to boys and encourage them more. Teachers give more praise for achievement to boys and call on girls less often than they call on boys. Teachers also respond to inappropriate behavior from boys and girls in different ways. Aggression is tolerated more in boys than in girls. Disruptive talking, however, is tolerated more in girls than in boys. Boys are reprimanded more than girls, and teachers use more physical means of disciplining boys.

Some physical education teachers believe that girls cannot perform at a level similar to boys, even though research shows otherwise. Particularly in elementary school, differences in strength, endurance, and physical skills are minimal. An effective physical education environment helps all children find success. Using the following teaching behaviors minimizes stereotyping by gender:

- Reinforce the performances of all students regardless of gender.

- Provide activities that are developmentally appropriate and allow all students to find success.

- Design programs that ensure success in coeducational experiences. Boys and girls can challenge each other to achieve higher levels if the atmosphere is positive.

- Do not use—and do not accept—students' stereotypical comments such as, "You throw like a girl."

- Include activities in the curriculum that cut across typical gender stereotypes so that students learn, for example, that rhythms are not just for girls, and football is not just for boys.

- Arrange activities so that the more aggressive and skilled students do not dominate. Little is learned if students are taught to be submissive or to play down their ability.

- Arrange practice sessions so that all students receive equal amounts of practice or opportunity to participate. Practice sessions should not give more practice opportunities to the skilled while the unskilled stand aside and observe.

- Expect all boys and girls to perform equally well. Teacher expectations communicate much about a student's ability level. Students view themselves through the eyes of their teacher.

Encourage Creative Responses

An effective lesson includes more than planned experiences. Giving students an opportunity to create and modify new experiences is an important part of the total learning environment. Effective lessons include opportunities for creative expression and student input regarding the implementation of the lesson.

By encouraging creativity in the classroom, a teacher helps students develop habits of discovery as well as reflective and abstract thinking. Self-discovered concepts are often better retained and retrieved for future use. To encourage creativity, set aside time for students to explore. For example, offer a hoop and the challenge, "See how many movements you can do with it." Offer time for creative responses during appropriate segments of the instructional sequence. Ask children to add on to a movement progression just presented or to expand it in a new direction. Make the lesson plan flexible enough to allow creativity at teachable moments. Stimulate creativity with a show-and-tell demonstration. After a period of exploration, have students demonstrate movement patterns they have created.

Teach Students How to Make Decisions

Decision making is a large part of behaving responsibly, but responsibility is a learned skill that takes practice. The decision-making process involves learning the consequences of decisions, including their effect on others. Cognitive development in students can be enhanced by allowing them to be an integral part of the lesson—choosing content, implementing the lesson, and assessing each other's techniques and development. When students are allowed to make decisions at a young age, incorrect decisions result in much less serious con-

sequences and offer an opportunity to learn. If children are always told how to behave when they are young, they may not know how to make serious decisions affecting their future as they age. Give them the opportunity to make decisions and choose from various alternatives, even if they make poor choices. The following strategies can help students learn to make decisions in a safe environment:

1. Limit the number of choices. Using this strategy, the teacher retains ultimate control but gives students a chance to decide, in part, how the outcome is reached. Use this technique when learners have had few decision-making opportunities. If you have a new class and know little about the students, limit their choices. For example, give students the choice of practicing either a drive or a pass shot in a hockey unit. The desired outcome is that students practice striking skills, but they can decide which striking skill to practice.

2. Let students modify activities. This strategy reduces pressure because the teacher no longer has to make exceptions and listen to student complaints that "It's too hard to do!" or "I'm bored." Modification allows learners to change activities to suit their personal skill level. The following are among the many ways to modify activities:

6

Creating different movement variations.

a. Use a slower-moving family ball rather than a handball.

b. Increase the number of fielders in a softball game.

c. Lower the basket in a basketball unit.

d. Decrease the length of a distance run or the height of hurdles.

3. Offer open-ended tasks. This approach offers wide latitude for making decisions about the content of the lesson. You decide the educational outcome, and students determine how to reach it. Here are a few examples:

a. Develop a game that requires four passes before a shot on goal.

b. Plan a floor exercise routine that contains a forward roll, a backward roll, and a cartwheel.

c. Design a rope-jumping routine that involves a long rope, four people, and two pieces of manipulative equipment.

The problem-solving approach has no predetermined answers. Students apply principles they already know and transfer them to new situations. Ultimately, the problem is solved through a movement response that has been guided by cognitive involvement.

Develop Positive Attitudes

The performing arts (e.g., physical education, music, and drama) offer opportunities for affective domain development. These opportunities include learning to share, express feelings, set personal goals, and function independently. Teamwork—learning to be subordinate to a leader, as well as being a leader—is achieved. Effective instruction includes teaching the whole person rather than just physical skills. It is disappointing to hear a teacher say, "My job is just to teach skills. I'm not going to get involved in developing attitudes. That's someone else's job." Physical education offers an opportunity to develop positive attitudes and values. Much is lost when students leave physical education with well-developed physical skills but negative attitudes toward physical activity and participation. Ponder the following situations:

1. A teacher asks everyone to run a mile, knowing that overweight students will run slowest. Faster students who finish first will hurry slower students to finish—an embarrassing situation. Obese students cannot change the outcome of the run even if they want to. When running in such an environment, these students experience failure and belittlement, so it is small wonder they hate physical activity.

2. Students are asked to perform skills in front of the class. Lesser-skilled students feel unsure and perform more poorly because of the pressure. Many of them vow never to perform these skills again.

3. A student pitches in a softball game only to find he or she is unable to throw strikes. The teacher refuses to remove the student from the situation, admonishing him or her to "Concentrate!" This student may never want to pitch again.

Few people have positive feelings about an activity if they are embarrassed or fail miserably. How students feel about a subject affects their motivation to learn. So, when planning, analyze whether the lesson will result in experiences that help students develop positive attitudes and values.

Students have to sense that you care about their feelings and that you try to avoid placing them into embarrassing situations. Caring about students is not a sign of weakness. Knowingly placing students into

TEACHING TIP

Do you teach students to make decisions that will be useful throughout life? Physical education can teach people how to make proper exercise decisions and healthy eating choices. Other decisions that will be important to students are stress management and substance abuse. If teachers always tell students what and how to do things, where do they learn to make decisions and accept the consequences of their choices? Students often make poor decisions when responsible adults are not around to help them. Help students learn to make decisions and accept the positive or negative consequences that come with their choices.

embarrassing situations is never justified and results in negative student attitudes. The teacher's attitude, not the lesson plan, fosters positive feelings toward activity. The attitudes and values that students form are based partly on how their teachers and peers treat them. To enhance the affective domain, how you teach is as important as what you teach. Your students are human beings with needs and concerns; treat them with courtesy and respect. Discover how students feel by asking them. If you ask, however, be aware that the feedback may not always be positive. Learn to listen without taking it personally or making negative judgments about students when they are honest. Concern for others' feelings creates an atmosphere that fosters positive attitudes and values.

Personalize Instruction

Though most instruction is conducted as a group activity, students' ability levels vary widely. As students mature, the range of ability increases because many students participate in extracurricular activities such as Little League baseball, YBA basketball, and private tutoring in gymnastics. In physical education classes, this range of experiences demands that tasks be modified so that all students find success and equity. Some ways to personalize instruction and accommodate developmental differences among students follow:

1. Modify the conditions. Adjust tasks and activities to help all children succeed. If students are learning to catch, move partners closer together, have them use a slower-moving object, such as a beach ball or a balloon, use a larger target, change the size of boundaries or goal areas, let students toss and catch individually, or use a larger striking implement. Try to minimize error and maximize success for the activity. When students find little success, they engage in off-task behavior to draw attention away from their subpar performance.

2. Use self-competition. As surprising as it sounds, if the success rate is too high, students become bored. Ask students to set personal goals—for example, to see if they can beat their personal best performance. Challenge students by asking them to accomplish higher levels of performance, such as by using a faster moving object, increasing the distance to the goal, or decreasing its size. Students respond best to challenges that are personal and slightly above their current skill level. Try to avoid holding all students to a single standard of performance.

3. Offer different task challenges. During the lesson, allow students to work on different tasks. Task cards and station teaching help students learn at an optimum rate. Present several tasks of varying complexity so that students can find personal challenges. For example, students with limited upper-body strength will have difficulty with inverted balances. Include some activities using the legs so that all students can achieve some success as they work on balance skill challenges.

Employ Effective Communication Skills

Communicating with learners is critical, and communication skills can always be improved. For children to learn essential information, the teacher must communicate in a way that encourages students to listen.

Students want to communicate openly and honestly with adults. Behavior used in talking to students can help keep relationships strong. When talking with students, assume a physical pose that expresses interest and attention. Kneel at times, so that children do not always have to look up. Check to see if your facial and verbal cues reinforce your interest and concern. The following suggestions can help teachers establish a positive bond with students and create a learning environment enjoyed by everyone.

1. Focus on specific behavior rather than making general comments that are personal and insulting. The following is an example of speaking about a student's behavior: "Talking when I am talking is unacceptable behavior." Such feedback identifies behavior that can be improved on and avoids questioning the student's self-worth. In contrast, saying something like, "Why are you always talking and acting foolish?" negatively reflects on the child's character and undermines his or her self-esteem. It is also nonspecific, so the student does not know what behavior you are reprimanding. Identify the specific misbehavior and then state the type of behavior you expect.

2. Understand the child's viewpoint. Imagine if someone embarrassed you in front of a class. How would you feel if you were inept and trying to learn a new skill with others watching? When suggesting ways to improve performance, do so privately (so that other students cannot hear you)

and allow the student to practice without scrutiny. Asking students to try something new and then watching over them until they do it correctly can be intimidating and cause resentment.

3. Identify your feelings about the learner. Teachers sometimes send their students mixed messages. You may be unhappy with a student because of a previous incident yet be unwilling to confront him or her. Because of these pent-up feelings, you might then offer the student unkind or sarcastic feedback about a skill performance. Usually, when you have negative feelings toward a student, that student cannot understand your unhappiness. Communicate how you feel (even if it is negative) but make sure that such communication is directed at specific, correctable behavior in a caring manner.

4. Accentuate the positive. When teaching key instructional points of a skill, emphasize positive performance points rather than incorrect actions. For example, stress that children "land lightly," rather than saying, "Don't land so hard." An easy way to emphasize key points positively is to say, "Do this because . . ." If movement patterns can be performed in several different and acceptable ways, be explicit with your points.

5. Optimize speech patterns. Avoid giving sermons at the least provocation. Sermons seldom work in the teaching environment. In addition, a period of silence can be effective because it gives students time to digest the information.

6. Conduct lengthy discussions in a classroom setting. Students expect to move around in the activity area, whereas they have learned to sit and interact cognitively in the classroom. Presenting lengthy explanations in the classroom before students go to the activity area makes maximum use of activity time. Explain rules, outline procedures and responsibilities, and draw formations on the chalkboard. In the activity area, try to limit discussions to 30 seconds.

7. Respect student opinion. Avoid humiliating a child who gives a wrong answer. Teachers can deal with this issue in several ways. Pass over inappropriate answers by directing attention to more appropriate responses. Alternatively, suggest that the student has offered a good answer but that the question was not asked correctly. Ask the student to save that answer and then go back to that student when the answer is correct for another

question. When injecting your personal opinion into the question-and-answer process, label it as such and avoid making it sound more valuable than student opinion. Try not to be surprised or offended if children comment negatively in response to a query asking for candid opinions about an activity or procedure. When opinions are honest, some are bound to be negative.

Be an Effective Listener

Effective listening skills are harder to learn than speaking techniques. Teachers are trained to impart knowledge to students and have practiced speaking for years. Many students view teachers as people who speak but do not listen. Poor communication often occurs because of a breakdown in listening. There is truth in the adage "You were given two ears and one mouth so you could listen twice as much as you speak." Do the following to promote effective listening skills:

1. Be an active listener. Active listeners convince the speaker they are interested in what the speaker is saying. Much of this interaction occurs through nonverbal behavior such as eye contact, nodding the head in agreement, facial expressions, and moving toward the speaker.

2. Listen to the hidden message of the speaker. Young children sometimes find it difficult to express their feelings clearly. The words expressed may not signal what the child is actually feeling. For example, a child may say, "I hate P.E." Most children do not hate all phases of physical education, and most likely a more current activity (such as jumping rope) is the problem. Try acknowledging their feelings with a response such as, "You sound angry; are you having a problem you want to discuss?" This helps students realize that their feelings are important and gives them an opportunity to clarify concerns.

3. Paraphrase what the student said. Paraphrasing is restating in your own words what was said to you, including your interpretation of the other person's feelings. For example, you might respond, "Do I hear you saying you are frustrated and bored with this activity?" If the paraphrasing is correct, the student feels validated and understood. If the interpretation is incorrect, the student has an opportunity to restate his or her concern.

Being an active listener.

4. Let students know you value listening. Teachers who listen to students learn about their students' feelings. Let students know you will listen, and then do something about what they say. If you are a good listener, you will not always hear positive things. For example, students may honestly tell you which activities they do not enjoy. If not taken personally, this communication can be constructive. It may not be valid criticism of the program or your procedures, but it opens the door to good communication. A word of caution: If you find it difficult to accept such feedback, it is best to ask students to keep their comments to themselves. Avoid such interactions if the feedback will affect your confidence.

Evaluate Your Instructional Effectiveness

Evaluating how you teach is every bit as important as monitoring how you treat students. This section accentuates the importance of finding ways to evaluate your teaching as a primary avenue for improvement.

Without a regular and measurable means of checking how you teach, becoming a better teacher is nearly impossible. This section offers methods for evaluating teaching behavior that are observable and therefore measurable. The do-it-yourself approach to evaluation is recommended because you can set personal goals and chart your performance in the privacy of your office. This method is in contrast to the resistance that some teachers feel when principals, supervisors, and peers evaluate them.

The first step is to select a teaching behavior to evaluate and decide how you will record and monitor the data. Generally, you should start by evaluating a single teaching behavior because recording more than one variable at a time can be frustrating and confusing. Examples of coding forms designed for different teaching behaviors are included in this section. Areas on the sheet allow you to record your name, the date, the lesson focus and content, the grade level and competency of the students, the duration of the lesson, and a short description of the evaluation procedure. These forms can be modified to meet your specific needs. Maintaining a consistent format for the coding sheets makes it easier to compare your performance throughout the year. The next section offers coding forms for gathering data on various teaching behaviors.

There are many ways to gather data about your teaching. For example, students who are not participating can gather the data, another teacher can gather the data, or the data can be gathered after recording the lesson. Because daily teaching behavior is least affected when outside observers are not present, self-evaluation techniques are recommended because they are more likely to reveal your actual teaching behavior.

Instructional Time

How much time do you devote to instruction? Are you instructing too much or not enough? To analyze instructional time, record the number of instructional episodes and the length of each episode. The average length of an instructional episode can be evaluated as well as what percentage of the lesson was used for instruction. Generally, episodes should be short and frequent. The goal should be to limit each episode to 30 seconds or less.

How to Do It

1. Design a form for duration recording (figure 6.2).

2. Video record the lesson and time the instructional episodes at the end of the day. Establish consistency in identifying the difference between instructional and management episodes.

3. Total the amount of time spent on instruction.

4. Convert the amount of time to a percentage of the total lesson time by dividing the total lesson time into the time spent on instruction. The average length of an instructional episode can be deter-

mined by dividing the amount of instructional time by the number of instructional episodes.

Management Time

Management time includes episodes that occur when students are moved into various formations, when equipment is gathered or put away, and when directions are given relative to these areas. Disciplining a class is another example of time used for management. As a rule of thumb, if you are talking and not giving instructions, you are managing students. These data are useful for analyzing how much of the lesson is devoted to management. Viewing your video may help you identify inefficient organizational schemes or find that students are not responding quickly to management requests.

How to Do It

1. Design a form to gather the desired data (figure 6.3).

2. Record the lesson. Time the episodes of management and note the length of each episode on the form.

3. Total the amount of management time and divide it by the length of the period to determine the fraction of management time in the lesson (multiply this number by 100 to see the number as a percentage).

4. Total the number of episodes and divide this number into the amount of time devoted to management to find the average length of a management episode.

 TECH TIP

Quite possibly the most valuable piece of technology for improving teacher effectiveness is for a teacher to have a video of himself or herself teaching. A video can help improve teaching in two ways. One, a teacher can watch the video and conduct a self-assessment. This chapter discussed many systematic tools that teachers can use to evaluate their teaching. With no risk of ridicule or judgement, teachers can sit by themselves and observe, watching for behaviors, such as using first names, providing positive feedback, teacher movement, length of instructions, and types of corrective feedback, to name a few. Watching a video of yourself teaching may be the single most powerful form of professional development available. A close second is to have a colleague observe the video. This approach takes some courage because teachers become vulnerable when someone else watches their teaching. But if that barrier can be overcome, much can be gained from this process. Having a colleague who can be trusted with watching and providing productive feedback opens the doors to other conversations regarding physical education. Often physical educators are isolated in their gymnasium and are the only teacher in the school who teaches physical education. For this reason, collaborations such as this can be extremely valuable for many aspects of teaching—and it all can start with technology and a desire to be a better teacher.

INSTRUCTIONAL TIME

Teacher: __Charlene Darst__   Observer: __Bob Pangrazi__

Class: __1st period__   Grade: __5th__   Date and time: __3/22 - 9:05__

Lessons focus: __Basketball__   Comments: __1st class meeting of unit__

Starting time: __9:30__   Ending time: __10:00__   Length of lesson: __30 min__

15	10	8	35	17	1:03	31	9	8
14	21	10	21	43	7			

Total instruction time: __5 min 12 sec__

Percentage of class time devoted to instruction: __17%__

Number of episodes: __15__   Average length of episodes: __20.8 sec__

FIGURE 6.2   Sample form for calculating instructional time.

6

MANAGEMENT TIME

Teacher: __Don Hicks__   Observer: __Connie Orlowicz__

Class: __6th period__   Grade: __3rd__   Date and time: __10/29 - 1:30__

Lessons focus: __Manipulative skills__   Comments: _____

Starting time: __1:30__   Ending time: __2:00__   Length of lesson: __30 min__

55	10	21	20	35	18	29	10	10	21	9	19	21
11												

Total management time: __4 min 49 sec__

Percentage of class time devoted to management: __16%__

Number of episodes: __14__   Average length of episodes: __20.6 sec__

FIGURE 6.3   Sample form for calculating management time.

Practice Time (Time on Task) and Dead Time

To state the obvious, to learn physical skills, students have to practice. Practice time, or time on task, is often referred to as academic learning time in physical education (ALT-PE). Practice time is the amount of time students spend practicing skills that result in the accomplishment of program objectives. Gathering data to show the amount of time that students are involved in on-task activity reveals time allotted to skill learning. Duration recording is most often used for evaluating practice time. Figure 6.4 shows the results of a duration recording for practice time. Strive to increase the amount of time devoted to skill practice by using more equipment, implementing drills that limit standing in line, or streamlining verbal instructions.

The amount of dead time in a lesson also can be measured. Dead time occurs when students are off task or doing something unrelated to practice, management, or instruction. Examples might be waiting in line for a turn, doing nothing because instructions were not understood, or standing still waiting for the ball to come to them during a game.

How to Do It

1. Design a form for collecting the data (figure 6.5).

2. Identify a student whom you will time during practice sessions. This step is critical. The student chosen should be neither exceptional nor below par and should give a realistic picture of the amount of practice time allotted to the entire class. You can record dead time by timing when the selected student is not involved in on-task practice, management, or instructional activity.

Teacher: Debbie Massoney School: Whittier Elementary		
Parts of the lesson	Practicing	Inactive, off-task, listening
Introductory activity	1.5 min	0.5 min
Fitness development	6.5 min	1.5 min
Lesson focus	10.0 min	4.0 min
Game	5.0 min	1.0 min
Total	23.0 min	7.0 min

FIGURE 6.4 Results of a duration recording for practice time.

Another way to calculate dead time is to subtract the combined amounts of time used for practice, management, and instruction (assuming that all have been timed) from the total length of the lesson.

3. Turn on the stopwatch when the student is involved in practice (or dead) activity. Stop the watch when the student stops (or starts) practicing. Record the amount of practice (or dead) time. Time all practice (or dead) episodes.

4. Total the amount of time devoted to student practice (in minutes) and divide it by the length of the lesson to find the percentage of practice time in a lesson. To compute the percentage of dead time, total the amount of dead time and divide it by the length of the lesson.

Response Latency

Response latency is the amount of time it takes for students to respond to instructions or management tasks. Record the amount of time that elapses between the moment a command is given to when the student actually begins or stops. The amount of elapsed time is the response latency.

The average duration of response latency can be calculated. A certain amount of response latency should be expected, but most instructors feel strongly about how long they are willing to tolerate. After more than a five-second response latency, most teachers become uneasy and expect the class to respond faster.

How to Do It

1. Develop a form for gathering the data (figure 6.6).

2. Record your class in action. Time the response latency that occurs when the class is asked to stop (or start). The clock should run from the time your directions are given until the class is involved in productive behavior. Starting (an activity or management instruction) and stopping latency (stopping an activity) are two separate behaviors that must be recorded separately.

3. Calculate the average episode length by tallying the number of response latency episodes and dividing this number into the total amount of time devoted to response latency.

PRACTICE TIME

Teacher: __Eugene Peterson__   Observer: __P.W. Darst__

Class: __2nd period__   Grade: __4th__   Date and time: __11/15 - 9:15__

Lessons focus: __Gymnastics skills__ Comments: __Week 2__

Starting time: __9:25__   Ending time: __10:00__   Length of lesson: __35 min__

35	10	2:04	25	29	1:39	17	55	34
43	1:55	1:01	33	10	10	18	1:17	4:50
24	39	31	34					

Total practice time: __20 min 13 sec__

Percentage of class time devoted to practice: __57.8%__

Number of episodes: __22__   Average length of episodes: __55.1 sec__

FIGURE 6.5 Sample form for collecting data on practice time.

Student Performance

The percentage of students performing a desired task is an excellent indicator of a well-managed class. Placheck recording is a technique used to observe group behavior at different times during a lesson. At regular intervals while reviewing a video of your class, scan the class from the left to the right side of the instructional area and record the number of students who are not performing the desired behavior. (Recording the smaller number of students exhibiting a behavior is easier. For example, if you are interested in identifying the percentage of students on task, generally it is easier to record the number of students not on task.) Each student in the class is observed only once during a scan. Do not go back and change your count, even if a student changes behavior during the interval. Intervals should last for 10 seconds and be randomly spaced throughout the lesson, with 8 to 10 observation intervals. Signals to scan the class can be recorded at random intervals to cue the observer.

The placheck is used to monitor behavior that is yes or no in nature—either students are performing the desired behavior or they are not. Examples of areas that might be evaluated are on-task behavior, active behavior, or effort while practicing an activity. After the results are determined, a goal can be set to increase the percentage of students involved in the desired observable behavior.

How to Do It

1. The sample form in figure 6.7 can be used to identify three different types of student performance. The data gathered indicate on-task and off-task student behavior.

2. Place 8 to 10 beeps at random intervals on a recording to signal when to conduct a placheck.

3. Scan your class in a specified, consistent direction from left to right each time you hear the recorded signal. Scan the class for 7 to 10 seconds and record the number of students engaged in the desired behavior.

4. Convert the data to a percentage by dividing the total number of students into the number of unproductive students and then multiplying the result by 100. Four to six plachecks spaced throughout a class period will yield valid information about class conduct.

RESPONSE LATENCY

Teacher: **Jim Roberts**   Observer: **Bob Pangrazi**

Class: **2nd period**   Grade: **2nd**   Date and time: **2/5 - 9:00**

Lessons focus: **Movement concepts**   Comments: _____

Starting time: **9:05**   Ending time: **9:35**   Length of lesson: **30 min**

Starting response latency

3		7	5	9	15	3	3	4	9	7	5	3	
2		4	10	7									

Stopping response latency

10		12	9	8	8	15	8	6	2	9	10	11	15
14		5	5	13									

Total amount of starting response latency: **1 min 42 sec**

Percentage of class time devoted to response latency: **5.7%**

Number of episodes: **16**   Average length of episodes: **6 sec**

Total amount of stopping response latency: **2 min 41 sec**

Percentage of class time devoted to stopping response latency: **8.9%**

Number of episodes: **17**   Average length of episodes: **9.5 sec**

FIGURE 6.6 Sample form for evaluating response latency.

Instructional Feedback

Feedback given to students strongly affects the instructional presentation. Feedback can be defined and measured so that meaningful goals for improvement can be established. The following areas can be evaluated to give direction for implementing personal change.

Praise and Criticism

When students are engaged, regular feedback should be directed to their performance. Feedback can either be positive and constructive or negative and critical. Tally the occurrence of praise and criticism so that you can calculate the ratio of positive to negative comments. With this information, goals can be set for increasing the number of comments per minute and modifying the ratio of positive to negative comments.

General Versus Specific Feedback

Feedback to students can be general or specific. "Good job," "Way to go," and "Cut that out" are examples of general feedback. General feedback can be positive or negative; it does not specify the behavior being reinforced. In contrast, specific feedback identifies the student by name and reinforces an actual behavior; it also might be accompanied with a valuing statement, such as, "Michelle, that's the way to keep your head tucked! I really like that forward roll!"

Using first names is important in personalizing feedback and directing it to the proper individual. The number of times first names are used can be totaled. Valuing statements can also be evaluated. Divide the data gathered in these categories by the length of the lesson (in minutes) to render a rate per minute.

STUDENT PERFORMANCE

Teacher: __Albert Santillan__   Observer: __Ms. Estfan__

Class: __8th period__   Grade: __6th__   Date and time: __5/5 - 2:30__

Lessons focus: __Rhythmic movement skills__   Comments: _____

Starting time: __2:30__   Ending time: __3:00__   Length of lesson: __30 min__

Active or inactive

On-task or off-task

5	4	12	7	3	3	2	5	6	5
4	3								

Effort or noneffort

Number of plachecks: __12__

Total number of students: __30__

Average number of students not on desired behavior: __4.9__

Average percentage of students not on desired behavior: __16%__

FIGURE 6.7 Sample form for placheck observation.

6

Corrective Instructional Feedback

Effective teachers help students achieve higher levels of performance. Part of this process involves giving performers meaningful corrective feedback. Corrective feedback focuses on improving a student's performance. Corrective instructional feedback should be specific so that students know what they must correct. An example of corrective instructional feedback is saying, "You struck the soccer ball above center. Try to strike it a little lower this time." This type of feedback tells the student what was incorrect about the skill attempt and how to perform the skill correctly.

Nonverbal Feedback

Much performance feedback is given nonverbally. Nonverbal communication is meaningful to students and is often as effective as verbal forms of communication. Examples of nonverbal feedback after a desired performance are a pat on the back, a wink, a smile, a nod of the head, the thumbs-up sign, and clapping the hands. Nonverbal feedback can also be negative: a frown, shaking the head in disapproval, walking away from a student, and laughing at a poor performance.

How to Do It

1. Design a form to collect the data (figure 6.8).

2. To evaluate instructional feedback, record a lesson to play back and evaluate later.

3. Identify the data to be analyzed. At first, it is best to take one category at a time. For example, analyze the use of first names during the first playback and then play the video again to evaluate corrective feedback.

4. Convert the data to a form that you can compare lesson to lesson (i.e., rate per minute, rate per lesson, or ratio of positive to negative interactions).

INSTRUCTIONAL FEEDBACK

Teacher: _____   Observer: _____

Class: _____   Grade: _____ Date and time: _____

Lessons focus: _____   Comments: _____

Starting time: _____   Ending time: _____ Length of lesson: _____

Interactions unrelated to skill performance	+									
	–									
General instructional feedback	+									
	–									
Corrective instructional feedback										
First names										
Nonverbal feedback	+									
	–									

Ratio + to –, nonskill related: _____

Ratio + to –, skill related: _____

FIGURE 6.8 Sample form for feedback observation.

Active Supervision and Student Contact

Effective instructors actively supervise students by moving throughout the area and offering personalized feedback. Count the number of times you personally engage with a student. One-on-one feedback differs from total class interaction and offers insight into each student's behavior and concerns.

Allied to this area is the relationship between teacher movement and active supervision. Many instructors develop a habit of moving to a spot in the teaching area where they feel most comfortable. This consistent movement pattern can cause students to drift to different areas, depending on how they feel about the activity or the instructor. Students who like the instructor will move closer, whereas students who dislike the teacher or are uneasy about the activity may move as far away as possible. As a result, the better performers typically are near the instructor and students who may be somewhat less able are farther away and harder to observe.

The teacher can avoid these problems by moving throughout the teaching area. A way to evaluate movement is to divide the area into quadrants and tally the number of times you move into each quadrant. A tally in the quadrant is made when you speak to a student or the class as a whole. Simply passing through a quadrant does not count. The amount of time spent in each quadrant can also be evaluated. Try to spend similar amounts of time in each area. When students cannot predict where you will be next, they have a greater tendency to remain on task.

Movement related to the use of lesson time can be determined by the amount of time you stay in a quadrant. The amount of time that a teacher spends in each quadrant can be recorded in corresponding locations on the form and analyzed at the end of the lesson. Another technique is to code the type of behavior that occurs each time the instructor moves into a new quadrant. For example, an "M" might signify management activity, an "I" instructional activity, and a "P" practice time. This approach reveals the location and amount of time spent on each behavior.

How to Do It

1. Develop a coding form similar to the one in figure 6.9.

2. Record your lesson and evaluate it later.

3. Evaluate the data by calculating the number of moves per lesson and the number of moves during instruction, management, and practice.

Are you a better teacher today than you were yesterday? What data do you have to show whether you are systematically improving your instructional skills? Many

ACTIVE SUPERVISION

Teacher: Alan Scarmazzo

Observer: Debbie Pangrazi

Class: 5th period

Grade: 1st   Date and Time: 3/7 - 1:05

Lessons focus: Movement concepts

Comments: _____

Starting time: 1:15

Ending time: 1:45   Length of lesson: 30 min

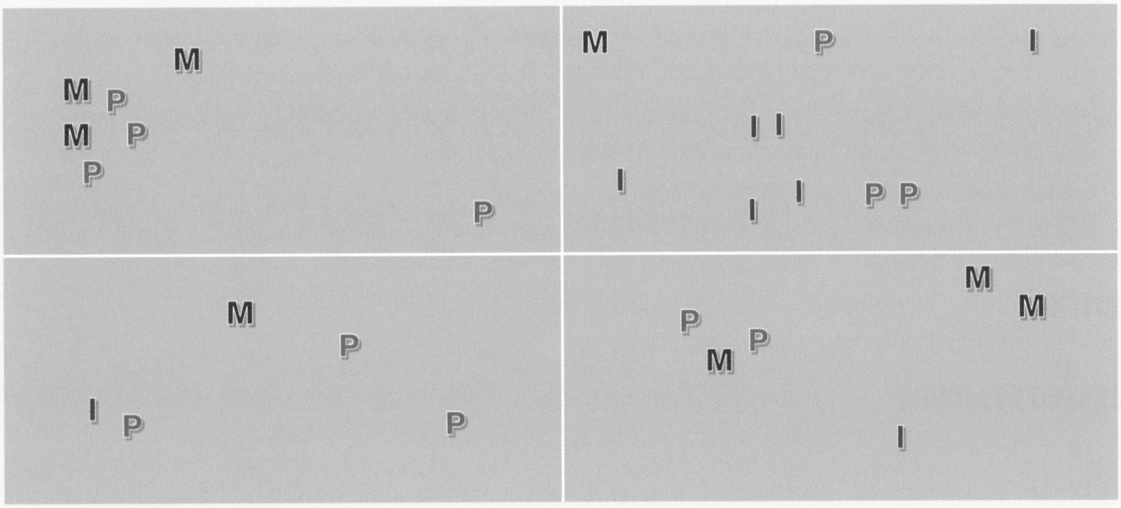

Total number of moves: 28

Number of moves (I): 8   Number of moves (M): 8   Number of moves (P): 12

Average moves per minute: .93

FIGURE 6.9 Sample form for evaluating supervision and student contact (M = management activity, I = instructional activity, and P = practice time).

professions have outcome measures to show whether they are more or less successful. But teaching is more subtle, and it is difficult to judge how much the quality of teaching affects the amount that students learn and retain. Today, politicians and school administrators expect teachers to improve, but they look only at how students perform on standardized tests. Unfortunately, your students haven't performed well, and during a conference with the principal you are told that it is your responsibility to see that your students improve in the future. After much thought, you decide that how

you teach matters as much as what you teach, and you want to change. Who is going to help you improve? The uncomfortable truth is that you are going to have to help yourself. The section Evaluate Your Instructional Effectiveness will help you gather objective data related to how you teach. You can evaluate yourself, analyze your data over time, and ultimately see the results of your hard work. Great teachers become great because they want to be the best and are willing to take personal responsibility for improving their instructional skills. Go for it!

LEARNING AIDS

HOW AND WHY

1. State whether the characteristics of a quality lesson were present for all students in your elementary physical education classes as a child.

2. Using teacher talk, list five meaningful feedback statements. Use statements other than those presented in this chapter and discuss why your statements are meaningful.

3. Describe how you can promote diversity in your classes. Why is this important?

4. Discuss your strengths and weaknesses when communicating.

5. Would you rather self-evaluate a lesson using videotape or have a peer evaluate you during the lesson? Why?

6. Why might the ability to be self-critical be important for physical education teachers and physical education curriculum designers?

CONTENT REVIEW

1. List and explain the characteristics of a quality elementary physical education program.

2. Explain the importance of several essential elements of instruction.

3. State the key components of instructional feedback. Discuss each component.

4. Describe ways to make instruction personal and meaningful for students.

5. Discuss several important communication skills for teachers.

6. Explain how teachers can use self-evaluation.

7. Explain four areas of teaching that can be evaluated; describe how to assess the specific areas.

WEBSITES

Nonverbal communication, http://nonverbal.ucsc.edu

SUGGESTED READINGS

Banks, J.A. (2009). *Teaching strategies for ethnic studies* (8th ed.). Boston, MA: Allyn & Bacon.

Bennett, C.L. (2011). *Comprehensive multicultural education: Theory and practice* (7th ed.). Boston, MA: Allyn & Bacon.

Buck, M.M., Lund, J.L., Harrison, J.M., & Blakemore Cook, C.L. (2007). *Instructional strategies for secondary physical education* (6th ed.). Boston, MA: McGraw-Hill.

Cushner, K.H. (2006). *Human diversity in action: Developing multicultural competencies for the classroom* (3rd ed.). Boston, MA: McGraw-Hill.

Hunter, R. (2004). *Madeline Hunter's mastery teaching: Increasing instructional effectiveness in elementary and secondary schools.* Thousand Oaks, CA: Corwin Press.

Hunter, R. (2004). *Madeline Hunter's mastery teaching: Increasing instructional effectiveness in elementary and secondary schools.* Thousand Oaks, CA: Corwin Press.

Koppelman, K., & Goodhart, L. (2014). *Understanding human differences: Multicultural education for a diverse America* (4th ed.). Boston, MA: Allyn & Pearson.

Mosston, M., & Ashworth, S. (2004). *Teaching physical education* (5th ed.). San Francisco, CA: Benjamin Cummings.

Rink, J.E. (2010). *Teaching physical education for learning* (6th Ed.). Boston, MA: WCB/McGraw-Hill.

Siedentop, D., & Tannehill, D. (1999). *Developing teaching skills in physical education* (4th ed.). Boston, MA: McGraw-Hill.

Tiedt, P.L., & Tiedt, I.M. (2010). *Multicultural teaching: A handbook of activities, information, and resources* (8th ed.). Boston, MA: Allyn & Bacon.

Wardle, F., & Cruz-Janzen, M.I. (2004). *Meeting the needs of multiethnic and multiracial children in schools.* Boston, MA: Allyn & Bacon.

REFERENCES

Alderman, B., Beighle, A., & Pangrazi, R.P. (2006). Enhancing physical activity motivation in a quality physical education program. *Journal of Physical Education, Recreation, and Dance, 77*(2), 41–45, 51.

Fronske, H. (2012). *Teaching cues for sport skills for secondary school students* (5th ed.). San Francisco, CA: Benjamin Cummings.

Kilpatrick, M., Hebert, E., & Jacobsen, D. (2002). Physical activity motivation: A practitioner's guide to self-determination theory. *Journal of Physical Education, Recreation, & Dance, 73*(4), 36–41.

Manning, M.L., & Baruth, L.G. (2009). *Multicultural education of children and adolescents* (5th ed.). Boston, MA: Allyn & Bacon.

Pangrazi, R.P., Beighle, A., & Pangrazi, D.L. (2009). *Promoting physical activity and health in the classroom.* San Francisco, CA: Pearson Benjamin Cummings.

Pangrazi, R.P., Beighle, A., & Sidman, C. (2007). *Pedometer power* (2nd ed.). Champaign, IL: Human Kinetics.

Weiss, M.R. (2000). Motivating kids in physical activity. *The President's Council on Physical Fitness and Sports Research Digest, 3*(11), 1–8.

Management and Discipline

7

Effective instruction is characterized by quality management and discipline. This chapter presents effective class management skills that improve the efficiency and productivity of instruction. Dealing with behavior involves two major parts: (1) modifying and maintaining acceptable behavior and (2) applying an approach to decreasing unacceptable behavior. Procedures such as time-outs, reprimands, and removing privileges are described. Ways to minimize the use of criticism and punishment are reviewed and specific recommendations are provided.

Learning Objectives

▶ Describe the role of the teacher as it pertains to managing children in a physical education setting.

▶ Implement management and discipline skills that result in a positive and constructive learning environment.

▶ Identify techniques used to start and stop the class; organize the class into groups, formations, and squads; and prepare students for activity.

▶ Cite acceptable and recommended procedures for dealing with inappropriate behavior.

▶ Describe techniques to increase or decrease specific behaviors.

▶ Explain the role of teacher reaction in shaping and controlling student behavior.

▶ Design or modify games that effectively change student behavior.

▶ Recognize the shortcomings of criticism and punishment when used to change and improve student behavior.

▶ Understand the legal consequences of expelling a student from school.

Successful teachers can effectively manage a class. In fact, classroom management has more influence on student learning than home environment, cognition, and policies (Wang, Haertel, & Walberg, 1994). Interestingly, classroom management has nearly the same effect on learning as student aptitude. Thus, the importance of classroom management cannot be ignored and should be the foundation of quality teaching. Effective teachers make three assumptions: teaching is a profession, students are in school to learn, and the teacher's challenge is to promote learning. These assumptions imply a responsibility to teach students who accept instruction and those who do not. Successful teachers teach all students. Competent teachers maintain faith in students who have not yet found success and maintain the expectation for them to do so eventually. Most children in a class are relatively easy to teach but being able to motivate low-aptitude and indifferent students is the result of effective instruction.

A smoothly functioning class is a joy to watch.

Effective Management and Discipline: A Coordinated Approach

Managing student behavior is not easy. A class of children is a group of individuals, each requiring unique treatment and understanding. Some teachers question the importance of effective management and discipline. The most basic reason for management and discipline is to help children learn effectively without infringing on other children's rights. Children can enjoy freedom as long as their behavior is consistent with educational expectations and does not prevent other students from learning.

The effective management of behavior means maintaining an environment in which all children have the opportunity to learn. Students who choose to be disruptive and off task compromise the rights of students who choose to cooperate. Typically, most students cooperate with the teacher. When a teacher has to spend a great deal of time working with children who are disorderly, students who want to learn are shortchanged. Thus, an efficient approach is to minimize disruptions that are distractions from learning

A smoothly functioning class is a joy to watch. Teachers behave in ways that promote positive student behavior, and students perform in a positive, caring way. Management and discipline techniques are interrelated; one affects the other. Throughout this chapter, *management* is defined as "organizing and controlling the affairs of a class." It refers to how students are organized, started and stopped, grouped, and arranged during class. Effective management means that students are moved quickly, called by their names, moved into instructional formations, taught using efficient bouts of instruction, and so on. Discipline is defined as "modifying student behavior when it is unacceptable." When things do not go smoothly, and some students decide not to follow the teacher's management requests, these behaviors must be addressed. Discipline techniques are required to create a constructive teaching environment and to shape behavior.

When working with children in any environment, discipline problems will occur. Successful teachers have strategies and skills to address these issues in an appropriate and productive manner. Teachers can apply the following strategies to develop a well-managed and disciplined class:

1. Use proper teaching behaviors.

2. Define class procedures, rules, and consequences.

3. Incorporate efficient management skills.

4. Teach acceptable student behavior.

5. Use behavior management to increase acceptable behavior.

6. Decrease unacceptable behavior with discipline.

Use Proper Teaching Behaviors

In a well-managed class, teacher and students assume dual responsibility for learning. The presentations and instructional strategies used should be appropriate for the capabilities of the students and the nature of the activity sequences. Remember that behavior issues may be a result of teaching behaviors and are not always derived from unacceptable choices by students. For example, unclear instructions may result in what is perceived by the teacher as off-task behavior. A quick reflection by the teacher may reveal that the students are not off task but rather confused by the directions.

Teachers who put time into thinking about what they are going to teach and how they are going to teach based on the class and students tend to have more success. Just as efficient instructors plan for their content, they also plan for their management, putting much thought into how the lesson will be implemented and how potential behavior issues will be addressed. When a skillful instructor prevents problems before they occur, less time is spent dealing with deviant behavior. *Your* behavior influences students. How students learn and behave reflects your personality, outlook, ideals, and background. Recognize your personal habits and attitudes that affect students negatively. Unsure of your habits? Video record yourself teaching. Although initially uncomfortable for some, this practice will shed light on to your mannerisms and attitudes. Try to model the behavior you desire from students. Hustle if you demand that students hustle. Use "please" and "thank you" frequently if you value politeness. Listen carefully to students and perform fitness activities from time to time. Modeling acceptable behavior strongly affects students. Your actions speak louder than your words.

Develop an Assertive Communication Style

You can benefit by hearing how you speak to students. Recording class sessions will help you identify the approach you take when interacting with students. Your communication style is often revealed when you are under pressure or unsure of yourself. At that point, teachers who are not assertive may become aggressive or passive in trying to get students back in line. Generally, a teacher communicates in three ways when dealing with management and discipline scenarios. Each style is discussed in detail here, the goal being for teachers to learn to develop and use an assertive style of communication when dealing with management and discipline issues.

Passive Communicator

To avoid becoming upset at students, a passive teacher hopes to make all children happy. Passive means "trying to avoid all conflict and pleasing others." Directly or indirectly, the passive teacher is constantly thinking, "Like me, appreciate what I do for you." Many passive teachers want to be perfect so that everybody will like them and their students will behave perfectly.

Passive teachers often relinquish their power to students, particularly the least cooperative students. They will say things like, "We are not going to start until everyone is listening!" Some students may interpret that to mean, "Terrific. We don't have to start until we are finished with our conversation." Passive teachers also ignore unacceptable behavior and hope it will disappear. Ignoring seldom causes behavior to disappear; rather, it becomes worse over time. Passive teachers often say things but never follow through. For example, "If you do that one more time, I am going to call your parents." When there is no follow-through or it is impossible to follow through, the threats become meaningless, and students soon learn disrespect for the teacher. Passive teachers, moreover, typically ask questions that result in useless information, such as, "What did you do that for?" or "Why are you doing this?" or "Don't you know better than that?" When students respond with "I don't know," teachers often become frustrated and angry.

Adopting a passive style of communication can also result in frustration and lashing out. When students go off task, a passive teacher can become upset and angry because he or she typically lets behavior slide until he or she can't take it anymore. Then the teacher loses composure and shouts at the class in anger. When the anger subsides, the passive teacher wants to make up and again starts the cycle of letting things go and trying to be liked. This cycle is frequently repeated. Thus, in some situations, a passive communicator can momentarily change into an aggressive communicator.

Aggressive Communicator

An aggressive teacher wants to intimidate students by coming on strong. Aggressive people feel that discussions are a form of competition that they must win at all costs. A common trait of aggressive communicators is that they use the word "you" all the time. These statements keep students feeling defensive and attacked: "You never listen to me; you are always in trouble; you are the problem here; you are always talking." Aggressive responders often think they have all the answers and try to express others' viewpoints. They may say to a student, "You think that because you did that last year in Mr. Jones' class, you can do it in my class." No one knows what another person is thinking, and communicating this way serves no purpose.

Aggressive teachers often use the words "always" and "never." These labeling words can make students believe they are bad people who always behave in certain ways or never do anything right. Words that generalize and label create problems in communication and often result in alienation rather than respect for a teacher. Aggressive teachers often see students as personally attacking them and focus on labeling and putting down the student rather than dealing with the behavior. Typically, these teachers do not reveal how they feel and are unwilling to express their thoughts. If students never know how a teacher feels, they will likely develop little empathy for them. Keep in mind that any statement about a student other than your own feelings or thoughts will give your communication an aggressive quality.

Assertive Communicator

An assertive teacher does not beg, plead, or threaten. Rather, he or she expresses feelings and expectations straightforwardly. Assertive people are not afraid to say what they want and do not worry about what others think of them. Teachers who want to be liked are concerned about what their students think. An assertive teacher wants what is best for students and does not worry about what they think. Assertiveness comes across to students as a no-nonsense approach that needs to be followed. The approach is clear, direct, and concrete (requiring little interpretation by students). For example, an assertive teacher might say to a student talking out of turn, "It upsets me when you talk while I am talking." This teacher is expressing feelings and making it clear what the unacceptable behavior is. The teacher can then follow that statement with an assertive statement that expresses the acceptable behavior: "That is your second warning; please go to time-out." Assertive communication emphasizes clarity without anger. Assertive responding does not involve high emotion, which turns assertion into aggressiveness.

One way to make messages more assertive is to use "I" instead of "you." Talking about your own feelings and emotions makes the messages sound more reasonable and firm: "When you are playing with equipment while I am talking, it bothers me and makes me forget what I planned on saying. Please leave your equipment alone

when I talk." Such messages identify the disrupting or annoying behavior, offer how you feel, and direct the student to behave properly. An excellent reference on this topic is *Assertive Discipline* (Canter, 2010).

Create a Personal Behavior Plan

A key element of an effective management approach is to understand and plan for how you will behave when disciplining students. Serious misbehavior can cause some teachers to become angry, others to feel threatened, and others to behave tyrannically. Personal behavior plans usually include these points:

1. *Maintain composure.* Students do not know your hot buttons unless you reveal them. If you lose it, students lose respect for you and believe you are an ineffective teacher.

2. *Acknowledge your feelings when student misbehavior occurs.* Do you feel angry, threatened, challenged, or fearful? How do you typically respond when a student defies you?

3. *Design a plan for yourself when such feelings occur.* For example, provide positive feedback to a nearby student immediately or take a deep breath. Avoid dealing with a student's misbehavior until you know how you feel and have created a plan.

4. *Know the options you have for dealing with the deviant behavior.* Talking with students is best done after class if you will need more than a few seconds. When time is limited, some options are to warn the student quietly, remove the student quietly from class, or send another student for help if the situation is severe.

Be a Leader, Not a Friend

Students want a teacher who is knowledgeable, personable, and a leader. They are not looking for a new friend; in fact, most students feel uncomfortable if they think you are trying to be one of them. Let students know what they will learn during the semester. Do not try to be a part of their personal discussions. You must keep a comfortable distance between you and your students. You can still be friendly and caring; it is important to be empathetic toward students as long as you express concern in a professional way. Being a leader means knowing where and how to direct a class. You are responsible for what is learned and how it is presented. Student input is important, but ultimately, it is your responsibility to lead a class to acceptable objectives.

Communicate High Standards

Students respond to your expectations. If you expect students to perform at high levels, most of them will strive to do so. That is, you get what you ask for. If you expect students to perform to the best of their abilities, they likely will do so. On the other hand, if you don't expect and reinforce quality behavior, some students will do as little as possible. Although these standards may fluctuate slightly from lesson to lesson, high expectations should be the norm.

Understand Why Students Misbehave

Students misbehave for various reasons, including the following:

- The student may be testing the teacher.
- The student may have some type of learning disability that causes the behavior problem.
- The student may be looking for reinforcement from the teacher.
- The student may have low self-esteem, which causes the student to misbehave while trying to become the center of attention.
- The student may not understand the directions given.
- The student may be bored and unchallenged by the activities.
- Performing the activities may result in continuous failure, so the student misbehaves to avoid revealing a lack of ability.
- Parents may deal with their children in a manner completely unlike the methods used in physical education.
- The teacher may not like the student, thus forcing the student to be combative and angry.
- Failure in other subjects may carry over to physical education.

Understanding these reasons and being able to identify them when the misbehaviors occur will help you anticipate and prevent many behavior problems. Students sometimes misbehave because they did not understand the instructions. Give instructions and then proceed with the activity. If some students are not performing correctly, perhaps they still did not understand. Clarify the instructions and proceed. This two-tiered approach usually ensures that directions are clear and that ample opportunity is given for all to understand.

Privately Deliver Negative and Corrective Feedback

When you deliver negative and corrective feedback, make it private and direct it to the particular student for whom it is intended. Few people want to have negative or corrective comments delivered publicly for others to hear. Besides, not all students should be punished for the behavior of a few misbehaving classmates. Negative feedback directed to a group can have contrary results. For example, a student may talk back to you in front of other students, which may cause you to lose the respect and admiration of students who were behaving properly.

Avoid Feedback That Offers the Possibility for Backlash

Some types of verbal interaction may work in the short term but have long-term negative consequences. Some types of feedback may work immediately (the behavior

7

Deliver negative or corrective feedback privately.

Clark and Company/iStock/Getty Images

stops) but cause greater problems over the long haul. If students become resentful, they tend to be deviant when the teacher is not looking. The following are some approaches to avoid:

- *Preaching or moralizing.* The most common example of moralizing is telling students, "You should know better than that!" Students make mistakes because they are young and still learning, and part of learning is making mistakes. Correct mistakes in a quiet and caring way.

- *Threatening.* Threats are ultimatums that attempt to terminate unacceptable behavior, even though you know the threat will be impossible to carry out. For example, "If you do not stop that, I'm going to kick you out of class" sounds tough but is usually impossible to enforce. You are not in a position to expel students, and some students know you cannot carry out the threat. If students hear enough idle threats, they will start to tune out, and their respect for you will gradually wane.

- *Ordering and commanding.* If you are bossy, students begin to think they are nothing more than pawns to be moved around the area. Request that students carry out tasks. Courtesy and politeness are requisites for effective teacher–student relationships.

- *Interrogating.* When a problem arises (such as a fight between students), an initial reaction is to try to discover who started the fight rather than deal with the combatants' feelings. Little is gained by trying to learn who started it. Students often shirk the blame and suggest it was not their fault. Try calmly saying, "You know that fighting is unacceptable behavior. You must have been very angry to place yourself in this situation." This statement encourages students to talk about their feelings rather than place blame. It also communicates a caring and concerned attitude toward children even when they do something wrong.

- *Refusing to listen.* This approach commonly manifests itself by the teacher saying, "Let's talk about it some other time." During instruction, this response may be necessary to keep students focused. But if you always refuse to listen, students will avoid interacting with you and will believe you do not care.

- *Labeling.* Labeling is characterized by telling children, "Stop acting like babies" or "You're behaving like a bunch of first graders." On an individual level, such feedback might sound like,

"You're always the troublemaker." Using labels is degrading and dehumanizes children. Teachers often think labeling will improve performance, but it is usually destructive and leaves students with negative feelings instead.

Define Class Procedures, Rules, and Consequences

Effectively managing is dependent on the teacher's ability to clearly articulate expectations. Without guidelines and routines, students have to guess what the teacher expects every day. This situation makes students uneasy. Suppose, for example, that students are outdoors for a physical education lesson, and their teacher tells them not to get too far away so that they can hear all the directions. Sure enough, some students stray beyond a distance the teacher deems acceptable, and they are disciplined. Unfortunately, the teacher was at fault because he or she did not set up clear guidelines. How can students judge what is too far away? What if they thought they could hear the directions, but the teacher did not think so? Can the teacher be consistent in applying this rule when even he or she does not know how far is too far? If the teacher had set up cones around the perimeter of the area and asked students to stay inside them, he or she could have eliminated the problem. The following steps will minimize misunderstandings and make all parties feel comfortable.

Step 1: Determine Management Routines for Students

Children like structure. Students feel best when they know your expectations and are most comfortable when they have established routines to follow. Explain your routines so that students understand why you are using them. Here are some routines that teachers often use:

1. How students are supposed to enter the teaching area

2. How the teaching area is defined

3. Where and how they should meet—in sitting squads, moving and freezing on a spot, in a semicircle, and so on

4. What they should do if equipment is located in the area

5. What signal is used to "freeze" a class

6. How they procure and put away equipment

7. How they will be grouped for instruction

Teachers should establish routines early in the school year and review them as needed. For example, if equipment has not been placed around the perimeter of the gymnasium for several weeks, a first-grade class may need to be reminded of the expectations before entering the teaching area. After establishing and practicing these class management routines, teachers and students can work together comfortably.

Step 2: Create Rules and Procedures for the School Year

Rules are an expected part of the school environment. School administrators typically judge teachers' effectiveness by how well they manage students rather than by how much they know about the subject matter. Teachers want students to show respect—to teachers and to other students. Expecting students to behave in an acceptable manner is reasonable. If you cannot manage students, you cannot teach them. When creating your rules, select general categories rather than specific behaviors. For example, "Respect your neighbor" means many things, from not pushing to not swearing at another student. Post rules in the teaching area where all students can easily read them. The following are some examples of general rules:

- *Stop, look, and listen.* This rule involves freezing on signal, looking at the instructor, and listening for instructions.
- *Take care of equipment.* This item includes caring for equipment and distributing, gathering, and using it properly.
- *Respect the rights of others.* This rule covers behavior such as not pushing others, leaving others' equipment alone, not fighting or arguing, and not physically or emotionally hurting others.

Students will have difficulty remembering all the details of more than three to five general rules. Too many rules can cause students to become rule specific. A child may choose to chew gum in the multipurpose room because the rule is "No gum chewing in the halls." When students become rule specific, they do not think about right, wrong, and the spirit of the rule; rather, they look for exceptions to the rule. Effective rules are general, positively phrased guidelines to direct acceptable behavior rather than negative statements that tell students what they cannot do. A great approach is to display your rules prominently for easy reference and show others what your expectations are in physical education (figure 7.1). Consider the following points when designing rules:

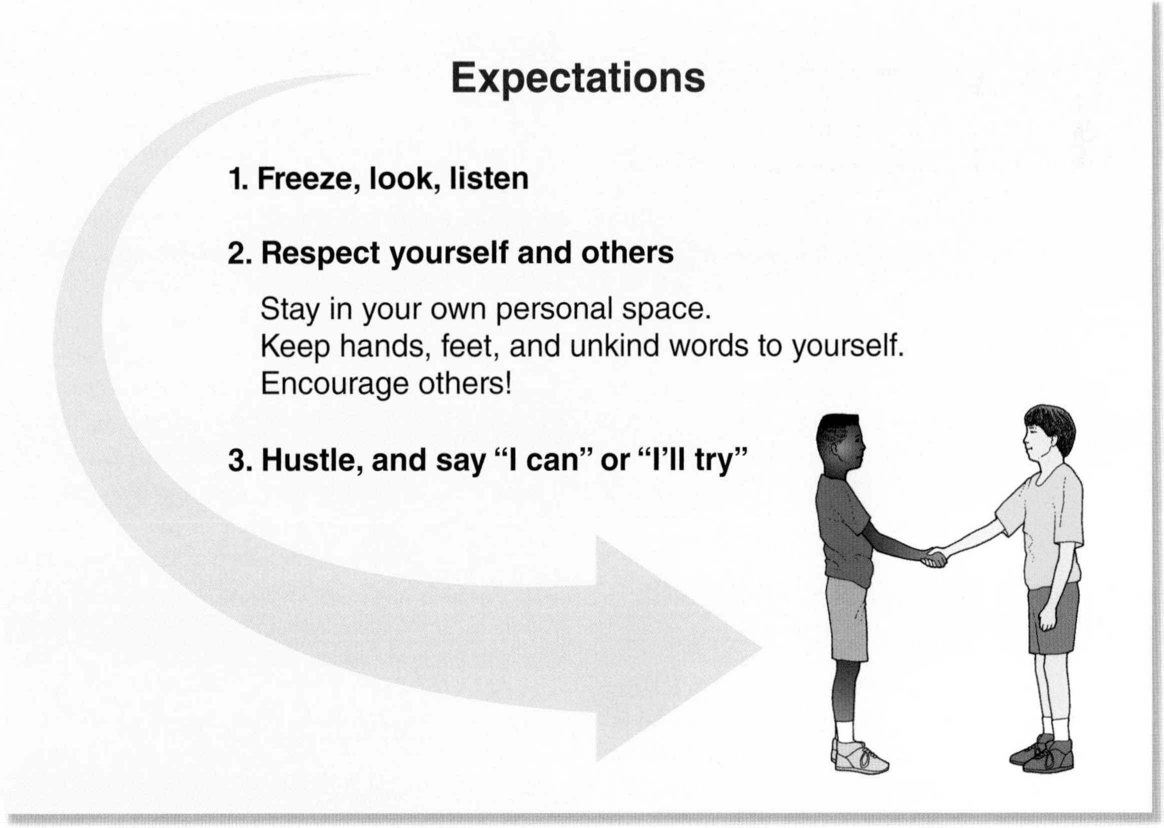

7

Expectations

1. **Freeze, look, listen**

2. **Respect yourself and others**

   Stay in your own personal space.
   Keep hands, feet, and unkind words to yourself.
   Encourage others!

3. **Hustle, and say "I can" or "I'll try"**

FIGURE 7.1 Sign displaying physical education rules.

- Select major categories of behavior rather than a multitude of specific rules, such as how to behave toward peers or how to treat the teacher.
- Identify observable behavior. Make it easy to determine whether a student is following a rule by not involving subjective judgment. "Do your best" is a common rule that is difficult, if not impossible, to determine whether a student is following.
- Make rules reasonable for the students' age level. Meaningful rules cut across all ages and are useful throughout the elementary school years (e.g., "Respect yourself and others").
- Limit the number of rules (three to five is usually best).
- State rules briefly and positively. Writing a rule that covers all situations and conditions is impossible. Make the rule brief yet broad.

Step 3: Develop Consequences When Rules Are Not Followed

When rules are broken, students must learn to accept the consequences of their misbehavior. Post the consequences for unacceptable behavior prominently in the teaching area. Discuss the rules and consequences with students to make sure they understand and see the need for behavior guidelines. Having students agree on rules and consequences helps create buy-in. One of the best ways to earn students' respect is to treat them all in a fair and caring way. Most students are willing to accept the consequences of their misbehavior if they think that their treatment will be consistent with and equal to that of other students. Animosity occurs when students sense that you play favorites. Physical education teachers commonly favor gifted athletes and students who are physically attractive. Be aware of such behavior and prevent it from occurring. One reason for defining consequences before misbehavior is that it allows you to administer the consequences equitably. When a student chooses to break a rule, apply the consequences without judging his or her character or making a derogatory statement about him or her. The student's misbehavior, not you, has triggered the consequences. Examples of consequences are addressed later in the chapter.

Step 4: Share Your Rules With Parents, Teachers, and Administrators

It is not enough to share your rules with students. If there is truth in the saying "It takes a village to raise a child," then make sure that all concerned parties know and understand your rules. A newsletter to parents at the start of the year explaining your program and your approach to class management will set the tone for students immediately. Parents have little room for complaint should their child have a problem, if routines, rules, and consequences were clearly explained from the outset. Sharing your rules with classroom teachers and administrators also helps clarify your expectations. Classroom teachers will then be able to reinforce your approach. Principals will also clearly understand what you expect, and it will be easier to work together to achieve common goals.

Step 5: Have the Class Practice Rules Systematically

Rules stipulate expected class behavior. If you have a rule for proper care of equipment, give students the opportunity to practice how you want equipment handled. If a situation requires students to stop and listen, practice and reinforce the correct behavior. Student behavior is not always correct, regardless of rules. It is common to hear teachers say to students, "How many times have I told you not to do that?" This question assumes that telling students once will result in perfect adherence to rules. But that is not the case. Continue to allow time for students to practice management behaviors throughout the school year.

Incorporate Efficient Management Skills

Class management skills are prerequisites to effective instruction. To move and organize students quickly and efficiently, teachers must implement various techniques and students must accept them. Students enjoy a learning environment that is organized, efficient, and devotes nearly all of the class time to learning skills.

Teach class management skills like you teach physical skills. All skills need to be learned through practice and repetition until they become second nature. Viewing class management skills in this light makes it easier to have empathy for students who do not perform well. Just as students make mistakes when performing physical skills, some will perform management skills incorrectly. A simple, direct statement, such as "It appears that you have forgotten how to freeze quickly; let's practice," is much more constructive than indicting a class for its carelessness and lack of interest.

Deliver Instruction Efficiently

If students are not listening when instructions are given, little learning occurs. Deliver instructions in small doses,

MAJOR FACTORS IN STUDENT ACHIEVEMENT

7

Although it is commonly believed that students from high socioeconomic status backgrounds have higher academic achievement because their parents have higher education levels, because their parents read to them, and because they have access to better programs, that is not necessarily the case. When it comes to student achievement, classroom management is the single most powerful variable influencing student learning (both in the gymnasium and in the classroom). Classroom management includes gaining students' attention, holding students accountable for learning, using efficient transitions, and having teacher awareness, or "with-it-ness."

Gaining student attention in physical education involves starting and stopping a class using consistent signals. The signals should not be the same. For example, students can become confused if blowing a whistle one time means they should begin an activity and blowing it another time means they should end it. When stopping the class, give students something to do with their hands or equipment (e.g., put hands on waist and volleyball between feet) so that these will not become distractions. Holding students accountable for learning in physical education can be accomplished in a variety of ways, and a number of assessment strategies are advocated. To be most efficient, teacher checklists, self-assessments, and peer checklists can be used as formal assessments. Informal assessments can be conducted simply by teacher observation, questioning, and asking students to give a thumbs-up or thumbs-down to signal their response. Transitions in physical education should be smooth and well organized. Grouping students can be completed using the toe-to-toe method and others from the chapter. One way to maintain physical activity for students is to have them walk, gallop, or slide in their own personal space inside the boundaries during transition times. If the teacher needs to gather his or her thoughts momentarily, this approach keeps the students active and eliminates opportunities for them to become bored and resort to off-task behaviors. Finally, teacher awareness is key to classroom management. Managing students involves using a *proactive* approach as opposed to a *reactive* approach to student behavior. Reading the students is crucial to maintaining on-task behavior and, in turn, greater student achievement. Teacher location and proximity is important to managing behavior; keeping your back to the wall allows the you to see all students and observe any inappropriate student activity. Additionally, if the teacher approaches a student who is off task, that student generally shifts his or her behavior as the teacher moves closer.

Although student aptitude, climate, program design, school organization, and state or district characteristics are all crucial factors that influence student learning, classroom instruction and climate is the most important. Within that category, classroom management is the number one variable affecting student achievement. Teachers do matter!

focusing on one or two points at a time. Instructions should be specific and seldom last longer than 20 to 30 seconds. An effective approach is to alternate short instructional episodes with periods of activity. This method contrasts with the common practice of delivering long, involved technical monologues on skill performance, only to find that many students have forgotten most of the information by the time practice begins. In a series of spoken items, people usually remember only the first and last; thus, most students will be able to integrate and concentrate on only one or two points when practicing a skill. Minimizing the amount of content per instruction helps eliminate students' frustration and allows them to focus on stated goals. This caution is not to suggest that information should not be delivered to students but that the "tell it all at the start" style should be replaced by the more effective "input, practice, feedback" model.

When giving instructions, tell students when to perform an activity before stating what the activity is. An effective way to implement "when before what" is to use a keyword, such as "Begin!" or "Start!" to start an activity. For example, "When I say, 'Start!' I'd like you to . . ." or, "When I say, 'Go!' I want you to jog to a beanbag, move to your own space, and practice tossing and catching." The keyword is not given until all directions have been issued, so students must listen to all instructions before starting.

Stop and Start a Class Consistently

The most basic and important management skill is being able to stop and start a class. Use a loud audio signal to stop a class and a voice command to start the class (see the previous discussion). Many teachers like to have students assume a specific position when they stop. Freezing in the ready position with hands on knees helps keep students' hands in their own space so that they do not distract other students. Using both an audio signal (e.g., a whistle) and a visual signal (e.g., raising the hand overhead) is effective because some children may not hear the audio signal when engrossed in activity. If children do not respond to the signal to stop, take time to practice the procedure. Reinforce students when they perform management behavior properly. Often, skill performance is reinforced but correct management behavior is not. Any behavior that is not reinforced regularly will not be performed well.

Expect 100% compliance when students are asked to stop. If only some students stop and listen to directions, class morale degenerates. Students begin to wonder why they have to stop but other students do not. If you settle for less than full attention, students will fulfill those expectations for you. Strategies for addressing unacceptable behavior are discussed later in the chapter.

Move Students Into Groups and Formations Quickly

Teachers must regularly move students into small groups and instructional formations. Simple techniques can be used to help students enjoy this process and do it quickly. Any grouping technique should require students to match up with someone near them rather than running and looking for their best friend. Place some rubber marking spots in the center of the area and call them the "friendship spots." Students who need a partner run to a friendship spot and raise their hands. After finding a partner, they move out of the friendship spot area. This approach keeps students from feeling left out.

Finding Partners

Use the activity Toe-to-Toe to teach children to find partners quickly. The goal of the game is to get toe-to-toe with a partner as fast as possible. Other challenges are to get elbow-to-elbow or shoulder-to-shoulder or look into a partner's eyes. Students without a partner must go to the friendship area and find someone else without a partner. To keep children from looking for a favorite friend or refusing to be someone's partner, tell them they must quickly find the nearest person. A sample cue to teach this might be to say, "If you have to take more than two or three steps, come to the middle." If students insist on staying near a friend, have the class move around the area and find a different partner each time you call, "Toe-to-toe!" This technique will help children meet many more students.

Dividing a Class in Half

To divide a class into two equal groups, have students get toe-to-toe with a partner. For Developmental Level I students, have one partner sit down while the other remains standing. Those standing are asked to go to one area, after which those sitting are then moved to the desired location. With students in Developmental Levels II and III, have one partner raise a hand. Move the students with their hands up to one side of the area.

Creating Small Groups

Another activity for arranging students in groups of a selected size is Whistle Mixer. When the whistle is blown a certain number of times, students form groups corresponding to that number and sit down to show that their group has the correct number. Students left out go to the friendship area, find the needed number of members, and move to an open area. After mastering this skill, students will be able to move quickly into groups with the correct number

Class in freeze position.

©Robert Pangrazi or Aaron Beighle

of students. Teachers should use hand signals along with the whistle to show the desired number of students per group. To arrange students in equal-sized groups, place an equal number of different-colored beanbags or hoops on the floor. Ask students to move throughout the area and, on signal, to sit on a beanbag. All students with a red beanbag are in the same group, those with green beanbags make up another group, and so on.

Creating Circles or Single-File Lines

An effective technique for moving a class into a single-file line or circle is to have students run randomly in the area until a signal is given. On the signal "Fall in," students continue jogging, move toward the perimeter of the area, and fall in line behind someone. Everyone jogs in the same direction as the teacher. As long as students continue to move behind another person, a circle forms automatically. Either you or a student leader can lead the line into an acceptable formation or position.

Another method of moving a class into formation is to ask students to get into various formations without talking. They can use visual signals but cannot ask someone verbally to move. Have groups hustle to see how quickly they can form the acceptable formation. Another method is to hold up a shape drawn on a large card to signal the acceptable formation. Young students learn to visualize shapes through this technique.

Using Squads to Expedite Class Organization

Some teachers find that placing students into squads helps them manage a class effectively. Squads offer a place for students to meet, keep certain students from being together, group students into prearranged teams of equal ability, and make it easier to learn students' names. Here are some guidelines for using squads to maximize teaching effectiveness:

1. Squads or groups should be selected so that a child who might be chosen last is not embarrassed. In all cases, avoid using an auction approach, in which student leaders look over the group and pick their favorites. A fast way to form squads is to use the Whistle Mixer technique described earlier.

2. Designate a location for assembling students into squad formation. On signal, children move to the designated area, with squad leaders in front and the rest of the squad behind.

3. Use squad leaders so that students have an opportunity to learn leadership and following skills among peers. Examples of leadership activities

are moving squads to a specific location, leading squads through exercises or introductory activities, and appointing squad members to certain positions in sport activities.

4. The composition of squads can be predetermined. Having equal representation of the sexes on each squad may be important. The makeup of squads may be determined by ability level so that you can quickly organize games with teams of similar ability. Squads can also be used to separate certain students so that they will not disrupt the class. Change squad members regularly so that students can work with all students in the class.

5. In most cases, an even number of squads should be formed so that the class can be broken quickly into halves for games. Dividing a class of 30 students into six squads of 5 members each ensures a small number of students for each piece of apparatus and minimizes waiting in line for group activities.

6. Using squads should be an exciting activity that encourages movement and creativity. For example, place numbered cones in different locations around the activity area. Write the numbers in a different language or hide them in a mathematical equation or story problem. When students enter the gym, instruct them to find their squad number and assemble. Another method is to distribute task cards specifying how the squads are arranged. The first squad to follow instructions correctly can be awarded a point or be acknowledged by the rest of the class. Examples of tasks for squads might be arranging the members in a circle, sitting with their hands on their heads, or assuming crab positions in a straight line facing northwest. Task cards can also be used to specify an introductory activity or tell students where to move for the fitness development activity.

7. An effective way to use squads is called home base. Place a number of marking spots on the floor throughout the area. When the teacher calls, "Home base," the captains quickly find the closest spot, and their squad members line up behind them. If an even number of squads has been created, half of the spots can be put in each half of the area. When the teacher calls, "Home base," the class quickly divides in half. This method is handy for station teaching as well; place a spot at each of the teaching stations and call, "Home base" to line up a squad at each station.

7

Know Students' Names

Effective class management requires learning the names of your students. Develop a system to help you learn names. One approach is to memorize three or four names per class period. Write the names on a note card and identify those students at the start and throughout the period. At the end of the period, identify the students again. Each time the class meets, continue in this way until you know everyone's name.

Tell students you are trying to learn their names. Ask them to say their name before performing a skill or answering a question. After learning a student's name, you can use it during activities; for example, say, "Mary, it's your turn to jump."

Another approach to learning names is to photograph each class, in squads, and identify students by matching names to the picture. Before class, identify a few students whose names you know and a few you do not know. Set personal goals by calculating the percentage of students whose names you know after each period.

Establish Pre-and Postteaching Routines

Children appreciate the security of knowing what to do from the time they enter the instructional area until they leave. Effective teaching demands routine handling of certain procedures. The following situations occur before and after teaching and need to be planned for before the lesson.

Nonparticipation

An efficient system should be devised for screening children who cannot participate in the lesson. The school nurse or classroom teacher should make the decision about whether a child should participate in physical education. This practice avoids a situation in which the physical education teacher encourages students to participate even though they have a written excuse from parents or a physician. A note from the classroom teacher or school nurse, listing the names and health problems of those who are to sit out or to take part in modified activity, can be delivered as children enter the room. Accept the information at face value and avoid questioning students about their reason for nonparticipation. A student with a note from home or from a physician should never be allowed to participate without parental permission.

Entering the Teaching Area

Nothing is more difficult than trying to start a class when students enter in a loud, disorderly way. Meet your class at the door. Explain how students should enter the area and what they are supposed to do. Alternatively, have the class enter the area and begin jogging around the teaching space. On the signal to freeze, students stop and listen as the day's activities are described. Another, less desirable method is to have students enter the area and sit in squads behind their cones or floor markers. Instruction starts when all students are in position. Regardless of the

Students can jog around the teaching space when class starts.

method used, students should enter the area under control, knowing where they are supposed to meet.

When a classroom teacher lets students straggle in late or brings the entire class in late, it disrupts the instructional process. Discuss the problem of tardiness with the teacher and try to find a solution. Try designating a couple of responsible students in each class to remind the classroom teacher that physical education begins in five minutes. Alternatively, designate an area away from the teaching area where classes can assemble and request that they line up at the gym door as soon as the entire group is ready. Resolve this problem quickly even if it requires asking the school's administrator to intervene.

Starting the Lesson

Students enter the activity area wanting to move. Take advantage of their urge to move by engaging them in some activity before discussing the lesson. Students are more willing to listen after they have participated in vigorous activity. Let them try an activity before instructing them on points of technique; this time gives you an opportunity to assess their performance level. Many students listen to instruction better after trying an activity and finding that they need help.

Closing the Lesson

Following a regular routine for closing the lesson is beneficial. It allows time for concluding the instructional content as well as a procedure for leaving the teaching area. If you want the students to arrive in an orderly fashion, they should leave physical education in an orderly fashion. A closing routine helps calm and quiet students, and classroom teachers picking up their class appreciate it. Another way to calm students is to take a few minutes for relaxation activities.

Equipment Procedures

Make students responsible for securing the equipment they use. Teach students how you want them to get the equipment and how you want them to return it at the end of the lesson. This method minimizes the amount of equipment rearrangement you will have to do. Place your equipment around the perimeter of the teaching area so that all students have easy access. Using students to assist in distributing and gathering equipment before and after school makes it possible to work closely with students who need special attention.

Passing Time for Discussing Student Behavior Issues

Children who misbehave during class need to be talked to after class, so teachers need to schedule a minimum of five minutes of passing time between classes. Scheduling classes back to back makes it impossible to talk with students, rearrange equipment, and take care of personal matters. If time between classes is unavailable, give a "meeting appointment" form to the classroom teacher and student to remind both parties of the student's obligation to meet with you at the end of the school day.

Use Equipment Effectively

When using small equipment such as balls, hoops, and jump ropes, be sure that every student has a piece for personal use. For large equipment or apparatus, establish as many stations or groups as possible. A class of 30 requires a minimum of six benches, mats, or jumping boxes to keep waiting time short. One way to cut students' waiting time is to use return activities, so that students can perform a task or tasks while returning to their squad.

Teach students where to place the equipment during instruction. Equipment should be in the same (home) position when the class is called to attention. For example, beanbags are placed on the floor, basketballs between the feet, and jump ropes folded and placed at the feet. Placing the equipment in home position avoids the problem of children striking one another with the equipment, dropping it, or practicing activities when they should be listening. To keep students from playing with the equipment when it is placed on the floor, ask them to take a giant step away from it.

Distribute equipment to students as rapidly as possible. When they have to wait in line for a piece of equipment, time is wasted and behavior problems occur. Many teachers assign student leaders to get the equipment for their squad, but this approach results in many students sitting and waiting. A better, faster method is to have the equipment placed around the perimeter of the area (figure 7.2). On signal, students move to acquire a piece of equipment, take it to their personal space, and begin practicing an assigned skill. This approach takes advantage of the natural urge to try the equipment and reinforces students who procure equipment quickly. Use the reverse procedure to put equipment away. *Any* method beats the often-used practice of placing the equipment in the middle of the area in a container and having students "run and get a ball." This approach raises children's chances of being aggravated or hurt. Similarly, handing equipment to each individual student is inactive, inefficient, and tends to yield behavior problems.

7

Pearson Education

FIGURE 7.2   Equipment placed around the perimeter.

Regardless of how students acquire equipment, clearly explain what to do with the equipment after they get it. Waiting for all students to get equipment before starting allows the slowest and least cooperative students to set the pace. Do not make students who have hustled to get their equipment wait for the laggards. Rather, reward them by letting them start practicing as soon as they get their equipment to provide incentive to hustle and be efficient. Interact with those students who are slow and less cooperative while the others are practicing.

Teach Acceptable Student Behavior

Teaching acceptable behavior has always been a basic reason that societies developed schools. By implementing a program that focuses on behavior, a school shows parents and students that this school outcome is important. This section outlines several programs used in physical education that focus on acceptable and responsible behavior.

Responsibility Through Physical Activity

Concern about student behavior and lack of discipline has increased the need to teach responsible behavior to stu-

dents. Hellison (2011) developed strategies and programs for teaching responsibility skills in physical education. A premise for learning responsible behavior is that it must be planned for, taught, and reinforced. Responsible behavior takes time and practice to learn, much like any other skill.

Levels of Responsible Behavior

Hellison (2011) suggests a hierarchy consisting of five levels of responsible behavior students can learn. The hierarchy, with examples of typical student behavior at each level, is as follows.

Level 0: Irresponsibility

Level 0 students are unmotivated and undisciplined. Their behavior includes discrediting other students' involvement and interrupting, intimidating, manipulating, and verbally or physically abusing other students and perhaps the teacher.

Behavior Examples

- *At home.* Blaming brothers or sisters for problems; lying to parents.
- *On the playground.* Calling other students names; laughing at others.
- *In physical education.* Talking to friends when the teacher is giving instructions; pushing and shoving when selecting equipment.

Level 1: Self-Control

Students at this level do not participate in the day's activity or show much mastery or improvement. These students control their behavior enough that they do not interfere with other students' right to learn or the teacher's right to teach.

Behavior Examples

- *At home.* Refraining from hitting a brother or sister even though angry.
- *On the playground.* Standing and watching others play; not getting angry at others because they upset you.
- *In physical education.* Waiting until an appropriate time to talk with friends; having control and not letting others' behavior bother them.

Level 2: Involvement

These students show self-control and are involved in the subject matter or activity.

Behavior Examples

- *At home.* Helping clean up the dishes after dinner; taking out the trash.

- *On the playground.* Playing with others; participating in a game.
- *In physical education.* Listening and performing activities; trying even when they dislike an activity; doing an activity without complaining or saying, "I can't."

Level 3: Self-Responsibility

Level 3 students take responsibility for their choices and for linking these choices to their own identities. They are able to work without direct supervision, eventually taking responsibility for their intentions and actions.

Behavior Examples

- *At home.* Cleaning up without being asked.
- *On the playground.* Returning equipment after recess.
- *In physical education.* Following directions; practicing a skill without being told; trying new activities without encouragement.

Level 4: Caring

Students behaving at this level are motivated to extend their sense of responsible behavior by cooperating, giving support, showing concern, and helping.

Behavior Examples

- *At home.* Helping take care of a younger brother or sister or a pet.
- *On the playground.* Asking others (not just friends) to join them in play.
- *In physical education.* Helping someone who is having trouble; helping a new student feel welcome; working with all students; showing that all people are worthwhile.

Responsible behavior is taught by using various strategies. Post the levels of responsibility in the teaching area. Explain the different levels of behavior and identify acceptable behaviors at each level. Finally, implement the program by reinforcing acceptable behavior and redirecting inappropriate behavior. The program is based on a two-pronged approach: (1) catch students behaving responsibly and reinforce them, and (2) redirect students behaving at level 0 by asking, "At what level are you performing, and what level would be more acceptable?" An example is the following discussion between teacher and student:

You see a student behaving at level 0, so you initiate a conversation with the student in a nonconfrontational and nonadversarial manner:

Teacher: Johnny, it appeared you were making fun of Sarah.

Student: I wasn't making fun of anyone!

Teacher: Maybe not, but if you were, what level of behavior would that be?

Student: Zero!

Teacher: Is that the kind of person you want to be or the level of behavior you want to show?

Student: No!

Teacher: If you were at level 0, do you think you could make some changes? Perhaps you could move to level 1 and have self-control even if someone else makes you mad or even if you do not like that person.

Strategies for Increasing Responsible Behavior

Teacher feedback forms the core of the responsibility approach, but many strategies can be used to increase responsible behavior in the instructional setting:

- *Model acceptable behavior.* How you interact with students encourages responsible behavior. It has been said, "Students do not care about how much you know until they know how much you

TECH TIP

Digital badges are also a way reinforce acceptable behavior. Traditionally, students can earn a badge or certificate for efforts or accomplishments and then sew onto a jacket or shirt. With technology, badges can also be given digitally. A wide variety of systems can be developed to determine how badges are earned. Examples include responsible behavior, kindness, effort, and so on. Badges can be self-created on a variety of websites and then shared with students. These badges can be sent digitally through a variety of programs such as a school learning management system. From there, they can be shared through student digital portfolios that are often shared with parents. Thus, digital badges offer a strategy for engaging students and parents while educating parents about some of the happenings in physical education.

care." Treat children with dignity and respect, and follow through with responsible action and words. In return, expect students to treat you and others with the same dignity and respect.

- *Use reinforcement.* Give students specific, positive feedback about the quality of their behavior. When giving corrective feedback, make sure that it identifies the acceptable level of behavior. If you are reinforcing acceptable behavior, explain why the behavior is acceptable and say that you appreciate it. In some cases, it may be beneficial to identify a super-citizen or give a "happy-gram" for special

behavior. Although these gestures may seem trivial to adults, they mean a great deal to students and can serve greatly to shape acceptable behaviors.

- *Offer time for responsibility and reflection.* Give students time to think about the attitudes and behaviors associated with each of the levels. Ask them to fill out a self-responsibility checklist (figure 7.3) at different times of the year.
- *Allow student sharing.* Let students give their opinions about responsible behavior. Accept all students' feelings as important. Focus on ways to encourage higher levels of responsible behavior. Brainstorming with your students to identify consequences of high and low behavior is effective, as is asking different students to give examples of responsible behavior at different levels. Give students time to share how they feel when someone uses a high- or low-level behavior around them.
- *Encourage goal setting.* Help students set goals for responsible behavior they want to exhibit. This can be done at the start of the lesson by asking students to tell a partner the behavior they want to use today. At the end of the lesson, partners evaluate each other to see if the behavior was exhibited. Examples of behaviors are listening, hustling, following directions, being courteous, and complimenting others.
- *Offer opportunities for responsibility.* Students often can be given responsibility in a class setting. Being a group leader, team captain, referee, scorekeeper, rule maker, or dispute resolver are roles that encourage students to exhibit high-level behavior. Because responsible positions affect other students, effective leaders have to behave responsibly.
- *Allow student choice.* Responsible behavior is best learned when students make choices. The natural consequences of self-selected choices are often the best teachers. Students can choose games, decide on fitness activities, and select partners. Discussing how to make meaningful health choices (see chapter 3) is an important phase of learning to make responsible choices.

MY SELF-RESPONSIBILITY CHECKLIST

Name: _____

Date: _____

Self-Control:

_____ I did not call others names.

_____ I had self-control when I became mad.

_____ I listened when others were talking.

_____ Other (describe) _____

Involvement:

_____ I listened to all directions before starting.

_____ I was willing to try all activities.

_____ I tried activities even when I didn't like them.

_____ Other (describe) _____

Self-Responsibility:

_____ I followed directions without being told more than once.

_____ I did not blame others.

_____ I worked on activities by myself.

_____ Other (describe) _____

Caring:

_____ I helped someone today.

_____ I said something nice to someone.

_____ I asked someone to do something with me.

_____ Other (describe) _____

FIGURE 7.3 Example of a responsibility checklist.

Use Conflict Resolution to Reduce Bullying

Nearly one-third of U.S. elementary school students say they are frequently bullied at school (Bradshaw, Sawyer, & O'Brennan, 2007). Bullying is described by Swearer, Espelage, and Napolitano (2009) as the use of either observable or unobservable aggressive behavior where an imbalance of power exists between the offender and the offended. The aggressive behavior usually occurs repeatedly. The American Psychological Association dictionary defines bullying as "persistent threatening and aggressive behavior directed toward other people, especially those who are smaller or weaker" (VandenBos, 2007, p. 139). Bullying often leads to conflict between students that can result in violence. Differences of opinion are part of daily life, so children must be taught how to deal with them effectively. Students must learn to respect others' opinions and feelings while maintaining their own worth and dignity. In addition, students who bully to get their way must be dealt with in ways that curb the behavior without causing a total loss of self-esteem.

Everyday conflicts can be resolved in various ways, but the most common methods involve three types of behavior—dominating, appeasing, and cooperating. Students who use the dominating style are often unsure of their standing in the group. They want things done their way but are afraid that others will reject them. They often lack confidence and try hard to get others to accept their way of doing things. Students who are appeasers lack confidence but want to be accepted by others. They do not like conflict and are willing to set aside their feelings to placate others.

Neither the dominating nor the appeasing approach for solving conflicts is effective in the long run. No one likes to be dominated or put in the position of having to appease others. Teaching students how to solve conflicts peacefully, cooperatively, and with no apparent losers will reduce the amount of bullying and intimidation that occurs in schools. Using cooperative skills to solve problems builds positive feelings between students and leads to better group cohesiveness. Use the following steps to resolve conflicts and minimize bullying:

1. *Stop the aggressive behavior immediately*. Separate students in conflict immediately and give them an opportunity to cool down. Time-out boxes are an excellent place to send students to relax and unwind.

2. *Gather data about what happened and define the problem*. Ask what happened, who was involved, and how each child is feeling. Ask open-ended questions such as, "What happened?" and "How did you feel about . . . ?" to help students talk freely about the problem.

3. *Brainstorm possible solutions*. Keep in mind that brainstorming is a nonjudgmental process that accepts all solutions regardless of their perceived value. Encourage students to think of as many options as possible by asking open-ended questions such as, "How could we solve this problem?" or "What other ways could we deal with this?"

4. *Test the solutions generated through brainstorming*. Ask a question such as, "What solutions might work best?" Help students understand the implications of the solutions and how the solutions can be implemented. Accept solutions that may differ from your way of solving the problem.

5. *Help implement the plan*. Walk students through the solution to help them understand the approach. Guide them through the steps by asking, "Who goes first?" and "Who will take the next step?" As the solution is implemented, it may need to be changed or modified. Changes must be agreed on by the students involved.

6. *Evaluate the approach*. Observe to make sure that the plan is accomplishing the accepted outcome. Encourage students to change the plan again if necessary.

Learning to solve problems through dialogue and cooperation takes practice and time. Bullying is a learned behavior, and teaching students that this behavior is

TECH TIP

One strategy for increasing positive behavior is to highlight that behavior and share it with parents. Schools use various platforms and systems to communicate with parents. These platforms allow students to take pictures or videos of themselves during lessons and then explain what they are doing to the camera. These bits of video can then be shared with the individual student's parents through their portfolio. Parents hearing about physical education lessons and student behavior is great, but parents seeing their child engaged in an activity during physical education leaves a powerful impression and is a great advocacy tool.

both unacceptable and unproductive will take some time. This process of negotiation should not focus on placing blame, because doing that will only encourage defensive behavior such as appeasing or being aggressive. Students must trust that the process will be equitable and objective and that they will get a fair shake if they deal with the issue cooperatively.

Peer Mediation

Peer mediation is similar to conflict resolution except that it is student directed. Students resolve their own disputes and conflicts, and a neutral peer acts as moderator. In peer mediation, the goal is to work out differences constructively. Mediation gets students involved in the problem-solving process, as either mediators or disputants, and teaches them a way of handling conflicts. A text by Cohen (2005) is an excellent resource for a step-by-step approach to student peer mediation.

Students are trained to help their classmates identify the problems behind the conflicts and find solutions. Peer mediation is not about who is right or wrong. Instead, students are encouraged to move beyond the immediate conflict and learn to get along with each other. Peer mediators ask the disputing students to tell their stories and ask the students questions for clarification.

A key component to any mediation process is letting all students tell their own story, so that they believe that someone understands their perspective. Common situations involving name-calling, spreading rumors, bumping into students in the hallways, and bullying are often best resolved through peer mediation. The two parts to the mediation process are establishing ground rules and following the steps of mediation.

Ground Rules

All parties (including the mediator) participate in reviewing, and agreeing to follow, the ground rules. When agreement is reached, mediation begins. Students must agree to the following basic ground rules:

- *The problem will be solved.* Participants must agree that a solution will be found in the session. Leaving without solving the problem is unacceptable.
- *The truth will be told.* Students must agree to tell the truth regardless of its effect on the situation. Because students are solving the problem without adult supervision and the session is confidential, telling the truth will not result in negative consequences.

- *The full story will be heard without interruption.* Both parties must be able to tell their side of the story without interruption. Each person must believe that her or his side of the story has been completely and fairly presented.
- *All parties will act in a respectful manner.* Students need to learn to state their case without excessive emotion and anger.
- *All discussion will be confidential.* Both the arbitrator and the parties in conflict must agree not to discuss the situation with nonparticipants.
- *The solution will be implemented.* Both parties must carry out the agreement regardless of whom the solution favors.

Mediation Steps

When the ground rules are agreed on, mediation led by a trained peer begins. The problem is not discussed while reviewing ground rules. The mediation steps are about solving the actual problem and doing so in a manner dictated by the ground rules that the students agreed to follow. The steps to finding a mediated solution are as follows:

- *Tell your story or grievance.* Both students have a chance to tell their side of the story. This step should be an opportunity to "lay it on the table" and believe that the problem is clearly understood by both the other party and the mediator.
- *Verify the story.* The mediator and the other party have the opportunity to ask questions to clarify and verify the story. The mediator is responsible for finding out exactly what happened and how each party feels.
- *Discuss the conflict.* The mediator conducts a discussion about the situation and the emotions involved.
- *Brainstorm solutions to the problem.* All parties discuss various ways to solve the problem. The mediator emphasizes the need to find solutions that resolve the situation for both parties.
- *Discuss and implement the agreed-upon solution.* Both parties have already agreed to follow the ground rules. One rule was to solve the problem, so leaving without coming to a solution is unacceptable.
- *Sign a contract.* After agreeing to a solution, the offended parties must sign a contract agreeing to carry out the solution.

Use Behavior Management to Increase Acceptable Behavior

Positive discipline focuses on reinforcing acceptable behavior by acknowledging a child's positive attributes. Increasing positive behavior may help reduce negative behavior because the student receives more feedback and attention. Lavay, French, and Henderson (2006) provide an excellent resource for taking a systematic approach to positive behavior management. This section presents an action plan for modifying and maintaining acceptable behavior. The program involves three phases: (1) increasing acceptable behavior, (2) prompting acceptable behavior, and (3) sharing acceptable behavior. Keep in mind that thinking of behavior as acceptable or unacceptable rather than positive or negative is usually best. The terms "unacceptable" and "acceptable" speak only to the behavior, not to the demeanor of the child. Avoid characterizing the child as bad, because this descriptor can erode self-esteem and self-worth.

Increase Acceptable Behavior

Catch them doing what you want them to do is one secret to increasing acceptable behavior. Behavior that is followed by appropriate positive reinforcement will occur more often in the future. This principle is the key for increasing acceptable behavior. Its strength is that it focuses on positive, acceptable educational outcomes. Key points for implementing the principle lie in deciding what to use as reinforcers, selecting those that effectively reinforce individuals, and properly using the reinforcers.

Social Reinforcers

Well before starting school, most children experience an environment filled with social reinforcers. Hart and Riley (1995) reported that by the age of three, children in professional families had received 500,000 encourages and 80,000 discourages. In contrast, children from lower-income families received only 80,000 encourages and 200,000 discourages. Teachers, therefore, cannot treat all children the same, because children arrive at school with entirely different backgrounds and experiences.

Parents use praise, physical contact, and facial expressions to acknowledge children's acceptable behavior. Here are some reinforcers to use with students in physical education class:

Words of Praise

Great job.	Nice going.
Exactly right.	I really like that effort.
Perfect arm placement.	That's the best one yet.
Way to go!	Nice hustle.

Physical Expressions

Smiling	Holding a clenched fist overhead
Nodding	Giving thumbs-up
Clapping	Winking

Physical Contact

Handshake	High five
Fist bump	

Find out what type of social reinforcers students are accustomed to responding to in the school setting. Certain reinforcers may embarrass students or make them uncomfortable. For example, some students may not want to be touched, even to the point of receiving a high five. Students, particularly those of the opposite sex, may incorrectly interpret a hug or pat on the back. If you are unsure, ask the school administrator to clarify which social reinforcers can be used.

TEACHING TIP

In some instances a teacher may observe acceptable behavior from across the gymnasium. In these cases, providing feedback from across the gymnasium may be appropriate. Saying, "Darion, I saw that. I like that leadership" is appropriate. If you think that kind of comment might embarrass a specific student, a simple thumbs-up to the student would be effective as well. Keep in mind that positive feedback is the only type of feedback provided publicly.

Activity Reinforcers

Various types of activities that children enjoy can be used as reinforcement. To determine activities that can be used as reinforcers, see what children do during their free time. Activities that will reinforce a class include offering free time to practice a skill, the opportunity to play a game, extra time in physical education class, or an extra physical education lesson during the physical education teacher's planning time. Also, consider having some children help administer equipment, act as teacher's aides, be peer teachers in a cross-aged tutoring situation, or serve as team captains. Students might receive special privileges such as being student of the day, getting to choose the game to play, or having lunch with the teacher.

Token Reinforcers

Because physical education is closely related to athletic competition, where winners often receive awards and trophies, many teachers feel a need to offer some type of token as a reinforcer. The less favorable aspect of giving tokens (i.e., points, ribbons, or certificates) is that when only the winners get them, other students are less likely to be motivated to perform in the future. Some teachers give participation certificates or ribbons to all students, but this practice reduces the reinforcement value of the token. In addition, some studies show that extrinsic rewards may actually decrease a child's intrinsic desire to participate (Greene & Lepper, 1975; Whitehead & Corbin, 1991). Token reinforcers work best with primary-grade children, who are motivated by receiving the tokens. After the age of nine, however, students begin to see tokens as a form of bribery to behave in a certain manner. Generally, it is best to use token reinforcers only if it appears that social reinforcers are ineffective.

Selecting Reinforcers

How do you know what will be reinforcing to your students? Fortunately, most children respond to praise, attention, smiles, games, free time, and privileges. A practical way to identify effective reinforcers is to observe children during free time, analyzing the things they enjoy doing. Another simple solution is to ask them what they would like to do. Most children will tell you that they would like more recess, free time, or other enjoyable activity.

Using Social Reinforcers

Effective use of social reinforcers requires giving praise and making positive statements. You may feel uncomfortable when learning to offer students positive reinforcement because learning new behavioral responses feels inauthentic. Trying new ways of communicating with a class (e.g., with more energy or more calmly) requires a period of adjustment. New patterns of praise and reinforcement often feel contrived and insincere (fortunately, most students do not know the difference), and you cannot avoid the discomfort. Teachers who are unwilling to experience the uneasiness of learning usually do not change. Do not assume that patterns of speech you learned as a child will be effective in an instructional setting. Teachers are made, not born; success comes

through hard work and dedication. If practiced regularly, new behavioral patterns can become a natural part of your repertoire.

Praise is especially effective when it refers to specific behavior exhibited by a student. Avoid using general statements such as "Good job" or "You are an excellent performer." Nonspecific statements do not tell a student what he or she did well. They leave the student wondering what behavior you meant. If the student's thoughts do not align with your intent, incorrect behavior may be reinforced. To improve the specificity and effectiveness of feedback, describe the behavior to be reinforced instead of judging it. This approach reinforces the student and tells the other students what behavior you expect. For example, compare the following statements for the same performance of a skill:

- *Describing.* "I saw your excellent forward roll, James; you tucked your head just right. Keep those knees tucked too."

- *Judging.* "That's not how I told you to do it. You can do better."

In the describing example, the student is identified and the specific behavior performed is reinforced. In the judging situation, identifying what the behavior is or who is getting the feedback is impossible. In most cases, if a question can be asked about delivered praise or criticism (such as what was good or why the performance was incorrect), the feedback is nonspecific and open to misinterpretation. To increase acceptable behavior, verbally or physically describe what made the performance effective, good, or noteworthy. This method reinforces the student and communicates to the rest of the class what behavior is expected by the instructor.

Premack Principle

The Premack principle (Premack, 1965) is often used unknowingly to motivate students. This principle states that a highly desirable activity can be used to motivate students to learn an activity they find less desirable. In practice, this principle allows students to participate in a favorite activity after performing a less enjoyable one. The Premack principle is often called the "Eat your peas if you want dessert" rule. Here are some examples of the Premack principle in use:

- "You may shoot baskets [preferred] after you complete the passing drill [less desirable]."

- "Once we get through the first few moves without music [less desirable], we'll turn on the music and do that part of the dance [preferred]."

- "Those who raise their hand [less desirable] will be selected to answer the question [preferred]."

Prompt Acceptable Behavior

Prompts are used to remind students to behave acceptably and to encourage the development of new patterns of behavior. Here are some common ways to prompt children in physical education class:

- *Modeling.* You or a student performs the acceptable behavior with the expectation that the other students will respond similarly. For example, placing your piece of equipment on the floor when stopping a class reminds the class to do likewise. Modeling is an effective prompt for acceptable behavior because young students emulate their teacher.

- *Verbal cues.* Verbal cues can help maintain the lesson pace, increase the performance level, or motivate students to stay on task. Using cues like "Hustle" and "Keep going" reminds students of acceptable behavior.

- *Nonverbal cues.* Many physical cues are given through body language to communicate concepts like "Hustle," "Move over here," "Great performance," "Quiet down," and so on. When learning skills, students can receive nonverbal physical cues to move into proper position, follow the correct pattern, or properly align body parts.

Avoid using prompts so much that students will not perform without them. The process of gradually removing the prompt so that behavior is self-motivated is called fading. Although you are likely to keep giving some prompts, use the weakest (least intrusive) prompt possible to stimulate the behavior. Instead of a prompt, you could give students a long lecture about the importance of staying on task, but lectures are time consuming, unsuited for repetitive use, and ineffective in the long run. Select a short, distinctive cue that students can easily identify with the acceptable skill.

Also, be sure that the prompt identifies the task being prompted. If you prompt the class to hustle and the prompt is not tied to an acceptable behavior, confusion may result. Some children may think that your prompt means to perform the skill as fast as possible; others may think it means to stop what they are doing and hustle to the teacher. To make sure that students clearly understand your prompt, use it consistently to stimulate the desired behavior.

TEACHING TIP

Create colorful posters that clearly outline your safety procedures and post them in the activity space. Review the rules as necessary with your students through warm-up activities and games.

Shape Acceptable Behavior

When behavior is unacceptable, use shaping techniques—extinction and reinforcement—to create new behavior. Two steps are followed when shaping behavior.

1. *Use differential reinforcement to increase the incidence of acceptable behavior.* Reinforce responses that reach a predetermined criterion, and ignore those that do not meet the criterion (extinction). For example, suppose you want students to put their equipment on the floor within 5 seconds after a signal. Using differential reinforcement, reinforce the students whenever they meet the 5-second criterion and ignore their performance when it takes longer than 5 seconds.

2. *Expand the criterion that must be reached for reinforcement to occur.* This step involves gradually shifting the criterion toward the desired goal. If the acceptable behavior is for the class to get quiet within 5 seconds after receiving a signal, you may have to start with a 12-second interval. Why the longer interval? Expecting an inattentive class to quiet down quickly is unreasonable. If you start with a 5-second interval, you and your students will most likely fail to meet the criterion. What's more, students will not often achieve this stringent standard of behavior, giving you few opportunities to reinforce them. Consequently, you and the class feel unsuccessful. To avoid this outcome, expand the criterion by starting with a 12-second interval. When the class reaches this goal, shift to 10 seconds and ask the class to conform to this new standard. Repeat the process gradually until the class reaches the 5-second interval.

Changing behavior can be accomplished in a similar way by taking a systematic approach to behavior modification. See A Plan for Changing Misbehavior sidebar for a step-by-step plan for changing unacceptable behavior.

7

A PLAN FOR CHANGING MISBEHAVIOR

Changing behavior can be done if teachers are willing to experiment and be patient. Teachers want to change behavior quickly and on the spot and at times make incorrect decisions because they don't have time to think of an effective solution. In-class misbehavior can be temporarily stopped, but it may often go unchanged for the future. Realize that change will require long-term action that must be planned ahead of time. The following steps can be used to develop a plan for changing behavior:

- Identify a single behavior that needs to be changed, improved, or strengthened. Don't pick more than one behavior because monitoring change will be much more difficult.
- Identify a behavior that will be substituted for the behavior to be changed.
- Determine what positively reinforces the student. Have a discussion with the student to see what is reinforcing.
- Decide whether a negative reinforcer is needed to give momentum to the change process.
- Develop a plan for getting the desired behavior to occur. This will generate a behavior that can be reinforced and used to replace the undesirable behavior.
- Put the plan into effect and set a time frame for evaluation of the plan. Decide what modifications are needed to make the plan more effective. This modification may demand a different set or schedule of reinforcers or negative consequences. If an entirely different plan is needed (because the behavior hasn't decreased or changed), make such changes and proceed.
- Continue evaluating and modifying the plan.

Decrease Unacceptable Behavior With Discipline

Corrective feedback and the use of consequences can be effective in decreasing unacceptable behavior. Consequences are actions that follow misbehavior and teach students that their behavior results in some action from the environment, peers, or teacher.

Use Corrective Feedback

First, as described earlier, try using positive reinforcement to increase acceptable behavior so that it will replace unacceptable behavior. If a skilled student is always criticizing less able students, ask the student to help others and serve as a student assistant. The intent is to teach the student to deliver positive, constructive feedback rather than criticism. An effective rule of thumb before using corrective feedback is to reinforce the acceptable (desired) behavior twice. For example, suppose that a child is slow to stop on signal whereas most other students are stopping and listening properly. Ask the class to move and freeze again. Reinforce students who are on task. (With older students, reinforce the class as a whole rather than individuals.) If the result is unacceptable, try it again. In primary-grade classes, misbehaving students frequently emulate those who are being reinforced. If not, you may have to use corrective feedback.

TEACHING TIP

When teachers, especially young teachers, read about disciplining students, they often become anxious. View this process as teaching students to be self-disciplined and responsible. Remember that the strategies discussed in this book, when practiced, will provide you with the skills necessary to address 99% of the behavior issues you will see in physical education. And the vast majority of students will respond favorably to these strategies. Be consistent and patient.

Corrective feedback should be clear and specific. Students must know exactly what behavior they are to stop and what acceptable behavior they are to start. Use corrective feedback as soon after the misbehavior as possible and deliver positive reinforcement immediately following the acceptable behavior.

After being disciplined or corrected—especially if such feedback is not delivered correctly—students may respond negatively and disrupt the class. Whether delivering corrective feedback or consequences, use the following steps to avoid teacher–student conflicts that embarrass students and yourself.

1. *Do not address the student publicly.* Buy some time to talk with the student privately by giving the class a task to perform. It may be as simple as jogging around the area or quickly asking them to pick their equipment and practice a task. While they are engaged, you are in control and have time to discuss the situation quietly with the misbehaving student.

2. *Isolate the student and yourself.* Do not correct a student where others can hear what you are saying. The problem is a private matter between you and the student.

3. *Deal with one student at a time.* Often, a few students are misbehaving together. Separate them and deal with their unacceptable behavior one on one. If you do not separate them, they may form a consensus about what happened that disagrees with your perceptions.

4. *State your position once; repeat it once if you believe that the student did not understand.* Do not argue or try to prove your point. Take no more than 10 or 15 seconds to tell the student the unacceptable behavior and state the acceptable behavior you would like to see. "Samarie, holding your bean-bag during instruction is unacceptable. I need your beanbag on the ground when you freeze. That is a warning."

5. *Deliver and move away.* Avoid glaring eyeball to eyeball at a student when delivering corrective feedback. Such behavior is confrontational and serves only to intimidate the student. Approach from the rear of the student and softly deliver your feedback to avoid scaring the student. Walk away after you have delivered the feedback. By walking away, you show the offender that you are not interested in discussing what the student has to say. Do not eyeball a student after repri-

manding him or her—you may see things you don't want to see. Get yourself back on track by positively reinforcing one or two students who are behaving acceptably.

6. *Do not threaten or bully the student.* This tactic builds resentment in students and may cause greater problems in the future.

7. *Avoid touching the student.* Even if you have positive intentions, touching can send mixed messages. Some students do not want to be touched and will aggressively pull away and make a scene in front of the class.

8. *Do not be sarcastic or raise your voice excessively.* Instead, clearly state the acceptable behavior you expect the student to exhibit.

When corrective feedback fails to change unacceptable behavior, students need to understand that such behavior brings negative consequences. Becoming responsible for one's behavior may be the most important social behavior learned from the school experience. Consequences of unacceptable behavior include reprimands, removal of positive consequences, and time-out.

Try Reprimands

Reprimands are commonly used to decrease unacceptable behavior. If given in a caring and constructive way, they can serve as effective reminders to behave.

- Identify the unacceptable behavior, state briefly why it is unacceptable, and communicate to students what behavior is acceptable. For example, "You were talking while I was speaking. It is unacceptable behavior and bothers me and other students, so please listen when others are speaking."

- Do not reprimand in front of other students. Doing so embarrasses students and can diminish their self-esteem. When students feel belittled, they may lash out and behave even more unacceptably.

- Speak about the unacceptable behavior, not the person, when reprimanding. Ask that the behavior stop rather than saying to a student, "You are always causing problems in this class." Avoid general and negative statements related to the student's personality.

- After reprimanding and asking for acceptable behavior, reinforce it when it occurs. Be vigilant in looking for the acceptable behavior because reinforcing such behavior will cause it to occur more often in the future.

Remove Positive Consequences

Parents often use this tactic when their children misbehave, so many students are familiar with it. The idea is to remove something positive from the student when misbehavior occurs. For example, have students who misbehave give up some of their free time, lose grade points, or sit out an activity they enjoy. This approach is ineffective unless students really value the privilege or activity that has been removed. Said another way, sitting in time-out is a consequence only when physical education is an enjoyable experience for the student. Here are a few key principles for using this technique:

- Be sure that the magnitude of the consequence fits the crime.

- Be consistent in removal; treat all students and occurrences fairly.

- Make sure that students understand the consequences of their misbehavior before they receive the penalties. This approach avoids applying penalties in an emotional, unthinking way. Students who know the consequences are choosing to accept the penalty for misbehaving.

- Chart a student's misbehavior to see if the frequency is decreasing. Regardless of the method used, if the behavior is not decreasing—or is increasing—change methods until a decrease in frequency occurs.

Use Time-Out From Reinforcement

The time-out procedure is an equitable technique for dealing with children in a manner consistent with social values. Rules are clearly posted, and consequences are clear and easy to comprehend. Teachers find time-out effective for dealing with unacceptable behavior that occurs randomly on an individual basis. During time-out, students who misbehave leave the activity and go to a designated area within the teaching area (e.g., gymnasium) for a specific time. Time-out means "time out from reinforcement." It does not mean the student is a "bad person," only that he or she has behaved unacceptably and needs a time-out to reconsider and redirect the student's misbehavior. When placing students in time-out, tell children they are valued as individuals but that their misbehavior is unacceptable.

Most students receive time-out because they have disrupted the class and must be removed so that the class can continue without interruption. Children can also voluntarily use the time-out area as a cooling-off spot when they become angry, embarrassed, or frustrated.

Students who are in time-out for fighting or arguing should be at opposite ends of the area so that the behavior does not escalate. After a time-out for fighting, students should stay in their half (or quadrant) of the teaching area for the rest of the class period to prevent recurring agitation between the two combatants and the possibility of increased hostility.

Discuss your time-out plan with students so that they know exactly what constitutes acceptable and unacceptable behavior, as well as the consequences of misbehaving. Be sure to post a list of acceptable behavior (rules) and consequences for unacceptable behavior. Some teachers want to have students stay in the time-out area for five minutes before returning. That method is fine if you have a way to keep track of the time, but it is difficult to manage when several children go to time-out at different times. Some teachers use the "You can return when I say you can" method. The problem with this approach is that it is arbitrary, and you may leave a student in time-out longer than you had planned. This approach can also result in unequal amounts of time in time-out for the same unacceptable behavior. If a student is a chronic offender, you may leave the child in time-out longer for the same behavior than you would a student

Student assigned to time-out.

TIME OUT

1. Please sit down.

2. Face this sign.

3. Think about making good choices.

©Robert Pangrazi or Aaron Beighle

who seldom misbehaves. This sends a message that you have favorites and like some students better than others. An effective behavior management system should be fair and consistent.

Time-out does not change behavior if the child is reinforced by this consequence. Time-out means receiving as little reinforcement as possible. If class participation is a negative experience for students, taking them out of class will be a positive consequence. The physical location for time-out must be considered to make it effective. For some students, sitting at the side of the teaching area and looking on as a spectator may be more reinforcing than participating in class activities. If you put someone in time-out, make sure the student is not facing the class and interacting with peers. Remember—if students do not enjoy being in class, time-out does not work. Other techniques will have to be used.

Consequences for Unacceptable Behavior

Just as with rules, consequences for unacceptable behavior should be listed and posted in the teaching area. Discuss each of the consequences until you reach general class consensus that the rules are fair and necessary. A possible set of consequences for unacceptable behavior is as follows:

First Misbehavior

The student is warned quietly that the unacceptable behavior must stop. Students are not always aware that they are bothering others, and a gentle reminder will refocus them. A private conversation with the student might be as follows: "John, you were talking while I was talking. That is unacceptable behavior. I will appreciate your listening in the future. This is your first warning."

Second Misbehavior

The student goes to a time-out spot and stays there until ready to return and behave acceptably. Place time-out stations in each of the four corners of the instructional area. When outdoors, delineate the instructional area with four cones and place a time-out sign on each cone. The student can go to the time-out area and return immediately to physical education class, but the assumption is that the student has agreed to behave properly and understands the consequences for a third misbehavior.

Third Misbehavior

The student goes to the time-out area for the rest of the period. Each time a student starts a new class, he or she should receive a fresh start on the consequences. A teacher

may tell a student at the start of class, "If you do one thing wrong, you are going to time-out for the rest of the period." This student is therefore treated differently from all the other students. Establishing a positive relationship with a student is hard if the child believes that you are unfair or uncaring.

If the unacceptable behavior continues each time the class meets, most schools have an in-school suspension program to deal with severe behavior. In-school suspension requires the student to leave the classroom and move into another room of students (of a different grade level). This practice ensures that the student receives little, if any, reinforcement. The foregoing steps assume that you have communicated with the student about the unacceptable behavior and the way that you expect him or her to behave.

If these consequences are ineffective, the next step is to talk with the principal about more serious consequences. The last resort is to call in the parents for a conference with you and the principal. Use discretion when deciding to call parents. Doing so may further alienate you from the student because of parental pressure and punishment at home. Another possibility is that parents will disagree with your assessment. If parents cannot or will not support you, dealing with the behavior in a school setting may be a better option. Along the same lines, do not ask the principal to solve all your problems with misbehaving students. The principal will soon believe that you cannot effectively manage students. Ultimately, your behavior will erode the principal's confidence in your teaching ability.

TEACHING TIP

Avoid using physical activity, such as running laps, for punishment. You may not be aware of a student's health issues that could be triggered by excessive or unusual activity.

Implement Behavior Contracts With Older Students

A behavior contract is a written statement specifying certain student behaviors that must occur for students to earn certain rewards or privileges. The contract is drawn up after a private conference to decide on appropriate behaviors and rewards. It is agreed upon and signed by the student and teacher. This approach allows students to make decisions that will improve their behavior.

The behavior contract may be a successful strategy for intermediate-grade students with severe behavior problems. Every attempt should be made to find activities in physical education class (such as jump-rope games, aerobics, or basketball) that are naturally rewarding. If this is not possible, different types of rewards may have to be used. For example, a student who is interested in music could be allowed to spend some time selecting music to be used in class during the next week. As behavior improves and the student's attitude becomes more positive, rewards should be switched to physical education activities. The contract is gradually phased out as the child gains control of his or her behavior and can participate in normal class environments.

Contracts can be written for a small group of students or for an entire class with similar problems, but teachers must be careful about setting up a reward system for too many students. The system can become too complex or time consuming to supervise properly. The contract is best used with a limited number of students who have severe problems. Examples of behavior contracts are shown in figures 7.4 and 7.5. The contract in figure 7.5 can be used with an individual, a small group, or an entire class of students.

Incorporate Behavior Games for Overall Class Behavior

Behavior games are an effective strategy for changing class behavior in the areas of management, motivation, and discipline. These activities use the shaping technique and are useful in changing whole-class behavior (in contrast to individual student behavior). If you are having problems in any of these areas, a well-conceived behavior game may quickly turn around the situation. These games can be organized so that a group of students compete against each other or against an established criterion. The goal of the game is to use group contingencies to develop behaviors that enhance the learning environment and to eliminate behaviors that detract from the environment.

This behavior game was used successfully with sixth graders in an effort to improve management behaviors:

1. Divide the class into four to six squads. Each squad has a designated color for identification. Mark a starting area by arranging four boundary cones in appropriate colors.

2. The rules of the game are as follows:

   a. Each squad member must be ready for activity and in proper position at a designated starting time. *Reward*: 2 points.

   b. Each squad member must move from one activity to another activity within the specified time (10, 20, or 30 seconds) and begin the appropriate behavior. *Reward*: 1 point for each activity.

   c. Each point earned is rewarded with one minute of free activity time on Friday. Free activity time includes basketball, rope jumping, or any other activity popular with students.

   d. The squad with the most points for the week earns a bonus of 5 points.

3. Explain the allotted time for each management episode (10, 20, or 30 seconds), and give a "Go" signal. At the end of the time, give the signal for "Stop" and award points for appropriate behavior.

Date: _____

I, _____, agree to follow the rules listed below:

1. Listen when the teacher is talking.
2. Do not touch others during class.

If I follow all the rules during physical education class, I will earn 10 minutes of basketball activity for me and a friend after school on Thursday anytime between 3:00 and 3:45 p.m..

Signed: _____, Student

Signed: _____, Teacher

FIGURE 7.4 Individual behavior contract.

Our squad agrees to follow the rules listed below:

1. Listen when the teacher is talking.
2. Take care of the equipment.
3. Treat others as we would like to be treated.

One point is earned each time the music stops and every member of the squad is following the rules. No points are awarded if one or more members of the squad are not following the rules. Each point is worth one minute of free activity time to be awarded every other Friday.

Signed: Squad Number _____ _____

_____ _____

_____ _____

_____ _____

FIGURE 7.5 Group behavior contract.

4. Successful squads are praised, and their points are recorded on a small card. Unsuccessful squads are not hassled or criticized, just reminded that they did not earn a point.

5. On Fridays, award the appropriate squads the special free-time activities while the other squads continue with the regularly scheduled class activities.

6. Slowly phase out (fade) the game as students begin to manage themselves more quickly.

Research used to evaluate behavior games showed the following results:

- The use of group contingencies and free-time activities reduced overall class management time.

- The free-time activities were within the physical education curriculum objectives and served as a break from regular activities.

- The free-time activities gave the teacher an opportunity to interact with students on a personal level.

- Students enjoyed the competition and the feeling of success when they behaved appropriately.

- Students enjoyed the free times with novelty activities.

- The positive approach of the game seemed to improve the overall teaching–learning atmosphere. Students were more attentive and cooperative.

- Teachers estimated that more time was available for instruction because of decreased management time.

When designing behavior games, be sure to structure them so that any student or squad is able to win the game. Each game need not generate one winner and many losers. Be aware that one or two students may find it reinforcing to cause their team to lose the behavior game. They will try to break every game rule to make sure that their team loses consistently. In these cases, hold a special team discussion with a vote to eliminate those students from the team and the game. These students are then sent to a time-out area or to in-school suspension. They can be asked to sit out the rest of the behavior game.

Another effective behavior game can be used to help students persist at learning activities in a station-type approach. Often, four to six learning stations are used for instruction. Performance objectives or learning tasks are posted at each station for students to practice. Some students may not be motivated, however, and will not use their time productively until you rotate to the station where they are working. Overall, this environment is unproductive, and you will quickly tire of hassling unmotivated

students. A possible solution to this situation is this game:

1. Divide the class into four to six squads. Let the students pick a name for their squad.

2. Set up the learning stations with the activities to be practiced. Each squad needs its own learning station.

3. Make a recording of music with irregularly spaced gaps of silence throughout the tape.

4. Inform students that if everyone in their squad is practicing the appropriate task, the squad will earn a point at each gap in the music. If one or more persons are not engaged, a point will not be awarded.

5. Exchange points for minutes of time in selected activities such as juggling or rope jumping. Fridays can be designated as reward days, when the accumulated time is used.

6. Change the music regularly. Also change and slowly increase the intervals between gaps until the gaps are eliminated. The music then serves as a discriminative cue for future practice time.

Students enjoy exercising and practicing skills while listening to music. The music enhances the motivational level and productivity of the environment. Students can be allowed to bring their own music as a special reward for productive behavior. (Make sure that the music is not offensive to others because of sexual, ethnic, or religious connotations.)

Use Criticism Sparingly

Use criticism and punishment with caution and good judgment. Criticism is sometimes used with the belief that it will improve student performance. Some teachers make scolding and criticism the behavior control tools of choice because these tools give the impression that the results are effective and immediate. Usually, misbehavior stops and the teacher assumes that the situation has been rectified. Unfortunately, this is not always the case. Criticism and punishment lend a negative air to the instructional environment and negatively affect both student and teacher. The old saying "It hurts me more than you" often applies. Most teachers feel uncomfortable when they must criticize or punish students. Having to do so makes them think that they cannot handle students and that the class is incorrigible. This feeling of incompetence leads to a destructive cycle in which students feel negative about the instructor and the instructor feels negative about the students. In the long run, criticism and punishment can have a debilitating effect.

As mentioned, another negative aspect of criticism is that it does not offer a solution. In one study (Thomas, Becker, & Armstrong, 1968), a teacher was asked to stop praising a class. Off-task behavior increased from 8.7% to nearly 26%. When the teacher was asked to increase criticism from 5 times in 20 minutes to 16 times in 20 minutes, students demonstrated more off-task behavior. On some days the percentage of off-task behavior increased to more than 50%. When teachers criticize off-task behavior and do not praise on-task accomplishment, off-task behavior increases dramatically. Using criticism makes teachers feel effective (students respond to the request of the criticism), but students do not actually change. In fact, the students are reinforced (they receive attention from the teacher) for their off-task behavior. Furthermore, because their on-task behavior is not praised, it decreases. The net result is exactly the opposite of what is desired.

Make Punishment a Last Resort

Deciding whether to use punishment in an educational setting is a difficult issue. Punishment can have negative side effects because fear is the primary motivator. Consider the long-term need for punishment. If the long-term effects of using punishment are more beneficial than not using it, it is unethical not to use punishment. In other words, if a child is going to be in a worse situation because punishment was not used to deter self-destructive behavior, not using it is wrong. Punishing a child for protection from self-inflicted harm (e.g., using certain apparatus without supervision) may be necessary. Likewise, punishing children so that they learn not to hurt others may be necessary. Punishment in these situations will cause discomfort to both teacher and child in the short run, but it may allow the student to participate successfully in society later.

Most situations in the educational setting do not require punishment, because they are not as severe as those just described. A major reason for not using punishment is that it can have negative side effects. When children are punished, they learn to avoid the source of punishment. They must become more covert in their actions. They spend time finding ways to avoid being caught. Instead of encouraging students to discuss problems with teachers and parents, punishment teaches them to avoid these people for fear of retribution. Punishment also teaches

 CASE STUDY

Connect With Students . . . All of Them

During his third year of teaching, Mr. Alex Holden had the most challenging class, Ms. Luski's fifth grade, in his short teaching career. For four lessons he tried to pinpoint the cause of the many behavior disruptions in the class. After discussing this issue with a peer mentor, Alex had several strategies to try. The first strategy was to be more consistent with the students. Upon reflecting, Mr. Holden believed he was not consistent with this class and that his expectations and tolerance for misbehavior fluctuated. In lessons, he began addressing all misbehavior more consistently and assertively. This approach took time to adjust to but seemed to improve the overall environment of the class. But one student, Nolan, was still consistently off task and somewhat defiant. Again, Mr. Holden sought advice from a peer regarding strategies for working with Nolan.

Nolan transferred to the school at the beginning of the year, so not much was known about him. But Alex did find out that in just three months, Nolan's behavior had resulted in his being removed from all other specials. Essentially, he was confined to the classroom for most of the day. Although Nolan's behavior in physical education was unacceptable, it was far better than his behaviors in other classes. Mr. Holden, while frustrated, took this as a signal that maybe physical education could be used as a tool, so he decided to meet with the classroom teacher. Together, they met with Nolan and developed a plan. When meeting with Nolan they found out he loves physical education. Thus, his behavior incentive was to serve as a peer teacher for a first-grade class on Friday afternoon. If he met his behavior goals in the classroom and was not put in time-out during physical education, he helped Mr. Holden teach the first-grade class. He was allowed to blow the whistle to "freeze" the students, provided short instructions, and chose the game at the end of class. In the classroom, the teacher placed three whistles on Nolan's desk to remind him of his goals. If he was demonstrating unacceptable behavior, Ms. Luski quietly walked by and took a whistle. His goal was to have at least one whistle left each day. The incentive was not successful at first, so Mr. Holden decided that he needed to let Nolan feel what it was like to lead and teach physical education. He loved it! Although the process went slowly, over a few weeks Nolan's behavior slowly improved. In the next two months he was slowly allowed to return to other specials, and all his teachers reported limited behavior concerns.

In Alex's three years of teaching, this experience was by far his most rewarding: "That feeling of getting to a kid and impacting him positively—you can't beat that. It's why we do this." Although effective teaching strategies work for the vast majority of students, at times there are students who require a bit more care and individual attention.

children to be aggressive toward others. Children who have been physically or emotionally punished by parents treat others the same way. The result is a child who is secretive and aggressive with others—certainly undesirable traits. Finally, if punishment is used to stop certain behavior, the behavior will return as soon as the punishment stops. Thus, little has been learned, and the punishment has led only to short-term change.

If using punishment is necessary, remember the following points:

1. *Be consistent and make the punishment fit the misbehavior.* Students quickly lose respect for a teacher who treats others with favoritism. They view the teacher as unfair if punishment is extreme or unfair. Peers quickly side with the student who is treated unfairly, causing a class morale problem for the instructor.

2. *Offer a warning signal, as discussed previously.* A warning may prevent excessive use of punishment, because students often behave after receiving a warning. In addition, they probably view the teacher as caring and fair.

3. *Do not threaten students.* Offer only one warning. Threats have little effect on students and make them feel that you cannot handle the class. One warning gives students the feeling that you are not looking to punish them and are fair. Follow through; do not challenge or threaten students and then fail to deal with the behavior.

4. *Make sure that the punishment follows the misbehavior as soon as possible.* When delayed, punishment is much less effective and more often viewed as unfair.

5. *Punish quietly and calmly.* Do not seek revenge or be vindictive. If you expect responsible behavior from students, be sure you reprimand and punish in a responsible way. Studies (O'Leary & Becker, 1968) show that quiet reprimands are more effective than loud ones.

Try to avoid developing negative feelings toward a student because you internalize the misbehavior. Being punitive when handling deviant behavior destroys any chance for a worthwhile relationship with the student. Handle misbehavior in a manner that contributes to the development of responsible, confident students who understand that people who function effectively in society must adjust to certain limits. Forget about past bouts of deviant behavior and approach the student with a positive mindset at the start of each class. If you do not, students will feel labeled and changing their behavior will be more difficult. Students may also learn to live up to the teacher's negative expectations.

If you use punishment, make sure that it applies only to those students who misbehave. Punishing an entire class for the deviant behavior of a few students is unfair and may trigger unacceptable side effects. Students become hostile toward those who caused the loss of privileges, and this peer hostility lowers the level of positive social interaction with the students who have misbehaved.

Expulsion: Legal Considerations

The information in this chapter is designed to address the majority of behavior problems encountered in physical education. If serious problems occur, discuss them with the classroom teacher and principal. Deviant behavior frequently is part of a larger, more severe problem that is troubling a child. A cooperative approach may provide an effective solution. A group meeting involving parents, classroom teacher, principal, behavior specialist, and physical education specialist may open avenues that encourage understanding and increase productive behavior.

Legal concerns involving the student's rights in disciplinary areas are an essential consideration. Although minor infractions may be handled routinely, expulsion and other substantial punishments can be imposed on students only after due process. The issue of student rights is complicated, and most school systems have established guidelines and procedures for dealing with students who have been removed from the class or school setting. Students should be removed from class only if they are disruptive to the point of interfering with the learning experiences of other children and if all other means of altering behavior have been unsuccessful. Sending a child out of class is a last resort and means that both teacher and student have failed.

LEARNING AIDS

HOW AND WHY

1. How would you respond to a child who consistently misbehaves?
2. How does it make you feel when a professor knows your name?
3. How might pre- and postteaching routines change depending on the school?
4. Why is it important for teachers to know their own trigger points? What are your trigger points? How would you feel when a student does not listen to you?

5. What rules would you have in your classes?
6. What types of emotions might you feel when placing a child in time-out?
7. As an adult, how does criticism make you feel?

CONTENT REVIEW

1. What class management skills are necessary to be an effective teacher?
2. What is the importance of using efficient instruction, a consistent stop signal, and moving students into formation quickly in an effective lesson?
3. How can knowing the names of students help teachers?
4. What types of routines do successful teachers establish?
5. What is the effective use of equipment?

WEBSITES

Classroom management, www.pecentral.org/climate/index.html
Assertive discipline, http://maxweber.hunter.cuny.edu/pub/eres/EDSPC715_MCINTYRE/AssertiveDiscipline.html
Positive discipline, www.positivediscipline.com
Compassionate discipline, www.amle.org

SUGGESTED READINGS

Canter, L., & Canter, M. (1993). *Succeeding with difficult students*. Bloomington, IN: Solution Tree.

Charles, C. (2011). *Building classroom discipline* (10th ed.). Upper Saddle River, NJ: Prentice Hall.

Charles, C. (2008). *Today's best classroom management strategies: Paths to positive discipline*. Upper Saddle River, NJ: Prentice Hall.

Fields, M., Perry, N., & Fields, D. (2010). *Constructive guidance and discipline: Preschool and primary education* (5th ed.). Upper Saddle River, NJ: Merrill.

Jones, F.H. (2007). *Tools for teaching* (2nd ed.). Santa Cruz, CA: Fredric H. Jones.

Plevin, R. (2018). *Connect with your students: How to build positive teacher-student relationships the #1 secret is effective classroom management*. Author: Independent.

Wong, H.K, & Wong, R.T. (2009). *The first days of school: How to be an effective teacher*. Mountain View, CA: Harry K. Wong.

REFERENCES

Bradshaw, C., Sawyer, A., & O'Brennan, L. (2007). Bullying and peer victimization at school: Perceptual differences between students and school staff. *School Psychology Review, 36*, 361–382.

Canter, L. (2010). *Assertive discipline: Positive behavior management for today's classroom*. Bloomington, IN: Solution Tree Press.

Cohen, R (205). *Students resolving conflict*. Tucson, AZ: Good Year Books.

Greene, D., & Lepper, M. (1975). Turning play into work: Effects of adult surveillance and extrinsic rewards on children's internal motivation. *Journal of Personality and Social Psychology, 31*, 479–486.

Hart, B., & Risley, T. (1995). *Meaningful differences in the everyday experience of young American children*. Baltimore, MD: Paul H. Brookes.

Hellison, D. (2011). *Teaching personal and social responsibility through physical activity* (3rd ed.). Champaign, IL: Human Kinetics.

Lavay, B.W., French, R., & Henderson H.L. (2006). *Positive behavior management in physical activity settings* (2nd Ed.). Champaign, IL: Human Kinetics.

O'Leary, K.D., & Becker, W.C. (1968). The effects of intensity of a teacher's reprimands on children's behavior. *Journal of School Psychology, 7*, 8–11.

Premack, D. (1965). Reinforcement theory. In D. Levine (Ed.), *Nebraska symposium on motivation*. Lincoln, NE: University of Nebraska Press.

Swearer, S.M., Espelage, D.L., & Napolitano, S.A. (2009). *Bullying prevention and intervention: Realistic strategies for schools*. New York, NY: Guilford Press.

Thomas, D.R., Becker, W.C, & Armstrong, M. (1968). Production and elimination of disruptive classroom behavior by systematically varying teachers' behavior. *Journal of Applied Behavior Analysis, 1*, 35–45.

VandenBos, G.R. (2007). *APA dictionary of psychology*. Washington, DC: American Psychological Association.

Wang, M.C., Haertel, G.D., & Walberg, H.J. (1994). What helps students learn? *Educational Leadership, Dec/Jan*, 74–79.

Whitehead, J.R., & Corbin, C.B. (1991). Effects of fitness test type, teacher, and gender on exercise intrinsic motivation and physical self-worth. *Journal of School Health, 61*, 11–16.

Assessment

8

Methods to assess student learning include checklists, self- and peer assessments, and written assessments. Assessing physical activity levels during physical education is also advocated. Pedometers offer a cost-effective, efficient tool for students to monitor physical activity. Grading in elementary physical education is a complex process with many issues to consider. A program checklist can be used to score the total physical education setting.

Learning Objectives

▶ Differentiate between standards, grade level outcomes, and lesson outcomes.
▶ Explain and understand the differences between process and product evaluation.
▶ Discuss the three type of assessments: diagnostic, formative, and summative.
▶ Cite several ways to assess student learning.
▶ Discuss the use of pedometers in physical education.
▶ Describe arguments for and against grading in physical education.
▶ Recognize the key elements of an effective physical education evaluation form.

Assessment involves gathering data or information that offers information about teaching effectiveness and student learning. Assessment is a process designed to determine whether progress is being made toward specified outcomes. In turn, evaluation uses assessment data to place a value on student outcomes and performance. For example, after assessment data are used for grading, it becomes an evaluation process. Both of these processes encompass all phases of education, including pupil progress, program effectiveness, and instructional progress. Both assessment and evaluation can be formal or informal and can focus on individual or group progress. Most of this chapter will focus on assessment because elementary school physical education emphasizes teaching and learning, and evaluation takes a great deal of time and energy.

Assessment

The purpose of assessment in this chapter is to help teachers obtain knowledge about student performance that can be used for making instructional decisions and programmatic changes. In simple terms, assessment gathers data about student learning, the results of the assessment are then used for evaluation of students, and, finally, decision making follows based on how students performed and where they may be subpar. Assessment for assessment's sake makes little sense. For example, too often students are assessed on fitness parameters or skill performance, but the data are never used. Data are worthwhile only if they help teachers diagnose student deficiencies or improve their instructional techniques. Assessment data can also help with curriculum modifications and updates. Before any assessment takes place, it is important to determine why it is being done and how it will be used to improve the educational process.

Physical education assessment is often difficult because classes are bigger than those in traditional classroom settings, the instructional area is more expansive, and rarely is a permanent record of work produced (like an essay in an English class or a lab report in a science class). Assessment instruments can be used for several purposes, including the following:

- *Feedback.* Assessing students provides an excellent opportunity to provide them with immediate, specific feedback on their performance. Students should receive feedback on the process of performing the skill. For example, they should receive feedback on their performance of parts of the skills, or cues, such as "Yes! Way to keep that elbow up. Keep working on it." Without some type of assessment, this type of feedback could not happen.

- *Diagnosis.* Assessment can help document problems or deficiencies. When teaching an entire class, teachers find it difficult to gauge each student's ability and progress. Often, the teacher expends more energy monitoring student behavior than observing student performance. Assessment focuses that energy on the progress of individual students and identifies those students who are deficient or performing skills incorrectly.

- *Curricular change.* Using data accrued during assessments, teachers can determine if changes to the curriculum need to be made. For instance, an assessment reveals that only a few students can jump an individual rope while demonstrating appropriate cues. This finding may suggest the curriculum needs to be modified to emphasize this skill more or provide more progressions with the skill.

- *Motivation.* Many students are motivated by personal improvement. When improvement can be documented through assessment, it shows that effort has been rewarded. The extent (or lack) of improvement is unclear if assessment is not part of the program. Another factor that motivates students is setting reachable goals. If students are unaware of their performance level and ability, then they will find it difficult to identify realistic goals they can achieve.

The three major types of assessment are diagnostic, formative, and summative. A brief discussion of each follows. Let it be clear that these are not clearly defined; a formative assessment can often be used as a summative assessment when values or grades are placed on the data.

Diagnostic Assessment

Diagnostic assessment is used to identify students' knowledge and skill level. The data gleaned through diagnostic assessment can help you understand the strengths and weaknesses of students. On a larger setting, it can help determine how much the class knows and at what level you should gear your instruction. Examples of diagnostic assessments are pretests, rubrics related to skill performance, and short Q & A sessions with individual students.

Formative Assessment

Formative assessment provides feedback and information while students are involved in the learning process. It is often somewhat informal and can be done in a quick and easy manner. The purpose should be for you to match your instruction better to student needs. Formative assessment also can let you know where your students are not performing well so that you can focus on rectifying the shortcomings. Typically, formative assessments are used to identify areas that may need improvement, rather than grading students. The following are examples of formative assessment tools:

- *Observations of student performance.* Experienced teachers often look for outliers to see who may be having issues.
- *Question-and-answer sessions.* Do a check for understanding or check how students feel about their performances. Self-evaluation with a peer can often help students better understand where they are deficient.
- *Hand signals or plickers to signal immediately how well all members of the class understand.* This information can immediately be used to modify the instruction to improve performance levels.
- *Rubrics that can be used to identify components of a skill.* Students can evaluate each other, or the teacher can check each student independently.
- *Short written evaluations.* Students identify their strong and weak points, how they feel about the activity, and how they could improve.

Summative Assessment

Summative assessment is done after a unit of instruction is completed. It provides information that shows how effective the teaching and learning process was. As is often the case with evaluation, little learning takes place during summative assessment. Instead, students are showing how much they have learned up to the assessment. Summative assessment is more difficult in elementary school because students are not involved in long units of study and they may have physical education only once or twice a week. Because units are short and students are in the early stages of motor development, summative assessment may not be possible or even meaningful. Summative assessment is product oriented toward a final outcome. If students do a two-day unit of throwing, their chances of developing mature throwing form are slim in the early grades and the results of a summative assessment may not be valid. In this case, a formative evaluation using a throwing skill rubric may be more meaningful.

Assessment Considerations

Physical education demands physical and cognitive performance. In reading or math, after a student masters a skill, he or she is ready to use that skill to develop new skills in somewhat of a building-block manner. Once

mastered, the ability to add numbers or read words stays with people throughout life. In physical education, however, skills are lost if not practiced. Thus, physical education assessment requires a different perspective compared with academic evaluation. In addition, one focus in physical education is to help students develop a positive attitude toward physical activity. This goal is different from those used in other areas in which the emphasis is strictly on cognitive performance.

Process Versus Product

Assessing the process of learning implies focusing on the performance of movement patterns and skills with emphasis on correct technique. The technique used during the execution of the skill is the focus of formative assessment. Typically, the technique is taught using performance cues. These cues are short statements that break the performance into essential components and are easy to remember. For example, cues for throwing might be "T, elbow, step, throw." The teacher emphasizes these cues, and the assessment would then be on the performance of each cue. In contrast, product or summative assessment focuses on the outcome of the skill performance. For example, when applying product assessment to ball skills, the teacher could measure how many times a target is hit with a thrown ball regardless of throwing form. The process assessment, on the other hand, focuses on the technique of throwing. This approach also allows children to experience success because most students can perform the four parts of the throw, although they may not be accurate in early stages of throwing. Emphasizing the product could also result in children using poor technique (e.g., stepping with the same foot) in an effort to hit the target.

As mentioned earlier, a clear demarcation between formative and summative assessment doesn't exist. A rubric containing the four components of throwing could be used as a formative assessment of their understanding the parts of throwing. The same rubric could be used as a summative assessment instrument if students were graded on how many of the parts they mastered.

Skilled Performers Versus Competency for All

Do you want to develop high-quality performers or focus on designing experiences for all students regardless of their ability level? Physical education should offer less skilled students skill instruction and the opportunity to learn the benefits of lifetime activity. Physical education may be the last time that less gifted students get a chance to practice and learn lifetime skills. Most adults are too busy to devote the time required to learn new skills.

Remember that physical education differs from

TEACHING TIP

Consider your teaching cues when creating your evaluations. For example, "Elbow in" could be a cue for shooting a basketball. To emphasize and evaluate the process of the movement, first teach the cues and then evaluate performance of the cues. Some students may never learn to shoot a jump shot, but most students can experience success by performing a cue such as "Elbow in."

academics when it comes to assessment and grading. Physical education teaches a handful of skills, that is, the locomotor and nonlocomotor skills, specialized sport skills, and manipulative skills. Motor skills are never perfectly learned; errors, misses, incomplete passes, and so on always occur in the arena of motor performance. This sort of performance is unacceptable in academic areas because math problems have only one solution and learning to read requires accurate recognition of words every time. Thus, academic areas rely much more on summative evaluation because concepts and skills must be mastered before the student can move on to a higher level of learning. In PE and sport, however, achieving perfection is impossible, and we practice the same skills at every grade level. In fact, the focus at every grade is repetition and refinement of the same skills.

Imperfect Nature of Motor Skill Learning

Skill perfection rarely occurs in physical education or sport. Even the best athletes miss half of the baskets they shoot or make an out in baseball about 70% of the time. Teaching skills as though reaching perfection is realistic and reasonable can lead students to believe that focusing on the outcome (such as making a basket) is more important than learning the skill correctly. Teachers encourage such

TEACHING TIP

Encourage students when they excel in physical activity, but avoid pressuring them beyond their developmental readiness. Pressure may cause them to dislike the activity or push themselves to the point of mental or physical stress.

thinking when they reinforce correct skill performance yet fail to comment on a student's quality of performance.

Refining a skill is not the same as improving performance. Many teachers believe that the effectiveness of their teaching is based on how many students reach product benchmarks, such as making a certain number of baskets or jumping rope a certain number of times without a miss. Unfortunately, they promise a product that is nearly impossible to achieve. For example, a golf pro can guarantee that she will teach with enthusiasm, know the latest techniques, and devote the time and energy necessary to help refine her client's skills. But she cannot guarantee improved scores, because she cannot control her client's genetic makeup or psychological willingness to change, practice, and improve. Teachers can teach students how to perform skills properly, but they cannot guarantee that all students have what it takes to be a high-level performer.

Assessment of Students

Student performance can be assessed in many ways. Almost all assessment in an elementary school setting is formative, meaning that standardized instruments are not used to evaluate students. In contrast to reading and math, which have standardized instruments, physical education teachers generally generate their own tools for monitoring student performance. Such alternative assessments have been developed because teachers are expected to assess and report student progress toward program standards (Chepko & Arnold, 2000; Hopple, 2005). Using these alternative assessment instruments as evidence that the program is reaching stated outcomes is difficult because they are not standardized. More on this can be found in the section on program accountability later in the chapter.

A number of alternative assessments are discussed in this section that can be used to measure learning in the three major learning domains. The domains are briefly described here (see chapter 4 for more information).

1. *Psychomotor domain.* This area is related to learning motor skills. Students are most often assessed in this domain because physical education focuses on skill development. The checklist in figure 8.1 shows one way to evaluate skills in the psychomotor domain.

2. *Cognitive domain.* This area focuses on understanding concepts of movement performance and related fitness and activity knowledge. Figure 8.2 is an example of a knowledge assessment related to pedometers.

Dr. Robert Pangrazi's	Assessment Method	Grade / Level	Lesson
DYNAMIC PE ASAP	TEACHER CHECKLIST	K-2 / 1	KICKING, TRAPPING, BOWLING, ROLLING

KICKING

Outcome: I can kick a stationary ball demonstrating 3 of 4 cues.

	STUDENT	Other Foot Beside	Favorite Foot Back	Shoelaces	Kick Through	TOTAL
1						
2						
3						
4						
5						
6						
7						
8						
9						
10						
11						
12						
13						
14						
15						
16						
17						
18						
19						
20						
21						
22						
23						
24						
25						
26						
27						
28						
29						
30						
	TOTAL FOR CUES					

FIGURE 8.1 Teacher checklist to assess the psychomotor domain.

Reprinted by permission from R.P. Pangrazi, *Dynamic PE ASAP* (Owatonna, MN: Gopher Sport).

3. *Affective domain.* This area involves responsibility and attitudes toward physical education and physical activity—that is, how a student feels and how a student behaves. This domain deals with a set of internal feelings, so it is often best to allow students to evaluate themselves. Knowing how students feel about their physical education experiences is important. Figure 8.3 is an example of an instrument that teachers can use for Developmental Level I students to allow students to explore and better understand the role of challenge in physical education.

These types of alternative assessment tools are not standardized instruments for determining program accountability because individual teachers decide what elements to include and the reliability and validity of the assessment are not determined. In short, a valid instrument accurately measures what it purports to measure, and its validity must be tested in various settings. A reliable instrument measures the same behaviors accurately over and over, yielding the same results when the same student is tested. Student assessment tools have value because they are an inventory of skills and behaviors that each teacher believes students should learn. They give teachers a systematic way to collect information that lets students and their parents know whether expected instructional outcomes are being met. The following are examples of alternative assessments.

Teacher Questioning

This strategy is particularly useful when looking to generate discussion, probe student understanding beyond a simple test item, and provide students a time to reflect. The questions are typically designed to assist teachers in their prompting of students to reflect on a specific concept or lesson purpose. These questions are modifiable to fit the needs of specific classes or students. See figure 8.3 for an example of teacher questioning.

Teacher Checklists

The teacher checklist provides multiple criteria related to a task or motor skill performance. This rubric is most often used to evaluate skill performance outcomes. The criteria focus on techniques students should use to perform skills correctly. In most cases, the criteria are the cues used when teaching the motor skill. A basic question common to most assessments is "Can the child perform the stated motor pattern using proper techniques?" Teachers using this type of assessment require accurate knowledge of the critical elements of the skills. For example, a nine-year-old child might be expected to demonstrate all four components of catching. If a child of this age exhibits only two of the components, a developmental deficiency is indicated. See figure 8.1 for an example of a checklist rubric for kicking skills. This rubric lists four critical elements required for kicking a stationary ball. In most cases, the quality of behavior is not judged; the behavior is marked simply as present or absent. This checklist could be modified and used with older students as well. For instance, rather than kicking a stationary ball, students could be asked to kick a rolling ball. Or in upper grades, students could be observed during game play to see if they are performing each of the cues.

Anecdotal Notes

Another alternative assessment is anecdotal notes that provide space for notes for each class. These notes can be written or voice recorded on a recording device. This latter idea may work best because teachers are always on the move and may not have access to a place to take notes during a lesson. Teachers often get busy and forget to document notes at the end of lessons. Such records can be reinforcing to both student and teacher because remembering how much progress has been made is often difficult. Anecdotal records enable teachers to inform students of their initial skill level compared with their present performance.

TECH TIP

Technology can assist in making assessments like checklists more user friendly and useful. Tablets or smartphones offer tools for assessing students while moving around the gymnasium. For instance, set up a teacher checklist like those provide in this chapter to display on a touch screen tablet. As students are observed, teachers can quickly touch the cell of the cue or cues not being performed. Using formulas, the worksheet will immediately populate the totals at the right and at the bottom. At that point, quickly look for students who are struggling with a skill (by looking at the student's total) or see what cues the class is struggling with (by looking at the cue totals at the bottom). This real-time feedback allows teachers to make instructional modifications.

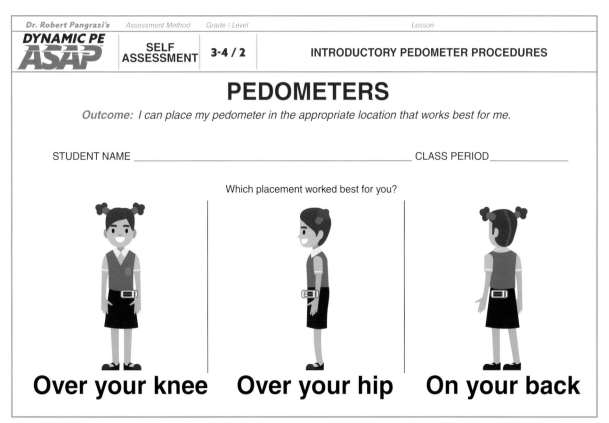

FIGURE 8.2   Written exit to assess the cognitive domain.

Reprinted by permission from R.P. Pangrazi, *Dynamic PE ASAP* (Owatonna, MN: Gopher Sport).

Dr. Robert Pangrazi's   *Assessment Method*   *Grade / Level*   *Lesson*

DYNAMIC PE ASAP | **TEACHER QUESTIONING** | **K-2 / 1** | **THROWING**

THROWING

Outcome: I can identify activities that might be challenging for me.

During the throwing portion of the lesson use prompts and questions such as these. These can be used for the whole class or asked individually as you circulate during practice time.

1. What does it mean if something is easy?
2. What if something is hard?
3. What are activities that are hard or challenging for you?
4. Is everyone good at everything? The secret is to keep trying, especially when a skill is challenging.

FIGURE 8.3   Teacher questioning to assess the affective domain.

Reprinted by permission from R.P. Pangrazi, *Dynamic PE ASAP* (Owatonna, MN: Gopher Sport).

ASSESSMENT TOOLS

The Dynamic Physical Education website curriculum provides teachers with many options for assessments. In fact, many of the figures in this chapter are directly from the website. All of the assessments are lesson specific and driven by the outcomes created just for the curriculum. New teachers are often confused and reluctant to assess because they simply don't know what to do. The assessments on this website offer turnkey easy-to-use assessments. Just pull up the lesson, find the assessment, print it out, and you are ready to teach, assess, and gain valuable data related to student learning.

Another form of evaluation for physical educators is *PE Metrics: Assessing Student Performance Using the National Standards & Grade-Level Outcomes for K-12 Physical Education, Third Edition*. This new edition aligns with SHAPE America's national standards and grade-level outcomes for K-12 physical education, was created by SHAPE America and its writing team, and was reviewed by researchers and teachers with expertise in assessment. Written for physical educators, administrators, and curriculum writers (and for physical education majors and minors), it offers:

- 130 ready-to-use assessments for kindergarten through grade 12
- Worksheets, checklists, and rubrics that support the assessments
- Guidance on creating your own assessments for any lesson or unit

For more information on *PE Metrics*, see https://us.humankinetics.com/products/pe-metrics-3rd-edition.

Another use for anecdotal record sheets is to monitor behavior in the affective domain. For example, teachers may have behavior expectations of students who exhibit behavior problems. Teachers can write short notes about how these students behaved each day. These notes create a record of how long the behavior has occurred and when it started to improve (or not improve). The teacher can then share this information with parents or students.

Student Logs

Intermediate-grade students are capable of maintaining a log that indicates their progress toward goals over time. Suppose, for example, that students want to increase the amount of physical activity they accomplish each day. Teacher and students can cooperatively create goals to help the students become more active. Another approach is to ask students to develop behaviors they need to reach their goals. The log should include goal behaviors they have accomplished over time—decisions and choices made, time spent on goal behaviors, and a reflection area to record their perceptions of the experience.

Students can share their experiences and feelings about things they have tried. The logistics of activities each student has tried can be shared. Examining how well the stated outcomes were reached is the most common way to evaluate logs. For students trying to increase their activity outside school, for example, a high score would go to

children who were active 30 minutes each of five days a week. An acceptable score would go to students who were active three days a week. An unacceptable score would go to those who were active one day or less. A nationally used recall log (available at www.presidentschallenge.org) for adults and children is the Presidential Active Lifestyle Award (PALA+). The PALA+ focuses on recalling physical activity and healthy eating goals. This award program is coordinated by the President's Council on Fitness, Sports, and Nutrition (2011), which also offers the Presidential Physical Fitness Award.

Classroom teachers often favor reflection logs because they encourage students to write—a major emphasis in the classroom. Without appropriate planning, however, student logs can take time away from physical activity. To avoid this issue, physical education teachers can collaborate with the classroom teacher to allow time for reflection and writing in the classroom following physical education. This method may require the development of writing prompts for students, but it is worth the time. If this approach is not possible, develop routines for students to retrieve writing materials, so that they can do their reflection and writing outside school.

Self-Assessments

For self-assessment, students can evaluate their own performance during a lesson. Figure 8.4 is an example of a self-assessment for a lesson involving dance. Students are given this document and asked to circle the level that best describes their performance that day. *Learning* means they are just starting to understand the idea and are looking forward to improving. *Practicing* means they are doing better but still working to get better. *Refining* suggests that their performance was good but they understand that, as with all skills, they can always get better. Using this approach sends the message that learning all skills is a process. A student may learn to throw, to throw to a partner, to throw to a moving partner, to throw in a game, and so on. The point is that we always have room for improvement with skills either in performance or in applying the skill in a different setting. An alternative to paper-and-pencil assessment would be to have students touch the sign that best describes their performance that day as they leave the gymnasium after a lesson. Student self-assessments are particularly useful for affective domain behavior. Use them to monitor how students feel about certain activities or about their behavior. Having students assess themselves forces a look inward that may help both the teacher and student understand why the behavior is occurring. Teachers can also learn about activities students enjoy and how they

behave when they do not like an activity. Figure 8.5 is an example of a self-assessment in which students rank the activities they enjoy. This assessment helps reinforce the notion that physical activity choices are personal.

Peer Assessments

Peer assessment is another way of teaching students how to recognize quality performances. Students must be taught how to evaluate and know what is expected of them before they begin the process. Peer assessment takes practice and feedback from teachers and peers. A good way to teach the evaluation process is to have the class observe a skill performance by a similarly aged student. Upper-grade students can examine the performance and determine what should be assessed and how success should be defined. Discussion should follow that helps peers understand how they would communicate their evaluation scores to fellow students.

Figure 8.6 is an example of a peer assessment sheet to allow students to share their knowledge of active living with a peer. In a "walkie-talkie" fashion, pairs of students walk for a few minutes and discuss the question provided. Next, they create a speech to persuade a friend

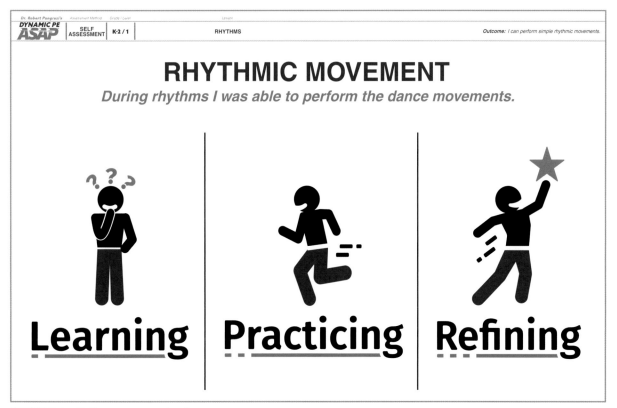

FIGURE 8.4 Self-assessment for dance.

Reprinted by permission from R.P. Pangrazi, *Dynamic PE ASAP* (Owatonna, MN: Gopher Sport).

Dr. Robert Pangrazi's	Assessment Method	Grade / Level	Lesson
DYNAMIC PE ASAP	**WRITTEN EXIT SLIPS**	**3-4 / 2**	**SOCCER SKILLS**

RANKING ACTIVITIES

Outcome: I can rank my enjoyment of soccer compared to other physical education activities.

STUDENT NAME _____ CLASS PERIOD _____

Rank the following activities one through six.

	Tennis			Frisbee
	Softball			Dancing
	Soccer			Parachute

FIGURE 8.5 Self-assessment for ranking enjoyment of activities.

Reprinted by permission from R.P. Pangrazi, *Dynamic PE ASAP* (Owatonna, MN: Gopher Sport).

to be active. This assessment not only demonstrates whether they know content but also allows them to apply that knowledge. Figure 8.7 is a peer assessment for the tennis forehand and backhand. Typically, students are taught the cues during a lesson and then those cues are used on the peer assessment sheet. This process allows teachers to evaluate skill performance as well as the observer's cognitive understanding of the skill. For example, if the performer is not performing a cue and the peer observer checks that square, the observer may not know what the cue means.

Students can also benefit from using rubrics or checklists to guide their assessments. At first, these tools can be designed by the instructor; after the students have more experience, they can develop personal rubrics. Checklists should remind peer evaluators to comment primarily on the skill performance rather than on items unrelated to the skill. For peer evaluation to be effective, students must feel comfortable and trust one another to provide honest and constructive feedback.

Written Assessments

Written assessments are administered to assess a variety of concepts. Use true-or-false or multiple-choice tests to minimize sedentary time and simplify correction. One approach is to use exit slips (figure 8.8). After a lesson, students quickly retrieve an exit slip and pencil, complete the items, and return the slips to the teacher. By offering only one to three items focusing on the key cognitive concepts of the day, you can check student learning while minimizing interference with activity

TECH TIP

Video can also be used for self-assessment. Allowing students to observe themselves performing a skill can be a valuable learning experience. This approach is best set up as a learning station. As an example, let's use kicking. A tablet is set up to video the students kicking for 10 seconds. The student then moves to the tablet to observe. This approach is simple. But by using an app that allows simultaneous recording and displaying of a video, the next student can kick while the first student observes. This setup can be used as a self-assessment, or a peer can watch the video with the performer and discuss his or her performance. Ideally, the station should contain a peer assessment highlighting the performance cues for kicking.

Dr. Robert Pangrazi's	Assessment Method	Grade / Level	Lesson
DYNAMIC PE ASAP	**PEER ASSESSMENT**	**5-6 / 3**	**WALKING ACTIVITIES**

ACTIVE LIFESTYLE

Outcome: I can persuade others to adopt an active lifestyle.

STUDENT NAME 1 _____ CLASS PERIOD_____

STUDENT NAME 2 _____ CLASS PERIOD_____

As you walk with your partner, address the following:

Step 1: What are three reasons you should be active?

Step 2: Based on your three reasons, create a stairwell speech to persuade a friend to be active.
(see below for a review of a stairwell speech criteria)
Stairwell Speech
1. State your reasons
2. Include an invitation to join you
3. Less than one minute

FIGURE 8.6 Peer assessment related to active lifestyles.

Reprinted by permission from R.P. Pangrazi, *Dynamic PE ASAP* (Owatonna, MN: Gopher Sport).

time. When composing exit slips, consider the students' reading level to ensure that you are testing for knowledge, not comprehension. Oral questions are often best for younger students. Remember that written tests give little to no indication of how a child will perform a motor skill. Avoid grading solely on written tests that examine cognition, because physical education is primarily based on physical skill.

Bike Racks

Another strategy for assessing is the use of "bike racks." Using bike racks involves providing designated places

TEACHING TIP

Just as you establish routines for retrieving and returning equipment, you can create routines for retrieving assessment tools. As opposed to setting out a pile of paper or handing out the forms individually, spreading out the papers and writing instruments around the teaching area will expedite the assessment and allow more time for physical activity.

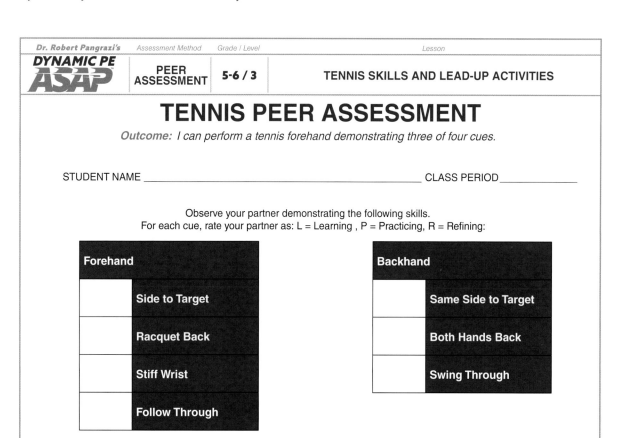

FIGURE 8.7 Peer assessment for tennis.

Reprinted by permission from R.P. Pangrazi, *Dynamic PE ASAP* (Owatonna, MN: Gopher Sport).

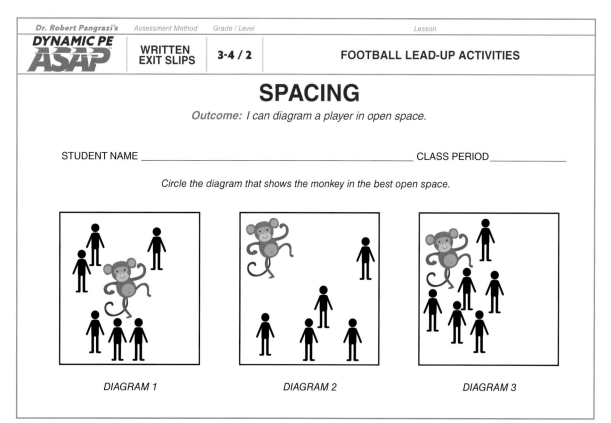

FIGURE 8.8 Exit slip related to spacing.

Reprinted by permission from R.P. Pangrazi, *Dynamic PE ASAP* (Owatonna, MN: Gopher Sport).

for students to go to answer a question or address an outcome for the lesson. For instance, in figure 8.9, the class is engaged in fitness stations, or a circuit. One of the stations is a white board. While at this station, students are instructed to write as many activities that work cardiovascular endurance as they can. When the station time is up, they cap their markers and move to the next station. Teachers can quickly walk by, read the activities, and gauge student understanding of the concept. Figure 8.10 is another example called Compliment Corner for Developmental Levels II or III. The outcome for this assessment is "I can compliment others during physical education." Students are instructed that if they hear a compliment for themselves or someone else, at any time during the lesson, they quickly write what they heard on the post it and stick it to the wall. Throughout the lesson the teacher can remind the students about the wall or praise their many compliments. At the end of the lesson or day, the teacher can quickly take a picture of the compliments and use this artifact to demonstrate student learning. This assessment can mean a great deal for changing the climate of a lesson or class.

Monitoring Physical Activity

As the field of physical education looks to promote lifelong physical activity, it makes sense that measuring physical activity during physical education, during the school day, and throughout the day is advocated. Pedometers are an excellent tool for measuring the amount of physical activity that a person accumulates. Pedometers generally measure the quantity of physical activity, although newer models can measure the intensity and duration of activity. The majority of pedometers detect movement through a spring-loaded, counterbalanced mechanism that records vertical acceleration at the hip.

FIGURE 8.9 A whiteboard station is one way to use a bike rack assessment.

FIGURE 8.10 A bike rack assessment like Compliment Corner can help create a positive climate in the class.

 TECH TIP

Classroom polling apps are also an efficient tool to gauge student learning. Although each platform can work differently, in most polling systems a teacher can use one device, such as a tablet or phone, to scan student cards. For instance, using a projector the teacher may project the question "Which of the following is a cardiovascular activity?" on the screen. Possible answers might be tag, sitting, sleeping, and push-ups. Students then hold up an answer card provided by the teacher with the correct answer up. These cards are premade specific to the app in use. The teacher scans the class with the tablet or phone and the responses are collected and tabulated. Instant feedback is provided regarding student responses. This method could be used for prompts such as "Today I was able to follow the teacher during the dance" or "Today I was able to select the appropriate challenge for me when juggling." These tools are an effective way to engage students, assess, and provide instant feedback associated with lesson outcomes.

New and more accurate models count steps using a piezoelectric sensor. Acceleration is measured by converting strain on the sensor to electricity, which is converted to a step count. Pedometers are small, unobtrusive, and easily fastened to a belt or waistband. In their most basic form, pedometers measure the number of steps a person takes. Counting steps is an effective way to measure how active a person is throughout the day, even though pedometers can't measure all types of activity. For example, because pedometers are not waterproof, they can't measure swimming activity. In addition, pedometers don't accurately measure activities on wheels such as bicycling, skateboarding, and in-line skating. However, because 90% of the physical activity people accumulate is over land, pedometers are an inexpensive and accurate way to measure physical activity for young and old alike. Using pedometers to measure the physical activity levels of youth is now an accepted instructional and research methodology (Bassett, Toth, LaMunion, & Crouter, 2017; Pangrazi, Beighle, & Sidman, 2007).

A number of pedometers on the market have features for measuring factors other than steps. Some of the more common measures include distance covered and caloric expenditure. To measure distance covered, the length of the step must be entered into the pedometer. The pedometer then calculates distance covered by multiplying the step length times the number of steps. To measure energy expenditure, a number of factors must be entered into the pedometer, such as weight and stride length. Based on the number of steps taken, the pedometer calculates the number of kilocalories expended. Newer pedometers have a function that measures activity time. Every time a person moves, the pedometer accumulates activity time. When the person stops moving, the timing function stops. This function shows the total hours and minutes of activity time accumulated throughout the day. Activity time is a much better variable for monitoring and comparing student activity because it is not affected by stride length.

One of the criticisms of pedometers has been that they are not able to monitor the intensity of physical activity. But a few pedometers, such as the Gopher FITstep (view the Gopher FITstep Pro at gophersport.com) pedometer now measure moderate to vigorous physical activity (MVPA). Most experts agree that MVPA activity offers greater health benefits than low-intensity activity. The FITstep pedometer identifies a personalized MVPA level based on steps per minute (SPM). For example, a person with short strides will take more steps per minute than one who takes long strides. The following steps explain how to teach students to determine their personal MVPA level:

1. Walk (two to three minutes) to warm up and get ready for MVPA.

2. After the warm-up, have students practice walking at a brisk pace (the current ACSM definition of MVPA). A brisk walk is a pace that can be continued for an extended time. It is characterized by swinging the arms and walking with a purpose. On the other hand, it should not be so fast that students quickly become fatigued. In addition, students should not walk with other students because their walking speeds may be different. When students have identified their personal brisk walking pace, go to step 3.

3. Have the class put their pedometers in the step mode, clear and close them, and walk briskly for one minute. At the end of one minute, stop the class and open the pedometers to see the number

TECH TIP

When purchasing pedometers to monitor student activity, make sure they can monitor both steps and time. Steps are necessary for validating the pedometer and making sure it is counting accurately. Step goals for students, however, can lead to unfair comparisons and expectations. For example, consider a teacher who sets a goal of 10,000 steps for students in her class. Stride lengths of students in her elementary school class vary from 18 to 30 inches (45 to 75 cm). The students with longer stride lengths will have to cover greater distances to reach 10,000 steps. In most cases, students with shorter stride lengths are smaller, so they burn fewer calories while they are walking. These differences are what make step goals an inequitable approach for students. Now consider a teacher who uses pedometers that measure activity time. Tall and short students walk together for 30 minutes and accumulate the same amount of activity time, but the students will likely have different step counts while covering the same distance. Therefore, when setting activity goals for students, avoid step counts and focus on activity time.

of steps they accumulated while walking. Round down the number to the nearest 10s group. That number is their SPM level.

4. Enter the SPM level into the pedometer. The FITstep pedometer can be set at nine levels, starting with a low value of 80 SPM to a high value of 160 SPM. When users move at a pace over their selected MVPA level, they accumulate both MVPA time and total activity time. When they move at a speed slower than their selected MVPA threshold, they accumulate only total activity time.

Accuracy of Pedometers

Activity recommendations in terms of daily minutes of physical activity for youth and adults (USDHHS, 2018) have created an interest in accurately measuring personal movement. When people recall and report the amount of activity they performed throughout the previous day, most find it difficult to quantify how active they were. Additionally, it may be that the recall was done on a day that is not typical, resulting in an underestimation or overestimation of physical activity. Some type of objective measuring tool is helpful for documenting activity levels because it avoids dependency on recollection and reading of questionnaires. The pedometer is an objective activity-measuring instrument that has been studied by a number of researchers.

Quality pedometers leave the factory with a high degree of accuracy. When tested on a shake machine, they exhibit a high degree of accuracy. Accuracy issues arise if the pedometer is not attached properly during use. Newer and more accurate models of pedometers now use a piezoelectric counter instead of a mechanical pendulum. The result is that the pedometer is much more accurate even when placement issues occur. In addition, they are more accurate with overweight and slow-moving people. Piezoelectric pedometers have no moving parts, which makes them much more resistant to breakage.

Pedometers depend on a small and consistent up-and-down motion with each step. Over the years, manufacturers have tried to design pedometers that measure distance and caloric expenditure. Unfortunately, these two measurements are not very accurate because stride length changes (distance is calculated by multiplying steps time stride length) when people are walking at different speeds, uphill, and downhill. Caloric expenditure is most often overestimated. These errors in distance and energy expenditure are not surprising considering they are all based on consistency of step length and walking speed.

When using a pendulum pedometer, undercounting errors may occur with highly overweight students because of the placement of the pedometer. On these students, the orientation of the pedometer is often tilted away from the vertical plane and moved toward the horizontal plane by excess body fat around the waist. If the pedometer is not parallel with the upright plane of the body, its accuracy is affected. Fortunately, the newer piezoelectric pedometers are much more tolerant of placement variations. Most will continue to count even with orientation changes in all planes. This makes piezoelectrics an accurate and reasonably priced tool for measuring physical activity in a group setting.

Funding Pedometers

Teachers are often concerned about the cost of pedometers and lack of budget. The first step is to offer the rationale for purchasing pedometers. They can be used as an accountability measure for their program in addition to teaching kids to focus on daily physical activity. Technology, such as pedometers to encourage physical activity, is often funded by parent–teacher groups. Many pedometers have been funded by parent groups when they learn how their children benefit from this measurement tool. Another option is a shareware program whereby companies sell pedometers at a reduced price to school employees, who in turn sell the pedometers to parents and others to raise money. A number of Internet companies are willing to sell pedometers to schools at wholesale so that they can resell them to parents and students at a profit. Certainly, selling pedometers is a much healthier fund-raising activity than selling candy or cookie dough.

One pedometer per student for a class is a minimal requirement. The pedometers can be used with all classes in physical education. The cost of pedometers ranges from $7 to $50 depending on the quality and functions of the pedometers. As discussed earlier, newer technology in pedometers like that of the Gopher FITstep allows the measurement of steps, activity time, and moderate to vigorous physical activity (MVPA). In addition, the pedometer comes with a dock that allows each student to upload his or her activity data to a computer (figure 8.11). Software allows the data to be charted, analyzed, and printed. If activity is being used as an accountability measure, quick and easy uploading saves a great deal of time and assures greater accuracy.

FIGURE 8.11 Students uploading pedometer data.

©Robert Pangrazi or Aaron Beighle

Pedometer Placement and Accuracy

Quality pedometers are accurate when they are validated at the factory, but measurement errors occur if they are not placed on the user correctly. Many people believe they can place the pedometer in their pocket or on a shoe and get an accurate reading. To date, all pedometers need to be fastened securely near the waist in an upright position to get the most accurate count. An accurate placement point must be identified for each individual. This process is a validity check to see whether the pedometer is monitoring the correct number of steps before activity data are collected. For years, the standard placement for pedometers was the waistline over the midpoint of the front of the thigh and kneecap. However, an article by Graser, Pangrazi, and Vincent (2007) showed that the right (or left) side (midaxillary line) is a slightly better place for the initial position. The thing to remember here is that no single placement point works for all people.

Students should be taught how to identify the placement point that offers them an accurate step count. The following protocol is designed to teach students how to find the placement point where the pedometer measures accurately.

1. Place the pedometer on the waistband on the right side of the body, midway between the front and back of the body (over the hip). Place the pedometer parallel to the body and upright. If it is angled in any direction, pendulum pedometers will not measure accurately. To measure the number of steps accurately, open the pedometer without removing it from the waistband, reset it to zero steps, and then gently close the pedometer without moving. Begin walking at a normal cadence while counting the number of steps you are taking. Stop immediately when you have counted 30 steps. Gently open the pedometer without removing it and check the step count. If the step count is between 27 and 33 steps, this placement is an accurate location for the pedometer. This range represents a 10% measurement error, which is acceptable for free-living activity research. If the step count does not fall in this range, perform the next step.

2. Move the pedometer so that it is positioned over the midpoint of the right (or left) thigh. Open the pedometer, clear it, and take 30 steps as described in step 1. Again, if the step count is within the range of 27 to 33 steps, this new placement is an accurate measurement spot. If not, try the next step.

3. Pedometers must remain in an upright plane (with the pedometer display perpendicular to the floor and parallel to the body) to register step counts accurately. Loose-fitting clothing will affect accuracy because the clothing absorbs the slight vertical force that occurs with each step. Excess body fat can tilt the pedometer and negate accuracy. In these cases, placement at waist level just to the right or left of the spine will offer an accurate measurement. Research (Graser, Pangrazi, & Vincent, 2007) showed that placing the pedometer on an adjustable Velcro belt resulted in more accurate readings because more precise adjustments could be made. Repeat the 30-step process outlined in step 1 until an accurate placement point has been identified.

When students and teachers are experienced at using pedometers and want an accurate reading, they should perform a validity check each day. Different clothing will often result in an inaccurate reading. The validity check assures the user (and the teacher) they are gathering accurate and meaningful data.

Pedometers and Personal Goal Setting

A common approach in physical education uses the idea that one standard fits all. It assumes that one goal will be meaningful for all types of students regardless of age, gender, or health. This practice of mass prescription often turns off students who need activity the most. For example, an often-referenced standard is 10,000 steps per day (Hatano, 1993). A common standard for boys and girls ages 6 to 19 is 12,000 steps. This standard is used for the Presidential Active Lifestyle Award (PALA+) (PCPFS, 2018), which is awarded to students who accumulate 60 minutes of MVPA or 12,000 steps most days over a six-week period. The 12,000-steps recommendation is based on research equating step counts to minutes of moderate to vigorous physical activity (MVPA) in youth. Children and adolescents participating in the Canadian Health Measures Survey (Colley, Janssen, & Tremblay, 2012) wore pedometers and accelerometers so that activity intensity and step counts could be analyzed. Because most activity recommendations for youth are 60 minutes of MVPA per day, the data were reviewed to see how steps per day would equate to 60 minutes of MVPA daily. Prediction equations were developed for the entire sample as well as separate groups defined by age and gender. The researchers concluded that a single minimal daily step target of 12,000 steps per day for both boys and girls was the most practical choice (but not necessarily the best fit for all students because of size and stride length differences).

The problem with a single-standard goal is that it does not account for the substantial individual differences among people of all ages and gender. Some students may be predisposed to be active and will easily reach the step criteria; others may find it next to impossible because they are naturally less active. How many steps should be set as a standard? Should it be set high, so that only those who are already active can reach it? Should it be set low, so that most people can reach it? Should it be set high enough to offer a proven health-related benefit? If you currently accumulate more than 12,000 steps, is there any benefit to moving beyond the 12,000-step threshold? If you accumulate 4,000 steps each day, does 12,000 steps seem an impossible goal? In addition, stride length strongly affects the number of steps that a student accumulates. Covering the same distance, a person with a long stride will accumulate significantly fewer steps than a person with shorter legs and stride length. Setting one goal that benefits everyone in a large population is a difficult proposition at best and can result in discouragement or lack of challenge.

The approach recommended here is the *baseline and goal-setting* technique (Pangrazi, Beighle, & Sidman,

2007). This method requires everyone to identify his or her average daily activity (baseline) level. For preadolescent youth, four days of monitoring step counts (or activity time) are required to establish an average activity level (Clemens & Biddle, 2013). The days do not have to be consecutive. In fact, nonconsecutive days over time may give a more accurate snapshot of a student's activity level. Baseline data can be entered in a chart like the one shown in figure 8.12.

After establishing the baseline level of activity, each student has a reference point for setting a personal goal. The personal goal is established by taking the baseline activity level and adding 10% more steps (or time in whole minutes) to that level. For example, assume a baseline of 6,000 steps per day. The personal goal for the first two weeks is 6,000 steps plus 600 more steps for a total of 6,600 steps. If the goal is reached on most days in this two-week period, another 10% (600 steps) is added to the goal and the process repeated. For most people, a top goal of 4,000 to 6,000 steps above their baseline level is a reasonable expectation. Using the example of 6,000 baseline steps here, a final goal of 10,000 to 12,000 steps would be the goal.

This baseline and goal-setting approach allows for individual differences. It gradually increases personal goals so that they seem achievable to even inactive individuals. Most people want to be compared against their own level of activity and are motivated when they find that goals are based on their activity level rather than compared with a group standard.

A third way to establish step levels for youth is to define a healthy activity zone (HAZ). This method sets no one standard for each child to reach and has been used by the FitnessGram (Cooper Institute, 2017) to specify a range of scores (the healthy fitness zone) that students should score on fitness test items. Some of the FitnessGram test items (e.g., PACER run and BMI) are based on health-related criteria, whereas others are based on improvement because of training. For physical activity, a range of steps (or activity time) can be established for each gender and can serve as the HAZ. For example, because the most often quoted standard is 12,000 steps per day, the HAZ range might be 10,000 to 16,000 steps. This method requires further research, but it may be an acceptable way to establish a range of scores that can apply to the vast majority of children and adults. Ultimately, a combination of methods, such as baseline goal setting and HAZ standards, may be the best solution.

Step 1: Calculate Your Baseline Step Counts

Name: _____

Date: _____

Day 1 step count: _____

Day 2 step count: _____

Day 3 step count: _____

Day 4 step count: _____

Total step count: divided by four equals _____. This number is your average baseline step count and will be used to determine your personal activity goal.

Step 2: Calculate Your Step Count Goal

The next step is to calculate your personal step count goal. A couple of examples are shown below. The first person discovered that she had a baseline step count of 4,000 steps. After 10 weeks her step count goal increases to 6,000 steps. For the person who has a baseline of 6,000 steps, his step count goal will increase to 9,000 steps by the final weeks. Thus, both individuals will increase their number of steps by one-third.

Baseline	Personal goal (10% of your baseline plus your baseline)	Weeks	Total step counts
4,000 steps	$4{,}000 \times 0.10 = 400$; $400 + 4{,}000 = 4{,}400$ Every 2 weeks thereafter, the goal will be increased by 400 steps.	1 & 2	4,400
		3 & 4	4,800
		5 & 6	5,200
		7 & 8	5,600
		9 & 10	6,000
6,000 steps	$6{,}000 \times 0.10 = 600$; $600 + 6{,}000 = 6{,}600$ Every 2 weeks thereafter, the goal will be increased by 600 steps.	1 & 2	6,600
		3 & 4	7,200
		5 & 6	7,800
		7 & 8	8,400
		9 & 10	9,000
	___ × 0.10 = ___; ___ + ___ = ___ Every 2 weeks thereafter, the goal will be increased by ____ steps.	1 & 2	
		3 & 4	
		5 & 6	
		7 & 8	
		9 & 10	

FIGURE 8.12 Setting personal activity goals using pedometers.

Using Pedometers in Physical Education

Proper management strategies are necessary if you are going to use pedometers with your students. Teachers resist using technology if it takes too much effort or causes discipline issues. For example, if students fuss with their pedometers or drop them while the teacher is delivering instruction, the teacher will soon become frustrated and quit monitoring activity. Guidelines for proper use need to be delineated. If students refuse to

FUND-RAISERS FOR PURCHASING PEDOMETERS

8

We live in an era of decreased budgets at the national level, the state level, and the local level. If purchasing a class set of pedometers exceeds your current physical education budget, then teachers should consider creative ways to obtain or earn the necessary money for their program; one possibility is a fund-raiser. Before you move ahead with your plans, though, your first step should be to speak with the administration about your fund-raising ideas. They will know what fund-raisers already take place within the school and whom to contact regarding the implementation of a new initiative.

The next step is to educate administrators, staff, parents, and community members about healthy fund-raising ideas. For instance, instead of selling cookie dough or providing pizza and a movie for the class that raises the most money, a number of healthier alternatives exist, such as healthy food items or nonfood items that can be sold, and things that students can do to earn money. Nonfood items include calendars, candles, cookbooks, products with the school logo, magazine subscriptions, wrapping paper, and plants, among others. Food items that can be sold include frozen bananas, trail mix, oranges, and fiber bars. These healthy food items often earn more profit than candy bars or bake sales. Finally, things that students can do to fund-raise include walk-a-thons, dances, talent shows, and skate nights, among others. Some physical education equipment companies, such as Gopher Sport, even offer assistance for fund-raising efforts.

After seeking approval to conduct a physical education fund-raiser and educating people about healthy fund-raiser ideas, the next step is to work with the most active groups in the school to make sure that the fund-raiser takes place and is a success. In general, the PTO or PTA has members who are the most involved with the school, and they would likely be the most supportive group for the cause. This organization or association may already have a number of fund-raisers occurring within the school, and they may be open to donating a portion of their proceeds to purchasing a class set of pedometers. For example, many PTO or PTA groups run school-wide competitions to see which class or grade can bring in the most Box Tops for Education or Tyson Foods A+ labels. These companies reward with points toward school products or with a specific amount of money back per label received. Other fund-raisers that schools may conduct each year are school carnivals or field days with the proceeds benefiting different content areas of the school. Schools can also sell spirit cards that offer discounts at a variety of local businesses.

Regardless of the type of fund-raiser that is conducted, with adequate planning, positive connections, and a bit of hard work, a significant amount of money can be raised for the physical education program. Purchasing pedometers with those funds not only allows the physical educator to monitor students' physical activity but also provides a form of assessment for the program and gives back to the students for their hard work in supporting physical education.

use the pedometer properly, they lose their pedometer privileges.

Here is an often-used procedure that minimizes pedometer preparation time. Before distribution, permanently number each pedometer and place it in a container that allows easy distribution (figure 8.13). Place the same number of pedometers in each container so that it is easy to see when a pedometer (and corresponding student) is missing. Students arrive and, on signal, go to their assigned box, secure a pedometer, and put it on while moving around the area. On signal, they freeze, reset their pedometers, and class begins as

usual (figure 8.14). At the end of class, students remove their pedometers, put them back in the same container, record their steps or activity time on the sheet next to their container, and prepare to exit class. Procedures for securing, fastening, and putting away the pedometers is critical for successful integration of pedometers into the program. Allied to this procedure are two basic rules:

1. "You shake it, I take it." Pedometers require a gentle up-and-down motion to count steps and activity time. The purpose of using pedometers is to record steps accurately, and falsely recording steps in any manner is strongly discouraged.

In most cases, the pedometer is taken from the student, but he or she can use it at the next class meeting.

2. "Once off, forever off." This rule stipulates that after the pedometer is placed on the waistband (at the start of class), it is not to be removed for the remainder of the period. The pedometer can be read from the waistband. If students are allowed to take their pedometers on and off, they will drop and break them and distract others. As in rule 1, the pedometer is available again at the next class period.

Pedometers are a novelty when they are first introduced to students. Students naturally want to explore how a pedometer works. Give them time to open and

FIGURE 8.13 Pedometer distribution.

close the pedometer, move it gently up and down and watch it count, and learn what stops the pedometer from measuring accurately. Also, see the earlier section Pedometer Placement and Accuracy for guidelines for teaching students appropriate pedometer placement. A related problem in the introduction phase is that the rate of pedometer loss may be excessively high if they are allowed to leave physical education classes. Introduce pedometers in a controlled setting, that is, physical education class, where students can be taught appropriate use and held accountable.

After the pedometers become a regular part of each student's lifestyle, fewer pedometers are lost or misplaced. Many schools put in place a replacement policy before giving students the freedom to take the pedometers out of the school environment. A letter is sent home explaining the activity program and the use of pedometers. If a pedometer is lost, the student must pay a fee to replace it. Another important point about using pedometers is the novelty phase. If the pedometers are not carefully monitored, especially in the introductory phase, many of them will be damaged.

Collecting Daily Physical Activity

After students have used pedometers during physical education and have shown they can be responsible with this equipment, teachers may wish to collect physical activity data beyond physical education. Of course, with this effort comes the chance of loss. Loss can be minimized in several ways. For at least the first six to eight weeks of school, use the pedometers only in physical education classes. This time will depend on the age and responsibility level of students. We recommend keeping pedometers in physical education for Developmental Level I. In Developmental Level II a next step might be to use the pedometers to evaluate how much activity students accumulate while in school. This approach keeps the pedometers in the school; students can check them out at the beginning of the day and bring them back at the end. Next, students can use the pedometers to carry out 24-hour monitoring. Each morning, they put on the pedometers and clear them. The next morning upon arriving at school, students record their activity and reset the pedometers. Recording

FIGURE 8.14 Students resetting their pedometers.

is conducted only Monday through Friday morning because accurate weekend readings are hard to obtain and more pedometers are lost when students take them home for the weekend.

Pedometers are valuable tools for testing hypotheses. Teachers can challenge students to answer questions such as "Are students more active than parents?" and "Do you take more steps during a football class or an Ultimate class?" Students can modify or invent a game based on pedometer-determined steps. Students also can use pedometers to determine their leisure-time physical activity with an aim of establishing personal goals or engaging in daily physical activity.

Lesson Ideas Using Pedometers

The following activities illustrate various ways to use pedometers in school. They are explained in more detail in the resource book *Pedometer Power* (Pangrazi, Beighle, & Sidman, 2007).

Moving Across the State or the United Sates

Students accumulate steps and measure their stride length to find out how far they have traveled across a state or U.S. map. As students reach different checkpoints, conduct class discussions about foods, art, and various cultural sites. A number of interactive web-based programs are designed to promote physical activity and allow students to log their steps each day.

Active or Inactive

Students can participate in various physical education lessons and try to predict which lessons are high activity and which are low activity. An enjoyable related activity is to have students guess how many steps they will take in the activity. With time, they will begin to understand the activity value of different sports and games.

School Steps Contest

All classes participate in this school-wide contest. Each class adds the step counts of all students and the teacher and then divides the total count by the number of students. Finding the average number of steps for the entire class makes this a group competition and avoids focusing on less active students. A gentle reminder here: Let students decide whether to reveal their step counts. A sensitive approach is to have the students place their step counts anonymously on a tally sheet.

The President's Council on Physical Fitness and Sports sponsors the Presidential Active Lifestyle Award (PALA+; www.presidentschallenge.org). At this website,

students can log their activity time or steps. By accumulating 60 minutes or 12,000 steps on most of the days of the week for six weeks, students can earn a PALA+ patch. If 35% of the students in a school earn the PALA+ twice or more during the year, the school can become an Active Lifestyle Model School. These schools receive a certificate and are recognized on the website.

Pedometers and Program Accountability

A common issue for physical education teachers is finding criteria they can be held accountable for. Many teachers have chosen fitness or skill development as outcomes they are willing to use as a measure of their success. But before choosing fitness or skill development as their success criterion, teachers may want to consider several issues. Fitness is most commonly used because tests have long been used in the school setting. Such tests may not be a good choice, however, because the increase in obesity among today's youth decreases fitness test performance. Common sense indicates that aerobic endurance and various strength measures are directly affected by the increase in body fat among youth. Besides, genetics strongly influences a person's ability to respond to training (Timmons et al., 2010), and some children will show little or no improvement. Growth also confounds fitness results; it is hard to tell if students' performance improved because of the training or because they grew older and stronger. Another problem in using fitness as an outcome is the amount of time currently available for physical activity during the school day. Students' chances of improving their fitness are limited to the extent measurable by fitness testing. Many students will improve their fitness test scores purely by maturing, but this result does not account for the teacher's contribution to student fitness. Using fitness as the main indicator of teaching success may be inviting failure.

Skill development is an important assessment outcome for physical education, but a large part of skill performance is genetically endowed too. Physical skills may also be difficult to evaluate because of time constraints and the large number of students seen by the physical education teacher. Physical skills are never perfected; even the world's best basketball and soccer players miss as many shots as they make. Baseball players strike out 3 in every 10 times at bat. Rugby players fumble the ball and miss kicks. Skills do need to be emphasized or assessed, but because students' performance will always be imperfect, it is asking a lot of teachers to base the success of their program on their students' skill performance. In addition, for evaluating skill development, few instruments are valid, reliable, and easy to administer in a limited time. Teachers also know that taking a lot of time to assess skill performance leaves little time to teach those skills.

Why not base program success on a school increase in physical activity? What could be more important for health and wellness than increasing the amount of activity that students accumulate daily? All students can move and be physically active both in and out of school. Barring physical disability, all students can monitor their physical activity levels using pedometers. Most parents are delighted when their children are learning to live an active lifestyle. That accomplishment might be one of the best legacies of a quality physical education program.

When the school year starts, use pedometers to evaluate the students' baseline activity levels. Follow this with regular monitoring several times during the school year. Students, regardless of genetic predisposition, can raise their goals for increasing daily physical activity. Physical education teachers can establish goals for various subgroups, including classes, grade levels, and gender. School administrators might accept a 2% increase in physical activity, accumulated as a school-wide goal over an 18-week period. Use activity levels both in and out of school as separate outcomes. Out-of-school activity can be regarded as physical education homework. A program designed to increase the amount of physical activity that students accumulate each day is a valuable contribution to the health of all students.

Pedometers can also be used to demonstrate teacher accountability. One indicator of a quality physical education lesson is having students engaged in physical activity for at least 50% of the lesson. That is, in a 30-minute lesson, students should be moving for at least 15 minutes. Although being active for half of the lesson is a seemingly easily obtainable goal, the research suggests that students are active on average only 34% of the lesson (Fairclough & Stratton, 2005, 2006). Fortunately, when teaching strategies based on those presented in this book are used, the research suggests that students can be active at least 50% of the time (McKenzie et al., 1997). Given the ability of pedometers to measure physical activity time, teachers can easily determine the activity level of students in minutes and thus calculate the percentage of lesson time spent engaged in physical activity. For example, if on average students spend 20 minutes being physically active during a 30-minute lesson, they are active 67% of lesson time. When students are inactive for at least 50% of the time, teachers can reflect and analyze their teaching by asking questions such as these: Did I talk too much? Could the activities be modified to be more active? Was I active? Were my transitions efficient? These are just a few of the questions that could be asked based on pedometer data. Thus, pedometers offer useful data for physical education teachers to use to improve and reflect on instruction.

Other Tools to Measure Physical Activity

As mentioned earlier, various tools are available to measure physical activity in physical education. Accelerometers, heart rate monitors, and direct observation, along with pedometers, all provide objective measures of physical activity that can be used in physical education. *Objective* simply means that the tools are unbiased and require little judgment by the data collector. That is, the PE teacher's opinion or preconceived notions about the physical activity levels of children will not influence the outcome of the data.

Accelerometers are similar in size to pedometers and measure physical activity in activity counts by measuring body movement. Two advantages of accelerometers are that they measure the intensity of physical activity and they can store data over time. Two disadvantages of accelerometers, which tend to limit their use in physical education, are their cost (as much as $300 each) and the need for sophisticated software and data analysis procedures. Heart rate monitors are advantageous because they are relatively unobtrusive and estimate minutes of time spent engaged in activity of varying intensity. They can be costly (approximately $100 each), however, and tend to place value on activity based on intensity. That is, activity within the target heart zone is deemed better than activity above or below that range. In physical education, the belief is that all activity counts, not just activity of a certain intensity. Lastly, because of the nature of heart rate, heart rate monitors do not allow for the lag in heart rate as movement intensity changes. This concern is of particular concern given the intermittent nature of children's activity, especially in physical education. Finally, direct observation involves observing children in an activity setting. A common tool in physical education is SOFIT (System for Observing Fitness Instruction Time). See http://activelivingresearch.org/sofit-system-observing-fitness-instruction-time for a description and protocol for SOFIT. Although this tool has the potential to offer valuable information about student activity levels, the percentage of time spent in various parts of a lesson, and teacher behaviors associated with physical activity promotion, SOFIT does have limitations. For example, using SOFIT requires time to observe lessons and is best completed after training and practice using the tool.

Grading

Grading is the process of taking an assessment, evaluating the assessment, and giving a grade to the evaluation based on a set of criteria. An example is giving a test (assessment), marking incorrect responses (evaluating), and assigning a grade based on the number of items missed (grading). Physical education grading policies in elementary schools vary widely, ranging from no grading at all to letter grades, as in high school classes. So, is it better to grade or not to grade? Each system has merits, and there is no definitive answer. If a decision is made to grade, then what grading system should be used? For an in-depth review of grading systems and ideas for evaluation, see the text by Lacy (2011).

Points Against Using a Grading System

- Grades can vary between teachers and schools. When a student moves to a different school, the meaning of the grade might not transfer, and teachers at the new school may view it differently.

- Physical education does not emphasize content and product. Rather, it judges success by improvement on skills. Grades in academic areas reflect achievement and accomplishment; because grades in physical education reflect improvement and effort, they may be interpreted incorrectly.

- Physical education classes in elementary schools often meet only once or twice a week. Regularly testing for grade requirements is time consuming. Physical educators in this setting are trying to squeeze as much learning and movement as possible into the class period, and grading reduces their instructional time.

- Physical education is diverse and broad. Instruction covers all three learning domains—skill development, attitude formation, and content knowledge. Trying to grade all three domains is difficult and time consuming. Furthermore, which of these three domains is most important, and can any of them be overlooked?

- Grading usually occurs in areas where standardized instruments have been developed. Fitness testing is the major area in elementary physical education where such tests have been developed. Because of the lack of standardized tests in other areas, teachers may give excessive attention to fitness testing.

- Physical education emphasizes physical fitness and skill performance. Performance in these areas is strongly controlled by genetics, making it difficult for every child to achieve, even with his or her best effort. In addition, when grades are given for physical fitness performance, some students feel discouraged because they trained and still did not reach standards of high performance.

Points for Using a Grading System

- When grades are not given, academic respect is lost. Physical education already suffers from the misguided perception that physical educators do not teach anything—they just roll out the ball. Lack of a grading system may make others think that little learning is occurring.

- Grades inform parents about their child's performance. Parents have a right to know how their children perform in physical education. Grades are used by teachers in other areas and are easily understood and interpreted by parents; therefore, they should be used in physical education, too.

- A grading system provides accountability. When grades are given, administrators and parents often assume that teaching and student accomplishment have occurred.

- A grading system rewards students who perform well. Students are rewarded in academic areas for their intelligence and performance. They should be similarly rewarded for accomplishment in physical education settings.

TEACHING TIP

When grading, consider focusing on student improvement and attitude toward physical activity. Joy in movement and the desire to improve are important for students to learn during physical education.

Grading Issues

If you decide to implement a grading system, difficult issues follow. There are different ways to grade, and many issues have to be examined before developing a grading approach. Consider the following points when determining how you will assign grades.

Educational Outcomes Versus Administrative Tasks

It is generally agreed that physical education should help students achieve in various areas, including skill development, cultivating personal values, and cognitive development. Some systems assign weight to each of these areas when compiling a grade. Regardless of the emphasis that each area receives, the final grade depends on accomplishing educational objectives. This approach contrasts with grading on the completion of administrative tasks, whereby students earn some or all of their grade by attendance, participation, and attitude. This latter approach grades students on tasks that have little to do with accomplishing physical education objectives. Furthermore, these tasks are usually documented at the beginning of the period and have little effect on holding students accountable for their in-class performances.

Consider the conflicts arising when students are graded on achieving educational objectives versus accomplishing administrative tasks. Assume that a student in a math class regularly forgets to bring a pencil and is tardy but earns an A grade on all math exams. Does this student earn a final grade of A, or is the student penalized for doing poorly on administrative tasks (tardiness and so on) and given a C grade? Reverse the situation and assume that the student has an outstanding attitude, is never tardy, and always brings the proper supplies to class. At the end of the semester, the student has earned a C grade on exams yet performed all administrative tasks at a high level. Does this student receive a final grade of A? If grades in other curricular areas of the school are earned by accomplishing educational objectives or performing administrative tasks, following suit in physical education is probably wise.

Attitude Versus Skill Performance

Another area of concern when grading is whether attitude or skill performance should be the focal point. Those who emphasize attitudes stress the importance of students leaving school with positive feelings toward physical activity. These educators often say, "I am not concerned about how many skills my students learn; I just want them to walk out of my class with positive feelings about physical activity." They assume that students who feel positive about physical activity will be willing to be active throughout their lifetimes. These teachers assign grades based on the process of trying rather than on reaching skill outcomes. Students who receive higher grades may not be the most skilled but have shown good behavior and a positive attitude throughout the semester.

Teachers who reside in the product camp focus primarily on student accomplishment and see effort as something that is laudable but not part of the grading process. They would say, "I don't really care whether students like me or physical education. What is ultimately important is their performance. After all, the students who are best in math earn the highest grades, so why should it be any different in physical education?" Teachers who focus on performance give the highest grade to the best performer, regardless of other factors. Less skilled students, no matter how hard they try, will not receive an above-average grade.

This issue is a difficult, hotly debated problem to resolve in physical education. One viewpoint is that students should learn from the grading system how society works. People are rewarded in life for their performance, not for how hard they try. For example, if real estate agents try hard but never sell a house, they make no money. The payoff is for selling houses, not for trying hard to sell houses. An opposing viewpoint is that many people in society are rewarded for effort, so doing your best should be rewarded.

A solution to consider is to grade on performance while focusing the instruction on students' attitudes toward physical activity and skill learning. Much is to be said for teaching that helps students develop a positive attitude toward activity. Attitude development depends largely on how teachers present the material rather than on how students perform skills. Help students understand that they also perform differently from each other in math or science and receive a respectively higher or lower grade.

Relative Improvement

Some physical educators believe that effort, or just doing the best that you can, should be the most important factor in assigning grades. To reward effort, these teachers base student grades on how much a student improves. This approach involves pretesting and posttesting to determine the amount of progress made throughout the grading period. Grades are not based on absolute performance; the best performer in the class quite possibly will not receive the highest grade because she or he may have improved less.

Grading on improvement is time consuming and requires that the same test be given at the beginning and end of the semester or unit. The test may or may not accurately reflect what has been learned in the class, and it may not be sensitive enough to reflect improvement made by both poor and outstanding performers. Testing at the beginning of a unit can be discouraging and demoralizing if a student performs poorly in front of peers. It can also be hazardous in activities such as gymnastics or golf that require intensive instruction to prevent accident or injury.

Another consideration is the issue of performing for a grade. Students learn quickly to perform at a low level on the pretest so that they can demonstrate a higher degree of improvement on the posttest. A related problem is that improvement is sometimes easier at beginning levels of skill than at high levels of performance. Most teachers are aware of the rapid improvement that beginners make before reaching a learning plateau. A skilled performer may be at a level where improvement is difficult to achieve. Lack of improvement in this situation results in a skilled performer receiving a lower grade than a beginner.

Grading on Potential or Effort

Some teachers choose to grade on whether students reach their potential. Such teachers decide what a student's potential performance level should be and then assign a grade based on whether the student reached that level. The grade that a student receives depends on the teacher's subjective perception of that student's genetic abilities and limitations. How can any teacher really know a student's absolute potential?

This approach often depends on the teacher's feelings about the student in question. It is based on intangibles, and a student may receive a grade because he or she is "just like her brothers or sisters." When grades are based on a teacher's subjective beliefs rather than on criteria that are measured and evaluated, they are difficult to defend. How would a parent react to a teacher's statement that "Your child received a failing grade because he just didn't live up to his potential"? To be defensible, grading systems need to be based on tangible data gleaned from observable behavior and performance.

Negative Versus Positive Grading

To make the grading system defensible and concrete, some teachers have used point systems. In most point systems, both performance objectives and administrative factors are listed as grade components. A student earns a grade through performance, attitude, and knowledge. Point systems can become a negative influence if handled incorrectly. For example, some teachers give students 100 points at the start of the semester and then "chip off" points for various unsatisfactory levels of performance. A student may lose points for not trying, not performing, or not knowing answers on a test. Students soon realize that they need to concentrate on negative behaviors that lose points rather than on educational objectives.

In contrast, some teachers use a point system that rewards positive behavior. Students receive points for performing well, and they can earn their grades through self-direction. In a negative system, teachers make all the judgments about points lost and receive, in turn, the negative feelings of the student. In a positive system, students can behave in a positive way to earn points. Teachers are constantly rewarding positive behavior, which fosters positive feelings toward physical education and teachers. Rewarding positive behavior makes students believe that the teacher cares about their welfare and growth.

A negative system tends to focus teachers on what students cannot do, rather than on what they can or should do. Energy is spent on policing students and threatening to take away points if they do not behave. Students respond poorly to this approach, because losing points does not require an immediate change in behavior and a redirection. The loss of points results in a lower final grade, a consequence that is usually six to nine weeks away. Few students respond positively to grade leverage through a negative system. Students who care about grades are performing well in the first place. Threatening to lower the grade of a student who does not like physical education or school in general only further alienates the student. Moreover, such a practice is based on a system of negative reinforcement. The grading system should positively encourage students to perform.

Letter Grades Versus a Student Progress Report

Letter grades tell parents little about their children's performance in physical education. Frequently, the grade reflects the student's behavior, but the parents interpret it as an indicator of their student's physical skill level. A letter grade does not communicate progress or performance related to other students at a similar developmental level. A student progress report takes more time to compile but gives parents much more information and helps communicate program goals.

Figure 8.15 is an example of a progress report that could be used to share information with parents. The seven areas of evaluation represent the five major content standards of the program (see chapter 1). If desired, some of the grade-level outcomes under each standard could also be included. Note that program standards are divided into two major areas: (1) physical education skills and (2) social skills and responsible behavior. Most teachers want to separate behavior and skill performance when grading. This progress report allows students to be rewarded for effort and proper behavior regardless of their skills and physical abilities. Evaluating a student based on developmental level gives parents an idea of how their child is performing compared with others of similar development and maturity. This report helps parents understand the skill performance of other children

PROGRESS REPORT FOR PHYSICAL EDUCATION

Name: _____ Class: _____

Students are expected to learn a wide variety of skills in physical education. The following areas reflect major program standards. Expectations are that your child will perform at or above developmental level (compared with other students the same age). If you are interested in discussing the progress of your child, please arrange a meeting with the physical education instructor.

Physical Education Assessment

Program Standards	Developmental Level Performance		
	Above	At	Below
Exhibits motor skills and movement competence			
Able to monitor and perform physical fitness activities			
Understands human movement principles			
Uses lifestyle and healthy eating habits that foster wellness			
Independently uses lifetime physical activity skills			

Social Skills and Responsible Behavior Assessment

Students are evaluated on social skills and responsible behavior in physical education classes. Behavioral consequences are recorded daily. Evaluations (see below) are based on how students perform in these areas.

Program Standards	O	S	N
Develops quality social skills			
Exhibits responsible behavior			

O = Outstanding. Exhibits effort and a positive attitude about participating in physical activities on a regular basis. Cooperates with classmates and receives no more than one behavior consequence during the nine-week grading period.

S = Satisfactory. Willingly attempts activities. Puts forth average effort, displays a positive attitude, cooperates with classmates, and receives two to five behavior consequences during the nine-week grading period.

N = Needs improvement. Consistently exhibits off-task behavior or a negative attitude. Has difficulty cooperating with classmates. Parents are notified by midterm of the grading period if their child is in jeopardy of receiving a grade of N.

Physical Activity Assessment (Average Minutes Per Day)

Students are expected to average 60 minutes or more of physical activity each day. The following scale is used to evaluate your child's level of activity.

Program Standards	O	S	N
Physical activity behavior			

O = Outstanding. Average of more than 90 minutes of physical activity per day.

S = Satisfactory. Average of 60 to 90 minutes of physical activity per day.

N = Needs improvement. Average of less than 60 minutes of physical activity per day.

Instructor's comments:

FIGURE 8.15 Sample progress report.

who are similar developmentally or who are above, at, or below their child's skill level. Such feedback may help temper unrealistic expectations of parents and coaches who do not have the perspective of seeing many children at similar developmental levels.

Completing a progress report takes more time than assigning letter grades, so a progress report cannot be sent home as often as a simple letter grade. Most elementary school teachers are responsible for 350 to 600 or more students, so completing a progress report for each student four times a year would be an unrealistic expectation. A solution is to offer a comprehensive, meaningful progress report once a year or once every second or third year. This approach alerts teachers to students they will have to grade for the forthcoming year and gives them time to review these students in detail throughout the year.

Program Accountability

Program outcomes are goals that the state, school district, superintendent, school board, and parents want to reach. They are referred to as accountability outcomes or are developed as answers to the question "What should the physical education program contribute to the total school environment?" Another common question related to accountability is "What skills do we want our students to have when they graduate?" The most common set of outcomes discussed in physical education are the five SHAPE America standards for physical education (SHAPE America, 2013) that are used throughout this text. They are global in nature and have many smaller grade-level outcomes listed for each standard.

Having national standards for physical education is one thing, but having standardized instruments to measure whether programs are meeting the standards is another. To evaluate institutional goals, a test needs to be valid and respected both within and outside the school setting. The best examples of tests for monitoring accountability in schools today are the high-stakes tests used for measuring math, science, and reading outcomes. In some cases, students are not allowed to graduate without passing these exams. If a large number of students do not pass these tests, their failure reflects poorly on the institution, so the tests become an important catalyst for change.

Refocusing SHAPE Standards

SHAPE America has been instrumental in developing standards for the profession. Most states have adopted or modified the five SHAPE America standards (2013), so it is safe to say that administrators and teachers accept these as important.

1. The physically literate individual demonstrates competency in a variety of motor skills and movement patterns.

2. The physically literate individual applies knowledge of concepts, principles, strategies, and tactics related to movement and performance.

3. The physically literate individual demonstrates the knowledge and skills to achieve and maintain a health-enhancing level of physical activity and fitness.

4. The physically literate individual exhibits responsible personal and social behavior that respects self and others.

5. The physically literate individual recognizes the value of physical activity for health, enjoyment, challenge, self-expression or social interaction.

The five SHAPE America standards reflect what most professionals believe should be accomplished in a quality physical education program. For all the standards, however, finding and implementing valid and reliable instruments is difficult, if not impossible, during physical education classes. Therein lies a fundamental issue. Whenever teachers are asked to offer some evidence of accountability for their program, they usually select physical fitness because it is one of the few standardized tests (Cooper Institute, 2010) that cut across all grades. If skill development is chosen as the outcome measure, then teachers discover that no standardized tests can be used across ages, sex, and grades. Unfortunately, no data are available to show that students have improved their fitness and skill competency over time. Today the United States is more overweight as a society compared with when all the concern for fitness was voiced in the 1950s. Why would we want to advocate physical fitness as a measure of accountability if we have no evidence of success?

The SHAPE America standards should be refocused so that some are used as standards for accountability and the remainder are used to guide instruction. This approach results in two categories of standards.

Instructional Standards Guide Instruction

Physical fitness, motor skill competency, and responsible personal and social behavior are standards that are difficult to evaluate. Improvement in these areas is related to growth and development (as children grow older, they improve in fitness and physical skill performance). Additionally, physical fitness and skill performance are controlled by genetic makeup (Bouchard, 1999; Timmons et al., 2010). As previously mentioned, little progress in these areas has been made over the last 60 years (Corbin & Pangrazi, 1992). Why would physical educators want to hold their programs accountable for standards that are, in part, out of their control? Teachers have done an excellent job of teaching fitness and skill development for many years, but little data are available to show long-term change.

Fitness, skill development, and character development should be taught in every physical education program. Instructional standards should guide the program so that every child receives instruction and the opportunity to learn in these areas. Parents want to be assured that all children receive instruction in fitness, skill development, and character development. The point here is that these instructional standards should be taught, but they should not be used as accountability measures for physical education.

Accountability Standards Guide Program Evaluation

School boards and administrators want to see whether programs are accomplishing written standards. Accountability standards for physical education should be within reach of all students if they have received effective instruction and put forth regular effort. If standards are used for accountability, valid, meaningful, and feasible evaluation instruments must be in place. In many cases, standards have been suggested for accountability only to find that the evaluation tools are sorely lacking or ineffective (see earlier remarks). Mandating that a standard be measured and then asking teachers to make up their own assessment instruments and rubrics does not make sense.

The SHAPE America standards that should be used for accountability purposes are physical activity participation and valuing physical activity for life. The concerns that many have about the state of America's health focus on inactivity and negative attitudes toward daily physical activity. The continuing saga of weight management for the majority of Americans revolves around increasing physical activity levels and decreasing or changing food intake. If physical education is to make a difference and become a centerpiece for America's health, teachers and schools must be held accountable for these important standards. If a healthy eating habits standard is added in the future, parents could be assured that their children will leave school with a positive attitude toward activity, an active lifestyle, and healthy eating habits. That outcome should be the legacy of a meaningful physical education program.

Accountability and Pedometers

Pedometers were discussed earlier in this chapter. Accountability data can be gathered in a number of ways with pedometers. Research has shown that four days of physical activity data can be used to calculate a student's average activity level. A set of pedometers can be rotated between classrooms to establish the average level of activity for each classroom. Goals for classes and schools can be established using this objective data set. Physical activity is a more achievable outcome measure (as compared with physical fitness outcomes) for elementary school students. Students can be monitored for four days at the start of the school year and again near the end of the year. An excellent outcome of monitoring physical activity is that all students can become more active. Contrast this outcome with physical fitness, in which most of the performance in elementary school students is controlled by their genetic endowments and physical growth. Most pretest versus posttest fitness gains shown in elementary school result from children becoming eight to nine months older.

Attitude Toward Physical Activity

A child's attitude about physical activity can help drive his or her physical activity levels now and into adulthood. For this reason, teachers need to be cognizant of their program's influence on student attitude toward physical activity. The Children's Attraction to Physical Activity (CAPA) instrument is used to assess the attraction of children ages 8 to 12 to physical activity (Brustad, 1996). The CAPA has been used for research purposes and validated by Brustad (1995). It is a 15-item pencil-and-paper instrument that assesses the extent of children's interest in physical activity by having them consider two opposing viewpoints. Children first choose the point of view that describes them and then select the strength of that feeling ("sort of true" or "really true") for each of the 15 items. The instrument is scored on a scale of 1 to 4 points, with a 4 reflecting the most positive attraction to physical activity. Figure 8.16 shows the CAPA instrument.

Because the CAPA is a standardized instrument, schools can use the results to see if the physical education program is positively influencing the students' affective domain. Schools and classrooms can be compared to see how students feel about physical activity. If attitudes toward physical activity are low, teachers and parents can develop strategies to improve the students' feelings.

Evaluate Your Program

Your program should be evaluated regularly to ensure that it is achieving stated program goals. Evaluation instruments reflect the program philosophy and objectives of individual districts. Figure 8.17 is a sample instrument that may be adapted for your use,

What I am like

Please look at the sample question first. Choose only one answer to each question. There are no right or wrong answers. Simply choose the statement you think is most true for you.

Really true for me	Sort of true for me	**Sample**			Really true for me	Sort of true for me
A	B	Some kids like to eat ice cream more than anything else.	BUT	Other kids like other foods more than ice cream.	C	D

Really true for me	Sort of true for me				Really true for me	Sort of true for me
1. A	B	Some kids have more fun playing games and sports than anything else.	BUT	Other kids like doing other things.	C	D
2. A	B	Some kids don't like to exercise very much.	BUT	Other kids like to exercise a whole lot.	C	D
3. A	B	Some kids get told by other kids that they are not very good at games and sports.	BUT	Other kids are told that they are good at games and sports.	C	D
4. A	B	Some kids get teased by other kids when they play games and sports.	BUT	Other kids don't get teased when they play games and sports.	C	D
5. A	B	Some kids think that the more exercise they get the better.	BUT	Other kids think that it is not good to get too much exercise.	C	D
6. A	B	Some kids don't enjoy exercise very much.	BUT	Other kids enjoy exercise a whole lot.	C	D
7. A	B	Some kids try hard to stay in good shape.	BUT	Other kids don't try hard to stay in good shape.	C	D
8. A	B	Some kids don't like getting out of breath when they play hard.	BUT	Other kids don't mind getting out of breath when they play hard.	C	D
9. A	B	Some kids think it is very important to always be in good shape.	BUT	Other kids don't think it is so important to always be in good shape.	C	D
10. A	B	For some kids, games and sports is their favorite thing.	BUT	Other kids like other things more than games and sports.	C	D
11. A	B	Some kids are popular with other kids when they play games and sports.	BUT	Other kids are not very popular with others when they play games and sports.	C	D
12. A	B	Some kids look forward to playing games and sports	BUT	Other kids don't look forward to playing games and sports.	C	D
13. A	B	Some kids really don't like to exercise.	BUT	Other kids do like to exercise.	C	D
14. A	B	Some kids feel bad when they run hard.	BUT	Other kids feel good when they run hard.	C	D
15. A	B	Some kids don't like to run very much.	BUT	Other kids do like to run a whole lot.	C	D

8

FIGURE 8.16 Children's Attraction to Physical Activity (CAPA) instrument.

Based on Brustad (1996).

depending on the needs and goals of your district. This instrument can be used to expose serious program deficiencies and operational difficulties. The results, including program strengths and weaknesses, can be shared with administrators or used by teachers to evaluate a program they have developed. The instrument can also be used to compare programs or to identify effective programs.

In the sample instrument, evaluative statements are written as a set of standards that, when met, ensure an effective program. The four areas evaluated are (1) program philosophy, (2) instructional procedures, (3) curricular

PHYSICAL EDUCATION PROGRAM EVALUATION

Program Philosophy

1. Physical education is regarded by the administration as an integral part of the total curriculum and is dedicated to the same curricular goal, the fullest possible development of each pupil for living in a democracy.   0   1   2
2. A written and up-to-date sequential curriculum is available and used by all instructors.   0   1   2
3. Lesson plans are developed from the course of study and are used as the basis for instruction.   0   1   2
4. A meaningful progression of activities is evident between developmental levels.   0   1   2
5. Students are scheduled in the physical education program on a regular basis.   0   1   2
6. Music, field trips, and extracurricular activities are not accepted as substitutes for physical education.   0   1   2
7. Students are excused from physical education on a long-term basis only when they can submit a physician's statement indicating the medical condition and the duration of the excuse.   0   1   2
8. Appropriate arrangements are made for students with medical, religious, or temporary health excuses.   0   1   2
9. A nurse, teacher, or staff member with suitable first aid training is available in case of accident.   0   1   2
10. The budget specified for physical education equipment and supplies is adequate.   0   1   2
11. Physical education demonstration programs are offered regularly for purposes of public relations and general information.   0   1   2
12. The minimum amount per class of time allotted for physical education activity is 30 minutes.   0   1   2
13. Each class receives physical education instruction a minimum of three times per week, excluding recess and supervised play.   0   1   2
14. Class sizes are the same as those allotted to classroom teachers.   0   1   2
15. Program activities are coeducational in nature.   0   1   2
16. Classroom teachers do not keep students from physical education classes for disciplinary reasons.   0   1   2

Comments:

Instructional Procedures

1. The teacher is prepared before the class. A written set of instructional activities is carried into the lesson on a small note card.   0   1   2
2. Equipment is correctly arranged around the perimeter of the activity area before class.   0   1   2
3. Proper procedures are used for acquiring and putting away equipment.   0   1   2
4. The instructor constantly moves and repositions him- or herself so that all students are in the line of sight. Instruction is conducted from different areas in the activity area.   0   1   2
5. Children in need receive special help during the lesson. The level of instruction is geared to the needs of students who lack skill.   0   1   2
6. Students understand why they are practicing skills.   0   1   2

FIGURE 8.17   Sample evaluation form for physical education program (0 = no compliance, 1 = partial compliance, and 2 = full compliance).

offerings, and (4) facilities, equipment, and supplies. The entire instrument can be used, or any of the four areas can be evaluated individually. Read each statement, determine the level of compliance with the accepted standard, and circle the appropriate score on the rating scale. Include any comments at the end of each section. Rate and assign points on the following basis: 2 indicates full compliance (the program meets the standard fully without deficiencies), 1 indicates partial compliance with room for improvement, and 0 indicates no compliance (the deficiency is serious and detrimental to an effective program).

8

7. Teacher enthusiasm and energy are adequate. Teacher movement and personal involvement are evident. 0 1 2

8. Positive encouragement is given to all students. Youngsters are encouraged to do their best. 0 1 2

9. Students are directed to be responsible for their learning and personal behavior. Content instruction is stopped when there is a need to improve behavioral skills. 0 1 2

10. Instruction is focused on developing quality skills rather than on changing activities often in an attempt to keep students on task. Adequate opportunity is given for repetition and refinement of skills. 0 1 2

11. Closure of the lesson is a positive experience. Students are encouraged to evaluate their level of responsibility. The pitfall of nagging students about their poor class performance is avoided. 0 1 2

12. Discipline and management problems are handled effectively. The self-esteem of students is preserved during behavior correction episodes. 0 1 2

13. Disciplinary measures in physical education instruction do not include physical punishment. 0 1 2

14. Procedures for dealing with accidents, including administration of first aid, reporting, and follow-up, are in written form. 0 1 2

15. Knowledge of liability concerns related to physical education instruction and programming is evident. 0 1 2

16. Facilities, equipment, and activity areas that could be liabilities are reported in writing to appropriate administrators. 0 1 2

17. Bulletin boards, charts, pictures, and other visual materials are posted and used in the instructional process. 0 1 2

18. Teaching aids such as instructional signs, videos, and posters are used to enrich and supplement instruction. 0 1 2

Comments:

Curricular Offerings

1. The physical education program provides learning experiences to help each child attain the following:

    a. Refinement of motor skills and movement competence 0 1 2

    b. Development of lifestyle habits that foster wellness 0 1 2

    c. Ability to monitor and maintain physical activity 0 1 2

    d. Understanding and applying human movement principles 0 1 2

    e. Enjoyment of a lifetime of physical activity 0 1 2

    f. Acquisition of quality social skills 0 1 2

    g. Ability to demonstrate responsible behavior 0 1 2

2. All children are considered important and the program is adjusted to suit the maturity and skill levels of youngsters. 0 1 2

3. Each lesson has a portion of time (7 to 10 minutes) devoted to physical fitness activities. 0 1 2

(continued)

4. The physical education program emphasizes and allocates enough time at the appropriate grade level for each of the following areas:

    a. Educational movement concepts   0   1   2

    b. Fundamental skills, including locomotor, nonlocomotor, manipulative, and specialized skills   0   1   2

    c. Rhythmic activities   0   1   2

    d. Gymnastics activities   0   1   2

    e. Games and relays   0   1   2

    f. Sports and lead-up activities   0   1   2

5. Both indoor and outdoor teaching stations are available for physical education instruction.   0   1   2

6. Units of instruction last no longer than three weeks and include skill instruction.   0   1   2

Comments:

Facilities, Equipment, and Supplies

1. Facilities include teaching stations that allow all students a minimum of three classes per week.   0   1   2

2. Outdoor facilities include the following:

    a. A physical education instructional area that is isolated from playground activities   0   1   2

    b. Areas where different age groups can play without interference from each other   0   1   2

    c. Areas for court games   0   1   2

    d. Cement or asphalt spaces marked with a variety of game patterns   0   1   2

    e. Backstops and goals for softball, soccer, and basketball   0   1   2

    f. Suitable fencing for safety and control   0   1   2

    g. Outdoor playground equipment, including climbing apparatus, turning bars, and tetherball areas   0   1   2

3. The outdoor area is free from rocks, sprinkler heads, and other hazards that might cause injury.   0   1   2

4. Indoor facilities meet the following standards:

    a. Clean, sanitary, and free from hazards   0   1   2

FIGURE 8.17 *(continued)*

LEARNING AIDS

HOW AND WHY

1. In a music or art class, would you want to be evaluated based on the product or the process? Why? How does this relate to your grading as a physical education teacher?

2. How is giving a child on-the-spot feedback about his or her performance a form of evaluation?

3. How are you evaluated as a college student? Do you believe you are evaluated fairly? Explain.

4. How could you use a pedometer to evaluate your current physical activity levels in a variety of settings? Why would that be important?

5. How can progress reports be more effective tools for communicating with parents?

6. Does the use of technology always improve the evaluation process? Provide examples when it would or would not.

CONTENT REVIEW

1. Discuss the significance of focusing on the process in physical education. Comment on how physical education and other academic areas differ regarding evaluation.

2. Identify and describe several methods of assessing lesson outcomes.

b. Well lighted, well ventilated, heated, cooled, and treated for proper acoustics	0	1	2
c. Surfaced with a nonslip finish and painted game area lines	0	1	2

5. All facilities and equipment, both indoor and outdoor, are periodically inspected and a written report is filed with appropriate administrators.   0   1   2

6. Storage facilities are adequate for supplies and portable equipment.   0   1   2

7. An office that is located near the instruction area is provided for the physical education instructor.   0   1   2

8. Basic supplies are sufficient in the following areas:

     a. Manipulative equipment (one piece for each child): fleece balls, small balls, beanbags, wands, hoops, and jump ropes   0   1   2

     b. Sport and game balls: softballs, footballs, volleyballs, basketballs, soccer balls, floor hockey sticks and pucks, tetherballs, and cageballs in sufficient numbers   0   1   2

     c. Sport and game supplies: cones, pinnies, track and field standards, jumping pits, and hurdles   0   1   2

     d. Testing equipment: measuring tapes, stopwatches, calipers to measure skinfold thickness, and specialized apparatus   0   1   2

9. Sufficient materials are available for a varied rhythmic program: CD or tape player, tapes and CDs, tom-toms, and tambourines.   0   1   2

10. Capital-outlay items for the indoor facility include the following:

     a. Minimum of six tumbling mats (4 by 8 feet [1.2 by 2.4 m] or larger)   0   1   2

     b. Individual mats (one per student)   0   1   2

     c. Sufficient climbing apparatus so that at least one-half of the class can be active at one time; should include wall bars, chinning bars, horizontal bars, climbing ropes on tracks, and ladders   0   1   2

     d. Balance-beam benches (at least six)   0   1   2

     e. Jumping boxes (at least eight)   0   1   2

     f. Basketball goals, volleyball nets, and hockey goals   0   1   2

     g. Equipment carts (at least two)   0   1   2

Comments:

8

3. Discuss how you could use pedometers in a physical education setting.

4. Describe advantages and disadvantages of a grading system and the steps for implementing one.

5. Discuss the pros and cons of using technology in education.

WEBSITES

PhysEdReviews assessments, https://physedreview.weebly.com/assessments.html

Assessments and grading, www.pelinks4u.org (now PHE America)

Pedometers in physical education, www.gophersport.com

SUGGESTED READINGS

Beighle, A, Pangrazi, R.P., & Vincent, S.D, (2001). Pedometers, physical activity, and accountability. *Journal of Physical Education, Recreation, and Dance, 72*(9), 16–19.

Block, M.E., Lieberman, J.L., & Connor-Kuntz, F. (1998). Authentic assessment in adapted physical education. *Journal of Physical Education, Recreation, and Dance, 69*(3), 48–55.

Brustad, R J. (1993). Who will go out and play? Parental and psychological influences on children's attraction to physical activity. *Pediatric Exercise Science, 5,* 210–223.

Brustad, R J. (1996). Attraction to physical activity in urban schoolchildren: Parental socialization and gender influences. *Research Quarterly for Exercise and Sport, 67,* 316–323.

Corbin, C.B., Pangrazi, R.P., & Franks, B.D. (Eds). (2004). *Toward a better understanding of physical fitness & activity: Selected topics, vol. 2.* Scottsdale, AZ: Holcomb Hathaway.

Crouter, S.E., Schneider, P.L., Karabulut, M., & Bassett, Jr., D.R. (2003). Validity of 10 electronic pedometers for measuring steps, distance, and energy cost. *Medicine and Science in Sports and Exercise, 35*(8), 1455–1460.

Darst, P.W., Zakrajsek, D.B., & Mancini, V.H. (1989). *Analyzing physical education and sport instruction* (2nd ed.). Champaign, IL: Human Kinetics.

Kilanowski, C.K., Consalvi, A.R., & Epstein, L.R. (1999). Validation of an electronic pedometer for measurement of physical activity in children. *Pediatric Exercise Science, 11*, 63–68.

Lambert, L.T. (1999). *Standards-based assessment of student learning: A comprehensive approach.* Reston, VA: National Association for Sport and Physical Education.

Morgan, C.F., Beighle, A., Pangrazi, R.P., & Pangrazi, D.L. (2004). Using self-assessment for personal fitness evaluation. *Teaching Elementary Physical Education, 15*(1), 1–3.

Wood, T.M., & Zhu, W. (Eds.). (2006) *Measurement practice and theory in kinesiology.* Champaign, IL: Human Kinetics.

Zhu, W., Safrit, M.J., & Cohen, A. (1999). *FitSmart test user manual.* Champaign, IL: Human Kinetics.

REFERENCES

Bassett, D.R., Toth, L.P., LaMunion, S.R., & Crouter, S.E. (2017). Step counting: A review of measurement considerations and health-related applications. *Sports Medicine, 47*(7), 1303–1315.

Bouchard, C. (1999). Heredity and health related fitness. In *Toward a better understanding of physical fitness & activity*, ed. Charles B. Corbin & Robert B. Pangrazi, 11–18. Scottsdale, AZ: Holcomb Hathaway.

Chepko, S.F., & Arnold R.K. (Eds.). (2000). *Guidelines for physical education programs: Grades, K–12 standards, objectives, and assessments.* Boston, MA: Allyn & Bacon.

Clemens, S.A., & Biddle, S.J.H. (2013). The use of pedometers for monitoring physical activity in children and adolescents: Measurement considerations. *Journal of Physical Activity and Health, 10*, 249–262.

Colley, R.C., Janssen, I., & Tremblay, M.S. (2012). Daily step target to measure adherence to physical activity guidelines in children. *Medicine & Science in Sports and Exercise, 44*(5), 977–982

Cooper Institute. (2017). *FitnessGram/ActivityGram test administration manual* (5th ed.). M. Meredith & G. Welk, Eds. Champaign, IL: Human Kinetics.

Corbin, C.B., & Pangrazi, R.P. (1992). Are American children and youth fit? *Research Quarterly for Exercise and Sport, 63*(2), 96–106.

Fairclough, S., & Stratton, G. (2005). Physical education makes you fit and healthy: Physical education's contribution to young people's physical activity levels. *Health Education Research, 20*(1), 14–23.

Fairclough, S., & Stratton, G. (2006). A review of physical activity levels during elementary school physical education. *Journal of Teaching in Physical Education, 25*(2), 239–257.

Graser, S.V., Pangrazi, R.P., & Vincent, W.J. (2007). Effects of placement, attachment, and weight classification on pedometer accuracy. *Journal of Physical Activity & Health, 4*(4), 359–369.

Hatano, Y. (1993). Use of the pedometer for promoting daily walking exercise. *International Council for Health Physical Education and Recreation, 29*, 4–28.

Hopple, C. (2005). *Elementary physical education teaching and assessment: A practical guide* (2nd ed.). Champaign, IL: Human Kinetics.

Lacy, A. (2011). *Measurement and evaluation in physical education and exercise science.* San Francisco, CA: Benjamin Cummings.

McKenzie, T.L., Sallis, J.F., Kolody, B., & Faucette, F. (1997). Long term effects of a physical education curriculum and staff development program: SPARK. *Research Quarterly for Exercise and Sport, 68*, 280-291.

Pangrazi, R.P., Beighle, A., & Sidman, C. (2007). *Pedometer power.* Champaign, IL: Human Kinetics.

President's Council on Fitness, Sports, and Nutrition. (2011). *The President's Challenge handbook.* Washington, DC: Author.

SHAPE America. (2013). National standards & grade-level outcomes for K–12 physical education. Reston, VA: SHAPE America and Champaign, IL: Human Kinetics.

Timmons, J.A., Knudsen, S. Tuomo Rankinen, T., Koch, L.G., Sarzynski, M., & Jensen, T. (2010). Using molecular classification to predict gains in maximal aerobic capacity following endurance exercise training in humans. *Journal of Applied Physiology, 108*, 1487–1496.

USDHHS. (2018). Physical activity guidelines for Americans (2nd ed.). Washington, DC: Author.

Children With Disabilities

In the United States, every child has the right to free and appropriate education. To ensure that an appropriate education is provided, federal law requires the identification and evaluation of all children with disabilities. Based on the assessment, an individual education plan (IEP), if applicable, must be developed and implemented. The IEP, moreover, must include physical education. According to federal law, students with disabilities must be educated in the least restrictive environment appropriate for their individual needs. This chapter provides background information pertaining to legislation and education environments, an overview of the IEP process, strategies for the successful inclusion of students with disabilities (as well as a summary table including a variety of special needs), characteristics of students with these disabilities, and strategies for educating students with these disabilities in physical education. To develop and implement an adapted physical education program, physical educators must refer to other resources for more in-depth discussion.

Learning Objectives

▶ Understand the implications of Public Laws 94-142 and 105-17 for physical education.

▶ Explain due process guidelines associated with assessment procedures.

▶ Develop a plan for identifying, locating, and evaluating all children with disabilities.

▶ Cite standards associated with assessment procedures for children with special needs.

▶ Identify essential elements of an individualized education program and list the stages of development.

▶ List strategies for the successful inclusion of all students.

▶ Describe characteristics of specific special needs and ways to modify learning experiences in physical education to accommodate children with disabilities.

▶ Locate nationally validated programs to assist in the screening, assessment, and curriculum development for children with special needs.

Providing a quality education for all students is the responsibility of the educational system. All professionals should view this responsibility as an ethical and professional duty regardless of the legal requirements. It is the appropriate thing to do for all children—and all children come to school with varying ability levels, disabled or not. Dr. Claudine Sherrill (2004) states, "In a sense, all good physical education is adapted physical education."

The Education for All Handicapped Children Act (Public Law [PL] 94-142) was passed by Congress in 1975. In short, the law requires that all youth with disabilities, ages 3 to 21, receive a free and appropriate education in the least restrictive environment:

> It is the purpose of this act to assure that all handicapped children have available to them . . . a free appropriate public education which emphasizes special education and related services designed to meet their special needs, to assure that the rights of handicapped children and their parents or guardians are protected, to assist states and localities to provide for the education of all handicapped children, and to assess and assure the effectiveness of efforts to educate handicapped children.

The law includes students in public and private care facilities and schools. Youth with disabilities who can learn in regular classes with the use of supplementary aids and services must be educated with children in the regular class. Physical education is the only specific area mentioned in PL 94-142. According to the law, the term "special education" means "specially designed instruction, instruction in physical education, home instruction, and instruction in hospitals and institutions." A 1997 amendment, Public Law 105-17 (also known as IDEA—Individuals with Disabilities Education Act), continues with the objective of providing individuals with disabilities with the least restrictive environment in the school setting. The Individuals with Disabilities Education Act states, "Physical education services, specially designed if necessary, must be made available to every child with a disability receiving a free appropriate public education." Such disabilities include a child diagnosed with mental impairment, deafness or other hearing impairment, speech or language impairment, blindness or other visual impairment, serious emotional disturbance, orthopedic impairment, autism, traumatic brain injury, a learning disability, deaf-blindness (the condition of little or no useful sight *and* little or no useful hearing), multiple disabilities, or other health impairments that require special education (Office of

Special Education and Rehabilitation Services, 2007). Adapted physical education may also include children with developmental delays as well as any physical or mental impairment that limits one or more major life activities (Winnick & Porretta, 2017).

To comply with PL 94-142, schools must locate, identify, and evaluate all students who might have a disability. A screening process must be followed by a formal assessment procedure. An assessment must be made and an IEP developed for each student before placement into a special program can be made. The law states who will be responsible for developing the IEP and what the IEP will contain.

Before 1970, students with disabilities had limited access to schools. They certainly did not have an equal opportunity to participate in school programs. The passage of PL 94-142 shows that a strong commitment has been made to equality and education for all Americans. The government also ensured that funding would be made available to provide quality instruction. The law authorizes a payment to each state of 40% of the average per pupil expenditure in U.S. elementary and secondary schools, multiplied by the number of children with disabilities who are receiving special education and related services. The federal mandate reveals public concern for comprehensive education programs for *all* students, regardless of disability. Regardless of the ability level of youth, quality physical education should make adaptations for all students to have success, especially those with a disability.

According to Section 504 of the Rehabilitation Act of 1973 (PL 93-112), no person with a disability can be discriminated against and must be provided equal opportunity to those provided to individuals without disabilities if the program or activity is federally funded. Because most schools are federally funded, this legislation is relevant to schools and physical education. Specifically, the physical education provided to students with disabilities must be comparable with that offered to nondisabled students. Thus, students with special needs who do not require special education programs are still entitled to services that allow them to benefit from all programs available to nondisabled students. In other words, all students identified with a disability by IDEA are also covered by Section 504, but not all students protected under Section 504 are disabled according to IDEA. Generally speaking, Section 504 plans (often called 504s) are not as rigorous as IEPs, and schools often develop their own forms. But this does not suggest that these plans should be ignored. They are equally important and assist physical educators in providing students with quality physical education that fits their special needs.

Least Restrictive Environment

PL 105-17 uses the term "least restrictive environment" (LRE) to help determine the best placement for students with disabilities. This concept refers to the idea that not all individuals can do all the same activities in the same environment. However, the concept of zero reject entitles everyone of school age to some aspect of the school program. No one can be totally rejected because of a disability. All students, regardless of ability level, must have access to physical education. Thus, after it is established that a child has special physical education needs, the most appropriate educational setting must be determined. During this process, the focus should be on placing students into settings that offer the best opportunity for educational advancement. Conversely, in a situation where the success of others will be disrupted, placing a young person in an environment where success is impossible is inappropriate.

For a given student, the LRE can vary from day to day and could change within a given lesson. It will also vary depending on the unit of instruction and the teaching style. For a student in a wheelchair, for example, a jump-rope activity might be very restrictive, whereas basketball or disc activities would be less restrictive. For a student with emotional disabilities, the direct style of instruction might be the LRE, whereas a problem-solving method with group cooperation may be too difficult and would end up being more restrictive. Consistent and ongoing judgments need to be made because curriculum content and teaching styles can change the type of environment that the student enters. In physical education, the environment is more than the physical surroundings (e.g., the equipment, the students, and the gym); it includes the environmental climate created by teacher choices and attitudes. It is shortsighted to place students into a situation and then forget about them or to assume that one teaching style or activity will always create the LRE. Evaluation and modification of environments need to be continuous. These evaluations will assist the physical education teacher in determining the LRE. The LRE will likely change over time; the goal is to create opportunities for the student to experience more regular programs offered by schools.

Inclusion

Inclusion refers to educating students with and without disabilities in a regular education setting. For physical education, therefore, a student with a disability will attend physical education with peers without disabilities. As figure 9.1 suggests, this can occur at varying levels along a continuum, depending on the needs of the student. For example, a child with cerebral palsy may attend a regular physical education class one day a week and one adapted physical education class per week with other students with disabilities. Another child who uses a wheelchair may attend a regular physical education class and have a classroom aide. Research examining the use of inclusion during physical education has found many benefits, including increased learning time, increased opportunities to respond, improved social skills, enhanced peer acceptance between students, and enhanced personal development (Lieberman & Houston-Wilson, 2009). Although some have argued that inclusion may result in the student with disabilities receiving less attention or that schools use this as a strategy for saving money, the evidence is clear that inclusion has many benefits. It is also the law.

Understanding the relationship between inclusion and LRE is important. Complete inclusion (i.e., full-time physical education in a regular physical education class) is not necessarily the LRE. To be the LRE, it must be the *most* integrated and appropriate. Some appropriate placements will not be in the regular physical education class. Great care needs to be taken when matching the LRE for a student with the most appropriate environment on the inclusion continuum (see figure 9.1). This process should be revised as the student progresses through the physical education program.

Segregated physical education classes (i.e., classes consisting only of students with disabilities) should be maintained only when it is in the student's best interests. Segregated physical education programs are intended to establish a level of skill and social proficiency that will eventually enable the special student to be transferred to a less restricted learning environment. Again, the goal of the process is to place students in the LRE that offers them the most benefit. Students with disabilities working on their own have often been denied opportunities to interact with peers and become part of the social and academic classroom network.

Students with disabilities need contact with support personnel regardless of the LRE. The physical education teacher is responsible for the students during class time, but these students may still require access to special education teachers, school psychologists, speech therapists, and paraeducators. Although these support personnel may view physical education as a break from their students, they are a source of information and support for the physical education teacher in charge

9

Physical education classes with no IEP needed	Physical education classes with curricular modifications	Physical education with class restrictions such as class size	Physical education classes with special services (e.g., trained peer tutor, peer educator)	Physical education with a trained adapted physical education specialist	Physical education with a part-time adapted physical education specialist	Full-time adapted physical education with a specialist	Full-time physical education in a school for students with unique needs only

FIGURE 9.1 Physical education inclusion continuum.

TEACHING TIP

Be sure that students with disabilities understand what is to be accomplished before an activity begins, especially when working with children who have an intellectual disability or an auditory impairment.

and should be there upon request. The physical education teacher must communicate regularly with these personnel to involve them in the students' learning as much as possible. Oftentimes, these individuals do not have the expertise to know what to do with the students during instruction or practice time. See the later section Recruiting Paraeducators and Volunteers.

Screening and Assessment

The screening process is the first step taken to identify students who are eligible for adapted physical education. This process, sometimes referred to as the "child find" process, per IDEA, must include the screening of all students entering a school, all students annually, all students with disabilities, and any students who are referred to adapted physical education. The physical educator usually conducts screening tests, which may include commonly used test batteries such as the FitnessGram (Cooper Institute, 2017) or the Brockport Physical Fitness Test (Winnick & Short, 2014). Skill performance checklists are also used for screening. Students who do not demonstrate developmentally appropriate or age-appropriate skill levels are referred for further testing.

All referrals from the initial screening are made to a district-level committee, typically called the Committee on Special Education (CSE). This referral does not have to come from a teacher. Any person who has an interest in the well-being of the child can make this referral. The CSE then determines if further testing is needed. At this point, the physical educator could be called on to assess the child using evaluation tools to determine the child's special needs. Based on this formal assessment, students with special needs warranting a specialized program for longer than 30 consecutive days are referred to an adapted physical education program. To examine the extensive variety of criteria available to determine special needs, see the reference list at the end of this chapter. Finally, after the child is determined to be eligible, decisions regarding the most appropriate educational environment (see LRE and inclusion discussed previously) are made. All vested parties (parents, teachers, physical therapists, occupational therapists, physicians, physical educators, and so on) need to be kept abreast of the progress of the student throughout the screening and evaluation process as well as during the implementation of the individualized education program.

Procedures for Effective Assessment

As discussed, the physical education teacher is likely to be approached to perform both screening and more formal evaluations of students during the "child find" process. Thus, all physical education teachers must be knowledgeable and skilled in appropriate assessment tools and protocol. Furthermore, PL 94-142 requires that assessment is held to certain standards to ensure fair and objective results. For the most accurate, effective, and useful evaluation, consider the following components.

Selection of Assessment Tools

A variety of assessment tools have been published and are available to physical educators (see references). First, any assessment tool selected must be valid. That is, it must measure what it purports to measure. Thus, when selecting instruments, all parties must understand how the tests were developed and how they will correctly measure the area of possible disability. Validated measurements for reflexes, reaction time, fundamental movements, specific sports skills, physical fitness, and physical activity are available (see Winnick, 2017, for details). In addition to these standardized tools, authentic assessment has been advocated (Jackson & Larkin, 2002). This type of assessment is conducted in real situations and provides data pertaining to student performance during the physical education program. Examples of authentic assessments are rubrics and portfolios.

An appropriate assessment tool must be selected for each student. The tools must be designed to measure the child's special needs rather than simply label the student's shortcomings. Although labeling is discouraged, students must be labeled to receive the services they have a right to. For this reason, appropriate tools must be used, not to label a child, but to ensure that accurate conclusions are drawn regarding the child's special needs.

Administration Procedures

Even the protocol for standardized, validated assessment tools can be compromised by the special needs of students. For example, a motor ability assessment tool may reveal that the child is low performing in a motor skill when in reality he or she simply was not able to process the entire instruction because of an intellectual disability. Fortunately, many of the tools designed for adapted physical education will account for these issues in their protocol, but the physical educators must become familiar with the protocol before using the assessment. When standardized instruments are validated, they are done so using a highly prescriptive protocol that must be followed to maintain validity and the usefulness of the data. This practice will ensure accurate data and decrease the likelihood of draw-

ing inaccurate conclusions about the needs of and most appropriate environment for the child.

Team Evaluation

The physical educator should not be the only professional involved in the evaluation process. Various experts should be used for assessment in a variety of areas. Providing a multidisciplinary team helps ensure that all facets of the child are reviewed and evaluated. Evaluation professionals must be well trained and qualified to administer the various tests. The team must work with the best interest of the student in mind and be aware of a number of typical barriers to effective team evaluation. Common barriers include communication problems, not understanding the individualized education program or the student's disability, and not accepting another team member's input. The school district is responsible for ensuring that a proper evaluation occurs.

Understanding an Individualized Education Program (IEP)

PL 94-142 requires that an IEP be developed for each child with a disability who is receiving special education and related services. Physical education is a requirement of the IEP, so the physical educator must be familiar with the IEP to be a contributing participant. Based on data from the formal assessment, the IEP must be developed

9

Physical education can and should include all students.

by a committee, as stipulated by the law. The committee must include a local education association representative who is qualified to provide and supervise the administration of special education, the child's parents or guardians, the teachers who have direct responsibility for implementing the IEP, and, when appropriate, the student. Other people may be included at the discretion of the parents or the school district.

The IEP identifies the child's special qualities and determines educationally relevant strengths and weaknesses. A plan is then devised based on the diagnosed strengths and weaknesses. The IEP must contain the material listed here (figure 9.2 provides examples of content specific to physical education for the following IEP components):

1. *Current status of the child's present level of performance.* This portion of the IEP is the foundation of the entire document. For physical education, the focus of the present level of performance will be physical skills and is typically a summary of the formal evaluation results. The focus of this section should be on what the student is currently able to accomplish.

2. *A statement of annual goals and short-term instructional objectives.* Annual goals define what a child is expected to achieve in a year. They are traditionally written in general terms (e.g., Jose will improve his abdominal strength) with subsequent short-term measurable objectives (e.g., perform 10 consecutive curl-ups using the FitnessGram cadence and technique during two consecutive classes). Revisions to the IDEA legislation in 2004 removed the requirement of short-term objectives. For this reason, annual goals are now being written in a manner that makes them more measurable.

3. *A statement of the processes that will be used for assessment, measuring progress, and reporting progress to parents.* As discussed earlier, parents must be informed of their child's progress. This statement should include how the parents will be notified, the type of information reported, how the information is collected, how it will be reported, and the frequency of reporting. Parents should be notified of their child's progress at least as frequently as the parents of students without disabilities are notified.

4. *A statement of the special education services, related services, and supplementary aids to be provided.* Based on the child's level of performance, the services, equipment, and materials needed to meet IEP goals are determined and delineated

in this section. In addition, the most appropriate educational setting and LRE are included. Physical education is a special education service. Related services include occupational therapists, recreational therapists, and speech therapy.

5. *A statement describing the educational setting placement.* Although mentioned earlier, the educational setting is described in more detail here. More detail includes how the LRE may change, depending on the unit, and the percentage of time that the child will be in regular physical education or other physical education environments. This section should also discuss where the physical education program will take place.

6. *Assessment accommodations that will be provided.* Based on the annual goals developed, this section discusses the assessment tools used to measure progress toward those goals. If modifications to the protocol are made, this section will discuss those modifications. In addition, if applicable, rationale for a specific assessment tool is provided here.

7. *Dates for initiation of services and anticipated duration of the services.* This section provides the anticipated start of the implementation of the IEP and its components. In addition, details related to the frequency and minutes of physical education and other services are provided. Specific times of these services can also be provided.

8. *A discussion of transitional activities and requisite services.* This section on transitional services is a crucial part of the IEP. The law requires that this section be included as a part of the IEP no later than when the child turns 16, and it must be updated annually. This section must include measurable, assessment-based goals related to training, education, vocation, and daily, independent living skills, if appropriate. In addition, information related to the services needed to meet these goals after the student leaves the public education system should be provided. In short, these goals assist the student in transitioning from the education program to community-based programs. For physical education, this assistance involves setting goals for the student to continue engaging in postsecondary physical activities. This might include assisting the student in joining community-based physical activity offerings.

SAMPLE IEP COMPONENTS

1. Present levels of performance

   - Performs Crab Walk and Puppy Walk for 10 feet (3 m).
   - Throws a yarn ball 20 feet (6 m) using mature pattern.
   - Performs jumping jacks moving his or her feet apart 10 out of 10 times and feet together 5 out of 10 times.
   - Performs one modified crunch using good form.
   - Jumps forward and backward over a 7-foot (2 m) rope lying on the ground 10 consecutive times.
   - Accumulates an average of 1,200 steps over five physical education lessons.
   - Averages three episodes of inappropriate social behaviors during six physical education lessons.

2. A statement of annual goals

   - By March 2020, Jose will be able to catch a tossed 8-inch (20 cm) gator ball using his hands and not closing his eyes three out of four times.
   - By September 2020, Faith will average two episodes of hitting or pushing peers during a 45-minute physical education class.
   - By May 2021, Libby will demonstrate a score of 6 inches (15 cm) for both left and right sides won the back-saver sit and reach.
   - By December 2021, Arnov will be able to kick an 8-inch (20 cm) gator ball while seated on a chair.

3. A statement of processes for assessment, measuring progress, and reporting progress to parents

   - LaShanda's progress will be evaluated based on progress toward the annual goals outlined in the IEP. Progress toward these goals will be measured monthly, and final evaluation will be conducted during the month presented in the goal. Information about progress toward these goals or final evaluation will be presented to the parents in written form at least quarterly. A final report will be provided during the last week of school each year. The sit and reach, PACER test, pedometer, and throwing-skill rubric will be used to provide feedback regarding progress toward the annual goals for flexibility, cardiovascular endurance, steps during physical education, and throwing performance, respectively.

4. A statement of special education services, related services, and supplementary aids to be provided

   - DeMarcus will receive regular physical education for 30 minutes, two times per week with a third-grade class consisting of 28 students. During physical education, behavioral expectations will be clearly defined at the beginning of each lesson and throughout the lesson. Behavior issues will be discussed privately and positive reinforcement for acceptable behavior will be provided. Short instructions will be provided with directional cues such as "listen" used at the beginning of the instruction. When appropriate, a trained peer tutor will be paired with DeMarcus to model acceptable behavior. No other special services are required.

5. A statement describing the educational setting placement

   - A combination of regular physical education with an aide and adapted physical education will be used to meet Hope's needs. She will receive 100% of her physical education in a regular physical education classroom during lessons focusing on individual skills including individual jump rope, movement skills, dance, and gymnastics. Because of her deficits with social interactions, during lessons that focus on partner or group activities she will participate in adapted physical education lessons.

6. Assessment accommodations that will be provided

FIGURE 9.2 Physical education content of an IEP.

(continued)

- Emily will participate in assessments with accommodations. Currently, she is able to complete one lap on the PACER. Modifications to the PACER will have Emily participating with a trained peer tutor. Her time to complete five laps will be measured. Standard protocol will be used to measure progress on all other annual goals.

7. Dates for initiation of services and anticipated duration of the services

- The requisite services will begin on September 1, 2020. Rashim will participate in regular physical education with a trained peer tutor from 8:00 to 8:35 a.m. on Tuesdays and Fridays. He will also be working with the district-based physical therapist one day per week to improve flexibility in his right arm. The date and time of this session will vary each week. These services will be provided throughout the remainder of the academic year.

8. Discussion of transitional activities and requisite services

- Sarah loves dancing. This summer she will be enrolled in a ballet and tap dance class at a local studio. In anticipation of this class, the focus of the adapted physical education class will be on the development of balance and foundational dance movements. These skills will be determined in consultation with the new dance instructor.

FIGURE 9.2 *(continued)*

Due Process Guidelines

Typically the IEP is an extensive document with information related to the child's needs in a variety of areas. The IEP is created by the school and parents and must be agreed upon by both parties before it is signed and implemented. If agreements cannot be reached, IDEA provides processes for coming to agreements. Referred to as due process, these procedures protect the rights of all parties, including the child, the parents, and the school. To ensure that due process is offered to parents and students, the following guidelines must be followed.

1. *Written permission.* A written notice must be sent to parents stating that their child has been referred for assessment (a referral may be made by either the parent or school personnel). The notice explains that the district requests permission to conduct an evaluation to determine if special education services are required for the child. Also included in the permission letter must be reasons for testing and the tests to be used. Before assessment can begin, the letter must be signed by the parents and returned to the district.

2. *Interpretation of the assessment.* Results of the assessment must be interpreted in a meeting that includes the parents. Persons knowledgeable of test procedures need to be present to answer questions that parents ask. At the meeting, parents are told whether their child has any disabilities and what services will be provided.

3. *External evaluation.* If parents are not satisfied with the results of the assessment, an evaluation outside school can be requested. The district must provide a list of agencies that can perform such assessments. If the results differ from the school district evaluation, the district must pay for the external evaluation. If the results are similar, parents have to pay for the external testing.

4. *Negotiation and hearings.* If parents and the school district disagree on the results of the assessment, the district is required to negotiate the differences. When negotiations fail, an impartial hearing officer listens to both parties and renders an official decision. This review is usually final, but both parties do have the right to appeal to the state department of education, which renders a binding and final decision. Civil action through the legal system can be pursued should the district or parents still disagree. Few cases, however, ever reach this level of long-term disagreement, and educators should not hesitate to serve the needs of students with disabilities based on this concern.

5. *Confidentiality.* As is the case with other student records, only parents of the child or authorized school personnel can review the student's evaluation. Review by other parties can be done only after the student's parents have given written permission.

Successful Inclusion

Regardless of the LRE or the location of education placement on the inclusion continuum, the role of the physical education teacher is to provide every student with a physical education experience that assists the child in meeting the annual goals spelled out in the IEP. To do this, the physical educator must be skilled in instructional strategies that ensure successful physical education for all students. The attitude that the physical educator uses to approach physical education for students with special needs is also important. As stated earlier, all quality physical education is adapted physical education because quality physical educators are constantly adapting lessons, equipment, and activities to meet the needs of all students, with or without disabilities.

One approach to adapted physical education that follows this philosophy is universal design for learning (Rose & Meyer, 2002). Adopted from the field of architectural design, in education "universal design" means that the entire learning environment (e.g., the physical education program) is created to support and meet the needs of diverse learners, including students with and without disabilities. Rather than rigidity, this approach is characterized by flexibility and modification. This approach designs the learning environment such that teaching strategies, instructional practices, equipment, and student participation are fluid and flexible, with alternatives to each woven throughout the curriculum. The goal of this approach is to meet the needs of all students continuously and simultaneously.

Use Appropriate Instructional Methods

The success of the student largely depends on the physical education teacher's choice of appropriate instructional methods. Developmentally appropriate activities in the appropriate LRE are unlikely to be a successful and enjoyable experience for the student if they are implemented with inappropriate instructional methods. The following are examples of instructional methods to use when working with students with special needs. These suggestions are general in nature but can apply to a variety of activities and can be used when working with students with a variety of disabilities. Figure 9.3 also provides a model for ensuring all students receive successful experiences.

- Provide immediate, appropriate feedback based on performance.
- Modify equipment use to increase the students' chances for success; examples include beeper balls, Velcro baseball gloves, and lighter, softer balls.
- If possible, ask the students for their input regarding any modifications.
- Provide the students with options, if feasible. For example, ask the students if they would rather use a beach ball or a balloon to practice volleying.
- Modify rules to ensure success and maximize repetition. Allowing multiple bounces during a tennis lesson increases the number of repetitions that a child will receive.
- Create a welcoming environment for success by making changes such as increasing lighting, decreasing noise or other potential distractions, or making the teaching area easily accessible.
- Model or provide physical assistance as necessary. Be sure to ask the student if physical assistance is OK when appropriate.
- When making modifications, always consider the safety of the modification and the fidelity of the activity.
- Make modifications as needed if a child is not experiencing success with an activity.
- Encourage social interactions between everyone in the physical education lesson. This can be accomplished with group or partner work, discussion, or stations.
- Include modifications in the lesson-planning process and not as an afterthought during the lesson.

9

 TECH TIP

Teachers can use technology to create learning materials such as teaching signs. Instructional signs can be made with easily accessible software such as PowerPoint, designed to produce visual products. For stations, unless a school has enough iPads, the signs can be printed, laminated, and placed on a cone. Signs with pictures are particularly helpful for students who are not able to read or have reading delays because pictures with words are useful to assist with word association.

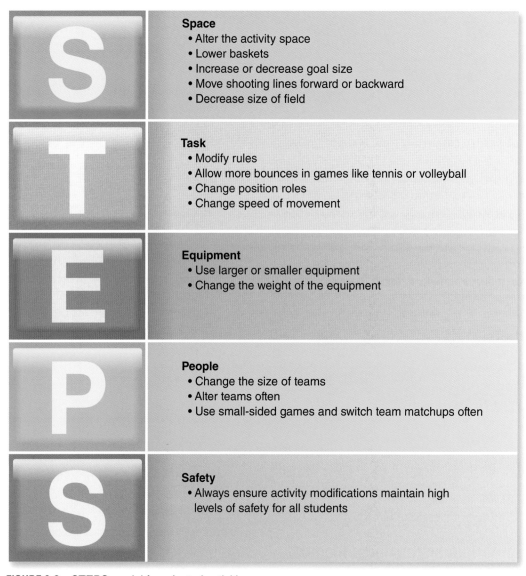

Space
- Alter the activity space
- Lower baskets
- Increase or decrease goal size
- Move shooting lines forward or backward
- Decrease size of field

Task
- Modify rules
- Allow more bounces in games like tennis or volleyball
- Change position roles
- Change speed of movement

Equipment
- Use larger or smaller equipment
- Change the weight of the equipment

People
- Change the size of teams
- Alter teams often
- Use small-sided games and switch team matchups often

Safety
- Always ensure activity modifications maintain high levels of safety for all students

FIGURE 9.3 STEPS model for adapted activities.

Determine Appropriate Content to Teach

Although determining how to teach is important, considering what to teach is important as well. When examining the curriculum and the appropriate content for each student, the special needs of the student must be considered. Depending on the extent of these needs, curricular modifications can range from no changes in the curriculum, to slight modification, which is what quality physical educators do on a daily basis, to using an entirely different curriculum. All curricular modifications will depend on the overall goal of the program. At the elementary level, a focus on teaching students a variety of skills that can be applied to other activities as they age is typically advocated. These skills are then used as the student transitions to postsecondary physical activities. When making curricular content decisions, the goal should always be to find appropriate activities that can be modified to meet the needs of all students. The teacher's intent and responsibility should be to individualize activities as much as possible, so that children with disabilities are smoothly integrated into lessons engaging in appropriate activities.

Reflection Check

As decisions about instructional methods and curriculum content are made, teachers need to pause and reflect on these decisions. Lesson modification will affect the students with special needs, students without disabilities, and the teacher. In addition, the impact of the modifications on the integrity of the curriculum and entire physical education environment must be evaluated. When thinking about ways to accommodate all students, take some time to reflect on the total experience.

Table 9.1 and figure 9.4 highlight physical education considerations for a variety of special needs that can be referred to during the reflection process. The table is divided by special needs and lists characteristics of students with each special need. Finally, physical education considerations based on the characteristics of students with each special need are provided. The range of abilities of students with these special needs is great, making the inclusion of every characteristic and every consideration for physical education unfeasible for this table. Although this table is not exhaustive, it provides an overview of a variety of special needs and is intended to be a starting point for physical education teachers when deciding what to teach and how to teach students with special needs.

As you formulate modifications, consider the following questions:

1. Do the changes allow the student with special needs to participate successfully yet still be challenged?

2. Does the modification make the setting unsafe for the student with special needs as well as for those students without disabilities?

3. Does the change negatively affect the quality of the educational experience for any student? Is learning seriously hampered because of the change that was made?

4. Does the change cause an undue burden on the teacher? This point is important; many teachers come to resent students with special needs because they believe that the burden is too great. Certainly, change needs to be made, but it has to be reasonable for all parties.

Activities need to be modified because all students have special needs. In fact, when teachers seldom or never modify activities, they probably are not meeting the needs

TABLE 9.1 Considerations for Students With Special Needs

Special need	Characteristics	PE considerations
Autism spectrum (pervasive developmental disorders)	• Impaired social interaction and communication • Delays or dysfunction in language use (autism only) • Stereotypic and repetitive behavior patterns • Difficulty processing sensory information • Short attention span	• Understand the specific disorder within the autism spectrum. • Provide a structured routine. • Use picture and communication boards. • Use parallel talk (e.g., As Tyler throws the ball, the teacher says, "Tyler is throwing the yarn ball."). • Inform the students of transitions ahead of time. • Use demonstration and physical assistance when appropriate. • Isolate one task at a time. • Be cautious of group activities. • Minimize or eliminate wait time. • Develop appropriate behavior reinforcement and use consistently. • Use short instructional bouts. • Speak softly and avoid loud noises. • Use activity stations with pictorial instructions.
Behavioral or emotional disabilities	• Odd or improbable ideas expressed • Temper tantrums or other disruptive behaviors to garner attention • Attention issues such as short attention span, blurting out responses, and inattentiveness • Inappropriate behavior or feeling given a specific context • General feeling of unhappiness • Ongoing, extreme behavior • Inability to relax, restless	• Provide structure and establish routines. • Create a positive, student-friendly physical education environment. • Identify triggers for each student. • Provide contexts for learning social skills. • Create leadership opportunities for students when feasible. • Provide lots of praise and positive reinforcement to the students. • Catch the student doing something positive. • Work with the student on conflict resolution. • Use behavior contracts when appropriate. • Avoid showing negative emotion when dealing with inappropriate behavior. • Allow students to make choices among given activities. • Encourage appropriate verbal expression when frustrated.

(continued)

TABLE 9.1 *(continued)*

Special need	Characteristics	PE considerations
Brain injury (cerebral palsy, traumatic brain injury, and stroke)	• Increased muscle tone or spasticity, possibly leading to permanent contractions and bone deformity • Slow, writhing movements such as facial grimacing and difficulty controlling the head • Classified from I to VIII, with class I being the most involved and class VIII the least • Lack of coordination • Difficulty coordinating movement patterns • Various sensory impairments such as vision • Spasticity • Headaches • Cognitive deficiencies • Seizures • Communication issues • Motor impairment	• Focus on strengthening extensor muscles for spasticity. • Modify activities involving speed or quick movements. • Consider teaching students who fall regularly a safe way to fall. • Assist students with planning movements and allow time to plan. • Minimize loud noises and speak quietly. • Allow rest time because students may fatigue easily. • Incorporate strategies for relaxation into lessons. • Use peer teaching when appropriate. • Allow students to stabilize using an apparatus when performing motor skills. • Use soft equipment to minimize injury. • Provide accommodation for activities involving balance. • Teach body awareness (e.g., "Which foot are you using?"). • Use simple directions. • Minimize distractions by creating routines. • Do not assume that the student has an intellectual delay.
Deaf, hard of hearing, and deaf-blind	• Degree of hearing loss classified by hearing threshold in decibels • Profound hearing loss (deaf) • Hearing loss that makes understanding speech difficult (hard of hearing) • Motor skills of deaf children equal to those of their peers given equal opportunity • Distorted visual and auditory input	• Use visual cues. • Speak normally and avoid yelling. • Use paper and pencil to assist with conversation if needed. • Avoid interruptions to the conversation. • Maintain eye contact. • Use hand-over-hand demonstration for students who are deaf-blind. • Allow students who are deaf-blind to touch equipment. • Learn basic sign language applicable to physical education (see figure 9.4 for samples). • Use a peer tutor to promote social inclusion of students in the class who are deaf. • If applicable, work with an interpreter to enhance the student's experience. • Minimize background noise. • Ensure that the student can see you and your facial expressions. • Include students in class discussion.
Health-impaired conditions (asthma, diabetes mellitus, epilepsy, heart condition, and so on)	• Low blood sugar possibly an issue during activity • Relatively frequent occurrence of seizures (epilepsy) • Breathing issues triggered by external allergens or internal factors	• Refer to the student's health management plan or IEP. • Monitor nutrition intake before PE and physical activity level during PE. • Be aware that for some students physical activity positively affects seizures whereas for others it can trigger seizures in high humidity. • Know symptoms of asthma and treatment of each student. • Consult parents, physicians, and school medical staff to determine appropriate PE activities.
Intellectual disabilities	• Classified from mild mental retardation to profound mental retardation • Wide variety of skills, abilities, and potential • Varied learning rates, which may be slower than peers • Inappropriate social and emotional responses at times • Greater motor delays	• Use peer tutoring. • Move from familiar activities to unfamiliar activities. • Progress slowly with instruction and motor skills. • Allow the student time to process instructions before beginning an activity. • Allow slow transitions between activities. • Develop routines and structure and use consistently. • Teach developmentally appropriate activities rather than age-appropriate activities. • Limit words and use just cues when feasible.

Special need	Characteristics	PE considerations
Les autres (amputations, dwarfism, arthritis, muscular dystrophy, multiple sclerosis)	• Congenital or acquired loss of limb or portion of a limb • Being shorter than 98% of other children that age • Inflammation of joints	• Maintain a positive environment for all students. • Avoid jarring activities. • Ensure successful experiences in all activities. • Integrate strength and endurance activities (including aquatic activities) frequently to combat muscle atrophy. • Use regular stretching and activities that foster flexibility. • Be cautious of twisting activities. • Use balance and agility activities to assist with gait issues.
Specific learning disabilities (learning disabilities, attention deficit/hyperactive disorder, developmental coordination disorder)	• Problems processing, storing, and producing information, which results in issues understanding written or spoken words • Learning difficulties in a specific area such as reading or math • Usually not easy to identify by outward physical signs	• Ensure a safe physical and psychological environment. • Choose instructional practices that support behavior management. • Provide class structure so that the child knows what to expect. • Avoid complex instructions and use only one skill cue at a time. • Use supportive positive feedback. • Provide adequate processing time after instruction. • Be aware of potential behavioral issues that may be a product of learning challenges. • Use peer tutoring when appropriate. • Allow students to learn through movement as much as possible. • Include relaxation activities such as yoga and stretching. • Use thoughtful, smooth, and efficient transitions to minimize down time.
Spinal cord disabilities (quadriplegia, paraplegia, polio, spina bifida, scoliosis)	• Classification of spinal cord injuries by location of the injury on the spinal column • Quadriplegia (or tetraplegia)—a spinal injury that affects all four limbs • Paraplegia—a spinal cord injury that affects the lower limbs • A form of paralysis caused by a viral infection that affects the spinal cord • Loss of motor function	• Emphasize developing appropriate motor skills. • Use stretching to assist with spasticity or increase in muscle tone. • Consider the social needs of students. • Maintain an inclusive PE environment as much as possible because these students have similar interests as peers. • Avoid tumbling rolls and contact if the child has a shunt.
Visual impairments	• Impairment to vision that affects the educational experience • Ranges from visual impairment to total blindness • Fearfulness and apprehension • Fewer social networks • Delays in motor skills • Holding the head in special positions to improve vision • Posture problems	• Incorporate socialization during PE. • Use peer tutoring. • Ask the student what will work or what he or she needs to succeed. • Maximize the use of the tactile sense, such as touching the foot when teaching how to kick. • Allow the child to touch equipment. • Describe the setting and allow the child to walk through the area and around the boundaries. • Allow the student to take your arm when guiding him or her. • Use brightly colored equipment and beeper balls. • Keep the teaching area free of clutter. • Ensure that appropriate support services are present. • Support the student in becoming independent in a safe manner.

9

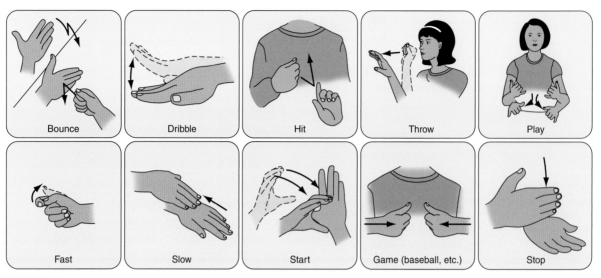

FIGURE 9.4 Learning basic physical education signs is helpful if working with a student who is deaf or hard of hearing.

of many students. Effective teachers always examine an activity and know that they are responsible for making the environment better for all students. Doing the most good for the most students is a good concept to follow.

Optimize Support and Services

The delineation of requisite services is included in the IEP process. Because physical education is a required component of the IEP, the physical education teacher must be aware of the services, materials, and assistance that the student needs. Thus, consultation and communication between the physical education teacher and the special education supervisor are of prime importance. The reception and acceptance of students cannot be left to chance. A scheduled plan of inclusion of the student is necessary. In addition, the entire implementation of the IEP, as it relates to physical education, must be carefully planned to optimize all available resources to provide the best possible experience for the student.

A key component of the services available to many students, and possibly the service that physical educators

will have the most exposure to, is access to a paraeducator (also referred to as support personnel or a teacher's aide) during physical education. The physical educator must develop a sound working relationship with the paraeducator to get the most from this service. The physical educator can consult with the paraeducator to learn more about the student's experiences outside physical education and must communicate the objectives of each physical education experience. This type of give-and-take relationship will allow physical education teachers to feel comfortable in telling the support personnel what kind of help they need and not feel as though they are burdening the support personnel. At times, the physical education teacher may need to be direct and tell the support person exactly what to do to assist the child. The support person and the physical education teacher must work together to provide assistance that is best for the child. If the physical educator thinks that students with special needs were dropped into his or her class before being asked what kind of help was required to integrate them properly, he or she will have negative feelings about those students.

In certain situations, the physical education teacher may feel as though the paraeducator is not providing the best services for the child. If this is the case, the teacher should consult with the paraeducator and express these concerns. If this conversation does not remedy the issues, the special education supervisor or principal should be notified. Although these discussions may not always be comfortable, the focus should always be on providing the student with the best experience possible.

Peer tutoring is also a common support service that can be provided in physical education. Peer tutor-

TEACHING TIP

Student abilities can change throughout the school year. You may need to modify your lesson plans to ensure that the physical education environment is still safe and appropriate for students with disabilities as the year progresses.

ing involves the peer receiving formal training. This approach has been found to be effective in helping students with special needs develop socially and improve skill (Copeland et al., 2002; D'Arripe-Longueville, Gernigon, Huet, Cadopi, & Winnykamen, 2002). Peer tutoring is not simply matching a child with special needs with a peer to help during a lesson. A peer-tutoring program should be created with formal training in a variety of types of peer-tutoring approaches.

Teach Tolerance to All Students

All students must learn and respond to issues related to being disabled. Students without disabilities must learn to understand, accept, and live comfortably with persons with disabilities. They should recognize that students with disabilities are functional and worthwhile people who have innate abilities and can make significant contributions to society. The concept of understanding and appreciating individual differences merits positive development and should concentrate on three aspects:

1. Recognize the similarities among all people—their hopes, rights, aspirations, and goals.

2. Understand human differences and focus on the concept that all people are disabled in various ways. Some people's disabilities are severe enough to interfere with normal living.

3. Explore ways to deal with those who differ without over helping them and stress the acceptance of all students as worthwhile people. While it's important to seek understanding of an individual with disabilities' needs, it's equally important to avoid a patronizing attitude and to affirm the individual's abilities and self-efficacy.

Integrate Students With Special Needs Into the Class Setting

Careful thought should be given to the process of including the child with special needs into the educational setting. When correctly implemented, inclusion allows the student to make educational progress, achieve in those areas outlined in the IEP, learn to accept limitations, observe and model appropriate behavior, and become socially accepted by others. The following are guidelines for successfully integrating students with disabilities into physical education:

1. Help students with disabilities meet target goals specified in the IEP and participate in the regular program of activities. This task may call for resources beyond the physical education class, including special work and homework.

2. Stress what the child is capable of doing and focus on accomplishments. Eliminate established practices that unwittingly contribute to embarrassment and failure.

3. Foster peer acceptance by treating each student as a functioning, participating member of the class.

4. Concentrate on the student's physical education needs and not on the disability. Stress fundamental skills and physical fitness qualities.

9

Peers with and without disabilities should work together.

WORKING WITH STUDENTS WHO ARE OVERWEIGHT OR OBESE

All students, regardless of gender, race, age, place of residence, or ability, have special needs. A physical education teacher must respond to each child's needs on an individual basis. Obesity is an epidemic in the United States, where 16 to 33% of children aged 6 to 12 are considered overweight or obese. These students may need additional monitoring or encouragement. Moreover, these students tend to feel helpless in terms of being active and feeling successful in physical education and other physical activity settings. The school may need to provide one-on-one training for students who are classified as overweight or obese. This personalized tutoring may need one of the roles of the physical education teacher beyond that of teaching motor skills and physical activity. This tutor would use his or her break time or other allotted time during the school day to work one-on-one or in small groups with any students identified as overweight or obese.

The first step is to find out what physical activities the students like to do. Although running a boot camp can result in short-term weight loss, this approach is generally ineffective in the long run because the activities that led to weight loss may not have been enjoyable to the students. Therefore, they are unlikely to continue performing those activities unless the physical educator is present to motivate. The goal of working with these youngsters is for them to be able to make independent decisions that will positively affect their health. Depending on what equipment and facilities are available, the physical educator can give the students choices of activities and work with them to participate in those activities during their individual or small-group time.

The physical educator can also work with the students to set goals for engaging in physical activity at home and in the neighborhood. Involving parents, other family members, and friends may help increase the amount of physical activity that these students accumulate. If people who surround the students are engaging in activities that require them to expend effort, the student who is overweight is more likely to take part in those activities as well.

Nutrition can also be addressed. Helping these students (and their parents) make healthy choices during mealtimes and snack times can help with weight management. Ultimately, engaging in appropriate physical activities and practicing healthy eating strategies can improve these students' physical, emotional, and social well-being.

5. Provide continual monitoring and periodically assess the student's target goals. Anecdotal and periodic record keeping are implicit in this guideline.

6. Be constantly aware of students' feelings and anxieties concerning their progress and integration through consistent communication. Provide positive feedback as a basic practice.

Recruiting Paraeducators and Volunteers

The use of paraeducators and volunteers can be an effective way to increase the amount of instruction and practice that students receive. Lieberman (2007) identifies ways to work with paraeducators and volunteers in the physical education arena. Volunteers are often available from various community organizations, such as parent–teacher associations, foster grandparents, and local colleges. High school students who volunteer have proved effective with elementary school students.

An initial meeting with volunteers should explain the type of special needs that their students will have and clarify their responsibilities. Volunteers must learn how to be most effective in assisting the instructor. Training should cover working effectively with different individuals, recording data, and developing special materials and instructional supplies. In addition, the potential volunteers should receive a trial experience with young people to see if they are capable and enjoy such work. Look for advice about how to work with volunteers. Oftentimes, physical educators find the task of organizing and supervising aides time consuming if they have not learned to supervise and organize.

Volunteers and paraeducators can assume roles that increase the effectiveness of the instructional situation. For example, they may gather and locate equipment and supplies before the lesson. They may officiate games and ensure that they run smoothly. Seasoned volunteers enjoy and are capable of offering one-on-one or small-group instruction to students. Using paraprofessionals and volunteers should not be viewed as a replacing the physical educator. Paraprofessionals and volunteers should only implement instruction strategies that have been organized and developed by the professional educator. In addition, the physical educator is responsible for assuring that presentations made by the paraprofessionals are of high quality.

Continue to Learn

Quality educators continue to learn about best practices, instructional modifications, and strategies for maximizing the effectiveness of their teaching. Continuing to educate yourself is a vital component of working with students with special needs. Numerous national, state, and local organizations can assist with this process. These organizations include the Society for Health and Physical Education (SHAPE America), the International Federation for Adapted Physical Activity (IFAPA), the National Consortium for Physical Education and Recreation for Individuals With Disabilities (NCPERID), and the North American Federation of Adapted Physical Activity (NAFAPA). These organizations offer useful, current documents, including journals, such as the *Journal of Physical Education, Recreation, and Dance* (*JOPERD*) and *Adapted Physical Activity Quarterly* (*APAQ*), to assist physical educators. In addition, countless quality textbooks that expand on many of the ideas and concepts presented here are available. See the references and suggested readings section at the end of the chapter.

If you wonder why inclusion is an important practice in schools, think about this. Suppose that you had a child or a brother or sister who had a disability. You would care about your sibling or child regardless of whether he or she had some type of disability. Suppose that you were told that your brother could never do the things that other children do because of his disability that he could never be placed in a regular school and would have to be isolated with others who had the same disability. Certainly, you understand that the disability would place limits on your brother, but wouldn't you want him to be around other students in a regular school setting? Inclusion offers students with disabilities a chance for socialization and the opportunity to learn how to cope in society. Many people with disabilities have accomplished a great deal. We all want the best for all students. Although inclusion seems to make your job harder at times, don't forget that your helping someone who didn't have the same opportunities you had may be your shining moment. Taking care of others less fortunate is the mark of a great teacher and a great society.

LEARNING AIDS

HOW AND WHY

1. How do you feel about teaching students with disabilities?
2. Why is it important for children with disabilities to participate in physical education?
3. Do all children have disabilities? Explain your answer.
4. How can teachers generate parental and social support for children with disabilities?

CONTENT REVIEW

1. Identify the implications of PL 94-142 and IDEA for physical education teachers.
2. Discuss the screening and assessment procedures for evaluating students.
3. Describe how individualized education programs are developed. Include comments on who is involved and what the IEP contains.
4. Discuss guidelines for successful inclusion.
5. Identify methods of modifying activities for inclusion.
6. Identify several special needs and discuss considerations for modifying activities to accommodate students with these needs.

WEBSITES

Adapted physical education, https://js.sagamorepub.com/palaestra
Adapted P.E. assessment tools, www.pecentral.org/adapted/adaptedinstruments.html

Children's Disabilities Information, www.childrensdisabilities.info
Legal issues, www.ed.gov/offices/OSERS/Policy/IDEA/the_law.html
National standards, http://apens.org

SUGGESTED READINGS

Auxter, D., Pyfer, J., & Huettig, C. (2005). *Principles and methods of adapted physical education and recreation* (10th ed.). Boston, MA: McGraw-Hill.

Bruininks, Robert H., & Bruininks, Brett D. (2005). *Bruininks-Oseretsky Test of Motor Development Proficiency* (2nd ed.). Circle Pines, MN: American Guidance Services.

Folio, M. Rhonda, & Fewell, Rebecca R. (2000). *Peabody Developmental Motor Scales* (2nd ed.). Austin, TX: PRO-ED.

Dunn, J.M., & Leitschuh, C.A. (2006). *Special physical education* (8th ed.). Dubuque, IA: Kendall Hunt.

Horvat, M., Kalakian, L.H., Croce, R., & Dahlstrom, V.H. (2011). *Developmental/adapted physical education: Making ability count* (5th ed.). San Francisco, CA: Benjamin Cummings.

National Consortium for Physical Education for Individuals with Disabilities & Kelly, L. (ed.). (2020). *Adapted Physical Education National Standards* (3rd ed.). Champaign, IL: Human Kinetics.

Ulrich, Dale A. (2000). *The test of gross motor development.* Austin, TX: PRO-ED.

Winnick, Joseph P., & Short, Francis X. (2014). *The Brockport Physical Fitness Test manual: A health-related test for youths with physical and mental disabilities* (2nd ed.). Champaign, IL: Human Kinetics.

REFERENCES

Cooper Institute (ed.) (2017). *FitnessGram/ActivityGram test administration manual.* Champaign, IL: Human Kinetics.

Copeland, S.R., McCall, J., Williams, C.R., Guth, C., Carter, E.W., & Fowler., S.E. (2002). High school peer buddies: A win-win situation. *The Council for Exceptional Children,* September/October, 16–21.

D'Arripe-Longueville, F., Gernigon, C., Marie-Laure Huet, M-L, Cadopi, M., & Winnykamen, F. (2002). Peer tutoring in a physical education setting: Influence of tutor skill level on novice learners' motivation and performance. *Journal of Teaching in Physical Education, 22*(1), 105–123.

Education for All Handicapped Children Act of 1975, Pub. L. No. 94-142.

Jackson, C.W., & Larkin, M.J. (2002). Teaching students to use grading rubrics. *Teaching Exceptional Children, 35,* 40–44.

Lieberman, L., (2007). Para-educators in Physical Education: At training guide to roles and responsibilities. Champaign, IL: Human Kinetics.

Lieberman, L., & Houston-Wilson, C. (2018). *Strategies for inclusion: Physical education for everyone* (3rd ed.). Champaign, IL: Human Kinetics.

Office of Special Education and Rehabilitation Services. (2007). 34 CFR 300.

Rehabilitation Act of 1973, Pub. L. No. 93-112 (Section 504).

Rose, D.H., & Meyer, A. (2002). *Teaching every student in the digital age: Universal design for learning.* Alexandria, VA: Association for Supervision and Curriculum Development.

Sherrill, C. (2004). *Adapted physical activity, recreation and sport* (6th ed.). Boston, MA: WCB/McGraw-Hill.

Winnick, J.P., & Porretta, D.L. (2017). *Adapted physical education and sport* (6th ed.). Champaign, IL: Human Kinetics.

Winnick, Joseph P., & Short, Francis X. (2014). *The Brockport Physical Fitness Test manual: A health-related test for youths with physical and mental disabilities* (2nd ed.). Champaign, IL: Human Kinetics.

Integrating Health Concepts

10

More and more physical educators are being asked to integrate health content into physical education lessons, which can be challenging for a couple of reasons. One, many physical educators are not trained to teach health education. Two, physical education time is already limited, making it difficult to teach all the necessary physical education content. Now health content is added to the mix. This chapter discusses integration of health concepts into physical education. In addition, strategies and activities for teaching health skills and concepts during quality physical education lessons will be provided.

Learning Objectives

▶ Define *integrating health concepts* and explain its importance.

▶ Understand the role of integrating health concepts in physical education.

▶ Explain the benefits and limitations of integrating health concepts in physical education.

▶ Present models for integrating health concepts and discuss how they can be used.

▶ Describe several activities that integrate either personal health, nutrition, mental and emotional health, or sun safety into a quality physical education lesson.

To cut to the chase, health education is an essential part of the education experience for youth. Note that ideally, health education would be its own subject matter within the elementary school curriculum and all students would receive standards-driven, cutting-edge, skills-based health education early in their education experience. The goal here is to provide physical educators with strategies and activities designed to supplement the health education content taught in the classroom. These activities are not intended to stand alone as a student's health education experience while in elementary schools. In some instances, however, this may be the only time students have the opportunity to be exposed to any health education content, so physical educators need to integrate this content as feasible.

What Is Integration?

Students often learn concepts that combine two seemingly unrelated academic areas. Reading about the habitats of animals, for example, combines reading (language arts) and biology (science). Calculating the distance from their town to the state capital uses concepts from both math and social studies. Instruction designed to integrate two or more concepts from different areas to enhance learning is referred to as *integration*. Other terms to describe this process are *interdisciplinary*, *multidisciplinary*, and *cross-disciplinary*. Although each term has a specific definition, for the purpose of this chapter and book, the term *integration* is used throughout.

Many health skills and concepts are easily connected to physical education content. Although health concepts can be integrated into a quality physical education curriculum, physical education instruction should not be centered on health integration. Health integration should be secondary to the five SHAPE America standards. Physical education is the only area in the school where children are taught how to care for their bodies,

so integrating health concepts makes sense but not at the expense of physical activity and physical education objectives.

Physical education offers an outstanding setting for the integration of health concepts. When done effectively, integration has only a minimal impact on the integrity of the physical education curriculum. For instance, as discussed in earlier chapters, we recommend a four-part lesson in which every lesson ends with a closing activity or game. Typically, this activity is related to the lesson focus of the day. But it doesn't always align with lessons such as gymnastics and jump rope. Often the game after those lesson foci is unrelated to the focus. During these lessons, games that teach a health concept or skill could easily be used. In addition, tag games are used as introductory activities at the beginning of the lessons. As you will see, these games can easily be modified to teach family and social health concepts or personal health concepts. All these examples are simple adjustments to common instructions that physical education teachers use.

When integrating health concepts, activities that ensure that physical education outcomes are reached should be planned first, and then the health concepts that can be integrated into the physical activities can be determined. Suppose, instead, that a teacher decides first to integrate a health concept and then chooses relays to do so. In this activity, teams of five to six students, one student at a time, use a specific locomotor movement to move the length of the gym, retrieve a fact card, and bring it back to the team. After all team members finish, the class uses the facts from the fact cards to determine the disease. In this example, only 20% of the class is engaged in activity at any given time, and during relays the emphasis is often on speed rather than appropriate locomotor movement, making the physical education outcome seem minimal. Thus, this activity sacrifices physical education outcomes for health integration. When integrating health content into the physical

 TEACHING TIP

Don't say it once! Say it over and over! Physical educators often feel marginalized because their subject matter isn't appreciated. Appreciating an area outside academics is difficult for those who don't know much about it. You are responsible for telling teachers and administrators all the benefits they receive by having a quality physical education program. Although you may be reluctant to "blow your own horn," how else will others learn about your program? Tell your staff on a regular basis about the benefits of quality physical education. Public relations is everything!

education curriculum, maintain the integrity of the physical education program. In addition, integration should occur *after* establishing a solid, well-planned, quality physical education program.

Physical education makes unique contributions to the total school curriculum: motor skill development, understanding and maintaining physical fitness, and learning how to live an active lifestyle. Considering that these outcomes for the physical well-being of youth cannot be developed elsewhere in the school curriculum, physical educators should work hard to sell their program on these merits. Physical educators can justify inclusion of their program based on its unique contributions. The public has shown support for a physical education program if it aids, nurtures, and shows concern for the physical development of all students.

Why Integrate Health Concepts?

In an era of accountability that places great pressure on classroom teachers to increase academic achievement by improving high-stakes test scores, physical educators can support classroom teachers by offering to supplement the classroom content related to health educations. This proposal shows classroom teachers that physical educators are team players concerned with student learning. Integrating also motivates classroom teachers to observe or visit the physical education setting to see how concepts are being integrated. Lastly, if physical educators are integrating health content and showing an interest in the classroom, classroom teachers may be inclined to integrate physical activity into their classroom instruction. If this situation arises, the physical educator should assist classroom teachers with ideas and strategies for teaching physically active students (Pangrazi, Beighle, & Pangrazi, 2009). Specifically, classroom teachers may need assistance with management strategies and equipment.

Integration in physical education has benefits and limitations. The benefits include building goodwill in the school, helping students who are kinesthetic learners, teaching content in a new setting through a different method, demonstrating that physical educators are educators too, and increasing students' activity level when classroom teachers integrate physical activity into their instruction. The limitations most often cited are finding time to develop the lessons, planning for integration that does not sacrifice the physical education lesson, and feeling uncomfortable teaching outside an area of expertise. These concerns are legitimate, but with some practice and the belief that integration can supplement classroom learning, physical education teachers can create effective integration activities.

Types of Integration

Several models are available to guide the planning of health integration. Models range from the physical education teacher working alone to a group of teachers working together to develop learning experiences in various settings. The individual model involves the physical education teacher working to develop ideas for integrating health content. For example, the teacher might integrate concepts related to stress during the game part of a four-part lesson. This idea requires reviewing information about stress and determining how best to integrate that content in a game. Again, the stress-related game must contribute to the physical education lesson outcomes.

Another model is the partner model. In this model, the physical education teacher collaborates with a classroom teacher or other special-area teacher. This collaboration can be as simple as the physical education teacher and classroom teacher working on vocabulary words for the week that relate to a health concept. A more complex use of this model would be two teachers developing a yearly

10

TECH TIP

Social media is an excellent way to use technology to connect with other teachers and learn from each other. Professional learning communities (PLC) are typically thought of as a group that meets face to face, but social media opens the doors to meetings of teachers from around the world. These virtual PLCs allow teachers to share teaching strategies, curriculum ideas, and other programmatic ideas. This collaboration is accomplished through posts, instant messaging, and video calling as well. The beauty of social media is that when a teacher is struggling with an issue, needs an activity idea, or simply wants to connect with others in similar situations, a PLC is at their fingertips.

calendar that teaches similar concepts during the same time. For example, a physical education dance lesson that includes a dance to a song that reinforces nutrition concepts could be taught during the same week that the students work on making healthy choices in the classroom. For the physical education lesson, the teacher could use key terms during instruction and reinforce that nutrition choices can be healthy choices. Such changes do not compromise the physical education curriculum because the rhythm and dance are a part of a well-balanced, quality curriculum; instead, they enrich the educational experience and reinforce health concepts learned in other areas.

The group collaboration model usually involves a group of classroom teachers from a common grade level and the physical educator. This model involves a fair amount of planning that usually centers on a health theme. Teachers take the theme and generate learning activities that cut across health areas. For example, during a set period, the student activities can be related to a hygiene theme. Classroom teachers and the physical education teacher worked together to determine the key concepts and skills to cover. Examples might include bathing, brushing teeth, and combing hair. The teachers then develop classroom learning experiences tied to these concepts and skills, and the physical education teacher creates games and activities that reinforce this concept.

TEACHING TIP

Many of the integration ideas here seem complex at first glance. But if a number of teachers are involved in the project, the ideas can be implemented without excessive effort. On another note, sometimes just a few small things done by the physical educator to help support classroom teachers will make a huge difference in how physical education is perceived. Reach out whenever possible.

How to Integrate Health Content

As stated earlier, integrating health content must be carefully and thoughtfully planned to ensure that the activity is a quality learning experience and that it maintains the integrity of the physical education curriculum. The following topics are a series of steps for initiating integration in physical education, identifying what to

integrate, and learning how to enhance the effectiveness of the integration activities. These suggestions are most suited if the classroom teachers are teaching health education in the classroom as well.

Step 1: Decide on the Integration Model

The individual model requires a fair amount of research to determine what lessons to teach, at what level it should be taught, and how to teach it. The partner model requires you to choose a potential teacher to partner with. The key is to find a fellow teacher who is equally interested in what is being taught in physical education. Ideally, the classroom teacher is also interested in strategies for teaching health concepts through physical activity in the classroom. Choosing the group model requires that you select teachers who are generally interested in all the activities, not just those they are teaching.

Step 2: Ask Teachers What Concepts They Will Be Teaching

Take an interest in the concepts that classroom teachers are teaching. Doing so shows that you are an interested, supportive teacher who wants to help students reach health outcomes. Classroom teachers can provide a calendar that lists the concepts being taught in the coming weeks. From this calendar, you can generate integration ideas. Classroom teachers may also have ideas about concepts that could be taught through physical education.

Step 3: Ask How Concepts Are Being Taught

After the health concepts to be integrated are established, find out how those concepts are being taught, if at all, in the classroom. Using key terms or similar ideas and slightly modifying them may be helpful when teaching the integrated material. Approach the classroom teacher to find out what concepts students are having trouble with in the classroom. Physical education may offer an excellent opportunity to teach the same concepts with a different strategy—namely, teaching the concepts with movement. If this is the case, discuss the idea with the classroom teacher. In some cases, teaching the same concept with two different methodologies or perspectives may confuse children rather than help them learn.

Step 4: Share What You Teach With Classroom Teachers

Invite the classroom teacher to a lesson involving integration. This offer serves two purposes. First, the classroom teacher can provide feedback concerning the integration activity that you might use to make the activity more effective. Inviting the classroom teacher also exposes the teacher to physical education. Often, classroom teachers have little knowledge of what is being taught during physical education. Having them observe a lesson will show them that physical education is educational and makes an important contribution to the school curriculum.

Step 5: Reflect

When reflecting on your instruction, review integration activities you taught as well. For example, did the integration activity sacrifice any of the activity planned for the physical education lesson? Could you have integrated the concept with less interference? Did the students understand the health content? How could you change the integrated activity to make it more effective? Would the integrated concept fit better in another part of the lesson or in another lesson?

Health Education

The remainder of this chapter provides learning experiences for children that can be integrated into physical education lessons without sacrificing time allocated for

physical education outcomes. Note again that what is presented here is not a health education curriculum but activities designed to supplement a health education curriculum. Just as physical education has national standards, health education has the national health education standards (Joint Committee on National Health Education Standards, 2007). These standards (figure 10.1) are written to guide curriculum development for skills-based health education. This approach seeks to provide students with life skills, such as decision making, goal setting, communication, and advocacy, that can be applied to a variety of health issues such as nutrition, sun safety, and hygiene. Note that physical education also provides students with the chance to learn decision making, goal setting, communication, and advocacy in a physical activity setting. For instance, as was seen in chapter 8, a simple "walkie-talkie" assessment at the end of a lesson can be used for students to share strategies for advocating for physical activity in the schools. Pedometers are a great tool for teaching students skills such as goal setting. Communication skills, and the fact that communicating is much more than talking, are learned and taught in many lessons, particularly lessons that emphasis cooperative skills in physical education. In this sense, many of our desired outcomes are similar to those of health education and allow effective integration across disciplines. With

10

NATIONAL HEALTH EDUCATION STANDARDS

Standard 1: Students will comprehend concepts related to health promotion and disease prevention to enhance health.

Standard 2: Students will analyze the influence of family, peers, culture, media, technology, and other factors on health behaviors.

Standard 3: Students will demonstrate the ability to access valid information, products, and services to enhance health.

Standard 4: Students will demonstrate the ability to use interpersonal communication skills to enhance health and avoid or reduce health risks.

Standard 5: Students will demonstrate the ability to use decision-making skills to enhance health.

Standard 6: Students will demonstrate the ability to use goal-setting skills to enhance health.

Standard 7: Students will demonstrate the ability to practice health-enhancing behaviors and avoid or reduce health risks.

Standard 8: Students will demonstrate the ability to advocate for personal, family, and community health

FIGURE 10.1 National Health Education Standards.

Reprinted with permission from the American Cancer Society, Inc. *National Health Education Standards: Achieving Excellence,* Second Edition. (Atlanta, GA: American Cancer Society, 2007), cancer.org/bookstore.

INTEGRATING CONTENT WITHOUT SACRIFICING PHYSICAL ACTIVITY TIME

Physical education is the only area in the school curriculum devoted to developing motor skills and fostering physical activity in students. Therefore, although integrating other content is feasible and often encouraged by administrators, physical educators need to remember that the physical education program and curriculum should be standards-based and focused on maximizing physical activity. That being said, physical education is a prime location for integrating health content for students because many of them are kinesthetic learners. A physical education teacher can make learning more effective for these students by incorporating movement with content.

One strategy for physical educators is to use specific content (e.g., nutrition) in lead-up games or various locomotor activities. Use efficient transitions during integration time and think of physical activity as the primary outcome when introducing these activities. Several examples of physically active games that deal with sun safety, relationships, and refusal skills are provided in the chapter. Although each of these games focuses on specific content, they are meant be taught in a way that also maximizes physical activity.

The physical educator is not the only teacher in the school who can and should effectively integrate content. Another strategy that a physical education teacher might use is to train classroom teachers how to integrate physical activity with the content they are teaching. This training should include effective ways for teachers to manage student behavior in the classroom while leading the students efficiently in physical activity. The same principles used during physical education should apply in the classroom (e.g., freezing students, grouping, short instructions, and efficient equipment distribution). The physical educator and classroom teacher have the opportunity to collaborate, thereby earning some respect for the physical educator and bringing greater awareness to the physical education program. Thus, when considering integrating traditional health content with physical education content, a teacher should first consider the needs and objectives of the physical education program. Integration should be a secondary goal after establishing effective physical education lessons focusing on physical education standards and maximizing skill practice and physical activity.

respect to health education integration in physical education, our goal is to provide further experiences and activities that reinforce student knowledge related to topics or skills associated with healthy living.

Instructional activities in this chapter are organized into the areas of nutrition, personal health, safety, sun safety, mental and emotional health, and family and social health. These broad areas cover the primary topics in most elementary school health education curricula. Note that within each of these areas are activities that provide health information or reinforce a health skill. For each integration activity that follows, these four components are listed: the health concept, the PE concept, the PE lesson part, and the equipment necessary to teach the concept. "Health concept" is the general concept (or skill) being taught or reinforced through the activity. "PE concept" states the general physical education concepts

being taught during the activity. "PE lesson part" shows where the integration activity can be taught during a four-part lesson. Finally, the "Equipment" needed to teach the activity is provided.

Health Activities

More elementary physical educators are being asked to teach health content. Fortunately, many health concepts can easily be integrated into the physical education curriculum and can be taught using physical education. Presented here are a few examples of games and activities that physical educators can use to integrate health content into their lessons. Pangrazi, Beighle, and Pangrazi (2009) offer many other activities related to nutrition, sun safety, and various other health concepts.

Family and Social Health

Who Helps Us?

Health concept: Occupations that serve our community

PE concept: Chasing and fleeing, strategy

PE lesson part: Game

Equipment: None

Two teams are formed and gather on opposite sides of the area. The teams form a huddle and choose an occupation that serves the community. (Teachers may need to discuss this before the activity and provide students with a list of such occupations.) Next, teams move to the middle of the area approximately 3 feet (1 m) from each other. One team at a time, students act out the duties of the chosen occupation. Members of the other team are chosen to guess the occupation. When the correct occupation is guessed, members of the guessing team attempt to tag members of the acting team before they can take three steps backward. Players who are tagged join the other team. Both teams act or guess, and new occupations are selected.

That's My Family

Health concept: Families all look different

PE concept: Walking, cooperating

PE lesson part: Closing activity

Equipment: List of interview questions

Students join partners using toe to toe. Each set of partners is given a list of interview questions. The questions relate to student families. Examples include the following:

- How many people live with you?
- Who are the people who live with you?
- What are their names?

Partners then walk around the teaching area answering questions and talking about members of their family and family traditions. Students do this with two or three different partners. At the end of the activity the teacher leads a discussion about families and how families come in different forms. Some people live with aunts, uncles, one parent, and so on, and that's what makes families unique and special.

Help a Friend

Health concept: Empathy

PE concept: Manipulative skills, locomotor skills

PE lesson part: Focus

Equipment: Yarn balls, foam-coated balls

This activity can be added to any lesson in which students are working with a partner. Each set of partners is given an index card with a disability written on it (e.g., visually impaired, hearing impaired, has the use of only one arm). One partner takes the role of the child with a disability, and the other student must teach the partner to perform a skill (throwing, kicking, skipping, and so on) Partners then switch roles. Finally, the teacher leads a discussion about empathy, patience, and helping others.

Mental and Emotional Health

Emotional Freeze and Go

Health concept: Emotion recognition

PE concept: Locomotor movements, spacing, following directions

PE lesson part: Introductory activity

Equipment: None

Students move around the classroom using a teacher-determined movement. On signal, students freeze. The signal for "Go" during this activity is an emotional expression made by the teacher. An example of a teacher's instruction would be, "When I have a happy look on my face, begin skipping around the classroom." The teacher then smiles or shows another emotion on his or her face. But the students should wait until they see a happy face before they move. The teacher can also choose to use emotional sounds such as crying or laughing as the stop signal.

Emotional Movement

Health concept: Emotion recognition and the way that emotions affect behavior

PE concept: Locomotor movements, spacing

PE lesson part: Introductory activity

Equipment: None

Students are instructed to move around the area as if they are angry, sad, happy, confused, or scared. This activity allows for a brief discussion about different emotions and reinforces that emotions such as anger and sadness are OK. But how we act when angry or happy is important.

Mystery Emotion

Health concept: Emotion recognition

PE concept: Animal movements, spacing

PE lesson part: Introductory activity

Equipment: Pictures representing different emotions

10

Without looking at the picture, the teacher holds it up for the class to see. Students are then instructed to use a locomotor movement and move around the room as if they are feeling the emotion in the picture. The teacher then attempts to guess the emotion. Teachers can also make signs that give a movement and an emotion such as "Happy Bear Crawl" or a picture of a frowning face and a crab.

Stress Tag

Health concept: Stress and stress relief

PE concept: Chasing and fleeing

PE lesson part: Closing activity, game, or introductory activity

Equipment: Stress balls or beanbags

Three to four students are selected as taggers, or "stressors." The teacher may ask, "What's a stressor?" When tagged by a stressor, students freeze. After 30 to 40 seconds, the teacher then mentions that like in the game, stressors slow us down and affect our health. Briefly explain that activity helps release stress. For the next game of tag, three or four students are stressors and three or four students are stress relievers. The stress relievers carry the stress balls. When a student is tagged, he or she freezes and raises a hand. The stress reliever then tags the student to unfreeze him or her and allow him or her to move again. New stressors and stress relievers are selected for the next round. The teacher may select to have more stressor than stress relievers to illustrate that having more stressors can affect our health.

Refusal Tag

Health concept: Refusal skills

PE concept: Chasing and fleeing

PE lesson part: Closing activity or introductory activity

Equipment: None

Students (four or five) are chosen to be taggers, and three students are selected to be "unhealthy choices." When students are tagged, they must freeze. Unhealthy choices move around to frozen students and ask questions such as, "Do you want to smoke?" or "Do you want this beer?" Frozen students must reply with a confident, "No!" followed by a reason such as the following:

- I want to be healthy.
- I want to follow the laws.
- I want to be safe.
- I want to be a responsible person.

After frozen students say, "No!" and give their reason, they may return to play the game.

Relax to the Max

Health concept: Relaxation skills

PE concept: Cool-down

PE lesson part: Closing activity

Equipment: Soft music

In scattered formation, students are instructed to close their eyes. Using a calm voice, the teacher instructs them, "Squeeze your feet and relax," and then moves onto the calves and other various body parts.

Next, students are encouraged to make their lungs big by pretending to smell their favorite food and then exhale slowly as if they are blowing a feather. Students then lie on their back and "melt into the floor." After they are relaxed, students can pretend they are on a raft floating down a river or on a magic carpet in the sky.

Nutrition

Food Group Hustle

Health concept: Food groups

PE concept: Chasing and fleeing, cooperation, locomotor skills

PE lesson part: Closing activity

Equipment: Pictures of food (or plastic food) and five boxes

Pictures of foods are placed throughout the room. Each box is labeled with one of the five food groups identified by MyPlate. On signal, using a designated locomotor movement, students retrieve a food picture and place it in the appropriate box. This process continues as students try to find a different food group each time. When all the pictures have been placed in a box, students stop. The teacher then goes through the boxes with the class. Each time the food is in the appropriate box, students jump and say, "Yes," or perform another cheer. The number of pictures, or pieces of food, used will determine the length of the activity. Have students bring in labels and wrappers to provide a cost-effective alternative.

Meal Planners

Health concept: Applying nutrition concepts to meals

PE concept: Moving in personal space, strategy

PE lesson part: Closing activity

Equipment: Six hoops and pictures of food or food labels (or plastic food)

The class is divided into six equal teams, and each team is assigned a hoop. Hoops are placed evenly around the area with 10 to 15 pictures of foods in each. For the first round, students quickly move to the hoops of other teams and collect as many food items as possible in their hoop (plate). They may only carry one item at a time. For the next round, teams attempt to have as few of food items as possible on their plate by taking food to the other teams' plates. In the next round, teams collect only one food group. The team can choose the group, or the teacher can have the entire class collecting a specific group. Finally, students attempt to create a balanced meal on their plate.

Hi-Lo Nutrient

Health concept: Food nutrients

PE concept: Locomotor movements spacing

PE lesson part: Introductory activity

Equipment: Food labels or poly spots with various food pictures on them

Students begin by moving about the area using a predetermined locomotor movement.

Students should be careful not to step on the index cards, which have been spread out on the floor. When the teacher gives a signal, students quickly find the closest card and pick it up. If the card has a high-nutrient food on it, the student Crab Walks. If the card has a low-nutrient food on it, the student bear crawls. When the teacher says, "Walk," students leave the card on the floor and begin walking, waiting for the signal to grab another card.

Anytime and Sometimes

Health concept: Healthy food choices

PE concept: Chasing and fleeing, cooperation

PE lesson part: Closing activity

Equipment: None

Two teams face each other in parallel lines approximately 3 feet (1 m) apart. One team is Everyday foods, and one team is Sometimes foods. Anytime foods are foods you can eat any time you are hungry, and sometimes foods are foods you can eat sometimes when you are hungry. If the teacher calls out an everyday food (e.g., apple, lettuce), the Anytime team quickly takes three steps backward before being tagged by a member of the other team. If the teacher calls out a sometimes food (e.g., candy bar, potato chips), the Sometimes team quickly takes three steps backward without being tagged by the other team, who are chasing them.

Nutrition Volleyball

Health concept: Healthy food choices

PE concept: Volleying, cooperation, spacing

PE lesson part: Closing activity

Equipment: One balloon per group of four students

Teams of four students stand in a circle with one player holding a balloon. The goal of the game is to keep the balloon up for as many consecutive hits as possible. For a hit to count, the player must call out a different food each time he or she strikes the balloon. To begin, any food can be called out. As students learn the game, the teacher specifies a food group. All foods that are called out must be in that food group.

Food Benefits

Health concept: Food benefits and nutrients

PE concept: Spatial awareness, cooperation, locomotor movements

PE lesson part: Closing activity

Equipment: Pairs of index cards, one with a food and one with the benefits of that food

The class is divided in half. One half has index cards with foods on them, and the other half has index cards with food benefits on them. A line is made in the middle of the classroom, and half the students are on one side and half on the other. Students move in scattered formation on their designated side of the area. On signal, students run to the middle line and find the classmate with the corresponding card. A food matches with a food benefit. After everyone has found a match, student return to moving in scattered formation, switching cards while they move. Another round is played, and students find their new match.

Red Light Green Light—Food Edition

Health concept: Healthy food choices

PE concept: Spatial awareness, locomotor skills, balance

PE lesson part: Closing activity or introductory activity

Equipment: Pictures of food (optional)

Students stand on a line at one end of the teaching area. The teacher stands 15 to 20 feet (5 to 6 m) in front of the line. When the teacher calls out (or holds up a picture of) a green-light food (healthy food), students

10

move toward the teacher. When the teacher calls out (or holds up a picture of) a red-light food (unhealthy food), students stop. Students who do not stop within one step must return to the starting line. The first player to reach an imaginary line even with the teacher wins

The teacher may also use yellow-light foods (foods to think about). If a yellow-light food is called or shown, students must move slowly and act as if they are thinking.

Food Labels

Health concept: Reading food labels

PE concept: Fitness activities

PE lesson part: Fitness

Equipment: Food labels and a white board

Various labels are spread throughout the class. On the white board the teacher writes directions such as the following:

- Calories = clap
- Fat = abdominal challenge
- Carbohydrate = jumping jacks
- Protein = biceps curls
- Fiber = high fives

Students quickly find a food label and complete the activities according to the label. If the food has 75 calories, the child claps 75 times and then looks at the fat content. If it has 7 grams of fat, he or she chooses an abdominal challenge and does it 7 times, and so on. After one minute, the teacher stops the class and instructs them to find a new label. This time they start on the food label component they were last working on. This process continues for seven to eight minutes with students changing food labels every minute. At the end of this activity the teacher holds a brief discussion reviewing how to read a food label.

Personal Health

Splish Splash

Health concept: Healthy routines

PE concept: Rhythmic movements

PE lesson part: Introductory activity

Equipment: Music—"Splish Splash" or other fun music

The activity begins with students lying on the floor pretending to be asleep.

When the music starts, the teacher leads students through the following activities to get ready for school:

- Jump out of bed.

- Stretch to the ceiling.
- Take a shower.
- Comb hair.
- Eat breakfast.
- Floss and brush teeth.
- Travel to school (walking, biking, riding in a car or bus, and so on).
- Bike riders must remember to put their helmet on.
- Car riders must remember to put their seatbelt on.

Following this activity, the teacher reminds students of the healthy behaviors they do on a daily basis.

Hygiene Move and Go

Health concept: Personal hygiene

PE concept: Spatial awareness, following class protocol

PE lesson part: Introductory activity

Equipment: None

Students use a favorite locomotor movement to move around the area. On signal, they freeze and look at the teacher. The teacher then instructs the students that the "Go" signal for this activity is "I brush my teeth like you should do two or three times a day." The teacher then gives a locomotor movement and begins either brushing his or her teeth or, to see if students are listening, pretends to brush his or her hair. Students have to wait until the teacher brushes his or her teeth to move.

The teacher can change the signal to other health-related actions such as flossing or taking a shower. Following the introductory activity, the teacher can then use these freeze signals throughout the lesson or during other lessons.

Healthy Choices

Health concept: Recognizing healthy behaviors

PE concept: Spatial awareness, jumping and landing

PE lesson part: Introductory activity or fitness

Equipment: Pictures of healthy and unhealthy choices

The teacher holds up a picture. If the picture depicts a healthy choice, students jump up and down. If the picture shoes an unhealthy choice, they jump side to side. Examples of pictures include the following:

- A child looking both ways before crossing the road
- A child eating a healthy breakfast
- A child skateboarding without a helmet
- A child helping to clean the house

Each time, the teacher can change the activities for students to do. Using a variety of fitness activities would work well during the fitness component of the lessons. Because this activity can be vigorous, after every three to four signs stop and have a 30- to 45-second discussion about why the activities are healthy or unhealthy.

Germs Everywhere

Health concept: Importance of hand washing

PE concept: Lesson specific

PE lesson part: All

Equipment: Glow in the dark gel, black light

Each student is given a small amount of gel to rub on their hands like lotion. Students then move around the classroom giving as many high fives as they can before the teacher stops them. This activity is done two or three times. Next, students participate in their normal lesson as usual. At the end of the lesson the teacher turns out the lights and shows the students how the gel has spread throughout the gym and on equipment and their hands. Finally, the teacher leads a brief discussion on the importance of hand washing to prevent the spread of germs (the gel).

Clogged Artery

Health concept: Importance of heart health

PE concept: Chasing and fleeing, spatial awareness, cooperation

PE lesson part: Closing activity

Equipment: None

One student is King or Queen Cholesterol and stands in the middle of the area. The remainder of the class (called blood) stands in a line on one end. The area is called the blood vessel (typically defined as the activity area). On signal, the blood attempts to move through the blood vessel to the other end without being tagged by King or Queen Cholesterol. Tagged students freeze and become cholesterol. They can pivot on one foot to tag other students. After one round, students attempt to move back to the original starting line, again without being tagged by cholesterol.

After two or three rounds, the passage from one side to the other will be crowded with cholesterol. Before starting over, students are taught that when cholesterol builds up, blood cannot easily get through a blood vessel.

Risk Factor Tag

Health concept: Risk factors of heart disease

PE concept: Chasing and fleeing

PE lesson part: Closing activity

Equipment: Index cards with one risk factor of cardiovascular disease on each

Taggers are given an index card. Players that are tagged by a tagger must freeze. One student is the activator, who can unfreeze frozen students. After 60 to 90 seconds the teacher changes taggers and the activator. Throughout the game the teacher alters the number of activators and taggers.

The teacher then asks, "What did the risk factors of cardiovascular do to you?" "How did I decrease the effect of the risk factors? That's right; I added more physical activity."

The important concept for students to learn is that to maximize cardiovascular health, they should decrease risk factors and increase activity.

Strong Heart

Health concept: Importance of heart health

PE concept: Heart rate, locomotor skills

PE lesson part: Introductory activity

Equipment: None

Teach students to take their pulse for 10 or 15 seconds. Teach students that the heart is the size of their fist and is a muscle that squeezes, or beats, to push blood throughout the body. Next, as the students count their heart beats, they squeeze their fists. Students then participate in jumping jacks or other vigorous activity. Following the vigorous activity, students again take their pulse and squeeze their fists with each beat. Remind students to squeeze hard. After 20 to 30 seconds, ask students if their hands are getting tired. Follow this by asking, "What will you do when your hand gets tired? Stop. But can your heart stop?" "So what do we have to do so that our hearts are healthy and strong? Exactly, we have to be active and eat healthy foods."

Senses

Health concept: Recognition of body senses

PE concept: Cooperation, following directions, nonlocomotor and locomotor skills, manipulative skills

PE lesson part: Closing activity

Equipment: Any type of balls and blindfolds

Students find a partner using toe to toe. Partners teach each other skills using the following conditions:

- The teaching partner can only speak. The partner being taught is blindfolded (or has eyes closed).
- The teaching partner may not speak. He or she must teach with modeling.
- The teaching partner must teach the skill by moving the partner's body through the movement.
- The teacher then discusses the importance of all senses.
- Fundamental skills such as jogging, skipping, throwing, kicking, and bending work best for this activity.

Safety

Falling

Health concept: Personal safety when falling

PE concept: Rolling

PE lesson part: Focus

Equipment: Tumbling mats

This activity can easily be integrated into a gymnastics lesson. Among other rolls, students can be taught how to roll when falling. The idea is to try to land on larger parts of the body as opposed to putting all the weight on the hands or arms. Students can learn this by starting on their knees, simulating a fall forward, and practicing rolling to their back. Students who seem fearful or unsure should not be forced to try this activity.

Get Low and "Go!"

Health concept: Fire safety

PE concept: Spatial awareness, animal movements

PE lesson part: Introductory activity

Equipment: None

Students perform a specific locomotor skill around the teaching area. When the teacher says, "Get low," students get into a crawling position and say, "Get low." The teacher then says, "Go," which signals the students to crawl. As the students crawl the teacher reminds them that if they are ever in a smoky room, they "get low and go" to the nearest safe way out. This activity is also an excellent opportunity to discuss the importance of family exit plan in case of emergency.

Medicine or Candy Shuffle

Health concept: Recognition of medicine versus candy

PE concept: Animal movements, spatial awareness

PE lesson part: Closing activity or fitness

Equipment: Prepare 10 to 15 index cards with pictures of either an over-the-counter medication or a small piece of candy that resembles medicine

The index cards are scattered on the floor throughout the teaching area. Students begin moving from card to card in a random pattern. If they come to a medicine, they bear crawl to the next card. If the come to a card with candy glued to it, they Crab Walk to the next card. Intermittently, the teacher stops the activity and discusses the importance of asking adults before eating something they think may be medicine. The movements should be changed frequently.

Hand Signals

Health concept: Bicycle safety

PE concept: Spatial awareness, lifetime activity

PE lesson part: Introductory activity

Equipment: None

This activity teaches students bicycle safety signals. Students give the following signals with the left arm:

- Left turn: arm straight out, parallel to the ground
- Right turn: elbow at a right angle, hand up
- Stop: elbow at a right angle, hand down

Students move around the area. Each time they turn or stop, they must give the appropriate hand signal. Classroom teachers can use this activity throughout the school year as they walk through the halls with their class. Teachers can also make reminders of other bicycle safety behaviors such as wearing a helmet.

Stop, Look, and Listen

Health concept: Pedestrian safety

PE concept: Following directions, personal spacing

PE lesson part: Introductory activity or closing activity

Equipment: Cones

This activity can be taught in the gymnasium with cones used to mark streets or in the school hallways with halls serving as streets. Students are taught that they should stop, look both ways twice, and listen before crossing the street. First, the entire class lines up on one side of the teaching area. They are challenged to move to the other side safely. To move safely they must walk as well as stop, look, and listen. Next, streets or hallways are used so that students can practice these skills independently. Students move around the area. When they come to the street they must stop, look both ways two times, listen, and then cross the street walking. After they reach the other side, they continue moving.

Sun Safety

Sun Safety Tag

Health concept: Importance of sun protection

PE concept: Chasing and fleeing

PE lesson part: Closing activity

Equipment:

- Props to represent sun protection (long sleeve shirt, hat, sunscreen, sunglasses)
- Yellow jersey (optional)

One student, who wears the yellow jersey, is the sun and serves as the tagger. If tagged by the sun, students must stop. Five students are selected to be the sun protectors. Each sun protector carries or wears an item that protects us from the sun. Sun protectors allow students who are stopped to reenter the game by tagging them. To let the sun protectors know they need help, stopped students call out, "I need sun protection" and pretend to shade themselves.

Stopped students can also be asked to answer a sun safety question before reentering the game. Examples include the following:

- What helps prevent getting sunburned?
- What SPF number sunscreen should be used?

Sunburn

Health concept: Sun safety

PE concept: Tossing, catching

PE lesson part: Closing activity

Equipment: One ball for five to six students

Groups of five to six students form circles with one player holding the ball. Each group begins passing the ball in hot potato fashion. When the teacher yells, "Sunburn," the person with the ball rotates to the next circle. When the student arrives at the circle he or she must provide a sun safety fact and then begin passing the ball. The teacher may choose to use music and yell, "Sunburn," when he or she turns off the music. The same sun safety fact cannot be used twice in a row. Provide a poster of sun safety facts for students to refer to if they get stuck.

Sunny Mime

Health concept: Activities that require sun protection

PE concept: Spatial awareness, following directions

PE lesson part: Introductory activity

Equipment: None

With music playing, the teacher asks students to call out activities that require sun safety. The teacher then quickly chooses an activity, and students pretend to do it. For example, the teacher says, "I heard swimming; let's pretend we are swimming." After 20 to 30 seconds, the teacher asks for more examples. After a series of movements, the teacher holds a discussion on why those activities require sun safety. The music is turned back on, and more examples are given.

LEARNING AIDS

HOW AND WHY

1. Why should physical education teachers integrate health concepts into their lessons?
2. How can physical education teachers go about integrating health content?
3. Why might physical education teachers be apprehensive about integrating health content?

CONTENT REVIEW

1. Discuss the models of integration available to physical educators.
2. Explain some of the issues that a physical educator should consider when deciding whether to integrate health content.
3. List and discuss strategies that teachers should use when integrating health content into physical education.
4. Discuss several ways to integrate mental and emotional health into physical education.

5. Explain three strategies or activities that can be used to integrate personal health into physical education.

6. List four ways to integrate nutrition into physical education.

7. Describe several methods of integrating family and social health into physical education.

WEBSITES

National Health Education Standards, www.cdc.gov/healthyschools/sher/standards/

Activities to teach health concepts in physical education, www.pecentral.org

Characteristics of an effective health education curriculum, www.cdc.gov/healthyschools/sher/characteristics/

Skills-based health education ideas, www.shapeamerica.org/publications/resources/skills-based_health_education.aspx

SUGGESTED READINGS

Benes, S., & Alperin, H. (2016). *The essentials of teaching health education*. Reston, VA: SHAPE America.

Benes, S., & Alperin, H. (2016). *Lesson planning for skills-based health education*. Reston, VA: SHAPE America.

Blaydes, J. (2004). *Thinking on your feet* (2nd ed.). Murphy, TX: Action Based Learning.

Connolly, M. (2020). *Skills-based health education* (2nd ed.). Burlington, MA: Jones & Bartlett Learning.

Placek, J.H. (2003). Interdisciplinary curriculum in physical education: Possibilities and problems. In *Student learning in physical education: Applying research to enhance instruction*. Silverman, S.J., & Ennis, C.D. (Eds.), 255–271. Champaign, IL: Human Kinetics.

REFERENCES

Joint Committee on National Health Education Standards. (2007). *National health education standards achieving excellence* (2nd ed.). Atlanta, GA: American Cancer Society.

Pangrazi, R.P., Beighle, A., & Pangrazi, D. (2009). *Promoting physical activity and health in the classroom*. San Francisco, CA: Benjamin Cummings.

Legal Liability, Supervision, and Safety

11

This chapter explains the various legal terms and situations associated with physical education as well as instructional and administrative procedures common to the responsible and prudent conduct of a physical education program. The teacher has a legal responsibility to create a safe environment that minimizes risk and the possibility for injury and to provide a standard of care that any reasonable and prudent professional with similar training would apply under the given circumstances. Safety instruction is designed to prevent accidents and should be included in lesson plans to ensure coverage. A comprehensive safety checklist is included to be sure that beginning teachers understand how to establish an accident-free environment.

Learning Objectives

- ▶ Define *tort*, *negligence*, *liability*, *malfeasance*, *misfeasance*, *nonfeasance*, and other terms common to legal suits brought against educators.
- ▶ List major points that must be established to determine teacher negligence.
- ▶ Explain how to examine all activities, equipment, and facilities for possible hazards and sources of accidents.
- ▶ Identify common defenses against negligence.
- ▶ Describe the supervisory responsibilities expected of all teachers.
- ▶ List guidelines for the proper supervision of instruction, equipment, and facilities.
- ▶ Describe aspects of sport programs that often give rise to lawsuits.
- ▶ Understand how to ensure safety, with an emphasis on prevention.
- ▶ Outline an emergency care plan.

Fancy/Veer/Corbis/Getty Images

School district personnel, including teaching and non-teaching members, are required to provide appropriate care for student safety. This duty is manifested as the ability to anticipate reasonably foreseeable dangers and the responsibility to take necessary precautions to prevent problems from occurring. Failure to do so may make the district the target of lawsuits.

Compared with other subject matter areas, physical education is particularly vulnerable to accidents and resultant injuries. More than 50% of all accidents in the school setting occur on the playground and in the gymnasium. Even though schools cannot be held financially accountable for costs associated with the treatment of injuries, they can be forced to pay those expenses if the injured party sues and wins judgment. Legal suits are conducted under respective state statutes. Principles underlying legal action are similar, but certain regulations and procedures vary among states. You should acquire a copy of the legal liability policy for your district. Districts usually have a written definition of situations in which teachers can be held liable.

All students have the right to freedom from injury caused by others or by participating in a program. Courts have ruled that teachers have the duty to protect their students from harm. Teachers must exercise the teaching skill, discretion, and knowledge that members of the profession in good standing normally display in similar situations. When citizens believe this standard of care was not exercised, lawsuits may result.

Liability is the responsibility to perform a duty to a particular group. For teachers it is an obligation to provide a standard of care required by law and enforced by court action. Teachers are bound by contract to carry out their duties reasonably and prudently. Liability is always a legal matter. Before a teacher can be held liable, it must be proved in a court of law that negligence occurred.

Torts

In education, a *tort* is concerned with the teacher–student relationship and is a legal wrong that results in direct or indirect injury to another individual or to property. *Black's Law Dictionary* (Garner, 2009) defines a tort as

> a private or civil wrong or injury, other than breach of contract, for which the court will provide a remedy in the form of an action for damages. Three elements of every tort action are: existence of legal duty from defendant to plaintiff, breach of duty, and damage as proximate result.

As the result of a tort, the court can award money for damages that occurred. The court can also award money for punitive damages if a breach of duty can be established. Usually, the court awards the offended individual for damages that occurred because of the negligence of the instructor or other responsible person. Punitive damages are much less common.

Negligence and Liability

Legal liability is usually concerned with a breach of duty through negligence. To determine liability, lawyers can examine the situation that led to injury. Four major points examined in deciding whether a teacher is liable because of negligence are duty, breach of duty, proximate cause, and damages.

Determination of Liability

1. *Duty.* The first point considered is that of duty owed to the participants. Did the school or teacher owe students a duty of care that implies conforming to certain standards of conduct? To determine a reasonable standard, the court compares the conduct of other teachers who are members of the profession in good standing.

2. *Breach of duty.* A teacher must commit a breach of duty by failing to conform to the required duty. After it is established that a duty was required, it must be proved that such duty was not performed. Two situations are possible: (*a*) the teacher did something that was not supposed to be done (e.g., putting boxing gloves on students to resolve their differences), or (*b*) the teacher did not do something that should have been done (e.g., failing to teach expected safety procedures for an activity).

3. *Proximate cause.* The teacher's failure to conform to the required standard must be the proximate cause of the resulting injury. It must be proved that the injury was caused by the teacher's breach of duty as well as by his or her failure to provide a reasonable standard of care. The plaintiff's expert tries to convince the court that a requisite standard was not met that caused injury, and the defendant's expert tries to show that the teacher met the proper standard of care.

4. *Damages.* Actual harm must occur if liability is to be established. If no injury or harm occurs, there is no liability. It must be proved that the injured party is entitled to compensatory damages for

A CASE OF FORESEEABILITY?

A common game in many school settings is bombardment, or dodgeball. During the game, a student is hit in the eye by a ball and loses vision in that eye. Was this a foreseeable accident that could have been prevented? Were the balls being used capable of inflicting severe injury? Were students aware of rules that might have prevented this injury? Were the students' abilities somewhat equal, or were some able to throw with such velocity that injury was predictable? Were all students forced to play the game? These questions would likely be considered in court in attempting to prove that the teacher should have predicted the excessively dangerous situation.

11

financial loss or physical discomfort. Actual damages can be physical, emotional, or financial, but the court offers only financial awards.

Foreseeability

A key to the issue of negligence is *foreseeability*. Courts expect a trained professional to foresee potentially harmful situations. Could the teacher have anticipated the danger of the harmful act or situation and used appropriate measures to prevent it? If the injured party can prove that the teacher should have foreseen the danger involved in an activity or situation (even in part), the teacher will be found negligent for failing to act reasonably and prudently. This potential outcome underscores the need to examine all activities, equipment, and facilities for possible hazards and sources of accident.

Types of Negligence

The courts define *negligence* as conduct that falls below a standard of care established to protect others from unreasonable risk or harm. This section examines several types of negligence—namely, malfeasance, misfeasance, nonfeasance, contributory negligence, and comparative or shared negligence.

Malfeasance

Malfeasance occurs when a teacher does something improper by committing an unlawful and wrongful act with no legal basis (often referred to as an act of commission). Malfeasance can be illustrated as follows: A male student frequently misbehaves. In desperation, the teacher gives him a choice of punishment—a severe

spanking in front of the class or running many laps around the field. He chooses the former and suffers physical and emotional damage. Even though the student chose the punishment of spanking, the teacher is still liable for any physical or emotional harm caused.

Misfeasance

Misfeasance occurs when a teacher follows proper procedures but does not perform according to the required standard of conduct. Misfeasance is usually the subpar performance of an act that might otherwise have been lawfully done. An example would be a teacher's offering to spot a student during a tumbling routine and then not doing the spotting properly. If the student is injured because of a faulty spot, the teacher can be held liable.

Nonfeasance

Nonfeasance is based on lack of action in carrying out a duty. This is usually an *act of omission*—the teacher knew the proper procedures but failed to follow them. Teachers can be found negligent if they act or fail to act. In contrast to the misfeasance example, nonfeasance occurs when a teacher knows that he or she should teach appropriate progressions but fails to do so. Courts expect teachers to behave with more skill and insight than parents do because teachers are educated to give students a higher standard of professional care than are parents.

Contributory Negligence

The situation is different when the injured student is partially or wholly at fault. Students are expected to exercise sensible care and to follow directions or regulations designed to protect them from injury. When improper behavior by the injured party causes the accident, it is

DOES STUDENT SIZE MAKE A DIFFERENCE?

Students are playing a game of Diagonal Soccer. On signal, three students from each team run to the center, trying to get the ball first and gain scoring advantage. One of the students weighs about 70 pounds (32 kg), whereas a student on the other team is mature and weighs nearly 160 pounds (72 kg). As they approach the ball, the large student runs over the small student, knocking him down and causing a head injury. Within two weeks the student has a seizure, and the parents plan to sue. Should the students have been matched for size? For maturity and ability? Does gender make a difference? Could the game have been modified to avoid this injury? Is the teacher guilty of malfeasance?

usually ruled to be *contributory negligence* because the injured party contributed to the resulting harm. For example, a student is repeatedly told not to walk in a certain area, yet she does it anyway, resulting in injury. This responsibility is directly related to the child's maturity, ability, and experience. Most states have laws specifying that a child under seven years of age is incapable of contributory negligence (Baley & Matthews, 1988).

Comparative or Shared Negligence

Under the doctrine of comparative negligence, the injured party can recover only if found to be less negligent than the defendant (the teacher). Where statutes apply, the amount of recovery is generally reduced in proportion to the injured party's participation in the circumstances leading to the injury.

Common Defenses Against Negligence

Negligence must be proved in a court of law. Teachers are frequently negligent in carrying out their duties, yet the injured party does not take the case to court. If a teacher is sued, some of the following defenses are used to show that the teacher's action was not the primary cause of the accident.

Act of God

The act-of-God defense places the cause of injury on forces beyond the teacher's or school's control. This defense claims that predicting an unsafe condition was impossible, but through an act of God, the injury occurred. Typical acts would be a gust of wind that blew over a volleyball standard or a cloudburst of rain that made a surface slick. The act-of-God defense can be used only in cases when the injury would have occurred even if reasonable and prudent action had been taken.

Proximate Cause

The defense of proximate cause attempts to prove that the accident was not due to teacher negligence. The breach of duty by the teacher and the injury must be closely related. This defense is common in cases dealing with proper supervision. Suppose that a student is participating in an activity supervised by a teacher. When the teacher leaves the playing area to get a cup of coffee, the student is injured. The defense lawyer will try to show that the accident would have occurred regardless of the teacher's location.

Assumption of Risk

Physical education is a high-risk activity when compared with most other curriculum areas. When choosing to be part of an activity, participants assume the accompanying risk. Physical education teachers seldom use the assumption-of-risk defense because they typically do not give students a choice between participating or not. An instructor for an elective program who allows students to choose desired units of instruction might find this a better defense than one who teaches a totally required program. Athletic and sport club participation is by choice, and players must assume greater risk in activities such as football and gymnastics.

Contributory Negligence

The defense often claims contributory negligence in attempting to convince the court that the injured party

I TOLD THEM, BUT THEY DID IT ANYWAY!

A physical education instructor teaching a class of fourth-grade students has thoroughly covered softball hitting and related safety rules and marked out clearly visible restraining lines. During class, students are engaged at various softball stations. One student runs through the restricted area and is hit by an aluminum baseball bat. Who is to blame? Was the student old enough to know better? Were too many stations being taught at the same time? Should the teacher have foreseen that an accident might happen even if students were warned? Are aluminum or wood bats an appropriate choice for physical education classes? Is there an assumption of risk in all physical education activities that these situations occasionally will occur?

11

acted in a manner that was not typical of students of similar age and maturity. The defense attempts to demonstrate that the activity or equipment in question had been used for years with no record of accident. A case is made based on how students were taught to act safely and on the premise that the injured student acted outside the parameters of safe conduct. A key point in this defense is whether the activity was suitable for the participant's age and maturity level.

Areas of Responsibility

A two-tiered approach for analyzing injuries is useful for determining responsibility. The first tier includes duties that the administration must assume in support of the program. The second tier defines duties of the instructor or staff member charged with teaching or supervising students. Each party has a role to fill, but some overlap occurs. The following example illustrates the differences.

A student is hurt while performing a tumbling stunt. A lawsuit ensues, charging the teacher with negligence for not following safe procedures. The administration could also be included in the suit, being charged with negligence for hiring an incompetent (unqualified) instructor. Three levels of responsibility should be considered when delegating responsibility because

1. they identify different functions and responsibilities of the teaching staff and administration,

2. they provide a framework for reducing injuries and improving safety procedures, and

3. they provide perspective for following legal precedents.

The following sections consider both administrative and instructional duties for the responsibilities described.

Supervision

All activities in a school setting must be supervised, including recess, lunchtimes, and field trips. For supervision to function properly, the school's responsibilities are critical.

Administration

Two levels are identified in supervision: general and specific. General supervision (e.g., playground duty) refers to broad coverage when students are not being controlled directly by a teacher or designated individual. A supervision plan should exist, designating the areas to be covered and including where and how the supervisor should rotate. This plan, kept in the principal's office, covers rules of conduct governing student behavior, expected supervisor duties, and required supervisor-to-student ratios. Rules should be posted prominently on bulletin boards, especially in classrooms. Besides the plan, administrators must select qualified personnel, provide necessary training, and monitor the plan properly.

The general supervisor is concerned primarily with student behavior, focusing on the student's right to a relaxing recreational experience. Supervisors must observe the area, looking for breaches of discipline, particularly when an individual or group picks on or bullies another child. The supervisor needs to look for protruding sprinkler heads, broken glass, and debris on the play area. Before leaving the area, the supervisor must find a qualified substitute to keep supervising the area.

MAINTAINING STUDENT SAFETY AT RECESS

Although principals and administrators are generally in favor of physical education and other sources of physical activity for students (i.e., recess or playtime), one of their biggest concerns about these aspects of the school day has to do with supervision and safety. Instructional personnel are responsible for providing supervision at all times, regardless of whether or not instruction is taking place. Therefore, school employees must actively monitor all students by having them within sight and hearing distance. One way that the school physical educator can facilitate this task is to encourage recess staff to walk constantly around the perimeter of the area. This action not only allows staff to see all the students at once but also provides staff extra physical activity and allows them to model healthy behaviors for the students.

Recess equipment and facilities need to be checked for safety on a weekly basis. The physical educator can take on this responsibility, and the students can be taught and instructed to assist with this process by reporting any unsafe equipment or potential hazards. Checklists are available for these weekly walk-throughs.

Equipment and facilities should be appropriate for the age levels of the students, and the play area should be set up so that all students can be active with known boundaries for specific activities. One way to establish this kind of suitable environment is to create activity zones, or defined areas, for different types of play. For instance, the physical educator may set up cones with signs and appropriate equipment for a variety of recess activities (e.g., jumping rope, playing soccer, walking a trail, playing with hoops, or throwing with a partner). After sharing the rules and having students practice proper procedures at recess, children know where they can participate in specific activities. In turn, invasion types of games are kept at a distance from individual and low-intensity activities, thus helping to maintain safety.

Offer modifications to the games that students play on the playground. The factors that can be adapted include distance, equipment, rules, and time to decrease likelihood of potential safety issues. The distance from the child to the target or the length of the playing area can be decreased or increased to make a task easier or more challenging. Modify the task by using a larger or smaller ball, for instance, or by deflating a ball if it is moving too quickly for the student. Rules can always be adjusted to meet the safety needs of the students. If a supervisor notices that some students are not receiving any passes during an impromptu soccer game, the game can be modified so that *all* team members must touch the ball before someone can shoot the ball or a second game can be started in a different space to allow smaller groups of students at different skill levels to play. With regard to time, the purpose or goal of a game can be modified to allow completion within the time available; this change can potentially result in fewer accidents because students won't try to attain an impossible result in a limited time. Fewer complaints will be heard that a game is always interrupted before it can be finished.

Instructional Staff

General supervision is necessary during recess, immediately before and after school, during lunch break, and during certain other sessions when instruction is not offered. The supervisor should know the school's supervision plan and emergency care procedures in case of an accident. Supervision is an overt act; supervisors are actively involved and moving throughout the area. The number of supervisors depends on the type of activity, the size of the area, and the number and ages of the students. At least two supervisors should be on duty to ensure that supervision will be uninterrupted if an emergency or situation requires close attention by one of the supervisors.

Specific supervision requires the instructor to be with a certain group of students (a class). If certain pieces of apparatus require special care and proper use, post rules and regulations near the apparatus (for upper-grade children). Make students aware of the rules and give them appropriate instruction and guidance in applying the rules. When rules are modified, rewrite them in proper form. Documentation is invaluable when the need to defend policies and approaches arises.

When teaching, arrange and teach the class so that all students are in view. This guideline implies supervising from the perimeter of the area. Standing at the center of the student group with many students behind you makes it impossible to supervise a class safely and effectively. Teachers should be in the teaching area at all times. Leaving students to retrieve something from an office or equipment room is unacceptable. Never leave equipment and apparatus unsupervised when it is accessible to students in the area. For example, never leave equipment on the playing field between classes. If other students in the area have easy access to the equipment, then they may use it unsafely, and the teacher can be found liable if an injury occurs.

Do not agree to supervise activities for which you are unqualified to anticipate possible hazards. If this situation arises, send a written memo to the department head or principal stating your lack of insight and qualification. Maintain a copy for your files.

Merriman (1993) proposes the following five recommendations to ensure that adequate supervision occurs:

1. The supervisor must be in the immediate vicinity (i.e., within sight and hearing of the students).

2. If required to leave, the supervisor must have an adequate replacement before departing. Adequate replacements do *not* include paraprofessionals, student teachers, custodial help, or untrained teachers.

3. Supervision procedures must be planned and incorporated into daily lessons.

4. Supervision procedures should include what to observe and listen for, where to stand for the most effective view, and what to do if a problem arises.

5. Supervision requires that participants' ages, maturity, and skill abilities always be considered, as well as the inherent risk of the activity.

Instruction

Instructional responsibility rests primarily with the teacher, but administrative personnel have certain defined functions as well.

Administrators

Administrators should review and approve the curricular plan. The curriculum should be reviewed regularly to keep it current. Be sure that the curriculum includes activities that meet program objectives and contribute to students' growth and development. Saying in a court of law that an activity was included "for the fun of it" or "because students liked it" makes little sense. Instead, activities should be placed in the curriculum because they contribute to program outcomes. Administrators are obligated to support the program with adequate finances to assure a safe environment. The principal and higher administrators should be requested to visit the program periodically.

Physical Education Teachers

During instruction, teachers have a duty to protect students from unreasonable physical or mental harm. This duty includes avoiding any acts or omissions that might cause such harm. You are educated, experienced, and skilled in physical education and must foresee possibly harmful situations.

The major area of concern involving instruction is whether all students are adequately instructed before or during participation in an activity. Adequate instruction means (1) teaching children how to perform activities correctly and use equipment and apparatus properly, and (2) teaching students necessary safety precautions. If this is not done, the instructor can be held liable. The risk involved in an activity must be communicated to the learner.

Students' ages and maturity play an important role in activity selection. Younger students require more care, simple instructions, and clear restrictions in the name of safety. Some students lack appropriate fear, and the teacher must be aware of this when discussing safety factors. Remember that children seven years old or younger are not held responsible for unsafe behavior. The entire responsibility falls on the teacher to give adequate instruction and supervision.

Careful planning is necessary. Written curriculum guides and lesson plans can offer a well-prepared approach that other teachers and administrators gladly support. Lesson plans should include proper sequence and progression of skills. Teachers are on defensible grounds if they can show that their progression of activities was based on presentations designed by experts and followed carefully when teaching. District and state guidelines enforcing instructional sequences and restricted activities should be checked and followed closely.

Students must not be forced to participate. If a child is required to perform an activity unwillingly, his or her

NEED FOR A CURRICULUM AND LESSON PLAN

A former gymnast who is now an elementary school physical education teacher decides to teach her classes gymnastics. The school has no curriculum guide, and the teacher does not write lesson plans. She decides to have students try a headspring over a tumbling mat. A student is seriously hurt (severe neck injury that causes paralysis), and his parents file a $1.5 million lawsuit. What argument would she use to defend herself in this situation? Would it help if she could say that gymnastics was part of the school curriculum? What will happen if the plaintiff's lawyer brings in an expert witness who says that the instructional sequence was inappropriate? Can the teacher show her written lesson plan that delineates the proper instructional sequence based on what expert instructors recommend? Can teachers be experts in every activity they teach, or do they need to rely on other experts for the proper sequence of activities to teach?

teacher may be open to a lawsuit. For older students, posting the proper sequence of skills and lead-up activities offers evidence the skills were presented properly. Tread the line carefully between offering encouragement and forcing students to try new activities. Offer students the choice of trying something they fear or think they cannot do. If they say no, offer a new challenge.

The following points will help you develop lessons that ensure safe instruction:

1. Sequence all activities in units of instruction and develop written lesson plans. Problems occur when snap judgments are made under the daily pressure and strain of teaching.

2. Scrutinize high-risk activities to ensure that all safety procedures are implemented. If in doubt, discuss the activities with experienced teachers and administrators.

3. Ensure that activities taught are adapted to the developmental levels of all students. Students display a wide range of maturity and physical development, so activities must be modified or adjusted to assure that all students can safely participate. For example, overweight students may not be able to play positions that demand high amounts of aerobic activity.

4. If students' grades are based on the number of activities they attempt, some students may feel forced to try all activities. Make it clear to students that the choice to try an activity they fear

belongs to them. If they are afraid of getting hurt, they should be able to choose not to perform an activity.

5. Include all necessary safety equipment in written lesson plans. The lesson plan should detail and diagram how equipment is arranged (e.g., how the mats are placed) and where the instructor carries out supervision.

6. If a student claims injury or brings a note from parents asking that the student not participate in physical activity, honor the request. Teachers usually receive excuses at the start of the period, when they are busy with many other duties (getting equipment ready, taking roll, and opening lockers). Making a thoughtful judgment during this time is difficult. The school nurse is qualified to make these judgments when they relate to health and should be expected to make such decisions. If the excuses continue for a long time, the teacher or nurse should schedule a conference with the parents to rectify the situation.

7. Make sure that the instruction includes activities that are in line with available equipment and facilities. For example, a soccer lead-up activity may no longer be safe and appropriate if it is brought indoors because of inclement weather unless you change the rules and types of balls used.

8. If spotting is required for safe completion of an activity, always do it yourself. Students spotting

I KNOW WE HAD A SUPERVISOR OUT THERE!

At lunch, students have free time to play on the activity field or in the gymnasium. One teacher is assigned to supervise the students on the playing field, and one supervises the gym. The playing field is large, and an injury occurs opposite where the teacher is standing. She hustles to help the student. While busy attending the injured student, the teacher does not notice a fight that breaks out. A larger student severely beats a smaller student. Is the teacher liable because she did not see the fight? Can one teacher adequately supervise a playground full of students? Is the administrator responsible because only one teacher was assigned to supervise? Did the teacher have a way to communicate with the front office to ask for additional help?

11

students is not recommended because they are not professionally trained. If an accident occurs while they are spotting, you will be held responsible.

9. If students are working independently at stations, distribute carefully constructed and written task cards to help eliminate unsafe practices.

10. Have a written emergency care plan posted in the gymnasium. This plan should be approved by health care professionals and followed to the letter when an injury occurs.

Teachers who incorporate punishment into the instructional process should carefully examine its consequences before using it. Physical punishment that leads to permanent or long-lasting damage is indefensible. The punishment used must be in line with the physical maturity and health of the student involved. A teacher's practice of having students run laps when they have misbehaved might go unchallenged for years. What might happen if an asthmatic student or a student with congenital heart disease is told to run and suffers injury or illness? What might happen if the student is running unsupervised and is injured from a fall or suffers heat exhaustion? In these examples, defending such punitive practices is hard. Making students perform physical activity for misbehavior is indefensible under any circumstance and does not serve to promote physical activity. If a child is injured while performing physical punishment, teachers are usually found liable and held responsible for the injury.

Safety

The major thrust of safety is to prevent situations that cause accidents. Studies estimate that more than 70% of injuries in sport and related activities can be prevented through proper safety procedures. On the other hand, some accidents occur despite precautions, and proper emergency procedures should be established for such situations. The U.S. Consumer Product Safety Commission (2010) conducted a comprehensive study of injuries received in sport and related activities gathered through a network of computers in 119 hospital emergency rooms. The sports and activities that produced the most injuries were, in order, football, touch football, baseball, basketball, gymnastics, and skiing. The facility that produced the most disabling injuries was the swimming pool.

Learning to recognize potential high-risk situations is an important factor in preventing accidents. Teachers must clearly understand the hazards and potential dangers of an activity before they can establish controls.

TEACHING TIP

When you modify safety rules or rules of familiar games, clearly communicate the revisions to your students so that everybody is aware of safe use of space.

RUNNING FOR PUNISHMENT—THE RIGHT CHOICE?

Children participating in a physical education class are unruly. They talk when they shouldn't and generally do not cooperate. The teacher, in a fit of controlled anger, has two students run laps around a large field until they decide to behave. It is a hot fall day and, after 15 minutes of running, one student falls and goes into convulsions on the far side of the field (1/3 mile [1/2 km] away from the teacher). The teacher doesn't see the child go down until another student tells him about it. Has malfeasance occurred? Is running an acceptable choice for punishment? Was the weather considered? Did the youth have a preexisting health condition? Were the students under the teacher's watchful eye or out of sight? Could you defend yourself in this situation?

Instructors must not assume that participants are aware of the dangers and risks involved in various activities but instead must thoroughly inform students before participation. See Guidelines for Creating a Safe Environment for specific guidelines and recommendations.

Safety Committee

Safety should be publicized regularly throughout the school. Students, parents, and teachers also need a process for voicing concerns about unsafe conditions. A safety committee can meet regularly to establish safety policies, rule on requests to allow high-risk activities, and analyze serious injuries that have occurred in the school district. This committee should develop safety rules that apply district-wide to all teachers. Some activities may be deemed too risky for the return in student benefit. The committee may establish acceptable criteria for sports equipment and apparatus.

Include one or more high-level administrators, physical education teachers, health officers (nurses), parents, and students on the safety committee. School administrators are usually indicted when lawsuits occur; because they are held responsible for program content and curriculum, their representation on the safety committee is important. Students on the committee may be aware of possible hazards, and parents may often voice concerns overlooked by teachers.

Emergency Care Plan

Before any emergency arises, teachers should prepare themselves by learning about any special health and physical conditions of their students (Gray, 2007). Most schools have a method for identifying such students. If a student has a problem that may require treatment, a consent-to-treat form should be on file in case the parent or guardian is unavailable. Keep necessary first aid materials and supplies available in a readily accessible kit.

Establishing procedures for emergency care and the notification of parents in case of injury is of utmost importance in providing a high standard of care for students. To plan properly for emergency care, all physical education teachers should have first aid training. First aid is the immediate and temporary care given at an emergency before a physician is available. Its purposes are to save lives, prevent the aggravation of injuries, and alleviate severe suffering. If life-threatening bleeding is occurring or if the victim is unconscious or has stopped

TEACHING TIP

A note of caution is warranted here about confidentiality of school records. The Family Education Rights and Privacy Act of 1974 (FERPA) is a federal law that protects the privacy of student educational records. Even though medical records are not considered educational records, check with your school administrator regarding the confidentiality of school medical records.

GUIDELINES FOR CREATING A SAFE ENVIRONMENT

1. Conduct in-service sessions in safety. Experienced, knowledgeable teachers should lead these sessions. Department heads may be responsible for the training, or outside experts can be employed and assigned responsibility. Give in-district credit to participating teachers to demonstrate the district's concern for using proper safety techniques.

2. Review medical records. Reviews should occur at the start of each school year. Identify students with disabilities and note them within each class listing before the first instructional day. Check the IEPs of students (see chapter 9) because they often contain relevant information. If necessary, the classroom teacher or school nurse can call the doctors of students with disabilities or students with activity restrictions to inquire about the situation and discuss special needs. Check with the classroom teacher or school nurse regarding students who have a special condition such as epilepsy or temporary health issues (e.g., medications).

3. Provide student safety orientations. Throughout the school year, safety discussions should cover potentially dangerous situations, class conduct, and rules for proper use of equipment and apparatus. Teachers should urge students to report any condition that might cause an accident.

4. Discuss safety rules. At the start of each instructional unit, cover specific safety issues. Post rules and regularly bring them to students' attention. Posters and bulletin boards can promote safety in an enjoyable and stimulating way.

5. Train paraprofessionals, volunteers, or students who serve as instructional aides. Aides must be properly instructed before being part of the educational process. Supervise aides carefully, because teachers are held responsible even if an aide performs a duty incorrectly.

6. Monitor instructional practices for possible hazards. For example, match students in competitive situations by size, maturity, and ability. Supply instruction required for safe participation before an activity begins. Instructors should be certified physical educators to ensure they are adequately trained to give instruction in various activities. Prepare the instructional area for safe participation; if the area lacks necessary apparatus and safety devices, modify instruction to meet safety standards.

7. Include a safety checklist with the inventory of equipment and apparatus. Whenever necessary, send equipment that needs repair to proper repair sources. If the repair cost is more than 40% of the replacement cost, discarding the equipment or apparatus is usually a more economical choice. Report equipment in need of repair to the chain of command for approval.

8. Record and report injuries in student files. Immediately file an injury report by type, such as ankle sprain or broken arm. To facilitate analysis at regular intervals, a report should list the activity and the conditions. Analysis may show that injuries occur regularly during a specific activity or on a certain piece of equipment. This process can give direction for creating a safer environment or for defending the safety record of a sport, activity, or equipment type.

9. Ensure that teachers have up-to-date first aid training and CPR certification. Automated external defibrillator (AED) training should be included as part of CPR certification. Administrators should be sure that teachers meet these standards and should provide training sessions when necessary.

11

breathing, the teacher must administer first aid. Do not move already injured persons unless further injury may result if they are not moved. As a rule, however, do not move an injured person unless necessary. If a back or neck injury is indicated, immobilize the victim's head and do not move him or her without using a spine board. Remember that the purpose of first aid is to save life. The emergency care plan should consist of the following steps:

1. *Administer first aid to the injured student as the first priority.* Treat only life-threatening injuries. Contact the building administrator or school safety officer and school nurse immediately. Most schools have an emergency action or care plan and chain of command to follow. Be sure to know these policies before the school year starts.

2. *Notify parents as soon as possible when emergency care is required.* Each student's file should list home and emergency telephone numbers where parents can be reached. If possible, the school should have an arrangement with local emergency facilities so that a paramedic unit can be called immediately to the scene of a serious accident.

3. *Release the student to a parent or a designated representative.* Policies for transporting injured students should be established and documented.

4. *Promptly complete a student accident report while the details of the accident are clear and fresh.* Figure 11.1 is an example of an accident form covering the required details. The principal and the nurse should each retain copies, and the physical education teacher should receive a copy.

Equipment and Facilities

School responsibility for equipment and facilities is required for both noninstructional and class use.

Administrators

The principal and the custodian oversee the fields and playground equipment used for recess and outside activities. Instruct students to report broken and unsafe equipment, as well as hazards (e.g., glass, cans, and rocks) to the principal's office. If the equipment is faulty, remove it from the area. Have the physical education specialist or custodian regularly (perhaps weekly) inspect

equipment and facilities. File the inspection results by formal letter with the school district safety committee. Replace sawdust, sand, or other shock-absorbing material regularly. For use in recording safety inspections, administrators should have a written checklist of equipment and apparatus. Note the date of inspection and be sure that inspection occurs regularly. If a potentially dangerous situation exists, post rules or warnings to inform students and other teachers of the risk. Even if the safety inspection is not your responsibility, if you see a problem, immediately report it to administrators by memo or letter. If an accident occurred and it was discovered that you had not reported an unsafe situation, you might be held liable for the accident.

Proper installation of equipment is critical. Have a reputable firm that guarantees its work install climbing equipment and other equipment that must be anchored. When examining apparatus, inspection of the installation is important. Maintenance of facilities is also important. Keep grass cut short and inspect the grounds for debris. Fill any holes in the ground and remove loose gravel. Repair or eliminate hazards found on playing fields. On indoor floors, use a proper finish that prevents excessive slipping. Shower rooms should have a roughened floor finish to prevent falls when the floors are wet.

Safe participation in an activity can be enhanced by the selection of equipment and facilities. Base the choice of apparatus and equipment on the students' growth and developmental levels. For example, allowing elementary school children to use a horizontal ladder that was designed for high school students may result in a fall that causes injury. The legal concept of an *attractive nuisance* implies that some piece of equipment or apparatus, usually left unsupervised, was so attractive to children that they could not be expected to avoid using it. When an injury occurs, even though students may have been using the apparatus incorrectly, teachers and school administration are often held liable because the attractive nuisance should have been removed from the area when unsupervised.

Physical Educators

Indoor facilities are of primary concern to physical education instructors. Even though the administration is charged with overall responsibility for facilities and equipment, including periodic inspection, instructors should regularly inspect the safety of the instructional area. If corrective action is needed, notify the principal or other designated administrator in writing. Verbal noti-

STUDENT ACCIDENT REPORT

_____ School

In all cases, this form should be filed through the school nurse and signed by the principal of the school. The original will be forwarded to the superintendent's office, where it will be initialed and sent to the head nurse. The second copy will be retained by the principal or the school nurse. The third copy should be given to the physical education teacher if the accident is related.

Name of injured _____ Address _____

Phone _____ Grade _____ Home room _____ Age _____

Parents of injured _____

Place of accident _____ Date of accident _____

Hour _____ a.m./p.m. Date reported _____ By whom _____

Parent contact attempted at _____ a.m./p.m. Parent contacted at _____ a.m./p.m.

Describe accident, giving specific location and condition of premises _____

_____

Nature of injury _____

(Describe in detail)

Care given or action taken by nurse or others _____

_____

Reason injured person was on premises _____

(Activity at time—i.e., lunch, physical education, etc.)

Staff member responsible for student supervision at time of accident _____

_____

Is student covered by school-sponsored accident insurance? _____ Yes _____ No

Medical care recommended _____ Yes _____ No

Place taken after accident _____

(Specify home, physician, or hospital, giving name and address)

By whom _____ **At what time** _____ a.m./p.m.

Follow-up by nurse to be sent to central health office

Remedial measures taken _____

(Attach individual remarks if necessary)

School _____ Principal _____

Date _____ Nurse _____

On the back of this sheet, list all persons familiar with the circumstances of the accident, giving name, address, telephone number, age, and location with respect to the accident.

FIGURE 11.1 Sample accident report form.

fication is insufficient to protect the instructor legally.

Arrange facilities with safety in mind. Often, the sidelines and endlines of playing fields for sports such as football, soccer, and field hockey are placed too close to walls, curbs, or fences. Adjust the boundaries to allow adequate room for deceleration, even if the size of the playing area is reduced. In the gymnasium, do not have students run to a line that is close to a wall. Another common hazard is placing basketball hoops too close to the playing area. Be sure that the poles that support the baskets are padded.

Proper use of equipment and apparatus is important. Regardless of the condition of equipment, misuse may result in injury. Instruct students on how to use equipment and apparatus before they are used. To ensure that all points are covered, include all safety instruction in the written lesson plan.

Equipment should be purchased based on quality and safety as well as potential use. Many lawsuits occur because of unsafe equipment and apparatus. The manufacturer may be held liable for such equipment, but this liability has to be proved. Thus, the teacher must state, in writing, the exact specifications of the desired equipment. The process of bidding for lower-priced items may result in the purchase of less safe equipment. If teachers have specified proper equipment in writing, however, the possibility of their being held liable for injury is reduced.

Personal Protection: Minimizing the Effects of a Lawsuit

Despite proper care, injuries do occur, and lawsuits may be initiated. Two courses of action are necessary to minimize the effects of a suit.

Liability Insurance

The school district's liability insurance may cover its teachers, but most often teachers buy their own policies. Many physical education professionals join the Society for Health and Physical Education (SHAPE America) and purchase liability insurance at a reasonable cost. Members can obtain a group liability policy for a modest amount. Most policies provide for legal services to contest a suit and will pay indemnity up to the limits of the policy (liability coverage of $500,000 is most common). Most policies give the insurance company the right to settle out of court. Unfortunately, when a settlement occurs, some people may infer that the teacher was guilty even though the circumstances indicate otherwise. Insurance companies usually settle out of court to avoid the excessive legal fees required to try the case in court.

Record Keeping

The second course of action in minimizing lawsuits is to keep complete records of *all* accidents. Teachers may fail to document an accident because they perceive it to be minor. A look through the legal literature shows many cases that began as a minor bump on the head that led to problems later. Besides, many lawsuits occur months or even years after the accident, when memory of the situation is fuzzy. Fill out an accident report immediately after an injury occurs. Take care to provide no evidence, oral or written, that others could use in a court of law. In the report, do not try to make a diagnosis or define the supposed cause of the accident. Simply record what happened by completing the student accident report (see figure 11.1).

If newspaper reporters probe for details, refuse comment and direct the reporter to a district administrator. When discussing the accident with administrators, focus only on the facts recorded in the accident report. Remember that school records can be subpoenaed in court proceedings. The point here is not to dissemble, but to be cautious and to avoid self-incrimination.

Safety and Liability Checklists

Use the following checklists to monitor the physical activity (i.e., the physical education, recess, and playground) environment. Immediately rectify any situations that deviate from safe and legally sound practices.

Supervision and Instruction

1. Are teachers adequately trained in all the activities they are teaching?

2. Do all teachers and recess supervisors have the necessary level of first aid training?

3. When supervising, do personnel have access to a written plan of the areas to be observed and the responsibilities to be carried out?

4. Have students been warned of potential dangers and risks and advised of rules and the reasons for the rules?

5. Are safety rules posted near areas of increased risk?

6. Are lesson plans written? Do they include provisions for proper instruction, sequence of activities, and safety? Are all activities that are taught listed in the district curriculum guide?

7. When introducing a new activity, do teachers always instruct the class in safety precautions and instructions for correct skill performance?

8. Are the activities taught in the program based on sound curriculum principles? Could the activities and units of instruction be defended based on their educational contributions?

9. Do the methods of instruction recognize individual differences among students, and are the necessary steps taken to meet all students' needs regardless of gender, ability, or disability?

10. Are substitute teachers given clear and easy to comprehend lesson plans so that they can maintain the scope and sequence of instruction?

11. Is the student evaluation plan based on actual performance and objective data rather than on favoritism or arbitrary and capricious standards?

12. Is appropriate dress required for students? This guideline does not imply wearing uniforms, only dress (including shoes) that ensures the safety of all students.

13. When necessary for safety, are students grouped according to ability level, size, or age?

14. Is the class left unsupervised when the teacher visits the office, lounge, or bathroom? Is one teacher ever asked to supervise two or more classes at once?

15. If students are used as teacher aides or to spot other students, are they properly instructed and trained?

16. Are playground supervisors appropriately trained?

17. Is adequate supervision taking place? Is the supervisor-to-student ratio adequate?

Equipment and Facilities

1. Is all equipment (physical education, recess, and playground) inspected regularly, and are the inspection results recorded on a form and sent to the proper administrators?

2. Is a log maintained recording the regular occurrence of inspections, the equipment in need of repair, and the times when repairs were made?

3. Are attractive nuisances eliminated from the gymnasium, playing field, and playground?

4. Are specific safety rules posted on facilities and near equipment?

5. Are the following inspected periodically?

    a. Playing field for the presence of glass, rocks, and metal objects

    b. Fasteners holding equipment such as climbing ropes, horizontal bars, baskets, and swings

    c. Goals for games such as football, soccer, and field hockey to be sure they are fastened securely

    d. Padded areas, such as goal supports

6. Are mats placed under apparatus from which a fall is possible?

7. Are playing fields arranged so that participants will not run into each other or be hit by a ball from another game?

8. Are landing pits filled and maintained properly?

Emergency Care

1. Is a written procedure for emergency care in place? Is a person who is properly trained in first aid available immediately following an accident? Are cell phones or walkie-talkies available for physical education teachers and recess supervisors?

2. Are emergency telephone numbers readily accessible?

3. Are parents' telephone numbers available?

4. Is an up-to-date first aid kit available? Is ice immediately available?

5. Are health folders listing restrictions, allergies, and health problems of students maintained?

6. Are health folders routinely reviewed by instructors?

7. Are students who participate in extracurricular activities required to have insurance? Is the policy number recorded?

8. Is a plan in place for treating injuries that involve the local paramedics?

9. Are accident reports filed promptly and analyzed regularly?

Transportation of Students

1. Have parents been informed that their students will be transported off-campus?

2. Are detailed travel plans approved by the site administrator and kept on file?

3. Are school vehicles used whenever possible?

4. Are drivers properly licensed and their vehicles insured?

5. If teachers or parents use their own vehicles to transport students, are the students, drivers, and car owners covered by an insurance rider purchased by the school district?

After-School Sports Programs

Physical educators are often responsible for after-school sports programs. For this reason, they should understand the legal issues associated with such programs. The administration should set minimum requirements for program leaders and ensure that incompetent individuals are removed from such duties. When students are involved in extracurricular activities, teachers and leaders are responsible for the safe conduct of activities. The areas that often give rise to lawsuits if not handled carefully include mismatched opponents, waiver forms, medical examinations, weather issues, and the transportation of students.

Mismatched Opponents

If an injury occurs, the instructor is liable even when competitors are the same gender and choose to participate. The question that courts examine is whether an effort was made to match students according to height, weight, and ability. Courts are less understanding about mismatching in the physical education setting compared with an athletic contest, but mismatching is to be avoided in any situation.

Waiver Forms

Require participants in extracurricular activities to sign a responsibility waiver form. The form should explain the risks involved in voluntary participation and briefly discuss the types of injuries that have occurred in the past during practice and competition. Supervisors should remember that waiver slips do not waive the rights of participants, and that teachers and coaches still can be found liable if injuries occur. The waiver form should clearly communicate the risks involved and may be a strong assumption-of-risk defense.

Medical Examinations

Participants must have a medical examination before participating. Keep records of the examination on file and mark them prominently when physical restrictions or limitations exist. A common practice is to "red dot" the folders of students who have a history of medical problems. Students must not be allowed to participate unless they purchase medical insurance, and evidence of such coverage should be kept in the folders of athletic participants.

Weather Issues

Be aware of guidelines dealing with heat and humidity. In Arizona, for example, guidelines advise avoiding strenuous activity when the temperature exceeds 85 degrees Fahrenheit (29.5 degrees Celsius) and the humidity exceeds 40%. When these conditions are exceeded, running is curtailed to 10 minutes and active games to 30 minutes. Students should be hydrated before activity, and drinking water made available on demand.

Transportation of Students

Whenever students are transported to play teams from other schools, program leaders are responsible for their safety both en route and during the activity. Transportation liability can be avoided by having participants arrange their own transportation to the event (Pittman, 1993). If the school must provide transportation, it should always use licensed drivers and school-approved vehicles. Travel plans should include official approval from the appropriate school administrator. Teachers or program leaders who transport students and receive reimbursement should purchase a special insurance rider that provides liability coverage for this situation.

LEARNING AIDS

HOW AND WHY

1. Should teachers have professional insurance?
2. How can effective classroom management help teachers avoid legal issues?
3. How can teachers protect themselves from lawsuits?
4. Why is a safety and liability checklist important?

CONTENT REVIEW

1. Define *tort*.
2. Identify four major points that must be established to determine whether a teacher is negligent. In addition, discuss the importance of foreseeability.
3. List and explain different types of negligence.
4. Describe common defenses against negligence.
5. Discuss the importance of supervision and instruction when examining responsibility.
6. Identify who is responsible for equipment and facilities.
7. List some issues related to sports programs that often result in lawsuits.
8. Briefly describe several guidelines for safety in physical education.
9. Explain the importance of an emergency care plan and discuss the steps in the plan.

11

WEBSITES

Playground safety, www.cpsc.gov/s3fs-public/325.pdf
Playground design, www.playdesigns.com
Playground programs, www.peacefulplaygrounds.com
School safety and security, www.schoolsecurity.org

SUGGESTED READINGS

Appenzeller, H. (2012). *Risk management in sport: Issues and strategies* (3rd ed.). Durham, NC: Carolina Academic Press.

Appenzeller, H. (2003). *Managing sports and risk management strategies* (2nd ed.). Durham, NC: Carolina Academic Press.

Carpenter, L.J. (2008). *Legal concepts in sport: A primer* (3rd ed.). Champaign, IL: Sagamore.

Dougherty, N.J. (Ed.). (2009). *Principles of safety in physical education and sport* (4th ed.). Reston, VA: AAHPERD.

Dougherty, N.J., Goldberger, A.S., & Carpenter, L.J. (2007). *Sport, physical activity, and the law* (3rd ed.). Champaign, IL: Sagamore.

Pittman, A.T., Spengler, J.G., & Young, S.J. (2016). *Case studies in sport law* (2nd ed.). Champaign, IL: Human Kinetics.

Zimmerman, S., Kramer, K., & Trowbridge, M.J. (2013). Overcoming legal liability concerns for school based physical activity promotion. *American Journal of Public Health, 103*(11), 1962–1967.

REFERENCES

Baley, J.A., & Matthews, D.L. (1988). *Law and liability in athletics, physical education, and recreation*. Boston, MA: Allyn & Bacon.

Garner, B.A. (Ed.) (2009). *Black's law dictionary* (9th ed.). St. Paul, MN: West Group.

Gray, G.R. (2007). Providing adequate medical care to program participants. *Journal of Physical Education, Recreation, and Dance, 64*(2), 56–57.

Merriman, J. (1993). Supervision in sport and physical activity. *Journal of Physical Education, Recreation, and Dance, 64*(2), 20–23.

Pittman, A.T. (1993). Safe transportation—A driving concern. *Journal of Physical Education, Recreation, and Dance, 64*(2), 53–55.

U.S. Consumer Product Safety Commission. (2010). *Public playground safety handbook*. Washington, DC: U.S. Government Printing Office.

12 Facilities, Equipment, and Supplies

This chapter presents procedures associated with the design, purchase, maintenance, and construction of physical education facilities, equipment, and supplies. Equipment is defined here as items that are rather fixed in nature, such as swings and basketball goals. Equipment has a relatively long-life span, needs periodic safety checks, and requires planned purchasing. Supplies are nondurable items with a limited period of use, such as volleyballs and jump ropes. When resources are limited, some equipment can be constructed. This chapter has a comprehensive section on how to build equipment and supplies.

Learning Objectives

▶ Identify standards to follow when constructing outdoor and indoor physical education facilities.

▶ Understand that safety is an essential consideration in the design of facilities.

▶ Illustrate floor lines and markings that enhance management potential and increase ease of instruction.

▶ List the essential equipment and the supplies needed for teaching elementary school physical education.

▶ List the recommended equipment for outdoor and indoor physical education areas.

▶ Outline a systematic plan for storing physical education equipment and supplies.

▶ Describe procedures for the care and repair of physical education equipment and supplies.

▶ Be able to construct selected physical education equipment and supplies.

Physical education facilities should be planned for the maximum projected enrollment. Too often, planning is done for the present situation. Later, when the school adds classrooms, the physical education areas are not expanded accordingly. Thus, what once was an adequate arrangement becomes a scheduling problem. Adding physical education facilities is difficult because of generally escalating costs and the relatively high cost of physical education facilities compared with the cost of adding regular classroom space.

Outdoor Facilities

Outdoor areas should include field space for games, a track, hard-surfaced areas, apparatus areas, play courts, age-specific play areas, covered play space, and a jogging trail. Fields should be leveled, drained, and turfed because grass is the most usable field surface. An automatic sprinkler system is desirable, but sprinkler heads must not protrude (in which case they become safety hazards). Automatic systems permit sprinkling during the evening and night so that the fields are not too soggy for play the next day.

Mark a hard-topped area for various games such as tetherball, volleyball, and basketball. Other markings for this area might include four-square courts, hopscotch layouts, and circles for games. Simple movement pattern courses can also be marked. Some research suggests that painting playground surfaces with bright, attractive art (e.g., castles or dragons) may help increase activity levels during recess (Stratton & Mullan, 2005). Some administrators prefer a hard surface for the entire play area because it eliminates the mud problem and the need for sprinkling, thus lowering maintenance costs. Hard surfaces are used when play space is limited and when the number of students makes it difficult to maintain a turf surface. As a minimum, the outdoor facility should have a track, located where it will not interfere with other activities. If a permanent installation is impractical, a temporary track can be laid out each spring.

In the planning, designate separate play spaces for different age groups. These areas should contain apparatus and equipment designed for each age group. Locate the play area for primary-level children well away from areas where footballs and softballs are used. Place small, hard-surfaced play courts near the edges of the outdoor area, thus spreading out the play groups. These courts, approximately 40 by 60 feet (12 by 20 m), can be equipped for basketball, volleyball, or both. A covered shed can be divided for use by different age groups. Climate conditions dictate the need for such facilities.

A walking–jogging trail can stimulate interest in walking or jogging. Small signs indicating the distances covered and markers outlining the trail are all that are needed. Stations for different exercises, such as a specified number of push-ups or sit-ups, can be placed at intervals. Such a circuit is popularly called a parcourse or fitness stations course.

An area set aside as a developmental playground is an important part of the total play space. The area should contain equipment and apparatus and be landscaped to have small hills, valleys, and tunnels for children. A recommended approach is to divide the playground into various developmental areas so that children must use different body parts in different areas of the play space. One area might contain climbing equipment to reinforce arm–shoulder girdle development, and another area might challenge the leg and trunk regions. Equipment and apparatus should be abstract, leaving creation and imagination to the children. Apparatus can be manipulated and changed to suit children's needs and desires.

Safety on the Playground

Studies by the U.S. Consumer Product Safety Commission (2010) show that most injuries are caused when children fall from an apparatus and strike the underlying surface. Injuries range from minor bruises to skull fractures, concussions, and brain damage. Falls onto paved surfaces result in a disproportionately high number of severe injuries, including some deaths.

The choice of materials for the surface under equipment needs to be based on local conditions and the availability of funds. Concrete, asphalt, and other paved surfaces require little maintenance, which is why they are so commonly used. Hard surfaces, however, do not soften the impact of accidental falls and thus are unsuitable for playground use. Organic materials such as pine bark nuggets, pine bark mulch, shredded hardwood bark, and cocoa shell mulch are recommended instead. Other suitable materials are wood chips, shredded tires, and sand. If hard surfaces are already in place, outdoor interlocking tiles or dense synthetic turf may be laid over them.

If loose, organic materials are used, provide at least a 6-inch (15 cm) layer of material to cushion the impact of falls. Continuous, proper maintenance is as important as selecting the proper material. Because children will move the material away from the area, frequent leveling, grading, and replacement are required. The material also needs to be screened routinely to eliminate insects, animal excrement, and concealed sharp objects. Unfortunately, organic materials decompose, become pulverized and dusty, and mix with dirt, thus losing their cushioning properties. In rainy or humid weather, they can absorb moisture and pack down, resulting in loss of resiliency. Select materials that do not harden during freezing temperatures. As part of the maintenance of these materials, you will need a checklist of procedures to be followed and filled out regularly.

Outdoor Apparatus and Equipment

Promoting physical activity should dictate the selection of outdoor equipment. Equipment that offers sit-and-ride experiences (e.g., swings, merry-go-rounds, and teeter-totters) does not meet this criterion. A second criterion is safety. Each piece of equipment should minimize the potential for injury. In general, if equipment has moving parts, its potential for injury increases. This section offers suggestions for equipment based on their potential to develop various components of fitness. Remember that safety is the highest priority with play-

ground equipment because it is often left unsupervised. If a playground is unrestricted during nonschool hours, it may be best to stick to traditional equipment. An excellent website on adventure playgrounds covers this topic in detail (http://adventureplaygrounds.hampshire.edu/index.html).

Equipment for Upper-Body Development

Most children lack the opportunity to develop upper-body strength. To develop arm–shoulder girdle strength on the playground, students need to climb, swing, and elevate their bodies. Climbing is important for physical development and for helping children overcome their fear of new situations. The following equipment can help develop arm–shoulder girdle strength:

- Large telephone cable spools, fastened securely so they will not move or tip over. Children can climb on and jump off the spools.

- Climbing poles placed next to platforms that children can reach by climbing the poles.

- Logs and clean railroad ties, positioned vertically, with handholds or handles placed in strategic locations for climbing.

Soft organic surfaces are safest for playgrounds.

- Tires attached to telephone poles or logs for climbing through and around.
- Jungle gyms that are attached securely.
- Horizontal ladders in various combinations and forms. Arched ladders are popular and allow children to reach the rungs easily. Uniladders, consisting of a single beam with foot pegs on each side, give children a different ladder challenge.
- Logs anchored vertically with handholds for climbing.

Equipment for Lower-Body Development

Equipment and apparatus for enhancing lower-body development should encourage children to use loco-motor movements. Allow enough distance and area to ensure movement. Here are suggestions for developing lower-body strength:

- Provide large spaces, which encourage free movement and running games.
- Anchor railroad ties vertically at varying heights and distances to encourage children to walk, run, hop, and jump from one to the other.
- Fasten used automobile tires to the ground in different patterns to stimulate moving in and out, around, and over the tires using different movements.
- Construct stairways and platforms for climbing on and jumping off.
- Offer stepping-stones to encourage movement patterns. Create a design that leads to oppositional patterning while moving.
- Design miniature challenge courses containing tires to move over and through, sand pits to run and jump into, and poles or cones for moving around and dodging.

Equipment for Balance Skills

Balance is a skill that can be improved through regular practice. Encourage children to move under control while practicing balance. Here are some suggestions for balance challenges:

- Balance beams made of 4-by-4-inch (10 by 10 cm) beams can be permanent installations. Arrange them in various patterns, but no more

than 12 to 18 inches (30 to 45 cm) above the ground.
- Logs, anchored securely, can be used as balance beams.
- Provide balance beams that start at 6 inches (15 cm) wide and progress in difficulty to 1-1/2 inches (3.8 cm) wide.
- Wooden ladders secured 6 inches (15 cm) above the ground can offer students opportunities to walk on the rungs and rails.

Equipment for Sport Skills

- *Basketball goals.* Outdoor basketball goals may or may not be combined with a court. Children play a lot of one-goal basketball, which does not require a regulation court. The goals, however, should be in a surfaced area. For elementary school use, place outdoor baskets at a height of 8 or 9 feet (2.4 or 2.7 m).
- *Volleyball standards.* Volleyball standards should have flexible height adjustments, including a low height of 30 inches (75 cm) for use in paddleball.
- *Softball backstops.* Softball backstops can be either fixed or portable.
- *Tetherball courts.* Tetherball courts should have fastening devices for the cord and ball so that they can be removed from the post for safekeeping.
- *Track and field equipment.* Jumping standards, bars, and pits should be available but must be maintained properly.

Indoor Facilities

The combination gymnasium–auditorium–cafeteria facility leaves much to be desired and often creates more problems than it solves. Although it may be labeled a multipurpose room, a better description is probably "multiuseless." The cafeteria poses a particular problem. The gymnasium must be vacated before the lunch hour so that chairs and tables can be set up, and the facility is unavailable again for physical education activities until it has been cleaned, which usually involves mopping. This schedule eliminates noontime recreational use and leaves little play area for children during inclement weather. In

12

extreme cases, a lack of help postpones gymnasium use for the early part of the afternoon, until the custodian has completed cleaning chores. Special programs, movies, and other events requiring chairs and the use of the area also complicate the situation.

Ideally, the gymnasium is located in a separate wing, connected to the classrooms by a covered corridor. This sort of facility provides ready access to play areas. Isolating the gym from the rest of the school minimizes the noise problem and allows after-school and community groups to use the facilities without access to other parts of the school. The indoor facility is planned so that athletic contests can be scheduled there at times, but its primary purpose is not to be an athletic facility. Consideration for spectators is not a major planning concern. Only after basic physical education needs have been met are the needs of spectators considered.

The gymnasium floor should have markings and boundaries outlining convenient areas for common activities. The markings should be painted on the floor after applying the first or second sealer coat. A finish coat

is then applied on top of the markings. Figure 12.1 shows how floor markings can maximize a facility's usefulness.

Temporary lines needed occasionally during the year can be applied with pressure-sensitive tape or white shoe polish. Other surfaces limit community use and create safety and maintenance problems.

For safety reasons and for rebound practice, gym walls should have a smooth surface 8 to 10 feet (2.4 to 3 m) up from the floor. Walls and ceilings need acoustical treatment to minimize noise. Exposed beams should be available for attaching apparatus. When planning a new facility, include a recessed storage location for each set of ropes on tracks.

The gym should be well lit, with fixtures recessed to prevent damage. Arrange lights so that they can be serviced from the floor. All walls should have electrical outlets. A permanent overhead public address system is desirable, as is a means of playing audio (Bluetooth speaker, CD player, and so on). In a new facility, place windows high on the long sides of the gymnasium. Include protection from glare and direct sun.

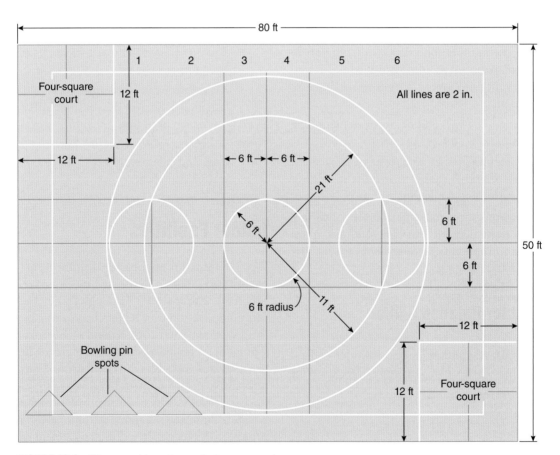

FIGURE 12.1 Floor markings to maximize gymnasium use.

The facility's storage space must be carefully planned. Equipment and instructional supplies require much storage space, and they must be readily available. One problem frequently associated with a combination auditorium–gymnasium facility is the use of the physical education storeroom for bulky auditorium equipment such as portable chairs on chair trucks, portable stages, lighting fixtures, and other paraphernalia for dramatic productions. Unless the storage facility is quite large—and most are not—an unworkable and cluttered facility is the result. The best solution is two separate storerooms for the dual-purpose facility, or at least one very large storeroom. Figure 12.2 shows an ideal physical education storage area.

A separate storage area of cabinets is essential for outside groups who use the facility. These groups should not have access to the regular physical education supply room. Sharing equipment with outside organizations will ultimately create ill will as equipment starts to disappear. Each group and the physical education teacher will blame each other with no solution in sight. If you choose to do so, make sure you have a checkout system so that others can be held accountable. Remember that your equipment is critical to your teaching success; they are the tools of your trade.

Many storage areas in European schools have doors on tracks, similar to overhead garage doors in the United States. One particular advantage of this design is that the overhead opening simplifies the handling of large apparatus. Most architects are unaware of the storage needs of a typical physical education program. Teachers can only hope that the architects designing a new school can be persuaded to provide sufficient storage. For the physical education specialist, an office–dressing room with toilet and shower is desirable.

If contract or task styles of teaching are important in the instructional process, an area that houses instructional materials is useful. Children can go to this area, search through materials, and view loop films and videos as they complete their learning packets.

Equipment and Supplies

As mentioned at the beginning of the chapter, equipment (sometimes referred to as capital outlay items) refers to more or less fixed items, whereas supplies are nondurable items with a limited life span. For example, a softball is a supply, but a softball backstop is equipment. Equipment needs periodic replacement, and budget

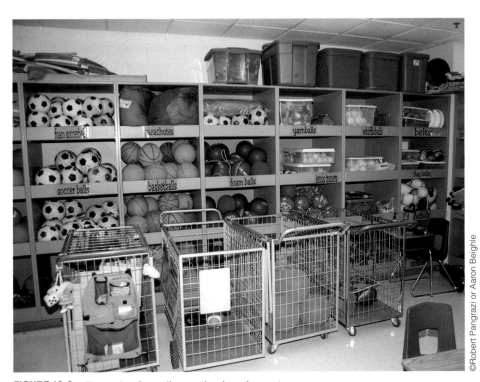

FIGURE 12.2 Example of a well-organized equipment room.

©Robert Pangrazi or Aaron Beighle

TEACHING TIP

If you don't have enough equipment or supplies, use peer coaching or teaching so that equipment is shared, students practice taking turns, and you don't need to split your focus and risk the occurrence of incidents through lack of supervision. Another option is station teaching whereby each small group uses different equipment. Any approach used to overcome equipment shortages, however, is never a good long-term solution. Equipment is what you use to teach skills, and quality instruction requires that all students have a piece for their own use.

planning must consider the life span of each piece of equipment. Supplies generally are purchased once a year. Having adequate financing for equipment and supplies is important, as is spending funds wisely.

To meet physical education program objectives, sufficient instructional materials must be available. Be sure that enough equipment is available so that children can use practice time well rather than wait in line.

Policies covering the purchase, storage, issuance, care, maintenance, and inventory of supplies are required to make optimum use of the program budget. Decide on program features first and then implement a purchasing plan based on these features. Having a minimal list of instructional supplies stabilizes the teaching process.

Some articles—yarn balls, hoops, Lummi sticks, balance beams, and bounding boards, for instance—can be made satisfactorily by school staff, by parents, and sometimes by students. The problem with homemade equipment is that it may not be tested for safety. Additionally, it communicates to leaders that funding is not required for physical education. In most cases, homemade equipment is usually a temporary solution only, undertaken in a program's early phases when equipment costs are high and cannot all be met immediately.

Purchasing Policies

Purchasing supplies and equipment involves careful study of need, price, quality, and material. The safety of the children who will use the equipment is paramount. Quantity buying by pooling the funds of an entire school district generally results in better use of tax dollars. Cooperative purchasing, however, may require compromises on equipment type and brand to satisfy different users in the system. If bids are requested, careful specifications are necessary. Request bids for specified items only, and do not accept "just as good" merchandise in their place.

Make one person at the school responsible for obtaining physical education supplies and keeping records of equipment, supplies, and purchasing. Needs vary from school to school, and it is practical for school district authorities to deal with a single person at each school. This system enables prompt attention to the need to repair and replace supplies. The designated person can also be responsible for testing various competing prod-

TECH TIP

Music is an excellent way to get students engaged and learning. In years gone by, playing music involved record albums, cassette tapes, and CDs, which were great but very limiting compared with the technology available today. Apps and websites that offer music at a cost-effective rate are plentiful. Some even offer mixed music for free. Teachers are encouraged to monitor songs for appropriate lyrics. Even if instrumentals are used, check the lyrics of the songs for appropriateness. Of obvious importance when using music is the sound system. The volume that the system can produce and that is needed depends on the teaching space. In some cases, a cart or a system on wheels is helpful to transport the system. Apps are available not only to play music but also to control the music. These apps allow teachers to turn music on or off, switch songs, change the tempo, and change the volume, all from a phone or even a watch. One last comment about music as a motivator is warranted. Music can certainly be motiving and energizing, but with young students, it may be too energizing. If the music seems to be yielding off-task behavior, consider turning it off until students can demonstrate proper behavior.

ucts to determine which ones give the best service over time. The materials must be labeled or marked in some way to complete such testing.

An accurate inventory of equipment is required at the start and end of each school year. A sound inventory system tracks the durability of equipment and supplies and accounts for lost or misplaced supplies. Order supplies and equipment by the end of the school year, or earlier if possible. To allow time for checking orders and making any necessary adjustments before the school year begins, specify an early delivery date.

Most quality equipment can be expected to last 7 to 10 years, thus keeping replacement costs to a minimum. School district purchasing agents who select low-cost items with little regard for quality are applying financially unsound policies. Budgetary practices should include an allotment for the yearly purchase of instructional supplies as well as for the major replacement and procurement costs for large items, which are usually staggered over several years. After obtaining sufficient equipment and supplies, the program's budget considerations will be for replacement and repair only.

Indoor Equipment

Several principles govern the choice of indoor equipment. First, a reasonable variety and amount of equipment should be available to keep children active. Include items to facilitate arm–shoulder girdle development (e.g., climbing ropes, climbing frames, ladders, and similar apparatus). A criterion for selection is that most, if not all, indoor equipment be of the type that children can carry, assemble, and disassemble.

Mats for Tumbling and Safety

Mats are basic to any physical education program. Enough mats—at least eight—must be available to provide a safe floor for climbing apparatus. Light, folding mats are best because they are easy to handle and store (figure 12.3). They stack well and can be moved on carts. Mats should have fasteners so that several can be joined. Plastic covers allow easy cleaning. (The one objection to plastic covers is that they are not as soft as the type of mat cover used for wrestling.) Mats should be 4 feet (1.2 m) wide and 7 or 8 feet (2.1 or 2.4 m) long. Heavy hand-me-down mats from the high school program may prove difficult for younger students to handle and are bulky to store.

FIGURE 12.3 Tumbling mats stored on wall with Velcro fasteners.

©Robert Pangrazi or Aaron Beighle

Other mats to consider are thick, soft mats (somewhat like mattresses) and inclined mats. Soft mats are generally at least 4 inches (10 cm) thick and may entice the timid to try activities they otherwise would avoid. Inclined mats are wedge-shaped and provide downhill momentum for rolls.

Individual Mats

The primary-level program requires a supply of 30 to 35 individual mats. The mats, which can be 20 by 40 inches (50 by 100 cm) or 24 by 48 inches (60 or 120 cm), are useful for practicing many movements and introductory tumbling activities and can serve as a home base for many activities.

Portable Speaker

A portable speaker with wireless capabilities is a great tool for teachers. It can be connected to a phone or other device to play music.

Balance-Beam Benches

Balance-beam benches have a double use. They can serve as regular benches for many types of bench activity, and, when turned over, can be used for balance-beam activities. Wooden horses or their supports can serve as inclined benches. Six benches are a minimum for class activity.

Balance Beams

A wide beam (4 inches [10 cm]) is recommended for kindergarten and first grade. Otherwise, a 2-inch (5 cm) beam can be used. Balance beams in two widths (i.e., 2 and 4 inches) can be constructed from common building materials.

Chinning Bar

The chinning bar is especially useful for physical fitness testing and in body support activities. A portable chinning bar, properly installed in the gym doorway, is an acceptable substitute.

Climbing Ropes

Climbing ropes are essential to the program. At least eight ropes are required but having more than eight allows better group instruction. Climbing ropes on tracks are the most efficient to handle (figure 12.4). With little effort or loss of time, the ropes can be pulled out for activity.

Quality climbing ropes made of synthetic fibers are now available. The best are olefin fiber ropes that are nonallergenic and have nonslip qualities, thus forestalling the problem of slickness—a characteristic of plastic ropes and even of older cotton ropes. Ropes should be either 1-1/2 or 1-3/4 inches (3.8 or 4.4 cm) in diameter. Climbing ropes on tracks and other large apparatus can be purchased from companies such as Gopher Sport.

Volleyball Standards

Volleyball standards should adjust to various heights for different grade levels and games.

Supply Cart

A cart to hold supplies is desirable. Other carts can be used for the audio equipment and for regular and individual mats.

Jumping Boxes

Small boxes used for jumping and related locomotor movements extend students' opportunities to work on basic movement skills. Boxes should be 8 and 16 inches (20 and 40 cm) high. If the boxes are made by staff, specify about 16 by 16 inches (40 by 40 cm) with

FIGURE 12.4 Climbing ropes on tracks.

©Robert Pangrazi or Aaron Beighle

a skidproof rubber surface on the bottom for stability. Holes drilled through the sides provide fingerholds for ease of handling. Eight boxes, four of each size, are a minimum number for the average-sized class.

Horizontal Ladder Sets

Horizontal ladders that fold against the wall make an excellent indoor equipment addition. The ladder may be combined with other pieces of apparatus in a folding set.

Other Indoor Items

A portable chalkboard is desirable, as is a wall screen for displaying visual aids. To display announcements or notes, hang a large bulletin board and a wall chalkboard near the gym's main door. An audiovisual cart or stand for projectors is helpful. Be sure that it includes enough electrical cord to reach wall outlets.

Rebound nets for throwing and kicking, while difficult to store, are useful. Substitute goals for basketball and related games can be designed. One suggested goal is 4 feet (1.2 m) square, with the rim 5 feet (1.5 m) above the ground. Beginners can be successful with this goal design. The frame can be made of 1-inch (2.5 cm) pipe or plastic (PVC) tubing.

Equipment and Supplies for Physical Education

Knowing what equipment to obtain for your program and where to find it can be an obstacle, but it need not be a major one. Figure 12.5 identifies the equipment, supplies, and capital-outlay items needed to teach a quality physical education program. The items are listed by priority based on cost, need, and versatility of the equipment. The first piece of equipment listed, playground balls, can be used to teach the greatest number of units, so it has the highest priority. The quantity of equipment is also listed to ensure that the proper amount is ordered to facilitate a normal class size. Some of the equipment can be constructed rather than purchased, as described later in this chapter.

Most of the equipment listed is available from Gopher Sport (www.gophersport.com). The author has worked

Priority	Material and supplies	Quantity
1	8-1/2 in. (22 cm) inflatable rubber playground balls	36
1a	8 in. (20 cm) foam balls (can be substituted for playground balls)	36
1b	8 in. (20 cm) polyurethane-coated foam balls (A substitute for balls; they are much more durable and give a true bounce. They can be used for all types of sport activities.)	36
2	6 in. × 6 in. (15 cm × 15 cm) beanbags, assorted colors	72
3	Jump ropes (plastic segments for beginners and speed ropes for experienced jumpers)	
	7 ft (2.1 m) length	36
	8 ft (2.4 m) length	36
	9 ft (2.7 m) length	18
	16 ft (5 m) length (long rope-jumping)	12
4	Hoops (solid or segmented)	
	30 in. (75 cm) diameter	36
	36 in. (90 cm) diameter	36
5	Wands (36 in. [90 cm] length, 3/4 in. [19 mm] diameter hardwood)	36
6	Game cones (12 in. [30 cm] bright orange vinyl)	20
7	Tambourine, single head, double ring	1
8	Plastic rackets (sized for elementary children)	36
9	Foam balls for racket skills (2-1/2 in. [6 cm])	36
10	Fleece balls (3 to 4 in. [7.5 to 10 cm] diameter)	36
11	Floor hockey sticks and pucks—36 of each	36
12	Wiffle balls (use for throwing, hockey, softball, and so on)	36
13	Individual mats (23 in. × 48 in. × 1/2 in. [58 × 120 × 1.25 cm])	36
14	Partner tug-of-war ropes (handles on both ends made with nylon webbing or garden hose and 3/8 in. [9.5 mm] nylon rope)	18

FIGURE 12.5   Basic equipment and supplies needed for quality physical education. *(continued)*

Priority	Material and supplies	Quantity
15	Juggling scarves	108
16	Beach balls (18 to 20 in. [45 to 50 cm] diameter)	36
17	Soccer balls (junior size or trainers)	18
18	Basketballs (junior size)	18
19	Footballs (junior size or foam rubber)	18
20	Volleyballs (lightweight trainer balls)	18
21	Softballs (extra soft)	18
22	Softball bats (wood or aluminum)	3
23	Discs (9 to 10 in. [23 to 25 cm] diameter)	36
24	Magic stretch ropes	12
25	Cageball (24 in. [60 cm])	1
26	Pinnies (four colors—12 each)	48
27	Ball bags (nylon see-through mesh)	12
28	Team tug-of-war rope (3/4 in. × 50 ft [19 mm × 15 m] nylon with sealed ends)	1
29	Stopwatches (digital)	6
30	Batons (for track and field relays)	12
31	Scooter boards (12 in. [30 cm] with handles)	18
32	Bowling pins	30
33	Lummi sticks	72

Priority	Capital-outlay items	Quantity
1	Tumbling mats (4 ft × 8 ft × 1-1/4 in. thick [1.2 m × 2.4 m × 3.2 cm thick]; four sides of Velcro fasteners)	12
2	Portable speaker with blue tooth	1
3	Parachute and storage bag (28 ft [8.5 m] diameter)	1
4	Electric ball pump	1
5	Heavy-duty equipment (ball) carts	4
6	Balance-beam benches (12 ft [3.6 m] length)	6
7	Jumping boxes (8 in. [20 cm] height)	6
8	Jumping boxes (16 in. [40 cm] height)	6
9	Audiovisual cart with electrical outlet, and so forth)	1
10	Sit-and-reach box (to measure flexibility)	2
11	Utility gym standards (for volleyball nets, and so on)	2
12	Field marker (for chalking lines)	1

FIGURE 12.5 *(continued)*

closely with this company to develop a Dynamic Physical Education equipment list. This list offers all the equipment and teaching materials needed for a high-quality program.

Storage Plans

When a class goes to the gymnasium for physical education, the teacher has a right to expect enough supplies to be available to conduct the class. A master list stipulating the kinds and quantities of supplies in storage should be maintained. A reasonable turnover is to be expected, and supply procedures must consider this. Supplies in the storage facility should be available for physical education classes and for organized after-school activities. These supplies are not to be used for games played during recess or for free play periods; each classroom should have its own supplies for such purposes. Establish a system for storing equipment and supplies. "A place for everything and everything in its place" is the key to good housekeeping. Label bins, shelves, and other assigned areas where supplies and equipment are to be kept. Principals are more favorably inclined toward purchase requests of instructional materials when the materials are taken care of in an obvious and routine manner.

Some schools use small supply carts, as pictured in figure 12.6. The carts, which hold the most frequently used supplies, take up some additional space but save students time in accessing needed items. The carts can be built inexpensively to meet specific needs, or they can be purchased from a commercial manufacturer. A cart for audio equipment and carts that store and move mats and balls are helpful.

Establish an off-season storage area for equipment not in present use, and keep this area locked. Knowing who has keys to the storage area is important so that if equipment goes missing, those with access to the area can be identified.

Care, Repair, and Marking

Balls must be inflated to proper pressures, so an accurate gauge must be used to check the pressures periodically. Instruct children to kick only those balls made specifically for kicking (soccer balls, footballs, and playground balls). Repair cuts, abrasions, and breaks in rubber balls immediately. Some repairs can be made with a vulcanized patch, like those used to repair tire tubes. For other repairs, a hard-setting rubber preparation is best. For off-season storage, deflate balls somewhat, leaving just

FIGURE 12.6 Portable ball cart.

©Robert Pangrazi or Aaron Beighle

enough air in them to retain their shape. Clean leather balls with an appropriate conditioner.

Mats are expensive and need proper care if they are to last. Establish a place where they can be stacked properly, or, if the mats have handles or Velcro, hang them (see figure 12.3) to serve as padding for the walls. A mat truck is another storage option if space is available for the truck. Periodically clean the newer plastic or plastic-covered mats with a damp, soapy mopping solution.

For small items, clean 5-gallon (20 L) buckets are adequate storage receptacles. Most hardware stores have these and other containers that can be used in the storage room to keep order. Small wire or plastic baskets also make good storage containers.

Mark all equipment and supplies. This practice is particularly important for equipment issued to different classrooms. Use indelible pencil, paint, an engraver, or stencil ink for marking. Few marking systems are permanent, however, and remarking at regular intervals is necessary. Sporting goods stores have marking sets. An electric burning pencil works well when used carefully to avoid damaging the equipment.

Rubber playground balls come in different colors, and their assignment to classrooms can be based on the color. A code scheme with different colored paints also can be used. A color system designating the year of issue can also facilitate the process of documenting the usage and care of equipment.

Constructing Equipment and Supplies

This section is divided into two parts. The first part offers recommendations for sources and materials needed to construct equipment and supplies. The second part provides diagrams and specifications for building equipment economically. If the recommended equipment can be described adequately without an illustration, it is included in the first part.

Recommendations for Constructing Equipment and Supplies

A good supply of ropes for jumping is essential. The newer, plastic-link jump ropes are recommended for younger children because they have enough weight to carry them over the jumper's head. For upper-grade

AUTHOR'S NOTE ON CONSTRUCTING EQUIPMENT

The next section shows how to construct equipment, because doing so can be a short-term solution when starting a new program or unit of instruction. But this text does not actively promote self-constructed equipment, for several reasons.

- Constructed equipment is usually second rate and does not last long. It also gives teachers and students a feeling of being second-rate citizens because little money is spent for their teaching and learning tools.

- Constructed equipment is often a rough equivalent of the commercial product. Therefore, less skilled students are using the lowest quality equipment to learn, whereas more advanced (generally high school) athletes have the best quality equipment. Unskilled students, however, need the benefit of the best possible equipment if they are to succeed.

- Safety and liability can become problems depending on who constructed the equipment and whether it meets minimal safety standards. If an accident occurs, and it can be proved that the constructed equipment does not meet safety standards of commercially built equipment, the school may be held liable for the injury.

- If your building administrator knows that you can get by without a budget because you construct your own equipment, you will never have an adequate budget.

Homemade equipment should be a last resort and a short-term solution.

students, the spaghetti or speed rope is a better choice. It can be turned faster, which is helpful when performing stunt jumping. Enough ropes should be available in the suggested lengths for each child to have a rope of the correct length. Developmental Level I students use mostly 7-foot (2.1 m) ropes, with a few 6- and 8-foot (1.8 and 2.4 m) ropes. Developmental Levels II and III students use mostly 8-foot (2.4 m) ropes, with a few 7- and 9-foot (2.1 and 2.7 m) ropes. Instructors will require 9- or 10-foot (2.7 or 3 m) ropes. The supply of ropes should include 8 to 10 long (14- to 16-foot [4.3 to 4.9 m]) ropes for long-rope jumping activities. A jump-the-shot rope can be made by tying an old, completely deflated volleyball to one end of a long rope.

Beanbags can be made using bright-colored muslin as a covering. Some teachers have asked parents to save the lower legs of worn-out denim jeans; this material wears extremely well and is free. Other instructors prefer a beanbag with an outer liner that snaps in place to allow washing. Another idea is to sew three sides of the beanbag permanently. The fourth side is used for filling and has an independent stitch. The beans can be removed through this side when the bag is washed. Beanbags should be about 4 by 4 inches (10 by 10 cm) or 6 by 6 inches (15 by 15 cm) and can be filled with small pebbles, glass beads, or sand.

For games requiring boundary markers, use pieces of rubber matting; small sticks or boards, painted white, are also excellent. A board 1 by 2 inches (2.5 by 5 cm) across and 3 or 4 feet (90 or 120 cm) long makes a satisfactory marker.

Schools near ski areas may be able to get discarded towropes. These make excellent tug-of-war ropes.

Bowling pins or clubs can be turned in the school shop, or suitable substitutes can be made. For example, pieces of 2-by-2-inch (5 by 5 cm) lumber cut short (i.e., 6 to 10 inches [15 to 25 cm]) stand satisfactorily. Lumber companies usually have dowels 1 to 1-1/2 inches (2.5 to 3.8 cm) in diameter. Sections of these dowels make a reasonable substitute for clubs. Broken bats also can be made into good substitute clubs.

White shoe polish has many marking uses and can be removed from the floor with a little scrubbing.

Three-pound (1.4 kg) plastic coffee cans make excellent targets. Empty half-gallon (2 L) milk cartons also have a variety of uses.

Inner tubes can be cut in strips and used as resistance exercise equipment. The tube should be cut crosswise into 1-inch-wide (2.5 cm wide) strips.

Old bowling pins can be obtained from most bowling alleys free of charge. Because the standard pins are too large for children to handle easily, cutting 2 to 4 inches (5 to 10 cm) off the bottom is recommended. Parallel cuts through the body of the pin provide shuffleboard disks. For kindergarten and first-grade children, make improvised balls from crumpled newspaper bound with cellophane tape. Papier-mache balls are also useful. Light foam-rubber cubes can be trimmed to make interesting objects for throwing and catching.

Diagrams and Specifications for Constructing Equipment and Supplies

Safety standards should apply to all school-constructed equipment; be sure the construction and the materials used do not create safety hazards. The design must be educationally sound and utilitarian.

Balance Beam

The balance beam is used for many kinds of activities. Two types of stands for a 2-by-4-inch (5 by 10 cm) beam are shown in figure 12.7. The beam can be placed with the wide or the narrow side up, depending on the

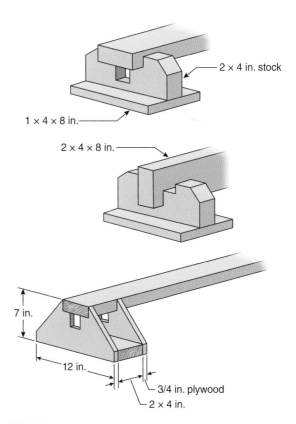

FIGURE 12.7 Balance beam with stand.

12

student's skill. If the beam is longer than 8 feet (2.4 m), place a third stand in the middle. To prevent splintering and cracking, carefully sand the beam and then apply multiple coats of finish.

Balance-Beam Bench

The balance-beam bench is a versatile piece of equipment. Its dimensions can be modified depending on the students' age (figure 12.8). It should be made of hardwood or hardwood plywood and it must be well finished.

Balance Boards

Many styles of balance board can be constructed, depending on the materials available and individual needs (figure 12.9). Glue a piece of rubber matting to

the top of the board to prevent slipping and place it on an individual mat or on a piece of heavy rubber matting. A square board is easier to balance than a round one, because its corners touch the floor and give it more stability.

Batting Tee

Ideally, the batting tee should be adjustable to accommodate batters of various heights (figure 12.10). Constructing an adjustable tee takes time, however, and the results are not always satisfactory. An alternative is to make several nonadjustable tees of different heights.

Materials:

- One piece of 1-inch (2.5 cm) pipe, 24 to 28 inches (60 to 70 cm) long
- One piece of radiator hose, 8 to 12 inches (20 to 30 cm) long, with an inside diameter of 1-1/2 inches (3.8 cm)
- One block of wood, 3 by 12 by 12 inches (7.5 by 30 by 30 cm)
- One pipe flange for 1-inch (2.5 cm) pipe, to be mounted on the block
- Screws and hose cement

Directions: Mount the flange on the block and screw the pipe into the flange. Place the radiator hose on the pipe. Paint as desired. To secure a good fit for the radiator hose, take the pipe to the supply source. If the hose is to remain fixed, then secure it with hose cement.

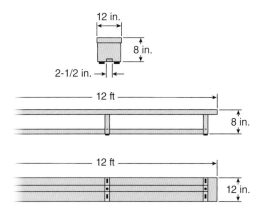

FIGURE 12.8 Balance-beam bench.

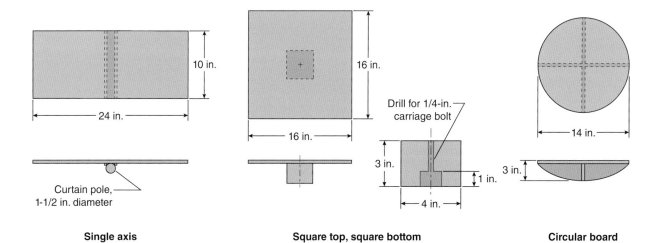

Single axis

Square top, square bottom

Circular board

FIGURE 12.9 Styles of balance board.

An alternative method is to drill a hole in the block and mount the pipe directly in the hole with mastic or good-quality glue. Note that a 1-inch (2.5 cm) pipe has an outside diameter of approximately 1 inch, allowing the hose to fit properly over it.

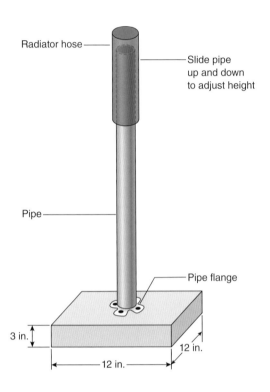

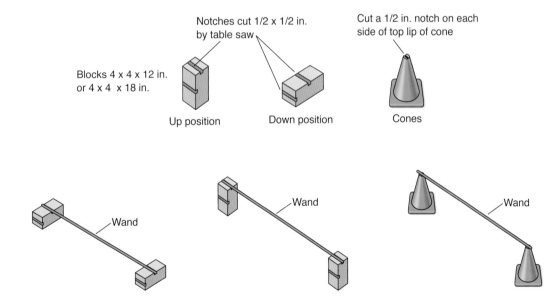

FIGURE 12.10 Batting tee construction.

Blocks and Cones

Blocks with grooves on the top and on one side are excellent for forming hurdles with wands. A 4-by-4-inch (10 by 10 cm) board cut in lengths of 6, 12, and 18 inches (15, 30, and 45 cm) yields several hurdle sizes. Cones can be notched and used in place of the blocks (figure 12.11).

Bowling Pins

Bowling alleys give away old pins, which can be used for many purposes, such as for field and gymnasium markers, for bowling games, and for relays. The bottom 2 inches (5 cm) of the pin should be cut off and the base sanded smooth (figure 12.12). Pins can be numbered and decorated with decals, colored tape, or paint.

Conduit Hurdles

Conduit hurdles are lightweight and easy to store. Because they are not weighted and fall over easily, children have little fear about hitting them. The elastic bands can be moved up and down to create different heights and different challenges. Conduit can be purchased at most electrical supply houses.

Materials:

- One piece of 1/2-inch (13 mm) electrical conduit pipe, 10 feet (3 m) long
- One piece of 1-inch (25 mm) stretch elastic tape
- Wooden dowel, 1/2-inch (13 mm) diameter

12

FIGURE 12.11 Blocks and cones.

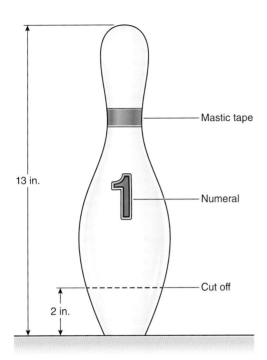

FIGURE 12.12 Bowling pin.

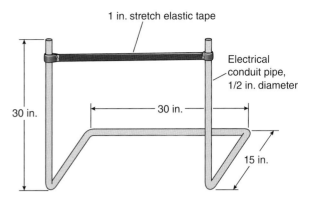

FIGURE 12.13 Conduit hurdle construction.

Directions: Bend the piece of conduit to the following dimensions: Uprights are 30 inches (75 cm) high, the base is 30 inches (75 cm) wide, and the sides of the base are 15 inches (38 cm) long. A special tool for bending the conduit usually can be purchased from the supply house where the conduit was bought. Sew loops on each end of the elastic tape so the tape slides over the ends of the hurdles with a slight amount of tension. If necessary, put short pieces of dowel into the ends of the conduit to raise the height of the hurdle (figure 12.13).

Footsies

Footsies can be made economically by the children and provide an excellent movement challenge. The activity requires coordination of both feet to keep the footsie rotating properly.

Materials:

- Plastic bleach bottle, half-gallon (2 L) size
- One piece of 1/8-inch (3.2 mm) clothesline rope
- Old tennis ball
- Large fishing swivel, preferably with ball bearings

Directions: Cut a circular strip about 2 inches (5 cm) wide out of the bottom of a bleach bottle. Cut two holes in the strip about 1 inch (2.5 cm) apart. Thread a 3-foot (90 cm) piece of clothesline through the holes and tie a knot on the outside of the strip. Cut the clothesline in half and tie the swivel to each end of the cut cord. The swivel prevents the rope from becoming twisted.

Puncture the tennis ball with an ice pick, making two holes directly across from each other. Thread the line through the holes with a piece of wire or a large crochet hook. Tie a large knot near the outer hole so the line cannot slip back through (figure 12.14).

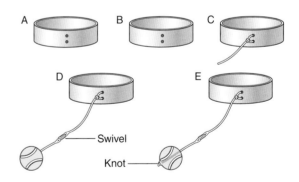

FIGURE 12.14 Footsie construction.

Gym Scooters

Scooters are easily constructed from readily available materials and can be made in many sizes and shapes. The casters should be checked to make sure they do not mark the floor. Scooters have many activity applications and can be used to move heavy equipment.

Materials:

- One piece of 2-inch (5 cm) yellow pine board, 12 by 12 inches (30 by 30 cm)
- Four ball-bearing casters with 2-inch (5 cm) wheels of hard rubber
- Protective rubber stripping, 4 feet (1.2 m) long
- Cement
- Screws and paint

Directions: The actual dimensions of the board are around 1-5/8 by 11-3/8 inches (4.1 by 29.5 cm). Two pieces of 3/4-inch (19 mm) plywood glued together can be substituted. Cut and round the corners, smoothing them with a power sander. Sand all edges by hand and apply two coats of paint. Fasten the four casters approximately 1-1/2 inches (3.8 cm) diagonally in from the corners. A rubber strip fixed around the edges with staples and cement (figure 12.15) will cushion the impact of the scooter on other objects.

FIGURE 12.15   Gym scooter construction.

Hoops

Hoops can be constructed from 1/2-inch plastic water pipe (PVC), which unfortunately is available in drab colors only. Hoops can be constructed in different sizes. A short piece of dowel, fixed with a power stapler or tacks, can be used to join the ends together (figure 12.16). An alternative joining method is to use special pipe connectors. Weather-stripping cement helps make a more permanent joint.

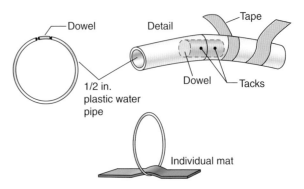

FIGURE 12.16   Hoop construction.

Hurdle and High-Jump Rope

The weighted hurdle and high-jump rope are ideal for beginning hurdlers and high jumpers who may fear hitting the bar. The rope can be hung over the pins of the high-jump standards; the weights keep the rope fairly taut.

Materials:

- One piece of 3/8-inch (9 mm) rope, 10 feet (3 m) long
- Two rubber crutch tips (number 19)
- Tacks (number 14) and penny shingle nails
- Sand

Directions: Drive a carpet tack through the rope approximately 3/4 inch (19 mm) from each end. Drive three nails into the bottom of each of the two rubber crutch tips. Place the rope ends inside the crutch tips and fill the tips with sand. Tape shut the top of the tips (figure 12.17).

Individual Mats

Individual mats can be made from indoor-outdoor carpeting with a rubber backing. This prevents the mat from sliding on the floor and offers some cushion. The mats can also be washed when they become soiled. Mats of different colors are preferable, because they can be used for games, for color tag, and for easily dividing the class by mat color. Carpet stores often have small pieces and remnants that they will sell cheaply or give away.

Another type of individual mat is designed to fold (figure 12.18). These mats are useful for aerobic dance classes because they are lighter and easier to handle than carpet mats. The major drawback is that folding mats are more expensive.

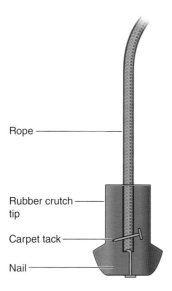

Rope

Rubber crutch tip

Carpet tack

Nail

FIGURE 12.17 Weighted hurdle and high-jump rope construction.

©Robert Pangrazi or Aaron Beighle

FIGURE 12.18 Folding individual mat.

Jumping Boxes

Jumping boxes are used to develop a wide variety of body management skills. The dimensions can be varied to satisfy individual needs, but 8- and 16-inch (20 and 40 cm) boxes seem to be the most useful.

Materials:

- 3/4-inch (19 mm) marine plywood
- Wood screws, paint, and glue

- Carpet pad remnants
- Naugahyde or similar material to cover box top
- Upholstery tacks

Directions: Cut the four sides to similar dimensions and then sand them together to make sure they are exactly the same size. Use a countersink and drill the screw holes, apply glue at the joints, and screw the sides together. When the box is assembled, sand all edges to remove any sharpness. Paint the boxes, preferably with a latex-based paint because it chips less than oil-based enamel does. If handholds are desired, drill holes and then cut them out with a saber saw (figure 12.19). Covering is optional. If desired, cut a carpet pad remnant the size of the top of the box and cover it with Naugahyde. The Naugahyde should overlap about 4 inches (10 cm) on each side of the box so that it can be folded under to make a double thickness and then tacked down.

Jumping Standards

Jumping standards are useful for hurdling, jumping, and over-and-under activities. Many shapes and sizes are possible (figure 12.20).

Materials:

- Two pieces of 3/4-inch (19 mm) plywood 24 inches (61 cm) long, cut as shown
- Two blocks of wood, 2 by 4 by 6 inches (5 by 10 by 15 cm)
- Glue and paint
- Broomstick, 48 inches (120 cm) long

Directions: Mortise the wood blocks lengthwise, about 1 inch (2.5 cm) deep. After cutting the uprights to form, set them with glue into the blocks—making sure that the uprights are plumb. Paint as desired. For quick positioning of the crosspiece, mark corresponding notches of the uprights with small circles of the same color.

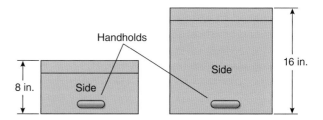

Handholds

8 in.

Side

Side

16 in.

FIGURE 12.19 Jumping-box construction.

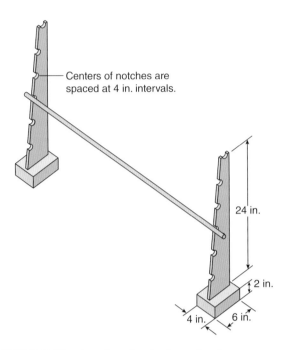

FIGURE 12.20 Jumping-standard construction.

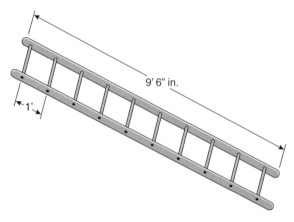

FIGURE 12.21 Ladder construction.

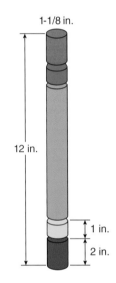

FIGURE 12.22 Lummi stick construction and decoration.

Ladder

A ladder laid on the floor or on a mat provides a floor apparatus for various movement experiences and has value in remedial programs and programs for exceptional children. Sizes may vary (figure 12.21).

Materials:

- Two straight-grained 2-by-4-inch (5 by 10 cm) timbers, 9-1/2 feet (2.9 m) long
- Ten 1-1/4 or 1-1/2-inch (3.2 or 3.8 cm) dowels, 20 inches (50 cm) long
- Glue
- Paint or varnish

Directions: Round the ends and sand the edges of the timbers. Center holes for the ladder rungs 12 inches (30 cm) apart, beginning 3 inches (7.5 cm) from one end. Cut the holes for the rungs 1/16 inch (1.6 mm) smaller than the diameter of the rungs. Put glue in all the holes on one timber, and drive in all the rungs. Next, glue the other timber in place. Varnish or paint the ladder.

Lummi Sticks

Lummi sticks are excellent tools for developing rhythmic skills. The sticks can also be used as relay batons.

Materials:

- 1-inch (2.5 cm) dowel, in 12-inch (30 cm) lengths
- Paint and varnish

Directions: Notches and different colors are optional, but these decorations do make the sticks more attractive. If desired, use a table saw to cut notches 1/8 inch (3.2 mm) wide and 1/8 inch deep. Round off the ends and sand the entire stick. Paint and varnish the stick as shown in figure 12.22.

Magic Ropes and Jump Bands

Common clothing elastic can also be used to make the ropes (figure 12.23). Some teachers have had success with shock cord, which usually can be purchased at a boating marina or hardware store. Bungee cord of the proper length may also be used. Like shock cord, it can be found at many sports equipment outlets.

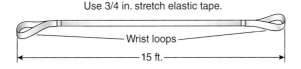

Use 3/4 in. stretch elastic tape.

Wrist loops

15 ft.

FIGURE 12.23 Magic rope construction.

Outdoor Bases

Bases for softball, baseball, and so on can be made in many ways. Use heavy canvas, folding it over three or four times and stitching it together. Cut heavy rubber matting to size. For more permanent bases, cut and paint pieces of outdoor plywood (figure 12.24).

Materials:

- Exterior 3⁄4-inch (19 mm) plywood
- One 1/2-inch (13 mm) carriage bolt, 14 inches (36 cm) long
- Paint

Directions: Cut the plywood into 12-by-12-inch (30 by 30 cm) squares. Bevel and sand the top edges. Drill a 1/2-inch (13 mm) hole in the center of the base and then paint the base. When the paint dries, place the carriage bolt into the center hole and drive it into the ground. To make the base more secure, use more holes. Large spikes can be substituted for carriage bolts.

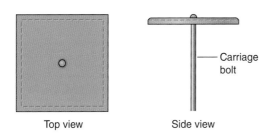

Top view   Side view

Carriage bolt

FIGURE 12.24 Outdoor base construction.

Paddles

Paddles can be made in many sizes and with different thicknesses of plywood (figure 12.25). Usually, 1/4-inch (6 mm) plywood is recommended for kindergarten through grade 2, and 3/8-inch (9 mm) plywood for grades 3 through 6. Paint or varnish the paddles, and tape the handles for a better grip. Drill holes into the paddle area to make it lighter and decrease air resistance.

For hitting lightweight foam-rubber or newspaper balls, nylon-stocking paddles work well. They are lightweight and do not cause injuries, so they are excellent for primary-grade use. Students can use a badminton birdie with the paddle for activities, such as hitting over a net, and for many individual stunts.

Materials:

- Old nylon stocking
- Wire coat hanger
- Masking tape or athletic tape
- String or wire

Directions: Bend the hanger into a diamond shape. Bend the hook into a loop, which becomes the handle of the paddle (figure 12.26). Pull the stocking over the hanger, beginning at the corner farthest from the handle, until the toe of the nylon is as tight as possible against the corner point of the hanger. Hold the nylon at the neck of the hanger and stretch it as tight as possible.

Tie the nylon securely with a piece of heavy string or light wire. Wrap the rest of the nylon around the handle

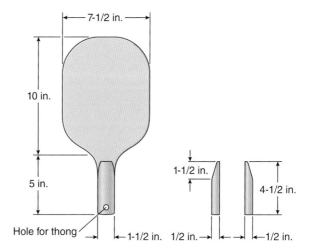

7-1/2 in.

10 in.

5 in.

Hole for thong

1-1/2 in.

1/2 in.

1-1/2 in.

4-1/2 in.

1/2 in.

FIGURE 12.25 Paddle construction.

FIGURE 12.26 Frame for nylon-stocking paddle.

to make a smooth, contoured surface. Complete the paddle by wrapping tape around the entire handle to prevent loosening.

Paddle Tennis Net Supports

Paddle tennis net supports can be made to stand by themselves on the floor and still provide proper net tension. The stands come apart easily and quickly and can be stored in a small space. For lengths up to 8 feet (2.4 m) or so, use a single center board with holes on each end, thus eliminating the need to bolt two pieces together (figure 12.27).

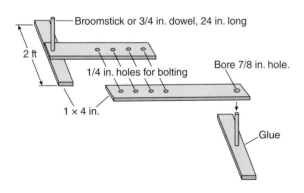

FIGURE 12.27 Paddle tennis net support construction.

Materials:

- Two broomsticks or 3⁄4-inch (19 mm) dowels, 2 feet (60 cm) long
- Two 1-by-4-inch (2.5 by 10 cm) boards, 2 feet (60 cm) long
- One or more additional 1-by-4-inch (2.5 by 10 cm) boards
- Glue

Directions: For the upright supports, drill a 3/4-inch (19 mm) diameter hole in the center of each 1-by-4-inch (2.5 by 10 cm) board. Drive the dowel into the hole, fixing it with glue. Notch the dowels at intervals for different net heights.

The crosspiece length depends on the court width. For a single crosspiece, bore holes into each end. Make the holes big enough (7/8 inch [22 mm]) for the dowel to slide through easily. If the crosspiece is in two sections, use 1/4-inch (6 mm) bolts to join the sections (see figure 12.27).

Partner Tug-of-War Ropes

Partner tug-of-war ropes can be made from garden hose and ropes (figure 12.28). Cheaper, plastic garden hose

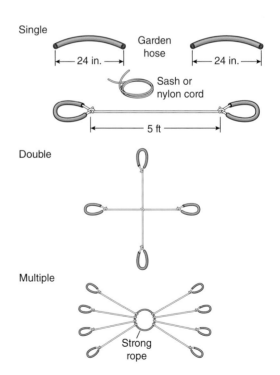

FIGURE 12.28 Partner tug-of-war construction.

259

(5/8-inch [16 mm] in diameter) works much better than more expensive rubber hose. Plastic hose creases less and protects the hands better than rubber hose does. White, soft, braided nylon rope (3/8-inch [9 mm] diameter) is strong enough and much easier to handle than other types of rope. Use a bowline knot that does not slip and tighten around the hands. To prevent the rope ends from fraying, melt them over a flame.

Plastic Markers and Scoops

One-gallon (4 L) plastic jugs filled halfway with sand and recapped make fine boundary markers. Paint the markers different colors to signify goals, boundaries, and division lines. The jugs can also be numbered and used to designate different teaching stations. Plastic bottles can be cut down to make scoops (figure 12.29) for use in many activities.

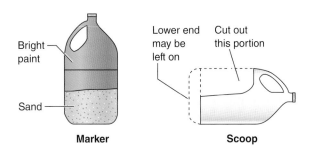

FIGURE 12.29 Plastic marker and scoop.

Rings, Deck Tennis (Quoits)

Deck tennis is a popular recreational net game that requires only a ring as basic equipment. Students can easily make the rings and use them in playing catch and for target throwing. They can be made from heavy rope by braiding the ends together, but the method shown in figure 12.30 is easier. Weather-stripping cement helps strengthen the joints.

Ringtoss Target

Many ringtoss targets can be made from a piece of 1-by-4-inch (2.5 by 10 cm) lumber or an old broom handle. Targets can be either hung on the wall or placed flat on the ground. The quoits constructed from garden hose are excellent for throwing at the targets. To signify different point values, paint the target pegs in different colors.

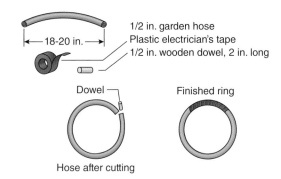

FIGURE 12.30 Ring construction.

Materials:

- Two 1-by-4-inch (2.5 by 10 cm) boards, 18 to 20 inches (45 to 50 cm) long
- Five pegs, 6 inches (15 cm) long (old broom handles)
- Screws and paint

Directions: Glue and screw the 1-by-4-inch (2.5 by 10 cm) boards together, as shown in figure 12.31. Bore holes in the boards with a brace and bit, and glue or screw the pegs into the holes. Screw two small blocks under the ends of the board placed on top so that the target stands level. Paint the base and the sticks and, if desired, number the sticks to show point values.

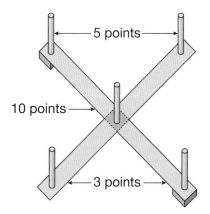

FIGURE 12.31 Ringtoss target construction.

Sit-and-Reach Box

Sit-and-reach boxes are used for measuring flexibility in fitness tests (figure 12.32). The basic sit-and-reach box is a 12-inch (30 cm) cube with a top 21 inches (53 cm) long. Sit-and-reach boxes require the top of the box to be marked in centimeters or inches. Check the specifications of your fitness test before marking.

Tire Stands

Tire stands keep tires in an upright position (figure 12.33). The upright tires can be used for movement problems, over-and-through relays, vaulting activities, and as targets. Tires are much cleaner and more attractive when they are painted both inside and out.

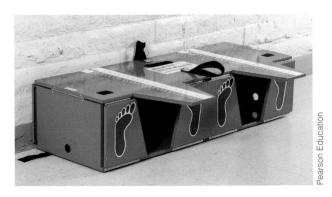

FIGURE 12.32 Sit-and-reach box.

Pearson Education

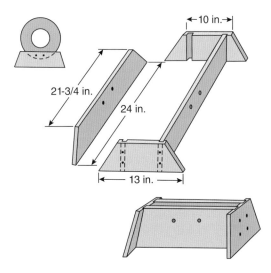

FIGURE 12.33 Tire stand construction.

Materials:

- Two 1-by-6-inch (2.5 by 15 cm) boards, 24 inches (60 cm) long, for side pieces
- Two 1-by-6-inch (2.5 by 15 cm) boards, 13 inches (33 cm) long, for end pieces
- Four 3/8-inch (9 mm) carriage bolts, 2 inches (5 cm) long
- Glue, screws, and paint
- One used tire

Directions: Cut the ends of the side boards at a 70-degree angle. Dado each end piece with two grooves 3/4 inch (19 mm) wide and 1/4 inch (6 mm) deep. The distance between the grooves depends on the width of the tire. Round off the board corners and sand the edges. Glue and screw the stand together. Install the tire in the frame by drilling two 3/8-inch (9 mm) holes in each side of the frame and in the tire. Secure the tire inside the frame with the bolts. Paint both the tire and the frame a bright color. For better stability when using large tires, increase the overall stand size.

Track Starter

The track starter simulates a gun report. Provide many starters so that the children can start their own races.

Materials:

- Two 2-by-4-inch (5 by 10 cm) boards, 11 inches (28 cm) long
- Two small strap hinges
- Two small cabinet handles

Directions: Cut the boards to size and sand off any rough edges. Place the two blocks together and apply the two hinges with screws. Add the two handles on the outsides of the boards. Open the boards and then slam them together quickly to create a loud bang (figure 12.34).

Wands

Handles from old brooms make excellent wands (figure 12.35). The handles may have different diameters, but this discrepancy is not important. Sand the ends and paint the wands in different colors. If noise is a concern, place rubber crutch tips on the wand ends.

12

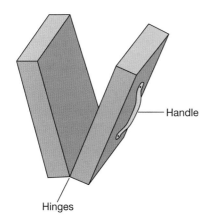

FIGURE 12.34 Track starter.

5/8 in. or 3/4 in. dowel

Lengths: grades K–1 = 30 in., 2–3 = 36 in.,
4–6 = 42 in. or 1 m

FIGURE 12.35 Wand dimensions.

Yarn Balls

Yarn balls can be used to enhance throwing and catching skills as well as for many games. Yarn balls do not hurt when they hit students, and they can be used in the classroom or in other areas of limited space. Two construction methods are offered here; both work well. When possible, use wool or cotton yarns because the balls will shrink and become tight when soaked in hot water or steamed. Nylon and other synthetic yarns do not shrink and bond.

Materials for Method 1:

- One skein of wool or cotton yarn per ball
- One piece of box cardboard, 5 inches (12.5 cm) wide and about 12 inches (30 cm) long
- Strong, light cord for binding

Directions for method 1: Wrap the yarn 20 to 25 times around the 5-inch-wide (12.5 cm wide) dimension of the cardboard. Slide the yarn off the cardboard and bind it in the middle with the cord to form a tied loop of yarn. Continue this procedure until all the yarn is used up and tied in looped bunches. Next, take two of

CASE STUDY

Equipment and supplies are the tools that teachers use to educate their students. Without equipment, students will have little chance to learn how to throw, catch, kick, and strike. Physical educators know that limited equipment means more standing in line and less time for repetition and refinement of skills. Even though they know better, however, many teachers settle for inadequate equipment and funding. Many teachers often state that they shouldn't have to beg for minimal equipment. The result of such an attitude is that little funding comes their way and they end up feeling marginalized and bitter.

In almost all business and educational settings, employees must have a systematic plan for securing an adequate budget for equipment and supplies. If you don't ask and present a well-organized budget based on need, you will be offered a minimal amount that is left over after more thoughtful requests have been funded. Note that many teachers become cynical and resentful when they believe they haven't been funded on par with other teachers. Here are a few points to help assure that you are successful in acquiring adequate funding.

- Have a priority list of items you would like funded. A good way to prioritize your list is to put equipment and supplies that offer the greatest utility at the top of your list. For example, a set of quality foam rubber balls would probably be of more use than climbing ropes because you can use them in a number of units of instruction.

- Attach all the information required to purchase the equipment to your budget request. This presentation makes it clear that you have been thoughtful in stating your needs, making your case more convincing. When the request is funded, everything is in place, making the ordering process fast and efficient.

- No one ever gets everything he or she wants. Above all, don't become discouraged. Ask for funding every time the opportunity arises. Avoid becoming negative and thinking that there is no use in trying anymore. That approach is a sure way to lose out to others who are more persistent and able to deal with minor setbacks.

the tied loops and tie them together at the center, using several turns of the cord. This forms a bundle of two tied loops, as illustrated in figure 12.36. Continue tying the bundles together until all are used. Now cut the loops carefully so that the yarn lengths are quite even. Trim the resulting ball.

Materials for Method 2:

- Two skeins of yarn per ball
- Two cardboard doughnuts, 5 or 6 inches (12.5 or 15 cm) in diameter
- Strong, light cord for tying

Directions for method 2: Make a slit in the doughnuts so that the yarn can be wrapped around the cardboard (figure 12.37). Holding strands from both skeins, wrap the yarn around both doughnuts until the center hole is almost completely filled with yarn. Lay the doughnut of wrapped yarn on a flat surface, insert a pair of scissors between the two doughnuts, and cut around the entire outer edge. Carefully insert a double strand of the light cord between the two doughnuts and catch all the individual yarn strands around the middle with the cord. Tie the cord as tightly as possible with a double knot. Remove the doughnuts and trim the ball if necessary.

12

FIGURE 12.36   Yarn ball, method 1.

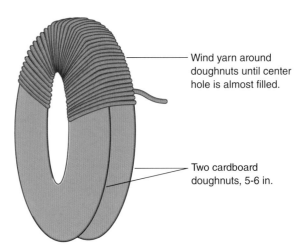

Wind yarn around doughnuts until center hole is almost filled.

Two cardboard doughnuts, 5-6 in.

FIGURE 12.37   Yarn ball, method 2.

LEARNING AIDS

HOW AND WHY

1. Do the school facilities in your area meet the standards for outdoor facilities?
2. How might teachers have to adapt because of the many non-PE uses of the indoor physical education facilities?
3. Why would homemade equipment be necessary for some schools?
4. How can teachers ensure that the equipment is appropriately maintained?

CONTENT REVIEW

1. Present several standards for outdoor facilities. Comment, in particular, on playgrounds.
2. Identify four pieces each of outdoor equipment for upper-body development, lower-body development, and balance skills.
3. Discuss the standards for indoor facilities for physical education.
4. Discuss the difference between equipment and supplies. List examples of each.
5. List equipment used primarily indoors.
6. Discuss the importance of purchasing policies, storage plans, and maintenance for equipment.

WEBSITES

Physical education, athletics, and fitness equipment, www.gophersport.com

Homemade equipment ideas, www.pecentral.org/preschool/prekhomemadeequipmentmenu.html

Homemade stuff ideas, http://igreen.tripod.com/gerpe/id18.html

Playground safety education, www.cpsc.gov/safety-education/safety-guides/playgrounds

Playground safety, www.playgroundsafety.org

SUGGESTED READINGS

Carpenter, Linda J. (2008). *Legal concepts in sport: A primer* (3rd ed.). Champaign, IL: Sagamore.

Dougherty, Neil J. (ed.). (2009). *Principles of safety in physical education and sport* (4th ed.). Reston, VA: AAHPERD.

Dougherty, Neil J., Goldberger, Alan S., & Carpenter, Linda J. (2007). *Sport, physical activity, and the law* (3rd ed.). Champaign, IL: Sagamore.

Greenberg, Jayne D., & LoBianco, Judy L. (2020). *Organization and administration of physical education.* Champaign, IL: Human Kinetics.

Hinson, Curt. (2001). *6 steps to a trouble-free playground.* Hockessin, DE: PlayFit Education.

Sullivan, Teresa, et al. (2012). *Build it so they can play: Affordable equipment for adapted physical education.* Champaign, IL: Human Kinetics.

REFERENCES

Stratton, Gareth, & Mullan, Elaine. (2005). The effect of multicolor playground markings on children's physical activity level during recess. *Preventive Medicine, 41*, 828–833.

U.S. Consumer Product Safety Commission. (2010). *Handbook for public playground safety.* Publication No. 325. Washington, DC: Author.

Introductory Activities

This chapter provides many activities designed to begin the lesson on an active note. Introductory activities, also called warm-ups or instant activities, help kickstart a dynamic lesson while establishing rules and procedures. Some activities that require no equipment and others involve equipment exploration. Furthermore, activities that can be done alone, with a partner, or in small groups are described. A variety of tag games are presented as well.

Learning Objectives

▶ Define the role of the introductory activity during a lesson.

▶ Teach two introductory activities that use locomotor movements.

▶ List introductory activities that involve rhythmic movements.

▶ Identify introductory activities that can be completed with a partner or in a small group.

▶ Teach an introductory activity that requires equipment.

▶ Describe at least two different tag games.

An introductory activity is the first movement that students experience when entering the teaching area. Such activities usually last two to three minutes and involve vigorous fundamental motor skills and minimal instruction. They help children warm up physiologically and prepare them for the physical activity to follow. A truism in teaching is "A lesson that starts well, ends well."

Introductory activities are inherently upbeat and active, and they will excessively arouse a poorly managed class. Use the "rule of three freezes" to check the students' disposition and prepare them for instruction. Have the class enter the teaching area on the move and then freeze on signal. Move the children a second time and privately correct off-task behavior (while students are on the move). Freeze the class two more times to correct off-task behavior and see if students are ready to learn. If the class is still not with you after three corrective episodes, teaching the introductory activity is usually not best; instead, focus on a management activity such as moving and freezing on signal.

Introductory activities are used for several reasons:

1. To offer students immediate activity when entering the gym (This satisfies their desire to move and helps teachers establish a positive learning attitude [purposeful movement done under control] for the class.)

2. To help children warm up physiologically and prepare them for the activity to follow

3. To practice management skills to be used in other parts of the lesson (For example, if partners or small groups will be used, the introductory activity might entail finding partners quickly and getting a new partner each time.)

Slow down the introductory activities at first, for safety reasons and as a way to warm up. For example, if you are using Rhythmic Running, start first with walking. As the class warms up, increase the pace to a jog. If you are using Curl and Around, begin by having students move around each other at moderate speed. After a short warm-up period, have them do the activity at full speed.

Introductory Activities Using Locomotor Movements

Locomotor movements used in introductory activities involve the body as a whole and change abruptly from one movement pattern to another. A routine can begin with running and then change to another movement pattern specified by the teacher or chosen by students. Supply signals for change with a voice command, whistle, drumbeat, or handclap. Children enjoy being challenged by having to change with the signal. Continue each part of a routine long enough for good body challenge and involvement but not so long that it becomes tiresome.

Running is the basis of many gross movement activities, but other vigorous activities can be used. The following suggested activities are classified roughly according to type and whether they are individual, partner, or group oriented.

Free Running

Students run in any direction, changing direction at will.

Running and Changing Direction

Children run in any direction, changing direction on signal. As a progression, specify the type of angle (right, obtuse, 45-degree, or 180-degree). Alternate right and left turns.

Running and Changing Level

Children run high on their toes and change to a lower level on signal. Instruct runners to touch the floor sometimes when at the lower level.

Running and Changing the Type of Locomotion

On signal, runners change from running to free choice or to a specific type of locomotion (walking, jumping, hopping, skipping, sliding, or galloping).

Running and Stopping

Students run in various directions and, on signal, freeze. Stress stopping techniques and an immobile position. On signal, have children stop running and assume a statue pose.

Move and Perform Athletic Movements

Students move and stop on signal. They then perform an athletic skill move, such as a basketball jump shot, leaping football pass catch, volleyball spike, or soccer kick. Have students focus on correct form and timing. Students can move with a partner and throw a pass on signal, punt a ball, or shoot a basket. The partner catches the ball or rebounds the shot.

Tortoise and Hare

The teacher calls out, "Tortoise," and the children run slowly in general space. On the command "Hare," they change to a rapid, circular run. Stress good knee lift during the run.

Ponies in the Stable

Each child has a stable—a place on the floor marked with a beanbag or hoop. On the first signal, children gallop lightly (like ponies) in general space. On the next signal, they trot lightly to their stable and continue trotting in place.

High Fives

Students move in different directions throughout the area. On signal, have them run toward a partner, jump, and give a high five (slap hands) while moving. Stress timing, so that the high five occurs at the top of the jump. Develop combinations of changing the level as well as speed of the movement.

Move and Perform a Task on Signal

Students move and perform a task on signal. During a signaled stop, they can perform several fitness challenges. Another variation is to perform individual or partner activities. Examples are Seat Circle, Wring the Dishrag, Partner Hopping, Partner Twister, and Back-to-Back Get-Up (see chapter 20).

Run, Stop, and Pivot

Students run, stop, and then pivot. This activity is excellent for developing game skills. Children enjoy it especially when asked to imagine they are basketball or football players.

Triple-S Routine

The triple s's are *speed*, *style*, and *stop*. Children are in scatter formation throughout the area. On the command "Speed," they run in general space rapidly while avoiding contact with others. On the command "Style," all run with style (easy, light, loose running) in a large, circular, counterclockwise path. On the command "Stop," all freeze quickly under control. Repeat as necessary.

Agility Run

Pick two lines or markers 5 to 10 yards (meters) apart. Students run (or use other locomotor movements) back and forth between the lines for a specific time (10, 15, or 20 seconds). Students can challenge themselves by seeing how many times they can move back and forth in the given time limit.

Moving on Twos and Fours

Students begin with a movement in upright position and change to one on all fours.

Secret Movement

From a stack of cards, each naming various movements, the teacher selects one and says, "I want you to show me the secret movement." Students decide on a movement and keep doing it until signaled to stop. The teacher then identifies students who did the movement on the card. Those children demonstrate the movement, and all do it together. If no one does the movement, repeat the activity by asking the children to try other movements.

Airplanes

The class pretends to be airplanes. When told to takeoff, they zoom with arms out, swooping, turning, and gliding (figure 13.1). When told to land, they drop to the floor facedown, simulating a plane at rest. To start their engines and takeoff, they can do a series of push-ups and move up and down while simulating engine noise.

FIGURE 13.1 Performing Airplanes.

©Robert Pangrazi or Aaron Beighle

Combination Movements

Combination movements can involve specified movements or allow some choice. The limitation might be to run, skip, and roll, or to jump, twist, and shake. Try setting a number for the sequence and letting the children select the activities. Say, "Put three different kinds of movements together in a smooth pattern."

Countdown

The teacher and class do a countdown to blastoff: "10, 9, 8, 7, 6, 5, 4, 3, 2, 1—blastoff!" The children are scattered during the countdown, and each makes an abrupt, jerky movement on each count. On the word *blastoff*, they jump up in the air and run in different directions until signaled to stop.

Magic-Number Challenges

The teacher issues a challenge like this: "10, 10, and 10." Children then put together three movements, doing 10 repetitions of each. With older students the teacher could say, "Today we are going to play our version of Twenty-One." Twenty-one becomes the magic number to be fulfilled with three movements, each done seven times.

Crossing the River

Set up a "river" as the space between two parallel lines about 40 feet (12 m) apart, or use the crosswise area in a gym. Each time the children cross the river, they use a different locomotor movement. Encourage them not to repeat a movement. Play is continuous for 30 to 60 seconds or so.

Four-Corners Movement

Lay out a square with a cone at each corner. As students pass each corner, they change to a different locomotor movement with an agility emphasis. Challenge students with some sport agility movements (backward running, leaps, grapevine step, front crossover, back crossover, high knees, and slide steps), or change the qualities of movement (i.e., soft, heavy, slow, fast, and so on). Students doing faster movements can pass to the outside of the area.

Jumping and Hopping Patterns

Each child has a home spot. The teacher provides jumping and hopping sequences to take children away from and back to their spot. The teacher could say, "Move with three jumps, two hops, and a half turn. Return to home the same way." Have on hand a variety of sequences. Action can go beyond simply jumping and hopping.

Leading With Body Parts

Students move throughout the area, with some body part leading. They can use various body parts (elbows, fingers, head, shoulders, knees, and toes). They can try the same exercise with different body parts trailing and then try leading or trailing with two and then three different body parts. Children can jog with some body part leading or trailing. On signal, have them make a different body part lead or trail.

Move, Rock, and Roll

Each child takes a mat and places it on the floor. Challenge students to move around, over, and on the mats. On signal, children move to a mat and try different ways of rocking and rolling. Specify rocking on different parts of the body and suggest various body rolls. As another challenge, tell the children to rock or roll (or both) on a mat, get up and run to another mat, and repeat the sequence. Older children enjoy seeing how many mats they can move to in the allotted time.

Rhythmic Introductory Activities

European Rhythmic Running

In many European countries, Rhythmic Running opens the daily lesson. The European style is light, rhythmic running to the beat of a drum or tambourine. Skilled runners do not need the beat, but keep time with a leader. Much of the running is circular (figure 13.2), but it can be done in scatter formation. To introduce a group of children to Rhythmic Running, have them clap to the drumbeat. Next, as they clap, have them shuffle their feet in place, keeping time. Then have them run in place without clapping. Finally, the class can run in single file. The running is light, bouncy, and in step with the beat. When running in single file, children stay behind the person in front, maintain proper spacing, and lift the knees in a light, prancing step.

©Robert Pangrazi or Aaron Beighle

FIGURE 13.2 European Rhythmic Running.

Other movements can be combined with Rhythmic Running.

1. On signal (a whistle or double drumbeat), runners freeze in place. They resume running when the regular beat begins again.

2. On signal, runners make a full turn in four running steps, lifting the knees high while turning.

3. Children clap hands every fourth beat as they run. Instead of clapping, runners call a brisk, "Hey!" on the fourth beat, raising one arm with a fist at the same time.

4. Children run in squads, following their leader.

5. On signal, children run in general space, being careful not to bump into each other. Again on signal, they return to running in a circle.

6. Students alternate between running with high knee action and regular running.

7. Runners change to a light, soundless run and back to a heavier run. The drum tone controls the quality of the movement.

8. Students use Rhythmic Running while handling a parachute.

9. On the command "Center," children run four steps toward the center, turn around (four steps), and run outward four steps to resume the original circular running pattern.

10. On signal, runners go backward, changing the direction of the circle.

11. Students carry a beanbag or a ball. Every fourth step, they toss the item up and catch it while running.

12. A leader moves the class through various formations. An enjoyable and challenging task is crossing two lines of children, alternating one child from one line in front of one child from the other line.

13. On signal, the class moves into various shapes (e.g., a square, rectangle, triangle, or pentagon). Rhythmic Running continues as students move into position.

14. On signal, each class member changes position with another student and then resumes the activity. For example, students opposite each other in the circle change places.

15. Because the movement is rhythmic, students can practice certain skills, such as a full turn. The turn can be done to a four-count rhythm and is more deliberate than a quick turning movement.

16. When the beat stops, children scatter and run at random. When the beat resumes, they return to circular formation and proper rhythm.

Musical Relaxation

Conduct musical relaxation with a drum or appropriate recorded music. Children run in time to the rhythm. When the rhythm stops, all children lie on their backs, close their eyes, and relax until the music begins again.

Moving to Rhythm

Rhythm has many possibilities for guiding locomotor movements. Tempo changes can be part of the activity, and sound intensity can be translated into light or heavy movements.

Moving to Music

Pieces like the "Bleking" song and "Pop Goes the Weasel" can be a basis for creative movement. These pieces have two parts, so students can do a nonlocomotor movement in the first part and a locomotor movement in the second.

Folk Dance Movement

Use a music recording to stimulate different types of rhythmic movement such as polka, schottische, and two-step. Have students move around the room while practicing the steps.

Introductory Activities With Equipment

Individual Rope Jumping

Each child runs with rope in hand. On the signal to change, the child stops and begins to jump.

Hoop Activities

Each child runs while holding a hoop. On signal, students either start twirling the hoop around the body or put the hoop on the floor and use it for hopping and jumping patterns.

Wand Activities

Wands can be used in movements similar to those done with jump ropes and hoops. After running and stopping, students do wand stunts.

Milk Carton Fun

Each child has a milk carton stuffed with crumpled newspapers and taped shut. Students kick the cartons in different directions for one minute.

Ball Activities

Students dribble balls as in basketball or as in soccer. On signal they stop, balance on one leg, and pass (or kick) the ball under the other leg, around the back, and overhead, keeping both control and balance. Suggest other challenges involving both movement with the ball and manipulative actions performed in place.

Beanbag Touch-and-Go

Beanbags are spread throughout the area. On signal, students move and touch as many beanbags as possi-

13

ble with their hands. Specify different body parts for children to use in touching. Select different colors of beanbags and issue commands such as "Touch as many blue beanbags as possible with your elbow."

Children can also move to and around a beanbag. Movement can be varied; for example, they might skip around the yellow beanbags with the left side leading. Change the movement as well as the direction and leading side of the body. Another enjoyable activity is to trace a shape (e.g., triangle, circle, square) while moving from beanbag to beanbag.

A variation on this activity is called Vanishing Beanbags. Students move around the beanbags as described earlier. While they are moving, the teacher or a student picks up one or two bags. On signal, students move to a beanbag and sit on it. The goal is not to be left out. Repeat, with all students participating each time.

Long-Rope Routine

Students begin in a loose column of four, all holding a single long jump rope in their right hands at waist level. The teacher gives a series of four signals: (1) Students jog lightly in a column; (2) the group shifts the rope overhead from the right to left side of the body while jogging; (3) the two inside students release the rope and begin jumping when the two students at the end of the rope start turning the rope; (4) the turners become jumpers, and vice versa. Repeat the series several times.

Disappearing Hoops

Each child gets a hoop and places it on the floor. Give challenges like "Move through five blue hoops, jump over four yellow hoops, and skip around six green hoops." On signal, the children move to a hoop and balance inside it. As they move, take away two or three hoops. At the signal, some students will not find a hoop. Those left out then offer the class the next movement challenge. Specify different challenges and stunts inside the hoops.

Partner and Small-Group Introductory Activities

Marking

Each child has a partner about equal in ability. Under control, one partner runs, dodges, and tries to lose the other, who must stay within 3 feet (1 m) of the runner. On signal, both stop. Chasers must be able to touch their partners to say they have marked them. Partners then change roles.

Following Activity

One partner leads and does various kinds of movements. The other partner must do the same movements. This idea can be extended to squad organization.

Fastest Tag in the West

Every player is a tagger. The object is to tag other players without being tagged. Players who are tagged must sit or kneel and await the next game (start new games frequently). If two or more players tag each other simultaneously, they are all out.

Medic Tag

Three or four students are designated as taggers who try to tag other students. When tagged, a student kneels as if injured. Another child (not one of the taggers) can "rehabilitate" the injured student with a touch, so that the student can resume play.

Hospital Tag

Every player is a tagger. Any player who is tagged must cover with one hand the body area that was touched. Students may be tagged twice but must be able to hold both tagged spots and keep moving. A student who is tagged three times must freeze. Restart the game when most of the students are frozen.

Curl and Around

Half of the class is scattered. Each child is in a curled position, facedown. The other half of the class moves around these children (figure 13.3). On signal, reverse the groups quickly. Instead of being curled, the students can form arches or bridges, and the moving children go around them. Try having the children on the floor alternate between curled and bridge positions; if a moving

FIGURE 13.3   Curl and Around.

child goes around the curled position, the child on the floor changes immediately to a bridge. Another challenge: Ask the moving half of the class to move backward and sideways using different locomotor movements.

Living Obstacles

This activity is similar to Curl and Around, except that the children on the floor are in a bridged position and moving slowly. The children moving over and around must move quickly, because the obstacles are moving. Change positions after a designated time.

Popcorn

Half the class is scattered throughout the area and assumes the push-up position. The other half moves and "pops the popcorn." They do this by moving over and around the students who are in push-up position. When a student moves around a child doing a push-up, that child lowers to the floor. When a student moves over a child lying on the floor, that child raises to the push-up position. Moving students change places with those on the floor after a designated time.

Pyramid Power

Students move throughout the area. On signal, they find a partner and build a simple pyramid or partner stand. Examples are the hip–shoulder stand, double-crab stand, double-dog stand, and shoulder stand. Remind students to select a partner of similar size and to stand on the proper points of support.

Bridges by Threes

Three children in a group can set up an interesting movement sequence using bridges. Two of the children make bridges, and the third child goes under both bridges and sets up a bridge. Each child in turn goes under the bridges of the other two. Teachers can specify different kinds of bridges and arrange the bridges so that a change in direction is made. An over-and-under sequence also is interesting. The child vaults or jumps over the first bridge and then goes under the next bridge before setting up the third bridge.

Rubber Band

Students gather around the teacher in the center of the area. On signal, students move away from the teacher with a specific movement such as run, hop sideways, skip backward, double-lame dog, or grapevine step. On signal, they sprint back to the central point, jump, and shout.

New Leader Movements

Squads or small groups run around the area, following a leader. On signal, the last person goes to the head of the line to lead. Groups of three are ideal for this activity.

Manipulative Activities

Each child has a beanbag. They move around the area, tossing the bags up and catching them. On signal, they drop the bags to the floor and jump, hop, or leap over as many bags as possible. On the next signal, they pick up a nearby bag and resume tossing it to themselves. Having one fewer beanbag than children adds to the fun. Hoops can also be used this way. Children begin by using hoops in rope-jumping style or for swinging around the hips. On signal, they place the hoops on the floor and jump in and out of as many hoops as they can. Next, they pick up a nearby hoop and resume the original movement pattern. The activity also can be done with jump ropes.

Body Part Identification

Enough beanbags for the whole class are scattered on the floor. Students either run between or jump over the beanbags. When a body part is called out, the children place that body part on the nearest beanbag.

Drill Sergeant

The drill sergeant leads the squad, which marches in line. At will, the drill sergeant commands the squad to do a specific movement sequence: "Walk, jump twice, land, and roll." "Run, jump-turn, and freeze (pose)." "Shake, jump-turn, land, and roll." "Seal Walk, Log Roll, and jump." The sergeant can be given cards indicating suggested patterns. For more realism, the sergeant can call the squad members to attention, give them the command, and then call, "March!"

Creative Introductory Activities

Another interesting approach is to give children creative and exploratory opportunities at the beginning of a lesson. Some examples follow.

1. Set out a variety of equipment (hoops, balls, wands, beanbags) and have each child take one piece to explore. This activity can be open exploration, or the movement can follow the trend of a prior lesson, thus extending the lesson.

2. Set out some manipulative items. Children select any item they wish and decide whether to play alone, with a partner, or as part of a small group.

13

3. Provide a range of apparatus, such as climbing ropes, climbing apparatus, mats, boxes, balance beams, balance boards, and so on. Manipulative items also can be part of the package. Students decide where they want to participate.

Tambourine-Directed Activities

The tambourine can signal changes of movement because it makes two different sounds: the tinny noise made by vigorous shaking and the percussive sound made by striking the instrument. Signal movement changes by going from one sound to the other.

Shaking Sound

1. The children remain in one spot but shake all over, using gross movements.
2. The children shake and gradually drop to the floor.
3. The children scurry in every direction.
4. The children run lightly with tiny steps.

Drum Sound

1. Students make jerky movements to the percussive beat.
2. They jump in place or through space.
3. Students do locomotor movements in time with the beat.
4. Responding to three beats, the children collapse on the first beat, roll on the second, and form a shape on the third.

Combinations

To form a combination of movements, select one from each category in the preceding lists (shaking or percussive). When the shaking sound is made, the children perform that movement. When the drum sound is made, the children react accordingly.

Games and Miscellaneous Activities

Selected games are quite suitable for introductory activities if they keep all children active, are simple, and require little teaching. To minimize teaching time, use one of these familiar games:

- Addition Tag (page 546)
- Airplanes (page 267)
- Barker's Hoopla (page 557)
- Circle Touch (page 558)
- Couple Tag (page 550)
- Curl and Around (page 270)
- European Rhythmic Running (page 268)
- Loose Caboose (page 553)
- One, Two, Button My Shoe (page 541)
- Squad Tag (page 555)
- Touchdown (page 564)
- Whistle Mixer (page 557)

Physical Fitness

An understanding of the difference between health- and skill-related fitness helps clarify the need for emphasizing lifetime activity. High-level fitness performance is not a reasonable expectation for most children. Instead, the goal is to increase the activity and health-related fitness level of all students to improve their health status. Fitness activities for children can be moderate in intensity and still offer many health benefits. This chapter includes suggestions for developing a fitness module, motivating children to maintain fitness, and developing positive attitudes toward fitness activities. Also described are some exercises and proper performance techniques for inclusion in a health-related program that meets all students' needs.

Learning Objectives

► Differentiate between skill- and health-related physical fitness.
► Describe the fitness status of youth in the United States.
► Explain the role that a broad program of physical fitness and activity plays in the elementary school curriculum.
► Identify the various components of health- versus skill-related physical fitness.
► List guidelines for developing and maintaining physical fitness.
► Develop a fitness module.
► Cite strategies and techniques for motivating children to maintain physical fitness.
► Discuss the importance of fitness testing and cite several tests that can be used to measure fitness in children.
► Categorize various exercises by the muscle group involved.
► Characterize isotonic, isometric, and isokinetic exercises.
► Identify harmful physical activities and exercises.
► Plan and demonstrate many activities and exercises that can improve the physical fitness of children.

Definitions of Physical Fitness

Physical activity is a process that involves accumulating a wide variety of movement. Physical fitness is often measured to see if an adequate standard is in place to ensure good health. The general definition of physical fitness is offered by Howley and Franks (2007) as "a state of well-being with a low risk of premature health problems and energy to participate in a variety of physical activities."

The two types of physical fitness most often identified are health-related physical fitness and skill-related physical fitness. The difference between functional fitness (health related) and fitness related to athletic ability (skill related) is shown in figure 14.1.

Health-related fitness is characterized by moderate to vigorous physical activity, as discussed in chapter 3. Health-related fitness is a better match for people who are generally unwilling to exercise at high intensities. Health-related fitness activities can be integrated into everyday activities that are often characterized as lifetime activities. In contrast, skill-related physical fitness includes health-related components, but it also covers components related to physical performance. Skill-related fitness is the right choice for people who can and want to perform at a high level, but it is less acceptable to most people because it requires training and exercising at high intensities.

Health-Related Physical Fitness Tests

Health-related fitness benefits all students (regardless of athletic ability) by improving their health status through daily physical activity. Health-related fitness is for all students, regardless of their ability level and genetic limitations. Students learn that if they are willing to be active, they can improve their health-related fitness. In contrast, skill-related fitness is strongly influenced by genetic traits and abilities. A primary reason for teaching health-related fitness is to help all students develop positive lifetime activity habits.

Health-related physical fitness includes aspects of physiological function that protect students from diseases related to a sedentary lifestyle. Health-related fitness is an important marker shown to predict cardiovascular disease, morbidity, and mortality (Morrow, Tucker, Jackson, Martin, Greenleaf, & Petrie, 2013). Such fitness can be improved or maintained through regular physical activity. Specific components include aerobic capacity, body composition (ratio of leanness to fatness), flexibility, and muscular strength and endurance. The FitnessGram (Cooper Institute, 2017) is the most-used test found in today's schools.

The FitnessGram uses criterion-referenced health standards related to good health. Criterion standards specify a level of fitness needed to help protect students from diseases related to sedentary living. The Fitness-

FIGURE 14.1 Components of physical fitness.

Gram classifies fitness performance into three categories: needs improvement high risk, needs improvement some risk, and healthy fitness zone (HFZ). All students are encouraged to score in the HFZ, but few benefits result from scoring beyond the HFZ. Criterion-referenced health standards are not designed to compare students. The goal is for all students to achieve and move their personal performance into the HFZ. What follows is a brief description of how each of the four components of health-related physical fitness (i.e., aerobic capacity, body composition, flexibility, and muscular strength and endurance) is evaluated.

Aerobic Capacity

Aerobic capacity offers many health benefits and is often seen as the most important element of fitness. Aerobic capacity is the ability of the heart, the blood vessels, and the respiratory system to deliver oxygen efficiently for an extended time. Continuous, rhythmic activities require the delivery of a constant supply of oxygen to the muscle cells. Activities that benefit this aerobic capacity are paced walking, jogging, biking, rope jumping, aerobics, and swimming.

The mile (1.6 km) run or the PACER (Progressive Aerobic Cardiovascular Endurance Run) is most often used to measure aerobic capacity. For elementary-aged youth, the PACER is an excellent alternative to the mile run—it involves a 15- or 20-meter shuttle run that can be performed indoors. This progressive test starts at a level that allows all students to succeed and gradually increases in difficulty. The test objective is to run back and forth across the 15- or 20-meter distance within a specified time. The amount of time allowed to complete the distance gradually decreases so that students have to run faster. The 15- or 20-meter distance does not intimidate students (compared with the mile) and avoids the problem of teaching students to pace themselves rather than run all out and fatigue rapidly.

Body Composition

Body composition is an integral part of health-related fitness. Body composition is the proportion of body fat to lean body mass. Skinfolds are still used to measure body composition, but lately the body mass index (BMI) has come into favor because it is less invasive. BMI is calculated from a child's height and weight. The easiest way to calculate BMI is to use a BMI calculator for children. The Center for Disease Control and Prevention (CDC) offers a calculator at the following website: http://app .nccd.cdc.gov/dnpabmi/Calculator.aspx.

Flexibility

Flexibility is the range of movement through which a joint or sequence of joints can move. Inactive people lose flexibility, whereas frequent movement helps retain the range of movement. Stretching activities increase the length of muscles, tendons, and ligaments. The ligaments and tendons retain their elasticity through constant use. Flexibility is important to fitness because a lack of flexibility can create health problems. People who are flexible usually have good posture and may have less low-back pain. Many physical activities demand a range of motion to generate maximum force, such as serving a tennis ball or kicking a soccer ball.

The back-saver sit-and-reach test is similar to the traditional sit-and-reach test, but it is performed with one leg flexed so that students avoid hyperextending. Measurement is made on both the right and left legs.

Muscular Strength and Endurance

Muscular strength is the ability of muscles to exert force. Most activities do not build strength in areas where it is needed—namely, the arm–shoulder girdle and the abdominal–trunk region. Muscular endurance is the ability to exert force over an extended period. Endurance postpones the onset of fatigue so that activity can continue for longer. Sport activities require muscular endurance because participants must perform throwing, kicking, and striking skills many times without fatigue. The three areas of strength that are most often measured are abdominal strength, upper-body strength, and truck extensor strength and flexibility.

Abdominal Strength

The curl-up test uses a cadence (one curl-up every three seconds). The maximum limit is 75. Students lie faceup with their knees bent at a 140-degree angle. The hands are placed flat on the mat alongside the hips. The objective is to sit up gradually and move the fingers down the mat a specific distance.

Upper-Body Strength

The push-up test is done to a cadence (one every three seconds). A successful push-up is counted when the arms are bent to a 90-degree angle. The goal is to complete as many push-ups as possible. Alternative tests include the modified pull-up, the pull-up, and the flexed-arm hang.

Trunk Extensor Strength and Flexibility

The trunk lift test is done from a facedown position. This test involves lifting the upper body 6 to 12 inches (15 to 30 cm) off the floor using the muscles of the back. The position must be held until the measurement can be made.

14

Skill-Related Physical Fitness

Skill-related fitness is related to athletic ability. Speed, reaction time, agility, balance, coordination, and power are the basis for excelling in sports. Because skill-related fitness is strongly influenced by a child's natural or inherited traits, many students will not be able to perform at the highest level. Skill-related fitness components are useful for performing motor tasks related to sport and athletics. The ability to perform well on fitness or skill tests is related to a child's genetic endowment. In fact, a recent study by Timmons et al. (2010) showed that about 20% of subjects fail to improve aerobic capacity with intense endurance training and 30% do not enhance their insulin sensitivity. These authors concluded that lifestyle interventions must be tailored to each person's genotype. This study was conducted with adults, who respond to training much more than children do. It shows the importance of explaining to students why some will perform well with little effort, whereas others, no matter how hard they try, will never perform at a high level. Many examples illustrate genetic differences, such as speed, jumping ability, strength, and physical size in individuals. Understand that a few students will work hard to improve their fitness performance, but most will be satisfied to play, be active, and enjoy their bodies in a less demanding way.

Few test batteries for children related to skill-related physical fitness attributes are available. The traits most often identified as being related to athletic ability are agility, balance, coordination, power, and speed:

- Agility is the body's ability to change position rapidly and accurately while moving in space. Sports requiring agility include wrestling and football.

- Balance is the body's ability to maintain a state of equilibrium while either stationary or moving. Maintaining balance is essential to all sports and is especially important in gymnastics.

- Coordination is the body's ability to perform more than one motor task at a time. In football, baseball, tennis, soccer, and other sports that require eye–hand and eye–foot skills, coordination can be developed by repeatedly practicing the skill to be learned.

- Power is the ability to transfer energy explosively into force. Developing power requires performing strength activities with maximum force and as quickly as possible. Skills requiring power include high jumping, long jumping, shot putting, throwing, and kicking.

- Speed is the body's ability to move rapidly. Usually associated with running forward, speed is essential for success in most sports and general locomotor movement skills.

Children and Fitness Testing

Many physical education teachers believe that today's youth are less fit than they were in the past. Comparative research (Corbin & Pangrazi, 1992) examined the last four national surveys (1957 to 1985) of youth fitness conducted by AAHPERD (now SHAPE America) or the President's Council on Physical Fitness and Sports. The only test items included in all four surveys were pull-ups and the flexed-arm hang. When these two items were compared over four decades, both boys and girls showed increased upper-body strength. Unfortunately, other areas of fitness are harder to compare because of variation in survey test items. Because the national testing programs revealed little about the comparative fitness levels of children, the surveys were discontinued.

What does appear to be true is that youth have shown a serious and documented increase in body fat. Childhood obesity has more than doubled in children and tripled in adolescents in the past 30 years (Ogden, Carroll, Kit, & Flegal, 2012). The latest reports show that 18% of youth ages 6 through 11 years old are obese. (Hales et al., 2017) Sex-specific BMI-for-age growth charts are used to classify children as obese or overweight. Those children above the 85th percentile are classified as overweight, and children above the 95th percentile are considered obese. This excess body fat negatively affects fitness scores. Common sense dictates that if a student can do 20 push-ups at normal weight, putting 20 pounds (10 kg) of sand on his or her back will decrease the number of push-ups the student performs. Body fat is dead weight that does not contribute to muscular or cardiovascular performance. Thus, strength in relationship to body size and aerobic performance scores decrease as obesity increases rapidly among youth.

Is it realistic to expect all children to reach specified fitness standards? What factors control fitness performance, and how much control do children have over their fitness accomplishments?

Physical fitness tests often lead students down a path of failure regardless of how much they train to improve. Heredity directly affects all aspects of health-related fitness (Corbin, Welk, Corbin, & Welk, 2011). Various factors, such as environment, nutrition, heredity, and maturation, affect fitness performance as reflected in physical fitness test scores. Research clearly shows that heredity and maturation strongly affect fitness scores (Corbin, 2012; Corbin & Pangrazi, 1992). In fact, these factors may have more to do with youth fitness scores than activity level does. Lifestyle and environmental factors can also make a difference. For example, nutrition is a lifestyle factor that can influence test scores, and environmental conditions (heat, humidity, and pollution) strongly modify test performances. Fitness performance is only partially determined by activity and training.

Beyond heredity lies another factor that predisposes some children to high (or low) performance. Recent research has shown that differences in trainability are strongly influenced by genetic predisposition (Bouchard, 2012). Trainability explains why some people benefit from training (regular physical activity) more than others do. Suppose that two children perform the same workload throughout a semester. Child A improves dramatically, but child B does not. Child A simply responds more favorably to training than does child B; that is, child A inherited a body that responds to exercise. Child A improves her fitness and scores well on the test, and she concludes, "The activity works—it makes me fit." Child B scores poorly, receives negative or no feedback, and concludes, "Activity doesn't improve my fitness, so why bother?" Child B's fitness actually may improve (but less than child A's), although it will take longer to show. Because of genetic limitations, child B will probably never achieve child A's level of fitness. Trainability and genetic endowment differences limit or enhance performance, highlighting the importance of having different expectations for students.

FITNESS, PHYSICAL ACTIVITY, AND HEALTHY EATING HABITS FOR YOUTH

Physical activity and physical fitness are not the only variables related to childhood obesity; of equal importance is healthy eating. To teach children about all the factors that affect fitness, teachers must teach them not only about physical activity but also about the nutritional value of the foods they eat. The physical education teacher of the school can work together with school staff and the food services personnel to address healthy eating for children in a variety of ways.

First, the physical education teacher can integrate nutrition content into the physical education curriculum. Specifically, physical activities can incorporate food group concepts as well as caloric intake versus caloric expenditure. (Example health integration activities can be found in chapter 10.)

Second, the physical educator can address healthy eating practices with staff so that they can model positive practices as well as encourage the students to choose healthy options at breakfast and lunch and during snack time, if applicable. Additionally, policies for nutritious school parties can be established. Instead of allowing students to bring cupcakes or cookies for birthday celebrations, healthy food alternatives or nonfood treats can be enforced. These same principles can be applied to rewards for student behavior or academic performance.

Third, healthy eating at mealtimes can be promoted with point-of-decision prompts posted around the cafeteria and throughout the school. The purpose of these posters or signs is to encourage students to make healthy choices. Other ideas include food labeling in the cafeteria (e.g., "slow, whoa, and go" foods) and rewarding students for making healthy choices during meals. Food labeling may be as simple as placing foods with higher nutrient density on a green food tray and those with less nutritional value on a red food tray. Some food service personnel label healthy food choices with certain colored sticker dots so that children will be aware of the choices they are making. Finally, cafeteria employees, teachers, and staff may randomly reward students whom they spot consuming healthy foods by giving them a sticker or providing some other healthy incentive.

In 2011 the United States Department of Agriculture unveiled MyPlate, which is a guide focusing on balancing calories; increasing consumption of foods such as fruits, vegetables, whole grains, and low-fat milk; and reducing intake of sodium and sugary drinks. The figure is a plate with a section each for vegetables, fruits, protein, and grains, and a circle of dairy on the side. The section sizes vary based on the suggested portions and proportionality of each of the food groups. For more information on the MyPlate initiative, see www.choosemyplate.gov.

Nutrition is a vital part of the energy balance equation and addressing these concepts with children is important in the ongoing battle against childhood obesity.

Other factors that influence fitness performance in children are physical maturation and age. A quick look at a table of fitness test standards shows that performance levels increase as children grow older. Because age does not accurately reflect physical maturity, an immature, active child might score lower than a more mature, less active child of the same age. Maturation and age can override the effects of activity among young children. Most of the improvement in fitness test scores from the beginning to end of the school year occurs because kids are eight to nine months older. Expect older students in the same classroom to perform better than their peers who are three or more months younger.

Children want to succeed. They try to behave in ways that please the teacher and impress their friends. When the teacher says that fitness scores can be improved by working hard each day, most children are believers. Students who have been exercising regularly expect to do well on the fitness tests—and teachers expect the same. But if their scores are lower than expected, students can be disappointed. They are discouraged if the teacher concludes that their low fitness scores reflect inactivity and lack of exercise. Conclusions such as "You weren't as fit as some of your peers, therefore you must not have worked hard enough" can be destructive. Conversely, it can be incorrect to assume that students who score high on fitness tests are active. Students who are genetically gifted may be inactive yet still perform well on fitness tests. If teachers do not teach otherwise, these students incorrectly develop the belief that they can be fit and healthy without being active.

Fitness-Testing Issues

When fitness testing children, the overriding consideration should be to make the experience positive and educational. Help children learn about improving personal fitness and developing a lifestyle that maintains good health without being turned off by the testing experience. Imagine the embarrassment of unfit children

if their fitness test results are announced to the class. Because many schools test children twice a year, every year, some students are labeled unfit for an entire school career. How could this practice be a positive experience for inactive children who need the most motivation?

Reporting Body Mass Index to Parents

Some states require that each student's body mass index (BMI) be calculated and sent home to parents. The purpose is to inform parents about the status of their child's weight. BMI scores, which are calculated from a child's weight and height, are often controversial among professionals. BMI is an indicator of body fat for most, but not all, children and teens. BMI does not measure body fat directly, but research has shown that BMI correlates to direct measures of body fat, such as underwater weighing. Because it is inexpensive and easy to do, BMI is used as an alternative to direct measures of body fat.

For children, the BMI is age- and sex-specific; it is often referred to as BMI-for-age. The easiest way to determine BMI is to use the Centers for Disease Control and Prevention's (CDC) calculator for teens and children at www.cdc.gov/healthyweight/bmi/calculator.html. The calculator requires date of birth, date of measurement, sex, and height and weight without shoes and heavy clothes. The calculator reports the BMI and the BMI-for-age percentile and their weight status category as shown in table 14.1. Percentiles are the most commonly used indicator to assess the size and growth patterns of individual children in the United States. The percentile indicates the relative position of the child's BMI number among children of the same sex and age.

Teachers can use the CDC's BMI-for-age percentile charts to show parents how their child's BMI score compares with those of other students of the same age and sex (figures 14.2 and 14.3). Parents can see if their child falls into healthy weight percentiles or decide whether they want to consult a professional if their child falls into the other categories. The teacher must remember that the BMI is an estimate and that health professionals

TABLE 14.1 CDC Weight Status Categories With BMI-for-Age Percentile Rankings

Weight status	BMI-for-age percentile range
Underweight	Less than the 5th percentile
Healthy weight	5th percentile to less than the 85th percentile
Overweight	85th percentile to less than the 95th percentile
Obese	Equal to or greater than the 95th percentile

2 to 20 years: Boys
Body mass index-for-age percentiles

NAME _____

RECORD # _____

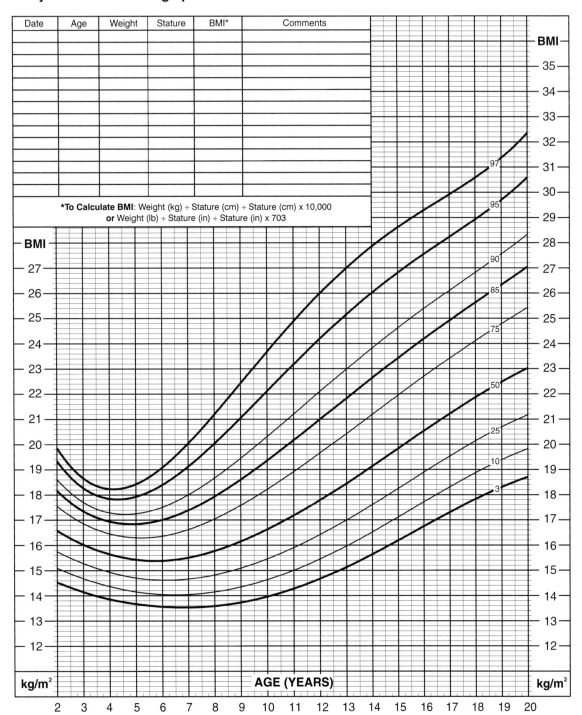

*To Calculate BMI: Weight (kg) ÷ Stature (cm) ÷ Stature (cm) x 10,000
or Weight (lb) ÷ Stature (in) ÷ Stature (in) x 703

Published May 30, 2000 (modified 10/16/00).
SOURCE: Developed by the National Center for Health Statistics in collaboration with
the National Center for Chronic Disease Prevention and Health Promotion (2000).
http://www.cdc.gov/growthcharts

FIGURE 14.2 Boys' body mass index-for-age percentiles: 2 to 20 years.

Reprinted from Center for Disease Control and Prevention. www.cdc.gov/growthcharts/data/set2clinical/cj41l073.pdf

2 to 20 years: Girls
Body mass index-for-age percentiles

NAME _____

RECORD # _____

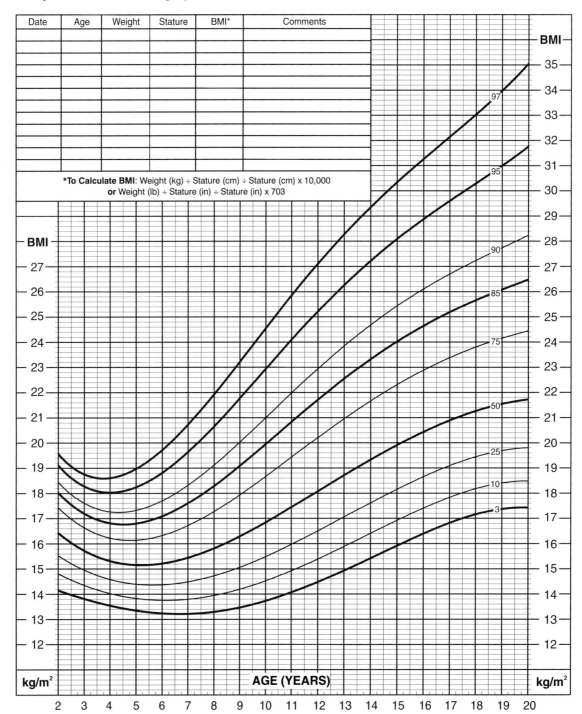

Date	Age	Weight	Stature	BMI*	Comments

*To Calculate BMI: Weight (kg) ÷ Stature (cm) ÷ Stature (cm) x 10,000
or Weight (lb) ÷ Stature (in) ÷ Stature (in) x 703

Published May 30, 2000 (modified 10/16/00).
SOURCE: Developed by the National Center for Health Statistics in collaboration with
the National Center for Chronic Disease Prevention and Health Promotion (2000).
http://www.cdc.gov/growthcharts

FIGURE 14.3 Girls' body mass index-for-age percentiles: 2 to 20 years.

Reprinted from Center for Disease Control and Prevention. www.cdc.gov/growthcharts/data/set2clinical/cj41l073.pdf

need to do further analysis and use different methods to see if other issues need to be addressed. The major purpose of sharing BMI with parents is to alert them to potential issues.

Should Rewards for Performance Be Used?

For years, reward systems have been used to recognize students who demonstrate high levels of fitness performance. Originally, such systems were thought to motivate students to improve their fitness level; evidence shows, however, that performance awards usually motivate only students who believe they can earn them. Many students find it impossible to earn such awards and often believe that there is no use in trying. Fitness awards focus on a single episode of accomplishment, making the act of participating in daily activity less important than earning an award. Students learn that the only thing that counts with fitness is their performance on the yearly test.

Reward systems that focus on improvement look at short-term changes. Fitness awards are given for a snapshot of fitness but do not recognize long-term behaviors. Studies show that students who achieve at an elite level on fitness tests do so because they are genetically gifted (Bouchard, 2012). Gifted students often pass the test without training and believe they do not have to exercise regularly to reap the benefits of an active lifestyle. If you do choose to offer awards, the best approach is to reward participation in daily activity (behavior) such as accumulating 60 minutes of activity. The physical education teacher's role is to encourage lifelong habits. When the focus is on long-term behaviors, participation in regular and moderate activity becomes the outcome of importance.

When awards and rewards are extrinsic and not available to all children, care must be taken to assure they do not undermine students' intrinsic motivation. If you choose to use them, consider the following points:

1. Base rewards on achievement of challenging, yet attainable goals. Difficult goals fail to elicit effort from students. Students least likely to try for an award are those with low self-esteem; they are probably the students who most need to achieve such goals.

2. If fitness goals do not seem attainable to students, learned helplessness sets in. This phenomenon occurs when children believe that there is no use in trying to reach the goals. Learned helplessness often occurs when performance rather than participation or effort is rewarded.

3. Teachers often use extrinsic rewards to get behavior started. With younger children this method can be an effective way to get students thinking about new behavior patterns. But the system should be phased out over time. Rewards do motivate primary-grade children, but by age 9 or 10, children start to see them as bribery to do something. Gradually removing rewards helps students learn that they should participate for intrinsic and personal reasons.

4. Develop an alternative, long-term approach that focuses on behavior rather than a single outcome by giving recognition for daily participation in activity. All students can earn these awards as they begin to establish lifelong activity habits.

Effective Uses of Fitness Tests

Fitness tests are designed to evaluate and educate students about the status of their physical fitness. Despite continued research and improvement, fitness tests—particularly field-based tests—have limitations and most show low validity. Validity is the extent to which a measurement is well-founded and corresponds accurately to the real world. In other words, does the test item accurately measure a fitness trait such as strength, aerobic capacity, and flexibility? How the tests are used becomes an important issue. Fitness tests can be used in three major ways: (1) to teach personal self-testing, (2) to establish personal-best fitness performances, and (3) to evaluate institutional fitness goals. The personal self-testing program is most strongly advocated in the elementary school physical education program. It takes the least amount of time, is educational, and can be done in an unthreatening manner. Little instructional time is lost, and students learn how to evaluate their fitness—a skill that will serve them for a lifetime. Many people have experienced fitness testing many times, but few people ever learn how to evaluate their personal fitness level.

Personal Self-Testing

The personal self-testing program is student centered, concerned with the process of fitness testing, and emphasizes learning to self-evaluate one's fitness level. Students can work on this program individually or with a friend. Partners evaluate each other and develop their own fitness profiles. The goal is to understand the process of fitness testing so that students will evaluate their health status during adulthood. Students are asked to do their best, but the teacher does not interfere in the process. The results are the student's property and

14

are not posted or shared with other students unless an individual chooses to do so. The personal self-testing program is an educational endeavor; it also allows more frequent evaluation because it can be done quickly, privately, and informally.

Figure 14.4 shows a self-evaluation FitnessGram form for student use. Students check the “HFZ” column to indicate whether they have met the minimum criterion-referenced health standard for each test item. Recording the data helps students learn to self-evaluate without the stigma of others viewing or knowing about it. A final note: It is acceptable for some students to choose not to test themselves on a certain item because they fear embarrassment (skinfolds) or failure (PACER). Think

FITNESSGRAM®

Personal Fitness Record A

Name ____________________ **School** __________________ **Grade** _____

Age _____ **Height** __________ **Weight** __________

	Date:		Date:	
	Score	**HFZ**	**Score**	**HFZ**
Aerobic capacity: ____________	______	______	______	______
Curl-up	______	______	______	______
Trunk lift	______	______	______	______
Upper-body strength: ____________	______	______	______	______
Flexibility: ____________	______	______	______	______
Activity questions: Days of aerobic activity ____________	______	______	______	______
Days of muscle-strengthening activity ____________	______	______	______	______
Days of bone-strengthening activity ____________	______	______	______	______

Note: HFZ indicates you have performed in the Healthy Fitness Zone.

I understand that my fitness record is personal. I do not have to share my results. My fitness record is important because it allows me to check my fitness level. If it is low, I will need to do more activity. If it is acceptable, I need to continue my current activity level. I know that I can ask my teacher for ideas for improving my fitness level.

FIGURE 14.4 My personal fitness record.

Reprinted by permission from The Cooper Institute, *FitnessGram Administration Manual Web Resource,* 5th ed (Champaign, IL: Human Kinetics, 2016).

about the psychological effect on the student; it might be worse for him or her to be tested and embarrassed than not to be tested at all. Morgan, Beighle, Pangrazi, & Pangrazi (2004) offer a detailed description of how to implement fitness self-testing.

Personal-Best Testing

The personal-best testing approach appeals to gifted performers and to motivated students. The objective is to achieve a maximum score in each of the test items. This approach has been used for years with most fitness tests. Unlike the self-testing approach discussed earlier, this approach is a formal testing program. Test items must be performed correctly, following test protocol to the letter. Testing also requires a considerable amount of time to administer.

Personal-best testing should be an elective program that requires maximal performance, so less capable students do not often choose to do it. Some students are threatened and fear the embarrassment of failing to perform well in front of peers. To avoid embarrassing these students, administer the test outside class time. Offer testing opportunities before or after school and on a weekend when school is not in session. Alternatively, some city recreation departments offer fitness-testing opportunities outside the physical education program. This approach is much less threatening; students can choose to participate in the personal-best testing session or decide to forgo it entirely.

Institutional Evaluation

The institutional evaluation program involves examining students' fitness levels to see if the institution (school) is reaching its desired objectives. Caution is urged in using any fitness test for this purpose because elementary school children show little response to fitness training. A common approach for institutional goal setting is to establish a percentage of the student body that must meet or exceed criterion-referenced health standards for a fitness test. Keep in mind that much of the improvement will occur because of the maturation of students.

Because this type of testing affects teachers and programs, it is done in a formal, standardized way. A common approach is to train a team of parents to administer tests throughout the system. This practice ensures accuracy and consistency across all schools in the district. Each test item is reviewed separately, because objectives may be reached for some but not all of the items. To avoid testing all students every year, some districts evaluate only during entry-level years into middle and high school. This schedule minimizes the amount of formal testing that students have to endure during their school career.

Evaluating Students With Disabilities

If a school-wide fitness-testing program is used, students with disabilities should have the same opportunity. People with disabilities often are less likely to engage in regular moderate physical activity than are people without disabilities, yet they have similar needs to promote health and prevent unnecessary disease. For most children with disabilities, the FitnessGram test (Cooper Institute, 2017) meets their needs for identifying health-related fitness. But if the FitnessGram test is unsuitable for specific students, alternatives are available—such as the Brockport Physical Fitness Test by Winnick and Short (2014). This test has been standardized for students with intellectual disabilities, spinal cord injuries, and visual impairments. An excellent resource covering these issues in more depth is *Developmental and Adapted Physical Activity Assessment* (Horvat, Kelly, Block, & Croce, 2019). The authors examine assessment issues related to motor development and motor skill performance, physical fitness, posture and gait, and behavior and social competencies.

This topic requires more coverage than the present text can offer. Regardless of the fitness test used, all students must receive equal treatment and consideration related to health and fitness issues. A final caveat is that children with disabilities usually fail to accumulate enough daily activity. Increasing their daily physical activity may be more important than evaluating fitness levels because physical activity is a lifestyle change that will serve them throughout life.

Create Positive Attitudes Toward Fitness

Fitness activity is neither good nor bad. The way you teach fitness activities determines how students feel about making fitness a part of their lifestyles. The following are strategies for making physical activity a positive learning experience.

Personalize Fitness Activities

Students who cannot perform exercises are unlikely to develop a positive attitude toward physical activity. For example, children in grades 1 through 5 are top heavy. Their oversized heads (in relation to their bodies) make it difficult to do fitness activities such as push-ups or

14

sit-ups. (The abdominal and upper-body strength activities later in this chapter offer a chance for all children to succeed.) To develop positive attitudes toward activity, fitness experiences should allow children to determine personal workloads. Use time as the workload variable, and ask children to do the best they can within a time limit. People dislike and fear experiences they view as forced on them from an external source. Voluntary long-term exercise is more likely to occur when people are internally driven to do their best.

Expose Children to a Variety of Fitness Activities

By offering children a variety of fitness opportunities, teachers can help students discover fitness activities they enjoy. Students are willing to accept activities they dislike if they know they will soon experience some they enjoy. A yearlong routine of calisthenics and 1-mile (1.5 km) runs forces children, regardless of ability and interest, to participate in the same routine. Systematically changing fitness activities is a significant way to help students feel positive about fitness.

Give Students Positive Feedback About Their Effort

Teacher feedback contributes to the way children view fitness activities. Immediate, accurate, and specific feedback regarding effort encourages continued participation. When offered in a positive way, feedback can stimulate children to extend their participation beyond the gym. Reinforce all children, not just those performing at high levels. All children need feedback and reinforcement even if they cannot perform at an elite level.

Teach Physical Skills and Fitness

Fitness and skill development are two important components of physical education. Skills are the tools that many adults use to maintain personal fitness. These people maintain fitness through skill-based activities such as tennis, badminton, swimming, golf, basketball, aerobics, bicycling, and so on. People who feel competent in an activity are much more likely to participate as adults. Some states mandate fitness testing, leading teachers to worry that their students will not pass. Unfortunately, some teachers sacrifice skill development to gain more time for teaching fitness. Fitness development is not enough; school programs must graduate students with requisite entry skills in a variety of activities.

Be a Role Model

Appearance, attitude, and actions speak loudly about teachers and their values regarding fitness. Teachers who display physical vitality, take pride in being active, participate in activities with children, and are physically fit positively influence children to maintain an active lifestyle. Of course, teachers cannot complete fitness routines nine times a day, five days a week, but by periodically exercising with your classes, you show your willingness to do what you ask students to do. Related to modeling positive fitness behavior is to point out how many adults enjoy fun runs, the social aspects of fitness activities, and being part of fitness club programs. Many adults use fitness clubs as a focal point for social experiences.

Care About Children's Attitudes

Attitudes dictate how students participate in activity. Too often, adults force fitness on children in a well-meaning effort to make them physically fit. But this approach is often used without considering the effect it has on students. Training does not result in lifetime fitness. When students are trained without concern for their feelings, the result may be fit children who hate physical activity. A negative attitude is difficult to change. Students should participate in fitness activities, but they must enjoy the experience. Do not funnel all students into one type of fitness activity. Running may harm the health of obese children, and lean, uncoordinated students may not enjoy contact activities.

The fitness experience works best when it is a challenge rather than a threat. A challenge is an experience that participants believe they can accomplish. A threat is a task that seems impossible no matter what the student does. The student, not the teacher, decides whether an activity is a challenge or a threat. Listen carefully to students rather than telling them they should do it for their own good.

Start Easy and Progress Slowly

Developing fitness is a journey, not a destination. No teacher wants students to become fit and then quit being active. A rule of thumb is to have students start at a level they can accomplish successfully. This usually means self-directed workloads within a specific period. Do not force students into excessive workloads too soon. Start easy, ensure success, and gradually increase the workload. This approach prevents the discouragement of failure and excessive muscle soreness. When students successfully accomplish activities, they develop a system of self-talk and feel positive about their exercise behavior. Students thus minimize self-criticism and the feeling that they are not living up to their own or others' standards.

Use Low-Intensity Activity

Prescribe activity appropriate to the child's developmental level. The amount of activity needed for good health is dictated by intensity and duration. Most children participate in high-volume, low-intensity activity because they have several opportunities for activity each day. This naturally occurring activity is consistent with their developmental level. In contrast, most adults are involved in low amounts of high-intensity, low-volume activity because they have little time for activity each day. This contrast of activity styles leads adults to believe that children need to participate in high-intensity activities to receive health benefits.

Adults often think children are unfit because they do not like to participate in high-intensity fitness activities. This focus on high-intensity activity can discourage some children and burn them out at an early age. Children are the most active segment of society (Rowland, 2005), and this trait should be maintained and encouraged through moderate to vigorous activity. When teachers and parents reinforce regular, low-intensity activity, fitness follows to the extent possible for each child, given heredity and maturation level.

Develop an Understanding of Physical Fitness Principles

Physical education instruction should teach activity habits that carry over to out-of-school activities. No matter how often students participate in physical education, they need to learn the principles of physical fitness as well as the practice of physical activity. When students are not taught fitness activities, they learn that such activities are unimportant or not valued by teachers and the school. Children are experiential; they learn by participating, and they develop perceptions based on those experiences. If physical activities are taught in school, students begin to learn the role of daily activity in a healthy lifestyle. Children are taught to brush their teeth at a tender age so that they learn a habit that will last a lifetime. Teaching children the habit of being active so that they retain their physical health throughout life is just as important.

Teaching students different ways to develop and maintain fitness (even if only one day per week) demonstrates that the school values health and exercise as part of a balanced lifestyle. What better outcome can students attain than learning how to maintain a balanced fitness program for life? Consider the following suggestions for integrating fitness concepts into the physical education program.

1. Provide basic explanations of rudimentary anatomy and kinesiology. Children can learn the names and locations of major bones and muscle groups, including how they function in moving various joints.

2. Provide an understanding of how fitness is developed. Explain the value of the procedures followed in class sessions so that children understand the purpose of all fitness development tasks. Additionally, teach children the components of a lifelong personal fitness program.

3. Bring the class together at the end of a lesson to discuss key fitness points that help students understand why fitness is important. To share cognitive information, teachers can establish a muscle of the week, construct educational bulletin boards to illustrate fitness concepts, or send home handouts on principles of fitness development.

4. Develop cognition of the importance of fitness to health. Help students understand how and why to perform fitness activities. They need to know the benefits of maintaining a minimal fitness level.

5. Place bulletin boards in the teaching area to explain components of the physical education program to parents and students. Bulletin boards can feature skill techniques, motivational reminders, and upcoming fitness activities. Classroom teachers are required to develop bulletin boards for their classes; physical education teachers can enhance their credibility by designing visual aids for the gymnasium.

6. Use music to accompany fitness routines and motivate the students. Exercise videos are an excellent medium for learning a new fitness activity.

7. Help children understand the values of physical fitness and the physiology of its development and maintenance. Homework dealing with the

14

cognitive aspects of fitness development communicates to parents that their children are gaining knowledge for a lifetime.

8. Emphasize self-testing programs that teach children to evaluate personal fitness levels without concern that others may be judging them. Fitness and activity are personal matters for most adults, and children should receive the same consideration.

Avoid Harmful Practices and Exercises

The following points contraindicate certain exercise practices and should be considered when offering fitness instruction. For in-depth coverage of contraindicated exercises, see Corbin, Welk, Corbin, and Welk (2011).

1. The following techniques (Macfarlane, 1993) should be avoided when performing abdominal exercises that lift the head and trunk off the floor:

   - Avoid placing the hands behind the head or high on the neck. This position may cause hyperflexion and injury to the discs when the elbows swing forward to help pull the body up.

   - Keep the knees bent. Straight legs cause the hip flexor muscles to be used earlier and more forcefully, making it difficult to maintain proper pelvic tilt.

   - Do not hold the feet on the floor. Having another student secure the feet places more force on the lumbar vertebrae and may lead to lumbar hyperextension.

   - Do not lift the buttocks and lumbar region off the floor. This action also causes the hip flexor muscles to contract vigorously.

2. Two types of stretching activities have been used to develop flexibility. Ballistic stretching (strong bouncing movement), once the most common method, has been discouraged for many years because it was thought to increase delayed-onset muscle soreness. The other method, static stretching, involves increasing the stretch to the point of discomfort, backing off slightly until the position can be held comfortably, and stretching for an extended time. Static stretching has been advocated because it is thought to reduce muscle soreness and prevent injury. Both ballistic and static stretching produce increases in muscle soreness. Static stretching is an excellent choice, but ballistic stretching is not harmful as once thought.

3. If forward flexion is done from a sitting position in an effort to touch the toes, the bend should be from the hips, not from the waist, and it should be done with one leg flexed. In response to this concern, the FitnessGram back-saver sit-and-reach test item is now done with one leg flexed to reduce stress on the lower back.

4. Straight-leg raises from a supine position should be avoided because they may strain the lower back. The problem can be somewhat alleviated by placing the hands under the small of the back, but avoiding such exercises altogether is probably best.

5. Deep knee bends (full squats) and the duck walk should be avoided. They may damage the knee joints and have little developmental value. Flexing the knee joint to 90 degrees and returning to a standing position is more beneficial.

6. When stretching from a standing position, students should not hyperextend their knees. The knee joint should be relaxed rather than locked. Having students do their stretching with bent knees is often effective because it reminds them not to hyperextend the joint. In all stretching activities, allow students to judge their own range of motion. Expecting all students to be able to touch their toes is unrealistic. If you are concerned about touching the toes from this position, have them do so from a sitting position with one leg flexed.

7. Avoid activities that place stress on the neck. Examples of such activities are abdominal exercises with the hands behind the head.

8. Do not have students perform the so-called hurdler's stretch. This activity is done in the sitting position with one leg forward and the other leg bent and to the rear. This stretch places undue pressure on the knee joint of the bent leg. Substitute a stretch using a similar position with one leg straight in front and the other leg bent with the foot placed in the crotch area.

9. Avoid stretches that demand excessive back arching. An example: In a prone position, the student

reaches back and grabs the ankles. By pulling and arching, the exerciser can hyperextend the lower back. This action stresses the discs and stretches the abdominal muscles, which most people do not need to stretch.

Implement a Yearlong Fitness Plan

Developing a yearlong plan of fitness instruction helps ensure that students have a variety of experiences. It also allows for progression and offers a well-rounded program of instruction. Plan physical fitness instruction like you would plan skill development sequences. The Dynamic PE ASAP website offers a yearlong sequence of fitness units for children at all three developmental levels.

When organizing a plan for fitness instruction, consider these points. Fitness units should vary in length depending on the students' age. Children need to experience a variety of routines that maintain a high level of motivation. During the elementary school years, becoming familiar with different types of activities is more important than following progressive, demanding fitness routines. Adhere to one principle: No single method of developing fitness is best for all children. Offer a variety of routines and activities so that students learn that fitness is not lockstep and unbending. The yearlong plan should offer activities that allow all children to succeed at one time or another during the school year.

The yearlong plan contains more structured activities as children grow older. Most of the activities listed for Developmental Level I children are unstructured and allow wide variation of performance. For children in Developmental Levels II and III, emphasis on proper technique and performance increases. But do not expect every student to do every activity exactly the same. Thinking that an obese child will be able to perform at a level similar to that of a lean child is unreasonable. Allow for variation in performance while emphasizing the importance of "doing your best."

Implementing Fitness Routines

Fitness routines are exclusively dedicated to presenting a variety of fitness activities. Here are some suggestions for successfully implementing fitness routines:

1. Precede fitness instruction with a two- to three-minute warm-up period. Introductory activities are useful for this purpose because they allow students to prepare for strenuous activity.

2. Be sure that the fitness part of the daily lesson, including warm-up, lasts only about 10 to 13 minutes. Some will argue that more time is needed to develop adequate fitness, but most teachers have only a 20- to 30-minute instruction period. Because skill instruction is part of a balanced physical education program, compromise is necessary to ensure that all phases of the program are covered.

3. Use activities that exercise all body parts and cover the major fitness components. Children are capable performers when workloads are geared to their age, fitness level, and abilities.

4. Use a variety of fitness routines comprising sequential exercises for total body development as a recommended alternative to a yearlong program of regimented calisthenics. To replace the traditional approach of doing the same routine day in and day out, offer a diverse array of activities appealing to the children's interests and fitness levels.

5. Assume an active role in fitness instruction. Children respond positively to role modeling. Teachers who actively exercise with children, hustle to assist students having difficulty, and make exercise fun can instill in children the value of an active lifestyle.

6. When determining workloads for children, remember that the available alternatives are time or repetitions. Base the workload on time rather than on a specific number of repetitions, so that students can adjust their workload within personal limits. Beginning dosages for exercises should start at a level at which all children will succeed. The best way to ensure success is to allow students to adjust the workload to suit their capabilities. Using a specific amount of time per exercise allows less gifted children to perform successfully. Do not expect all children to perform exactly the same workload.

7. Take advantage of interval training with students. Most routines are effective in 30-second intervals; longer intervals cause students to become fatigued or bored and go off task. Alternate stretching and strength development exercises with aerobic exercises. This approach permits students to recover from an aerobic activity while stretching, and it allows for recovery time after strength development activities.

14

8. Use music to time fitness activity segments so that you are free to move throughout the area and offer individualized instruction. The easiest way to time segments is to alternate 30-second intervals of music and silence. When music is playing, it signals that students are to perform an aerobic activity. The silence interval signals stretching or strength development activity.

9. Never use fitness activities as punishment. Students should not learn that push-ups and running are things you do when you misbehave. The opportunity to exercise should be a privilege as well as an enjoyable experience. Think of the money adults spend to exercise. Take a positive approach and offer students a chance to jog with a friend when they do something well. This activity allows them to visit and to exercise with a positive feeling. Be an effective salesperson; sell your students on the joy of activity and the benefits of physical fitness.

Fitness Activities for Developmental Level I

Fitness activities for young children can teach components of physical fitness as well as exercise various body areas. All the fitness routines that follow alternate strength and flexibility activities with cardiovascular activity. Most routines include strength and flexibility activities. Together, the introductory and fitness activity offer broad coverage by including activities for each of these five areas: arm–shoulder girdle, trunk, abdomen, legs and cardiorespiratory system, and flexibility.

Modified Fitness Activities That Ensure a Successful Experience

Too often, students are asked to take on an impossible fitness load. For example, look at the developmental characteristics of five- through eight-year-old children. Their heads are about 90% of adult size, their trunks are 50% of adult size, and their legs are short (30 to 40% of adult size). These top-heavy, short-legged little people cannot possibly succeed at doing push-ups and sit-ups. Yet time and again, teachers ask children of this age to do these important exercises—only to see them fail. Small wonder that most children enter the intermediate grades hating push-ups and sit-ups. The following

fitness activities are modifications that can help ensure a successful experience. Present the activities early in the year to students in all grades. Then, when upper-body or abdominal strength activities are assigned, students can select any of the modified activities they believe they can perform successfully.

Students must be allowed to select activities they believe they can accomplish. The student, not the teacher, must dictate workload. No teacher knows how many repetitions of an activity a child can perform. Allowing each student to do his or her best is ideal. Fitness is ineffective when forced down a student's throat. Most people will avoid future activity if they feel pressured and unsuccessful in their early experiences with fitness activities.

Alternate 30 seconds of strength or flexibility activities with 30 seconds of aerobic activities to avoid fatiguing students. This simple form of interval training works well with young children. When pushed too long aerobically, children show their fatigue in many ways (i.e., complaining, quitting, misbehaving, or sitting out). Short bouts of activity are much more effective than long distance runs.

Arm–Shoulder Girdle Strength Activities

These activities precede push-up activities and should be learned first. All the challenges encourage students to support their body weight with the arms and shoulders.

1. Practice taking your weight completely on your hands.

2. In crab position (tummy toward the ceiling), keep your feet in place and make your body go in a big circle. Do the same from the push-up position.

3. In crab position, go forward, backward, and to the side. Turn around, move very slowly, and so on.

4. Successively from standing, supine, and hands-and-knees positions, swing one limb (arm or leg) at a time, in different directions and at different levels.

5. Combine two limb movements (arm-arm, leg-leg, or arm–leg combinations) in the same direction and in opposite directions. Vary the levels.

6. Swing the arms or legs back and forth and go into giant circles. In supine position, make giant circles with the feet.

7. In a bent-over position, swing the arms as if swimming. Try a backstroke or a breaststroke. What does a sidestroke look like?

8. Make the arms go like a windmill. Turn the arms in different directions. Accelerate and decelerate.

9. Show other ways you can circle your arms.

10. Pretend that bees are swarming around your head. Brush them off and keep them away.

Push-Up Lead-Up Activities

The push-up (figure 14.5) and crab positions are excellent for developing upper-body strength. Allow students to rest with one knee on the floor in the up position rather than lie on the floor. Let students select a challenge they believe they are able to accomplish rather than force them to fail at doing push-ups. Many of the directives listed for the push-up position also can be done in the crab position. As students develop strength, they make a controlled descent to the floor from the up position. The following activities can be done with one knee down (beginning) or in the regular push-up (more challenging) position.

1. Hold your body off the floor (in push-up position).

2. Wave at a friend. Wave with the other arm. Shake a leg at someone. Do these challenges in the crab position.

3. Lift one foot high. Now lift the other foot.

4. Bounce both feet up and down. Move the feet out from each other while bouncing.

5. Slowly move the feet up to the hands and go back again. Slowly move the feet up to the hands and then slowly move the hands out to return to the push-up position.

6. Reach up with one hand and touch the other shoulder behind the back.

7. Lift both hands from the floor. Try clapping the hands.

8. Turn over so that your back is to the floor. Now complete the turn to push-up position.

9. Walk on your hands and feet. Try two hands and one foot. Walk in the crab position.

10. With one knee on the ground, touch your nose to the floor between your hands. As you get stronger, move your head forward a little and touch your nose to the floor. (The farther the nose touches the floor in front of the hands, the more strength is demanded.)

11. Lower your body a small distance at a time until your chest touches the floor. Return to the up position any way possible.

12. Pretend you are a tire going flat. Gradually lower yourself to the floor.

Abdominal Strength Lead-Up Activities

The basic position for exercising the abdominal muscles is supine on the floor or on a mat. Challenges should lift the upper and lower portions of the body from the floor, either singly or together. Because young children are top heavy, they find it difficult to perform most abdominal exercises. Therefore, begin early abdominal development with students lying on the floor and lifting

14

FIGURE 14.5 Push-up position.

the head. Have students progress to a sitting position and gradually lower (with head tucked) the upper body backward to the floor.

1. Lift your head from the floor and look at your toes. Wink your right eye and wiggle your left foot. Reverse.
2. In a supine position, wave a leg at a friend. Use the other leg. Use both legs.
3. Lift your knees up slowly, an inch at a time.
4. Pick up your heels about 6 inches (15 cm) off the floor; swing them back and forth. Cross your feet and twist them.
5. Sit up any way you can and touch both sets of toes with your hands.
6. Sit up any possible way and touch your right toes with your left hand. Do it the other way.
7. In a sitting position, lean the upper body backward without falling. How long can you hold this position?
8. From a sitting position, lower your body slowly to the floor. Vary the positions of your arms (across the tummy, the chest, and above the head).
9. From a supine position, curl up by pulling up on your legs.
10. From a supine position, hold your shoulders off the floor.
11. From a supine position, lift your legs and head off the floor.

Trunk Development Activities

Movements that include bending, stretching, swaying, twisting, reaching, and forming shapes help develop trunk strength. No particular sequence exists, but the activity should move from simple to more complex. Vary the position the child is to take: standing, lying down, kneeling, or sitting.

Bending

1. Bend in different ways.
2. Bend as many parts of your body as you can.
3. Make different shapes by bending two, three, and four parts of your body.
4. Bend the arms and knees in different ways and on different levels.
5. Try different ways of bending your fingers and wrist of one hand with the other. Use some resistance (explain resistance). Add body bends.

Stretching

1. Keep one foot in place and stretch your arms in different directions; move with the free foot. Stretch at different levels.
2. Lie on the floor and stretch one leg different ways in space. Stretch one leg in one direction and the other in another direction.
3. Stretch as slowly as you can and then snap back to original position.
4. Stretch with different arm–leg combinations in several directions.
5. See how much space on the floor you can cover by stretching.
6. Combine bending and stretching movements.

Swaying and Twisting

1. Sway your body back and forth in different directions. Change the position of your arms.
2. Sway your body, bending over.
3. Sway your head from side to side.
4. Select a part of your body and twist it as far as you can in one direction and then in the opposite direction.
5. Twist your body at different levels.
6. Twist two or more parts of your body at the same time.
7. Twist one part of your body while untwisting another.
8. Twist your head to see as far back as you can.
9. Twist like a spring. Twist like a screwdriver.
10. Stand on one foot and twist your body. Untwist.
11. While seated, make different shapes by twisting.

Leg and Cardiorespiratory Development Activities

Leg and cardiorespiratory development activities include a range of movement challenges in general space or in place. Children fatigue and recover quickly. Take advantage of this trait by alternating cardiorespiratory activities with strength and flexibility exercises.

Running Patterns

- Running in different directions
- Running in place
- Ponies in the Stable
- Tortoise and Hare

- European Rhythmic Running
- Running and stopping
- Running and changing direction on signal

Jumping and Hopping Patterns

- Jumping in different directions back and forth over a spot
- Jumping or hopping in, out, over, and around hoops, individual mats, or jump ropes laid on the floor
- Jumping or hopping back and forth over lines, or hopping down the lines

Rope Jumping

- Individual rope jumping—allow choice

Combinations

Many combinations of locomotor movements can be used to motivate students. Here are some possible challenges:

1. Run in place. Do some running steps in place without stopping.
2. Skip or gallop for 30 seconds.
3. Slide all the way around the gymnasium.
4. Alternate hopping or jumping for 30 seconds with 30 seconds of rest.
5. Jump in place while twisting your arms and upper body.
6. Do 10 skips, do 10 gallops, and finish with 30 running steps.
7. Hold hands with a friend and do 100 jumps.
8. Jump rope as many times as possible without missing.
9. Hop back and forth over a line from one end of the gym to the other.
10. Try to run as fast as you can. How long can you keep going?

Animal Movements

Animal activities are enjoyable for Developmental Level I children, who enjoy mimicking animal sounds and movements. Most of the animal movements are done with the body weight on all four limbs, which helps develop the arms and shoulders. Challenge students to move randomly throughout the area, across the gym, or between cones set at a specific distance. Increase workload by extending the distance or the amount of time that students do each animal walk. To avoid excessive fatigue, alternate the animal movements with stretching

activities. Here are some animal movements that can be used (see chapter 20 for descriptions of more animal movements):

- Puppy Walk. Move on all fours (not the knees). Keep the head up and move lightly.
- Lion Walk. Move on all fours while keeping the back arched. Move deliberately and lift the "paws" to simulate moving without sound.
- Elephant Walk. Move heavily throughout the area, swinging the head back and forth in the way that elephants swing their trunks.
- Seal Walk. Move by using the arms to propel the body. Allow the legs to drag along the floor, as a seal would move.
- Injured Coyote. Move using only three limbs. Hold the injured limb off the floor. Vary the walk by specifying which limb is injured.
- Crab Walk. Move on all fours with the tummy facing the ceiling. Try to keep the back as straight as possible.
- Rabbit Jump. Start in a squatting position with the hands on the floor. Reach forward with the hands and support the body weight. Jump both feet toward the hands. Repeat the sequence.

Fitness Games

Fitness games are highly motivating and excellent for cardiovascular endurance. Instruct all students to keep moving during the game. A great way to be sure that this occurs is to play games that do not eliminate players. A player who tags someone is no longer "it," and the person tagged becomes the tagger. This rule makes it difficult for players to tell who the tagger is, and it ensures that players cannot stop and stand when the tagger is somewhere nearby. If various games stipulate a safe position, allow players to maintain this position for only five seconds. Because fitness games primarily focus on cardiovascular fitness, alternate the games with strength and flexibility activities. Here are some games that can be played:

- Stoop Tag. Players cannot be tagged when they stoop.
- Back-to-Back Tag. Players are safe when they stand back-to-back. Other positions can be designated (toe-to-toe, knee-to-knee, and so on).
- Train Tag: Form groups of three or four and have them make a train by holding the hips of the

14

other players. Three or four players are designated as "it" and try to hook onto the rear of the train. If they are successful, the player at the front of the train becomes the new it.

- Color Tag. Players are safe when they stand on a specified color. Leaders may change the safe color at any time.
- Elbow-Swing Tag. Players cannot be tagged as long as they are performing an elbow swing with another player.
- Balance Tag. Players are safe when they are balanced on one body part.
- Push-Up Tag. Players are safe when they are in push-up position. Other exercise positions, such as bent knee curl-up, V-up, and crab position, can be used.
- Group Tag: Players are safe from being tagged only when they are all in a group (its size specified by the leader) and holding hands. For example, the number might be 4, which means that students holding hands in groups of four are safe.

Miniature Challenge Courses

Miniature challenge courses (figure 14.6) can be set up indoors or outdoors. The distance between the start and finish lines depends on the type of activity. A good starting point is a distance of about 30 feet (10 m), but this can be adjusted. Mark the course boundaries with cones.

Each child performs the specified locomotor movement from the start to the finish line and then jogs back to the start. Movement is continuous. Give directions

in advance so that no delay occurs. Limit the number of children on each course to normal squad size or fewer. The following movements can be specified:

- All types of locomotor movements: running, jumping, hopping, sliding, and so on
- Movements on the floor: crawling, Bear Walk, Seal Crawl, and the like
- Movements over and under obstacles or through tires or hoops

Sample Routine

1. Crawl under a wand set on two cones.
2. Roll down an inclined mat.
3. Logroll up an inclined mat.
4. Move up and down on jumping boxes. Climb on the last box, jump, and roll.
5. Crawl through hoops or bicycle tires held by individual mats.
6. Walk a balance beam.
7. Pull the body down a bench in prone position.
8. Leap over five carpet squares.
9. Move through a tunnel created by four jumping boxes (or benches) covered with a tumbling mat.
10. Hang on a climbing rope for 10 seconds.
11. Crab Walk from one cone to another and back.
12. Run and weave around a series of five cones.

Parachute Fitness Activities

The parachute has long been a popular item in elementary physical education. Usually used to promote teamwork, provide maximum participation, stimulate interest, or play games, the parachute can also be a tool for developing physical fitness. Teachers can develop exciting fitness routines by combining vigorous shaking movements, locomotor circular movement, and selected exercises while holding onto the chute.

Use alternating segments (20 seconds each) of silence and music to signal the duration of exercise. Music segments indicate aerobic activity with the parachute, whereas intervals of silence signal using the chute to enhance flexibility and strength development. Space students evenly around the chute. Have them use different hand grips (e.g., palms up, down, mixed). Make sure that all movements are done under control. Instruct the faster and stronger students to moderate their performance.

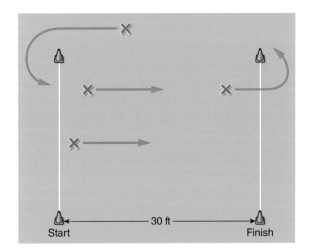

FIGURE 14.6 Miniature challenge course.

Parachute Fitness Activities

1. Jog while holding the chute in the left hand (music).
2. Shake the chute (no music.)
3. Slide while holding the chute with both hands (music).
4. Sit and perform curl-ups (no music).
5. Skip (music).
6. Freeze, face the center, and stretch the chute tightly. Hold for 8 to 12 seconds. Repeat five to six times (no music).
7. Run in place while holding the chute taut at different levels (music).
8. Sit with legs under the chute. Do a seat-walk toward the center. Return to the perimeter. Repeat four to six times (no music).
9. Place the chute on the ground. Jog away from the chute and return on signal. Repeat (music).
10. Move into push-up position holding the chute with one hand. Shake the chute (no music).
11. Shake the chute and jump in place (music).
12. Lie on back with feet under the chute. Shake the chute with the feet (no music).
13. Hop to the center of the chute and return. Repeat (music).
14. Sit with feet under the chute. Stretch by touching the toes with the chute. Relax with other stretches while sitting (no music).

Walk, Trot, and Jog

Four cones outline a square or rectangular area 30 to 40 yards (meters) on a side. (Indoors, use the perimeter of the gym.) Children are scattered around the perimeter, all facing the same direction. Use a whistle to give signals. On the first whistle, children begin to walk. On the next whistle, they change to a trot. On the third whistle, they jog faster but still under control. Finally, on the fourth whistle, they walk again. Repeat the cycle, allowing faster-moving students to pass on the outside.

Another way to signal change is by drumbeat. One beat signals walk, two beats signal trot, and three beats signal run. The three movements can be presented in random order. For variation, try other locomotor movements such as running, skipping, galloping, and sliding. At regular intervals, stop students and have them perform various stretching activities and strength development exercises. This routine allows short rest periods

between bouts of activity. Use alternating segments (30 seconds each) of silence and music to signal the duration of exercise. Music segments indicate walking, trotting, and jogging activities, whereas intervals of silence signal the strength and flexibility exercises.

Examples of activities are one-leg balance, push-ups, curl-ups, touching the toes, and any other challenges.

Walk, Trot, and Jog

Move to the following signals:

1. One drumbeat—walk.
2. Two drumbeats—trot.
3. Three drumbeats—jog.
4. Whistle—freeze and perform exercises.

Perform various strength and flexibility exercises between bouts of walking, trotting, and jogging. Exercises might include the following:

- Bend and Twist
- Sitting Stretch
- Push-Up challenges
- Abdominal challenges
- Body Twist
- Standing Hip Bend

Jump-Rope Exercises

Jump ropes can be used in many exercises and aerobic activities. Playing music followed by an interval of silence is an excellent way to alternate periods of rope jumping and exercises. During the periods of silence, students perform an exercise; when the music starts, children pick up their ropes and begin jumping.

Jump-Rope Routine

1. Jump rope for 30 seconds. If unable to jump, practice swinging the rope to the side while jumping.
2. Place the rope on the floor and do locomotor movements around and over the rope. Make different shapes and letters with the rope.
3. Hold the folded rope overhead. Sway from side to side. Twist right and left.
4. Jump rope for 30 seconds.
5. Lie on your back and hold the rope toward the ceiling with outstretched arms. Bring up one leg at a time and touch the rope with your toes.

14

Lift both legs together. Sit up and try to hook the rope over your feet. Release and repeat.

6. Touch your toes with the folded rope.

7. Jump rope for 30 seconds.

8. Place the rope on the floor and do various animal walks along or over the rope.

9. Do push-up variations with the rope folded and held between your hands.

10. Jump rope for 30 seconds.

Four-Corners Movement

Use four cones to mark off a rectangle. Students move around the perimeter of the rectangle. Each time they pass a corner, they change their movement pattern. On long sides, students do rapid movements, such as running, skipping, or sliding. On short sides, students hop, jump, or do animal walks. Have students vary clockwise and counterclockwise directions. On signal, students stop and perform flexibility and strength development challenges in place.

Using the four-corners ideas as a basis, devise other combinations. For example, the pattern in figure 14.7 requires running along one of the long sides and sliding along the other. One of the short sides has mats and requires three forward rolls; the other short side requires an animal walk on all fours. Another variation that stimulates children is to place different equipment at the perimeter of the area. On signal, students stop and pick up a piece of equipment and manipulate it for a specified time. By interspersing four-corners movement (aerobic movement) with equipment handling (resting), teachers can implement interval training. Students can use equipment such as beanbags, scooters, balance beams, benches, balls, and hoops.

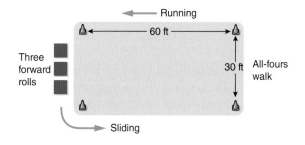

FIGURE 14.7 Four-corners movement formation.

Fitness Activities for Developmental Levels II and III

For Developmental Levels II and III, emphasis shifts to more structured exercises and routines. Start the year with teacher–leader exercises because these basic exercises will be used in other routines.

Exercises for Fitness Routines

Exercises in this section fall into seven categories: (1) flexibility, (2) arm–shoulder girdle, (3) abdominal, (4) leg and agility, (5) trunk twisting and bending, (6) partner resistance, and (7) yoga. Stress points, modifications, variations, and teaching suggestions are presented when appropriate. Include 6 to 10 exercises in a fitness routine, with 2 exercises from the arm–shoulder girdle group and at least 1 from each of the other categories. Remember that many students will not be able to perform some abdominal and arm–shoulder girdle exercises. Allow them to select some of the modified fitness activities (push-ups and abdominal modifications) described in the Developmental Level I section of this chapter.

Flexibility Exercises

Bend and Twist

Starting position: Stand with the arms crossed, hands on opposite shoulders, knees slightly flexed, and feet shoulder-width apart.

Movement: Bend forward at the waist (count 1). Twist the trunk and touch the right elbow to the left knee (count 2). Twist in the opposite direction and touch the left elbow to the right knee (count 3). Return to the starting position (count 4). Knees can be flexed.

Sitting Stretch

Starting position: Sit on the floor with one leg extended forward. Bend the other leg at the knee and place that foot against the opposite leg (figure 14.8).

Movement: Gradually bend forward and touch the toes, taking three counts to bend fully. Recover to sitting position on count 4.

Important point: Bend from the hips.

FIGURE 14.8 Sitting Stretch position.

FIGURE 14.9 Partner Rowing.

Partner Rowing

Starting position: Partners sit facing each other, holding hands with palms touching and fingers locked. The legs are spread and extended to touch the soles of partner's feet.

Movement: One partner bends forward, with the help of the other pulling backward, and tries to bring the chest as close to the floor as possible (figure 14.9). Reverse direction.

Variation: Steam Engine. With both partners in the sitting position, alternate pulling hands back and forth like a pair of steam engine pistons. Do eight sets, right and left combined twists.

Lower-Leg Stretch

Starting position: Stand facing a wall with the feet about shoulder-width apart. Place the palms of the hands on the wall at eye level.

Movement: Slowly walk away from the wall, keeping the body straight, until the stretch is felt in the lower portion of the calf. Keep the feet flat on the floor during the stretch.

Achilles Tendon Stretch

Starting position: Stand facing a wall with the forearms on it. Place the forehead on the back of the hands. Back away from the wall (2 to 3 feet [60 to 90 cm]), bend, and move one leg closer to the wall.

Movement: Flex the bent leg with the foot on the floor until the stretch is felt in the Achilles tendon. Keep the feet flat on the floor when flexing the leg closest to the wall. Repeat, flexing the other leg.

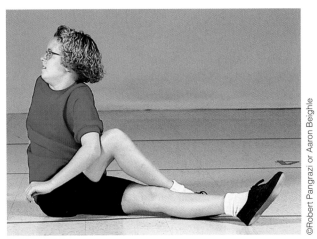

FIGURE 14.10 Body Twist.

Body Twist

Starting position: Sit on the floor with the left leg straight. Lift the right leg over the left leg and place it on the floor outside the left knee (figure 14.10). Move the left elbow outside the upper right thigh and use it to maintain pressure on the leg. Lean back and support the upper body with the right hand.

Movement: Rotate the upper body toward the right hand and arm. Reverse the position and stretch the other side of the body.

Standing Hip Bend

Starting position: Stand with the knees slightly flexed, one hand on the hip, and the other arm overhead.

Movement: Bend to the side with the hand resting on the hip. The arm overhead should point and move in the direction of the stretch with a slight bend at the elbow. Reverse and stretch the opposite side.

14

Arm–Shoulder Girdle Exercises

Arm–shoulder girdle exercises for this age group include both arm-support and free-arm activities.

Push-Ups

Starting position: Assume the push-up position (see figure 14.5), holding the body straight from head to heels.

Movement: Keeping the body straight, bend the elbows and touch the chest to the ground; then straighten the elbows, raising the body in a straight line.

Important points: The movement is in the arms. The head is up, and the eyes are looking ahead. The chest touches the floor lightly, without receiving the weight of the body. The body remains in a straight line throughout, without sagging or humping. Controlled movement is a goal; speed should not be encouraged. Push-ups are done at will, allowing each child to achieve individually within a specific time limit.

Variation: Some students develop a dislike for push-ups because they are asked to perform them without any modification. Allow students to judge their strength and choose a push-up challenge they believe they are able to accomplish. Instead of asking an entire class to perform a specific number of push-ups, personalize the workload by allowing each child to accomplish as many repetitions as possible of a self-selected push-up challenge in a specified amount of time.

Reclining Pull-Ups

Starting position: One student lies in supine position. Her partner is astride, with feet alongside the reclining partner's chest. Partners grasp hands with interlocking fingers, with an interlocked wrist grip, or with some other suitable grip.

Movement: The student on the floor pulls up with her arms until her chest touches the partner's thighs. The body remains straight, with weight resting on the heels (figure 14.11). Then she returns to the starting position.

Important points: The supporting student keeps the center of gravity well over the feet by maintaining a lifted chest and proper head position. The lower student maintains a straight body during the pull-up and moves only the arms.

Variation: Raise as directed (count 1), hold the high position isometrically (counts 2 and 3), and return to the starting position (count 4).

FIGURE 14.11   Reclining Pull-Ups.

©Robert Pangrazi or Aaron Beighle

Triceps Push-Ups

Starting position: Assume the inverted push-up position with the arms and body held straight.

Movement: Keeping the body straight, bend the elbows and touch the seat to the ground; then straighten the elbows and raise the body.

Important points: The fingers point toward the toes or are turned in slightly. The body is held firm with movement restricted to the arms.

Arm Circles

Starting position: Stand erect, with feet apart and arms straight out to the side.

Movement: Do forward and backward circles with palms facing forward, moving arms simultaneously. The number of circles executed before changing can be varied.

Important points: Avoid doing Arm Circles with palms down (particularly backward circles) because doing so stresses the shoulder joint. Maintain correct posture, keeping the abdominal wall flat and holding the head and shoulders back.

Crab Kick

Starting position: Assume crab position, with the body supported on the hands and feet and the back parallel to the floor. The knees are bent at right angles. For all crab positions, keep the seat up and avoid body sag.

FIGURE 14.12 Crab Kick.

Movement: Kick the right leg up and down (counts 1 and 2; figure 14.12). Repeat with the left leg (counts 3 and 4).

Crab Alternate-Leg Extension

Starting position: Assume crab position.

Movement: On count 1, extend the right leg forward so that it rests on the heel. On count 2, extend the left leg forward and bring the right leg back. Continue alternating.

Crab Full-Leg Extension

Starting position: Assume crab position.

Movement: On count 1, extend both legs forward so that the weight rests on the heels. On count 2, bring both feet back to crab position.

Crab Walk

Starting position: Assume crab position.

Movement: Move forward, backward, and sideways, and turn in a small circle right and left.

Flying Angel

Starting position: Stand erect, with feet together and arms at sides.

Movement: In a smooth, slow, continuous motion, raise the arms forward with elbows extended and then upward, at the same time rising up on the toes and lifting the chest, with eyes following the hands (figure

FIGURE 14.13 Flying Angel.

14.13). Lower the arms sideways in a flying motion and return to the starting position. Keep the abdomen flat throughout to minimize lower-back curvature. The head is back and well up. Do the exercise slowly and smoothly, under control.

Variation: Move the arms forward as if doing a breaststroke. Then slowly raise the arms, with hands in front of the chest and elbows out, to full overhead extension. Otherwise, the movement is the same as the Flying Angel.

Abdominal Exercises

For most exercises stressing abdominal development, start from the supine position on the floor or on a mat. When lifting the upper body, begin with a roll-up (curling) action, moving the head first so that the chin touches the chest, thus flattening and stabilizing the lower-back curve. Bend the knees to isolate abdominal muscles and avoid stressing the lower back. When doing abdominal exercises, avoid moving the trunk up to the sitting position (past 45 degrees) because doing so may cause pain and exacerbate back injury in susceptible people (Macfarlane, 1993).

14

Some children develop a dislike for abdominal work in the early school years because they are top heavy and unable to lift their upper body off the floor. To ensure success, allow students to choose an abdominal challenge they believe they are able to accomplish. Instead of asking an entire class to perform a specified number of curl-ups, personalize the workload by allowing students to accomplish as many repetitions as possible in a specific amount of time using a self-selected abdominal challenge.

Reverse Curl

Starting position: Lie on the back with the hands on the floor and to the sides of the body.

Movement: Curl the knees to the chest. The upper body remains on the floor. As abdominal strength increases, the child should lift the buttocks and lower back off the floor. Roll the knees to the chest and return the feet to the floor after each repetition. The movement is controlled, emphasizing the abdominal contraction.

Variations:

1. Hold the head off the floor and bring the knees to the chin.
2. Instead of returning the feet to the floor after each repetition, hold them 1 or 2 inches (2.5 to 5 cm) off the floor. This activity requires greater abdominal strength because there is no resting period (feet on floor).

Pelvis Tilter

Starting position: Lie on the back with feet flat on the floor, knees bent, arms out in wing position, and palms up.

Movement: Flatten the lower back, bringing it closer to the floor by tensing the lower abdominals and lifting up on the pelvis. Hold for 8 to 12 counts. Tense slowly and release slowly.

Knee Touch Curl-Up

Starting position: Lie on the back with feet flat, knees bent, and hands flat on top of thighs.

Movement: Leading with the chin, slide the hands forward until the fingers touch the kneecaps and gradually curl the head and shoulders until the shoulder blades are lifted off the floor (figure 14.14). Hold for eight counts and return to starting position. To avoid stress on the lower back, do not curl up to the sitting position.

FIGURE 14.14 Knee Touch Curl-Up.

Curl-Up

Starting position: Lie on the back with feet flat, knees bent, and arms on the floor at the side of the body with palms down.

Movement: Lift the head and shoulders to a 45-degree angle and then back in a two-count pattern. The hands should slide forward on the floor 3 to 4 inches (7.5 to 10 cm). The curl-up can also be done as an 8-count exercise, moving up on count 1, holding for 6 counts, and moving down on count 8.

Important points: Roll up, with the chin first. The hands remain on the floor.

Curl-Up With Twist

Starting position: Lie on the back with feet flat and knees bent. Arms are folded and placed across the chest with hands on shoulders.

Movement: Do a partial curl-up and twist the chest to the left. Repeat, turning the chest to the right (figure 14.15).

Variations:

1. Touch the outside of the knee with the elbow.
2. Touch both knees in succession. The sequence is up, touch left, touch right, and down.

Leg Extension

Starting position: Sit on the floor with legs extended and hands on hips.

Movement: With a quick, vigorous action, raise the knees and bring both heels as close to the seat as possible (figure 14.16). The movement is a drag with the toes touching lightly. Return to position.

Variation: Alternate bringing the knees to the right and left of the head.

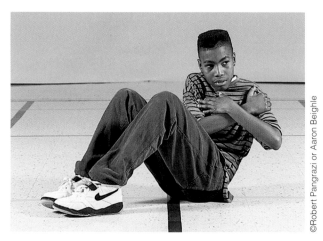

FIGURE 14.15 Curl Up With Twist.

FIGURE 14.16 Leg Extension.

Abdominal Cruncher

Starting position: Lie in supine position with feet flat, knees bent, and palms of hands cupped over the ears (not behind the head). An alternate position is to fold the arms across the chest and place the hands on the shoulders.

Movement: Tuck the chin and curl upward until the shoulder blades leave the floor. Return to the floor with a slow uncurling.

Variation: Lift the feet off the floor and bring the knees to waist level. Try to touch the right elbow to the left knee and vice versa while in the crunch position.

Leg and Agility Exercises

Running in Place

Starting position: Stand with arms bent at the elbows.

Movement: Run in place. Begin slowly, counting only the left foot. Speed up somewhat, raising the knees

to hip height. Then run at full speed, raising the knees hard. Finally, slow down. The run should be on the toes.

Variations:

1. Tortoise and Hare. Jog slowly in place. On the command "Hare," double the speed. On the command "Tortoise," slow the tempo to the original slow jogging pace.

2. March in place, lifting the knees high and swinging the arms up. Turn right and left on command while marching. Turn completely around to the right and then to the left while marching.

3. Fast Stepping. Step in place for 10 seconds as rapidly as possible. Rest for 10 seconds and repeat five or more times.

Jumping Jack

Starting position: Stand at attention.

Movement: On count 1, jump to a straddle position with arms overhead. On count 2, recover to the starting position.

Variations:

1. Begin with the feet in a stride position (forward and back). Change feet with the overhead movement.

2. Instead of bringing the feet together when the arms come down, cross the feet each time, alternating the cross.

3. After completing each set of eight counts, do a quarter turn right. (After four sets, the child is facing in the original direction.) Do the same to the left.

4. Modified Jumping Jack. On count 1, jump to a straddle position with arms out to the sides, parallel to the floor, and palms down. On count 2, return to the starting position.

Treadmill

Starting position: Assume push-up position, except that one leg is brought forward so that the knee is under the chest (figure 14.17).

Movement: Reverse the position of the feet, bringing the extended leg forward. Change back again so that the original foot is forward. Continue rhythmically alternating feet. Keep the head up. A full exchange of the legs is made, with the forward knee coming well under the chest each time.

14

FIGURE 14.17   Treadmill.

Power Jumper

Starting position: Begin in a semicrouched position, with knees flexed and arms extended backward.

Movement: Jump as high as possible and extend the arms upward and overhead.

Variations:

1. Jump and perform different turns (quarter, half, full).

2. Jump and perform different tasks (such as click heels, slap heels, clap hands, catch an imaginary pass, snare a rebound).

Trunk Twisting and Bending Exercises

Trunk Twister

Starting position: Stand with feet shoulder-width apart and pointed forward. Cup the hands and place them loosely over the shoulders (right hand on left shoulder; left hand on right shoulder), with the elbows out and the chin tucked.

Movement: Bend downward, keeping the knees relaxed. Recover slightly. Bend downward again and simultaneously rotate the trunk to the left and then to the right (figure 14.18). Return to the original position, pulling the head back, with chin in.

Bear Hug

Starting position: Stand with feet comfortably spread and hands on hips.

FIGURE 14.18   Trunk Twister.

FIGURE 14.19   Bear Hug.

Movement: Take a long step diagonally right, keeping the left foot anchored in place. Tackle the right leg around the thigh by encircling the thigh with both arms. Squeeze and stretch (figure 14.19). Return to the starting position. Tackle the left leg. Return to the starting position.

Important point: The bent leg must not exceed a right angle.

Side Flex

Starting position: Lie on one side with lower arm extended overhead. The head rests on the lower arm. The legs are extended fully, one on top of the other.

Movement: Raise the upper arm and leg diagonally (figure 14.20). Repeat for several counts and then change to the other side.

Variation: Side Flex, supported. Similar to the regular Side Flex but more demanding. The student maintains a side-leaning rest position throughout (figure 14.21).

FIGURE 14.20 Side Flex.

FIGURE 14.21 Side Flex, supported.

Body Circles

Starting position: Stand with feet shoulder-width apart, hands on hips, and body bent forward.

Movement: Make a complete circle with the upper body. Perform a specific number of circles to the right and the same number to the left.

Variations:

1. Circle in one direction until told to stop and then reverse direction.
2. Try placing the hands on the shoulders and spreading the elbows wide. Otherwise, the exercise is the same.

Windmill

Starting position: Stand with feet shoulder-width apart and arms extended sideways with palms down.

Movement: Bend and twist at the trunk, bringing the right hand down to the left toes. Recover to the starting position. Bend and twist again, but bring the left hand to the right toes. Recover to the starting position.

Partner Resistance Exercises

Partner resistance exercises are used in conjunction with activities that demand considerable endurance such as aerobic fitness routines, jogging, or astronaut exercises. The exercises are simple and enjoyable; children can do them as homework with parents or friends. Partners should be roughly matched in size and strength, so that they can challenge each other. The exercises are performed through the full range of motion at each joint and should take 8 to 12 seconds to complete. The partner providing the resistance counts the duration of the exercise; positions are then reversed.

Arm Curl-Up

The exerciser keeps the upper arms against the sides with the forearms and palms forward. The partner puts the fists in the exerciser's palms (figure 14.22). The exerciser attempts to curl the forearms upward to the shoulders. To develop the opposite set of muscles, partners reverse hand positions. They push down in the opposite direction, starting at shoulder level.

Forearm Flex

The exerciser extends the arms and places the hands, palms down, on the partner's shoulders. The exerciser attempts to push the partner into the floor. The partner may slowly stoop lower to allow the exerciser movement through the full range of motion. Then they try with the palms upward.

Fist Pull-Apart

The exerciser places the fists together in front of the body at shoulder level. The exerciser tries to pull the

FIGURE 14.22 Arm Curl-Up.

FIGURE 14.23 Back Builder.

hands apart while the partner forces them together with pressure on the elbows. As a variation, with fists apart, the exerciser tries to push them together. The partner applies pressure by grasping the wrists and holding the exerciser's fists apart.

Butterfly

The exerciser starts with arms straight down at the sides. The partner, from the back, attempts to hold the arms down while the exerciser lifts with straight arms to the sides. Then they try with arms above the head (partner holding) to move them down to the sides.

Camelback

The exerciser is on all fours with head up. The partner pushes on the exerciser's back, while the exerciser attempts to arch the back like a camel's hump.

Back Builder

The exerciser spreads the legs and bends forward at the waist with head up. The partner faces the exerciser and places the hands on top of the shoulders. The

exerciser attempts to stand upright, while the partner pushes downward (figure 14.23).

Scissors

The exerciser lies on one side, while the partner straddles the exerciser and holds the upper leg down. The exerciser attempts to raise the top leg. Then the exerciser reverses sides and lifts the other leg.

Bear Trap

Starting from a supine position on the floor, the exerciser spreads the legs and then tries to move them together. The partner provides resistance by trying to keep the legs apart.

Knee Bender

The exerciser lies in prone position with legs straight and arms extended for stability. The partner places the hands on the back of the exerciser's ankles. The exerciser tries to flex the knees while the partner applies pressure (figure 14.24). Then they try in the opposite direction, starting with the knee joint at a 90-degree angle.

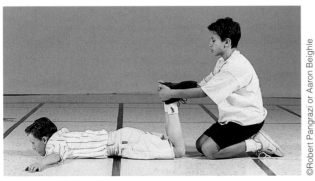

FIGURE 14.24 Knee Bender.

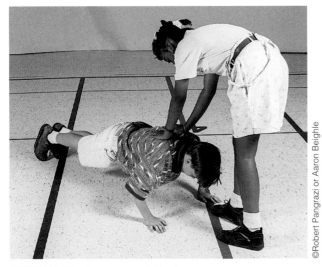

FIGURE 14.25 Push-Up With Resistance.

FIGURE 14.26 Lotus pose.

Each activity, called a posture in yoga, combines physical skills with breathing. These postures allow children to explore unique fitness movements that are not always taught in physical education.

Lotus Pose

Sit with legs crossed and spine erect as in figure 14.26. With the hands on the knees, close the eyes and slowly inhale and exhale deep breaths.

Sunrise and Sunset

Begin by standing tall and taking three deep breaths. Next, inhale and lift the arms overhead while pressing the feet into the ground. Reach to the sky for three to five seconds at the top. For the sunset, slightly bend the knees. While exhaling, bend forward from the hips as far as is comfortable. Focus on maintaining appropriate posture and a flat back. Finally, inhale, bringing the arms above the head, and exhale, bringing palms together and down to chest height with fingers pointing upward. In yoga, this is the namaste ("NAH-mah-stay") position.

Tree Pose

Start in namaste position. Lift the right foot and hold it against the inside of the left thigh (or calf). Raise both arms high and spread them like the branches of a tree (figure 14.27). After holding this pose for three breaths, return to the starting position. Do the same posture, this time lifting the left foot.

Push-Up With Resistance

The exerciser is in push-up position with arms bent, so that the body is about halfway up from the floor. The partner straddles or stands alongside the exerciser's head and puts pressure on the top of the shoulders by pushing down (figure 14.25). The amount of pressure takes judgment by the partner. Too much causes the exerciser to collapse.

Yoga Activities

Yoga has become a popular fitness activity largely because it appeals to people of varying physical skill levels. For adults, it provides a refuge, both mentally and physically, from busy lives. For students in physical education, yoga can expose them to yet another health-related fitness activity they can engage in now and for the rest of their lives. Teachers can use the yoga exercises described here as an introductory activity, during a fitness routine, or as a fun and relaxing closing activity at the end of a lesson.

14

FIGURE 14.27   Tree pose.

FIGURE 14.28   Up Cat pose.

FIGURE 14.29   Down Cat pose.

Up Cat

Start on hands and knees with fingers facing forward. Place the knees below the hips and the hands below the shoulders. While inhaling, assume the posture shown in figure 14.28. The key is to move the tailbone and shoulders up while moving the center of the torso downward into a backbend. Complete the posture by looking slightly up.

Down Cat

This posture is typically combined with the Up Cat. From the Up Cat position, inhale deeply and take the position shown in figure 14.29. The spine is rounded with the middle of the back pressed as high as possible. Tuck the head and look backward between the knees.

Fish

Begin on the back with legs straight, arms close to the body, and palms down. Slowly slide the arms under the body while inhaling and raising the chest upward. After two deep breaths, exhale and slowly move to the starting position. Once there, slowly bring the knees to the chest and hug them (figure 14.30).

Child's Pose

Start by sitting on the heels. Bend at the hips and move downward while slightly opening the knees so that the tummy is on the thighs. Bring the arms back to the feet with palms up and rest the forehead on the ground (figure 14.31). A continuation of this pose involves moving the arms forward with palms down.

FIGURE 14.30 Fish pose.

FIGURE 14.31 Child's pose.

Downward-Facing Dog

Begin on the hands and knees. Inhale deeply and then exhale while lifting the knees and pushing the toes into the floor. As the legs move backward, the bottom moves upward toward the sky and the head hangs down loosely, like fruit from a tree. Straighten the arms and legs and try to place the heels on the ground to stretch the hamstrings. This pose is typically followed immediately by the Child's pose.

Pilates Activities

Pilates, like yoga, has quickly become a popular fitness activity that attracts people of varying abilities. The program, which originated in Germany, focuses on breathing, good posture, and controlled exercises that strengthen and stretch muscles. Pilates movements are usually performed in sequence; at the elementary school level, however, when the exercises are just being learned, teach them as individual exercises until students are comfortable with them.

Stretch With Knees Sway

Start in a supine position and slowly bring the knees to the chest and hug the knees. Flatten the entire back to the ground and hold the position. Slowly sway the knees from side to side, holding for a second on each side.

Spinal Rotation

Sit in a straddle position with good posture and extend the arms out to the side. Rotate the upper body to one side and hold; then rotate to the other side and hold.

Rolling Ball

In a seated position on the floor, bring the knees to the chest and hug the ankles. From this position, roll backward while maintaining the curved spine.

14

Plank

This position is similar to a push-up, but the weight is placed on the elbows rather than the hands. The forearms and hands are pointed forward. Depending on strength, students may wish to have their knees resting on the ground rather than their feet. Keeping the abdominal muscles tight and the back and bottom in a straight line, try to balance in this position for as long as possible.

Star Positions

Similar to a yoga posture, the Star 1 exercise begins with the student in the Plank position. The first movement is to put all the weight on the right elbow and rotate the hips so that the left hip is higher and both feet are on the ground with the left hand raised in the air.

The Star 2 position requires raising the left leg off the ground and maintaining balance on only the right elbow and right foot. The third and final step in the Star sequence is to start in a traditional push-up position and move to the Star 1 position by balancing on the right hand.

Examples of Fitness Routines

When planning fitness routines, establish variety in activities and include different approaches. This plan minimizes the inherent weaknesses of any single routine. The routines should exercise all major parts of the body. When placing fitness activities into a routine, avoid overloading the same body part with two similar exercises. For example, if push-ups are being performed, the next exercise should not be crab walking, because it also stresses the arm–shoulder girdle.

Measure exercise dosage for students in time rather than repetitions. Expecting all students to perform the same number of exercise repetitions is unreasonable. As discussed earlier, fitness performance is controlled by several factors, including genetics and trainability, which make it impossible for all children to do the same workload. When time is used to determine the workload, each child can personalize the amount of activity performed within the time constraints. A gifted child can be expected to perform more repetitions in a certain amount of time than a less genetically endowed child does. An obese child may not be able to perform as many push-ups as a leaner peer can. Develop positive attitudes toward activity by asking students to do the best they can within the time allotted.

Student Leader Exercises

Students enjoy leading their peers in single exercises or in an entire routine. Students need time to practice before leading their peers effectively in a stimulating exercise session. Do not force children to lead; this can result in failure for the child as well as the class. The following routine is an example of student leader exercises.

Student-Led Routine

Encourage students to do the best they can within the specified time limit.

Arm Circles	30 seconds
Push-Up challenges	30 seconds
Bend and Twist	30 seconds
Treadmill	30 seconds
Sit-Up challenges	30 seconds
Single-Leg Crab Kick	30 seconds
Knee-to-chest curl	30 seconds
Running in Place	30 seconds
Spinal Rotation	30 seconds

Conclude the routine with two to four minutes of jogging, rope jumping, or other aerobic activity.

Squad Leader Exercises

Squad leader exercises give students an opportunity to lead exercises in a small group. This method is an effective way to teach students how to lead others and help them learn to put together a well-balanced fitness routine. A student from each squad is given a task card that has exercises and activities grouped by how they affect different parts of the body (figure 14.32). After leading the exercise for the desired amount of time, the first student passes the card to another squad member, who becomes the next leader. To ensure a balanced routine, each new leader must select an exercise from a different group. The following is an example of how to group exercises and activities for the squad leader exercise routine.

If a delay occurs in starting an exercise, advise the squad to walk or jog rather than stand in place.

Squad Leader Relay

Divide the class into groups of four or five students. Give each group a task card listing 8 to 10 exercises. One of the group members begins as the leader and leads the group through an exercise. Each time an exercise is

Task card for squad leader exercises	
Aerobic activities	**Aerobic strength exercises**
Running in Place	Reverse Curl
Jumping Jack	Pelvis Tilter
Treadmill	Knee Touch Curl-Up
Power Jumper	Curl-Up
Rhythmic jumping	Curl-Up with Twist
	Plank
Flexibility activities	**Upper-body strength exercises**
Bend and Twist	Star 1
Stretch with knee sway	Reclining Pull-Up
Partner Rowing	Triceps Push-Up
Lower-Leg Stretch	Arm Circles
Achilles Tendon Stretch	Crab Kick
Body Twist	Crab Full-Leg extension
Standing Hip Bend	Crab Walk

FIGURE 14.32   Sample task card for squad leader exercises.

completed, the card is passed to a new leader. Use alternating intervals of music to signal exercising (30 seconds) and silence (5 to 8 seconds) to indicate passing the card.

Exercises to Music

Exercises to music add another dimension to developmental experiences. Many commercial CD sets with exercise programs are available. Use a homemade music set with alternating intervals of silence and music to signal time for exercises and aerobic activity. For example, students can run or walk for 30 seconds while the music is playing and stretch or perform strength activities during the 30 second silent interval. Using music frees you from keeping an eye on a stopwatch. Many exercise modules work well with music, including circuit training, aerobic fitness routines, continuity exercises, astronaut exercises, squad leader exercises, and rope-jumping exercises. A set of music intervals on CD is available from Human Kinetics, P.O. Box 5076, Champaign, IL 61825-5076 (800-747-4457) or www.humankinetics.com. The CDs are titled *Physical Education Soundtracks, Vol. 1* and *Vol. 2*. A routine using music follows.

Sample Routine

Crab Kicks	25 seconds
Rope jumping	30 seconds
Windmills	25 seconds
Walk and do Arm Circles	30 seconds
Abdominal Crunchers	25 seconds
Jumping-Jack variations	30 seconds
Side Flex	25 seconds
Two-step or gallop	30 seconds
Triceps Push-Ups	25 seconds
Aerobic jumping	30 seconds
Push-Up challenges	25 seconds
Leg Extensions	30 seconds
Walking to cool down	30 seconds

Circuit Training

Circuit training incorporates several stations, each with a designated fitness task. Students move from station to station, generally in a prescribed order, completing the designated fitness task at each station. Exercises for the circuit focus on developing all parts of the body. Activities also involve the various components of physical fitness (i.e., strength, power, endurance, agility, and flexibility).

Instructional Procedures

1. Each station provides an exercise task to perform without assistance. Exercises that directly follow each other must make demands on different parts of the body. This sequence ensures that one task does not cause fatigue and affect students' ability to perform the next task.

2. Assign an equal number of students to each station to keep demands on equipment low and activity high. For example, if 30 children are performing a circuit of six stations, start 5 children at each spot.

3. Use music with intervals, whistle signals, or even verbal directions to signal students to the next station. The intervals provide time control and consistency to the circuit and allow you to help students without worrying about timing.

4. The number of stations can vary, but ideally it should be between six and nine (figures 14.33 and 14.34).

14

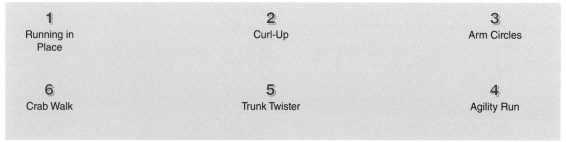

Supplies and equipment: mats for curl-ups (to hook toes)
Time needed: 4 minutes—based on 30-second activity limit, 10 seconds to move between stations

FIGURE 14.33   Sample six-station circuit-training course.

1		2		3
Rope jumping		Push-Up		Agility Run		Arm Circles

Supplies and equipment: jumping ropes, mats for knee push-ups (if used), hoops (if used)
Time needed: 6 minutes—based on 30-second activity limit, 10 seconds to move between stations

FIGURE 14.34   Sample nine-station circuit-training course.

Signs at the different stations can include the name of the activity and any necessary cautions or stress points for execution. When children move between lines as limits (as in the Agility Run), traffic cones or beanbags can be used to mark the designated boundaries.

Timing and Dosage

Setting a fixed time limit at each station is the easiest way to administer circuit training. Children do their personal best during the time allotted at each station. Give students a 10-second interval to move from one station to the next. Later, reduce the interval to 5 seconds. Students start at any station, as designated, but follow the established station order. A second method of timing is to sound only one signal for the change to the next station. With this plan, all students cease activity at their station, move to the next, and immediately begin the task at that station without waiting for another signal. Another effective method is to use alternating segments of silence and music to signal the duration of exercise. Music segments (begin at 30 seconds) indicate activity at each station; intervals of silence (10 seconds) announce that students should stop and move to the next station.

Making the exercises more strenuous can increase the activity demands of the circuit. For example, a station could specify knee or bench push-ups and later change to regular push-ups, a more demanding exercise. Another method of increasing intensity is to have each child run a lap around the circuit area between station changes. Dividing the class into halves can enhance cardiovascular endurance. One half exercises on the circuit, while the other half runs lightly around the area. On signal to change, the runners go to the circuit and the others run.

Another method of organizing a circuit is to list several activities at each station. The circuit then can be made more than once, and students do a different exercise each time they return to the same station. If students make the circuit only once, they can perform their favorite exercise from those listed. Exercises at each station should emphasize development of the same body part. A sample circuit-training routine follows.

Sample Routine

Ask students to do the best they can for 30 seconds at each station. This instruction implies that students will not perform similar workloads. Fitness is a personal challenge.

> Rope jumping
>
> Triceps Push-Ups
>
> Agility Run
>
> Body Circles
>
> Hula-hooping
>
> Reverse Curls
>
> Crab Walk
>
> Tortoise and Hare
>
> Bend and Twist

Conclude circuit training with two to four minutes of walking, jogging, rope jumping, or other self-paced aerobic activity.

Alternate Toe Touching

Begin on the back with arms extended overhead. Alternate by touching the right toes with the left hand and vice versa. Bring the foot and the arm up at the same time and return to the flat position each time.

Continuity Exercises

Children are scattered, each with a jump rope. They alternate between rope jumping and exercises. Make a music set that alternates music segments (25 seconds) with silent segments (30 seconds). While the music plays, students jump rope; when silence occurs, students do the flexibility and strength development exercises. At the signal to stop (or when the music stops), children drop their ropes and take the beginning position for the exercise selected. Many of the exercises use a two-count rhythm. When children are positioned for the exercise, the leader says, "Ready!" The class completes one repetition of the exercise and responds, "One, two!" This is the response for each repetition. A sample routine of continuity exercises follows.

Sample Routine

Rope jumping—forward	25 seconds
Double Crab Kick	30 seconds
Rope jumping—backward	25 seconds
Knee Touch Curl-Up	30 seconds
Jump and turn body	25 seconds
Push-Ups	30 seconds

Rocker Step	25 seconds
Bend and Twist	30 seconds
Swing-Step forward	25 seconds
Side Flex	30 seconds
Free jumping	25 seconds

Relax and stretch for a short time.

Hexagon Hustle

Using six cones, form a large hexagon. Students do the hustle by moving around the hexagon, changing their movement patterns every time they reach one of the six points in the hexagon. On signal, the hustle stops and students do selected exercises.

Instructional Procedures

1. To create a safer environment, have children move in the same direction around the hexagon.

2. Inform children of the new activity to be performed by placing laminated posters with colorful illustrations by the cones.

3. Instruct faster children to pass to the outside of slower children.

4. Change the direction of the hustle after every exercise segment.

Sample Routine

Use alternating segments of silence and music to signal the duration of exercise. Music segments (25 seconds) indicate moving around the hexagon, whereas intervals of silence (30 seconds) indicate flexibility and strength development activities.

Hustle	25 seconds
Push-Up from knees	30 seconds
Hustle	25 seconds
Bend and Twist (eight counts)	30 seconds
Hustle	25 seconds
Jumping Jacks (four counts)	30 seconds
Hustle	25 seconds
Curl-Ups (two counts)	30 seconds
Hustle	25 seconds
Crab Kick (two counts)	30 seconds
Hustle	25 seconds
Sit and stretch (eight counts)	30 seconds
Hustle	25 seconds
Power Jumper	30 seconds
Hustle	25 seconds
Squat Thrust (four counts)	30 seconds

Conclude the Hexagon Hustle with a slow jog or walk.

14

Astronaut Exercises

Astronaut exercises are performed in circular or scatter formation. Routines involve moving using various locomotor movements, alternated with stopping and performing exercises in place. Use alternating segments of music and silence to signal the duration of exercise. Music segments indicate aerobic activity, whereas intervals of silence indicate flexibility and strength development activities. Use scatter formation; ask students to change directions from time to time to keep spacing. Allow students to adjust the workload pace. Allow them to move at a pace that is consistent with their ability level.

The following movements and tasks can be used in the routine.

1. Various locomotor movements, such as hopping, jumping, running, sliding, skipping, taking giant steps, and walking high on the toes.

2. Movement on all fours—forward, backward, or sideways—with respect to the direction of walking. Repeat backward and forward using the Crab Walk.

3. Stunt movements, such as the Seal Walk, Gorilla Walk, and Rabbit Jump.

4. Upper-body movements and exercises that can be done while walking, such as Arm Circles, bending right and left, and body twists.

5. Various exercises performed in place when the music stops. Include a balance of arm–shoulder girdle and abdominal exercises.

6. Astronaut exercises can be adapted successfully to any developmental level. The movements selected will determine the intensity of the routine. More active children pass on the outside. Enjoyment comes from being challenged by a variety of movements.

Sample Routine

Walk and do Arm Circles	35 seconds
Crab Full-Leg Extension	30 seconds
Skip sideways	35 seconds
Body Twist	30 seconds
Slide and change lead leg	35 seconds
Jumping-Jack variations	30 seconds
Crab Walk	35 seconds
Curl-Ups With Twist	30 seconds
Hop to center and back	35 seconds
Push-Ups (four counts)	30 seconds
Gallop backward	35 seconds
Up Cat and Down Cat	30 seconds
Grapevine step (Carioca)	35 seconds
Trunk Twisters	30 seconds
Power Jumper	35 seconds

Cool down with stretching and walking or jogging for 1 to 2 minutes.

Challenge Courses

Challenge courses are popular as a tool for fitness development in elementary schools. Students move through the course with proper form rather than run against a time standard. The course is designed to exercise the entire body through a variety of activities. Equipment such as mats, parallel bars, horizontal ladders, high-jump standards, benches, and vaulting boxes can make effective challenge courses (figure 14.35). An array of courses can be designed, depending on course length and tasks included. Some schools have established permanent courses.

The following is the equipment list for the sample course shown in figure 14.35:

- Three benches (16 to 18 inches [40 to 45 cm] high)
- Four tumbling mats (4 by 8 feet [1.2 by 2.4 m])
- Four hoops
- One pair of high-jump standards with magic rope
- One climbing rope
- One jumping box
- Five chairs or cones

Aerobic Fitness Routines

Aerobics is a fitness activity that helps people of all ages develop cardiorespiratory fitness, strength, and flexibility. A leader is designated to perform a series of movements that the other students follow. There are few limits to the range of activities a leader can present. Manipulative equipment (including balls, jump ropes, hoops, and wands) can be integrated with movement activities.

Instructional Procedures

1. Base movement patterns on units of 4, 8, or 16 counts.

2. Vary movements so that stretching and flowing movements are alternated with the more strenuous aerobic activities.

3. Keep steps relatively simple. Focus on activity rather than developing competent rhythmic performers. Stress continuous movement (moving

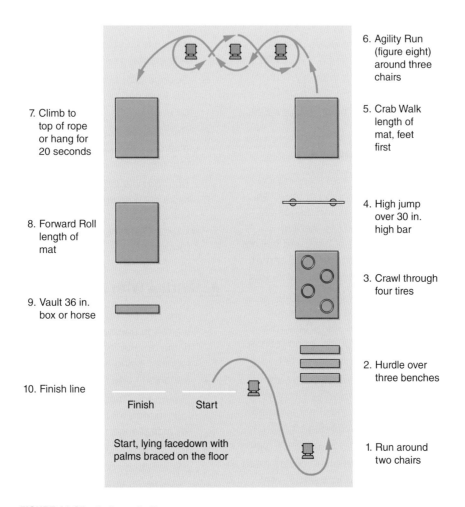

6. Agility Run (figure eight) around three chairs

7. Climb to top of rope or hang for 20 seconds

5. Crab Walk length of mat, feet first

4. High jump over 30 in. high bar

8. Forward Roll length of mat

3. Crawl through four tires

9. Vault 36 in. box or horse

2. Hurdle over three benches

10. Finish line

Finish   Start

1. Run around two chairs

Start, lying facedown with palms braced on the floor

FIGURE 14.35   Indoor challenge course.

14

with the flow) rather than perfection of the routines. Running and bouncing steps are easily followed and motivating.

4. Remember that routines are best when they are not rigid. Students should not have to worry about being out of step.

5. Establish cues to help students follow routines (e.g., "Bounce," "Step," "Reach," and "Jump").

Basic Steps

The following are some basic steps and movements for use in developing a variety of routines. Most steps are performed to four counts, although the count can vary.

Running and Walking Steps

1. Directional runs—forward, backward, diagonal, sideways, and turning.

2. Rhythmic runs with a specific movement on the fourth beat. Examples are knee lift, clap, jump, jump-turn, and hop.

3. Runs with variations. Run while lifting the knees, kicking up the heels, or slapping the thighs or heels; or run with legs extended, as in the goose step.

4. Runs with arms in various positions—on the hips, in the air above the head, and straight down.

Movements on the Floor

1. *Side leg raises.* Do these with a straight leg while lying on the side.

2. *Alternate leg raises.* While on the back, raise one leg to meet the opposite hand. Repeat, using the opposite leg or both legs.

3. *Rhythmic push-ups.* Do these in two- or four-count movements. A four-count would be as follows: halfway down (count 1), touch nose to floor (count 2), halfway up (count 3), and fully extend arms (count 4).

4. *Crab Kicks and Treadmills.* Do these to four counts.

Upright Rhythmic Movements

1. *Lunge variations.* Perform a lunge, stepping forward on the right foot while bending at the knee and extending the arms forward and diagonally upward (counts 1 and 2). Return to starting position by bringing the right foot back and pulling the arms into a jogging position (counts 3 and 4). Vary the lunge by changing its speed, depth, and direction.

2. *Side bends.* Begin with the feet apart. Reach overhead while bending to the side. This movement is usually done to four counts: bend (count 1), hold (counts 2 and 3), and return (count 4).

3. *Reaches.* Reach upward alternately with each arm. Reaches can be done sideways also and are usually two-count movements. Fast alternating one-count movements can be done too.

4. *Arm and shoulder circles.* Make Arm Circles with one or both arms. Vary the size of the circles and the speed. Do shoulder shrugs in a similar way.

Jumping-Jack Variations

1. *Jump with arm movements.* Alternately extend upward and then pull in toward the chest.

2. *Side Jumping Jacks.* Use regular arm action while the feet jump from side to side or forward and backward together.

3. *Feet variations.* Try different variations such as forward stride alternating, forward and side stride alternating, kicks or knee lifts added, feet crossed, or heel-toe movements (turning on every fourth or eighth count).

Bounce Steps

1. *Bounce and clap.* This step is like a slow-time jump-rope step. Clap on every other bounce.

2. *Bounce, turn, and clap.* Turn a quarter or halfway with each jump.

3. *Three bounces and clap.* Bounce three times and bounce and clap on count 4. Add some turns.

4. *Bounce and rock side to side.* Transfer the weight from side to side or forward and backward. Add clapping or arm swinging.

5. *Bounce with body twist.* Hold the arms at shoulder level and twist the lower body back and forth on each bounce.

6. *Bounce with floor patterns.* Bounce and make different floor patterns such as a box, diagonal, or triangle.

7. *Bounce with kick variations.* Perform different kicks such as knee lift and kick, double kicks, knee lift and knee slap, and kick and clap under knees. Combine the kicks with two- or four-count turns.

Activities With Manipulative Equipment

1. *Jump ropes.* Perform basic steps such as forward and backward steps with slow and fast time. Jump on one foot, cross the arms, and while jogging, swing the rope from side to side with the handles in one hand.

2. *Beanbags.* Toss and catch while performing various locomotor movements. Use different tosses for a challenge.

3. *Hoops.* Rhythmically swing the hoop around different body parts. Perform different locomotor movements around and over hoops.

4. *Balls.* Bounce, toss, and dribble, and add locomotor movements while performing tasks.

Sample Routine

These aerobic movements are suggestions only. When students begin to fatigue, stop the aerobic fitness movements and work on developing flexibility and strength to give students time to recover aerobically. Here are a few tips for creating routines.

1. Use music to stimulate effort. Any combination of movements can be used.

2. Keep the steps simple and easy to perform. Some students will become frustrated if they make slow progress in learning the steps.

3. Signs explaining the aerobic activities will help students remember performance cues.

4. Do not stress or expect perfection. Allow students to perform the activities as best they can.

5. Alternate bouncing and running movements with flexibility and strength development movements.

Rhythmic run with clap

Bounce turn and clap

Rhythmic four-count Curl-Ups (knees, toes, knees, back)

Rhythmic Crab Kicks (slow time)

Jumping-Jack combination

Double knee lifts

Lunges (right, left, forward) with single-Arm Circles (on the side lunges) and double-Arm Circles (on the forward lunge)

Rhythmic Trunk Twists

Directional run (forward, backward, side, turning)

Rock side to side with clap

Side leg raises (alternate legs)

Rhythmic four-count Push-Ups (if too difficult for students, substitute single-Arm Circles in the push-up position)

Partner Resistance and Aerobic Fitness Exercises

Partner resistance exercises combined with aerobic fitness routines make an excellent fitness activity. Partner resistance exercises develop strength but offer little aerobic benefit. Combining them with aerobic fitness routines offers a well-balanced program. The following exercises refer to partner resistance exercises. Allot enough time for each partner to resist as well as exercise.

Sample Routine

Students find a partner and lead each other in aerobic activities. Partners switch leader and follower roles after each partner resistance exercise. See Aerobic Fitness Routines for descriptions of activities. Use alternating segments of music and silence to signal duration of exercise. Music segments indicate aerobic activity (25 seconds), whereas intervals of silence signal partner resistance exercises (45 seconds).

Teach the exercises first. A sign with aerobic activities on one side and partner resistance exercises on the other helps students remember the activities. The signs can be held upright by cones and shared by two to four students. Take 6 to 10 seconds to complete a resistance exercise.

Bounce and clap	25 seconds
Arm Curl-Up	45 seconds
Jumping-Jack variations	25 seconds
Camelback	45 seconds

Lunge variations	25 seconds
Fist Pull-Apart	45 seconds
Directional runs	25 seconds
Scissors	45 seconds
Rhythmic Running	25 seconds
Butterfly	45 seconds
Bounce with Body Twist	25 seconds
Push-Up With Resistance	45 seconds

Walk, stretch, and relax for 1 to 2 minutes.

Sport-Related Fitness Activities

Many sport drills can be modified to place fitness demands on students. An advantage of sport-related fitness activities is that many children are highly motivated by sport activities. Thoughtful planning and creative thinking can result in drills that teach sport skills and confer fitness benefits. Here are some examples of fitness adaptations of sport skills:

Baseball and Softball

1. *Base running.* Set up several diamonds on a grass field. Space the class evenly around the base paths. On signal, students run to the next base, round the base, take a lead, and run to the next base. Faster runners may pass on the outside.

2. *Most lead-up games.* Children waiting on deck to bat and those in the field perform selected activities (skill or fitness related) while waiting for the batter to hit.

3. *Position responsibility.* Start children at various positions on the field. On signal, children are free to move quickly to any other position. After reaching that position, students must display the movement most frequently practiced at that position (for instance, shortstop fields a ball and throws to first base). Continue until all players have moved to each position.

Basketball

1. *Dribbling.* Each child has a basketball or playground ball. Assign one or more people to be "it." On command, everyone begins dribbling the ball and avoids being tagged by those who are "it." A child who is tagged becomes a new tagger. A variation would be for the taggers to begin the game without a ball. Their objective would be to steal a ball from classmates.

14

2. *Dribbling, passing, rebounding, shooting, and defense.* Using the concept of a circuit, assign selected basketball skills to be performed at each station. Be sure that each station has ample equipment to keep all students active. Movement from one station to another should be vigorous and may include a stop for exercise.

3. *Game play.* Divide the class into four teams. Two teams take the court and play a game of basketball. The other teams line up along respective sidelines and practice a series of exercises. After completing the exercise sequence, playing teams change positions with exercising teams.

Football

1. *Ball carrying.* Divide the class into four to six squads. The first person in line carries the ball while zigzagging through preplaced boundary cones. The rest of the squad does a specific exercise. After completing the zigzag course, the first person hands off the ball to the next person in line. This handoff signals a change in exercise for the rest of the squad.

2. *Punting.* One child punts the ball to a partner. After catching the ball, the object is to see which child can get to the receiver's original starting position first (because the punt will more than likely move the receiver). Repeat, with the receiver becoming the punter.

3. *Forward passing.* Divide the children into groups of four or fewer. Children practice running pass patterns. Rotate the passing responsibility after every six throws.

Volleyball

1. *Rotating.* Place students in the various court positions. Teach them the rotational sequence. As they reach a new court position, have them do several repetitions of a specific exercise. On command, they rotate to the next position. Select activities that exercise components of fitness to enhance volleyball skill development.

2. *Serving.* Divide the class evenly among available volleyball courts. Starting with an equal number of children and several balls on each side of the net, have them practice the serve. After each successful serve, the children run (around the net standard) to the other side of the net, retrieve a ball, and serve.

3. *Bumping and setting.* Using the concept of the circuit, establish several stations for practicing

the bump and set. Movement from station to station should be vigorous and may contain a special stop for exercise.

Soccer

1. *Dribbling.* With a partner, one child dribbles the ball around the playground as the partner follows close behind. On signal, the children reverse roles.

2. *Passing and trapping.* Devise routines for the players to move continuously (e.g., jogging, running in place, doing selected exercises while waiting to trap and pass the soccer ball) while working with partners or small groups.

3. *Game play.* Divide the class into teams of three or four players each. Organize the playground area to provide enough soccer fields for all teams to play. Make the fields as large as possible.

Sample Routine

Instructional activities	Teaching hints
Station 1: Soccer Lines Drill—Working with a beach ball, dribble the ball back and forth between two lines as quickly as possible. Use only dribbling skills; long kicks are not allowed.	Place even numbers of students at each station so that they can partner up for the sport activities.
Station 2: Push-Up challenges	Use intervals of music and silence to signal moves to the next station. Begin this routine with 60 seconds at the sport-related activities and 30 seconds at the strength and flexibility stations.
Station 3: Basketball Chest Pass—With a partner, practice the chest and bounce pass. If medicine balls are available, use them for strength development.	Ask students to store the equipment when the activity ends.
Station 4: Flexibility Activities	
Station 5: Volleyball Passing—Using a beach ball, practice passing and setting with a partner or partners. Keep the ball in the air as long as possible using two-handed passes and sets.	

Station 6: Abdominal challenges

Station 7: Hockey Circle Passing—One partner is stationary while the other circles around and passes to the partner. Change roles after five passes.

Station 8: Trunk challenges

Walking and Jogging

Jogging and walking, fitness activities for all ages, can lead to regular activity habits and a lifelong exercise program. Jogging is defined as easy, relaxed running at a pace that can be maintained for long distances without undue fatigue or strain. It is the first level of locomotion above walking. Jogging and walking are unique; they require no special equipment, can be done almost anywhere and anytime, are individual activities, and take relatively little time. For most people, this type of regular activity is an exercise in personal discipline that can enhance self-image and confidence.

Instructional Procedures

1. Let students find a friend to jog or walk with, usually a friend of similar ability level. A way to judge correct pace is to talk with a friend without undue stress. If students are too winded to talk, they are probably moving too fast. A friend helps ensure that the experience is positive and within the student's aerobic capacity.

2. Allow children to jog and walk in any direction to minimize comparisons of distance covered. Doing laps on a track is one of the surest ways to discourage less able students. They always finish last and are open to chiding by the rest of the class.

3. Have children jog and walk for a specific time rather than a specific distance. Why should all students have to run the same distance? Doing this goes against the philosophy of accommodating individual differences and varying aerobic capacities. Running or walking for a set amount of time allows less able children to move without fear of ridicule.

4. Do not be concerned about foot action, because children select a gait most comfortable to them. Arm movement should be easy and natural, with elbows bent. The head and upper body are held up and back. The eyes look ahead. The general body position in walking and jogging is erect but relaxed. Jogging on the toes should be avoided.

5. Do not turn jogging and walking into competitive, timed activities. Let students determine their own pace. Racing belongs in the track program. Another reason to avoid speed is that racing negates learning to pace during a run. For developing endurance and gaining health benefits, have children move for a longer time at a slower speed instead of running at top speed for a shorter distance.

Racetrack Fitness

Arrange five or six fitness activities in the center (the pit) of a large circle outlined with marking spots (the racetrack). If desired, mark the pit stop area by placing tumbling mats in the center of the racetrack. Students work with a partner and alternate running (or doing other locomotor movements) around the racetrack and going to the pit to perform a strength or flexibility exercise. Have students do a different exercise each time to vary the workout. Signal role changes by alternating 30 seconds of music with 10 seconds of silence. When the music stops, the partner who was running the track goes to the pit to exercise and vice versa.

Sample Routine

Instructional activities	Teaching hints
Here are some exercises that can be used in the pit:	Place exercise descriptions on signs in the pit area so that students can easily see the sequence of activities and know how to perform the exercises.
1. Arm Circles	
2. Bend and Twist	
3. Abdominal challenges	Place mats in the pit area to mark where students are to perform their exercises.
4. Knee-to-chest curl	
5. Push-Up challenges	To encourage students to do a variety of racetrack activities, post descriptions of different locomotor movements (e.g., jogging, sliding, skipping, and grapevine movements) at a corner of the track. Offer rope jumping as an alternative to running around the track.
6. Trunk Twist	

14

Fitness Orienteering

Students work together as members of a team. Set up 8 to 10 stations randomly around the area. Give each squad a laminated map card of exercise stations. Each map shows the stations in different order, so only one squad is at a landmark. Team members exercise together (at each child's own pace) and, on signal, hunt for the next exercise station listed on their map card. After completing a station activity, one squad member picks up a letter from the checkpoint, and the team moves to the next station. The goal is to complete the fitness orienteering stations, pick up a letter at each station, and return to the original starting point to unscramble the secret word. Intervals of music (30 seconds) and silence (15 seconds) signal when to exercise and when to change to a new station.

Here are some examples of checkpoint stations on the exercise map card:

1. Run to the northwest corner of the gym and pick up your letter now. When the music starts, continue running to a different corner until the music stops.

2. Move to the individual mats and do push-up challenges until the music stops.

3. Run to the benches and do step-ups until the music stops. The step count is "up, up, down, down."

4. Move to the red marking spots and do two different stretches until the music stops.

5. Run and find the jump ropes. When the music starts, pick up the ropes and do some jump rope tricks you learned earlier.

6. Skip to the tumbling mats. When the music starts, do abdominal challenges.

7. As a group, jog to the three green marking spots and pick up your letter. Jog and try to touch at least five walls, two different red lines, and three different black lines. Stay together with your group.

8. Jog to the jumping-jacks sign and do jumping jacks with at least four different variations in arm or foot patterns.

All-Around Jackpot Fitness

Around the teaching area set up three different jackpots (boxes) filled with fitness exercises and activities. One jackpot has various strength development activities written on small index cards. A second jackpot holds flexibility activities. The third jackpot contains aerobic activities. Students can work individually or with a partner. They begin at any jackpot and randomly pick out an activity to perform. If with a partner, they take turns selecting the card from the box. The only rules are that they must rotate to a different jackpot each time and they cannot select an activity they did earlier. If they draw an activity they have already performed, they return it to the jackpot and select another. A music interval of 30 seconds signals the duration of fitness activity, followed by a 10- to 15-second interval for selecting a new activity from a different jackpot. Instruct students to do as many repetitions as possible while the music is playing.

Here are some activities for the jackpot:

Aerobic Jackpot

1. Do the Carioca around the basketball court.
2. Perform a mirror drill with your partner for 30 seconds.
3. Jump rope using both slow and fast time.
4. Do Tortoise and Hare or Running in Place.
5. March with high steps around the area.

Strength Jackpot

1. Perform abdominal challenges.
2. Perform push-up challenges.
3. Do the Treadmill exercise.
4. Do as many Power Jumpers as possible.
5. Perform as many Crab Kicks as possible.

Flexibility Jackpot

1. Perform the Bend and Twist exercise.
2. Stretch using the Sitting Stretch.
3. Stretch using the Lower-Leg Stretch.
4. Do the Standing Hip Bend.
5. Improve your flexibility performing the Body Twist.

Partner Interval Fitness

Students pair up with a partner and perform these activities. The activities are designed so that one partner performs aerobic activity while the other is stretching or doing strength development activities. Use timed intervals of 30 seconds of music and 10 seconds of silence to signal changing positions (or activity). Have students perform all the activities.

1. *High Fives.* One partner runs around the area and gives as many high fives as possible to others who are running. The other partner remains stationary and performs push-up challenges. On signal, they switch roles. Various locomotor movements can be used as well as different high-five styles.

2. *Over and Around.* One partner makes a bridge on the floor while the other moves over and around the bridges of other students. To ensure that one child is moving (working) while the other is resting, they continue until a signal is given to change positions. Have students try different types of bridges and movements to vary the activity.

3. *Jump Rope and Exercise.* Each partner has a jump rope. One partner jumps the rope, while the other partner folds the rope and does strength or stretching activities. On signal, partners switch roles. An example of a stretching activity is to fold the rope in half and hold it overhead while stretching from side to side and to the toes.

4. *Stick and Stretch.* One partner tries to stick like glue to his or her partner, who tries to move as far away as possible. All movements are controlled. On signal, the other partner leads a stretching or strength development (resting) activity. On the next signal, the partners switch roles.

5. *Partner Swing and Exercise.* During the first music interval, partners swing each other under control. During the next music interval, one partner leads the other in a stretching or strength development activity. The partners swing again, and then the other partner leads a stretching or strength development activity.

Interval Training

All fitness routines in this chapter are based on interval-training principles. Interval training is effective for elementary school children because they fatigue and recover quickly. Interval training involves alternating work and recovery intervals. Intervals of work (large-muscle movement dominated by locomotor movements) and recovery (dominated by nonlocomotor activity or walking) are alternated at regular timed intervals. Teachers can use all the activities just described

in Partner Interval Fitness as well as the following motivating activity.

Rubber Band

Students move throughout the area. On signal, they time a move to the center of the area. After reaching the center simultaneously, they jump upward and let out a loud, "Yea!" or similar yell and resume running throughout the area. The key to the activity is to synchronize the move to the center. After several runs, students take a rest and stretch or walk.

After all work intervals, students participate in recovery intervals characterized by strength development or stretching activities. Using a series of timed intervals of music and silence is an effective approach for motivating students.

Partner Fitness Challenges

Partner challenges are fitness activities that can be used with intermediate-grade students to develop aerobic endurance, strength, and flexibility. Another advantage of partner challenges is that they can be done indoors as a rainy-day activity. Try to pair students with someone of similar ability and size. Telling students to pair up with a friend usually means they will select a partner who is caring and understanding. Emphasize continuous movement and activity. The following partner activities are challenging and enjoyable.

Circle Five

Partner 1 stands stationary in the center of the circle with one palm up. Partner 2 runs in a circle around 1 and gives a high five when passing the upturned palm. Students should see how many touches they can make in 15 seconds. They reverse roles on signal.

Knee Tag

Partners stand facing each other. On signal, they try to tag their partner's knees. Students score 1 point each time they make a tag. Have them play for a designated amount of time.

Mini Merry-Go-Round

Partners face each other with their feet nearly touching and their hands in a double-wrist grip. Partners slowly lean backward while keeping the feet in place until the arms are straight. Then they spin around as quickly as possible. Partners need to be of similar size.

14

Around and Under

One partner stands with the feet spread shoulder-width apart and hands held overhead. The other partner goes between the standing partner's legs, stands up, and slaps the partner's hands. They continue the pattern for a designated time.

Ball Wrestle

Both partners grasp an 8-inch (20 cm) playground ball and try to wrestle it away from each other.

Sitting Wrestle

Partners sit on the floor facing each other and grasp hands. The legs are bent and feet are flat on the floor with toes touching. The goal is to pull the partner's bottom off the floor.

Upset the Alligator

One partner lies facedown on the floor. On signal, the other partner tries to turn the "alligator" over. The alligator tries to avoid being turned over.

Seat Balance Wrestle

Partners sit on the floor facing each other with their knees raised and feet off the floor. If desired, they place their hands under their thighs to help support their legs. They start with the toes touching. Each student tries to tip the other backward using the toes.

Head Wrestle

Partners hold each other's left wrists with their right hands. On signal, they try to touch their partners' heads with their left hands. They then switch the handhold and try to touch with the opposite hand.

Pull Apart

One partner stands with the feet spread, arms bent at the elbows in front of the chest, and the fingertips touching. Partner 2 holds the other's wrists and tries to pull the fingertips apart. Jerking is not allowed; the pull must be smooth and controlled.

Pin Dance

Partners hold hands, facing each other, with a bowling pin (spot or cone) between them. On signal, each student tries to make the other touch the pin.

Finger Fencing

Partners face each other with their feet one in front of the other in a straight line. The toes of each partner's front foot should touch. Partners lock index fingers and try to make the other move either foot from the beginning position.

LEARNING AIDS

HOW AND WHY

1. Why are America's youth perceived as being unfit and inactive?
2. Why must physical education teachers understand various concepts related to physical fitness?
3. Should fitness-testing awards be used?
4. Why do so many students fail fitness tests? Defend your answer.
5. How can teachers make fitness fun?
6. Should physical education teachers be physically fit? Explain.

CONTENT REVIEW

1. Differentiate between health-related fitness and skill-related fitness, and identify the components of each.
2. Indicate whether American children are fit. Explain your answer.
3. Identify the purpose of physical fitness testing and the steps to implementing a fitness test battery. Include descriptions of several fitness tests and the fitness component for each measure.

4. Describe methods for fostering positive attitudes toward physical fitness.

5. Discuss guidelines for promoting fitness for children.

6. Cite several harmful exercises.

7. Create a developmentally appropriate fitness routine. Be sure to identify the developmental level that will use the routine.

8. Describe or demonstrate numerous activities and exercises designed to improve the fitness of children.

WEBSITES

Physical Activity and Fitness Assessment

www.fitnessgram.net
www.presidentschallenge.org/index.shtml

Physical Activity, Fitness, and Children

www.americanheart.org
www.cdc.gov\\HealthyYouth\\publications\\index.htm
www.nlm.nih.gov\\medlineplus\\exerciseforchildren.html

Physical Activity Reports

www.cdc.gov\\nccdphp\\dnpa\\physical\\recommendations\\index.htm
https://health.gov/our-work/healthy-people/
www.actionforhealthykids.org

Teaching Fitness Concepts

www.eatsmartmovemorenc.com

SUGGESTED READINGS

American College of Sports Medicine. (2009). *ACSM's guidelines for exercise testing and prescription* (8th ed.). Philadelphia, PA: Lippincott, Williams, & Wilkins.

Conkle, J., & SHAPE America. (2020). *Physical best: Physical education for lifelong fitness and health.* (4th ed.). Champaign, IL: Human Kinetics.

Corbin, Charles B., & Le Masurier Guy C. (2014). *Fitness for life—updated* (6th ed.). Champaign, IL: Human Kinetics.

National Association for Sport and Physical Education. (2004). *Physical activity for children: A statement of guidelines* (2nd ed.). Reston, VA: American Alliance for Health Physical Education, Recreation, and Dance.

Pangrazi, Robert P. (2016). *Dynamic physical education curriculum guide: Lesson plans for implementation* (18th ed.). San Francisco, CA: Benjamin Cummings.

President's Council on Physical Fitness and Sports. (2011). *The President's Challenge handbook*. Washington, DC: Author.

REFERENCES

Bouchard, Claude. (2012). Genomic predictors of trainability. *Experimental Physiology, 97*(3), 347–352.

Cooper Institute. (2017). *FitnessGram test administration manual: The journey to MyHealthyZone* (5th ed.). Champaign, IL: Human Kinetics.

Corbin, Charles B. (2012). C.H. McCloy Lecture: Fifty years of advancements in fitness and activity research. *Research Quarterly for Exercise and Sport, 83*(1), 1–11.

Corbin, Charles B., Welk, Greg, Corbin, William, & Welk, Karen. (2011). *Concepts of physical fitness: Active lifestyles for wellness* (16th ed.). Boston, MA: McGraw-Hill.

Corbin, Charles B., & Pangrazi. Robert P. (1992). Are American children and youth fit? *Research Quarterly for Exercise and Sport, 63*(2), 96–106.

Hales, Craig M., Carroll, Margaret D., Fryar, Cheryl D., & Ogden Cynthia L. (2017). Prevalence of obesity among adults and youth: United States, 2015–2016. *NCHS data brief, no 288.* Hyattsville, MD: National Center for Health Statistics.

Horvat, Michael, Kelly, Luke E., Block, Martin E., & Croce, Ron. (2019). *Developmental and adapted physical activity assessment* (2nd ed.). Champaign, IL: Human Kinetics.

14

Howley, Edward T., & Franks, B.D. (eds.). (2007). *Fitness professional's handbook* (5th ed.). Champaign, IL: Human Kinetics.

Macfarlane, Pamela A. (1993). Out with the sit-up, in with the curl-up. *Journal of Physical Education, Recreation, and Dance, 64*(6), 62–66.

Morgan, C.F., Beighle, A., & Pangrazi, R.P. & Pangrazi, D. (2004). Using self-assessment for fitness evaluation. *Teaching Elementary Physical Education, 15*(1), 19-22.

Morrow, James R. Jr., Tucker, Jacob S., Jackson, Allen W., Martin, Scott B., Greenleaf, Christy A., & Petrie, Trent A. (2013). Meeting physical activity guidelines and health-related fitness in youth. *American Journal of Preventive Medicine, 44*(5), 439–444.

Ogden, Cynthia L., Carroll, Margaret D., Kit, Brian K., & Flegal, Katherine M. (2012). Prevalence of obesity and trends in body mass index among U.S. children and adolescents, 1999–2010. *Journal of the American Medical Association, 307*(5), 483–490.

Rowland, Thomas W. (2005). *Children's exercise physiology*. Champaign, IL: Human Kinetics.

Timmons, James A., Knudsen, Steen, Rankinen, Tuomo, Koch, Lauren G., Sarzynski, Mark, Jensen, Thomas, et al. (2010). Using molecular classification to predict gains in maximal aerobic capacity following endurance exercise training in humans. *Journal of Applied Physiology, 108*, 1487–1496.

Winnick, Joseph P., & Short, Francis X. (2014). *The Brockport Physical Fitness Test manual* (2nd ed.). Champaign, IL: Human Kinetics.

Movement Concepts and Themes

This chapter is designed to help teachers and students understand movement concepts—namely, the classification and vocabulary of movement. Concepts and teaching strategies related to body awareness, space awareness, qualities of movement, and relationships are presented. Emphasis is placed on the process of moving rather than the product of correctly performing a skill. Students' creativity is rewarded, and their ingenuity is reinforced. Movement themes are designed to integrate the concepts into actual activities on the floor.

Learning Objectives

- ▶ Explain how movement themes are used to develop an understanding of movement concepts.
- ▶ Define the four major categories of human movement concepts.
- ▶ Explain the purpose of movement themes.
- ▶ Define the qualities of movement.
- ▶ Teach a variety of movement themes.
- ▶ Design a unique movement theme using the four-step approach.
- ▶ Specify individual cooperative partner activities and group activities to develop educational movement.

Physical education emphasizes skill development and learning the joy of physical activity in the elementary school years. Learning fundamental skills in the early years is important because they are the building blocks for more sophisticated skills. In addition, these skills can foster enjoyment in physical activity. This chapter explains the vocabulary and classification of human movement and offers teachers a framework for designing lessons that help students understand the relationship between their bodies and physical activity. In learning the movement concepts, teachers will need to consider three major components:

1. Knowing the classification scheme for movement.

2. Understanding how to design effective movement themes for instruction.

3. Using movement themes to bring the concepts of movement to life. This step integrates concepts and activities aimed at developing a physically literate youngster.

Chapters 15 through 18 cover the development of fundamental motor skills. These chapters form the foundation for developing a physically literate youngster by exploring movement concepts and themes, locomotor and nonlocomotor skills, manipulative skills, and body management skills. Even though all the skills and concepts are learned simultaneously, they are listed in separate chapters for the sake of organization and reference. Figure 15.1 shows the movement concepts and skills addressed in each chapter.

Movement Concepts and Themes

Chapter 15

Space, awareness, direction, level, pathways, planes

Locomotor and Nonlocomotor Skills

Chapter 16

Locomotor skills: Walking, hopping, jumping, sliding, running, leaping, skipping, galloping

Nonlocomotor skills: Bending, turning, balancing, pushing, twisting, rocking, stretching, pulling

The Foundational Skills of a Physically Educated Person

Body Management Skills

Chapter 18

Strength, balance, agility, flexibility, coordination

Manipulative Skills

Chapter 17

Striking, throwing, kicking, catching, dribbling, volleying, running, rolling, trapping

FIGURE 15.1 The components of movement concepts and fundamental motor skills.

With Developmental Level I children (ages four to nine), the emphasis is on developing an understanding of movement concepts and learning the vocabulary of movement. Skill technique and correct performance of skills receive less emphasis. Lessons are designed to help students understand and physically experience the classification of movement concepts, including body awareness, space awareness, qualities of movement, and relationships. That is, activities allow students to experience self-space, slow movements, fast movements, movements at a low level, and so forth. Instructional objectives are designed to show children how movements are classified (e.g., speeds) and how movement themes can turn concepts into concrete movements. Activities emphasize the process of moving rather than the product of correctly performing a skill.

Movement themes form the foundation of the movement experiences necessary for developing more specific fundamental skills. Through this process, children develop increased awareness and understanding of the body as a vehicle for movement, and they acquire a personal vocabulary of movement skills.

Classification of Human Movement Concepts

This text classifies movement themes according to body awareness, space awareness, qualities of movement, and relationship. These movement concepts offer structure and direction for planning new movement experiences. As youngsters experience movement, they learn the vocabulary of movement so that they are able to discuss and understand the unlimited possibilities for creative and productive movement.

Body Awareness

Body awareness defines what the body can perform, what shapes it can make, how it can balance, and how it can transfer weight to different body parts. Using these categories to develop challenges adds variety to movement.

1. *Shapes the body makes.* Many shapes can be formed with the body, such as long or short, wide or narrow, straight or twisted, stretched or curled, symmetrical or asymmetrical.

2. *Balance or weight bearing.* Different parts of the body support the weight or receive the weight. Different numbers of body parts can be involved in the movements and used as body supports.

3. *Transfer of body weight.* Body weight can be moved from one body part to another, such as in walking, leaping, rolling, and so on.

4. *Flight.* Unlike the transfer of body weight, flight is explosive movement that involves lifting the body weight from the floor or apparatus for an extended period. The amount of time off the floor distinguishes flight from transfer of weight. Examples include running, jumping onto a climbing rope, and hanging.

Space Awareness

Space awareness defines where the body can move. The spatial qualities of movement have to do with moving in different directions and at different levels. Youngsters learn to use space effectively when moving. Space can be modified and used in movement experiences in the following ways:

1. *General or personal space. Personal space* is the limited area that individual children use that is reserved for that individual only. *General space* is the total space that is used by all youngsters in an activity.

2. *Direction.* The desired route of movement, whether forward, backward, sideways, upward, or downward.

3. *Level.* The relationship of the body to the floor or apparatus, whether low, high, or in between.

4. *Pathways.* The path a movement takes through space. Examples are straight, zigzag, circular, and curved.

5. *Planes.* Somewhat specific pathways defined as circular, vertical, and horizontal, usually restricted in elementary school to performing simple activities in a specified plane.

Qualities of Movement

The qualities of movement define *how* the body moves. Rather than dealing with specific movements, the focus is on how movements are performed—for example, with speed or with great force or lightly. These qualities can be applied to many skills and activities.

1. *Time or speed.* Children learn to move at varying speeds and to control speed throughout a variety of movements. They should learn the relationship between body shape and speed and be able to use body parts to generate speed. The time factor may be varied by using different speeds—moving to a constant rhythm, accelerating, and decelerating.

15

2. *Force.* The effort or tension generated in movement. Force can be used effectively to aid in executing skills. Learning how to generate, absorb, and direct force is an important outcome. For example, catching requires absorbing the force of the object by bending the knees and elbows. Force qualities may be explored by using words such as *light*, *heavy*, *strong*, *weak*, *rough*, and *gentle*.

3. *Flow.* How movements are purposefully sequenced to create continuity of movement. Most often this quality is discussed in terms of interrupted (bound) or sustained (free) flow. *Interrupted flow* stops at the end of a movement or part of a movement. *Sustained flow* involves smoothly linking different movements or parts of a movement as in a basketball layup or a dance.

Relationship

Relationship defines with whom or to what the body relates. A *relationship* is defined as the position of the performer to a piece of apparatus or to other performers. Examples of relationships are near–far, above–below, over–under, in front–behind, on–off, and together–apart. In activities with other people, students can explore relationships such as leading–following, mirroring–matching, and unison–opposites. Additionally, relationships can define the body parts of a single performer, such as arms together–apart or symmetrical–asymmetrical.

Teaching Movement Skills and Concepts

Four steps are suggested for creating lessons that teach movement skills and concepts incorporating the problem-solving style. These steps include many specific ideas for developing movement tasks that promote a diversity of responses.

Step 1: Set and Define the Movement Task

Define a movement task for students so that they know what to solve. The task should include one or more of the following:

1. *What to do.* An action word directs the activity. Are children to move a certain way, go over and under, explore alternatives, or experiment with some nonlocomotor movement? Direct them to run, jump, or use a fundamental skill.

2. *Where to move.* What space is to be used—personal or general? What directional factors are to be employed—path or level?

3. *How to move.* What are the force factors (light–heavy)? What elements of time are involved (even–uneven, acceleration–deceleration, sudden–sustained)? What are the relationships (over–under–across, in front of–behind)? What body parts are involved for support? For locomotion?

4. *With whom or what to move.* With whom are children to work—by themselves, with a partner, or as a member of a group? Is a choice involved? With what equipment or on what apparatus are they to perform?

When initiating movement patterns, use the following partial sentences to frame the task. Unlimited movement tasks can be developed for students to solve.

Develop a Task to Solve

1. Show me how a(n) _____ moves. (Show me how an alligator moves.)

2. Have you seen a(n) _____? (Have you seen a kangaroo jump?)

3. What ways can you _____? (What ways can you hop over the jump rope?)

4. How would you _____? How can you _____? (How would you dribble a ball, changing hands frequently?)

5. See how many different ways you can _____. (See how many different ways you can catch a ball.)

6. What can you do with a(n) _____? What kinds of things can you _____? (What can you do with a hoop?)

7. Can you pretend to be a(n) _____? (Can you pretend to be an automobile with a flat tire?)

8. Discover different ways you can _____. (Discover different ways you can volley a ball against a wall.)

9. Can you _____? (Can you keep one foot up while you bounce the ball?)

10. Who can _____ a(n) _____ so that _____? (Who can bounce a ball so that it keeps time with the tom-tom?)

11. What does a(n) _____? (What does a leaf do in the wind?)

12. Show _____ different ways to _____. (Show four different ways to move safely across the floor.)

TEACHING TIP

Enthusiasm is essential when teaching youngsters movement concepts. Smiles, voice inflections, noises, and so on will serve you well. Consider the following instructions: "Can you walk like a bear?" versus "Oh, I have a great idea. First grade, can you walk like this animal I saw in the mountains last summer? Make sure you make their noise . . . . Wow! Listen to these bears!" Little bits of creativity and imagination will bring these experiences alive for children.

Step 2: Experiment and Explore

After defining the movement task, encourage youngsters to accomplish it through experimentation and exploration. Variety can also be achieved by setting limitations and by asking youngsters to develop the task in a different way. Present tasks in the form of questions or statements that elicit and encourage variety, depth, and extent of movement. Using contrasting terms is another way to increase the depth and variety of movement. Some examples follow.

Phrases that Encourage Exploration and Variety

1. Try it again another way. Try to _____. (Try to jump higher.)

2. See how far (many times, high, close, low) _____. (See how far you can reach with your arms.)

3. Find a way to _____ or find a new way to _____. (Find a new way to jump over the bench.)

4. Apply _____ to _____. (Apply a heavy movement to your run.)

5. How else can you _____? (How else can you roll your hoop?)

6. Make up a sequence _____. (Make up a sequence of previous movements, changing smoothly from one balance to the next.)

7. Now try to combine a(n) _____ with _____. (Now try to combine a locomotor movement with your catching.)

8. Alternate _____ and _____. (Alternate walking and hopping.)

9. Repeat the last movement and add _____. (Repeat the last movement and add a body twist as you move.)

10. See if you can _____. (See if you can do the movement with a partner.)

11. Trace (draw) a(n) _____ with _____. (Trace [draw] a circle with your hopping partner.)

12. Find another part of the body to _____. Find other ways to _____. (Find another part of the body to take the weight.)

13. Combine the _____ with _____. (Combine the hopping with a body movement.)

14. In how many different positions can you _____? (In how many different positions can you carry your arms while walking the balance beam?)

15. How do you think the _____ would change if _____? (How do you think the balance exercise we are doing would change if our eyes were closed?)

16. On signal, _____. (On signal, speed up your movements.)

Contrasting Terms to Stimulate Variety

Another way to increase the variety of movement responses is to use terms that stress contrasts. Instead of challenging children to move quickly, ask them to contrast a quick movement with a slow movement. The following list includes many common sets of contrasting terms for use in describing ways to move.

Above–below, beneath, under	On–off
Across–around, under	On top of–under, underneath
Around clockwise–around counterclockwise	Over–under, through
Before–after	Reach down–reach up
Between–alongside of	Right–left
Big–little, small	Round–straight
Close–far	Separate–together
Crooked–straight	Short–long, tall
	Sideways–forward, backward
Curved–flat, straight	Smooth–rough
Diagonal–straight	Standing upright–inverted

15

Fast–slow
Forward–back, backward
Front–back, behind
Graceful–awkward
Heavy–light
High–low

In–out
In front of–behind,
  in back of
Inside–outside

Into–out of
Large–small
Near–far

Sudden–sustained
Swift–slow
Tight–loose
Tiny–big, large
Top–bottom
To the right of–to the
  left of
Up–down
Upper–lower

Upside down–right
  side up
Upward–downward
Wide–narrow, thin
Zigzag–straight

Some of the terms may be grouped more logically in sets of three contrasts (such as forward–sideways–backward, up–down–in between, or over–under–through). Word meanings can also be emphasized according to rank or degree (as in near–nearer–nearest, or low–lower–lowest).

Step 3: Observe and Discuss Various Solutions

In this step, allow youngsters to observe some of the patterns created by others. Achievement demonstrations stimulate effort because children enjoy showing what they have put together. Focus discussions on how to put together different movements into flow and continuity. This time also can be an opportunity to point out that movement tasks can be solved in many ways.

Step 4: Refine and Expand Solutions to the Movement Task

The final step involves integrating various ideas students have developed and expanding their ideas into new solutions. Students can work together to develop cooperative partner and small-group skills. Make problems realistic, and allow opportunities for discussion and decision making between partners. Here are some activities that can be cooperatively developed:

1. One child is an obstacle, and the partner devises ways of moving around the positions that the "obstacle" takes (figure 15.2). To increase the challenge, have one partner hold a piece of equipment, such as a wand or hoop, to expand movements.

2. One partner partially supports the other's weight, or the two partners work together to form different kinds of figures or shapes.

3. One child does a movement, and the partner copies or provides a contrasting movement.

4. One child moves, and the partner attempts to shadow (do the same movements). They do it slowly with uninterrupted flow predominating.

5. One partner does a movement. The other partner repeats the movement and adds another. The first child repeats both movements and adds a third, and so on. Some limit on the number of movements can be set.

6. Children form letters or figures with their bodies on the floor or in erect positions.

7. Children practice copying activities. One child sets a movement pattern, and the rest copy the actions.

FIGURE 15.2 Going around a partner.

Movement Skills and Concepts Lesson Plans

The Dynamic PE ASAP website contains lesson plans for teaching movement skills and concepts. Each lesson plan contains four or five parts, thus presenting a variety of experiences in movement concepts and skills. This variety of activities offers children a broad spectrum of challenges, ensures a balance of experiences, and maintains student interest.

1. *Movement themes.* Two or more themes are developed to focus on teaching the concepts of movements. Locomotor and nonlocomotor movements are used as the medium for developing a movement vocabulary. Movement themes focus on a movement quality around which

children build patterns and sequences. Exploration is emphasized so that children develop body awareness and an understanding of movement concepts.

2. *Fundamental skills.* This section presents a wide variety of fundamental skills. Locomotor skills covered include walking, running, galloping, skipping, sliding, leaping, hopping, and jumping. Nonlocomotor skills covered are bending, rocking, swinging, turning, twisting, stretching, pushing, and pulling. Emphasis is on developing proper technique and using the skill in novel situations.

3. *Manipulative skills.* Manipulative skills are presented in each lesson using a variety of equipment. Skills practiced include throwing, kicking, striking, catching, bowling, and rolling.

Teaching Movement Themes

Children apply the concept of movement themes to create various movement patterns and sequences. Some themes involve only a single principle or factor, and others involve two or more. Themes in this chapter focus on exploring different concepts of movement. In practice, however, isolating a particular factor is difficult. For example, in exploring balance, movement possibilities are expanded through the application of body shape, level, and time factors. The following themes are classified into four major groups or concepts of human movement: body awareness, space awareness, qualities of movement, and relationship.

Body Awareness Themes

Body Shape

"Let's try making shapes and see whether we can name them. Make any shape you wish and hold it. What is the name of your shape, John? [Wide.] Try to make different kinds of wide shapes. Show me other shapes you can make. What is the name of your shape, Susie? [Crooked.] Show me different kinds of shapes that are crooked. Make yourself as crooked as possible."

"Make yourself wide and then narrow. Now tall and then small. How about tall and wide, small and narrow, tall and narrow, and small and wide? Show me some other combinations."

"Select three different kinds of shapes, and move smoothly from one to another. This time I will clap my hands as a signal to change to a different shape."

"Select four different letters of the alphabet. On the floor, one after the other, make your body shape like each of these letters. Try it with numbers. Make up a movement sequence that spells a word of three letters. Show us a problem in addition or subtraction."

"Use your jump rope and make a shape on the floor. Make a shape with your body alongside the rope."

"Pretend to be as narrow as an arrow or telephone pole. Pretend to be as wide as a house, store, or hippopotamus."

"Squeeze into a tiny shape; now grow slowly into the biggest shape you can imagine. Travel to a different spot on the floor, keeping the big shape. Quickly change to the tiny shape again."

"Move around the room in groups of three. On signal, form a shape with one person standing, one kneeling, and one sitting."

"Pretend you are at a farm. Make a barn with your body."

"Jump upward, making a shape in the air. Land, holding that shape. Begin with a shape, jump upward with a half turn, and land in another shape."

"What body shapes can you make while standing on one foot?"

"Show me what body shapes you can make with your tummy touching the floor."

"Look to see where your personal space is within the general space. When I say, 'Go,' run in general space. On the next signal, return to your personal space and sit down."

Figure 15.3 is an example.

FIGURE 15.3 Forming different shapes.

©Robert Pangrazi or Aaron Beighle

Balancing: Supporting Body Weight

"Show me different ways you can balance on different surfaces of your body. Can you balance on three different parts of your body? On two? On one? Put together sequences of three or four balance positions by using different body parts or different numbers of body parts."

"Can you balance on a flat body surface? What is the smallest part of the body you can safely balance on?

Support the body on two parts that are not the same, like one hand and one foot or an elbow and a foot. On three parts that are not alike. Support the body on different combinations of body flats and body points."

"Use two parts of the body far away from each other to balance. Shift smoothly to another two parts."

"Pretend you are in a circus. Who can balance on one foot with their arms stretched overhead? Out to the side?"

"Stand with feet together and eyes closed. Keep your balance while using different arm positions. Balance on one foot for 10 counts."

"From a standing position, raise one leg, straighten the leg in front of you, and swing the leg to the side and back without losing your balance."

"Move from a narrow, unstable base to a wide, stable base."

"Balance on parts of the body to form a tripod." (Explain the term.)

"Show different balance positions with part of your weight supported by the head."

"In a crab position balance on the right hand and right foot, the left hand and left foot, the right hand and left foot, the left hand and right foot."

"Stand on your toes and balance, using different arm positions."

"Place a beanbag on the floor. How many different ways can you balance over it? Try with a hoop. How many different ways can you balance inside the hoop? Two hands inside and one foot outside the hoop?"

"When I call out a body part or parts, you balance for five seconds on that part or part combination." (Use knees, hands, heels, flats, points, and a variety of combinations.)

"Keep your feet together and sway in different directions without losing your balance. Can you balance on one foot with your eyes closed? Can you bend forward while balancing on one foot? Can you lift both sets of toes from the floor and balance on your heels? Now sit on the floor. Can you lift your feet and balance on your seat without hand support? Can you balance on your tummy without your feet or hands touching the floor?"

"In a standing position, lift one leg out sideways and balance on the other foot."

"Make a sequence by balancing on a narrow surface, changing to a wide surface, and changing back again to a different narrow surface."

Figure 15.4 is an example.

Bridges

"Pretend a little stream is running by you. Show me a bridge over the water with your hands on one side and your feet on the other. What other kinds of bridges can you make? Suppose that the stream is a big river. Can you make a bridge using only three body parts? Only two?"

"Show me a wide bridge. A narrow one. A short bridge. A long one. How about a high bridge? A low one? Can you make a bridge that opens when a boat goes through? Get a partner to be the boat while you be the bridge. If you are the boat, choose three ways of traveling under a bridge. Each time the boat goes under the bridge, change the kind of bridge."

"As I touch you, go under a bridge and make another bridge."

"Show how you would make London Bridge fall down."

"With a partner, alternate going under a high bridge and going over a low bridge."

"Can you move one end of the bridge, keeping the other end still?"

"Make a bridge with one side of your body facing upward. Change to the other side."

"Show me a twisted bridge. A curved bridge."

"Be an inchworm and start with a long, low bridge. Walk the feet to the hands. Walk the hands forward while keeping the feet in one place."

"Show me a bridge at a high level. At a low level. In between."

"Make up a sequence of bridge positions, going smoothly from one to the next."

Figure 15.5 is an example.

FIGURE 15.4 Balancing on different body parts.

FIGURE 15.5 Making bridges.

Flight

"Show me three different ways you can go through space. Try again, using different levels. Lead with different parts of your body."

"See how high you can go as you move through space. What helps you get height?"

"Practice various combinations for take-off and landing. See if you can work out five different possibilities for taking off and landing, using one or both feet." (Possibilities are same to same [hop]; one foot to the opposite [leap]; one-foot takeoff, two-foot landing; two-foot takeoff, two-foot landing [jump]; two-foot takeoff, one-foot landing.)

"Run and jump or leap through the air with your legs bent. With your legs straight. With one leg bent and the other straight. Try it with your legs spread wide. With your whole body wide. With your whole body long and thin through the air."

"Project yourself upward, beginning with the feet together and landing with the feet apart. Run, takeoff, and land in a forward stride position. Repeat, landing with the other foot forward."

"With a partner, find ways to jump over your partner as he or she changes shape."

"Using your arms to help you, run and project yourself as high as possible. Practice landing with bent knees."

Moving With the Weight Supported on the Hands and Feet

"Pick a spot away from your personal space and travel to and from that spot on your hands and feet. Try moving with your hands close to your feet. Far away from your feet. Show me bilateral, unilateral, and cross-lateral movements. Build up a sequence."

"Move from your personal space for eight counts. Do a jump turn (180 degrees) and return to your space using a different movement for eight counts."

"Lie on your tummy. Move using only your hands."

"Experiment with different hand–foot positions. Begin with a narrow shape and with hands and feet as close together as possible. Extend your hands from head to toe until they are as far apart as possible. Extend the hands and feet as wide as possible and move. Now try with the hands wide and the feet together. Reverse."

"Practice traveling so that both hands and feet are off the ground at the same time. Go forward, backward, sideways."

"With your body straight and supported on the hands and feet [push-up position], turn the body over smoothly and face the ceiling. The body should remain straight throughout. Turn to the right and left. Return to your original position."

"What kinds of animal movements can you imitate? Move with springing types of jumps. What shapes can you make while you move?"

Figure 15.6 is an example.

FIGURE 15.6 Taking the weight on hands and feet.

©Robert Pangrazi or Aaron Beighle

TEACHING TIP

An effective approach to teaching movement concepts is to integrate several concepts into one lesson. For example, early in the lesson focus students on experiencing activities in various planes, activities involving balance, and weight transfer with no equipment. Then after retrieving a hoop, you can lead them through activities that move the hoop through various planes. Then students balance inside the hoop, outside the hoop, or with body parts inside and outside the hoop. Finally, you can teach activities involving weight transfer of weight inside, outside, and around the hoop. The key with teaching movement concepts is to be creative.

Receiving and Transferring Weight

"Support the weight on two different body parts and then transfer the weight smoothly to another pair of parts. Add another pair of unlike parts if you can."

"Take a deep breath, let out the air, relax, and drop to the floor, transferring the weight from a standing position to a position on the floor. Can you reverse the process?"

"While walking, show how the weight transfers from the heel to the ball of the foot with a push-off from the toes. In a standing position, transfer the weight from the toes, to the outside of the foot, to the heel, and back to the toes. Reverse the order."

"Using three different parts, transfer weight from one to another in a sequence."

"Travel with a jump or a leap and then lower yourself gently to your back after landing. Repeat, only lower yourself smoothly to your seat."

"From a standing position, bend forward slowly and transfer the weight partially to both hands. Lift one foot into the air. Return it to the ground gently. Repeat with the other foot. Lift a hand and a foot at the same time and return them smoothly."

"Lower yourself in a controlled way to take the weight on your tummy. Can you turn over and take the weight on your seat with your hands and feet touching the floor?"

"Move from lying on your back to a standing position without using your arms."

"Select a shape. See if you can lower yourself to the ground and return to your original position, keeping the shape."

"Try some jump turns, quarter and half. What is needed to keep your balance as you land?"

"Project yourself into the air and practice receiving your weight in different ways. Try landing without any noise. What do you have to do? See how high you can jump and still land lightly."

"See how many different ways you can transfer weight smoothly from one part of your body to another. Work up a sequence of three or four movements and go smoothly from one to another, returning to your original position."

Stretching and Curling

"In your own space, stretch out and curl. What different ways can you find to do this? Let's go slowly from a stretch to a curl and back to a stretch in a smooth, controlled movement. Curl your upper body and stretch your lower body. Now curl your lower body and stretch your upper body. Work out a smooth sequence between the two combinations."

"Show different curled and stretched positions on body points and on body flats. Go from a curled position on a flat surface to a stretched position supported on body points. Explore how many different ways you can support your body in a curled position."

"Stand in your personal space and stretch your arms at different levels. Lift one leg and stretch it to the front, side, and back. Repeat with the other leg."

"Stretch sideways with an arm and a leg until it pulls you over."

"In a sitting position, put your legs out in front. Bend your toes forward as far as possible. Bend them backward so that your heels are ahead of your toes. Turn both toes as far as you can inward. Turn them outward."

"Lie on the floor on your back. Stretch one leg at a time in different ways in space."

"Stand. Stretch to reach as far as you can with your hand. Try reaching as far as possible with your toe."

"Show how you can travel on different body parts, sometimes stretched, sometimes curled."

"Jump and stretch as high as possible. Now curl and roll on the floor." (Repeat several times.)

Taking the Weight on the Hands

Establishing proper hand positioning for taking the weight on the hands (and later for the headstand) is important.

"Put your hands about shoulder-width apart, with fingers spread and pointed forward. With knees bent, alternate lifting the feet silently into the air, one foot at a time. Pick a point ahead of your hands (2 feet [60 cm] or so) and watch it with your eyes. Keep from ducking your head between your arms."

"Place both hands on the floor. Kick up like a mule. Can you kick twice before coming down?"

"Take the weight on your hands. Make one foot go past the other while in the air."

"Do as many movements as you can while keeping your hands on the floor and kicking both feet in the air."

"See whether you can take the weight on your hands for a brief time. How do you get your body into the air? What different movements can you make with your feet while your weight is on your hands? See how long you can keep your feet off the ground. Repeat, and try to get your hips above your hands. Now add a twist at the waist to return your feet to the floor at a different spot."

"Try again, but shift the weight to one hand and land both feet at a different spot."

"Begin in a standing position and try to keep your feet over your head for as long as possible. Begin with the arms and hands stretched overhead, and repeat. Kick up one leg and then the other."

Figure 15.7 is an example.

FIGURE 15.7 Taking the weight on the hands.

©Robert Pangrazi or Aaron Beighle

Space Awareness Themes (Where the Body Moves)

Moving in General Space

Besides developing movement competence, these movement experiences should enhance the ability to (1) share space with other children, (2) move through space without bumping anyone, and (3) develop consideration for the safety of others.

"Run lightly in the area, changing direction without bumping or touching anyone until I call, 'Stop.' Raise your hand if you were able to do this without bumping into anyone."

"Let's try running zigzag fashion in the area without touching anyone. This time, when I blow the whistle, change your direction and change the type of movement."

"Run lightly in general space and pretend you are dodging someone. Can you run toward another runner and change direction to dodge?"

"Get a beanbag and drop it to mark your personal space. See how lightly, while under control, you can run throughout the area. When I give the signal, run to your spot, pick up your beanbag, put it on your head, and sit down [or give some other challenge]. Try this skipping."

"We are going to practice orienteering. [Explain the term.] Point to a spot on the wall, and see if you can run directly to it in a straight line. You may have to stop and wait for others to pass so as not to bump into anyone, but you cannot change direction. Stay in a straight line. When you get to your spot, pick another spot and repeat."

"What happens when general space is decreased? You had no problem running without touching anyone in the large space. Now let's make the area smaller with these cones. Run lightly inside the cones and try not to bump anyone. Now it's going to get more difficult. I'm going to make the space even smaller, but first let's try walking in the new area. Now, run lightly." (Decrease the area as feasible.)

"Get a beanbag and mark your personal space. Run around the beanbag until you hear a bang, and then explode in a straight direction until I call, 'Stop,' which means return to your personal space."

"From your beanbag, take five [or more] jumps [hops, skips, gallops, slides] and stop. Turn to face home and return with the same number of movements. Take the longest steps you can away from home and then return home with tiny steps."

"Show me how well you can move with these combinations in general space: run–jump–roll, skip–spin–collapse. Now you make up a series of any three movements and practice them."

"Today our magic number is five. Can you move in any direction with five repetitions of a movement? Change direction and pick another movement to do five times. Continue."

"Blow yourself up like a soap bubble. Can you huff and puff? Think of yourself as a big bubble that is floating around. When I touch you, the bubble breaks, and you collapse to the ground. This time, blow up your bubble and float around. When you are ready, say, 'Pop,' so that the bubble bursts."

"This time, see whether you can run rapidly toward another child, stop, and bow to each other. Instead of bowing, fist bump and say, '"How are you?"'"

"From your personal space, pick a spot on a wall. See whether you can run to the spot, touch it, and return without bumping anyone. This time, it's more difficult. Pick spots on two different walls, touch these in turn, and return."

Exploring Personal Space

Personal space is space that can be reached from a fixed base. Youngsters can take this personal space with them when they are moving in general space. A graphic way to illustrate personal space is to have youngsters take an individual jump rope and double it. From a kneeling position, they swing it in a full arc along the floor. It should not touch another child or rope.

"Show us how big your space is. Keeping one foot in place, outline how much space you can occupy with the other foot. Sit cross-legged and outline your space. Support your weight on different parts of your body and outline your space."

"Make yourself as wide [narrow, small, large, low, high] as possible. Try these from different positions—kneeling, balancing on the seat, and others. Show us what kinds of body positions you can make while you stand on one foot. While you lie on your tummy. On your seat. Try the same with one foot and one hand touching the floor."

"Stand tall in your space. To the beat of a drum, move beat by beat to a squat position. Reverse."

"Move from a lying position to a standing position without using your arms or hands. Return to lying."

"Can you stay in one place and move your whole body but not your feet?"

"Sway back and forth with your feet together and then with your feet apart. Which is better?"

"Sitting in your personal space, bend your toes forward; now backward. Bend your feet so that your heels move ahead of your toes."

"While lying on your back, move your arms and legs from one position slowly and then move them back quickly to where you started. Explore other positions."

"Keeping one part of your body in place, make as big a circle as you can with the rest of your body."

15

"Explore different positions while you keep one leg [foot] higher than the rest of your body. Work out a smooth sequence of three different positions."

"Pump yourself up like a balloon, getting bigger and bigger. Hold until I say, 'Bang!'"

"In your personal space, show me how a top spins. Keep your feet together in place. With your arms wide to the sides, twist and make your feet turn."

Circles and the Body

"Can you form full circles with your hands and arms at different joints—wrist, elbow, and shoulder? Now what circle can you make with your legs and feet? Try this lying on your back. Use other body joints to make circles."

"Travel in general space by skipping [running, hopping, sliding]. Stop on signal and make moving, horizontal [vertical, inclined] circles with an arm. Repeat, but on signal lie down immediately on your back and make the [specified] circle with one foot."

"Show how swimmers make circles with their arms when doing the backstroke. Alternate arms and also move them together. Reverse the arm direction to make the crawl stroke. Make vertical circles with one arm and both arms across the body."

"With one hand, make a circle on your tummy. At the same time, use your other hand to pat the top of your head. Reverse hands."

"Keep one foot fixed and make a circle with the other foot by turning completely around."

"Select a partner. Match the Arm Circles that your partner makes."

"Can you keep two different circles going at the same time? Make a circle turning one way and another circle turning the other way. Repeat, using the twisting actions of the body parts to make the circles."

Figure 15.8 is an example.

FIGURE 15.8 Forming circles.

©Robert Pangrazi or Aaron Beighle

Planes of Movement

"Show me a variety of movements in a horizontal plane. In a vertical plane. In a diagonal plane. Put together combinations so that you can transition from movements in one plane to another plane."

"Here's a challenge. When I call out a plane of movement, respond with a movement in the correct plane. Ready?" (Specify the plane of movement.)

"Using a jump rope doubled in one hand, make circles in the different planes. Try the same with a hoop."

"Crouch at a low level, spin upward toward the ceiling, and come back to the floor. Spin in the other direction."

Levels

"Choose one way of traveling at a high level and another at a low level. Again, move at a high level and stop at a low level. Move at a low level and stop at a high level. Choose one way of traveling at a medium level and add this somewhere in your sequence—beginning, middle, or end."

"Select three different kinds of traveling movements with the arms at a high, medium, and low level. Link these movements together in a smooth sequence."

"Travel around the room, raising your arms as high as possible. Travel on your tiptoes. Repeat with your arms as low as possible."

"Run at different levels. Run as high as you can. Run as low as possible. Run at a medium level."

"When I clap my hands, change direction and level."

"Move on all fours with your body at a high level, a medium level, and then as low as possible. Try these movements with your face turned to the ceiling."

"Use a jump rope or a line or board in the floor as your path to follow. Begin at the far end. Show me a slow, low-level movement down and back. What other ways can you go down and back slowly and at a low level? Change to a fast, high-level movement. On what other levels can you move?"

"Combine a low, fast movement down the path with a high, slow movement on the way back. Explore other combinations. Make different movements by leading with different parts of your body."

Moving in Different Ways

"Discover different ways you can make progress along the floor without using your hands and feet. See whether you can walk with your seat. Let your heels help you."

"What ways can you move sideways or backward? What rolling movements can you make? Look carefully before you move to make sure you have a clear space."

"Use large movements and travel through general space. Make your body into a straight line and move in straight lines, changing direction suddenly. With your body in a curved shape, move in a curved pathway."

"Each time you change direction, alternate a straight body and a straight path with a curved body shape and a curved path."

"Find ways of moving close to the floor with your legs stretched. Now move with your legs bent, keeping at a low level."

"As you travel forward, move up and down. As you travel backward, sway from side to side."

"Travel, keeping high in the air. Change direction and travel at a low level. Continue to alternate."

"Counting the four limbs [two arms, two legs], travel first on all four, then on three, next on an arm and a leg, and then on one leg. Now reverse the order."

"With your hands fixed on the floor, move your feet in different ways. Cover as much space as possible. With your feet fixed, move your hands around in different ways as far away from the body as you can. Move around general space the way that a skater does. The way that a person on a pogo stick does. Choose other ways. Change body direction as you move, but keep facing in the original direction."

Qualities of Movement Themes (How the Body Moves)

Time (Speed)

Speed involves the pace of action, which can be slow, fast, or any degree in between. Speed involves acceleration and deceleration; that is, the time factor can be constant, or it can speed up or slow down. Time can also be even or uneven.

"With your arms, do a selected movement slowly and then quickly. Move your feet slowly and then as rapidly as you can. Change your support base and repeat."

"In turn, stretch a part of your body slowly and then return it to place quickly, like a rubber band snapping. Stretch the entire body as wide as possible and snap it back to a narrow shape."

"Travel through the area without touching anyone. Speed up when there is an open area and slow down when it is crowded."

"Choose a way of traveling across the floor quickly and then do the same movement slowly. Do a fast movement in one direction and, on signal, change to a slow movement in another direction."

"Select a magic number between 10 and 20. Do that many slow movements and then do the same number of fast movements."

"With your partner a little bit away from you, begin moving quickly toward your partner and decelerate as you get close. Move away by beginning slowly and accelerate until you return to where you started. Repeat.

Select the kinds of movement you wish to use together."

"Staying in your own personal space, begin with some kind of movement and accelerate until you are moving as fast as you can. Reverse by beginning with a fast movement and then slowing down until you are barely moving. Put together a sequence of two movements by beginning with one and accelerating, and then changing to another movement and decelerating. Try doing two different body movements at the same time—one that accelerates and one that decelerates."

Contrasting Movements

Contrasting movements have wide and frequent applications in the development of other themes.

"Show me a fast movement. Now show me a slow one. Show me a smooth movement. Now show me a rough, jerky one."

"Find three ways to rise from the floor and three ways to sink to the floor. Choose one way to rise and one way to sink. Try to do this three times very smoothly."

"Make yourself as tall as possible. Now, get as short as you can while still on your feet."

"Move with a small and delicate skip. Change to a large skip."

"Show me a wide shape. Now, an opposite one. A crooked shape. Now, its opposite. Show me a high-level movement and its contrast. Can you do a balanced movement? What is its opposite?" (Use light–heavy and other contrasts as well.)

"Pick two contrasting movements. When I clap my hands, do one and then change to the other when I clap again. What movements did you do?"

Force

"Show me different kinds of sudden movements. Do a sudden movement and then repeat it slowly. Put together a series of sudden movements. Put together a series of sustained movements. Mix sudden and sustained movements."

"Pick a partner and do a quick, strong movement followed by a quick, light movement."

"Take five strong, slow jumps, changing your body for each jump."

"When the drum beat is loud, walk heavily. When the drum beat is soft, walk lightly."

"Reach in different directions with a forceful movement. Crouch down as low as you can and explode upward. Try again, exploding forward. Move as if you were pushing something very heavy. Pretend you are hitting a heavy punching bag."

"What kinds of movements can you do that are light movements? Can you make movements light and

15

sustained? Light and sudden? Heavy and sustained? Heavy and sudden? Which is easier? Why?"

"Try making thunder [big noise with hands and feet] and then lightning [same movements without any noise], timing each movement with five slow counts."

"Can you combine heavy movements in a sequence of sudden and sustained movements? Can you make one part of your body move lightly and another part heavily?"

Tension and Relaxation

"Make yourself as tense as possible. Now slowly relax. Take a deep breath and hold it tight. Let out the air and relax. How does that make you feel?"

"Hug yourself hard! Now harder. Follow this by relaxing your body. Shake your hands."

"Reach as high as possible with both hands, relax slowly, and drop to the floor. Tense one part of your body and relax another. Slowly shift the tension to the relaxed part and vice versa."

"Run forward, stop suddenly in a tensed position, and then relax. Run in a tensed manner, change direction, and then run in a relaxed manner."

"Walk forward with tight, jerky movements. Change direction and walk with loose, floppy movements. Pretend you are a boxer by using short, tense movements. Now move your arms like a floppy rag doll."

Relationship Themes (To Whom and to What the Body Relates)

Moving Over, Under, Around, and Through Things

This theme is flexible and can use any available equipment as obstacles to go over, under, around, and through. It can be used effectively in a rotating station system. Equipment can be already arranged, or the children can set it up themselves.

"Using the equipment, show me different ways you can go over, under, around, or through what you have set up. Lead with different parts of the body."

"In your group of three, use your jump ropes to make a triangle, a square, and a rectangle on the floor. Move in, out, and around the three figures."

"Toss your beanbag in the air. When I call out a body part, sit down quickly, and put the beanbag on that part."

Symmetrical and Asymmetrical Movements

Symmetrical movements are identical movements using similar body parts on opposite sides of the body.

Asymmetrical movements are different movements using similar body parts on opposite sides of the body. Symmetry increases stability because the two body halves are counterbalanced. Asymmetry, with the body weight distributed unequally, leads to quick starts and to easier sequential flow. Balancing on a balance beam with both arms to the side is a symmetrical movement. The arms are extended symmetrically to increase stability and balance. Running while alternately flexing and extending the legs is an asymmetrical movement.

"Show me different kinds of symmetrical movements. Now different kinds of asymmetrical movements. Put together sequences of symmetrical and asymmetrical movements."

"Taking the weight on your hands, show symmetrical and asymmetrical movements of your legs."

"Run and jump high in the air and place your limbs symmetrically in flight."

"Perform different movements like throwing, skipping, running, long jumping, and leaping and identify whether they are symmetrical or asymmetrical movements."

Relative Location of Body Parts

"We are going to try some special ways of body part touching. Raise your right hand as high as you can—now down. Raise your left hand as high as you can—now down. Touch your left [or right] shoulder [elbow, knee, hip, ankle] with the right [or left] hand." (Try many combinations.)

"Now, point to a door [window, ceiling, basket] with an elbow [thumb, toe, knee, nose]. Let's see if you can remember right and left. Point your left [or right] elbow to the window." (Try different combinations.)

"When I name a body part, let's see if you can make this the highest part of your body without moving from your place."

"Now, the next task is a little harder. Move in a straight line for a short distance and keep the body part named above all the other body parts. What body parts would be difficult to keep above all the others?" (Possibilities are the eyes, both ears, both hips.)

"Touch the highest part of your body with your right hand. Touch the lowest part of your body with your left hand."

"Let's see if you can locate some of the bones in your body. When I name a bone, hold that bone, move and touch a wall, and return to your spot." (These challenges depend on bones that the children can identify. The same procedure can be used to identify selected muscles.)

"Now move around the room, traveling any way you wish."

(The movement can also be limited.) "The signal to stop will be a word describing a body part. Can you stop and immediately put both hands on that part or parts?" (Or say, "On 'Stop,' hide the body part.") "You are to move around the room again. When I call out a body part, find a partner and place the body parts together."

"This time, when I call out a body part, you are to move around the room as you wish while holding with one hand a named body part. When I name another body part, change the type of movement and hold that part with the other hand as you move. Now I will call out two body parts. Have the parts touch each other."

Leading With Different Parts of the Body

"As you move between your beanbags [lines, markers], explore ways that different parts of your body can lead movements. Add different means of locomotion. Work at different levels."

"Have a partner make a bridge and you go under, leading with different parts of the body. Can you find five different ways to go under with different body parts lead-ing? Now try finding five ways to go over or around."

"What body parts are difficult to lead with?"

Figure 15.9 is an example.

FIGURE 15.9 Leading with a foot.

©Robert Pangrazi or Aaron Beighle

LEARNING AIDS

15

WEBSITES

Movement activities for young children, www.happalmer.com

SUGGESTED READINGS

Cleland-Donnelly, F., Mueller, S.S., & Gallahue, D. (2017). *Developmental physical education for all children* (5th ed.). Champaign, IL: Human Kinetics.

Cone, T.P., & Cone S. (2012). *Teaching children dance* (3rd ed.). Champaign, IL: Human Kinetics.

Graham, G., Hale, S.A., & Parker, M.A. (2019). *Children moving: A reflective approach to teaching physical education* (10th ed.). Boston, MA: McGraw-Hill.

Laban, R., & Lawrence, F.C. (1947). *Effort: A system analysis, time motion study.* London, United Kingdom: Union Brothers.

McGreevy-Nichols, S., Scheff, H., & Sprague, M. (2005). *Building dances: A guide to putting movements together* (2nd ed.). Champaign, IL: Human Kinetics.

Weikart, Phyllis S. (2007). *Teaching movement and dance* (6th ed.). Ypsilanti, MI: High Scope Press.

16 Locomotor and Nonlocomotor Skills

Fundamental skills in this chapter include two major categories: locomotor and nonlocomotor skills. These skills are the basis of nearly all physical activities that students will participate in throughout life. Locomotor skills define the many ways that the body can move through space. Nonlocomotor movements generally do not require moving through space; these skills are learned by repetition and refinement, and by offering many variations to keep students motivated.

Learning Objectives

▶ Explain why teaching fundamental movement is synonymous with providing instruction designed to learn a specific skill.

▶ Describe the differences between locomotor and nonlocomotor skills.

▶ Cite stress points, instructional cues, and suggested movement patterns to enhance the learning of locomotor and nonlocomotor skills.

▶ Specify activities designed to develop locomotor and nonlocomotor motor skills.

Fundamental Skills

Fundamental skills, sometimes called basic or functional skills, are the skills that children need to function effectively in the environment. Fundamental skills are basic human movements usually identified by a single verb, such as walking, twisting, running, jumping, or stretching. The pattern of development for learning physical skills develops from general (large motor) to specific (fine motor) movements. This chapter focuses on general motor skills involving the large-muscle groups. Fundamental skills are the tools that most adults use when participating in leisure activities. Without a learned set of fundamental skills and a positive feeling about being able to perform in activity settings, many people resign themselves to a lifetime of inactivity.

Learning fundamental skills requires practicing the basic locomotor and nonlocomotor skills through many repetitions. Repeating these skills over a wide range of activities helps assure that children can perform them in varying conditions. To help students learn the skills correctly and quickly, this chapter presents key stress points and instructional cues. Because all locomotor movements are rhythmic, each section also includes rhythmic activities. The skills are grouped for ease of teaching and comprehension by students. The skills are presented here individually, but they are most often performed in a seemingly infinite number of combinations, depending on the sport or activity.

Locomotor skills are used to move the body from one place to another or to project the body upward. They include walking, running, skipping, galloping, leaping, sliding, jumping, and hopping. They form the foundation of gross motor coordination and involve large-muscle movement.

Nonlocomotor skills are performed without appreciable movement from place to place. These skills are not as well defined as locomotor skills. They include bending and stretching, pushing and pulling, twisting and turning, rocking, swaying, and balancing, among others.

Locomotor Skills

The following locomotor skill descriptions include stress points to help teachers present correct techniques. Also included are instructional cues—short, concise phrases for reminding students how to perform activities correctly. Suggested learning activities fall into two categories: (1) basic activities, consisting of movement-oriented sequences that do not require rhythm, and (2) rhythmic activities, consisting of movements with rhythmic accompaniment.

Walking

When walking, each foot moves alternately, with one foot always touching the ground or floor. The stepping foot touches the ground before the other foot is lifted. Body weight is transferred from the heel to the ball of the foot and then to the toes for push-off. The toes point straight ahead, and the arms swing freely from the shoulders in opposition to the feet. The body is erect, and the eyes focus straight ahead and slightly below eye level. The legs swing smoothly from the hips, with knees bent enough to clear the feet from the ground. Marching is a precise type of walk accompanied by lifted knees and swinging arms.

Basic Activities

Stress Points

1. Toes are pointed reasonably straight ahead.
2. Arm movement is natural. The arms do not swing too far.
3. The head is up, and the eyes focus ahead.
4. Stride length is not excessive. Avoid unnecessary up-and-down motion.

Instructional Cues

1. Head up, eyes forward.
2. Point toes straight ahead.
3. Nice, easy, relaxed arm swing.
4. Walk quietly.
5. Hold tummy in, chest up.
6. Push off from the floor with the toes.

Suggested Movement Patterns

1. Walk in different directions, changing direction on signal.
2. While walking, lift each knee and slap with the hands on each step.
3. Walk on the heels, toes, and sides of feet.
4. Gradually lower your body while walking (going downstairs), and rise again slowly (going upstairs).
5. Walk with a smooth, gliding step.
6. Walk with a wide base of support on the tiptoes and rock from side to side.
7. Clap the hands alternately in front and behind. Clap the hands under the thighs while walking.

16

8. Walk slowly and gradually increase speed. Reverse the process.

9. Take long strides. Take tiny steps.

10. On signal, change levels (high, low, and so on).

11. Walk quickly and quietly. Walk heavily and slowly.

12. Change direction on signal but keep facing the same way.

13. Walk gaily, angrily, happily. Show other moods.

14. Hold the arms in different positions. Make an arm movement with each step.

15. Walk in different patterns—circle, square, triangle, figure eight.

16. Walk through heavy mud. On ice or a slick floor. Walk on a rainy day. Walk in heavy snow.

17. Walk like a soldier on parade, a giant, a robot.

18. Duck under trees or railings while walking.

19. Point your toes in different directions—in, forward, and out.

20. Walk with high knees. Stiff knees. One stiff knee. A sore ankle.

21. Walk to a spot, turn in place while stepping, and go in another direction.

22. Practice changing steps while walking.

23. Walk and change direction after taking the magic number of steps (selected by a student).

24. Tiptoe around the area and through puddles of water.

25. Walk as if you are on a balance beam. Walk across a tightrope.

26. Walk as if you are sneaking up on someone.

27. Walk with funny steps, as if you are a clown.

28. Take heel-and-toe steps forward. Without turning around, walk heel-and-toe backward.

Rhythmic Activities

When using rhythmic accompaniment, teach students to hear the phrasing in the selection. Have children use one kind of walk during a phrase and then use another kind of walk during the next phrase.

1. Walk forward one phrase (eight counts) and change direction. Continue to change at the end of each phrase.

2. Use high steps during one phrase and low steps during the next.

3. Walk forward for one phrase and sideways during the next. The side step can be a draw step, or a grapevine step. To do a grapevine, step to the left, lead with the left foot, stepping directly to the side. Cross the right foot behind the left and then cross the right foot in front of the left on the next step with that foot. The pattern is step left, cross right (behind), step left, cross right (in front), and so on.

4. Find a partner. Face each other and join hands. Pull your partner by walking backward as your partner resists a little (eight counts). Reverse roles. Now stand behind your partner and place your hands on your partner's shoulders. Push your partner by walking forward as your partner resists (eight counts). Reverse roles.

5. Walk slowly and then gradually increase the tempo. Now begin fast and decrease. (Use a drum for this activity.)

6. Walk in various directions while clapping your hands alternately in front and behind. Try clapping hands under a thigh at each step or clap hands above the head in time with the beat.

7. Walk forward four steps and turn completely around in four steps. Repeat, but turn the other way the next time.

8. While walking, lift each knee and slap with the hands on each step in time with the beat.

9. On any one phrase, take four fast steps (one count to each step) and two slow steps (two counts to each step).

10. Walk on the heels or toes or with a heavy tramp. Change every four or eight beats.

11. Walk with a smooth, gliding step or walk silently to the beat.

12. Walk to the music, accenting the first beat of each measure. Now sway your body to the first beat of the measure. (Use a waltz with a strong beat.)

Running

Running (figure 16.1), in contrast to walking, is moving fast so that both feet briefly leave the ground. Running varies from trotting (a slow run) to sprinting (a fast run for speed). The heels can take some weight in distance running and jogging. Running is done with the body leaning slightly forward. The knees are flexed and lifted, while the arms swing back and forth from the shoulders with a bend at the elbows. The track, field, and cross country running unit gives more pointers for sprinting (see chapter 29).

FIGURE 16.1 Running.

Basic Activities

Stress Points

1. The balls of the feet are used when sprinting.

2. The faster you want to run, the higher you must lift the knees. For fast running, bend the knees more.

3. For distance running, use less arm swing than when sprinting for speed. For greater comfort, less body lean is used in distance running. The weight is absorbed on the heels and transferred to the toes.

Instructional Cues

1. Run on the balls of the feet when sprinting.

2. Head up, eyes forward.

3. Bend your knees.

4. Relax your upper body and swing the arms forward and backward, not sideways.

5. Breathe naturally.

Suggested Movement Patterns

1. Run lightly throughout the area, changing direction as you wish. Avoid bumping anyone. Run zigzag throughout the area.

2. Run and stop on signal. Change direction on signal.

3. Run, turn around with running steps on signal, and continue in a new direction. Alternate turning direction.

4. Pick a spot away from you, run to it, and return without touching or bumping anyone.

5. Run low, gradually increasing the height. Reverse.

6. Run in patterns. Run between and around objects.

7. Run while slapping the knees.

8. Run with different steps—tiny, long, light, heavy, crisscross, wide.

9. Run with your arms in different positions—circling, overhead, stiff at your sides.

10. Run free, concentrating on good knee lift.

11. Run at different speeds.

12. Touch the ground at times with either hand while running.

13. Run backward, sideways.

14. Run with exaggerated arm movements. Run with a high bounce.

15. Run forward 10 steps and backward 5 steps. Repeat in another direction. (Other tasks can be imposed after the 10 steps.)

16. Run forward; then make a jump turn in the air to face in a new direction. Repeat. Be sure to use both right and left turns. Make a full reverse (180-degree) turn.

17. Run the Tortoise and Hare sequence and Ponies in the Stable.

18. Run with knees turned outward. Run high on your toes.

19. Show how quietly you can run. Pretend you are running through high weeds.

20. Run to a wall and back to place. Run and touch two walls.

21. Run lightly twice around your spot. Then explode (run quickly) to another spot.

Rhythmic Activities

Many of the walking patterns apply equally to running patterns. Here are some additional suggestions for running.

1. Walk during a phrase of music and then run for an equal length of time.

2. Run in different directions, changing direction on the sound of a heavy beat (or on a signal).

3. Lift the knees as high as possible while running, keeping time to the beat.

4. Do European Rhythmic Running to supplement the running patterns described earlier.

16

Hopping

Hopping involves propelling the body up and down on the same foot. The body lean, the other foot, and the arms help balance the movement. Students can practice hopping in place or try it as a locomotor movement.

Basic Activities

Stress Points

1. To increase height of the hop, swing arms rapidly upward.
2. Hop on the ball of the foot.
3. Small hops are used to start, and the height and distance of the hop increase gradually.

Instructional Cues

1. Hop with good forward motion.
2. Stay on your toes.
3. Use your arms for balance.
4. Reach for the sky when you hop.
5. Land lightly.

Suggested Movement Patterns

1. Hop on one foot and then on the other, using patterns such as 1rf–1lf, 2rf–2lf, 3rf–3lf; 2rf–1lf, 1rf–2lf, 3rf–2lf, 2rf–3lf; and so on (rf = right foot; lf = left foot). Have children practice each combination for 10 to 20 seconds.
2. Hop, increasing height. Reverse.
3. See how much space you can cover in two, three, or four hops.
4. Hop on one foot and do a heel-and-toe pattern with the other. Now change to the other foot. Try to follow a consistent pattern.
5. Make a hopping sequence by combining hopping in place with hopping ahead.
6. Hop forward, backward, sideways. Then hop in different patterns on the floor.
7. Hop while holding the free foot in different hand positions.
8. Hold the free foot forward or sideways while hopping. Explore other positions.
9. Hop with the body in different positions—try leaning forward, backward, sideways.
10. Hop lightly, so that no one can hear you. Then hop heavily.
11. While hopping, touch the floor with the hands—first one and then both.
12. Hop back and forth over a line, moving down the line as you hop.
13. Trace out numbers or letters by hopping.
14. Turn around while hopping in place.
15. Hop forward and then backward according to a magic number (selected by a student). Repeat in another direction. Now add sideward hopping instead of going backward.

Rhythmic Activities

Because students tire rapidly, combining rhythm with hopping patterns is harder than walking, running, or skipping to rhythm. The suggested patterns combine other locomotor movements with hopping.

1. Walk four steps, hop three times, and rest one count.
2. Walk four steps and then hop four times as you turn in place. Repeat in a new direction.
3. Hop eight times on one foot (eight counts) and then eight times on the other.
4. Hop forward and backward over a line to the rhythm, changing feet each phrase (eight counts).
5. Combine skipping, sliding, or galloping with hopping.
6. Practice the step-hop to music. (In two counts, the child steps and then hops on the same foot.)

Jumping

Jumping requires taking off with both feet and landing on both feet (figure 16.2). The arms move forward with an upswing, and body movement combined with force of the feet helps lift the weight. Jumping can be done in place or as a locomotor activity to cover ground.

Basic Activities

Stress Points

1. Knees and ankles are bent before takeoff to get more force from muscle extension.
2. Landing is on the balls of the feet, with knees bent to absorb the impact.
3. Arms swing forward and upward at takeoff to add momentum to the jump and to gain distance and height.

FIGURE 16.2 Jumping.

4. Legs must be bent after takeoff to prevent the feet from touching the ground too soon.

Instructional Cues

1. Swing your arms forward as fast as possible.
2. Bend your knees.
3. On your toes.
4. Land lightly with bent knees.
5. Jump up and try to touch the ceiling.

Suggested Movement Patterns

1. Jump up and down, trying for height. Try small and high jumps. Mix in patterns.
2. Choose a spot on the floor. Jump forward over the spot. Now jump backward and then sideways.
3. Jump with your body stiff and arms held at your sides. Jump like a pogo stick.
4. Practice jump turns in place—quarter, half, three-quarter, full.
5. Increase and decrease jumping speed. Increase and decrease jump height.
6. Land with feet apart and then together. Alternate with one foot forward and one backward.
7. Jump and land quietly. How is this done?
8. Jump, crossing and uncrossing the feet.
9. See how far you can go in two, three, and four consecutive jumps. Run lightly back to place.

10. Pretend you are a bouncing ball.
11. Clap hands or slap your thighs while in the air. Try different arm positions.
12. Begin a jump with your hands touching the floor.
13. Jump in various patterns on the floor.
14. Pretend you are a basketball center jumping at a jump ball. Jump as high as you can. Jump from a crouched position.
15. Combine a jump for distance with one for height.
16. Jump and click heels in the air. Try two clicks.
17. Jump like a kangaroo. A rabbit. A frog.
18. Combine opposite jumps: forward and backward. Big and little. Right and left. Light and heavy.
19. Try different ways of doing a jumping jack.
20. Jump and clap hands in front. Behind you. Overhead.
21. First swing your arms three times and then jump forward.
22. Jump. While in the air, touch your heels. Touch both knees. Touch both toes in front.
23. Half of the class is on the floor in selected positions. The other half jumps over those on the floor. Have the children switch positions.

Rhythmic Activities

Most of the activities suggested for hopping to rhythm are suitable for jumping. Other suggestions follow.

16

1. Begin jumping slowly to the drumbeat and then speed up. Then jump fast and slow down to the beat.

2. Toss a ball upward and jump in time to the bounce. (The ball must be a lively one.)

3. Do varieties of the jumping jack. First move your feet without moving your arms. Now lift arms to shoulder height; then lift arms straight overhead. Finally, add body turns and different foot patterns.

4. Take a forward stride position. As you jump, switch feet back and forth to the rhythm.

Sliding

Sliding is similar to a gallop, but it is done with the body moving sideways in a one-count movement; the leading foot steps to the side, and the other foot follows quickly. Slide on the balls of the feet while shifting weight from the leading to the trailing foot. Body bounce during the slide is minimal.

Basic Activities

Stress Points

1. Stress the sideways movement. Students may move forward or backward, which is actually galloping.

2. Slide in both directions, so that each leg can lead as well as trail.

3. The slide is smooth and graceful, stressing balance and stability.

Instructional Cues

1. Move sideways.

2. Do not bounce.

3. Slide your feet.

Suggested Movement Patterns

1. Go in one direction a specific number of slides, do a half turn in the air, and continue the slide by leading with the other leg in the same direction. (A four-plus-four combination is excellent.)

2. Begin with short slides and increase the length. Reverse.

3. Slide in a figure-eight pattern.

4. Change levels while sliding. Slide so that the hands touch the floor with each slide.

5. Slide quietly and smoothly.

6. Pretend to be a basketball defensive player and slide with good basketball position.

7. Do three slides and a pause. Change the leading foot and repeat.

8. In circle formation, facing in, the whole class does 10 slides one way and then pauses. They repeat, going in the other direction.

Rhythmic Activities

With proper accompaniment, many of the previous movement patterns can be set to rhythm. Use music phrases to signal a change of direction or issue another challenge.

Galloping

Galloping is similar to sliding, but the body faces forward. One foot leads and the other moves rapidly forward to it. The body has more upward motion than it does in sliding. Teach the gallop by having children hold hands and slide in a circle, responding to either verbal cues or a drumbeat. Have the class gradually face the direction that the circle is moving to take them naturally from a slide into a gallop.

Basic Activities

Stress Points

1. The movement is smooth and graceful.

2. Give each foot a chance to lead.

Instructional Cues

1. Keep one foot in front of the other.

2. Now lead with the other foot.

3. Make high gallops.

Suggested Movement Patterns

1. Do a series of eight gallops with the same foot leading; then change to the other foot. Change after four gallops. Change after two gallops. (Later in the rhythmic program, the gallop is used to teach the polka, so children need to learn to change the leading foot.)

2. Change the length of the gallops.

3. Gallop in a circle with a small group.

4. Pretend to hold reins and use a riding crop.

5. Gallop backward.

6. Gallop like a spirited pony. Like a heavy draft horse.

Rhythmic Activities

Because galloping is essentially rhythmic, many of the previously described patterns can be done to rhythm. Use music phrases to signal a change in the lead foot. Check previous sections on locomotor movements for other rhythmic movement suggestions.

Leaping

Leaping is an elongated step used to cover distance or move over low obstacles. It is usually combined with running, because doing a series of leaps alone is difficult (figure 16.3). Suggested movement patterns use combinations of running and leaping.

Basic Activities

Stress Points

1. Strive for height and graceful flight.
2. Landing is light and relaxed.

Instructional Cues

1. Push off and reach.
2. Up and over, landing lightly.
3. Use your arms to help you gain height.

Suggested Movement Patterns

1. Leap in different directions.
2. See how high you can leap.
3. Leap and land softly.
4. Vary your arm position when leaping. Clap hands as you leap.
5. Leap with the same arm and leg forward. Try the other way.
6. Try leaping in slow motion.
7. Leap and turn backward.
8. Leap over objects or across a specified space.
9. Practice by playing Leap the Brook.
10. Leap and move into a balanced position.

FIGURE 16.3 Leaping.

Rhythmic Activities

Because a leap is an explosive movement through space and children must gather themselves when preparing to leap, rhythm cannot easily be applied to this movement.

Skipping

Skipping is a series of step-hops done with alternate feet. To teach skipping, first have children do a step-hop on one foot and then a step-hop on the other. Skipping is done on the balls of the feet with arms swinging to shoulder height alternately with feet. Another way to teach skipping is to have children hold a large ball (9 inches [23 cm] or more) in front at waist height. Have them take a step with one foot and then raise the other knee to touch the ball. This movement stimulates the hop. They repeat with the other foot and opposite knee.

Basic Activities

Stress Points

1. Smoothness and rhythm, not speed and distance, are goals in skipping.
2. Weight is transferred from one foot to the other on the hop.
3. The arms swing alternately with the legs.

Instructional Cues

1. Step-hop.
2. Swing your arms.
3. Skip smoothly.
4. On your toes.

16

Suggested Movement Patterns

Many of the suggested movement patterns for walking and running can be applied to skipping, particularly those for changing direction, stopping, making floor patterns, and moving at different speeds.

1. Skip with exaggerated arm action and lifted knees.
2. Skip backward.
3. Clap as you skip.
4. Skip with a side-to-side motion.
5. Skip twice on one side (double skip).
6. Skip as slowly as possible. Skip as fast as possible.
7. Skip so lightly that your partner cannot hear the movement.
8. Skip to a chosen spot in as few skips as you can.

Rhythmic Activities

Most of the combinations suggested for walking and running are good for skipping movements, and many skipping, walking, and running combinations are possible. For example, "Pop Goes the Weasel" is great skipping music. On the "pop," specify a movement challenge.

Nonlocomotor Skills

Nonlocomotor skills include bending, twisting, turning (in place), moving toward and away from the center of the body, raising and lowering parts of the body, and other movements done in place. Flexibility, balance, and other movements leading to effective body control are important goals.

Bending

Bending is movement at a joint. Teach students how the body bends, why it needs to bend, and how to combine bends in various movements.

Basic Activities

Stress Points

1. Bending as far as possible to increase flexibility and range of movement is a key goal.
2. Explore the bending possibilities of many joints.
3. Timing can be introduced in slow and rapid bending.

Instructional Cues

1. Bend as far as possible.
2. Bend one part while holding others steady.

Suggested Movement Patterns

1. Bend your body down and up.
2. Bend forward and backward, left and right, north and south.
3. Bend as many ways as possible.
4. Bend as many body parts as you can below your waist. Above your waist. Bend with your whole body.
5. Sit down and see if you can bend differently from the ways you bent when standing.
6. Try to bend one body part quickly while bending another part slowly.
7. Lie down and bend six body parts. Can you bend more than six? Now bend fewer.
8. Make a familiar shape by bending two body parts. Add two more parts.
9. Think of a toy that bends; see if you can bend like that.
10. Find a partner and bend together. Have your partner make big bends while you make tiny bends.
11. Show how you would bend to look funny. To look happy or sad. Bend slowly or quickly.
12. Bend your largest part. Your smallest part.
13. Begin by bending one body part. While returning this part to its original position, bend another part.
14. Bend your fingers one at a time. Bend all of them at once.
15. Bend your knees while standing, sitting, and lying. What other joint has to bend in a standing position?

Rocking and Swaying

Rocking occurs when the center of gravity shifts fluidly from one body part to another. In rocking, the body is rounded where it touches the floor. Swaying is a slower movement and is somewhat more controlled than rocking.

Basic Activities

Stress Points

1. Rocking is done best on a rounded body surface. Arm movements and movements of other body parts can facilitate the motion.

2. Rocking is done smoothly and in a steady rhythm.

3. Rocking can begin with small movements and increase in extent, or vice versa.

4. Rocking and swaying are done to the full range of movement.

5. Swaying maintains a stable base.

Instructional Cues

1. Rock smoothly.

2. Rock in different directions. At varying speeds.

3. Rock higher (farther).

4. Sway until you almost lose your balance.

Suggested Movement Patterns

1. Rock in as many different ways as you can.

2. Show how you can rock slowly. Quickly. Smoothly.

3. Sit cross-legged with arms outstretched to the sides, palms facing the floor. Rock from side to side until the hands touch the floor.

4. Lie on your back and rock. Now point your arms and legs toward the ceiling as you rock.

5. Lie on your tummy with arms stretched overhead and rock. Hold your ankles and make giant rocks.

6. Try to rock while standing.

7. Rock and twist at the same time.

8. Lie on your back, lift your knees, and rock from side to side.

9. Show me two ways to have a partner rock you.

10. While standing, sway back and forth. Right and left. Try different foot positions. Sway slowly and rapidly. What effect does rapid swaying have?

11. Repeat swaying movements from a kneeling position.

12. Start with a little rocking motion and make it bigger and bigger.

13. Choose three (or more) ways of rocking and try to change smoothly between them.

14. Rock like a cradle. A rocking horse.

15. Sway like a tree in a heavy wind.

Swinging

Swinging involves moving body parts somewhat like a swinging rope or clock pendulum. Most swinging movements involve the arms and legs.

Basic Activities

Stress Points

1. Swinging is a smooth, rhythmic action.

2. The body parts involved in swinging are relaxed and loose.

3. The extent of the swing movement is the same on both sides of the swing.

4. Swinging movements are as full as possible.

Instructional Cues

1. Loosen up; swing easy.

2. Swing fully; make a complete movement.

3. Swing in rhythm.

Suggested Movement Patterns

1. Explore different ways to swing your arms and legs.

2. Make up swinging patterns with the arms. Combine them with a step pattern, forward and back.

3. Swing the arms back and forth, and go into full circles at times.

4. With a partner, work out different swinging movements (figure 16.4). Add circles.

5. Develop swinging sequences with swinging and full-circle movements (best done to waltz music with a slow or moderate tempo).

6. Swing like a clock pendulum. A cow's tail.

FIGURE 16.4 Partner swinging.

16

Turning

Turning is rotating around the long axis of the body. Turning and twisting are sometimes used interchangeably to designate the movements of body parts, but turning refers to moving the body as a whole. Most turns begin with a twist. In the movements suggested here, action involves moving the entire body. Movements of body parts are discussed in the section Twisting.

Basic Activities

Stress Points

1. Maintaining balance and body control is important.
2. Turning is tried in both right and left directions.
3. Standing turns can be made by jumping, hopping, or shuffling with the feet.
4. Most turns are made in multiples of quarter turns. Students should practice multiples.
5. Turns are practiced in body positions other than standing—seated, on the tummy or the back, and so on.

Instructional Cues

1. Keep your balance.
2. In jump turns, land loosely with the knees relaxed.
3. Be precise in your movement, whether it is a quarter, half, or full turn.

Suggested Movement Patterns

1. While standing, turn your body to the left and right, clockwise and counterclockwise.
2. Turn to face north, east, south, west. (Post directions on the wall.)
3. Stand on one foot and turn around slowly. Now turn around quickly. Now turn with a series of small hops. Try to keep good balance.
4. Show me how you can cross your legs with a turn and sit down. Can you get up again in one movement?
5. Every time you hear the signal, see if you can turn around once, moving slowly. Can you turn two, three, or four times slowly on signal?
6. Lie on your tummy on the floor, and turn your body slowly in an arc. Turn over so that you are on your back. Turn back to your tummy again.
7. Find a friend and see how many different ways you can turn each other. Take turns.
8. Play Follow the Leader with a partner. Take turns being the leader.
9. Begin with a short run, jump into the air, and turn to land facing in a new direction. Practice both right and left turns. Can you make a full reverse (180-degree) turn?
10. Lie on your back, turn, and rest on your side. Return. Repeat on the other side.
11. Lie on your back and turn over onto your tummy. Return. Turn over the opposite way.
12. Find a partner and see how many ways you can rotate each other.
13. Walk in general space and turn completely around on signal.
14. With your hands outstretched to the sides, pretend you are a helicopter.

Twisting

Twisting is rotating a selected body part around its own long axis (figure 16.5). Various joints can be used in twisting: spine, neck, shoulders, hips, ankles, and wrists.

FIGURE 16.5 Twisting movements.

Basic Activities

Stress Points

1. Twists extend as far as possible with good control.
2. The body parts the twist is based on are stabilized.
3. A twist in one direction is countered by a reverse twist.
4. Some joints are better for twisting than others. (Explain why.)

Instructional Cues

1. Twist as far as possible.
2. Twist the other way.
3. Hold the supporting parts firm.

Suggested Movement Patterns

1. Glue your feet to the floor. Can you twist your body to the left and right? Can you twist your body slowly? Quickly? Can you bend and twist at the same time? How far can you turn your hands back and forth?
2. Twist two or more parts of your body at once.
3. Twist one body part in one direction and another in the opposite direction.
4. Try twisting the lower half of your body without twisting the upper half.
5. What body parts can you twist while sitting on the floor?
6. Try to twist one body part around another part. Can you twist together even more parts?
7. Stand on one foot and twist your body. Can you bend and twist at the same time?
8. Show me some different shapes you can make by twisting your body.
9. Try to twist like a spring. Like a cord on a telephone.
10. Try to move and twist at the same time.
11. With the weight on your feet, twist as far as you can in one direction. Now take the weight on your hands and move your feet.
12. Twist like a pretzel. Like a licorice stick.
13. Twist as if you are hitting a home run with a baseball bat.
14. Twist as if you are hitting a golf ball.

Stretching

Stretching moves body parts away from the body center. Stretching sometimes involves moving a joint through the range of movement. Stretching is necessary for maintaining and increasing flexibility.

Basic Activities

Stress Points

1. Stretching is extended to the full range of movement.
2. Stretching exploration involves many body parts.
3. Stretching is done in many positions.
4. Stretching can be combined with opposite movements, such as curling.
5. Stretching is done slowly and smoothly.
6. Hold full stretching position for 10 seconds.

Instructional Cues

1. Stretch as far as possible. Make it hurt a little.
2. Find other ways to stretch the body part (joint).
3. Keep it smooth. Do not jerk.

Suggested Movement Patterns

1. Stretch as many body parts as you can.
2. Stretch your arms, legs, and feet in as many different directions as possible.
3. Try to stretch a body part quickly. Slowly. Smoothly.
4. Bend a body part and say which muscle or muscles are being stretched.
5. See how many ways you can stretch while sitting on the floor.
6. Lie on the floor and see if you can stretch two, three, four, or five body parts at once.
7. Try to stretch one body part quickly while stretching another part slowly.
8. While kneeling, see if you can stretch to a mark on the floor without losing your balance.
9. Stretch your right arm while curling your left arm.
10. Find a friend and see how many ways you can help each other stretch.
11. Try to stretch and become as tall as a giraffe. (Name other animals.)

16

12. Stretch and make a wide bridge. Find a partner to go under, around, and over your bridge.

13. Bend at the waist and touch your toes with your fingers. See if you can keep your legs straight while stretching to touch the toes.

14. Combine stretching with curling. With bending.

15. Stretch the muscles in your chest, back, tummy, ankles, wrists, fingers.

16. Make a shape with your body. Now stretch the shape to make it larger.

17. While moving at a low level, curl and stretch your fingers.

18. Find a position in which you can stretch one side of the body.

19. Find a position in which you can stretch both legs far apart in the air. Now make the legs as narrow as possible.

20. Stretch like a rubber band. When I say, "Snap!" move quickly back to original position.

Pushing

Pushing is a controlled, forceful action against an object to move the body away from the object or to move the object in a desired direction by applying force to it (figure 16.6).

FIGURE 16.6 Pushing.

Basic Activities

Stress Points

1. A forward stride position is used to broaden the base of support.

2. The body's center of gravity is low.

3. The line of force is directed toward the object.

4. The back is in reasonable alignment, and the body forces gather for a forceful push. Do not bend the waist.

5. The push is controlled and steady.

Instructional Cues

1. Broaden your foot base.

2. Use all your body forces.

3. Push steadily and evenly.

4. Lower yourself for a better push.

Suggested Movement Patterns

1. Stand near a wall and push it from an erect position; then push with the knees bent and one foot behind the other. In which position can you push harder?

2. Pretend you are pushing something very light. Now pretend to push something heavy.

3. Try to push a partner who is sitting on a jumping box; then try to push a partner who is sitting on a scooter. How does your body position change?

4. Push an object with your feet without using your arms or hands.

5. Sit down and push a heavy object with your feet. Can you put your back against the object and push it? See how many different ways you can find to push the object.

6. Find a friend and try to push each other over a line in turn.

7. Sit back-to-back with your partner and take turns seeing if you can push each other backward.

8. Lie on the floor and push your body forward, backward, and sideward.

9. Lie on the floor and push yourself with one foot and one arm.

10. Put a beanbag on the floor and push it with your elbows, shoulders, nose, or other body part.

11. Move in crab position and push a beanbag.

12. Show how you can push a ball to a friend.

Pulling

Pulling is a controlled, forceful action that moves an

object closer to the body or the body closer to an object. If the body moves while pulling an object, the object follows the body.

Basic Activities

Stress Points

1. For forceful pulling, the base of support is broad and the body's center of gravity is low.
2. The body's vertical axis provides a line of force away from the object.
3. Pulling is a controlled movement with little jerking and tugging.
4. Hand grips must be comfortable if pulling is to be efficient. Gloves or other padding can help.
5. Pulling movements can be isolated in the body, with one part of the body pulling against the other.

Instructional Cues

1. Get your body in line with the pull. Lower yourself.
2. Widen your base of support.
3. Gather your body forces and pull steadily.

Suggested Movement Patterns

1. Reach for the ceiling and pull an imaginary object toward you quickly. Pull it slowly and smoothly.
2. Use an individual tug-of-war rope and practice pulling against a partner. Try it with your hands and arms at different levels.
3. From a kneeling position, pull an object.
4. Try to pull with your feet while sitting on the floor.
5. Pretend to pull a heavy object while lying on the floor.
6. Clasp your hands together and pull as hard as you can.
7. Try pulling an object while standing on one foot.
8. Hold hands with a partner, and pull slowly as hard as you can.
9. Have your partner sit down and then see how slowly you can pull each other. Take turns.
10. With your partner sitting on the floor, take turns seeing if you can pull each other to your feet.
11. Pull with different body parts.
12. Pull your partner by the feet as your partner sits on a rug square.
13. Reach for the stars with both hands and pull one hand back to you.
14. Balance on one foot. Try to pull something. What happens?

Pushing and Pulling Combinations

Combinations of pulling and pushing movements should be arranged in sequence. Musical phrases can signal changes from one movement to the other. Balance beam benches are excellent for practicing pulling and pushing techniques. Partner tug-of-war ropes provide effective pulling experiences. Partner resistance exercises are also useful pulling and pushing experiences.

Fleeing, Chasing, and Tagging

Many physical education games involve fleeing, chasing, and tagging. Speed and reaction are essential in dodging, for both the person being chased and the chaser responding to the target child's movements.

Basic Activities

Stress Points

1. Run under control.
2. The fleeing child is in a moderate crouch position with feet wider apart than usual. This position enables moving quickly from side to side.
3. The fleeing child becomes adept at faking—moving briefly in one direction before going another way.
4. All runners move on the balls of their feet.
5. The chaser maneuvers the fleeing child into a confined area to facilitate tagging.
6. Eyes are focused on the center of the dodger's body to avoid falling for a fake.
7. The tag is a gentle yet firm touch between the knees and shoulders.

Instructional Cues (Chaser)

1. Run under control.
2. Move on the balls of the feet and stay slightly crouched when approaching the dodger.
3. Focus on the dodger's waistline.
4. Tag gently but firmly.

16

Suggested Movement Patterns

1. Run in general space toward other classmates and then dodge at the last moment. Avoid contact. To vary the activity, change direction on signal.

2. In general space, run and stop on signal.

3. In partners, have one person run and the other shadow (follow closely). Runners should change direction often. Switch roles.

4. Move into squads, with the leader 10 yards (meters) away from and facing the rest of the squad column. All members of the squad take turns running and dodging around a passive captain. Replace the squad captain regularly.

5. Partners mark a small area (12 feet by 12 feet [4 m by 4 m]) with cones. They chase and dodge within this area. Try it with two chasers and one dodger.

LEARNING AIDS

SUGGESTED READINGS

Cleland-Donnelly, F., Mueller, S.S., & Gallahue, D. (2017). *Developmental physical education for all children* (5th ed.). Champaign, IL: Human Kinetics.

Haywood, K.H., & Getchell, N. (2020). *Life span motor development* (7th ed.). Champaign, IL: Human Kinetics.

Colvin, A.V., Egner Markos, N.J., & Walker, P.J. (2016). *Teaching fundamental motor skills* (3rd ed.).

Magill, R.A. (2016). *Motor learning and control: Concepts and applications* (9th ed.). Boston, MA: McGraw-Hill.

Payne, V. Gregory, & Isaacs, Larry D. (2017). *Human motor development: A lifespan approach* (9th ed.). London, United Kingdom: Routledge.

Manipulative Skills

Activities in this chapter develop manipulative skills. A manipulative skill is one in which a child handles an object with the hands, feet, or other body parts. Manipulative skills are basic to the development of sport skills. Jump-rope activities develop specialized motor skills, particularly visual–tactile coordination. Rope-jumping activities in this chapter progress from individual movements using rope patterns to long-rope jumping with turners to individual rope-jumping challenges. Rhythmic gymnastics activities combine rhythmic and manipulative skills using a particular piece of manipulative equipment while moving to accompaniment.

Learning Objectives

▶ Demonstrate the various stages of development associated with throwing, catching, kicking, and striking.

▶ Identify instructional procedures related to different types of manipulative skills.

▶ Identify objects that can be used to help children succeed in manipulative skills.

▶ Outline skill progressions, activities, and instructional hints associated with using balloons, beanbags, balls, paddles, Frisbees, hoops, jump ropes, parachutes, and other objects to teach manipulative skills.

▶ Identify beginning, intermediate, and advanced rope-jumping skills and routines using individual and long ropes.

▶ List progressions to use when teaching rope jumping.

Manipulative skills involve using some type of implement, often with the hands but also with the feet or other body parts. Manipulative activities develop both eye–hand and eye–foot coordination as well as dexterity. Using equipment such as balloons, hoops, wands, beanbags, balls, tug-of-war ropes, Lummi sticks, Frisbees, and scoops, students can develop manipulative skills in many different settings. Activities with jump ropes are important in the program because they offer many possibilities for practicing multiple skills such as manipulative skills, rhythmic skills, and locomotor movements.

Balloons, beanbags, and yarn balls are used to teach throwing and catching activities for younger children. Soft, slow-moving objects reduce children's fear of being hurt while catching. Start children with an activity that allows all to achieve success. Based on that success, gradually increase the challenge of skills and experiences. Most activities begin with individual practice and then move to partner activity.

Manipulative Skills

Manipulative skills are basic to a number of specialized sport skills—catching, throwing, striking, and kicking, among others. General developmental stages have been identified for these complex motor patterns, from initial stages through mature performance patterns. Most complex skills should be practiced at normal speed. Although locomotor skills can be slowed down to promote learning, doing so with complex skills such as throwing, striking, or kicking destroys the rhythm of the skills. Provide the proper type of equipment and enough space for children to try these skills with maximum force. The following skills are sequenced by developmental stages rather than age, because of the wide maturity differences among children of similar ages. Major manipulative skills are described here and followed by many instructional activities, organized by equipment type, later in the chapter.

Throwing

In throwing, an object is thrust into space and accelerated using arm movement and total body coordination to generate force. Young children often go through two preliminary tossing stages before entering the stages of throwing. The first toss is a two-handed underhand throw involving little foot movement. A large ball, such as a beach ball, is best for teaching this type of throw, which begins with the ball held in front of the body at waist level. The toss is completed using only the arms.

The second preliminary toss is a one-handed underhand throw. In this toss, which resembles pitching a softball, body torque is generated and weight shifts from the rear to the front foot.

The following stages of skill analysis consider overhand throwing only. Velocity, not accuracy, is the primary goal in developing mature patterns characterized by a full range of motion and speed. Throwing for accuracy is practiced only after a mature form of the skill is in place.

Stage 1

Stage 1 throwing is generally seen between the ages of two and three years. This stage is restricted to moving the arm from the rear toward the front of the body. The feet are stationary and positioned at shoulder width, and little or no trunk rotation occurs (figure 17.1). Most of the movement force originates from flexing the hip, moving the shoulder forward, and extending the elbow.

Stage 2

Stage 2 throwing develops between the ages of three and five years. Some rotary motion is developed in an attempt to increase the amount of force. This stage is characterized by a lateral fling of the arm while rotating

FIGURE 17.1 Throwing form, stage 1.

the trunk (figure 17.2). Some children step into the throw, although many keep their feet stationary. This throwing style sometimes looks like a discus throw rather than a baseball throw. This toss requires a smaller object such as a beanbag, fleece ball, or small sponge ball.

Stage 3

Typically, stage 3 is seen in children at ages five and six years. The starting position is similar to that of stages 1 and 2 because the body is facing the target area, the feet are parallel, and the body is erect. In this stage, however, the child steps toward the target with the foot on the same side of the body as the throwing arm. This allows the body to rotate and the body weight to shift forward as the step occurs. The arm action is closer to overhand throwing than is the fling of stage 2, and hip flexion increases. Many students never mature beyond this stage without many opportunities for practice in throwing with velocity.

Stage 4

Stage 4 is a mature form of throwing; more force is applied to the object being thrown. The thrower uses the rule of opposition in this stage, stepping into the throw with the leg opposite the throwing arm. This method develops maximum body torque. Beginning with the weight on the back leg, the movement sequence is as follows: (a) step toward the target, (b) rotate the upper body, and (c) throw with the arm (figure 17.3). Use the cue phrase, "Step, turn, and throw." The elbow leads the way in the arm movement, followed by forearm extension and a final snapping of the wrist. Have students practice this pattern frequently to develop total body coordination. Through a combination of sound instruction and practice, most children can develop a mature pattern of throwing by age eight or nine years.

FIGURE 17.3   Throwing pattern, stage 4.

TEACHING TIP

1. Offer a variety of objects during throwing practice, so that students understand how varying weight and diameter affects throwing distance and speed.

2. When children are learning to throw, stress distance and velocity. Throwing for accuracy hampers development of a mature throwing form. Tell students to throw as hard and far as possible.

3. Avoid practicing throwing and catching at the same time. Many children's throws will be inaccurate and hard for a partner to catch. Have them practice throwing against a wall (velocity) or on a large field (distance).

4. Use carpet squares or circles drawn on the floor to teach children proper foot movement (stepping forward and off the square or out of the circle).

5. Beanbags and yarn balls are excellent for developing throwing velocity because they do not bounce.

©Robert Pangrazi or Aaron Beighle

FIGURE 17.2   Throwing form, stage 2.

Stress Points

1. Stand with the nonthrowing side of the body facing the target. The throwing arm side of the body is away from the target.

2. Step toward the target with the leg opposite the throwing arm.

3. Rotate the hips as the throwing arm moves forward.

4. Bend the arm at the elbow. The elbow leads the forward movement of the arm.

5. Body weight remains on the rear foot (away from the target) during early phases of the throw. Just before moving the arm forward, shift weight from the rear leg to the forward leg (nearer the target).

Catching

Catching uses the hands to stop and control a moving object. Catching is harder to learn than throwing, because children must track the object while moving into its path. Catching is also hard to master because of the fear of being hurt by an oncoming object. When teaching the early stages of catching, use balloons, fleece balls, and beach balls—because they move slowly, make tracking easier, and do not hurt if they hit a child in the face.

Stage 1

In stage 1 of catching, the child holds the arms in front of the body, with elbows extended and palms up, until the ball makes contact. The elbows are then bent in a trapping movement, and the arms press the ball against the chest (figure 17.4). Children often turn their heads away or close their eyes because of the fear response. Encourage them to focus on the object rather than the thrower.

Stage 2

Stage 2 catching is much like that in stage 1. Rather than waiting for the ball to contact the arms, however, the child makes an anticipatory reaching movement and cradles the ball somewhat.

Stage 3

In stage 3, the child prepares for the catch by lifting the arms and bending them slightly. The chest is used as a backstop for the ball. During this stage, the child makes contact with the hands first and then guides the object to the chest (figure 17.5).

Stage 4

In the fourth and final stage of catching, which occurs at about age nine years, the child catches with the hands. Encourage this skill by decreasing the size of the ball. Teach "giving" with the arms (reaching and bringing the

FIGURE 17.4 Catching form, stage 1.

FIGURE 17.5 Catching form, stage 3.

ball to the body, thus absorbing force) while catching. The legs bend, and the feet move in anticipation of the catch.

Stress Points

1. Maintain visual contact with the projectile.
2. Reach for the projectile and absorb its force by bringing the hands into the body. This "giving" makes catching easier by reducing the chance for the object to bounce out of the hands.
3. Place the feet in a stride position rather than a straddle position. A fast-moving object can cause a loss of balance if feet are in the straddle position.
4. Align the body with the object rather than reaching to the side of the body to make the catch.

Kicking

Kicking is a striking action made with either foot. Types of kicking include punting (dropping the ball from the hands and kicking before it touches the ground) and placekicking (kicking the ball in a stationary position on the ground). A third type, soccer kicking, is difficult because the ball is moving before the kick is executed.

Stage 1

In stage 1 the body is stationary, and the kicking foot is flexed to prepare for the kick. The kicking motion is carried out with a straight leg and little or no flexing at the knee. The arms and trunk do not move much, and concentration is on the ball.

Stage 2

In the second stage of kicking, the kicking foot swings backward by flexing at the knee. Usually, the child displays opposition of the limbs. When the kicking leg goes forward, the opposite arm moves forward. Unlike the first stage, in stage 2 the kicking leg moves farther forward in the follow-through.

Stage 3

In stage 3, movement toward the object to be kicked is added. The leg moves a greater distance, coupled with a movement of the upper body to counterbalance the leg movement.

Stage 4

Mature kicking styles involve a preparatory extension of the hip to increase the range of motion. The child runs to the ball and takes a small leap to get the kicking foot

TEACHING TIP

1. It is natural to dodge an object that may cause harm. Remove the fear factor by using projectiles that will not hurt children, such as foam balls, yarn balls, beach balls, and balloons.
2. Use smaller projectiles as students improve their catching skills. Larger objects move more slowly and are easier to track visually.
3. Prepare students for a catch by asking them to focus on the ball while it is in the thrower's hand. Use a verbal cue such as "Look (focus), ready (for the throw), catch (toss the ball)."
4. Balls and background colors should strongly contrast to increase visual perception.
5. Throwing the projectile at a greater height offers the child more opportunity to track it successfully. Beach balls move slowly throughout a high trajectory, giving children time to focus and move into the path of the oncoming object.
6. Bounce objects off the floor so that children learn to judge the rebound angle of a projectile.

in position. While swinging the kicking foot forward, the child leans backward and then takes a small step forward on the support foot to regain balance (figure 17.6).

Stress Points

1. Students need to step forward with the nonkicking leg. Have them stand behind and slightly to the side of the ball. They keep the eyes on the ball (head down) throughout the kick.

FIGURE 17.6 Kicking a soccer ball, stage 4.

2. Practice kicking with both feet.

3. Use objects that will not hurt children. For example, regulation soccer balls, which are heavy and hard, hurt young children's feet. Foam balls and beach balls are excellent objects for kicking practice.

4. Encourage kickers to move their leg backward in preparing for the kick. Beginners often fail to move the leg backward, making it difficult for them to generate kicking force.

5. Arms move in opposition to the legs during the kick.

6. After children develop kick speed and velocity, they should focus on altering the force of the kick. Many children learn to kick only with velocity; activities like soccer demand both soft "touch" kicks and kicks of maximum velocity.

Striking

Striking is hitting an object with an implement. Common forms of striking are hitting a softball with a bat, using a racket for striking in tennis and racquetball, and striking a ball with the hand as in volleyball.

Stage 1

In this stage, the child's feet are stationary and the trunk faces the direction of the oncoming object (or ball on a tee). The elbows are fully flexed, and extending them downward generates force. Little body force is generated because the trunk does not rotate and the motion is from back to front. The striking force comes from the arms and wrists.

Stage 2

In stage 2, the child's upper body generates force. The trunk is turned to the side in anticipation of the ball. The weight shifts from the rear foot to the forward foot before contacting the ball. The child's trunk and hips rotate into the ball during the swing. The elbows are less flexed, and force is generated by extending the flexed joints. Trunk rotation and forward movement are in an oblique plane.

Stage 3

In stage 3, mature striking skills, the child stands parallel to the path of the oncoming object. Weight shifts to the rear foot, and the hips rotate, followed by a weight shift toward the ball as it approaches the hitter. Striking occurs with the arms extended in a long arc. The swing ends with weight on the forward foot. Mature striking involves a swing through the full range of motion and a smooth transfer of weight from the rear to the front plane of the body.

Stress Points

1. Track the ball as soon as possible and keep tracking until it is hit. (It is impossible to see the racket hit the ball, but this is an excellent technique for training students to keep their eye on the ball as long as possible.)

2. Grip the bat with the hands together. For right-handed hitters, the left hand is on the bottom (near the small end of the bat).

3. Keep the elbows away from the body. Emphasis is on making a large swing and extending the elbows as the ball is hit.

4. Swing the bat in a horizontal (parallel to the ground) plane. Beginners tend to strike downward in a chopping motion.

Manipulative Skill Activities

Manipulative skills come into play when children handle an object, usually with their hands and feet. Other parts of the body can also be used. These skills lead to better eye–hand and eye–foot coordination, which are particularly important for tracking items in space. Manipulative skills are basic to many game skills. Throwing, batting,

TEACHING TIP

1. When teaching kicking skills, focus on velocity and distance rather than accuracy. Students who are asked to kick accurately will poke at the ball rather than develop a full kicking style.

2. Ensure that all students have a ball to kick. Beach balls (for primary grades) and foam balls are excellent because they do not travel far and children can kick and retrieve them quickly.

3. Stationary balls are easier to kick than moving balls. Use this progression when teaching beginners to kick.

4. Teach various types of kicks: the toe kick, instep kick, and side-of-the-foot kick.

TEACHING TIP

1. Striking is done with maximum force and bat velocity when the focus of instruction is on developing a mature striking form.
2. Practice hitting stationary objects before progressing to moving objects. Batting tees and balls suspended on a string are useful for beginners.
3. In the early stages of striking practice, use slow-moving objects such as balloons and beach balls. They are easier to track when moving.
4. As skill in striking increases, decrease the size of the projectile and bat (or racket).
5. To enhance visual perception, ensure that the ball contrasts with the background.
6. Use rubber footprints to help children learn to step into the ball.

kicking, and catching objects are important skills that can be taught by using beanbags and various balls. Rebounding or redirecting an object in flight (such as a volleyball) is another useful manipulative skill. Continuous control of an object, such as a wand or hoop, is also a manipulative activity.

Instructional Activities

Instructional activities for each unit progress from easiest to most difficult and are organized by major skill groups. This structure helps teachers focus on desired objectives. For example, the first group of skills to practice in beanbag activities is Tossing to Self in Place. The teacher can take either of two approaches: Develop the first group in depth, exhausting all the possibilities, or select two or more activities from several groups. In the latter case, when repeating the lesson the following day, use the same groups of activities but pose different challenges. By working within groups of activities, students focus on the same type of skill, but they stay motivated because of the many different challenges being offered. This approach offers random practice opportunities. Random practice results in better retention because students are mentally generating solutions and are less likely to become bored.

Why work on group activities around equipment rather than skills? Creating random practice sessions by using different types of equipment to practice the same skills is certainly possible. But this approach makes most lessons equipment intensive. Teachers often avoid units that demand too much equipment because of the difficulty of moving it to and from the instructional area. For example, if a teacher is working with first-graders

and sixth-graders during the same period and has to move equipment outside, twice as much equipment has to be moved. The same goal can be accomplished (random practice sessions) by bringing out one type of equipment and modifying the activities that focus on a single skill. The result will be effective and challenging random practice sessions.

Student-Developed Games

Skills can be reinforced and enhanced through games that students create involving the skills just learned. For example, ask students to create a game using a certain skill for which they are to select the equipment needed, outline the game space, specify the number of participants, and set the rules, including scoring. If desired, the teacher can outline certain conditions, such as using two hoops and two bowling pins, limiting space to two lines 20 to 30 feet (6 to 10 m) apart, and having competing sides of two against two. Within those parameters, students create and play a game.

Creative games can be designed for individuals, partners, or small groups. Keep the groups small, so that each child's input is considered. Specify different kinds of equipment (such as mats, wands, goals, or benches). Later, the new games can be demonstrated to the rest of the class. When students are in the learning phase of skill development, the games should focus on applying the skills rather than serious competition. Competition may reduce students' performance level if they focus on winning the game rather than correctly performing the skill.

17

Activities With Balloons and Beach Balls

Balloons provide safe, interesting movement experiences and emphasize eye–hand coordination. Students who are not ready for faster-moving ball skills can achieve success with balloons. Beach balls are larger, and they move more slowly and predictably. Both objects are harmless, so students can learn to catch without fear of being hurt. These objects move slowly, so students have ample time to learn proper footwork—preparing for a volley, catching, and striking, for example.

Instructional Procedures

1. Use the following instructional cues when teaching balloon and beach ball skills:

   a. Catch and control with the fingertips.

   b. Keep your eyes on the object.

   c. Move your body into the path of the oncoming object.

   d. Reach, catch, and move the object to the body (giving).

2. After blowing up each balloon, do not tie a knot in the neck of the balloon. Fix it with a twist tie used to close plastic bags, so that the balloon can be deflated easily and reused.

3. Beach balls last longer and are easier to control if they are a bit underinflated. Beach balls 16 to 20 inches (40 to 50 cm) in diameter are best for most students and can be used with older students for lead-up games in volleyball and soccer.

Recommended Progression

1. Begin with free exploration by having children practice controlling their balloon (figure 17.7). The objective is to have the children gain a sense of the balloon's flight.

2. Introduce specific hand, finger, and arm contacts. Include using alternate hands; contacting at different levels (low, high, in between); jumping and making high contact; using different hand contacts (palm, back, side, and different fist positions); using different finger combinations (two fingers, index finger, thumb only); and using arms, elbows, and shoulders.

©Robert Pangrazi or Aaron Beighle

FIGURE 17.7 Batting balloons from different body positions.

3. Establish contact sequences with three or four body parts. Use various levels and body shapes. Make some flash cards with names of body parts. Students must take their eyes off the balloon to see the named body part. This challenge helps young children learn to track a moving object.

4. Bat from various body positions—kneeling, sitting, lying.

5. Use an object to control the balloon (Lummi stick, ball, stocking paddle).

6. Restrict movement. Keep one foot in place. Keep one or both feet within a hoop or on a mat or carpet square.

7. Work with a partner by alternating turns, batting the beach ball back and forth, employing follow-the-leader patterns, and so on.

8. Introduce some aspects of volleyball technique, including the overhand pass, underhand pass, and dig pass. Begin with a volleyball serve. Make this informal and on a "let's pretend" basis. Check the volleyball unit (see chapter 30) for technique suggestions.

9. Toss a balloon up. Pick up a hoop from the floor, pass it around the balloon, place the hoop on the floor, and keep the balloon from touching the ground.

10. Have four to six children sit on the floor in a small circle. Each circle gets two balloons to be kept in the air. Children's seats are "glued" to the floor.

If a balloon hits the floor, it is out of play. Play for a specific time (30 to 60 seconds). Increase the challenge by using beach balls.

Activities With Beanbags

Beanbag activities provide valuable learning experiences for elementary school children at all levels. Challenging partner activities—juggling, different and unique methods of propulsion, and the Split-Vision Drill—are suitable activities for older students.

Instructional Procedures

1. Use these instructional cues when teaching beanbag activities:

   a. Catch the beanbag softly by giving with the hands, arms, and legs. "Giving" involves the hands going out toward the incoming beanbag and bringing it in for a soft landing.

   b. Keep your eyes on the beanbag when catching.

   c. When tossing and catching, toss slightly above eye level.

2. Make sure that beanbags are about 6 inches (15 cm) square. This size balances well and can be controlled on various parts of the body for a greater challenge to intermediate-level children.

3. Throwing and catching skills involve many intricate elements. Stress the principles of opposition, eye focus, weight transfer, and follow-through. Stress tracking the object when catching and focusing on the target when throwing.

4. Stress laterality and directionality when teaching throwing and catching skills. Teach children to throw, catch, and balance beanbags with both the left and right sides of the body. Have them learn to catch and throw at different levels.

5. Children throw at chest height to a partner, unless teachers specify a different type of throw. Teach all types of return: low, medium, high, left, and right.

6. In partner work, keep distances between partners reasonable, especially in introductory phases. A good starting distance is 15 feet (5 m) or so.

7. In partner work, emphasize skillful and varied throwing, catching, and handling of the beanbag.

Throwing too hard or out of range, to make the partner miss, should be avoided.

Most activities are classified as individual or partner activities. A few activities are for groups of three or more.

Individual Activities

Tossing to Self in Place

1. Toss with both hands, with right hand only, and with left hand only. Catch the same way. Catch with the back of the hands.

2. Toss the beanbag progressively higher and then progressively lower.

3. Hold the beanbag in one hand and make large Arm Circles (imitating a windmill). Release the bag so that it flies upward and then catch it.

4. Toss from side to side, right to left (reverse), front to back (reverse), and around various body parts in different combinations.

5. Toss upward and catch with hands behind the back. Toss upward from behind the body and catch in front. Toss upward and catch on the back, knees, toes, and other body parts.

6. Hold the bag at arm's length in front of the body, with palms up. Withdraw hands quickly from under the bag and catch it from on top in a palms-down stroke before it falls to the floor.

7. Toss upward and catch as high as possible. As low as possible. Work out a sequence of high, low, and in between.

8. Toss upward and catch with the body off the floor. Try tossing as well as catching with the body off the ground.

9. Toss in various ways while seated and while lying down.

10. Toss two beanbags upward and catch a bag in each hand.

Adding Stunts in Place

1. Toss overhead to the rear, turn around, and catch. Toss, do a full turn, and catch.

2. Toss, clap hands, and catch. Clap hands more than once. Clap hands around various body parts.

3. Toss, do pretend activities (e.g., comb hair, wash face, brush teeth, shine shoes), and catch.

4. Toss, touch different body parts with both hands, and catch. Touch two different body parts, calling out the name of the parts. Touch two body parts, clap hands, and catch.

17

5. Toss, kneel on one knee, and catch. Try this going to a sitting or lying position. Reverse the position, going from lying or sitting to standing to catch.

6. Toss, touch the floor, and catch. Explore with other challenges. Use Heel Clicks or balance positions.

7. Bend forward, reach between the legs, and toss the bag onto the back or shoulders.

8. Reach one hand over the shoulder, drop the beanbag, and catch it with the other hand behind the back. Reverse the hands. Drop the beanbag from one hand behind the back and catch it with the other hand between the legs. Put the beanbag on the head, lean back, and catch it with both hands behind the back. Catch it with one hand.

Locomotor Movements

1. Toss to self, moving to another spot to catch. Toss forward, run, and catch. Move from side to side. Toss overhead to the rear, run back, and catch.

2. Add various stunts and challenges described earlier. Vary with different locomotor movements.

Balancing the Beanbag on Various Body Parts

1. Balance the beanbag on the head. Move around, keeping the beanbag in place. Sit down, lie down, turn around, and so on.

2. Balance the beanbag on other parts of the body and move around. Balance on top of the instep, between the knees, on the shoulders, on the elbows, under the chin. Use more than one beanbag.

Propelling With Various Body Parts

1. Toss to self from various parts of the body: elbow, instep, knees, shoulders, between the feet, between the heels.

2. Sit and toss the bag from the feet to the hands. Practice tossing while lying on the back. While lying down, pick up the bag between the toes and place it behind the head, using a full curl position. Go back and pick it up, returning it to its original place.

Juggling

1. Begin with two bags and juggle them in the air.

2. Juggle three bags.

Other Activities

1. From a standing wide straddle, place the beanbag on the floor and push it between the legs as far back as possible. Jump in place with a half turn and repeat.

2. Take the position just described. Push the beanbag back as far as possible between the legs, bending the knees. Without moving the legs, turn to the right and pick up the beanbag. Repeat to the left.

3. Stand with feet apart and hold the beanbag with both hands. Reach as high as possible (with both hands), bend backward, and drop the beanbag. Reach between the legs and pick up the beanbag.

4. On all fours, put the beanbag in the small of the back. Wiggle and force the beanbag off the back without moving the hands or knees from place.

5. In crab position, place the beanbag on the tummy, and try to shake it off. On all fours, put it on the back and do a Mule Kick (see figure 20.41).

6. Push the beanbag across the floor with different body parts such as the nose, shoulder, or knee.

7. Each student drops a beanbag on the floor. See how many different ways students can move over, around, and between the beanbags. For example, jump three beanbags, Crab-Walk around two others, and cartwheel over one more.

8. Spread the legs about shoulder width. Bend over and throw the beanbag between the legs and onto the back. Next, throw the beanbag all the way over the head and catch it.

Partner Activities

Tossing Back and Forth

1. Begin with various kinds of two-handed throws: underhand, overhead, side, and over the shoulder. Change to one-handed tossing and throwing.

2. Throw at different levels, at different targets, right and left.

3. Throw under the leg, around the body, as a center in football. Try imitating the shot put and the discus throw. Try the softball (full arc) throw.

4. Have partners sit cross-legged about 10 feet (3 m) apart. Throw and catch in various styles.

5. Use follow activities, in which one partner leads with a throw and the other follows with the same kind of throw.

6. Jump, turn in the air, and pass to partner.

7. Stand back-to-back and pass the beanbag around both partners from hand to hand as quickly as possible. Try moving the beanbag around and through various body parts.

8. Toss in various directions to make partner move and catch.

9. Run around partner in a circle, tossing the beanbag back and forth.

10. Toss two beanbags back and forth. Each partner has a beanbag, and the beanbags go in opposite directions at the same time. Try having one partner toss both beanbags at once in the same direction, using various types of throws. Try to keep three beanbags going at once.

Propelling With Various Body Parts

1. From a sitting position, toss the beanbag to a partner with foot or toes, from on top of the feet, and from between the feet, with elbow, shoulder, head, and any other body part.

2. With back to partner, take a Rabbit Jump position. Hold the beanbag between the feet and kick it back to partner. Try kicking with both feet from a standing position.

3. Partners lie faceup on the floor with heads pointing toward each other, about 6 inches (15 cm) apart. One partner has a beanbag between the feet and places it between the partners' heads. The other partner picks up the beanbag with the feet (by reaching over the head) and places it on the floor by the feet after returning to original position. With both partners in a backward curl, try to transfer the beanbag directly from one partner to the other with the feet.

Group Activities and Games

Split-Vision Drill

This Split-Vision Drill from basketball is adapted to beanbags. An active player faces two partners about 15 feet (5 m) away. They stand side-by-side, not far apart. The active player holds a beanbag, and one of the partners holds a beanbag. The active player tosses to the open partner and at the same time catches the bag tossed by the other partner. The two bags move back and forth between the active player and the other two, alternately (figure 17.8). After a while, change positions.

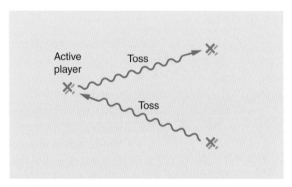

FIGURE 17.8 Split-Vision Drill for beanbags.

Target Games

Wastebaskets, hoops, circles drawn on the floor, and other objects can be used as targets for beanbag tossing. Target boards with holes cut out are available from commercial sources. Holes can be triangles, circles, squares, and rectangles, thus stressing form concepts.

Beanbag Quoits

This game is played like horseshoes. Draw a court by marking two spots (e.g., with masking tape) on the floor about 1 inch (2.5 cm) in diameter and 20 feet (6 m) apart. Each competitor has two beanbags, a different color for each player. Players toss from behind one spot to the other spot. The object is to get one or both beanbags closer to the mark than the opponent does. If a beanbag completely blocks out the spot, as viewed from directly overhead, the player scores 3 points. Otherwise, the bag nearest the spot scores 1 point. Games are played to 11, 15, or 21 points. In each round, the player winning the previous point tosses first.

Other Games

Children enjoy playing One Step, and Teacher Ball (see chapter 22) is also readily adaptable to beanbags.

Activities With Balls

This section focuses on ball skills in which the child handles balls without using other equipment, such as a bat or paddle. Ball skills are mostly of two types: (1) eye–hand skills, including throwing, catching, bouncing, dribbling (as in basketball), batting (as in volleyball), and rolling (as in bowling); and (2) eye–foot skills, including kicking, trapping, and dribbling (as in soccer).

17

Types of Balls

For younger children, sponge rubber, yarn, and fleece balls are all excellent for introductory throwing and catching, because they help overcome the fear factor. (Chapter 12 gives instructions on making balls from yarn.) The Wiffle ball, a hollow plastic ball with holes, is also useful. Scoops, either commercial or home constructed, are an extension of Wiffle-ball activities. Another useful ball is a soft softball, a much softer version of the regular softball. It is suitable for catching and throwing but does not hold up well if batted.

The inflated rubber playground ball (8.5-inch [22 cm] size) should be used for most ball-handling experiences. Inflate the balls so that they bounce well, but do not overinflate, which makes them difficult to catch and distorts their shape. Eight-inch (20 cm) foam balls last longer and have more utility for children. Foam balls are easier to catch and pass and do not hurt students who are accidentally hit by one. Many types of foam are used to make these balls, so make sure that the balls are dense and will bounce well. Many of the cheaper styles are extremely light and do not bounce. The best choice is the foam "tough-skin" ball. These foam balls have a tough plastic coating that makes the balls bounce better and protects the soft foam. In the long run, these tough-skin balls may be the best buy because they do not leak or develop punctures like the standard playground ball. Bright-colored balls add contrast to the background, so children can track and catch them easier.

Types of Organization

Instruction with younger children begins with individual work and progresses to partner and group activities. When propelling the ball back and forth, partners go from rolling the ball to throwing with one bounce to throwing on the fly. Be sure that partners with different skill levels can work well together.

Distance between partners is short at first and then lengthens gradually. Introduce the concept of targets by directing children to throw the ball to specific points. Later, to maintain progression, change from a stationary target to a moving target. Group activities are confined to small groups (of three to six), so that each child can be active, and they include activities not possible in individual or partner activity.

Instructional Procedures

1. Use these instructional cues when teaching ball skills.

   a. Keep your eyes on the ball.
   b. Catch and dribble the ball with the pads of the fingers.
   c. Use opposition and weight transfer when passing the ball.

2. When catching, receive the ball softly by "giving" with the hands and arms. The hands reach out to receive the ball and then cushion the impact by bringing the ball in toward the body in a relaxed way.

3. To catch a throw above the waist, hold the hands so that the thumbs are together. To catch a throw below the waist, keep the little fingers toward each other and rotate the thumbs outward.

4. When throwing to a partner, unless otherwise specified, try to reach the partner at about chest height. At times, specify different target points—high, low, right, left, at the knee, and so on.

5. Begin with basic skills within all children's reach and progress to more challenging activities.

6. Have students practice the skills on the right and left sides (laterality) of the body.

7. Incorporate split vision in bouncing and dribbling. Encourage students to look forward, rather than at the ball, when bouncing and dribbling.

8. Tactile senses can be enhanced by having children dribble or bounce the ball with their eyes closed.

9. Rhythmic accompaniment, particularly for bouncing and dribbling activities, adds another dimension to ball skills.

10. Have enough balls available so that each child has one.

11. Solve the problem of uncontrolled balls by telling children to ignore stray balls, because someone is sure to be coming after them.

Activities with balls are presented with a 6- to 8.5-inch (15 to 22 cm) ball in mind. Some modification is needed if the balls used are smaller or do not bounce.

Individual Activities

Each child has a ball and practices alone. In the first group of individual activities, the child stays in the same spot. Next, the child bounces the ball against a wall. (The wall should be reasonably free of projections and irregular surfaces so that the ball can return directly to the student.) In the third group of activities, the child performs alone while on the move.

Controlled Rolling and Handling in Place

1. In a standing wide straddle (other possible positions are seated, legs crossed or outstretched, and push-up position), place the ball on the floor and roll it with constant finger guidance between and around the legs.

2. Roll the ball in a figure-eight path in and out of the legs.

3. Reach as far to the left as possible with the ball and roll it in front of you to the other side. Catch it as far to the right of the body as possible.

4. Turn in place and roll the ball around with one hand in a large circle.

5. Roll the ball around while lying on top of it. Roll the ball around the floor while on all fours, guiding it with the nose and forehead.

6. With the back moderately bent, release the ball behind the head, let it roll down the back, and catch it with both hands.

7. Make different kinds of bridges over the ball while using the ball as partial support for the bridge.

8. Starting with one arm above the head, roll the ball down that arm, behind the back, down the other arm, and then catch it.

Bouncing and Catching in Place

1. Beginning with two hands, bounce and catch the ball. Bounce a given number of times. Bounce at different levels. Bounce one-handed in a variety of ways. Bounce under the legs. Close the eyes and bounce and catch.

2. Bounce, perform various stunts (a Heel Click, body turn, or handclap), and catch.

3. Bounce the ball around, under, and over the body.

4. Practice various kinds of bounces, catching all with the eyes closed.

5. Bounce the ball with various body parts, such as the head, elbow, or knee.

6. Bounce the ball, using consecutive body parts (such as the elbow and then the knee), and catch.

Tossing and Catching in Place

1. Toss and catch, increasing height gradually. Toss from side to side. Toss underneath the legs, around the body, and from behind. Add challenges while tossing and catching. Clap hands one or more times, make body turns (quarter, half, or full), touch the floor, click heels, sit down, lie down, and so on.

2. To enhance body part identification, toss and perform some of these challenges: Touch the back with both hands, touch the back with both hands by reaching over both shoulders, touch both elbows, touch both knees with crossed hands, touch both heels with a heel slap, and touch the toes. Be sure to catch the ball after completing each challenge. The teacher or a leader can quickly call out a body part, and the class must respond with a toss, touch, and catch.

3. Toss upward and catch the descending ball as high as possible and then as low as possible. Work out other levels, and create combinations. Catch with crossed arms.

4. From a seated position, toss the ball to self from various directions. Lie down and do the same. Toss with the feet.

5. Practice catching by looking away after tossing the ball upward. Experiment with different ways of catching with the eyes closed.

Striking to Self in Place

1. Strike the ball as in volleyball by using the fist, an open hand, or the side of the hand.

2. Strike and let the ball bounce. Catch in different ways.

3. Rebound the ball upward, using different parts of the body. Let it bounce. Practice serving to self.

4. Strike and rebound the ball so that it does not touch the ground. Change position while doing this.

5. Strike the ball, perform a stunt, and strike again.

Foot Skills in Place

1. Put the toes on top of the ball. Roll the ball in different directions, keeping the other foot in place but retaining control.

2. Use a two-foot pickup, front and back. Do this by putting the ball between the feet and hoisting it to the hands.

3. From a seated position with legs extended, toss the ball with the feet to the hands.

4. While lying on the floor, hold the ball between the feet. Try to bring the knees to the chest and then return to the starting position without losing control of the ball. Try bringing the ball to a point directly over the body. Next, with the arms out to the sides for support, touch the floor with the ball on the left and right sides of the body.

17

5. In a supine position, hold the ball on the floor above the head. Do a curl-up, bring the ball forward, touch the toes with it, and return to supine position.

6. Drop the ball, and immediately trap it against the floor with one foot. Try to bounce it with one foot.

Dribbling Skills With Hands in Place

1. Dribble the ball first with both hands and then with the right and the left. (Stress that the dribble is a push with good wrist action. Children should not bat the ball downward.) Use various number combinations with the right and left hands.

2. Dribble under the legs in turn and back around the body. Kneel and dribble. Go from standing to lying, maintaining a dribble. Return to standing position.

3. Dribble the ball at different levels and at various tempos.

4. Dribble without looking at the ball. Dribble and change hands without stopping the dribble. Dribble with the eyes closed.

Throwing Against a Wall (Catching on the First Bounce)

1. Throw the ball against the wall and catch the return after one bounce. Practice various kinds of throws: two-handed, one-handed, overhead, side, baseball, chest pass.

2. Throw at a target mounted on the wall.

Throwing Against a Wall (Catching on the Fly)

Repeat the throws used in the previous activity but catch the return on the fly. Moving closer and having the ball contact the wall higher may be necessary.

Striking Against a Wall (Handball Skills)

1. Drop the ball and bat it after it bounces. Keep the ball going as in handball.

2. Serve the ball against the wall as in volleyball. Experiment with different ways to serve.

Kicking Against a Wall and Trapping (Eye–Foot Skills)

1. Practice different ways to control kicking against the wall and stopping (trapping) the ball on the return. Try using the foot to keep returning the ball against the wall on the bounce.

2. Put some targets on the wall and kick the ball at them. See how many points are scored after 10 kicks.

Rolling on the Move

1. Roll the ball, run alongside it, and guide it with the hands in different directions.

2. Roll the ball forward; then run and catch up with it.

Tossing and Catching on the Move

1. Toss the ball upward and forward. Run forward and catch it after one bounce. Toss the ball upward in various directions (forward, sideward, backward), run under it, turn, and catch it on the fly.

2. Add various stunts and challenges, such as touching the floor, clicking the heels, or turning around.

Striking on the Move

With first the right and then the left hand, bat the ball upward in different directions and catch it on the first bounce or on the fly.

Practicing Foot Skills on the Move

Dribble the ball (soccer style) forward and in other directions. Dribble around an imaginary point. Make various patterns while dribbling, such as a circle, square, triangle, or figure eight.

Dribbling With Hands on the Move

1. Dribble (basketball style) forward using one hand and dribble back to place with the other. Change direction on a signal. Dribble in various directions, describing different pathways. Dribble around cones, milk cartons, or chairs.

2. Place a hoop on the floor. Dribble inside the hoop until a signal is sounded. Then dribble to another hoop and continue the dribble inside that hoop. Avoid dribbling on the hoop itself.

Practicing Locomotor Movements While Holding the Ball

1. Holding the ball between the legs, perform various locomotor movements.

2. Try holding the ball in various positions with different body parts.

Partner Activities

Rolling in Place

Roll the ball back and forth to a partner. Begin with two-handed rolls and proceed to one-handed rolls. When partner rolls the ball, pick it up with the toes and snap it up into the hands.

Throwing and Catching in Place

1. Toss the ball to a partner with one bounce, using various kinds of tosses. Practice various kinds of throws and passes to partner.
2. Throw to specific levels and points: high, low, right, left, at the knee, and so on. Try various throws: from under the leg, around the body, backward tosses, and centering as in football.
3. Throw and catch over a volleyball net.
4. Work in a threesome with one person holding a hoop between the two partners playing catch. Throw the ball through the hoop, held at various levels. Try throwing through a moving hoop.

Volleying in Place

1. Toss the ball upward to self and bat it two-handed to a partner, who catches and returns it in the same way. Serve as in volleyball to partner. Partner makes a return serve. Toss the ball to partner, who makes a volleyball return. Keep distances short and control the ball. Try to keep the ball going back and forth as in volleyball.
2. Bat the ball back and forth on one bounce. Bat it back and forth over a line, wand, jump rope, or bench.

Kicking in Place

1. Practice different ways of controlled kicking between partners and different ways of stopping the ball (trapping).
2. Practice a controlled punt, preceding the kick with a step on the nonkicking foot. Place the ball between the feet and propel it forward or backward to a partner.
3. Practice foot pickups. One partner rolls the ball, and the other hoists it to self with extended toes.

Throwing in Place from Various Positions

1. Practice different throws from a kneeling, sitting, or lying position. (Allow the children to be creative in selecting positions.)

2. Using two balls, pass back and forth, with balls going in opposite directions.

Follow Activities in Place

Throw or propel the ball in any manner desired. Partner returns the ball in the same way.

Throwing and Catching Against a Wall

Alternate throwing and catching against a wall. Alternate returning the ball after a bounce, as in handball.

Throwing on the Move

1. One child stays in place and tosses to the other child, who is moving. The moving child traces different patterns, such as back and forth between two spots or in a circle around the stationary child. (Spatial judgments must be good to anticipate where the moving child will be to receive the ball. Moderate distances are maintained between children.)
2. Practice different kinds of throws and passes as both children move in different patterns. (Considerable space is needed for this type of work.) Practice foot skills of dribbling and passing.
3. Partners hold the ball between their bodies without using the hands or arms. Experiment with different ways to move together.
4. Carrying a ball, run in different directions while partner follows. On signal, toss the ball upward so that the child following can catch it. Now change places and repeat the activity.

Juggling

Juggling is a novel and exciting task for elementary school children. Learning to juggle demands practice and repetition. An excellent medium for teaching beginners is sheer, lightweight scarves from 18 to 24 inches (45 to 60 cm) square. Scarves move slowly, allowing children to track them visually. Juggling with scarves teaches children correct patterns of object movement. But this skill does not transfer easily to juggling with faster-moving objects such as fleece balls or tennis balls. Therefore, two distinct sections for juggling are offered: a section that deals with learning to juggle with scarves and a second section that explains juggling with balls.

Most of the class will succeed at juggling with scarves. While acquiring this skill, however, students will experience many misses. Because children tire quickly if they

17

are not having success, it may be desirable to play a game and then return to juggling practice.

Juggling With Scarves

Scarves are held by the fingertips near the center. To throw the scarf, lift and pull it into the air above eye level. Scarves are caught by clawing, a downward motion of the hand, and grabbing the scarf from above as it is falling. Scarf juggling should teach proper habits (for example, tossing the scarves straight up in line with the body rather than forward or backward). Many instructors remind children to imagine they are in a phone booth or large refrigerator box—to emphasize tossing and catching without moving.

Cascading

Cascading is the easiest pattern for juggling three objects. The following sequence can be used to learn this basic technique.

1. *One scarf.* Hold the scarf in the center. Quickly move the arm across the chest and toss the scarf with the palm out. Reach out with the other hand and catch the scarf in a straight-down motion (clawing). Toss the scarf with this hand using the same motion, and claw it with the opposite hand. Continue, repeating the tossing and clawing sequence. The scarf moves in a figure-eight pattern as shown in figure 17.9.

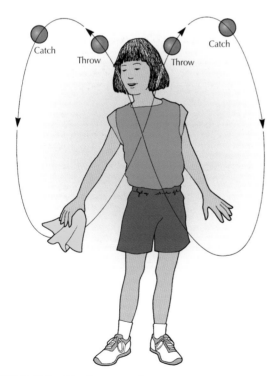

FIGURE 17.9 Clawing a scarf.

2. *Two scarves—two hands.* Hold a scarf with the fingertips in each hand. Toss the first one across the body as described in step 1. When it reaches its peak, look at it, and toss the second scarf across the body in the opposite direction. The first scarf thrown is clawed by the hand throwing the second scarf, and vice versa (figure 17.10). Use verbal cues such as "Toss, claw, toss, claw."

FIGURE 17.10 Tossing and clawing with two scarves.

3. *Two scarves—one hand.* Students must learn this sequence before trying to juggle three scarves. Start with both scarves in one hand (hold them as described next in three-scarf cascading). The important skill to learn is the sequence: tossing the first scarf, tossing the second scarf, and then catching the first and the second. Verbal cues to use are "Toss, toss, catch, catch." If students cannot toss two scarves before catching one, they cannot master juggling with three scarves. Practice tossing skills with both hands.

4. *Three-scarf cascading.* Hold a scarf in each hand by the fingertips, as described in step 2. Hold the third scarf with the ring and little fingers against the palm of one hand. Toss the first scarf from the hand that is holding two scarves. Toss this scarf from the fingertips across the chest as learned earlier. When the first scarf reaches its peak, toss the second scarf from the other hand and across the body. As this hand starts to come down, it catches the first scarf. When the second scarf reaches its peak, toss the third scarf in the same path as that of the first scarf. To complete the cycle,

as the hand comes down from throwing the third scarf, it catches the second scarf. Repeat the cycle by tossing the first scarf with the opposite hand. Figure 17.11 illustrates the figure-eight motion used in cascading. Tosses always alternate between left and right hands with a smooth, even rhythm.

FIGURE 17.11 Three-scarf cascading.

Reverse Cascading

Reverse cascading involves tossing the scarves from waist level to the outside of the body and allowing the scarves to drop down the midline of the body (figure 17.12).

1. *One scarf.* Begin by holding the scarf as described earlier. The throw goes away from the midline of the body over the top, releasing the scarf so that it falls down the center of the body. Catch it with the opposite hand and toss it in similar fashion on the opposite side of the body.

2. *Two scarves.* Begin with a scarf in each hand. Toss the first scarf as described in step 1. When it begins to fall, toss the second scarf. Catch the first scarf, catch the second scarf, and repeat the toss, toss, catch, catch pattern.

3. *Reverse cascading with three scarves.* Think of a large funnel at eye level directly in front of the juggler. The goal is to drop all scarves through this funnel so that they drop straight down the center of the body. Begin with three scarves as described for three-scarf cascading. Toss the first scarf from the hand holding two scarves.

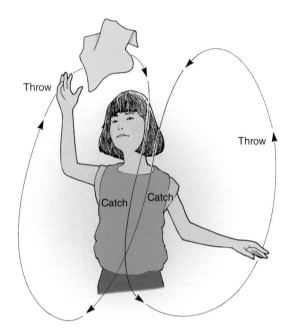

FIGURE 17.12 Reverse Cascading.

Column Juggling

Column juggling is so named because the scarves move straight up and down, as if they were inside a large pipe or column, and do not cross the body. To perform three-scarf column juggling, begin with two scarves in one hand and one in the other hand. From the hand that has two scarves, toss a scarf straight up the midline of the body and overhead. When this scarf reaches its peak, toss the other two scarves upward along the sides of the body (figure 17.13). Catch the first scarf with either hand and toss it upward again. Catch the other two scarves and toss them upward, continuing the pattern.

Showering

Showering is more difficult than cascading because the hands move rapidly and less time is available for catching and tossing. The scarves move in a circle following each other. For maximum challenge, students can practice in both directions

Start with two scarves in the right hand and one in the left. Begin by throwing the first two scarves from the right hand. Toss the scarves in a large circle away from the midline of the body and overhead as high as possible. As soon as the second scarf is released, toss the scarf across from the left hand to the right and then toss the scarf in the opposite hand and catch the first scarf with this hand also. Finish by tossing the last scarf (figure 17.14). All scarves are caught with the left hand and passed to the right hand.

17

FIGURE 17.13 Column Juggling.

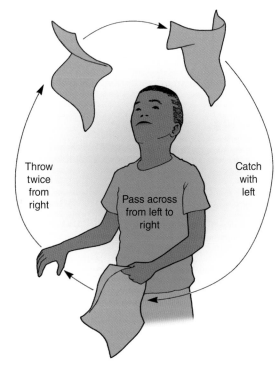

Throw twice from right

Pass across from left to right

Catch with left

FIGURE 17.14 Showering with scarves.

Juggling Challenges

1. While cascading, toss a scarf under one leg.

2. While cascading, toss a scarf from behind the back.

3. Instead of catching one of the scarves, blow it upward with a strong breath of air.

4. Begin cascading by tossing the first scarf into the air with a foot. Lay the scarf across the foot and kick it into the air.

5. Try juggling three scarves with one hand. Do not worry about establishing a pattern; just catch the lowest scarf each time. Try both regular and reverse cascading as well as column juggling.

6. While doing column juggling, toss up one scarf, hold the other two, and make a full turn. Resume juggling.

7. Juggle three scarves while standing alongside a partner with inside arms around each other. (This is actually easy to do, because it is regular three-scarf cascading.)

8. Try juggling more than three scarves (up to six) with a partner.

Juggling With Balls

Two balls can be juggled with one hand, and three balls can be juggled with two hands. Balls can be juggled using cascading or showering. Cascading, considered the easier of the two styles, should be the first one attempted.

Instructional Procedures

1. Juggling requires accurate, consistent tossing, which is the first emphasis. Toss the ball to the same height on both sides of the body—about 2 to 2.5 feet (60 to 75 cm) upward and across the body, because the ball is tossed from one hand to the other. Practice tossing the ball parallel to the body; the most common problem in juggling is that the balls are tossed forward and the juggler has to move forward to catch them.

2. Use the fingers, not the palms, when tossing and catching. Stress relaxed wrist action.

3. Instruct students to look upward and watch the balls at the peak of their flight, rather than watching the hands. Focus on where the ball peaks, not on the hands.

4. The balls are caught about waist height and released a little above this level.

5. Two balls must be carried in the starting hand, and the art of releasing only one must be mastered.

6. Students progress from working first with one ball, then two balls, and finally three balls (figure 17.15).

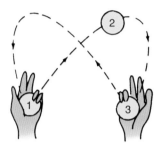

FIGURE 17.15   Cascading with three balls.

Recommended Progression for Cascading

1. Using one ball and one hand only, toss the ball upward (2 to 2.5 feet [60 to 75 cm]), and catch it with the same hand. Begin with the dominant hand and later practice with the other. Toss quickly, with wrist action. Then handle the ball alternately with right and left hands, tossing from one hand to the other.

2. Now, with one ball in each hand, alternate tossing a ball upward and catching it in the same hand so that one ball is always in the air. Begin again with a ball in each hand. Toss across the body to the other hand. To keep the balls from colliding, toss under the incoming ball. After acquiring some skill, try alternating the two kinds of tosses by doing a set number (four to six) of each before shifting to the other.

3. Hold two balls in the starting hand and one in the other. Toss one of the balls in the starting hand, toss the ball from the other hand, and then toss the third ball.

Recommended Progression for Showering

1. The showering motion is usually counterclockwise. Hold one ball in each hand. Begin by tossing with the right hand on an inward path and then immediately toss the other ball from the left directly across the body to the right hand. Continue this until the action is smooth.

2. Now, hold two balls in the right hand and one in the left. Toss the first ball from the right hand on an inward path and immediately toss the second

on the same path. At about the same time, toss the ball from the left hand directly across the body to the right hand (figure 17.16).

3. A few children may be able to change from cascading to showering, and vice versa. This skill is quite a challenge.

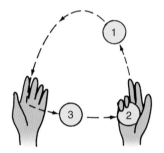

FIGURE 17.16   Showering with three balls.

Activities With Scoops and Balls

Scoops can be purchased (figure 17.17) or made with bleach bottles or similar containers (see chapter 12). They are excellent for practicing catching and tossing skills using an implement rather than the hands. The following activities are recommended.

FIGURE 17.17   Catching a ball with a scoop.

17

Individual Activities

1. Put the ball on the floor and pick it up with the scoop. Toss the ball up and catch it with the scoop. Throw the ball against a wall and catch it in the scoop. Put the ball in the scoop, throw it in the air, and catch it. Throw the ball against a wall with the scoop and catch it with the scoop.

2. Throw the ball, switch the scoop to the opposite hand, and catch in the scoop. Use the scoop to toss the ball up, do a stunt such as a Heel Click or a body turn, and catch the ball in the scoop.

3. Toss the ball up and catch it as low as possible. As high as possible. Toss it a little higher each time and catch it in the scoop. Tell students to toss the ball so that they have to stretch to catch it. (Most activities should begin with a toss from the free hand and later add a toss from the scoop.)

Partner Activities

1. One partner rolls the ball on the floor, and the other catches it in the scoop. Partners throw the ball back and forth and catch it in the scoop. Challenge students to play One Step while playing catch.

2. One partner tosses the ball from the scoop, and the other partner catches. Throw the ball from the scoop at different levels and catch it at different levels. Throw and catch from various positions, such as sitting, back-to-back, prone, and kneeling.

3. Work with more than one partner, with more than one ball, and with a scoop in each hand.

Games and Relays

Many games and relays can be played using scoops. Modified lacrosse can be played using the scoops and a Wiffle ball. Set up a lesson in which children devise games for themselves using the scoop and a ball.

Bowling Activities

Before bowling, younger children should practice informal rolling. As they mature, begin to emphasize bowling skills. Bowling skills begin with a two-handed roll and progress to one-handed rolls, alternating between the right and left hand. Various targets can be used—bowling pins, milk cartons, small cones, blocks, and even people.

The 8.5-inch (22 cm) foam or playground ball is excellent for teaching bowling skills. Volleyballs and soccer balls also can be used. Stress moderate speed in rolling the ball. The ball should roll off the fingertips with good follow-through.

The four-step approach is the accepted form for tenpin bowling. Here is the technique, in brief, for a right-handed bowler.

> **Starting position:** Stand with the feet together and the ball held comfortably in both hands in front of the body.
>
> **Step 1:** Step forward with the right foot, pushing the ball forward with both hands and a little to the right.
>
> **Step 2:** Step with the left foot, allowing the ball to swing down alongside the leg on its way into the backswing.
>
> **Step 3:** Step with the right foot. The ball reaches the height of the backswing with this step.
>
> **Step 4:** Step with the left foot and bowl the ball forward.

For instructional cues, the teacher can call out this four-step sequence: "Out," "Down," "Back," and "Roll."

Bowling activities are organized mostly as partner or group work. When using targets, have two children stand near the target end. One child resets the target, while the other recovers the ball. The following are partner activities unless otherwise noted. A fine game for rounding off the activities is Bowling One Step.

Recommended Activities

1. Use a wide-straddle stance and begin with two-handed rolls from between the legs.

2. Roll the ball first with the right and then with the left hand. The receiver can use the foot pickup, done by hoisting the ball to the hands using the extended toes.

3. Practice putting different kinds of spin (English) on the ball. (For a right-handed bowler, a curve to the left is called a hook ball and a curve to the right is a backup ball.)

4. Get into groups of three and use human straddle targets. Using a stick 2 feet (60 cm) long, make marks on the floor for the target child, who stands between the two bowlers. The target child stands with the inside edges of the shoes on the marks, thus standardizing the target spread. (Targets must keep their legs straight and motionless

during the bowling. Otherwise, they can make or avoid contact with the ball and upset the scoring system.) Start from a moderate distance (15 to 20 feet [4.5 to 6 m]), and adjust as proficiency increases. Scoring can be 2 points for a ball that goes through the legs without touching and 1 point for a ball that goes through but touches the leg.

5. Use milk cartons or bowling pins as targets. Begin with one and progress to two or three. (Plastic bowling pins are available. Other targets might be a wastebasket lying on its side—the ball is rolled into it—or a 3-pound [1.4 kg] coffee can for a smaller ball.)

Activities With Wands

Wands have been used in physical education programs for many years and now offer a wide variety of interesting and challenging activities. Wands can be made from 3/4-inch (19 mm) maple dowels or from broom and mop handles. If two lengths are chosen, make them 36 and 42 inches (90 and 105 cm). If only one size is to be used, a length of 1 meter (39 inches) is recommended. Wands are more interesting when painted with imaginative designs—this can be a class project. Wands are noisy when they hit the floor. Gluing rubber crutch tips on the ends of a wand alleviates most of the noise and makes it easier to pick up.

Instructional Procedures

1. Because wands are noisy when dropped, have the children hold their wands with both hands or put them on the floor during instruction.

2. Many wand activities require great flexibility, which means that not all children are able to do them. Girls usually perform better than boys at flexibility stunts.

3. Give each child adequate space because wand stunts demand room.

4. To avoid injuries, do not allow children to misuse wands (or other potentially dangerous equipment).

Recommended Activities

Wands can be used for challenge activities that offer a relatively unstructured approach. Here are some of the many possible challenges:

1. Can you reach down and pick up your wand without bending your knees?

2. Try to balance your wand on different body parts. Watch the top of the wand for cues on keeping it balanced.

3. Can you hold your wand against the wall and move over and under it?

4. Let's see if you can hold the wand at both ends and move through the gap.

5. Can you spin the wand and keep it going like a windmill?

6. See how many different ways you can move over and around your wand when it is on the floor.

7. Put one end of the wand on the floor and hold the other end. How many times can you run around your wand without getting dizzy?

8. Place one end of the wand against a wall. Holding the other end and keeping the wand against the wall, duck under it. Place the wand lower and lower on the wall and go under it.

9. Place the wand between your feet and hop around as though you are on a pogo stick.

10. Throw your wand into the air and catch it.

11. Hold the wand vertically near the middle. Can you release your grip and catch the wand before it falls to the floor?

12. Have a partner hold a wand horizontally above the floor. Jump, leap, and hop over the wand. Gradually raise the height of the wand.

13. Put your wand on the floor and try making different kinds of bridges over it.

14. Place the wand on the floor. Curl your body into a ball alongside it, just touching it. Curl your body at one end of the wand.

15. Balance the wand vertically on the floor. Release the wand and try some stunts—clap hands, do a Heel Click, touch different body parts—before the wand falls to the floor.

16. Put the wand on the floor and see how many ways you can push it, using different body parts.

Individual Wand Stunts

Wand Catch

Stand a wand on one end and hold it in place with the fingers on the tip. Loop the foot quickly over the stick, letting go of the wand briefly but catching it with the fingers before it falls. Do this with the right and left hand for a complete set. Try to catch the wand with just the index finger.

17

Thread the Needle (V-Seat)

Maintaining a V-seat position, with the wand held in front of the body with both hands, bend the knees between the arms and pass the wand over them and return, without touching the wand to the legs. Try with the ankles crossed.

Thread the Needle (Standing)

Holding the wand in both hands, step through the space, one leg at a time, and return without touching the wand. Step through again, but this time bring the wand up behind the back, over the head, and down in front. Reverse. Try from side to side with the stick held front and back.

Grapevine

Holding the wand near the ends, step with the right foot around the right arm and over the wand inward, toward the body (figure 17.18). Pass the wand backward over the head and right shoulder (figure 17.19), and continue sliding the wand down the body until you are standing erect with the wand between the legs. Reverse the process. Try with the left foot leading.

Back Scratcher

Hold the wand with an underhand grip (palms up), arms crossed in front of the body (figure 17.20). Bend the elbows so that the wand can go over and behind the head. Try to pass the wand down the length of the body from the back of the shoulders to the heels. Do not release the grip on the wand. The wand is worked down behind the back, while the arms stay in front of the body.

Wand Whirl

Stand the wand upright in front of the body. Turn around quickly and grasp the wand before it falls. Do the movement both right and left. Try making two full turns and still catching the wand before it falls.

Twist Under

Grasp the upright wand with the right hand. Twist around under the right arm without letting go of the wand, taking it off the floor, or touching the knee to the floor. Repeat, using the left arm.

FIGURE 17.18 Beginning the Grapevine.

FIGURE 17.19 Grapevine, stage 2 (head ducks under, and wand is pulled down the back).

FIGURE 17.20 Back Scratcher (wand has been passed overhead and is now being forced down the back).

Jump Wand

Holding the wand in front of the feet with the fingertips of both hands, jump over it. Jumping back is not recommended, because the wand can hit the heels and cause an awkward fall. (If children are having difficulty, replace the wand with a rope or a towel.)

Balancing the Wand

Balance the wand vertically with one hand. Experiment with different hand and finger positions. Walk forward, backward, and sideward. Sit down, lie down, and move into other positions while keeping the wand balanced. Keep the eyes on the top of the wand. Balance the wand horizontally on the hands, arms, feet, and thighs. Balance it across the back of the neck. In crab position, balance it across the tummy.

The Sprinter

Get into a sprinter's position, with the wand on the floor, between the feet, and perpendicular to the direction of the sprint. Change the feet rapidly, alternating over the wand. Try moving both feet together forward and backward over the wand.

Crab Leap

Place the wand on the floor. Get into crab position and attempt to move the feet back and forth over the wand without touching it. Try this with alternating feet.

Long Reach

Stand with legs extended and feet spread about 12 inches (30 cm) apart. Hold a wand in the left hand and use it like a third limb. With a piece of chalk in the right hand, reach forward as far as possible and make a mark. Use the wand as a support and see if the mark can be bettered.

Wand Bridge

On a mat, start in a straddle stance with legs straight. Hold a wand near one end, with the other end above the head and pointed toward the ceiling. Bend backward, place the wand on the mat behind you, and walk the hands down the wand. Return to standing position.

Wand Twirl

Children in the class who have baton-twirling experience can show the class some points of technique.

Partner Wand Stunts

Partner Catch

Partners face each other a short distance (5 feet [150 cm]) apart, each holding a wand in the right hand. On signal, each throws the wand to the partner with the right hand and catches the incoming wand with the left. Distances can be increased somewhat.

Partner Change

Partners face each other a short distance (5 feet [150 cm]) apart. Each has a wand standing upright, held on top by the right hand. On signal, each runs to the other's wand and tries to catch it before it falls. This activity can also be done in the same way as the Wand Whirl, with each whirling to the other's wand. Try with a small group of five or six. On signal, all move to the next wand.

Wring the Dishrag

Partners face each other and grasp a wand. When ready, they perform a dishrag turn.

Jump the Wand

One partner moves the wand back and forth along the floor, and the other partner jumps over it. To add challenge, partners can change the tempo and raise the wand.

17

Wand Reaction

One partner holds the wand horizontally. The other partner places one hand directly above the wand, palm down. When the first partner drops the wand, the second partner tries to catch it before it strikes the floor.

Cooperative Movements

Holding a wand between them, partners stand toe-to-toe and circle either way with light foot movements. Together, partners squat down and stand up. Sit down and come up. Kneel and hold the wand overhead as they face each other. Bend sideways and touch the wand to the floor.

Isometric Exercises With Wands

The isometric exercises (muscle contractions without movement) with wands presented here are mainly grip exercises. Have children use a variety of grips. With the wand horizontal, use either the overhand or underhand grip. With the wand vertical, grip with the thumbs pointed up, down, or toward each other. Repeat each exercise with a different grip. Exercises can also be repeated with the wand in different positions: in front of the body (either horizontal or vertical), overhead, or behind the back. Hold each exercise for 8 to 12 seconds.

Pull the Wand Apart

Place the hands 6 inches (15 cm) apart near the center of the wand. With a tight grip to prevent slippage and with arms extended, try to pull the hands apart. Change grip and position.

Push the Wand Together

Hold the wand as previously, except attempt to push the hands together.

Wand Twist

Hold the wand with both hands about 6 inches (15 cm) apart. Twist the hands in opposite directions.

Bicycle

Holding the wand horizontally using an overhand grip, extend the wand out and down. Bring it upward near the body, completing a circular movement. On the downward movement, push the wand together, and on the upward movement, pull the wand apart.

Arm Spreader

Hold the wand overhead with hands spread wide. At-

tempt to compress the stick. Reverse force and attempt to pull the stick apart.

Dead Lift

Partially squat and place the wand under the thighs. Place the hands between the legs and try to lift. Try also with hands on the outside of the legs.

Abdominal Tightener

From a standing position, place the wand behind the buttocks. With hands on the ends of the wand, pull forward and resist with the abdominal muscles.

Stretching Exercises With Wands

Wands are useful for stretching, bending, and twisting movements.

Side Bender

Grip the wand and extend the arms overhead with feet apart. Bend sideways as far as possible, maintaining straight arms and legs. Recover and bend to the other side.

Body Twist

Place the wand behind the neck, with arms draped over the wand from behind. Rotate the upper body first to the right as far as possible and then to the left. The feet and hips stay in position. The twist is at the waist.

Body Twist to Knee

Assume body twist position. Bend the trunk forward and twist so that the right end of the wand touches the left knee (figure 17.21). Recover and touch the left end to the right knee.

Shoulder Stretcher

Grip the wand at the ends in a regular grip. Extend the arms overhead and rotate the wand, arms, and shoulders backward until the stick touches the back of the legs. Keep the arms straight. Those who find the stretch too easy can move their hands closer to the center of the wand.

Toe Touch

Grip the wand with the hands about shoulder-width apart. Bend forward, reaching down as far as possible without bending the knees. The movement is slow and controlled. Try the same activity while sitting.

©Robert Pangrazi or Aaron Beighle

FIGURE 17.21   Body Twist to Knee.

Over the Toes

Sit down, flex the knees, pass the wand over the toes, and rest it against the middle of the arch on the bottoms of the feet. Grip the stick with the fingers at the outside edge of the feet. Slowly extend the legs forward, pushing against the stick and trying to extend the legs fully.

Activities With Hoops

Most hoops made in the United States are plastic, but Europeans sometimes use wooden ones. Plastic hoops are less durable but more versatile. Extra hoops are needed because some breakage will occur. The standard hoop is 42 inches (105 cm) in diameter, but smaller hoops (36 inches [90 cm]) work better with primary-grade children.

Instructional Procedures

1. Hoop activities are quite noisy. Have the children lay their hoops on the floor when they are to listen.

2. Hoops can be a creative medium for children. Give them free time to explore their own ideas.

3. Give the children enough space in which to perform, because hoops require much movement.

4. In activities that require children to jump through hoops, instruct the holder to grasp the hoop lightly, so as not to cause an awkward fall if a performer hits it.

5. Hoops can serve as a "home" for various activities. For instance, the children might leave their hoops to gallop in all directions and then return quickly to the hoop on command.

6. Hoops are good targets. To make a hoop stand up, place an individual mat over its base.

7. When teaching the reverse spin with hoops, have the students throw the hoop up, in place, rather than forward along the floor. After learning the upward throw, they can progress to the forward throw for distance.

Recommended Activities

Hoops as Floor Targets

Each child has a hoop, which is placed on the floor. Various movement challenges can give direction to the activity.

1. Show the different patterns you can make by jumping or hopping in and out of the hoop.

2. Do a Rabbit Jump and a Frog Jump into the center and out the other side.

3. Show the ways you can cross from one side of the hoop to the other by taking the weight on your hands inside the hoop.

4. What kinds of animal walks can you do around your hoop?

5. On all fours, show the kinds of movements you can do with your feet inside the hoop and your hands outside. With your hands inside the hoop and your feet outside. With one foot and one hand inside, and one foot and one hand outside.

6. (Set a time limit of 15 to 30 seconds.) See how many times you can jump in and out of your hoop during this time. Now try hopping.

7. Balance on and walk around the hoop. Try to keep your feet from touching the floor.

8. Curl your body inside the hoop. Bridge over your hoop. Stretch across your hoop. See how many different ways you can move around the hoop.

17

9. Pick up your hoop and see how many different machines you can invent. Let your hoop be the steering wheel of a car. What could it be on a train or a boat?

10. Jump in and out of the hoop, using the alphabet. Jump in on the vowels and out on the consonants. Use odd and even numbers in the same way. Vary the locomotor movements.

11. Get into the hoop by using two different body parts. Move out by using three parts. Vary the number of body parts used.

12. Get organized in squads or comparable groups and divide the hoops. Arrange the hoops in various formations and try different locomotor movements, animal walks, and other ways of maneuvering through the maze. (When the children are more experienced, this can become a follow-the-leader activity.)

Hoop Handling

1. Spin the hoop like a top. See how long you can make it spin. Spin it again and see how many times you can run around it before it falls to the floor.

2. Hula-hoop using various body parts such as the waist, legs, arms, and fingers. While hula-hooping on the arms, try to change the hoop from one arm to the other. Lie on the back with one or both legs pointed toward the ceiling and explore different ways that the legs can twirl the hoop. Hula-hoop with two or more hoops.

3. Jump or hop through a hoop held by a partner. For a greater challenge, vary the height and angle of the hoop.

4. Roll the hoop and run alongside it. On signal, change direction.

5. Hula-hoop on one arm. Throw the hoop in the air and catch it on the other arm.

6. Hold the hoop and swing it like a pendulum. Jump and hop in and out of the hoop.

7. Use the hoop like a jump rope. Jump forward, backward, and sideward. Do a crossover with the hands.

8. Roll the hoop with a reverse spin to make it return to you. The key to the reverse spin is to pull down (toward the floor) on the hoop as it is released. Roll the hoop with a reverse spin, jump over it, and catch it as it returns. Roll the hoop with a reverse spin; as it returns, hoist it with the foot and catch it. Roll the hoop with a reverse spin, kick it up with the toe, and go through the hoop. Roll the hoop with a reverse spin, run around it, and catch it. Roll the hoop with a reverse spin, pick it up, and begin hooping on the arm—all in one motion.

9. Play catch with a partner. Try with two or more hoops.

10. Hula-hoop. Attempt to change hoops with a partner.

11. Have one partner roll the hoop with a reverse spin and the other attempt to crawl through the hoop. (This is done most easily just after the hoop reverses direction and begins to return to the spinner. Some children can go in and out of the hoop twice.)

12. Tell partners to spin the hoops like tops and see who can keep theirs spinning longer.

Games With Hoops

Cooperative Musical Hoops

Hoops, one per student, are placed on the floor. Give players a locomotor movement to do. On signal, they cease the movement, find a hoop, and sit cross-legged in the center of it. Music can be used, with the children moving to the music and seeking a hoop when the music stops. The teacher can remove some hoops, challenging students to share hoops with each other. This activity can continue until all students are in three or four hoops.

Around the Hoop

Divide the class into groups of three; children in each group are numbered 1, 2, and 3. Each threesome sits back-to-back inside a hoop. Their heels may need to be outside the hoop. The leader calls out a direction (right or left) and names one of the numbers. The child with that number immediately gets up, runs in the indicated direction around the hoop, and then runs back to place and sits down. The winner is the first group sitting in good position after the child returns to place.

Hula-Hoop Circle

Four to six children hold hands in a circle, facing in, with a hoop dangling on one pair of joined hands. They move the hoop around the circle and back to the starting point. All bodies must go through the hoop. Hands can help the hoop move, but grips cannot be released.

Hula-Hoop Relay

Relay teams of four to six players, each with a hoop, are placed in line or circle formation. The hoop must be held upright with the bottom of the hoop touching the floor. On signal, designated starters drop their hoops and move through the hoops held by squad members. Repeat the sequence until every player has moved through the hoops.

Bumper Car Tag

Divide the class into pairs. Each pair stands inside a hoop held at waist level—the "bumper car." Three or more sets of partners are declared to be "it." The object is to tag other partners, who are also moving inside a bumper car. The game can also be played with three players in a hoop. This activity is challenging, because players will want to move in different directions.

Hoop Addition Relay

Divide the class into relay teams of four. On signal, the first person moves to the end marker (a hoop), returns, and takes the next person to the marker, and so on, until all four players are in the hoop. Players must sit down in the hoop when the relay is completed.

Activities With Jump Ropes

Rope jumping is an excellent activity for conditioning all parts of the body. It increases coordination, rhythm, and timing while offering a wide range of challenges. Rope jumping can be designed to suit the activity needs of all people regardless of age or condition. Workloads can easily be measured and modified by changing the amount of time jumped or the number of turns. It is a useful activity to teach children because of its carryover value for activity in later life.

Rope jumping has increased in popularity during the past decade. This nationwide movement has spawned school teams, exhibitions, and competition in the form of state and national tournaments. It is a creative medium with many possible variations. Rope-jumping skills in this chapter are suitable for use in an elementary school physical education program. Highly advanced and complex activities, such as those often used by competitive clubs, are not included because they are less suitable for giving success to all children in physical education programs. For more information about advanced activities, see the references at the end of the chapter. Rope-jumping activities in this chapter are grouped into three categories: (1) movements guided by rope patterns, (2) long-rope jumping, and (3) individual rope jumping.

Pre–Rope-Jumping Skills

As a prelude to rope-jumping skills, ropes can be placed on the floor in various ways to stimulate different locomotor and nonlocomotor movements. Teachers can interweave educational movement factors of space, time, force, and flow in the activity. Students can perform the challenges as individuals, with partners, or in a small group. Generally, a rope is placed in a straight line or in a circle. Geometric figures can also be formed, and numbers or letters of the alphabet can be featured.

Rope Forming a Straight Line

When the rope is placed in a straight line, one approach is for children to begin at one end and perform the activities along the length of the rope. Many of the movements are based on hopping or jumping. The children then return to the starting point and prepare for another activity. Here are some examples of pre–rope-jumping activities:

1. Jog around the rope forward and backward. Try other locomotor skills such as hopping, jumping, skipping, and sliding. Do the Crab Walk down and back. Use various animal walks, such as Bear Walk or Lame Dog Walk.

2. Hop back and forth across the rope, moving down the line. Return, using the other foot.

3. Jump lightly back and forth down the line. Return.

4. Hop slowly, under control, down the line. Hop rapidly back.

5. Jump so that the rope is between the feet each time, alternately crossing and uncrossing the feet.

6. Move on all fours, leading with different body parts.

7. Do Crouch Jumps back and forth across the rope. Vary with three points and then two points of contact.

8. Jump as high as possible while going down the line and as low as possible coming back.

9. Hop with a narrow shape down and a different shape back.

10. Walk the rope like a tightrope.

11. Begin with a bridge and move the bridge down the line. Return with a different bridge.

12. Lie across the rope, holding one end. Roll down the line, causing the rope to roll around the body. Unroll the rope back to position.

17

13. Do a movement with the rhythm slow-slow, fast-fast-fast, going down the line; repeat it coming back.

14. "Pull" yourself down the line and "push" yourself back.

For the following movements, the child is positioned close to the center of the line and simply moves back and forth across it without changing the relative position.

1. Hop back and forth across the line. Jump back and forth.

2. Go over with a high movement. Come back with a low one.

3. Do a Rabbit Jump across and back, a Frog Jump, and a Crouch Jump.

4. Lead with different parts of the body back and forth. Propel with different parts.

5. Get into a moderately crouched position over the rope. Jump the feet back and forth over the rope.

6. Take a sprinter's position with the rope between the feet. Alternate the feet back and forth over the rope.

7. Jump back and forth lightly on the tiptoes.

8. Go back and forth, using different shapes.

9. With toes touching the rope, drop the body forward across the rope, taking the weight on both hands. Walk the hands forward, out to the limit.

10. Pretend that the rope is a river. Show different kinds of bridges that you can make over the river.

11. Stand straddling the rope. Jump up, perform a Heel Click (or two), and return to original position.

Rope Forming a Circle

With the rope in a circle, children can move around the outside clockwise and counterclockwise—walking, skipping, hopping, sliding (facing toward and away from the circle), jumping, running, and galloping. These activities also can be done with hoops.

1. Hop in and out of the circle, moving around. Jump.

2. Jump directly in and then across. Jump backward.

3. Jump in, collapse, and jump out, without touching the rope.

4. Begin in the center of the circle. Jump forward, backward, and sideways, each time returning to the center.

5. Place the feet in the circle and walk the hands all around the outside of the circle. Place the hands inside and the feet outside. Face the floor, the ceiling, and to the side.

6. Inside the circle, make a small shape. Make a large shape so that you are touching all sides of the circle.

7. Try different balance stunts inside the circle. Close your eyes and balance.

8. Make a bridge over the circle. How many types of bridges can you make?

9. Do a pogo stick jump in and out of the rope circle.

10. Do a Tightrope Walk clockwise and counterclockwise.

11. Jump and click the heels, landing inside the circle. Repeat, going out.

12. Do jump turns (quarter, half, full) inside the circle without touching the rope.

13. Jump in with a Rabbit Jump. Jump out. Try with a Frog Jump.

14. Take the weight on the hands inside the circle so that the feet land on the other side. Try a cartwheel.

Rope Forming Various Figures

Have the rope form different figures, such as geometric shapes, letters, and numbers. Besides the following challenges, many of the previous ones can be applied here.

1. With the rope and your body, form a triangle, a square, a rectangle, a diamond shape, and a figure eight.

2. With the rope and your body, form a two-letter word. Form other words.

3. Get a second rope and make your own patterns for hopping and jumping.

4. Toss the rope in the air and let it fall to the floor. Try to shape your body into the same figure that the rope made on the floor.

Partner Activity

Partner activity with ropes is excellent. Partners can work with one or two ropes and do matching, following, or contrasting movements. Add-On is an interesting game: One partner does an activity, and the other adds on an activity to form a sequence. Using the suggested rope forms (multiple ropes) in figure 17.22, one partner makes a series of movements. The other partner then tries to duplicate the movements.

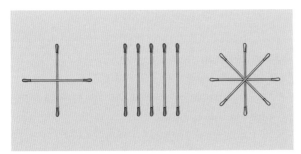

FIGURE 17.22 Suggested rope forms.

Group Activity

Group activity with jump ropes has many possibilities. Each child brings a rope to the group. Patterns for hopping, jumping, and other locomotor movements can be arranged with the ropes. An achievement demonstration after a practice period allows each group to show the patterns and movements they have devised. A further extension is to leave the patterns where they are and rotate the groups to different locations.

Long-Rope Jumping

Long-rope jumping is an excellent activity for beginning jumpers. Students can concentrate on jumping the rope without learning the skill of turning. Many activities with two or more long ropes add much variety to long-rope jumping and can make it challenging for the most skilled jumpers. Long jump ropes can be from 9 to 14 feet (2.7 to 4.3 m) and are typically 12 to 14 feet (3.7 to 4.3 m). The exact length depends on the children's age and skill; the longer the rope, the harder it is to turn. For primary-grade children, use individual jump ropes to teach beginning skills. Individual ropes are shorter and thus easier for young children to turn. Another alternative is to fasten one end of the rope with a snap to an eyebolt fixed on a post or to the side of a wall. This setup makes turning easier and allows more children to be actively jumping.

Chants are suggested for many of the jumping sequences. Rope-jumping chants represent a cultural heritage. In many cases, children have their own favorites. Traditionally, many chants used girls' names, because rope jumping was considered a feminine activity. Today, however, this has changed; both sexes participate in rope-jumping activities. Several of the chants included were modified to reflect this change.

Instructional Procedures

1. Groups of four or five children are best for practicing long-rope skills. Two members of the group turn the rope while the others practice jumping. A plan for rotating turners is important, so that all the children can practice jumping.

2. Turning the rope is a difficult skill for young children. Tell students they must learn to turn before learning to jump. Have them practice regularly until they can maintain an even, steady rhythm. Effective turning is one key to successful jumping. If turning is not rhythmic, even skilled jumpers will have problems.

3. When teaching students rope turning, focus on these points:

   a. Keep the elbow close to the body, and concentrate on turning the rope with the forearm.
   b. The thumb stays up during the turning motion of the hands. This positioning emphasizes turning with the forearm.
   c. Hold the rope in front of the body at waist level. Keep the body perpendicular to the rope.

4. Motivate students by having them turn the rope under a lively bouncing ball. Turners stand ready, and a third child tosses a ball upward so that it stays in one spot while bouncing. Turners adjust their turning as the bounces become smaller and faster. Turners can count the number of turns made before the ball stops bouncing.

5. Children of all ages can perform long-rope jumping. To check readiness, see if the children are capable of jumping in place with both feet leaving the ground simultaneously. They should be able to jump at least 2 to 3 inches (5 to 7.5 cm) off the ground, be well balanced, and land lightly with fairly straight knees.

6. Teach children the terms used to describe entering the long jump rope. Front door means entering from the side where the rope is turning forward and toward the jumper after it reaches its peak. Back door means entering from the side where the rope is turning backward and away

17

from the jumper. To enter front door, the jumper follows the rope in and jumps when it completes the turn. To enter back door, the jumper waits until the rope reaches its peak and moves in as the rope moves downward. Learning to enter at an angle is usually easier, but any path that is comfortable is acceptable.

7. Introduce students to long-rope jumping skills using the following steps:

   a. Use a shorter long rope (8 to 12 foot [2.4 to 3.7 m]). Lay the rope on the floor and have students jump back and forth across the rope. Stress making small, continuous jumps and learning to jump back and forth without stopping. Jumps are not high, just enough to clear the rope.

   b. Turners slowly move the rope back and forth along the floor while the jumper moves over the rope each time it moves near. The speed of the rope moving along the floor increases gradually. Encourage the jumper to jump up and down with as little forward-backward-sideways movement as possible. If necessary, use white shoe polish to mark an "X" on the floor and encourage the child to stay on target.

   c. The jumper stands near the center of the rope. The rope is moved like a pendulum back and forth, and the jumper clears the rope each time it hits the floor. This activity is often called Blue Bells.

   d. The jumper starts by facing the center of the stationary rope. Use three pendulum swings followed by a full turn of the rope, rotating from the jumper's back to the front. Continue jumping until a miss occurs. Verbal cueing helps most beginners find success; each time the rope hits the floor, say, "Jump." If students are having difficulty, have them stand behind a turner and jump (without the rope) each time the rope hits the floor.

   e. When jumpers have difficulty jumping rhythmically, they can practice off to one side without actually jumping over the rope. A drumbeat can reinforce the rhythm with alternating heavy (jump) and light (rebound) beats.

   f. Teach front-door and back-door entry, making sure that jumpers enter at an angle rather than perpendicular to the rope.

8. Instructional cues for long-rope jumping skills:

   a. Turn the rope with the forearm.

   b. Lock the wrist and keep the thumb up while turning.

   c. Stand perpendicular to the rope.

   d. Barely touch the floor with the turning rope.

   e. Do not cross the midline of the body with the forearm while turning the rope.

   f. Jump on the balls of the feet.

   g. To enter, stand near the turner and move to the center of the rope.

Introductory Skills

Some introductory skills and routines follow.

1. Holders grip the rope loosely, in a stationary position 6 inches (15 cm) above the ground. Jumpers jump over, back and forth. Raise the rope a little each time. This activity is called Building a House.

2. Ocean Wave is another stationary jumping activity. Holders make waves in the rope by moving the arms up and down. Jumpers try to time it so that they jump over a low part of the wave.

3. Holders stoop down and wiggle the rope back and forth on the floor. Jumpers try to jump over the rope and not touch it as it moves. This activity is called Snake in the Grass.

4. The jumper stands in the center between the turners, who carefully turn the rope in a complete arc over the jumper's head. As the rope completes the turn, the jumper jumps over it and exits immediately in the direction in which the rope is turned.

5. Children run through the turning rope (front door) without jumping, following the rope through.

6. While the rope is being turned, the jumper runs in (front door), jumps once, and runs out immediately.

7. Children can play school by trying to pass to the sixth grade. To pass kindergarten, run through

the turning rope. To pass first grade, run in, take one jump, and run out. For the second through sixth grades, increase the number of jumps by one for each grade. A jumper who misses becomes a turner.

8. When children can jump several times consecutively, add motivation by using some of the following chants.

Intermediate Skills, Routines, and Chants

Intermediate routines require jumpers to go in front door, jump, and exit front door, and to do the same sequence back door. Practice the simple jumping skills and exits enough to fortify students' confidence; they can then turn to more intricate routines. Entries and exits should be varied in the following routines.

1. Jumpers run in, jump a specified number of times, and exit.

2. Children can add chants that dictate the number of jumps, which are followed by an exit. Here are some examples:

   Tick tock, tick tock,

   What's the time by the clock?

   It's one, two, [up to midnight].

   I like coffee, I like tea,

   How many people can jump like me?

   One, two, three, [up to a certain number].

   Hippity hop to the butcher shop,

   How many times before I stop?

   One, two, three, [and so on].

   Bulldog, poodle, bow wow,

   How many doggies have we now?

   One, two, three, [and so on].

   Michael, Michael (student's name) at the gate,

   Eating cherries from a plate.

   How many cherries did he (she) eat?

   One, two, three, [and so on].

3. Children can label their first jump "kindergarten" and exit at any "grade." To graduate from high school, the exit is at grade 12. Have them call out each grade as they jump.

4. Kangaroo (or White Horse) gets its name from the jump required for back-door entry, in which the jumper resembles a kangaroo or a leaping horse. The jumper calls out, "Kangaroo!" enters through the back door, and exits. Next time, the same jumper calls out, "Kangaroo one!" and adds a jump. Successive jumps are called and added until reaching a designated number.

5. An interesting challenge is to turn the rope over a line parallel to it and have the jumper jump back and forth over the line. The jumper can vary foot position: feet together, feet apart, stride forward and back.

6. Jumpers can vary the pattern with turns. Make four quarter-turns until facing the original direction. Reverse the direction of the turns.

7. Students can add stunts as directed by selected chants.

   Teddy Bear, Teddy Bear, turn around.

   Teddy Bear, Teddy Bear, touch the ground.

   Teddy Bear, Teddy Bear, show your shoe.

   Teddy Bear, Teddy Bear, you better skidoo.

   Teddy Bear, Teddy Bear, go upstairs.

   Teddy Bear, Teddy Bear, say your prayers.

   Teddy Bear, Teddy Bear, turn out the light.

   Teddy Bear, Teddy Bear, say good night.

   Daddy, daddy (mommy, mommy), I am sick.

   Get the doctor quick, quick, quick.

   Daddy, daddy, turn around.

   Daddy, daddy, touch the ground.

   Daddy, daddy, are you through?

   Daddy, daddy, spell your name.

8. In Hot Pepper, turners turn the rope faster and faster, while the jumper tries to keep up. These chants are good for Hot Pepper.

   Charlie, Charlie (student's name), set the table.

   Bring the plates if you are able.

   Don't forget the salt and

   Red hot pepper!

17

(On the words Red hot pepper, the rope is turned as fast as possible until the jumper misses.)

Pease porridge hot, please porridge cold,

Pease porridge in a pot, nine days old.

Some like it hot, hot, hot!

Ice cream, ginger ale, soda water, pop.

You get ready 'cause we're gonna turn hot!

9. In Calling In, the first player enters the rope and calls in a second player by name. Both jump three times, holding hands, and then the first runs out. The second player then calls in a third player by name. Both jump three times, holding hands, and the second player exits. Players should be in an informal line, because the fun comes from not knowing when a player is to enter.

10. Children can enter and exit according to the call in the following chants.

    In the shade and under a tree,

    I'd like _____ to come in with me.

    She's (he's) too fast and I'm too slow.

    He (she) stays in and I must go.

    Calling in and calling out,

    I call (student's name) in and I'm getting out.

    House for rent,

    Inquire within.

    When I move out,

    Let (student's name) move in.

11. In High Water, the rope is turned so that it lifts higher and higher off the ground.

    At the beach, at the sea,

    The waves come almost to the knee.

    Higher, higher, [and so forth].

12. In Stopping the Rope, the jumper (*a*) stops and lets the rope hit the feet, (*b*) stops the rope by straddling it, (*c*) stops with the legs crossed and the rope between the feet, or (*d*) stops the rope by stamping on it. The following chant works well, with accompanying action as indicated.

    Junior, Junior, climb the tree.

    Junior, Junior, slap your knee.

    Junior, Junior, throw a kiss.

    Junior, Junior, time to miss.

13. Two, three, or four children can jump at a time. After achieving some skill, children in combination can run in, jump a specified number of times, and run out, keeping hands joined all the time.

14. Two, three, or four children can start as a small moving circle. They run in and jump in a circle, keeping the circle moving in one direction. They run out as a circle.

15. The jumper takes in a ball or other object. Bounce the ball while jumping. Try balancing a beanbag on a body part while jumping.

16. A partner stands ready with a ball and tosses it back and forth to the jumper.

17. For Chase the Rabbit, four or five jumpers are in single file with a leader, the Rabbit, at the head. The Rabbit jumps in any way he or she wishes, and all of the others must match the movements. Anyone who misses must go to the end of the line. A Rabbit who misses or stops the rope goes to the end of the line, and the next child becomes the new Rabbit. Set a limit on how long a Rabbit can stay at the head of the line.

18. In the activity On Four Cylinders, the challenge is to do activities in a series of fours—four of one kind of jump, four of another, and so on. Specify the number of series and let the children choose what they wish to include. (Tell the children that their "engines are running on four cylinders.")

19. In Begging, a jumper runs in and works his or her way up the rope toward one of the turners. As the jumper jumps, he or she says, "Father, Father, give me a dollar." The turner replies, "Go see your mother." The jumper works his or her way toward the other turner and says, "Mother, Mother, give me a dollar." The turner replies, "Go to your father." This continues until a miss occurs or until one of the turners says in reply, "Get out" or "Get lost," at which time the jumper exits.

20. In Setting the Table, a jumper enters and starts jumping. A partner stands ready with at least four beanbags. While the following verse is recited, the partner tosses in the beanbags one at a time, and the jumper catches and places them in a row on the side (with the upward swing of the rope) and then exits.

Debbie, Debbie (student's name), set the table (toss in one bag),

Bring the plates if you are able (toss in another bag),

Don't forget the bread and butter (toss in the other two bags).

21. Partners can go in and perform a number of stunts, such as Bouncing Ball (see figure 20.34), Wring the Dishrag, or Partner Hopping (see figure 20.73). Examine the partner stunts for other selections.

22. Children can enter and begin with a hop (one foot), then make a jump (two feet), add a hand touch next (two feet, one hand), and then jump with both hands and feet (two feet, two hands). Selected movements on hands and feet, such as Rabbit Jumps or Push-Ups, can be executed.

23. For jumping with the eyes closed, single or multiple jumpers enter and begin jumping to this chant.

Peanuts, popcorn, soda pop,

How many jumps before you stop?

Close your eyes and you will see

How many jumps that this will be!

The eyes remain closed during the jumping, which continues to a target number or a miss.

24. One or both turners can go inside and jump, turning with their outside hands. First attempts should begin with a pendulum swing and proceed to a full turn.

Double Dutch (Two-Rope) Jumping

Double Dutch rope jumping is popular on playgrounds and in gyms across the country. This type of jumping requires two rope turners using two long ropes that are turned in opposite directions. Turning two ropes at once requires practice, and time must be allotted for this. Handling two ropes is tiring, so rotate the turners frequently.

Instructional Procedures

1. Arm positions and turning motions are similar to turning a single long rope. In short, keep the upper arm stationary, rotate at the elbow with locked wrist, and keep the thumb up. Avoid crossing the midline of the body and establish an even cadence. Rotate the hands inward toward the midline of the body (right forearm counterclockwise and left forearm clockwise). Have students concentrate on the sound of the ropes hitting the floor so that they make an even, rhythmic beat.

2. Double Dutch turning takes considerable practice. Take time to teach it as a skill that is necessary for successful jumping experiences.

3. When entering, jumpers stand beside a turner and run into the ropes when the back rope (farther from the jumper) touches the floor. Teach the turners to say, "Go," each time the back rope touches the floor.

4. Concentrate on jumping in the center of the ropes facing a turner. Use white shoe polish to mark a jumping target.

5. Exit the ropes by facing and jumping toward one turner and exiting immediately after jumping. The exit is made as close to the turner's shoulder as possible.

6. Practice many of the skills listed in the section Long-Rope Jumping. Many of the chants and stunts provide challenge and variety to the unit.

Double Dutch Skills

- *Basic Jump on Both Feet.* Land on the balls of the feet, keeping ankles and knees together with hands across the tummy.

- *Turnaround.* Circle left or right using the basic jump. Begin circling slowly at first and then increase speed. To increase the challenge, try the Turnaround on one foot.

- *Straddle Jump.* Jump to the straddle position and return to closed position. Try a Straddle Cross Jump by crossing the legs on return to the closed position. Straddle Jumps are performed facing away from the turners.

- *Scissors Jump.* Jump to a stride position with the left foot forward and the right foot back, about 8 inches (20 cm) apart. Each jump requires reversing the position of the feet.

- *Jogging Step.* Run in place with a jogging step. Increase the challenge by circling while jogging.

- *Hot Peppers.* Use the Jogging Step and gradually increase the speed of the ropes.

- *Half-Turn.* Perform a half-turn with each jump.

17

Remember to lead the turn with the head and shoulders.

- *Ball Tossing*. Toss and catch a beanbag or playground ball while jumping.

- *Individual Rope Jumping*. Enter Double Dutch with an individual rope and jump. Face the turner and decrease the length of the individual jump rope.

Double Dutch Variations:

- *Double Irish*. Two ropes are turned in the reverse directions used in Double Dutch. The left hand turns counterclockwise and the right hand clockwise. Entry is made when the near rope hits the floor. Jumpers time their entry by following the near rope on its downward swing.

- *Egg Beater*. Two long ropes are turned at right angles simultaneously by four turners (figure 17.23). Entry is at the quadrant where both ropes are turning front doors. The number of ropes being turned can be increased to three or four. This activity is easier than jumping Double Dutch because the jumping action is similar to single-rope jumping, and it helps build confidence in jumping more than one long rope.

Formation Jumping

For formation jumping, four to six long ropes with turners can be placed in various patterns, with tasks specified for each rope. Ropes can be turned in the same direction, or the turning directions can be mixed. Several formations are illustrated in figure 17.24.

Individual Rope Jumping

Individual rope jumping should stress establishing basic turning skills and letting children create personal routines. Individual rope jumping is particularly valuable as part of the conditioning process for certain sports. It lends itself to prescribed doses based on number of turns, length of participation, speed of the turning rope, and various steps. Because rope jumping is rhythmic, adding music is a natural progression. Music enhances the activity and enables the jumper to create and organize routines to be performed to the musical pieces. The most effective approach is probably a combination of experiences with and without music.

Several types of jump ropes are on the market. All of them are satisfactory, depending on the instructor's likes and dislikes. The most popular appear to be the solid plastic speed (often called licorice) ropes and the beaded or segmented ropes. The speed rope is excellent for rapid turning and doing tricks. It does not maintain momentum as well as the segmented ropes do, which makes it more difficult to use with beginners. Beaded ropes are heavier and easier to turn for beginning jumpers, but these ropes hurt when they hit another student. In addition, if the segments are round, the rope rolls easily

FIGURE 17.23   Egg Beater.

©Robert Pangrazi or Aaron Beighle

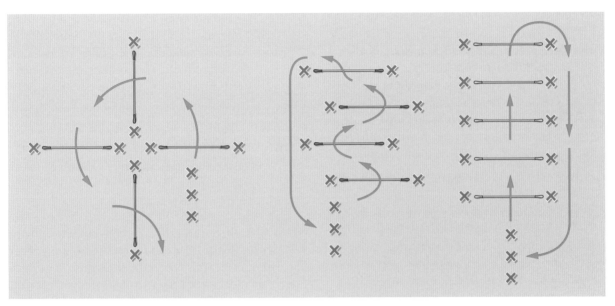

FIGURE 17.24 Formations for jumping rope.

on the floor and children may fall when they step on it. An ideal situation is to have a set of each type of rope.

Instructional Procedures

1. The rope length depends on the jumper's height. It should be long enough so that the ends reach to the armpits (figure 17.25) or slightly higher when the child stands on its center. Preschool children generally use 6-foot (1.8 m) ropes, and the primary-level group needs mostly 7-foot (2.1 m) ropes, with a few 6- and 8-foot (1.8 and 2.4 m) ropes. Grades 3 through 6 need a mixture of 7-, 8-, and 9-foot (2.1, 2.4, and 2.7 m) ropes. Tall students and teachers require a 9- or 10-foot (2.7 or 3.0 m) rope. Ropes or handles should be color-coded for length.

2. Posture is an important consideration in rope jumping. The body should be in good alignment, with the head up and the eyes looking straight ahead. The jump is made with the body held erect. A slight straightening of the knees provides the lift for the jump, which is low (about 1 inch [2.5 cm]). The wrists supply the force to turn the rope, and the elbows are kept close to the body and extended at a 90-degree angle. A pumping action and lifting of the arms is unnecessary. Jumpers land on the balls of the feet, with the knees bent slightly to cushion the shock. Usually, the feet, ankles, and legs are kept together, except when a specific step calls for a different position.

©Robert Pangrazi or Aaron Beighle

FIGURE 17.25 Correct jump-rope length.

3. The rope is held by the index finger and thumb on each side, and the hands make a small circle. The elbows are kept down and near the sides to avoid making large Arm Circles with the rope.

4. Introducing and teaching students individual rope-jumping skills can be accomplished by following these steps:

a. Students first jump without the rope until they learn the correct rhythm and footwork. For slow time, this is a jump and then a rebound step. Children can pretend they are turning the rope. Remember that rope jumping involves learning two separate skills: jumping a rope and turning a rope. Students who have difficulty need to practice the parts separately before trying them together.

b. Students turn the rope overhead and catch it with the toes.

c. The jumper holds the rope stationary in front of the body. Jump forward and backward over the rope. To increase the challenge, swing the rope slightly. Gradually increase the swing until a full turn of the rope is made.

d. Hold the rope to one side with one or both hands, swing the rope forward, and jump each time the rope hits the floor. If swinging the rope is a problem, practice without jumping first.

5. When jumpers have learned the basics of jumping, add music to motivate them to continue jumping.

6. In the primary-level group, some children cannot jump. By the third grade, nearly all children who have some experience can jump. Children who cannot jump may be helped by the pendulum swing of the long rope or by another student jumping with them inside an individual rope. Give cues such as "Jump" or "Ready–jump."

7. Most steps can be done with either rhythm: slow time or fast time. In slow-time rhythm, the child jumps over the rope, rebounds, and then does the second step (or repeats the original step) on the second jump. The rebound is simply a hop in place as the rope passes overhead. Better jumpers bend the knees only slightly, without actually leaving the floor on rebound. The rebound carries the rhythm between steps. The rope rotates slowly, passing underfoot on every other beat. The feet also move slowly, because a rebound occurs after each jump.

8. In fast-time rhythm, the rope rotates in time with the music, one turn per beat (120 to 180 turns per minute, depending on the tune's tempo), and the student does a step only when the rope is passing underfoot.

9. Instructional cues for improving jumping technique:

a. Keep the arms down and at the sides of the body while turning. (Many children lift the arms to shoulder level, trying to move the rope overhead. This makes it impossible for the child to jump over the elevated rope.)

b. Turn the rope by making small circles with the wrists.

c. Jump on the balls of the feet.

d. Bend the knees slightly to absorb the force of the jump.

e. Make a small jump over the rope.

10. To collect ropes after a rope-jumping activity, have two or three children act as monitors. They put both arms out to the front or to the side at shoulder level. The other children then drape the ropes over their arms (figure 17.26). The monitors return the ropes to the correct storage area.

Basic Steps

The basic steps presented here can be done in slow or fast time. After children have mastered the first six steps in slow time, teachers can introduce fast time. The Alternate-Foot Basic Step and Spread Legs Forward and Backward are two steps that work well for introducing fast-time jumping.

Side Swing

Swing the rope, held with both hands to one side of the body. Switch and swing the rope on the other side of the body.

Double Side Swing and Jump

Swing the rope once on each side of the body. Follow the second swing with a jump over the rope. The sequence should be swing, swing, jump.

Two-Foot Basic Step

Jump over the rope with feet together as it passes underfoot and then take a preparatory rebound while the rope is overhead.

Alternate-Foot Basic Step

As the rope passes underfoot, shift the weight alternately from one foot to the other, raising the free foot in a running position.

FIGURE 17.26 Collecting the ropes.

17

Bird Jumps

Jump with the toes pointed in (pigeon walk) and with the toes pointed out (duck walk). Alternate toes in and toes out.

Swing-Step Forward

This step is the same as the Alternate-Foot Basic Step, except that the free leg swings forward. The knee is kept loose, and the foot swings naturally.

Swing-Step Sideways

This step is the same as the Swing-Step Forward, but the free leg swings to the side. The knee is kept stiff. The sideways swing is about 12 inches (30 cm).

Rocker Step

In this step, one leg is always forward in a walking-stride position. As the rope passes underfoot, the weight shifts from the back foot to the forward foot. The rebound is on the forward foot while the rope is overhead. On the next

turn of the rope, the weight shifts from the forward foot to the back foot, repeating the rebound on the back foot.

Spread Legs Forward and Backward

Start in a stride position (as in the Rocker Step) with weight equally distributed on both feet. As the rope passes underfoot, jump into the air and reverse the position of the feet.

Straddle Jump

Alternate a regular jump with a Straddle Jump. The straddle jump is performed with the feet shoulder-width apart.

Cross Legs Sideways

As the rope passes underfoot, spread the legs in a straddle position (sideways) to take the rebound. As the rope passes underfoot on the next turn, jump into the air and cross the feet with the right foot forward. Then repeat with the left foot forward and continue alternating feet.

Toe-Touch Forward

Swing the right foot forward as the rope passes underfoot and touch the right toes on the next count. Then alternate, landing on the right foot and touching the left toes forward.

Toe-Touch Backward

This step is similar to the Swing-Step Sideways, except that the toes of the free foot touch to the back at the end of the swing.

Shuffle Step

Push off with the right foot and sidestep to the left as the rope passes underfoot. Land with the weight on the left foot and touch the right toes beside the left heel. Repeat the step in the opposite direction.

Skier

This double-foot jump is similar to a technique used by skiers. The jumper stands on both feet to one side of a chalked or painted line. Jumping is done sideways from side to side over the line. Have children try jumping forward and backward also.

Heel-Toe

As the rope passes underfoot, jump with the weight landing on the right foot while touching the left heel forward. On the next turn of the rope, jump, land on the same foot, and touch the left toes beside the right heel. This pattern is then repeated with the opposite foot bearing the weight.

Leg Fling

On the first jump, bring the right leg up so that it is parallel to the floor with the knee bent. On the second jump, kick the same leg out and up as high as possible. Try with the other leg.

Heel Click

Do two or three Swing-Steps Sideways, in slow time, in preparation for the Heel Click. When the right foot swings sideways, instead of a hop or rebound when the rope is above the head, raise the left foot to click the heel of the right foot. Repeat on the left side.

Step-Tap

As the rope passes underfoot, push off with the right foot and land on the left. While the rope is turning overhead, brush the sole of the right foot forward and then backward. As the rope passes underfoot for the second turn, push off with the left foot, land on the right, and repeat.

Skipping

Do a step-hop (skip) over the rope. Start slowly and gradually increase the rope speed.

Schottische Step

This step can be done to double-time rhythm, or it can be done with a varied rhythm. The pattern is step, step, step, hop (repeat), followed by four step-hops. In varied rhythm, three quick turns in fast time are made for the first three steps and then double-time rhythm prevails. Students practice the step first in place and then in general space. Schottische music is introduced.

Bleking Step

Turn the rope in the pattern slow-slow, fast-fast-fast. The Bleking Step begins with a hop on the left foot with the right heel forward, followed by a hop on the right with the left heel forward. Repeat this action with three quick changes: right, left, right. Start the sequence again, this time hopping on the right foot with the left heel extended. If music for the Bleking dance is used, students do four Bleking steps. The second part of the music (the chorus) allows children to create their own routine. They must listen for changes in the music.

Crossing Arms

After mastering the basic steps, children can try this interesting variation. Crossing the arms while turning the rope forward is easier than crossing them while turning backward. Crossing and uncrossing can be done at predetermined points after a specific number of turns. Crossing can be used during any of the routines.

Double Turning

The double turn of the rope is also challenging. The jumper does a few basic steps in preparing for the double turn. As the rope approaches the feet, give an extremely hard flip of the rope from the wrists, jump from 6 to 8 inches (15 to 20 cm) high, and let the rope pass underfoot twice before landing. The jumper must bend forward at the waist somewhat, which increases the speed of the turn. Challenge advanced rope jumpers to see how many consecutive double-turn jumps they can do.

Shifting From Forward to Backward Jumping

To switch from forward to backward jumping without stopping, use any of these techniques.

1. As the rope starts downward in forward jumping, rather than allowing it to pass underfoot, the performer swings both arms to the left (or right) and makes a half-turn of the body in that direction (i.e., facing the rope). On the next downward swing, the jumper spreads the arms and starts turning in the opposite direction. This method also works for shifting from backward to forward jumping.

2. When the rope is directly overhead, the jumper extends both arms, causing the rope to hesitate momentarily, and at the same time makes a half-turn in either direction and continues to skip with the rope turning in the opposite direction.

3. From a crossed-arm position, as the rope is going overhead, the jumper may uncross the arms and turn simultaneously. This starts the rope turning and the jumper going in the opposite direction.

Sideways Skipping

In Sideways Skipping, the rope is turned laterally with one hand held high and the other extended downward. The rope is swung around the body sideways. To accomplish this, the jumper starts with the right hand held high overhead and the left hand extended down the center of the body. Swing the rope to the left, at the same time raising the left leg sideways. Usually the speed is slow time, taking the rebound on each leg in turn. Later, better jumpers may progress to fast-time speed. The rope passes under the left leg, and the jumper then is straddling the rope as it moves around his or her body behind him or her. Take the weight on the left foot, raising the right foot sideways. A rebound step on the left as the rope moves to the front brings the jumper back to the original position.

Combination Possibilities

Many combinations of steps and rope tricks are possible in rope jumping. Here are some ideas:

1. Make changes in the speed of the turn—between slow time and fast time. Children should be able to shift from one speed to another, particularly when the music changes.

2. Developing expertise in various foot patterns and steps is important. Have children practice changing from one foot pattern to another.

3. Try the crossed-hands position both forward and backward. Many of the basic steps can be combined with crossed-hands position to add challenge.

4. Practice moving from a forward to a backward turn and returning. Perform the turn while doing a variety of basic steps.

5. Double turns combined with basic steps look impressive and are challenging. A few children may be able to do a triple turn.

6. Have children try to move forward, backward, and sideways, employing various basic steps.

7. Backward jumping is exciting, because it is a different skill from forward jumping. Most basic steps can be done backward or modified for the backward turn.

8. Practice doing speedy turns (Hot Peppers). Have children see how fast they can turn the rope for 15 or 30 seconds.

Individual Rope Jumping With Partners

Many interesting combinations are possible when one child turns the individual rope and one or more children jump it. For routines that call for a child to run into a jumping pattern, a more effective approach may to begin with the child already in position before proceeding to the run-in stage.

1. The first child turns the rope, and the other stands in front, ready to enter.

   a. Run in and face partner, and both jump (figure 17.27).

FIGURE 17.27 Rope jumping with a partner.

b. Run in and turn back to partner, and both jump.

c. Decide which steps are to be done; then run in and match steps.

d. Repeat with the rope turning backward.

e. Run in with a ball and bounce it during the jumping.

2. Partners stand side by side, clasp inside hands, and turn the rope with outside hands.

a. Face the same direction and turn the rope.

b. Face opposite directions, clasp left hands, and turn the rope.

c. Face opposite directions, clasp right hands, and turn the rope.

d. Repeat routines with inside knees raised.

e. Repeat routines with elbows locked. Try other arm positions.

3. The first child turns the rope, and the second is to the rear, ready to run in. The second child runs in and grasps the first child's waist or shoulders, and they jump together (engine and caboose).

4. Partners stand back-to-back, holding a single rope in the right hand.

a. Turn in one direction—forward for one and backward for the other.

b. Reverse direction.

c. Change to left hands and repeat.

5. Three children jump. One turns the rope forward; one runs in, in front; and one runs in behind. All three jump. Try with the rope turning backward.

6. Two jumpers, each with a rope, face each other and turn both ropes together, forward for one and backward for the other, jumping over both ropes at once. Turn the ropes alternately, jumping each rope in turn.

7. One partner jumps in a usual individual rope pattern. The other jumps to the side. The turning partner hands over one end of the rope, and the other maintains the turning rhythm and then hands the rope back.

a. Try from the other side.

b. Turn the rope backward.

8. Using a single rope held in the right hand, partners face each other and turn the rope in slow time. With the rope overhead, one partner makes a turn to the left (turning in) and jumps inside the rope, exiting by turning either way. See if both can turn inside.

Movement Sequences to Music

Opportunities for creative movement sequences performed to music are unlimited. Music must have a definite beat and a bouncy quality. Pieces with a two-part format (verse and chorus) are excellent. The change from the verse to the chorus signals a change in rope-jumping pattern. (Many of the recordings listed in chapter 19 are suitable for rope jumping to music.) Schottisches, marches, and polkas provide good background. Popular rock music motivates children if it has a strong, even rhythm. Special selections for rope jumping also are available from commercial sources. Suggested recordings include the following:

- "The Muffin Man"
- "Looby Loo"
- "Bleking"
- "Pop Goes the Weasel"
- Schottische
- Polka

Devising Sequences to Music

Devising jumping sequences allows children to create their own routines to selected music. Simple changes from slow time to fast time can introduce this activity. Later, students can try different steps, add crossing and uncrossing of arms, and vary the turning direction. Partner rope-jumping stunts can also be adapted to music. Suggestions for incorporating different steps in the sequences follow.

1. "Pop Goes the Weasel" has a definite verse and chorus change. Children can switch from slow-time jumping to fast-time jumping on the chorus.

2. Bleking music offers an interesting change in rope speed. The rhythm is slow-slow, fast-fast-fast (four times). The rope is turned with each beat. Later, the Bleking step can be added.

3. Using schottische music, children can do the Schottische Step in place twice and four moving step-hops in different directions during the chorus.

4. To "Little Brown Jug," students can do a four-part routine to four rounds of the music.

First verse: Two-Foot Basic Step (slow time)

Chorus: Two-Foot Basic Step (fast time)

Second verse: Alternate-Foot Basic Step (slow time)

Chorus: Alternate-Foot Basic Step (fast time)

Third verse: Swing-Step Forward (slow time)

Chorus: Swing-Step Forward (fast time)

Fourth verse: Swing-Step Sideways (slow time)

Chorus: Swing-Step Sideways (fast time)

Assessment of Individual Rope Jumping

Individual rope-jumping stunts, because of their specificity and individuality, can be adapted easily to learning packages and contract teaching. Skill assessment can be based on completing a stated maneuver in so many turns of the rope. The assessment can be organized progressively or grouped by beginning, intermediate, and advanced tests. An example of a beginning test follows. All test items are done first in slow time and then in fast time.

1. Two-Foot Basic Step: 10 turns

2. Alternate-Foot Basic Step: 10 turns

3. Turning Rope Backward: 10 turns

4. Alternate crossing arms: 10 turns

5. Running forward: 20 turns

Intermediate and advanced tests can be organized similarly.

Footbag Activities

A footbag is a specifically designed object used for footbag skills and games. Although the construction varies, most footbags are leather spheres about 2 inches (5 cm) in diameter and weighing about 1 ounce (28 g). These soft, flexible balls are stitched internally for durability and do not bounce. The object of the activities is to keep the bag in the air by means of foot contact.

The kicking motion used for footbag activities is new to most participants because of the lift, which is done by lifting the foot upward, not away from the body. The lifting motion directs the footbag upward to permit controlled, consecutive kicks and passes.

Several points contribute to successful footbag work. Start with the basic athletic stance (ready position): feet are about shoulder-width apart and point straight ahead. Knees are bent slightly, so that body weight is lowered.

Use both feet equally for lifting and kicking. The standing foot is important for maintaining balance and keeping the body in a crouched position. Eye focus on the footbag is essential. Kicking speed is slow; most beginners kick too quickly. Kicking speed is about that of the descending footbag. Slow and low are the key words in kicking.

Use the arms and upper body for balance and control. For the outside and back kicks, an outstretched arm, opposite to the kicking foot and in line with it, aids in maintaining balance. The near arm is carried behind the body so as not to restrict the player's vision. For inside kicks, the arms are relaxed and in balanced position.

To begin, start with a hand toss to self or with a courtesy toss from another player. Touching the footbag with any part of the body above the waist is a foul and interrupts any sequence of kicks. Three basic kicks are recommended.

1. *Inside kick.* Used when the footbag falls low and directly in front of both shoulders. Use the inside of the foot for contact by turning the instep and the ankle upward to create a flat striking surface. Curling the toes under aids in creating a flat striking surface. Contact with the footbag is made at about knee level.

2. *Outside kick.* Used when the footbag falls outside either shoulder. Use the outside of the foot by turning the ankle and knee in to create a flat striking surface. With the kicking foot now parallel to the playing surface, use a smooth lifting motion, striking the footbag at approximately knee level. Pointing the toes up aids in creating a flat surface.

3. *Back kick.* Somewhat similar to the outside kick, the back kick is used when the footbag goes directly overhead or is approaching the upper body directly. Rotate the hips and body parallel to the flight direction to enable the footbag to pass while still maintaining constant eye contact. Lean forward in the direction of the footbag's flight and allow it to pass by before executing the kick.

Play can take various forms.

17

1. *Individual play.* Individuals attempt to see how long they can keep the footbag in play. Score 1 point for each kick.

2. *Partner play.* Partners alternate kicking the footbag. Score 1 point for each alternate successful kick.

3. *Group play.* A circle of four or five children is the basic formation. Rules governing consecutive kicks are (*a*) all members of the circle must have kicked the footbag for a consecutive run to count, and (*b*) return kicks are prohibited; that is, kickers may not receive return kicks from the person to whom they kicked the footbag.

Footbag play is an enjoyable activity, but the skills are not easily learned. Persistence and patience are needed. Students will have many misses before slowly gaining control. Many physical education suppliers carry footbags; for further sources and information, write to World Footbag, http://worldfootbag.com.

Rhythmic Gymnastics

Rhythmic gymnastics became popular in the United States during the 1970s and was accepted as an official sport competition in the 1984 Summer Olympic Games. The activities are varied and merit much more explanation than can be presented in this context. Essentially, rhythmic gymnastics involves routines done to music by a performer using a particular type of manipulative equipment. The routine can be individual, partner, or team competition. Equipment used includes balls, jump ropes, hoops, ribbons, and clubs. Wands, flags, and scarves are sometimes used but not in national or international competition. The elements of competition are not discussed here.

Many movement qualities—balance, poise, grace, flow of body movement, coordination, rhythm, and kinesthetic sense—grow out of serious participation in rhythmic gymnastics. Fitness qualities of agility, flexibility, and proper posture are also developed. Furthermore, skill in handling the various pieces of manipulative equipment is enhanced, because these skills must be mastered before they can be organized into a routine set to music.

Participants, after developing the necessary skills, work with music. In competitive situations the music is restricted to one instrument. In the school setting the music should be instrumental, light, lively, and enjoyable to the gymnast. Most companies dealing in music for physical education stock specialized recordings for gymnastics movement, including specific selections for

various pieces of equipment. Most of these recordings contain directions for suggested routines. There is no substitute, however, for teacher ingenuity in helping children expand and create their routines.

This unit is excellent for developing group routines in which a class works together. Routines can be used for physical education demonstrations, back-to-school presentations, and at halftimes of athletic events. The routines are impressive and do not require a high level of skill. All children are capable of participating and will enjoy the opportunity to be involved in a team event.

Organizing the Program

The activities presented here focus on balls, jump ropes, hoops, and ribbons—all ordinarily covered in the elementary program. The club is a difficult hand apparatus to use and is not included in elementary school programs.

Rhythmic gymnastics strives for continuous body movement with the selected piece of equipment. Composition goals are originality, variety of movement, use of the performing area, performance presentation, and smoothness of transition. Harmony of movement with the music, the apparatus, and execution factors are also important. An individual competitive routine is 1 to 1-1/2 minutes long, but performing time should be shorter for children. Group routines last 2 to 3 minutes and may involve one or two types of equipment. The primary goal is the personal satisfaction that students receive from participating in the program. Introducing students to these activities is more important than having them compete.

A practical way to include rhythmic gymnastics in the curriculum is a dual approach. Teach the basic skills to all children in physical education classes, so that they can express themselves by composing creative routines. More refined work can take place through the intramural program or a sport club. Students can choose to participate in competition. Instructors often lack background in these activities. If possible, recruit dance instructors from private clubs to introduce the activities.

Developing Routines

Routines for the elementary level should be uncomplicated and based on learned skills. Aesthetics, although important as skill develops, is of secondary emphasis. Ballet, jazz, and modern dance movements, along with basic dance steps, are normally included in high-level competition.

In developing routines to music, remind children that most music is based on units of 8 or 16 counts.

Movements are performed in the sagittal, frontal, and horizontal planes. These terms are used when developing routines and should be learned by children. The sagittal plane is an imaginary division of the body into right and left halves. Movements "in the sagittal" are performed parallel to this plane on either side of the body. The horizontal plane involves movements that are parallel to the floor. The frontal plane divides the body into front and rear halves. Movements in this plane are performed parallel to this plane either in front of or behind the body.

An effective way to form a routine is to teach the beginning of a routine and then let students create the rest. For example, perform the following movements using ribbons. End each series with the hands in front of the waist.

> Sagittal forward circles on the right side (6 counts)
>
> Sagittal forward circles on the left side (6 counts)
>
> Elevator (4 counts)

This routine could consist of a number of 16-count units, each concluding with the Elevator (4 counts). Students can develop additional units. For any one piece of apparatus, certain skill areas can be specified. It is then up to the participant to include these skills at some point in the routine.

Rhythmic Gymnastics Ball Skills

The ball should be large enough that it cannot be grasped by the hand but must rest in the hand and be controlled by balance. For elementary school children, use either a 6-inch (15 cm) or an 8.5-inch (22 cm) ball, moderately inflated.

In handling the ball, the fingers are closed and slightly bent, and the ball is resting in the palm. In throwing, the ball can roll from the fingertips. After catching, the ball returns immediately to the palm.

Here are some ball skills that can be combined to develop a routine:

1. In a sitting position, try these activities: Roll the ball under the legs and around the back, around the body, down the arms, and down the legs. Lift legs, toss the ball off the toes into the air, and catch.

2. Combine basketball dribbling drills with graceful body movements; execute locomotor dance-type movements while bouncing.

3. Toss and catch the ball, employing different body positions.

4. Add locomotor movements to tosses and catches.

5. Perform body waves with the ball.

6. Throw or bounce the ball in a variety of ways.

7. Make swinging movements (also circular movements). Swinging movements are more difficult than they seem. The ball must be kept in the palm while doing the movements.

8. Try different balancing movements: spirals, curls, and other balances inherent to rhythmic gymnastics.

9. Allow opportunity for student exploration that combines several of these activities.

Figure 17.28 is an example of a simple routine using balls. The numbers refer to the floor area in the figure where each activity is performed.

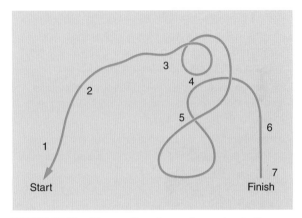

FIGURE 17.28 Floor pattern for routine using balls.

1. Bounce the ball in place.

2. Bounce the ball while moving forward slowly.

3. Run forward while making swing tosses from side to side.

4. Bounce the ball and make a full turn.

5. Run in a figure-eight pattern.

6. Toss the ball up and catch it with one hand.

7. Finish with a toss and catch behind the back.

Rhythmic Gymnastics Rope Routines

As with ball routines, jump-rope routines can be used in various ways. Most important is that the participant excels in the basic jumps. Ropes can be full length, folded in half, or folded in fourths. Knotting the end of the rope makes it easier to handle. Proper length is determined by standing on the center of the rope with one foot and extending the rope ends to the outstretched hands at shoulder level. Handles are not appropriate. Most rope jumping is done with the hands far apart. The rope should not touch the floor; it should pass slightly above it. Jumping techniques used for rhythmic gymnastics obviously differ from those taught in the physical education class. Here are some movements that can be performed using jump ropes:

1. Try single and double jumps forward and backward.

2. Circle the rope on each side of the body, holding both ends of the rope.

3. Make figure-eight swings by holding both ends of the rope or by holding the center of the rope and swinging the ends.

4. Swing the rope like a pendulum and jump it.

5. Run or skip over a turning rope. Try forward and backward.

6. Do a schottische step over a turning rope.

7. Holding the ends and center of the rope, kneel and horizontally circle the rope close to the floor. Stand and circle the rope overhead.

8. Perform a body wrap with the rope. (Hold one end on the hip and wrap the rope around the body with the other hand.)

9. After jumping over a backward-turning rope, toss the rope with both ends into the air and catch.

10. Run while holding both ends of the rope in one hand and circling the rope sagittally backward at the side of the body. Toss the rope and catch it while running.

11. While performing a dance step, toss and catch the rope.

12. Hold both ends of the rope and swing it around the body like a cape.

13. Perform leaps while circling the rope sagittally at one side of the body.

14. Try different balance movements. Balance movements add variety and permit the performer to catch his or her breath. These movements involve held body positions with the rope underneath the foot or hooked around a foot.

15. Hold the rope around the foot and make shapes with the body and foot–rope connection.

16. Explore and combine a number of the activities described.

Rhythmic Gymnastics Hoop Movements

The basic hoop stunts and challenges should first be mastered. The same hoop used in physical education classes is suitable for these routines. The hoop may be held, tossed, or caught in one or both hands and with a variety of grips (figure 17.29). Hoops may turn forward or backward. Some suggested rhythmic movements with hoops follow.

1. *Swinging movements.* A variety of swinging movements are possible. The swinging movement is very large. Good alignment between

FIGURE 17.29 Rhythmic gymnastics movements using hoops.

FatCamera/E+/Getty Images

body and hoop is important. Hoops can be swung in a frontal, sagittal, or horizontal plane. Do the movements in place or while moving. Here are some suggestions:

   a. Swing across the body.
   b. Swing with body lean.
   c. Swing around the body, changing hands.
   d. Swing across the body, changing hands.
   e. Swing overhead, change hands, and swing downward.
   f. Swing in a figure-eight pattern.

2. *Spinning movements.* Turn the hoop, usually with both hands but sometimes with one. The hoop also can be spun on the ground. Here are some suggestions:

   a. Spin in front of the body.
   b. Spin on the floor.
   c. Spin and kick one leg over the hoop. Add a full body turn after the kickover.

3. *Circling movements.* These movements are most characteristic of hoop activities. Hoops can be twirled using the hand, wrist, arm, leg, or body (hula-hooping). Changes are made from one hand or wrist to the other. Here are some suggestions:

   a. Extend the arm in front of the body. Circle on the hand between the thumb and first finger in the frontal plane.
   b. Circle the hoop while swaying from side to side.
   c. Circle the hoop horizontally overhead.
   d. Hold both sides of the hoop and circle it in front of the body.
   e. Circle the hoop around different parts of the body.

4. *Tossing and catching movements.* Toss the hoop high in the air with one or both hands. Catch it one-handed, between the thumb and index finger. Most tosses grow out of swinging or circling movements. Here are some suggestions:

   a. Try with one- and two-handed catches.
   b. Toss the hoop in different directions.
   c. Toss overhead from hand to hand.
   d. Circle the hoop on the hand, toss into the air, and catch.

5. *Rolling movements.* Roll the hoop on the floor—either forward or reverse (return) rolling—or roll it on the body in diverse ways. If the hoop is rolled along the floor, various jumps can be executed over it. Here are some suggestions:

   a. Roll the hoop and run alongside it.
   b. Roll the hoop and move through it.
   c. Roll the hoop and jump over it.
   d. Roll the hoop along one arm to the other, on the front or the back of the body.

6. *Jumping movements.* Use the hoop, turned forward or backward, like a jump rope.

Rhythmic Gymnastics Ribbon Movements

Ribbon movements are spectacular and make fine demonstrations. Official ribbon length is around 21 feet (6.4 m) with the first 3 feet (.9 m) doubled. For practical purposes, shorter lengths are used at the elementary school level.

Ribbons can be made easily in many colors. A rhythmic flow of movement is desired, featuring circular, oval, spiral, and wavelike shapes. A light, flowing movement is the goal, with total body involvement. The dowel or wand to which the ribbon is attached should be an extension of the hand and arm. Laterality is also a consideration. The following are basic ribbon movements.

1. *Swinging movements.* The entire body should coordinate with these large, swinging motions:

   a. Swing the ribbon forward and backward in the sagittal plane.
   b. Swing the ribbon across and in front of the body in the frontal plane.
   c. Swing the ribbon overhead from side to side.
   d. Swing the ribbon upward and catch the end of it.
   e. While holding both ends of the ribbon, swing it upward, around, and over the body.

2. *Circling movements.* Large circles involve the whole arm; smaller circles involve the wrist. Make circles in the frontal, sagittal, and horizontal planes.

   a. Circle the ribbon at different levels.
   b. Circle the ribbon horizontally, vertically, or diagonally.
   c. Circle the ribbon in front of the body, around the body, and behind the body.
   d. Run while circling the ribbon overhead; leap as the ribbon is circled downward and under the legs.
   e. Add dance steps and turns while circling the ribbon.

3. *Figure-eight movements.* Figure eights are also made in the three planes. The two halves of the figure eight should be the same size and on the

same plane level. Make the figure with long arm movements or with movements of the lower arm or wrist. While doing a figure eight, hop through the loop when the ribbon passes the side of the body.

4. *Zigzag movements.* Make these movements in the air or on the floor. Use continuous up-and-down hand movements, primarily with the wrist.

    a. Execute the zigzag in the air in front, around, and behind the body.
    b. Run backward while zigzagging the ribbon in front of the body. Perform at different levels.
    c. Run forward while zigzagging behind the body at different levels.

5. *Spiral movements.* The circles in the spiral can be the same size or in an increasing or decreasing progression. Make spirals from left to right or the reverse.

    a. Execute spirals around, in front of, or beside the body while performing locomotor dance steps.
    b. Execute spirals while performing forward and backward rolls.

6. *Throwing and catching movements.* These difficult skills are usually combined with swinging, circling, or figure-eight movements. Toss the ribbon with one hand and catch it with either the same hand or the other hand.

7. *Exchanges.* During group routines, hand or toss the ribbon to a partner.

LEARNING AIDS

WEBSITES

Footbag

http://worldfootbag.com

Frisbees

www.upa.org
www.vul.ca/learn

General Physical Education

www.pecentral.org

Jump Rope

www.worldofropejumping.com

SUGGESTED READINGS

Bibaud, R. (2008). *Complete fundamentals of rope jumping: A teaching guide* (DVD edition). Champaign, IL: Human Kinetics.

Bennett, J.P., & Riemer, P.C. (2006). *Rhythmic activities and dance* (2nd ed.). Champaign, IL: Human Kinetics.

Beckerman, C. (2012). *Juggling for beginner: 25+ tricks to astound your friends.* New York, NY: Sterling Innovation.

Cassidy, J., & Rimbeaux, B.C. (2007). *Juggling for the complete klutz.* Palo Alto, CA: Klutz Press.

Colvin, A.V., Egner Markos, N.J., & Walker, P.J. (2016). *Teaching fundamental motor skills* (3rd ed.). Champaign, IL: Human Kinetics.

Lee, B. (2010). *Jump rope training* (2nd ed.). Champaign, IL: Human Kinetics.

Wall, M. (2017). *So you want to learn: Juggling.* Lincoln, NE: Henderson.

Body Management Skills

18

Body management skills are usually large-muscle activities required for controlling the body in various situations. Body management skills integrate agility, coordination, strength, balance, and flexibility. Activities in this chapter help students learn to control their bodies while using a wide variety of apparatus. This chapter offers organizational hints, instructional strategies, and activities for helping students develop body management skills.

Learning Objectives

▶ Help students develop body management skills using large and small apparatus.

▶ Apply proper instructional procedures to a wide variety of apparatus activities.

▶ Design a safe environment when teaching large-apparatus activities.

▶ Teach a variety of activities on large apparatus, including climbing ropes, benches, balance beams, and jumping boxes.

▶ Teach activities using small apparatus, including magic ropes, individual mats, tug-of-war ropes, and gym scooters.

Body management skills are an important component of movement competency. Efficient movement demands integration of agility, balance, strength, flexibility, and coordination. Students also must learn how to control their bodies while on large apparatus such as beams, benches, and jumping boxes.

This chapter focuses on developing body management skills using large and small apparatus. The first half of this chapter describes large-apparatus activities such as climbing ropes, benches, balance beams, and jumping boxes. Large-apparatus activities enable students to learn body management skills while free of ground support. The second half of the chapter focuses on small-apparatus activities, including magic ropes, individual mats, and gym scooters. Small-apparatus activities help develop body control in space and on the ground.

Safe and Effective Use of Apparatus

Many of the body management skills require large apparatus. Have the apparatus in place before a class arrives, if possible. To ensure a safe environment, tell students they are not to use the equipment until the teacher gives approval. Establish procedures for setup, storage, and safe use of apparatus and mats. Here are guidelines for using apparatus in the instructional setting:

1. *Use tumbling mats to absorb shock.* Position tumbling mats for safety in dismounting and where falls are possible, such as under all climbing ropes.

2. *Students must carry, not drag, apparatus.* Teach students how to lift and carry the apparatus. For the pieces that require cooperation, designate the number of children and the means of carrying. Discuss proper setup and storage of apparatus and have students practice the procedures.

3. *Activity on apparatus occurs only when directed by teachers.* Instruct children to stay away from all apparatus in the area that has been positioned for later use.

4. *Instruction precedes activity on all apparatus.* Improper use of apparatus can result in injury. Signs emphasizing proper use can be placed on cones near individual pieces of equipment.

5. *Use return activities to increase the movement potential of apparatus.* Return activity requires children to do a movement task (jumping, hopping, skipping, animal walks, and so on) after performing on the apparatus. This approach reduces the time that children stand in line waiting for another

turn after completing their task on the apparatus. To increase the amount of time that children are actively engaged, increase the distance they have to travel. Return activities demand little supervision. For example, when teaching balance-beam activities, give the children this task: Walk across the beam, do a straddle dismount, and Crab Walk (the return activity) to a cone and back to the starting point.

6. *Have students move slowly when working on apparatus.* Many of the activities require balance and agility. Instruct students to aim for controlled and sustained movements.

7. *Place apparatus on teaching surface.* Apparatus such as jump boxes and balance beams should be placed directly on the teaching surface. Placing them on mats or carpet squares decreases their stability and increased their chances of moving or sliding.

Activities With Climbing Ropes

Climbing ropes offer high-level developmental possibilities for the upper trunk and arms as well as training in coordination of different body parts (figure 18.1). Adequate grip and arm strength are prerequisites for climbing. Becoming accustomed to the rope and gaining confidence are important early goals. Climbing rope sets can be purchased from Gopher Sport (www.gophersport.com).

Climbing-rope lessons are often a student favorite. As with any activity in physical education, the key is to provide appropriate progressions for students, and let students know you are not forcing them to perform all the activities. Many factors stop students from trying, including fear of failure in front of others. Allow students the option to choose from the current skill being taught or a previously taught, easier activity. Assure maximum activity by providing one rope for every two or three students.

Instructional Procedures

1. Place tumbling mats under all ropes.

2. The hand-over-hand method is used for climbing and the hand-under-hand method for descending.

3. Caution the children not to slide; sliding can cause rope burns on the hands and legs.

FIGURE 18.1 Rope climbing on an eight-rope set.

©Robert Pangrazi or Aaron Beighle

4. A climber who becomes tired should stop and rest. Proper rest stops are taught as part of the climbing procedure.

5. Teach children to go no higher than their strength allows. Marks to limit the climb can be put on the rope with adhesive tape. A height of 8 to 10 feet (2.4 to 3.0 m) above the floor is reasonable until a child demonstrates proficiency. A maximum height of 14 to 16 feet (4.3 to 4.9 m) is plenty for elementary school children.

6. Use spotters for activities in which the body is inverted.

7. Rosin in powdered form and magnesium chalk aid in gripping, which is particularly important when the rope becomes slippery.

8. Instruct children to make sure that other children are out of the way before swinging on the ropes.

Preliminary Activities

Progression is important in rope climbing. Teachers should follow these fundamental skill progressions.

Supported Pull-Ups

In supported pull-up activities, a part of the body remains in contact with the floor. The pull-up is hand-over-hand, and the return is hand-under-hand.

1. Kneel directly under the rope. Pull up to the tip-toes and return to kneeling position.

2. Start in sitting position under the rope. Pull up; weight is on the heels. Return to sitting position.

3. Start in a standing position. Grasp the rope, rock back on the heels, and lower the body to the floor. Keep a straight body. Pull up to a standing position using hand-over-hand.

Hangs

To do a hang, pull up the body in one motion and hold for a length of time (5, 10, or 20 seconds). Progression is important.

1. From a seated position, reach up as high as possible and pull the body from the floor, except for the heels. Hold.

2. Same as step 1, but pull the body completely off the floor. Hold.

3. From a standing position, jump up, grasp the rope, and hang. This is a Bent-Arm Hang, with the hands about even with the mouth. Hold.

4. Repeat step 3, but add leg movements—one or both knees up, bicycling movement, half lever (one or both legs up, parallel to the floor), full lever (feet up to the face).

Swinging and Jumping

The child reaches high and jumps to a bent-arm position. Landing is on the feet with bent knees.

1. Jump and swing. Add half turns and full turns.

2. Swing and return to the starting point. Add single and double knee bends.

3. Jump for distance over a cone or bowling pin.

4. Swing and pick up a bowling pin and return to the starting point.

5. Carry objects (beanbags, balls, or deck tennis rings). A partner, standing to the side away from the takeoff bench, can put articles to be carried back on the takeoff perch by placing each article between the knees or feet.

6. Run toward a swinging rope, grasp it, and gain momentum for swinging.

7. The previous activities can also be done using a bench, box, or stool as a takeoff point.

18

Pull-Ups

Repeatedly raise and lower the body. At the highest point of the Pull-Up, the chin touches the hands. Start by challenging students to accomplish one Pull-Up in the defined position and then slowly increase the number of repetitions. All the activities described for hangs are adaptable to Pull-Ups.

Inverted Hang

Both hands reach up high, and the rope hangs to one side. Jump to a bent-arm position, at the same time bringing the knees up to the nose to invert the body, which is now in a curled position. In a continuation of the motion, bring the feet up higher than the hands, and lock the legs around the rope. The body should now be straight and upside down. In the learning phase, teachers should spot.

Climbing the Rope

Scissors Grip

Approach the rope and reach as high as possible, standing with the right leg forward of the left. Raise the left leg, bend at the knee, and place the rope inside the knee and outside the foot (the rope will lay across the top of the foot). While hanging, move the right foot on top of the rope and left foot and straighten the legs with the toes pointed down (figure 18.2). This position should give a secure hold. The teacher can check the position.

To climb using the Scissors Grip, raise the knees up close to the chest, the rope sliding between them, while supporting the body with the hand grip. Lock the rope between the legs and climb up, using the hand-over-hand method and stretching as high as the hands can reach. Bring the knees up to the chest and repeat the process until you have climbed halfway. Later, strive for a higher climb.

Leg-Around Rest

Wrap the left leg completely around the rope, keeping the rope between the thighs (figure 18.3). The bottom of the rope then crosses over the instep of the left foot from the outside. The right foot stands on the rope as it crosses over the instep, providing pressure to prevent slippage. For additional pressure, release the hands and wrap the arms around the rope, leaning away from the rope at the same time.

FIGURE 18.2   Scissors Grip.

FIGURE 18.3   Leg-Around Rest.

To climb using the Leg-Around Rest, proceed as in climbing with the Scissors Grip but loosen the grip each time and grasp higher up on the rope.

Descending the Rope

There are four ways to descend the rope. The only differences are in the use of the leg locks, because the hand-under-hand is used for all descents.

Scissors Grip Descent

From an extended Scissors Grip position, lock the legs and lower the body with the hands until the knees are against the chest. Hold with the hands and lower the legs to a new position.

Leg-Around Rest Descent

From the Leg-Around Rest position, lower the body until the knees are against the chest. Lift the top foot, and let the feet slide to a lower position. Secure with the top foot and repeat.

Instep Squeeze Descent

Squeeze the rope between the insteps by keeping the heels together. Lower the body while the rope slides against the instep.

Stirrup Descent

Have the rope on the outside of the right foot and carry it over the instep of the left. Pressure from the left foot holds the position. To get into position, let the rope trail along the right leg, reach under, and hook it with the left instep. When the pressure from the left leg is reduced, the rope slides smoothly while the descent is made with the hands.

Climbing Without Using the Feet

This strenuous activity should be attempted only by the most skilled climbers. During early sessions, do not set the mark higher than the child's reach. Climbers start from a sitting position.

Stunts Using Two Ropes

Two ropes hanging close together are needed for the following activities.

Straight-Arm Hang

Jump up, grasp one rope with each hand, and hang with the arms straight.

Bent-Arm Hang

Do this like the Straight-Arm Hang but bend the arms at the elbows.

Arm Hangs With Different Leg Positions

1. Do single and double knee lifts.
2. Do a Half Lever. Bring the legs up parallel to the floor and point the toes.
3. Do a Full Lever. Bring the feet up to the face and keep the knees straight.
4. Do a Bicycle. Pedal as on a bicycle.

Skin the Cat

From a bent-arm position, kick the feet overhead and continue the roll until the feet touch the mat. Return to the starting position. A more difficult stunt is to start from a higher position with the feet not touching the mat. Reverse to original position.

Pull-Ups

Do a Pull-Up the same way as on a single rope, except that each hand grasps a rope.

Inverted Hang

1. Hang with the feet wrapped around the ropes.
2. Hang with the feet against the inside of the ropes.
3. Hang with the toes pointed and the feet not touching the ropes (figure 18.4).

FIGURE 18.4 Spotting an Inverted Hang on two ropes. (Holding the performer's hands ensures confidence and safety.)

18

Climbing

1. Climb up one rope, transfer to another, and descend.
2. Climb halfway up one rope, cross over to another rope, and keep climbing to the top.
3. Climb both ropes together without using the legs. This difficult activity requires climbers to slide one hand at a time up the ropes without completely releasing the grip.
4. Climb as on a single rope, with hands on one rope and feet on the other rope.

Activity Sequences

Rope-climbing activities offer sequences that help the child progress. The following sequence indicates the kind of progressive challenges that can be met.

1. Jump and hang (10 seconds).
2. Pull up and hold (10 seconds).
3. Scissors climb to blue mark (10 feet [3 m]).
4. Scissors climb to top (15 feet [5 m]).
5. Demonstrate Leg-Around Rest (10 feet [3 m]).
6. Do an Inverted Hang, with body straight (5 seconds).

Activities on Balance Beams

Balance-beam activities contribute to control in both static and dynamic balance situations (figure 18.5). The balance-beam side of a balance-beam bench, with its 2-inch-wide (5 cm wide) and 12-foot-long

©Robert Pangrazi or Aaron Beighle

FIGURE 18.5 Walking on a balance-beam bench.

(3.7 m long) beam, is ideal for such activities. Balance-beam benches can be purchased from Gopher Sport (www.gophersport.com). Balance beams come in many other sizes, however, and can be built from common lumber materials (see chapter 12). Some teachers prefer a wider beam for kindergarten and first-grade children and, in particular, for special education children. Students graduate to the narrower beam as soon as activities on the wider beam no longer challenge them.

Other ideas for balance equipment are available. For example, a beam that goes from 2 inches (5 cm) wide to 1 inch (2.5 cm) wide at the other end or beams of varying widths (from 1 to 4 inches [2.5 to 10 cm]) could be used. Children progress from the wider to the narrower beams. For children with disabilities, provide a variety of widths. Gymnasium lines can be used as a "beginning beam" for students learning balance activities.

Instructional Procedures

1. Children should move with controlled, deliberate movements. Speed is not a goal. Advise students to recover their balance before taking another step or making another movement.

2. Observing the principle of control, children should step slowly on the beam, pause momentarily in good balance at the end of the activity, and dismount with a small, controlled jump from the end of the beam after completing the routine.

3. Place tumbling mats at the end of the bench to cushion the dismount and allow rolls and stunts after the dismount.

4. Visual focus is important. Tell children to look straight ahead rather than down at the feet. Eye targets can be marked on or attached to walls to assist in visual focus. This focus allows balance controls other than vision to function more effectively. From time to time, have children do movements with the eyes closed, entirely eliminating visual control of balance.

5. Direct children to step off the beam immediately if they think they are losing their balance, rather than teetering and falling off awkwardly. Allow the child to step back on the beam and continue the routine.

6. Success in a balance-beam activity can be based on two levels. The lower level allows the child to step off the beam once during the routine. The higher level requires the child to remain on the

beam throughout. For both levels, ask students to pause in good balance at the end of the beam before dismounting.

7. Both laterality and directionality are important. Give the right and left feet reasonably equal treatment. A child naturally uses the dominant side and direction but must be encouraged to perform with both sides.

8. The child next in line begins when the performer ahead is about three-quarters of the distance across the beam.

9. Return activities are a consideration for enhancing the breadth of activity.

10. A child or the teacher can assist the performer. The assistant holds the hand palm up, ready to help the performer if help is needed.

Activity Sequences

Activities for the balance beam are presented as a progression of movement themes. The teacher can fully develop all activities and possibilities within a theme before proceeding to the next theme, or take a few activities from each theme and cover more.

Activities on Parallel Beams

Activities on two parallel beams are presented first as lead-up practice for the single-beam tasks. The beams are placed about 10 to 30 inches (25 to 75 cm) apart. The parallel-beam activities can be done alone or with a partner when more security is desired.

1. With a partner, join inside hands and walk forward, backward, and sideways. Walk sideways, using a grapevine step (step behind, step across). Hold a beanbag in the free hand.

2. Without a partner, do various animal walks, such as the Crab Walk, Bear Walk, Measuring Worm, and Elephant Walk.

3. With one foot on each beam, walk forward, backward, and sideways.

4. Step to the opposite beam with each step taken.

5. Progress the length of the beams with hands on one beam and feet on the other.

6. Progress to the middle of the beams and do various turns and stunts, such as picking up a beanbag, moving through a hoop, or stepping over a wand.

Movements Going the Full Length of a Single Beam

1. Do various locomotor tasks, such as walking, follow steps, heel-and-toe steps, side steps, tiptoe steps, the grapevine step, and so on.

2. Follow different directions—forward, backward, sideways.

3. Use different arm and hand positions—on the hips, on the head, behind the back, out to the sides, pointing to the ceiling, folded across the chest.

4. Move across the beam while assuming different shapes.

5. Balance an object (beanbag or eraser) on various body parts—on the head, on the back of the hands, on the shoulders. Try balancing two or three objects at once.

Half-and-Half Movements

These movements repeat the movements, arm positions, and balancing stunts described previously, except that the performer goes halfway across the beam using a selected movement and then changes to another type of movement on the second half of the beam.

Challenge Tasks or Stunts

The performer moves halfway across the beam with a selected movement, does a particular challenge or stunt at the center, and finishes the movements on the second half of the beam. Here are some suggestions:

1. *Balances.* Forward Balance, Backward Balance, Stork Stand, Seat Balance.

2. *Stunts.* Leg Dip, Finger Touch.

3. *Challenges.* Make a full turn, pick up a beanbag at the center, do a push-up.

More Difficult Movements Across the Beam

1. Hop the length of the beam—forward, sideways, backward.

2. Do the Cat Walk, Rabbit Jump, Lame Dog Walk, Seal Crawl, or Crab Walk.

3. Do various locomotor movements with the eyes closed.

4. Walk to the center of the beam and do a side-leaning rest. Try on the other side as well.

18

5. Walk to the center and do a complete body turn on one foot only.

Activities With Wands and Hoops

1. Carry a wand or hoop. Step over the wand or through the hoop in various fashions.
2. Step over or go under wands or hoops held by a partner.
3. Twirl a hoop on the arms or around the body while moving across the beam.
4. Balance a wand on various body parts while moving across the beam.
5. Balance a wand in one hand, twirl a hoop on the other hand, and proceed across the beam.

Solo Manipulative Activities

1. Using one or two beanbags, toss to self in various fashions—over the head, around the body, under the legs.
2. Using a ball, toss to self. Circle the ball around the body, under the legs.
3. Bounce a ball on the floor and on the beam. Dribble on the floor.
4. Roll a ball along the beam.

Partner Manipulative Activities

With a partner standing beyond the far end of the beam, throw a beanbag or ball back and forth. Have partner toss for a volleyball return. Bat the ball (as in a volleyball serve) to a partner.

Stunts with a Partner

1. Do a Wheelbarrow with the supporting performer keeping the feet on the floor.
2. Partners start on opposite ends of the beam and move toward each other with the same kind of movement, do a balance pose together in the center, and return to their respective ends of the beam.
3. Partners start on opposite ends of the beam and attempt to pass each other without losing their balance and without touching the floor. Find different ways to pass.

Activities on Benches

The balance-beam bench is effective in developing strength and balance. Bench activities are challenging to children and offer a variety of movement possibilities.

Instructional Procedures

1. Divide all activities on the benches into three parts: approaching and mounting the bench, doing the bench activity, and dismounting from the bench.
2. Place tumbling mats at each end of the bench to facilitate the dismount and various rolls and stunts done after dismounting.
3. Position benches either horizontally or inclined. For more variety and challenge, combine bench activities with other equipment.
4. Limit the number of children per bench to four to five.
5. The child next in turn begins when the performer ahead is about three-quarters of the way across the bench.
6. Return activities add to the activity potential.
7. Speed is not a goal in bench activities. Students move deliberately and carefully, paying attention to body control.
8. Students should also focus on laterality and directionality. For example, if a child hops on the right foot, the next move should be on the left foot. In jump turns, both right and left movements are used.

Activity Sequences

Animal Walks

Do various animal walks on the bench, such as the Seal Crawl, Cat Walk, Lame Dog Walk, and Rabbit Jump.

Locomotor Movements

Do various locomotor movements along the length of the bench, such as stepping or jumping on and off the side of the bench, hopping on and off the side of the bench, or skipping and galloping on the bench.

Pulls

Pull the body along the bench, using different combinations of body parts. Use the arms only, the legs only, the right leg and the left arm, or the left leg and the right arm. Use the following positions:

1. Prone position (head first; figure 18.6)
2. Supine position (feet first; figure 18.7)
3. Side position (head first and feet first)

FIGURE 18.6 Prone movements, head first.

FIGURE 18.7 Supine movements, feet first.

Have students use various leg positions (such as legs up in a half-lever position, knees bent, and so on) when doing pulls and pushes. Body parts not used in pulling can carry a piece of manipulative equipment (a beanbag, ball, or wand). Try different body shapes, like a submarine (one foot in the air like a periscope).

Pushes

Push the body along the bench, using different parts of the body as discussed for pulls. Use the following positions:

1. Prone position
2. Supine position
3. Side position

Movements Along the Side of the Bench

Move alongside the bench in the following positions. Keep the hands on the bench and the feet on the floor as far from the bench as possible.

1. Prone position
2. Supine position
3. Turn over (a movement along the bench, changing from prone to supine position)

Repeating these positions with the feet on the bench and the hands on the floor as far from the bench as possible

Scooting Movements

Sit on the bench and move along it without using the hands. Here are some suggestions:

1. Do a Scooter. Move with the feet leading the body. Try to pull the body along with the feet.
2. Do a reverse Scooter. Move with the legs trailing and pushing the body along the bench.
3. Do a Seat Walk. Move forward by walking on the buttocks. Use the legs as little as possible.

Crouch Jumps

Place both hands on the bench and jump back and forth over it. Move the length of the bench by placing the hands forward a few inches (about 10 cm) after each jump.

1. Do a regular Crouch Jump (figure 18.8). Use both hands and both feet. Jump as high as possible.
2. Do a Straddle Jump. Straddle the bench with the legs, take the weight on the hands, and jump with the legs as high as possible.
3. Use one hand and two feet. Do a Crouch Jump but use only one hand.
4. Use one hand and one foot. Do the Crouch Jump using only one hand and one foot.
5. Stand to one side, facing the bench, with both hands on it. With stiff arms, try to send the seat as high as possible into the air. Add the Mule Kick before coming down.

Basic Tumbling Stunts

Basic tumbling stunts can be incorporated into bench activities: the Back Roller, Backward Curl, Forward Roll (figure 18.9), Backward Roll, and Cartwheel.

18

FIGURE 18.8 Crouch Jump.

FIGURE 18.9 Preparing to do a Forward Roll on the bench.

Dismounts

All bench activities in which the child moves from one end of the bench to the other should end with a dismount. Many stunts can be used. Here are some suggestions:

1. Single jump (forward or backward; figure 18.10).
2. Jump with turns (half turn, three-quarter turn, full turn).
3. Jackknife. Jump, kick up the legs, and touch the toes with the fingertips. Keep the feet together.
4. Jackknife Split. Same as the Jackknife but spread the legs as far as possible.

5. Jump to a Forward Roll.
6. Backward jump to a Backward Roll.
7. Side jump to a Side Roll.
8. Judo Roll.
9. Jump with combinations of the stunts noted in this list.

FIGURE 18.10 Dismounting from a bench.

Additional Experiences on Benches

1. Extend the range of activities by adding balls, beanbags, hoops, and wands. Use wands and hoops as obstacles to go over, under, around, or through. Use balls and beanbags to incorporate basic balance and manipulative skills into the activity.

2. Two can perform at once; each child is near an opposite end of the bench doing different balance positions on the bench.

3. Children like to go over and under a row of benches arranged in a kind of obstacle course.

4. A bench can be supported by two jumping boxes and used as a vaulting box. Each bench is long enough to accommodate three children. They can jump off it, Mule Kick on it, and vault over it.

5. Four benches can be placed in a large rectangle (figure 18.11), with a squad standing at attention on top of each bench. On signal, each squad gets off its bench, runs around the outside of the other three benches, and then runs back to its own bench. The first squad back and at attention on the bench is the winner.

6. Place benches in a square formation, so that children can move around the square and try a different movement on each bench.

7. Place one end of the bench on a jumping box or on another bench. Children can practice jumping by running up the incline and striving for jump height at the end of the bench.

8. Benches are appropriate for some partner activities. Partners can start on each end and pass through or around each other, reversing original positions. Wheelbarrow walks are also suitable.

9. Another enjoyable activity is arranging the benches in a course as illustrated in figure 18.12. Have one student lead the squad or class through the challenge course. A different activity must be done at each bench.

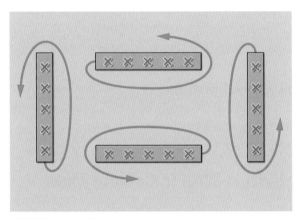

FIGURE 18.11   Rectangular bench activities.

Activities With Jumping Boxes

Jumping boxes give children opportunities to jump from a height and propel the body through space. Activities with jumping boxes are generally confined to the primary grades. Boxes can be of varying heights; 8 inches (20 cm) and 16 inches (40 cm) are suggested. Place a rubber floor pad under the box to protect the floor and prevent sliding. Jumping boxes can be built or purchased; chapter 12 includes plans for building boxes.

Instructional Procedures

1. Have students focus on landing in proper form. Stress lightness, bent-knee action, balance, and body control.

2. Use tumbling mats to cushion the landing.

3. Emphasize exploration and creativity; there are few standard stunts in jumping-box activities.

4. Assign no more than four or five children to each series of boxes.

5. Incorporate additional challenges by using hoops, wands, balls, and the like. Rolling stunts after the dismount extend the movement possibilities.

6. Return activities work well with boxes.

7. Children should strive for height and learn to relax as they go through space.

Activity Sequences

The following activities can be augmented easily. Let the children help expand the activity.

18

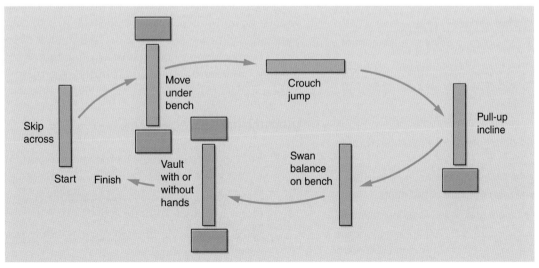

FIGURE 18.12   Challenge course using benches.

Various Approaches to the Boxes

Vary the approach to the boxes by using movements like the following:

1. Fundamental locomotor movements: run, gallop, skip, and hop

2. Animal walks: Bear Walk, Crab Walk, and so on

3. Moving over and under various obstacles: jumping over a bench, moving through a hoop held upright by a mat, doing a Backward Roll on the mat

4. Rope jumping to the box: Students try to continue jumping while mounting and dismounting the box

Mounting the Box

Students can use many different combinations to get onto the box.

1. Practice stepping onto the box (mounting) by taking the full weight on the stepping foot and holding it for a few seconds. This action develops a sense of balance and stabilizes the support foot.

2. Mount the box, using locomotor movements such as a step, jump, leap, or hop. Do various turns—quarter, half, three-quarter, and full—while jumping onto the box.

3. Use a Crouch Jump to get onto the box.

4. Back up to the box and mount it without looking at it.

5. Mount the box while a partner tosses you a beanbag.

6. Make various targets on top of the box with a piece of chalk and try to land on the spot when mounting.

Dismounting the Box

Use the following dismounts to develop body control.

1. Jump off with a quarter turn, half turn, or full turn.

2. Jump off with different body shapes: stretching, curling up in a ball.

3. Jump over a wand or through a hoop.

4. Jump off and do a Forward Roll or a Backward Roll.

5. Change the foregoing dismounts by substituting a hop or a leap in place of the jump.

6. Increase the height and distance of the dismount.

7. Dismount in various directions, such as forward, backward, sideways, northward, and southward.

8. Jump off using a Jackknife or wide straddle.

9. Do a balance stunt on the box and then dismount.

After the class has learned the basic movements used with jumping boxes, teachers can incorporate continuous squad motion. The squad captain is responsible for leading the group through different approaches, mounts, and dismounts. The same activity cannot be used twice in succession. Squad leaders are then rotated.

Addition of Equipment

Various pieces of equipment enhance box activities. Here are some suggestions:

1. Toss beanbags up while dismounting or try to keep one on your head while mounting or dismounting the box.

2. Try to dribble a playground ball while doing the box routine.

3. Jump through a stationary hoop held by a partner while dismounting or use the hoop as a jump rope and see how many times you can jump through it while dismounting.

4. Jump over or go under a wand.

Box Combinations

Arrange boxes in a straight line and in other patterns. Children do a different movement over each box as though running a challenge course.

Activities With Individual Mats

Individual mat activities originated in England and are the basis for many exploratory and creative movements. The mat serves as a base of operation or as an obstacle to go over or around. Mats vary in size, with the most popular being 24 inches by 48 inches (60 by 120 cm). Standard thickness is 3/4 of an inch (19 mm), but it can vary. The mat should have rubber backing to prevent slipping. Rubber-backed indoor-outdoor carpeting makes excellent mats; commercial mats also are available.

Instructional Procedures

1. Educational movement techniques are important in mat work.

2. Stress body management and basic skills of locomotor and nonlocomotor movement.

3. Place the mats far enough apart to allow free movement around them.

4. Each child should have a mat.

Activity Sequences

The sequence presented here is a suggestion only. The activities are quite flexible and require only fundamental skills.

Command Movements

In command movements, children change movement on command. Try these activities:

- *Stretch.* Stretch out your body in all directions as wide as possible.
- *Curl.* Curl into a tight little ball (figure 18.13).
- *Balance.* Form some kind of balanced position.
- *Bridge.* Make a bridge over the mat.
- *Reach.* Keeping the toes of one foot on the mat, reach out as far as possible across the floor in a chosen direction.
- *Rock.* Rock on any part of the body.
- *Roll.* Do some kind of roll on the mat.
- *Twist.* Make a shape with a part of the body twisted.
- *Shake.* Shake all over or shake designated parts of the body.
- *Melt.* Sink down slowly into a little puddle of water on the mat.
- *Fall.* Fall to the mat.
- *Collapse.* The movement is similar to a fall but follows nicely after a bridge.
- *Prone.* Lie facedown on the mat.

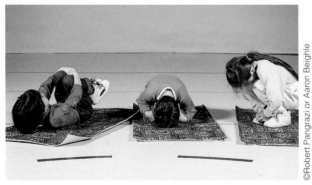

©Robert Pangrazi or Aaron Beighle

FIGURE 18.13　Curl activities on individual mats.

Sequencing can be established in several ways. The children can emphasize flow factors by changing at will from one movement to another, or they can make changes on a verbal signal or on the beat of a drum. Magic-number challenges can be used too.

Another means of exploration is selecting one of the movement challenges—say, "Stretch"—and changing from one type of stretch position to another. If balance is selected, the movement sequence can begin with a balance on six body parts; then the number can be reduced by one on each signal until the child is balancing on one body part. Have students explore different kinds of shapes.

Movements On and Off the Mat

Children do different locomotor movements on and off the mat in different directions. Turns and shapes can be added (figure 18.14).

1. Take the weight on the hands as you go across the mat.

2. Lead with different body parts as you go on and off the mat. Move on and off the mat and land by using a specific number (one to five) of body parts.

3. Jump backward, forward, sideways. Make up a rhythmic sequence. Move around the area, jumping from mat to mat.

©Robert Pangrazi or Aaron Beighle

FIGURE 18.14　Movements on and off the mat.

Movements Over the Mat

These movements are similar to the preceding movements, but the child goes completely over the mat each time.

Movements Around the Mat

Locomotor movements around the mat are done both clockwise and counterclockwise.

1. Do movements around the mat, keeping the hands on the mat. Now do movements around, keeping the feet on the mat.

2. Change to one foot and one hand on the mat. Vary with the crab position.

18

3. Work out combinations of stunt movements and locomotor activities, going around the mats. Reverse direction often.

4. Move throughout the area, running between the mats. On signal, jump over a specific number of mats.

Activities Using Mats as a Base

1. Stretch and reach in different directions to show how big the space is.

2. Do combination movements away from and back to the mat. For example, do two jumps and two hops or six steps and two jumps.

3. Use the magic-number concept.

4. See how many letters you can make. Find a partner, put your mats together, and make your bodies into different letters and numbers.

Mat Games

Each child sits on a mat. On signal, each rises and jumps over as many different mats as possible. On the next signal, each child sits on the nearest mat. The last child to sit can pay a penalty. The game can also be played by eliminating one or two mats so that one or two children are left without a home base. The teacher can stand on a mat or turn over mats to put them out of the game. To control roughness, make a rule that the first child to touch a mat gets to sit on it.

A variation is to have each child touch at least 10 mats and then sit cross-legged on the 11th, or have them alternate touching a mat and jumping over the next mat until reaching a total of 10. Challenge students: "See how many mats you can cartwheel or jump over in 10 seconds." Change the challenge and try again.

Developmental Challenges

1. Experiment with curl-ups (partial or full). (This can be done informally or as a challenge.)

2. From a sitting position on the mat, pick up the short sides of the mat and raise the feet and upper body off the floor. Try variations of the V-Up.

Manipulative Activities

Keeping one foot on the mat, maintain control of a balloon in the air, either with a hand, a nylon-stocking paddle, or a Lummi stick. Try the same activity with a stocking paddle and a paper ball. Children can count the number of touches or strokes. Try with both feet on the mat.

Activities With Magic Ropes (Jump Bands)

Magic rope activities originated in Germany. The ropes are similar to long rubber bands and are sometimes referred to as Jump Bands. Magic ropes can be made from ordinary 3/4-inch (19 mm) elastic tape available in most fabric stores. Children place their hands through loops on each end and grasp the rope. Another option is to place the foot through the loop, and the loop goes around the ankle. Ropes should be long enough to stretch to between 10 and 15 feet (3 and 4.5 m) and up to 30 to 40 feet (9 to 12 m) when stretched. A major advantage of the magic rope is its flexibility; children have no fear of hitting it or tripping on it while performing. Ropes should be stretched tight, with little slack.

Instructional Procedures

1. Two or more children are located at the end of ropes. They are referred to as holders. Teachers can develop a rotation plan for holders.

2. By changing the height or raising and lowering opposite ends of the ropes, many variations are possible.

3. The jumping activities are strenuous; alternate them with activities that involve crawling under the ropes.

4. Have students focus on not touching the rope. The magic rope can help develop body perception in space if it is treated as an obstacle to be avoided.

5. Better use can be made of the rope by using an angled approach, which involves starting at one end of the rope and moving to the other end by using jumping and hopping activities. In comparison, the straight-on approach allows the child to jump the rope only once.

6. From 8 to 12 ropes, 2 for each squad, are needed for a class. Squads are excellent groups for this activity because the leader can control the rotation of the rope holders.

7. The child next in turn begins when the child ahead is almost to the end of the rope.

Activity Sequences

Activities With Single Ropes

Start the ropes at a 6-inch (15 cm) height and gradually raise them to add challenge.

1. Jump over the rope.
2. Hop over the rope.
3. Jump and do various body turns while jumping.
4. Make different body shapes and change body size while jumping.
5. Crawl or slide under the rope.
6. Crouch-jump over the rope.
7. Hold the rope overhead and have others jump up and touch it with their foreheads.
8. Gradually lower the rope and do the limbo under it without touching the floor with the hands.
9. Jump over the rope backward without looking at it.
10. Do a Scissors Jump over the rope.

Activities With Double Ropes

Vary the height and spread of the ropes.

1. Do these activities with the ropes parallel to each other.

   a. Jump in one side and out the other (figure 18.15).
   b. Hop in one side and out the other.
   c. Crouch-jump in and out.
   d. Do various animal walks in and out of the ropes.
   e. Do a long jump over both of the ropes.
   f. Do a stunt while jumping in between the two ropes. Possible stunts are the Heel Click, body turn, and Straddle Jump.
   g. Jump or leap over one rope and land on the other rope

2. With the ropes crossed at right angles to each other, try these activities:

   a. Do various movements from one area to the next.
   b. Jump into one area and crawl into another.

3. With one rope above the other to resemble a fence, do these activities. Vary the height of the ropes and their distance apart. Challenging children not to touch the "barbed-wire fence" adds much excitement to the activity.

   a. Step through the ropes without touching.
   b. Crouch-jump through.

Miscellaneous Activities With Magic Ropes

Give students time to create their own ideas with the ropes and other pieces of equipment.

©Robert Pangrazi or Aaron Beighle

FIGURE 18.15 Jumping in and out of two magic ropes.

1. Do the various activities with a beanbag balanced on the head. Try them while bouncing a ball.
2. Use four or more ropes to create various floor patterns.
3. Add variety with a follow-the-leader activity.
4. Create a challenge course with many ropes for a relay.

Activities With Partner Tug-of-War Ropes

A partner tug-of-war rope is about 6 feet (2 m) long with a rubber hose covered loop on each end. (See chapter 12 for instructions on making partner tug-of-war ropes.) Tug-of-war activities develop strength, because students must use most of their strength. These strength demands may continue over a short time.

Instructional Procedures

1. Start and stop the tugging with clear signals. Tugging bouts should last no more than five to seven seconds. Problems occur when students become tired and one partner gets pulled around. Tell students not to pull until someone falls down but to have a good tug and stop.

2. Contests are between partners of comparable ability and size, so that each child has a chance to win.

18

3. Plan a system of rotation so that children meet different partners. If students stay with the same partner, the same person keeps winning.

4. Caution students not to let go of the rope. If the grip is slipping, they should ask the other student to stop pulling, renew the grip, and start over.

5. Individual ropes are excellent for partner resistance activities. Have students practice some of these activities each time they use the ropes.

6. Use a line on the floor, perpendicular to the direction of the rope, to signal a win. When one child pulls the other over the line, the contest ends. Another signal for a win could be for children to back up, while pulling, until they can pick up an object behind them.

Partner Activities

The tug-of-war rope offers good possibilities in movement exploration. Have partners try the following ways of pulling. Let them devise other ways to pull against each other.

1. Pull with the right hand only, the left hand only, both hands.

2. Grasp with the right hand, with the body supported on three points (the left hand and the feet). Change hands.

3. Pull with backs toward each other, with the rope between the legs, holding with one hand only.

4. Partners get down on all fours, with feet toward each other. Hook the loops around one foot of each partner. Each contestant pulls using both hands and the foot still on the floor.

5. Partners get into crab position and pull the rope by hooking a foot through the loop (figure 18.16).

6. Partners face each other and stand on one foot only. Students try to pull each other off balance without losing their own balance. If the raised foot touches the floor, the other person wins.

7. Partners stand with opposite sides toward each other. They hold a tug-of-war rope with opposite hands and move apart until the rope is taut. By pulling and giving on the rope, they try to make the other person move the feet. The legs must be kept straight, and only the arms can be used in the contest.

8. Students stand 10 feet (3 m) away from the rope, which is on the floor. On signal, they run to the rope, pick it up, and have a tug-of-war. Students can start from different positions, such as push-up, curl-up, or crab.

9. Instead of pulling each other across a line, each partner tries to pull the other toward a peg or bowling pin placed behind them and pick up the object.

10. Tie two individual ropes together at the center so that four loops are available for pulling. Use four cones to form a large square; four children stand inside it and compete to see who can pick up a cone first.

11. Two children pull against two others. Be sure that the rope loops are big enough so that two students can hold each end. They can use right hands only or left hands only.

12. For Frozen Tug-of-War, two children hold a rope, each with both hands on a loop. The children stand close enough together to give the rope some slack. A third child grasps the rope to make a 6-inch (15 cm) bend at the center, and the contestants then pull the rope taut so that there is no slack (figure 18.17). On "Go," the third child drops the loop, and the opponents try to pull each other off balance. The feet are "frozen" to the floor; the player who moves either foot loses.

13. Hawaiian Tug-of-War uses two parallel lines about 20 feet (6 m) apart. The game is between two people; as many pairs as are in a class can play. Lay a partner tug-of-war rope on the floor at right angles to, and midway between, the two lines. Each player stands about 1 foot (30 cm) from one end of the rope. On signal, they pick up the rope and pull against each other. The goal is to pull the other child far enough to be able to touch the line behind. Children must not reach down and pick up the rope until the teacher says, "Hula!" To assure that students are listening, use other commands, such as "Go" and "Begin!"

14. Group contests are possible. (See figure 12.28 for rope arrangements suitable for groups.)

FIGURE 18.16 Pulling in crab position.

©Robert Pangrazi or Aaron Beighle

FIGURE 18.17 Frozen Tug-of-War.

Partner Resistance Activities

In partner resistance activities, students follow exercise principles of using sufficient force (near maximum), maintaining resistance through the full range of motion for 8 to 10 seconds, and stabilizing the base so that the selected part of the body is exercised. The movements are controlled, not a tugging or jerky motion. The partner should not be compelled to move out of position. Much of the exercise centers on the hands and arms, but other parts of the body come into play as braces. Partners work together, both in the same position.

As in other activities, grip can be varied. The upper grip (palms down) and the lower grip (palms up) are usually used. Occasionally, a mixed grip—one hand palm down and one hand palm up—is used. Be sure that the right and left sides of the body receive equal treatment.

Partners Standing With Sides Toward Each Other

1. Use a lower grip. Do a flexed-arm pull, with elbows at right angles.
2. Use an upper grip. Extend the arm from the side at a 45-degree angle. Pull toward the side.
3. Use a lower grip. Extend the arm completely overhead. Pull overhead.
4. Place the loop around one ankle. Stand with feet apart. Pull with the closer foot.

Partners Standing, Facing Each Other

1. Use a lower grip. Do a flexed-arm pull with one hand and then both hands.
2. Use an upper grip. Extend the arms at the side or down. Pull toward the rear.
3. Use an upper grip. Pull both hands straight toward chest.
4. Use an upper grip. Extend the arms overhead. Pull backward.

Partners Sitting, Facing Each Other

1. Repeat the activities described for standing position (figure 18.18).
2. Place both feet in the loop. Pull.

FIGURE 18.18 Partner resistance activity in sitting position.

Partners Prone, Facing Each Other

1. Use an upper grip. Pull directly toward the chest.
2. Use a lower grip. Do a flexed-arm pull.

Partners Prone, Feet Toward Each Other

1. Hook the rope around one ankle. With knee joint at a right angle, pull.
2. Try with both feet together.

18

19 Rhythmic Movement Skills

Activities in this chapter are selected expressly for developing rhythmic movement skills. The activities progress from easy to more complex and from Developmental Levels I to III. Students develop social skills and a positive self-concept when rhythmic activities are taught in a sensitive, educational way. Schedule rhythmic activities as you would other phases of the yearly physical education program. Most dances use skills and steps that children learn in sequence.

Learning Objectives

- ▶ Know where to find sources of rhythmic accompaniment.
- ▶ Understand the inherent rhythmic nature of all physical activity.
- ▶ Outline components of the yearly rhythmic movement program and identify accompanying activities and skill progressions.
- ▶ Describe instructional procedures and ideas to help facilitate implementation of rhythmic movements into the yearly program.
- ▶ Cite creative rhythms, movement songs, folk dances, and other dance activities that are used as learning experiences in physical education.
- ▶ Describe dance progressions appropriate to the various levels of children's development

Rhythm is the basis of music and dance. Rhythm in dance is simply expressive movement either with or without music. All body movements tend to be rhythmic—from the beating of the heart to swinging a tennis racket to throwing a ball. Most movements in physical education class also contain elements of rhythm. Movement to rhythm begins early in the child's school career and continues throughout. Rhythmic activities are particularly appropriate for younger children. Much of the Developmental Level I program focuses on such activities. One problem in incorporating rhythmic activities is the vast amount of material available; teachers must judiciously make hundreds of choices to present a broad, progressive program. Another problem is that many teachers are hesitant about the subject area. But if you prepare properly, you soon will become comfortable with rhythmic activities and find that they are a favorite among children.

Early experiences center on functional and creative movement forms. Locomotor skills are inherently rhythmic in execution, and adding rhythm can enhance students' development of these skills. An important component of children's dance is these fundamental rhythms. Instruction begins with and capitalizes on locomotor skills that children already possess. Rhythmic activities are a vehicle for expressive movement. These activities offer opportunity for broad participation and personal satisfaction for all, because children personalize their responses to a movement and create unique rhythmic responses within action songs and dances.

Implementing the Rhythmic Movement Program

The rhythmic program should be balanced and include activities from each category of rhythmic movement. Table 19.1 shows recommended types of rhythmic activities for each developmental level.

Skill Progressions

Another factor in program construction is the progression of basic and specific dance steps. Dances employing the following skills and steps appear in each of the respective developmental level programs.

Developmental Level I

Children in Developmental Level I focus on creative rhythms and movement songs. Students learn simple folk dances and mixers with a focus on one or two locomotor movements. They also use simple mixers in learning to find

new partners and move rhythmically. At this level, teachers focus on activities requiring a minimum of instruction while giving students a positive experience with rhythms.

TABLE 19.1 Types of Rhythmic Activity

Activity	Developmental Level		
	I	II	III
Creative rhythms	X		
Folk dances	X	X	X
Line dances		X	X
Mixers	X	X	X
Aerobic dancing		X	X
Square dancing			X
Rope jumping to music	S	X	X
Musical games	S	S	S
Rhythmic gymnastics (refer to chapter 17)			

Note: X means that the activity is an integral part of the program. S means that the activity receives only minor emphasis.

Developmental Level II

At this level, greater practice on folk dances and line dances includes combinations of locomotor skills, such as the step-hop and the grand right and left. Marching, basic tinikling steps, and introductory square dancing steps are taught as skill improves. All the activities are taught with an emphasis on mastering simple locomotor skills rather than performing the dances perfectly.

Developmental Level III

Developmental Level III students learn more difficult steps such as the grapevine step, schottische, polka, intermediate tinikling steps, two-step, advanced tinikling steps, square dancing, and all steps introduced at earlier levels. Developmentally, some students may not be comfortable moving with partners of the opposite sex, so activities are modified to allow for individual activity.

Understanding Rhythmic Accompaniment

Music has essential characteristics that children should recognize, understand, and appreciate. These characteristics are also present to varying degrees in other purely percussive accompaniment.

Tempo is the speed of the music. It can be constant, show a gradual increase (acceleration), or decrease (deceleration).

19

Beat is the underlying rhythm of the music. Some musicians refer to the beat as the pulse of the music. The beat can be even or uneven. Music with a pronounced beat is easier to follow.

Certain notes or beats in a rhythmic pattern receive more force than others, and this quality defines *accent*. Accent is generally expressed by a more forceful movement in a sequence of movements.

A *measure* is a group of beats made by the regular occurrence of a heavy accent. Usually the accent is applied to the first beat of a measure. A measure represents the underlying beat enclosed between two adjacent bars on a musical staff.

The *intensity* of music is related to mood and can be loud, soft, light, or heavy. Music can reflect many moods—happiness, sadness, gaiety, fear, or stateliness.

A *phrase* is a natural grouping of measures. Phrases of music are put together into rhythmic *patterns*. Children should learn to recognize when a pattern repeats or changes.

Sources of Rhythmic Accompaniment

Essential to any rhythmic program is accompaniment that encourages desired motor patterns and expressive movement. Children are more likely to move to a rhythm that is stimulating, appropriate for the expected responses, and appealing. Skillful use of a drum or tambourine adds much to rhythmic experiences. A major use of the drumbeat is to guide the movement from one pattern to another by signaling tiny increments of change with light beats that control the flow. The motion in striking is essentially a wrist action, not an arm movement. Each school and teacher should build a collection of recorded music. Sets created especially for physical education movement patterns and dance are available from various sources (see information on Wagon Wheel Records later in this chapter). Physical education teachers should store their music in the physical education facility rather than the school library. Arrange storage so that each recording has its assigned place and is readily available.

Creative Rhythms

Creative rhythms are a special program area in which creativity is the goal and functional movement is secondary. The emphasis is on the process, not the movement outcomes. Guide the movement patterns by suggestions, questions, encouragement, and challenges that help children structure their ideas and add variety. Careful guidance is necessary to fan the spark of self-direction; freedom alone does not automatically develop creativity.

Instructional Procedures

1. Provide appropriate music or rhythmic background; otherwise, movement can become stilted. Establish an atmosphere of creative freedom, making the class comfortable and relaxed.

2. When analyzing the setting, ask, "What is the basic idea? What expressive movements can be expected? What are the guidelines or boundaries of movement? What space are the children to use?"

3. Listening is an important element, because children must understand the mood or sense of the rhythmic background. Examples of questions to ask are, "What does the music make us think of?" and "What does the music tell us to do?" If the movement or interpretation is preselected, waste no time in starting. Provide enough music so that children can grasp the effect. Have them clap the beat if necessary and then move into action.

4. Use action-directing statements such as, "Let's pretend we are . . . ," "Let's try being like . . . ," "Try to feel like a . . . ," and "Make believe you are . . ."

5. In some lessons, the initial focus may be on selecting appropriate rhythmic background. In this instance children formulate a creative rhythm of the dramatic type and then seek suitable music for their dance.

6. Give children time to develop and try their ideas. This open-ended process has a variety of solutions. Coaching and guidance are important aspects at this stage. Application of time, space, force, flow, and body factors is essential. Encourage large, free movement of all body parts. Use the entire area and fill in the empty places in general space. Allow time for exploration.

Expressive Movement

Children can express moods and feelings and show reactions to colors and sounds by improvising dances or movements that demonstrate different aspects of force or gestures that depict different feelings. After playing a piece of music, discuss its qualities and ask the children how it makes them feel. Children may interpret the music differently. Moods can be described as happy, lighthearted, sad, brave, fearful, cheerful, angry, solemn, silly, stately, sleepy, funny, cautious, bold, or nonchalant.

Identification

Endless sources are available for identification and interpretation. Children can assume the identity of a familiar character, creature, or object. These ideas may be useful: animals, people, play objects, make-believe creatures, machines, circus characters, and natural phenomena such as trees and tornadoes.

1. Animals—elephants, ducks, seals, chickens, dogs, rabbits, lions, and others

2. People—soldiers, firefighters, sailors, nurses, various kinds of workers, forest rangers, teachers, and cowboys and cowgirls

3. Play objects—seesaws, swings, rowboats, balls, various toys, and other common articles

4. Make-believe creatures—giants, gnomes, witches, trolls, dragons, pixies, and fairies

5. Machines—trains, planes, jets, rockets, automobiles, bicycles, motorcycles, tractors, and elevators

6. Circus characters—clowns, trained animals, trapeze artists, tightrope walkers, jugglers, acrobats, and bands

7. Natural phenomena—fluttering leaves, grain, flowers, rain, snow, clouds, wind, tornadoes, hurricanes, and volcanoes

Dramatization

Dramatization and rhythm are useful vehicles for group activity. Suitable background music or rhythmic accompaniment is required.

Here are some useful ideas for dramatic rhythms: build a house, fly a kite, go fishing, do chores like chopping wood, act out sports or stories about heroic characters like astronauts and firefighters.

1. Build a house, garage, or other structure.

2. Make a snowman, throw snowballs, go skiing.

3. Fly a kite, go hunting or fishing, go camping.

4. Act out stories about astronauts, cowboys and cowgirls, firefighters, explorers.

5. Interpret familiar stories, such as "Sleeping Beauty," "The Three Bears," or "Little Red Riding Hood."

6. Do household tasks such as chopping wood, picking fruit, mowing the lawn, cleaning the yard, washing dishes, and vacuuming.

7. Celebrate holidays such as Halloween, the Fourth of July, Thanksgiving, or Christmas; or dramatize the seasons.

8. Play sports such as football, basketball, baseball, track and field, swimming, tennis, and golf.

9. Divide the class in groups of three or four, and assign each group a sport other than one of the major sports. Have them develop a series of movements dramatizing that sport to the class. Have the remaining groups guess which sport is being presented. Slow-motion movements add to this activity.

10. Plan a trip through a haunted house. Use Halloween music for this activity.

11. Have the children make a motor. One student starts by getting into a position of choice in the middle of the floor and by putting one body part in motion. The motion should be a steady, rhythmic movement. The remaining students, one at a time, attach onto the first person, and each person puts one body part in motion. After all are attached, a machine with many moving parts is the result.

12. Act out the children's favorite parts in popular movies. Having the children perform to the original soundtrack makes the performance more realistic.

13. Select a favorite poem ("Old Mother Hubbard," "Pat-a-Cake," "The Giant"), and design a sequence of activities to fit the meaning of the poem. Stories have excellent appeal.

To learn how an idea can be exploited for a lesson on creative rhythm, consider an activity called the Wind and the Leaves. One or more children are chosen to be the wind, and the other children are the leaves. Two kinds of rhythm are needed: one fast for the wind, one slower and reactive for the trees. The students break into two teams; some act out the wind based on its rhythms, and the rest act out the trees. The first rhythm is high, fast, and shrill, indicating the blowing of the wind. The intensity and tempo illustrate the speed and force of the wind. The second rhythm is slow, measured, and light, to represent the leaves fluttering in the still air and finally coming to rest at various positions on the ground. During the first rhythm, children representing the wind act out a heavy gust. While this is going on, the leaves show what it is like to be blown about. During the second rhythm, the wind is still and the leaves flutter to the ground. Other characterizations can be added. For example, street sweepers can come along and sweep up the leaves.

Another lesson strategy is to divide the class into groups and ask each group to develop and act out an idea with percussive accompaniment. Each group then performs for the others. After each group performs, the other groups guess what they interpreted. In this game, keep the interpretations brief.

19

Folk Dances

A *folk dance* is defined as a traditional dance of a particular culture. In this concept, a definite pattern or dance routine is usually specified and followed. Folk dancing is one phase of a child's education that can assist in bringing about international understanding. A country's folk music often reflects its way of life and many other habits. From these dances, children gain an understanding of why people from certain countries act and live as they do, even though modern times may have changed their lifestyle from that of days gone by.

Folk dances in Developmental Level I consist of fundamental locomotor skills, either singly or in combination. Dances with more specialized steps, such as the two-step, polka, and schottische, are found in Developmental Levels II and III. The first consideration when teaching folk dance is to determine whether children know the basic skills required for the dance. If a skill needs to be taught, it can be handled in one of two ways. The first is to teach the skill separately, before teaching the dance. The second is to teach the dance in its normal sequence, giving specific instructions when the skill appears. The first method is often best, because children can concentrate solely on learning the skill.

Teaching New Dances

Learning to move rhythmically is the underlying goal of folk dancing. Unfortunately, many students (often boys) develop negative attitudes and feelings of failure about rhythmic activities. Effective teachers have long recognized the need to modify sport activities to ensure that students learn skills correctly and experience success. Modifications, such as using smaller balls, lower baskets, and slower-moving objects, are now commonplace in most elementary school physical education activities. But when teaching rhythmic activities, teachers often discard this approach. Dances are taught with precision and emphasis on "doing it right," instead of modifying them so that they are appealing and easier to learn. Here are some guidelines for modifying rhythmic activities to increase the likelihood of success.

1. *Slow down the music.* Children's first contact with the activity must be successful. No student wants to be embarrassed because he or she is out of step. If students are still not doing well, stop the music and walk them through it. Start from the beginning each time, so that students who are lost can begin anew.

2. *In general, if the dance is short, use the whole-teaching approach.* If the dance is longer and has several parts, use the part–whole method and teach one part at a time. For example, have children learn half of a two-part dance or one-third of a three-part dance and then put that part to music. After learning all the parts, students can try the complete dance.

3. *When introducing a new dance, place students in scatter formation.* Circles and formations make some students feel as if others are looking directly at them. If they are self-conscious about their ability, a circle formation may be intimidating. A scattered formation allows these children to move to an area where fewer peers can see them perform.

4. *Avoid the use of partners when teaching a new activity.* Because using partners makes many dances more complex, add them only after students master the basic steps. Let students who do not want to dance with a partner perform the steps alone.

5. *Avoid the left–right and clockwise-counterclockwise orientation when introducing a new dance.* Anytime students are asked to move in a specified direction, the possibility of error increases. Let students choose the direction they would like to move when learning new steps. Later, when students master the steps, teachers can add various orientations and formations.

6. *To avoid stressing students, perform a dance once or twice in a daily lesson.* Presenting several dances, rather than one or two in depth, allows students who are having difficulty to start with a clean slate on a new dance. Come back to a difficult dance and practice it in a later lesson. Some students panic when they experience difficulty, and the increased stress limits their ability to learn.

7. *Teach rhythmic activities in the same way that sport skills are taught.* Teachers expect that students will make mistakes, regardless of their ability level; baskets are missed and passes are dropped. Treat rhythmic activities like sport skills and know that perfection is virtually impossible to reach. Use rhythmic activities to teach students to move rhythmically, not to showcase one or two dances learned perfectly. If teachers accept student errors, students learn that rhythms are fun and worth trying.

8. *Dances that emphasize strong movements such as hand clapping and foot stomping appeal to boys.* Because boys are often hard to sell on rhythmic activities, introducing them to some activities that include strong, bold physical movements makes sense.

Modifying Rhythmic Activities

Folk dances are traditional rhythmic activities people have done for generations. The traditional music and style may not appeal to some children in a school setting, but with a few modifications, the dances are easier to learn. Table 19.2 shows how some common folk dances can be modified to increase student interest and increase the ease of learning.

Another way to motivate students is to use current music and change traditional dances into line dances. Line dances can motivate students to learn new steps without worrying about a partner. Here are some folk and popular dances that can be done as line dances.

- Popcorn
- Jiffy Mixer
- Cotton-Eyed Joe
- Jessie Polka
- Teton Mountain Stomp
- Alley Cat

Arranging for Partners

Arranging for partners can be hurtful or embarrassing for some children. To be acceptable, a method of arranging for partners must prevent any children from being rejected or overlooked. If this is not possible, modifying it for individual participation rather than forging ahead at all costs is probably best.

Music for Folk Dances

Quality recordings are difficult to find. Wagon Wheel Records is a reliable source of music accompaniment for all the dances included in this chapter. You can order materials from the following address or website:

> Wagon Wheel Records
> 16812 Pembrook Lane
> Huntington Beach, CA 92649
> Phone or fax: 714-846-8169
> Website: www.wagonwheelrecords.net
> Email: info@wagonwheelrecords.net

Each dance in this chapter includes a code indicating whether it is in CD (WWCD) or cassette (WWC) format; a catalog number (e.g., 7054) identifies the source for ordering.

TABLE 19.2 Examples of Dance Modifications

Dance	Skills	Modifications	Formation
The Bird Dance	Skipping or walking, elbow swing or star	Good introductory dance for all levels	Scattered
Shortnin' Bread	Sliding, turning with a partner, clapping	Slow music; practice without partner	Scattered first, then with partner
Jump Jim Jo	Jumping, running, draw step	No partner; move in any direction	Scattered
Eins Zwei Drei	Walking, heel-toe step, sliding	No partner, no numbering; slide any direction; play giant cymbals	Scattered, then facing center of area
Wild Turkey Mixer	Walking, elbow swing	Groups of three—scattered; center person with pinny; do not mix when learning	Scattered first, then circle formation
Irish Washerwoman	Walking, swinging, promenade position	No partners; swing and promenade the closest partner or move to the center for a partner; emphasize clapping and stomping	Facing center
Oh, Susanna	Walking, promenade, grand right and left	Half of class with pinnies; use a wild grand right and left; go to center and find partner if left without one	Facing center
Jessie Polka	Step and touch, two-step or polka	Slow down music; no partners; practice step and touch first	Scattered, students can hook on if they desire
Limbo Rock	Touch step, swivel step, jump-clap-clap	Slow down music; teach steps and add together	Scattered
Inside-Out Mixer	Wring the dishrag, walk, change partners	Practice without music; no mixing until learned	Groups of three
Teton Mountain Stomp	Walking, two-step	Do individually; emphasize clapping; move in any direction; no side car or banjo position	Scattered

19

Formations for Folk Dances

Figure 19.1 illustrates the formations used for folk dances in this chapter. Each folk dance description begins by listing the records, skills, and formation to be used. If you are unsure about how the class should be arranged, consult figure 19.1, which shows four types of formations: single-circle, double-circle, triple-circle, and others.

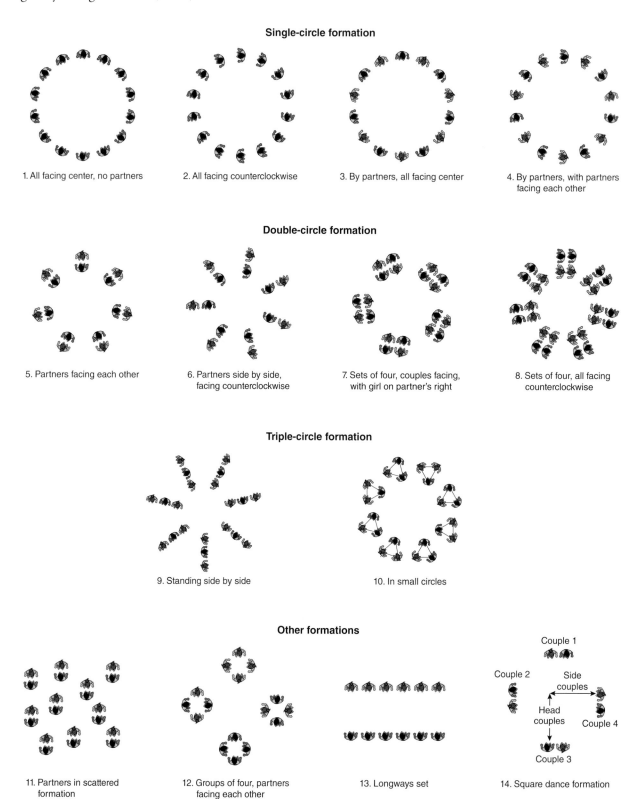

Single-circle formation

1. All facing center, no partners

2. All facing counterclockwise

3. By partners, all facing center

4. By partners, with partners facing each other

Double-circle formation

5. Partners facing each other

6. Partners side by side, facing counterclockwise

7. Sets of four, couples facing, with girl on partner's right

8. Sets of four, all facing counterclockwise

Triple-circle formation

9. Standing side by side

10. In small circles

Other formations

11. Partners in scattered formation

12. Groups of four, partners facing each other

13. Longways set

14. Square dance formation

Couple 1

Couple 2

Side couples

Head couples

Couple 4

Couple 3

FIGURE 19.1   Dance formations.

Dance Positions

In most dance positions, partner A holds a hand or hands palms up and partner B joins the grip with a palms-down position. The following dance positions or partner positions are common to many dances.

Partners-Facing Position

In partners-facing position, as the name suggests, the partners are facing. Partner A extends hands forward with palms up and elbows slightly bent. Partner B places hands in A's hands.

Side-by-Side Position

In side-by-side position (figure 19.2), partner A always has partner B to the right. Partner A offers the right hand, held above the waist, palm up. B places the left hand in A's raised hand.

Closed Position

Closed position is the social dance position. Partners stand facing each other, shoulders parallel, and toes pointed forward. Partner A holds partner B's right hand in A's left hand out to the side, at about shoulder level, with elbows bent. Partner A places the right hand on B's back, just below the left shoulder blade. B's left arm rests on A's upper arm, and B's left hand is on A's right shoulder.

Open Position

To go from closed to open position, partner A turns to the left and partner B to the right. Their arms stay in about the same position. Both face in the same direction and are side by side.

Promenade Position

Promenade position (figure 19.3) is a crossed-arm position in which dancers stand side by side, facing the same direction. The partners hold each other's right hand in their right hand and left hand in their left.

Varsouvienne Position

Partners stand side by side and face the same direction. Partner B is slightly in front and to the right of partner A. Partner A holds B's left hand in his or her left hand in front and at about shoulder height. B brings the right hand directly back over the right shoulder, and A reaches behind B at shoulder height and grasps that hand with his or her right hand.

FIGURE 19.2 Side-by-side position.

FIGURE 19.3 Promenade position.

19

Progression of Folk Dances

The dances in this section start with the easiest and end with the most difficult. Dances are grouped into the three developmental levels to give you the widest possible latitude in selecting dances that fit the students' maturity and skills. For a quick and clear overview of the total dance program, see the sidebar Alphabetical Listing of Folk Dances by Developmental Level, which lists all dances in alphabetical order by developmental level, notes skills required for the dance, and includes page numbers for quick reference.

ALPHABETICAL LISTING OF FOLK DANCES BY DEVELOPMENTAL LEVEL

Dance	Skills	Page
Developmental Level I		
Ach Ja	Walking, sliding	426
Ballin' the Jack	Sliding, do-si-do	425
Bleking	Bleking step, step-hop	430
Bombay Bounce	Hesitation step, side step	430
Carousel	Draw step, sliding	430
Children's Polka	Step-draw	428
Chimes of Dunkirk, Var. 1	Turning in a small circle with a partner, changing partners	427
Chimes of Dunkirk, Var. 2	Turning with a partner, skipping	429
Circassian Circle	Walking, skipping, promenade	433
Clapping Out	Rhythmic clapping	425
Danish Dance of Greeting	Running or sliding, bowing	426
Did You Ever See a Lassie?	Walking at 3/4 time, creativity	424
Eins Zwei Drei	Walking, sliding	429
Hitch Hiker, The	Chug step, skipping	432
Hokey Pokey	Body identification, nonlocomotor movements	424
How D'Ye Do, My Partner?	Bowing, curtsying, skipping	426
Jingle Bells, Var. 1	Elbow swing, skipping, sliding	432
Jolly Is the Miller	Marching	430
Jump Jim Jo	Jumping, running, draw step	428
Little Liza Jane	Marching, rope jumping, galloping	424
Looby Loo	Skipping or running, body identification	424
Movin' Madness	Keeping time, creativity	424
Muffin Man, The	Jumping, skipping	425
Nixie Polka	Bleking step	431
Rhythm Sticks—It's a Small, Small World	Rhythmic tapping, manipulation of sticks	433
Seven Jumps	Step-hop, balance, control	427
Seven Steps	Running, hopping	433
Shoemaker's Dance	Skipping, heel and toe	428
Shortnin' Bread	Sliding, turning with a partner	427
Skip to My Lou	Skipping, changing partners	425
Turn the Glasses Over	Walking, wring the dishrag	432
Yankee Doodle	Walking, galloping, sliding, bowing	429
Developmental Level II		
Apat	Walking, star hold	443
Bingo	Walking, grand right and left	437
Bird Dance, The (Chicken Dance)	Skipping or walking, elbow swing or star	434
Crested Hen	Step-hop, turning under	441

19

Regarding level of difficulty, teachers must be aware that if a group of students lacks a rhythmic background, some dances at their developmental level may be too difficult. For example, a sixth-grade class that lacks dance skills may need to begin with Developmental Level II dances. On the other hand, avoid boring a class by starting children on material below their maturity level.

Developmental Level I Dances

Dances in this section contain introductory movement songs and folk dances using simple formations and uncomplicated changes. The movements are primarily basic locomotor skills and hand gestures or clapping sequences. There are dances both with and without partners. As the dances increase in difficulty, patterns become more definite, and more folk dances are included. Movements are still primarily of the simple locomotor type, with additional and varied emphasis on more complicated patterns.

Movin' Madness (American)

Music source: WWCD-1044

Skills: keeping time, creativity

Formation: scattered

Directions: The music is in two parts.

Part I: The tempo is slow, slow, fast-fast-fast. The children do any series of movements of their choice to fit this pattern, repeated four times. The dance involves large motor movements.

Part II: During the second part (chorus) of the music, the children do any locomotor movement in keeping with the tempo. They can use a step-hop or a light run with the tempo of part II.

Did You Ever See a Lassie? (Scottish)

Music source: WWCD-7054; WWC-7054

Skills: walking at 3/4 time, creativity

Formation: single circle, facing halfway left, hands joined; one child in the center

Directions:

Measures	Action
1–8	All walk (one step per measure) to the left in a circle with hands joined. (Walk, 2, 3, . . . , 8.) The child in the center gets ready to demonstrate some type of movement.
9–16	All stop and copy the movement suggested by the child in the center.

As the verse starts over, the center child selects another to do some action in the center and changes places with him or her.

Looby Loo (English)

Music source: WWCD-7054; WWC-7054

Skills: skipping or running, body identification

Formation: single circle, facing center, hands joined

Directions: The chorus is repeated before each verse. During the chorus, all children skip around the circle to the right. On the verse part of the dance, the children stand still, face the center, and follow the directions of the words. On the words "and turn myself about," they make a complete turn in place and get ready to skip around the circle again. Movements are definite and vigorous. On the last verse, they jump forward and then backward, shake vigorously, and then turn about.

Make the dance more fun and vigorous by changing the tasks. Try these: Right side or hip, left side or hip, big belly, backside.

Hokey Pokey (American)

Music source: WWC-9126

Skills: body identification, nonlocomotor movements

Formation: single circle, facing center

Directions: During the first four lines, the children act out the words. During lines 5 and 6, they hold their hands overhead with palms forward and do a kind of hula while turning around in place. During line 7, they stand in place and clap their hands three times.

The basic verse is repeated by substituting, successively, the left foot, right arm, left arm, right elbow, left elbow, head, right hip, left hip, whole self, and backside. Encourage the students to make large, vigorous motions during the Hokey Pokey portions and during the turn around. Encourage the class to sing lightly while following the directions in the song.

Little Liza Jane (American)

Music source: WWCD-FFD

Skills: marching, rope jumping, galloping

Formation: single circle, facing center

Directions: Students do a different movement every 32 counts. After each movement, they perform the chorus.

Measures	Action
1–4	Introduction: Listen to the rhythm.
1–16	Feet together and bend the knees up and down.
17–32	Swing arm overhead as if swinging a lasso (16 counts in each hand).
33–48	March eight steps to the center and eight steps back (repeat).
49–64	Jump rope for 32 counts.
65–80	Do Arm Circles (16 forward and 16 backward).
81–96	Gallop around the circle (16 gallops in each direction).
97–112	Join hands and circle (16 steps in each direction).

Chorus: After each movement above, students perform the chorus. Roll the hands four times in front, then touch both hands to the knees, clap hands together, and push palms forward. Sing, "Roll Little Liza, Little Liza Jane" while performing the hand pattern. Perform this movement in 8 counts (roll, 2, 3, 4, knees, clap, palms for 2). Repeat the chorus four times.

The Muffin Man (American)

Music source: WWCD-YR002; WWC-YR002

Skills: jumping, skipping

Formation: single circle, facing center, hands at; one child, the Muffin Man, stands in the circle, in front of another child of the opposite gender

Directions:

- *Verse 1*: The children stand still and clap their hands lightly. The Muffin Man and his partner join hands and jump lightly in place while keeping time to the music. On the first beat of each measure, the partners take a normal jump, followed by a bounce in place (rebound) on the second beat.

- *Verse 2*: The Muffin Man and his partner then skip around the inside of the circle individually and, near the end of the verse, each stands in front of a child, thus choosing a new partner.

Verse 1 is then repeated, with two sets of partners doing the jumping. During the repetition of verse 2, four children skip around the inside of the circle and choose partners. This procedure continues until all children have partners.

Let the children choose the name of a street to put in the verses.

Clapping Out (American)

Music source: WWCD-FFD

Skills: rhythmic clapping

Formation: single circle, facing center

Directions:

Measures	Action

Short introduction (8 counts)

1–4	Hand pattern 1: Two hands touch own thighs, then touch knees of the person on the right, clap own knees, then touch knees of the person on the left. Repeat four times for 16 counts.
5–8	Hand pattern 2: Clap own knees, cross hands and clap own knees, uncross hands and clap own knees, clap out hands to the right and left of the person next to you at the same time. Other person's hands can pass over or underneath. Repeat four times for 16 counts.
9–12	Hand pattern 3: Clap own knees, clap own hands, snap fingers twice while bumping hips from side to side. Repeat four times.
13–16	Hand pattern 4: Clap own knees, clap own hands, snap fingers twice while bumping hips from side to side. Repeat four times.
17–32	Repeat entire dance with only the rhythm section of the music playing.
33–48	Repeat entire dance again. This time there is no music for hand patterns 1–3. The group continues clapping without accompaniment. On hand pattern 4, the music starts. If the group has maintained the correct rhythm, they are right in time with the music.

Skip to My Lou (American)

Music source: WWCD-7054; WWC-7054

Skills: skipping, changing partners

Formation: scattered with a partner

Directions: During the chorus, partners skip around the area. At the verse, everyone finds a new partner and continues skipping.

Ballin' the Jack (American)

Music source: WWCD-FFD

19

Skills: sliding, do-si-do

Formation: double circle, partners facing each other

Directions:

Measures	Action
1	Each person slaps own thighs twice.
2	Each person claps hands twice.
3	Each person does a scissors movement with hands twice (with palms down, slide right hand over left and then left hand over right).
4	Each person touches partner's hands twice.
5–16	Repeat the previous sequence three more times.
17–18	Holding hands, slide four steps (step-close) to the outside circle person's right.
19–20	Slide four steps (step-close) and return to the original position.
21	Slide two steps (step-close) to the outside circle person's right.
22	Slide two steps (step-close) and return to the original position.
23–26	Drop hands and do-si-do, passing right shoulders for eight counts back to the original position or partner.

Variation: To change partners after the do-si-do, outside people return to their original position. Inside circle partners move one space to the right after the do-si-do. On the last two beats of the do-si-do, move to the right diagonally to face a new partner.

How D'Ye Do, My Partner? (Swedish)

Music source: WWCD-1041; WWC-07042

Skills: bowing, curtseying, skipping

Formation: double circle, partners facing, partner A on inside

Directions: Words in parentheses are teacher cues.

Measures	Action
1–2	Partners A bow to their partner. (Bow.)
3–4	Partners B bow. (Bow.)
5–6	Partner A offers the right hand to B, who takes it with the right hand. (Join right hands.) Both turn to face counterclockwise. (Face counterclockwise.)

Measures	Action
7–8	Couples join left hands in promenade position, preparing to skip when the music changes. (Join left hands.)
9–16	Partners skip counterclockwise in the circle, slowing down on measure 15. (Skip.) On measure 16, partners B stop and partners A move ahead to secure a new partner. (New partner.)

Danish Dance of Greeting (Danish)

Music source: WWCD-1041; WWC-07042

Skills: running or sliding, bowing

Formation: single circle, all face center; partner A stands to the left of partner B

Directions:

Measures	Action
1	All clap twice and bow to partner. (Clap, clap, bow.)
2	Repeat but turn your back to partner and bow to neighbor. (Clap, clap, bow.)
3	Stamp right, stamp left. (Stamp, stamp.)
4	Turn around in four running steps. (Turn, 2, 3, 4.)
5–8	Repeat the action of measures 1–4.
9–12	All join hands and run to the left for four measures. (Run, 2, 3, . . . , 16.)
13–16	Repeat the action of measures 9–12, taking light running steps in the opposite direction. (Run, 2, 3, . . . , 16.)

Variation: Instead of a running step, use a light slide.

Ach Ja ("Oh Yes"; German)

Music source: WWCD-0860; WWC-0860

Skills: walking, sliding

Formation: double circle, partners facing counterclockwise, partners A on the inside, inside hands joined

Directions:

Measures	Action
1–2	Partners walk eight steps in the line of direction. (Walk, 2, 3, . . . , 8.)
3	Partners drop hands and bow to each other. (Bow.)

4	Each A then bows to the B on the left, who returns the bow. (Bow.)
5–8	Repeat measures 1–4.
9–10	Partners face each other, join hands, and take four slides in the line of direction. (Slide, 2, 3, 4.)
11–12	Partners take four slides clockwise. (Slide, 2, 3, 4.)
13	Partners bow to each other. (Bow.)
14	Partner A bows to the B on the left, who returns the bow. (Bow.) To start the next dance, A moves quickly toward this B, who is the next partner.

Seven Jumps (Danish)

Music source: WWCD-1043; WWC-3528

Skills: step-hop, balance, control

Formation: single circle, hands joined

Directions: The dance involves seven jumps, each preceded by an action.

Measures	Action
1–8	The circle moves to the right with seven step-hops, one to each measure. On measure 8, all jump high in the air and reverse direction. (Step-hop, 2-hop, 3-hop, . . . , 7-hop, change direction.)
9–16	Circle to the left with seven step-hops. Stop on measure 16 and face the center. (Step-hop, 2-hop, 3-hop, . . . , 7-hop, face center.)
17	All drop hands, put their hands on hips, and lift the right knee with the toes pointed downward. (Knee up.)
18	All stamp the right foot to the ground on the signal note and then join hands on the next note. (Stamp.)
1–18	Repeat measures 1–18, but do not join hands.
19	Lift the left knee, stamp, and join hands.
1–19	Repeat measures 1–19, but do not join hands.
20	Put the right foot back and kneel on the right knee. Stand and join hands.
1–20	Repeat measures 1–20, but do not join hands.
21	Kneel on the left knee. Stand and join hands.

1–21	Repeat measures 1–21, but do not join hands.
22	Put the right elbow to the floor with the cheek on the fist. Stand and join hands.
1–22	Repeat measures 1–22, but do not join hands.
23	Put the left elbow to the floor with the cheek on the fist. Stand and join hands.
1–23	Repeat measures 1–23, but do not join hands.
24	Put forehead on the floor. Stand, join hands.
1–16	Repeat the first measures.

Chimes of Dunkirk, Var. 1 (French–Belgian)

Music source: WWCD-1042; WWC-07042

Skills: turning in a small circle with a partner, changing partners

Formation: double circle, partners facing

Directions:

Measures	Action
1–2	Stamp three times in place, right-left-right. (Stamp, 2, 3.)
3–4	Clap hands three times overhead (chimes in the steeple). (Clap, 2, 3.)
5–8	Partner A places both hands on partner B's hips; B places both hands on A's shoulders. Taking four steps, they turn around in place. (Turn, 2, 3, 4.) On the next four counts, partner B (on the outside) moves one person to the left with four steps. (Change, 2, 3, 4.) Repeat the sequence from the beginning.

Variation: Instead of the turn described, students can do an elbow turn by linking right elbows.

Shortnin' Bread (American)

Music source: WWCD-7050; WWC-7050

Skills: sliding, turning with a partner

Formation: scattered with partner

Directions:

19

Measures	Action
1–2	Clap own hands.
3–41	Slap partner's hands, palms together.
5–6	Clap own hands.
7–8	Slap own thighs.
9–16	Repeat measures 1–8.
17–20	Couples slide to the right holding hands.
21–24	Circle holding hands.
25–32	Repeat measures 17–24, moving to the left.

Children's Polka (German)

Music source: WWCD-07042; WWC-07042

Formation: single circle, partners facing

Skills: step-draw

Directions:

Measures	Action
1–2	Take two step-draw steps toward the center of the circle, ending with three steps in place. (Draw, draw, step, 2, 3.)
3–4	Take two step-draw steps away from the center, ending with three steps in place. (Draw, draw, step, 2, 3.)
5–8	Repeat the pattern of measures 1–4.
9	Slap own knees once with both hands; clap own hands once. (Slap, clap.)
10	Clap both hands with partner three times. (Clap, 2, 3.)
11–12	Repeat the pattern of measures 9 and 10.
13	Hop, placing one heel forward, and shake the forefinger at partner three times. (Scold, 2, 3.)
14	Repeat the scolding pattern with the other foot and hand. (Scold, 2, 3.)
15–16	Turn once around in place with four running steps and stamp three times in place. (Turn, 2, 3, 4; stamp, 2, 3.)

Shoemaker's Dance (Danish)

Music source: WWCD-1042; WWC-07042

Skills: skipping, heel and toe

Formation: double circle, partners facing, with partner A's back to the center of the circle

Directions:

Measures	Part I action
1	With arms bent and at shoulder height, and with hands clenched to form fists, circle one fist over the other in front of the chest. (Wind the thread.)
2	Reverse the circular motion and wind the thread in the opposite direction. (Reverse direction.)
3	Pull the elbows back vigorously twice. (Pull and tighten the thread.)
4	Clap own hands three times. (Clap, 2, 3.)
5–7	Repeat the pattern of measures 1–3.
8	Tap own fists three times to drive the nails. (Tap, 2, 3.)
	Part II action
9–16	Partners face counterclockwise, inside hands joined. Skip counterclockwise, ending with a bow. (Skip, 2, 3, . . . , 15, bow.)

Variation: Dancers can try this variation of part II.

Measures	Variation of part II action
9	Place the heel of the outside foot forward (counts 1 and), and point the toe of the outside foot to the back (2 and).
10	Take three running steps forward, starting with the outside foot and pausing on the last count.
11–12	Repeat the pattern of measures 9–10, starting with the inside foot.
13–16	Repeat the pattern of measures 9–12, entire "heel and toe and run, run, run" pattern dance, four times while singing part II verse

Jump Jim Jo (American)

Music source: WWCD-1041

Skills: jumping, running, draw step

Formation: double circle, partners facing, both hands joined

Directions:

Measures	Action
1–2	Do two jumps sideways, progressing counterclockwise, followed by three quick jumps in place. (Slow, slow, fast-fast-fast.)

3–4	Release hands and turn in place once, using four jumps (two jumps per measure). Finish facing partner and rejoin hands. (Jump, turn, 3, 4.)
5	Take two sliding steps sideways, moving counterclockwise. (Slide, slide.)
6	Partners face counterclockwise with inside hands joined and tap three times with the toe of the outside foot. (Tap, tap, tap.)
7–8	Take four running steps forward; then face partner, join both hands, and end with three jumps in place. (Run, 2, 3, 4; Jump, 2, 3.)

Yankee Doodle (American)

Music source: WWCD-FDN

Skills: walking, galloping, sliding, bowing

Formation: scattered or open circle, facing counterclockwise

Directions:

Measures	Action
1–4	All gallop eight steps. (Gallop, 2, . . . , 8.)
5–8	All stop, face center, point to cap, and bow on word "macaroni." (Stop, point, bow.)
9–12	All join hands, take six slides to the right, and stamp feet two times on word "dandy." (Slide, 2, 3, . . . , 6; stamp, stamp.)
13–16	All slide six times to the left and clap hands two times on the word "candy." (Slide, 2, 3, . . . , 6; clap, clap.)

Variation: Change the locomotor movements to fit the group's age and interests. Have the class create new movement patterns.

Eins Zwei Drei ("One, Two, Three"; German)

Music source: WWCD-1042

Skills: walking, sliding

Formation: single circle (partner B to partner A's right) facing the center and numbered alternately couple 1, 2, 1, 2

Directions:

Measures	Part I action
1–2	Couples 1 take three steps toward the center of the circle as they clap their hands by brushing them vertically like cymbals. (Forward, 2, 3, pause.)

3–4	Couples 1 repeat measures 1 and 2, walking backward to place. (Back, 2, 3, pause.)
5–8	Couples 1 face, join both hands, and take four slides toward the center of the circle and four slides back to place. Partner A starts with the left foot, and partner B starts with the right. (Slide, 2, 3, 4.)
9–16	Couples 2 repeat measures 1–8.
	Part II action
17	Partner A turns and touches the right heel sideways while shaking the right index finger at partner. Partner B does the same with the left heel and left index finger. (Scold, 2, 3.)
18	Repeat measure 17 with the corner, reversing footwork and hands. (Scold, 2, 3.)
19–20	Repeat measures 17 and 18.
21–24	All join hands and circle left with eight slides. (Slide, 2, 3, . . . , 8.)
25–32	Repeat measures 17–24, reversing the direction of the slides. (Slide, 2, 3, . . . , 8.)

Variation: To facilitate learning, practice all steps individually in a scattered formation.

Chimes of Dunkirk, Var. 2 (French–Belgian)

Music source: WWCD-1042

Skills: turning with a partner, skipping

Formation: single circle, partners facing

Directions:

Measures	Action
1–2	Stamp three times in place. (Stamp, 2, 3.)
3–4	Clap own hands three times. (Clap, 2, 3.)
5–8	Do a two-hand swing with partner. Join both hands with partner and turn once clockwise with eight running or skipping steps. (Swing, 2, 3, . . . , 8.)
	Chorus action
1–8	Circle left, singing, "Tra, la, la, la, la, . . ." All join hands and circle left with 16 running or skipping steps, ending with a bow. (Run, 2, 3, . . . , 15; bow.)

19

TEACHING TIP

1. Use Chimes of Dunkirk, Var. 2 (French-Belgian) as a mixer by having all partners B advance one partner to the left. Instead of a two-hand swing with partner, have dancers use the shoulder–waist position. Partner A places a hand on B's waist, and B places both hands on A's shoulders.

2. To facilitate forming the circle for the chorus, use a four-step turn instead of an eight-step turn on measures 5–8. This gives the dancers four counts to get ready for the circle formation and four counts to make the circle.

Bombay Bounce

Music source: any music with a definite, moderately fast beat

Skills: hesitation step, side step

Formation: scattered, all facing forward

Directions:

Part I (16 counts): Perform a hesitation step to the left by taking a short step to the left and touching the right foot near the left while standing on the left foot. Do a hesitation step to the right by taking a step to the right and touching the left foot near the right. Start the dance by doing eight hesitation steps in place and a hand clap on each touch. (Left, touch and clap; right, touch and clap.) Repeat four times.

Part II (16 counts): Take two side steps to the left and then two to the right. Clap on counts 4 and 8. (Left, close; left, close and clap; right, close; right, close and clap.) Repeat the pattern.

Part III (16 counts): Take four side steps left and four side steps right. Clap only on count 8. (Left, close, left, close, left, close, left, close and clap.) Repeat to the right.

Part IV (16 counts): Take four steps forward and four steps backward; then take four steps forward and four steps backward. Clap on counts 4, 8, 12, and 16. (Forward, 2, 3, 4 and clap; backward, 2, 3, 4 and clap; forward, 2, 3, 4 and clap; backward 2, 3, 4 and clap.)

Variation: In part IV, instead of four steps, use three steps and a kick (swing).

Carousel (Swedish)

Music source: WWCD-1041

Skills: draw step, sliding

Formation: double circle, facing center; the inner circle, representing a merry-go-round, joins hands; the outer players, representing the riders, place their hands on the hips of the partner in front

Directions:

Measures	Verse action
1–16	Moving to the left, children take 12 slow draw steps and stamp on the last 3 steps. (Step, together, 2, 3, . . . , 12; stamp, stamp, stamp, rest.)
	Chorus action
17–24	Moving left, speed up the draw step until it becomes a slide or gallop. Sing the chorus. (Slide, 2, 3, . . . , 8.)
25–32	Repeat measures 17–24 while moving to the right. (Slide, 2, 3, …, 8.)

During the chorus, the tempo increases and the movement changes to a slide. Have children take short, light slides to keep the circle in control.

Variation: Students can do this dance while holding the edge of a parachute.

Jolly Is the Miller (American)

Music source: WWC-317

Skills: marching

Formation: double circle, partners facing counterclockwise, partners A on the inside with inside hands joined; a "miller" is in the center of the circle

Directions: All sing. Students march counterclockwise, with inside hands joined. During the second line, when "the wheel goes round," the dancers turn their outside arms in a circle to form a wheel. Children change partners at the line "right steps forward and the left steps back." The miller then tries to get a partner. The child left without a partner becomes the next miller.

Bleking (Swedish)

Music source: WWCD-1044; WWC-07042

Skills: Bleking step, step-hop

Formation: single circle, partners facing, both hands joined; partners A face counterclockwise, and partners B face clockwise

Directions:

Part I: The Bleking step; cue by calling, "Slow-slow, fast-fast-fast."

Measures	Action
1	Hop on the left foot and extend the right heel forward with the right leg straight. At the same time, thrust the right hand forward. Hop on the right foot, reversing the arm action and extending the left foot to rest on the heel. (Slow, slow.)
2	Repeat the action with three quick changes—left, right, left. (Fast-fast-fast.)
3–4	Beginning on the right foot, repeat the movements of measures 1 and 2. (Slow, slow, fast-fast-fast.)
5–8	Repeat measures 1–4.

Part II: The windmills; partners extend their joined hands sideways at shoulder height.

Measures	Action
9–16	Partners turn in place with a repeated step-hop. At the same time, the arms move up and down like a windmill. They turn clockwise, with A starting on the right foot and B on the left. After doing the step-hops (16), the partners are in their original places ready for part I again. (Step-hop, 2-hop, 3-hop, . . . , 16-hop.)

Variations:

1. Change from original positions to a double circle, partners facing, with partners A with their back to the center. Part I is as described. For part II, all face counterclockwise and partners join inside hands. Partners do the basic schottische of "step, step, step, hop" throughout part II.

2. An excellent variation is to do the dance with partners scattered. Part I is as described. In part II, the children leave their partners and step-hop in various directions around the dancing area. Just before the music changes back to part I, performers find a partner wherever they can and repeat the dance.

3. Bleking music is excellent for creative dance. Instruct the children to follow the Bleking rhythm of "slow, slow, fast-fast-fast" during part I and do any kind of movement in place. In part II, let them do a locomotor or other movement at will.

Nixie Polka (Nigarepolska; Swedish)

Music source: WWCD-1041; WWC-572

Skills: Bleking step

Formation: single circle, all facing center, with one or more children scattered inside the circle; one child is in the center for each 12 dancers

Directions:

Measures	Part I action
1–4	Bleking step: With hands joined, all spring lightly onto the left foot and extend the right foot forward, heel to ground, toe up. Next, spring lightly onto the right foot and extend the left foot forward. Do four slow Bleking steps. (Slow, slow, slow, slow.)
5–8	All clap hands once and shout, "Hey!" The center child then runs around the inside of the circle, looking for a partner and finally selecting one. They join both hands and run lightly in place until the music ends. This refrain is repeated, giving the children time to return to the center of the circle. (Clap, run.)

	Part II action
1–4	The center dancer and partner, with both hands joined, repeat the action of measures 1–4. All dancers in the circle also repeat the action of measures 1–4. (Slow, slow, slow, slow.)
5–8	On count 1, all clap hands, shouting, "Hey!" The center dancer then about-faces and puts both hands on the shoulders of partner, who becomes the new leader. In this position, both shuffle around the inside of the circle, looking for a third person to dance with. The music is repeated again so that partners can return to the center. (Clap, run.)

	Part III action
1–4	The action of measures 1–4 is repeated; the new dancer faces the circle, and the other two face the new dancer. (Slow, slow, slow, slow.)
5–8	On count 1, all clap hands, shouting, "Hey!" The two people in the center then about-face. All three now face the center to form a line of three dancers with a new leader, who looks for a fourth dancer. The music is repeated. (Clap, run.)

Students repeat the entire dance, accumulating dancers with each repetition.

19

Turn the Glasses Over (American–English)

Music source: WWCD-WOF1

Skills: walking, wring the dishrag

Formation: single circle, couples in promenade position; extra students are in the center

Directions:

Measures	Verse action
1–16	The couples walk forward, singing the verse. At the phrase "turn the glasses over," they raise their arms, keeping the hands joined, and turn under the raised arms, making one complete outward "dishrag" turn. Dancers must anticipate the turn and start in time to complete the movement by the end of the phrase.

Measures	Chorus action
1–16	Dancers in the outer circle continue walking, while those in the inner circle turn and walk in the opposite direction. An extra dancer or dancers join one of the circles and continues with the group. At the phrase "girl in the ocean," students take the nearest person for a new partner. Those without a partner move to the center.

Jingle Bells, Var. 1 (Dutch)

Music source: any version of Jingle Bells or WWCD-FFD

Skills: elbow swing, skipping, sliding

Formation: double circle, partners facing, with both hands joined

Directions:

Measures	Action
1–2	Partners take eight slides counterclockwise. (Slide, 2, 3, . . . , 8.)
3–4	Partners turn so that they are back-to-back and take eight more slides in the same direction. This move is best made by dropping the front hands and swinging the back hands forward until the dancers are standing back-to-back. They rejoin the hands that are now in back, making this move without losing rhythm. (Slide, 2, 3, . . . , 8.)
5–6	Repeat the action of measures 1 and 2. To get back to the face-to-face position, let go of the back hands and swing the front hands backward, allowing the bodies to pivot and face again. (Slide, 2, 3, . . . , 8.)
7–8	Repeat measures 3 and 4. (Slide, 2, 3, . . . , 8.)

Measures	Chorus action
1	Clap own hands three times. (Clap, 2, 3.)
2	Clap both hands with partner three times. (Clap both, 2, 3.)
3	Clap own hands four times. (Clap, 2, 3, 4.)
4	Clap both hands with partner once. (Clap both.)
5–8	Right elbow swing with partner. Partners hook right elbows and swing clockwise with eight skips. (Swing, 2, 3, . . . , 8.)
9–12	Repeat clapping sequence of measures 1–4.
13–16	Left elbow swing with partner for eight skips, finishing in the original starting position, ready to repeat the entire dance with the same partner. Or, left elbow swing with partner for four skips, which is once around; then all children in the inner circle skip forward to the outer dancer ahead and repeat the entire dance from the beginning with a new partner. (Swing, 2, 3, . . . , 8.)

The Hitch Hiker (American)

Music source: WWCD-FDN

Skills: chug step (a short backward jump with the feet together on the floor), skipping

Formation: double circle, partners facing each other with boys on inside facing out

Directions:

Measures	Action
1–2	Introduction (no movement.)
1–2	Take two chugs away from partner and clap hands on each step. Jerk right thumb over right shoulder while twisting right foot with heel on the floor. Repeat. (Chug, chug, right, right.)

3–4	Same as measures 1–2 except use left thumb and foot. (Chug, chug, left, left.)
5–6	Same as measures 1–2 except use both thumbs and feet. (Chug, chug, both, both.)
7–8	Skip diagonally forward and to the right toward a new partner with four skips; continue with four more skips around your new partner with right hands joined and get ready to repeat the dance. (Skip, 2, 3, 4; around, 2, 3, 4.)

Repeat the sequence eight times.

Circassian Circle (English)

Music source: WWCD-FDN

Skills: walking, skipping, promenade

Formation: large single circle of couples, facing center with all hands joined

Directions:

Measures	Action
1–2	Introduction. (no movement.)
1–2	All walk four steps forward to center and four steps backward to starting place. (Walk 2, 3, 4; back, 2, 3, 4.)
3–4	Repeat measures 1 and 2. (Walk 2, 3, 4; back, 2, 3, 4.)
5–6	Partners A walk four steps forward and four steps backward. (A, 2, 3, 4; back, 2, 3, 4.)
7–8	Partners B walk four steps forward, do a half-turn left, and walk diagonally clockwise four steps to a new partner. (B, 2, 3, 4; move to new partner.)
9–10	Using a crossed-arm grip, new partners lean away from each other and skip eight steps clockwise once around each other. (Skip, 2, 3, . . . , 8.)
11–12	Without dropping hands, couples promenade counterclockwise for eight steps. They take the last two steps to stop and face the center, ready to do the dance again. (Promenade, 2, 3, . . . , 6; face center.)

Students repeat the dance four times.

Seven Steps (Austrian)

Music source: WWCD-FDN

Skills: running, hopping

Formation: double circle, couples facing counterclockwise with inside hands joined

Directions:

Measures	Action
1–2	Introduction (no movement.)
1–2	Start with outside foot and run seven steps forward counterclockwise. Then pause with weight on outside foot on count 8. (Run, 2, 3, . . . , 7, pause.)
3–4	Start with inside foot and run seven steps backward (clockwise). Then pause with weight on inside foot on count 8. (Run, back, 3, 4, . . . , 7, pause.)
5	Release hands, turn away from partner; starting with the outside foot, run three steps away from partner and hop on the outside foot on count 4. (Away, 2, 3, hop.)
6	Turn and face partner; starting with the inside foot, run three steps toward partner and then hop on the inside foot on count 4. (Back, 2, 3, hop.)
7–8	Partners join right hands and run once around each other with eight running steps clockwise. (Swing, 2, 3, . . . , 8.)
9	Release hands and turn away from partner. Starting with the outside foot, run three steps away from partner; on count 4, hop and turn on the outside foot to face diagonally toward new partner. (Apart, 2, 3, hop.)
10	Take three running steps to a new partner (inside partner moves counterclockwise forward diagonally toward new partner; outside partner moves clockwise backward diagonally to next partner). Then hop on count 4.
11–12	New partners join left hands and run once around each other with eight running steps counterclockwise. Finish in starting position with inside hands joined.

Perform the dance five times.

Rhythm Sticks—It's a Small, Small World (American)

Rhythm sticks or Lummi sticks are 12 to 15 inches (30 to 38 cm) long. Activities may be done individually or in partners. This routine is done individually. Students hold the sticks with the thumb and the forefinger at about the bottom third of the stick.

19

Music source: WWCD-2015; WWC-2015

Skills: rhythmic tapping, manipulation of sticks

Formation: children sitting cross-legged individually scattered around the area

Directions:

Measures	Call	Action
1–2	Down, cross, down, cross	Tap ends of both sticks on the floor and then cross the arms over, tapping the sticks on the floor again.
3–4	Down, cross, down, cross	Repeat.
5–6	Down, cross, down, cross	Repeat.
7–8	Chorus: It's a small, small world.	Lean forward, touching head to knees. (Curl forward.)
9–10	Tap, tap, knees, knees.	Tap sticks two times in front of the chest and then lightly tap the knees twice.
11–12	Tap, tap, knees, knees	Repeat
13–14	Tap, tap, knees, knees	Repeat
15–16	Chorus: It's a small, small world.	Lean forward, touching head to knees. (Curl forward.)

Repeat the sequence several times with touches to the toes, shoulders, head, and nose.

Variation: Students can face a partner and tap both of their sticks to their partner's sticks.

Developmental Level II Dances

Developmental Level II activities focus on folk dance. Locomotor skills are still the basis of the movement patterns, but in most dances the patterns are more difficult than those in Developmental Level I. At this level, each dance always has at least two parts and may have three or more. Because the movement patterns are longer, at this level you will use the part–whole teaching method more often. These vigorous, fast-moving dances are exciting for children to perform.

Tinikling and Lummi sticks add challenge and novelty to the progression. Emphasize participation and enjoyment rather than perfection. Normal progress through the rhythms program will assure children's success.

The Bird Dance (Chicken Dance)

Music source: WWC-9126

Skills: skipping or walking, elbow swing or star

Formation: circle or scatter formation, partners facing

Directions: Have students perform the following Chicken Dance individually, with everyone moving to find a new partner on the skipping sequence. Vary the locomotor movements to include sliding or galloping.

Measures	Part I action
1	Four snaps—thumb and fingers, hands up.
2	Four flaps—arms up and down, elbows bent.
3	Four wiggles—hips, knees bent low.
4	Four claps.
5–16	Repeat action of measures 1–4 three times.

Measures	Part II action
1–8	With a partner, do either a right-hand star with 16 skips or 16 walking steps, or an elbow swing. (Skip, 2, 3, . . . , 15; change hands.)
9–16	Repeat with the left hand. On the last 4 counts of the last swing, everyone changes partners. If dancing in a circle formation, partners B advance forward counterclockwise to the next partner A. If dancing in a scattered formation, everyone moves to find a new partner. (Skip, 2, 3, …, 12; change partners.)

Csebogar (Hungarian)

Music source: WWCD-1042

Skills: skipping, sliding, draw step, elbow swing

Formation: single circle, partners facing center, hands joined with partners B on the right

Directions:

Part I:

Measures	Action
1–4	Take seven slides to the left. (Slide, 2, 3, . . . , 7, change.)
5–8	Take seven slides to the right. (Back, 2, 3, . . . , 7, stop.)

| 9–12 | Take three skips to the center and stamp on count 4. Take three skips backward to place and stamp on count 8. (Forward, 2, 3, stamp; backward, 2, 3, stamp.) |
| 13–16 | Hook right elbows with partner and turn around twice in place, skipping. (Swing, 2, 3, . . . , 8.) |

Part II: Partners face each other in a single circle with hands joined.

Measures	Action
17–20	Holding both of partner's hands, take four draw steps (step, close) toward the center of the circle. (Step-close, 2-close, 3-close, 4-close.)
21–24	Take four draw steps back to place. (Step-close, 2-close, 3-close, 4-close.)
25–26	Go toward the center of the circle with two draw steps. (In-close, 2-close.)
27–28	Take two draw steps back to place. (Out-close, 2-close.)
29–32	Hook elbows and repeat the elbow swing, finishing with a shout and facing the center of the circle in the original formation. (Swing, 2, 3, 4, 5, "Csebogar!")

Instead of an elbow swing, partners can use the Hungarian turn. Partners stand side by side, put their right arms around their partners' waist, and lean away from partner. They hold their left arms out to the side with the elbow bent, the hand pointing up, and the palm facing the dancer.

Patty Cake (Heel-and-Toe) Polka (International)

Music source: WWCD-FDN

Skills: heel-and-toe polka step, sliding, elbow swing, skipping

Formation: double circle, partners facing, partner A in the inner circle with back to the center; partners join both hands; partner A's left foot and B's right foot are free

Directions:

Measures	Part I action
1–2	Heel-toe twice with A's left and B's right foot. (Heel, toe, heel, toe.)
3–4	Take four slides sideways to A's left, moving counterclockwise. Do not transfer the weight on the last count. Finish with A's right and B's left foot free. (Slide, 2, 3, 4.)

| 5–8 | Repeat the pattern of measures 1–4, starting with A's right and B's left foot, moving clockwise. Finish with the partners separated and facing. (Heel, toe, heel, toe; slide, 2, 3, 4.) |

	Part II action
9	Clap right hands with partner three times. (Right, 2, 3.)
10	Clap left hands with partner three times. (Left, 2, 3.)
11	Clap both hands with partner three times. (Both, 2, 3.)
12	Slap own knees three times. (Knees, 2, 3.)
13–14	Right elbow swing with partner. Partners hook right elbows and swing once around with four walking steps, finishing with A's back to center. (Swing, 2, 3, 4.)
15–16	Move to the left toward a new partner with four walking steps. (Left, 2, 3, 4.)

Repeat the entire dance with the new partner.

Pop Goes the Weasel (American)

Music source: WWCD-1043; WWCD-FDN

Skills: walking, skipping, turning under

Formation: double circle of sets of four; couples facing with partner B on partner A's right; couples facing clockwise are number 1 couples; couples facing counterclockwise are number 2 couples

Directions:

Measures	Action
1–4	Join hands in a circle of four and circle left, once around, with eight skipping or sliding steps. (Circle, 2, 3, . . . , 8.)
5–6	Take two steps forward, raising the joined hands, and two steps backward, lowering the hands. (Forward, 2; back, 2.)
7–8	"Ones" pop the "Twos" under. Number 1 couples raise their joined hands to form an arch and pass the number 2 couples under. All walk ahead to meet a new couple. (Forward; pop through.)

Repeat as desired.

Variations:

1. Dancers are in sets of three, all facing counterclockwise. Each forms a triangle with one child in

front and the other two with joined hands forming the base. The front dancer reaches back and holds the outside hands of the other two dancers. The groups of three are in a large circle formation.

Measures	Action
1–2	Sets of three dancers skip forward four times. (Forward, 2, 3, 4.)
3–4	Sets of three skip backward four times. (Backward, 2, 3, 4.)
5–6	Sets of three skip forward four times. (Forward, 2, 3, 4.)
7–8	On "Pop goes the weasel," the two back dancers raise their joined hands and the front dancer backs up underneath to the next set. This set, meanwhile, has "popped" its front dancer back to the set behind it. (Raise and pop under.)

2. "Pop Goes the Weasel" is excellent for stimulating creative movement. The music actually consists of a verse and a chorus part. During the verse, children can slide, gallop, or skip until the "Pop" line, when they make a half or full turn in the air. During the chorus, they can do jerky nonlocomotor movements. Other options include ball routines, in which children dribble in time to the music during the verse and pass the ball around various parts of the body during the chorus. Another variation has children carry a jump rope while skipping, sliding, or galloping. During the chorus, they jump in time to the music, and on "Pop," they try to do a double jump.

Wild Turkey Mixer (American)

Music source: WWC-FFD or any music with a definite rhythm

Skills: walking, elbow swing, partner change

Formation: trios abreast, facing around the circle

Directions:

Measures	Action
1–8	In lines of three, with the right and left person holding the near hand of the center person, all walk 16 steps forward. (Walk, 2, 3, . . . , 16.)
9–12	The center person (Wild Turkey) turns the right-hand person once around with the right elbow. (Turn, 2, 3, . . . , 8.)
13–16	The Wild Turkey turns the left-hand person with the left elbow and then moves forward to repeat the dance with the two new people ahead. (Turn, 2, 3, 4; forward, 2, 3, 4.)

The same dance can be adapted to other pieces of music. With a faster tempo, dancers do elbow swings while skipping instead of walking.

La Raspa ("The Rasp"; Mexican)

Music source: WWCD-05117

Skills: Bleking step, running, elbow swing

Formation: partners facing, couples scattered around room

Directions: These dance movements are supposed to represent a rasp or file in action. Directions are the same for both partners.

Part I: To begin, the partners face each other, partner B with hands at sides and partner A with hands behind the back.

Measures	Action
1–4	Beginning right, take one Bleking step. (Slow, slow, fast-fast-fast.)
5–8	Turn slightly counterclockwise away from partner (right shoulder to right shoulder) and, beginning with a jump on the left foot, repeat measures 1–4. (Slow, slow, fast-fast-fast.)
9–12	Repeat action of measures 1–4, facing opposite direction (left shoulder to left shoulder). (Slow, slow, fast-fast-fast.)
13–16	Repeat action of measures 1–4, facing partner. (Slow, slow, fast-fast-fast.)

Part II: Partners hook right elbows; left elbows are bent, and left hands point toward the ceiling.

Measures	Action
1–4	Do a right elbow swing, using eight running or skipping steps. Release and clap the hands on count 8. (Swing, 2, 3, . . . , 7, clap.)
5–8	Do a left elbow swing, using eight running or skipping steps. Release and clap the hands on count 8. (Swing, 2, 3, . . . , 7, clap.)
9–16	Repeat the actions of measures 1–8.

Variations:

1. Face partner (all are in a single-circle formation for this version) and do a grand right and left around the circle. Repeat part I with a new partner.

2. All face center or face a partner and do the Bleking or raspa step. On each pause, clap own hands twice.

Polly Wolly Doodle (American)

Music source: WWCD-1041

Skills: sliding, turning, walking

Formation: double circle, partners facing with both hands joined, partner A with back to center of circle

Directions:

Measures	Part I action
1–4	All slide four steps—partners A to left, partners B to right, counterclockwise. (Slide, 2, 3, 4.)
5–8	Drop hands and all turn solo circle, partners A to left, partners B to right, with five stamps in this rhythm: 1-2-1, 2, 3. (Stamp on the word "Polly," stamp the other foot on the word "doodle," and do three quick stamps on the word "day.") (Turn, 2, stamp, 2, 3.)
9–16	Repeat measures 1–8 but in the opposite direction, partners A moving to right and partners B to left. (Slide, 2, 3, 4; turn, 2, stamp 2, 3.)
	Part II action
1–4	Both bow to each other, partners A with hands on hips, partners B with hands at sides. (A bows; B bows.)
5–8	With four walking steps (or skipping steps), both move backward, away from each other. (Back, 2, 3, 4.)
9–12	Both move diagonally forward to own left to meet a new partner. (Diagonal, 2, 3, 4.)
13–16	With the new partner, elbow swing in place using a skipping step. (Swing, 2, 3, 4.) Repeat the dance from the beginning with the new partner.

Bingo (American)

Music source: WWCD-FDN

Skills: walking, grand right and left

Formation: double circle, partners side by side and facing counterclockwise, partners A on the inside and inside hands joined

Note: "Bingo" is a favorite of young people. The singing must be brisk and loud. The dance is in three parts.

Directions:

Part I: Partners walk counterclockwise around the circle, singing the refrain. (Walk, 2, 3, . . . , 15; face center.)

Part II: All join hands to form a single circle, partner B on partner A's right. They sing (spelling out) with these actions.

Action:

1. All take four steps into the center.

2. All take four steps backward.

3. All take four steps forward again.

4. Take four steps backward, drop hands, and face partner.

Part III: Shake right hands with the partner, calling out "B" on the first heavy note. All walk forward, passing their partners, to meet the oncoming person with a left handshake, calling out "I" on the next chord. Continue to the third person with a right handshake, calling out "N." Pass on to the fourth person, giving a left handshake and a "G." Instead of a handshake with the fifth person, face each other, raise the arms high above the head, shake all over, and call out a long, drawn-out "O." The fifth person becomes the new partner, and the dance is repeated.

Variation: At the end of part II (the end of the line "And Bingo was his name"), partners A face the chute and hold it with both hands, lifting it to shoulder level. Partners B drop their hands from the parachute and get ready to move clockwise. On each of the letters B-I-N-G-O, they move inside the first A, outside the next, and so on, for five changes. They then take a new place as indicated and get ready to repeat the dance. The next sequence can have partners B remaining in place, holding the chute, while partners A move counterclockwise.

Grand March (American)

Music source: WWCD-WOF-2 or any good march or square dance music

Skills: controlled walking, marching, grand march figures

Formation: Partners B are on the left side of the room, facing the end, and partners A are on the right side,

19

facing the same end. This is the foot of the hall. The teacher or caller stands at the other end of the room, the head of the hall. An alternative formation is to put half of the class on each side of the room and have each half wear different-colored pinnies.

Directions:

Call	Action
Down the center by twos.	The lines march forward to the foot of the hall, turn the corner, meet at the center of the foot of the hall, and march in couples toward the caller (figure 19.4), with inside hands joined. The partners B's line should be on the proper side so that when the couples come down the center, A is on B's left. Odd couples are numbered 1, 3, 5, and so on. Even couples are numbered 2, 4, 6, and so on.
Twos left and right.	The odd couples go left and the even couples go right around the room and meet at the foot of the hall.
Down the center by fours.	The couples walk down the center, four abreast.
Separate by twos.	When they approach the caller, odd couples go left and even couples go right. They meet again at the foot of the hall.
Form arches.	Instead of coming down the center, odd couples form arches and even couples tunnel under. Each continues around the sides of the hall to meet at the head.
Other couples arch.	Even couples arch, and odd couples tunnel under. Each continues around the sides of the room to the foot.
Over and under.	The first odd couple arches over the first even couple and then ducks under the second even couple's arch. Each couple goes over the first couple and under the next. Continue around to the head of the hall.
Pass right through.	As the lines come toward each other, they mesh and pass through each other in the following fashion: All drop handholds. Each B walks between the A and B of the opposite couple and continues walking to the foot of the hall.
Down the center by fours.	Go down the center four abreast.
Fours left and right.	The first four go left around the room, and the second four go right. The fours meet at the foot of the hall.
Down the center by eights.	Go eight abreast down the center.
Grapevine.	All persons in each line join hands and keep them joined. The leader takes either end of the first line and starts around the room with the line trailing. The other lines hook on to form one long line.
Wind it up.	The leader winds up the group in a spiral formation, like a clock spring. The leader makes the circles smaller and smaller until he or she is in the center.
Reverse (unwind).	The leader turns and faces in the opposite direction and walks between the lines of winding dancers. The leader unwinds the line and leads it around the room.
Everybody swing.	After the line is unwound, everybody does a square dance swing.

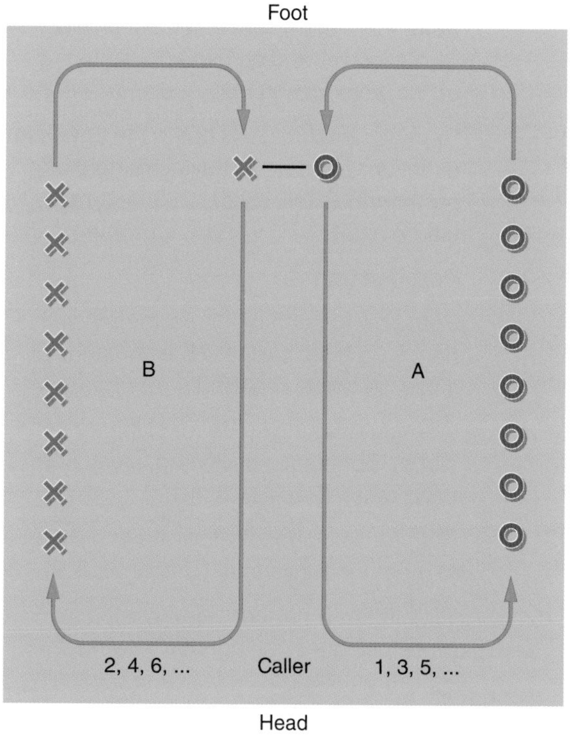

FIGURE 19.4 Formation and action for Grand March.

TEACHING TIP

The Grand March (American) leaders (couples 1 and 2) should maintain an even, steady pace and not hurry so that the march does not becomes a race. When one set of couples forms arches (as in movements 5 and 6) for the other set of couples to tunnel under, the arches should be made with the inside arms and the couples should continue marching while they form the arches.

Green Sleeves (English)

Music source: WWCD-1042

Skills: walking, star formation, over and under

Formation: double circle, couples in sets of four, facing counterclockwise; two couples form a set and are numbered 1 and 2; inside hands of each couple are joined

Directions:

Measures	Call	Action
1–8	Walk	Walk forward 16 steps.
9–12	Right-hand star	Each member of couple 1 turns individually to face the couple behind. All join right hands and circle clockwise (star) for eight steps.
13–16	Left-hand star	Reverse direction and form a left-hand star. This should bring couple 1 back to place facing in the original direction.
17–20	Over and under	Couple 2 arches, and couple 1 backs under four steps while couple 2 moves forward four steps. Couple 1 then arches, and couple 2 backs under (four steps for each).
21–24	Over and under	Repeat the action of measures 17–20.

Jingle Bells, Var. 2 (Dutch)

Music source: WWCD-FFD or any version of Jingle Bells

Skills: skipping, promenade position, sliding, elbow swing

Formation: single circle of couples facing counterclockwise, partner B on partner A's right; promenade position: hands crossed in front, right hands joined over left, right foot free

Directions:

Measures	Part I action
1–2	Take four skips forward and four skips backward, starting with the right foot free. (Forward, 2, 3, 4; Back, 2, 3, 4.)
3–4	Repeat the pattern of measures 1 and 2. (Forward 2, 3, 4; Back, 2, 3, 4.)
5	Do four slides to the right, away from the center of the circle. (Out, 2, 3, 4.)
6	Now do four slides left, toward the center. (In, 2, 3, 4.)
7–8	Skip eight times, making one turn counterclockwise, with partner A pivoting backward and partner B moving forward. Finish in a double circle, partners facing, with partners A back to the center. (Skip, 2, 3, . . . , 8.)

Measures	Part II action
1	Clap own hands three times. (Clap, 2, 3.)
2	Clap both hands with partner three times. (Both, 2, 3.)
3	Clap own hands four times. (Clap, 2, 3, 4.)
4	Clap both hands with partner once. (Both.)
5–8	Right elbow swing with partner. Partners hook right elbows and swing clockwise for eight skips. (Swing, 2, 3, . . . , 8.)
9–12	Repeat clapping pattern of measures 1–4.
13–16	Left elbow swing with partner using eight skips and finishing in the original starting position to repeat the entire dance with the same partner, or left elbow swing with partner once around; then all children in the inner circle skip forward to the outer dancer ahead and repeat the entire dance with a new partner. (Swing, 2, 3, . . . , 8.)

19

E-Z Mixer

Music source: WWC-FFD or any music with a definite rhythm

Skills: walking, elbow swing, swing in closed position

Formation: single circle, couples in promenade position, inside hands joined, facing counterclockwise

Directions:

Measures	Action
1–2	With partner B on the right, walk forward four steps. (Forward, 2, 3, 4.) Back out to face center in a single circle. (Circle, 2, 3, 4.)
3–4	Partners B walk to the center. (In, 2, 3, 4.) Back out of the center. (Out, 2, 3, 4.)
5–6	Partners A take four steps to the center and do a half turn to the left on count 4. (In, 2, 3; turn left.) They take four steps toward the corner. (Out, 2, 3, 4.)
7–8	Partners A swing the corner B twice around, opening up to face counterclockwise, back in starting position, to begin the dance again. (Swing, 2, 3, open.)

Any piece of music with a moderate 4/4 rhythm is appropriate for this basic mixer.

Ve David (Israeli)

Music source: WWCD-FFD; WWC-RM3

Skills: walking, pivoting, buzz-step turn

Formation: double circle, couples facing counterclockwise, partner B on partner A's right; inside hands joined, right foot free

Directions:

Measures	Part I action
1–2	All walk forward and form a ring. Take four walking steps forward, starting with the right foot and going counterclockwise; then back out, taking four walking steps to form a single circle, facing center, with all hands joined. (Walk, 2, 3, 4; single, circle, 3, 4.)
3–4	All forward and back. Four steps forward to center and four steps backward, starting with the right foot. (Forward, 2, 3, 4; back, 2, 3, 4.)

Part II action

1–2	Partners B forward and back; partners A clap. Partners B, starting with the right foot, walk four steps forward to the center and four steps backward to place, while partners A clap. (Partners B in, 2, 3, 4; out, 2, 3, 4.)

Part III action

1–2	Partners A forward, circle to the right, and move to a new partner; all clap. Partners A, clapping hands, walk four steps forward to the center, starting with the right foot. They do an about-face right on the last "and" count and walk forward four steps, passing their original partner and moving forward to the next. (Partners A in, 2, 3, 4; turn to new partner.)
3–4	Swing the new partner. The partner A and the new partner B swing clockwise with right shoulders adjacent, right arms around each other across in front, and left arms raised—pivoting with right foot for an eight-count "buzz-step" swing. (Swing, 2, 3, …, 8.)

Repeat the entire dance.

Irish Washerwoman (Irish)

Music source: WWCD-1043

Skills: walking, elbow swing, promenade

Formation: single circle, couples facing center, partner B to the right, hands joined

Directions: Dancers follow the call.

Action: Beginning left, take four steps to the center. (Center, 2, 3, 4.)

Stamp four times in place. (Stamp, 2, 3, 4.)

Take four steps backward to place. (Back, 2, 3, 4.)

Swing the corner and promenade in the line of direction. (Swing, 2, 3, promenade.)

Dancers keep promenading until they hear the call again to repeat the pattern.

Oh, Susanna (American)

Music source: WWCD-1043

Skills: walking, promenade position, grand right and left

Formation: single circle, all facing center, partner B on the right

Directions:

Measures	Part I action
1–4	Partners B walk forward four steps and back four, as partners A clap hands. (Forward, 2, 3, 4; back, 2, 3, 4.)
5–8	Reverse, with A walking forward and back, and B clapping time. (Forward, 2, 3, 4; back, 2, 3, 4.)

Part II action

1–8	Partners face each other, and all do a grand right and left by grasping the partner's right hand and passing to the next person with a left-hand hold. Continue until reaching the seventh person, who becomes the new partner. (Face, 2, 3, . . . , 8.)

Chorus action

1–16	All join hands in promenade position with the new partner and walk counterclockwise around the circle for two full choruses. (Promenade, 2, 3, . . . , 16.)

Repeat the dance from the beginning, each time with a new partner. For variety in the chorus, skip instead of walk, or walk during the first chorus and swing the partner in place during the second chorus.

Crested Hen (Danish)

Music source: WWCD-1042

Skills: step-hop, turning under

Formation: sets of three; one child is designated the center child

Directions:

Part I:

Measures	Action
1–4	Dancers in each set form a circle. Starting with a stamp with the left foot, each set circles to the left, using step-hops. (Stamp-and, 2-and, 3-and, 4-and, 5-and, 6-and, 7-and, stop.)
5–8	The figure is repeated. Dancers reverse direction, beginning again with a stamp with the left foot and following with step-hops. The dancers change direction vigorously and quickly, with the left foot crossing over the right. At the end of the sequence, two dancers release each other's hands to break the circle and stand on either side of the center person, forming a line of three while retaining joined hands with the center dancer. (Stamp-and, 2-and, 3-and, 4-and, 5-and, 6-and, 7-and, line.)

Part II: During this part, the dancers use the step-hop continuously while making the pattern figures.

Measures	Action
9–10	The dancer on the right moves forward in an arc to the left and dances under the arch formed by the other two. (Under-and, 2-and, 3-and, 4-and.)
11–12	After the right dancer has gone through, the two forming the arch turn under (dishrag) to form again a line of three. (Turn-and, 2-and, 3-and, 4-and.)
13–16	The dancer on the left then repeats the pattern, moving forward in an arc under the arch formed by the other two, who turn under to unravel the line. (Under-and, 2-and, 3-and, 4-and; turn-and, 2-and, 3-and; circle.)

As part II ends, dancers again join hands in a small circle. The entire dance is repeated. Another of the three can be designated the center dancer.

Troika (Russian)

Music source: WWCD-3528; WWC-3528

Skills: running step, turning under

Formation: trios face counterclockwise; start with hands joined in a line of three; body weight is on left foot and right foot is free

Directions:

Measures	Part I action
1	Take four running steps diagonally forward right, starting with the right foot. (Forward, 2, 3, 4.)
2	Take four running steps diagonally forward left, starting with the right foot. (Diagonal, 2, 3, 4.)
3–4	Take eight running steps in a forward direction, starting with the right foot. (Forward, 2, 3, . . . , 8.)
5–6	The center dancer and the left-hand partner raise joined hands to form an arch and run in place. Meanwhile, the right-hand partner moves counterclockwise around the center dancer with eight running steps, goes under the arch, and back to place. The center dancer unwinds by turning under the arch. (Under, 2, 3, 4; turn, 2, 3, 4.)

19

7–8	Repeat the pattern of measures 5 and 6, with the left-hand partner running under the arch formed by the center dancer and the right-hand partner. (Under, 2, 3, 4; turn, 2, 3, circle.)

Part II action

9–11	The trio joins hands and circles left with 12 running steps. (Run, 2, 3, . . . , 12.)
12	Three stamps in place (counts 1–3), pause (count 4). (Stamp, 2, 3, pause.)
13–15	The trio circles right with 12 running steps, opening out at the end to re-form in lines of three facing counterclockwise. (Run, 2, 3, . . . , 8, open, 10, 11, 12.)
16	The center dancer releases each partner's hand and runs under the opposite arch of joined hands to advance to a new pair ahead. Right- and left-hand partners run in place while waiting for a new center dancer to join them in a new trio. (Stamp, 2, line, pause.)

TEACHING TIP

Practice the Troika (Russian) running steps in groups of three. Then introduce turning under the arch and finish by practicing the running circle with accent stamps.

Gustaf's Skoal (Swedish)

Music source: WWCD-1044CD; WWCD-FDN

Skills: walking (stately), skipping, turning

Formation: Similar to a square dance set of four couples, each facing center. Partner A is on partner B's left. Couples join inside hands; outside hand is on the hip. Two of the couples facing each other are the head couples. The other two couples, also facing each other, are the side couples.

Directions: The dance has two parts. Part I music is slow and stately; dancers move with dignity. Part II music is light and represents fun.

Measures	Part I action
1–2	Head couples, inside hands joined, walk forward three steps and bow to the opposite couple. (Forward, 2, 3, bow.)
3–4	Head couples take three steps backward to place and bow to each other (meanwhile, side couples hold their places). (Back, 2, 3, bow.)
5–8	Side couples repeat action of measures 1–4; head couples hold their places. (Forward, 2, 3, bow; back, 2, 3, bow.)
9–16	Dancers repeat measures 1–8.

Part II action

17–22	Side couples raise joined hands to form an arch. Head couples skip forward four steps, release partners' hands, join inside hands with opposite person, and skip under the nearest arch with a new partner. After going under the arch, they drop hands and head back home to their original partner. (Head couples: Skip, 2, 3, 4; under, 2, 3, 4; around, 2, 3, 4.)
23–24	All couples join both hands with partners and swing once around with four skipping steps. (Swing, 2, 3, 4.)
25–30	Head couples form arches; side couples repeat the action of measures 17–22. (Side couples: Skip, 2, 3, 4; under, 2, 3, 4; around, 2, 3, 4.)
31–32	All couples then repeat the movements in measures 23–24. (Swing, 2, 3, 4.)

Variation: During the first action sequence of part I (the dancers take three steps and bow), dancers can shout, "Skoal!" and raise their right fists high overhead as a salute. The word "skoal" is a toast. (Partners release hands when raising their fists.)

Shoo Fly (American)

Music source: WWCD-FDN

Skills: walking

Formation: single circle, couples facing the center with all hands joined; about six couples to a circle

Directions:

Measures	Part I action
4	Introduction (no movement)
1–4	All walk four steps to the center and four steps back to place. (Center, 2, 3, 4; back, 2, 3, 4.)
5–8	Repeat action of measures 1–4. (Center, 2, 3, 4; back, 2, 3, 4.)

Measures	Action
9–12	Partners turn each other clockwise with a right forearm grasp using eight walking steps. (Turn, partner, 3, 4, . . . , 8.)
13–16	Partners turn each other counterclockwise with a left forearm grasp using eight walking steps. (Turn, partner, 3, 4, . . . , 8)

Part II action

Measures	Action
1–8	Repeat action of measures 1–8 in part I.
9–12	Keep hands joined. Choose a leading couple to form an arch by lifting inside joined hands and then move toward the center of the circle. The couple opposite the leading couple pulls the continuous circle through the arch using eight steps. (Through, arch, 3, 4, . . . , 8.)
13–16	When all have passed through the arch and are facing out, the leading couple turns under their joined arms to turn the circle inside out. (Inside, out, 3, 4, . . . , 8.)

Part III action

Measures	Action
1–8	Repeat the action of measures 1–8 in part I but all walk backward four steps to the center and then forward four steps back to place. Repeat. (Backward, 2, 3, 4, forward, 6, 7, 8; Repeat.)
9–12	Leading couple release joined hands (others keep joined hands) and separate, pulling dancers attached to them by joined hands around the circle with eight walking steps. (Release, 2, 3, . . . , 8.)
13–16	Continue following leaders with eight walking steps until in original places facing the center. Lead couple joins hands to form a circle again. (Circle, 2, 3, . . . , 8.)

Perform the dance twice.

Apat (Philippines)

Music source: WWCD-572; WWC-572

Skills: walking, star hold

Formation: double circle, partners facing counterclockwise with inside hands joined

Directions:

Measures	Action
Introduction	No movement
1	All face counterclockwise with inside hands joined and walk forward four steps. On count 4, release hands and do a half turn right to face clockwise. (Walk, 2, 3, turn.)
2	Take four walking steps forward clockwise. Release hands on the fourth step and face partner. (Walk, 2, 3, face.)
3	Walk four steps backward away from partner. (Away, 2, 3, 4.)
4	Walk four steps forward toward partner with each partner taking a quarter turn to the right on count 4. Partners now face opposite directions. (Forward, 2, 3, right turn.)
5	Walk four steps forward with partners moving in opposite directions. (Forward, 2, 3, 4.)
6	Walk four steps backward to meet partner. (Backward, 2, 3, 4.)
7	Face partner. With right-hand star (join right hands with elbows bent), walk clockwise around partner four steps in place. (Star, 2, 3, 4.)
8	Release hands; dancers inside circle walk forward four steps counterclockwise to meet next partner. Dancers outside circle do a half turn in place to wait for a new partner.

Repeat the dance.

Pata (African)

Music source: WWCD-3528; WWC-3528

Skills: toe touches, knee lift, quarter turns

Formation: single lines facing in one direction

Directions:

Measures	Action
1–2	Start with feet together; touch right foot sideways right and return next to left foot. (Right touch, together.)
3–4	Same as above with left foot. (Left touch, together.)
5	With feet together, move toes out, keeping heels on the ground. (Toes out.)
6	Turn heels out, keeping toes on the ground. (Heels out.)
7	Turn heels in, keeping toes on the ground. (Heels in.)
8	Turn toes in, keeping heels on the ground. The feet are now together. (Toes in.)

19

| 9–12 | Raise right knee diagonally in front of the body and then touch right foot next to left foot. Repeat for counts 11–12. (Lift, touch, lift, touch.) |
| 13–16 | Kick left foot forward while doing a quarter turn to the right with weight on the right foot. Step backward left, right, left. Feet are together at the end of count 16. (Kick, left, right, left.) |

Repeat the dance.

TEACHING TIP

After learning the Pata (African) footwork, students enjoy adding some arm movements to the dance. At count 5, with elbows close to the body, raise hands up and straight out, palms up. Count 6—turn palms down with elbows out. Count 7—turn palms up. Count 8—turn palms down.

Savila Se Bela Loza ("Grapevine Twined in Itself"; Serbian)

Music source: WWCD-572; WWC-572

Skills: running step, crossover step, hop

Formation: broken circle or line; joined hands are held down

Directions: *Savila se bela loza* is pronounced "SAH-vee-lah say BAY-lah LOH-zah."

Measures	Part I action
Introduction	No movement
1–20	Face slightly to right; move right starting with the right foot, taking 18 small running steps forward. Do a step-hop on steps 19 and 20. (Run, 2, 3, . . . , 18, step, hop.)
21–40	Face slightly left and repeat previous action starting with the left foot. Finish with a step-hop on the left foot. (Run, 2, 3, . . . , 18, step, hop.)
	Part II action
41–44	With right foot, take one schottische step moving right (this is a step to the right sideways on the right foot, a step with the left foot behind the right, and then a step-hop on the right foot). (Right, left, right, hop.)

| 45–48 | With left foot, take one schottische step to the left (step to the left sideways on left foot, step with the right foot behind the left, and do a step-hop on the left foot). (Left, right, left, hop.) |
| 49–64 | Repeat the action of counts 41–48 two more times. |

Repeat the dance. During the music for part I, the leader may lead the line anywhere, winding or coiling it like a grapevine.

Los Machetes (Mexico)

Central America and parts of Mexico are largely covered with dense jungle, and the workers (macheteros, both men and women) must clear the trails with machetes. Macheteros often do this dance at fiestas.

Music source: WWCD-FFD

Skills: marching, rhythmic clapping

Formation: two lines of partners facing forward

Directions:

Measures	Action
Introduction	No movement
1–4	March forward 16 steps while clapping or clicking sticks.
5–8	Do an about-face and march back 16 steps.
9–12	The two lines face each other. Partners walk backward four steps and bow on count 4. (One, 2, 3, bow.) An alternative to the bow is to click Lummi sticks on count 4. Walk forward to original position and clap on count 4.
13–16	Repeat measures 9–12.
17–18	Clapping sequence facing partner. Clap own hands once (1); clap right hand to partner's right hand (2); clap own hands once (3); clap left hand to partner's left hand (4); clap own hands once (5); clap both hands to partner's hands (6); clap own hands together three times fast (7–8).
19–20	Repeat clapping sequence (measures 17–18).
21–28	With partner, do a right-hand star for 8 counts; do a left-hand star for 8 counts. Repeat.
29–84	Repeat the entire dance two more times

Popcorn (American)

Music source: WWCD-RM7; WWC-RM7

Skills: toe touches, knee lifts, jumps, quarter turns

Formation: single lines of students, no partners

Directions:

Counts	Action
1–24	Wait 24 counts; gently bounce up and down by bending the knees during the introduction.
1–4	Touch right toe in front and return; repeat. (Right, together, right, together.)
5–8	Touch left toe in front and return; repeat. (Left, together, left, together.)
9–12	Touch right toe in back and return; repeat. (Back, together, back, together.)
13–16	Touch left toe in front and return; repeat. (Back, together, back, together.)
17–20	Lift right knee up in front of left knee and return; repeat. (Knee up, return, knee up, return.)
21–24	Lift left knee up in front of right knee and return; repeat. (Knee up, return, knee up, return.)
25–26	Lift right knee up in front of left knee and return. (Knee up, return.)
27–28	Lift left knee up in front of right knee and return. (Knee up, return.)
29–30	Clap both hands together once. (Clap.)
31–32	Jump and do a quarter turn to the right. (Jump and turn.)

Repeat entire dance to the end of the music.

Red River Valley (American)

Music source: WWCD-FDN

Skills: walk, buzz swing, do-si-do

Formation: triple circle with three dancers side by side in sets of six dancers—two trios facing each other; half the trios face counterclockwise, and half face clockwise

Directions:

Measures	Part I action
Introduction	No movement
1–4	Middle child in each trio leads partners forward to right to meet on coming trio using eight walking steps. (Walk, 2, 3, . . . , 8.)
5–8	Join hands with oncoming trio and circle to the left (clockwise) using four walking steps; reverse direction and circle right using four walking steps. (Circle, left, 3, 4; circle, right, 3, 4.)
9–12	Middle child swings around with child on left using eight buzz steps (shuffling). (Swing, 2, 3, . . . , 8.)
13–16	Middle child swings around with child on right using eight buzz steps (shuffling). (Swing, 2, 3, . . . , 8.)
	Part II action
1–8	Repeat action of measures 1–8 in part I. (Walk, 2, 3, . . . , 8.)
9–12	The four outside students form a right-hand star in the center of the set and walk around once to starting point using eight walking steps. (Star, 2, 3, . . . , 8.)
13–16	The two middle students do-si-do around each other, returning to own place using eight walking steps. (Do-si-do, 2, 3, . . . , 8.)
	Part III action
1–8	Repeat action of measures 1–8 in part I. (Walk, 2, . . . , 8.)
9–12	The two left-hand outside students change places diagonally across using eight walking steps. (Left, diagonal, 3, . . . , 8.)
13–16	The two right-hand outside students change places diagonally across using eight walking steps. The middle child now has different partners. (Right, diagonal, 3, . . . , 8.)

Repeat the entire dance twice.

Sicilian Circle (American)

Music source: WWCD-FDN

Skills: walking, two-hand swing (either walking or buzz turn), wheel turn

Formation: double circle, groups of two couples facing each other with partners side by side; couples are numbered 1 and 2; number 1 couples move counterclockwise and number 2 couples move clockwise

Directions:

Measures	Action
Introduction	No movement

19

1–4	The sets of two couples join hands, walk eight steps to the left, ending where they started, and drop hands. (Circle, left, 2, 3, . . . , 8.)
5–8	Partners join both hands and swing once around to the left using eight walking or buzz steps. (Swing, left, 2, 3, . . . , 8.)
9–12	Couples move toward each other and pass right shoulders through to opposite's place using four walking steps. As soon as they are across, couples do a wheel-turn with partner on the left, walking backward four steps and moving into place on partner's left, who turns in place using four steps. If desired, left partner can take partner's left hand in the left and put the right arm around partner's waist. Hands are dropped. (Pass, through, 3, 4; wheel, turn, 3, 4.)
13–16	Couples pass through again as described in measures 9–12. (Back, through, 3, 4; wheel, turn, 3, 4.)
17–20	Right-hand partners advance toward each other, join right hands briefly, pass each other by right shoulders, drop hands, and join left hand with opposite left partner using four steps. The opposite left partner does a wheel turn as described in measures 9–12 using four steps. (Right partner, chain, 3, 4; wheel, turn, 3, 4.)
21–24	Right-hand partners chain back again and turn as in measures 17–20 using eight steps and end with left hands joined with partner. (Chain, back, 3, 4; wheel, turn, 3, 4.)
25–28	Partners join hands in promenade position and advance four steps toward opposite and four steps backward to place. (Forward, 2, 3, 4; back, 2, 3, 4.)
29–32	Each couple with hands in promenade position advances to the left of the opposite couple to the next couple using eight steps. (New couple, 2, 3, . . . , 8.)

Repeat the dance three times.

Lummi Sticks

Music source: WWCD-2015 or 2014; WWC-2000

Skills: rhythmic tapping, flipping, catching of sticks

Formation: couples scattered throughout the area

Lummi sticks are smaller versions of wands; they are 12 to 15 inches (30 to 38 cm) long. Some believe that the Lummi Indians in northwest Washington first used these sticks; others credit South Pacific cultures. Their actual origin remains obscure.

Most Lummi stick activities use partners, although some can be done individually. Each child sits cross-legged, facing a partner at a distance of 18 to 20 (45 to 50 cm) inches. Children adjust this distance as the activities demand. They hold the sticks in the thumb and fingers (not the fist) at about the bottom third of the stick.

Routines are based on sets of six movements; each movement is completed in one count. Many routines are possible but only the basic ones are presented here. Use the following one-count movements to make up routines.

- *Vertical tap.* Tap both sticks upright on the floor.
- *Partner tap.* Tap partner's stick (right stick to right stick, or left to left).
- *End tap.* Tilt the sticks forward or sideways and tap the ends on the floor.
- *Cross-tap.* Cross hands and tap the upper ends to the floor.
- *Side tap.* Tap the upper ends to the side.
- *Flip.* Toss the stick in air, giving it a half turn, and catch the other end.
- *Tap together.* Hold the sticks parallel and tap them together.
- *Toss right (or left).* Toss the right-hand stick to partner's right hand, at the same time receiving partner's right-hand stick.
- *Pass.* Lay the stick on the floor and pick up partner's stick.
- *Toss right and left.* Toss stick to partner quickly, right to right and left to left, all within one count.

The following routines incorporate the basic movements and are listed in order of difficulty. Partners do each routine four times to complete the 24 beats of the chant.

TEACHING TIP

Lummi Sticks can be done by four children with a change in the timing. One set of partners begins at the start, and the other two start on the third beat. All sing together. In this way, the sticks are flying alternately.

1. Vertical tap, tap together, partner tap right, vertical tap, tap together, partner tap left.

2. Vertical tap, tap together, pass right stick, vertical tap, tap together, pass left stick.

3. Vertical tap, tap together, toss right stick, vertical tap, tap together, toss left stick.

4. Repeat routines 1–3 but substitute an end tap and flip for the vertical tap and tap together. Perform the stated third movement (i.e., end tap, flip, partner tap right, end tap, flip, partner tap left).

5. Vertical tap, tap together, toss right and left quickly, end tap, flip, toss right and left quickly.

6. Cross-tap, cross-flip, vertical tap (uncross arms), cross-tap, cross-flip, vertical tap (uncross arms).

7. Right flip side—left flip in front, vertical tap in place, partner tap right. Left flip side—right flip in front, vertical tap in place, partner tap left.

8. End tap in front, flip, vertical tap, tap together, toss right, toss left.

9. Vertical tap, tap together, right stick to partner's left hand, toss own left stick to own right hand. Repeat. This is the circle throw.

10. Same as routine 9 but reverse the circle.

Tinikling (Philippine Islands)

Music source: WWC/CD-8095; WWC/CD-9015

Skills: tinikling steps

Formation: sets of fours scattered around the room; each set has two strikers and two dancers (figure 19.5)

Note: The dance represents a rice bird as it steps with its long legs from one rice paddy to another. The dance is popular in many countries in Southeast Asia, where different versions are seen.

Directions: Two 8-foot (2.4 m) bamboo poles and two crossbars on which the poles rest are needed for the dance. A striker kneels at each end of the poles; both strikers hold the end of a pole in each hand. The music is in waltz meter, 3/4 time, with an accent on the first beat. The strikers slide and strike the poles together on count 1. On the other two beats of the waltz measure, strikers open the poles about 15 inches (38 cm) apart, lift them an inch (2.5 cm) or so, and tap twice on the crossbars in time to counts 2 and 3. The rhythm "close, tap, tap" continues throughout the dance, each sequence taking a measure.

Basically, the dance requires students to step outside the poles on the close (count 1) and two steps inside the poles (counts 2 and 3) when the poles are tapped

FIGURE 19.5 Tinikling set.

on the crossbars. Many step combinations have been devised.

Have students practice the basic tinikling step until they master it. The step is done singly, although two dancers can perform at once. The dancers stand at opposite ends with their right sides to the poles. Have students practice steps with stationary poles, with lines drawn on the floor or with jump ropes laid on the floor. Students handling the poles must concentrate on watching each other rather than the dancer to avoid becoming confused by the dancer's feet.

Count 1: Step slightly forward with the left foot.

Count 2: Step with the right foot between the poles.

Count 3: Step with the left foot between the poles.

Count 4: Step with the right foot outside poles to dancer's own right.

Count 5: Step with the left between the poles.

Count 6: Step with the right between the poles.

Count 7: Step with the left outside to the original position.

The first step (count 1) is used only to get the dance started. The last step (count 7) to the original position is actually the beginning of a new series (counts 7–12).

Because some tinikling dances and records guide the dancers with a different rhythm (tap, tap, close), they require adjusting the steps and patterns in these descriptions.

Tinikling steps also can be adjusted to 4/4 rhythm (close, close, tap, tap), so the poles are closed on two counts and open on the other two. The basic foot pattern is two steps outside the poles and two inside. For consistency, this text presents all routines in the original 3/4 time (close, tap, tap).

19

Dancers can go from side to side or can return to the side from which they entered. The dance can be done singly, with the two dancers moving in opposite directions from side to side, or the dancers can enter from and leave toward the same side. Dancers can do the same step patterns or different ones. They can dance as partners and move side by side with inside hands joined, or they can face each other with both hands joined.

To gain a sense of the movement pattern for 3/4 time, slap both thighs with the hands on the "close" and clap the hands twice for movements inside the poles. For 4/4 time, slap the right thigh with the right hand, slap the left thigh with the left hand, and clap two times. This routine should be done to music, with the poles closing and opening as indicated. Getting the feel of the rhythm is important.

Other Tinikling Steps and Routines

Straddle step: Dancers do a Straddle Jump outside the poles on count 1 and do two movements inside the poles on counts 2 and 3. Let the dancers explore the different combinations. Jump turns are possible.

Jump step: Dancers begin the side jump with their side toward the poles. They can do the jump from either side.

Measure 1:

- Count 1: Jump lightly in place.
- Counts 2 and 3: Jump twice between the poles.

Measure 2:

- Count 1: Jump lightly in place (other side).
- Counts 2 and 3: Jump twice between the poles.

Dancers keep the feet close together to fit between the poles. They can exit to the same side they entered from or alternate sides. Another way to enter and exit is by facing the poles and jumping forward and backward rather than sideways. When jumping sideways, dancers can keep one foot ahead of the other in a stride position. On the second jump inside the poles, they can reverse this position.

Rocker step: For the rocker step, dancers face the poles and begin with either foot. As they step in and out (forward and backward), they make a rocking motion with the body.

Crossover step: The crossover step is similar to the basic tinikling step, but the dancer begins with the right foot (forward step) and steps inside the poles with the left foot, using a cross-foot step. Each time, the dancer must step in or out using a cross-step.

Circling poles: For circling the poles, dancers position themselves as in the basic tinikling step (figure 19.6) and execute the following movements:

Measure 1:

- Count 1: Step slightly forward with the left foot.
- Count 2: Step with the right foot between the poles.
- Count 3: Step with the left foot between the poles.

Measure 2:

- Count 1: Step with the right foot outside the poles to the right.
- Counts 2 and 3: With light running steps, make a half circle to a position for the return movement.

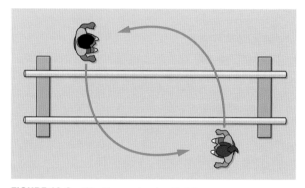

FIGURE 19.6 Circling poles for tinikling.

Measures 3 and 4: Dancers return to their original position using the same movements as in measures 1 and 2.

Fast tinikling trot: The fast tinikling trot is similar to circling the poles, but the step goes twice as fast and thus requires only two sets of three counts. Instead of having the side of the body to the poles, as in the basic tinikling step, the dancers face the poles. They do the following steps:

Measure 1:

- Count 1: Shift the weight to the left foot and raise the right foot.
- Count 2: Step with the right foot between the poles.
- Count 3: Step with the left foot outside the poles and begin turning to the left.

Measure 2:

- Count 1: Step with the right foot outside the poles, completing the left turn to face the poles again.

- Count 2: Step with the left foot inside the poles.
- Count 3: Step outside with the right foot.

Dancers do the next step with the left foot to begin a new cycle. The movement is a light trot with quick turns. Note that the step outside the poles on count 3 in each measure is made with the poles apart.

Cross-step: To do the cross-step, dancers begin with the basic tinikling position and use the following sequence:

Measure 1:

- Count 1: Cross-step across both poles with the left foot, hopping on the right side.
- Counts 2 and 3: Hop twice on the right foot between the poles.

Measure 2:

- Count 1: Hop on the left foot outside the poles to the left.
- Counts 2 and 3: Hop twice again on the right foot between the poles.

Line of poles: Place three or more sets of poles about 6 feet (2 m) apart. The object is to dance down the sets, make a circling movement (as in circling poles), and return down the line in the opposite direction (figure 19.7). Dancers keep their right sides toward the poles throughout.

During measure 1 (three counts), dancers do a basic tinikling step, finishing on the right side of the first set of poles. During measure 2 (three counts), they do three light running steps to position themselves for the tinikling step at the next set of poles. After reaching the end, dancers circle in three steps to get in position for the return journey.

Square formation: Four sets of poles can be placed in a square formation for an interesting dance sequence (figure 19.8). Four dancers are positioned as shown. During measure 1, each dancer does a tinikling step, crossing to the outside of the square. On measure 2, the dancers circle to position for a return tinikling step. During measure 3, the dancers do a tinikling step, returning to the inside of the square. On measure 4, they rotate counterclockwise to the next set of poles with three running steps.

Tell the dancers to look ahead (not at the poles), so that they learn by thinking and doing and not by gauging the pole distances visually.

Four-pole set: This arrangement features two longer crossbars on which two sets of poles rest, leaving a small space between the poles when the sets are open. Four strikers control the poles. Two dancers begin by facing each other and straddling a set of poles on opposite ends. They can change foot patterns every 16 measures, which for most selections is a full pattern of music. Here are some suggested routines.

1. Straddle, jump, jump, exiting on measure 16 to the left.
2. Do the basic tinikling step, exiting on the left foot.
3. Do the basic tinikling step, first on his or her own set of poles and then on the other set of poles. As the dancer comes out of the first set of poles with the right foot, he or she makes a half turn to do the tinikling step through the other poles. On the return, the dancer makes another half turn in the middle to face and return to his or her original position. Repeat the sequence twice.

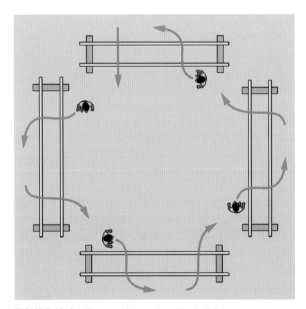

FIGURE 19.8 Square formation for tinikling.

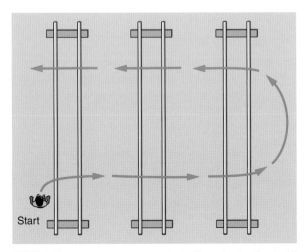

FIGURE 19.7 Movement through the line of poles for tinikling.

19

4. Do routine 3, but move diagonally, passing the oncoming dancer with right shoulder to right shoulder, in effect changing places. (Do not use half turns.) Turn around in six steps and return to position. Repeat.

5. Jump to a straddle position with one foot in each of the pole openings. On "close," jump to the space between the sets. On measure 16, the dancer jumps out to the left on both feet.

6. Two-footed step: Jump twice with both feet inside the first set of poles, to the space between, twice inside the second set, and out. Return. Repeat twice.

Developmental Level III Dances

Children at Developmental Level III are skillful, especially if they have participated in rhythmic activities for several years. If students do not have a well-developed dance background, have them start by learning dances from Developmental Levels I and II. Developmental Level III dances include patterns that students must perform with skill and finesse. At this level, patterns are longer and require more concentration and memorization. The difficulty level ranges from introductory square dance moves to dances featuring the two-step, polka step, and schottische.

Hora ("Hava Nagila"; Israeli)

Music source: WWCD-3528; WWC-3528

Skills: stepping sideways, step-swing

Formation: single circle, facing center, hands joined; the circle can be partial

Note: The hora is regarded as the national dance of Israel. It is a simple dance that expresses joy. The traditional hora is done in circle formation, with the arms extended sideways and the hands on the neighbors' shoulders. It is easiest to introduce the dance step individually. After learning the step, students can join hands and practice the circle formation counterclockwise or clockwise. The clockwise version is presented here.

Israelis perform an old and a new hora. The new hora is more energetic; dancers spring high in the air and whirl around with shouts of ecstasy. The hora can be danced to many tunes, but "Hava Nagila" (meaning "Come, let us be happy!") is the favorite.

Directions—old hora:

Measures	Action
1–3	Step left on the left foot. Cross the right foot in back of the left, keeping weight on the right. Step left on the left foot and hop on it, swinging the right foot forward. Step-hop on the right foot and swing the left foot forward. Repeat the same step over and over. (Side, behind, side, swing; side, swing.)

The circle also may move to the right; dancers use the same step, beginning with the right foot.

Directions—new hora:

Measures	Action
1–3	Face left and run two steps. Jump in place. Hop on the left foot, swinging the right foot forward. Take three quick steps in place. Continue in the same way, moving to the left. (Run, run, jump, hop-swing, step, step, step.)

The hora often begins with the dancers swaying in place from left to right as the music builds. The dance gradually increases in pace and intensity. Shouts accompany the dance as the participants call to each other across the circle.

Jiffy Mixer (American)

Music source: WWCD-FDN

Skills: heel-and-toe step, chug step

Formation: double circle, partners facing

Directions: The music includes an introduction. Directions are for partners A; B's actions are opposite. Introduce the dance by having all join hands in a single circle, facing inward. There are no partners and no progressions to new partners.

Measures	Introduction
1–4	Wait, wait, balance apart (push away on the left foot and touch the right). Balance together (forward on the right and touch the left).

Measures	Action
1–4	Strike the left heel diagonally out and return to touch the toe near the right foot. Repeat. Do a side step left with a touch. (Heel-toe, heel-toe, side-close, side-touch.)

| 5–8 | | Repeat while moving in the opposite direction, beginning with the right foot. (Heel-toe, heel-toe, side-close, side-touch.) |

| 9–12 | | Take four chug steps backward, clapping on the upbeat. (Chug-clap, chug-clap, chug-clap, chug-clap.) |

| 13–16 | | Starting with the left foot, take four slow, swaggering steps diagonally to the right, moving to a new partner. (Walk, 2, 3, 4.) |

The chug step is done by jumping and dragging both feet backward. The body is bent slightly forward.

Virginia Reel (American)

Music source: WWCD-05114

Skills: skipping, arm turn, do-si-do, sliding (sashay), reeling

Formation: six couples in a longways set of two lines facing; partners on one end of the set are designated the head couple

Directions:

Measures	Call	Action
1–4	All go forward and back.	Take three steps forward and curtsey or bow. Take three steps back and close.
5–8	Right hands around.	Move forward to partner, turn once in place using a right forearm grasp, and return to position.
9–12	Left hands around.	Repeat measures 5–8 with a left forearm grasp.
13–16	Both hands around.	Partners join both hands, turn once in a clockwise direction, and move backward to place.
17–20	Do-si-do your partner.	Partners pass each other right shoulder to right shoulder and then back-to-back and move backward to place.
21–24	All go forward and back.	Repeat the action of measures 1–4.
25–32	Head couple sashay.	The head couple, with hands joined, takes eight slides down to the foot of the set and eight slides back to place.
33–64	Head couple reel.	The head couple begins the reel with linked right elbows and turns one time to face the next couple in line. Each member in the head couple then links left elbows with the person facing and turns once in place. The head couple meets again in the center and turns once with a right elbow swing. The next dancers down the line are turned with a left elbow swing, and then the head couple returns to the center for another right elbow turn. The head couple thus progresses down the line, turning each dancer in order. After the head couple has turned the last dancers, they meet with a right elbow swing, turn halfway around, and sashay (slide) back to the head of the set.
65–96	Everybody march.	All couples face toward the head of the set with the head couple in front. The person on the right turns to the right; the person on the left turns to the left and goes behind the line, followed by the other dancers. When the head couple reaches the foot of the set, they join hands and make an arch for all other couples to pass under. The head couple is now at the foot of the set, and the dance is repeated with a new head couple.

Repeat the dance until each couple gets to be the head couple.

Teaching the Two-Step

Children can learn the forward two-step simply by moving forward on the cue "Step, close, step," starting on the left foot and alternating thereafter. The close-step is made by bringing the toe of the closing foot to a point even with the instep of the other foot. All steps are almost slides, a kind of shuffle step.

The two-step just described is nothing more than a

19

TEACHING TIP

1. Versions of Virginia Reel (American) vary. Some allow time at the beginning for a do-si-do after the "both hands around" (measures 13–16); others do not. Check the music for phrasing before presenting the dance to the class.

2. Technically, the dance is written for eight couples in each set. For the head couple to reel all couples in the set, they must not miss one beat of the music or they will be behind the phrasing for the reel section. When introducing the dance to a class for the first time, having only six couples in each set is helpful. Then, if a couple gets behind the music for the reeling section, they still can stay in time to the music and finish before the "casting off" section begins.

slow gallop, alternating the lead foot. One way to help students learn the step-close-step pattern is to put them in a single circle and have them gallop forward. Instruct them to start on the left foot and move forward eight slow gallops. Stop the class and have them put their right foot forward and repeat the gallops. Continue this pattern, and have students change from galloping with their left foot forward to galloping with their right foot forward without stopping. When making this change, students bring the right foot forward in a walking step, keeping their weight on the left foot. Reverse the procedure when moving the left foot forward. The movement is very smooth. When students master this pattern, repeat the sequence but have them do four gallops with each foot forward. After they master this pattern, repeat the pattern with two gallops on each foot. Students who can do this are performing the forward two-step.

Next, arrange the children by couples in a circle formation, partners A on the inside, all facing counterclockwise. Repeat the instruction, with both partners beginning on the left foot. Practice the two-step with a partner, with partner A beginning on the left foot and partner B starting on the right. In the next progression, the children move face-to-face and back-to-back.

Jugglehead Mixer (American)

Music source: any music with a definite, steady beat

Skills: two-step, elbow turn (forearm grasp)

Formation: double circle, facing counterclockwise in promenade position

Directions: Actions described are for partners on the inside circle; directions are opposite for partners on the outside circle.

Measures	Call	Action
1–4	Two-step left and two-step right. (Walk-2-3-4.)	Do a two-step left and a two-step right, and take four walking steps forward.
5–8	Two-step left and two-step right. (Walk-2-3-4.)	Repeat measures 1–4.
9–10	Turn your partner with the right.	Inside partner takes the outside partner's right hand and walks around to face the person behind.
11–12	Now turn your corner with your left.	Inside partner turns the person behind with the left hand.
13–14	Turn your partner all the way around.	Inside partner turns partner with the right hand going all the way around.
15–16	And pick up the forward lady.	Inside partner steps up one place to the outside person ahead, who becomes the new partner.

Teton Mountain Stomp (American)

Music source: WWCD-FDN

Skills: walking, banjo position, sidecar position, two-step

Formation: single circle, partners in closed dance position, partners A facing counterclockwise and partners B facing clockwise

Directions:

Measures	Action
1–4	Step to the left toward the center of the circle on the left foot, close right foot to the left, step again to the left
	On the left foot, stomp right foot beside the left but leave the weight on the left foot. Repeat this action, but start on the right foot and move away from the center. (Side, close; side, stomp; side, close; side, stomp.)

5–8	Step to the left toward the center on the left foot; stomp the right foot beside the left. Step to the right, away from the center on the right foot, and stomp the left foot beside the right. In "banjo" position (modified closed position with right hips adjacent), partner A takes four walking steps forward while partner B takes four steps backward, starting on the right foot. (Side, stomp, side, stomp; walk, 2, 3, 4.)
9–12	Partners change to sidecar position (modified closed position with left hips adjacent) by each making a one-half turn to the right in place, A remaining on the inside and B on the outside. Partner A walks backward, while B walks four steps forward. Partners change back to banjo position with right hips adjacent by each making a left-face one-half turn; then they immediately release from each other. Partner A walks forward four steps to meet the second B approaching, while B walks forward four steps to meet the second A approaching. (Change, 2, 3, 4; new partner, 2, 3, 4.)
13–16	New partners join inside hands and do four two-steps forward, beginning with A's right foot and B's left. (Step, close, step; repeat four times.)

TEACHING TIP

If the dancers are skillful enough, use the following action for measures 13–16 of the Teton Mountain Stomp (American): New partners take the closed dance position and do four turning two-steps, starting on A's left (B's right), and make one complete right-face turn while moving in the specified direction.

Cotton-Eyed Joe (American)

Music source: WWCD-FDN

Skills: heel-toe, two-step

Formation: double circle, partner B is on the right, holding inside hands and facing counterclockwise; varsouvienne position can also be used

Directions:

Measures	Action
1–2	Starting with the left foot, cross the left foot in front of the right foot and kick the left foot forward. (Cross, kick.)
3–4	Take one two-step backward. (Left, close, left.)
5–6	Cross the right foot in front of the left foot; kick the right foot forward. (Cross, kick.)
7–8	Do one two-step backward. (Right, close, right.)
9–16	Repeat measures 1–8.
17–32	Perform eight two-steps counterclockwise beginning with the left foot. (Step, close, step; repeat eight times.)

Teaching the Polka Step

Like the two-step, the polka has a step-close-step pattern. The two-step is simply step-close-step, but the polka is step-close-step-hop. Technically, the polka is usually described as hop-step-close-step (or hop-step-together-step). However, the first description is probably more helpful when working with beginning students.

The polka step involves four movements: (1) step forward left; (2) close the right foot to the left, bringing the toe up and even with the left instep; (3) step forward left; and (4) hop on the left foot. The series begins with the weight on the right foot.

Several methods can be used to teach the polka:

1. *Step-by-step rhythm approach.* Analyzing the dance slowly, have the class walk through the steps together in even rhythm. The cue is "Step, close, step, hop." Accelerate the tempo to normal polka time and add the music.

2. *Gallop approach.* Many elementary instructors prefer the gallop approach. Use the same approach as in the section Teaching the Two-Step, but add the polka hop and increase the tempo. When moving the right foot forward, students hop on the left foot. When moving the left foot forward, they hop on the right foot.

3. *Two-step approach.* Students begin with the left foot and two-step with the music, moving forward in the specified direction in a single circle. Accelerate the tempo gradually to a fast two-step and have students take smaller steps. Without stopping, have students change to a polka rhythm by following each two-step with a

hop. Use polka music for the two-step but slow it down considerably to start.

4. *Partner approach.* After learning the polka step individually by one of the three methods, children can practice the step with partners in a double-circle formation, partners A on the inside and all facing counterclockwise, with inside hands joined. Partners A begin with the left foot, and partners B begin with the right.

Klumpakojis (Swedish)

Music source: WWCD-1042

Skills: walking, stars, polka step

Formation: couples in a circle, side by side, all facing counterclockwise, with partner B to the right

Directions:

Measures	Part I action
1–4	With inside hands joined and free hand on hip, all walk briskly around the circle for eight steps counterclockwise. (Walk, 2, 3, . . . , 7; turn.)
5–8	Turn individually to the left, reverse direction, change hands, and walk eight steps clockwise. (Walk, 2, 3, . . . ,7; turn.)

	Part II action
9–12	Face partner and make a star by joining right hands (be sure that the right elbow is bent). The left hand is on the hip. With partner, walk around clockwise for eight walking steps. Change hands and repeat the eight steps, reversing direction. (Star, 2, 3, . . . , 8; reverse, 2, 3, . . . , 8.)

	Part III action
13–16	Listen to the musical phrase and then stamp three times on the last two counts. Listen to the phrase again and then clap own hands three times. (Listen, listen, stamp, 2, 3; listen, listen, clap, 2, 3.)
17–20	Shake the right finger in a scolding motion at partner. (Scold, 2, 3.) Shake the left finger. (Scold, 2, 3.)
21–24	Turn solo to the left, clapping partner's right hand once during the turn. Use two walking steps to make the turn and finish facing partner. (Turn, 2; stamp, 2, 3.)
25–32	Repeat the action of measures 13–24.

	Part IV action
33–40	With inside hands joined, do 16 polka steps (or two-steps) forward, moving counterclockwise. (Later, as the dance is learned, change to the promenade position.) On polka steps 15 and 16, partner A moves forward to take a new partner B while handing the original partner B to the A in back. New couple joins inside hands. (Step, close, step, hop; step, close, step, hop; repeat for a total of 16 polka steps.)

Alley Cat (American)

Music source: WWCD-9126; WWC-RM3

Skills: grapevine step, touch step, knee lifts

Formation: none, although all should face the same direction during instruction

Directions:

Measures	Action
1–2	Do a grapevine left and kick: Step sideways left, step right behind left, step left again, and kick. Repeat to the right. (Left, behind, left, kick; right, behind, right, kick.)
3–4	Touch the left toe backward, bring the left foot to the right, touch the left toe backward again, bring the left foot to the right, taking the weight. Repeat, beginning with the right toe. (Left-and, left-and; right-and, right-and.)
5–6	Raise the left knee up in front of the right knee and repeat. Raise the right knee up twice, similarly. (Left-and, left-and; right-and, right-and.)
7–8	Raise the left knee and then the right knee. Clap the hands once and make a jump quarter turn to the left. (Left-and, right-and, clap-and, jump.)

After repeating the routine three times, each dancer will be facing in the original direction.

Ten Pretty Girls (American)

Music source: WWCD-1042

Skills: walking, grapevine

Formation: circle of groups of any number, with arms linked or hands joined, all facing counterclockwise

Directions:

Measures	Action
1–2	Starting with the weight on the right foot, touch the left foot in front, swing the left foot to the left and touch, swing the left foot behind the right foot and put the weight on the left foot, step to the right, close the left foot to the right. (Front, side, back-side, together.)
3–4	Repeat, starting with the weight on the left foot and moving to the right. (Front, side, back-side, together.)
5–6	Take four walking or strutting steps forward, starting on the left foot. (Walk, 2, 3, 4.)
7–8	Swing the left foot forward with a kicking motion; swing the left foot backward with a kicking motion; stamp left, right, left, in place. (Swing, swing, stamp, stamp, stamp.)

Repeat the entire dance 11 times, starting each time with the alternate foot. The dance can be used as a mixer when performed in a circle by groups of three. On measures 7–8, have the middle person move forward to the next group during the three stamps.

Limbo Rock

Music source: WWCD-9126

Skills: touch step, swivel step, jump clap step

Formation: single circle or scattered

Directions:

Measures	Part I action
1–2	Touch left foot in. Touch left foot out. Three steps in place. (In, out, left, right, left.)
3–4	Repeat measures 1 and 2 beginning with opposite foot. (In, out, right, left, right.)
5–8	Repeat measures 1–4.
	Part II action
9–10	Swivel toes right, swivel heels right. Repeat and straighten feet. (Swivel, 2, 3, straighten.)
11–12	Repeat beats 1 and 2 beginning with swivel toes left.
13–14	Jump in, clap; jump out, clap. (Jump, clap, jump, clap.)
15–16	Repeat measures 13 and 14.

An easier version involves walking eight steps right during measures 9–16.

Jessie Polka (American)

Music source: WWCD-RM8

Skills: step and touch, two-step, polka step

Formation: single circle, couples facing counterclockwise with inside arms around each other's waist

Directions:

Measures	Part I action
1	Beginning left, touch the heel in front and then step left in place. (Left heel, together.)
2	Touch the right toe behind. Then touch the right toe in place or swing it forward, keeping the weight on the left foot. (Right toe, touch.)
3	Touch the right heel in front and then step right in place. (Right heel, together.)
4	Touch the left heel to the left side and sweep the left foot across in front of the right. Keep the weight on the right. (Left heel, crossover.)
	Part II action
5–8	Take four two-steps or polka steps forward in the line of direction. (Step, close, step; step, close, step; step, close, step; step, close, step.)

Variations: The dance may be done as a mixer by having partners B turn out to the right on the last two two-steps and come back to the A behind them. Partners A keep moving forward on the last two two-steps, making it easier to meet the B coming toward them. Another variation is to perform this activity as a line dance. Students place their hands on the waist or shoulders of the dancer in front of them.

Inside-Out Mixer

Music source: any music with a pronounced beat suitable for walking at a moderate speed

Skills: walking, wring the dishrag, change partners

Formation: triple circle (three children standing side by side), facing counterclockwise, inside hands joined; children in the center of each trio can wear pinnies

Directions:

Measures	Action
1–4	Take eight walking steps forward. (Forward, 2, 3, . . . , 8.)

19

5–8 Form a small circle and circle left in eight steps back to place. (Circle, 2, 3, . . . , 8.)

9–12 The center child walks forward under the raised arms opposite, pulling the other two under to turn the circle inside out. (Inside-out, 2, 3, . . . , 8.)

13–16 The trio circles left in eight steps, returning to place. When almost back to place, they drop hands. The center child walks forward counterclockwise, and the other two walk clockwise (the way they are facing) to the nearest trio for a change of partners. (Circle, 2, 3, 4; mix, 6, 7, 8.)

D'Hammerschmiedsgselln ("The Journey Blacksmith"; Bavarian)

Music source: WWCD-FFD; WWC-TC1

Skills: clapping routine, step-hops

Formation: circle of four

Directions:

Measures	Action
1–16	First opposites do a clapping pattern beginning on the first count of measure 1, while the other pair does a clapping pattern beginning on the first count of measure 2. The six-count pattern follows: With both hands, slap own thighs (count 1), slap own chest (count 2), clap own hands (count 3), clap right hands (count 4), clap left hands (count 5), and clap opposite's hands (count 6). (Thighs, chest, together, right, left, both.) Repeat the six-count pattern seven more times.

Part I

17–24 Join hands and circle left with eight step-hops. (Step-hop, 2-hop, . . . , 8-hop.)

25–32 Circle right in the same way. (Step-hop, 2-hop, . . . , 8-hop.)

33–48 Repeat the chorus action.

Part II—star

49–56 Right-hand star with eight step-hops. (Step-hop, 2-hop, . . . , 8-hop.)

57–64 Left-hand star in the same manner. (Step-hop, 2-hop, . . . , 8-hop.)

65–80 Repeat the chorus action.

Part III—big circle

81–88 Circles of four open to form one large circle, and circle left with eight step-hops. (Step-hop, 2-hop, . . . , 8-hop.)

89–96 Reverse direction, continuing with eight step-hops. (Step-hop, 2-hop, . . . , 8-hop.)

Variation: As a mixer, try the following sequence.

Measures	Action
1–16	Use the chorus clapping pattern described.
17–24	As in part I or II, circle left, or do a right-hand star with step-hops (or simple walking steps).
25–32	Do eight step-hops with the corner in general space or in any comfortable position, moving anywhere.

Repeat the entire sequence with a new foursome.

Kalvelis ("Little Blacksmith"; Lithuanian)

Music source: WWCD-WOF3

Skills: polka step, swing, clapping pattern, grand right and left

Formation: single circle of couples facing center, partner B on partner A's right, all hands joined in a single circle with the right foot free

Directions:

Measures	Part I action
1–8	Circle right with seven polka steps, ending with three stamps. (Circle-and, 2-and, 3-and, . . . , 7-and; stamp, stamp, stamp.)
9–16	Circle left with seven polka steps, ending with three stamps. (Circle-and, 2-and, 3-and, . . . , 7-and; stamp, stamp, stamp.)

Chorus action

1–2	Clap own hands four times, alternating left hand onto own right, then right hand onto own left. (Clap, 2, 3, 4.)
3–4	Right elbow swing with four skips. (Swing, 2, 3, 4.)
5–6	Repeat the clapping pattern of measures 1 and 2. (Clap, 2, 3, 4.)
7–8	Left elbow swing with four skips. (Swing, 2, 3, 4.)
9–16	Repeat the pattern of measures 1–8.

Part II action

1–8   Partners B dance three polka steps forward toward the center, ending with three stamps. They turn to face their partners and return to place with three polka steps forward, ending with three stamps, facing center again. (Step-close-step-hop; step-close-step-hop; step-close-step-hop; stamp, stamp, stamp.)

9–16   Partners A repeat the pattern of measures 1–8 but dance more vigorously, stamping on the first beat of each measure. (Step-close-step-hop; step-close-step-hop; step-close-step-hop; stamp, stamp, stamp.)

Chorus action

1–16   As described.

Part III action

1–16   Grand right and left around the circle with 16 polka steps, meeting a new partner on the last measure. (Step-close-step-hop; repeat 16 times.)

Chorus action

1–16   As described but with a new partner.

Doudlebska Polka (Czechoslovakian)

Music source: WWCD-572; WWC-572

Skills: polka step, walking, clapping pattern

Formation: one large circle or several smaller circles scattered around the floor; directions are for one large circle

Directions:

Measures   Part I action

1–16   Partners assume the varsouvienne position and do 16 polka steps around the circle, one couple following another. (Polka, 2, 3, . . . , 16.)

Part II action

17–32   Partner A puts his or her right arm around partner B's waist as they stand side by side, and B puts his or her left hand on A's right shoulder. A puts the left hand on the shoulder of the A in front. This closes the circle. Partners A move sideways to the center to catch up with the A ahead. In this position, all march forward counterclockwise and sing loudly, "La, la, la," and so forth. This takes 32 walking steps. (Walk, 2, 3, . . . , 32.)

Part III action

33–48   Partners A face the center, and partners B drop behind their partner. Partners B turn to face the other way, clockwise, and polka around the circle (around the partners A) with their hands on hips. At the same time, partners A, who face center, clap a rhythm as follows: Clap hands twice and then extend both hands, palms outward, toward the neighbor on each side, and clap hands once with the neighbor. Repeat this pattern over and over. For variation, partners A may slap a thigh occasionally, or duck down or cross their arms when clapping the neighbor's hand. (A: Clap, clap, out; repeat 16 times.) (B: Polka, 2, 3, . . . , 16.)

At the end of part III, partners A turn around, each taking the partner B behind her or him, and start the dance from the beginning. Children who are looking for a partner move to the center to find one.

Extra children can enter the dance during the clapping part for partners A, and some can join the ring to polka around the outside. Those left without a partner wait for the next turn. When the group is large, form several circles; it is perfectly fine for unpartnered children to steal into another circle. The polka in this case is done anywhere around the room. During the march, circles can have any number of people.

Teaching the Schottische Step

The schottische is actually a light run, but when students are learning, have them practice it as a walking step. (This is also true in polka instruction.) Lively music will quicken the step later. The cue is "Step, step, step, hop; step, step, step, hop; step-hop, step-hop, step-hop, step-hop." A full schottische pattern, then, is three steps and a hop, repeated once, followed by four step-hops. Partner A starts on the left foot, and partner B starts on the right. The step can be learned first in scattered formation, then in a single circle, and practiced later by couples in a double circle. The "Horse and Buggy Schottische" is a good introduction to this step.

Horse and Buggy Schottische (American)

Music source: WWCD-1046

Skills: schottische step

Formation: double circle, couples in sets of four, facing counterclockwise; couples join inside hands and join outside hands with the other couple (figure 19.9)

19

Directions:

Measures	Action
1–2	Moving forward, perform two schottische steps. (Step, step, step, hop; step, step, step, hop.)
3–4	Progress in specified direction, performing four step-hops. (Step-hop, 2-hop, 3-hop, 4-hop.)

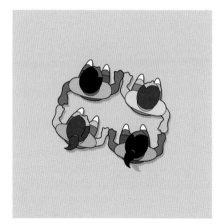

FIGURE 19.9 Horse and Buggy Schottische formation.

During the four step-hops, dancers can do one of three movement patterns.

1. The lead couple drops inside hands and step-hops around the outside of the back couple, who move forward during the step-hops. The lead couple then joins hands behind the other couple, and the positions are reversed.

2. The lead couple continues to hold hands and move backward under the upraised hands of the back couple, who untwist by turning away from each other.

3. Alternate 1 and 2.

Alunelul ("Little Hazelnut"; Romanian)

Music source: WWCD-FFD; WWC-TC1

Skills: step-behind step, grapevine step, stomping

Formation: single circle, hands on shoulders to both sides, arms straight ("T" position)

Directions: The title is pronounced "ah-loo-NAY-loo." The Romanians are famous for rugged dances. In this dance, the stomping action represents the breaking of hazelnuts. Stomps are made close to the supporting foot. When teaching the dance, scatter the dancers in general space so that they can move individually.

Measures	Part I action
1–2	Sidestep right, step left behind right, sidestep right, step left behind right, sidestep right, stomp left foot twice. (Side, back, side, back, side, stomp, stomp.)
3–4	Beginning with the left foot, repeat the action but with reverse footwork. (Side, back, side, back, side, stomp, stomp.)
5–8	Repeat the action of measures 1–4.
	Part II action
9-10	Sidestep right, left behind right, sidestep right, stomp. (Side, back, side, stomp.)
11–12	Sidestep left, right behind left, sidestep left, stomp. (Side, back, side, stomp.)
13–16	Repeat the action of measures 9–12.
	Part III action
17–18	In place, step right, stomp left; step left, stomp right; step right, stomp left twice. (Side, stomp, side, stomp, side, stomp, stomp.)
19–20	In place, step left, stomp right; step right, stomp left; step left, stomp right twice. (Side, stomp, side, stomp, side, stomp, stomp.)
21–24	Repeat action of measures 17–20.

Korobushka (Russian)

Music source: WWCD-572; WWC-572

Skills: schottische step, balance step, cross-out-together step, walking step

Formation: double circle, partner A's back to the center with partners facing and both hands joined; partner A's left and B's right foot are free

Directions:

Measures	Part I action
1–2	Take one schottische step away from the center (partner A moving forward, partner B backward) starting with A's left and B's right foot. (Out, 2, 3, hop.)
3–4	Repeat the pattern of measures 1 and 2, reversing direction and footwork. (In, 2, 3, hop.)

5–6	Repeat the pattern of measures 1 and 2, ending on the last count with a jump on both feet in place. (Out, 2, 3, jump.)
7–8	Hop on the left foot, touching the right toes across in front of the left foot (count 1). Hop on the left foot, touching the right toes diagonally forward to the right (count 2). Jump on both feet in place, clicking the heels together (count 1), pause, and release the hands (count 2). (Across, apart, together.)

Part II action

9–10	Facing partner and beginning with the right foot, take one schottische step right, moving sideways away from partner. (Side, back, side, hop.)
11–12	Facing partner and beginning with the left foot, take one schottische step left, returning to partner. (Side, back, side, hop.)
13–14	Joining right hands with partner, balance forward and back: Step forward on the right foot (count 1), pause (count 2), rock back on the left foot in place (count 3), pause (count 4). (Forward, hop; back, hop.)
15–16	Take four walking steps forward, starting with the right foot, and change places with partner. (Walk, 2, 3, 4.)
17–24	Repeat the pattern of measures 9–16, returning to place.

TEACHING TIP

To use Korobushka (Russian) as a mixer, during measures 19 and 20, move left to the person just before partner and continue with this new partner. Practice the schottische steps in different directions before trying the dance as a whole.

Oh Johnny (American)

Music source: WWCD-05114; WWC-57

Skills: shuffle step, swing, allemande left, do-si-do, promenade

Formation: single circle of couples facing inward with partner B on the right

Directions: A shuffle step is used throughout this dance. To simplify the dance, begin in scattered formation and teach each call with students changing from partner to corner using any nearby person. Because this is a fast-moving dance, slow down the music until students have learned it.

Action:

All join hands and circle for eight steps.
All stop and swing with partner.
Partners A turn to their left and swing the corner B.
Swing with partner again.
Partners A turn to their left and do an allemande left with their corner.
Partners A turn to their right and do-si-do with their partner.
Partners A promenade with the corner B, who becomes the new partner for the next repetition.

Shindig in the Barn (American)

Music source: WWC-FFD

Skills: walking, do-si-do, swinging, sliding

Formation: contra style (two lines with partners facing each other); music is for seven couples

Directions:

Measures	Action
2 (8 counts total)	Introduction (no movement).
1–2	Everybody walk forward four steps and back four steps. (Forward, 2, 3, 4; back, 2, 3, 4.)
3–4	All pass through to the other side by walking forward four steps toward partner, do a half turn while passing right shoulder of partner, and walk four steps backward. (Walk, 2, 3, 4; turn, 6, 7, 8.)
5–6	Everybody forward and back—repeat measures 1 and 2. (Forward, 2, 3, 4; back, 2, 3, 4.)
7–8	Everybody pass through to the other side with eight steps—repeat measures 3 and 4. (Walk, 2, 3, 4; turn, 6, 7, 8.)
9–10	All couples do-si-do by passing right shoulders and back. (Do-si-do, 2, 3, . . . , 8.)
11–12	All couples do a two-hand swing once around to the left in eight steps. After the swing, all couples except the head couple go back to their original position. Head couples remain in the middle with their hands joined and face each other. (Swing, 2, 3, . . . , 8.)

19

Measures	Action
13–14	The head couple takes eight sliding (sashay) or skipping steps to the foot of the line. All the other couples clap to the beat and watch. (Slide, 2, 3, . . . , 8.)
15–16	Head couple does a right elbow swing at the foot of the line for eight counts and remains at the foot of the line, creating a new head couple. (Swing, 2, 3, . . . , 8.)

Repeat dance to the end of the music.

Big Sombrero Circle Mixer (American)

Music source: WWC-FFD

Skills: circling, do-si-do, star, swing

Formation: Sicilian circle; couples facing couples clockwise and counterclockwise around the circle

Directions:

Measures	Action
2 (8 counts total)	Introduction (no movement).
1–2	Join hands with the facing couple and circle left using eight walking steps. (Circle, 2, 3, . . . , 8.)
3–4	Keeping hands joined, circle right using eight walking steps. (Circle right, 2, 3, . . . , 8.)
5–6	Face partner and do-si-do using eight walking steps. (Do-si-do, 2, 3, . . . , 8.)
7–8	Face opposite and do-si-do using eight walking steps. (Opposite, 2, 3, . . . , 8.)
9–10	All four circle while doing a right-hand star using eight walking steps. (Star, 2, 3, . . . , 8.)
11–12	All four circle while doing a left-hand star using eight walking steps. (Star, 2, 3, . . . , 8.)
13–14	Swing partner by linking right elbows and swinging once or twice. (Swing, 2, 3, . . . , 8.)
15–16	Pass through the opposite couple, passing right shoulders, and walk to the next couple using eight steps. (Pass, through, 3, 4, . . . , 8.)

Repeat the dance to the end of the music. Dancers return to starting positions after every eight-count movement.

Trio Fun Mixer (American)

Music source: WWC-FFD

Skills: walking, do-si-do, star

Formation: single large circle with lines of three facing lines of three

Directions:

Measures	Action
1–4	Facing threesomes (six dancers) join hands and circle left one time around back to place. (Circle, 2, 3, . . . , 16.)
5–6	Center students in each threesome do a do-si-do with each other. (Do-si-do, 2, 3, . . . , 8.)
7–8	Right students in each threesome move diagonally to do-si-do with each other. (Do-si-do, 2, 3, . . . , 8.)
9–10	Left students in each threesome move diagonally to do-si-do with each other. (Do-si-do, 2, 3, . . . , 8.)
11–12	Center student in each threesome faces the child on the right, turns that child with a right-hand star, turns the child on the left with a left-hand star, and goes back to place. (Star, 2, 3, 4; Left, 2, 3, 4.)
13–14	Lines of three go forward four counts and back four counts. (Forward, 2, 3, 4; Back, 2, 3, 4.)
15–16	Lines of three walk forward, passing right shoulders, and move forward to the next group of three. (Forward pass, 2, 3, . . . , 8.)

Repeat to the end of the music.

Circle Virginia Reel (American)

Music source: WWCD-57; WWC-57

Skills: star, swing, do-si-do, promenade

Formation: couples facing in a double circle with dancers about 4 feet (120 cm) apart

Directions:

Measures	Action
1–4	Partners walk forward four steps and backward four steps; repeat. (Forward, 2, 3, 4; back, 2, 3, 4; forward, 2, 3, 4; back, 2, 3, 4.)

5–8	Partners make a star by joining right hands (with bent elbows) and circling around once clockwise in eight steps. Reverse direction and star with left hands back to place in eight steps. (Right star, 2, 3, . . . , 8; left star, 2, 3, . . . , 8.)
9–10	Partners join hands with bent elbows held chest high and circle clockwise back to place in eight steps. (Circle, 2, 3, . . . , 8.)
11–12	Partners walk forward and do-si-do, passing right shoulders and stepping to the right when passing back-to-back. After passing, each partner moves diagonally (veers) to the right to end in front of a new partner. (Do-si-do, 2, 3, 4; veer, 2, 3, 4.)
13–16	Facing a new partner and joining hands, inside partner begins with left foot and outside partner begins with right foot, doing two heel-toe steps and four slide steps counterclockwise. Repeat to the other side, sliding clockwise. (Heel-toe, heel-toe, slide, slide, slide, slide; heel-toe, heel-toe, slide, slide, slide, slide.)
17–20	Partners do a right elbow swing in place for 12 counts using a walking step and use 4 counts to end in promenade position. (Swing, 2, 3, . . . , 12; promenade position 15, 16.)
21–24	In promenade position, partners walk forward counterclockwise 16 steps and end facing each other. (Promenade, 2, 3, . . . , 16.)

Introductory Square Dance

When teaching introductory square dance, do not expect elementary school children to become finished, accomplished square dancers. Instead, emphasize enjoyment and learning the basics within the students' maturity capabilities. Some dancers, however, will acquire considerable skill and polish. Square dancing is a varied, colorful activity with many figures, patterns, and dances. The abundance of materials (introductory, intermediate, and advanced) poses a selection problem given the limited amount of program time for the activity.

Square dance fun begins with an effective caller, and calling takes practice. Although a few children can develop into satisfactory callers, teachers may want to select square dance music that includes some selections with calls and some with the music only. Directions are

usually supplied with the CDs. Choose singing calls that an individual, a group, or the entire class can use. Singing calls are fun to dance to because they tell children what is coming next.

Square dance instruction can begin modestly in the fourth grade, with increased focus in the fifth and sixth grades. This method does not rule out using square dance-related figures in folk dances taught earlier. Square dance as a specialized dance activity requires an appropriate method. Some teaching suggestions follow.

1. In early figure practice or patter calls, one partner becomes the left partner and the other the right. In the following section, calls are given in their traditional forms, and gender references, where they appear, correspond with the traditional calls.

2. Use the shuffle step rather than the skipping or running step for beginners. The shuffle step makes a smoother and more graceful dance, has better carryover to other dancing, and conserves energy. It is a quick walk, almost a half glide, in time to the music and is done by reaching out with the toes in a gliding motion. Dancers have good posture and do not bounce up and down on each step.

3. Teach the dancers to listen to the call. They can have fun, but they must be quiet enough to hear the call.

4. Dancers must follow the caller's directions and not move too soon. Instruct children to be ready for the call and then move at the proper time.

5. Generally, the caller explains the figures, has the children walk through the patterns, and then calls the figures. It is important for children to know what the call means.

6. When teaching, remember that there are many ways to do different turns, swings, hand positions, and so on—and as many opinions on how they should be done. Settle on good principles and stick with them.

7. When a set becomes confused, have each couple return to home position and try to pick up from that point. Otherwise, have them wait until the dance is over or a new sequence starts.

8. Change partners at various times during the dancing. Have each partner A move one place to the right and take a new partner, or have all the partners A (or partners B) keep their positions and have their partners change to another set.

19

Individual Approach to Square Dance

Many square dance terms can be taught using an individual approach. Students scatter in general space, and boy or girl roles are not defined. A piece of country-and-western music with a strong beat is played. Anytime students hear the call, they perform it with the person nearest to them. Dancers use a two-handed swing instead of the regular buzz-step swing.

Two calls are basic. "Hit the lonesome trail" directs students to promenade individually in general space in diverse directions. Use this call at any time to move the students in new directions. The other basic call is, "Stop where you are and keep time to the music." Students stop and beat time to the music with light claps. Here are some other calls.

1. *Right (or left) arm round.* With a forearm grasp, turn your partner once around and return to place.

2. *Honor your partner, honor your corner.* Bow to one person, then bow to another.

3. *Do-si-do your partner, do-si-do your corner.* Pass around one person, right shoulder to right shoulder, and go back to place. Repeat with another person.

4. *Right- (or left-) hand star.* Place indicated hands (palm to palm with fingers pointed upward) about shoulder height with elbow somewhat bent. The next call indicates how far to turn the star.

5. *Two-hand swing.* Partners grasp both hands, lean away from each other, and circle clockwise once around.

6. *Go forward and back.* Move forward with three steps and a touch toward another person, who is moving toward you the same way. Move back to place with three steps and a touch.

Another teaching strategy is to divide the class into groups of four. Use a call such as, "Circle up, four hands round." Groups of four circle clockwise. There are usually extra children. If there are three extras, one child can pretend to have a partner. Rotate the extras in and out.

Circle fours until all groups are formed. With the call, "Break and swing," the fours separate into pairs within the foursome. Position the pairs so that they face each other. Call "left partner" and "right partner" instead of "boy" and "girl." If convenient when there are mixed pairs, the girl is on the right.

These figures can be practiced in fours.

1. *Circle to the left (or right).* Join hands and circle once around as indicated.

2. *Form a right- (or left-) hand star.* Hold right hands at about shoulder height and turn clockwise. A left-hand star turns counterclockwise.

3. *Swing your opposite and swing your partner.* Left partners walk toward their right partner opposite and swing. They walk back to their own partner and swing. The call can be reversed.

4. *Birdie in the cage and three hands round.* One child (the birdie) goes to the center, while the other three join hands and circle left once around.

5. *The birdie hops out and the crow hops in.* The birdie joins the circle and another child goes in the center.

6. *Go into the middle and come back out; go into the middle and give a little shout.* This figure is done from a circle-right or circle-left formation. The dancers face center and come together. Repeat, but with a light shout.

7. *Round and round in a single file; round and round in frontier style.* Circle left (or right), drop hands, and move into a single file.

8. *Dive for the oyster, dig for the clam.* Usually after circling left once around, one couple goes partially under the raised joined hands of the other couple. The other couple repeats the same maneuver. (In, 2, 3, touch; out, 2, 3, touch.)

Square Dance Formation

Each couple's position is numbered, going counterclockwise around the set. Couples need to know their position. The couple with their backs to the music is generally couple 1, or the head couple. The couple to their right is number 2, and so on. While the head couple is number 1, the term *head couples* includes both couples 1 and 3; couples 2 and 4 are the side couples.

For any one left-hand partner (gent), the following terms are used in traditional calls (adjust references to gender as necessary):

Partner: the other (right-hand) dancer of the couple

Corner or corner lady: the right-hand partner on the left

Right-hand lady: the right-hand partner in the couple to the right

Opposite or opposite lady: the right-hand partner directly across the set

Callers also use these terms:

Home: the couple's original or starting position

Active or leading couple: the couple leading or visiting the other couples for different figures

After introducing the square dance formation, have children practice the figures and pattern calls in the full formation of four couples. Some of this material is presented in the section Individual Approach to Square Dance, but the following figures merit discussion regarding square dance formation.

American Square Dance Figures

Here are some common square dance figures:

1. *Honor your partner*. Partners bow to each other.

2. *Honor your corner*. Left-hand dancer bows to corner, who returns the bow.

3. *Shuffle step*. Dancers do a light walking step on the ball of the foot, holding the body upright and moving in time with the music.

4. *Do-si-do your partner (or corner)*. Partners face and pass each other right shoulder to right shoulder, move around each other back-to-back, and return to the original position facing their partner.

5. *Promenade*. The couple walks side by side, right hand joined to right hand and left to left in a crossed-arm promenade position. They walk around the square once and return to home position.

6. *Circle right (or left)*. All eight dancers join hands and circle. The caller can add, "Into the center with a great big yell!" Dancers can break circle with a swing at home place.

7. *Grand right and left*. All face their partner, join right hands, walk past the partner, and join left hands with the next person in the ring, and so on down the line. This causes left-hand partners to go in one direction (counterclockwise) around the circle and right-hand partners to go in the other direction, alternately touching right and left hands until partners meet again. Grand right and left starts with your partner and ends with your partner, and then another call is given.

8. *Allemande left*. Left-hand dancer faces corner, grasps corner with a left-forearm grip, walks around corner, and returns to partner.

9. *Arm swing*. Left-hand dancer turns partner with a right-arm swing, using a forearm grasp.

10. *Swing your partner (or corner)*. Partners stand side by side with right hip against right hip. The dancers are almost in social dance position, but the left-hand partner's right arm is more around to the side than back at the shoulder blade. The dancers walk around each other with a slight lean away from each other until they reach their starting position.

11. *Do Paso*. Starting position is a circle of two or more couples. Partners face, grasp left forearms, and turn each other counterclockwise until facing the corner. Turn corner with right forearm grasp until facing partner. Take partner with the left hand; left-hand partner turns the other with a courtesy turn.

12. *All around your left-hand lady, seesaw your pretty little taw*. Corners move one time around each other in a loop pattern, left-hand dancer starting behind the corner, on moving around corner and back to place, right-hand dancer starting in front of corner and moving around back to place. Repeat with partner to complete the other half of the loop.

13. *Ladies chain*. From a position with two couples facing each other, the girls cross over to the opposite boy, touching right hands as they pass each other. Upon reaching the opposite boy, they join left hands with him. At the same time, each boy places his right arm around the girl's waist and turns her once around to face the other couple. On "Chain right back," the girls cross back to their partner in a similar figure.

14. *Right-and-left through (and back)*. Two couples face each other. Dancers join right hands and pull past opposite, passing right shoulder to right shoulder. Couples are back-to-back. Courtesy turn to face again and repeat to original place.

Selecting Square Dances and Music

In the past, elementary students learned traditional square dances using a patter call. Today, square dancing is a popular form of adult recreation. Singing calls and modern music help make square dancing popular among adults, but more important is the change from traditional to modern calls. In traditional square dancing, everyone knew what the next call was. In modern square dancing, only the caller knows the next call.

Two popular series of albums with different developmental levels and proper progression are the *Wagon Wheel Fundamentals of Square Dancing, Levels 1, 2, and*

19

3, and *Square Dance Party for the New Dancer, No. 1 and No. 2*. Both series feature the calling of Bob Ruff. They can be ordered from Wagon Wheel Records.

Culminating Events for the Rhythms Unit

When students in all grade levels are reasonably accomplished dancers, the school can sponsor a culminating event. Here are a few suggestions.

Country-Western Day

On country-western day, teachers and students wear country-western clothing all day. For the last hour of the school day, the student body attends a square dance. Include activities that everyone, from third graders to sixth graders, can do together. The movement approach presented earlier can help achieve this goal.

May Festival

In the spring, as the rhythm program draws to a close, a May festival featuring all the dances learned can be an exciting event. This activity includes everyone; each class or grade level presents a dance. Have an announcer describe the history and background of each dance (consult specialty dance books for a description of the various dances). End the festival with the entire school performing the maypole dance.

LEARNING AIDS

WEBSITES

Dance ideas, www.pecentral.org
Multicultural dances, www.centralhome.com/ballroomcountry/video_store.htm
Music sources, www.wagonwheelrecords.net
Square dancing, www.dosado.com

SUGGESTED READINGS

Carline, S. (2011). *Lesson plans for creative dance.* Champaign, IL: Human Kinetics.

Durden, E. M. (2019). *Beginning hip-hop dance.* Champaign, IL: Human Kinetics.

Gilbert, A.G. (2019). *Brain-compatible dance education.* (2nd ed.). Champaign, IL: Human Kinetics.

Gilbert, A.G. (2015). *Creative dance for all ages.* (2nd ed.). Champaign, IL: Human Kinetics.

Laufman, D., & Laufman J. (2009). *Traditional barn dances with calls and fiddling.* Champaign, IL: Human Kinetics.

Lozano, S., & Canamar, K. (2016). *Mexican folkloric dance.* DVD with music CD. Champaign, IL: Human Kinetics.

Paine, L., & NDTA. (2014). *Complete guide to primary dance.* Champaign, IL: Human Kinetics.

Scheff, H., Sprague, M., & McGreevy-Nichols, S. (2010). *Exploring dance forms and styles.* Champaign, IL: Human Kinetics.

Gymnastics-Related Skills

Gymnastics-related activities contribute significantly to children's flexibility, agility, balance, strength, and body control. This chapter is not about the sport of gymnastics and the traditional Olympic events. Rather, these lead-up activities develop body management skills without the need for equipment and apparatus. Students learn specialized motor skills such as body rolling, balance skills, inverted balances, and basic tumbling skills. Various partner and group activities offer opportunity for social interaction and cooperation. Finding success in gymnastics-related activities, developing a positive attitude, and overcoming personal limitations are more important than skill technique.

Learning Objectives

▶ List progressions and specify developmental levels for gymnastics activities.

▶ Understand the techniques of spotting when teaching gymnastics activities.

▶ Organize a comprehensive lesson of gymnastics activities, including the six basic groups: (1) animal movements, (2) tumbling and inverted balances, (3) balance stunts, (4) individual stunts, (5) partner and group stunts, and (6) partner support activities.

▶ Identify effective management techniques when teaching gymnastics activities.

▶ Cite safety considerations essential to the gymnastics program.

▶ Describe appropriate tumbling activities for elementary school children.

Gymnastics-related activities are an important part of every child's physical education experience, and they can contribute significantly to physical education goals. The gymnastics program helps strengthen children's dedication and perseverance, because stunts are seldom mastered quickly. Because much of the work is individual, students face challenges and have the opportunity to develop resourcefulness, self-confidence, and courage. When children master a challenging stunt, satisfaction, pride in achievement, and a sense of accomplishment can improve their self-esteem. Students benefit from social interplay, cooperating in various partner and group stunts. A caring and accepting environment will nurture the social attributes of tolerance, helpfulness, courtesy, and appreciation for the ability of others.

Important physical values also emerge from a gymnastics program. Teachers offer body management opportunities for students to enhance coordination, flexibility, and agility. Many activities give children an opportunity to practice balance. By holding positions and executing stunts, students develop strength and power in diverse parts of the body. Many stunts demand support—wholly or in part—by the arms, and thus help strengthen the musculature of the arm–shoulder girdle.

Progression and Developmental Level Placement

Progression is important in the gymnastics program. This book presents the activities in progression within three developmental levels. To avoid safety problems, the order of these activities should be reasonably maintained. Adhering to a developmental level is secondary to the principle of progression. If children have little or no experience in these activities, start them on activities specified in a lower developmental level.

Activities in this chapter are in six basic groups: (1) animal movements, (2) tumbling and inverted balances, (3) balance stunts, (4) individual stunts, (5) partner and group stunts, and (6) partner support activities. This arrangement allows teachers to pick activities from each group for a well-balanced lesson. Often, too much time is spent on tumbling activities, and children become bored and fatigued. Choosing activities from all the categories will help children who do not like tumbling activities find something they enjoy. At the heart of a gymnastics program are the standard tumbling activities, such as rolls, stands, springs, and related stunts. As your students perform these activities, emphasize exposure and overcoming fear. Perfect technique is less important than developing positive approach behaviors. Here is the suggested progression of basic activities for each developmental level.

Developmental Level I
- Log Roll (Rolling Log)
- Side Roll
- Forward Roll (Tuck Position)
- Back Roller
- Forward Roll (Straddle Position)
- Backward Curl
- Climb-Up
- Three-Point Tip-Up
- Mountain Climber
- Switcheroo

Developmental Level II
- Forward Roll to a Walkout
- Backward Roll (Regular)
- Frog Handstand (Tip-Up)
- Half Teeter-Totter
- Cartwheel
- Forward Roll (Pike Position)
- Forward Roll Combinations
- Backward Roll Combinations
- Teeter-Totter
- Handstand

Developmental Level III
- Forward and Backward Roll Combinations
- Back Extension
- Headstand Variations
- Handstand Against a Wall
- Freestanding Handstand
- Cartwheel and Round-Off
- Judo Roll
- Advanced Forward and Backward Roll Combinations
- Straddle Press to Headstand
- Headspring
- Walking on the Hands
- Walk-Over

The Developmental Level I program relies on simple stunts, with a gradual introduction to tumbling stunts classified as lead-ups or preliminaries to more advanced stunts. Stunts requiring exceptional body control, critical balancing, or substantial strength are best for higher levels of development. The Developmental Level II and III programs are built on activities and progressions developed earlier. Most stunts at Developmental Level I have a wide range of acceptable performance; at Developmental Levels II and III, the activities place higher demands on strength, control, form, agility, balance, and flexibility. Most students can perform the activities at Developmental Level I, at least in some fashion; but certain activities at Developmental Levels II and III may be too challenging for some students. Design lessons to include a variety of activities ranging from easy to more challenging to keep all students motivated and able to succeed.

Instructional Methodology for Gymnastics

Warm-Up and Flexibility Activity

Normal introductory activity and fitness development activities are usually sufficient as a warm-up for the gymnastics lesson. If additional stretching seems warranted, instruct students to take a wide straddle position with their feet about 3 feet (90 cm) apart and toes pointed ahead. With arms out to the sides, bend, twist, and generally stretch in all directions. Next, touch the floor with the hands to the front, sides, and back, with some bending of the knees. Extra flexibility may be required in the wrists, ankles, and neck. Have students do these activities before participating in gymnastics activities.

Wrists

1. Extend one arm forward. With the other hand, push the extended hand down, thus stretching the top of the wrist and forearm muscles. Hold the position for eight counts. Next, pull the hand backward and hold for eight counts to stretch the wrist flexor muscles.

2. Clasp the fingers of both hands in front of the chest. Make circles with both hands and stretch the wrists.

Ankles and Quadriceps

1. Kneel and sit on both feet. Smoothly and gently lean backward over the feet, using the arms to support the body.

2. In a sitting position, cross one leg over the other. Use the hands to help rotate each foot through its full range of motion. Reverse legs and repeat.

Neck

1. In a sitting position, slowly circle the head in both directions through the full range of motion.

2. In the same position, hold the chin against the chest for eight counts. Repeat with the head looking backward as far as possible. Look to each side and hold for eight counts.

Lower Back and Shoulders

Begin in a supine position. Raise both arms overhead; bend elbows and place the hands facing backward on the mat with fingers pointing toward the toes. Form a bridge by extending the arms and legs. While in the bridge position, slowly rock back and forth.

Effective Class Management

Here are some guidelines for keeping children engaged during gymnastics-related activities.

1. Whenever possible, all children should be active and performing. Activities not requiring mats can be done anywhere in the gymnasium. Use individual mats for simple balances and rolling stunts, particularly at Developmental Level I. When larger mats are required, be more ingenious. Ideally, provide one mat for each group of three students. When students in groups of three are doing return activities, few children are standing around.

2. If the number of mats is limited, students can perform sideways on them. An 8-foot-long (2.4 m long) mat is large enough for three performers at the same time. This arrangement allows for single rolls but does not rule out an occasional series of rolls lengthwise on the mat. Use the ends of the mats as a cushion for various headstands, as long as children are aligned so that they do not fall toward each other.

3. Consider station teaching if equipment is limited. Make plans that ensure that the experience

20

stresses progress and diligence. You can include a few tumbling and inverted balance stations as well as other stations featuring less demanding activities. Wall charts listing the activities in progression provide excellent guidance.

Formations for Teaching

For best effect in a particular lesson, choose from these standard formations.

1. *Squad formation.* Mats are laid end to end, and squads line up behind the mats. Each child takes a turn and then goes to the end of the squad line as the others move up. An alternative method is for each child to perform and then return to a seated position.

2. *Semicircular formation.* Students and mats are positioned in a semicircular arrangement. This formation directs attention toward the teacher, who stands in the center.

3. *U-shaped formation.* The mats are placed in a large U shape. This formation offers an excellent view for the teacher and allows children to see what their classmates are doing.

4. *Demonstration mat.* One mat is placed in a central position and used exclusively for demonstrations. Little student movement is necessary to see demonstrations.

Description and Demonstration of New Gymnastics Activities

To enhance student learning when presenting an activity, try the three-step approach:

1. *Significance of the name.* Most activities have a characteristic name that students should learn. If the stunt is of an imitative type, briefly discuss the animal or character represented.

2. *Description of the activity.* Most stunts have three parts: starting position, execution, and finishing position. Most stunts have a defined starting position, which is part of the performance. First, tell students how to assume the starting position. Next, teach the key points for properly executing the activity. Technical points include how far to travel, how long to balance, and how many times to do a movement. In some gymnastics activities, a definite finishing position or action is part of the stunt. Balancing stunts require performers to return to standing (or some other) position without losing balance and moving the feet.

3. *Demonstration of the activity.* Three levels of demonstration are recognized: (1) minimal demonstration in the form of the starting position; (2) slow, step-by-step demonstration of the entire stunt, with an explanation of what is involved; and (3) execution of the stunt as it is normally done. Remember that children need to analyze and solve problems. Because too much demonstration defeats this process, cover just a few points in your explanation. Show only the points necessary to get the activity going. Add further details and refinements as the activity progresses.

Opportunities for Practice and Improvement

The character of each stunt determines the amount of practice needed and the number of times the stunt should be performed. Analyze the stunt thoroughly enough to explain the points necessary for proper performance. Practice and repetition are essential in establishing effective movement patterns. To maximize activity and minimize standing in line, allow time for the class to practice the activity. On signal, the class stops whatever they are doing without returning to formation. After receiving directions for the next activity, the class resumes practicing. This method decreases the amount of management time spent waiting for each squad to finish and return to formation.

Safety Considerations

Safety is a foremost consideration in the gymnastics program. The inherent hazards of an activity must be emphasized in the instructional procedures.

You will have to decide whether you feel qualified and confident enough to teach activities that require spotting; if you do not, you should probably avoid spotting children. Because tumbling and inverted balance activities make up only about 10% of the activities in this chapter, you can offer many other stunts and balance activities to teach students body management skills. Never force children to participate in tumbling and inverted balance activities. This chapter offers spotting techniques for competent teachers who are knowledgeable about stunts and tumbling.

The purpose of spotting is twofold. First is assisting the performer, helping support the body weight, and preventing a hazardous fall. Second is guiding the performer through the stunt to help develop proper body awareness. Here are two major considerations to consider regarding spotting.

1. *Should teachers spot students?* In most cases, a child who has to be spotted for a basic tumbling or balance activity should not be asked to do the activity. A better alternative is to let students choose one of several activities. For example, allow children to choose between the Forward Roll and a Log Roll. Students who are fearful or do not want to do a Forward Roll can still have a successful and enjoyable experience.

   Because teachers can spot only one child at a time, many children will be standing around waiting for a turn, which is an unacceptable practice. Teachers also have to be aware that some children do not want an adult's hands on them. Finally, some children, because of their strength or other physical limitations, may never be able to do a Forward Roll, Backward Roll, or Headstand. Fortunately, there are many other ways to provide physical education to these students.

2. *Should students spot their peers?* If an accident were to occur while a student was spotting, the teacher would probably be liable. Legal authorities might try to show that you were not supervising the spotting carefully or that students are too young and not responsible enough to fulfill the duties of correct spotting. Rarely are students trained enough to be able to perform quality spotting. If your only recourse is to have students spot each other, avoid teaching those activities.

Instructional Procedures

1. Mats are not needed for some stunts, but you should include stunts requiring mats in every lesson. Children like to perform on mats, and rolling stunts using mats are vital to the gymnastics program.

2. Many partner stunts work best when partners are about the same size. If the stunt requires partner support, be sure that the support child is strong enough to hold the other's weight.

3. No two children are alike. Respect individual differences and allow different levels of success.

4. Relating new activities to those learned earlier is important. An effective approach is to review the lead-up stunt for an activity.

5. When a stunt calls for a position to be held for a number of counts, use a standard counting system (e.g., "One thousand one, one thousand two, . . .").

6. When appropriate, have children work in pairs, with one child performing and the second providing a critique.

7. Shifting of mats should not be necessary during the instruction. When arranging a gymnastics routine for a day's lesson, group the mat stunts. The tumbling mats should be bordered with Velcro for fastening them together.

Start-and-Expand Technique

When feasible, use the start-and-expand technique to teach stunts. Consider this example for teaching a simple Heel Click.

1. *Start.* "Let's see all of you jump high in the air and click your heels together before you come down."

2. *Expand.* "Now, to do the stunt properly, you will jump into the air, click your heels, and land with your feet apart with a nice bent-knee action to absorb the shock." To expand further, have students add a quarter or half turn before landing, clap the hands overhead while clicking the heels, or click the heels twice before landing.

The start is generally simple, so that all children can experience some success. The instruction then expands to other elements of the stunt, adding variations and refining movements.

Basic Mechanical Principles

Certain mechanical principles are basic to gymnastics techniques. Teaching children to build on these principles can facilitate learning.

1. Momentum needs to be developed and applied, particularly for rolls. Tucking, starting from a higher point, and preliminary raising of the arms are some ways to increase momentum.

2. The center of weight must be positioned over the center of support in balance stunts, particularly in the inverted stands.

3. In certain stunts, such as the Headspring, the hips should be projected upward and forward to raise the center of gravity for better execution.

4. When hands wholly or partially support the body, proper hand position is essential to effective performance. The hands should be approximately shoulder-width apart, and the fingers should be spread and pointed forward.

20

Basic Gymnastics Positions

Teach your students to recognize and demonstrate the basic positions unique to gymnastics. At the elementary level, children focus on learning the basic form of the activity rather than pure technique.

Tuck Position

Perform the tuck with the legs bent and the chin tucked to the chest. Cue students to "Curl up like a ball." Students should know all three of the tuck positions: Sitting Tuck (figure 20.1), Standing Tuck, and Lying Tuck.

Pike Position

Perform the pike by bending forward at the hips and keeping the legs straight. The three basic pike positions are the Sitting Pike (figure 20.2), Standing Pike, and Lying Pike.

Straddle Position

Perform the straddle position by bending forward at the hips and spreading the legs to the sides as far as possible. Keep the legs straight. Variations of the straddle position are the Sitting Pike Straddle (figure 20.3), Standing Pike Straddle, and Lying Pike Straddle.

Front-Support Position

This position is similar to the push-up position. Hold the body straight and the head up (figure 20.4).

Back-Support Position

This is an inverted push-up position. Keep the body as straight as possible (figure 20.5).

FIGURE 20.3 Straddle position.

©Robert Pangrazi or Aaron Beighle

FIGURE 20.4 Front-support position.

©Robert Pangrazi or Aaron Beighle

FIGURE 20.1 Tuck position.

©Robert Pangrazi or Aaron Beighle

FIGURE 20.2 Pike position.

©Robert Pangrazi or Aaron Beighle

FIGURE 20.5 Back-support position.

©Robert Pangrazi or Aaron Beighle

Gymnastics Dance Positions

Attitude

Assume this position by supporting the body weight on one leg while lifting the other leg and bending it at the knee (figure 20.6). Hold the arm on the side of the lifted leg overhead and extend the other arm to the side.

Lunge Position

Perform the lunge by straightening the rear leg and bending the forward, supporting the leg at the hip and knee. Most of the weight is on the forward leg. Extend the arms and keep the head up with eyes forward (figure 20.7).

Plié

Plié ("plee-AY") means "a bending of the knees." Bend both knees, extend the arms at right angles to the sides, and tuck the seat to hold the abdomen flat. There are different plié positions, but in gymnastics instruction, the plié is used to teach landing with grace and control.

Relevé

The relevé ("rell-uh-VAY") is an extension movement from the plié position. The movement goes from the plié (knees bent) position to the extended position (legs straight). Extension is complete through all of the joints, stretching upward from the balls of the feet.

Arabesque

Perform the Arabesque by supporting the weight on one leg while extending the other leg to the rear. Keep the extended leg with the toe pointed and hold the torso erect (figure 20.8). The Back Extension and the Cartwheel are often brought to completion with an Arabesque.

Jumps

Gymnastics dance commonly uses three jump variations: the Tuck Jump, Pike Jump, and Straddle Jump. These jumps are simply a jump with the prescribed position added. The arms are raised in a lifting motion to increase the height of the jump and to enhance balance. The impact of the landing is absorbed at the ankles and knee joints.

Chassé

The chassé ("shah-SAY") is a slide. This basic locomotor movement involves one leg chasing the other out of position. It is done close to the floor with a light spring in the step.

Stunts and Tumbling Activities

This chapter presents the stunts and tumbling activities, in order of difficulty, within three developmental levels. A brief discussion of each developmental level follows.

FIGURE 20.6 Attitude.

FIGURE 20.7 Lunge position.

FIGURE 20.8 Arabesque.

20

Developmental Level I Activities

Developmental Level I activities consist primarily of imitative walks and movements, as well as selected balance stunts and rolls. The Forward Roll is practiced but refined only in later levels. The Back Roller is a prelude to the Backward Roll.

Animal Movements

Alligator Crawl

Lie facedown on the floor with elbows bent. Move along the floor like an alligator, keeping the hands close to the body and the feet pointed out (figure 20.9). First, use unilateral movements—that is, right arm and leg moving together—and then change to cross-lateral movements.

FIGURE 20.9   Alligator Crawl.

Kangaroo Jump

Carry the arms close to the chest with the palms facing forward. Place a beanbag or ball between the knees. Move in different directions by taking small jumps without dropping the object.

Puppy Dog Run

Place the hands on the floor, bending the arms and legs slightly. Walk and run like a happy puppy. Look straight ahead. Keep the head up, in good position, to strengthen the neck muscles. Go sideways, backward, and so on. Turn around in place.

Variations:

1. *Cat Walk.* Use the same position to imitate a cat. Walk softly. Stretch at times like a cat. Be smooth and deliberate.

2. *Monkey Run.* Turn the hands and feet so that the fingers and toes point in (toward each other).

Bear Walk

Bend forward and touch the ground with both hands.

Travel forward slowly by moving the hand and foot on the same side together (that is, first the right hand and foot, and then the left hand and foot) (figure 20.10). Make deliberate movements.

Variation: Lift the free foot and arm high while the support is on the other side.

FIGURE 20.10   Bear Walk.

Gorilla Walk

Bend the knees and carry the trunk forward. Let the arms hang at the sides. Touch the fingers to the ground while walking.

Variation: Stop and beat on the chest like a gorilla. Bounce up and down on all fours with hands and feet touching the floor simultaneously.

Rabbit Jump

Crouch with knees apart and hands placed on the floor. Move forward by reaching out with both hands and then bringing both feet up to the hands. Look straight ahead.

   Tell students that this action is a jump rather than a hop because both feet move at once. Note that the jump is a bilateral movement.

Variations:

1. Try with knees together and arms on the outside. Try alternating with knees together and apart on successive jumps. Go over a low hurdle or through a hoop.

2. Experiment with taking more weight on the hands before the feet move forward. To do this, raise the seat higher in the air when the hands move forward.

Elephant Walk

Bend well forward, clasping the hands together to form a trunk. Swing the end of the trunk close to the ground. Walk slowly and deliberately, keeping the legs straight and swinging the trunk from side to side (figure 20.11). Stop and throw water over the back with the trunk. Recite the following verse while walking and move the trunk appropriately.

The elephant's walk is steady and slow,
His trunk like a pendulum swings to and fro.
But when there are children with peanuts around,
He swings it up and he swings it down.

FIGURE 20.11   Elephant Walk.

Variation: With a partner, decide who is the mahout (elephant keeper) and who is the elephant. The mahout walks to the side and a little in front of the elephant, with one hand touching the elephant's shoulder. The mahout leads the elephant around during the first two lines of the poem. During the last two lines, the mahout walks to a spot in front of the elephant and tosses it a peanut when the trunk sweeps up. The Mahout returns to the elephant's side and repeats the action.

FIGURE 20.12   Twin Walk.

Twin Walk

Stand back-to-back with a partner. Lock elbows (figure 20.12). Walk forward, backward, and sideways in unison.

Tightrope Walk

Select a line, board, or chalked line on the floor as the high wire. Pretend to be on the high wire and do various tasks, exaggerating loss of control of balance. Add tasks such as jumping rope, juggling balls, and riding a bicycle. Pretend to hold a parasol or a balancing pole while performing. Children can give good play to the imagination. The teacher can set the stage by discussing what a circus performer on the high wire might do.

Lame Dog Walk

Walk on both hands and one foot. Hold the other foot in the air as if injured. Walk a distance and change feet. The eyes should look forward. Move backward and in other combinations. Try moving with an injured front leg.

Crab Walk

Squat down and reach back, putting both hands on the floor without sitting down. With head, neck, and body level, walk forward, backward, and sideways (figure 20.13). Because children tend to lower the hips, emphasize keeping the body in a straight line.

Variations:

1. As each step is taken with one hand, slap the chest or seat with the other.

2. Move the hand and foot on the same side simultaneously.

3. Try balancing on one leg and the opposite hand for five seconds.

FIGURE 20.13   Crab Walk.

20

473

Tumbling and Inverted Balances

To avoid risk of injuries, never encourage or force children to perform an activity they are uncomfortable with. If a child lacks the neck and shoulder-girdle strength to do tumbling or inverted balances, substitute an alternate activity. Spotting techniques are offered for teachers who feel capable of helping children who can perform the activities. Spot only children who can and want to perform an activity.

Log Roll (Rolling Log)

Lie on the back with arms stretched overhead (figure 20.14). Roll sideways the length of the mat. The next time, roll with the hands pointed toward the other side of the mat. To roll in a straight line, keep the feet slightly apart.

FIGURE 20.14   Log Roll.

Variation: Alternately curl and stretch while rolling.

Side Roll

Start on the hands and knees, with one side toward the direction of the roll. Drop the shoulder, tuck both the elbow and the knee, and roll over completely, returning to the hands-and-knees position. Momentum is needed to return to the original position. Practice rolling back and forth from one hand-and-knee position to another.

Forward Roll (Tuck Position)

Stand facing forward, with the feet apart. Squat and place the hands on the mat, shoulder-width apart, with elbows against the inner thighs. Tuck the chin to the chest and make a rounded back. A push-off with the hands and feet provides the force for the roll (figure

20.15). Carry the weight on the hands, with the elbows bearing the weight of the thighs. By keeping the elbows against the thighs and bearing the weight there, the force of the roll transfers easily to the rounded back. Try to roll forward to the feet. Try with knees together and no weight on the elbows.

FIGURE 20.15   Forward Roll.

Spotting: The spotter kneels beside the child and places one hand on the back of the child's head and the other under the thigh (figure 20.16). As the child moves through the roll, the spotter lifts upward on the back of the neck to assure that the neck does not absorb the body's weight. Use this technique for all Forward Roll variations.

FIGURE 20.16   Spotting the Forward Roll. (One hand is on the back of the head, and one is under the thigh.)

Back Roller

Begin in a crouched position with knees together and hands resting lightly on the floor. Roll backward, gaining momentum by bringing the knees to the chest and clasping them with the arms (figure 20.17). Roll back and forth rhythmically. On the backward movement, go well back on the neck and head. Try to roll forward to the original position. If students have difficulty rolling back to the original position, have them cross the legs and roll to a crossed-leg standing position. (This stunt is a lead-up to the Backward Roll.)

FIGURE 20.17   Back Roller.

Forward Roll (Straddle Position)

Start with the legs spread in the straddle position. Bend forward at the hips, tuck the head, place the hands on the mat, and roll forward. To return to the standing position, students must push with the hands at the end of the roll.

Forward Roll Practice and Variations

Review the Forward Roll (tucked), with spotting and assistance as necessary. Work on coming out of the roll to the feet. Grasping the knees at the end of the roll helps.

Variations:

1. Roll to the feet with ankles crossed.
2. Try to roll with knees together.

Backward Curl

Approach this activity in three stages. The first stage begins in a sitting position with the knees drawn up to the chest and the chin tucked. Clasp the hands and place them behind the head, holding the elbows out as far as possible. Gently roll backward until the weight is on the elbows (figure 20.18). Roll back to starting position.

In stage 2, perform the same action as before but place the hands beside the head on the mat while rolling back. Point the fingers in the direction of the roll, with palms down on the mat. (A good cue is, "Point your thumbs toward your ears and keep your elbows close to your body.")

©Robert Pangrazi or Aaron Beighle

FIGURE 20.18   Backward Curl, stage 1.

For stage 3, perform the same action as in stage 2 but start in a crouched position on the feet with the back facing the direction of the roll. Gain momentum by sitting down quickly and bringing the knees to the chest. This, like the Back Roller, is a lead-up to the Backward Roll. Teach children to push against the floor to take pressure off the back of the neck.

Climb-Up

Begin on a mat in a kneeling position, with hands about shoulder-width apart and the fingers spread and pointed forward. Place the head in front of the hands, so that the head and hands form a triangle on the mat. Walk the body weight forward so that most of it rests on the hands and head. Using the knees, climb to the top of the elbows. (This stunt is a lead-up to the Headstand.) Overweight children or those lacking strength may need to perform an alternate activity.

Variation: Lift the knees off the elbows.

Three-Point Tip-Up

Squat down on the mat, placing the hands flat with fingers pointing forward. The elbows are inside and pressed against the inner part of the lower thighs. Lean forward, slowly transferring body weight to the bent elbows and hands until the forehead touches the mat (figure 20.19). Return to starting position.

FIGURE 20.19   Three Point Tip-Up.

The Three-Point Tip-Up ends in the same general position as the Climb-Up, but with the elbows held inside the thighs. Some children may have better success by turning the fingers in slightly, thus making the elbows point outward more and offering better support at the thigh contact point. This stunt is a lead-up to the Headstand and the Handstand done at later levels.

Variation: Tuck the head and do a Forward Roll as an alternative finishing act.

Mountain Climber

This activity is similar to the Treadmill. Take the weight on the hands with one foot forward and one foot extended back, similar to a sprinter's start. When ready, switch foot position by moving both feet simultaneously. As a lead-up to the Handstand, this activity teaches children to support the body weight briefly with the arms.

Switcheroo

This Handstand lead-up activity begins in the front lunge position with the arms overhead. In one continuous movement, bend forward at the hips, place the hands on the mat, and raise the legs overhead. Scissor the legs in the air and then reverse the position of the feet on the mat. Repeat in a smooth and continuous motion.

Balance Stunts

One-Leg Balance

Lift one leg from the floor. Later, bring the knee up. The arms are free at first and then assume specified positions: folded across the chest, on the hips, on the head, or behind the back.

Double-Knee Balance

Kneel on both knees, with feet pointed to the rear. Lift the feet from the ground and balance on the knees. Experiment with different arm positions.

Head Touch

On a mat, kneel on both knees, with feet pointed backward and arms outstretched backward for balance. Lean forward slowly and touch the forehead to the mat. Recover to the original position (figure 20.20). Vary the arm position.

FIGURE 20.20   Head Touch.

Head Balance

Place a beanbag, block, or book on the head (figure 20.21). Walk, stoop, turn around, sit down, get up, and so on. Maintain good upper-body posture while balancing the object. Keep the hands out to the sides for balance. Later, vary the position of the arms—fold across the chest, place behind the back, or hold down at sides. Link together a series of movements.

©Robert Pangrazi or Aaron Beighle

FIGURE 20.21   Head Balance.

One-Leg Balance Stunts

Try each of these stands with different arm positions, starting with the arms out to the sides and then folded across the chest. Have children devise other arm positions.

Have students hold each stunt first for three seconds and then for five seconds. Later, they can close the eyes during the count. Children should recover to the original position without losing balance or moving excessively. Repeat these stunts, using the other leg.

1. *Kimbo Stand.* Keeping the left foot flat on the ground, cross the right leg over the left until the right foot points partially down and the toe touches the ground.

2. *Knee-Lift Stand.* From a standing position, lift one knee up so that the thigh is parallel to the ground and the toe points down. Hold. Return to starting position.

3. *Stork Stand.* From a standing position, shift all the weight to one foot. Place the other foot so that the sole is against the inside of the knee and thigh of the standing leg (figure 20.22). Hold. Recover to standing position.

FIGURE 20.22 Stork Stand.

and the arms out to the sides, bend forward, balancing on the other leg (figure 20.24). Hold for five seconds without moving. Reverse legs. (This is also called a Forward Scale.)

FIGURE 20.24 Forward Balance.

Balance Touch

Place an object (block, beanbag) one yard (meter) away from a line. Balancing on the line on one foot, reach out with the other foot, touch the object (without placing weight on it; figure 20.23), and recover to the starting position. Reach sideways, backward.

FIGURE 20.23 Balance Touch.

Variation: Try placing the object at various distances. On a gym floor, count the number of boards to establish the distance for the touch.

Single-Leg Balances

1. *Forward Balance.* Extend one leg backward until it is parallel to the floor. Keeping the eyes forward

2. *Backward Balance.* With knee straight, extend one leg forward, with toes pointed. Keep the arms out to the sides for balance. Lean back as far as possible. Bend back far enough to look at the ceiling.

3. *Side Balance.* Standing on the left foot, bend to the left until the right (top) side of the body is parallel to the floor. Put the right arm alongside the head and in line with the rest of the body. Reverse, standing on the right leg (students may need support briefly to get into position).

Hand-and-Knee Balance

Start on all fours and take the weight on the hands, knees, and feet (toes point backward). Lift one hand and the opposite knee (figure 20.25). Keep the free foot and hand from touching during the hold. Reverse hand and knee positions.

FIGURE 20.25 Hand-and-Knee Balance.

Single-Knee Balance

Perform the Hand-and-Knee Balance, this time balancing on one knee (and leg) with both arms outstretched to the sides (figure 20.26). Use the other knee.

FIGURE 20.26 Single-Knee Balance.

©Robert Pangrazi or Aaron Beighle

Individual Stunts

Directional Walk

For a left movement, begin in standing position (feet together). Do all these actions simultaneously: Take a step to the left, raise the left arm and point left, turn the head to the left, and state crisply, "Left." Return to standing position. Take several steps left and then reverse. The Directional Walk is designed to aid in establishing right–left concepts. Definite and forceful simultaneous movements of the arm, head (turn), and leg (step) coupled with crisply stating the direction are the ingredients of this stunt.

Line Walking

Use a line on the floor, a chalked line, or a board. Walk forward and backward on the line as follows. First, take regular steps. Next, try follow steps—the front foot moves forward and the back foot moves up. The same foot always leads. Then do heel-and-toe steps, bringing the back toe up against the front heel on each step. Finally, hop along the line on one foot. Change to the other foot. The eyes look forward.

Fluttering Leaf

Keeping the feet in place and the body relaxed, flutter to the ground slowly, like an autumn leaf. Swing the arms back and forth loosely to accentuate the fluttering.

Elevator

With arms out level at the sides, pretend to be an elevator going down. Lower the body bit by bit, bending the

knees but keeping the upper body erect and eyes forward. Return to position. Add a body twist to the downward movement. (Use a drum to signal movements.)

Cross-Legged Stand

Sit with the legs crossed and bend the body partially forward. Respond appropriately to these six commands.

- "Touch the right foot with the right hand."
- "Touch the left foot with the right hand."
- "Touch the right foot with the left hand."
- "Touch the left foot with the left hand."
- "Touch both feet with the hands."
- "Touch the feet with crossed hands."

Vary the sequences of these commands. Students must remember that their right foot is on the left side and vice versa. If this seems too difficult, have children start with the feet in normal position (uncrossed).

Variation: Do the stunt with a partner, one child giving the commands and the other following.

Walking in Place

Pretend to walk vigorously, using the same movements as in walking but not making any progress. This is done by sliding the feet back and forth. Exaggerated arm movements are made. (Children can gain or lose a little ground. Two children can walk alongside each other, with first one and then the other going ahead.)

Jump Turns

Do jump turns (use quarter turns and half turns) right and left, as directed. Keep the arms outstretched to the sides. Land lightly without a second movement. Jump turns reinforce directional concepts. Teachers can use jump turns to develop number concepts. Call out the number as a preparatory command and then say, "Move." Number cues are "One" for a left quarter turn, "Two" for a right quarter turn, "Three" for a left half turn, and "Four" for a right half turn. Give children a moment after calling the number and before giving the "Move" command.

Rubber Band

Start in a squat position and clasp the hands and arms around the knees. On the command "Stretch, stretch, stretch," stretch as tall and as wide as possible. On the command "Snap," snap back to the original position.

Variation: *Pumping Up the Balloon.* One child, the

pumper, is in front of the other children, who are the balloons. The pumper pretends to use a bicycle pump to inflate the balloons, making a "shoosh" sound for every pumping motion. The balloons get larger and larger until the pumper shouts, "Bang!" The balloons then collapse to the floor.

Rising Sun

Lie on the back. Using the arms for balance only, rise to a standing position.

Variation: Fold the arms over the chest. Experiment with different foot positions: crossed, spread wide, both to one side, and so on.

Heel Click

Stand with the feet slightly apart, jump up, and click the heels, coming down with the feet apart (figure 20.27). Try with a quarter turn right and left.

FIGURE 20.27 Heel Click.

Variations:

1. Clap the hands overhead while clicking the heels.
2. Join hands with one or more children. Count, "1, 2, 3!" and jump on the third count.
3. Begin with a cross-step to the side; then click the heels. Try both right and left.
4. Try to click the heels twice before landing. Land with the feet apart.

Lowering the Boom

Start in push-up (front-leaning rest) position. Lower the body slowly to the floor. Control the movement, keeping the body rigid.

Variations:

1. Pause halfway down.
2. Go down in stages, inch by inch (2.5 cm). (Show children what you mean by an inch.)
3. Go down slowly, accompanied by a noise that simulates air escaping from a punctured tire. Try representing a blowout, starting with an appropriate sound.
4. Go down in stages by alternately lowering the right and left arms.
5. Vary the stunt with different hand-base positions, such as fingers pointed in, thumbs touching, and others.

Turnover

From a front-leaning rest position, turn over so that the back is to the floor. The body does not touch the floor. Continue the turn until the original position is reassumed. Reverse the direction. Turn back and forth several times. Keep the body as rigid as possible while turning.

Thread the Needle

Touch the fingertips together in front of the body. Step through with one foot at a time, keeping the fingers in contact (figure 20.28). Step back to the original position. Next, lock the fingers in front of the body and repeat the stunt. Finally, step through the clasped hands without touching them.

©Robert Pangrazi or Aaron Beighle

FIGURE 20.28 Thread the Needle.

Heel Slap

From an erect position with hands at the sides, jump upward and slap both heels with the hands (figure 20.29).

FIGURE 20.29 Heel Slap.

Variation: Use a one-two-three rhythm with small preliminary jumps on the first and second counts. Make a quarter or half turn in the air. During a jump, slap the heels twice before landing.

Pogo Stick

Pretend to be on a pogo stick by keeping a stiff body and jumping on the toes. Hold the hands in front as if grasping the stick (figure 20.30). Move in various directions. (Teachers: Stress upward propelling action by the ankles and toes, keeping the body stiff, particularly at the knees.)

©Robert Pangrazi or Aaron Beighle

FIGURE 20.30 Pogo Stick.

Top

From a standing position with arms at the sides, try jumping and turning to face the opposite direction, turning three-quarters of the way around or making a full turn to face the original direction. Land in good balance with hands near the sides. Do not move the feet after landing. Turn both right and left. (Stress number concepts by having children do half turns, three-quarter turns, and full turns.)

Variation: Fold the arms across the chest.

Sitting Stand

Stand with feet apart and arms folded in front. Pivot on the balls of both feet and face the opposite direction. The legs are now crossed. Sit down in this position. Reverse the process. Get up without using the hands for aid and uncross the legs with a pivot to face in the original direction. The feet do not move much (figure 20.31).

FIGURE 20.31 Sitting Stand.

Push-Up

From a front-leaning rest position, lower the body and push up, back to the original position. Focus on moving only the arms, and keep the body rigid. (Because the Push-Up is used in many exercises and testing programs, children need to learn proper execution early.)

Variation: Stop halfway down and halfway up. Go up and down by small increments.

Crazy Walk

Move forward in an erect position by bringing one foot behind and around the other to gain a little ground each time (figure 20.32). (Teachers can set a specified distance and see which children cover the distance in the fewest steps.)

FIGURE 20.32 Crazy Walk.

Variation: Reverse the movements and go backward. This means bringing the foot in front and around to gain distance in back.

Seat Circle

Sit on the floor with knees bent and hands braced behind. Lift the feet off the floor and push with the hands so that the body spins in a circle with the seat as a pivot (figure 20.33). Spin right and left.

FIGURE 20.33 Seat Circle.

Variation: Place a beanbag between the knees or on the toes and spin without dropping it.

Partner and Group Stunts

Bouncing Ball

Toss a lively utility ball into the air and watch how it bounces lower and lower until it comes to rest on the floor. From a bent-knee position with the upper body erect, imitate the ball by beginning with a high bounce and gradually lowering the height of the jump to simulate the ball coming to rest. Have children push off from the floor with the hands to gain additional height and absorb part of the body weight with their hands as well. Toss a real ball into the air and move with the ball.

Variation: Try this with a partner by having one partner serve as the bouncer and the other as the ball (figure 20.34). Reverse positions. Try having one partner dribble the ball in various positions.

FIGURE 20.34 Bouncing Ball.

Seesaw

Face and join hands with a partner. Move the seesaw up and down, one child stooping while the other rises. Recite the words to this version of "Seesaw, Margery Daw."

Seesaw, Margery Daw,
Maw and Paw, like a saw,
Seesaw, Margery Daw.

Variation: Jump upward at the end of the rise each time.

Wring the Dishrag

Face a partner and join hands. Raise one pair of arms (right for one and left for the other) and turn under, continuing a full turn until back to the original position. Take care not to bump heads. Reverse.

Variation: Try the stunt using a crouched position.

481

Partner Toe Toucher

Partners of about the same height lie on their backs with heads near each other and feet in opposite directions. They join arms, using a hand-wrist grip, and bring the legs up so that their toes touch. They stay high on the shoulders and touch the feet high (figure 20.35). Partners should strive to reach the high shoulder position, which is the most difficult.

FIGURE 20.35   Partner Toe Toucher.

Variation: One child carries a beanbag, a ball, or similar object between the feet. The student transfers the object to the partner, who lowers it to the floor.

Double Top

Face a partner and join hands. Experiment to see which type of grip works best. With straight arms, lean away from each other while moving the toes close to partner's (figure 20.36). Spin around slowly in either direction, taking tiny steps. Increase speed.

FIGURE 20.36   Double Top.

Variations:

1. Use a stooped position.
2. Instead of holding hands, hold a wand and increase the body lean backward. Try the stunt while standing right side to right side.

Roly Poly

Review the Log Roll. Four or five children lie facedown on the floor, side by side. The last child does a Rolling Log over the others and then takes a place at the end. Continue until all have rolled twice.

Developmental Level II Activities

Developmental Level II activities focus more on form and quality of performance than do those at Level I. Stunts such as the Frog Handstand, Mule Kick, Teeter-Totter, and Handstand give children experience in taking the entire weight on the hands. Partner support stunts are introduced. Flops or falls are another addition.

Animal Movements

Cricket Walk

Squat. Spread the knees. Put the arms between the knees and grasp the outsides of the ankles with the hands. Walk forward or backward. Chirp like a cricket. Turn around right and left. What happens when both feet are moved at once?

Frog Jump

From a squatting position, with hands on the floor slightly in front of the feet, jump forward a short distance, landing on the hands and feet simultaneously (figure 20.37). Note the difference between this stunt and the Rabbit Jump. Emphasis eventually is on both height and distance. The hands and arms absorb part of the landing impact to prevent excessive strain on the knees.

FIGURE 20.37   Frog Jump.

Seal Crawl

Start in the front-leaning rest position, with the weight on straightened arms and toes. Keeping the body straight, walk forward, using the hands for propelling force and dragging the feet (figure 20.38). Keep the body straight and the head up.

Variations:

1. Crawl forward a short distance and then roll over on the back, clapping the hands like a seal, with appropriate seal barks.
2. Crawl with the fingers pointed in different directions, out and in.
3. *Reverse Seal Crawl.* Turn over and attempt the crawl, dragging the heels.
4. *Elbow Crawl.* Assume the original position but with weight on the elbows. Crawl forward on the elbows (figure 20.39).
5. Use the crossed-arm position for a more challenging stunt.

Measuring Worm

From a front-leaning rest position, keeping the knees stiff, inch the feet up as close as possible to the hands. Regain position by inching forward with the hands. Keep the knees straight, and bend at the hips as necessary (figure 20.40).

Mule Kick

Stoop down and place the hands on the floor in front of the feet. The arms are the mule's front legs. Kick out with the legs while briefly supporting the weight on the arms (figure 20.41). Taking the weight on the hands is important. Students can learn the stunt in two stages: (1) practice taking the weight momentarily on the hands; (2) add the kick.

Variation: Make two kicks before the feet return to the ground.

FIGURE 20.38 Seal Crawl.

©Robert Pangrazi or Aaron Beighle

FIGURE 20.39 Elbow Crawl.

©Robert Pangrazi or Aaron Beighle

FIGURE 20.40 Measuring Worm.

20

FIGURE 20.41 Mule Kick.

Walrus Walk

Begin in a front-leaning rest position, with fingers pointed outward. Progress by moving both hands forward at the same time (figure 20.42). Try to clap the hands with each step. Before doing this stunt, review the similar Seal Crawl and its variations.

FIGURE 20.42 Walrus Walk.

Variation: Move sideways so that the upper part of the body describes an arc while the feet hold position.

Double-Lame Dog

Support the body on one hand and one leg (figure 20.43). Move forward in this position, maintaining balance. Keep the distance short (5 to 10 feet [1.5 to 3 m]) because this stunt is strenuous. Have students try different leg–arm combinations, such as cross-lateral movements (right arm with left leg and left arm with right leg).

FIGURE 20.43 Double-Lame Dog.

Variation: Keep the free arm on the hip.

Turtle

Hold the body in a wide push-up position with the feet and hands widely spread (figure 20.44). From this position, move in various directions, keeping the body always about the same distance from the floor. Move the hands and feet only in small increments.

FIGURE 20.44 Turtle.

Walrus Slap

From the front-leaning rest position, push the body up in the air quickly by force of the arms, clap the hands together, and recover to position. Before doing this stunt, review the Seal Crawl and the Walrus Walk.

Variations:

1. Try clapping the hands more than once.
2. Move forward while clapping the hands.
3. Reverse Walrus Slap. Turn over and do a Walrus Walk while facing the ceiling. Clapping the hands in this position is not easy; only the more skilled students should try it while on a mat.

Tumbling and Inverted Balances

To reduce risk of injuries, never encourage or force children to perform an activity they are uncomfortable with. If a child lacks the neck and shoulder-girdle strength to do tumbling or inverted balances, substitute an alternate activity. Spotting techniques are offered for teachers who feel capable of helping children who can perform the activities. Spot only children who can and want to perform an activity.

Forward Roll to a Walkout

Perform the Forward Roll as described earlier, but walk out to a standing position. The key to the Walkout is to develop enough momentum to enable a return to the feet. Bend the leg that first absorbs the weight while keeping the other leg straight.

Spotting: Same as the Forward Roll.

Backward Roll (Regular)

Begin in the Forward Roll squat position but with the back to the direction of the roll. Push off quickly with the hands, sit down, and start rolling over onto the back. Bring the knees to the chest, tucking the body and thus increasing momentum. Quickly bring the hands up over the shoulders, with palms up and fingers pointed backward. Continue rolling backward with knees close to the chest. The hands touch the mat at about the same time as the head does. At this point, push hard with the hands to release pressure on the neck. Continue rolling over and pushing off the mat until the roll is completed (figure 20.45). Teachers can emphasize proper hand position by having children point their thumbs toward their ears and spread their fingers for better push-off control.

FIGURE 20.45 Regular Backward Roll.

Spotting: Rather than spotting a child who is having trouble doing the Backward Roll, have the child try an activity like the Log Roll. If you choose to spot this activity, never push a child at the hips or buttocks, thus forcing the roll. This action puts undue pressure on the back of the neck. The proper way to aid a child who has difficulty with the stunt is as follows: The spotter stands in a straddle position, with the near foot alongside the spot where the student's hands and head will make contact with the mat (figure 20.46). The

FIGURE 20.46 Spotting the Backward Roll. (The lift is at the child's hips. Lift the student rather than force her over.)

Pearson Education

other foot is one stride in the direction of the roll. The critical point is for the spotter to lift the hips just as the child's head and hands contact the mat. This is done by taking the back hand and reaching across to the child's far hip, getting under the other hip with the near hand. Apply the lift on the front of the hips and just below the beltline to ensure that pressure on the neck is released.

Backward Roll (Handclasp Position)

Clasp the fingers behind the neck, holding the elbows out to the sides (figure 20.47). From a crouched position, sit down rapidly, bringing the knees to the chest for a tuck to gain momentum. Roll completely over backward, taking much of the weight on the forearms (figure 20.48). This method, which protects the neck, brings children early success in learning the backward roll. Remind children to keep their elbows back and out to the sides to ensure maximum support and minimal neck pressure. This is a lead-up activity to the regular backward roll. Allow children who cannot roll over to practice rocking back and forth with the elbows out. In no case should another person apply force to a child's hips in attempting to force him over.

©Robert Pangrazi or Aaron Beighle

FIGURE 20.47 Handclasp Position.

FIGURE 20.48 Backward Roll.

Frog Handstand (Tip-Up)

Squat down on the mat, placing the hands flat, with fingers pointing forward and elbows inside and pressed against the inner knees. Lean forward, using the leverage of the elbows against the knees, and balance on the hands (figure 20.49). Hold for five seconds. Return

20

to position. The head does not touch the mat at any time. The hands may be turned in slightly if this makes better contact between the elbows and the insides of the thighs. (This stunt follows from the Three-Point Tip-Up.)

FIGURE 20.49 Frog Handstand.

©Robert Pangrazi or Aaron Beighle

Half Teeter-Totter

This activity is part of the continued lead-up for the Handstand. Begin in the lunge position and shift the weight to the hands. Kick the legs up in the air to a 135-degree angle; then return to the feet. This activity is similar to the Switcheroo, but the feet are kicked higher without switching foot position.

Cartwheel

Start with the body in an erect position, arms outspread and legs shoulder-width apart. Bend the body to the right and place the right hand on the floor. Follow this, in sequence, by the left hand, the left foot, and the right foot (figure 20.50). Each body part touches the floor at evenly spaced intervals. The body is straight and extended when in the inverted position. The entire body stays in the same plane throughout the stunt, and the feet pass directly over the head.

FIGURE 20.50 Cartwheel.

Instruct children who have difficulty with the Cartwheel to concentrate on taking the weight of the body on the hands in succession. They need to learn to support their weight and later concentrate on getting the body into proper position. After the class has had some practice in doing Cartwheels, add a running approach with a skip before takeoff.

Forward Roll (Pike Position)

Begin the piked Forward Roll in a standing pike position. Keep the legs straight and bend forward at the hips. Place the hands on the mat, bend the elbows, and lower the head to the mat. Keep the legs straight until nearing the end of the roll. Bend at the knees to facilitate returning to the feet.

Forward Roll Combinations

Review the Forward Roll, focusing on proper form. Introduce some of these combinations:

1. Do a Forward Roll preceded by a short run.
2. Do two Forward Rolls in succession.
3. Do a Leapfrog and a Forward Roll.
4. Do a Forward Roll to a vertical jump in the air and repeat.
5. Do a Rabbit Jump and a Forward Roll.
6. Hold the toes while doing a Forward Roll.

Backward Roll Combinations

Review the Backward Roll. Continue focusing on the push-off with the hands. Teach students these combinations:

1. Do a Backward Roll to a standing position. Push strongly with the hands to create enough momentum to land on the feet.
2. Do two Backward Rolls in succession.
3. Do a Crab Walk into a Backward Roll.
4. Add a jump in the air at the end of a Backward Roll.

Teeter-Totter

The Teeter-Totter is the final lead-up activity for the Handstand. It is performed like the Half Teeter-Totter, but the feet are held together for a moment in the handstand position before the child returns to the standing position.

Handstand

Start in the lunge position. Do a Teeter-Totter to the inverted position. The body extends in a straight line from the shoulders through the feet, and the head is down. Teach the correct position first in a standing position with the arms overhead and the ears between the arms.

Spotting: The spotter takes a stride position, with the forward knee bent somewhat (figure 20.51). The performer's weight is transferred over the hands, and the body goes into the handstand position with a one-two kick-up. The spotter catches the legs and holds the performer in an inverted position (figure 20.52).

FIGURE 20.51　Single spotting for the Handstand, stage 1.

FIGURE 20.52　Single spotting for the Handstand, stage 2. (Note knee pressure against performer's shoulder.)

Balance Stunts

One-Leg Balance Reverse

Assume a forward balance position. Moving quickly to gain momentum, swing the free leg down and change to the same forward balance position facing in the opposite direction (a 180-degree turn; figure 20.53). No unnecessary movement of the supporting foot occurs after completing the turn. The swinging foot does not touch the floor.

FIGURE 20.53　One-Leg Balance Reverse.

Tummy Balance

Lie prone on the floor with arms outstretched forward or to the sides, with palms down. Raise the arms, head, chest, and legs from the floor and balance on the tummy (figure 20.54). Keep the knees straight.

FIGURE 20.54　Tummy Balance.

Leg Dip

Extend both hands and one leg forward, balancing on the other leg. Lower the body to sit on the heel and return without losing the balance or touching the floor with any part of the body. Try with the other foot. (Another child can assist from the back by pressing upward on the performer's elbows.)

Balance Jump

With arms out to the sides and body parallel to the ground, extend one leg back and balance the weight on the other leg (figure 20.55). Quickly change to the other foot and balance in the initial position (figure 20.56). Keep the body

20

parallel to the ground when switching legs. Try with arms outstretched forward. Working in pairs might be helpful. One student critiques the other's performance to ensure that the arms and body are straight and parallel to the floor.

FIGURE 20.55   Balance Jump, starting position.

©Robert Pangrazi or Aaron Beighle

FIGURE 20.56   Balance Jump.

Seat Balance

Sit on the floor, holding the ankles in front, with elbows inside the knees. The feet are flat on the floor, and the knees are bent at almost a right angle. Raise the legs (toes pointed) so that the knees are straight (figure 20.57) and balance on the seat for five seconds.

FIGURE 20.57   Seat Balance.

Face-to-Knee Touch

Begin in a standing position with feet together. Placing the hands on the hips, balance on one foot, with the other leg extended backward. Bend the trunk forward and touch the knee of the supporting leg with the forehead (figure 20.58). Recover to the original position.

FIGURE 20.58   Face-to-Knee Touch.

Teachers can have children begin by keeping the arms away from the sides for balance and then try the hands-on-hips position later. In the learning stages, assist a student from behind by supporting the leg extended backward, or have students place one hand against a wall.

Finger Touch

Put the right hand behind the back with the index finger straight and pointed down. Grasp the right wrist with the left hand. From an erect position with the feet about 6 inches (15 cm) apart, squat down and touch the floor with the index finger (figure 20.59). Regain the erect position without losing balance. Reverse hands. (In the learning stages, teachers can use a book or the corner of a mat to decrease the distance and make the touch easier.)

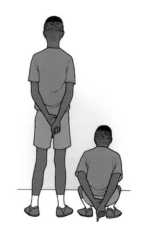

FIGURE 20.59   Finger Touch.

Individual Stunts

Reach-Under

Take a position with the feet pointed ahead (about 2 feet [60cm] apart) and toes against a line or a floorboard. Place a beanbag two boards in front of, and midway between, the feet. Without changing the foot position, reach one hand behind and between the legs to pick up the beanbag. Now pick up with the other hand. Repeat, moving the beanbag a board farther away each time.

Variation: Allow the heels to lift off the floor. Use the other hand.

Stiff Person Bend

Stand with feet about shoulder-width apart and pointed forward. Place a beanbag a few inches (about 10 cm) behind the right heel. Grasp the left toes with the left hand, thumb on top. Without bending the knees, reach the right hand outside the right leg and pick up the beanbag without releasing the hold on the left toes. Gradually increase the distance of the reach. Reverse sides (figure 20.60).

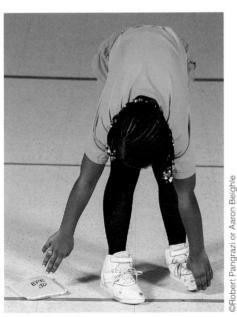

FIGURE 20.60   Stiff Person Bend.

Coffee Grinder

Put one hand on the floor and extend the body to the floor on that side in a side-leaning rest position. Walk around the hand, making a complete circle and keeping the body straight (figure 20.61). The stunt is done slowly, with controlled movements.

FIGURE 20.61   Coffee Grinder.

Scooter

Sit on the floor with legs extended, arms folded in front of the chest, and chin held high. To scoot, pull the seat toward the heels, using heel pressure and lifting the seat slightly (figure 20.62). Extend the legs forward again and repeat the process. (This activity is excellent for abdominal development.)

FIGURE 20.62   Scooter.

Hip Walk

Sit in the same position as for the Scooter, but with arms in thrust position and hands making a partial fist. "Walk" by using alternate leg–seat movements. Arm–leg coordination is unilateral.

Long Bridge

Begin in a crouched position with hands on the floor and knees between the arms. Push the hands forward a little at a time until reaching an extended push-up position (figure 20.63). Return to the original position. (Teachers: Challenge children to extend as far as they can in this position.)

20

FIGURE 20.63 Long Bridge.

Variation:

1. Begin with a forward movement; then change to a sideways movement, spreading as wide as possible.
2. Work from a crossed-hands position.

Heelstand

Begin in a full squat with the arms dangling at the sides. Jump upward to full leg extension with the weight on both heels and fling the arms out diagonally. Hold momentarily and then return to the original position (figure 20.64). Several movements can be done rhythmically in succession.

FIGURE 20.64 Heelstand.

Wicket Walk

Bend over and touch the floor with the weight evenly distributed on the hands and feet, thus forming a wicket. Walk the wicket forward, backward, and sideways. Keep the arms and legs as nearly vertical as possible (figure 20.65). This stunt loses much of its flexibility value if students bend their knees too much. A common error in the execution of this stunt is to place the hands too far forward of the feet. (The stunt is named for the child's body position, which resembles a wicket in a croquet game.)

FIGURE 20.65 Wicket Walk.

©Robert Pangrazi or Aaron Beighle

Knee Jump to Standing

Kneel, with seat touching the heels and toes pointing backward (shoelaces against the floor). Jump to a standing position with a vigorous upward swing of the arms (figure 20.66). Jumping from a smooth floor is easier than jumping from a mat, because the toes slide more readily on the floor.

FIGURE 20.66 Knee Jump to Standing.

Variation: Jump to a standing position, doing a quarter turn in the air in one quick motion. Try a half turn.

Individual Drops, or Falls

Drops, or falls, can challenge children to achieve good body control. Mats must be used. The hands and arms absorb the impact of a forward fall. During the fall, keep the body in a straight-line position. Little change in body angles occurs, particularly at the knees and waist.

Knee Drop

Kneel on a mat, with the body upright. Raise the feet up, off the floor, and fall forward, breaking the fall with the hands and arms (figure 20.67).

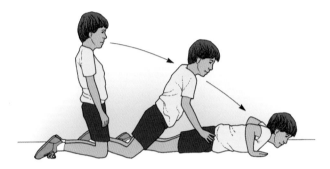

FIGURE 20.67   Knee Drop.

Forward Drop

From a forward balance position, on one leg with the other leg extended backward and the arms extended forward and up, lean forward slowly, bringing the arms toward the floor. Continue to drop forward slowly until overbalanced; then let the hands and arms break the fall (figure 20.68). The head is up, and the extended leg is raised high; knee joints are reasonably straight. Repeat, changing position of the legs.

FIGURE 20.68   Forward Drop.

Dead Body Fall

Fall forward from an erect position to a down push-up position (figure 20.69). A slight bend at the waist is permissible, but keep the knees straight and do not move the feet forward.

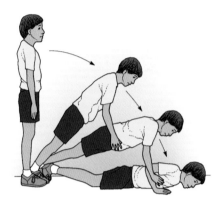

FIGURE 20.69   Dead Body Fall.

Stoop and Stretch

Hold a beanbag with both hands. Stand with heels against a line and feet about shoulder-width apart. Keeping the knees straight, reach between the legs with the beanbag and place it as far back as possible. Reach back and pick it up with both hands.

Variation:

1. Bend at the knees, using more of a squatting position during the reach.

2. Use a piece of chalk instead of a beanbag. Reach back and make a mark on the floor. Try writing a number or drawing a small circle or some other shape.

Tanglefoot

Stand with heels together and toes pointed out. Bend the trunk forward and wrap arms between the knees and around behind the ankles. Bring the hands around the outside of the ankles from behind and touch the fingers to each other (figure 20.70). Hold for five seconds.

Variation: Instead of touching, clasp the fingers in front of the ankles. Hold this position in good balance for five seconds without releasing the hands.

FIGURE 20.70   Tanglefoot.

20

Egg Roll

While sitting, assume the same clasped-hands position as for Tanglefoot. Roll sideways over one shoulder, then to the back, then to the other shoulder, and finally back up to the sitting position (figure 20.71). Repeat the movements in turn to make a full circle back to the original position. The key to performing this stunt is a vigorous sideways movement to gain initial momentum. If mats are used, place two side by side to cushion the entire roll. (Some children can do this stunt better from a crossed-ankle position.)

FIGURE 20.71 Egg Roll.

Toe Touch Nose

While sitting on the floor, touch the toes of either foot to the nose with the help of both hands. First do one foot and then the other. More flexible students will be able to place the foot on top of the head or even behind the neck. Although this exercise promotes flexibility, caution students not to force the leg too far.

Variation: Perform from a standing position. Touch the toes to the nose and return the foot to the original position without losing balance. Try the standing version with eyes closed.

Toe-Tug Walk

Bend over and grasp the toes with thumbs on top (figure 20.72). Keep the knees bent slightly and the eyes forward. Walk forward without losing the grip on the toes. Challenge students to walk backward and sideways. Walk in various geometric patterns, such as a circle, triangle, or square. (Teachers can introduce an easier version of this stunt by having children grasp the ankles, thumbs on the insides, and perform the desired movements.)

FIGURE 20.72 Toe Tug Walk.

Variation: Try doing the walk with the right hand grasping the left foot, and vice versa.

Partner and Group Stunts

Depending on the maturity and nature of the class, separating boys and girls may be more effective for some of the partner and group stunts. Students enjoy these activities, but some of the requisite touching may cause problems for some classes.

Partner Hopping

Partners coordinate hopping movements for short distances and in different directions and turns. Three combinations are suggested.

1. Stand facing each other. Extend the right leg forward to be grasped at the ankle by partner's left hand. Hold right hands and hop on the left leg (figure 20.73).
2. Stand back-to-back. Lift the leg backward, bending the knee, and have partner grasp the ankle. Hop as before.
3. Stand side by side with inside arms around each other's waist. Lift the inside foot from the floor and move by hopping on the outside foot.

If either partner begins to fall, the other releases the leg immediately. Reverse foot positions.

FIGURE 20.73   Partner Hopping.

©Robert Pangrazi or Aaron Beighle

Partner Twister

Partners face and grasp right hands as if shaking hands. One partner swings the left leg over the other's head and turns around, taking a straddle position over the partner's arm (figure 20.74). The other swings the right leg over the first partner, who has bent over, and the partners are now back-to-back. First partner continues with the right leg and faces in the original direction. Second partner swings the left leg over the partner's back to return to the original face-to-face position. Partners need to duck to avoid being kicked during the leg swings.

FIGURE 20.74   Partner Twister.

Variation: Introduce the stunt by having students grasp a wand instead of holding hands.

Partner Pull-Up

Partners sit facing each other in a bent-knee position, with heels on the floor and toes touching. Pulling cooperatively, they come to a standing position (figure 20.75).

FIGURE 20.75   Partner Pull-Up.

Variation: Try with feet flat on the floor.

Back-to-Back Get-Up

Partners sit back-to-back and lock arms. From this position, they try to stand by pushing against each other's back (figure 20.76). They sit down again. If the feet are sliding, do the stunt on a mat.

FIGURE 20.76   Back-to-Back Get-Up.

Variation:

1. Try with three or four children.

2. Try from a halfway-down position and move like a spider.

20

Rowboat

Partners sit on the floor or on a mat, facing each other with legs apart and feet touching. Both grasp a wand with both hands and pretend to row a boat. Seek a wide range of movement in the forward–backward rowing motion. (The stunt can be done without a wand by having children grasp hands.)

Leapfrog

One student bends over forward, forming a base. A leaper takes a running start, lays hands flat on the back at the shoulders, and vaults over the first student. Bases are formed at various heights (figure 20.77). To form a low base, crouch down on the knees, curling into a tight ball with the head tucked well down. To form a medium base, reach down the outside of the legs from a standing position and grasp the ankles. The feet are moderately spread, and the knees are straight. The position must be stable to absorb the shock of the leaper. To form a high base, stand stiff-legged, bend over, and brace arms against the knees. The feet are spread, the head is down, and the body is braced to absorb the vault.

FIGURE 20.77   High, medium, and low Leapfrog positions.

Leapfrog is a traditional physical education activity, but the movement is actually a jump-and-vault pattern. The takeoff is made with both feet. At the height of the jump, the chest and head are held erect to avoid falling forward. Teachers should emphasize a forceful jump to achieve height, coordinated with light hand pressure to vault over the back. Landing is light and under good control, with a bent-knee action.

Variation:

1. Work in pairs. Alternate leaping and forming the base while moving around the room.

2. Have more than one base for a series of jumps.

3. Using the medium base, vault from the side rather than from the front. The vaulter's legs must be well spread, and the base must keep the head well tucked down.

4. Following the Leapfrog, do a Forward Roll on a mat.

Wheelbarrow

One partner gets down on the hands with feet extended to the rear and legs apart. The other partner (the pusher) grasps partner's legs about halfway between the ankles and the knees. The wheelbarrow walks forward on the hands, supported by the pusher (figure 20.78). Movements should be under good control.

FIGURE 20.78   Wheelbarrow.

Children tend to grasp the legs too near the feet. The pusher must not push too fast. The wheelbarrow holds the head up and looks forward. Fingers are pointed forward and well spread, with the pads of the fingers supporting much of the weight. The pusher carries the legs low and keeps the arms extended.

Wheelbarrow Lifting

Partners assume the wheelbarrow position. The pusher lifts partner's legs as high as possible without changing the hand position. The pusher must lift the legs enough so that the lower child's body is about at a 45-degree angle to the floor.

Variation: The pusher brings the legs up to the level described, changes the handgrip to a pushing one, and continues raising the lower child toward a handstand position. The lower child keeps arms and body straight.

Camel Lift and Walk

In the wheelbarrow position, the wheelbarrow raises the seat as high as possible, forming a camel. Camels can lower themselves or walk in the raised position.

Dump the Wheelbarrow

Get into the wheelbarrow position. Walk the wheelbarrow over to a mat. The lower child ducks the head (chin to waist), raises the seat (bending at the waist), and exits from the stunt with a Forward Roll. The pusher gives a little push and a lift of the feet to help create momentum.

Dromedary Walk

One child (the support) gets down on the hands and knees. The other child sits on the support, facing the rear, and fixes the legs around the support's chest. The top child leans forward, to grasp the back of the support's ankles. The top child's arms are reasonably extended (figure 20.79). The support takes the weight off the knees and walks forward with the top child's help.

FIGURE 20.79 Dromedary Walk.

©Robert Pangrazi or Aaron Beighle

Centipede

A strong, large child gets down on hands and knees. The other child faces the same direction, places the hands about 2 feet (60 cm) in front of the support's, and places her legs and body on top of the support. The knees are spread apart, and the heels are locked together. The centipede walks with the top child using hands only and the supporting child using both hands and feet. The support gathers the legs well under while walking and is not on the knees.

Variation: More than two can do this stunt (figure 20.80). After getting into position, the players keep step by calling out, "Right" and "Left."

FIGURE 20.80 Centipede.

Double Wheelbarrow

Two children form a Centipede, but the support child extends his legs to the rear and spreads his feet apart. A third child stands between the support's legs, reaches down, and picks them up (figure 20.81). The Double Wheelbarrow moves forward with right and left arms moving together. Three children usually do this stunt but more can do it.

FIGURE 20.81 Double Wheelbarrow.

Partner Support Stunts

Several considerations are important for partner support stunts at this level. The lower child (the support) needs to keep the body as level as possible. The support child must widen the hand base to make the shoulders more nearly level with the hips, and he or she must be strong enough to handle the support chores. Spotters are needed, particularly when the top position involves a final erect or inverted pose. The top child must avoid stepping on the small of the support's back. In the Lighthouse and the Hip–Shoulder Stand, the top performer can remove his or her shoes, making the standing position more comfortable for the support. When holding the final pose, the top child fixes his or her gaze forward and relaxes as much as possible while maintaining the position.

20

Another consideration is the students' size. Avoid obvious mismatches and try to ensure that students of nearly equal size are partnered. Some students may be designated as bases only, because their size restricts their ability to be supported by others. In addition, in some settings, pairing students of the same sex may be best to avoid the touching issues when performing these activities.

Double Bear

The bottom child gets down on the hands and knees. The top child assumes the same position directly above the support, with hands on the shoulders and knees on the hips of the support (figure 20.82). Improve the final position by holding heads up and backs straight.

FIGURE 20.82   Double Bear.

Table

The bottom performer assumes a crab position. The top performer straddles this base, facing the rear, and positions the hands on the base's shoulders, fingers pointing toward the ground. The top child then places the feet on top of base's knees, forming one crab position on top of another (figure 20.83). As a final touch, the performers look up toward the ceiling and lift their seats so that their backs are straight.

Statue

The first child gets down in crab position. The second child straddles either foot, facing the first child. With a spotter's help, the second child mounts the base child's knees and stands erect (figure 20.84). Hold the position for a few seconds. The top child must not mount with her back toward the base child. (Spotters are important; students must use them until they master the stunt.)

FIGURE 20.83   Table.

FIGURE 20.84   Statue.

Lighthouse

The support gets down on the hands and knees. The top child completes the figure by standing on the support's shoulders and facing in the same direction. The lighthouse stands erect with arms out to the sides (figure 20.85).

Variation: The support turns around in a small circle, while the partner keeps the standing balance.

Hip–Shoulder Stand

The support child is on the hands and knees, with hands spread out to make the back level. The top child faces to the side and steps up, first with one foot on the support's hips and then with the other on the shoulders (figure 20.86). A spotter stands on the opposite side and aids in the mounting. Caution the top child to avoid stepping on the small of the support's back.

Developmental Level III Activities

Expecting all children to accomplish the entire list of stunts at this level is unrealistic. In fact, some children will likely never become outstanding at the tumbling and inverted stunts. Such activities are difficult for students who are heavier and less strong. Some children at this level will become skillful at both the Forward and the Backward Rolls. The Judo Roll, Cartwheel and Round-Off, and Double Roll continue the tumbling activities. Improvement in the Headstand is expected. Such stunts as the Headspring, Front Seat Support, Elbow Balance, Straddle Press to Headstand, and Walk-Over provide sufficient breadth for even the most skilled.

Tumbling and Inverted Balances

To prevent serious injuries, never encourage or force children to perform an activity they are uncomfortable with. If a child lacks the neck and shoulder-girdle strength to do tumbling or inverted balances, substitute an alternate activity.

Forward and Backward Roll Combinations

Have students review combinations from Developmental Level II. The following routines can be added.

1. Begin with a Forward Roll, coming to a standing position with feet crossed. Pivot the body to uncross the feet and to bring the back in the line of direction for a Backward Roll (figure 20.87).

FIGURE 20.85 Lighthouse.

FIGURE 20.86 Hip–Shoulder Stand.

FIGURE 20.87 Alternating Forward and Backward Rolls.

Pearson Education

©Robert Pangrazi or Aaron Beighle

20

2. Hold the toes, heels, ankles, or a wand while rolling. Use different arm positions, such as out to the sides or folded across the chest. Use a wide straddle position for both the Forward Roll and the Backward Roll.

Back Extension

Carry the Backward Roll to the point where the feet are above and over the head. Push off vigorously with the hands, shoot the feet into the air, and land on the feet.

Headstand Variations

Review the various aspects of the Headstand, using the single-spotter technique as needed. Vary with different leg positions. Add the two-footed recovery. After holding the headstand, a student recovers by bending at the waist and knees, pushing off with the hands, and landing on the feet in the original position.

Handstand Against a Wall

Using a wall as support, do a Handstand. The arms must be kept straight, with the head between the arms (figure 20.88). Some performers like to bend the knees and place the soles of the feet against the wall.

FIGURE 20.88 Handstand Against a Wall.

©Robert Pangrazi or Aaron Beighle

A critical point in the Handstand Against a Wall is to position the hands the correct distance from the wall. Being too close is better than being too far. Being too far can cause the performer to collapse before the feet gain the support of the wall. Use spotters and a mat in the preliminary stages.

Headstand

Two approaches are suggested for the Headstand: (1) relate the Headstand to the Climb-Up; and (2) go directly into a Headstand, using a kick-up to achieve the inverted position. In either case, maintaining the triangle position of the hands and the head is essential.

In the final inverted position, the legs are straight with feet together and toes pointed. The weight is evenly distributed among the three points—the two hands and the forward part of the head. The body is as straight as possible.

The safest way to come down from the inverted position is to return to the mat in the same direction used in going up. To ease recovery, bend at the waist and the knees. In the case of overbalancing, have students tuck their heads under and go into a Forward Roll. When presenting the instructional sequence, explain both methods of recovery from the inverted position.

Headstand Climb-Up

Take the inverted position of the Climb-Up and move the feet slowly upward to the headstand position (figure 20.89).

FIGURE 20.89 Headstand based on the Climb-Up.

Spotting: The spotter stands directly in front of the performer and steadies the performer as needed. The spotter must be ready to move out of the way when the performer goes into a Forward Roll to come out of the inverted position.

Headstand Kick-Up

Keeping the weight on the forward part of the head and maintaining the triangle base, walk the feet forward until the hips are high over the body (similar to the Climb-Up position). Keep one foot on the mat, bending the knee of that leg and extending the other leg backward. Kick the back leg up to the inverted position, following quickly with a push by the other leg, thus bringing the two legs together in the inverted position (figure 20.90). The timing is a quick one–two movement.

FIGURE 20.90　Headstand based on the a kick-up.

Emphasize the importance of forming a triangle with the hands and the head as well as centering the weight on the forward part of the head. Most difficulties with the Headstand come from an incorrect head–hand position. The correct positioning has the head placed the length of the performer's forearm from the knees and the hands placed at the knees. To help children form the proper triangle, mark the three spots on the mat with chalk.

Spotting: When learning, students can try the stunt with a spotter on each side. Each spotter kneels, placing the near hand under the performer's shoulder. The performer then walks the weight above the head and kicks up to position. The spotter on each side supports by grasping a leg (figure 20.91). The performer is responsible for getting into the inverted position.

Headstand Practice and Variations

Continue work on the Headstand. Try the following variations. (Spot as needed.)

1. Clap the hands and recover. The weight shifts momentarily to the head for the clap. (Some children will be able to clap the hands twice before recovery.)

2. Use different leg positions: legs split sideways, legs split forward and backward, and knees bent.

FIGURE 20.91　Spotting the Headstand.

3. Holding a utility ball or a beanbag between the legs, go into the Headstand, retaining control of the ball.

Freestanding Handstand

Perform a Handstand without support. Students must learn to turn the body when a fall is imminent, so that they land on their feet. (Use spotters to prevent an awkward fall.) Move the hands to help control the balance.

Cartwheel and Round-Off

Practice the Cartwheel, adding a light run with a skip for a takeoff. To change to a Round-Off, place the hands somewhat closer together during the early Cartwheel action. Bring the feet together and make a quarter turn to land on both feet, with the body facing the starting point. The Round-Off can be followed by a Backward Roll.

Judo Roll

For a left Judo Roll, stand facing the mat with the feet well apart and the left arm extended at shoulder height. Bring the arm down and throw the left shoulder toward the mat in a rolling motion, making the roll on the shoulder and upper part of the back (figure 20.92). Reverse for a right Judo Roll. Practice the rolls on both sides. Later, start the Judo Roll with a short run and a two-footed takeoff. The Judo Roll is a basic safety device to prevent injury from tripping and falling. Rolling and taking the fall

20

lessen the chances of injury. The Judo Roll is essentially a Forward Roll with the head turned to one side. The point of impact is the back of one shoulder and the finish is a return to the standing position.

FIGURE 20.92   Judo Roll.

Variation:

1. Roll to the feet and to a ready position.
2. Place a beanbag about 3 feet (90 cm) in front of the toes and go beyond the bag to start the roll.

Advanced Forward and Backward Roll Combinations

Develop different combinations of Forward Rolls and Backward Rolls. Emphasize choice, exploration, and self-discovery. Variations can involve different approaches, execution acts, and finishes. Try these variations of the Forward Roll.

1. Roll while holding the toes, heels, ankles, or a wand.
2. As before, but cross the hands.
3. Roll with hands on the knees or with a ball between the knees.
4. Roll with arms at the sides, folded across the chest, or on the back of the thighs.
5. Press forward from a front-leaning rest position and go into the roll.

Try these suggestions with the Backward Roll.

1. Begin with a Stiff-Legged Sit-Down and go into the roll.
2. Push off into a Back Extension, landing on the feet.
3. Roll to a finish on one foot only.
4. Roll with hands clasped behind the neck.
5. Roll with a ball between the knees.
6. Walk backward using a Crab Walk and then roll.

Finally, try combining Forward Rolls with Backward Rolls in various ways.

Straddle Press to Headstand

Begin by placing the hands and head in the Triangular Headstand position. The feet are in a wide straddle, and the hips are up. Raise the hips slowly by pressing to a point over the base of support. Slowly raise the legs to a straddle position and finish with the legs brought together in regular Headstand position. Do all movement as a slow, controlled action. (This stunt is more difficult than a regular Headstand.)

Handstand Variations

Review the first two stages of the Handstand, done with double spotting and then single spotting with knee support. Progression can then follow this order.

1. Single spotting, without knee support
2. Handstand against a wall
3. Freestanding Handstand
4. Walking on the hands
5. Stunts against a wall

Spotting: For single spotting without knee support, the performer and the spotter face each other at 4 to 5 feet (120 to 150 cm) apart. The performer lifts both arms and the left leg as a preliminary move; the weight shifts to the right leg. The lifted arms and forward leg come down forcefully to the ground, as the weight shifts first to the left leg and then to the arms. For momentum, the performer kicks the right leg backward and upward, followed quickly by the left leg. The downward thrust of the arms, coupled with the upward thrust of the legs, inverts the body to the handstand position. The performer's hands are about 2 feet (60 cm) in front of the spotter, who reaches forward and catches the performer between the knees and the ankles.

Headspring

With forehead and hands on the mat and knees bent, lean forward until almost overbalanced. As the weight begins to overbalance, raise the feet sharply and snap forward, pushing with the hands. As the feet begin to touch the ground, snap the body to a bent-knee position (figure 20.93). Keep control of balance and rise to a standing position.

FIGURE 20.93   Headspring.

Spotting: Use two spotters, one on each side of the performer. Each spotter places one hand under the performer's back and the other hand under a shoulder. The spotters give the performer a slight lift under the shoulders to help in snapping to the standing position.

Walking on the Hands

Walk on the hands in a forward direction, bending the knees slightly, if desired, for balance. (Walking can be done first with a spotter supporting, but this support should be minimal.)

Variation: Walk on the hands, using a partner. The performer does a Handstand, and the partner catches the feet. The performer then walks the hands forward until they are on the partner's feet. The two walk cooperatively.

Walk-Over

Do preliminary movements as if for the Handstand. Let the legs continue beyond that position and contact the floor with a one-two rhythm. Keep the body well arched as the leading foot touches the floor. Push off with the hands and walk out.

Spotting: The spotter supports the small of the performer's back.

Balance Stunts

V-Up

Lie on the back, with arms overhead and extended. With the knees straight and feet pointed, bring the legs and upper body up at the same time to form a V shape. The entire weight balances on the seat (figure 20.94). Hold for five seconds. This exercise, like the Curl-Up, is excellent for developing the abdominal muscles. It is much like the Seat Balance, except for the starting position.

FIGURE 20.94 V-Up.

Variation: Place the hands on the floor in back for support. (This makes the stunt easier for some students.)

Push-Up Variations

Begin the development of Push-Up variations by reviewing proper Push-Up techniques. The only movement is in the arms. The body does not quite touch the floor. Explore the following variations.

Monkey Push-Up: Point the fingers toward each other. Next, bring the hands close enough for the fingertips to touch.

Circle-O Push-Up: Form a circle with each thumb and forefinger.

Fingertip Push-Up: Get up high on the fingertips.

Different Finger Combinations: Do a Push-Up using the thumb and three (or two) fingers only.

Extended Push-Up: Extend the position of the hands progressively forward or to the sides.

Crossed Push-Up: Cross the arms. Cross the legs. Cross both.

One-Legged Push-Up: Lift one leg from the floor.

One-Handed Push-Up: Use only one hand, with the other outstretched or on the hip.

Exploratory Approach: Try creating other types of Push-Ups or combinations.

Flip-Flop

From a push-up position, propel the body upward with the hands and feet, doing a Turnover (figure 20.95). Flip back. Do this stunt on a mat. (Review the Turnover before students try this stunt.)

FIGURE 20.95 Flip-Flop.

Long Reach

Place a beanbag about 3 feet (90 cm) in front of a line. Keeping the toes behind the line, lean forward on one hand and reach out with the other hand to touch the beanbag (figure 20.96). Recover in one clean, quick movement to the original position, lifting the supporting hand off the floor. Increase the distance of the bag from the line.

20

FIGURE 20.96 Long Reach.

Toe Jump

Hold the left toes with the right hand (figure 20.97). Jump the right foot through without losing the grip on the toes. Try with the other foot. (Do not be discouraged if only a few students can do this stunt; it is quite difficult.)

FIGURE 20.97 Toe Jump.

Handstand Stunts

Try these challenging activities from the handstand position against a wall.

1. Turn the body in a complete circle, maintaining foot contact with the wall throughout.
2. Shift the support to one hand and hold for a moment.
3. Do an inverted push-up, lowering the body by bending the elbows and then returning to handstand position by straightening the elbows.

Front Seat Support

Sit on the floor, with the legs together and forward. Place the hands flat on the floor, somewhere between the hips and the knees, with fingers pointed forward. Push down so that the hips come off the floor, with the weight supported on the hands and heels. Next, lift the heels and support the entire weight of the body on the hands for three to five seconds. (Someone can help the performer get into position by giving slight support under the heels.)

Elbow Balance

Balance the body facedown horizontally on two hands, with elbows supporting the body in the hip area. To get into position, support the arched body with the toes and forehead. Work the forearms underneath the body for support, with fingers spread and pointed backward. Try to support the body completely on the hands for three seconds, with elbows providing the leverage under the body (figure 20.98). (Slight support under the toes can be provided.) The Elbow Balance is challenging. The teacher should take time to discuss the location of the center of gravity. The elbow support point should divide the upper and lower body mass.

FIGURE 20.98 Elbow Balance.

Individual Stunts

Wall Walk-Up

From a push-up position with feet against a wall, walk up the wall backward to a handstand position (figure 20.99). Walk down again.

FIGURE 20.99 Wall Walk-Up.

Skier's Sit

Assume a sitting position (as if in a chair) against a wall with the thighs parallel to the floor and the knee joints at right angles. Place the hands on the thighs with the feet flat on the floor and the lower legs straight up and down (figure 20.100). Try to sit for 30 seconds, 45 seconds, and 1 minute. The Skier's Sit is an isometric activity and is excellent for developing the knee extensor muscles. Skiers use it to develop the muscles used in skiing.

FIGURE 20.100   Skier's Sit.

©Robert Pangrazi or Aaron Beighle

Variation: A more difficult stunt is to support the body on one leg and extend the other leg.

Rocking Horse

Lie facedown on a mat with arms extended overhead, palms down. Arch the back and rock back and forth (figure 20.101). (Some children may need someone to start them rocking.)

FIGURE 20.101   Rocking Horse.

Variation: Reach back and grasp the insteps with the hands. (The body arch is more difficult to maintain in this position.) Also, try rocking from a side position.

Heel Click (Side)

Balance on one foot with the other out to the side. Hop on the supporting foot, click the heels, and return to balance. Try with the other foot. Good form dictates recovering to the one-footed balance position with little foot movement.

Variation:

1. Take a short step with the right foot leading. Follow with a cross-step with the left and then a hop on the left foot. During the hop, click the heels together. To hop on the right foot, reverse these directions.

2. Jump as high as possible before clicking the heels.

3. Combine right and left clicks.

Walk-Through

From a front-leaning rest position, walk the feet through the hands, using tiny steps, until the body is fully extended with the back to the floor (figure 20.102). Return to the original position. The hands are on the floor throughout.

FIGURE 20.102   Walk-Through.

Jump-Through

Starting in a front-leaning rest position, jump the feet through the arms in one motion. Reverse with another jump and return to the original position. The hands must push off sharply from the floor, so that the body is high enough off the floor to allow the legs to jump under. (Students may find it easier to swing a little to the side with one leg, going under the lifted hand, as indicated in figure 20.103.)

FIGURE 20.103   Jump-Through.

20

Circular Rope Jump

Crouch down in a three-quarter knee bend, holding a folded jump rope in one hand. Swing the rope under the feet in a circular fashion, jumping it each time (figure 20.104). Reverse the direction of the rope. Work from both right and left sides, turning the rope either counterclockwise or clockwise.

FIGURE 20.104   Circular Rope Jump.

Variations:

1. Perform the rope jump with a partner.
2. Jump using different foot patterns (one foot or alternate feet) and using slow and fast time.
3. Establish standards for declaring a class champion in different areas, such as maximum number of turns in 30 seconds, most unique routine, and most jumps without a miss.

Bouncer

Start in a push-up position. Bounce up and down with the hands and feet leaving the ground at the same time. Try clapping while doing this. Move in various directions. Turn around.

Pretzel

Touch the back of the head with the toes by raising the head and trunk and bringing the feet to the back of the head (figure 20.105). First try to get the toes within a hand span (the distance between the thumb and little finger when spread) of the head. If this distance is met, then try touching one or both feet to the back of the head.

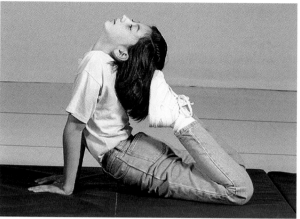

FIGURE 20.105   Pretzel.

Jackknife

Stand erect with hands out level to the front and a little to the side. Jump up and bring the feet up quickly to touch the hands. Vary by starting with a short run. The feet must come up to the hands; do not move the hands down to the feet (figure 20.106). Do several Jackknives in succession. The takeoff is with both feet and at a good height.

FIGURE 20.106   Jackknife.

Heel-and-Toe Spring

Place the heels against a line. Bend over, grasp the toes, and jump backward over the line. (Before jumping, lean forward slightly to gain momentum.) Try jumping forward to the original position. To be successful, students must retain the grasp on the toes. Teachers can make the stunt easier by having children grasp their ankles when first making the jumps.

Single-Leg Circle (Pinwheel)

Assume a squatting position, with both hands on the floor, left knee between the arms, and right leg extended to the side. Swing the right leg forward and under the lifted right arm, under the left leg and arm, and back to starting position (figure 20.107). Make several circles in succession. Reverse position and try with the left leg.

FIGURE 20.107   Single-Leg Circle.

Partner and Group Stunts

Depending on the maturity and nature of the class, teachers may decide to separate boys and girls for some of the partner and group stunts. Students enjoy these activities, but some of the requisite touching may cause problems for some students.

Double Scooter

Two children about the same size face each other, sitting on each other's feet (figure 20.108). With arms joined, they scoot forward or backward with cooperative movements. As one child moves her seat, the other child helps by lifting with her feet. They move by alternately flexing and extending the knees and hips. Review the Scooter before doing this stunt.

Double Roll

One child lies on a mat with his feet in the direction of the roll. The other places his feet on either side of the partner's head. The first child reaches back and grasps the other's ankles with thumbs on the inside and then raises his own feet, so that the other child can similarly grasp his ankles. The second child propels his hunched body forward, while the first sits up and takes the position originally held by the other (figure 20.109). Positions are then reversed, and the roll continues.

Be sure that the top child hunches well and ducks the head to cushion the roll on the back of the neck and shoulders. In addition, when the top child propels himself forward, bent arms should momentarily take the weight. The lower child must keep the knees bent.

©Robert Pangrazi or Aaron Beighle

FIGURE 20.108   Double Scooter.

20

FIGURE 20.109   Double Roll.

Tandem Bicycle

One child forms a bicycle position with back against a wall and knees bent, as if sitting. The feet are placed under the body. The second child backs up and sits down lightly on the first child's knees. Other children may be added in the same fashion, their hands around the waist of the child immediately in front for support (figure 20.110). Progress is made by moving the feet on the same side together.

FIGURE 20.110   Tandem Bicycle.

Circle High Jump

Stand in circles of three, each circle having children of roughly equal height. Join hands. One child tries to jump over the opposite pair of joined hands (figure 20.111). To be completely successful, each circle must have each child jump forward in turn over the opposite pair of joined hands. (Jumping backward is not recommended.) To reach good height, an upward lift is necessary. Try two small preliminary jumps before exploding into the jump over the joined hands.

FIGURE 20.111   Circle High Jump.

Variation: Precede the jump with a short run by the group. Sound a signal to let all groups know when to stop and jump.

Stick Carry

Children of similar weight stand in groups of three. Each group has a sturdy broom handle about 4 feet (120 cm) long. Using movement exploration techniques, two of the children carry the third with the broom handle (figure 20.112). The child who is carried may be partially or wholly supported by the handle. Exchange positions. (Use special sticks for this purpose because ordinary wands may break.)

FIGURE 20.112   Stick Carry.

Two-Way Wheelbarrow

One child holds two wheelbarrows, but with one in front and one behind. The child lifts the front wheelbarrow first in a normal wheelbarrow position. The back wheelbarrow then places one leg on each side of the holder, hooking the ankles over the front wheelbarrow's legs (figure 20.113). (Review the various wheelbarrow activities before doing this stunt.)

FIGURE 20.113   Two-Way Wheelbarrow.

Partner Rising Sun

Partners lie facedown on the floor with heads together and feet in opposite directions. They hold a volleyball or a basketball (or a ball of similar size) between their heads (figure 20.114). Working together, they stand up and then return to position while retaining control of the ball. Do not touch the ball with the hands. A slightly deflated ball works best. Some caution is necessary to prevent bumping heads if the ball is suddenly squeezed out.

FIGURE 20.114   Partner Rising Sun.

Triple Roll

Three children are on hands and knees on a mat, all facing the same side. The performers are about 4 feet (120 cm) apart. Child 1 is in the center, 2 is on the right, and 3 is on the left. Child 1 starts rolling toward and under child 2, who lifts up and over child 1. Child 2 is then in the center and rolls toward child 3, who lifts up and over 2. Child 3, in the center, rolls toward and under child 1, who, after clearing child 3, is back in the center. Each performer in the center thus rolls toward and under the outside performer (figure 20.115). (Review the Side Roll before doing this stunt.)

Teach children that as soon as they roll to the outside, they must get ready to go over the oncoming child from the center. They cannot delay. The upward lift of the body to allow the rolling child to go under is important.

FIGURE 20.115   Triple Roll.

Quintuplet Roll

Five children can make up a roll series. They are numbered 1 through 5, as shown in figure 20.116. Children 3 and 5 begin by going over 2 and 4, who roll under. Child 1 goes over child 3 as soon as possible. Each child then continues to go alternately over and under.

FIGURE 20.116   Quintuplet Roll.

Dead Person Lift

One child lies facing the ceiling, with body stiff and arms at the sides. Two helpers stand, one on each side of the "dead" person, with hands at the back of the neck and fingers touching. Working together, they lift the child, who remains rigid, to a standing position (figure 20.117). From this position, the child is released and falls forward in a Dead Body Fall.

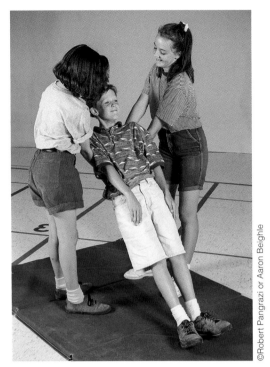

FIGURE 20.117   Dead Person Lift.

Injured Person Carry

The "injured" child lies on the back. Six children, three on each side, kneel down to do the carry. The lifters slide their hands, palms up, under the person to form a human stretcher and then lift up (figure 20.118). (The injured child must maintain a stiff position.) The lifters walk a short distance and set the child down carefully.

FIGURE 20.118   Injured Person Carry.

Merry-Go-Round

From 8 to 12 children are needed. Half of the children form a circle with joined hands, using a wrist grip. The other children, the riders, stand within the circle and each one leans back against a pair of joined hands. The riders stretch out their bodies, faces up, toward the center of the circle, with the weight on the heels. Each rider then connects hands, behind the circle of standing children, with the riders on either side. There are two sets of joined hands—the first circle, or merry-go-round, and the riders (figure 20.119). The Merry-Go-Round moves counterclockwise. The support children use sidesteps. The riders keep pace, taking small steps with their heels.

FIGURE 20.119   Merry-Go-Round.

Partner Support Stunts

Teachers should review instructional procedures that ensure safety and proper class organization for partner support stunts.

Front Sit

The support gets down in the same position as for the Back Layout. The top child straddles the support, facing him. The top child backs up to sit on the support's feet. As the support raises the top child into a seated position, the top child extends the legs forward so the support can reach up and grasp him to stabilize the seated position (figure 20.120). (Spotting should be done from behind.)

FIGURE 20.120   Front Sit.

Flying Dutchman

The top child takes a position facing the support, grasping the support's hands while bending over the support's feet. The support then raises the top child from the floor by extending the knees. The top child arches the back and can then release the grip and put the arms out level to the sides in a flying position (figure 20.121). A little experimentation determines the best place for the foot support. (Spotting should be available for getting into position and for safety.)

FIGURE 20.121   Flying Dutchman.

All-Fours Support

The bottom child lies on the back with legs apart, the knees up, and the hands close to the shoulders with palms up. The top child stands on the support's palms and leans

forward, placing the hands on the support's knees. The support raises the top child by lifting with the arms. The top child is then in an all-fours position, with feet supported by the bottom child's extended arms and hands supported by the bottom child's knees (figure 20.122).

FIGURE 20.122   All-Fours Support.

Angel

The top child stands in front of the support partner. Both face the same direction. The support squats down, placing the head between the top child's legs. The support rises, so that the top child is sitting on the support's shoulders. The top child then takes a position with the feet on the support's knees. The support must lean well back for balance, removing the head from between the top child's legs. The top performer stands erect on the support's knees, holding arms out to the side and level. The support takes hold of the top child's thighs and leans back to place the pose in balance (figure 20.123). They hold for five seconds. (Children need to experiment to determine the best way to achieve the final position.)

FIGURE 20.123   Angel.

20

Side Stand

The support partner gets onto the hands and knees to form a rigid base. The top child stands to the side, bends over the support's back, and hooks the hands, palms up, well underneath the support's chest and waist. The top child leans across, steadying with the hands, and kicks up to an inverted stand (figure 20.124). (Spotters are needed on the far side.)

Variation: The top child, instead of hooking hands underneath, grasps the bottom performer's arm and leg.

FIGURE 20.124 Side Stand.

©Robert Pangrazi or Aaron Beighle

Pyramids

Children enjoy making pyramids, which use skills learned in the gymnastics program. Pyramids promote creativity, because children can make a variety of figures. These activities focus on pyramid groups of three or fewer (figure 20.125); larger groups are not recommended at this developmental level. To decrease potential for accidents, have students practice stunts using only one performer or pair before trying to make pyramids with three students.

FIGURE 20.125 Pyramid formation.

Pearson Education

Developing Gymnastics Routines

Teachers can design sequences of stunts and other movements and present them as movement problems. The problems might be structured as follows.

1. Specify the number and kind of stunts and movements to be done and the sequence to be followed. For example, tell the child to do a balance stunt, a locomotor movement, and a rolling stunt.

2. Arrange the mats in some prescribed order to provide the key to the movement problems. For example, place two or three mats in succession, three or four in a U shape, or four in a hollow square. Leave some space between mats, depending on the problem. You could present the problem like this: "On the first mat, do a Forward Roll variation and then a movement to the next mat on all fours. On the second mat, do some kind of balance stunt and then proceed to the next mat with a jumping or hopping movement. On the third mat, you choose the activity." You can also state the problem in more general terms, and children can do a different stunt or variation on each mat and a different movement between mats.

3. Have partners design a series of stunts. Ensure that paired children are of equal size and strength, so that they can alternate as the support. If children are of different sizes, the larger child can provide support for the smaller, and a third child may act as a spotter. After practicing for a while, each pair demonstrates the routines they have created.

LEARNING AIDS

WEBSITES

USA Gymnastics, www.usa-gymnastics.org

SUGGESTED READINGS

Broomfield, L. (2011). *Complete guide to primary gymnastics.* Champaign, IL: Human Kinetics.

Redhead, L. (2016). *Coaching youth gymnastics: An essential guide for coaches, parents, and teachers* (Kindle ed.). Ramsbury, Marlborough, United Kingdom: Crowood Press.

USA Gymnastics. (2011). *Coaching youth gymnastics ebook.* Champaign, IL: Human Kinetics.

Werner, P.H., Williams, L., & Hall, T. (2012). *Teaching children gymnastics* (3rd ed.). Champaign, IL: Human Kinetics.

Cooperative Skills

Cooperative activities teach students to work together for their group's common good. By participating in these activities, students can learn the skills of listening, discussing, thinking as a group, group decision making, and sacrificing individual wants for the common good. The activities also offer students unique, rewarding challenges. The parachute activities in this chapter require an entire class to work together to accomplish desired outcomes with the parachute. Students have many opportunities to learn cooperative skills while using the parachute to perform various fundamental motor and fitness skills.

Learning Objectives

- ▶ Understand the role of cooperative activities in physical education.
- ▶ Understand the steps involved in teaching cooperative activities.
- ▶ Communicate the importance of questioning and discussion following cooperative activities.
- ▶ Describe several group challenges appropriate for elementary school children.
- ▶ Discuss various parachute activities and explain their role as cooperative activities.

Role of Cooperative Activities

Terms such as *team building, cooperative learning, cooperative,* and *adventure education* are used interchangeably to describe a variety of activities. Each term has subtle differences, but when applied in elementary physical education, most of them focus primarily on teaching cooperation. This chapter uses the term *cooperative activities* to describe such activities.

Two primary objectives guide the teaching of cooperative activities. First, cooperative activities allow students to apply a variety of fundamental motor skills in a unique setting. Students are typically asked to perform motor skills in a specific way, such as "skip in general space" or "balance on one foot and one elbow." Rarely are students asked to skip with their hands on the shoulders of someone in front of them, or walk with big steps while placing their feet on small spots, or walk across an area blindfolded while someone directs their moves. Because of the uniqueness of such experiences, students find cooperative activities exciting and thus enjoyable.

Second, cooperative activities are a wonderful medium for teaching social and emotional learning (SEL). SEL is a process where students can learn to understand and manage their emotions. In addition, such activities offer an opportunity to show empathy for others and develop positive relationships. Cooperative activities demand that all students play a role in completing the task or solving the movement problem. Every student is important and contributes to group goals.

Cooperation requires students to manage their personal needs, be aware of how others feel, and develop social awareness, which is certainly emotional intelligence at its best. An example of integrating SEL into instruction can be exemplified in a simple parachute activity. The first-grade class is challenged to get a tennis ball to fall through the hole in the center of the chute. After trying many different approaches, the class decides to have everyone raise the chute above their heads and watch the ball fall through the hole. Barbara would rather make waves with the chute by her waist. But when she does that, the ball rolls to her and not into the hole. Managing her personal needs and thinking of others would require her to raise her hands above her head and help the class make the ball fall through the chute.

Cooperative activities also teach other social skills. In many classes, students become members of cliques and rarely interact with other students, even in their own class. Effectively implemented cooperative activities teach all students to work together. By working together, students learn that all students are important, that everyone has similarities and differences, and that all students can contribute to the group's effort to accomplish a common goal. Obvious roles include leader and follower, but other student roles, such as being responsible for organizing a plan, keeping the group focused, and remembering specific rules, will emerge. Note that the teacher will likely have to point out and teach these roles. With their varied roles and unique tasks, most cooperative activities allow all students to contribute and experience success. This outcome is especially helpful for less physically skilled students, who often benefit greatly from enhanced self-confidence. In summary, cooperative activities teach social skills, such as teamwork, communication, decision making, and conflict resolution, while using fundamental motor skills in unique situations.

Teaching Cooperative Activities

A common misconception is that teaching cooperative activities and skills simply means providing students with the appropriate activities. In fact, presenting the activities without adequately introducing and summarizing them can do more harm than good. Without a series of concluding questions or effective teacher monitoring, negative outcomes may emerge. The usual role of quiet, less skilled students—"stay in the back and don't be embarrassed"—may be reinforced as dominant students continue to control the activities while learning nothing about group dynamics and cooperation. Explaining what cooperative skills the group will be using before the activity can also limit its effectiveness. By doing so, you may cause students to begin focusing on specific skills, preventing them from learning other skills that may present themselves. Students who are told that the activity requires them to communicate will focus on listening and talking but may lose sight of the different roles that other students are assuming to help accomplish the goal. Similarly, telling the group what they learned after the cooperative activity may diminish its effectiveness. For example, after students have participated in an activity that requires discussion about methods of accomplishing a task, the teacher says, "In that activity you had to think and then explain your ideas to your teammates. That is communication, which is important in cooperation." But one student may have figured out that he or she had to listen more or that he or she did not explain clearly. As with all education, remember that all children are individuals who approach challenges differently. To encourage individuality and maximize the effectiveness of cooperative activities in teaching cooperative skills, teachers can use the following steps.

Steps to Teaching Cooperative Activities

1. *Set the stage.* The teacher's job is to sell the activity by giving students the following information:

   What is the challenge?

   What are the rules?

   What are the consequences for breaking the rules?

   Do any safety issues need to be addressed?

   During this step, provide only the information needed to get the group going. This information is best presented in the form of a descriptive and often imaginary story. For example, rather than framing a challenge as getting the entire group to go through a hoop hanging from a basketball basket, place the students in an imaginary jungle where they find a time-traveling cell. They are lost and their only way out of the jungle is to get everyone in the group through the cell. But when anyone touches the cell, it pushes out everyone who is already through and they have to start over. These types of stories pique students' interest and help them exercise imagination and creativity.

2. *Facilitate.* After setting the stage, the teacher must step back and let the students work. Many teachers find this step difficult because they want to tell students how to accomplish the task or at least give them a few hints. But the best approach is simply to answer questions and monitor the group's safety. Often, time may run out before the class has time to complete the challenge. In cooperative activities, success does not always mean accomplishing the task; learning to cooperate is more important. Much can be learned and gained from simply working on the task. But teachers must allow time for the final step—debriefing.

3. *Debrief.* This may be the most important step in effectively implementing cooperative activities. So far during the activity, little has been said about cooperation. This step of the cooperative activity process allows students to share their experiences and gives teachers the opportunity to meet their own objectives (e.g., to discuss listening) and to connect what was learned to daily living.

   The foundation of debriefing is open-ended questions. Questions like "Did that work?" or "Would you do that again?" require a yes or no response and do not foster discussion. Here are some examples of open-ended questions:

   What did you have to do to accomplish the goal?

   What does communicate mean?

   What happened that was positive?

   What happened that could have been better?

   How could you have changed things?

   What does it mean to be patient?

   How can you compromise?

   What would you have done differently? The same?

   An important part of the debriefing is discussing how students can use the skills learned in the activity outside PE class. Again, open-ended questions—"When would you have to be patient outside of PE?" or "How would good communication skills help you at home?"—are helpful in discussing these ideas.

Group Challenges

Group challenges are designed to place students in a unique situation that requires some form of cooperation. The activities and rules are created in such a way that students cannot complete the tasks alone; they must cooperate. Many of these activities are most effective with small groups and can be taught in one of three ways:

1. The entire class works on the same task or activity, such as Pig Ball.

2. All groups work independently on the same task. For example, groups A and B can work on Group Juggling in separate areas. Teachers using this approach must ensure that the activities do not become races, which is best accomplished by downplaying speed and stressing cooperation. When a team accomplishes a task, challenge them with another.

3. Teach through stations and provide one station per team. Each team reports to a station and begins the challenge by reading the task card. Task cards allow teachers to integrate reading into physical education without sacrificing physical education time.

21

Group challenges in this chapter are designed for Developmental Levels II and III. In Developmental Level I, students learn basic cooperative skills—sharing, listening, and individual or partner decision making—throughout the curriculum. These skills are further taught and reinforced throughout the curriculum for older students. The following cooperative activities specifically focus on basic as well as more advanced cooperative skills such as group decision making and group communication.

Lifeboats

Formation: groups of 8 to 12 students

Supplies: two to three individual mats or hoops, two scooters, and one long jump rope per group

Teams stand on one side of the gym (a slowly sinking ship). Each team has a scooter (lifeboat) and a long jump rope. The objective is to get the entire team from the sinking ship to the mainland (the other side of the gym) using only the lifeboat (figure 21.1). Spaced randomly between the ship and mainland are three individual mats or hoops (islands in the ocean). Any students who touch the gym floor (water) must return to the starting point or island they were on (if hoops are used as islands, inside the hoop counts as land). All students must stay on a mat at all times unless they are traveling across the ocean in a lifeboat (scooter). Students may be pulled while holding the jump rope and sitting on the scooter. They may not be pushed and the rope cannot be tied to the scooter. Students

who reach the mainland must stay there; they cannot return to the island or lifeboats. But if they step into the water when trying to rescue a teammate, they must return to the final island.

Mat Folding

Formation: groups of four to five students

Supplies: one tumbling mat for each group

Give each team one tumbling mat and instruct them to stand on it. While keeping their feet on the mat at all times, teams work on the following challenges:

1. Rotate the mat 360 degrees.
2. Move the mat 15 feet (5 m).
3. Without using any hands, fold the mat into fourths.
4. Unfold the mat without using any hands.

Attached at the . . .

Formation: partners

Supplies: one beanbag or ball for each set of partners

Partners stand on one side of the activity area. Challenge them to get to the other sideline or endline while attached at the hip, back, ankle, elbow, hamstring, and so on. Locomotor movements can be specified for moving across the area. For a more difficult activity, instruct the students to hold a beanbag or ball between the "attached" body parts.

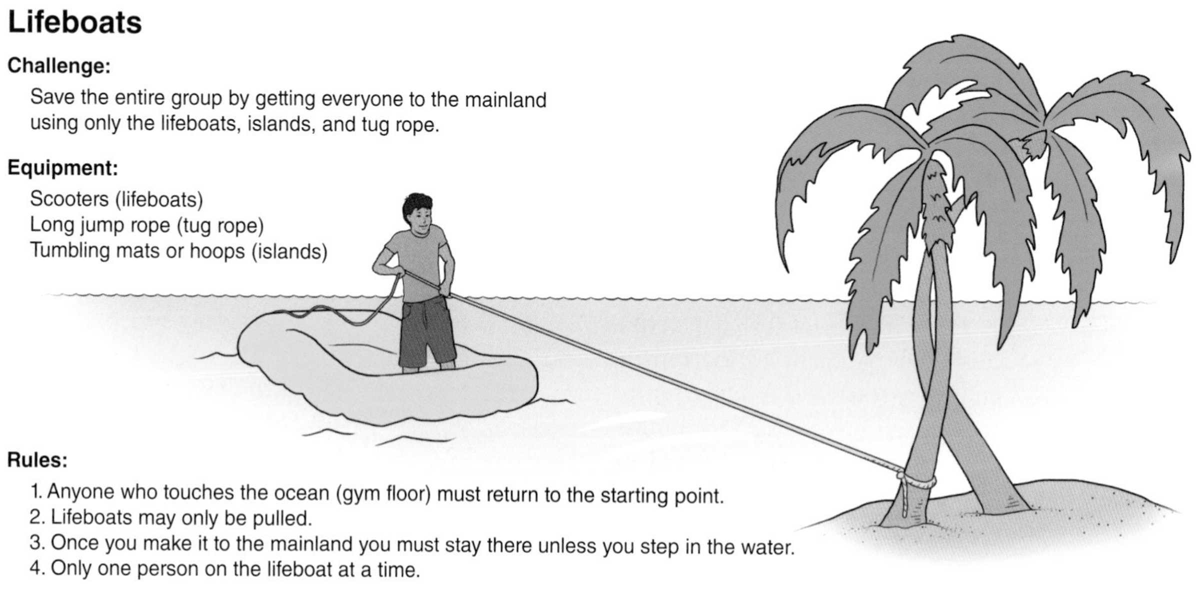

Lifeboats

Challenge:
Save the entire group by getting everyone to the mainland using only the lifeboats, islands, and tug rope.

Equipment:
Scooters (lifeboats)
Long jump rope (tug rope)
Tumbling mats or hoops (islands)

Rules:
1. Anyone who touches the ocean (gym floor) must return to the starting point.
2. Lifeboats may only be pulled.
3. Once you make it to the mainland you must stay there unless you step in the water.
4. Only one person on the lifeboat at a time.

FIGURE 21.1 Task card for Lifeboats.

Variation: To add difficulty after students complete partner tasks, challenge them to work in groups of three, four, or more.

Moving Together

Formation: groups of four students

Supplies: none

Teams stand on the sidelines of the teaching area. The objective is for the team to move to the other sideline with the following stipulations:

1. Six feet touching the floor and all team members touching an ankle.
2. Eight body parts (no heads) touching the ground at all times.
3. Half the team at a high level and half the team at a low level.
4. Every foot touching one other foot.
5. Only four feet can touch the ground.
6. Four feet and one hand must be on the ground.
7. Move with the fewest number of feet possible touching the floor.
8. Move with the largest number of hands and fewest number of feet touching the floor.

Variations: Pose additional challenges by having the teams carry different pieces of equipment while attempting the challenges. To minimize competition and ensure continuous activity, give each team its own list of challenges. After completing a challenge, teams choose a new challenge from their list.

Balance Beam Mixer

Formation: groups of 8 to 10 students

Supplies: one low balance beam or bench per group

Students stand shoulder-to-shoulder on a low balance beam or bench (for younger students) with mats alongside the beam for safety (figure 21.2). Challenge groups, while remaining on the balance beam or bench, to get in order based on these criteria:

1. Alphabetical order by first name from left to right
2. Alphabetical order by first name from right to left
3. Tallest to shortest
4. Month of birth date (January to December or vice versa)

FIGURE 21.2 Balance Beam Mixer.

Pearson Education

Quiet Cooperation

Formation: groups of 10 to 12 students

Supplies: one marking spot for each student

Students stand in a line, shoulder-to-shoulder, with a marking spot under their feet. Without talking, making any noise, or touching the gym floor, students get in order using these criteria:

1. Number of pets (fewest to most)
2. Alphabetical by first name (or father's, mother's, or pet's name)
3. Alphabetical by last name
4. Month of birthday (January to December or vice versa)
5. Shortest to tallest

All Aboard

Formation: entire class scattered; hoops spread throughout area

Supplies: 15 hoops

Challenge students to get as many students as possible into one hoop placed on the ground. A person is considered "on board" when one foot touches the ground inside the hoop and no body parts touch the floor outside the hoop.

A lead-up to All Aboard is to play musical hoops Scatter hoops throughout the gym and play some music. When the music stops, students move to a hoop, placing at least one foot inside the hoop. More than one student can be in a hoop. Each time the music plays, the teacher removes one or two hoops until only enough hoops remain for all students to be aboard.

Human Spelling Bee

Formation: groups of five to six students

Supplies: none

21

Challenge teams to spell out words, letter by letter, with their bodies while lying on the floor. All team members must be in the letter, and the team's result must differentiate between the top and bottom of the letter.

Moving the World

Formation: entire class, scattered throughout area

Supplies: one large cageball

Using a cageball or other large ball as the world, challenge the class to move the world to different locations in the gym. The ball may not be kicked, thrown, or struck, and all class members must be involved:

1. No hands can touch the ball.
2. Only feet can touch the ball.
3. Half of the team must be lying on their backs.
4. Only backs can touch the ball.
5. Only elbows can touch the ball, and no talking is allowed (figure 21.3).
6. Students must crabwalk.

Variation: Use directions such as "move the ball 30 feet (10 m) northwest" or "move the world 25 feet (8 m) in the same direction you would travel from Arcanum to New Madison."

FIGURE 21.3 Moving the World.

Group Juggling

Formation: groups of five to six students

Supplies: one ball or beanbag for each student

Each student in every team has a ball or beanbag. Using a variety of balls makes this activity more exciting. On signal (e.g., "1, 2, ready, toss"), each team mem-

ber tosses his or her ball to another teammate and then catches a ball tossed to him (figure 21.4). The goal is to see how many successful tosses can be made in unison. Often, students will toss to the same person each time. A successful juggle occurs when all team members catch the ball tossed to them. After several tosses, the teacher gives each team the responsibility of selecting one member to give the signal for their team.

FIGURE 21.4 Group Juggling.

Stranded

Formation: groups of five to six students

Supplies: one tumbling mat, three hoops (or volleyball standards), two scooters, and one long jump rope per team

In this challenge, all team members must get from a capsized but floating boat (represented by a tumbling mat), across the river via three islands, and onto the shore (a line on the opposite side of the area). Islands (the hoops) are about 15 feet (5 m) apart, and one team member is placed on each island. These students' other team members are on the boats. The students on the boat have two scooters and a 16- to 20-foot-long (5 to 6 m) jump rope. While on the scooters, students may not be pushed by other students or pulled using the rope; they must find a way to move without touching the "water." The rope may not be tied to the scooter. Any student touching the water must return to the boat.

Scoop Ball

Formation: groups of six to eight students

Supplies: four basketballs, one hoop, four tinikling poles (or 10- to 15-foot [3 to 5 m] sections of PVC pipe), and two scoops for every team

Using tinikling poles and scoops, the teams try to move four basketballs about 50 feet (15 m). Without touching the basketballs with any body parts, they must place the balls into a hoop. The following rules apply:

1. If a ball touches the floor or a student, the ball must be returned to the starting point.
2. Players may not walk with the balls.
3. The balls may not be thrown, kicked, or passed.
4. Balls that roll or bounce out of the hoop must be returned to the starting point.
5. Students are permitted to hold only one scoop at a time.

Centipede

Formation: entire class, shoulder-to-shoulder

Supplies: none

All students stand on a sideline, facing the same direction, with feet touching the person next to them. The entire class must move to the other sideline without breaking the chain of touching feet. If the chain breaks, the class must take three steps back. Students may put their arms around each other if desired. Some classes may require a progression starting with partners, then small groups, and finally the entire class.

Flippers

Formation: entire class, divided into two teams

Supplies: 30 to 40 flying disks

Spread the flying disks throughout the teaching area. Instruct one team to flip the disks faceup; instruct the other team to flip the disks facedown. After a practice game, add the following stipulations.

1. No hands
2. Feet only
3. Students must crab walk or bear crawl
4. Feet only, and only one foot can touch the disk at a time
5. Knees only
6. Heel only

Circle Up

Formation: groups of six to eight students in circle formation

Supplies: three or four hoops per group

Students in each team join hands or wrists to close the circle. Two students release hands, and the teacher places a hoop between them. The students then rejoin hands inside the hoop. Without releasing hands, teams must pass the hoop around the circle. That is, each student must pass through the hoop without letting go of their neighbors' hands. After the students get the hang of going through the hoop, add more hoops. If a slightly smaller hoop is available, have team members pass it in the opposite direction.

When teaching Circle Up, give teams one or two hoops and time them to see how fast they can pass the hoop around the circle. After letting the teams briefly discuss how to move the hoop faster, challenge them to beat their own record. Emphasize that the activity is group challenge, not a race against other groups.

Is It Raining?

Formation: entire class in a circle

Supplies: none

This activity works well at the end of a vigorous lesson. Standing in the circle, the teacher initiates a movement that makes a sound; then the child immediately to his or her right imitates the movement, and so on, like a wave at a stadium sporting event. When the "wave" gets back to the teacher, another movement is started. The students keep making the previous sound until the next one gets around to them. The movements can be any sounds that mimic those heard in nature during a storm:

- Clapping
- Snapping
- Patting quadriceps
- Stamping
- Patting the chest
- Rubbing the hands on the legs
- Rubbing the hands together
- Clucking the tongue
- Making hollow whistles
- Making "shhhhh" sounds

Variations:

1. Allow students to create movements and lead the changes.
2. Instruct students to close their eyes and rely on their hearing to listen for the sound to come around while trying to figure out what the new movement is.

21

Be Careful

Formation: groups of six to eight students

Supplies: for each group of eight students: 4 blindfolds, 10 beanbags, 10 yarn balls, 8 poly spots, 8 cones, and 3 jump ropes

Mark off a 10-by-10-foot (3 by 3 m) area with four cones. Next, scatter the beanbags, yarn balls, poly spots, jump ropes, and remaining cones inside the area so that no straight paths lead from any one side to another. In partners, students decide who will be the walker and who will be the driver. Roles will be reversed later. The walker is blindfolded and tries to get from one side of the area to the opposite side without touching any of the equipment. The driver stands on the opposite side giving directions such as, "Walk forward" to the walker (figure 21.5). Thus, the walker must trust the driver and follow strict directions. The team gets 1 point for each piece of equipment that the walker touches. The goal is to get to the other side with no points. As students experiment with the activity, directions will become more specific.

FIGURE 21.5 Be Careful.

Pearson Education

Variation: For an advanced activity, start one walker on each side of the square and add 1 point for each walker who is touched. To motivate each set of partners to move faster, allow them to time how long it takes to cross. Then multiply the number of items touched by 10 and add their time in seconds. For example, if a team touches two items and takes 30 seconds to cross, their score is $2 \times 10 + 30 = 50$. These partners would then attempt to cross and achieve a better score.

Zap

Formation: groups of 4 to 10 students

Supplies: one tumbling mat, one magic rope or jump rope, two volleyball standards or device to attach the ropes

Attach the rope on either side of the mat, about 3 to 4 feet (90 to 120 cm) off the ground (height depends on the children's age). Challenge students to get their entire team over the rope and to the other side without touching, or getting "zapped" by, the rope. To enhance the challenge and keep it safe, do not permit students to jump over the rope. In addition, to start, each team forms a circle and joins hands to form a "closed chain." This chain must remain closed throughout the challenge. If anyone is zapped by the rope or the chain is broken (two people release hands), the entire team must go back to the other side and start over.

Keep It Floating

Formation: groups of four to eight students

Supplies: for each group, two balloons, one beach ball, and one hoop for every two students

Students form a circle and join hands. Their challenge is to keep a balloon up for as many hits as possible without releasing hands (figure 21.6). After a few rounds, add another balloon to increase the difficulty. Finally, add a beach ball and one balloon.

Variation: For advanced classes, place one hoop between each team. Team members must keep one foot in each hoop on either side of them. This advanced challenge is best with only one balloon. To integrate other academic content, have the teams do the following while participating in the basic challenge:

1. State a different fruit or vegetable with each hit.
2. Count in a foreign language.
3. Count by twos, threes, fours, and so on.
4. Try to strike the balloon with a different bone or muscle each time and call out the name of that body part.
5. Call out a different lifetime activity with each hit.

FIGURE 21.6 Keep it Floating

Pearson Education

Shoe Tying

Formation: partners

Supplies: shoes with shoelaces

This activity is good for the end of a highly active lesson. Partners sit side by side, and one of them unties one shoe. Each partner then puts one hand behind his or her back. Using the two remaining hands cooperatively, the partners must then tie the shoe. After tying the shoe, the partners must try using the other hand. Finally, still using only one hand each, have them try to tie the shoe with their eyes closed.

Students tie their shoes in several different ways. For this reason, some partners may become frustrated simply because their method of tying shoes is different. This teachable moment is good for dealing with frustration, learning the importance of communication, and personal differences, even with shoe tying.

Pig Ball

Formation: two equal teams

Supplies: a rubber pig (or, if not available, a deflated playground ball)

This activity is a continuous version of Alaskan Baseball. Team A stands in single file with the last person in line holding the pig. That child starts the game by throwing the pig anywhere in the teaching area (the teacher marks this area). Team B then hustles to the pig and stands in single file behind the first child to reach the pig. When the entire team is in line, they hand the pig to the back of the line, alternating between passing it overhead and between the legs. This part is best described as "over and under, over and under." While team B is

doing this, the child who threw the pig hustles around his or her team, which is still in single file. Each time the student passes an end of the line, his or her team scores 1 point. This part allows all children to score at least 1 point for their team. When the pig gets to the last child on team B, the team yells, "Pig!" and that child throws the pig anywhere in the teaching area. The child who threw the pig then begins running around his or her teammates, who stay in single file. At the same time, team A hustles to the pig and begins the over-and-under passing. The game continues for as long as desired.

Because this game is rigorous, stop after three to four rounds and give students some type of instruction. You might talk about cardiovascular health and why the heart is beating faster, why Pig Ball is cooperative, or what strategy they might use for the game. Soon, however, students will be ready to resume play. This time, have all students use a specific locomotor movement or animal movement when running around their teammates.

Pretzel

Formation: groups of 6 to 10 students

Supplies: none

Students stand shoulder-to-shoulder in a circle with arms extended in front. Each student must grasp two other hands, one in each hand. The hands that each student grasps cannot be of the same child, and they cannot be of the child beside them. The team must then undo the pretzel they have just created and form a circle—without releasing hands. After the pretzel unravels, some children may be facing toward the center and some away from the center. Figure 21.7 is a task card for a Pretzel station.

FIGURE 21.7 Task card for the Pretzel.

Pretzel

Challenge:

Untangle the group pretzel you create to form a circle, with each person standing next to the person they are holding hands with.

Directions:
1. Make a circle standing shoulder-to-shoulder.
2. Put your hands in the middle.
3. Join hands with two different people.
4. You may not join hands with the person next to you.

Rules:

Hands must stay together.

21

Who's Leading?

Formation: entire class in a circle

Supplies: none

The entire class stands shoulder-to-shoulder in a circle. One student volunteers to go into the middle and cover his or her eyes. The teacher then selects a volunteer to lead the class in movements while remaining in the circle. This choice must be made quietly so that the child in the middle does not know who the leader is. The teacher suggests some movements to the leader (jogging or skipping in place, biceps curls, jumping jacks, and so on) and instructs the leader to change activities every few seconds. The child in the middle then opens his or her eyes and watches the movements. The student must stay in the middle but may scan the entire class in an effort to find the leader as he or she changes movements.

Variations:

1. To add difficulty, encourage the leader to make small changes in movements. For example, start with normal jumping jacks, move to skier jacks, then to skiers with no arm movements, and finally to walking in place.

2. Suggest that the guesser watch only half of the circle. If the activity changes and the child in the middle does not see anyone do it first, the leader is probably in the other half of the circle. Remind followers not to give the leader away by staring at him or her.

How Are We Alike?

Formation: partners

Supplies: none

This activity is good for the physical education orientation held at the beginning of the school year, when students are getting to know each other and the teacher. Students join with a partner and discuss, "How are we alike?" The teacher provides a few categories—such as appearance, family, favorite activities, and birthdays—and then lets students talk. Before grouping students with a different partner or a group of four to repeat the activity, allow volunteers to share their findings.

After "How are we alike?" have students find out "How are we different?" This activity sets the tone for a physical education setting in which children understand that we all have similarities and differences, and that is OK. Students need to understand early on that respecting similarities and differences is crucial to working with others.

Lily Pads

Formation: groups of 6 to 15 students

Supplies: one poly spot per child

Students begin by standing on their poly spots, or lily pads, in a straight line. The lily pads are about 12 inches (30 cm) apart. The team's challenge is to reverse their order so that the two students on the end switch places, the second to last switch places, and so on (see visual explanation). The catch is that each team member must have at least one foot on a lily pad at all times. If this rule is broken, the team must start over in the original order. If poly spots are not available, use a line or a long piece of tape for this activity. Simply make the rule that all team members must keep one foot on the tape at all times.

Start	Finish
1 2 3 4 5 6 7 8	8 7 6 5 4 3 2 1

The Cell

Formation: groups of five to six students

Supplies: one tumbling mat and one hoop suspended from a basketball hoop, about 2 to 4 feet (30 to 60 cm) above the mat at its lowest point

Students are charged with the task of getting everyone on the team through the hoop, or cell. No team member may touch the hoop. Jumping through the hoop is not allowed. Students may step through, or the group may "hand" team members through.

Variation: The height of the hoop determines the difficulty of the challenge. For an additional challenge, require all team members to hold hands throughout the activity.

Dot Bridge

Formation: groups of five to six students

Supplies: one poly spot per player plus one additional poly spot

The challenge is for students to get from one side of the "river" (teaching area) to the other, but they cannot touch the "water" (the floor). The only tools they have are their floating dots (the poly spots). If anyone touches the water, the entire team must start over.

Variations: To add difficulty and prevent teams from moving straight across, place hazards (hoops, cones, and so on) that the students must avoid throughout the river. Also, add the rule that if at any time a dot is not being touched, it sinks and can no longer be used.

Activities With Parachutes

Children of all ages enjoy parachute play, and at the same time they learn a variety of skills, including cooperation skills. Unless all students work together, many of the tasks are difficult to accomplish. Activities must be selected carefully for younger children, because some of the skills required are difficult for them. One parachute about 24 to 32 feet (7 to 10 m) in diameter is generally suitable for a class of 30 children. Each parachute has an opening near the top to allow trapped air to escape and to keep the parachute shaped properly. Most parachutes are constructed of nylon. A parachute should stretch tight and not sag in the middle when pulled on by children spaced around it. One that sags has limited usefulness.

Values of Parachute Play

For most adults and children, parachute activities rank high on the scale of all-time enjoyable physical education activities. Besides being enjoyable, parachute play holds many educational opportunities. Students learn movement concepts and practice fundamental motor skills in a unique context. Teachers can incorporate and reinforce levels of movement, speed, weight transfer, force, direction, balancing, pulling, bending, twisting, and all locomotor movements. Parachute play is effective in teaching cooperation. The success and enjoyment gained from many parachute activities depend on group and individual cooperation.

Grips

Students can handle the parachute with grips similar to those used in hanging activities on an apparatus. Grips can be with one or two hands, overhand (palms facing down), underhand (palms facing upward), or mixed (one hand underhand and the other overhand). Design activities requiring students to use various grips.

Instructional Procedures

1. Carefully explain the terms relating to parachute activity. Define words such as *inflate*, *deflate*, *float*, *dome*, and *mushroom* the first time the terms are used.

2. For preliminary explanations, spread out the parachute on the ground in its circular pattern and provide brief, yet concise instructions. Have the children sit around the parachute, just far enough away so that they cannot touch it. Allow students to hold the parachute during later explanations, but instruct them to hold it lightly, letting the center drop to the ground. Teach children to exercise control and not to manipulate the parachute while listening to explanations.

3. Explain the activity, demonstrating as needed. Start the activity with a command such as "Ready—begin!"

4. Teams are useful for competitive units in game activity. During parachute activities use parachute colors to generate teams.

This section presents activities by type, along with variations and tips for supplementary activities. Unless otherwise specified, activities begin and halt on signal. Children's suggestions can broaden the scope of activity.

Exercise Activities

Exercises are done vigorously and with enough repetitions to challenge the children. Teachers also can adapt other exercises to parachute play.

Toe Toucher

Sit with feet extended under the parachute and hold the chute taut with a two-hand grip, drawing it up to the chin. Bend forward and touch the grip to the toes. Return the parachute to stretched position.

Abdominal Curl-Up (Good Morning and Good Night)

Extend the body in supine position under the parachute in curl-up position, so that the chute comes up to the chin when held taut. Do curl-ups, returning each time to the stretched chute position. Students say, "Good morning!" when rising to the sitting position and "Good night!" when returning to the supine position.

Dorsal Lift

Lie prone, with head toward the parachute and feet pointed back, away from it. Grip the chute and slide it toward the feet until there is some tension on the chute. Raise the chute off the ground with a vigorous lift of the arms, until head and chest rise off the ground. Return.

V-Sit

Lie supine, with head toward the chute. Do V-Sits by raising the upper and lower parts of the body simultaneously into a V-shaped position. Keep the knees straight.

21

Backward Pull

Face the parachute and pull back, away from its center. Pulls can be made from a sitting, kneeling, or standing position.

Other Pulls

With arm flexed, do side pulls with either arm. Devise other variations of pulling.

Hip Walk and Scoot

Begin with the parachute taut. Move forward with the Scoot or Hip Walk. Move back to place with the same movement until the chute is taut again.

Elevator

Begin with the chute taut and at ground level. On the command "Elevator up," lift the chute overhead while keeping it stretched tight. On the command "Elevator down," lower the chute to starting position. Lowering and raising are done quickly or in increments. Levels can also bring in body part identification; have children hold the chute even with their head, nose, chin, shoulders, chest, waist, thighs, knees, ankles, and toes.

Running in Place

Students run in place while holding the chute at different levels.

Isometrics

Hold the chute taut at shoulder level and try to stretch it for 10 seconds. Many other isometric exercises can be performed with the parachute to develop all body parts.

Dome Activities

To make a dome, children begin with the parachute on the floor, holding with two hands and kneeling on one knee. To trap air under the chute, children stand up quickly, thrusting their arms overhead (figure 21.8a), and then return to starting position (figure 21.9b), holding the parachute tight to the ground. Some or all the children can move inside of the chute on the down movement. Try making domes while moving in a circle.

Students Under the Chute

Specify tasks to do under the chute, such as turning a certain number of turns with a jump rope, throwing and catching a beanbag, or bouncing a ball a number of times. Place the needed objects under the chute before making the dome.

©Robert Pangrazi or Aaron Beighle

FIGURE 21.8 (a) Making a dome; (b) holding the air inside a dome.

Number Exchange

Children are numbered from 1 to 4. The teacher calls a number as the dome is made, and those whose number is called must get under the chute before it comes down. Locomotor movements can be varied.

Punching Bag

Children make a dome and stand on the edges. They then punch at the chute while slowly and gently walking the edges of the chute toward the center.

Tidal Wave or Bubble

Students create a dome and then stand on the edges. The teacher then pushes the chute to the left while still standing on the edges. The child to the teacher's left follows and pushes the parachute to the left. Each child then continues pushing the parachute in the same direction immediately after the child before them while keeping his or her feet on the edges. After a few rounds a bubble, or wave, of air will begin quickly circulating around the chute.

Blooming Flower

Children make a dome and kneel with both knees on

the edge of the chute. Students hold hands around the chute and lean in and out to represent a blooming flower opening.

Lights Out

While making a dome, the children take two steps toward the center and sit inside the chute. The chute can be held with the hands at the side or by sitting on it.

Class Picture

After making a dome, students carefully move to their knees and then to their tummies. While lying on their tummies and with the parachute in their hands, students bring their hands to their shoulders. This action leaves only their heads inside the chute.

Mushroom Activities

To form a mushroom, students begin with the chute on the ground, kneeling on one knee and holding with two hands. They stand up quickly, thrusting the arms overhead. Keeping the arms overhead, each child walks forward three or four steps toward the center. Students hold their arms overhead until the chute deflates.

Mushroom Release

All children release the chute at the peak of inflation and either run out from under it or move to the center and sit down. The chute descends over them.

Mushroom Run

Children make a mushroom. After moving into the center, they release the chute and run once around the inside, counterclockwise, back to place.

Activities With Equipment

Ball Circle

Place a basketball or a cageball on the raised chute. Make the ball roll around the chute in a large circle, controlling it by raising or lowering the chute. Try the same with two balls. A beach ball works well too.

Popcorn

Place from 6 to 10 beanbags on the chute. Shake the chute to make the bags rise like corn popping (figure 21.9).

Cageball Elevator

Place a 2-foot (60 cm) cageball on the chute. On signal, the class lifts the chute and makes a mushroom. Just before the chute with the ball on it reaches its apex, stu-

FIGURE 21.9 Popping Popcorn.

©Robert Pangrazi or Aaron Beighle

dents snap the chute to the floor. If the "elevator" works correctly, the cageball rises up to the ceiling.

Team Ball

Divide the class in half and have each team defend half of the chute. Put from two to six balls of any kind on the chute. Teams try to bounce the balls off their opponents' side.

Poison Snake

Divide into two teams. Place from 6 to 10 cotton jump ropes on the chute. Shake the chute and try to get the ropes off (entirely or hanging over) the parachute. Each time a rope touches a team member, 1 point is scored against that team. The lowest scoring team wins.

Circular Dribble

Each child has a ball suitable for dribbling. The object is to run around the chute counterclockwise, holding onto it with the left hand and dribbling with the right hand while retaining control of the ball. As an equalizer for left-handers, try the dribbling clockwise. Students start the dribble first and then, on signal, they start to run. Children who lose a ball must recover it and try to hook on at their original place.

Hole in One

Use four or more plastic Wiffle balls the size of golf balls (half of the balls in one color, half in another color). Divide the class into two teams on opposite sides of the chute. Each team tries to shake the other team's balls into the hole in the center of the chute.

Other Activities

Merry-Go-Round Movements

Merry-Go-Round Movements, in which children rotate the chute while keeping the center hole over the same

21

523

spot, offer many opportunities for locomotor movements, either free or to the beat of a tom-tom. Use fundamental movements, such as walking, running, hopping, skipping, galloping, sliding, draw steps, and grapevine steps. Have students hold the parachute at different levels, using one- or two-handed grips.

Shaking the Rug and Making Waves

Shaking the Rug involves rapid movements of the parachute, either light or heavy. Making Waves involves large movements to send billows of cloth up and down. Waves can be small, medium, or high. Children can make different types of waves by alternating their up-and-down motions or by working in small groups around the chute. These small groups take turns showing what they can do. For a more demanding activity, children can perform locomotor movements while shaking the rug.

Chute Crawl

Half the class, either standing or kneeling, stretches the chute at waist level parallel to the ground. The other children crawl under the chute to the opposite side from their starting position.

Kite Run

The class holds the chute on one side with one hand. The leader points in the direction they are to run while holding the chute aloft like a kite.

Running Number Game

The children around the chute count off by fours; then they run lightly, holding the chute in one hand. The teacher calls out one of the numbers. Children with that number immediately release their grip on the chute and run forward to the next place vacated. They must use a burst of speed to move ahead.

Routines to Music

Like other routines, parachute activities can be adapted to music. Base each sequence on eight counts and design the routine for an appropriate number of sequences.

Tug-of-War

For team tug-of-war, divide the class into halves. On signal, teams pull against each other and try to reach a line located behind them (figure 21.10). Primary-grade children often enjoy pulling individually, in any direction they desire.

FIGURE 21.10 Parachute Tug-of-War.

Action Songs and Dances

Children can perform many action songs, games, and dances while holding onto a parachute. Here are some suggestions: Carousel, Bingo, and Seven Jumps.

LEARNING AIDS

WEBSITES

PE Central cooperative lessons, www.pecentral.org/lessonideas/searchresults.asp?subcategory=cooperative+learning

Project Adventure, www.pa.org

Team-Building Activities

www.corporategames.com
www.teachingideas.co.uk\\pe\\contents.htm

SUGGESTED READINGS

Anderson, L., Midura, D.W., & Glover, D.R. (2020). *Team building through physical challenges* (2nd ed.). Champaign, IL: Human Kinetics.

Hastie, P. (2010). *Student-designed games.* Champaign, IL: Human Kinetics.

Midura, D.W., & Glover, D.R. (2005). *Essentials of team building: Principles and practices.* Champaign, IL: Human Kinetics.

Orlick, T. (2006). *Cooperative games and sports—joyful activities for everyone* (2nd ed.). Champaign, IL: Human Kinetics.

Strong, T., & LeFevre, D. (2006). *Parachute games with DVD* (2nd ed.). Champaign, IL: Human Kinetics.

Game Skills

22

Games are a laboratory where children can apply physical skills in a game setting. Through games, children can experience success and accomplishment. They can develop interpersonal skills, understand rules and limitations, and learn how to behave in various competitive and cooperative situations. Many games help develop large-muscle groups and enhance the child's ability to run, dodge, start, and stop under control while sharing space with others. By applying strategy in games, children learn the importance of alertness and the mental aspect of participation. Eliminate or modify games that involve only a few children, allow some children to dominate, or offer little opportunity for skill development. Offer children the opportunity to create and modify games to meet their needs.

Learning Objectives

▶ Explain various ways to create or modify games.
▶ Understand safety precautions associated with the teaching of games.
▶ Cite various ways to teach games effectively.
▶ Identify games that offer maximum participation and many opportunities to develop skills.
▶ List games that can be explained and implemented quickly.
▶ Classify various games according to developmental levels.

As an important part of the physical education program, games must be scrutinized and evaluated based on what they offer children. Many traditional games can be modified to make a meaningful contribution to the program. Offering students a chance to create and modify games helps them understand that game components can be changed to improve the play experience for all.

Evaluating Games

Factors affecting the worth of games include the physical skills required, number of participants, complexity of rules, and amount of strategy involved. Game skills are best learned in a practice setting where the outcome of the game is not a high priority. Children may be able to throw with proper form, but throwing accurately in a game setting is different. They may be able to hit a stationary object but not a moving target.

Students also have to learn how to cooperate with teammates and compete against peers. The greater the number of teammates and competitors is, the more difficult the game becomes. Cooperating with teammates is just as difficult as competing in a meaningful way. Moving from partners to a small group to team games is a natural progression and a formula for success. Many games are more effective when played in small groups because the players handle objects more often and get more chances to contribute actively.

The rules and strategies for a game increase its difficulty. Developmental Level I children find it difficult (and uninteresting) to play a game that has many rules. If cognitive strategy is required, students must have overlearned the required physical skills previously so that they can concentrate on the mental aspects of the game rather than the skills. Elementary school children cannot concentrate on skill performance and strategy simultaneously. Complex games require team members to play specific roles, some of which (i.e., goalkeeper or line positions) may not appeal to many children. In contrast, many of the more popular games are spontaneous and demand little concentration on strategy.

Games require a combination of skills. Games that call for children to sequence many skills may result in failure or frustration for many. Lead-up games are developed expressly to limit the number of skills needed to participate successfully. Evaluate the skills required and build a progression of games that gradually increases the use of skill combinations.

Be sure that children find games to be a positive experience. The younger the children are, the less willing they are to wait for the outcome; feedback must be immediate. Children become bored and tire of playing long games. Fatigue is also a factor in children's interest level; watch carefully for such signs.

Creating or Modifying Games

Students, working with your help or individually, can modify games and create new variations. For example, after noticing that a specific game is not meeting the desired objectives, you may decide to modify or change it to facilitate skill development. Stop the class and ask them to think of a way to make the game better. Students can suggest alternatives and then test the newly created activity to see if it is more effective. With Developmental Level II and III students, you can offer some parameters for developing a game and then give the class time to create and test the activity. Establish ground rules that facilitate group dynamics. For example, suggest voting on a rule change or specify a maximum number of changes allowed per period.

To make meaningful modifications, you and your students must understand how to analyze a game. The most recognized elements of game structure are desired outcomes, skills, equipment, rules or restrictions, number of players, and scheme of organization. Stiehl, Morris, and Sinclair's (2008) approach to game analysis may be helpful if you are interested in modifying games. Students need to learn how and what to modify, and they need to practice the process. Here are some suggestions to start children thinking:

1. Change the distance to be run. For example, in Star Wars, go around once instead of twice.

2. Change the means of locomotion.

3. Play the game with one or more partners. The partners can move and act as if they were a single person.

4. Change the method of tagging in simple tag games. Call out, "Reverse" to signal that the chaser is to become the tagger and vice versa.

5. Make goals or restricted areas larger or smaller.

6. Vary the boundaries of the game by making them larger or smaller, as dictated by the number of players.

7. Change the formation in which the game is played. For example, play Circle Kickball in a square or triangular shape.

8. Change the requirements necessary for scoring.

9. Increase the number of players, taggers, or runners. Also, try increasing the amount of equipment.

10. Change the rules or penalties of the game. For example, set a maximum of three dribbles or allow players to hold the ball for no more than three seconds.

Cooperation and Competition

Games require cooperation before competition can be an outgrowth of an activity. If participants chose not to follow the rules and play with teammates, playing games would be impossible. *Cooperation* involves two or more children working together to achieve a common goal. *Competition* is characterized by opponents working against each other as each person tries to reach a common goal or reward. Because cooperation precedes competition and is more difficult for students to learn, focus on this phase of game activity. Through games, players can develop a spirit of working together, a concern for teammates, and an appreciation for the collective skills of the group.

Safety

Safety is a primary consideration in game situations. Check the play area for dangerous objects and hazards. Tables, chairs, equipment, and apparatus can become dangerous during a high-speed game. Teach children to move in a controlled way, using the entire playing area to avoid collisions. Learning to stop play immediately when a signal is given prepares students for games with referees and assures safety. This prerequisite is important for later sports experiences.

Teaching Games Effectively

1. *Put students in the formation they are going to use before presenting a new game to a class.* If students can sit in game formation, they will more easily understand instructions. Make directions as brief as possible and begin the game quickly. Give minimal instruction and gradually add more subtle rules. Try the game first before answering any questions students may have. This approach gives them some idea of how the game is played and answers many questions without taking more time and boring students who already understand.

2. *Use a trial period (no scoring) when students are first learning a game.* This trial prevents children from feeling resentful about losing a point or being caught off guard because they did not understand the activity.

3. *Do not use games that isolate one child.* Games like these may create a negative experience for students who have low self-esteem. The common sport lead-up game called Birdies in the Cage traditionally puts one child in the center of the circle and requires him or her to intercept or touch passes made by circle players. A child who reacts slowly or is overweight may never succeed, and this game makes his or her failure especially public. Placing several students in the

---

TEACHING TIP

Many games involve fast movements. Teach students that their safety and the safety of their classmates are much more important than winning a game.

Achieving a balance between offense and defense helps participants understand that both phases are important. In tag and capture games, offer opportunities to remain safe as well as a challenge to be at risk and elude capture. Evaluate game components continually and modify them to ensure an enjoyable experience. Because children's motivation fades when they have no chance to succeed, teachers must ensure that teams are somewhat equal. Rotate students regularly so that they have a chance to play with different classmates and be on a winning team. Emphasizing cooperation reinforces the need to play with all classmates regardless of ability. Include children with disabilities in all rotation plans.

center makes it a team game and spreads the responsibility among more players.

4. *Develop a rotation plan to give all children equal time to play.* Avoid letting winners stay on the court while the losers sit out, receiving much less practice than better players get. Likewise, do not play elimination games until only one or two children remain. The least skilled students are eliminated early and have to sit the longest. Remember that games are played to keep students involved in physical activity. Sitting out does not contribute to physical education goals.

5. *Give all children an equal chance to participate in games that require taking turns.* For games in which numbers are called, write the numbers on a card so that no one is left out. If a game eliminates children from play, have them sit out for only one or two turns so that they can get back in the game quickly.

6. *Plan carefully before teaching a new game.* Identify safety hazards, anticipate difficult concepts, and adapt the game to the class and the situation. Make physical preparations before teaching. Mark boundaries and have equipment ready for distribution. The children's skill and age usually dictate the size of the playing area. If you plan to do some instruction during a game, make the playing area smaller so that students are closer to you.

7. *When playing low-organized and sport lead-up games, avoid using the out-of-bounds rule.* Instead, make a rule that whoever gets to the ball first gains possession. This speeds up the game and offers a strong incentive for getting the ball quickly back into play. If the game involves a goal line or running to a line, establish a safety zone. Instead of using the wall or a line near the wall as the goal, draw safety lines 10 feet (3 m) from the wall to allow adequate space for deceleration. Mark the deceleration zone with cones or spots. Try to play as many games as possible.

8. *Change the makeup of the teams often and play relatively short games.* Nobody likes to lose all the time. Playing short games means that more games can be played, so more children can be winners. If a team wins twice in a row, that is usually a signal to form new teams. Everybody gets a fresh start, and more students stay motivated.

9. *To identify teams, use pinnies, crepe paper armbands, colored shoulder loops, or team belts worn around the waist.* Have a standing rule that the team that puts on the pinnies gets the ball first. Students usually dislike wearing pinnies, and this rule gives them some incentive.

10. *Games are an excellent vehicle for learning social skills.* Encourage children to call infractions or penalties on each other and on themselves. Teach them to accept calls made by officials as an integral part of any game situation. When disagreements occur, adopt the role of arbitrator, rather than taking one side or the other. Encourage players to learn negotiation skills and resolve differences rather than have a teacher decide each issue.

11. *Help students understand that learning to perform skills correctly is more important than winning the game.* Continue instruction throughout the early phases of a game. Look for opportunities to stop the game briefly and offer instruction or correction. Give coaching hints to improve skill techniques.

12. *Use the rule of three as a way of simplifying rules.* Apply the rule of three to mean that students can hold the ball for only three seconds, or take three steps, or miss three catches, and so on. This convention reduces the number of rules that students have to remember and makes games easier to play. It also seems to diminish the disagreements children have about rules.

Selection of Games

The games selected for this chapter require minimal skill and offer activity for all children. Analyze the skills that children must practice before playing. Drills and skill practice become more meaningful when children know they will use the skill in a game situation. Games are sorted by difficulty and placed into three developmental levels. Table 22.1 lists each of the games alphabetically by developmental level and gives its page number in text. The table also describes the skills required for successful play. Games in Developmental Level I do not require competency in sport skills. Most use basic locomotor skills and offer children opportunities to practice and participate successfully. You can easily modify these games so that all children will enjoy them.

TABLE 22.1 Alphabetical Listing of Games by Developmental Level

Games	Skills	Page
Developmental Level I games		
Animal Tag	Imagery, running, dodging	534
Aviator	Running, locomotor movements, stopping	534
Ball Passing	Object handling	534
Blindfolded Duck	Fundamental locomotor movements	534
Bottle Bat Ball	Batting, retrieving balls	535
Bottle Kick Ball	Kicking, trapping	535
Cat and Mice	Running, dodging	535
Change Sides	Body management	535
Charlie Over the Water	Skipping, running, stopping, bowling (rolling)	536
Circle Stoop	Moving to rhythm	536
Circle Straddle Ball	Ball rolling, catching	536
Colors	Color or other perceptual concepts, running	536
Corner Spry	Light, silent walking	537
Firefighter	Running	537
Flowers and Wind	Running	537
Forest Ranger	Running	538
Freeze	Locomotor movements to rhythm	538
Hill Dill	Running, dodging	538
Hot Potatoes	Object handling	539
Jack Frost and Jane Thaw	Running, dodging, holding position	539
Leap the Brook	Leaping, jumping, hopping, turning	539
Marching Ponies	Marching, running	539
May I Chase You?	Running, dodging	539
Midnight	Running, dodging	540
Mix and Match	Fundamental locomotor movements	540
Mousetrap	Skipping, running, dodging	540
Musical Ball Pass	Passing, handling	541
One, Two, Button My Shoe	Running	541
Popcorn	Curling, stretching, jumping	541
Red Light	Fundamental locomotor movements, stopping	542
Right Angle	Rhythmic movement, body management	542
Rollee Pollee	Ball rolling, dodging	542
The Scarecrow and the Crows	Dodging, running	542
Sneak Attack	Running	543
Soap Bubbles	Body management	543
Squirrel in the Trees	Fundamental locomotor movements	543
Statues	Body management, applying force, balance	543

(continued)

22

TABLE 22.1 *(continued)*

Games	Skills	Page
Developmental Level I games		
Stop Ball	Tossing, catching	544
Tag Games (Simple)	Fundamental locomotor movements, dodging	544
Back-to-Back		544
Bowing		544
Frozen		544
Locomotor		544
Nose-and-Toe		544
Skunk		544
Stoop		544
Stork		544
Turtle		544
Teacher Ball (Leader Ball)	Throwing, catching	544
Toe-to-Toe	Fundamental locomotor movements	545
Tommy Tucker's Land	Dodging, running	545
Twins (Triplets)	Body management	545
Up Periscope	Fundamental locomotor movements	545
Where's My Partner?	Fundamental locomotor movements	546
Developmental Level II games		
Addition Tag	Running, dodging	546
Alaska Baseball	Kicking, batting, running, ball handling	546
Arches	Moving rhythmically	547
Bat Ball	Batting, running, catching, throwing	547
Beach Ball Bat Ball	Batting, tactile handling	547
Bird Catcher	Chasing, fleeing, dodging	548
Bounce Ball	Throwing, ball rolling	548
Box Ball	Running, ball handling	548
Busy Bee	Fundamental locomotor movements	548
Cageball Kick-Over	Kicking	549
Club Guard	Throwing	549
Competitive Circle Contests	Throwing, catching	549
Circle Club Guard		550
Touch Ball		550
Couple Tag	Running, dodging	550
Crows and Cranes	Running, dodging	550
Fly Trap	Fundamental locomotor movements	551
Follow Me	All locomotor movements, stopping	551

Games	Skills	Page
Developmental Level II games		
Fox Hunt	Running, dodging	551
Galloping Lizzie	Throwing, dodging, running	551
Hand Hockey	Striking, volleying	552
Home Base	Reaction time, locomotor movements, body management	552
Indianapolis 500	Running, tagging	552
Jump the Shot	Rope jumping	552
Keep 'Em Movin'	Body management	553
Loose Caboose	Running, dodging	553
Nine Lives	Throwing, dodging	553
Nonda's Car Lot	Running, dodging	554
One Behind	All locomotor and nonlocomotor movements	554
One Step	Throwing, catching	554
Partner Stoop	Marching rhythmically	554
Ricochet	Rolling	555
Squad Tag	Running, dodging	555
Steal the Treasure	Dodging	555
Trades	Imagery, running, dodging	556
Trees	Running, dodging	556
Whistle March	Moving rhythmically	556
Whistle Mixer	All basic locomotor movements	557
Developmental Level III games		
Air Raid	Throwing	557
Barker's Hoopla	Running	557
Cageball Target Throw	Throwing	558
Chain Tag	Running, dodging	558
Circle Touch	Dodging, body management	558
Clean-Up	Throwing	558
Fast Pass	Passing, catching, moving to an open area	559
Flag Chase	Running, dodging	559
Galactic Empire and Rebels	Chasing, fleeing, dodging	559
Guess the Leader	Body management	559
Jolly Ball	Kicking	560
Jump-the-Shot Variations	Rope jumping	560
Mushrooms	Rolling, throwing	560
Octopus	Maneuvering, problem solving	560
One-Base Tagball	Running, dodging, throwing	561
Over the Wall	Running, dodging	561

(continued)

22

TABLE 22.1 *(continued)*

Games	Skills	Page
Developmental Level III games		
Pacman	Fleeing, reaction time	561
Partner Dog and Cat	Chasing, fleeing, dodging	562
Pin Knockout	Rolling, dodging	562
Right Face, Left Face (Streets and Alleys)	Running, dodging	562
Scooter Kickball	Striking with various body parts	563
Star Wars	Running	563
Strike the Pins	Throwing	563
Sunday	Running, dodging	564
Touchdown	Running, dodging	564
Triplet Stoop	Moving rhythmically	564
Whistle Ball	Passing, catching	565
Wolfe's Beanbag Exchange	Running, dodging, tossing, catching	565
Four Square	Batting a ball	565
Team Handball	Running, dribbling, passing, throwing, catching	566
Tetherball	Batting a ball	567
Two Square	Batting a ball	567
Volley Tennis	Most volleyball skills	567

Many of the games in Developmental Levels II and III require specialized sport skills. Ball-handling and movement skills, emphasizing agility, are important for success in many of these games. Give children opportunities to practice required game skills before they start to compete.

Sport Lead-Up Games

Games in Developmental Levels II and III are separated into two categories: sport lead-up games and low-organization games. This chapter includes low-organization games only, but sport lead-up games can also be integrated into the games program. Sport lead-up games limit the number of skills required for successful participation, thus helping children experience success in a sport setting. For example, Five Passes is a game designed to develop passing skills. Children do not have to perform other skills (such as dribbling or shooting) required by the regulation sport to achieve success. The sidebar Lead-Up Games From Sport, Chapters 24 Through 30 lists all sport-related lead-up games presented in those chapters. If you are teaching soccer skills and want to finish the lesson with a lead-up game, consult this list to find an appropriate activity. Many of the lead-up games are excellent choices for skill development, particularly with Developmental Level III students. Many of these games are used as culminating activities with sport lesson plans.

Developmental Level I

Games in the early part of Developmental Level I feature individual games and creative play. Few of these games emphasize team play or have scoring systems. The games are simple, easily taught, and not demanding of skills. Many games feature dramatic elements, and others help establish number concepts and symbol recognition. As children mature, they enjoy running, tag, and ball games. Ball games at this level require the skills of throwing and catching.

LEAD-UP GAMES FROM SPORT CHAPTERS 24 TO 30

Animal Tag

Supplies: none

Skills: imagery, running, dodging

Mark off two parallel lines about 40 feet (12 m) apart. Divide children into two groups, each standing along one of the lines. Children in one team get together with their leader and decide what animal they wish to imitate. After choosing the animal, they move over to within 5 feet (1.5 m) or so of the other team's line. There they imitate the animal, and team 2 tries to identify the animal correctly. After doing so, team 2 chases team 1 back to its line, trying to tag as many opponents as possible. Those caught must go over to the other team. Team 2 then selects an animal, and the roles are reversed. If the guessing team cannot guess the animal, however, the performing team gets another try. To avoid confusion, children must raise their hands to take turns at naming the animal. Otherwise, many false chases will occur. If children have trouble guessing, the leader of the performing team can give the initial of the animal.

Aviator

Supplies: none

Skills: running, locomotor movements, stopping

Players are parked (in push-up position) at one end of the playing area. The air traffic controller (ATC) is in front of the players and calls out, "Aviators, aviators, takeoff!" Students takeoff and move like airplanes to the opposite side of the area. The first person to move to the other side and land the plane (get into push-up position facing the ATC) becomes the new ATC.

If the ATC yells out some type of stormy weather, all planes must return to the starting line and resume the parked position. Examples of stormy weather commands are lightning, thunder, hurricane, and tornado. Each ATC is allowed to give stormy weather warnings once.

Ball Passing

Supplies: five or six different kinds of balls for each circle, a whistle

Skill: object handling

Formation: circles with 15 or fewer in each circle

Divide the class into two or more circles, with no more than 15 children in any one circle. Each circle consists of two or more teams, but team members need not stand together.

The teacher starts a ball around the circle; it passes from player to player in the same direction. The teacher introduces more balls until five or six are moving around the circle at the same time and in the same direction. If a child drops a ball, he or she must retrieve it, and a point is scored against the student's squad. After a specific time, a whistle is blown, and the points against each team are totaled. The team with the lowest score wins. Beanbags, large blocks, or softballs can be substituted for balls.

Blindfolded Duck

Supplies: a wand, broomstick, cane, or yardstick

Skills: fundamental locomotor movements

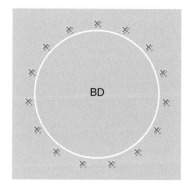

One child, designated the duck (Daisy if a girl, Donald if a boy), stands blindfolded in the center of a circle and holds a wand or similar article. Daisy taps on the floor and tells children to hop (or do some other locomotor movement). Children in the circle act accordingly, all moving in the same direction. Daisy then taps the wand twice on the floor to signal all children to stop. She moves forward with her wand, still blindfolded, to find a child in the circle. She asks, "Who are you?" The child responds, "Quack, quack." Daisy tries to identify this student. If she is correct, that child becomes the new duck. If she is wrong, Daisy must take another turn. After two unsuccessful turns, choose another child to be the duck.

Bottle Bat Ball

Supplies: a plastic bottle bat, Wiffle ball, batting tee (optional), home plate, base marker

Skills: batting, retrieving balls

Formation: scattered

Batters get three pitches (or swings if a batting tee is used) to hit a fair ball. If they fail, they are out. The pitches are easy (as in slow-pitch softball), so that the batter has a chance to hit the ball. The batter hits the ball and runs around the base marker and back to home. If the ball is returned to the designated pitcher's mound before the batter reaches home, the batter is out. Otherwise, the batter has a home run and bats again. One fielder other than the pitcher is needed, but another can be used. The running distance to first base is critical. It can either remain fixed or be made progressively (one step) longer until it grows so long that the fielders are heavily favored. Establish a rotation system for players after an out is made. Limit the number of home runs per at bat to three.

Bottle Kick Ball

Supplies: plastic gallon jugs (bleach or milk containers), 8-inch (20 cm) foam balls

Skills: kicking, trapping

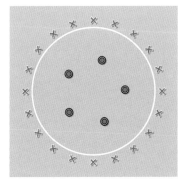

Players form a large circle around 10 to 12 plastic gallon (4 L) jugs (bowling pins) standing in the middle of the circle. Students kick the balls and try to knock over the bottles. Use as many foam balls as necessary to keep all children active. If the group is large, make more than one circle of players.

Cat and Mice

Supplies: none

Skills: running, dodging

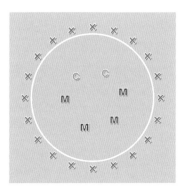

Form a large circle. Two or three children are the cats, and four others are the mice. The cats and mice cannot leave the circle. On signal, the cats chase the mice inside the circle. As they are caught, the mice join the circle. The last three mice caught become the cats for the next round. Start at one point in the circle and go around the circle selecting mice, so that each child gets a chance to be in the center. Sometimes, children have difficulty catching the last mouse or any of the mice. If this happens, children forming the circle can take a step toward the center, thus constricting the running area. Regardless, cut off any prolonged chase sequence.

Change Sides

Supplies: none

Skill: body management

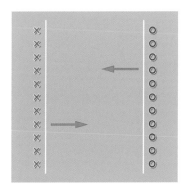

Establish two parallel lines 30 feet (10 m) apart. Half of the class stands on each line. On signal, all players cross through to the other line, face the center, and stand at attention. The first group to do all three things correctly wins a point. Caution children to use care when passing through the opposite group. They should be spaced well along each line, allowing room to move through each group. Vary the locomotor movements used by specifying skipping, hopping, long steps, sliding, and other movements. The final position also can be varied.

Charlie Over the Water

Supplies: volleyballs or playground balls

Skills: skipping, running, stopping, bowling (rolling)

Formation: single large circle

Place two or more children in the center of the circle, each holding a ball. Introduce one of the center players as Charlie (or Sally). The class skips around the circle, reciting this chant:

> *Charlie over the water,*
> *Charlie over the sea,*
> *Charlie caught a bluebird,*
> *But can't catch me!*

On the word *me*, the center players toss their balls in the air while the rest of the class runs and scatters throughout the area. When Charlie catches his ball, he shouts, "Stop!" All the children stop immediately and must not move their feet. Each center player rolls their ball and tries to hit one of their scattered classmates. When a ball is rolled into a scattered player, that player becomes a new Charlie. If center players miss, they remain in the center, and the game is repeated. If a center player misses twice, however, he or she joins the circle and picks another child as a replacement.

Circle Stoop

Supplies: music or tom-tom

Skills: moving to rhythm

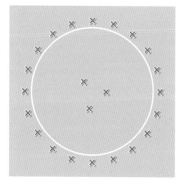

Children are in a single circle, facing counterclockwise. Use a march or similar music, or a tom-tom beat, to signal movement. The class marches until the music stops and then they stoop and touch both hands to the ground without losing balance. The last child to touch both hands to the ground, and the children who lost balance, pay a penalty by going into the mush pot (the center of the circle) for one turn. Vary the length of the music so that children cannot anticipate the signal.

Variations:

1. Using suitable music, have children try different locomotor movements, such as skipping, hopping, or galloping.

2. Vary the stopping position. Instead of stooping, use positions such as the push-up, crab, Lame Dog, balancing on one foot, or touching with one hand and one foot.

Circle Straddle Ball

Supplies: two or more 8-inch (20 cm) foam balls

Skills: ball rolling, catching

Formation: circles of 10 to 15 students, facing in

Each player stands in a wide straddle with the side of each foot against their neighbors'. Their hands are on the knees. The object of the game is to roll a ball between another player's legs before that player can get hands down to stop the ball. Keep the circles small to give students more ball-handling opportunities. Players must catch and roll the ball, rather than bat it. They must keep their hands on their knees until a ball is rolled at them. After some practice, try the following variation.

Variation: Two or more children are in the center, each with a ball. The other children are in the same formation as before. The center players try to roll the ball through any child's legs, masking intent by using feints and changes of direction. Any child allowing the ball to go through becomes "it."

Colors

Supplies: colored paper (construction paper) cut in circles, squares, or triangles for markers

Skills: color or other perceptual concepts, running

Use five or six different-colored markers, so that several children have the same color. Children stand or sit in a circle, each with a marker in front of them. The teacher (or another player) calls out a color. Everyone having that color runs counterclockwise around the circle and back

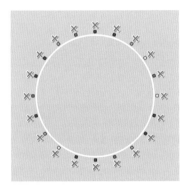

to place. The first player seated upright and motionless is declared the winner. Specify different kinds of locomotor movement, such as skipping, galloping, walking, and so on. After playing for a while, the children leave the markers on the floor and move one place to the left.

Variation: Use shapes (circles, triangles, squares, rectangles, stars, and diamonds) instead of colors or try numbers and other articles or categories, such as animals, birds, or fish.

Corner Spry

Supplies: blindfold
Skills: light, silent walking

One person is blindfolded and stands in the center of the square. The other players are scattered in the corner areas. On signal, they travel as quietly as possible from corner area to corner area. The blindfolded person, when ready (less than 20 seconds), calls out, "Corner Spry!" All players finish their trips to the corner nearest them. The blindfolded person then picks (by pointing) a corner, trying to select the one with the most players. A new player is then selected to be blindfolded.

Variation: Number the corners 1, 2, 3, and 4, and have the blindfolded person call out the corner number.

The blindfolded child can also start class movement by naming the locomotor movement to be used.

Firefighter

Supplies: none
Skill: running

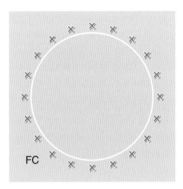

A fire chief runs around the outside of a circle of children and taps several of them on the back, saying, "Firefighter" each time. After making the round of the circle, the chief goes to the center. When the chief says, "Fire," the firefighters run counterclockwise around the circle and back to place. The one who returns first and can stand motionless in place becomes the winner and the new chief.

The chief can use other words to fool children, but they run only on the word "fire." This rule merely adds some fun, because a false start carries no penalty. Children in the circle can sound the siren as the firefighters run.

Variation: Have children stand while the chief is circling. All children not tapped drop to their knees, as they would do if there was a fire.

Flowers and Wind

Supplies: none
Skill: running

22

Draw two parallel lines, about 30 feet (10 m) apart and long enough to accommodate the children. Divide children into two groups: the flowers and the wind. Each team stands on one of the lines, facing the other team. The flowers secretly select the name of a common flower. When ready, they walk over to the other line and stand about 3 feet (1 m) away from the wind. The players on the wind team begin calling out flower names—trying to guess the flower chosen. When the flower has been guessed, the flowers run to their goal line, chased by the players of the other team. Any player caught must join the other side. The roles are reversed, and the game is repeated. If one team has trouble guessing, the other team can offer a clue about the color or size of the flower or the first letter of its name.

Variation: Change the object that students choose to integrate other academic areas (i.e., trees, spelling words, math functions).

Forest Ranger

Supplies: none

Skill: running

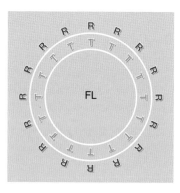

Half of the class forms a circle and faces the center. These students are the trees. The other students are forest rangers who stand behind the trees. An extra child, the forest lookout, is in the center. The forest lookout starts the game by calling, "Fire in the forest. Run, run, run!" Immediately, the forest rangers run around the outside of the circle to the right. After a few moments, the lookout steps in front of one of the trees. On this signal, each of the rangers steps in front of a tree. One player is left out and becomes the new forest lookout. The trees and the rangers switch roles. Establish the circle before playing a new game because the formation narrows when the rangers step in front of the trees.

Freeze

Supplies: music or tom-tom

Skills: locomotor movements to rhythm

Formation: scattered

When the music starts, players move throughout the area, guided by the music. They walk, run, jump, or use other locomotor movements, depending on the selected music or beat. When the music stops, they freeze and do not move. Any child caught moving after the rhythm stops receives a point. The goal is to avoid accumulating points. A tom-tom or a piano is a fine accompaniment for this game, because the rhythmic beat can be varied easily and the rhythm can be stopped at any time.

This game is useful for practicing management skills because it reinforces freezing on a stop signal.

Variations:

1. Specify the pose in which children must freeze.

2. Have children fall to the ground or balance or go into a different position (push-up, crab, Lame Dog, and so on).

Hill Dill

Supplies: None

Skills: running, dodging

Mark two parallel lines, 50 feet (15 m) apart. Choose two or more players to be "it" and stand in the center between the lines. The other children stand on one of the parallel lines. One of the center players calls,

Hill dill! Come over the hill,
Or else I'll catch you standing still!

Children run across the open space to the other line, while the players in the center try to tag them. Anyone caught helps the taggers in the center. When children cross over to the other line, they must await the next call. Start a new game after most of the students are tagged.

Hot Potatoes

Supplies: one to three balls or beanbags for each group

Skill: object handling

Formation: circles with 8 to 12 players

Players stand in small circles so that they can pass balls, beanbags, or both around the circle. The teacher or a selected student, who stands with his or her back to the class, randomly shouts, "Stop!" The point of the game is to avoid being the player who passes the object to the child who caught it when the signal occurred. If this happens, the player or players who passed the object get up and move to the next circle. Begin the game with one object and gradually add objects if the class is capable. Call out, "Reverse" to signal players to pass the object in the other direction.

Jack Frost and Jane Thaw

Supplies: blue streamers or pinnies for Jack Frosts and red ones for Jane Thaws

Skills: running, dodging, holding position

Formation: scattered

The class moves to avoid being frozen (tagged) by two or three Jack Frosts, who carry a blue pinny or streamer in one hand. Frozen children remain immobile until touched (thawed) by the Jane Thaws, who carry a red streamer or pinny.

Leap the Brook

Supplies: none

Skills: leaping, jumping, hopping, turning

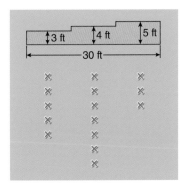

Mark off a brook across the floor as shown in the diagram. Children line up on one side of the area. On the signal "Cross the Brook!" players pick a challenge and try to jump across the brook. The wider the brook is, the greater the challenge is. Use different styles of locomotor movements such as hopping, jumping, and leaping

over the brook. The distances are arbitrary and can be changed if unsuitable for your group of children.

Variation: Use different types of turns while jumping the brook, such as right or left; quarter, half, three-quarter, or full. Use different body shapes, different arm positions, and so on.

Marching Ponies

Supplies: none

Skills: marching, running

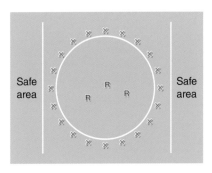

Two or three children are ringmasters who crouch in the center of a circle of ponies formed by the rest of the class. Two goal lines on opposite sides of the circle are established as safe areas. The ponies march around the circle in step, counting as they do so. At a predetermined number (the teacher whispers it to the ringmasters) the ringmasters jump up and try to tag the others before they can reach the safety lines. Anyone tagged joins the ringmasters in the center and helps catch others. Reorganize the game after six to eight children have been caught. Try other characterizations, such as lumbering elephants, jumping kangaroos, and the like.

May I Chase You?

Supplies: none

Skills: running, dodging

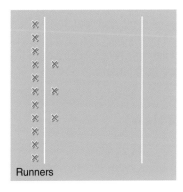

22

539

The class stands behind a line long enough to accommodate all. Two or three runners stand about 5 feet (1.5 m) in front of the line. The class asks, "May I chase you?" One of the runners (designated by teacher) replies, "Yes, if you are wearing . . ." and names a color, an article of clothing, or a combination of the two. All who qualify immediately chase the runners until one is tagged. New runners are chosen and the game is repeated. Encourage players to think of other ways to identify those who run.

Midnight

Supplies: none

Skills: running, dodging

Mark off a safety line about 40 feet (12 m) from a den in which two or three players, the foxes, are standing. The others stand behind the safety line and ask, "What time is it, Mr. Fox?" Choose one of the foxes to answer in various ways, such as "1 o'clock," "4 o'clock," and so on. When the fox says a certain time, the class walks forward that number of steps. For example, if the fox says, "6 o'clock," the class has to move forward six steps. The fox continues to draw the players toward him or her. Eventually, the fox answers the question by saying, "Midnight," and chases the others back to the safety line. Any player who is caught becomes a fox in the den and helps to catch others.

Variation: *Lame Wolf.* The wolf is lame and advances in a series of three running steps and a hop. Other children taunt, "Lame Wolf, can't catch me!" or "Lame Wolf, tame wolf, can't catch me!" The wolf may give chase at any time. Children who are caught join the wolf and must also move as if lame.

Mix and Match

Supplies: none

Skills: fundamental locomotor movements

Mark off a line through the middle of the area. Half of the children stand on each side. Two or three extra children stand on one side of the line. The teacher signals children to move as directed on their side of the line. Instruct them to run, hop, skip, or make some other movement. On signal, players run to the dividing line and reach across to join hands with a player on the opposite side. The goal is to find a partner and not be left out. Children may reach over but cannot cross the line. The players left out move to the opposite side, so that players left out come from alternating sides of the area. To speed up the process, encourage students to raise their hands if they need a partner.

Variation: Try playing the game to music or a drumbeat. Players rush to the centerline to find partners when the rhythm stops.

Mousetrap

Supplies: none

Skills: skipping, running, dodging

Half of the class forms a circle, joining hands and facing the center. This grouping is the trap. The other children, the mice, are on the outside of the circle. The game involves three signals (word cues or other signals). On the first signal, the mice skip around, outside the circle, playing happily. On the second signal, the trap opens (players in the circle raise their joined hands to form arches). The mice run in and out of the trap. On the third signal, the trap snaps shut (the arms come down). All mice caught inside join the circle. The game is repeated until most of the mice are caught. The players then exchange places, and the game begins anew.

Musical Ball Pass

Supplies: one or two playground balls per group, music

Skills: passing, handling

Break the class into small groups (six to seven players) in circle formation facing the center. Each team receives a ball and passes it around their circle when the music starts. When the music stops, the player with the ball (or the last player to touch the ball) takes the ball and moves to another circle. To avoid arguments, a player must move to the next circle if the ball is in the player's hands or on the way to him or her. Try using more than one ball.

One, Two, Button My Shoe

Supplies: none
Skill: running

Mark off two parallel lines on opposite sides of the playing area. Choose two or three players to be leaders and stand in front of the class. The rest of the class stands behind one of the lines. When the leaders say, "Ready," the following dialogue begins.

Children: One, two.
Leader: Button my shoe.
Children: Three, four.
Leader: Close the door.
Children: Five, six.
Leader: Pick up sticks.
Children: Seven, eight.
Leader: Run, or you'll be late!

As children carry on the conversation with the leaders, they toe the line, ready to run. When the leaders say, "Late," players run to the other line and return. Choose new leaders after each run. The leaders can give the last response ("Run, or you'll be late!") in any timing desired—pausing or dragging out the words. No player can leave before hearing the word "late" spoken.

Popcorn

Supplies: none
Skills: curling, stretching, jumping

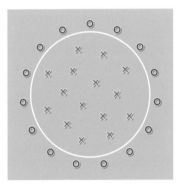

Choose half of the class to be popcorn; they crouch down in the center of the circle formed by the rest of the class. Children in the circle also crouch to represent the heat. Choose one of them to be the leader, whose actions will guide the other children. Children in the circle gradually rise to a standing position, extend their arms overhead, and shake them vigorously to indicate the intensifying heat. In the meantime, the popcorn in the center starts to pop. This begins slowly and increases in speed and height as the heat is applied. In the final stages, children are popping up rapidly. After a time, the groups change places and repeat the game.

22

Red Light

Supplies: none

Skills: fundamental locomotor movements, stopping

Mark off a goal line at one end of the area. The object of the game is to move across the area successfully without being caught. Two or three players are leaders and stand on the goal line. The leaders turn away from the players. One of the leaders claps five times. All leaders turn around on the fifth clap. Meanwhile, the players move toward the goal line, timing their movements to end on the fifth clap. If any of the leaders catch any child moving, that child returns to the starting line and begins anew. After the clapper turns away, he or she can turn back immediately to catch any movement. After the clapper begins clapping, however, he or she has to clap five times before turning around. The first child to reach the goal line successfully without being caught moving is the winner. Choose new leaders for the next game.

Variations:

1. An excellent variation of the game is to have the leaders face the oncoming players. The designated leader calls out, "Green light" for them to move and "Red light" for them to stop. When the leader calls other colors, the players should not move.

2. Explore different types of locomotion. The leader names the type of movement (e.g., hop, crawl, skip) before turning his or her back to the group.

3. Have the leader specify how those caught must go back to place—walk, hop, skip, slide, crawl.

4. Divide the area into quadrants and have four games with one or two leaders.

Right Angle

Supplies: music

Skills: rhythmic movement, body management

Formation: scattered

To provide the rhythm for this activity, use a tom-tom. Children quickly change direction at right angles on each heavy beat or change of music. The object of the game is to make the right-angle change on signal and not to bump into other players.

Rollee Pollee

Supplies: many 8-inch (20 cm) foam balls

Skills: ball rolling, dodging

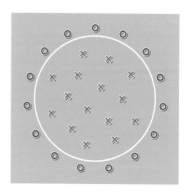

Half of the class forms a circle; the other half is in the center. Give balls to the players forming the circle. These players roll the balls at the feet and shoes of the center players, trying to touch them with a ball. The center players move around to avoid the balls. A center player who is touched leaves the center and joins the circle. After a specific time, or when all of the children have been touched, the teams trade places.

Balls that stop in the center are dead and must be taken back to the circle before being put into play again. The preferable procedure is to have players who recover balls roll them to a teammate rather than return to place with the ball.

The Scarecrow and the Crows

Supplies: none

Skills: dodging, running

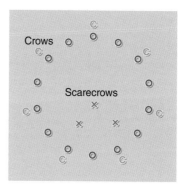

Children form a large circle to outline the garden, which is guarded by two or three players who are the scarecrows. Six to eight crows scatter on the outside of the circle, and the scarecrows assume a characteristic pose inside the circle. Players in the circle raise their joined hands and let the crows run through, into the garden, where they pretend to eat. The scarecrows try to tag the crows. The circle children help the crows by raising their joined hands and allowing them to leave the circle, but they try to hinder the scarecrows. If the scarecrows run out of the circle, all the crows immediately run into the garden and start to nibble at the vegetables while the circle children hinder the scarecrows' reentry.

When the scarecrows have caught one or two crows, choose new players. If, after a reasonable time, the scarecrows fail to catch any crows, change players.

Sneak Attack

Supplies: none

Skills: running

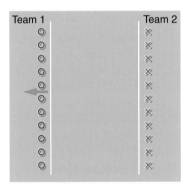

Draw two parallel lines about 60 feet (20 m) apart. Divide the class into two teams. Team 1, the chasers, stands along one line with their backs to the area. Team 2, the sneak team, is on the other line, facing the area. The sneak team moves forward on signal, moving toward the chasers. When they get reasonably close, a signal is given, and the sneak team turns and runs back to its line, chased by the other team. Anyone tagged before reaching the line becomes a chaser. The game is then repeated, with the roles exchanged.

Soap Bubbles

Supplies: cones to delineate space, music

Skills: body management

Formation: scattered

Use four cones to mark off the movement area. Each player is a soap bubble floating throughout the area.

Call out a locomotor movement for students to perform while moving within the four cones. As the game progresses, move the cones toward the center of the area to make it smaller. The object of the game is not to touch or collide with another bubble. When this occurs, both bubbles burst and sink to the floor, becoming as small as possible. Keep making the area smaller, until only a few players have not been touched. Players who are broken bubbles can go to the area outside the cones and move. This game teaches the concept of moving in general space without touching.

Squirrel in the Trees

Supplies: none

Skills: fundamental locomotor movements

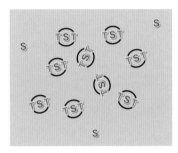

Form several trees by having two students face each other and hold hands or put hands on each other's shoulders. A squirrel is in the center of each tree, and one or two extra squirrels are outside. On signal, the trees open up and let the squirrels move around the area. The trees stay together and move throughout the area. On signal, the trees freeze in place and the squirrels find any available tree. Only one squirrel is allowed in a tree. Quickly begin another game to avoid drawing attention to those who did not find a tree.

Rotate students so that everyone gets to be a squirrel. After the squirrels are in a tree, ask them to face one of the tree players. The child they are facing becomes the partner for a tree; the other child becomes a new squirrel.

Statues

Supplies: none

Skills: body management, applying force, balance

Formation: scattered in pairs

One partner in each pair is the swinger, and the other is the statue. The teacher calls a directive, such as "Pretty," "Funny," "Happy," "Angry," or "Terminator." The swinger takes the statue by one or both hands, swings it around

22

in a small circle two or three times (the teacher specifies), and releases it. The statue then takes a pose that follows the directive, and the swinger sits on the floor.

A committee of children can decide on the best statues. Statues must hold the position without moving or they are disqualified. After the winners are announced, the partners reverse positions.

Variation: In the original game, partners swing until they hear the directive. The swinger then immediately releases the statue, who takes the pose as called. This gives the statue little time to react. Statues are more creative if the directive is given earlier.

Stop Ball

Supplies: a ball

Skills: tossing, catching

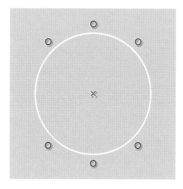

Divide the class into small circles of five to seven players. One player, with hands over the eyes, stands in the center of each circle. Players toss a ball clockwise or counterclockwise around the circle. When he or she chooses, the center player calls, "Stop!" The player caught with the ball (or the ball coming to him or her) takes the ball to the next circle and plays with a new team. Give the center players three or four turns each.

Tag Games (Simple)

Supplies: none

Skills: fundamental locomotor movements, dodging

Formation: scattered

Tag has many variations. The following are "give up the tag" games; a player is no longer "it" after tagging another child, who then becomes "it." Children are scattered, and several players are taggers. When making a tag, that player says, "You're it." The new tagger can chase any player other than the person who tagged him or her (no tagbacks). Eliminating tagbacks keeps students from always being "it" because they are slower than the child who tagged them.

Variations:

1. Touching a specific object (such as wood or iron), color, or the floor can make a runner safe.

2. Children can be safe by doing a particular action or by striking a certain pose.

   a. *Stoop Tag.* Players touch both hands to the ground.
   b. *Stork Tag.* Players stand on one foot. (The other cannot touch.)
   c. *Turtle Tag.* Players get on their backs, feet pointed toward the ceiling.
   d. *Bowing Tag.* Players bow with forehead to the ground.
   e. *Nose-and-Toe Tag.* Players touch the nose to the toe.
   f. *Back-to-Back Tag.* Players stand back-to-back with any other child.
   g. *Skunk Tag.* Players reach an arm under one knee and hold the nose.

3. *Locomotor Tag.* The child who is "it" says how the others should move—skipping, hopping, jumping. The tagger must use the same kind of movement.

4. *Frozen Tag.* Two children are "it." The rest are scattered over the area. When tagged, they are frozen and must keep both feet in place. Any free player can tag a frozen player and thus release him or her. The tagger's goal is to freeze all players. Frozen players can be required to hop in place until released.

Teacher Ball (Leader Ball)

Supplies: a volleyball or rubber playground ball

Skills: throwing, catching

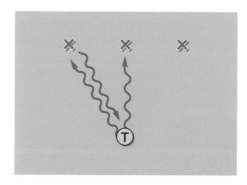

One child, the "teacher," stands about 10 feet (3 m) in front of three other students, who are lined up facing the teacher. The object of the game is to move up to the teacher's spot by not making bad throws or missing catches. The teacher throws to each child in turn, beginning with the child on the left, who must catch and return the ball. Any child making a throwing or catching error goes to the end of the line, on the teacher's right. Those in the line move up, filling the vacated space.

A teacher who makes a mistake goes to the end of the line, and the child at the head of the line becomes the new teacher. Teachers score 1 point by remaining in position for three rounds (three throws to each child). After scoring a point, the teacher goes to the end of the line, and the first child becomes the teacher.

Variation: The "teacher" can suggest specific methods of throwing and catching, such as "Catch with the right hand only" or "Catch with one hand and don't let the ball touch your body."

Toe-to-Toe

Supplies: none

Skills: fundamental locomotor movements

Formation: scattered

Students perform a locomotor movement around the area. On signal, each child must find a partner and stand toe-to-toe (one foot only) with that person. An important skill is to take the nearest person for a partner instead of searching for a particular friend. Students who cannot find a partner in their immediate area must run quickly to the center of the area (marked with a spot or cone) to find one. The goal is to find a nearby partner as quickly as possible and avoid being the last pair formed. If the number of students playing is uneven, the teacher can join in and play. Change locomotor movements often.

Tommy Tucker's Land

Supplies: about 10 beanbags for each game

Skills: dodging, running

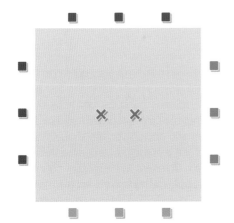

Two students, Tommy and Tammy Tucker, stand in the center of a 15-foot (5 m) square, within which the beanbags are scattered. The Tuckers are guarding their land and treasure. The other children chant,

I'm on Tommy Tucker's land,
Picking up gold and silver.

Children try to pick up as much of the treasure as they can while avoiding being tagged by the Tuckers. Any child who is tagged must return the treasure and retire from the game. The game ends when only three children are left or when all beanbags are successfully filched. The teacher may wish to stop the game earlier if it reaches a stalemate. In that case, select new Tuckers.

Twins (Triplets)

Supplies: none

Skills: body management, running

Formation: scattered with partner

Have students pair with a partner (twin). The teacher gives commands such as "Take three hops and two leaps" or "Walk backward four steps and three skips." When the pairs are separated, the teacher says, "Find your twin!" Players find their twin and stand frozen toe-to-toe. The goal is not to be the last pair to find each other and freeze. Make sure that students move away from each other when following commands. One alternative is to find a new twin each time. Another variation is to separate twins in opposite ends of the playing area.

Variation: For greater challenge, have students play in groups of three (triplets). For this variation, children select new partners each time.

Up Periscope

Supplies: none

Skills: fundamental locomotor movements

Formation: scattered

Children move around the area pretending to be ships. Remind the ships to not contact another ship and stay as far away as possible. When the teacher says, "Submarines," players quickly lower their bodies and move at a low level. On "Up periscope," students move to their backs and put one leg in the air to imitate a periscope. On "Double periscope," they raise both legs to imitate two periscopes. While students are in double periscope position, the teacher can quickly give the previous commands to keep students moving. When the teacher says, "Surface," the students resume moving through the area as ships.

22

Where's My Partner?

Supplies: none
Skills: fundamental locomotor movements

Children are in a double circle by couples, with partners facing. The inside circle has two or three more players than the outside. On signal, the circles skip (or walk, run, hop, gallop) to the right. This means they are skipping in opposite directions. On the command "Halt," the circles face each other to find partners. The players left without a partner go to the friendship spot (the center area of the circle) for one turn. The circles are reversed after a time.

Developmental Level II

Compared with the games in Developmental Level I, the games program in Level II is distinctly different. Chase and tag games are more complex and demand more maneuvering. Introductory lead-up games make an appearance. Children at this level become more interested in games with a sports slant, and kicking, throwing, catching, batting, and other sport skills start to mature.

Addition Tag

Supplies: none
Skills: running, dodging

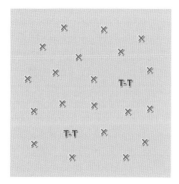

Two or more pairs are it, and each stands with inside hands joined. These children are the taggers. The other children run individually. The pairs move around the area, trying to tag with their free hands. The first child tagged joins the couple, making a trio. The three then chase until they catch a fourth. After catching a fourth child, the four divide and form two pairs, adding another set of taggers to the game. This process continues until most of the players are tagged.

If pairs are having problems catching the runners, establish some area restrictions. For a faster game, start with more pairs. A tag is legal only when the pair or trio keeps their hands joined.

Alaska Baseball

Supplies: a volleyball or soccer ball
Skills: kicking, batting, running, ball handling

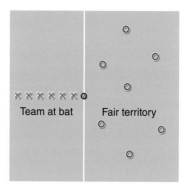

Players form two teams; one is at bat and the other is in the field. A straight line is the only out-of-bounds line. The team at bat is behind this line at about the middle. The other team scatters around the fair territory. One player propels the ball, either by batting a volleyball or kicking a stationary soccer ball. Teammates are in a close file formation behind the batter. After sending the ball into the playing area, the batter starts running around the line of teammates. Each time the runner passes the head of the file, the team gives a loud count.

There are no outs. The first fielder to get the ball stands still and starts passing the ball back overhead to the nearest teammate, who moves directly behind to receive it. The rest of the field players must run to the ball and form a file behind it. Teammates pass the ball back overhead, and each player handles the ball. When the last field player in line has a firm grip on it, he or she shouts, "Stop!" A count is then made of the number of times the batter ran around his or her team. To score more closely, count half rounds. When five batters (or half of the team) have batted, the teams change places. This approach is better than having an entire team bat before changing to the field, because players in the field tire from many consecutive runs.

Variation: Set up regular bases for the batters to run. Score points whether or not the batter makes a home run, or have the batter continue around the bases, scoring 1 point per base.

Arches

Supplies: music

Skills: moving rhythmically

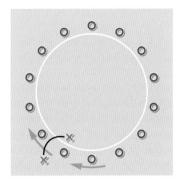

The game is similar to London Bridge. In the playing area, two students form an arch by facing one another with hands joined and arms raised. When the music starts, the other players move in a circle, passing under the arch. Suddenly, the music stops, and the arch closes as the two students lower their arms. All players caught in the arch immediately pair off to form other arches, staying in a general circle formation. If a caught player has no partner, he or she waits in the center of the circle until one is available. The last players caught (or left) form arches for the next game. Warn the arches not to bring down their hands and arms so forcefully that they hit children passing under.

Variation: Try using different types of music and have children move to the pattern of each piece.

Bat Ball

Supplies: an 8-inch (20 cm) foam ball

Skills: batting, running, catching, throwing

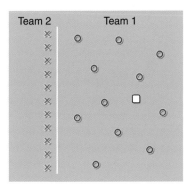

Mark off a serving line across one end of the field and set up a 3-by-3-foot (1 by 1 m) base about 50 feet (15 m) from the serving line. Divide children into two teams. Team 1 is scattered over the playing area. Team 2 is behind the serving line, with one player at bat. The batter puts the ball into play by batting it with a hand into the playing area. To be counted as a fair ball, the ball must land in the playing area or be touched by a member of team 1. As soon as the ball is hit, the batter runs to the base and back across the serving line. In the meantime, team 1 fields the ball and tries to complete five passes before the team 2 runner gets back across the line.

Fielders may not run with the ball. It must be passed from fielder to fielder. A pass may not be returned to the fielder it was received from. Violation of any of these rules constitutes a foul.

A run is scored each time the batter hits a fair ball, touches the base, and gets back to the serving line. A run is also scored if the fielding team commits a foul.

The batter is out when the ball is caught on the fly. Two consecutive foul balls also put the batter out. The batter is out when hit by a thrown ball in the field of play. Sides change when three outs are made.

Beach Ball Bat Ball

Supplies: four to six beach balls

Skills: batting, tactile handling

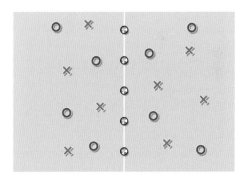

Divide players into two teams. Begin the game by placing the balls on the centerline of the court area. All beach balls are in play at the same time. Players score by batting a ball over the endline. Balls that cross the endline are dead. Players use the remaining balls in play. Balls on the floor are picked up and batted into play. Balls may never be carried. The game ends when all four balls score. Teams then switch places and start a new game.

22

Bird Catcher

Supplies: hoops or cones

Skills: chasing, fleeing, dodging

Formation: class in line formation with two to four players in the bird nest

Choose two to four players to be bird catchers and stand in the center of the teaching area. One child is the mother or father bird and stands on an endline. (Alternatively, use cones to mark the bird's nest.) The rest of the class stands on the other endline. Students on the endline quickly choose the type of bird they will be for the game. On signal, the mother or father bird commands a specific type of bird to fly, such as by saying, "Cardinals fly." All students who are cardinals then try to reach the bird's nest without being tagged by a bird catcher. Students who are tagged help the bird catcher until the game ends.

Bounce Ball

Supplies: volleyballs or rubber playground balls of about the same size

Skills: throwing, ball rolling

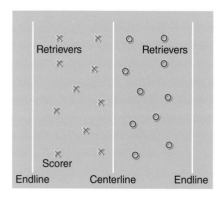

Children form two teams. Each team occupies half of the court and has several balls. Two players from each team are assigned to retrieve balls behind their own endlines. Teams try to bounce or roll the ball over their opponents' endline. A ball thrown across the line does not count. Two scorers are needed, one at each endline. Players can move wherever they wish in their own area but cannot cross the centerline. After the starting signal, students bounce and roll the balls back and forth at will.

Box Ball

Supplies: a sturdy box, 2 feet (60 cm) square and about 12 inches (30 cm) deep; four volleyballs (or similar balls)

Skills: running, ball handling

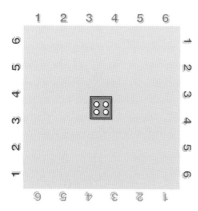

Divide the class into four even teams of 6 to 10 players. Each team stands along one side of a hollow square at an equal distance from the center. Players face inward, and each team numbers off consecutively from right to left. Place a box containing four balls into the center. When the teacher calls a number, the player from each team who has that number runs forward to the box, takes a ball, and runs to the head of his or her line, taking the place of player 1. Meanwhile, the players in the line have moved to the left just enough to fill in the space left by the runner. On reaching the head of the line, the runner passes the ball to the next child, and so on down the line to the end child. The last child runs forward and returns the ball to the box. The first team to return the ball to the box scores a point.

Runners must not pass the ball down the line until they are in place at the head of the line. Each child must receive and then pass the ball. Teams failing to follow these rules are disqualified. Runners stay at the head of the line, retaining their original number. The lines do not stay in consecutive number sequence.

Busy Bee

Supplies: none

Skills: fundamental locomotor movements

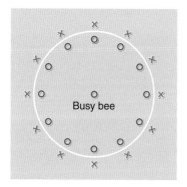

Half of the students form a large circle, facing in, and are the stationary players. The other students seek partners from this group and stand in front of the stationary players. An extra child in the center is the busy bee. The bee calls out directions such as "Toe-to-toe," "Face-to-face," "Shake hands," "Kneel on one knee [or both]," and "Hop on one foot." All the children in the double circle follow these directions. When the bee calls out, "Busy bee," stationary players stand still. Their partners seek new partners, and the bee also tries to get a partner. The child without a partner becomes the new busy bee.

Teach students various movements they can call out if they become the busy bee. When changing partners, children must select a child other than the stationary player next to them. After a specific time, rotate the active and stationary players.

Cageball Kick-Over

Supplies: an 18-, 24-, or 30-inch (45, 60, or 75 cm) cageball

Skill: kicking

Players are divided into two teams and sit facing each other, with legs outstretched and soles of the feet about 6 to 12 feet (2 to 4 m) apart. All players support their weight on the hands, which are placed slightly to the rear. The teacher rolls the cageball between the two teams. Players try to kick the ball over the other team and score a point. When a team scores, the teacher rolls the ball into play again. Rotate players by having a player on the left side of the line take a place on the right side after a point is scored, thus moving all players one position to the left. If players kick the ball out at either end, no score results. The teacher returns the ball into play. Let children use their hands to stop the ball from going over them.

Club Guard

Supplies: a juggling club or bowling pin, foam rubber ball
Skill: throwing

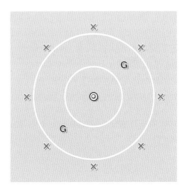

Draw a circle about 15 feet (5 m) in diameter. In the center of that circle, draw an 18-inch (45 cm) circle and place the club in it. Two or three students guard the club. The other players stand outside the large circle, which is the restraining line for them. The circle players throw the ball at the club and try to knock it down. The guards try to block the throws with the legs and body but must stay out of the small inner circle. The circle players pass the ball around rapidly so that one of the players can get an opening to throw as the guards maneuver to protect the club. Rotate in new guards after a short time (15 to 20 seconds). The guards are disqualified if they step into the small circle.

Variations:

1. Place more than one club in the center.
2. Play multiple games to increase the activity level for all players.

Competitive Circle Contests

Supplies: volleyballs or 8-inch (20 cm) foam rubber balls, two bowling pins

Skills: throwing, catching

Formation: two circles with the same number of students in each

Two teams arranged in separate circles compete against each other. Draw lines on the floor to ensure that the circles are the same size. Consecutively number each team's players, using the same numbers for both teams. Two consecutively numbered players go to the center of the opponents' circle to compete for their team in one of the following activities.

22

1. *Circle Club Guard.* The two center players guard a bowling pin. Players roll the ball at the club. The team that knocks down the club first wins a point. They must pass the ball to three different players before rolling it at the club.

2. *Touch Ball.* The circle players pass the ball from one to another while the two center players try to touch it. The center player who touches the ball first wins a point for his or her team. If neither player can touch the ball within a reasonable time, stop the action without awarding a point.

After all players have competed, the team with the most points wins.

Couple Tag

Supplies: none

Skills: running, dodging

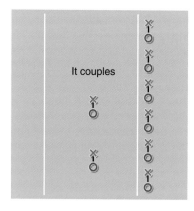

Mark two goal lines on opposite sides of an area. Players run in pairs, with inside hands joined. All pairs, except two, line up on one of the goal lines. The pairs in the center are "it." When they call, "Come," all pairs, with hands joined, run to the other goal line. The pairs in the center, also keeping hands joined, try to tag any other pair. As soon as a couple is caught, they help the center couples. The game continues until all are caught. The last two couples caught are "it" for the next game.

Variation: *Triplet Tag.* Try playing the game with sets of threes. Tagging is done with any pair of joined hands. If a triplet breaks joined hands, they are caught.

Crows and Cranes

Supplies: none

Skills: running, dodging

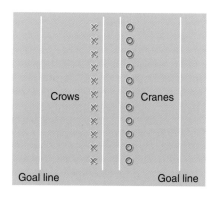

Establish two goal lines on opposite sides of an area. The class is divided into two groups—crows and cranes. The groups face each other at the center of the area, about 5 feet (1.5 m) apart. The leader calls out either "Crows" or "Cranes," using a *cr-r-r-r-r* sound at the start of either word to mask the result. If "Crows" is the call, the crows chase the cranes to the goal line. If "Cranes" is the call, then the cranes chase. Any player caught goes over to the other side and becomes a member of that group. The goal is to capture the most players.

Variations:

1. *Toe-to-Toe.* Instead of facing each other, children stand back-to-back, about a foot (30 cm) apart, in the center.

2. *Red and Blue.* Instead of using calls, throw a piece of cardboard (red on one side and blue on the other) into the air between the teams. If red comes up, the red team chases and vice versa.

3. *Nouns and Verbs.* When the leader calls out any verb, the nouns team chases and vice versa.

4. *Odd and Even.* Throw large foam rubber dice in the air. If they come up even, the even team chases. If they come up odd, the odd team chases.

5. *Blue, Black, and Baloney.* On the command "Blue" or "Black," the game proceeds as described. On the command "Baloney," no one is to move. The caller draws out the *bl-l-l-l* sound in giving one of the three commands.

6. Have a leader tell a story using as many words beginning with *cr–* as possible (e.g., *crazy, crunch, crust, crown, crude, crowd, crouch, cross, croak, critter*). Each time the leader says one of these words, he or she lengthens the beginning with a drawn-out *cr-r-r-r* sound. No one may move on any of the words except crows or cranes.

Fly Trap

Supplies: none

Skills: fundamental locomotor movements

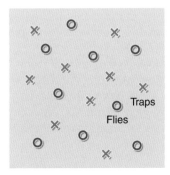

Half of the class is scattered around the playing area, sitting cross-legged on the floor. These children form the trap. The rest of the players are the flies, and they buzz around the seated children. On signal, the flies must freeze where they are. If any of the traps can touch a fly, that fly sits down at that spot and becomes a trap. The traps must keep their seats glued to the floor. The game continues until all flies are caught. To add realism, have the flies make buzzing sounds and move their arms like wings. When most of the flies are caught, the groups trade places. Occasionally change the method of locomotion.

Follow Me

Supplies: a marker for each child (squares of cardboard or plywood, individual mats, or beanbags)

Skills: all locomotor movements, stopping

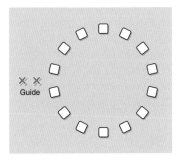

Arrange the class in a rough circle, each child standing or sitting with one foot on a marker. Two extra players are guides. They move around the circle, pointing at different players and asking them to follow until all players are selected. Each player chosen falls in behind the guide who pointed at him or her. The guides then take their group on a tour, and each group member does just what the guide does. The guide may hop, skip, and do stunts or other movements; the group following must do the same. At the signal "Home," all run for places with a marker. Two players will be left without a marker. They can become guides or choose other guides.

Fox Hunt

Supplies: none

Skills: running, dodging

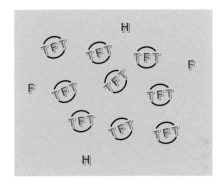

Pairs of players form trees by facing each other and holding hands. A third member of each group is a fox and stands between the hands of the trees. Two players are foxes without trees, and two players are hounds. The hounds try to tag foxes who are not in trees. The extra foxes may move to a tree and displace the fox who is in that tree. The foxes in trees may leave the safety of their trees at any time. If the hound tags a fox, their roles are reversed immediately.

Stop the game at regular intervals to allow the players who are trees to change places with the foxes and hounds. Vary the game by specifying different locomotor movements.

Galloping Lizzie

Supplies: a fleece ball

Skills: throwing, dodging, running

Formation: scattered

Two or more players are "it" and have fleece balls. The other players are scattered around the playground. The players with the balls run after the others and try to hit them below the waist with the fleece ball. The person hit becomes "it," and the game continues. Taggers must throw the ball, not just touch another child with it.

22

Hand Hockey

Supplies: 8-inch (20 cm) gray foam ball

Skills: striking, volleying

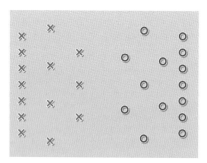

Players are divided into two teams. Half of the players on each team are guards and stand on the goal line as defenders. The other half are active players and are scattered throughout the playing area in front of their goal line.

The ball is put into play by being rolled into the center of the field. The object of the game is to bat or push the ball with either hand so that it crosses the goal line defended by the other team. Players may move the ball as in hockey but may not throw, hoist, or kick it. Defensive goal line players are limited to one step into the playing field when playing the ball. When a team scores, or after a specific period, guards become active players and vice versa. An out-of-bounds ball goes to the opposite team and is put into play by being rolled from the sidelines into the playing area. If the ball is trapped among players, the teacher stops play and puts the ball into play again.

Players must play the ball and not resort to rough tactics. Players who use unnecessary roughness or illegally handle the ball must go to the sidelines (as in hockey) and stay in the penalty area until the players change positions. Players should scatter and try to pass to each other rather than bunch around the ball. After students learn the game, increase the activity by adding more balls.

Variation: *Scooter Hockey*. The active center players from each team are on gym scooters. Specify the position (e.g., kneeling, sitting, on tummy) that each child takes on the gym scooter or allow a free choice. Because scooters require a hard surface, this version is usually played indoors on a basketball court.

Home Base

Supplies: cones to delineate the area, four pinnies

Skills: reaction time, locomotor movements, body management

Formation: groups of five or six, in single file

Place several marking spots on the floor throughout the area. Each team quickly lines up behind one child who stands on a marking spot. This child is the team captain. When the teacher calls out a locomotor movement, all players perform this movement throughout the area. When the teacher calls, "Home base," the captains quickly find the closest spot and their respective team members line up behind them. The first team to return to proper position (standing in a straight line) is the winner. Avoid calling "home base" until the students are thoroughly mixed. You can specify many different formations for teams to assume after they return to home base.

Indianapolis 500

Supplies: none

Skills: running, tagging

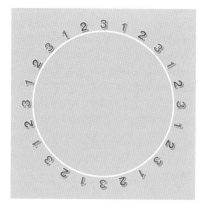

Children start in a large circle and are numbered off by threes or fours. A race starter says, "Start your engines," and then calls a number. Children with the corresponding number run the same way around the circle and try to tag players in front of them. If the starter yells, "Pit stop," all runners have to stop and return to their original position. If the starter calls, "Car wreck," all runners change direction and keep running until they hear "Pit stop" called. Change the starter often.

Jump the Shot

Supplies: jump-the-shot ropes

Skill: rope jumping

Divide the class into four or five small circles. One player with a long rope stands in the center. Tie a soft object to the free end of the rope to give it some weight. A de-

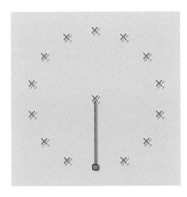

flated ball or beanbag makes a good weight (use duct tape to keep it from becoming untied). The center player turns the rope for the circle players, who must jump over it. A player who touches the rope with the feet must move up to the next group.

Variations:

1. Change the center player after one or two misses. Caution center players to keep the rope close to the ground. The rope speed can be varied. A good way to turn the rope is to sit cross-legged and turn it overhead. Students can do different tasks such as hopping, jumping and turning, or jumping and clapping.

2. Teams line up in spoke formation. Each member does a specified number of jumps (three to five) and then exits. The next team member in line must come in immediately without missing a turn of the rope. Players score a point for the team by coming in on time, jumping the prescribed number of turns, and exiting successfully. The team with the most points wins.

3. Couples line up in the same formation. They join inside hands and stand side by side when jumping.

Keep 'Em Movin'

Supplies: tennis balls, Wiffle balls, foam balls

Skills: body management

Formation: scattered throughout the teaching area

Scatter many tennis balls or Wiffle balls (10 to 15 more than the number of students) throughout the teaching area. On signal, students begin tapping the tennis balls with their feet or hands to get them moving or "alive." Balls may not be picked up or kicked. While the students try to keep all balls moving, the teacher looks for balls that are stationary. Upon seeing three different balls not moving, the teacher yells, "Dead bugs," and all students

move to their backs with their arms and legs up and moving like a bug. After several seconds, the teacher signals for the game to resume.

Loose Caboose

Supplies: none

Skills: running, dodging

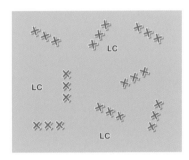

Choose two or three children to be loose cabooses that try to hook onto a train. Trains are formed by three or four children standing in single file with their hands on the shoulders of the child immediately in front. The trains, by twisting and turning, try to keep the caboose from hooking on. Should the caboose manage to hook on, the front child in the train becomes the new caboose. Each train also tries to keep together. If a train breaks while being chased, it goes to the side and counts to 25 before reentering.

Nine Lives

Supplies: fleece balls

Skills: throwing, dodging

Formation: scattered

Any number of fleece balls can be used—the more the better. On signal, players get a ball and hit as many children below waist level as possible. Players who are hit nine times leave the game and stay out of bounds until they have counted to 25. Players may run anywhere with a ball or to get a ball, but they may possess only one ball at a time. All throwers who hit players in the head are out. Children often fudge the number of times they are hit. A few words about fair play may be necessary, but high activity is the focus of the game.

Variations:

1. Players who catch a ball on the fly may deduct a specific number of hits.

2. Specify either left- or right-hand throwing.

Nonda's Car Lot

Supplies: none

Skills: running, dodging

Two or three players are "it" and stand in the center of the area between two lines at opposite ends of the playing area. The class selects four brands of cars (e.g., Honda, Corvette, Toyota, Cadillac). Each student then selects a car from the four but keeps it a secret.

One of the taggers calls out a car name. All students who chose that name try to run to the other line without being tagged. The tagger calls out the cars until all students have run. Children (cars) who are tagged must sit down at the spot of the tag. They cannot move but may tag other students who run too near. When a tagger calls out, "Car lot," all the cars must go. Change taggers often.

One Behind

Supplies: none

Skills: all locomotor and nonlocomotor movements

Formation: scattered

Students are instructed to watch a leader's activities and stay one move behind. As the leader begins an activity, the children watch. After 10 to 15 seconds, the leader changes movements and the students begin the first leader movement. Each time the leader changes movements, the students do the "one behind." The leader can trick students by doing an activity with his or her eyes closed. Thus, when the students begin this activity, they have no way of knowing when to change activities or what the next leader activity is. Use this activity for any skills or with any piece of equipment.

One Step

Supplies: a ball or beanbag for each pair of children

Skills: throwing, catching

Two children stand facing each other about 3 feet (1 m) apart. One has a ball or a beanbag. The object of the game is to throw or toss the item in the specified way so that the partner can catch it without moving the feet on or from the ground. After successfully completing the throw, the thrower takes one step backward and waits for the throw from his or her partner. Children can try to increase their distance to an established line, or the two children who move the greatest distance apart can be declared the winners. When either child misses, moves the feet, or fails to follow directions, the partners move forward and start over. Variables offering interest and challenge are type of throw, type of catch, and kind of step. Throwing can be underhand, overhand, two-handed, under one leg, around the back, and so on. Catching can be two-handed, left-handed, right-handed, to the side, and so on. The step can be a giant step, a tiny step, a hop, a jump, or a similar movement.

Variation: *Bowling One Step.* In groups of four to six, each of the players in turn gets a chance to roll the ball at a bowling pin. Use a minimal distance (5 to 10 feet [1.5 to 3 m]), so that most bowlers can hit the pin on the first try. Players take a step backward each time the pin is knocked down and keep rolling until they miss. The winner is the child who moves the farthest from the pin.

Partner Stoop

Supplies: music, a whistle

Skills: marching rhythmically

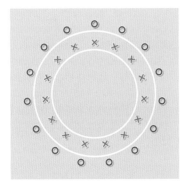

The game follows the same basic principle of stooping as in Circle Stoop but is played with partners. The group forms a double circle, with partners facing counterclockwise; one partner is on the inside, and one is on the outside. When the music begins, all march in the line of direction. After a short period of marching and on signal (whistle), the inside circle reverses direction and marches the other way—clockwise. The partners are thus separated. When the music stops, the outer circle stands still, and the partners making up the inner circle walk to rejoin their original partners. As soon as children reach their partner, they join inside hands and stoop without losing balance. The last couple to stoop and those who lose balance go to the center of the circle and wait out the next round. Start the game with walking and gradually increase the speed of movements when the class moves under control.

Ricochet

Supplies: foam balls, fleece balls

Skills: ball rolling

Formation: circle

Place several foam balls in the center of a large circle of students. Also, give the class several fleece balls. On signal, the class begins rolling the fleece balls at the foam balls, trying to move them out of the circle. Children may move outside the circle to retrieve fleece balls but may not enter the circle. The game is over when all or most of the foam balls are out of the circle.

Variations:

1. Time the students and challenge them to beat their best class time.

2. Play several games at once.

3. Use beach balls rather than foam balls.

Squad Tag

Supplies: pinnies or markers for one squad, stopwatch

Skills: running, dodging

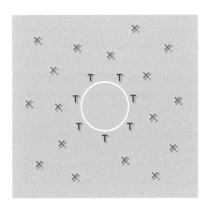

Mark the running area with cones. An entire squad acts as taggers. The object is to see which squad can most quickly tag the remaining class members. The tagging squad, which is marked, stands in a football huddle in the center of the area with their heads down. The rest of the class scatters at will throughout the area. On signal, the tagging squad scatters and tags the other class members. A class member who is tagged stops in place and remains there. Time is recorded when the last person is tagged. Each squad gets a turn at tagging. Caution children to move under control. Definite boundaries are needed.

Steal the Treasure

Supplies: a bowling pin

Skill: dodging

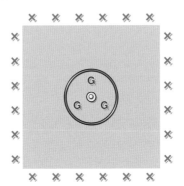

Outline a playing area about 20 feet (6 m) square, with a small circle (hoop) in the center. Inside the hoop is a bowling pin—the treasure. Choose two or more guards to protect the treasure. The guards can move as far from the treasure as they like to tag a player. Anyone tagged is out until the next game. To steal the treasure, a player must pick it up cleanly without being tagged. The guards tag players who come too near. If the treasure is knocked over by a player trying to steal it, that player must also wait out a turn. The guards must find the balance between being too far from the treasure and staying too near the treasure and never tagging anyone. If the guards tag all players, they are declared billionaires.

Variation: *Bear and Keeper.* Instead of treasure, a bear (seated cross-legged on the ground) is protected by two keepers. Anyone who touches the bear without being tagged becomes the new keeper.

Trades

Supplies: none

Skills: imagery, running, dodging

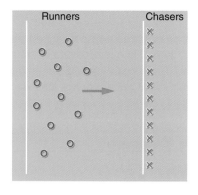

Divide the class into two teams of equal number, each team with a goal line on opposite sides of the area. One team, the chasers, stays behind its goal line. The other team, the runners, approaches from its goal line, marching to the following dialogue:

Runners: Here we come.

Chasers: Where from?

Runners: New Orleans.

Chasers: What's your trade?

Runners: Lemonade.

Chasers: Show us some.

Runners move up close to the other team's goal line and begin acting out a selected occupation or a specific task. The opponents try to guess what the pantomime represents. On a correct guess, the running team must run back to its goal line chased by the others. Any runner tagged must join the chasers. The game is repeated with roles reversed. The team ending with the most players wins.

If a team has trouble guessing the pantomime, the other team should provide hints. Remind students to raise their hand and be selected to make a guess. If a guess is just shouted out, the pantomiming team gets to take another turn.

Trees

Supplies: none

Skills: running, dodging

Two parallel lines are drawn at opposite ends of the playing area. All players, except two or three taggers, are on one side of the area. On the signal "Trees," the players run to the other side of the area. The taggers try to tag as many players as possible. Any player tagged becomes a tree, stopping where tagged and keeping both feet in place. Trees cannot move their feet but can tag any runners who come close enough. The taggers keep chasing the players as they cross on signal until only a few remain. New players are selected to be taggers.

Whistle March

Supplies: music, a whistle

Skill: moving rhythmically

Formation: scattered

Use brisk marching music for this game. Children are scattered around the room, walking in various directions and keeping time to the music. When the teacher blows a whistle several times, players form lines of that exact number of children. To form the lines, children stand side by side with locked elbows. As soon as players form a line of the proper number, they begin marching to the music counterclockwise around the room. Any children left over go to the center of the room and stay there until the next signal. On the next whistle signal (a single blast), the lines break up and all walk individually around the room in various directions.

Before children form new lines, instruct them not to use the same players as in the previous line.

Whistle Mixer

Supplies: a whistle

Skills: all basic locomotor movements

Formation: scattered

Children are scattered throughout the area. To begin, they walk around in any direction they wish. The teacher blows several short, sharp whistle blasts. Children then form small circles with the number in the circles exactly equal to the number of whistle blasts. The goal is not to be left out or caught in a circle with an incorrect number of students. Encourage players to move to the center of the area and raise their hands to find others without a group. When the circles are formed, the teacher calls, "Walk," and the game continues.

Variation: This game can be played with the aid of a tom-tom. Different beats indicate different locomotor movements—skipping, galloping, slow walking, normal walking, running. The teacher uses a whistle to signal the number for each circle.

Developmental Level III

Games at Developmental Level III are more complex and organized. Greater cooperation is needed to make the activities enjoyable. Strategy is important for successful play at this level, thus encouraging cognitive development.

Air Raid

Supplies: four to eight tumbling mats, fleece balls, foam balls

Skills: throwing

Formation: class divided into two teams

Two teams are in opposite halves of the teaching area. Each team has two tumbling mats that are fastened together and set on end to form an upright cylinder or target. The target is then placed near the back wall in the center of the gym (if baskets are obstructing the flight of balls, move the cylinder). Teams also have fleece balls and foam balls to throw. On signal, teams try to throw as many balls into the target as possible. The team with the most balls in at the end of the game wins.

Variations:

1. Use two targets for each side.

2. Place the target in a corner and score 2 points for balls that ricochet in.

3. Have the students decide where to place the target.

4. Allow students to guard their target. This may require setting cones around the target to keep guards from colliding with it.

Barker's Hoopla

Supplies: hoops, beanbags

Skill: running

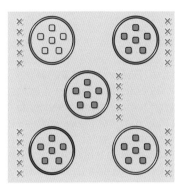

Arrange five hoops as illustrated. Use any distance between hoops (25 to 30 feet [8 to 10 m] is a challenge). Place 6 to 10 beanbags in each hoop. Divide the class into five equal teams; one team is near each hoop, which is their home base. The teams then try to take beanbags from other hoops and return them to their own home base. Here are the rules:

1. Players can take only one beanbag at a time. They must take the beanbag to their team's home base before returning for another one.

2. Beanbags cannot be thrown or tossed to the home base. Players must set each bag on the floor in the hoop.

3. No player can protect the home base or its beanbags with any defensive maneuver.

4. Beanbags may be taken from any hoop.

5. When signaled to stop, every player must freeze immediately and release any beanbags in possession. Any follow-through of activities to get a better score is penalized.

6. The team with the most beanbags in their home base is the winner.

22

Cageball Target Throw

Supplies: a cageball (18- to 30-inch [45 to 75 cm]), 12 to 15 smaller balls of various sizes

Skill: throwing

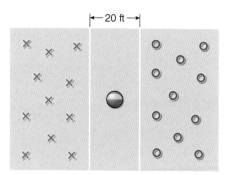

Mark an area about 20 feet (6 m) wide across the center of the playing area and place a cageball in the center. Form two teams. Players must throw the smaller balls against the cageball, thus forcing it across the line in front of the other team. Players may come up to the line to throw, but they may not throw while inside the cageball area. A player may enter the area, however, to recover a ball. No one is to touch the cageball at any time or with any object (such as a ball). If the cageball seems to roll too easily, deflate it slightly. The throwing balls can be of almost any size (e.g., soccer balls, volleyballs, or playground balls).

Chain Tag

Supplies: none

Skills: running, dodging

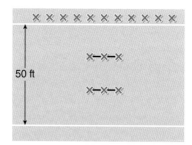

Mark two parallel lines at opposite ends of the playing area. Two groups of three players form a chain with joined hands and occupy the center. The players with free hands on either end of the chain do the tagging. All other players line up on one of the parallel lines. The center players call, "Come on over," and children cross from one line to the other. The chains try to tag the run-

ners. Anyone caught joins the chain. When the chain grows to six players, it divides into two groups of three players.

Variation: *Catch of Fish.* The chain catches runners by surrounding them like a fishing net. The runners cannot run under or through the links of the net.

Circle Touch

Supplies: yarn balls, marking spots

Skills: dodging, body management

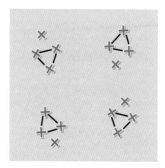

One child plays against three others, who form a small circle with joined hands. The object of the game is for the lone child to touch a designated child (on the shoulders) in the circle with a yarn ball. The other two children in the circle, by moving side to side, try to keep the tagger away from the third member of the circle. The circle players may circle in any direction but must not release hand grips. The circle cannot move across the floor; they must circle back and forth around a marking spot. The tagger, in trying to touch the protected circle player, must go around the outside of the circle. He or she cannot go underneath or through the joined hands of the circle players. To avoid roughness, play the game in short, seven-second bouts and then rotate in a new tagger.

Variation: *Grab the Flag.* A piece of cloth, a handkerchief, or a flag is tucked into the belt in back of the protected child. The fourth child, the tagger, tries to pull the flag from the belt.

Clean-Up

Supplies: volleyball net or magic rope, fleece balls or foam balls

Skill: throwing

Formation: scattered in two large groups

Use a volleyball net to divide the gym in half and place one team on each side of the net. Scatter many fleece balls around each side of the gym (the more balls, the better). On signal, students begin throwing balls over the net one at a time. After throwing one ball, students quickly find another ball and throw it over the net. This process continues until the game is stopped. The team with the fewest balls on their side of the gym is the winner.

Variation: Track scoring individually, awarding children 1 point for each ball they throw over the net. Balls that hit the back wall are worth 2 points.

Fast Pass

Supplies: one 8-inch (20 cm) foam rubber ball, pinnies

Skills: passing, catching, moving to an open area

Formation: scattered

One team begins with the ball. The object is to make five consecutive passes without letting the ball touch the floor. The team without the ball tries to intercept it or recover an incomplete pass. Each time a pass is caught, that team shouts the number of consecutive passes completed. Each time a ball touches the floor or is intercepted, the count starts over. When a team makes five consecutive passes, they immediately turn the ball over to the other team.

Players may not contact each other. Emphasize spreading out and using the entire court area. If players do not spread out, break the area into quadrants and restrict players to one quadrant.

Flag Chase

Supplies: flags, stopwatch

Skills: running, dodging

Formation: scattered

One team wears flags tucked in the back of the belt. The flag team scatters throughout the area. On signal, the chasing team tries to capture as many flags as possible in a specific amount of time. Players give the flags to the teacher or place them in a box. Players cannot use their hands to ward off a chaser. Roles are reversed. The team pulling the most flags is the winner.

Galactic Empire and Rebels

Supplies: none

Skills: chasing, fleeing, dodging

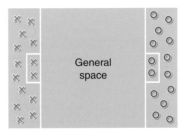

This game can be played indoors or outdoors in a square that is about 100 feet (30 m) on each side. Each team's spaceport is behind the endline, where the single space fighters are stationed, waiting to emerge against the enemy. To begin, one or more space fighters from either team move from their spaceport to entice enemy flyers for possible capture. A flyer leaving the spaceport may capture only opposing flyers who previously have left their respective spaceport. This is the basic rule of the game. A flyer may go back to his or her spaceport and be eligible immediately to emerge again to capture an opponent who was already in general space. The technique of the game is to entice enemy flyers close to the spaceport so that fellow flyers can go out and capture (tag) an opposing flyer.

Here is an example of how the game proceeds: Rebel flyer 1 moves into general space to entice Empire flyer 1 so that he can be captured. Rebel flyer 1 turns back and heads for her spaceport, chased by Empire flyer 1. Rebel flyer 2 now leaves her spaceport and tags Empire flyer 1 before the Empire flyer can tag Rebel flyer 1. The Empire flyer is now a prisoner.

A player captured by an opposing flyer goes to the tagger's prison—both captor and captive have free passage to the prison. In prison, the captives form a chain gang, holding hands and extending the prisoners' line toward their own spaceport. The last captive is always at the end of the prisoners' line with one foot in the prison. Captives can be released if a teammate can get to them without being tagged. The released prisoner (only the end one) is escorted back to his or her own spaceport, and both players are given free passage.

The game becomes one of capturing opposing flyers and freeing captured teammates. Flyers stepping over the sideline automatically become prisoners. Assign one or two players in the spaceport to guard the prison. Set a time limit of 10 minutes and declare the team with the most prisoners the winner.

Guess the Leader

Supplies: none

Skills: body management

22

The class forms a large circle and chooses two or three students, the guessers, to be in the middle. While the guessers have their eyes closed, a leader in the circle is chosen. After this child leads the class in an exercise, the guessers open their eyes and try to guess who the leader is. As the guessers watch the class, the leader continues to lead the class in various exercises. The guessers are watching for the student who changes first (the leader). The guessers have three chances to identify the leader. A new leader is then chosen.

Jolly Ball

Supplies: a cageball 24 inches (60 cm) or larger (or a 36- to 48-inch [90 to 120 cm] pushball)

Skill: kicking

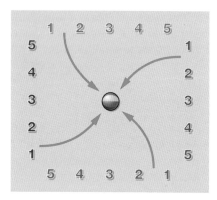

Organize four teams, each forming one side of a hollow square. Children sit down, facing in, with hands braced behind them (crab position). Consecutively number each team's members. Children wait until their number is called. Four active players (one from each team) move in crab position and try to kick the cageball over any one of the three opposing teams. Sideline players can also kick the ball. Allow players to use their hands when learning the game; later, the hands are not used.

A point is scored against a team that allows the ball to go over its line. A ball that goes out at the corner between teams is dead and must be replayed. When a point is scored, the active players return to their teams and the teacher calls another number. The team with the fewest points wins the game. This game is strenuous for the active players, so rotate them after a reasonable length of time when there is no score.

Variation: Call two active players from each team.

Jump-the-Shot Variations

Supplies: a jump-the-shot rope
Skill: rope jumping

Before students try these variations, have them review the Jump-the-Shot routine and variations listed earlier.

1. Two or more teams are in file formation facing the rope turner. Each player runs clockwise (against the turn of the rope), jumping the rope as often as necessary to return to the team.

2. Each player runs counterclockwise and tries to run around the circle before the rope catches up with him or her. If this happens, the player must jump to allow the rope to go under him or her. The best time to start the run is just after the rope passes.

3. Players can try some stunts in which the hands and feet are on the ground, to see if they can have the rope pass under them. The Rabbit Jump, push-up position, Lame Dog, and others are possibilities.

Mushrooms

Supplies: 10 to 16 cones, 10 to 16 discs, fleece balls (or foam balls)

Skill: rolling, throwing

Formation: class divided into two equal teams; scattered formation

Each team occupies half of the gym. On the endline of each half are five to eight cones with a disc balanced on top of the cone (to resemble mushrooms). Each team member has a foam ball. On signal, team members try to roll (or throw) their balls and knock off the discs. Students may not guard the cones, and any disc knocked off has to stay off, even if touched by a team's member. The game ends when discs are knocked off.

Octopus

Supplies: none

Skills: maneuvering, problem solving

Formation: groups of six to nine, holding hands, tangled

This game gets its name from the many hands joined together. Children stand shoulder-to-shoulder in a tight circle. Everyone thrusts the hands forward and reaches through the group of hands to grasp the hands across the circle. Players must make sure that they do not hold both hands of the same player. Players also may not hold the hand of an adjacent player. The object is to untangle the mess created by the joined hands by going under, over, or through fellow players. No one is permitted to release a hand grip during the unraveling. What is the end result? Perhaps one large circle or two smaller connected circles.

If, after a while, the knotted hands do not seem to unravel, call a halt and administer "first aid." The teacher and group can decide where the difficulty is and allow a change in position of those hands until the knot is dissolved. This cooperative game demands teamwork.

One-Base Tagball

Supplies: one base (or standard) and a volleyball (8-inch [20 cm] foam ball for younger children)

Skills: running, dodging, throwing

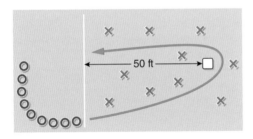

Draw a home line at one end of the playing space. Place a base or standard about 50 feet (15 m) in front of the home line. Use two teams, one scattered around the fielding area (whose boundaries are determined by the number of children). Have the other team form a single file behind the home line. The object of the game is for the fielding team to tag the runners with the ball. Two runners at a time try to round the base and head back for the home line without being tagged. The game is continuous—as soon as a running team player is tagged or crosses the home line, another player starts immediately.

The fielding team may run with the ball and pass it from player to player, trying to tag one of the runners. The running team scores a point for each player who runs successfully around the base and back to the home line. When the game begins, the running team has two players ready at the right side of the home line. The others on the team are in line, waiting for a turn.

The teacher throws the ball anywhere in the field, and the first two runners start toward the base. They must run around the base from the right side. After all players have run, the teams exchange places. The team that scores the most points wins.

To facilitate tagging a runner, instruct the players of the fielding team to pass the ball to a child close to the runner. They must be alert, because two children at a time are running. The next player on the running team must watch carefully and start the instant one of the two active runners is back behind the home line or has been hit.

Over the Wall

Supplies: none

Skills: running, dodging

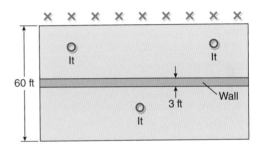

Mark off two parallel goal lines about 60 feet (20 m) apart. In the middle of the game area, lay out two parallel lines about 3 feet (1 m) apart. This is the wall. Two or three players are "it" and stand on, or behind, the wall. All other players are behind one of the goal lines. One of the taggers calls, "Over the wall." All the players must then run across the wall to the other goal line. The taggers try to tag any crossing players. Anyone caught helps catch the others. Taggers can step on or run through the wall at will, but other players who step on the wall are caught. They must clear it with a leap or a jump and cannot step on it anywhere, including on the lines. After crossing over to the other side safely, players wait for the next call. For a more difficult game, make the wall wider.

Pacman

Supplies: markers in the shape of Pacman

Skills: fleeing, reaction time

Three students are "it" and carry the Pacman marker. The rest of the class scatters throughout the area, standing on a floor line. Players can move only on a line. Begin the game by placing the three taggers at the cor-

22

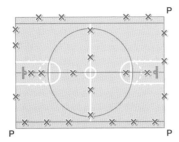

ners of the perimeter lines. Play is continuous; a player who is tagged takes the marker and becomes a new tagger. If a player leaves a line to escape being tagged, that player must secure a marker and become an additional tagger. Tagbacks are not allowed—players cannot tag the person who tagged them.

Partner Dog and Cat

Supplies: none

Skills: chasing, fleeing, dodging

Formation: partners

Partners stand toe-to-toe on a line in the center of the area. Partner A begins the game by saying, "Dog." Partner B can then say, "Dog" or "Cat." If partner B says, "Cat," partner A chases him or her to a designated line. If partner A tags him or her, he or she gets a point and the game starts over.

Variation: Try varying the number of "Dogs" that partners must say before they can call, "Cat." Using four or five "Dogs" makes the game more enjoyable.

Pin Knockout

Supplies: many playground balls, 12 bowling pins

Skills: rolling, dodging

Formation:

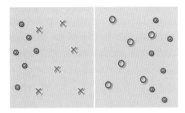

Two teams of equal number play the game on a court 30 by 60 feet (10 by 20 m) or larger (its size depends on the number of players). Each team has many playground balls and six bowling pins. The object of the game is to knock down all the opponents' bowling pins. The balls are used for rolling at the opposing team's pins. Each team stays in its half of the court.

Players are eliminated in these cases:

1. Being touched by any ball at any time, regardless of the situation (other than picking up a ball).
2. Stepping over the centerline to roll or retrieve a ball (Any opposing team member hit because of such a roll is not eliminated.)
3. Trying to block a rolling ball with a ball in their hands and being touched by the rolling ball in any way.

A foul is called when a player holds a ball longer than 10 seconds without rolling it at the opposing team. Play stops, and the ball goes to the opposing team.

The bowling pins are put anywhere in the team's area. Players may guard the pins but must not touch them. When a pin is down, even if a defending team member knocked it over unintentionally, it is removed immediately from the game. The game is over when all pins on one side have been knocked down.

Right Face, Left Face (Streets and Alleys)

Supplies: none

Skills: running, dodging

Children stand in rows, aligned from front to rear and from side to side. Two runners and two chasers are chosen. Players all face the same way and join hands with the players on either side. The chasers try to tag the runners, who run between the rows with the restriction that they cannot break through or under the arms. The teacher helps the runners by calling, "Right face" or "Left face" at various times. On command, the children drop hands, face the new direction, and join hands with the players on each side, thus making new passages available. When runners are caught or when children become tired, choose new runners and chasers.

Variations:

1. Use directions (north, south, east, west) instead of right or left commands.
2. *Streets and Alleys*. The teacher calls, "Streets," and the children face in one direction. He or she calls, "Alleys," and they face the other way.

3. Give the command, "Air raid," and children drop to their knees and make themselves into small balls, tucking their heads and seats down. This gives taggers and runners unlimited movement.

Scooter Kickball

Supplies: a cageball, gym scooters for active players

Skill: striking with various body parts

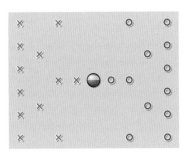

Divide each team into active players (on scooters) and goal defenders. The active players sit on the scooters, and the goal defenders sit on the goal line with feet extended. The object of the game is to kick the cageball over the goal line defended by the opposite team. The players are positioned as shown in the diagram in the left column. The game starts with a face-off of two opposing players on scooters at center court. The face-off is also used after a goal is scored. The players on scooters propel the ball mainly with their feet. Touching the ball with the hands is a foul and results in a free kick by the opposition at the spot of the foul. Players also may use the head and body to stop and propel the ball.

The goal defenders may not use their hands either; but they can use the feet, body, and head. (If scoring seems too easy, allow the defenders to use their hands.) Defenders must remain seated at the goal line and cannot enter the field of play to propel or stop the ball.

The number of scooters determines the number of active players. The game works well if half of the players from each team are in the center on scooters and the other half are goal defenders. After a goal or after a specific time, active players and goal defenders exchange places. Active players must be seated on the scooter before propelling the ball.

Variation: If every child has a scooter, the game can be played like soccer. Use standards to mark a more restricted goal (perhaps half of the endline). A goalie defends this area. All other players are active and can move anywhere on the floor. The area must be large enough to allow some freedom of play.

Star Wars

Supplies: four bowling pins

Skill: running

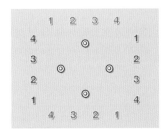

Four teams, each occupying one side facing in, form a hollow square about 10 yards (meters) on each side. Each team's members are numbered consecutively from right to left; thus, four players (one on each team) have the same number. At the center of the square, place four bowling pins, one in front of each team and spaced to keep players from colliding.

When the teacher calls their number, four children run to the right, around the outside of the square, and through their own vacated space to the center of the square. The first child to place their team's bowling pin on its side is the winner.

Keep score by using letters in the words *Star Wars*. The player who puts the pin down first gets two letters; the second player gets one. The first team to spell *Star Wars* wins, and a new game begins. Because numbers are not called in order, be sure to call every number.

Strike the Pins

Supplies: 8 to 12 bowling pins per team, 15 to 20 foam rubber balls

Skill: throwing

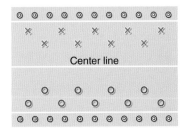

Divide the floor into two courts, each occupied by one team. Each court has another line, 25 feet (8 m) from the centerline, where each team spaces its bowling pins. Each team has at least five balls. The object of the game is to knock over the other team's pins by rolling

the balls. Players roll the balls back and forth but cannot cross the centerline. Remove pins that are knocked over by a ball or player (accidentally or not). The team with the most pins standing at the end of the game is the winner. Out-of-bounds balls can be recovered but must be rolled from inside the court.

Variation: Pins can be reset instead of removed. Two scorers, one for each pin line, are needed.

Sunday

Supplies: none
Skills: running, dodging

Three or more players are "it" and stand in the center of the area between the two parallel lines. The rest of the class is on one of the two lines. The object is to cross to the other line without being tagged or making a false start.

All line players stand with their front foot on the line. The line players must run across the line immediately when the tagger calls, "Sunday." Anyone who does not run immediately is caught. The tagger can call other days of the week to confuse the runners. Players cannot make a false start if another day of the week is called. Clearly define "making a false start." To begin, define it as a player moving either foot. Later, when children get better at the game, define it as any forward movement of the body.

Touchdown

Supplies: a small object (coin, thimble) that can be concealed in the hand
Skills: running, dodging

Two teams face each other, each standing on one of the parallel lines in the playing area. One team (offen-

sive) huddles as the members choose a player to carry an object to the opponent's goal line. The offensive team moves out of the huddle and spreads out along the line. On the signal "Hike," the offensive players move toward the opponent's goal line, each player holding the hands closed as if carrying the object. The opponents (defense) also run forward and try to tag the players. On being tagged, players must stop immediately and open both hands to show whether they have the object. If the player carrying the object reaches the goal line without being tagged, that player calls, "Touchdown!" and scores 6 points. The defensive team then goes on the offense.

Triplet Stoop

Supplies: music
Skill: moving rhythmically

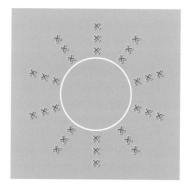

The game is played in groups of three players, who march abreast in the same direction. On signal, the outside player of the three continues marching in the same direction. The middle player stops and marches in place. The inside player reverses direction. When the music stops, the groups of three try to reunite at the spot where the middle player stopped. The last three to join hands and stoop move to the center to wait out one turn.

Whistle Ball

Supplies: a ball for each group of six to eight players

Skills: passing, catching

Formation: circles of six to eight

Eight or fewer children stand in circle formation. They pass a ball rapidly back and forth among them in any order. The object is to stay in the game as long as possible. A player sits down in place after making any of these errors:

1. Either holding the ball or catching it as the stop signal occurs. (Signal time intervals with music on–music off in 5- to 15-second segments.) Another way to control the time intervals is to appoint a student as timer.

2. Making a poor throw or not catching the ball after a catchable throw.

3. Passing the ball back to the player who threw it.

4. To avoid having anyone sit out for too long, restart the game when four or five players are left standing.

Wolfe's Beanbag Exchange

Supplies: one beanbag per child

Skills: running, dodging, tossing, catching

Formation: scattered

Identify five or six children as taggers. The remaining children start scattered throughout the area, each with a beanbag in hand. The taggers chase the players with beanbags. Tagged players must freeze, keeping their feet still and beanbag in hand. To unfreeze a player, a nonfrozen player can exchange his or her beanbag with one held by a frozen player. If two frozen players are within tossing distance, they can thaw each other by exchanging their beanbags through the air using a toss and catch. Both tosses have to be caught. If the players fail to make successful catches, they must retrieve the beanbags and try again.

Variation: After students have learned the game, tell the taggers they may interfere with the tossing of beanbags between two frozen players by batting them to the floor. The frozen players then have to try the toss again, and they are frozen until both players make successful catches.

Miscellaneous Playground Games

The following playground games are useful only for small groups, but children do enjoy playing them.

Four Square

(Developmental Levels II and III)

Supplies: 8-inch (20 cm) playground ball or volleyball

Skill: batting a ball

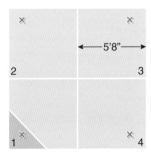

Lines are drawn as shown in the diagram. The squares are numbered 1, 2, 3, and 4. A service line is drawn diagonally across the outer corner of square 1. The player in this square always serves and must stay behind the line when serving.

Serve the ball by dropping and hitting it underhanded from the bounce. If the serve hits a line, the server is out. The server can hit the ball after it has bounced once in his or her square. The receiver directs it to any other square with an underhand hit. Play continues until one player fails to return the ball or commits a fault. Any of the following constitutes a fault:

1. Hitting the ball sidearm or overhand

2. Landing a ball on a line between the squares (A ball landing on an outer boundary is considered good.)

3. Stepping into another square to play the ball

4. Catching or carrying a return volley

5. Letting the ball touch any part of the body except the hands

A player who misses or commits a fault goes to the end of the waiting line, and all players move up. The player at the head of the waiting line moves into square 4.

Variations:

1. Draw a 2-foot (60 cm) circle at the center of the area. Hitting the ball into the circle constitutes a fault.

2. Change the game by varying the method of propelling the ball. The ball can be hit with a partially closed fist, the back of the hand, or the elbow. A foot or knee also can be used to return the ball. The server calls, "Fisties," "Elbows," "Footsies," or "Kneesies" to set the pattern.

22

3. *Chain Spelling*. The server names a word, and each player returning the ball must add the next letter in the sequence.

4. For Developmental Level I students, use cooperative scoring. Players see how many consecutive hits they can make without missing.

Team Handball

(Developmental Levels II and III)

Supplies: team handball, foam rubber ball, or volleyball; cones; pinnies

Skills: running, dribbling, passing, throwing, catching

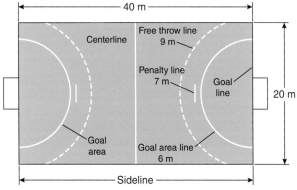

Outdoor field markings

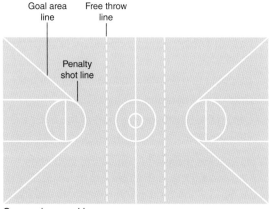

Gymnasium markings

The regulation handball court is shown in the diagram. Only the goalie occupies the goal area inside the six-meter line. Players use the seven-meter line for a major penalty shot and the nine-meter line for a minor penalty shot. Boundary cones, tape on the wall, rope through a chain-link fence, soccer goals, or field hockey goals can be substituted for actual team handball goals. For indoor play, modify a basketball court for team handball by running a line from the corners of the court to the top of the key.

The object of the game is to move a small soccer ball down the field by passing and dribbling and then throw the ball into a goal area three meters wide by two meters high. In regulation play, each team has six court players and one goalie. The six court players cover the entire court. A player is allowed three steps before and after dribbling the ball. There is no limit on the number of dribbles. Dribbling is discouraged, however, because passing is more effective. A double dribble is a violation. Players can hold the ball for only three seconds before passing, dribbling, or shooting. Only the goalie can kick the ball.

One point is awarded for a goal. Violations and penalties are similar to those in basketball. Free throws are taken from the point of the violation, and defense must stay three meters away from that player while protecting the goal. A penalty throw is awarded from the seven-meter line for a major violation, such as fouling an offensive player who is inside the nine-meter line in a good shooting position. During a penalty throw, all players must be behind the nine-meter line.

For more in-depth coverage of rules, order a teaching resource kit from USA Team Handball, One Olympic Plaza, Colorado Springs, CO 80909 (www.usateamhandball .org).

The offensive team starts the game with a throw-on from the centerline. A throw-on also starts play after each goal. All six offensive players line up at the centerline, and a teammate throws the ball to a teammate. The defense is in position, using either a zone or person-to-person defense. Offensive strategy is similar to basketball with picks, screens, rolls, and movement to open up shots on the goal. With a zone defense, players make short, quick passes in an overloaded portion of the zone.

The defensive strategy is also similar to basketball, commonly using person-to-person and zone defense. Beginning players should start with the person-to-person defense and learn how to stay with an offensive player. In zone defense, the back players in the zone are back against the goal line, and front players are just inside the nine-meter line. The zone rotates with the ball as passes are made around the court.

Variation: *Sideline Team Handball*. Try this game when space is limited and the class is large. Extra team members spread out along each sideline (one team on each side). These sideline players can receive passes from teammates and help pass the ball downcourt. Sideline members can only pass the ball, however, and the three-second rule applies to them. A challenging variation might have different team members on each sideline. This distribution forces the active players to sharpen their passing skills.

Tetherball

(Developmental Levels II and III)

Supplies: a tetherball assembly (pole, rope, ball)

Skill: batting a ball

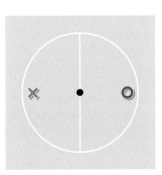

One player stands on each side of the pole. The server puts the ball into play by tossing it into the air and hitting in the direction he chooses. The opponent must not strike the ball on the first swing around the pole. On its second swing around the pole, he or she hits the ball back in the opposite direction. Each player tries to hit the ball so that the rope winds completely around the pole in the direction they are hitting the ball. The winner is the player who succeeds in doing this or whose opponent forfeits the game by making a foul. A foul is any of the following:

1. Hitting the ball with any part of the body other than the hands or forearms
2. Catching or holding the ball during play
3. Touching the pole
4. Hitting the rope with the forearms or hands
5. Throwing the ball
6. Winding the ball around the pole below the 5-foot (1.5 m) mark

After the opening game, the winner of the preceding game serves. Winning four games wins the set.

Two Square

(Developmental Levels II and III)

Supplies: a playground ball or volleyball

Skill: batting a ball

The basic rules and lines are the same as for Four Square, but only two squares are used. If players are waiting for a turn, the active player who misses or fouls can be eliminated as in Four Square. If only two players wish to play, they can keep score. The ball must be served from behind the baseline.

TEACHING TIP

Set up learning stations for passing, shooting, goal tending, dribbling, and defensive work. Performance objectives are useful for structuring practice time at each station. Students can use nerf balls, playground balls, and volleyballs to practice goal attempts while helping goalies perfect their skills. Group drills from basketball apply to team handball defense, offense, passing, and dribbling. Include various instructional devices for targets in passing, timing for dribbling through cones, or narrowing the goal area for shots to the corners. Have students practice penalty shots. Competitive drills are enjoyable and motivating for most students.

Volley Tennis

(Developmental Levels II and III)

Supplies: volleyball and net

Skills: most volleyball skills

Formation: scattered

The game can be played as a combination of volleyball and tennis. The net touches the ground, as in tennis, and the ball is put into play with a serve. It may bounce once or be passed directly to a teammate. Players must hit the ball three times before sending it over the net. Spiking is common because of the low net. A point is scored when the ball cannot be returned over the net to the opposing team.

Relays

Relays offer children opportunities to learn cooperative skills because they must follow rules and directions and work with fellow team members. Relays are appropriate when they feature skills children have overlearned, such as running, jumping, balancing, and so forth Relays can be used at opportune times as motivational activities. The following procedures will assure that all students have the opportunity to participate and contribute to a group outcome.

1. Restrict teams to four or five players. Too many on a team increases the amount of time spent waiting for a turn.
2. Change teams often so that all youngsters have a chance to win. Reserve the right to change team

22

makeup and the order in which the students are placed on individual teams. No team should have to lose more than twice in a row.

3. Placing less skilled players in the first or last position of the relay team can create an uncomfortable situation by spotlighting their ability level. Use discretion and move both skilled and lesser skilled players to avoid this situation.

4. Infractions of rules should be briefly discussed. Make relays a social learning experience. Children are in a situation where they have to conform to rules if the experiences are to be enjoyable for all. Discuss how cooperation precedes competition; competing is impossible if players choose not to cooperate and follow the rules.

5. Designate a deceleration zone with cones or spots to prevent students from running into the wall. Place the markers at least 10 feet (3 m) from the wall.

6. Concentrate on the process of enjoying relays rather than identifying a winner each time. Add other incentives to the relay so that the focus isn't only on speed or skill. For example, the winning team must have all players sitting and in a straight line to be eligible for a win.

7. Always conduct a trial run so that each team clearly understands the procedures. If a new relay does not start properly, stop the activity and review the instructions. The trial run assures that all students understand how to perform. If youngsters do not understand the relay, they might be embarrassed.

8. Clarify traffic rules. In most cases, the way to the right governs. When runners go around the turning point, they do it from the right (counterclockwise), returning past the finish line on the right side. Team members are not to leave the restraining line until they are tagged by the returning runner. Exchanging a baton or a beanbag can also be used to restrain runners from leaving too early.

Most of the relays presented here can be used successfully with children in Developmental Levels II and III. The relays incorporate previously learned fundamental motor skills and are arranged in order of increasing difficulty. If youngsters have not previously learned the skills required for a relay, practice the skills first.

Beanbag Relays

Beanbag relays are a good starting point for younger children, because beanbags are easier to handle than balls.

Beanbag Handoff Relay

Players are in a line, standing side by side. The player on the right starts the beanbag, which is handed from one player to the next down the line. When it gets to the end of the line, the relay is over. Children should rotate positions in line.

In the next stage, a revolving relay can be developed in which each member of the team rotates from the right of the squad to the left. When each child has had an opportunity to be the lead member of the group, the relay is complete. This relay can be varied with an under-leg pass. The child passes the beanbag underneath one leg to the next player.

Circle Beanbag Handoff Relay

Players stand in a circle, facing out, but close enough so that the beanbag can be handed from player to player. One circuit begins and ends with the same player. The under-leg pass can be used in this formation also.

Carry-and-Fetch Relay

Players are in closed squad formation, with a hoop or circle positioned up to 30 feet (10 m) in front of each team. The first runner on each team has a beanbag. On the command "Go," this player carries the beanbag forward, puts it inside the hoop, and then returns and tags off the next runner. The second runner goes forward, picks up the beanbag, and hands it off to the third runner. One runner carries the beanbag forward, and the next runner fetches it back. Different locomotor movements can be specified.

Beanbag Circle Change Relay

Players are in lane formation. Two hoops or circles are about 15 and 30 feet (5 and 10 m) in front of each team. A beanbag is placed in the far hoop. The first runner runs forward, picks up the beanbag, and moves it to the hoop closer to the team. The next player picks it up and takes it back to the farthest hoop. The beanbag must be placed inside the hoop.

The Farmer and the Crow Relay

Runners are in lane formation. A line is drawn about 20 feet (6 m) in front of the teams. The first runner of each team is the farmer, the second runner the crow, and so on. The farmer has five beanbags. On the signal "Go," the farmer hops forward and drops the five beanbags in a randomly spaced fashion, placing the last beanbag beyond the drawn line. The farmer then runs back and tags the next player, the crow. The crow runs to the farthest beanbag and begins hopping, picking up the beanbags. The crow hands the five beanbags to the third runner, another farmer, who puts the objects out again.

Whenever players have a beanbag, they hop; when they have no beanbags, they run. The last beanbag should be placed beyond the far line, because this determines how far each player has to move. The relay can be done with only hopping allowed.

Lane Relays Without Equipment

In lane relays, each runner runs in turn. The race is over when the last runner finishes. Lane relays are usually regular relays. Different types of movements can be used to challenge the runners.

1. Locomotor movements: walking, running, skipping, hopping, galloping, sliding, jumping.

2. Stunt and animal movements: Puppy Dog Run, Seal Crawl, Bear Walk, Rabbit Jump, Frog Jump, Crab Walk.

3. Restricted movements: Heel-and-toe walk, sore toe walk (hold the left foot with the right hand), walking on the heels, Crazy Walk, Toe Tug Walk.

4. Children run (walk, skip, gallop, hop) with partners (inside hands joined) just as a single runner would.

5. Children face each other with hands joined (as partners), slide one way to a turning point, and slide back to the starting point—leading with the other side.

6. *Wheelbarrow Relay.* One person walks on his or her hands while the partner holds him or her by the lower legs, wheeling down to a mark. Positions are switched for the return. Distances should not be too long.

Lane Relays With Equipment

1. All Up, All Down Relay. Three bowling pins are set in a small circle about 20 feet (6 m) in front of each team. The first player runs forward and sets up the pins one at a time, using only one hand. The pins must stand. The next player puts them down again, and so on.

2. A short line (24 inches [60 cm]) is drawn about 20 feet (6 m) in front of each team. A bowling pin stands on one side of the line. Each player must run forward and stand the pin on the other side of the line, using one hand only.

3. Two adjacent circles are drawn about 20 feet (6 m) in front of each team. Three bowling pins stand in one of the circles. A player runs forward and moves the pins, one at a time, standing each pin in the other circle. The next player moves the pins back, one at a time, to the original circle, and so forth.

4. Roll-and-Set Relay. Each team has a mat and a bowling pin. The mat is placed lengthwise in front of the team (40 to 60 feet away [12 to 18 m]), and the pin is between the team and the mat. The first player runs toward the mat, picking up the pin. Carrying the pin in one hand, he or she does a Forward Roll, sets the pin beyond the far edge of the mat, and runs back and tags off the next player. This player runs to the pin, picks it up, does a Forward Roll on the way back, and sets the pin in the original spot. The players alternate in this fashion until all have run. The pin must stand each time, or the player must return and make it stand.

5. Three-Spot Relay. Three parallel lines are drawn in front of the teams to provide three spots for each team. Each player is given three tasks to perform, one at each spot. The player then runs back and tags off the next player, who repeats the performance. Suggestions for the tasks are the following:

   - Lie prone.
   - Lie supine.
   - Do an obeisance (touch the forehead to the floor).
   - Do a nose-and-toe (touch the toe to the nose from a sitting position).
   - Do a specified number of hops, jumps, push-ups, or curl-ups.
   - Perform a designated stunt, such as the Coffee Grinder or Knee Dip.
   - Jump rope for a specified number of turns.

The runner must perform according to the directions at each spot, completing the performance before moving to the next spot. Other task ideas can be used. The winning team selects the requirements for the next race.

22

6. Potato Relay. A small box about a foot square is placed 5 feet (1.5 m) in front of each lane. Four 12-inch (30 cm) circles are drawn at 5-foot (1.5 m) intervals beyond the box. The last circle is therefore 25 feet (7.5 m) from the starting point. Four blocks or beanbags are needed for each team.

To start, the blocks are placed in the box in front of each team. (The race can also be done with bowling pins. Instead of being placed in a box, they are in a large circle at the start.) The first runner goes to the box, takes a single block, and puts it into one of the circles. He or she repeats this performance until there is a block in each circle; then the first runner tags off the second runner. This runner brings the blocks back to the box, one at a time, and tags off the third runner, who returns the blocks to the circles, and so on.

Using a box to receive the blocks makes a definite target. When the blocks are taken to the circles, some rules must be made regarding placement. The blocks should be considered placed only when they are inside or touching a line. Blocks outside need to be replaced before the runner can continue. Paper plates or pie plates can be used instead of circles drawn on the floor.

Gym Scooter Relays

Each team has a gym scooter. Scooters lend themselves to a variety of movements, both with individuals and with partners. Scooters should not, however, be used as skateboards. Some suggestions for individual movements follow:

1. Sit on the scooter and propel with the hands or feet.
2. Kneel and propel with the hands.
3. Lie facedown and move in alligator or swimming fashion.

Partner activity can feature any of several approaches. Partners can operate as a single unit, doing the task and passing the scooter to the next pair, or one partner can push or pull the other to the turning point, where they exchange roles and return to the starting line. A third approach is for the pusher to become the rider on the next turn.

1. Rider kneels, and partner pushes or pulls.
2. Rider sits in a Seat Balance, and partner pushes or pulls on the rider's feet.

3. Rider does a Tummy Balance, and partner pushes on his or her feet.

A wheelbarrow race also can be done with the down person supporting the hands on the scooter.

Lane Relays With Balls

A number of interesting lane relays (some regular and some revolving) feature ball-handling skills. The balls should be handled crisply and cleanly. A mishandled ball must reenter the race at the point of error. (See chapters 24 and 27 for some suggested basketball and soccer ball dribbling relays.)

Bounce Ball Relay

A circle is drawn 10 to 15 feet (3 to 5 m) in front of each team. The first player runs to the circle, bounces the ball once, runs back to the team, and gives the ball to the second player, who repeats the routine. Each player has a turn, and the team whose last child carries the ball over the finish line first wins. To vary the relay, players can bounce the ball more than once.

Kangaroo Relay

The first player in each lane holds a ball between the knees. He or she jumps forward, retaining control of the ball, rounds the turning point, jumps back to the head of the file, and hands the ball to the next player. If a player loses the ball from between the knees, he or she must stop and replace it. Slightly deflated balls are easier to retain.

Bowling Relay

The player at the head of each team has a ball. A line is drawn 15 to 20 feet (5 to 6 m) in front of each team. The first player runs to the line, turns, and rolls the ball back to the second player. The second player must wait behind the starting line to catch the ball and then repeats the pattern. The race is over when the last player has received the ball and carries it over the forward line.

Crossover Relay

The Crossover Relay is similar to the Bowling Relay, except that the ball is thrown instead of rolled.

Obstacle Relays

Over-and-Under Relay

A magic rope is stretched about 18 inches (45 cm) above the floor to serve as the turning point. Each runner jumps over the rope and starts back immediately by going under the rope.

Figure-Eight Relay

Three or four cones are spaced evenly in front of each team. Players weave in and out in figure-eight fashion.

Iceberg Relay

Teams are in lane formation, with each team having two rubber marking spots (small rubber mats). The mats represent icebergs, and the task is to use the spots as stepping-stones. Each player moves his or her own icebergs by placing one in front, jumping on it, and reaching back to pick up the one from which he or she jumped. A player who touches the floor (falls in the ocean) must go back to the previous spot and try again. As soon as the player reaches the opposite end, he or she can pick up his or her spots and run them back to the next competitor.

Jack Rabbit Relay (Jump Stick Relay)

The relay starts with the first player in line running forward around the turning point and back to the head of the line. In the meantime, the next person in line holds a 36-inch (90 cm) wand. The runner returns and grabs one end of the wand from the player at the front of the line. These two runners then move the stick under the rest of the team members in line who jump it. When the stick has passed under all players, the previous stick holder hands the stick to the next person in line, runs around the turning point, and returns. He or she then helps the next player in line hold the stick, who becomes the next runner, and so on. When the stick is being jumped, it should be held close to the ground.

Hoop Relay

Each team consists of a file of five or six children who join hands. The leader, in front, holds a hoop in the free hand. The object is to pass the hoop down the line so that all bodies go through it, until the last person holds the hoop. The last person takes the hoop to the head of the line, and the process is repeated until the original leader is again at the head. Children may manipulate the hoop with their hands as long as they keep their hands joined. They should lock little fingers if necessary. All team members must pass through the hoop, including the last person.

The hoop can be moved around a circle of children with hands joined. The hoop starts on a pair of joined hands. When it has gone around the circle, over all the bodies, and returned to the same spot, the race is over.

Revolving Team Ball Relays

Arch Ball Relay

Each team is in lane formation. Each player, using both hands, passes a ball overhead to the next person, and so on to the back player. The last player, on receiving the ball, runs to the head of the column, and the activity is repeated. The race is over when the original front player comes back to his or her spot at the head of the line. Each player must clearly handle the ball.

Right and Left Relay

The action is the same as for Arch Ball, except that the ball is handed to the person behind with a side turn. The first turn is to the right, and the next person turns to the left.

Straddle Ball Relay

Players are in lane formation. Each player takes a wide straddle stance, forming an alley with the legs. The ball is rolled down the alley to the back person, who runs to the front with it and repeats the activity. Players may handle the ball to help it down the alley, but it is not required that each person do so.

Over and Under Relay

Players take a straddle position in lane formation. The first player hands the ball overhead with both hands to the player behind, who in turn hands the ball between his or her legs to the next player. The ball goes over and under down the line.

Pass and Squat Relay

One player (number 1) with a ball stands behind a line 10 feet (3 m) in front of his or her teammates, who are in lane formation. Number 1 passes the ball to number 2, who returns the ball to number 1. As soon as he or she has returned the ball to number 1, number 2 squats down so that the throw can be made to number 3, and so on down the file. When the last person in line receives the ball, he or she does not return it, but carries it forward, straddling the members of his or her team, including number 1, who has taken a place at the head of the file. The player carrying the ball forward then acts as the passer. The race is over when the original number 1 player receives the ball in the back position and straddles the players to return to his or her original position.

Some care must be taken that the front player in the file is behind the team line as the passing starts. After the straddling, repositioning the file is necessary. Each player should form a compact ball during the straddling activity. This relay is interesting, but some practice is needed for it to function properly.

Circle Pass Relays

Simple Circle Relay

Each team forms a separate circle of the same size. At first, the circle should be small enough so that players can hand the ball to each other. The leader of each group starts the ball around the circle by handing it to the player on his or her right. As soon as the ball gets back to the leader, the entire team sits down. The first team to be seated in good formation wins.

Later, the circle can be enlarged so that the ball must be passed from player to player. More than one circuit of the circle can be specified. The leader can hold the ball aloft to signal completion.

Circle-and-Leader Relay

A circle 15 to 20 feet (5 to 6 m) in diameter is formed. One player is in the center with a ball. The ball is passed in succession to each of the players. The race is over when the ball is returned to the center player by the last circle player. Different passes can be specified.

Corner Fly Relay

The players are in a line or semicircle facing the leader , who has a ball. The ball is passed to and received from each player, beginning with the player on the left. When the last player receives the ball, he or she calls out, "Corner fly." The player then takes the position of the leader. The leader takes a position in the line to the left. In the meantime, all players adjust positions to fill the spot vacated by the new leader. The relay continues, with each player becoming the leader in turn. When the original leader returns to the spot in front of the team, the relay is over.

A marker can be placed behind the leader so that the last player in line, when he or she receives the ball, runs around the marker to the leader's spot. This gives a little more time for the team to shift places and get ready for the new leader.

If a team is one person short of the number of players on the other teams, two consecutive passes could be made by the leader to the first person. Alternatively, the initial leader might take two turns (first and last), which means that another person comes forward after the second turn to provide the finish.

Tadpole Relay

One team forms a circle, facing in, and has a ball. Another team is in lane formation about 10 feet (3

m) behind the circle. The object of the game is to see how many times the ball can be passed completely around the circle while the other team completes a relay. Each player from the team in lane formation runs in turn around the outside of the circle and tags off the next runner until all have run. In the meantime, the ball is being passed around the circle on the inside. Each time the ball makes a complete circuit, the circle players count the number loudly. After the relay is completed and the count established, teams trade places and the relay is repeated. The team making the higher number of circuits by passing the ball is the winner. The relay gets its name from the shape of the formation, which resembles a tadpole.

Miscellaneous Relays

Pass the Buck Relay

Players are facing sideways, with teams about 5 feet (1.5 m) apart. All players of a team are linked by joined hands. The leader is on the right of each team. On signal, the leader "passes the buck" to the next player by squeezing his or her hand. This player in turn passes the squeeze to the next, and so on down the line. The end player, when he or she receives the buck, runs across the front of the team and becomes the new leader. The player starts the squeeze, and it is passed down the line. Each player in turn comes to the front of the line, with the original leader finally returning to the head position.

Rescue Relay

Lane formation is used, with the first runner behind a line about 30 feet (10 m) in front of the team. The first runner runs back to the team, takes the first player in line by the hand, and "rescues" the player by leading him or her back to the 30-foot (10 m) line. The player who has just been rescued then runs back to the team and gets the next player, and so on, until the last player has been conducted to the line.

Around-the-Bases Relay

Four bases are laid out as in a baseball diamond. Two teams, lined up at opposite bases on the inside of the diamond, compete at the same time. The leadoff player for each team makes one complete circuit of the bases. Each player on the team follows in turn.

The same type of relay can be run indoors by using chairs or bowling pins at the four corners. Further variations can require children to run more than one lap or circuit on a turn.

Modified Relays

In modified relays, players are numbered and run as individuals. These activities are not relays in the true sense of the term.

Attention Relay

The players on each team are facing forward in lane formation with team members about arms' distance apart. The distance between the teams should be about 10 feet (3 m). Two turning points are established for each team—one 10 feet (3 m) in front of the team and the other 10 feet behind. Players are numbered consecutively from front to rear. The teacher calls, "Attention." All come to the attention position. The teacher calls out a number. The player on each team holding that number steps to the right, runs around the front and the back markers, and returns to place. The rest of the team runs in place. The first team to have all members at attention, including the returned runner, wins a point. The numbers should not be called in consecutive order, but all numbers should be called. Distance between the teams must be sufficient to prevent runners from colliding.

Variations:

1. Different means of locomotion can be used.

2. The teams can be organized by pairs, and two can run at one time, holding inside hands.

3. *Under the Arch*. The leader calls two consecutive numbers, say, numbers 3 and 4. Immediately, numbers 3 and 4 on each team face each other and form an arch by raising both hands. The players in front of the arch (numbers 1 and 2) run forward around the front marker, around the back marker, and then back to place, passing under the arch. The players behind the arch run under the arch first, around the front marker, around the back marker, and back to place. When all have returned to place, the arch players drop hands and resume position. The first team to be at attention is the winner. The running is always forward at the start. Each player follows the person ahead, keeping in numbered order. Each goes around the front marker, around the back marker, and back to place after passing under the arch.

4. Each team stands on a bench. With the teams standing at attention, a number is called, and that team member jumps down from the bench, runs completely around it, and runs back to place on top of the bench.

Circular Attention Relay

Two teams form a circle, with players facing counterclockwise and each team occupying half of the circle. The players of each team are numbered consecutively. The teacher calls the group to attention and then calls a number. Children with that number (one on each team) immediately run counterclockwise around the circle back to place and stand at attention. The first to get back to place scores a point for the team. All numbers should be called.

Variation: *Circle Leapfrog*. All players crouch on their knees, facing counterclockwise and supporting the forehead in cupped hands on the floor. When a number is called, the runner straddles or leapfrogs all children around the circle, returns to place, and resumes the original position. Scoring is the same as in Circular Attention.

Supine Relay

Players lie supine on the floor, in a circle, with their heads toward the center of the circle and hands joined. The members of each team are numbered consecutively. When a number is called, the player with that number runs around or over the players on his or her team and then returns to his or her place, assuming the supine position with hands rejoined. The first player back scores a point for the team. The game can continue to a definite score or until all numbers are called.

Variations:

1. *Human Hurdle*. Each team forms a small circle and sits with backs to the center. The action is the same as for Supine Relay.

2. *Cyclone*. This activity is a team race; the team getting back to original place first is declared the winner. At the signal, the first player gets up and starts around the group. Immediately after the first player passes him or her, the second player follows. The third player follows as soon as the first two have passed. The remaining players follow in the same manner. When the first player gets back to place, he or she takes his or her original seated position. Each player in turn goes around until the player is back to his or her original place. The last player cannot move until all the other players have gone by. When the player gets back to place, the race is over.

22

LEARNING AIDS

SUGGESTED READINGS

Dowson, A. (2009). *More fun and games.* Champaign, IL: Human Kinetics.

Hastie, P. (2010). *Student-designed games.* Champaign, IL: Human Kinetics

Horowitz, G. (2009). *International games.* Champaign, IL: Human Kinetics.

LeFevre, D. (2012). *Best new games* (updated edition). Champaign, IL: Human Kinetics.

Pangrazi, R.P., Beighle, A., & Pangrazi, D.L. (2009). *Promoting physical activity and health in the classroom.* San Francisco, CA: Benjamin Cummings.

Tomporowski, P., McCullick, B., & Pesce, C. (2015). *Enhancing children's cognition with physical activity games.* Champaign, IL: Human Kinetics.

REFERENCES

Stiehl, J., Morris, D., & Sinclair, C.D. (2008). *Teaching physical activity: Change, challenge, and choice.* Champaign, IL: Human Kinetics.

Lifetime Activities

Lifetime activities are activities used to maintain an active lifestyle throughout the life span. Too often, physical education curricula offer a narrow scope of experiences and do not offer activities that students can use as they become adults. This chapter is designed to introduce students to various activities they can perform alone or in small groups. These activities can be played in highly competitive situations or enjoyed in recreational settings with limited competition. Rather than creating outstanding performers, this chapter focuses on introducing students to activities not always found in elementary school settings.

Learning Objectives

▶ Explain why lifetime physical activities should be taught in physical education.
▶ Identify characteristics of lifetime physical activities.
▶ Discuss the importance of teaching walking in elementary schools.
▶ Design an orienteering course for students and list the skills that students will need to know before attempting the course.
▶ List a variety of racket skills and lead-up games involving rackets.
▶ Discuss various disc activities that can be taught in elementary schools.

Lifetime physical activities can be enjoyed throughout the lifespan. A primary role of physical education is to promote lifetime physical activity for all students. Thus, physical education teachers need to understand the activities that adults engage in as well as the popular activities in the school community (such as disc golf and tennis). When thinking of lifetime activities, most people immediately envision activities for the elderly, such as gardening, shuffleboard, and walking. After all, such activities are participated in throughout life, including those in the older adulthood stage of life. Because older people typically engage in less intense activities, the thought process might go something like this: "An 80-year-old woman can walk for exercise; therefore, walking is a lifetime activity" or "Basketball requires large amounts of intense running, so you probably can't play if you are in your 70s; therefore, it's not a lifetime activity." Although this thinking is logical, it is not entirely accurate. Lifetime activities usually meet all or most of these criteria:

- They offer opportunity for participation at various intensities, including low and vigorous.
- They can be noncompetitive; they are enjoyable even if competition is not the focus of participation.
- They can be done alone or with a partner or small group.
- They can contribute to the participant's overall health.

As most of us grow older, our desire and ability to engage in intense physical activity decrease. Thus, the physical activities we enjoy will change. At age 20, we may like playing football and rugby, but after age 25, we do not typically choose to play these games. In fact, we do not think of most traditional team sports as lifetime activities because they are usually quite vigorous. Physical education traditionally has focused on team sports, but the data suggest that the types of activities that adults participate in are not team sports. Of the top 20 physical activities for adults, only 2 are team sports (basketball at 13 and soccer at 20).

1. Exercise walking
2. Exercising with equipment
3. Swimming
4. Camping
5. Bicycle riding
6. Bowling
7. Aerobic exercising
8. Hiking
9. Workout at club
10. Running or jogging
11. Fishing
12. Weightlifting
13. Basketball
14. Billiards or pool
15. Golf
16. Yoga
17. Boating (motor or power)
18. Target shooting (net)
19. Hunting with firearms
20. Soccer

Data from *Sports Participation in 2010: Series I* (Mt. Prospect, IL: National Sporting Goods Association.)

Note that not all of the top 20 activities are appropriate for elementary children or the physical education setting. These are not the only activities that should be included in physical education; they are merely the most popular for adults. Physical education can certainly teach team sports, especially modified versions of team sports. But if the role of physical education is to promote lifelong physical activity, we must take these data into account and include lifetime physical activities when developing our curricula.

The feasibility of including physical activity in a typical day also plays a role in lifetime activity. Most adults work at least an eight-hour day, care for children, and run errands—leaving little time for physical activity. Those who deem physical activity important must work it into their schedules when time permits. Trying to find a group of six to eight adults who can work physical activity into their schedules at the same time and on the same day is even more difficult, although it can be done. For example, at universities, small groups of faculty and staff often participate in sports during lunch. But most adults do not work on a campus that has facilities such as gyms and fields. For these scheduling and logistics reasons, most lifetime physical activities require only one or two participants.

The role of physical education is to promote lifetime physical activity for all students. Because all students have unique needs and desires, offering a variety of activities is important. Thus, physical educators should use a balanced curriculum, including gymnastics, rhythms, traditional sports, and lifetime activities.

Walking

Walking is by far the most popular physical activity for adults (NPR et al., 2015). It requires minimal equipment, can be done almost anywhere and at any time, causes few injuries, and can be enjoyed alone or in small groups. For these reasons, walking is likely the activity that most physical education students will engage in as adults. Walking is an often overlooked, but important, component of any physical education curriculum designed to promote lifetime physical activity.

Instructional Procedures

1. Delineate the walking route with cones.
2. Emphasize appropriate posture and technique using these cues: head up, eyes forward, and smooth arm swing.
3. Check the course before student use; watch for irregular sidewalks and other hazards
4. If an outside course is used, emphasize safety.
   a. Use crosswalks.
   b. Walk on the left, looking toward oncoming traffic.
   c. Ensure appropriate supervision
5. During the walking lessons, emphasize the excellent health benefits gained from walking.
6. Students can participate in walking activities alone, with a partner, or in small groups. For most activities, encourage students to walk with a friend. Being able to socialize is a great motivator for children.
7. Teach "Pace, don't race." Many students want to start out fast, even to jog, only to tire out quickly. Pacing is a difficult concept for some students to grasp, and thus it must be taught.
8. Avoid counting laps and having children walk in the same direction. Doing so conveys the message that winning, finishing last, and lap counting are important.
9. Let students walk in any direction they choose within the marked course.
10. Use time as the workload rather than number of laps. Have students walk for a set number of minutes. This approach helps minimize the ridicule that many slower students face.

TEACHING TIP

Thoroughly investigate designated walking routes to ensure they are safe and easy to follow. Are there sidewalks or wide shoulders on the road? Is it a low-traffic area? Are aggressive dogs found in the area? Are there obvious distractions that would tempt students to stray from the route?

11. Some students may enjoy walking with a piece of equipment, such as a beanbag, hoop, jump rope, or basketball.
12. After the walking activity, let students choose an activity such as basketball, hopscotch, jump rope, or Four Square.

Walking Activities

Move to the Beat

Playing area: gymnasium or outside teaching area
Players: individuals
Supplies: cones, one tambourine or drum
Skills: walking, pacing

Begin with students walking in general space to the beat of the drum and then begin modifying the pace of the drum. Next, have students walk to the drumbeat around the perimeter (marked by cones) of the teaching area. Directions such as "Take a step with each beat" help students learn to move at the correct pace.

After students have grasped the concept of fast, medium, and slow walking through an activity such as Move to the Beat, pacing can be introduced. Explain that the goal is to move from one cone to the next in a designated number of steps, reaching each cone neither before nor after the last beat, but "just in time." Start students at different places on a path marked by cones, and repeat this activity.

Variations: Challenge students to move from cone to cone in a specific amount of time by using a beat per second and then ultimately removing the beat. Progressively increase the distance that students move by increasing the number of cones they have to pass.

23

Walking Interviews

Playing area: gymnasium or outside walking course

Players: partners

Supplies: 4-by-6-inch (10 by 15 cm) index cards with interview questions

Skills: walking, communication, pacing

Children choose a partner. Give each set of partners an index card with a series of questions. For this activity, students simply walk with their partners and interview them using the questions provided (figure 23.1). After the first partner's interview, the partners switch roles using the questions on the backside of the card. Here are some possible interview questions:

- What is your favorite physical activity? Why?
- What is your favorite movie and why?
- Who are the people in your family? Describe them.
- What do you usually do after school?
- What do you like about school?
- What is your favorite fruit or vegetable?

Pearson Education

FIGURE 23.1   Walking Interviews.

Use just a few interview questions, so that students can change partners often and get to know other children. Another motivating idea is to let students create their own questions.

Bank Walk

Playing area: gymnasium or outside walking trail

Players: individuals or partners

Supplies: cones, fake money, or other tokens

Skills: walking, pacing, counting money, communication

Students choose a partner and begin walking a planned route. The teacher walks the route in the opposite direction. Each time the students meet the teacher, they receive money. After a set amount of time, students count their money. Next, they give the money back to the teacher and begin again, this time trying to beat the total they earned the first time.

To promote politeness, pay extra money to students who are polite (e.g., those who say, "Please" and "Thank you"). To prevent students from saying, "Thank you" just to get money, keep this bonus a secret by not telling the class what the extra money is for until after the lesson.

Giant Map Construction

Playing area: gymnasium or defined teaching area

Players: groups of two or three students

Supplies: one sheet of paper and a pencil for each set of partners

Skills: walking, map reading, cooperation

In an activity setting marked by cones, each set of partners maps a route they will walk together. They can use shapes, words, or letters as routes. They then walk the route with their partner. For example, a spelling word for the week may be *intensity*. Using the entire activity area as their mapping area, the partners walk and spell out the word *intensity* from left to right.

The key to this activity is to get students to use the entire teaching area for the route they will map and walk. If pedometers are used, have students guess the number of steps that one or both partners will take to finish the route. Sets of partners can test the number of steps or amount of activity time they need to walk the route and then swap maps with another group.

New Engineer

Playing area: gymnasium or defined activity area

Players: groups of six to eight students

Supplies: a small piece of equipment (beanbag or baton) for a group of four to six students

Skills: walking, pacing

Teams of students stand in single-file and begin walking with the leader (engineer) holding the piece of equipment and leading the group throughout the teaching area. On signal, the leader hands the piece of equipment to the second person, who hands it to the third, and so on. They do all this while the line is still walking. When the equipment gets back to the last person (caboose), the caboose speed-walks to the front of the line and becomes the new engineer.

Challenge students to walk briskly. At intervals, stop and change the makeup of the teams to provide renewed interest.

Just Walk

Playing area: outside walking area

Players: groups of one to four students

Supplies: cones

Skills: walking, pacing

Use cones to set up a walking course. If desired, draw a map of the path directions for students. With the map, this activity is a precursor to an orienteering lesson presented later. Students can walk alone, with a partner, or in groups. The only rules are (1) they must keep moving, and (2) they must stay on the course for a predetermined time. This activity is not intended to take an entire period; 10 to 15 minutes is sufficient. This activity is an excellent opportunity for teachers to walk with students and get to know them as individuals.

Walking Club

Walking clubs are great for getting youth moving both in and out of school. To provide more opportunity for participation, they can be conducted before school, after school, and even during recess. After a motivating walking unit in physical education, students may be excited to start walking whenever possible. Physical educators can create school walking courses, changing them often to add excitement. Emphasize safety when starting a walking club:

- Always tell an adult where you will be walking.
- Always walk with a friend or small group.
- Use the sidewalk.
- Cross the street only where there is a sidewalk.
- Obey traffic signs.
- Avoid crowded areas.
- Wear bright-colored clothes with safety reflective material.
- Look left, right, left, right before crossing.
- Avoid dangerous areas such as construction sites.

Careful planning helps ensure the success of a walking club. Programs that are hastily put together tend to disappear quickly. Here are some steps for starting a walking club.

1. Envision what a walking club should look like at the elementary level.

   a. How many students will participate?
   b. What grades will be invited?
   c. When will the club meet?
   d. Who will be responsible for administering the program?
   e. Will volunteers be needed?

2. Discuss the possibilities and options with the principal.

3. Recruit other teachers who may be interested in cosupervising the club.

4. Develop a plan for inclement weather. Most schools have hallways or a gym or cafeteria where students could walk in case of rain, snow, and the like. The club should meet even during long stretches of poor weather.

5. Create and post a schedule. The schedule will depend on the number of supervisors and participants. Rotating grades may be necessary—with one or two participating each day—especially for before- and after-school clubs. Starting with one grade level, or even one classroom, may also help work out any problems before taking the club school-wide.

6. Advertise the club with school announcements, during physical education lessons, in a physical education newsletter to parents, and at open houses. As the first club meeting approaches, letters home inviting parents to participate will help in recruiting participants.

7. Create a system for tracking participation. Sheets can be designed to track laps or minutes of participation. Given the number of laps that equals 1 mile, students can track their progress on a map of their city, state, or country. Devise a similar system for minutes of movement. For example, 15 minutes of walking equals a mile. Granted, each child's pace affects this formula, but the idea is simply to get students moving.

8. Consider calling your club a Physical Activity Club (PAC) and include a variety of activities, either structured or unstructured. You can thus address the interests of a variety of students, especially those who may enjoy activities other than walking.

9. Approach local businesses about sponsoring the club. Hosting a Family Walk-a-Thon is a great fund-raiser and public relations event for the physical education program.

23

10. If funds are available, buy pedometers for club use. Also, purchase walking-club T-shirts for all club members. Local sporting goods stores may be willing to help with T-shirts.

11. Using activities from the following section, teachers and students can create challenging orienteering courses for the walking club.

Orienteering

Orienteering is a navigation and sport activity that incorporates walking or jogging, determining directions, and map reading. The object of the activity is to use a map and perhaps a compass to locate specific points in a given area. Competitive orienteering can involve skills such as skiing, mountain biking, compass reading, and point tracking while navigating a wilderness course designed to test participants' skills. At the elementary level, orienteering focuses on teaching students basic concepts such as recognizing directions (north, south, east, west) and map reading. Orienteering can also be integrated with walking, disc golf, challenge courses, or other activities that involve map reading. Students will actively learn the skills necessary to navigate an area such as the gymnasium, a classroom, the school, the playground, or a local park.

Instructional Procedures

1. Introduce map directions by placing a large N, S, E, and W on the appropriate walls.

2. Refer to the walls as the east wall or the north wall when giving directions. For example, say, "When I say 'Go,' hustle to the red line closest to the east wall."

3. To introduce directional travel, use short instructions such as by saying, "If we run from this wall (pointing to the east wall) to that wall (pointing to the west wall), what direction are we moving?" Presenting this information in a variety of lessons leading up to orienteering will help set the stage for those lessons. For example, if you are working on basketball passing with a partner, you might say, "When I say go, work on your overhead pass with one partner facing north and one facing south."

4. Introduce students to basic symbols used to designate landmarks and controls. Controls refer to the specific locations students are challenged to find on an orienteering course. See figures 23.2 and 23.3 for examples of maps with symbols.

5. If pencils are needed, for safety reasons have students carry their materials (maps, pencils, and so on) in a pencil box or folder.

Orienteering Skills

Determining Directions

Many students have difficulty learning directions. One strategy is to mark the gym walls with N, S, E, and W to identify compass directions. These signs allow students to learn the relationship of one direction to another (e.g., when they face east, north is to the left). Another strategy is to mark landmarks on the school grounds—paint an S on the slide on the south side of the playground; paint or hang an E on the fence on the east side of the school grounds. These strategies allow teachers to teach directions inside and outside. Teach older children to determine directions by looking at the sun. The sun always rises in the east. Thus, if students are looking at the sun in the morning, west is always behind them. Another way to teach this concept is to know that in the morning, shadows point west. Next, students can transfer what they learned in the gym and know that if they face east, then north is to the left and south is to the right. Conversely, in the afternoon, when students face the sun, their shadows point east; north is to the right and south is to the left. Students will need time to process and understand this information. Because most physical education classes are at the same time each day, students can learn one method before going on to another.

Reading a Map

Most classrooms have maps and globes that help students understand the idea of map reading. Reading a map involves determining landmarks and directions. For elementary students in a gym, this process could be recognizing symbols such as doors, the clock, or posters on a wall when shown a map of the gym. Figure 23.2 shows a gymnasium map with symbols. Students will ultimately read the map to find specific locations called controls.

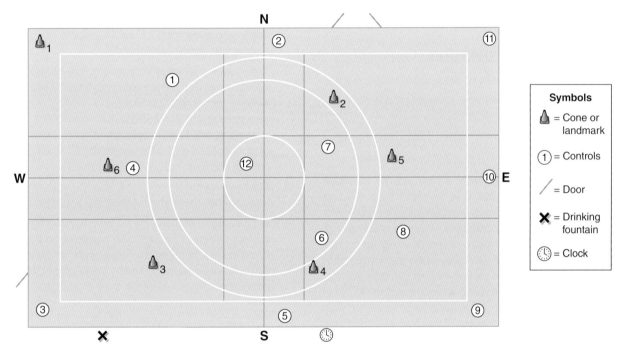

FIGURE 23.2 Gymnasium orienteering map.

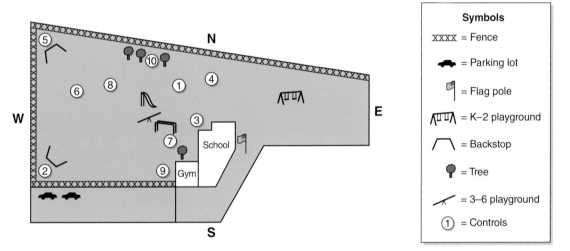

FIGURE 23.3 School grounds orienteering map.

Before reading a map, students must orient it. They do this by turning the map until it matches what they are facing in the gym. For example, using figure 23.2, students may be standing in the southeast corner of the gym facing the side door on the west wall. They would then turn the map until the southeast corner of the gym on the map is closest to them and the west wall is farthest away. Teachers can give instruction such as by saying, "Standing where you are, orient your map to the clock." Students can also learn to keep their thumb where they are on the map and move their thumb as they move, a method called thumbing.

23

Orienteering Activities

Gymnasium Orienteering

Playing area: gymnasium or designated teaching area

Players: individuals, partners, or small groups (three or four students)

Supplies: map of the gymnasium, cones, poly spots

Skills: map reading, problem solving, cooperation

Because orienteering is likely a new activity for most students, the best approach is to begin map reading and learning to find controls in a controlled environment like the gym. Introduce concepts like map reading and compass directions in short pieces leading up to orienteering activities. For example, when teaching circuit training, give students a simple map of the stations and ask them to find their stations when prompted. Alternatively, use poster board and draw a large map that students can see from a distance. This activity introduces students to map reading while searching for controls. These steps will aid in planning this activity.

1. Get a drawing of the gym and lay out an orienteering course on paper (see figure 23.2). Be sure to mark N, S, E, and W on the map. Figure 23.2 uses numbered circles to designate control points and numbered triangles to designate

cones or landmarks. If a gym has few landmarks, add some numbered cones. Poly spots (also numbered) represent controls.

2. Next develop a set of instructions that students will follow to get to the next control point; see the sidebar for sample instructions. Print each set of instructions, cut it into individual instructions, and tape each one to the appropriate control marker or poly spot (e.g., tape instructions for finding control number 2 on control number 1).

3. After writing the instructions, use the map to walk through them and ensure they are accurate.

4. On the day of instruction, be sure to have the correct number of cones with numbers on them and the correct number of poly spots, or controls, with numbers on them. Using the map, set the cones and control points in their proper locations.

Divide the class into small groups. Give each group a map and instruct them to report to any numbered control. Review concepts that have been taught leading up to this lesson. For example, ask, "If I am walking from the south wall to the north wall, in what direction am I traveling?" A refresher on map orienting may also be helpful. Signal the teams to begin, following the instructions at their control. This way, all teams are searching for a different control.

GYM ORIENTEERING SAMPLE INSTRUCTIONS

Control	Instruction
1	Move directly east to find control 2.
2	To find control 3, go to the southwest corner of the gym.
3	Control 4 is close to landmark 6.
4	Find control 5 in the middle of the south wall.
5	Control 6 is just north of landmark 4.
6	To find control 7, walk directly north of control 6.
7	You will find control 8 directly south of landmark 5.
8	Control 9 is in the southeast corner of the gym.
9	Walk directly north of control 9 to find control 10.
10	To find control 11, go to the northeast corner of the gym.
11	Control 12 is in the middle of the gym.
12	Control 1 can be found by walking northwest from control 12.

School Grounds Orienteering

Playing area: school grounds

Players: individuals or groups of two to four students

Supplies: map of school grounds with landmarks and controls

Skills: map reading, cooperation

This activity is a follow-up to Gymnasium Orienteering, so the planning process is identical. Depending on students' familiarity with finding N, S, E, and W outside, the instructions may change. For example, instead of reading, "Move northwest from control number 7 to find control number 8," the instruction may say, "From control number 7, move toward the slide to find control number 8." Figure 23.3 is an example of a school grounds orienteering map. Notice that the teacher can see all controls—and thus all students—from anywhere on the grounds. Before starting this activity, give students instructions about the area they will use. For example, if using the map in figure 23.3, tell students there are no controls on the K–2 playground or in front of the school.

Variation: For additional challenge, remove the numbers from each control. Similar to Gymnasium Orienteering, students will have to use the instructions and their map-reading skills to find the controls.

Scavenger Hunt

Playing area: entire gymnasium or designated teaching area

Players: individuals, partners, or small groups of three to four

Supplies: an orienteering map, instructions, an envelope for each control, a clue for each control

Skills: map reading, problem solving

Devise an orienteering course similar to those shown earlier. This activity is taught and participated in like an orienteering course; but at each control, students find a clue that is part of a series to be collected at each control. At the end of the course, each team uses the clues to solve the puzzle. Here are some possible puzzles to be solved.

- At each control, students collect an index card with a single letter. Together, the letters spell out O-R-I-E-N-T-E-E-R-I-N-G.

- Paste a picture onto stiff paper and cut it into the same number of pieces as there are controls. At each control, teams collect a piece of the puzzle that they will assemble into a picture after completing the course.

TEACHING TIP

1. To add difficulty, remove the control numbers from the map. Students then have to use the directions on the control and the map, rather than just the map.

2. At each control, place a pencil box. After finding each control and before moving on to the next, students draw a line from the previous control to the current one. With some extra planning, these lines could form an object, make a letter, or spell a short word.

3. Each control also could present a trivia question, a skill to perform, or a fitness challenge. Orienteering is thus integrated with other physical education lessons.

- At each control, students find an index card bearing one word. When put together, the words form a question such as "What is an important part of a healthy lifestyle?" for teams to answer. Each team will probably come up with a different answer, such as "physical activity," "a balanced diet," or "not smoking."

- On separate index cards, print the letters used in two or three of a class's spelling words. Students must then unscramble the letters to spell the words. This is an excellent way to reinforce classroom content without sacrificing physical education objectives.

Tennis

Tennis is a popular activity worldwide. Because it can be played at varying levels and intensities, it is a lifetime activity that many older adults enjoy. Fortunately, the United States Tennis Association has developed a school tennis program that allows play and games in a physical education setting. The Physical Education Guide for Teaching Tennis in the Schools (USTA, 2017) is available to physical educators and offers a curriculum, instructional materials and station signs, and a DVD that shows management and instructional skills. The role of the physical educator is to present modified activities that allow children to explore the game of tennis and use a racket successfully. Practice in tennis should move from individual skills to partner activities as quickly as is feasible.

23

Tennis Skills

Grip

An easy method for teaching the grip is to have the student hold the paddle perpendicular to the floor and "shake hands" with it (figure 23.4). Young people tend to revert to the inefficient hammer grip, so named because it is similar to the grip used on a hammer. Students should practice picking up their racket using a handshake grip. Spinning the racket and stopping in a handshake grip is excellent practice.

FIGURE 23.4 Handshake grip.

Pearson Education

Ready Position

Getting ready to hit is the first step to successful tennis strokes. This skill is often overlooked because it is usually missed by spectators who are watching the other player hit the ball. Preparing to hit involves being in a solid athletic position with heels slightly raised (just enough to get a piece of paper under the heels) and ready to move. The racket is gripped in the handshake grip with the other hand just below the strings. This position enables students to move quickly to the ball. Use these instructional cues to aid skill development:

1. Athletic position.
2. Paper under your heels.
3. Racket in front.
4. Little jump.

Forehand

The forehand shot is the most frequently used tennis shot and the easiest for most people to learn. For this reason, many students will want to make every shot a forehand. Be sure to encourage students to try other shots as their skills improve. For the forehand stroke, the body is turned sideways; for a right-handed player, the left side points in the direction of the hit. Contact is made slightly before the ball reaches the plane of the body. Instructional cues for a proper forehand shot follow.

1. Ready position.
2. Opposite side to target.
3. Racket back.
4. Watch the ball.
5. Step and swing through the ball with a stiff wrist.
6. Ready position.

Backhand

The backhand is a more difficult stroke to learn than the forehand. Forehand resembles other motions that students often perform, such as throwing and swinging a baseball bat, but backhand is just the opposite. It thus feels unnatural and must be practiced before it feels comfortable. For the backhand stroke, the thumb is placed against the racket handle for added support and force, and the body turns sideways so that the shoulder on the side of the racket hand points in the direction of the stroke. The racket strikes the ball even with, or slightly before, it reaches the front leg (figure 23.5).

FIGURE 23.5 Tennis backhand sequence.

1. Ready position.
2. Same side to target.
3. Both hands back.
4. Watch the ball.
5. Step and swing through the ball.
6. Follow through high.
7. Ready position.

Serve

The serve is a difficult skill for children to perform accurately. When teaching serving, begin by allowing any serve that crosses the net to be played, regardless of location. With beginners, the goal of playing activities is to maximize repetitions and refinement. Instruct your students to put the ball into play with a bounce and forehand or backhand stroke.

Volley

A volley is made with a sort of punch stroke. The hitter faces in the direction of the hit, pushing the racket forward rather than stroking. In modified courts and activities, children often use this stroke. For many, it is their primary stroke. Provide these skill cues to help develop the volley:

1. Ready position.
2. Step and push the racket toward the ball.
3. Back to ready position.

Individual Tennis Drills

Racket Spin

Stand the racket on its frame with the grip up. On signal, spin the racket like a top; quickly grab and turn it until it is in a handshake grip.

Racket Roll

All students place a ball on their racket. On signal, they begin rolling the ball around the racket while sitting, standing, or walking. The challenge is for the ball to touch every hole on the racket. After a short time, have students let the ball bounce off the floor once and catch it on the other side of the racket.

Bounce-Downs

In scattered formation, each child has a racket and a tennis ball. They use the racket to dribble the ball on the ground, trying to bounce the ball waist high. Instruct students to switch hands periodically. Bouncing the ball and catching can also be allowed.

Bounce-Ups

As the name suggests, this activity is the opposite of bounce-downs. Each student has a ball and bounces the ball into the air. Instruct students to keep the ball eye high. When students are comfortable with this, let them invent their own bouncing routine.

Edgies

In scattered formation, each child has a ball and racket. On signal, they begin bouncing the ball, either up or down, using the edge of the racket. Encourage them to switch hands and try using different edges of the racket.

Flip-Flops

Every student starts with a racket and a ball in scattered formation. Using bounce-ups, students rally the ball with alternating sides of the racket. Notice the positioning of the hand in figures 23.6 and 23.7. If necessary, the ball can bounce on the floor. Instruct students to switch hands often.

Pearson Education

FIGURE 23.6 Tennis flip.

23

FIGURE 23.7 Tennis flop.

Invent-a-Bounce

After players are comfortable with basic bouncing, encourage them to invent different ways of bouncing the ball. First, offer some examples such as around the back, under the leg, using the handle, or balancing on one foot. To modify an activity, students develop a dribbling routine such as two bounce-downs, two bounce-ups, two edgies, and two flip-flops.

Racket Stunts

Each student has a ball and racket. When instructed, they hit the ball into the air and try to touch the floor—or do a heel click, clap their hands, or turn around—before the ball hits the floor. Emphasize controlled rackets and bounces. For this activity, students can use beanbags rather than balls. If they use balls, after the ball hits the floor, have students try to absorb the force of the bounce by dribbling the ball back down until it is rolling on the racket. After the ball is rolling, have them try another stunt.

Self-Rally

With a ball and racket, students try to rally the ball as many times as possible. Bounce-ups, bounce-downs, edgies, and flip-flops can be used. Students can also choose if they want to allow a bounce. The primary goal is for students to develop personal challenges and try to better previous self-rally scores.

Pick It Up

All students start with the racket in hand and the ball on the floor. The challenge is to get the ball on the racket without touching it with the other hand. One strategy is to scoop up the ball with the racket. An easier alternative is to get the ball rolling by tapping it with the racket and then scooping it up. Students may also choose to trap the ball between the outside of their foot and the racket. They then lift the foot and racket, raising the ball to a level where it can be dropped. The ball then bounces, and they try to balance it on the racket. Lastly, students can start dribbling the ball, gradually bouncing it higher and higher. They can then catch the ball on the racket by placing the racket under the ball and "giving" with the knees as the ball touches the racket.

Wall Rally

Introducing the forehand and backhand by using Wall Rally allows students many repetitions. Standing with their opposite side to the wall, students bounce the ball with their other hand and lightly tap the ball to the wall. Stop the class periodically to introduce the next cue. You might say, "If you want to continue working on bringing your racket back, that's great. If you are ready, go ahead and work on stepping toward the wall when you hit the ball. Remember, watch the ball. Go." Wall Rally can be used to teach every tennis stroke, with instruction progressing to students counting the number of times they can rally the ball without missing. Emphasize a controlled, soft racket.

Partner Tennis Drills

Racket Grab

Partners stand about 3 feet (1 m) apart with their racket on its frame with the grip standing up. On signal, partners let go of their racket and move forward toward their partner's racket. The goal is to grab the partner's racket before it hits the ground and quickly take a handshake grip. With each success, partners take one step back.

Partner Toss

One partner has a racket, and the other partner stands about 8 feet (2.5 m) away with the ball. The partner with the ball lightly tosses the ball to the other partner's forehand side. The racket partner turns with the opposite side to the target and lightly hits the ball back. Be sure to emphasize the importance of the toss. After five hits, partners switch roles. Challenge each pair of partners to see how many times they can execute a toss to the forehand side followed by a correct forehand hit. This activity can be used for backhand and volley strokes as well. As the students' skills progress, increase the distance and use a line in the area as the net.

Partner Rally

Players are paired up, each with a racket and one ball. The partner with the ball bounces it and hits a forehand or backhand shot. After striking the ball, that player returns to the ready position. Meanwhile, the receiving partner moves from the ready position to a striking position and hits a forehand or backhand shot. This activity teaches players to return to ready position after stroking the ball. To increase the challenge, have students find a line on the floor and use it as a net.

Step Back

This drill is like Partner Rally, with one exception. For every four consecutive hits, each player takes one step back. Be sure that all students are in a formation that allows them to step back without getting in the others' way. Figure 23.8 shows where partners might be during a Step Back game.

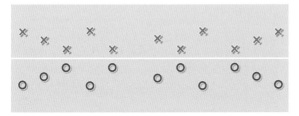

FIGURE 23.8 Step Back formation. Partners are across the line from each other and are the same distance from the line.

Juggle Rally

Each set of partners has two rackets and one ball. The partner with the ball starts the rally with two individual drills, such as two bounce-downs or an edgie and a bounce-up. After the two hits, the third hit is to his or her partner. The partner then receives the ball with one hit, executes another individual activity, and then hits it back to his or her partner. Children may choose to use floor bounces, the wall, or any other creative idea. The only rule is to hit the ball three times during each rally.

Toss and Catch

Partners stand about 8 feet (2.5 m) apart, one with a racket and one with a ball. The partner with the ball tosses the ball to the partner with the racket, who uses his or her hand and racket to catch the ball against the racket strings. The partner then tosses the ball back to the tosser, and they repeat the drill. The object of this activity is to teach students to move to the ball. The tosser attempts to move the catcher forward, backward, left, and right.

Toss, Hit, Catch

One partner starts with a ball and the other with a racket. The partner with the ball tosses the ball to the partner with the racket, who hits it back; the tosser then tries to catch the ball. As a variation, the tosser can have a racket and try to trap the ball against the racket with the nondominant hand. The game can also be changed to Hit, Hit, Catch, or ultimately Hit, Hit, Hit, which is essentially a tennis rally.

Tennis Activities

Racket Roll Tag

Playing area: gymnasium or specified playing area

Players: entire class

Supplies: one racket and ball per student

Skills: racket awareness, dodging, fleeing

Every player has a racket with a ball balanced on it. Designate two to four students as taggers. All players must move with the ball balanced on their racket. If tagged by a tagger, that person becomes "it," and the previous tagger is no longer "it." If the ball falls off, the child quickly grabs the ball, places it on the racket, and continues. The tagger's ball must be on his or her racket when tagging someone. Before beginning, define how students may be tagged (e.g., only tapped on the shoulder with the hand not holding the racket). Stop and start the game often to keep students from getting frustrated if they cannot tag someone or if they keep getting tagged.

Racket Red Light

Playing area: gymnasium or specified playing area

Players: entire class

Skills: one racket and ball per student

Skills: racket awareness, cooperation

23

This game is played like regular Red Light, with two twists. The traffic controller holds a red piece of paper and a green piece of paper. Rather than yell, "Red light" to stop students' movement or "Green light" to start them, the controller holds up the red or green paper. Therefore, students have to keep their eyes up and not focused on the ball. If this activity is too challenging, use the traditional method of calling out commands. Also, all players must have their ball balanced on their racket. If the ball falls off, they must return to the starting line. As in the original game, the first person to reach the line that the traffic controller is standing on becomes the traffic controller. Another variation is to command left turn, right turn, and caution.

Wall Rally

Playing area: gymnasium or playing area with wall sections of 5 to 6 feet for each group

Players: groups of two to four students

Supplies: one racket per child, one ball for each group, masking tape to mark off wall space

Skills: forehand, backhand, court movement

Assign each group to a section of wall designated with tape. For this activity, students in all teams on the court are working together to see how many times they can consecutively rally without the ball being called dead. One player puts the ball in play by bouncing it and hitting a forehand or backhand (figure 23.9). After the ball

hits the wall, the second player must return the ball to the same section. Although there is no limit to the number of hits or the number of bounces allowed before the ball is hit back to the wall, encourage students to hit it back after the first bounce. To keep the rally going, allow even rolls. Each team's players must also maintain the order in which they hit the ball to the wall (first player, second player, third player, fourth player). Remind players that they are all a team and can help each other. For example, player 1 hits the ball off the wall and player 2 is unable to reach it, but player 3 can. Player 3 can stop the ball with his or her racket and set it up for player 2. The only thing that player 3 cannot do is hit it to the wall until after player 2 does. The rally is over if any of the following occur:

1. The ball stops rolling.
2. The ball is hit toward the wall and is not between the tape lines.
3. The ball is hit to the wall but not in the correct order of players.

One-Wall Tennis

Playing area: gymnasium or playing area with wall sections of 5 to 6 feet (1.5 to 1.8 m) for every group (figure 23.10)

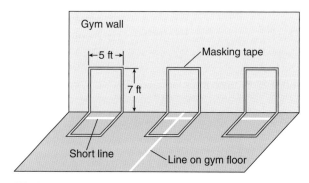

FIGURE 23.10 One-Wall Tennis setup.

Players: Groups of two to four students

Supplies: one racket per child, one ball for each group, masking tape to mark off wall space

Skills: forehand, backhand, score keeping, court movement

Player 1 serves the ball to the wall. The ball must hit the wall and come off the wall past the short line. The short line is 3 feet (1 m) from the wall. Player 2 then must

FIGURE 23.9 Wall Rally.

Pearson Education

return the ball to the wall before it bounces twice and before his or her third hit. Thus, after player 1 hits it off the wall, player 2 can let it bounce once, hit it in the air, let it bounce again, and then hit it to the wall. Emphasize using short strokes. Do not allow spiking and hitting the ball downward. Score points as follows:

- If the ball bounces more than twice before being returned to the wall
- If the ball is hit more than twice before being returned to the wall
- If the ball hits the wall but not in the space designated by tape
- If the ball hits the wall but does not come back past the short line

Tennis Volleyball

Playing area: volleyball court

Players: two teams of 8 to 10 students

Supplies: one training ball, one racket per child, a net

Skills: forehand, backhand, volley, score keeping

A team 1 player puts the ball in play by hitting it to team 2's half of the court. After the ball hits the floor on team 2's side, all team 2 players can hit the ball. They can hit the ball to their teammates or directly over the net to team 1's side. Teams can hit the ball any number of times before hitting it back over the net. The opposing team scores a point each time the ball is not hit back to them. Bounces are unlimited, but a rolling ball is considered dead. No boundaries, other than the net, are used. Students play to 11 points and then start over. As in most games, frequently change the makeup of teams.

Tennis Over the Line

Playing area: teaching area divided into 5-by-10-foot (1.5 by 3 m) squares with masking tape

Players: partners

Supplies: one training ball, one racket for each student, one line, strips of masking tape

Skills: forehand, backhand, volley

Before class, mark off the teaching area using masking tape and existing lines to create two 5-foot (1.5 m)

squares with a common middle line. One child stands in one square, and his or her opponent stands in the other. The game is a combination of two square and tennis. Only underhand shots are permitted. Player 1 puts the ball in play by dropping the ball and hitting a forehand or backhand off the bounce into player 2's square. Before the ball bounces twice, player 1 must return the ball, again using only an underhand stroke, to player 2's square. If a player cannot return the ball into his or her opponent's square or does not hit the ball before it bounces twice, his or her opponent scores 1 point. Player 1 serves five times in a row, regardless of scoring, and then player 2 serves.

USA School Tennis

Playing area: gymnasium divided so that each group of six students has a court

Players: three students per team

Supplies: one racket per student; one training ball per group of six; tumbling mats, stretched magic rope or other equipment to use as a net for each court (figure 23.11)

Skills: forehand, backhand, volley, score keeping

This team game of tennis has no more than three players on a side. The focus of the game is controlled swings. All balls must move upward when leaving the racket, and no spiking is allowed. Again, racket control is important. Each game is played to 5 points, by ones. Scoring is as follows:

- If the ball rolls, it is dead; the other team scores.
- If the first bounce after the ball crosses the net is out-of-bounds, the other team scores.
- If the ball is spiked, the other team scores.

Start play with a drop serve—one player drops the ball and hits a forehand or backhand over the net. If players are having difficulty with spacing and staying in their own area, divide the halves of the court into three equal areas and instruct all players to stay in their area. Teams can hit the ball any number of times before sending it back to the other side. Similarly, bounces are unlimited. A modification of the game allows a rolling ball to be in play. This variation requires students to scoop up the ball and continue play.

23

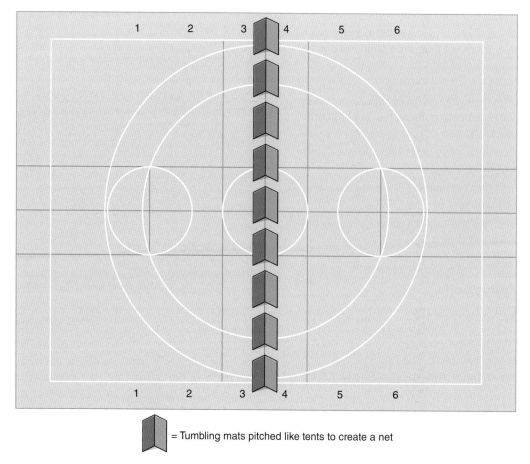

| 1 | 2 | 3 | 4 | 5 | 6 |

| 1 | 2 | 3 | 4 | 5 | 6 |

= Tumbling mats pitched like tents to create a net

FIGURE 23.11 USA School Tennis diagram.

Badminton

People around the world enjoy playing badminton. Although this sport is less popular in the United States, it still ranks as one of students' favorite activities in many physical education programs. The game is played with a shuttlecock, or birdie, rackets (figure 23.12), and a net. Its regulation court is unique to badminton (figure 23.13). Badminton is considered a lifetime activity because it can be played at a fast pace when at competitive levels or at a slower pace as a recreation or leisure activity. The basic badminton strategy is to use finesse, and moving the opponent up, back, and side-to-side is an effective strategy. At the elementary level, the goal is to expose students to striking a birdie with a badminton racket. Tracking and striking a birdie is somewhat difficult because of the trajectory of a birdie. The birdie will fall straight down as opposed to the trajectory a ball takes. To increase children's success,

several equipment manufacturers now offer larger birdies. Also, students can use smaller paddles or rackets at first and then progress to the longer badminton rackets. After learning this skill, students will experience greater success in other skills, and they can enjoy badminton as a lifetime activity.

Pearson Education

FIGURE 23.12 Birdie and badminton racket.

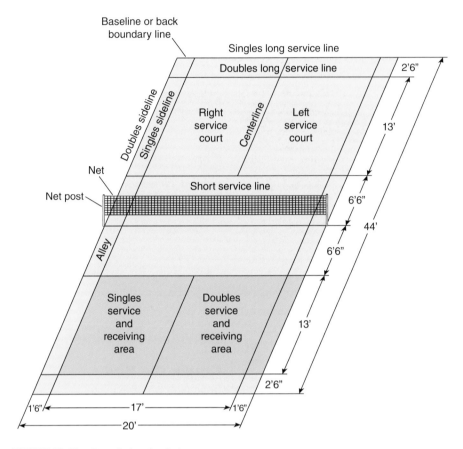

FIGURE 23.13 Regulation badminton court.

Badminton Skills

Racket Control

Elementary students must first learn to control the racket. Before striking the racket they should first learn the appropriate grip. For beginning purposes, the shakes hands grip as seen in figure 23.4 is appropriate and easy to learn. Using this grip, students learn to manipulate the racket using a variety of challenges.

Serve

For beginners, the most appropriate serve is the underhand forehand serve (figure 23.14). This serve can be used for long and short serves. Teach this skill first, for two reasons: (1) for children to succeed early and learn the basic underhand motion, they must drop the birdie to themselves; and (2) to progress to partner rallying,

students must be able to put the birdie into play. The easiest way to do this is the underhand serve.

For this serve, the child begins with the opposite foot forward; the student's dominant foot is back with the weight shifted to the back foot. In his or her nondominant hand, the child holds the birdie by the tip in front of his or her body. The racket goes straight back in the backswing. As the student swings the racket forward, the

FIGURE 23.14 Badminton serve sequence.

23

student shifts his or her weight to the front foot, drops the birdie, and makes contact about at knee level. The student hits through the birdie and stops when his or her arm is parallel to the ground. Here are instructional cues for the serve:

1. Favorite foot back with weight on back foot.
2. Birdie by tip and out in front.
3. Backswing, shift weight, drop, swing.
4. Racket follows birdie.

Forehand Underhand Clear

The underhand clear on the forehand side is a common shot in badminton and an easy stroke to learn. The major difference between this forehand and forehands in other racket activities is the step. For the forehand underhand clear, the player reaches with the dominant foot and the dominant hand, which has the racket in it. This allows for a greater reach for the birdie. The shot begins with the student in ready position. After seeing that the birdie will fall in front on the dominant side, the player quickly steps toward the birdie. If necessary, he or she takes a few shuffles or slide steps. The player then swings with an upward motion with the palm of the hand up. Here are teaching cues for the forehand underhand clear:

1. Ready position.
2. Move toward birdie with dominant side.
3. Reach with dominant hand and foot.
4. Swing low to high.
5. Back to the ready position.

Forehand Overhead Clear

The forehand overhead clear uses a motion similar to throwing. When the player sees that the serve is a high one that he or she can return, the player moves into position as if to make a throw with the nonstriking side closest to the net. The player draws back the racket as if scratching the back. Next, he or she swings forward, trying to contact the birdie as high as possible. The follow-through is down to the waist. The trajectory of this shot is either straight or upward. These instructional cues will help develop this skill:

1. Ready position.
2. Opposite side to net.
3. Scratch your back.
4. Swing high to low.
5. Back to the ready position.

Backhand Underhand Clear

The backhand underhand clear shot is executed when the birdie is on the nondominant side and cannot be hit above the head. The shot starts with the player stepping with the dominant foot toward the birdie and placing his or her side or back to the net. As this is taking place, the player shifts his or her thumb from the handshake grip to on top of the racket. Next, the player reaches back and swings to strike the birdie using an upward motion. Here are some useful cues for teaching this skill:

1. Ready position.
2. Step with dominant foot toward birdie.
3. Back to net.
4. Swing low to high.
5. Back to the ready position.

Individual Badminton Drills

Cradle the Birdie

Beginning with the racket in hand and the birdie on the ground, each student tries to scoop up the birdie from the ground using only the racket. The goal is to get the birdie on the racket and balanced. After this happens, the child drops the birdie and does this activity again. Combine this activity with Birdie Balance and Bird Bounce, which follow.

Birdie Balance

Each student has a racket and a birdie. When instructed, students place the birdie on their racket and move around the teaching area using various locomotor skills. At first, most students will place the birdie on the racket with feathers down. Next, instruct students to put the birdie on its side and continue moving. Challenge students to jump, jump while turning, sit down, lie down, stand up, bend their arm at different angles, and do other movements while balancing the birdie.

Bird Bounce

All students begin with a racket and a birdie. On signal, they begin bouncing the birdie with their racket. They can start by standing still and then progress to moving. Challenge students to make each bounce with alternating sides of the racket. Also, encourage students to try using their nondominant hand and to switch hands between bounces. As a lead-up to other activities, ask students to catch the birdie in the nondominant hand after every third hit.

Flip and Catch

With a birdie and a racket, students balance the birdie on the racket by standing it on its feathers. Next, they toss the birdie into the air with the racket and catch it with the other hand. Have them practice this skill with the racket in the nondominant hand as well. Next, students toss the birdie in the air and catch it on the racket. Remind them that "giving" with the birdie, by bending their knees, creates a "soft" racket and helps with catching. Controlled low flips are encouraged to make catching easier. Have students stand in hoops to emphasize safe, controlled flips.

Flip and Hit

This drill is a continuation of Flip and Catch. Rather than catch the birdie, the student tries to hit it using the appropriate stroke. This drill is an excellent opportunity to review the best strokes for use in particular situations. To ensure that students have ample space and remember the importance of safe, low tosses, have them stand inside a hoop while flipping and hitting.

Partner Badminton Drills

Hit and Catch

Birdies move differently from balls and tend to drop at a steeper angle, so players must learn to track their flight. For this activity, one partner has a birdie and a racket. The player uses an underhand serve to hit it to his or her partner, who then tracks the birdie and catches it with his or her hands. Encourage the serving partners to hit high shots, low shots, short shots, and long shots. After 5 to 10 serves, partners reverse roles. Next, the receiving partner gets a racket and traps the birdie with one hand and the racket. Finally, the receiver tries to catch the birdie with just the racket.

Bounce, Bounce, Hit

Both partners have rackets, and they get one birdie. The first partner bounces the birdie twice on his or her racket, just as in Birdie Bounce. After the second bounce, he or she hits it to his or her partner. The partner receives the birdie and tries to bounce it twice before hitting it back. The partners try to see how many times they can hit the birdie back and forth in this way.

Partner Rally

Partners begin with a racket each and one birdie. The partner with the birdie begins the rally with an underhand serve. The receiving partner sends the birdie back to his or her partner with one stroke. The partners try to see how many times they can hit it back and forth, or rally, without a mistake. A line on the floor can be used to simulate a net. The birdie must also pass over the line to count. After teams reach 20 to 25 times, challenge them to use two birdies—each partner starts with a birdie and serves at the same time. From then on, each partner strikes the birdie at about the same time and then quickly finds the returning birdie.

Badminton Activities

Badminton Conveyer

Playing area: gymnasium or designated teaching area

Players: groups of 8 to 10 students

Supplies: one racket per student, one birdie, one cone

Skills: racket awareness, cooperation

Students, with racket in hand, begin in a line on one end of the teaching area. Their challenge is to get the birdie to the other end of the teaching area and set it on the cone. These rules apply:

1. The birdie must be touching a racket at all times.
2. The birdie cannot be touching more than two rackets at a time.
3. The birdie may touch rackets only until it is set on a cone.
4. If the birdie is on your racket, your feet may not move.

If students pick up on this activity quickly, they can move the cone as a group. Encourage them to experiment by putting the racket in their nondominant hand, or even by blindfolding them so that they must communicate to move the birdie.

Shuttle

Playing area: courts, 8 by 20 feet (2.5 by 6 m)

Players: six per court

Supplies: one racket per student, one birdie per court, nets or lines, lines or tape for boundaries

Skills: forehand strokes, backhand strokes, serving, court movement

Three players are on each side of their court. One player from each side is in bounds, and the other two wait by the back line (figure 23.15). The first player puts the birdie in play by serving to the other side. Immediately after striking the birdie, the player quickly runs out of bounds, around the net or line, and to the other side, quickly get-

23

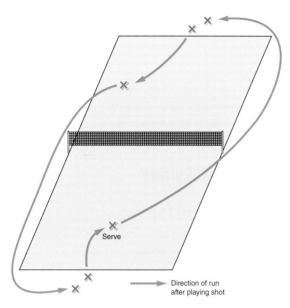

FIGURE 23.15 Shuttle diagram. Each X represents a student.

ting in line behind the two players out of bounds. The receiving player returns the birdie and hustles over to stand behind the players on the side the first player just hit it to. All players on the court work together to see how many times they can rally the birdie in this way. The rally is over if the birdie hits the ground. Double hits are allowed.

Badminton 500

Playing area: gymnasium or designated teaching area

Players: groups of two to four students

Supplies: one racket per student, one birdie

Skills: serving, tracking

One student is the server, and the other students are scattered about 20 feet (6 m) in front of him or her. The server serves the birdie to the other students, who try to catch the birdie with their racket for points. For safety and order, students either alternate turns catching or let the first player to call it attempt the catch. Students score points as follows:

1. Clean catch with the racket with no hands and no bounces = 100

2. Catch with no hands and one bounce = 75

3. Catch with no hands and two bounces = 50

4. Catch using racket and the other hand or more than two bounces = 25

Each catcher quickly serves the birdie back to the server for another round. The first player to earn 500 points becomes the server.

Discs

Disc activities are popular with children of all ages. Basic skills are used for Disc Golf, Disc Bowling, and Ultimate. Manipulating a disc is a novel skill for elementary school children, and they will require considerable guidance to develop skills.

Instructional Procedures

1. Allow students to toss and catch the disc individually first. Otherwise, they spend more time chasing than they do throwing and catching.

2. Use these instructional cues:

    a. Release the disc parallel to the ground. (Tilting it results in a curved throw).

    b. Step toward the target and follow through on releasing the disc.

    c. Snap open the wrist to make the disc spin.

    d. If space is limited, have students throw all disc in the same direction. They can line up on each side of the area and throw across to each other.

    e. To maximize practice time, give each child a disc at first. Later, most activities are best practiced by pairs of students using one disc.

    f. Children can develop both sides of the body by learning to throw and catch with either hand. Design the activities so that students get both right-hand and left-hand practice.

    g. Because a disc is somewhat different from other objects that children usually throw, devote some time to teaching form and style in throwing and catching. Avoid drills that reward speed in throwing and catching.

Disc Skills

Backhand Throw

The backhand grip is used most often. The thumb is on top of the disc, the index finger along the rim, and the other fingers underneath. To throw the disc with the right hand, stand sideways with the right foot toward the target.

Step toward the target with the right foot, and throw the disc in a sideways motion across the body, snapping the wrist and trying to keep the disc flat on release.

Underhand Throw

The underhand throw uses the same grip as in the backhand throw, but the thrower faces the target and holds the disc at the side of the body. Step forward with the leg opposite the throwing arm while bringing the disc forward. When the throwing arm is out in the front of the body, release the disc. The trick to this throw is learning to release the disc so that it is parallel to the ground.

Thumb-Down Catch

The thumb-down catch is used for catching the disc at waist level or above. The hand is shaped like a C with the thumb pointing toward the ground. To see any tilt on the disc that may cause it to curve, the catcher tracks the disc from the thrower's hand (figure 23.16).

Thumb-Up Catch

Pearson Education

FIGURE 23.16   Thumb-down catch.

The thumb-up catch is used when the disc is received below waist level. The thumb points up, and the fingers are spread. As with the thumb-down catch, the hand forms a C and then clamps the disc.

Sandwich Catch

The catcher holds one hand at chin level and the other at tummy level. As the disc approaches and the catcher can see where it will arrive, the catcher moves his or her hands closer to that spot. The catcher catches the disc by sandwiching it between both hands (one above and one below the disc).

Trick Catches

Discs can be caught in various positions. The two most popular trick-catch positions are behind the back and between the legs. The behind-the-back catch uses the thumb-up technique; the disc is caught with the arm farthest from the thrower. The between-the-legs catch also uses the thumb-up catch; the catcher can lift one leg to facilitate the catch.

Individual Disc Drills

Throw and Catch

Each with a disc, students practice the appropriate throws and catches individually. They toss the disc into the air using the backhand grip and the underhand throw. Throwers must release the disc at a sharp angle or completely vertical to get it to boomerang back. This activity offers an excellent chance to try the thumb-up, thumb-down, and sandwich catches. In addition, challenge students to throw and catch the disc with their nondominant hand. Students can try more difficult stunts such as throwing the disc under their leg or behind their back, doing a trick while the disc is in the air, and catching the disc under the leg, on the foot, and so on. Throughout this activity, emphasize controlled throwing.

Throw to a Wall

Each student has a Disc and practices a soft underhand throw to a wall about 3 feet (1 m) away. This activity allows students many repetitions and prevents them from having to spend most of their time chasing the disc. Early on, performing many repetitions in throwing is important.

Outside Throwing and Catching

If outside, students can move through the Throw and Catch activity just described and then try other drills. Have them throw the disc like a boomerang. Also, challenge students to throw the disc into the air and then run and catch it. Each time, they can increase the throwing distance and still try to make the catch before the disc touches the ground.

Partner and Small-Group Disc Drills

Tossing and Catching

After practicing Disc grips and catches individually, students can do these drills to practice the skills more authentically. Again, emphasize controlled throws. Each set of partners has one disc and is about 15 to 20 feet

23

(4.5 to 6 m) apart. Offer these challenges:

- Throw the disc at different levels to a partner.
- Catch the disc, using various catching styles and hand positions.
- Throw a curve by tilting the disc. Try curving it to the left, right, and upward. Throw a slow curve and then a fast slider.
- Throw a bounce pass to a partner. Throw a low, fast bounce. Throw a high, slow bounce.
- As the catcher, do various stunts after the disc leaves the partner's hand. Examples are a full turn, heel click, handclap, or touching the ground.
- Throw the disc with the nondominant hand. Try to throw for accuracy first and then strive for distance.
- Have the partner hold a hoop as a target. See how many times you can throw the disc through the hoop. Play a game of One Step, in which you move back a step each time you throw the disc through the hoop. When you miss twice in a row, your partner gets a turn.
- Place a series of hoops on the ground. Different-colored hoops can signify different point values. Challenge your partner to see who earns more points in five throws.
- Play catch while both partners are moving. Try to throw the disc so that your partner does not have to break stride to catch it.
- Throw for distance. Try to throw farther than your partner by adding up a series of four throws.
- Throw for both distance and accuracy. Using a series of four or more throws, try to reach a goal that is a specific distance away. Many objects can be used as goals, such as basket standards, fence posts, and trees. (This activity could be the start of playing Disc Golf, which is becoming a popular recreational sport.)
- Set a time limit of 30 seconds. Within this time, students see how many successful throws and catches they can make. Partners must stand a set distance apart, and missed catches do not count as throws.
- Working in groups of three, students try to keep the disc away from the person in the middle. Let them make their own rules about when someone else must move to the middle.

Disc Activities

Keepaway

Playing area: gymnasium, 10 by 10 feet (3 by 3 m)

Players: groups of four to five students

Supplies: one disc per group

Skills: throwing, catching

Two players start on defense. The other players spread out around the designated area and are the offense. Use cones to establish boundaries if necessary. The players on offense try to make three consecutive throws. Defensive players try to break up the consecutive throws by knocking the disc down or catching it. After the disc is caught, it cannot be taken away or knocked to the ground. If the disc is caught or knocked from the air to the ground, the player who threw the disc becomes a member of the defense, and the defensive player who knocked the disc down or caught it is on offense. After making three consecutive throws, two players from offense switch with the defensive players and the game continues.

Step Back

Playing area: gymnasium or designated activity area

Players: partners

Supplies: one disc per set of partners

Skills: throwing, catching

Partners begin standing 1 to 2 feet (30 to 60 cm) apart with the gym's centerline between them. The partner who makes a successful catch gets to take one step backward. If either partner drops the disc, they return to the centerline and begin again.

Disc Bowling

Playing area: gymnasium or outside, in 8-by-15-foot (3 by 5 m) lanes

Players: groups of three students

Supplies: 2 discs and 6 to 10 bowling pins (or rectangular blocks or plastic two-liter soda bottles) per group

Skills: throwing

Each group gets 2 discs, a bowling lane, and 6 to 10 bowling pins. Two students take on the role of pinsetters and stand beside the pins. The third student is the bowler. He or she stands 15 feet (5 m) from the pins and has two throws to knock down as many pins as possible.

After the first throw, the setters remove only the disc. All pins are left as they are. After the second throw, the setters quickly tell the bowler how many pins were knocked down. One setter then collects both discs and reports to the bowling line, while the other setter sets up the pins. At first, the pins are set to form a triangle; later, allow the students to choose the pin setup. The only rule is that they must use the same setup for each bowler. When the pins are set, the next bowler begins. The game continues until every student rotates to each role. Setters can also retrieve errant throws when they see they are not going to hit the pins. Give students safety reminders throughout this activity—students must look before throwing and before stepping in front of someone on the bowler's end of the lane.

Disc Golf

Playing area: large outside playing area

Players: groups of two to four students

Supplies: 1 disc per child, 8 to 10 hoops, 8 to 10 cones

Skills: throwing

Disc Golf is played exactly like golf except that players throw the disc rather than hitting a ball with a club. Before students play, give them an overview of golf. Explain that they must get their disc from the cone (called the tee) to the hoop (the hole) in the fewest number of throws. To minimize waiting after each hole, assign each group a starting tee. One at a time, each child in the group throws his or her disc. Students then hustle to their disc for the second throw. The child farthest from the hole goes first. For safety reasons, remind all group members to watch the throw. This process continues until all players have thrown the disc into the hoop. The next tee is near the previous hole. Teach students to move to hole 2 after playing hole 1, or to hole 6 after playing hole 5. If they start on hole 6, then hole 5 is the end of their course. Students can track their own score or use a scorecard. Do not have students carry pencils, which creates a safety hazard; instead, place pencils at each tee. Before starting the next hole, they record their score from the previous hole. Students must wait until the group in front of them is finished and has moved on to the next hole. If desired, make inexpensive flags (see figure 23.17) with 1-inch (2.5 cm) PVC pipe or wands and plastic triangles and put them into cones. The flags help students locate the hole. To integrate orienteering with disc activities, give students a map of the course (figure 23.18). Printing the scorecard on the back of the map may be easiest.

FIGURE 23.17 Disc Golf tees and flags.

©Robert Pangrazi or Aaron Beighle

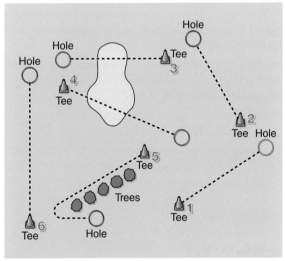

FIGURE 23.18 Disc Golf course.

Ultimate

Playing area: gymnasium or outside area, 40 by 50 feet (12 by 15 m)

Players: teams of 8 to 10 students

Supplies: one disc, cones to mark boundaries, pinnies

Skills: throwing, catching, moving to open spaces, cooperation

Ultimate is a combination of basketball, soccer, and football, played with a disc. At the elementary school

23

level, rules are minimized and activity is emphasized. Teams try to move the disc down the field or court by throwing it to teammates. These rules apply:

1. The disc can be stolen only when it is in the air; it cannot be taken from someone's hands.

2. The player with the disc can take only three steps.

3. The player with the disc can hold it for only five seconds.

4. If the disc is dropped or hits the ground after a throw, it goes to the other team.

5. A point is scored when the disc is thrown across a team's endline and caught by an opposing player.

After each score, the scoring team quickly throws the disc downfield. The opposing team either catches the disc or picks it up and begins moving it downfield in an effort to score.

Bowling

Bowling is a recreational activity dating back to ancient Egypt. Modern bowling typically takes place in bowling alleys with lanes, automatic pin setting, and automatic scoring. The game involves rolling balls down slightly oiled wooden lanes in an attempt to knock down 10 pins set in a triangular pattern. Many rules exist regarding the approach before bowling the ball, the number of times a bowler bowls during a game, and scoring. But at the elementary level, the emphasis is on exposing students to fundamental bowling skills and giving them basic knowledge about the game.

Bowling Skills

Gripping the Ball

Regulation bowling balls weigh 8 to 16 pounds (3.5 to 7 kg) and have three finger holes. For elementary physical education, use small 7-inch (18 cm) foam balls. Besides their obvious safety benefits, smaller, lighter balls allow children to hold the ball in a way that leads to successful performance and appropriate technique in bowling. Students simply pick up the ball using one hand and a stiff wrist.

Stance

The player begins standing with shoulders and head up, and feet shoulder-width apart and pointing toward the

pins. The knees are bent, and the ball is held at waist level slightly toward the dominant hip. The dominant hand is under the ball, and the elbow is bent. The other hand is on the side of the ball, and that elbow is bent as well. Here are cues for the bowling stance:

1. Stand tall.

2. Toes pointed at pins.

3. Ball at waist.

4. Dominant hand under ball.

5. Other hand on the side.

Approach and Delivery

In elementary schools, teach the one-step delivery. Advanced players use three-, four-, and five-step approaches. To begin the approach, the bowler extends the bowling hand and slowly drops it to the side while stepping toward the target with the other foot. As the bowling arm moves backward to waist level, the knees begin to bend. The bowling arm reaches a peak at waist level and begins moving forward. Meanwhile, the knees continue to bend; the dominant knee approaches the ground as it moves forward. When the ball reaches the front thigh, it should be low enough to allow the bowler to release the ball safely (so that the ball is only briefly in the air and does not bounce). As the bowler releases the ball, the bowling arm follows through to eye level. Here are cues for the approach and delivery:

1. Stance.

2. Step and take arm back with a stiff wrist.

3. Bend and bring arm forward.

4. Roll the ball.

5. Follow through.

Bowling Drills

Wall Bowling

Each child has a ball and stands 5 to 6 feet (1.5 to 1.8 m) away from the wall. Challenge students to bowl the ball to the wall and have it bounce straight back to them. This activity allows the teacher to reinforce the appropriate cues and see whether students are bowling the ball straight. Angled bowling results in the ball not coming straight back to the child. As children get comfortable with the activity, they can move back a few feet (a meter) at a time.

Partner Bowl

Partners stand 8 to 10 feet (2.5 to 3 m) apart facing each other. The partner with the ball begins by bowling the ball to the other partner, who stands with his or her feet shoulder-width apart. After partners have success, challenge them to roll the ball between their partner's legs in various ways. For example, one partner might challenge the other partner to bowl the ball so that it hits his or her left leg. Within limits, partners can also take steps back for added challenge.

Triangle Bowl

Groups of three form a triangle with 8 to 10 feet (2.5 to 3 m) between them. In the same order each time, partners bowl the ball to a group member and try to get the ball between their feet. The third child serves as the coach and watches the bowler. After the ball is bowled, the coach quickly gives the bowler appropriate feedback. Feedback can be as simple as "You followed through well" or as detailed as "Try to bend your knee more so that the ball doesn't bounce." This activity works well with peer assessment. After a few rounds, change the order to allow feedback from a different partner.

Bowling Activities

Red Pin

Playing area: gymnasium or outside area, 50 feet by 80 feet (15 by 25 m)

Players: groups of two or three students

Supplies: five pins (or two-liter bottles), one with red tape; one 7-inch (18 cm) foam ball per group; cones to mark lanes

Skills: rolling

Throughout the area, mark enough 5-by-15-foot (1.5 by 5 m) lanes for groups of two or three. At one end of the lane, have students set up the six pins (one with red tape) in any way they choose. Two players stand by the pins (the closest acting as pinsetter), while the first bowler bowls one time. Bowlers score 1 point for knocking down the red pin. Players rotate from bowler to pinsetter to next bowler in line.

Three Pins

Playing area: gymnasium or outside area, 50 feet by 80 feet (15 by 25 m)

Players: groups of two or three students

Supplies: three pins (or two-liter bottles), one 7-inch (18 cm) foam ball per group, cones to mark lanes

Skills: rolling

Set up lanes as in previous activities. Each player begins with 20 points. In turn, each player bowls the ball once. They subtract 1 point for each pin knocked down. The first player to reach exactly 0 wins. But if a player has 1 point left and knocks down two pins, he or she returns to 5 points and play continues.

Soccer Bowling

Playing area: gymnasium or outside area, 50 by 80 feet (15 by 25 m)

Players: groups of two or three students

Supplies: 10 pins (or two-liter bottles), one 7-inch (18 cm) foam ball per group, cones to mark lanes

Skills: kicking

Lane size for this activity depends on the students' kicking skills. Each player has two chances to kick the ball and knock down all the pins. Players score 1 point for each pin knocked down. Players who knock down all pins on the first try score 5 bonus points. For safety reasons, any ball that becomes airborne before touching the pins does not count; that player forfeits a turn and his or her points for the round.

Aerobic Bowling

Playing area: gymnasium or outside area, 50 feet by 80 feet (15 by 25 m)

Players: groups of three players (one bowler, one retriever, and one pinsetter)

Supplies: six pins (or two-liter bottles), one 7-inch (18 cm) foam ball per group, cones to mark lanes

Skills: rolling

Play begins with the bowler at one end of the lane and the retriever and setter at the other end by the pins. The bowler rolls the ball toward the pins and receives 1 point for each pin he or she knocks down. The retriever quickly picks up the ball, runs down the lane, and becomes the bowler. In the meantime, the setter and the bowler quickly reset the pins. As soon as the pins are set, the ball is bowled. Players rotate from bowler to setter, setter to retriever, and retriever to bowler.

LEARNING AIDS

WEBSITES

Walking

http://walking.about.com
www.orcasinc.com/products/walk-smart/

Orienteering

www.us.orienteering.org
www.orienteering.org
www.4orienteering.com
www.orienteeringunlimited.com

Tennis

www.usta.com

Badminton

www.worldbadminton.com

Discs

www.discgolf.com
www.whatisultimate.com

Bowling

www.bowl.com/youth/

SUGGESTED READINGS

American Sport Education Program. (2008). *Coaching youth tennis* (4th ed.). Champaign, IL: Human Kinetics.

Brown, J., & Soulier, C. (2013). *Tennis: Steps to success* (4th ed.). Champaign, IL: Human Kinetics.

Darst, P.W., & Pangrazi, R.P. (2015). *Dynamic physical education for secondary school students* (7th ed.). San Francisco, CA: Pearson Benjamin Cummings.

Grice, T. (2008). *Badminton: Steps to success* (2nd ed.). Champaign, IL: Human Kinetics.

Mood, D.P., Musker, F.F., & Rink, J.E. (2013). *Sports and recreational activities* (15th ed.). Boston, MA: McGraw-Hill.

Mullen, M. (2014). *Bowling fundamentals* (2nd ed.), Champaign, IL: Human Kinetics.

Ferguson, C., & Turbyfill, R. (2013). *Discovering orienteering*. Champaign, IL: Human Kinetics.

USA Pickleball Association. (2015). *Pickleball fundamentals*. Champaign, IL: Human Kinetics.

Wiedman, D. (2016). *Bowling: Steps to success* (2nd ed.). Champaign, IL: Human Kinetics.

REFERENCES

NPR, The Robert Wood Johnson Foundation, & Harvard T.H. Chan School of Public Health. (2015). *Sports and Health in America*. Retrieved from https://media.npr.org/documents/2015/june/sportsandhealthpoll.pdf.

United States Tennis Association. (2017). *Net Generation Physical Education Tennis Curricula*. White Plains, NY: USTA.

Basketball

Skills instruction for basketball is introduced primarily during the intermediate grades after children have mastered the basic prerequisite skills. The teaching of rules and strategies for basketball should be an integral part of the instructional process. Using proper progression is a key to success when teaching fundamental skills and lead-up games associated with basketball. Lead-up games provide an opportunity to emphasize development of selected basketball skills in a setting compatible with children's ability.

Learning Objectives

► Know the basic rules of basketball.

► Develop a unit plan and lesson focus for basketball.

► Identify safety precautions associated with teaching basketball.

► Describe essential elements for a successful lead-up game.

► Cite assessment procedures for evaluating basketball skills.

FatCamera/E+/Getty Images

Basketball is an activity enjoyed by many boys and girls. The thrill of making a basket and the exhilaration of running up and down the court makes it an attractive game. Along with the joy of playing, its positive effects on children's cardiorespiratory systems make basketball a strong contributor to the total curriculum. Basketball instruction in the elementary school focuses on developing skills and competence so that students can participate later in life. Emphasize lead-up games so that all students can experience success and enjoyment. The physical education setting, which emphasizes instruction and skill development, allows little time for regulation basketball during school hours. More skilled and interested students should be given additional opportunities through intramural programs, recreational leagues (such as the Youth Basketball Association), or an educationally sound interschool competitive league.

Modifying equipment used by elementary school children is important. Smaller balls and lower baskets help develop technically correct patterns, increase students' success, and maintain motivation. Children cannot practice the ball control drills if the ball is too large for their hands.

Instructional Emphasis and Sequence

Table 24.1 shows the sequence of basketball activities, divided into two developmental levels. In most cases, children are not ready to participate in this chapter's activities until age eight.

Developmental Level II

Little emphasis is placed on regulation basketball at Developmental Level II. Teaching focuses on the fundamental skills of passing, catching, shooting, and dribbling. Lead-up games such as Birdies in the Cage and Circle Guard and Pass allow students to learn skills in a setting that offers both enjoyment and success. Movement of players is somewhat limited, increasing the opportunity for a positive experience. As children mature at this level, a goal is to develop a range of skills, including passing, catching, dribbling, and shooting. Have them work on the layup shot and the one-hand push shot. Captain Ball adds elements of simple defense, jump balls, and accurate passing.

Developmental Level III

Several lead-up activities are introduced at Developmental Level III. Shooting games, such as Twenty-One and Freeze-Out, become favorites. Sideline Basketball and Captain Basketball offer meaningful competition. To ensure a good base of motor development, have students continue practicing fundamental skills. Drills to enhance skill performance and rules for regulation basketball are presented. Teach officiating so that students can learn to appreciate the importance and difficulty of refereeing. Allow players to conduct some games through self-officiating.

Basketball Skills

Basketball skills at the elementary level are divided into the following categories: passing, catching, dribbling, shooting, defending, stopping, pivoting, and feinting.

Passing

All passes have some common elements. For firm control, handle the ball with the thumb and finger pads, not with the palms of the hands. Step forward in the direction of the receiver while extending the arms and wrists. After releasing the pass, the palms face the floor.

Instructional Cues

1. Fingers are spread with thumbs behind the ball.
2. Elbows are in; extend through the ball.
3. Step forward, extend arms, and rotate hands slightly inward.
4. Throw at chest level to the receiver.
5. For bounce passes, bounce the ball past the halfway point closer to the receiver.

Chest (or Two-Hand) Pass

For the chest pass, place one foot ahead of the other, with the knees flexed slightly. Release the ball at chest level, with the fingers spread on each side of the ball. Pass the ball by extending the arms and snapping the wrists as one foot moves toward the receiver (figure 24.1).

TABLE 24.1 Suggested Basketball Program

Developmental Level II	Developmental Level III
Skills	
Passing	
Chest (or two-hand) pass	All passes to moving targets
One-hand push pass	Two-hand overhead pass
Bounce pass	Long passes
Two-hand overhead pass	Three-player weave
Catching	
Above the waist	While moving
Below the waist	
Dribbling	
Standing and moving	Figure eight
Down and back	Pivoting
Right and left hands	Individual dribbling skills
Shooting	
One-hand (set) push shot	Free-throw shot
Layup, right and left	Jump shot
Defending and Stopping	
Pivoting	Parallel stop
Feinting	Stride stop
Knowledge	
Dribbling	Held ball
Violations	Personal fouls
• Traveling	• Holding
• Out-of-bounds	• Hacking
• Double dribbling	• Charging
	• Blocking
	• Pushing
	Conducting the game
	Officiating
Activities	
Circle Guard and Pass	Sideline Basketball
Dribblerama	Twenty-One
Captain Ball	Lane Basketball
Around the Key	Freeze-Out
	One-Goal Basketball
	Three-on-Three
	Paper Clip Basketball
Skill Tests	
Straight Dribble	Figure-eight dribble
	Wall pass test
	Baskets per minute
	Free throws

24

FIGURE 24.1 Chest pass.

FIGURE 24.2 Two-hand overhead pass.

One-Hand Push Pass

To make a one-hand push pass, support the ball with the left hand and place the right hand behind the ball. Using the right hand, push the ball forward with a quick wrist snap.

Bounce Pass

Any of the preceding passes can be adapted for a bounce pass. The object is to get the pass to the receiver on the first bounce, with the ball coming to the receiver's outstretched hands at about waist height. Some experimentation determines the distance. Bounce the ball a little more than halfway between the two players to make it rebound efficiently to the receiver.

Two-Hand Overhead Pass

The two-hand overhead pass is effective against a shorter opponent. The passer is in a short stride position, holding the ball overhead (figure 24.2). The momentum of the pass comes from a forceful wrist and finger snap. The pass should take a slightly downward path.

Catching

When catching, the receiver moves toward the pass with the fingers spread and relaxed, reaching for the ball with elbows bent and wrists relaxed. To absorb the ball's force, the hands give as the ball comes in.

Instructional Cues

1. Move to the ball.
2. Spread the fingers and catch with the fingertips.
3. Reach for the ball.
4. Give with the ball (bring the ball to the chest).

Dribbling

Use dribbling to advance the ball, break for a basket, or maneuver out of a difficult situation. The dribbler's knees and trunk are slightly flexed (figure 24.3), with hands and eyes forward. Peripheral vision is important. The dribbler looks beyond the ball and sees it in the lower part of the visual area. Dribble the ball using the fingertips and a downward wrist action. Younger children tend to slap at the ball rather than push it. Have students practice dribbling with both hands.

Instructional Cues

1. Push the ball to the floor. Don't slap it.
2. Push the ball forward when moving.
3. Keep the hand on top of the ball. (Carrying the ball is illegal.)
4. Keep eyes forward and head up.

604

FIGURE 24.3 Dribbling.

Shooting

Shooting is an intricate skill, and students need to develop consistent and proper technique rather than just be satisfied that they made a basket.

1. Body position is important. Both the toes and the shoulders are facing the basket. The weight is evenly distributed on both feet. When preparing to shoot, hold the ball between shoulder and eye level.

2. A comfortable grip, with fingers well spread and the ball resting on the pads of the fingers, is essential. The palms of the hand do not touch the ball. The shooting elbow is held near the side, so the hand moves up through the ball toward the basket.

3. When shooting, focus on the front of the rim for the entire shot.

4. As the shot starts, cock the wrist.

5. The follow-through gives the ball a slight backspin. The arms are fully extended, the wrist is completely flexed, and the hand drops down toward the floor ("make a swan's neck"). The arc should be 45 degrees or a little higher.

Instructional Cues

1. Use the pads of the fingers. Keep the fingers spread.
2. Keep the shooting elbow in (near the body).
3. Shoot through the ball by extending the elbow.
4. Bend the knees and use the legs for more force.
5. Release the ball off the fingertips.

One-Hand (Set) Push Shot

The one-hand shot is usually a jump shot at short distances and a set shot at longer distances for young children. Most elementary school children find it difficult to shoot a jump shot. The one-hand set shot can be a prelude to the jump shot as students mature. At the beginning level, stress proper technique rather than accuracy. Hold the ball at shoulder–eye level with both hands; keep the body erect and the knees slightly flexed in preparation for a jump. For a jump shot, the shooter executes a vertical jump, leaving the floor slightly (figure 24.4). (In a set shot, the shooter rises on the toes.) The supporting (nonshooting) hand stays in contact with the ball until the top of the jump is reached. The shooting hand then takes over with fingertip control, and the ball rolls off the center three fingers. The hand and wrist follow through.

FIGURE 24.4 One-hand push shot.

Layup Shot

The layup is a short shot, taken when going to the basket, either after receiving a pass or at the end of a dribble. In a shot from the right side, the player takes off with the left foot and vice versa. The ball is carried with both hands early in the shot and then shifted to one hand for the final push. The ball, guided by the fingertips, should gently rebound off the backboard with a minimum of spin.

Free-Throw Shot

The one-hand set shot is the shot of choice for free throws. Some players find it helpful to bounce the ball several times before shooting. Others like to take a deep

24

breath and exhale completely just before shooting. The mechanics of the shot are the same as those of any shot at a comparable distance.

Jump Shot

The jump shot has the same upper-body mechanics as the one-hand shot described earlier. The main difference is the jump height. The jump is straight up, rather than at a forward or backward angle. The ball is released at the height of the jump (figure 24.5). Because the legs cannot increase the force applied to the ball, the jump shot is difficult for most elementary school children. It may be best to postpone teaching this type of shot to children who lack the strength to shoot the ball correctly and thus resort to throwing it. If the jump shot is taught, move the basket to the lowest level and use a junior-sized basketball to develop proper shooting habits. Another way to practice proper form with the jump shot is to use foam balls and cardboard boxes or garbage cans for goals. The balls are light and easy to shoot. Concentrate on proper form rather than on making baskets. Reinforce students who use proper technique.

FIGURE 24.6   The defensive position.

Defending

Defending involves a characteristic stance. The defender, with knees bent slightly and feet comfortably spread (figure 24.6), faces the opponent at a distance of about 3 feet (1 m). Distributing body weight evenly on both feet allows movement in any direction. Sideways movement is done with a sliding motion; the feet should not cross. The defender can wave one hand to distract the opponent and to block passes and shots. A defensive player needs to learn to move quickly and not be caught flat-footed.

Instructional Cues

1. Keep the knees bent.
2. Keep the hands up.
3. Don't cross the feet when moving.

Stopping

To stop quickly, a player lowers the center of gravity (figure 24.7). In the parallel stop, the body turns sideways and both feet brake simultaneously. The stride stop comes from a forward movement and is done in a 1–2 count. On the first count, one foot hits the ground with a braking action; the other foot is planted firmly ahead on the second count. The knees are bent, and the center of gravity lowers. From a stride stop, the player can move into a pivot by picking up the front foot and carrying it to the rear.

FIGURE 24.5   Jump shot.

FIGURE 24.7 Stopping.

Pivoting

Pivoting protects the ball by keeping the body between the ball and the defensive player. The ball is held firmly in both hands, with elbows out to protect it. One foot, the pivot foot, must always be on the floor. Turning on that foot is permitted, but it must not be dragged away from the pivot spot. The lead foot, however, may step in any direction (figure 24.8).

FIGURE 24.8 Pivoting.

If a player has received the ball in a stationary position or during a jump in which both feet hit the ground simultaneously, either foot may become the pivot foot. If a player stops after a dribble on a 1–2 count, the pivot foot is the foot that made contact on count 1.

Feinting

Feinting (faking) masks the intent of a maneuver or pass and is essential to basketball. Feinting is faking motion in one direction and then moving in another direction. It can be done with the eyes, the head, a foot, or the whole body. In passing, feinting means faking a pass in one manner or direction and then passing in another.

Instructional Procedures

1. Many basketball skills do not require the use of basketballs. Other balls, such as volleyballs or rubber balls, can be used successfully.

2. Many skills can be practiced individually or in pairs with a variety of balls. This approach allows all children to develop at their own pace, regardless of skill level. Dribbling, passing, and catching skills receive more practice when many balls are used.

3. Lower baskets to 7, 8, or 9 feet (210, 240, or 270 cm), depending on the students' age and height. If the facility is a community center, adjustable baskets—preferably power-driven—are a necessity. Baskets of 5- or 6-foot (150 or 180 cm) height are good for children in wheelchairs. This height also allows younger children to develop proper shooting form.

4. The program should concentrate on skills and include many drills to give it variety and breadth. Basketball offers endless possibilities. Be sure that each child has an opportunity to practice all skills. Achieving this objective is not possible when much of class time is spent playing regulation basketball on a full-length court.

Basic Basketball Rules

Basketball as played at the elementary school level is similar to the official game played in the junior and senior high schools, but it is modified to assure the opportunity for success and proper skill development. A team is made up of five players, including two guards (positions 1 and 2), two forwards (positions 3 and 4), and a center (position 5). When someone refers to a position by number, as in "Let's have the student play a 5," he or she is talking about the center. The game is divided into four quarters, each

24

six minutes in length. The game is controlled by referees, each having an equal right to call violations and fouls. The following rules apply to the game for elementary school children. (Note: The rules are seldom strictly followed in physical education or intramural settings with young children. Modifying the rules assures more activity and success for young people.)

Putting the Ball Into Play

The game starts with a jump ball at the center circle. The loser of the jump ball get the ball out of bounds at mid court to start the second quarter, then the other team gets it to start the third quarter and the it rotates back to the other team to start the fourth quarter. However, we recommend the USA Basketball rules that do not use a jump ball to start the game. Instead, a coin flip is used to award the ball at midcourt. For the following quarters, the ball is awarded as described above. Throughout the game, a jump ball is called when the ball is tied up between two players or when it is not clear which team caused the ball to go out-of-bounds. Although these situations are called a jump ball, the ball is alternately awarded to each team rather than jumped off between the two players. In other words, the first called jump ball goes to team A, the second called jump ball goes to team B, and so on. After each successful basket or free throw, the team that was scored against puts the ball into play at the end of the court under the basket.

Violations

The penalty for a violation is to award the ball to the opponents near the out-of-bounds point. The following are violations:

1. Traveling—that is, taking more than one step with the ball without passing, dribbling, or shooting (sometimes called "walking" or "steps")

2. Stepping out-of-bounds with the ball or making the ball go out-of-bounds

3. Taking more than 10 seconds to cross the center-line from the back to the front court (After the ball is in the front court, it may not be returned to the back court by the team in control.)

4. Dribbling violations—when a player takes a second series of dribbles without another player handling the ball, or when the ball is palmed (carried) or dribbled with both hands at once

5. Stepping on or over a restraining line during a jump ball or free throw

6. Kicking the ball intentionally

7. Remaining more than three seconds in the area under the offensive basket bounded by the two sides of the free-throw lane, the free-throw line, and the end of the court (This area is called the *lane* or *key*.)

To equalize scoring opportunities, a time limit (30 seconds) may be established during which the offensive team must score or give up the ball.

Fouls

Personal fouls are called for holding, pushing, hacking (striking), tripping, charging, blocking, and unnecessary roughness. When a foul is called, the ball is awarded to the team that was fouled. After five fouls in a half, the team that was fouled is awarded one shot and a bonus shot (if the first foul shot was made). If a player is fouled in the act of shooting and misses the basket, the fouled player receives two shots. If, despite the foul, the player makes the basket, the basket counts and one free throw is awarded. A player who has five personal fouls is out of the game and must go to the sideline.

Scoring

A basket from the field scores 2 points; a free throw scores 1. In most cases, the 3-point goal is not a consideration because of the distance of the shot. Teachers may want to create a shorter 3-point line to simulate the game played by older students. If the score is tied, an overtime period of two minutes is played. If the score is still tied after this period, the next team to score (1 or 2 points) wins. Some teachers alter the rules to offer more scoring opportunities: Teams can score 1 point for hitting the backboard, 2 points for hitting the basket (rim), and 3 points for making a basket.

Substitutes

Substitutes must report to the official scorer and await a signal from the referee or umpire before entering the game. The scorer will indicate when the ball is not in play, so the official on the floor can signal the player to enter the game. In physical education classes, involve all students in multiple games so that they all have equal opportunity to learn.

Basketball Drills

Drills should simulate actual game situations. Teach students that practice is ineffective unless it is purposeful and correct. For drills, instructors should use the technique suggestions for the skill being practiced and apply movement principles. The drills presented here cover both individual skills and combinations of skills.

Ball-Handling Drills

Ball-handling drills are practiced continuously for about 30 seconds. The ball is handled with the pads of the fingers. The drills are listed in order of difficulty.

Around-the-Body Drills

1. *Around the waist*. Hold the ball in the right hand, circle it behind the back, and transfer it to the left hand. The left hand carries it to the front of the body for a transfer to the right hand. Start with the left hand and move the ball in the opposite direction.

2. *Around the head*. With shoulders back, circle the ball around the head much as described for the first drill. Try it in both directions.

3. *Triple play*. First circle the ball around the head; then circle it at waist level and knee level. Try it in the opposite direction.

Figure Eight

1. Begin by squatting with the ball in the right hand. Move the ball around the leg to the right and bounce the ball between the legs to the left hand. Circle the ball around the left leg and through the legs to the right hand.

2. Bounce the ball through the legs front to back, followed by the figure-eight pattern.

Speed Drill

Place the feet shoulder-width apart. Hold the ball between the legs with one hand in front and the other behind the back in contact with the ball. In a quick motion, flip the ball slightly upward and reverse the hand positions. Using a quick exchange of the hands, make a series of rapid exchanges. The ball will appear to be suspended between the legs (figure 24.9).

Double-Circle Drill

Start with the ball in the right hand. Go around both legs, with an assist from the left hand. When the ball returns to the right hand, move the left foot away from the right foot. With the ball moving in the same direction, circle the right leg. Move the leg back to the starting position and circle both legs; then move the legs apart and circle the left leg (figure 24.10). In short, circle both legs; circle the right leg; circle both legs; circle the left leg. Try moving the ball in the opposite direction.

FIGURE 24.9 Speed drill.

FIGURE 24.10 Double-circle drill.

24

Two-Hand Control Drill

Start from a semicrouch with the feet shoulder-width apart. Hold the ball with both hands between the legs in front of the body (figure 24.11). Let go of the ball, move the hands behind the body, and catch the ball before it hits the floor. Flipping the ball upward slightly may be helpful. Reverse the action, moving the hands to the front of the body. Perform continuously.

FIGURE 24.11 Two-hand control drill.

Changing Hands Control Drill

Begin with the ball in the right hand. Move the ball around the back of the right leg and catch it with both hands. The right hand is in front, and the left hand is behind. Drop the ball and quickly change position of the hands on the ball after it has bounced once (figure 24.12). Immediately after the catch, bring the ball to the front of the body with the left hand and switch the ball to the right hand. Repeat continuously. Try moving the ball in the opposite direction.

FIGURE 24.12 Changing hands control drill.

Individual Dribbling Drills

Students can practice dribbling only or combine it with other skills. When dribbling a basketball, students should be taught to keep their head up rather than watch the ball. Here are some individual drills.

Hoop Dribbling Drill

Each child has a ball and hoop. Place the hoop on the floor and practice dribbling the ball inside the hoop while walking outside the hoop. Dribble counterclockwise using the left hand and clockwise using the right hand. Repeat by dribbling outside the hoop while walking inside the hoop.

Random Dribbling

Each child has a ball. Dribble in place, using the left and then the right hand. Develop a sequence of body positions (standing, kneeling, lying on the side, on two feet and one hand). Encourage players to develop a sequence by dribbling a certain number of times in each selected position. Dribble with each hand.

One-Hand Control Drill

Hold the ball in the right hand. Make a half circle around the right leg to the back. Bounce the ball between the legs (back to front), catch it with the right hand, and move it around the body again (figure 24.13). Try the drill with the left hand.

FIGURE 24.13 One-hand control drill.

Figure-Eight Dribbling Drill (Speed)

Start with either hand. Dribble outside the respective leg, between the feet, and continue in front with the opposite hand in a figure-eight pattern. Begin slowly and gradually increase dribbling speed.

Figure-Eight Dribbling Drill (One Bounce)

Stand in a semicrouch with feet shoulder-width apart. Start with the ball in the right hand and bounce it from the front of the body between the legs. Catch it with the left hand behind the legs (figure 24.14). Bring the ball to the front of the body with the left hand and start the sequence over with that hand.

FIGURE 24.14 Figure-eight dribbling drill (one bounce).

Figure-Eight Dribbling Drill (Two Bounces)

Begin in the same position as described in the preceding drill. Using the right hand, take one dribble outside the right leg (angled toward the back) and a second dribble between the legs to the left hand in front of the body (figure 24.15). Repeat, starting with the left hand.

FIGURE 24.15 Figure-eight dribbling drill (two bounces).

Group Dribbling Drills

Children can practice these drills in groups of various sizes.

File Dribbling

Players dribble forward around an obstacle (such as a bowling pin, a cone, or a chair) and back to the line, where the next player starts the drill (figure 24.16). A variation has each player dribbling down with one hand and back with the other.

FIGURE 24.16 File dribbling.

Shuttle Dribbling

Students stand in files. The head player dribbles across to another file and hands the ball off to the player at the head of the second file. The first player then takes a place at the end of that file (figure 24.17). The player receiving the ball dribbles back to the first file. Various shuttles can be arranged for dribbling crossways over a basketball court.

FIGURE 24.17 Shuttle dribbling.

Obstacle, or Figure-Eight, Dribbling

Position three or more obstacles about 5 feet (1.5 m) apart. The first player at the head of each file dribbles in and around each obstacle, changing hands so that the hand opposite the obstacle is the one always used (figure 24.18).

24

FIGURE 24.18 Obstacle, or figure-eight, dribbling.

Dribbling and Pivoting Drills

Dribbling and pivoting drills focus on stopping and turning.

File Drill

Each player in turn dribbles forward to a designated line, stops, pivots, faces the file, passes back to the next player, and runs to a place at the end of the line (figure 24.19). The next player repeats the pattern.

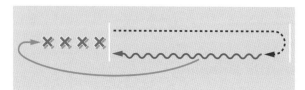

FIGURE 24.19 File drill.

Dribble-and-Pivot Drill

Players scatter in pairs around the floor (figure 24.20). Each pair has one ball. On the first whistle, the front player of the pair dribbles in any direction. On the second whistle, the player stops and pivots back and forth; on the third whistle, he or she dribbles back and passes to the partner, who immediately dribbles forward, repeating the drill.

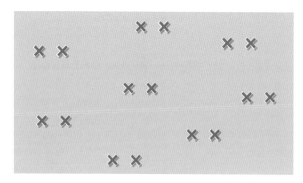

FIGURE 24.20 Dribble-and-pivot drill.

Passing Drills

In passing practice, make regular use of the various movement and shuttle formations (chapter 5) two-line, circle, circle-and-leader, line-and-leader, shuttle turnback, and so on.

Slide Circle Drill

A circle of four to six players slides around a person in the center. The center person passes to and receives from the sliding players. After the ball has gone around the circle twice, another player takes the center position.

Circle-Star Drill

This drill is particularly effective for five players, and it works well as a relay. Players pass to every other player, and the path of the ball forms a star (figure 24.21). Any odd number of players ensures that the ball goes to everyone so that they all receive equal practice.

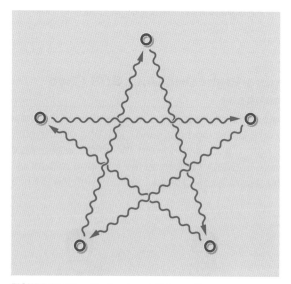

FIGURE 24.21 Circle-star drill formation.

Triangle Drill

Four to eight players can participate in this drill. The ball begins at the head of a line and is passed forward to a player away from the line. This player then passes to a teammate out at a corner, who then passes back to the head of the line (figure 24.22). Players take turns passing and then moving to the spot where they passed the ball, thus constantly changing positions.

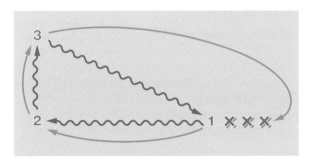

FIGURE 24.22   Triangle drill formation.

Squad Split-Vision Drill

This drill requires two basketballs. The center player holds one ball; player 1 (figure 24.23) has the other. The center player passes the ball to player 2 while receiving the other ball from player 1. The center player now passes to player 3 and receives the other ball from player 2 until the balls move completely around the semicircle. To rotate players, the player with the ball moves to the center and the first center player becomes player 1. All other players shift one space to the right.

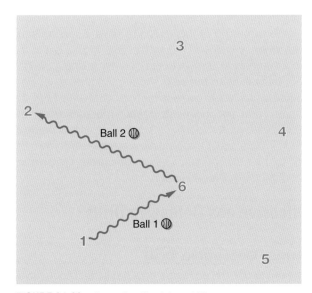

FIGURE 24.23   Squad split-vision drill.

Three-Lane Rush

This drill leads up to the three-player weave, which is difficult for elementary school children. Students are in three lines across one end of the area. The first three players move in parallel down the court, passing the ball back and forth to each other. As they near the basket, one player can try a layup.

Three-Player Weave

This drill requires practice and should be learned at slow speed. Walking students through the drill sometimes helps. If it is too difficult for a class, do not use it. The player in the center always starts the drill. The player passes to another player coming across in front and then goes behind that player. As soon as the player goes behind and around the player, he or she heads diagonally across the floor until he or she receives the ball again. The pass from the center player can start to either side.

Shooting Drills

Shooting drills may involve only shooting or a combination of shooting and other skills.

Simple Shooting Drill

In one simple shooting drill, players form files of no more than four people and take turns shooting a long and then a short shot or some other prescribed series of shots.

File-and-Leader Drill

The first player in each file has a ball and is the shooter. He or she passes the ball to the leader, who returns the ball to the spot that the shooter has selected for the shot (figure 24.24).

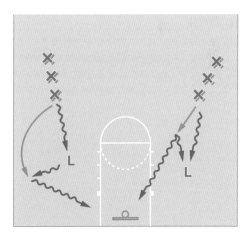

FIGURE 24.24   File-and-leader drill.

Dribble-and-Shoot Drill

Students form two files at one end of the floor. One file has a ball. The first player dribbles in and shoots a layup. A member of the other file recovers the ball and passes it to the next player (figure 24.25). As each person in turn either shoots or retrieves, he or she goes to the

24

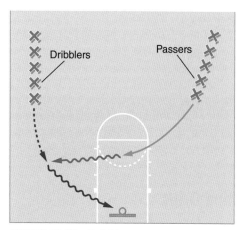

FIGURE 24.25 Dribble-and-shoot drill.

rear of the other file. When students develop some proficiency in the drill, two balls can be used to provide more shooting opportunities.

Shoot-and-Rebound Drill

Players are scattered an equal distance around the basket in a semicircle. Have them stand close enough to the basket so that they can shoot accurately. All shooters have a ball and must rebound their own shots. Inject a bit of competition by allowing successful shooters to take one step back for the next shot.

Layup Drill

This drill is a favorite. One line passes to the other line for layup shots (figure 24.26). Shooters come in from the right side first (this is easier), then from the left, and finally from the center. Each player goes to the end of the other line.

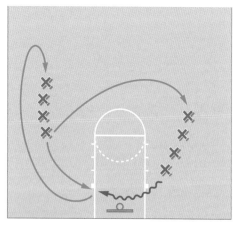

FIGURE 24.26 Layup drill.

Jump-Shot Drill

This drill is like the layup drill, except that the incoming shooter receives the ball from a passer, stops, and takes a jump shot. The line of shooters should move back to allow room for forward movement to the shooting spot. As soon as the passer releases the ball to the shooter, he or she moves to the end of the shooter's line. The shooter goes to the passer's line after shooting (figure 24.27).

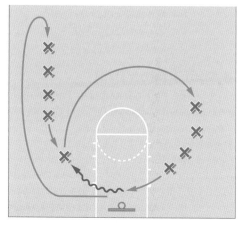

FIGURE 24.27 Jump-shot drill.

One extension of this drill is to allow a second jump shot when a shooter makes the first. In this case, the incoming passer throws to the shooter taking a second shot as well as to the next shooter. Another extension, which simulates a game situation, is having both the shooter and the incoming passer rebound when the shot is missed. As soon as the follow-up shot is made or the followers make three misses, the passer throws the ball to the new shooter. Encourage children to practice shooting from different spots.

Offensive and Defensive Drills

Group Defensive Drill

The entire class is scattered on a basketball floor, facing one of the sides (figure 24.28). The instructor or the student leader stands on the side, near the center. The drill can be done in several ways.

1. The leader points in one direction (forward, backward, or to one side) and gives the command "Move." When the students have moved a short distance, the leader commands, "Stop." Players keep good defensive position throughout.

2. Commands can be changed so that movement is continuous. Commands are "Right," "Left,"

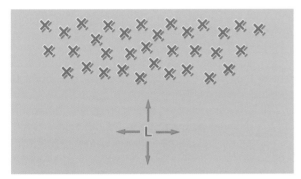

FIGURE 24.28 Group defensive drill.

"Forward," "Backward," and "Stop." The leader must watch that players do not move so far in any one direction that they run into obstructions. Commands can be given in order and be accompanied by pointing.

3. The leader is a dribbler with a ball who moves forward, backward, or to either side. The defensive players reacting accordingly.

Stress good defensive position and movement. Movement from side to side should be a slide. Movement forward and backward is a two-step, with one foot always leading.

Offensive–Defensive Drill With a Post

This drill consists of an offensive player, a defensive player, and another player acting as a passing post. The post player usually stands still and receives the ball from and passes to the offensive player. The player on offense tries to maneuver around or past the defensive player to find a good shot (figure 24.29). Players can be confined to one side of an offensive basket area so that

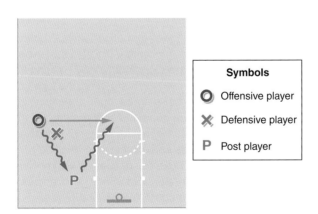

Symbols	
O	Offensive player
X	Defensive player
P	Post player

FIGURE 24.29 Offensive–defensive drill with post.

two drills can occur at the same time on one end of the court. If side baskets are in place, many drills can occur at once. After a basket attempt, all players, including any waiting player, rotate.

The defensive player's job is to cover the offensive player well enough to prevent shots in front of him or her. The drill is nonproductive when players' skill levels are not well matched.

Basketball Activities

Developmental Level II

Games at this level focus on the basic skills of passing, catching, shooting, and dribbling.

Circle Guard and Pass

Playing area: any smooth surface with circle markings

Players: 8 to 10 per team

Supplies: a basketball or playground ball

Skills: passing, catching, guarding

The offensive team is in formation around a large (30-foot [10 m] diameter) circle. Two or more offensive players move into the center. The defensive team is positioned around a smaller (20-foot [6 m] diameter) circle inside the larger circle. On signal, the offensive team tries to pass the ball to the center players. They may pass the ball around the circle to each other before attempting a pass to the center. The defensive team tries to bat the ball away but cannot catch it. After a specific time (one minute), offensive and defensive teams trade positions. If score is kept, 2 points are awarded for each successful pass.

Variation: Use more than one ball and specify different types of passes. The defensive team also can earn points for each time a team member touches the ball.

Dribblerama

Playing area: any smooth surface with a large circle or square, clearly outlined

Players: entire class

Supplies: one basketball for each player

Skills: dribbling and protecting the ball

The playing area is a large circle or square. Dribblerama can be played at three levels of difficulty.

24

- *Level 1*: All players dribble throughout the area, controlling their ball so that it does not touch another ball. If a touch occurs, both players go outside the area and dribble around the area. After students have completed dribbling around the area, they reenter the game.

- *Level 2*: The area is divided in half, and all players move to one of the halves. While dribbling and controlling a ball, each player tries to make other players lose control of the ball. Players who lose ball control take their ball and move to the opposite half of the area. Play continues against other players who have lost control. When five or six players remain, bring all players back into the game and start over.

- *Level 3*: The class is divided into four teams, and the area is divided into equal quadrants. Each of the four teams goes to one of the quadrants. After losing ball control, players move to the next quadrant and begin play. This variation is more controlled and keeps students involved continuously.

Captain Ball

Playing area: playground or gymnasium area, about 30 by 40 feet (10 by 12 m)

Players: seven or more on each team

Supplies: a basketball, pinnies, mats or spots

Skills: passing, catching, guarding

Two games can be played crosswise on a basketball court. A centerline is needed (figure 24.30); otherwise, normal boundary lines are used. Use spots to mark where forwards and captains must stay. Each team has a captain, three or more forwards, and three or more guards. The guards are free to move in their half of the playing area and try to keep the ball from being thrown to the opposing captain. The captain and forwards are each assigned to their respective spots and must always keep one foot on their assigned spot.

The game starts with a tip-off jump at the centerline by two guards from opposing teams. Guards can roam in their half of the court but may not touch the opposing forwards. When points are scored by getting the ball to the captain, an opposing guard immediately puts the ball into play with an in-bounds throw. Guards try to throw the ball to their forwards, who maneuver to be open while keeping a foot on their spot. The forwards can throw the ball to their guards and forwards or to the captain. Score 3 points when two forwards handle the ball and it is passed to the captain. Score 2 points when the ball is passed to the captain but has not been handled by two forwards. No points are scored when a guard throws the ball to the captain.

Stepping over the centerline is a foul. A guard stepping on a forward's marking spot or making personal contact with a player on a spot is also a foul. The penalty for a foul is a free throw. For a free throw, an unguarded forward gets the ball and has five seconds to pass successfully to the guarded captain. If the throw succeeds, score 1 point. If it does not, the ball is in play. Rotate free-throw shooting among all the forwards.

As in basketball, when the ball goes out-of-bounds, it is awarded to the team that did not make it go out. If a forward or a captain catches a ball without a foot touching his or her spot, the ball is taken out-of-bounds by the opposing guard. For violations such as traveling or kicking the ball, the ball is awarded to an opposing guard out-of-bounds. No score may be made from a ball that is thrown in directly from out-of-bounds.

Variations:

1. Try a five-spot formation like that on a die. Each team has nine players: four forwards, four guards, and one captain. Depending on space and the size of the courts, teams can have even more players.

2. Use more than one captain on each side to make scoring easier.

3. An effective offensive formation places guards spaced along the centerline (figure 24.31—only the offensive team is diagrammed). By passing the ball back and forth among the guards, the forwards have more opportunity to be open, because the passing causes the guards to shift position. To advance the ball, guards may dribble, but only three times. The forwards and captain may shift back and forth to become open for passes, but they must keep one foot on the spot. Short and accurate passing uses both chest and bounce passes. Forwards and centers may jump for the ball but must come down with one foot on their spot.

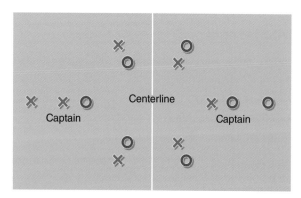

FIGURE 24.30   Formation for Captain Ball.

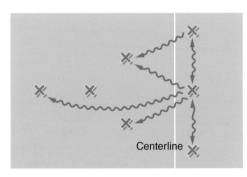

FIGURE 24.31 An effective offensive formation in Captain Ball.

Around the Key

Playing area: one end of a basketball floor

Players: three to eight

Supplies: a basketball

Skills: shooting

Spots are arranged for shooting as indicated in figure 24.32. A player begins at spot 1 and continues around the key, shooting from each spot. When the player misses, he or she can stop and wait for the next opportunity, starting from the spot where he or she missed. Rather than waiting, the player can risk taking another shot immediately from that spot. If the player makes the shot, he or she continues. If the player misses, he or she must start from spot 1 on the next turn. The winner is the player who completes the key first or makes the most progress.

Variations:

1. Each child shoots from each spot until a basket is made. Limit players to three shots from any one

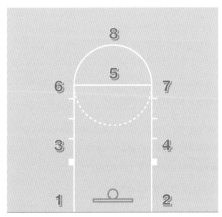

FIGURE 24.32 Shooting positions for Around the Key.

spot. The child finishing the round of eight spots after taking the lowest number of shots is the winner.

2. Change the order of the spots. Players can start on one side of the key and move back along the line, around the free-throw circle, and down the other side of the key.

Developmental Level III

Games at this level give students lead-up practice in all basketball skills.

Sideline Basketball

Playing area: basketball court

Players: entire class

Supplies: a basketball, pinnies

Skills: all basketball skills

Divide the class into two teams, each lined up along one side of the court and facing the other. Three or four active players from each team enter the court to play regulation basketball. The other players, who stand on the sideline, can catch and pass the ball to the active players. Sideline players may not shoot or enter the court. They must keep one foot completely out of bounds at all times.

The active players play regulation basketball but may not shoot until they pass and receive the ball three times from sideline players. Sideline players may pass to each other but must pass back to an active player after three sideline passes. The team that was scored on takes the ball out of bounds under its own basket. Play continues for a specific period (30 to 60 seconds). Teams do not change after a score, only at the end of the period. The active players then go to the end of their line, and three new active players come out from the front. All other players move down and adjust to fill the space left by the new players.

No official out-of-bounds on the sides is called. Players on that side simply put the ball into play with a quick pass to an active player. Out-of-bounds on the ends is the same as in regular basketball. If any sideline player enters the court and touches the ball, it is a violation; the ball is awarded out-of-bounds on the other side to a sideline player of the other team. Active players who are fouled get free throws.

Variation: Use a modified scoring system so that all students can help win the game. Hitting the backboard: 1 point; hitting the rim: 2 points; making a basket: 3 points.

24

Twenty-One

Playing area: one end of a basketball court

Players: three to eight in each game

Supplies: a basketball

Skills: shooting

Players are in file formation by teams. Each player attempts a long shot (from a specified distance) and a follow-up shot. The long shot, if made, is 2 points; the follow-up shot is 1 point. Players must shoot the follow-up shot from where they recovered the ball after the first shot. Allow the normal one- to two-step rhythm on the follow-up shot. The first player scoring a total of 21 points is the winner. Players who miss the backboard and basket altogether on the first shot must take their second shot from the corner.

Variations:

1. Start with a simpler game that permits dribbling before the second shot.

2. Let players shoot until they miss. Players who make both the long and the short shot go back to the original position for a third shot. Count all shots made.

3. Use various combinations and types of shots.

4. For more activity time and practice in rebounding, use this modified version. Score 1 point for hitting the backboard, 2 points for hitting the rim, and 3 points for a made basket. Players who make the basket or hit the rim get a free long shot that must make a basket to count. If the shooter misses, the player who gets the rebound tries to score. If that shot misses, the shooter gets 1 point for hitting the backboard or 2 points for hitting the rim, and play continues. Because players are learning these skills, standing and waiting for long shots seldom occurs.

Lane Basketball

Playing area: basketball court divided into six or more lanes

Players: five per team

Supplies: a basketball, pinnies, cones to mark zones

Skills: all basketball skills

Divide the court into six lanes as shown in figure 24.33. Players must stay in their lane and cannot cross the midcourt line. Regular basketball rules prevail, but players cannot dribble more than three times. Play starts with a jump ball. At regular intervals, players rotate to the next lane so that they get to play offense and defense.

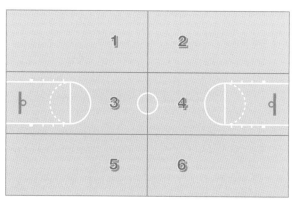

FIGURE 24.33 Court markings for Lane Basketball.

To change the game's focus, teachers can adapt the rules. For example, require three passes before shooting may occur. Also, for increased activity, permit students to move the entire length of the floor within their lane.

Freeze-Out

Playing area: one end of the basketball court

Players: four to eight

Supplies: a basketball

Skills: shooting under pressure

Among the many types of freeze-out shooting games is this interesting one, which ends quickly and allows players back into the game with little waiting time. Each player gets three misses before being out. After the first miss, the player gets an O; after the second, a U; and after the third, a T. This spells "OUT" and puts the player out. The last player remaining is the winner.

The first player shoots a basket from any spot desired. If the basket is missed, there is no penalty and the next player shoots from any spot desired. If the basket is made, the next player must make a basket from the same spot or it is scored as a miss (and a letter).

One-Goal Basketball

Playing area: an area with one basketball goal

Players: two to four on each team

Supplies: a basketball, pinnies (optional)

Skills: all basketball skills

This class activity is excellent if four or more baskets are available. The game is played by two teams using basketball rules, but with these exceptions:

1. A defensive player who recovers the ball, either from the backboard or on an interception, must take the ball out past the foul-line circle before starting offensive play and attempting a goal.

2. After a basket is made, the ball is again taken to the center of the floor, where the other team starts offensive play.

3. Regular free-throw shooting can be used after a foul, or the offended team can take the ball out-of-bounds.

4. An offensive player who is tied up in a jump ball loses the ball to the other team.

5. Individuals are responsible for calling fouls on themselves.

Three-on-Three

Playing area: half of a basketball court

Players: many teams of three players each

Supplies: basketballs

Skills: all basketball skills

Three teams of three are assigned to a basket. The offensive team stands at the top of the key, facing the basket. The defensive team starts at the free-throw line. The third team waits their turn beyond the endline. Use regular basketball rules. The offensive team plays until they score or the defense steals the ball. The defensive team then moves to the center of the floor and becomes the offensive unit. The waiting team moves onto the floor and plays defense. The first offensive team goes to the end of the line of waiting players. All teams keep their own score. A team wins by scoring 3 points. Winning teams can rotate to games at other baskets. Many games can go on at once, depending on the baskets available.

Paper Clip Basketball

Playing area: basketball court

Players: entire class

Supplies: basketballs, hoops, paper clips, discs

Skills: shooting, passing, dribbling

Form four equal teams, each standing on the sideline of one quadrant of the basketball floor (figure 24.34). Each team has a basketball and a hoop that has been placed near the center of the gym. Allow enough room between the hoops so that players do not collide. On signal, the first three players for each team must hustle for their ball and then pass and dribble toward one bas-

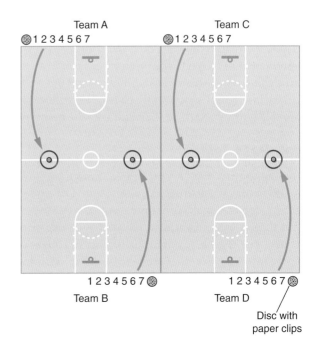

FIGURE 24.34 Paper Clip Basketball.

ket. Each player must receive the ball before that group can shoot. After making a basket, or after three tries, the players return the ball to their team's hoop, return to their sideline, and give a high five to the next three players. These three players repeat the process, moving toward the other basket. On the sideline, each team also has a disc and several paper clips. If any of the three players makes a basket, the team places one paper clip into the disc after returning to the sideline. The game continues for several minutes, after which the team with the most paper clips in their disc is the winner. To allow different combinations of players to work together, use team numbers not divisible by three.

Basketball Skill Tests

Tests in basketball cover dribbling, passing, shooting, and making free throws. The first four tests presented here are timed, so a stopwatch is needed.

Straight Dribble

Place a marker 15 yards (meters) down the floor from the starting point. The dribbler must dribble around the marker and back to the starting position, where he or she finishes by crossing the starting line. If the marker falls over, the test is disqualified. Allow two or three trials and take the best time.

24

Figure-Eight Dribble

Place four obstacles (bowling pins, bases, or cones) 5 feet (1.5 m) apart in a straight line beginning 5 feet from the starting line. The student must dribble in and out of the markers in a figure-eight pattern, ending where he or she started. Allow two or three trials and take the best time.

Wall-Pass Test

A player stands 5 feet (1.5 m) from a smooth wall. Use a board or mat as a definite restraining line. The student has 30 seconds to make as many catches as he or she can from throws or passes against the wall. The two-hand or chest pass is generally used. Balls must be caught on the fly to count. Another student does the counting. Allow only one trial.

Baskets Made in 30 Seconds

A player stands near the basket in any position he or she wishes. On signal, the player shoots and continues shooting for 30 seconds. The player's score is the number of baskets he or she makes during the 30-second period. Another student does the counting. Allow only one trial.

Free Throws

Count the number of free throws made out of 10 attempts. The player gets three or four warm-up trials and announces when he or she is ready. Another student keeps score with pencil and paper, making an X for a basket and an O for a miss.

LEARNING AIDS

WEBSITES

Teaching and Coaching Basketball

www.breakthroughbasketball.com/coaching/youthbasketball.html
www.coachesclipboard.net/CoachingYouthBasketball.html
www.basketballcoaching101.com
www.yboa.org

SUGGESTED READINGS

American Sport Education Program. (2012). *Coaching youth basketball* (5th ed.). Champaign, IL: Human Kinetics.

Goodson, R. (2016). *Basketball essentials.* Champaign, IL: Human Kinetics.

Krause, J., Meyer, D., & Meyer, J. (2008). *Basketball skills and drills* (3rd ed.). Champaign, IL: Human Kinetics.

Miniscalco, K., & Kot, G. (2015). *Survival guide for coaching youth basketball* (2nd ed.). Champaign, IL: Human Kinetics.

Mood, D.P., Musker, F.F., & Rink, J.E. (2012). *Sports and recreational activities* (15th ed.). Boston, MA: McGraw-Hill.

Paye, B., & Paye, P. (2013). *Youth basketball drills* (2nd ed.). Champaign, IL: Human Kinetics.

Wissel, H. (2012). *Basketball: Steps to success* (3rd ed.). Champaign, IL: Human Kinetics.

Football

Skills instruction for football is introduced during the intermediate grades with teaching of football rules and strategies an integral part of the instructional process. Progression is a key to success when teaching fundamental skills and lead-up games associated with football. Lead-up games offer an opportunity to emphasize development of selected football skills in a setting compatible with students' abilities.

Learning Objectives

► Teach the basic rules of football that can translate to informal play and watching football as a spectator or participant.
► Structure learning experiences efficiently regarding appropriate formations, progressions, and coaching techniques.
► Develop a unit plan and lesson focus for football.
► Identify safety precautions associated with teaching football.
► Describe instructional procedures for implementing a successful lead-up game.
► Cite assessment procedures for evaluating football skills.

Specialized throwing, catching, and kicking skills are needed if students are to enjoy participating. Touch and Flag Football are modifications of the game of American football. A ball carrier usually is considered down in Touch Football when touched by one hand (though some leagues require a two-hand touch). In Flag Football, a player wears one or two flags that opponents must seize to down the ball carrier, hence the name. Flag Football has advantages over Touch Football; it involves more twisting and dodging, so the game is more interesting and challenging. Also in Flag Football, players are less likely to argue over whether the ball carrier was downed.

Instructional Emphasis and Sequence

Table 25.1 shows the sequence of football activities, divided into two developmental levels. Regular and junior-sized footballs are difficult to throw and catch.

The ends of the football are hard and can hurt children who have not mastered catching skills. For this reason, the use of foam footballs is encouraged. Students show a greater tendency to participate if they know that the projectile won't harm them.

Developmental Level II

Passing, centering, and catching receive the greatest focus at this level. Teachers need to spend most of the instructional time on skills. Five Passes and Football End Ball are lead-up games that make use of the skills listed.

Developmental Level III

At this level, emphasis shifts to passing skills, with moving receivers in football drills. Punting and kicking games are introduced. More specialized skills, such as blocking, carrying the ball, exchanging the ball, and football agility skills, provide lead-up work for the game of Flag Football.

Football Skills

Forward Pass

Skillful forward passing is needed in Flag Football, and in the lead-up games, passing is a potent weapon. The ball is gripped lightly behind the middle with the fingers on the lace. The thumbs and fingers are relaxed (figure 25.1).

TABLE 25.1 Suggested Football Program

Developmental Level II	Developmental Level III
Skills	
Forward pass	Stance
Centering	Pass receiving
Catching	Punting
	Blocking
	Carrying the ball
	Running and dodging
	Handing off the ball
	Lateral pass
Knowledge	
Football rules	Plays and formations
Activities	
Football End Ball	Kick-Over
Five Passes	Fourth Down
	Football Box Ball
	Flag Football
	Pass Ball
	Speed Football
Skill Tests	
Passing for distance	Kicking for distance
Centering	Passing for distance
	Passing for accuracy

©Robert Pangrazi or Aaron Beighle

FIGURE 25.1 Preparing to pass.

When passing, the opposing foot points in the direction of the throw, with the body turned sideways. In preparation for the pass, the ball is raised up and held over the shoulders. The ball is delivered directly forward with an overhand movement of the arm and with the index finger pointing toward the line of flight. Figure 25.2 shows a left-handed passer.

FIGURE 25.2   Passing (left-handed thrower).

Instructional Cues

1. Nonthrowing side turns in the direction of the pass.
2. Grasp the ball with the pads of the fingers.
3. Throw the ball with an overhand motion.
4. Step toward the pass receiver.
5. Follow through with the arm after releasing the ball.

Lateral Pass

A lateral pass is a simple underhand toss of the ball to a teammate (figure 25.3). The ball must be tossed sideways or backward to qualify as a lateral. It is tossed with an easy motion, not trying to make it spiral like a forward pass.

Catching

Catching a football requires the receiver to keep both eyes on the ball and catch with the hands with a slight give. After being caught, the ball is tucked into the carrying position. The little fingers are together for most catches.

FIGURE 25.3   Preparing for a lateral pass.

Instructional Cues

1. Keep eyes on the ball.
2. Thumbs are together for a high pass (above shoulder level).
3. Thumbs are apart for a low pass (below shoulder level).
4. Reach for the ball, catch with the hands, and bring it to the body.

Handing Off the Ball

Children enjoy making plays in which one player gives the ball to another, as with a reverse. The reverse play starts as the player with the ball goes one direction and then hands the ball to another player heading the opposite way. The ball can be handed backward or forward. The player with the ball holds the ball with both hands but always makes the exchange with only the inside hand—the one near the receiving player. When the receiver is about 6 feet (2 m) away, the carrier shifts the ball to the hand on that side, with the elbow bent partially away from the body. The receiver comes toward the carrier with the near arm bent and carried in front of the chest, the palm down. The other arm is about waist high, with the palm up (figure 25.4). As the ball is handed off (not tossed), the receiver clamps down on the ball to secure it. As quickly as possible, the receiver then changes to a normal carrying position.

A fake reverse, sometimes called a bootleg, is made when the quarterback pretends to make the exchange but keeps the ball instead and briefly hides it behind one leg.

25

FIGURE 25.4   Handing off the ball.

Carrying the Ball

Carry the ball with the arm on the outside and the end of the ball tucked into the notch formed by the elbow and arm. The fingers add support for the carry (figure 25.5).

FIGURE 25.5   Carrying the ball securely.

Centering

Centering involves transferring the ball, on signal, from a lineman to the quarterback. Elementary schools most often use the shotgun formation, which requires snapping the ball a few yards (meters) backward to the quarterback. In a direct snap, the quarterback holds his or her hands under the center's buttocks. The center lifts the ball, rotates it a quarter turn, and snaps it into the quarterback's hands.

The centering player bends his knees with the feet well spread and toes pointed straight ahead. He is close enough to the ball to reach it with a slight stretch. The right hand takes about the same grip as is used in passing. The other hand is on the side near the back of the ball and merely acts as a guide (figure 25.6). On signal from the quarterback, the center extends his arms backward through the legs and hands the ball to the quarterback.

FIGURE 25.6   Centering (note the hand and finger positions).

Instructional Cues

1. Keep legs spread and toes straight ahead.
2. Reach forward for the ball.
3. Snap the ball with the dominant hand.
4. Guide the ball with the nondominant hand.

Stance

The two-point stance is the stance used in Flag Football for both offense and defense. The feet are about shoulder-width apart and facing toward the line of scrimmage. The weight is centered over the feet with the knees bent, back flat, and head up. Place hands above the knees so they're ready for movement. In the past, the three- and four-point stances were used, but many youth football organizations have rules against using them to prevent head injuries (figure 25.7).

FIGURE 25.7   Two-point stance.

©Robert Pangrazi or Aaron Beighle

Blocking

Blocking requires the player to maintain balance and not fall to the knees. The elbows are out, and the hands are held near the chest. The block is more like a pick in basketball but you can move but can't leave your feet (figure 25.8). Making contact from the rear in any direction is a penalty (clipping) because it could cause injury.

Punting

The kicker stands with the kicking foot slightly forward. The fingers extend in the direction of the center. The eyes are on the ball from the time it is centered until it is kicked—the kicker should actually see the foot kick the ball. After receiving the ball, the kicker takes a short step with the kicking foot and then a second step with the other foot. She swings the kicking leg forward and, at impact, straightens the leg to create maximum force. The toes are pointed, and the long axis of the ball makes

FIGURE 25.8   Blocking position.

©Robert Pangrazi or Aaron Beighle

contact on the top of the instep. The leg follows through well after the kick (figure 25.9). Emphasize dropping the ball properly. Beginners tend to throw it in the air rather than drop it, making the punt more difficult.

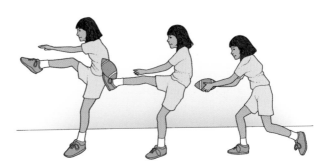

FIGURE 25.9   Punting.

Instructional Cues

1. Drop the football; do not toss it upward.
2. Keep the eyes focused on the ball.
3. Kick upward and through the ball.
4. Contact the ball on the outer side of the instep.

Place Kicking

The kicker stands 5 to 7 feet (1.5 to 2 m) behind the ball and slightly to the left (if a right-footed kicker). The ball is held upright by a teammate or a kicking tee. As when kicking a long soccer pass, the kicker approaches the ball at an angle and sets his opposite foot beside the ball. At this point, the kicking leg is at the height of its

25

backswing. The kicker's head is down as the kicking foot comes forward, making ball contact with the inside part of the shoelaces. To create loft, the kicker leans back slightly and strikes the ball below the middle, close to the ground. The kicking foot continues up and forward after contact (figure 25.10).

FIGURE 25.10   Place kicking.

Instructional Cues

1. Approach and plant.
2. Foot back, knee bent.
3. Head down and lean back.
4. Swing through the ball.

Instructional Procedures

1. All children need the opportunity to practice all football skills. To ensure this, set up a rotation system.
2. Drills should be performed with attention to proper form, and they should approximate game conditions. For example, when students practice going out for passes, have them start the pattern in the proper stance.
3. Use junior-sized or foam footballs. Provide at least six to eight footballs for football drills. The best teaching situation is to have one football for each pair of children.
4. Control roughness and unfair play by supervising play and strictly enforcing rules.

5. To prevent rough contact and decrease the possibility of injuries, use flag belts or soft touching (with the back of the hand on the shoulder) as the method to "down" students during football lessons

Football Drills

Ball Carrying

Formation: scattered

Players: four to six students

Supplies: a football, a flag for each player, cones to mark the zones

The ball carrier stands on the goal line ready to run. At 20-yard (meter) intervals, three defensive players wait; each one is stationed on a zone line of a regular Flag Football field, facing the ball carrier (figure 25.11). Each defender is assigned to the zone he or she is facing and must down the ball carrier by pulling a flag while the carrier is still in the zone. The ball carrier runs and dodges, trying to get by each defender in turn without having his or her flag pulled. If the flag is pulled, the runner continues, and the last defender uses a two-handed touch to down the ball carrier. After completing the run, the ball carrier goes to the end of the defender's line and rotates to a defending position.

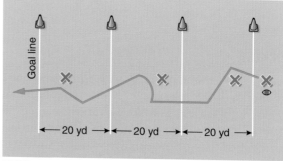

FIGURE 25.11   Ball-carrying drill.

Ball Exchange

Formation: shuttle, with the halves about 15 yards (meters) apart

Players: 4 to 10 students in two files

Supplies: a football

The two halves of the shuttle face each other across the 15-yard (meter) distance. A player at the head of one of the files has a ball and carries it over to the other file, where he or she makes an exchange with the player at the front of that file (figure 25.12). The ball is carried back and forth between the shuttle files. Receiving players do not start until the ball carrier is almost up to them. A player, after handing the ball to the front player of the other file, continues around and joins that file. A simpler way to practice ball exchanges is to use scatter formation in which half the class has a ball and the other half does not. On signal, students without a ball run toward those who have a ball. Handoffs continue as students alternate delivering and receiving the handoff.

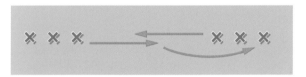

FIGURE 25.12 Ball exchange drill.

Combination

Formation: regular offensive formation with passer, center, end, and ball chaser

Players: four to eight students

Supplies: a football

This drill combines passing, centering, and receiving skills. Each player, after his or her turn, rotates to the next spot. At least four players are needed. The center player hikes the ball to the passer; the passer passes the ball to the end; the end receives the pass; the ball chaser retrieves the ball if missed by the end, or takes a pass from the end (if he or she caught the ball) and carries the ball to the center spot, which is his or her next assignment (figure 25.13).

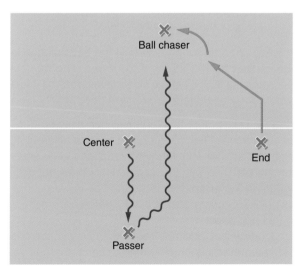

FIGURE 25.13 Combination drill.

The rotation follows the path of the ball—the rotation system moves from center to passer to end to ball chaser and back to center. Extra players are stationed behind the passer waiting their turns.

One-on-One Defensive Drill

Formation: center, passer, end, defender

Players: 8 to 10 students

Supplies: a football

This drill is as old as football itself. A defensive player stands about 8 yards (meters) back, waiting for an approaching end. The passer tries to complete the pass to the end, while the defender tries to break up the pass or intercept the ball. One defender practices against all the players and then rotates (figure 25.14). The passer must be able to pass well or this drill has little value.

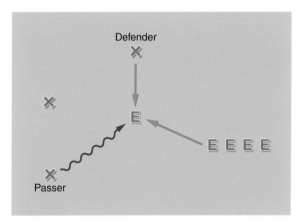

FIGURE 25.14 One-on-one defensive drill.

Variation: Play the drill with two ends and two defenders. The passer throws to the end who seems the most unguarded.

Punt Return

Formation: center, kicker, two lines of ends, punt receivers

Players: 10 to 20 students

Supplies: a football, a flag for each player

In this drill the receiver must catch a punted ball and return it to the line of scrimmage while two ends try to pull a flag or make a tag. Two ends are ready to run downfield. The center snaps the ball to the kicker, who punts the ball downfield to the punt receiver. The ends cannot cross the line of scrimmage until the ball has

25

been kicked. Each end makes two trips downfield as a "tackler" before rotating to the punt-receiving position. This drill requires an effective punter. The ends must wait until the ball is kicked, or they will be downfield too soon for the receiver to have a fair chance of making a return run.

Stance

Formation: squads in extended file formation

Players: six to eight students in each file

Supplies: none

The first player in each file performs the drill and then goes to the end of his or her file. On the command "Ready," the first child in each file assumes a football stance. The teacher can correct and make observations. On the command "Hike," the players charge forward for about 5 yards (meters) (figure 25.15). The new player at the head of each line gets ready.

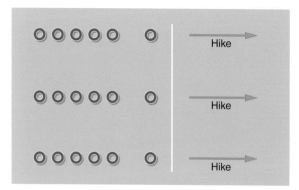

FIGURE 25.15 Stance drill.

Football Activities

Developmental Level II

Football End Ball

Playing area: court 20 by 40 feet (6 by 12 m)

Players: two teams of 9 to 12 students each

Supplies: footballs

Skills: passing, catching

The court is divided in half by a centerline. End zones are marked 3 feet (1 m) wide, completely across the court at each end. Divide players on each team into three groups: forwards, guards, and ends. The object is for a forward to throw successfully to one of the end-zone players. Position players from each team as shown in figure 25.16. End-zone players take positions in one of the end zones. Their forwards and guards then occupy the half of the court farthest from this end zone. The forwards are near the centerline, and the guards are back near the end zone of their half of the court.

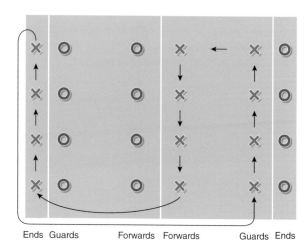

Ends Guards   Forwards Forwards   Guards Ends

FIGURE 25.16 Player positions and rotation for Football End Ball.

When a team gets the ball, the forwards try to throw over the heads of the opposing team to an end-zone player. To score, a player with both feet inside the end zone must catch the ball. No players may move with the ball. After each score, resume play with a jump ball at the centerline.

A penalty results in loss of the ball to the other team. Penalties are assessed for these actions:

1. Holding a ball for more than five seconds
2. Stepping over the endline or stepping over the centerline into the opponent's territory
3. Pushing or holding another player

In case of an out-of-bounds ball, the ball belongs to the team that did not cause it to go out. The nearest player retrieves the ball at the sideline and returns it to a player of the proper team.

Variation: Using more than one ball increases activity and throwing repetitions but requires a different rotation system. When a throw is completed to an end, he or she switches with the forward who threw the ball. Throughout the game, play is stopped as forwards and ends quickly become guards while guards become forwards and ends.

Encourage fast, accurate passing. Players in the end zones must practice jumping high to catch the ball yet land with both feet inside the end-zone area. A rotation system is desirable. After making a score, players on that team can rotate one player (see figure 25.16).

To outline the end zones, some instructors use folding mats (4 by 7 feet or 4 by 8 feet [1.2 by 2.1 m or 1.2 by 2.4 m]). Three or four mats for each end zone define the area and eliminate the problem of defensive players (guards) stepping into the end zone.

Five Passes

Playing area: football field or other defined area

Players: 6 to 10 students on each team

Supplies: a football; pinnies or other identification

Skills: passing, catching

Players scatter on the field. The object is for one team to make five consecutive passes to five different players without losing control of the ball. This sequence scores 1 point. The defense may play the ball only and cannot make personal contact with opposing players. If a player takes more than three steps when in possession of the ball, traveling is called and the ball is awarded to the other team.

The ball is given to the opponents at the nearest out-of-bounds line for traveling, minor contact fouls, after a point has been scored, and for causing the ball to go out of bounds. No penalty is assigned when the ball hits the ground. It remains in play, but the five-pass sequence is interrupted and must start again. Jump balls are called when the ball is tied up or when a pileup occurs. Players should call out the pass sequence.

Developmental Level III

Kick-Over

Playing area: football field with a 10-yard (meter) end zone

Players: 6 to 10 students on each team

Supplies: a football

Skills: kicking, catching

Teams are scattered on opposite ends of the field. The object is to punt the ball over the other team's goal line. If the ball is caught in the end zone, no score results. A ball kicked into the end zone and not caught scores a goal. If the ball is kicked beyond the end zone on the fly, a score is made whether or not the ball is caught.

Play is started with a punt from 20 to 30 feet (6 to 10 m) in front of the goal line. On a punt, if the ball is not caught, the team must kick from the spot of recovery. If the ball is caught, players can take three long strides to advance the ball for a kick. The player kicking next should move quickly to the area where the ball is to be kicked. Players are numbered and kick in rotation. If the players do not kick in rotation, one or two aggressive players will dominate the game.

Fourth Down

Playing area: half of a football field or equivalent space

Players: six to eight students on each team

Supplies: a football, pinnies

Skills: most football skills, except kicking and blocking

Every play is a fourth down—the play must score or the team loses the ball. No kicking is permitted, but players may pass at any time from any spot and in any direction. A series of passes can occur on any play, either from behind or beyond the line of scrimmage.

The teams line up in an offensive football formation. To start the game, the ball is placed at the center of the field; a coin toss decides which team has the chance to put the ball into play. The ball is put into play by centering. The back receiving the ball runs or passes to any of his or her teammates. The one receiving the ball has the same privilege. No blocking is permitted. After each touchdown, the ball is brought to the center of the field, and the team that did not score puts the ball into play.

Players can down a runner or pass receiver by making a two-handed touch above the waist. The back first receiving the ball from the center has immunity from tagging, providing he or she does not try to run. All defensive players must stay 10 feet (3 m) away unless he or she runs. The referee waits for a reasonable length of time for the back to pass or run. If the player holds the ball beyond that time, the referee calls out, "Ten seconds." The back must then throw or run within 10 seconds or be rushed by the defense.

Defensive players scatter to cover the receivers. They can use either a one-on-one defense, with each player covering an offensive player, or a zone defense.

Because the team with the ball loses possession after each play, use the following rules to determine where the ball is placed when the other team takes possession.

1. If a ball carrier is tagged with two hands above the waist, the ball goes to the other team at that spot.

2. If an incomplete pass is made from behind the line of scrimmage, the ball is given to the other team at the spot where the ball was put into play.

3. When a player beyond the line of scrimmage makes an incomplete pass, the ball is brought to the spot from which it was thrown.

25

TEACHING TIP

The team in possession must pass by the count of 10, because children tire from running around to become free for a pass. The defensive team can score by intercepting a pass. Because passes can be made at any time, on interception, the player should look down the field for a pass to a teammate.

Football Box Ball

Playing area: football field 50 yards (meters) long

Players: 8 to 16 students on each team

Supplies: a football, pinnies

Skills: passing, catching

Five yards (meters) beyond each goal is a six-by-six foot (two by two meter) square, which is the box. Teams are marked so they can be distinguished. The game is similar to End Ball because the teams try to make a successful pass to the captain in the box.

To begin the play, players are onside (on opposite ends of the field). The team losing the toss kicks off from its own 10-yard line to the other team. The game then becomes keep-away—teams try to secure or retain possession of the ball until a successful pass can be made to the captain in the box. The captain must catch the ball on the fly and still keep both feet in the box. This scores a touchdown.

A player may run sideways or backward when in possession of the ball. Players may not run forward but are allowed momentum (two steps) if receiving or intercepting a ball. The penalty for illegal forward movement while in possession of the ball is loss of the ball to the opponents, who take it and immediately begin play.

The captain is changed after three unsuccessful attempts or when a goal is scored. If either occurs, another player is rotated into the box. On any incomplete pass or failed attempt to get the ball to the captain, the team loses the ball. If a touchdown is made, the team brings the ball back to its 10-yard line and kicks off to the other team. If the touchdown attempt is not successful, the other team receives the ball out-of-bounds on the endline.

Any out-of-bounds ball is put into play by the team that did not send it out-of-bounds. No team can score from a throw-in from out-of-bounds.

In case of a tie ball, a jump ball is called at the spot. The players face off as in a jump ball in basketball.

Players must play the ball and not the individual. For unnecessary roughness, a player is sidelined until a pass is thrown to the other team's captain. The ball is awarded to the offended team out-of-bounds.

On the kickoff, all players must be onside (behind the ball when it is kicked). If the kicking team is called offside, the ball goes to the other team out-of-bounds at the centerline. After the kickoff, players may move to any part of the field. On the kickoff, the ball must travel 10 yards (meters) before either team can recover it. A kickoff outside or over the endline is treated like any other out-of-bounds ball.

A ball hitting the ground remains in play as long as it is inbounds. Players may not bat or kick a free ball. The penalty is loss of the ball to the other team out-of-bounds.

Falling on the ball also means loss of the ball to the other team.

Variation: Use a folding tumbling mat (about 4 by 7 feet [1.2 by 2.1 m]) as the box where the captain must stand to catch the ball for a score.

Flag Football

Playing area: field 30 by 60 yards (meters)

Players: six to nine students on a team

Supplies: a football, two flags per player (about 3 inches [7.5 cm] wide and 24 inches [60 cm] long), pinnies

Skills: all football skills

Divide the field into three zones by marking off lines at 20-yard (meter) intervals. Also mark two end zones, from 5 to 10 yards (meters) wide, defining the area behind the goal where passes may be caught. Flag Football is played with two flags on each player. The flag is a length of cloth hanging from the side at each player's waist. Opposing players can down (stop) a player with the ball by pulling one of the flags.

Avoid playing Flag Football with 11 players on a side. This many players results in a crowded field and leaves little room to maneuver. If 6 or 7 are on a team, 4 players must stand on the line of scrimmage. For 8 or 9 players, 5 offensive players must be on the line.

The game consists of two halves. Each half involves 25 plays. All plays count in the 25, except the try for the point after a touchdown and a kickoff out-of-bounds.

The game begins with a kickoff. The team winning the coin toss can either select the goal it wishes to defend or choose to kick or receive. The loser of the toss takes the option not chosen by the first team. The kickoff is from the goal line, and all players on the kicking team must be onside. The kick must cross the first zone line, or it does not count as a play. A kick that flies out-of-bounds (and is not touched by the receiving team) must be kicked again. A second consecutive kick out-of-bounds gives the ball to the receiving team in the center of the field. The kicking team cannot recover the kickoff unless the receivers catch and then fumble it.

A team has four downs to move the ball into the next zone, or they lose the ball. If they legally advance the ball into the last zone, the team has four downs to score. A ball on the line between zones is considered to be in the more forward zone, and the team with the ball may continue to advance it.

Time-outs are permitted only for injuries or when called by the officials. Unlimited substitutions are permitted. Each substitute must report to the official.

The team in possession of the ball usually huddles to make up the play. After any play, the team has 30 seconds to put the ball into play after the referee gives the signal.

Blocking is done with the arms close to the body. Blocking must be done from the front or side, and blockers must stay on their feet.

A player is down if one of his or her flags has been pulled. The ball carrier must try to avoid the defensive player and is not permitted to run over or through the defensive player. The tackler must focus on making physical contact with the flags, not with the ball carrier. Good officiating is needed, because defensive players may try to hold or grasp the ball carrier until they can remove one of his or her flags.

All forward passes must be thrown from behind the line of scrimmage. All players on the field are eligible to receive and intercept passes.

All fumbles are dead at the spot of the fumble. The first player who touches the ball on the ground is ruled to have recovered the fumble. When the ball is centered to a back, he or she must gain definite possession of it before a fumble can be called. The player is allowed to pick up a bad pass from the center when he or she does not have possession of the ball.

All punts must be announced. Neither team can cross the line of scrimmage until the ball is kicked. Kick receivers may run or use a lateral pass. They cannot make a forward pass after receiving a kick.

A pass caught in an end zone scores a touchdown. The player must have control of the ball in the end zone. A ball caught beyond the end zone is out-of-bounds and is considered an incomplete pass.

A touchdown scores 6 points, a completed pass or run after touchdown scores 1 point, and a safety scores 2 points. A point after touchdown is made from a distance of 1 yard (meter) from the goal line. One play (pass or run) is allowed for the extra point. Any ball kicked over the goal line is ruled a touchback and is brought out to the 20-yard (meter) line to be put into play by the receiving team. A pass intercepted behind the goal line can be a touchback if the player does not run it out, even if he or she is tagged behind his or her own goal line.

A penalty of 5 yards (meters) is assessed for these actions:

1. Being offside
2. Delaying the game (too long in huddle)
3. Failure of substitute to report to the official
4. Passing from a spot not behind line of scrimmage (also results in loss of down)
5. Stiff-arming by the ball carrier, or not avoiding a defensive player
6. Failing to announce intention to punt
7. Shortening the flag in the belt, or playing without flags in proper position
8. Faking the ball by the center, who must center the pass on the first motion

The following infractions are assessed a 15-yard (meter) loss:

1. Holding, illegal tackling
2. Illegal blocking
3. Unsportsmanlike conduct (also can result in disqualification)

TEACHING TIP

Specifying 25 plays per half eliminates the need for timing and avoids arguments about a team's taking too much time in the huddle. Using the zone system makes the first-down yardage point definite and eliminates the need for a chain to mark off the 10 yards (meters) needed for a first down.

Pass Ball

Playing area: field 30 by 60 yards (meters)

Players: six to nine students on a team

Supplies: a football, flags (optional), pinnies

Skills: all football skills, especially passing and catching

Pass Ball is a more open game than Flag Football, but the rules are similar except for these differences.

1. The ball may be passed at any time. It can be thrown at any time beyond the line of scrimmage, immediately after an interception, during a kickoff, or during a received kick.
2. Four downs are given to score a touchdown.

25

3. Players use a two-handed touch on the back instead of pulling a flag. Flags can be used, however.

4. If the ball is thrown from behind the line of scrimmage and results in an incomplete pass, the ball is down at the previous spot on the line of scrimmage. If the pass originates otherwise and is incomplete, the ball is placed at the spot from which this pass was thrown.

5. Because the ball can be passed at any time, no downfield blocking is permitted. A player may screen the ball carrier but cannot make a block. Screening is defined as running between the ball carrier and the defense.

Speed Football

Playing area: football field 30 by 60 yards (meters), divided into three equal sections

Players: entire class divided into two teams

Supplies: a football, flag for each player

Skills: passing, catching, running with ball

The ball is kicked off or started at the 20-yard (meter) line. The object is to move the ball across the opponent's goal by running or passing. If the ball drops to the ground or if a player's flag is pulled when carrying the ball, it is a turnover and the ball is set into play at that spot. Interceptions are turnovers, and the intercepting team moves on offense. Teams must make at least four complete passes before being eligible to move across the opponent's goal line. No blocking is allowed. To speed up the game, a team can immediately (without waiting for the opponents to set up) kick or throw off after the other team scores. This motivates all players to hustle after a score.

Variation: To allow more students to be actively involved, use smaller fields and let your class play more than one game at a time. Students also enjoy playing this game with discs.

Football Skill Tests

Tests for football skills cover centering, passing, and kicking (punting).

Centering

Each player is given five trials to center the ball at a target. The target is stationed 6 yards (meters) behind the center. Some suggestions for targets follow.

1. Suspend an old tire so that the bottom of the tire is about 2 feet (60 cm) above the ground. Players score 2 points for centering the ball through the tire. They score 1 point for hitting the tire but not going through it. Possible total: 10 points.

2. Use a baseball pitching target from the softball program. Scoring is the same as with the tire target.

3. Have a player hold a 2-by-3-foot (60 by 90 cm) piece of plywood at the target line in front of his or her body, keeping the target's upper edge even with the shoulders. The target is not to be moved during the centering. Players score 1 point for hitting the target. Possible total: 5 points.

Passing for Accuracy

To test accuracy in passing, each player attempts five throws from a minimum distance of 15 yards (meters) at a tire suspended at about shoulder height. (To stabilize the tire, suspend it from goal posts or volleyball standards.) As skill increases, increase the distance.

Players score 2 points for throwing through the tire and 1 point for hitting the tire but not passing through. Possible total: 10 points.

Passing for Distance

Each player is allotted three passes to determine how far he or she can throw a football. Measure the longest throw to the nearest foot (half meter). Reserve the test for a relatively calm day, because the wind can be quite a factor (for or against the player) in this test.

The passes are made on a field marked off in 5-yard (meter) intervals. Use markers made from tongue depressors to indicate the first pass distance. If a later throw is longer, move the marker to that point. When individual markers are used, team members can complete the passing turns before measuring.

Kicking for Distance

Punting, place kicking, and drop kicking can be measured for distance by using techniques similar to those described for passing for distance.

Flag Football Formations

There are various offensive formations for Flag Football, including the T-formation. The T-formation has limited use in Flag Football, because the passer (the quarterback) is handicapped by being too close to the center. Emphasize using a variety of formations including spread formations, with flankers and ends positioned out beyond normal placement.

The following formations are based on a nine-player team (four in the backfield and five on the line). The formations will vary if the number on each team is decreased. Presenting a variety of formations to players makes the game more interesting. Backfield formations can be right or left.

Offensive Line Formations

Figure 25.17 depicts only formations to the right. The center is indicated by an X, backs by B, ends by E, and line positions by O.

Offensive Backfield Formations

The formations diagrammed in figure 25.18 can be combined with any of the offensive line formations. For clarity, however, the illustrations for all formations show a balanced line with tight ends.

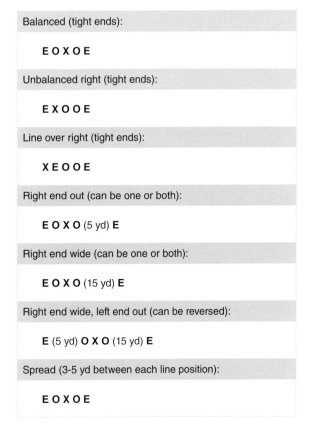

FIGURE 25.17 Offensive line formations.

Single wing:	Wing right, flanker right:
E O X O E B B B B	E O X O E B B B B
Double wing:	T-formation (regular):
E O X O E B B B B	E O X O E B B B B
Punt:	Wing T:
E O X O E B B B B	E O X O E B B B B
Flanker right:	Spread:
E O X O E B B B B	E O X O E B B B B
Wing right, flanker left:	Shotgun:
E O X O E B B B B	E O X O E B B B B

FIGURE 25.18 Offensive backfield formations.

Pass Patterns

The pass patterns illustrated in figure 25.19 may be run by the individual pass catcher, whether he or she occupies a line position or is a back. The patterns are particularly valuable in practice, when the pass receiver informs the passer of his or her pattern.

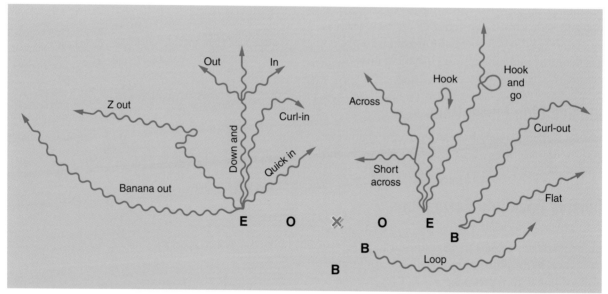

FIGURE 25.19 Pass patterns.

LEARNING AIDS

WEBSITES

American Flag Football League, www.affl.com
International Women's Flag Football Association, www.iwffa.com
Youth Flag Football, www.youthflagfootballplays.com

SUGGESTED READINGS

American Youth Football With Joe Galat. (2017). *Coaching youth football* (6th ed.). Champaign, IL: Human Kinetics.
Colby, G. (2013). *Football: Steps to success*. Champaign, IL: Human Kinetics.
Dougherty, J., & Castel, B. (2010). *Survival guide for coaching youth football*. Champaign, IL: Human Kinetics.
Mood, D.P., Musker, F.F., & Rink, J.E. (2012). *Sports and recreational activities* (15th ed.). Boston, MA: McGraw-Hill.
Wein, H. (2007). *Developing youth football players*. Champaign, IL: Human Kinetics.

Hockey

Skills instruction for hockey is introduced during the intermediate grades. Teaching the rules and strategies for hockey is an integral part of the instructional process. Using proper progression is a key to success when teaching fundamental hockey skills and lead-up games. Lead-up games allow teachers to emphasize development of selected hockey skills in a setting compatible with their students' abilities.

Learning Objectives

▶ Structure learning experiences efficiently using appropriate formations, progressions, and coaching techniques.

▶ Develop a unit plan and lesson focus for hockey.

▶ Identify safety precautions associated with teaching hockey.

▶ Describe instructional procedures used for directing a successful lead-up game.

▶ Cite assessment procedures used for evaluating hockey skills.

Hockey is a fast-moving game that can be adapted for use in the elementary school. Hockey at the elementary level is a lead-up to ice hockey as well as field hockey. With a plastic puck or yarn ball, children can play hockey indoors (figure 26.1). Outdoors, they can use a lightweight hard plastic ball. Success at hockey demands much running and team play. Teach fundamental skills and position play rather than the disorganized "everyone chase the puck" style of hockey.

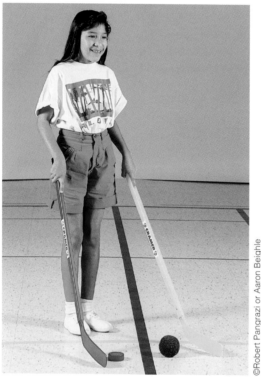

FIGURE 26.1 Hockey equipment.

©Robert Pangrazi or Aaron Beighle

Table 26.1 shows the sequence of hockey activities for two developmental levels. Actual use of activities is dictated by the students' maturity and experience.

Developmental Level II

Instruction at Developmental Level II involves little strategy. Use drills to develop fundamental skills with focus on learning to carry the ball loosely, receive the ball, and make short passes.

Developmental Level III

Skill development continues at Developmental Level III, with more emphasis on ball control and passing accuracy. Review and practice skills by using selected

TABLE 26.1 Suggested Hockey Program

Developmental Level II	Developmental Level III
Skills	
Gripping and carrying the stick	Controlled dribble
Loose dribble	Side field
Passing	Tackle
Front field	Dodging
Goalkeeping	Face-off
	Driving
	Jab shot
Knowledge	
Hockey rules	Ball handling and passing
	The game of hockey
	Team play and strategy
Activities	
Stick-Handling Competition	Goalkeeper Hockey
Circle Keep-Away	Sideline Hockey
Five Passes	Regulation Elementary Hockey
Star Wars Hockey	
Lane Hockey	
Modified Hockey	
Skill Tests	
Passing for accuracy	Dribbling for speed
Fielding	Driving for distance

drills and lead-up games. Drills are designed to foster team play, and lead-up games introduce strategy and field positioning. At this level, students learn regulation hockey rules and play the actual game.

Hockey Skills

Gripping and Carrying the Stick

The hockey stick is held with both hands and carried as low to the ground as possible. The basic grip puts the left hand at the top of the stick and the right hand 6 to 12 inches (15 to 30 cm) below the left (figure 26.2). Players must learn to carry the stick to the right of the body, with the blade close to the ground, while running. To ensure accuracy as well as safety, instruct players not to swing the stick above waist height.

FIGURE 26.2 Gripping and carrying.

©Robert Pangrazi or Aaron Beighle

Passing

Regardless of the pass used, players carry and grip the stick the same way. For a right-handed player, the basic grip has the left hand at the top of the stick and the right hand 6 to 12 inches (15 to 30 cm) below the left. The stick is carried with both hands and low to the ground at all times. Passers should avoid telegraphing the direction of the pass. They must learn to use peripheral vision and keep their eyes moving from place to place to develop an awareness of their teammates' positions. At the same time, they must anticipate the direction that a teammate will move to receive the pass.

Here are instructional cues to help players focus on correct passing techniques:

1. When first learning to pass, keep the eyes and head down and look toward the puck.
2. Keep the stick below the waist at all times.
3. Transfer the weight from the back foot to the front foot.
4. Drive through the puck.
5. Keep the stick on the ground until the puck is struck.

TEACHING TIP

During all hockey lessons, the stick should never rise above the child's knees (no high-sticking). Strictly enforce this rule.

Forehand Pass

The forehand pass is a short, accurate pass. It is the pass most often used, typically during stick handling. The player approaches the puck with the stick held low. He then pulls the stick back in line with the desired direction of the pass and no higher than waist level. The hands remain in the carrying position as the right hand guides the stick through the puck. After contacting the puck, the stick makes a small follow-through (figure 26.3).

FIGURE 26.3 Forehand pass.

Receiving

Receiving and controlling the ball is known as receiving and is an important basic skill. Many turnovers involve failure to handle a pass properly.

Here are some instructional cues for receiving:

1. Keep soft hands and stick.
2. Give as the puck hits the stick. Receive the pass; do not just stop it.
3. Maintain the carrying grip.

26

Receiving a Pass From the Front

To receive a pass from the front, the player must first move to a point in line with the path of the puck. He then extends the flat part of the blade toward the puck. The puck is received in front of the player (figure 26.4).

FIGURE 26.4   Receiving a pass from the front.

Receiving a Pass From the Side

Receiving a pass coming from the side is a more difficult skill. To field a puck from the side, the player must field the puck on her stick side (figure 26.5). Thus, a right-handed player fielding the puck from the left must allow the puck to pass in front of her before controlling it with the stick. Her body and feet remain facing the direction she wishes to move after controlling the pass.

Stick Handling

Stick handling is used to advance the puck, break for the goal, or maneuver out of a difficult situation.

Here are some instructional cues for stick handling:

1. Keep the puck under control (within a stick length).
2. Move under control.
3. Keep the head up.
4. Keep the elbows out (away from the body).

FIGURE 26.5   Receiving a pass from the side.

Loose Stick Handling

Loose stick handling is the easiest type of stick handling. Typically used in open-field play with no defenders around, loose stick handling involves the player pushing the puck 10 to 15 feet (3 to 5 m) ahead and then "chasing" after the puck. But controlled taps should be stressed, not "slap and chase" hockey. Loose stick handling allows players to move at a faster speed.

Controlled Stick Handling

Controlled stick handling (figure 26.6) consists of a series of soft taps in the desired direction of movement. Players must keep the puck away from their feet but less than one stride ahead, to allow for control.

FIGURE 26.6   Controlled stick handling.

Shooting

Hockey players use three basic shots—the wrist shot, the slap shot, and the one-timer.

Wrist Shot

Wrist shots are similar to the forehand pass. Use these instructional cues to help players focus on executing a proper wrist shot:

1. Keep the stick below the waist; a backswing is not used on a wrist shot.

2. Transfer weight from back foot to front foot as you carry the puck forward.

3. Release the puck from the toe of the stick. The higher the stick blade is when the puck is released, the higher the shot will go.

Slap Shot

Use these instructional cues to help players focus on executing a proper slap shot:

1. Stand with feet shoulder-width apart, with the nondominant side of the body facing the net. Place the puck about 1 to 2 feet (30 to 60 cm) in front (board side) of your front foot.

2. Keep the backswing below waist level.

3. Transfer weight from back to front foot as you swing, making contact with the playing surface 1 to 2 inches (2.5 to 5 cm) behind the puck. Follow through the puck, slapping it toward the net.

4. Hitting the playing surface before hitting the puck causes the stick to whip, creating a harder shot.

One-Timer

The one-timer is simply a redirection of an existing pass. It is a very fast shot meant to catch the goalie by surprise. During a one-timer, the player receiving a pass does not actually receive it; instead, he or she shoots it immediately on net. This shot is basically a slap shot with a shorter backswing designed to redirect the puck. Here are some instructional cues to help players focus on executing a proper one-timer:

1. Take a short knee- to waist-level backswing.

2. Time your swing to arrive when the puck reaches the spot you want to shoot from.

3. Just concentrate on making contact and sending it to the goal. This shot is typically inaccurate, so do not worry about aiming it.

4. Fire through the puck, releasing it quickly.

Defense

Stick Check

In hockey, stick checking is a means of taking the puck away from an opponent. While moving toward the opponent with the puck, the defensive player times the check so that his or her stick contacts the puck when the opponent's stick is off the puck. After knocking the puck away, the player quickly stick-handles or passes the puck in the desired direction. Throwing the stick or slapping at the puck carelessly is discouraged. Players can also use the stick to lift an opponent's stick off the ground to take the puck from him or her.

Poke Check

The poke check, an attempt to steal the puck from the opponent, involves a quick poke toward the puck (figure 26.7). As in stick checking, careless swinging and jabbing with the stick is discouraged.

©Robert Pangrazi or Aaron Beighle

FIGURE 26.7 Poke check.

Face-Off

The face-off is used at the start of the game, after a goal, or when the ball is stopped from further play by opposing players. The face-off involves two players, each facing a sideline, with their right sides facing their team's goal. Players simultaneously hit the ground three times with their sticks (on their side of the base). After the third hit

26

on the ground, the ball is played and each player tries to control the ball or pass it to a teammate. The right hand can be moved down the stick to facilitate a quick, powerful movement. Another method of starting action is for a referee to drop the ball between the players' sticks.

Goalkeeping

The goalie may kick the puck, stop it with any part of the body, or let it rebound off his or her body or hand. The goalie may not, however, hold the puck or throw it toward the other end of the playing area. The goalkeeper is positioned in front of the goal line and moves between the goal posts. When a puck is hit toward the goal, the goalie tries to move in front of the puck and keep the feet together. This stance allows the body to block the puck should the stick miss it. After the block, the goalie immediately passes the puck to a teammate.

Instructional Procedures

1. For many children, hockey is a new experience. Few have played the game, and many may never have seen a game. Showing a video clip of a hockey game may be helpful.

2. Because few children have the opportunity to develop skills elsewhere, teach the basic skills in sequence and give students ample practice sessions.

3. Hockey can be a rough game if children do not learn the proper methods of stick handling. Remind them often to use caution and good judgment when handling hockey sticks.

4. Ample equipment increases individual practice time and facilitates skill development. Try to provide each child with a stick and a ball or puck.

5. If hockey is played on a gym floor, use a plastic puck or yarn ball. If played on a carpeted area or outdoors, use a Wiffle ball. An 8-foot (2.4 m) folding mat set on end makes a satisfactory goal.

6. Hockey is a team game that is more enjoyable for all when the players pass to open teammates. Discourage excessive control of the ball by one player.

Hockey Drills

Stick-Handling Drills

1. *Phantom stick handling.* Successful hockey play demands good footwork and proper stick handling. To develop these skills, spread players on the field, carrying the stick in proper position, in a group mimetic drill. On command, players move forward, backward, and to either side. Quick reactions and footwork are the focus.

2. *Direction stick handling.* Each player with a ball practices handling it individually. Practice first at controlled speeds and increase speed as skill develops. On signal, players change direction while maintaining control of the ball.

3. *Change-of-direction stick handling.* Players are spread out on the field, each with a ball. On command, they carry the ball left, right, forward, and backward. On the command "Change direction," the players move away from an imaginary tackler. Players should concentrate on ball control and dodging in all directions.

4. *Down, around, and pass.* Players can practice in pairs, with partners standing about 20 feet (6 m) apart. One player carries the ball toward a partner, goes around the partner, and returns to the starting spot (figure 26.8). The ball is then passed to the partner, who moves in a similar manner. A shuttle type of formation can be used with three players.

FIGURE 26.8 Down, around, and pass drill.

Passing and Receiving Drills

1. *Partner passing.* In pairs, about 20 feet (6 m) apart, players pass the ball quickly back and forth. Emphasize passing immediately after receiving the ball. Cue phrase: "Receive and pass."

2. *Pass and carry.* One player passes the ball to a partner, who carries the ball a few steps left or right and passes it back to the other. Players can try receiving passes from various angles and from the right and left sides.

3. *Sliding circle drill.* In this drill, a circle of four to six players skates around a player in the center. The center player passes to and receives from the skating players. After the puck has gone around the circle twice, another player takes the center position.

4. *Triangle drill.* From four to eight players can participate in this drill. The puck begins at the head of a line and is passed forward to a player off to one side of the line. This player then passes to a teammate out at a corner, who then passes back to the head of the line. Each player passes and then moves to the spot to where he or she passed the puck, thus making a continual change of positions. This drill replicates the motion of cycling the puck.

5. *Circle-star drill.* This drill is particularly effective for five players. Players pass to every other player, and the path of the puck forms a star. Any odd number of players will cause the puck to go to all participants, assuring that all receive equal practice.

6. *Downfield drill.* This drill is useful for polishing passing and receiving skills while moving. Three files of players start at one end of the field. One player from each file moves downfield, passing to and fielding from the others until he or she reaches the other end of the field. The player can make a goal shot at this point. Players remain close together for short passes until they reach a higher skill level.

7. Practice driving for distance and accuracy with a partner.

FIGURE 26.9 Cone dodge drill.

Dodging and Checking Drills

1. *Cone dodge.* Three players form the drill configuration (figure 26.9). Player 1 has the puck in front, approaches the cone (which represents a defensive player), dodges around the cone, and passes to player 2, who repeats the dodging maneuver in the opposite direction. Player 2 passes to layer 3, and the drill continues.

2. *Partner stick checks.* Players work in pairs. One partner dribbles toward the other, who tries to make a stick check. Reverse the roles at regular intervals. Have students start by practicing this drill at moderate speeds.

3. *Three on three.* A three-on-three drill affords practice in many skill areas. Three players are on offense, and three are on defense. The offense concentrates on passing, stick handling, and dodging, while the defense concentrates on checking. The offense scores 1 point for reaching the opposite side of the field. Reverse offensive and defensive roles at set times.

Shooting Drills

1. *Give-and-go drill.* Each player has a partner. The first partner has a puck and is the shooter. He or she passes the puck to the wing (partner), who passes the puck to the spot the shooter has selected for the shot. To increase difficulty, have players try one-timers.

2. *Three-player rush.* For this drill, establish three lines of players at one end of the ice. One line has a puck. One player from each line moves down the ice, passing to the other two players. As the players near the goal, one of the players shoots on goal. The other players retrieve the puck, and all three players hustle back to the starting point and start again.

Hockey Activities

Developmental Level II

Stick-Handling Competition

Playing area: any clearly defined area

Players: entire team

Supplies: a stick and puck (or ball) for each player

Skills: stick handling and protecting the puck

This activity can be played at two levels of difficulty.

- *Level 1:* All players stick-handle throughout half of the area, controlling their puck so that it does not touch another puck. If a touch occurs, both players go to the other half of the area and stick-handle around its perimeter. After stick handling around the second area, these players reenter the game.

- *Level 2:* Divide the area and have all players move to one of the halves. While stick handling and controlling a puck, each player tries to make another player lose control of his or her puck. Players who lose control take their puck and move to the other area. Play continues against other players who have lost control. When five or six players remain in the first area, all players return to the game and start over.

Circle Keep-Away

Playing area: a 20- to 25-foot (6 to 8 m) circle

Players: 8 to 10 students

Supplies: one stick per player, a puck or ball

Skills: passing, receiving

Players are spaced evenly around the circle, and two or more players are in the center. The object is to keep the players in the center from touching the puck. Players pass the puck back and forth, focusing on accurate passing and receiving. Center players see how many touches they can make during their turn. Change the center players after a set time so that all students get to be center players.

Five Passes

Playing area: any defined area

Players: teams of five or more students each

Supplies: a puck (or ball) and a stick for each player, pinnies

Skills: passing, guarding

Two teams play. To have several games at once, divide the area into smaller areas. The object is to complete five consecutive passes and score a point. The game starts with a face-off in the center of the area. The teams observe regular hockey rules. The team with the puck counts aloud as it completes each pass. Players cannot pass the puck back to the player who made the pass. No stick handling is allowed. If for any reason a player fumbles and recovers the puck or passes it improperly, the count starts over. After scoring, a team immediately turns over the puck to the other team. A foul draws a penalty shot, which can score a point. Mark teams well to avoid confusion.

Variations:

1. After each successful point (five passes), the team is awarded a penalty shot, which can score an additional point.

2. When a team scores a point, restart the game by giving the puck to the other team out-of-bounds.

Star Wars Hockey

Playing area: playground or gymnasium

Players: four teams of equal size

Supplies: one stick per player, four pucks or balls

Skills: stick handling

Each team forms one side of a square formation. The game is similar to Star Wars, with these exceptions:

1. Four pucks (or balls) are used. When a number is called, all players with that number go to a puck and stick-handle it out of the square through the spot previously occupied, around the square counterclockwise, and back to the original spot. Draw circles 12 inches (30 cm) in diameter on the floor to mark where players must return the puck. If the game is played outdoors, use hoops to mark the spot.

2. No player is allowed to use anything other than the stick in making the circuit and returning the puck to the spot. The penalty for infractions is disqualification.

Lane Hockey

Playing area: hockey field or gymnasium, 60 by 100 feet (18 by 30 m)

Players: nine players on each team

Supplies: one stick per player, puck, two goals

Skills: all hockey skills

The field is divided into eight lanes (figure 26.10). Assign a defensive and an offensive player to each of the eight lanes. Each team also has a goalkeeper, who stands in front of the goal area. Players may not leave their lane during play. They cannot shoot on the goal until they complete at least two passes. This rule encourages looking for teammates and passing to someone in a better position before taking a shot on goal.

FIGURE 26.10 Field markings for Lane Hockey.

Encourage players to maintain their spacing during play. The purpose of the lanes is to force them to play within a zone rather than rush to the puck. Rules used for regulation hockey enforce situations not described here. Players who are fouled receive a free shot (unguarded). Rotate players at regular intervals.

Modified Hockey

Playing area: hockey field or gymnasium

Players: teams of 7 to 11 students each

Supplies: one stick per player, a puck or ball

Skills: stick handling, passing, dodging, checking, face-off

The teams may take any position on the field as long as they remain inside the boundaries. The object is to hit the puck through the opponent's goal. No goalies are used. Players face off at the start of the game and after each score. Each goal scores 1 point.

The distance between goal lines is flexible but should be on the long side. If making goals is too easy or too difficult, adjust the width of the goals.

Developmental Level III

Goalkeeper Hockey

Playing area: a square about 40 by 40 feet (12 by 12 m)

Players: two teams of equal size

Supplies: one stick per player, a puck or ball

Skills: passing, receiving, goalkeeping

Each team occupies two adjacent sides of the square (figure 26.11). Team members are numbered consecutively from left to right. When the teacher calls two or three numbers, those players enter the playing area and try to capture the ball, which is at the center of the square, and pass it through the opposing team. A team scores 1 point when the ball goes through the opponent's side. Sideline players are goalies and should concentrate on goalkeeping skills. After a short time (1 minute), the active players return to their sidelines, and new players are called. Keep track of the numbers called to give all players an equal opportunity to play.

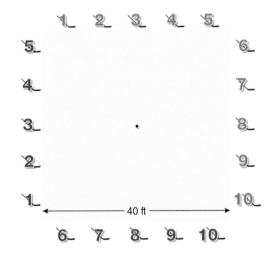

FIGURE 26.11 Team positions for Goalkeeper Hockey.

Sideline Hockey

Playing area: hockey field or gymnasium area, 60 by 100 feet (18 by 30 m)

Players: teams of 6 to 12 players each

Supplies: one stick per player, a puck or ball, two 4-by-8-foot (1.2 by 2.4 m) folding tumbling mats

Skills: most hockey skills, except goalkeeping

26

Divide each team into two groups. Position them as shown in figure 26.12, which has eight players on each team. Three to six players from each team move onto the court; these are the active players. The others actively participate on the sidelines. No goalkeeper is used. A face-off at the center starts the game and puts the ball into play after each score. Each team on the field, aided by sideline players, tries to score a goal. The sideline players help keep the ball inbounds and can pass it onto the court to the active players. Sideline players may pass to an active player or to each other.

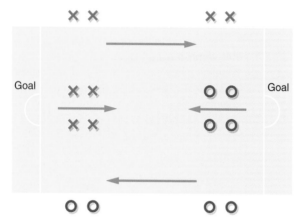

FIGURE 26.12 Team positions for Sideline Hockey.

Any puck that goes out-of-bounds on a sideline belongs to the team guarding that sideline and is immediately put into play with a pass. An out-of-bounds shot over the endline that does not score a goal is put into play by the team defending the goal. After a set time, the active players on a team change places with the sideline players.

Encourage team play and passing strategies rather than have all players charge and swarm the puck. An effective rule is to require active players to make three passes to their sideline teammates before taking a shot on goal. This rule makes all players an important part of the game.

Illegal touching, sideline violations, and other minor fouls result in loss of the ball to the opposition. Players who commit roughing fouls and illegal striking are sent to the sideline until the game period ends.

Regulation Elementary Hockey

Playing area: hockey field or gymnasium area, approximately 40 to 50 feet (12 to 15 m) by 75 to 90 feet (23 to 27 m)

Players: teams of six or more students each

Supplies: one stick per player, a puck or ball

Skills: all hockey skills

In a small gym, use the walls as boundaries. In a large gym or on an outdoor field, mark off the playing area with traffic cones. Divide the area in half, with a 12-foot (4 m) restraining circle centered on the midline. Play begins here at the start of a period, after goals, or after foul shots. The official goal is 2 feet high by 6 feet wide (60 by 180 cm), with a restraining area 4 by 8 feet (120 by 240 cm) around the goal to protect the goalie (figure 26.13). Each team has a goalkeeper, who stops shots with his or her hands, feet, or stick; a center, who is the only player allowed to move full court and who leads offensive play (the center's stick is striped with black tape); two guards, who cannot go beyond the centerline into the offensive area and are responsible for keeping the ball or puck out of their defensive half of the field; and two forwards, who work with the center on offensive play and cannot go back over the centerline into the defensive area.

FIGURE 26.13 Regulation Elementary Hockey playing field.

A game consists of three periods of eight minutes each, with a three-minute rest between periods. Play begins with a face-off by the centers at midcourt. Other players cannot enter the restraining circle until the ball has been hit by the centers. The clock starts when the ball is put into play and runs continuously until a goal is scored or a foul is called. Substitutions can be made only when the clock is stopped. If the ball goes out-of-bounds, the team that did not hit it last puts it back into play.

Whenever the ball passes through the goal on the ground, 1 point is scored. If, however, the ball crosses the goal line while in the air, it must strike against the mat or back wall to count for a score. Under no circumstances can a goal be scored on a foul. The ball can deflect off a player or equipment to score, but it cannot be kicked into the goal.

The goalkeeper may use his or her hands to clear the ball away from the goal, but the goalie may not hold it or throw it toward the other end of the playing area. He or she is charged with a foul for holding the ball. The goalkeeper may be pulled from the goal area but cannot go beyond the centerline. No other player may enter the restraining area without being charged with a foul.

The following actions are fouls that are penalized by losing the ball at the spot of the foul:

1. Illegally touching the ball with the hands
2. Swinging the stick above waist height (called high sticking)
3. Guards or forwards moving across the centerline
4. Player other than the goalie entering the restraining area
5. Goalie throwing the ball
6. Holding, stepping on, or lying on the ball

Defenders must be 15 feet (5 m) back when the ball is put into play after a foul. If the spot where the foul occurred is closer than 15 feet to the goal, only the goalkeeper may defend. The ball is then put into play 15 feet directly out from the goal.

Personal fouls include any action or rough play that endangers other players. A player committing a personal foul must retire to the sidelines for two minutes. The following are personal fouls:

1. Hacking or striking with a stick
2. Tripping with either the foot or the stick
3. Pushing or blocking

Hockey Skill Tests

Passing for Accuracy

In passing for accuracy, the player has five attempts to pass the puck or ball into a 3-by-3-foot (1 by 1 m) target. Draw or tape the target on the wall, or use a 3-foot square of cardboard. The player must pass from a distance of 30 feet (10 m). The player can approach the 30-foot restraining line in however he or she chooses. Each successful pass scores 2 points.

Receiving

Three players are designated as passers and pass from different angles to a student being tested for receiving. The puck must be definitely stopped and controlled. The teacher can judge whether the pass was a fair opportunity for the player to field. Six passes, two from each angle, are given, and players score 1 point for each successful field.

Stick Handling for Speed

To test carrying for speed, line up three cones 8 feet (2.5 m) apart. The first cone is 16 feet (5 m) from the starting line. The player carries the puck around the cones in a figure-eight pattern to finish at the original starting line. Use a stopwatch for timing and record scores to the nearest tenth of a second. Players get two trials, and the faster trial is recorded as the score.

Shooting for Distance

Evaluate shooting for distance outdoors only. Use a restraining line as a starting point. Give each player five trials to see how many goals can be scored from an established distance. Adjust the distance to the goal depending on the players' ability level. Line up players in four or five squads behind the restraining line. After taking their five trials, players can exchange places with someone who is returning pucks.

LEARNING AIDS

WEBSITES
Field hockey information, www.fieldhockey.com
Hockey news and information, www.letsplayhockey.com
In-line hockey, www.usahockey.com
In-line hockey drills, www.whockey.com/work/cirsa/drillbook/
USA Field Hockey, www.teamusa.org/usa-field-hockey

SUGGESTED READINGS
Anders, E. (2008). *Field hockey: Steps to success* (2nd ed.). Champaign, IL: Human Kinetics.
Bertagna, J. (2016). *The hockey coaching bible.* Champaign, IL: Human Kinetics.
Chambers, D. (2016). *The hockey drill book* (3rd ed.). Champaign, IL: Human Kinetics.
Mood, D.P., Musker, F.F., & Rink, J.E. (2012). *Sports and recreational activities* (15th ed.). Boston, MA: McGraw-Hill.
Walter, R., & Johnston, M. (2010). *Hockey plays and strategies.* Champaign, IL: Human Kinetics.

26

27 Soccer

Skills instruction for soccer begins during the intermediate grades after children have mastered basic prerequisite skills. Teaching the basic rules and beginning strategies for soccer is an integral part of the instructional process. Proper progression is the key to teaching fundamental skills and lead-up games associated with soccer. Lead-up games allow teachers to emphasize development of selected soccer skills in a setting compatible with their students' abilities.

Learning Objectives

▶ Structure learning experiences efficiently using appropriate formations, progressions, and coaching techniques.

▶ Develop a unit plan and a lesson focus for soccer.

▶ Identify safety precautions associated with teaching soccer.

▶ Describe instructional procedures used for directing a successful lead-up game.

▶ Cite assessment procedures used for evaluating soccer skills.

Soccer is the most popular—and probably the most active—sport in the world for youth. Globally this sport is called "football" and there are many "football" or "futbal" clubs in the U.S. that adopt the international name. Effective soccer instruction stresses position play, in contrast to a group of children chasing the ball. To improve their playing ability, students must have organized practice that involves handling the ball as often as possible. Offer students many opportunities on offense to kick, control, dribble, volley, and shoot the ball and many opportunities on defense to mark, guard, tackle, and recover the ball. Success in soccer depends on how well individual skills are coordinated in team play.

Modifications of Soccer for Children

A regulation soccer ball is too large and heavy for young soccer players who are learning the sport. Many students avoid contact with the regulation ball for fear of injury. Several manufacturers produce smaller-sized soccer balls that move and rebound exactly like regulation balls. Using foam balls covered with a tough plastic skin that looks like a soccer ball can calm players' fear of being hurt. Beach balls are excellent for teaching beginning skills because they move slowly and do not hurt when they strike someone.

To give students more chances to practice skills, use fewer players per game. The 11-person team is not suitable for beginning players, but Mini-Soccer is an excellent game with 6 or 7 players per team. Two games can be played crosswise on a regulation soccer field, and only a penalty area and the out-of-bounds lines are marked. The regulation soccer goal (24 feet wide by 8 feet high [7.3 m wide by 2.5 m high]) is too large for elementary school play. Modify the size to give teams a reasonable chance of scoring as well as preventing a score. The suggested size is from 18 to 21 feet (5.5 to 6.5 m) wide by 6 to 7 feet (1.8 to 2.1 m) high. Depending on the game, the goal size can be even smaller. Another strategy is to use more than one ball to increase activity, ball touches, and team play.

Instructional Emphasis and Sequence

Table 27.1 shows the sequence of soccer activities divided into two developmental levels. Based on the skills children have acquired through community sports programs, the actual sequence may differ in certain areas

TABLE 27.1 Suggested Soccer Program

Developmental Level II	Developmental Level III
Skills	
Dribbling	Dribbling
Inside-the-foot pass	Outside-the-foot pass
Long pass	Ball control (trapping)
Foot trap	Passing
Passing	Tackling
Goalkeeping	Kicking goals
Defensive maneuvers	Kickoff (placekicking)
Soccer rules	Punting
	Volleying
	Heading with beach balls
	Ball control and passing
	The game of soccer
	Team play and strategy
Activities	
Circle Kickball	Manyball Soccer
Diagonal Soccer	Sideline Soccer
Dribblerama	Over the Top
Bull's-Eye	Lane Soccer
	Line Soccer
	Mini-Soccer
	Six-Spot Keep-Away
	Regulation Soccer
Skill Tests	
Passing against a wall	Figure-eight dribbling
Kicking for accuracy	Controlling (three types)
Placekicking for distance	Punting for distance
	Penalty kicking

and communities. Although using the feet to control a ball, dribble, and kick are taught during Developmental Level I as a part of manipulative lessons, these skills are further refined within the context of soccer now.

Developmental Level II

Basic soccer skills for this level are dribbling, trapping, and passing the ball with the foot to another player or to a target. These skills are basic in that they are precursors to other skills used in soccer games. Activities

27

at Developmental Level II stress games and drills that facilitate practicing and using basic skills. To maximize involvement, provide at least one ball for every two players. For many drills, one ball per student is optimal.

Developmental Level III

To enhance control of the ball, in Developmental Level III students are taught to manipulate the ball with other body parts, such as the thigh and chest. Lessons continue to focus on passing, dribbling, and trapping, and teachers can introduce games with two to five players per team. Players learn the basic goalkeeping skills of catching low and high balls. Further development of basic skills is recommended, along with instruction on shooting, tackling, heading, jockeying, and the concept of two-touch soccer for more advanced players. Students learn the basics of team and positional play as well as regular soccer rules. Explaining to students that soccer is an international game is valuable because few U.S. children realize how important this game is in other countries.

Soccer Skills

Offensive skills taught in the elementary grades are passing, kicking, controlling, dribbling, volleying (including heading), and shooting. Shooting is defined as taking a shot at the goal with the intent to score. Defensive skills include marking, guarding, jockeying, tackling, and recovering the ball.

Dribbling

Dribbling involves moving the ball with a series of taps or pushes to cover ground while still retaining control. It allows a player to change direction quickly and avoid opponents. The best contact point is the inner side of the foot, but the outer side of the foot is used at faster running speeds. Players must keep the ball close to maintain control. Use these instructional cues to emphasize proper dribbling form:

1. Keep the head up to see the field.
2. Move on the balls of the feet.
3. Contact the ball with the inside, outside, or instep of the foot.
4. Keep the ball near the body so it can be controlled. (Do not kick it too far in front of the body.)
5. Dribble the ball with a controlled tap.

Passing

Balance and timing are the keys to accurate passing. Players use passes to advance the ball to a teammate and to shoot on goal. Occasionally, teams use a pass to send the ball downfield so that they can regroup—although their opponents have an equal chance to recover the ball. Here are instructional cues to enhance accurate passing:

1. Place the nonkicking foot alongside the ball.
2. Keep the head down and the eyes focused on the ball during contact.
3. Spread the arms for balance.
4. Follow through with the kicking leg in the intended direction of the ball.
5. Make contact with the outside or inside of the foot rather than with the toe.
6. Practice kicking with both the left and right foot.

Inside-the-Foot Pass (Push Pass)

The inside-the-foot pass is used for accurate passing over distances of up to 15 yards (meters). Because of the technique used, this pass is sometimes known as the push pass. The passer places the nonkicking foot well up alongside the ball. As the passer draws back the kicking foot, she turns the toe out. During the kick, the toe remains turned out, keeping the inside of the foot perpendicular to the line of flight. The sole stays parallel to the ground. At contact, the knee of the kicking leg is well forward, over the ball, and both knees are slightly bent (figure 27.1).

Outside-the-Foot Pass (Flick Pass)

The player's nonkicking foot is more to the side of the ball than it is for the inside-the-foot kick, and the kicking leg approaches from directly behind the ball. The kicking foot is fully extended, and contact with the ball is on the outside of the foot between the laces and the sole line. This pass is useful for running without breaking stride or for flicking the ball to the side.

Long Pass (Shoelace Kick)

The long pass is the power pass in soccer, used to kick for distance or to kick the ball past a goalie. Rather than the top of the foot (shoelace area), beginners often use the toes when making this pass; this technique can cause injury or an inaccurate kick. For a long pass, the player approaches the ball in a full running stride at an angle to the line of flight. As the player sets the nonkicking foot alongside the ball, his or her kicking leg is cocked

FIGURE 27.1 The inside-the-foot pass.

FIGURE 27.2 Controlling with the inside of the foot.

in the backswing. Just before contact, the ankle of the kicking foot is fixed with the toes pointed down. As with all passes, the head is down and the eyes focus on the ball. Contact is made at the shoelace area of the foot. The passer crisply snaps the lower leg forward at the knee, completing the pass with a normal follow-through in the direction of the pass. To lift the ball, the passer contacts the ball below the midline, close to the ground, with the body leaning slightly backward. The nonkicking leg is to the side and slightly behind the ball so that the kicking foot makes contact just as the leg begins its upswing. The lofted pass is aimed over the heads of opposing players.

When teaching students the long pass, ample spacing should be provided in setting up because students who are learning the activity often have difficulty controlling the location of the pass.

Ball Control (Trapping)

Learning to receive a ball and get it into the ideal position for making a pass or shot is vital. In fact, one of the best measures of skilled players is how quickly they can bring the ball under control with the feet, legs, or torso. Advanced players achieve control in one smooth movement with one touch of the ball. The second touch occurs when they make the pass.

For efficient control, present a large surface of the body to the ball. On contact, briefly withdraw the surface to produce a sponge-like or shock-absorbing action that decelerates the ball and allows it to drop into an ideal position about a yard (meter) in front of the body. Then make the pass or shot. These instructional cues will help students develop ball control skills:

1. Move in line with the path of the ball.
2. Reach to meet the ball and give with the contact.
3. Stay on the balls of the feet.
4. Keep the eyes on the ball.

Inside-the-Foot Trap

This method of control is the most common; it is used when the ball is either rolling along the ground or bouncing up to knee height. Present the full surface of the foot, from heel to toe, alongside the ball (figure 27.2).

Chest and Thigh Traps

Soccer players also use the chest and inner thigh to deflect the ball downward when it is bouncing high. For the chest trap, the player aligns his body with the path of the ball (figure 27.3). On contact, he draws back the

27

FIGURE 27.3 Chest trap.

chest and waist so his body leans forward and the ball drops directly to the ground in front of him. For the thigh trap, the player turns his body sideways to the flight of the ball. He contacts the ball with the inner thigh, which he then relaxes and draws backward. This action absorbs the force of the ball, which drops to the ground ready to be played.

Sole-of-the-Foot Trap

This method of control is not used as often to stop the ball. For beginners, it is less successful than the inside-the-foot trap, because the ball can roll easily under the foot. Players also use the sole to roll the ball from side to side in dribbling and to adjust for a better passing position.

Heading

Heading is a special kind of volleying in which players change the ball's path by hitting it with the head. Recent research has shown that heading might cause some brain damage. With this in mind, use beach balls—and most specially, avoid regulation soccer balls—if teaching heading skills.

In heading, teach players to use the neck muscles to help reduce the impact of the blow. When executing the header, students must keep their mouths shut to avoid

chipping teeth or biting their tongue. They must keep the eyes on the ball until the moment of impact. The point of contact is the top of the forehead at the hairline. In preparing to contact the ball with the head, the player stands in stride position, with knees relaxed and trunk leaning backward at the hips. At the moment of contact, the trunk moves forward abruptly, driving the forehead into the ball. Advanced heading is achieved in midair and is especially useful in beating other players to the ball. Midair heading can be done by using a running one-footed takeoff or a standing two-footed jump.

Defensive Maneuvers

Tackling, different from American football tackling, is a move to take the ball away from an opponent who is dribbling. The most common tackle is the front block, which involves contacting the ball with the inside of the foot just as the opponent touches it. The tackler presents a firm instep to the ball, his or her weight behind it. The stronger the ball contact is, the better the chance is of controlling it. Body contact is avoided because it may constitute a foul. Other tackles may be made when running alongside the player with the ball.

How much tackling should be taught in elementary school programs? In most cases, it is probably best to teach tackling skills that involve the defensive player remaining upright. Methods like the hook slide and split slide have little value in elementary school programs.

Jockeying

Knowing when to make a tackle, and when not to, is one of the most difficult skills to learn. A failed tackle may mean that an attacker breaks through with a free shot on goal. Often, defenders keep jockeying until defensive support arrives. Jockeying means backing off while staying close enough to pressure the advancing player. Defenders stay on their toes, watching the ball rather than the opponent's feet and staying within 1 or 2 yards (meters) of the ball.

Throw-Ins

The throw-in is the only time field players can handle the ball with their hands. Players must closely follow throw-in rules to avoid a turnover to the other team. The rules are as follows:

1. Both hands must be on the ball.
2. The ball must be released from over the thrower's head.

3. The thrower must face the field.

4. The thrower cannot step onto the field until after the throw-in.

5. Both feet must be in contact with the ground until the ball is released.

6. The thrower cannot play the ball until another player on the field touches it.

The throw-in from out-of-bounds may be executed from a standing or running position. Teach beginning players how to make the throw without a running start. The feet often are placed one behind the other, with the rear toe trailing along the ground. Delivery of the ball is from behind the head, using both arms equally. Release is in front of the forehead with arms outstretched. Instructional cues to help students perform correctly are "Drag your back foot" and "Follow through with both hands pointing toward the target."

Shooting

Scoring is the purpose of the game, and players need to practice shooting skills while stationary as well as on the run. As with passing, players can use the inside, outside, and top of the foot. See the earlier sections related to passing for instructional cues. The primary difference is that for shooting, the ball is driven in a line and less loft is typically sought.

Goalkeeping

Goalkeeping involves blocking shots by catching, stopping, or otherwise deflecting the ball. Goalkeepers should become adept at catching low-rolling balls, diving on rolling balls, catching airborne balls at waist level and below (figure 27.4), and catching airborne balls at waist height and above.

Have students practice catching low-rolling balls much like a baseball outfielder does. The goalie gets down on one knee, with his body behind the ball to act as a backstop, and catches the ball with both hands, fingers pointing toward the ground.

When catching a ball below the waist, goalies point the thumbs outward ("pinkies together") as the arms reach for the ball; the body and arms give while bringing the ball into the abdomen. For balls above waist level, the goalie's thumbs turn inward ("thumbs together") as the arms reach to meet the ball and give while guiding it to the midsection. When diving for the ball, the goalie always tries to throw his body behind it and cradle it with his hands. Drills for goalies should offer opportu-

FIGURE 27.4 Goalie catching a ball below waist level.

nities to catch different shots. All students should receive goalkeeping practice.

Punting

The punt, used by the goalkeeper only, can be stationary or done on the run. The ball is held in both hands at waist height in front of the body and directly over the kicking leg. For the stationary punt, the kicking foot is forward. A short step is taken with the kicking foot, followed by a full step with the other foot. With the knee bent and the toe extended, the kicking foot swings forward and upward. As contact is made with the ball at the instep, the knee straightens, and additional power is secured from the other leg through a coordinated rising on the toes or a hop (figure 27.5).

The goalkeeper who can develop a strong punt has an advantage. Distance and accuracy are important in setting up the next attack. Over shorter distances,

FIGURE 27.5 Punt.

27

throwing underhand or overhand can be more accurate than kicking. In those cases, goalies must use a straight arm for rolling or throwing the ball to players.

Instructional Procedures

1. In practices, emphasize controlling the ball and passing. Organize drills and activities to keep all children involved and active. One ball is needed per two children.

2. Include many combination drills featuring both offense and defense. Enjoyment is the key to continued learning. Use drills and lead-up activities to make the skills challenging, but be sure that all activities are appropriate to the players' developmental level.

3. Use small-group games (two to five players per team) to ensure maximum activity. As players' skill improves, use larger teams.

4. Lead-up games are designed to use the skills practiced in drills. For example, if long passing is the skill of the day, have students play lead-up games requiring and rewarding long passing. In the early stages of teaching soccer, prohibiting tackling may be best.

5. The grid system is useful when organizing drills, activities, and small-sized games. With cones or chalk, mark a grid system of 10-yard (meter) squares on the playing field. The number of squares needed depends on class size, but at least one square for every three students is recommended (figure 27.6 shows two layouts). Use the squares as boundaries for tackling, keeping possession, and passing diagonally or sideways. Drill and game areas can be defined easily, allowing several small-sized games to be played simultaneously.

6. Use balls smaller and lighter than the regulation soccer ball. An excellent alternative for novices is the tough-skin foam rubber training ball. It withstands heavy usage and does not hurt students on impact. Another alternative is a beach ball. They are light and move slowly, making them an excellent choice for unskilled players. Junior-sized soccer balls (number 4) are also excellent but more expensive. The key to soccer practice is to have plenty of balls available.

7. Soccer, with its attack and defense, can be a rough game. Control rough play such as pushing, shoving, kicking, and tripping. Teachers need to enforce rules strictly.

8. Modify the scoring to make the activity more enjoyable for more children. Scoring must be a challenge—neither too easy nor too difficult. To avoid arguments when the ball is to be kicked through a line of children, limit the height of the kick to shoulder level or below. Mark goal outlines with cones and designated spots. Regulation soccer goals are not needed for an elementary school program.

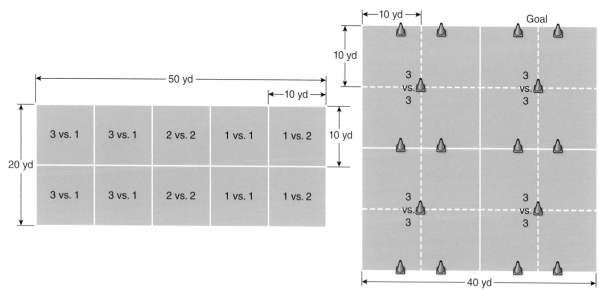

FIGURE 27.6 Examples of grid layouts and usage.

Soccer Drills

Teachers typically use two types of soccer drills: (1) players practice technique without opposition from any defense, and (2) players practice skills in a drill involving both offensive and defensive players and perhaps a target. Some drills begin by practicing technique and then move to using skills. Individual practice is excellent, particularly with dribbling techniques, but drill work should lead to activities in combinations of two or three players and small groups.

The playing surface greatly affects the quality of soccer practice. Grass is the most desirable surface, but some schools have only hardtop surfaces. In that case, deflate the balls slightly to simulate how they travel on grass. When space is restricted, outline areas with cones, beanbags, jugs, or boundary boards.

Note: The following symbols are used in soccer game formation diagrams:

Defensive player: X

Offensive player: O

Player moving without the ball: solid arrow

Player dribbling: dashed arrow

Player passing, kicking, or shooting on goal: wavy arrow

Individual Work

Dribbling practice is best done individually. Activity can begin by having students dribble in various directions and signaling them to make right and left turns. As a variation call out, "Left," which means turn left, "Right," and "Reverse." Scatter some cones around the area and have players dribble around one cone clockwise and around the next cone counterclockwise.

Have students practice heading skills by tossing a beach ball overhead and heading it. Alternate heading with a short period of dribbling practice. To teach trapping skills, drop a ball and show students how to smother it with a foot. Another drill is to have players toss the ball into the air, let it bounce, and then kick it to themselves with an instep (inside-the-foot) pass. Yet another activity is to toss the ball high and use the instep kick to control it.

Rebounding to oneself continuously, although not actually used in the game of soccer, is an excellent way to learn ball control. (This activity is sometimes called foot juggling.) Students begin by dropping the ball so that it bounces to waist height and then practice the following skills:

1. Rebound the ball with alternating feet, letting it bounce between contacts.

2. Play the ball twice with one foot, let it bounce, and then play it twice with the other foot.

3. Toss the ball so that it can be handled with the thigh and then catch it. Add successive rebounds with the thigh.

4. Play ball with the foot, thigh, head, thigh, foot, and catch it.

The foot pickup is another skill that can be taught in two ways. The first is to have students put the ball between their feet, jump up, and hoist the ball so it can be caught. The second is the toe pickup. Students put a toe on top of the ball and pull the toe back and down so that the ball spins up the instep, from which it can be hoisted to the hands. Another bit of individual work is toe changing on top of the ball. Students put the ball of the foot on top of the ball. On signal, they change feet.

Drills for Two Players

Many introductory drills are best practiced with a partner. The grid system, mentioned earlier, is a fine way to organize partner drills. The distance between the grid lines depends on the skills to be practiced. Partners position themselves opposite each other, thus forming two lines of players and giving the teacher a clear view of the class in action (figure 27.7). This approach is recommended for introducing all new skills, such as passing with both sides of the foot and ball control. Skill combinations can be used, such as throw-ins by one partner and control-and-pass by the other. Within the grids, partners can work on passing, dribbling, keep-away, and one-on-one games.

Here are some drills that can be used in partner formation.

FIGURE 27.7 Class organized along grid lines.

27

1. *Dribbling, marking, and ball recovery.* Pairs are scattered, and one player in each pair has a soccer ball. That player dribbles in various directions as the second player tries to stay close to the first (marking). As skill improves, the defensive players try to recover the ball from the dribblers. If they succeed, roles are reversed.

2. *Dribbling.* One player of the pair has a ball and dribbles in different directions. On signal, the player passes to his or her partner, who repeats the dribbling, continuing until another signal is given.

3. *Dribbling, moving, and passing.* Two lines of paired children face each other across a 40- to 60-foot (12 to 20 m) distance (figure 27.8). Each child in one of the lines has a ball and works with a partner directly across from him or her. The teacher calls one of the following challenges, and a player with a ball from line A moves forward to perform it. When the player moves near his or her partner, the player passes to him or her, and the partner (line B) repeats the same maneuver back to line A. Both players are then in their starting places.

   a. Dribble across to partner, using the outside of either foot.
   b. Gallop across, handling the ball with the front foot only. On return, lead with the other foot.
   c. Skip across, dribbling at the same time.
   d. Slide across, handling the ball with the back foot. On return, lead with the other foot.
   e. Hop across, using the lifted foot to handle the ball. Be sure to change feet halfway across.
   f. Dribble the ball to a point halfway across. Stop the ball with the sole of the foot and leave it there. Continue to the other line. Meanwhile, the partner from line B moves forward to dribble the ball back to line A.
   g. Player A dribbles to the center and passes to player B. Player A now returns to line A. Player B repeats and returns to line B.

4. *Volleying and controlling.* Pairs of players are scattered. One player in each pair has a ball and acts as a feeder, tossing the ball to practice various receptive skills including different kinds of volleying and controlling balls in flight. Controlled tossing is essential to this drill.

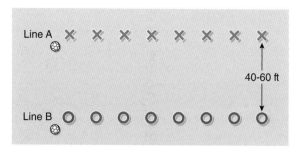

FIGURE 27.8 Dribbling, moving, and passing.

Drills for Three Players

With one ball for three players, many of the drills suggested for pairs are still possible. Drills for three players require fewer balls.

1. *Passing and controlling.* The trio of players sets up a triangle with players about 10 yards (meters) apart. They practice controlled passing and ball control.

2. *Volleying and controlling.* One player acts as a feeder, tossing to the other two players, who practice volleying and controlling in-flight balls.

3. *Dribbling and passing.* Structure a shuttle-type drill as shown in figure 27.9. Players go back and forth continuously. Player 1 has the ball and dribbles to player 2, who dribbles the ball back to player 3, who in turn dribbles to player 1. Players can dribble the entire distance, or dribble partway and then pass the ball to the end player. Obstacles can be set up to challenge players to dribble through or around each obstacle.

4. *Dribbling and stopping the ball.* Three dribblers are in line, each with a ball. The leader moves in various directions, followed by the other two players. On signal, each player controls his or her ball. The leader circles around to the back ball,

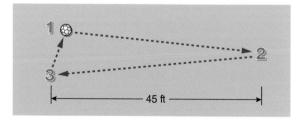

FIGURE 27.9 Shuttle-type dribbling drill.

and the other two move one ball forward. The dribbling continues for another stop. A third stop returns the players to their original positions.

5. *Passing.* Players stand in three corners of a 10-yard (meter) square. After passing, a player moves to the empty corner of the square, which may be a diagonal movement (figure 27.10).

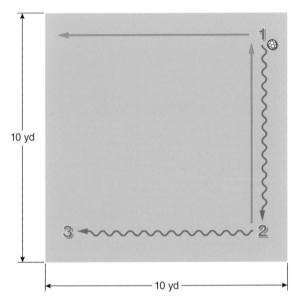

FIGURE 27.10 Passing drill.

6. *Passing and defending.* One player is the feeder and rolls the ball to either player. After rolling the ball, he or she tries to block or tackle the player receiving the ball to prevent a pass to the third player, who—if the pass is completed—tries to pass back (figure 27.11).

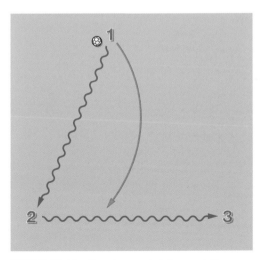

FIGURE 27.11 Passing and defense drill.

Drills for Four or More Players

Organize drills for four or more players using a rotation system that gives all players an equal chance to practice skills.

1. *Dribbling.* Four players are in line, as shown in figure 27.12. Each player in front has a ball. Both front players dribble to the center, where they exchange balls and continue dribbling to the other side. The next players do the same. A variation is to have the two players meet at the center, exchange balls, and dribble back to their starting point. Action is continuous.

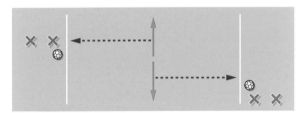

FIGURE 27.12 Dribble exchange drill.

2. *Passing, guarding, and tackling.* Four players occupy the four corners of a square (figure 27.13). One player has a ball. Practice begins with one player rolling the ball to the player in the opposite corner, who, in turn, passes to either of the other two players. The player rolls the ball twice per round, so that passes are made both ways. The next progression calls for the player who rolled the ball to move forward rapidly to block the pass to either side. The player gets several tries before another player takes over the rolling duties.

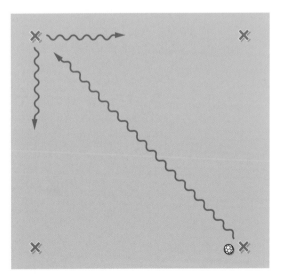

FIGURE 27.13 Passing, guarding, and tackling drill.

27

3. *Shooting, goalkeeping, and defense.* A shooting drill against defense can be coordinated with four players and a 15-foot (5 m) goal set off with cones or other markers (figure 27.14). One player has the ball. The player advances and tries to maneuver around a second player so that he or she can shoot past the goalkeeper guarding the goal. A fourth player acts as the retriever. Rotate positions.

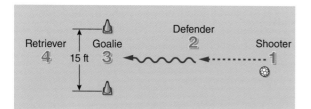

FIGURE 27.14 Shooting, goalkeeping, and defense.

4. *Dribbling.* Four or five players, each with a ball, form a line. A "coach" stands about 15 yards (meters) in front of the line. Each player, in turn, dribbles up to the coach, who indicates with a thumb in which direction the player should dribble. The coach gives the direction at the last possible moment.

5. *Passing, controlling, and defense.* Four players stand in the four corners of a square, 10 yards (meters) on a side. Two defensive players are inside the square. The corner players stay in place within the square and try to pass the ball between them while the two defenders try to recover the ball (figure 27.15). After a set time, another two players take over as defenders.

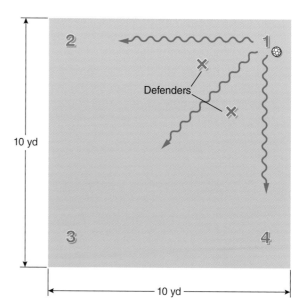

FIGURE 27.15 Passing, controlling, and defense.

6. *Shooting.* For two-way goal practice, use two teams of two to six players and assign each team to one side of the goal. The goal width can vary, depending on the players' skill. Players practice two types of shooting: (1) kicking a stationary ball from 10 to 20 yards (meters) out and (2) preceding a kick with a dribble. The second type requires a restraining line 12 to 15 yards (meters) out. Mark this line with cones, as shown in figure 27.16. Use at least four balls for this two-way drill. After a period of kicking, the groups change sides. Ball chasers are the players at the end of each line.

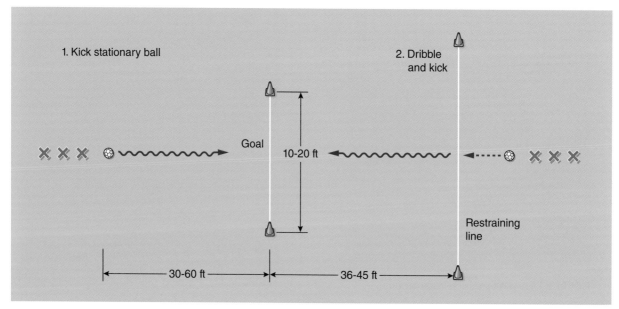

FIGURE 27.16 Shooting drill.

7. *Shooting and goalkeeping.* Players can also practice scoring with a goalkeeper (figure 27.17). Players use a stationary ball from 12 yards out (penalty distance) by doing kicks preceded by a dribble. The goalie and the chaser complete one round and then rotate. Having a second ball to play with saves time because play can continue while the chaser recovers the previous ball.

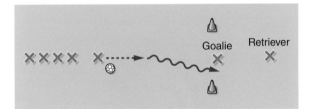

FIGURE 27.17 Shooting and goalkeeping.

8. *Kicking and trapping.* This activity is an excellent squad drill. About eight players form a circle 15 yards (meters) in diameter. They pass two balls back and forth independently. Passes are kept low, using primarily the side-of-the-foot kick. Players can try using three balls.

9. *Passing and shooting.* The drill can be done with four to six players and two balls. A passer stands about 15 yards from the goal, and a retriever is behind the goal. The shooters are in line, 20 yards (meters) from the goal and to the right. The first shooter passes to the passer and then runs forward. The passer returns the ball to the shooter. The shooter tries to time his or her run forward so that he or she successfully shoots the pass through the goal. Both the passer and the retriever stay in position for several rounds of shooting and then rotate to become shooters. The first pass can be from a stationary ball. Later, however, the kicker can be allowed to dribble forward a short distance before making the first pass. Reverse the field and practice from the left, shooting with the nondominant leg (figure 27.18).

10. *Tackling and ball handling.* A defender is restricted to tackling in the area between two parallel lines spaced 1 yard (meter) apart. The field is 20 by 40 yards (meters; figure 27.19). Four to six players can practice this drill. Player 1 advances the ball by dribbling and tries to maneuver past the defender. After evading the defender, player

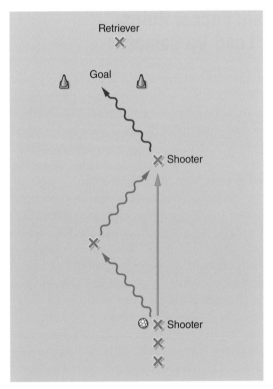

FIGURE 27.18 Passing and shooting.

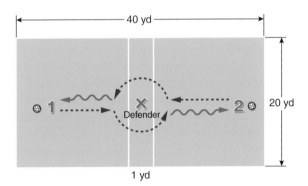

FIGURE 27.19 Tackling and ball-handling drill.

1 passes to player 2 and takes his or her place at the other side of the field. Player 2 repeats the routine, passing the ball off to the next player in the line. If the ball goes out of control or is stopped by the defender, it is rolled to the player whose turn is next. Play is continuous, with the defender maintaining his or her position for several rounds.

27

Basic Soccer Rules for Lead-Up Games

Teach players not to handle the ball deliberately with the hands or arms, but in the early stages, ignore incidental or unintentional handling of the ball. Eventually, a violation leads to a direct free kick—the ball is placed on the ground with the opposition a specific distance away (10 yards [meters] on a full-sized field). A goal can be scored directly from this type of kick.

The goalkeeper is allowed to handle the ball within his or her area by catching, batting, or deflecting with the hands. If the goalie has caught the ball, opponents cannot charge him or her. While the goalie is holding the ball, official rules limit him or her to four steps. In elementary school play, teachers should insist on the goalkeeper getting rid of the ball immediately by throwing or kicking. This removes the temptation to touch or harass the goalie. In some lead-up games, several students may have the same ball-handling privileges as the goalie. The rules need to be clear, and ball handling is done within a specific area.

All serious fouls—tripping, kicking a player, holding, or pushing—result in a direct free kick. If a defender commits one of these fouls or handles a ball in his or her own penalty area, the other team gets a penalty kick. Only the goalkeeper may defend against this kick, which is shot from 12 yards (meters) out. All other players must be outside the penalty area until the ball is kicked. In lead-up games, devise rules for penalty fouls committed in a limited area near the goal by the defensive team. Award the attacking team a kick or an automatic goal.

The ball is out of play and the whistle blown when the ball crosses any of the boundaries, when a goal is scored, or when a foul is called. The team that last touched the ball or sent it out-of-bounds on the side of the field loses possession. The ball is put into play with an overhead throw-in using both hands (figure 27.20).

If the attacking team touches the ball last before it goes over the endline, the defending team is awarded a kick from any point chosen near the endline of that half of the field. If the defense last touched the ball going over the endline, the attacking team gets a corner kick. The ball goes to the corner on the side where the ball went over the endline, where the player takes a direct free kick and may score a goal.

The game is normally started by a kickoff with both teams onside. In lead-up games, the ball can be dropped for a free ball. In some games, the teacher may decide

FIGURE 27.20 Throwing in from out-of-bounds.

©Robert Pangrazi or Aaron Beighle

simply to award the ball for a free kick in the backcourt to the team not making the score.

Lead-up games can continue for a specific time (by halves) or until one team reaches a predetermined score. In a regular soccer game, the play is timed.

When the ball is ensnarled by several players or when someone has fallen, a quick whistle is needed. Put the ball into play by dropping it between players of the opposing teams.

The offside rule has little value in elementary school play, but children should understand the rule and the reasons for it. It prevents the cheap goal (scored by a player on offense who waits near the goal, takes a pass behind the defenders, and scores easily against the goalie). Although the concept of offsides involves various details, it basically means that a player on offense who is ahead of the ball must have two defensive players between his or her and the goal when the ball is kicked forward. One of these players is, of course, the goalie. The offside rule does not apply when the player receives the ball directly from an attempted goal kick or from an opponent, on a throw-in or corner kick, or when the player is in his or her own half.

Instruct players not to raise their feet high or show the soles or cleats of their shoes when other players are nearby. This action constitutes dangerous play, and the other team receives an indirect free kick.

Soccer Activities

Developmental Level II

Circle Kickball

Playing area: playground or gymnasium

Players: 10 to 20 students

Supplies: two beach balls or 8-inch (20 cm) foam rubber balls

Skills: blocking (goalie skills), kicking

Players are in circle formation. Using the sides of their feet, players kick the balls back and forth inside the circle. The object is to kick the ball out of the circle beneath the shoulder level of the other players. Circle players can use their hands and feet to block the ball because they are goalies. All players score 1 point if a ball leaves the circle between them. If, however, a lost ball is clearly one player's fault, then only that player scores a point. Any player who kicks a ball higher than the shoulders of the circle players scores a point. Players scoring the fewest points win. A player is not penalized if he or she leaves the circle to recover a ball and the second ball goes through the vacated spot.

Diagonal Soccer

Playing area: A square about 60 by 60 feet (20 by 20 m)

Players: 20 to 30 students

Supplies: soccer ball, beach ball, or 8-inch (20 cm) foam rubber ball and pinnies (optional)

Skills: kicking, passing, dribbling, some controlling, defending, blocking shots

Mark off two corners with cones 5 feet (150 cm) from the corners on both sides, outlining triangular dead areas. Each team lines up (figure 27.21) and tries to protect two adjacent sides of the square. To start play, three students from each team move into the playing area in their own half of the space. These active players may roam anywhere in the square. Only active players may score; the other players act as goalkeepers.

The object is for active players to kick the ball through the opposing team's line (beneath shoulder height) to score. After 30 to 45 seconds, active players rotate to the sidelines and new players take their place. Players on the sidelines may block the ball with their bodies and use their hands. The team that was scored against

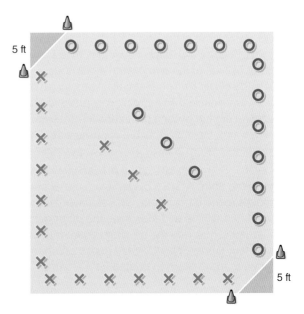

FIGURE 27.21 Formation for Diagonal Soccer.

starts the ball for the next point. Scoring is much the same as in Circle Kickball—the opponents score 1 point when any of these actions occur:

1. A team allows the ball to go through its line below the shoulders.
2. A team touches the ball illegally.
3. A team kicks the ball over the other team above shoulder height.

Dribblerama

Playing area: playground

Players: 10 to 20 students

Supplies: soccer ball or 8-inch (20 cm) foam rubber ball for each player

Skills: dribbling, protecting the ball

The playing area is a large circle or square, clearly outlined. All players dribble within the area. The game is played on three levels.

- *Level 1*: Each player dribbles throughout the area, controlling the ball so that it does not touch another ball. If a touch occurs, both players go outside the area and dribble around the area. After dribbling one lap, these players may reenter the game.

27

- *Level 2*: Mark off two equal playing areas. All players start in one of the areas. While dribbling and controlling the ball, each player tries to kick any other ball out of the area. When a ball is kicked out, the player owning that ball takes it to the other area and dribbles. As more players move to the second area, a second game ensues. Players in this area move back to the opposite side. This keeps all players actively involved in the games.

- *Level 3*: Start with one game on each half of the teaching area. When a player is out, he or she moves to the other game. Or, the player takes one lap dribbling and then joins the other game. Alternatively, divide the area into quadrants and play four games; players can choose another game to move to when ousted from a game.

Bull's-Eye

Playing area: playground

Supplies: soccer ball or 8-inch (20 cm) foam rubber ball for each player

Skills: dribbling, protecting the ball

The playing area is a large outlined shape—circle, square, or rectangle. Two players hold a ball in their hands, which serves as bull's-eyes. The other players dribble within the area. The players with the bull's-eye try to throw their balls (basketball push shot) at any other ball. A player whose ball is hit becomes a new bull's-eye player. The old bull's-eye player becomes one of the dribblers. A new bull's-eye cannot hit back immediately at the old bull's-eye. No score is kept, and no one is eliminated.

Variation: Specify that the bull's-eyes must keep one foot on a marking spot.

Developmental Level III

Manyball Soccer

Playing area: soccer field

Players: entire class

Supplies: six foam rubber or soccer balls, cones, pinnies

Skills: all soccer skills

Players are divided into two teams and begin in the defensive half of the field. Players can freely roam the entire field except for the two goalie boxes, which are marked with cones. Only the goalie is allowed in the goalie box, and only goalies can touch the ball with their hands. Goal-

ies try to keep the balls from going between the cones and can return the ball to play by punting or throwing. To make scoring more difficult, use several goalies.

The object is to kick one of the six balls through the goal. If a ball goes through the goal, the player who scored (not the goalie) retrieves the ball and returns it to the midline for play. All balls are in play at once except when being returned after a goal. Basic soccer rules control the game.

Sideline Soccer

Playing area: rectangle about 60 by 100 feet (20 by 30 m)

Players: teams of 10 to 12 students each

Supplies: a soccer or foam rubber ball, four cones, pinnies (optional)

Skills: most soccer skills, competitive play

Teams line up on the sidelines of the rectangle. Call three or four active players from the end of each team's line (figure 27.22). These players remain active until a point is scored; then they rotate to the other end of the line. The object is to kick the ball between cones (goals) that define the scoring area. The active players on each team compete against each other, aided by their teammates on the sidelines.

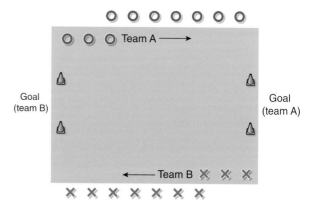

FIGURE 27.22 Formation for Sideline Soccer.

To start play, give the ball to one team or drop it between two opposing players at the center of the field. Only active players can score a goal—by kicking the ball through the goal at or below shoulder height. A goal counts as 1 point. Sideline players can pass to other sideline players or an active teammate, but they cannot score.

Regular soccer rules generally prevail, with special attention to restricting pushing, holding, tripping, or other rough play. Rough play is a foul; the other team receives 1 point. For an out-of-bounds ball, the team on that side of the field gets a free kick near that spot. No score can result from a free kick. Violation of the touch rule also results in a free kick.

Rotate in a new set of active players after 30 to 45 seconds; use more active players when the class is large. Rule that sideline players must receive a set number of passes before active players can take a shot on goal. When players become more skilled, make the goal area narrower. If the ball goes over the endline but not through the goal area, a defender puts the ball into play with a kick.

Over the Top

Playing area: playground

Players: two teams of five to seven students each

Supplies: a ball for each player on offense

Skills: dribbling, ball control, guarding, tackling

One team is on offense and the other is on defense, placed as shown in figure 27.23. Defensive players stay in their respective areas. On signal, all offensive players dribble through the three areas. A player is eliminated if his or her ball is recovered by a defensive player or goes out-of-bounds. The offensive team scores 1 point for each ball dribbled across the far endline. Have the

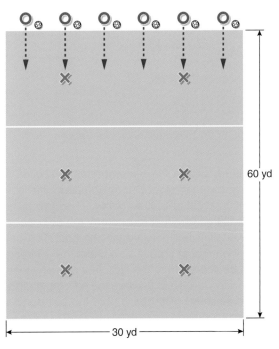

60 yd

30 yd

FIGURE 27.23 Over the Top.

teams reverse roles to give the other team a chance to score. Field markings need to be definite to keep the defensive players in their respective zones. A variation is to use neutral zones between the active zones.

Lane Soccer

Playing area: soccer field

Players: 9 students per team

Supplies: soccer, foam rubber, or beach balls; pinnies

Skills: all soccer skills

Divide the field into four lanes (eight equal sections), as shown in figure 27.24. Place a defensive and an offensive player in each of the eight areas. A goalkeeper guards each goal, following regulation soccer rules. At least two passes must be made before taking a shot on goal. Basic soccer rules guide play. Only the goalie can handle the ball with the hands. Failing to stay within a lane also results in a free kick. Players must rotate after a goal is scored or a specific time has elapsed. This rotation enables all students to play four positions: defense, midfield defense, midfield offense, and offense.

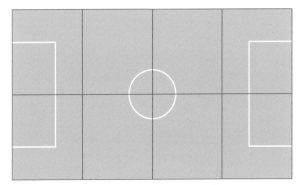

FIGURE 27.24 Field markings for Lane Soccer.

Variations:

1. Vary the number of lanes depending on the number of players and the field size.

2. Allow players to choose an opponent for their lane. Usually, they will choose an opponent of equal ability.

3. Increase the number of balls, goals, and goalies.

Line Soccer

Playing area: soccer field

Players: teams of 8 to 10 students each

Supplies: a soccer, foam rubber, or beach ball; four cones; pinnies

Skills: most soccer skills, competitive play

Each team stands on, and defends, one of two goal lines drawn 80 to 120 feet (25 to 35 meters) apart. A restraining line is drawn 15 feet (5 m) in front of and parallel to each goal line. Field width can vary from 50 to 80 feet (15 to 25 m). The referee stands in the center of the field and holds a ball (figure 27.25). At the whistle, three players (more if the teams are large) run from the right side of each line to the center of the field and become the six active players. The referee drops the ball to the ground, and the players try to kick it through the team defending the goal line. The players in the field may advance by kicking only.

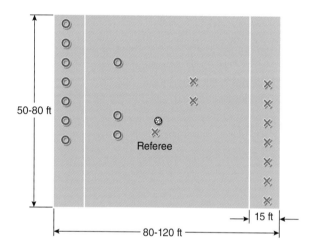

FIGURE 27.25 Line Soccer.

A team scores 1 point when an active player kicks the ball through the opposing team and over the endline (the kick must be made from outside the restraining line). Place cones at the field corners to define the goal line. Teams score 1 point for kicking the ball over the opponent's goal line below shoulder level. A team is awarded 1 point in the case of a personal foul involving pushing, kicking, tripping, and so on.

Line players act as goalies and are allowed to catch the ball. After catching the ball, however, the goalie must put it down immediately and either roll or kick it. It cannot be punted or drop-kicked.

For illegal touching by the active players, the opposing team gets a direct free kick from a point 12 yards (meters) in front of the penalized team's goal line. All active players on the defending team must stand to one side until the ball is kicked. Only goalies can defend. An out-of-bounds ball is awarded to the opponents of the team last touching it. Use the regular soccer throw-in from out-of-bounds. If the ball goes over the shoulders of the defenders at the endline, any endline player may retrieve the ball and put it into play with a throw or kick.

Set a time limit of 1 minute for any group of active players. When time is up, stop play and rotate the players so that all participants get to play.

Mini-Soccer

Playing area: any large area 100 by 150 feet (30 by 45 m), with goals

Players: two teams of seven students each

Supplies: a soccer ball, pinnies or colors to mark teams, four cones for the corners

Skills: all soccer skills

Each end of the field has a 21-foot-wide (6.5 m) goal marked by jumping standards. A 12-yard (meter) semicircle on each end outlines the penalty area. The center of the semicircle is at the center of the goal (figure 27.26).

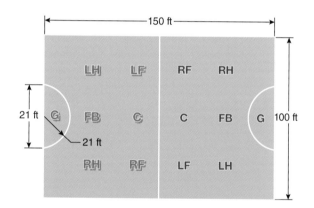

FIGURE 27.26 Formation for Mini-Soccer.

The game follows the general rules of soccer, with one goalie for each side. One new feature, the corner kick, is incorporated in this game. This kick is used when a ball that was last touched by the defense goes over the endline but not through the goal. The ball is taken to the nearest corner for a direct free kick, and a goal can be scored from the kick. In a similar situation, if the attacking team last touched the ball, the goalkeeper kick is awarded. The goalie puts the ball down and placekicks it forward.

The players are designated as center, right forward, left forward, right halfback, left halfback, fullback, and goalie. Players should rotate positions. The forwards play in the front half of the field, and the halfbacks play in the back half. Neither position, however, is restricted to these areas entirely; all players may cross the center-line without penalty.

A foul by the defense within its penalty area (semi-circle) results in a penalty kick, taken from a point 12 yards distant, directly in front of the goal. Only the goalie is allowed to defend. The ball is in play; the others wait outside the penalty area.

Emphasize position play, and encourage the lines of three to spread out and stay in their area. The number of players can vary; games may use as few as three on a side in a more restricted area.

Six-Spot Keep-Away

Playing area: playground, gymnasium

Players: two teams, one with six offensive players and one with three defensive players

Supplies: a soccer ball, stopwatch

Skills: passing, ball control, guarding

Five offensive players stand in a pentagon formation, and the sixth player is in the center (figure 27.27). The pentagon is about 20 yards (meters) across. The game begins with the ball in possession of the center player. Three defenders from the other team enter the penta-gon and try to interrupt the offensive team's passing the ball from one to another. Offensive players should stay reasonably in position. Players may not pass the ball back to the player who passed it to them.

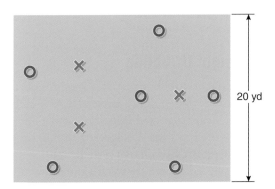

FIGURE 27.27 Six-Spot Keep-Away.

The object is to make as many good passes as possible against the three defenders. After one minute, three offensive players become defensive players and repeat the activity. One more rotation occurs so that all players have been on defense. The threesome scoring the most points is the winner.

Regulation Soccer

Playing area: soccer field (figure 27.28)

Players: 11 students on each team

Supplies: a soccer ball, pinnies

Skills: all soccer skills

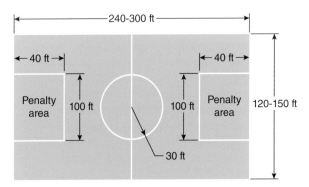

FIGURE 27.28 Regulation Soccer field.

A team usually consists of three forwards, three midfield players, four backline defenders, and one goalkeeper. Teams can have more players, depending on class size. Forwards are the main line of attack and focus primar-ily on scoring. Midfield players need good passing and tackling skills as well as good cardiovascular fitness. Defenders work to keep the opponent from scoring. They try to keep the ball away from their own penalty area and avoid dribbling or passing toward their own goal unless it is absolutely safe to do so. Goalkeepers are usually quick, agile, and have good ball-handling skills.

After a coin toss, the winning team gets to kick off or choose a goal to defend. The loser exercises the option not selected by the winner.

On the kickoff, the ball must travel in any direction at least 1 yard (meter), and the kicker cannot touch it again until another player has kicked it. The defensive team must be 10 yards (meters) away from the kicker. After each score, the team not winning the point gets to kick off. Both teams must be onside at the kickoff. The defensive team must stay onside and out of the center circle until the ball is kicked. Regular soccer rules call for scoring by counting the number of goals made.

Elementary school children usually play 6-minute quarters, but this time can vary depending on the play-ers' skill. Provide a rest period of 1 minute between quarters and 10 minutes between halves.

When the ball goes out-of-bounds on the sideline, it is put into play with a throw-in from the spot where it crossed the line. A goal may not be scored nor may the thrower play the ball a second time until another player

27

has touched it. All opponents are to be 10 yards back at the time of the throw.

If the attacking team causes the ball to go out-of-bounds on the endline, a goal kick is awarded. The ball is placed in the goal area and kicked beyond the penalty area by a defending player, who may not touch the ball twice in a row. If a player touches the ball before it goes out of the penalty area, it is not yet in play and is kicked again.

If the defensive team sends the ball out-of-bounds over the endline, the other team gets a corner kick. The ball is placed 1 yard from the corner of the field and kicked into the field of play by an attacking player. The 10-yard restriction also applies to defensive players.

If two opponents touch the ball at the same time and it goes out-of-bounds, a drop ball is called. The referee drops the ball between two opposing players, who cannot kick it until it touches the ground. A drop ball is also called when the ball is trapped among downed players.

If a player is closer to the opponent's goal line than to the ball when the ball is played in a forward direction, it is an offside infraction. Exceptions exist, and a player is not offside when he or she is in the player's half of the playing field, when two opponents are nearer their goal line than the attacking player at the moment the ball is played, or when the ball is received directly from a corner kick, a throw-in, or a goal kick.

Personal fouls involving unnecessary roughness are penalized. Tripping, striking, charging, holding, pushing, and jumping an opponent intentionally are forbidden.

It is a foul for any player, except the goalkeeper, to handle the ball with the hands or arms. The goalkeeper is allowed only four steps and must then get rid of the ball. After the ball has left the player's possession, the goalkeeper may not pick it up again until another player has touched it. Players are not allowed to screen or obstruct opponents, unless they are in control of the ball.

Penalties are as follows:

1. A direct kick is awarded for all personal fouls and handled balls. A goal can be scored from a direct free kick. Examples of infringements are pushing, tripping, kicking a player, and holding.

2. A penalty kick is awarded if a defender in his or her penalty area commits direct free-kick infringements.

3. An indirect free kick is awarded for offsides, obstruction, dangerous play such as high kicking, a goalkeeper's taking more than four steps or repossessing the ball before another player has touched it, and playing the ball twice after a dead-ball situation. A second player must touch the ball before a goal can be scored. A referee signals if the kick is indirect by pointing one arm upward vertically.

From an early stage, players must learn to give information to each other during the game. Valuable help can be given by shouting instructions, such as "Man on," "You have time," or "Player behind," and by calling for the ball when in position to receive a pass.

Encourage players to use the space on the field to the best advantage. When a team is in possession of the ball, players should try to find a position where they can pass either behind the player with the ball to give support or toward the goal to be in a better position to shoot. When a team is forced into defense, the defenders should get goal side of attackers (between the attackers and their own goal) to prevent them from gaining an advantage.

Soccer Skill Tests

The tests for soccer skills cover various kinds of kicks, dribbling, and controlling. These tests are best used as self-testing stations. Signs will tell students how to test themselves. Students rotate from station to station after a designated amount of time.

Passing Against a Wall

Players pass the ball from behind a line drawn 5 to 10 yards (meters) away from a wall. Encourage students to control the ball before kicking. The score consists of the number of passes made from behind the line in one or two minutes. This is an excellent test of general ball control and short passing skill.

Figure-Eight Dribbling

For a figure-eight dribbling test, arrange three obstacles or markers in a line, 4 yards (meters) apart, with the first marker 4 yards (meters) from the starting line. The finish line is 4 yards wide. Using a stopwatch, time the players to the nearest tenth of a second.

Each player gets three trials, and the fastest trial is recorded. On each trial, the player dribbles over the figure-eight course and finishes by kicking or dribbling the ball over the 4-yard (meter) finish line, and the watch is then stopped. The test is best done on a grass surface. If a hard surface must be used, deflate the ball somewhat so that players can control it.

Controlling

For the controlling test, the formation is a file plus one. A thrower stands 15 to 20 feet (5 to 6 m) in front of the file and rolls or bounces the ball to the player at the head of the file. Players get three trials each for sole-of-the-foot control, foot control, and body control. The ball must be definitely stopped and controlled. The highest possible total score is 9 points.

The thrower should adopt one type of throw for all controls and for all players. If the scorer judges that the roll was not a good opportunity, the trial is taken over. Five trials can be allowed.

Punting and Placekicking for Distance

To test punting for distance, a football field or any other field marked in gridiron fashion at 5- or 10-yard (meter) intervals is needed. One soccer ball is required, but using three saves considerable time. A measuring tape (25 or 50 feet [10 or 15 m]) and individual markers complete the supply list.

Each player takes three kicks from behind a restraining line. One child marks the kick for distance, and one or two others act as ball chasers. Each player's marker is left at the spot of their longest kick. This location is determined by marking where the ball first touched the ground after the kick.

Kicks are measured to the nearest foot (half meter), and each student in the small group should kick before the distances are measured. The punt must be from a standing, not a running, start. If a child crosses the line during the kick, it counts as a trial and is not marked.

Placekicking for distance is tested in the same way as punting for distance, with two exceptions. First, the ball is kicked from a stationary position and must be laid on a flat surface and not elevated by dirt, grass, or other means. Second, the child gets credit for the entire distance of the kick, including the roll. Kicking should be done on a grassy surface, because the ball will roll indefinitely on a smooth, hard surface. If the surface presents a problem, the test can be limited to the distance the ball traveled in flight.

Penalty Kicking and Kicking for Accuracy

In the penalty-kicking test, the kicker faces a target area from a point 12 yards out, where the ball has been placed. The target area is formed by a rope stretched tight 6 feet (180 cm) above the ground. Four ropes, set 5 feet (150 cm) apart, are dropped from the stretched rope. This setup outlines three target areas 6 feet high and 5 feet wide. The center target area scores 1 point, and the side areas score 2 points (figure 27.29). (This scoring system reflects the principle that a penalty kick should be directed away from a goalkeeper and toward either corner of the goal.) Each child is allotted five kicks at the target. Possible score: 10 points.

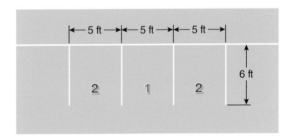

FIGURE 27.29 Penalty-kicking target area.

The same target is used for kicking for accuracy, but the center area scores 2 points and the side areas score 1 point each. A chalk line is about 20 feet (6 m) from the target, and the child stands back another 20 feet for the start. The student dribbles the ball forward and must kick the ball as it is moving and before it crosses the chalk line. Five trials are given. Possible score: 10 points.

27

LEARNING AIDS

WEBSITES

Soccer Information

www.soccerhelp.com

www.gotsoccer.com

www.usyouthsoccer.org

www.saysoccer.org

www.socceramerica.com

SUGGESTED READINGS

American Sport Education Program with Snow, S. (2011). *Coaching youth soccer* (5th ed.). Champaign, IL: Human Kinetics.

Blom, L., & Blom, T. (2009). *Survival guide for coaching youth soccer*. Champaign, IL: Human Kinetics.

Garland, J. (2013). *Youth soccer drills* (3rd ed.). Champaign, IL: Human Kinetics.

Hanlon, T. (2014). *The sports rule book* (3rd ed.). Champaign, IL: Human Kinetics.

LaPrath, D. (2009). *Coaching girls' soccer successfully*. Champaign, IL: Human Kinetics.

Mood, D.P., Musker, F.F., & Rink, J.E. (2012). *Sports and recreational activities* (15th ed.). New York, NY: McGraw-Hill.

Softball

Skills instruction for softball begins during the intermediate grades after children have learned throwing, catching, and striking skills. Teaching the rules and strategies for softball is an integral part of the instructional process. Using proper progression is key to successful teaching of fundamental skills and lead-up games associated with softball. Lead-up games allow teachers to emphasize development of selected softball skills in a setting compatible with their students' abilities.

Learning Objectives

▶ Structure learning experiences efficiently using appropriate formations, progressions, and coaching techniques.

▶ Develop a unit plan and lesson focus for softball.

▶ Identify safety precautions associated with teaching softball.

▶ Describe instructional procedures used for directing a successful lead-up game.

▶ Cite assessment procedures used for evaluating softball skills.

Instructional Emphasis and Sequence

Table 28.1 shows the sequence of softball activities divided into two developmental levels. The activities are listed in progression. Students can practice many softball skills but may not be ready to participate in this chapter's activities until age eight.

Developmental Levels I and II

Developmental Levels I and II emphasize the basic skills of batting, throwing, and catching. Batting receives

TABLE 28.1 Suggested Softball Program

Developmental Level II	Developmental Level III
Skills	
Throwing	
Gripping the ball	Throw-in from outfield
Overhand throw	
Underhand toss	
Around the bases	
Catching and fielding	
Catching thrown balls	Catching flies from fungo bat
Catching fly balls	Infield practice
Grounders	
Fielding grounders in infield	
Sure stop for outfield	
Batting	
Simple skills	Different positions at plate
Tee batting	Bunting
Fungo hitting	
Fielding positions	
Infield practice	Backing up other players
How to catch	Double play
Base running	
To first base and turn	Fast start off base
Circling the bases	Tagging up on fly ball
	Sacrifice

Developmental Level II	Developmental Level III
Pitching	
Simple underhand	Target pitching
Application of pitching rule	Slow pitches
Knowledge, Rules	
Strike zone	Pitching rule
Foul and fair ball	Position
Safe and out	Illegal pitches
Foul tip	Infield fly
Bunt rule	Keeping score
When batter is safe or out	Base running
	Situation quiz
Activities	
Throw-It-and-Run Softball	Five Hundred
Two-Pitch Softball	Home Run
Hit and Run	Scrub (Work-Up)
Kick Softball	Slow-Pitch Softball
Beat Ball	Hurry Baseball (One-Pitch Softball)
Steal a Base	Three-Team Softball
Skill Tests	
Throwing for distance	Pitching
Throwing for accuracy	Circling the bases
	Fielding grounders

much attention, because softball is little fun unless children can hit. Proper form and technique in all three basic skills are parts of the instruction, paying attention to the how as well as the why. Lead-up games introduce students to the basic rules of the game. As children mature, lessons focus on specific skills for pitching, infield play, base running, and batting.

Developmental Level III

Children at Developmental Level III acquire the background to play the game of regulation softball. Tee Ball offers an opportunity for developing all softball skills except pitching and catching. Home Run and Scrub

(Work-Up) provide a variety of experiences, and Batter Ball stresses hitting skills. Students practice batting, throwing, catching, and infield play. Teachers add new pitching techniques, situation play, and double-play work. Slow-Pitch offers lots of action. Babe Ruth Ball emphasizes selective hitting.

Softball Skills

Children can find many ways to execute softball skills effectively, by trial and error and through instruction. Teach proper technique but allow for individual variation.

Gripping the Ball

The standard softball grip, which is difficult for elementary school children, calls for the thumb on one side, the index and middle fingers on top, and the other fingers supporting the ball along the other side (figure 28.1). Children with small hands can use a full-hand grip, spacing the thumb and fingers rather evenly (figure 28.2). Regardless of the grip used, the pads of the fingers control the ball.

Throwing (Right-Handed)

Softball requires accurate throwing. To play softball well, players must develop proper throwing technique. Of all the team sports, softball is probably the most difficult for children because of the fine motor coordination required. Use these instructional cues to help students develop proper throwing technique:

1. Place the throwing-arm side of the body away from the target.
2. Step toward the target with the foot opposite the throwing hand.
3. Rotate the hips as the throwing arm moves forward.
4. Bend and raise the arm at the elbow. Lead with the elbow.
5. Shift the weight from the rear foot to the front foot (nearest the target) before the arm moves forward.

Overhand Throw

To prepare for throwing, the child firmly grips the ball, raises the throwing arm to shoulder height, and brings

FIGURE 28.1 Gripping the ball, two-finger grip.

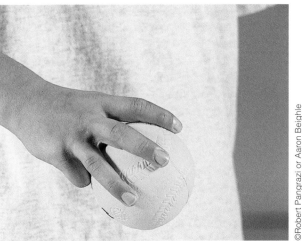

FIGURE 28.2 Gripping the ball, full grip. (The little finger supports on the side.)

the elbow back. For the overhand throw, the hand with the ball then moves back over the head until it is well behind the shoulder at about shoulder height. The left side of the body turns in the direction of the throw, and the left arm is raised in front of the body. The weight is on the rear (right) foot, with the left foot advanced and the toe touching the ground. The arm comes forward with the elbow leading, and the ball is thrown with a downward snap of the wrist (figure 28.3). The body weight is shifted forward into the throw, transferring the weight to the front foot. The player follows through so that the palm of the throwing hand faces the ground after the throw. The eyes are on the target throughout, and the arm is kept free and loose during the throw.

28

669

FIGURE 28.3 Throwing overhand.

Underhand Throw

For the underhand throw, the player draws back the throwing hand and arm—with the ball in his or her palm, facing up—in a downward swing. The elbow is bent slightly; weight is mostly on the back foot. The arm comes forward in a bowling motion, and the weight shifts to the front foot during the toss. The flight of the ball stays low and arrives at about waist height.

Pitching

Official rules call for the pitcher to have both feet in contact with the pitcher's rubber, but few elementary schools have one. Instead, the pitcher can stand with both feet about even, facing the batter, and hold the ball briefly in front with both hands. The pitcher takes one hand from the ball, extends the right arm forward, and brings it back in a pendulum swing, positioning the ball well behind the body. A normal stride taken with the left foot toward the batter begins the throwing sequence for a right-handed pitcher. The arm swings forward with an underhanded slingshot motion, and the weight shifts to the leading foot. Only one step is permitted. The follow-through motion is important (figure 28.4).

FIGURE 28.4 Pitching.

The windmill is an alternate pitching motion in which the arm makes a full arc overhead, moving behind the body and then forward toward the batter. The arm goes into full extension on the downward swing in the back, gathering momentum as the forward motion begins. The pitch is otherwise the same as the normal motion. The windmill is difficult for students to master. Here are instructional cues for pitching:

1. Face the plate.
2. Keep your eyes on the target.
3. Swing the pitching arm backward and step forward.
4. Keep the pitching arm extended.

Fielding

Infielders should assume the ready position—a semi-crouch, with legs shoulder-width apart, knees bent slightly, and hands on or in front of the knees (figure 28.5). As the ball is delivered, the weight shifts to the balls of the feet. The outfielder's position is a slightly more erect semicrouch. Here are instructional cues for fielding:

1. Move into line with the path of the ball.
2. Give when catching the ball.
3. Use the glove to absorb the force of the ball.
4. For grounders, keep the head down and watch the ball move into the glove.

FIGURE 28.5 Ready position for the infielder.

Fly Balls

There are two ways to catch a fly ball. For a low ball, the fielder keeps the fingers together and forms a basket with the hands (figure 28.6). For a higher ball, the thumbs are together, and the ball is caught overhead (figure 28.7).

FIGURE 28.6 Catching a low fly ball.

FIGURE 28.7 Catching a high fly ball.

The fielder must absorb the force of the ball with the hands. The eye is on the ball continually until the ball hits the glove or hands. The knees are flexed slightly when receiving and aid in absorbing force when the ball is caught.

Grounders

To field a grounder, the fielder moves as quickly as possible into the path of the ball (figure 28.8). The eyes focus on the ball, following it into the hands or glove. The feet are spread, the seat stays down, and the hands are held low and in front (figure 28.9). Weight is on the balls of the feet or on the toes, and the knees are bent to lower the body. After catching the ball, the fielder straightens up, takes a step in the direction of the throw, and makes the throw.

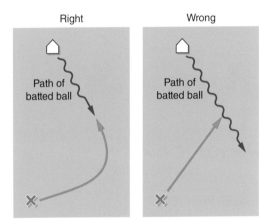

FIGURE 28.8 Fielding a grounder correctly.

FIGURE 28.9 Fielding a grounder.

28

Sure Stop for Outfield Balls

To keep the ball from going through the hands and thus allowing extra bases, the outfielder can use her body as a barrier. She turns halfway to the right and lowers one knee to the ground at the point toward which the ball is traveling (figure 28.10). The hands catch the rolling ball, but if the ball is missed, the body stops it.

FIGURE 28.10 Sure stop.

First-Base Positioning

When a ball is hit to the infield, the first-base player moves to the base until his foot is touching it. He then judges the path of the ball, stepping toward it with the left foot (if right-handed) and stretching forward. The right foot remains in contact with the base (figure 28.11).

FIGURE 28.11 First-base player stretching for a catch.

Catcher's Position

The catcher crouches with the feet about shoulder-width apart and the left foot slightly ahead of the right foot. A glove and a mask must be used, and a body protector is desirable. The catcher is positioned just beyond the swinging range of the bat.

Batting (Right-Handed)

The batter stands with the left side of the body toward the pitcher. The feet are spread, and weight is on both feet. The body faces the plate. The bat is held over the right shoulder, pointing both back and up. The left hand grasps the bat below the right hand. The elbows are away from the body (figure 28.12). The swing begins with hip rotation and a short step toward the pitcher. The bat is then swung level with the ground at the height of the pitch. The eyes focus on the ball.

FIGURE 28.12 Batter's position.

Batters should avoid the following habits: lifting the front foot high off the ground, stepping back with the rear foot, dropping the rear shoulder, chopping down on the ball, golfing, dropping the elbows, and crouching or bending forward. Failing to keep the eyes on the ball is a serious error. Players should practice the choke grip, the long grip, and the middle grip. In all three, the grip is relaxed. Beginning batters can start with the choke grip. Here are instructional cues for batting:

1. Keep the hands together.
2. Swing the bat horizontally.
3. Swing through the ball.
4. Hold the bat off the shoulder.
5. Watch the ball hit the bat.

Students should be taught never to swing a bat unless they have looked all around them and they are standing in the area designated for swinging the bat. Similarly, students should be taught never to walk in the designated bat-swinging area unless no one in the area is holding a bat.

Bunting (Right-Handed)

To bunt, the batter turns to face the pitcher, setting the right foot alongside home plate. As the pitcher releases the ball, the batter runs his upper hand about halfway up the bat. He holds the bat loosely in front of the body and parallel to the ground to meet the ball (figure 28.13). Bunts can be directed down the first- or third-base line.

The surprise, or drag, bunt is done without squaring around to face the pitcher. The batter holds the bat in a choke grip. When the pitcher lets go of the ball, the batter runs the right hand up the bat and directs the ball down either foul line, keeping it as close as possible to the line in fair territory.

FIGURE 28.13 Regular bunt position.

Pearson Education

Base Running

A batter who hits the ball runs hard and purposefully toward first base, no matter what kind of hit it is. The runner runs past the bag, touching it in the process, and steps on the foul-line side of the base to avoid colliding with the first-base player.

Because a runner on base must hold the base position until the pitcher releases the ball, quickly leaving the base is essential. With either toe touching the base, the runner leans his or her body, keeping his or her weight on the ball of the leading foot and eyes on the pitcher. After the pitch, the runner takes a few steps away from the base in the direction of the next base.

Instructional Procedures

1. Safety is of the utmost importance. Teachers must take these precautions:

   a. Throwing the bat is a constant danger. Have members of the batting team stand well back from the baseline, preferably behind a fence or in a dugout if available.

   b. Try these techniques for teaching batters not to throw the bat:

      Have the batter touch the bat to the ground before dropping it.

      Call the batter out if the bat is thrown.

      Have the batter carry the bat to first base.

      Have the batter change ends of the bat before dropping it.

      Have the batter place the bat in a 3-foot (1 m) circle before running.

   c. Sliding can lead to injury and destruction of clothing. With unskilled players, the best approach is to forbid sliding.

   d. A catcher who stands close behind the plate while catching must wear a mask. A body protector is also recommended.

   e. To prevent players from colliding while running for a fly ball, teach them to call for the ball and stay out of another player's area.

   f. When changing fields at the beginning of an inning, the batting team stays on the first-base side of the infield. The fielding team goes to bat via the third-base side of the infield.

   g. Use soft softballs, particularly in the early

28

stages of development. Fleece balls are excellent for introductory fielding skills. Because many children fear batted balls, using balls that will not hurt them is a necessity.

2. Emphasize batting skills. No experience is more ego shattering for a child than standing at the plate and showing an ineptness that draws scorn and ridicule from peers. Make sure that students know the correct stance and proper mechanics of batting. Improved hitting will come with practice.

3. The spoiler of many softball games is the pitcher–batter duel. If this confrontation becomes prolonged, the other players become justifiably bored while standing around. To eliminate the problem, have a member of the batting team pitch or give each batter only two or three swings.

4. Players should rotate positions often. In physical education classes, have everyone—including the pitcher—rotate to another position at the start of each inning.

5. The distance between bases greatly affects the game. Adjust the distance according to the game and the players' abilities.

6. Appoint umpires or have the team at bat umpire. A convenient method is to appoint the person who made the last out of the previous inning as the umpire for the next inning. Teach all students how to umpire.

7. Encourage players to recognize and give approval and support to less skillful players. Because students vary widely in ability, take the opportunity to teach tolerance. Do not let an error become a tragedy to a player.

8. Have each player run out a hit, no matter how hopeless it seems.

9. Analyze the purpose of lead-up games. Have students practice needed skills before using them in a game.

10. Players must learn to respect officials and accept the umpire's judgment. Do not allow the disreputable practice of baiting the umpire to be a part of children's softball experiences.

Organizing for Instruction

Students must develop skills in softball and acquire knowledge about the various phases of the game. The amount of field space and the equipment available determine the instructional organization. To cover the various phases of the game, a multiple-activity or station pattern is effective. Here are some guidelines for instruction:

1. Give children many opportunities to practice different skills. Even with rotation, use as many small groups as possible. For example, two children can practice throwing and fielding grounders.

2. Address differences in ability. Because some players have practiced more, they are often more skilled than others in the class. Teachers can use skillful players (first giving them sufficient direction) in various phases of instruction.

3. Carefully plan and communicate to all students the activities and procedures to be followed at each station. Covering appropriate softball rules in meetings with captains and other helpers is valuable.

4. Complete rotation of stations is not necessary at each class session. During a class session, teams may practice at one station for part of the time and use the remaining time to participate in an appropriate lead-up game.

5. Provide directions at each station to help students make the most of the skill development opportunities. Post signs offering instructional strategies on cones at each station.

6. Using the rotational station system does not rule out whole-class activities. Mimetic drills (i.e., drills without equipment) help establish basic movement patterns for most skills. Have students practice batting, pitching, throwing, and fielding without worrying about results.

7. Station teaching offers an excellent opportunity for older students to help. In some school systems, high school students visit elementary schools for cross-age tutoring.

8. Having students move from one station to another gives them encouragement, correction, coaching, and motivation for learning.

9. Motivate players by comparing the rotational system to varsity or major league practices. This gives the activity an adult flavor.

10. Let students choose from the list of lead-up games, particularly for team or small-group activities.

Basic Softball Rules

Most sporting goods establishments have copies of the official softball rules, which students should use when learning the game. This section describes the basic rules.

The official diamond has 60-foot (18.3 m) baselines and a pitching distance of 46 feet (14.0 m). Elementary school students should use a diamond with baselines no longer than 45 feet (14 m) and a pitching distance of 35 feet (11 m) or less. The nine players on a softball team are the catcher; the pitcher; first-, second-, and third-base players; the shortstop; and left, center, and right fielders. The right fielder is the outfielder nearest first base.

Batting Order

Players may bat in any order, but having them bat according to their positions in the field can be convenient in class. Once established, the batting order cannot be changed, even if the player changes to another position in the field.

Pitching

The pitcher must face the batter with both feet on the pitching rubber, holding the ball in front with both hands. The pitcher can take one step toward the batter and must deliver the ball during that step. The ball must be pitched underhanded. The pitcher cannot fake a pitch or make any motion toward the plate without delivering the ball. Rolling or bouncing the ball to the batter is illegal. No quick return is allowed before the batter is ready. To be called a strike, a pitch must be over the plate and between the batter's knees and shoulders. A ball is a pitch that does not go through this area.

Batting

The bat must be a softball bat. The batter cannot cross to the other side of the plate when the pitcher is ready to pitch. If a player bats out of turn, he or she is out. A bunt that goes foul on the third strike is an out. A pitched ball that touches or hits the batter entitles the batter to first base if he or she does not strike or bunt at the ball.

Striking Out

A batter who misses the ball on the third strike is out. This is called striking out.

Batter Safe

A batter who reaches first base before the fielding team can field the ball and throw it to first is safe.

Fair Ball Types

A fair ball is any batted ball that settles on fair territory between home and first base and home and third base. A ball that rolls over a base or through the field into fair territory is a fair ball. Fly balls (including line drives) that drop into fair territory beyond the infield are fair balls. Foul lines are in fair territory.

Foul Ball

A foul ball is a batted ball that settles outside the foul lines between home and first or between home and third. A fly ball that drops into foul territory beyond the bases is a foul.

Fly Ball

Any fly ball (foul or fair), if caught, is an out. A foul fly, however, must rise over the batter's head or it is ruled a foul tip. A foul tip caught on the third strike, then, puts the batter out.

Base Running

Base runners cannot lead off. On penalty of being called out, the runner must stay on base until the ball leaves the pitcher's hand. On an overthrow when the ball goes into foul territory and out of play, runners advance one base beyond the one they were headed toward when the overthrow occurred. On an overthrow at second base, when the ball rolls into center field, the runners may advance as far as they can. The runner may try to avoid being tagged on a baseline but must stay within 3 feet (90 cm) on either side of a direct line from base to base. A runner hit by a batted ball while off the base is out. The batter, however, is entitled to first base. Base runners must touch all bases. If a runner fails to touch a base, an appeal play can occur; the fielding team must call the oversight to the umpire's attention before she will rule on the play.

Runners may overrun first base without penalty. On all other bases, however, the runner must maintain contact with the base or be tagged out. To score, the runner must make contact with home plate.

Scoring

A run is scored when the base runner makes the circuit of the bases (i.e., first, second, third, and home) before the batting team has three outs. If the third out is a force out, no run is scored, even if the runner crossed home plate before the out was actually made.

28

The situation needing the most clarification occurs when a runner is on base with one out and the batter hits a fly ball that is caught, making the second out. If the runner does not return to the base previously occupied before the ball reaches that base, the runner, too, is out. If he or she makes the third out by failing to return to the base in time, no run is scored.

Softball Drills

Softball drills lend themselves to a station setup. For a regular class of 30 students, four to six squads are suggested. Activities at each station can emphasize a single skill or a combination of skills. Situational drills can also be incorporated. Remind children that constant repetition is necessary to develop, maintain, and sharpen softball skills.

The multitude of softball skills to be practiced allows for many different combinations and setups. Here are some examples for use in station teaching:

1. Batting can be organized in many ways. Ensure that each child has many opportunities to hit the ball successfully.

   a. Have students use a batting tee. For each station, two tees are needed, with a bat and at least two balls per tee. Assign three to five children to each station: a batter, a catcher to handle incoming balls, and fielders. When only three children are in a unit, omit the catcher. Give each batter a certain number of swings before rotating to the field. The catcher becomes the next batter, and a fielder moves up to catcher.

   b. Organize informal hitting practice. A batter, a pitcher, and fielders are needed. Assign two batting groups to each station. A catcher is optional.

   c. Have students practice hitting a foam rubber ball thrown underhand. The larger ball is easier to hit.

   d. Have students practice bunting in groups of three: a pitcher, a batter, and a fielder.

2. Have students practice throwing and catching using these drills:

   a. Throw back and forth, practicing various throws such as ground balls.

   b. A player acting as a first-base player throws grounders to the other infielders and receives the put-out throw.

   c. Throw flies back and forth. Hit flies, with two or three fielders catching.

   d. Establish four bases and throw from base to base.

3. Have players use proper pitching and catching form for pitching practice.

   a. Pitch to another player over a plate.

   b. Call balls and strikes. One player is the pitcher, the second is the catcher, and the third is the umpire. A fourth player can be a stationary batter to offer a more realistic pitching target.

4. For infield drills, place children at normal infield positions—behind the plate, at each base, and at shortstop. One child acts as the batter and gives directions. The play begins with practice in throwing around the bases in either direction. Next, the batter can roll the ball to the different infielders, starting at third base and continuing in turn around the infield, with each player throwing to first to retire an imaginary runner. A skillful batter can hit the ball instead of rolling it to infielders, thus making the drill more realistic. Using a second softball saves time when the ball is thrown or batted past an infielder, because players do not have to wait for the ball to be retrieved before continuing play. After the ball is thrown to first base, other throws around the infield can take place. The drill also can be done with only a partial infield.

5. Organize various situations for practicing base running.

   a. Bunt and run to first base. A pitcher, a batter, an infielder, and a first-base player are needed. The pitcher serves the ball up for a bunt, and the batter, after bunting, takes off for first base. A fielding play can be made on the runner.

   b. Bunt and run to second base. The batter bunts the ball and runs to first base and then on to second, making a proper turn at first.

6. Play Pepper. (This is one of the older skill games in softball.) A line of three or four players stand about 10 yards (meters) in front of and facing

a batter. The players toss the ball to the batter, who tries to hit controlled grounders back to them (figure 28.14). The batter stays at bat for a specified time and then rotates to the field.

7. At stations, schedule some game-type activities like Batter Ball, Steal a Base, Five Hundred, and Scrub. Stations might be organized as follows. (Numbers and letters refer to the drills just listed.

> *Station 1: batting (see 1a)*
>
> *Station 2: throwing and fielding grounders (see 2c)*
>
> *Station 3: base running—Steal a Base*
>
> *Station 4: bunting and base running (see 5a)*

Here is another example of station arrangement:

> *Station 1: batting and fielding—Pepper (see 6)*
>
> *Station 2: pitching and umpiring (see 3b)*
>
> *Station 3: infield practice (see 4)*
>
> *Station 4: batting (see 1b)*

Stations might also be arranged as follows:

> *Station 1: fly ball hitting, fielding, and throwing (see 2e)*
>
> *Station 2: bunting and fielding (see 1d)*
>
> *Station 3: pitching to targets (see 3c)*
>
> *Station 4: batting (see 1a and 1b)*

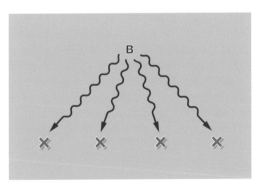

FIGURE 28.14 Play Pepper.

Softball Activities

Developmental Level II

Throw-It-and-Run Softball

Playing area: softball diamond reduced in size

Players: two teams of 7 to 11 (usually 9) students each

Supplies: a softball or similar ball

Skills: throwing, catching, fielding, base running

Throw-It-and-Run Softball is played like regular softball, with one exception: With one team in the field at regular positions, the pitcher throws the ball to the batter, who, instead of batting the ball, catches it and immediately throws it into the field. The ball is then treated as a batted ball, and regular softball rules prevail. No stealing is permitted, however, and runners must hold their bases until the batter throws the ball. A foul ball is an out.

Variations:

1. Under-Leg Throw. Instead of throwing directly, the batter can turn to the right, lift the left leg, and throw the ball under the leg into the playing field.

2. Beat-Ball Throw. The fielders, instead of playing by regular softball rules, throw the ball directly home to the catcher. The batter, in the meantime, runs around the bases. The player scores 1 point for each base he or she touches before the catcher receives the ball. A ball caught on the fly means no score. Similarly, a foul ball does not score points but counts as a turn at bat.

Two-Pitch Softball

Playing area: softball diamond

Players: two teams of 7 to 11 students each

Supplies: a softball, bat

Skills: most softball skills, except regular pitching

Two-Pitch Softball is played like regular softball but with these changes:

1. A member of the team at bat pitches. Set up a rotation system that gives every child a turn as pitcher.

2. The batter has only two pitches in which to hit the ball, and he or she must hit a fair ball on one of these pitches or is out. The batter can foul the first ball, but if he or she fouls the second, he or she is out. Do not call balls or strikes.

28

3. The pitcher does not field the ball. A member of the team in the field acts as the fielding pitcher.

4. If the batter hits the ball, teams follow regular softball rules. Stealing is not allowed.

Variation: Three Strikes. In this game, the batter gets three pitches (strikes). Otherwise, the game proceeds as in Two-Pitch Softball.

Hit and Run

Playing area: softball field or gymnasium

Players: two teams of 6 to 15 students each

Supplies: a volleyball, soccer ball, or playground ball; home plate; base markers

Skills: catching, throwing, running, dodging

One team is at bat, and the other is scattered in the field. Boundaries are established, but the area does not have to look like a baseball diamond. The batter stands at home plate with the ball. In front of the batter, 12 feet (4 m) away, is a short line over which the ball must be hit to be in play. In the center of the field, about 40 feet (12 m) away, is the base marker.

The batter bats the ball with the hands or fists so that it crosses the short line and lands inside the area. The batter then tries to run down the field, around the base marker, and back to home plate without being hit by the ball (figure 28.15). The other team's members field the ball and try to tag the runner. The fielders may not run or walk with the ball but may throw to teammates closer to the runner.

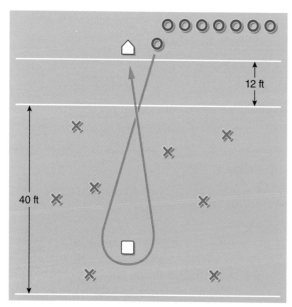

FIGURE 28.15　Hit and Run.

A run is scored each time a batter runs around the marker and back to home plate without getting tagged by the ball. A run is also scored if a foul is called on the fielding team for walking or running with the ball.

The batter is out in any of these situations:

1. A fly ball is caught.
2. The ball is not hit beyond the short line.
3. The team touches home plate with the ball before the runner returns. (This out is used only when the runner stops in the field and does not continue.)

The game can be played in innings of three outs each, or teams can change positions after all members of one team have batted. Depending on players' abilities, you may have to adjust the distance from home plate to the base marker.

Variation: Five Passes. The batter is out when a fly ball is caught, or when the ball is passed among five different players of the fielding team and the last pass is to a player at home plate that beats the runner to the plate. Passes must not touch the ground.

Kick Softball

Playing area: regular softball field with a 3-by-3-foot (1 by 1 m) home base

Players: two teams of 7 to 11 students each

Supplies: a soccer ball or another ball to be kicked

Skills: kicking a rolling ball, throwing, catching, running bases

The batter stands in the kicking area, a 3-foot-square (1 m) home plate. The batter kicks the ball rolled on the ground by the pitcher. The ball is rolled at moderate speed. An umpire calls balls and strikes. A strike is a ball that rolls over the 3-foot square. A ball rolls outside this area. Strikeouts and walks are called as in regular softball. The number of foul balls allowed should be limited. No base stealing is permitted. Otherwise, the game is played like softball.

Variations:

1. The batter kicks a stationary ball. This method saves time, because there is no pitching.
2. Punch Ball. The batter can hit a volleyball as in a volleyball serve or punch a ball pitched by the pitcher.

Beat Ball

Playing area: softball diamond, bases approximately 30 feet (10 m) apart

Players: two teams of 5 to 12 students each

Supplies: soft softball, bat, batting tee (optional)

Skills: all softball skills

One team is at bat, and the other team is in the field. The object is to hit the ball and run around the bases before the fielding team can catch the ball, throw it to first base, and then throw it to the catcher at home plate. If the ball beats the hitter home or a fly ball is caught, it is an out. If the hitter beats the ball to home plate, a run is scored. All players on a team get to bat once before switching positions with the fielding team. The ball must be hit into fair territory before the hitter can run. Each hitter gets three pitches.

Variations:

1. Depending on the players' maturity, a batting tee may be used. Give hitters the option of using the batting tee or hitting a pitched ball.

2. Select the pitcher from the batting team. This rule ensures that the player will try to make pitches that can be hit.

3. Vary the distance so that hitters have a fair opportunity to score. If hitters score too easily, add another base.

Steal a Base

Playing area: any 40-by-20-foot (12 by 6 m) flat area, or larger with more skilled students

Players: 6 to 10 students

Supplies: hoops, softball, gloves (optional)

Skills: throwing, catching, tagging, running

Space the hoops about 20 feet (6 m) apart in a rectangular shape. Hoops are used as bases to prevent collisions. One player, serving as a fielder, stands at each hoop to begin the game. All other players are on a base; more than one runner is permitted on a base. On signal, runners begin accumulating runs by running to another base without being tagged. Fielders work together to tag as many runners as possible. Fielders may leave their base and chase runners if necessary. If a fielder leaves his or her base, other fielders may rotate to the vacant base. Fielders and runners change positions every two to three minutes.

Variation: Runners may not move to an adjacent base.

Developmental Level III

Five Hundred

Playing area: field big enough for fungo hitting

Players: 3 to 12 (or more) students

Supplies: a softball, bat

Skills: fungo batting, catching flies, fielding grounders

There are many versions of the old game Five Hundred. A batter stands on one side of the field and bats the ball to several fielders, who are scattered. The fielders try to become the batter by reaching a score of 500. Fielders earn 200 points for catching a ball on the fly, 100 points for catching a ball on the first bounce, and 50 points for fielding a grounder cleanly. When the batter changes, all fielders lose their points and must start over. Let players hit the ball off a batting tee if fungo hitting is too difficult.

Variations:

1. The fielder's points must total exactly 500.

2. Points are subtracted from the fielder's score for mishandling a ball. Fielders who drop a fly ball, for example, lose 200 points.

Home Run

Playing area: softball diamond (only first base is used)

Players: 4 to 10 students

Supplies: a softball, bat

Skills: most softball skills, modified base running

The crucial players are a batter, a catcher, a pitcher, and one fielder. Any other players are fielders; some can take positions in the infield. The batter hits a regular pitch and on a fair ball must run to first base and back home before the ball can be returned to the catcher.

The batter is out in these situations:

1. A fly ball (fair or foul) is caught.

2. The batter strikes out.

3. On a fair ball, the ball beats the batter back to home plate.

Variations

1. This game can be played like softball—allowing the batter to stop at first base if another batter is up.

2. A fielder who catches a fly ball goes directly to bat. The preceding batter then goes to the end of the rotation, and the other players rotate up to the position of the fielder who caught the ball. This

28

rule has one drawback—it may cause children to scramble and fight for fly balls, which is not desirable in softball. The ball belongs to the player in whose territory it falls.

3. Triangle Ball. First and third bases are moved toward each other, thus narrowing the playing field. Second base is not used. The game gets its name from the triangle formed by home plate and the two bases. The batter must circle first and third bases and return home before the ball reaches home plate. This game can be played with as few as three players, with the pitcher covering home plate.

TEACHING TIP

1. To keep skillful players from staying too long at bat, make a rule that after a certain number of home runs, the batter automatically moves to the field. Devise a rotation (work-up) system. The batter goes to right field, moves to center, and then goes to left field. The rotation continues through third base, shortstop, second base, first base, pitcher, and catcher. The catcher is the next batter. Naturally, the number of positions depends on the number of players in the game. If there are enough players, an additional batter can be waiting to take a turn.

2. The game can be played with only three students and no catcher. With only one fielder, the pitcher covers home plate. Make the first-base distance far enough away to be a challenge but close enough so that a well-hit ball scores a home run. The distance depends on the number playing and the players' abilities.

Scrub (Work-Up)

Playing area: softball field
Players: 7 to 15 students
Supplies: a softball, bat
Skills: most softball skills

The main feature of Scrub is player rotation. The game follows regular softball rules, although individuals are more or less playing for themselves. At least two batters, and generally three, are needed. A catcher, a pitcher, and a first-base player are essential. The remaining players assume the other positions. A batter who is out goes to a position in right field. All other players move up one position, with the catcher becoming the batter. The first-base player becomes the pitcher, the pitcher moves to catcher, and all others move up one place. You can also add a rule that if a fly ball is caught, the fielder and batter exchange positions.

Slow-Pitch Softball

Playing area: softball diamond
Players: two teams of 10 students each
Supplies: a softball, bat
Skills: most softball skills

The major difference between regular softball and Slow-Pitch Softball is in the pitching, but there are other differences. With slower pitching, players make more hits and thus create more action on the bases and in the field. Outfielders are an important part of the game, because many long drives are hit. Official softball rules are modified as follows:

1. The pitch must be a slow pitch. Any other pitch is illegal and is called a ball. The pitch must have an arc of 1 foot (30 cm) but must not rise over 10 feet (3 m) from the ground. Pitch legality depends on the umpire's call.

2. The game uses 10 players instead of 9. The extra one, called the roving fielder, plays in the outfield and handles line drives hit just over the infielders.

3. The batter must take a full swing at the ball and is out if he or she chops at the ball or bunts.

4. If the batter is hit by a pitched ball, he or she is not entitled to first base. The pitch is merely called a ball. Otherwise, balls and strikes are called as in softball.

5. The runner must stay at his or her base until the pitch has reached or passed home plate. No stealing is permitted.

Hurry Baseball (One-Pitch Softball)

Playing area: softball diamond
Players: two teams of 8 to 12 students each
Supplies: a softball, bat
Skills: slow pitching, most softball skills except stealing bases and bunting

Hurry Baseball demands rapid changes from batting to fielding, and vice versa. The game is like regular softball, with these exceptions:

1. The pitcher is from the team at bat and must not interfere with, or touch, a batted ball on penalty of the batter's being called out.

2. The team coming to bat does not wait for the fielding team to get set. It has its own pitcher, who gets the ball to the batter just as quickly as the batter can grab a bat and get ready. The fielding team has to hustle to get out to their places.

3. Each batter gets only one pitch. The batter must hit a fair ball, or he or she is out. The pitch is made from about two-thirds of the normal pitching distance.

4. No stealing is permitted.

5. No bunting is permitted.

The batter must take a full swing. The game offers much activity in the fast place changes that must be made after the third out. Teams in the field learn to make the next hitter a catcher, so that he or she can bat immediately when the third out is made. Batters must bat in order. Scoring follows regular softball rules.

Three-Team Softball

Playing area: softball diamond

Players: 12 to 15 students

Supplies: a mask, ball, bat

Skills: all softball skills

Three-Team Softball works well with 12 players, a number considered too small to divide into two effective fielding teams. The players are instead divided into three teams. Softball rules apply, with these exceptions:

1. One team is at bat, one team covers the infield (including the catcher), and the third team consists of the outfielders and the pitcher.

2. The team at bat must bat in a definite order. Because of the small number of batters on each side, the person due to bat may sometimes be on base. To take a turn at bat, the runner must be replaced by a player not on base.

3. After three outs, the teams rotate; the outfield moves to the infield, the infield takes a turn at bat, and the batters go to the outfield.

4. An inning is over when all three teams have batted.

5. The pitcher is limited to only one inning. A player may repeat as pitcher only after all members of that team have had a chance to pitch.

Softball Skill Tests

Throwing for Accuracy

To test accuracy in throwing, make a target on a wall. Draw three concentric circles of 54, 36, and 18 inches (135. 90, and 45 cm). Scoring is 1, 2, and 3 points, respectively, for the circles. Five trials are allowed, for a possible score of 15. Balls hitting a line score the higher number.

Instead of the suggested target, hang a tire. Scoring allows 2 points for a throw through the tire and 1 point for simply hitting the tire. Highest possible total: 10 points.

Throwing for Distance

In the test of throwing for distance, give each child three throws and record the longest throw on the fly.

Fielding Grounders

A file of players stands behind a restraining line. A thrower is about 30 feet (10 m) in front of this line. Each player in turn tries to field five ground balls. The score is the number of balls fielded cleanly. Inconsistencies will occur in the throw and bounce of the ground balls served up for fielding. If a throw is obviously not fair, give the child another chance.

Circling the Bases

Runners are timed as they circle the bases. A diamond with four bases and a stopwatch for timing are needed. Two runners can run at once by starting from opposite corners of the diamond; two stopwatches are needed with this system. The batter can bunt a pitched ball and run around the bases. The timing starts with the bunt and ends when the batter touches home plate.

Pitching

Pitching is one of the easier skills to test in softball and certainly one of the most popular with children. Testing is done in two basic ways. In the first, each child makes a certain number of pitches at a target. Scoring is based on the number of strikes thrown. In the second, each child pitches regularly—as if to a batter—and balls and strikes are counted. Batters are either struck out or walked. The score is the number of batters the child is able to strike out from a given number at bat. This score is recorded as a percentage.

28

Both methods require a target. It should be 19 inches (48 cm) wide and 42 inches (107 cm) high. The bottom of the target should be about 18 inches (45 cm) above the ground or floor. If the target is made from plywood or wood, it will need to be supported or hung up. A target also can be outlined temporarily on a wall with chalk or paint. Balls that hit the edges of the target count as strikes. Use a normal pitching distance (35 feet [11 m]) and observe regular pitching rules.

LEARNING AIDS

WEBSITES

USA Softball, www.teamusa.org/USA-Softball.aspx
Softball Manitoba, www.softball.mb.ca
Softball Skills by Howard Kabota, https://kobatastyle.com/

SELECTED READINGS

American Sport Education Program. (2007). *Coaching youth softball* (4th ed.). Champaign, IL: Human Kinetics.

Benson, R., & Benson, T. (2010). *Survival guide for coaching youth softball*. Champaign, IL: Human Kinetics.

Garman, J. (2011). *Softball skills and drills* (2nd ed.). Champaign, IL: Human Kinetics.

Mood, D.P., Musker, F.F., & Rink, J.E. (2012). *Sports and recreational activities* (15th ed.). New York, NY: McGraw-Hill.

National Fastpitch Coaches Association. (2016). *Practice perfect softball*. Champaign, IL: Human Kinetics.

Noren, R. (2008). *Softball fundamentals ebook*. Champaign, IL: Human Kinetics.

Walker, K. (2009). *The softball drill book*. Champaign, IL: Human Kinetics.

Track, Field, and Cross Country Running

Using proper progression is vital to successful teaching of fundamental skills and lead-up games associated with track, field, and cross country running. Teaching the rules and strategies for track, field, and cross country running is an integral part of the instructional process. Lead-up activities allow teachers to emphasize development of selected track, field, and cross country running skills in a setting compatible with their students' abilities.

Learning Objectives

▶ Structure learning experiences efficiently using appropriate formations, progressions, and coaching techniques.

▶ Develop a unit plan and lesson focus for track, field, and cross country running.

▶ Identify safety precautions associated with teaching track, field, and cross country running.

▶ Describe instructional procedures used for directing a successful lead-up game.

▶ Cite assessment procedures used for evaluating track, field, and cross country running skills.

Track and field is a diverse sport that allows students to apply a wide variety of skills. For this reason, students can find an activity they enjoy and experience success. The elementary track and field program consists of short sprints (40 to 100 yards [m]); running and standing long jumps, high jumps, and hop-step-and-jumps; and relays. Jogging and distance running are encouraged throughout the program. The primary focus is on practice and personal accomplishment, but modified competition in cross country running is acceptable. Hurdling can be included when the equipment is available.

Children should experience the differences between walking, sprinting, running, striding (for pace), and jogging. Sprinting techniques are particularly important; instruction centers on correct form for starting, accelerating, and sprinting. Speed and quickness are important attributes that affect the degree of success in many play and sport activities. Teach the rules for different events. Because few elementary schools have a permanent track, laying out and lining the track each year are valuable educational experiences.

Instructional Emphasis and Sequence

Table 29.1 divides track and field activities into two developmental levels. The activities are listed in progression. Because many track and field skills involve locomotor movements, students of all ages can enjoy and participate in these activities.

TABLE 29.1 Suggested Track, Field, and Cross Country Program

Developmental Levels I and II	Developmental Level III
Track and Cross Country Skills	
40- to 60-yard (m) sprints	50- to 100-yard (m) sprints
Standing start	Distance running
Sprinter's start	Relays
Jogging and cross country running	Hurdling
	Baton passing
Field Skills	
Standing long jump	High jump
Long jump	Hop-step-and-jump

Developmental Levels I and II

Because children can easily master running and jumping, these skills are introduced in Developmental Level I. Early experiences at this level stress running short distances, learning different starting positions, and participating in the two types of long jump. Some running for distance is included, and cross country meets are introduced. Relays offer exciting experiences and involve many students in a team activity.

Developmental Level III

More serious efforts to achieve proper form begin at Developmental Level III. The scissors style of high jumping can be introduced, and students can be encouraged to experiment with other styles. Students should begin to use check marks with the running long jump. Running for distance and cross country activities are emphasized. Hurdling using modified hurdles is an exciting event. In the high jump, students learn critical points of the Straddle Roll and the Western Roll. Teachers encourage developing pace in distance running without strong elements of competition. The hop-step-and-jump extends the range of jumping activities. Relays and baton passing receive increased coverage at this level.

Track and Field Skills

Standing Start

Have students practice the standing start because it has several uses in physical education activities. Many children find it more comfortable than the sprinter's start. As soon as is practical, however, children should accept the sprinter's start for track work.

In the standing start, the feet are in a comfortable half-stride position. An extremely long stride is to be avoided. The body leans with the center of gravity forward. Weight is on the toes, and the knees are flexed slightly. The arms can be down or hanging slightly back (figure 29.1).

Norwegian Start

The Norwegian start is a standing start, which is useful when the running surface makes it difficult to use the sprinter's start. On the command "On your mark," the runner takes a position at the starting line with the right foot forward. On "Get set," the left hand is placed on the right knee and the right hand is carried back for a thrust (figure 29.2). On "Go," the right hand comes forward, coupled with a drive by the right foot. The advantage claimed for this start is that it forces the body to lean and uses the forward thrust of the arm coordinated with stepping off on the opposite foot.

Sprinter's Start

The kinds of sprinter's starts vary, but teachers are advised to concentrate on a single one. The "On your mark" position places the toe of the front foot from 4 to 12 inches (10 to 30 cm) behind the starting line. The thumb and first finger are just behind the line, and other fingers add support. The knee of the rear leg is placed just opposite the front foot or ankle.

For the "Get set" position, the seat lifts so that it is nearly parallel to the ground. The knee of the rear leg rises off the ground, and the shoulders move forward over the hands. Weight is evenly distributed over the hands and feet (figure 29.3). The head is not raised; the runner should be looking at a spot a few feet (a meter or so) in front of the starting line.

On the "Go" signal, the runner pushes off sharply with both feet and the front leg straightens as the back leg comes forward for a step. The body rises gradually rather than pops up suddenly. Teachers should watch for

FIGURE 29.2 Norwegian start.

FIGURE 29.1 Standing start.

FIGURE 29.3 Sprinter's start—"Get set!"

29

a stumbling action on the first few steps. This problem results from too much weight resting on the hands in the "Get set" position.

Running

Sprinting

In proper sprinting form, the body leans forward, with the arms swinging in opposition to the legs. The arms are bent at the elbows and swing from the shoulders in a forward and backward plane, not across the body (figure 29.4). Forceful arm action aids sprinting. The runner lifts his knees sharply forward and upward and brings them down with a vigorous motion, followed by a forceful push from the toes. Sprinting is a driving and striding motion, as opposed to the inefficient pulling action displayed by some runners.

FIGURE 29.4 Proper sprinting form.

Distance Running

In distance running, as compared with sprinting, the body is more erect and arm motion is less pronounced. Pace is an important consideration. Runners should try to concentrate on the qualities of lightness, ease, relaxation, and looseness. Good striding action, a slight body lean, and good head position are also important. Encourage runners to strike the ground with the heel first and then push off with the toes (figure 29.5).

FIGURE 29.5 Proper running form.

Relays

Children's track and field programs usually include two types of relays. Instruction in baton passing is incorporated into relay activity. On the track, students always run in a counterclockwise direction.

Circular (Pursuit) Relays

Circular relays occur on the regular circular track. The baton exchange technique is important, and students need to practice it. On a 220-yard (200 m) track, relays can be organized in various ways, depending on how many runners are spaced for one lap. Four runners can do a lap, each running one-fourth of the way; two can do a lap, each running one-half of the distance; or each runner can complete a whole lap. In these races, each member of the relay team runs the same distance. A medley relay allows for individual differences because members of the team run different distances (e.g., the first person runs 110 yards [100 m], the second 220 yards [200 m], and so on).

Shuttle Relays

Because children are running toward each other, one great difficulty in running shuttle relays is controlling the exchange. In the excitement, the next runner may leave too early, and the tag or exchange is then made ahead of the restraining line. A high-jump standard or cone can be used to prevent early exchanges. The next runner awaits the tag with an arm around the standard or a hand on a cone.

Baton Passing

Two methods of baton passing are commonly used. The first, known as the right to left-hand method, is used in longer-distance relays. It is the best choice for elementary school children because it is easy and offers a consistent passing method. This pass allows the receiver to face the inside of the track while waiting to receive the baton in the left hand. The oncoming runner holds the baton in the right hand like a candle when passing it to a teammate. The receiver reaches back with the left hand, fingers pointing down and thumb to the inside, and begins to run as the runner comes within three to five yards (meters). The receiver grasps the baton and shifts it from the left to the right hand while moving. A dropped baton must be picked up, or the team is disqualified. An alternative way to receive the baton is to reach back with the hand facing up, but the fingers-down method is considered more suitable for sprint relays.

The second style of passing, the alternating handoff, is often used in the 440- and 875-yard [400 and 800 m] relays. The first exchange is right to left, the second exchange is left to right, and the third exchange is right to left, a method that prevents the runner from having to switch the baton from hand to hand while sprinting. This method is used in high-level competition in short distances but is less effective with elementary-age children.

Receivers can look over their shoulders to see the oncoming runner or can look forward in the direction of the run. Looking backward is called a *visual pass* and is slower than passing while looking forward (a *blind pass*). But the chance of error increases when the receiver is not looking backward and at the baton during the pass. The visual pass is recommended for elementary school children.

Horizontal Jumping

For both the standing and the running long jump, distance is measured from the front of the takeoff board or line to the nearest point (from takeoff) on the ground touched by the jumper. To help children improve their jump distances, teach them the importance of not falling or stepping backward after making a jump.

Standing Long Jump

In the standing long jump, the child toes the line with feet flat on the ground and fairly close together. He brings his arms forward in a preliminary swing and then swings down and back (figure 29.6). He jumps with both feet while swinging his arms forcibly forward to assist in lifting his body upward and forward. In the air, he brings his knees upward and forward while holding his arms forward for balance.

©Robert Pangrazi or Aaron Beighle

FIGURE 29.6 Standing long jump. (Note position of hands and arms.)

Long Jump

The running long jump begins with a short run. The run ends when the toes of the runner's jumping foot contact the board in a natural stride. The runner takes off from one foot and strives for height. The runner lands on both feet after bringing the knees forward. A proper landing is in a forward direction, not sideways.

Using a checkpoint results in more efficient jumping. Set up the checkpoint about halfway down the run. Competitors can help each other mark checkpoints. Each jumper should know the number of steps from the checkpoint to the takeoff board. In running for the jump, the student hits the mark with the appropriate foot (right or left) to reach the board with the correct foot in a normal stride for the jump. The student should arrive at the checkpoint at full speed. The last stride can be shortened somewhat (figure 29.7).

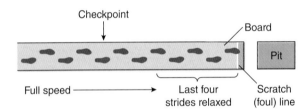

FIGURE 29.7 Long jump.

A fair jump takes off behind the scratch line. A foul (scratch) jump is called if the jumper steps beyond the scratch line or runs into or through the pit. Each contestant gets a certain number of trials (jumps). A scratch jump counts as a trial. Distance is measured from the scratch line to the nearest point of touch.

Hop-Step-and-Jump

The hop-step-and-jump event is gaining popularity, particularly because it is now included in Olympic competition. A takeoff board and a jumping pit are needed. Place the takeoff board close enough to the pit so that all jumpers can reach the pit. Like the running long jump, this event typically begins with a run, but beginners should start from a standing, stationary position. They can then progress from standing to a walking approach and then to the running approach. Regardless of the approach, the sequence of skills is the same. The jumper takes off with one foot and must land on the same foot to complete the hop. The jumper then takes a step (skilled performers take a leap) followed by a jump. The jumper ends by landing on both feet, as in the long jump (figure 29.8). Left-handers can change the pattern to begin with the left foot. This event also uses a checkpoint.

29

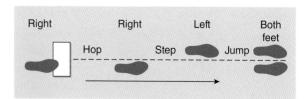

FIGURE 29.8 Hop-step-and-jump.

To avoid fouling, the jumper must not step over the takeoff board in the first hop. Distance is measured from the front of the takeoff board to the closest place that the body touches. This location is usually a mark made by one of the heels, but it could be a mark made by an arm or another part of the body if the jumper landed poorly and fell backward.

High Jumping

High-jump techniques are developed by practice. Place the bar at a height that challenges students but allows them to focus on technique rather than height. Too much emphasis on competition for height quickly eliminates the poorer jumpers, who need the most practice. Safety is of utmost importance. Prevent injury by using a flexible elastic rope as a crossbar and having the students avoid any type of flop. Children often want to use the Fosbury Flop technique. But if this technique is not taught and performed correctly, it can result in a neck or back injury. Include it only if taught by a knowledgeable instructor and supervised closely. Use a crash pad to absorb the force of the landing for Straddle Roll and Western Roll techniques.

Scissors Jump

In the Scissors Jump, the student approaches the high-jump bar from a slight angle. The takeoff is by the leg farthest from the bar. The near leg is lifted and goes over, followed quickly by a looping movement of the far leg. Students should focus on an upward kick with the front leg and an upward thrust of the arms. The knees should be straightened at the highest point of the jump. The landing is made on the lead foot followed by the rear foot.

Straddle Roll

In the Straddle Roll (figure 29.9), the jumper approaches from the left side at an angle of no more than 45 degrees. The jump has four key parts to be coached:

1. *Gather.* The last three steps are fast and vigorous, with the body leaning back a bit. The takeoff is on the left foot.

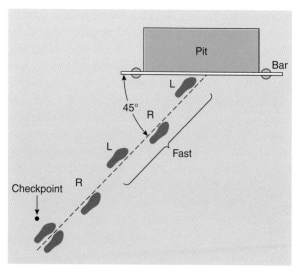

FIGURE 29.9 Straddle Roll.

2. *Kick.* The right leg is kicked vigorously as the jumping foot is planted.

3. *Arm movement.* Both arms are quickly lifted, and the left arm reaches over the bar as the right arm moves straight up. This movement puts the jumper in a straddle position while going over.

4. *Back leg clearance.* The jumper clears the bar by straightening the body, rolling the hips to the right (over the bar), or dropping the right shoulder.

Western Roll

In the Western Roll, the approach, gather, and kick are the same as for the Straddle Roll; but instead of being facedown, the jumper clears the bar by lying parallel to it on his or her side. The left arm points down at the legs while crossing the bar and then is lowered. The jumper's head is turned toward the pit after clearance, and he or she lands on both hands and the left (takeoff) foot.

Hurdling

For safety, students should use hurdles designed specifically for elementary schools. The hurdles should tip over easily when struck by runners. Children often want to jump hurdles in the wrong direction. This can cause a serious fall because the hurdles do not give when crossed from the wrong side. Hurdles can be made from electrical conduit pipe. Wands supported on blocks or cones also can be used as hurdles. To begin, set hurdles at 12 inches (30 cm) high and increase to 18 (45 cm) inches. Place hurdles about 25 feet (8 m) apart. Using six hurdles, you can set up a 180-foot (55 m) course as shown in figure 29.10.

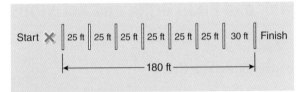

FIGURE 29.10 Hurdling course.

Several key points govern hurdling technique. The runner must adjust his or her stepping pattern so that the takeoff foot is planted 3 to 5 feet (90 to 150 cm) from the hurdle. The lead foot extends straight forward over the hurdle; the rear (trailing) leg is bent, with the knee to the side. The lead foot reaches for the ground, quickly followed by the trailing leg. A hurdler may lead with the same foot over consecutive hurdles or may alternate the leading foot. Some hurdlers like to thrust both arms instead of a single arm forward. Encourage students to develop a consistent step pattern.

Instructional Procedures

1. Spiked running shoes are not permitted. They create a safety problem and give an unfair advantage to children whose parents can afford them.

2. Stress good form at all times, but make it appropriate to the individual. Encourage students to develop good technique within their own style. Observing participants in any event at a track meet proves that many individual styles are successful.

3. Be sure that the program offers something for all boys and girls the highly skilled and the less skilled, and those with physical problems. Children with weight problems need particular attention. They must be stimulated and encouraged to participate. Set special goals for overweight children and establish special events and goals for children with disabilities.

4. Progressively increase the amount of activity, particularly distance work. A period of conditioning should precede any competition or all-out performance. If this procedure is followed, children will show few adverse effects.

5. Provide warm-up activities before track and field work, and design warm-ups to include jogging as well as bending and stretching exercises.

6. Ensure that pits for the long jump and the high jump are maintained properly. They should be filled with fresh sand of a coarse variety. For high jumping, commercial impact landing pads are necessary though expensive. If they are not available, restrict high jumping to the scissors style and use tumbling mats for the landing area.

7. A metal high-jump crossbar is economical in the long run, although it will bend. A satisfactory crossbar can be made of nylon cord with a weight on each end to keep it taut yet allow it to give. Magic ropes (rubberized stretch ropes) can be adapted for low-level jumping practice.

8. The use of a track starter signal is recommended. The clapboard track starter approximates the sound of the usual starter's gun and does not have the drawback of requiring expensive ammunition.

9. Make the goal of the program to allow students to develop at their own rate. Instructional sessions should be strenuous enough to ensure some overload but not enough to make students discouraged or physically ill. Watch students closely to determine whether they are working too hard or too little. Pay special attention to students who seem disinterested, dejected, emotionally upset, or withdrawn.

Organizing for Instruction

Track, field, and cross country running differ from other areas of the elementary school program in that they require considerable preparation before the classes begin.

1. If the school has no permanent courses, a track or a cross country course must be laid out. This can be done with marking lime. Sprinting lanes are useful but not required.

2. Outline a hurdling area (use marking lime) in an appropriate location.

3. Make separate pits for the running long jump, the high jump, and the hop-step-and-jump. Space the pits well apart to minimize interference.

4. Obtain the high-jump equipment. Standards with pins, crossbars (or cord substitutes), and cushioned landing pads are needed.

5. Be sure that takeoff boards for the long jump and the hop-step-and-jump are in place. Jumping without a takeoff board is not a satisfying experience.

29

6. Gather accessory materials including batons, starter clapboards, watches, hurdles, and yarn for the finish line.

7. Decide whether to use starting blocks (their value is debatable). Starting blocks add interest to the program, but elementary school students may find them difficult to use.

Organizing students is as important as organizing equipment. Children's height and weight affect the degree of physical performance in track, field, and cross country activities. Grouping students by height and weight allows for more efficient instruction. Students also can be arranged by gender. These groups may serve as a basis for instruction: (1) heavier and taller boys, (2) shorter and lighter boys, (3) heavier and taller girls, and (4) shorter and lighter girls. A simple way to form groups is to rank boys and girls separately according to the following formula, which yields a standard number: Score = 10 × (age to the nearest half year) + weight in pounds (kilograms).

After ranking the boys, assign the upper 50% to group 1 and the rest to group 2. Do the same with the girls. You may have to make some decisions in borderline cases.

Some track and field skills can be practiced with a single-activity organization. Starting skills can be practiced with perhaps one-fourth of the children at a time. Four groups can practice baton-passing skills at a time. Striding for distance can be practiced with each group running as a unit.

Station Teaching

The overall organization plan should include multiple activities. Four stations can make use of the selected group organization, but more stations are desirable. If eight stations are used, assign two stations to each group. Choose stations from these skill areas: (1) starting and sprinting, (2) baton passing, (3) standing and running long jump, (4) hop-step-and-jump, (5) high jump, (6) hurdles, (7) striding for distance and pace judgment, and (8) the Potato Shuttle Race.

Having children practice at all stations in any one class session is generally not a sound approach. They can complete the entire circuit during additional sessions. Posting written directions at each station is helpful. The directions can describe the activity and offer points of technique.

In later instruction, students can select the skills they want to practice. With guidance, the choice system could embrace the entire program and be used at every session. This system can be related to individualized or contract instruction.

Track and Field Drills and Activities

Potato Shuttle Race

The Potato Shuttle Race is an adaptation of an old U.S. custom during frontier harvest celebrations. For each competitor, several potatoes were placed in a line at various distances. The winner was the one who brought in his potatoes first, one at a time. He won a sack of potatoes for the best effort.

The modern version of this race uses blocks instead of potatoes, and each runner runs the following course: A box is placed 15 feet (5 m) in front of the starting line, followed by four blocks in individual circles set the same distance (15 feet) apart (figure 29.11). The box is 12 by 12 inches (30 by 30 cm), with a depth of 3 to 6 inches (7.5 to 15 cm). The runner begins behind the starting line and brings the blocks, one at a time, back to the box. The runner can bring the blocks back in any order desired but must put all blocks inside the box. Blocks must be placed or dropped, not thrown, into the box.

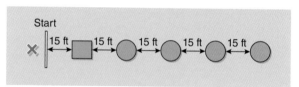

FIGURE 29.11   Potato Shuttle Race.

The most practical way to organize competition in this race is to time each runner and then award places based on elapsed time, because the race is physically challenging. Competitors must understand that each child is running individually and that they are striving for their best time, regardless of position or place of finish in the race. Timers can act as judges to see that the blocks are not thrown into the box. A block that lands outside the box must be placed inside before going after another.

The race can be run as a relay: The first runner brings in all the blocks, one at a time, and then tags the second team member, who returns the blocks, one at a time, to the respective spots. The third relay runner brings in the blocks again, and the fourth puts them out again. This race requires pie tins, floor tiles (9 by 9 inches [23 by 23 cm]), or some other items besides the box. When the second and fourth runners put out the blocks, they will place them precisely at these spots (e.g., pie tins) before going on to the next block.

Running for Pace

To learn pacing, children need some experience in running moderate distances. The running should be loose and relaxed. Distances up to 1,600 meters may be part of the work. To check his or her time, each runner needs a partner. Someone with a stopwatch loudly counts the elapsed time, second by second, and the partner notes the runner's time as he or she crosses the finish line.

Children can be motivated by estimating their pace and time. On a circular track, at a set distance, let the runners stipulate their own target time and see how close they can come to it.

Interval Training

Children should know the technique of interval training, which consists of running at a set speed for a specific distance and then walking back to the starting point. On the 1/8-mile (200 m) track, children can run for 110 yards (100 m) and then walk to the starting point, repeating this procedure several times. They can also run the entire 220 yards (200 m), take a timed rest, and then repeat. Allow the runners' breathing to return to near normal before they run the next 220-yard interval.

Suggested Track Facility

Having a track facility is a boon to any program. Few elementary schools have the funds or space for a quarter-mile (800 m) track. A shorter track facility that can be installed permanently with curbs or temporarily with marking lime is suggested. Use discarded fire hoses to mark curbs; they can be installed each spring and fastened with spikes.

The short facility is 1/8 mile (220 yards [200 m]) long and has a straightaway of 66 yards (60 m), which is ample for the 60-yard (55 m) dash (figure 29.12). It offers flexibility in relays, allowing for relay legs of 55, 110, and 220 yards (50, 100, and 200 m). In keeping with international practice, a 200-meter track may be preferable (figure 29.13). Running on a track is always counterclockwise.

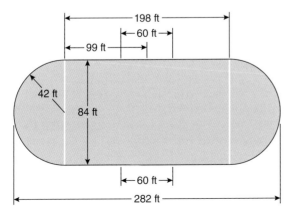
FIGURE 29.12 220-yard (1/8-mile) track.

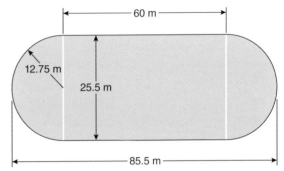
FIGURE 29.13 200-meter track.

Conducting Track and Field Days

Track and field days can range in organization from single-classroom competition to competition among several classes and from an all-school playday meet to a meet between neighboring schools or an area-wide or all-city meet. In informal meets within a class or between a few classes, ensure that all children participate in one or more events. Each student can be limited to two individual events plus one relay event, with no substitutions permitted. An additional condition could be imposed that competitors for individual events enter only one track event and one field event.

For larger meets, two means of qualification are suggested:

1. At the start of the season, set qualifying times and performance standards. Any student meeting or bettering these times or performances is qualified to compete.

2. In an all-school meet, first- and second-place winners in each class competition qualify for entry. For a district or all-city meet, first- and second-place winners from each all-school meet become eligible.

Generally, competition is organized for each event by sex and grade or age. This rule does not preclude mixed teams competing against mixed teams in relays. Height and weight classifications can be used to equalize competition.

Planning the Meet

Determine the order of events by the type of competition. Relays are usually last on the program. If preliminary heats are necessary, these relays are run off first. Give color-coded cards to the heat qualifiers. This system helps get them into the correct final race.

The local track coach can give advice about details of

29

organizing the meet. Helpers can be secured from among school patrons, secondary students, teacher-training students, and service clubs. Adequate and properly instructed help is essential. A list of key officials and their duties follows.

1. *Meet director.* The meet director records the winners and makes final decisions if there are any disputes. Position the meet director at a convenient point near the finish line, with a table on which all official papers are kept.

2. *Announcer.* The announcer is in charge of the public address system. Much of the meet's success depends on the announcer's abilities.

3. *Clerk of course.* The clerk, of course, is in charge of all entries and places the competitors in their proper starting slots.

4. *Starter.* The starter works closely with the clerk of course.

5. *Head and finish judges.* There should be one finish judge for each place awarded, plus one extra. In case of a disqualification, judges identify the first competitor "out of the money." The head judge casts the deciding vote if there is doubt about the first- and second-place winners.

6. *Timers.* Use three timers for first place, although fewer can be used. Another timer, if available, can time second place. Timers report their times to the head timer, who determines the correct winning time. Accurate timing is important if records are a factor.

7. *Messenger.* A messenger takes the entry card from the clerk of course to the finish judge, who records the correct finish places and the winner's time. The messenger then takes the final record of the race to the meet director's table.

8. *Field judges and officials.* A sufficient crew, headed by a designated individual, should manage each field event. Provide each crew head with a clipboard and full explanation of the rules of the particular event.

9. *Marshals.* Appoint several marshals to keep general order. They are responsible for keeping noncompetitors from interfering with the events. Competitors can be kept under better control if each unit has an assigned place, either in the infield or in the stands.

Ensure that only the assigned officials and competitors are at the scenes of competition. In smaller meets, first, second, and third places are usually awarded, with scoring on a 5-, 3-, and 1-point basis. Relays, because of multiple-student participation, should count double in the place point score. For larger meets, more places can be awarded, and the individual point scores can be adjusted.

Ribbons can be awarded to winners but need not be elaborate. The ribbon bears the meet title, the individual event, and the place. After each event, award blue ribbons for first place, red for second, and white for third. Awarding ribbons at the end of a large interschool meet is anticlimactic, because many spectators will have left.

An opening ceremony, including a salute to the flag, is desirable for larger meets. After introducing each group of competitors, the announcer can emphasize or clarify announcements and instructions. Holding the event on a school morning or afternoon gives status to the affair and allows all children to participate.

Having competitors wear numbers is helpful. Use safety pins, not straight pins, to keep the numbers in place. Numbers can be made at the individual schools before the meet, following clear instructions for materials, colors, and sizes.

Organizing the Competition

The overriding goal of elementary school competition is to have many children take part and experience some success. Determining individual champions and meet winners has lower priority. Track and field competition can take many forms.

In informal competition, competitors are assigned to different races and compete only in those races. There are no heats as such, nor is there advancement to a final race. Races are chosen so that students on the same team usually do not run against each other. Points may or may not be given toward an overall meet score. The informal meet is more like a playday and can include nontrack events such as the softball throw, football kick, and disc throw.

Track and field competition can be focused on individuals or teams. In individual competition, team scoring is not used and only individuals are declared winners. Team competition results in individual as well as team winners. Points scored by individual winners, such as 5 points for first place and 3 points for second place, are credited to respective teams. The team with the highest score wins. Team winners can be determined for different grades or levels.

Relay competition is a carnival consisting of several relays. Performances can be combined for several individuals if field events are to be included. Few, if any, uncombined scores are considered. Some relays should be part of track and field days under any plan. Relays increase student participation. Mixed relays are another possibility.

Cross Country Running

Running laps around a track motivates some students. Others soon tire of these circular efforts, however, and can be motivated by cross country running. Students can run marked or unmarked courses and enjoy the competition. By focusing on improving personal time rather than on winning, all students have personalized goals and an ongoing incentive for running.

Cross country courses can be marked with a chalk line and cones so that runners follow the course as outlined. Checkpoints every 220 yards (200 m) offer runners a convenient reference point for accurately gauging how far they have run. Three courses of differing lengths and difficulty can be laid out. The beginning course can be 1 mile (1.5 km) long, the intermediate 1.25 miles (2 km), and the advanced 1.5 miles (2.5 km). Including sandy

or hilly areas in the course increases the challenge. When students run cross country, they can select the course that challenges them appropriately.

Students who are running long distances need to learn pacing. One teaching method is to place cones at similar intervals and challenge students to run from cone to cone at a specified rate. A student or the instructor can call out the time at each cone, and students can adjust their running to the desired pace. Another method is to break down long-distance runs into smaller segments and times, thus helping students get a feel for how fast they must run the shorter distances to attain a certain cumulative time over the longer distance. Tables 29.2 and 29.3 gives times for the 40- and 100-yard dashes and 50- and 100-meter dashes, respectively.

Cross Country Meets

Cross country meets provide a culminating activity for students involved in distance running. The attraction of cross country competition is that it is a team activity, and the success of the team depends on all its members. Runners should learn how to score a meet. Probably

TABLE 29.2 Times for 40- and 100-Yard Dashes

To run a mile in:	Runner has to run 40-yard dash 44 times—each dash run in:	Runner has to run 100-yard dash 17.6 times—each dash run in:
3:44 minutes (near world-record time)	5.18 seconds	12.95 seconds
5:00 minutes	6.81 seconds	17.04 seconds
6:00 minutes	8.18 seconds	20.45 seconds
7:00 minutes	9.55 seconds	23.87 seconds
8:00 minutes	10.90 seconds	27.25 seconds
10:00 minutes	13.62 seconds	34.08 seconds

TABLE 29.3 Times for 50- and 100-Meter Dashes

To run 1.5 km (1,500 m) in:	Runner has to run 50-meter dash 30 times—each dash run in:	Runner has to run 100-meter dash 15 times—each dash run in:
3:26 minutes (world-record time)	6.86 seconds	13.73 seconds
5:00 minutes	10.0 seconds	20.0 seconds
6:00 minutes	12.0 seconds	24.0 seconds
7:00 minutes	14.0 seconds	28.0 seconds
8:00 minutes	16.0 seconds	32.0 seconds
10:00 minutes	20.0 seconds	40.0 seconds

29

the easiest way to keep team scores is to assign seven (depending on class size) members to each team. Finishers receive points based on their placement in the race. For example, the 1st-place runner receives 1 point, the 10th-place runner receives 10 points, and so on. The points for all team members are totaled, and the team with the lowest score is declared the winner.

To equalize the teams, have students run the course before the meet and record their times. Form teams whose abilities are somewhat balanced. As a guideline, table 29.4 offers suggested competitive divisions and distances to be run. Divisions 5 and 6 are classed as open divisions, which any child in the elementary school may enter, even if under age 12. Ages are defined by birthdays; that is, a child is classified as being a certain age until the next birthday.

A primary concern is for children to gauge their running pace so that they can finish the race. Improving personal times should be the focus of the activity, and place at the end of the race should be a secondary goal. The timekeeper can voice the time as each runner finishes so that children can evaluate their performance.

A funnel made of cones at the finish line prevents tying times (figure 29.14). As runners go through the funnel, the meet judges and helpers can hand each one a marker with the place of finish on it. This practice simplifies scoring at the end of the meet. Each team captain can total the scores and report the result.

Teach cross country runners to cool down on completing a race. Children tend to fall down rather than keep moving. They should jog gently until they are somewhat rested. Because runners do not all finish at once, setting out some recreational activities near the track to keep the students moving as they cool down is sometimes helpful.

TABLE 29.4 Suggested Divisions for Cross Country Meets

Division	Age	Sex	Distance in miles (kilometers)
1	8–9	M	1 (1.5)
2	8–9	F	1 (1.5)
3	10–11	M	1.25 (2.0)
4	10–11	F	1.25 (2.0)
5	12–13	M	1.5 (2.5)
6	12–13	F	1.5 (2.5)

©Robert Pangrazi or Aaron Beighle

FIGURE 29.14 Funneling runners at the finish line.

LEARNING AIDS

WEBSITES

American Track and Field, www.american-trackandfield.com
Cross Country, www.crosscountryforyouth.org
Youth Track and Field, www.usatf.org

SUGGESTED READINGS

American Sport Education Program. (2008). *Coaching youth track and field*. Champaign, IL: Human Kinetics.
Grant, M., & Molvar, J. (2014). *The youth and teen running encyclopedia: A complete guide for middle and long distance runners ages 6 to 18*. Seattle, WA: Amazon.
Hershey Corporation. (2014). *Hershey's track & field official rule book and manual*. Hershey, PA: Hershey.
Mood, D.P., Musker, F.F., & Rink, J.E. (2012). *Sports and recreational activities* (15th ed.). New York: McGraw-Hill.
USA Track & Field. (2015). *Track & field coaching essentials*. Champaign, IL: Human Kinetics.

Volleyball

Skills instruction for volleyball begins during the intermediate grades after students have mastered basic skills. Teaching the rules and strategies for volleyball is an integral part of the instructional process. Lead-up games allow teachers to emphasize development of selected volleyball skills in a setting that is compatible with their students' abilities.

Learning Objectives

▶ Structure learning experiences efficiently using appropriate formations, progressions, and coaching techniques.

▶ Develop a unit plan and lesson focus for volleyball.

▶ Identify safety precautions associated with teaching volleyball.

▶ Describe instructional procedures used for implementing a successful lead-up game.

▶ Cite assessment procedures used for evaluating volleyball skills.

Volleyball requires practicing serving and passing skills and developing eye–hand and body coordination for effective ball control. Informal practice begins with activities that mimic volleyball skills—passing, serving, and rebounding of all types. Blocking is an important skill that students can perform if they anticipate correctly. Setting and hitting or spiking (also called attacking) are challenging skills for most students, so teachers should spend little time on these techniques.

Instructional Emphasis and Sequence

Indoor facilities sometimes pose a problem for volleyball play. In some gyms, the lack of court space means playing with 12 to 15 children on a side in a single game. This arrangement results in little activity for most participants because a few skilled players on each side dominate the game. A basketball court can be divided into two volleyball courts where players play crosswise. Lowering nets to 6 feet (180 cm) or less ensures success. Raise the nets gradually as children mature. Attach nets so that both the upper and lower net cords are tight. A loose net restricts ball recovery from the net.

In the primary grades, children can practice ball-handling activities related to volleyball skills. Rebounding and controlling balloons are excellent related experiences, particularly for younger children. These preliminary experiences in visual tracking are helpful when learning volleyball skills in the upper grades.

Regulation volleyballs are of little value when introducing students to the basic skills. For practice, beach balls and foam balls of comparable size will increase success because they move slower and are of lighter weight. Many practice activities do not require a net, so they can be used outdoors. Normally, in physical education classes, the program focuses on keeping the ball in play, thereby increasing activity, skill development, and enjoyment. As a matter of game orientation, however, students should be introduced to setting, attacking, and blocking techniques.

Table 30.1 shows a sequence of volleyball activities divided into two developmental levels. In most cases, children are not ready to participate in this chapter's activities until age eight.

Developmental Level II

Experiences at Developmental Level II are based on using a beach ball and culminate in the game of Beach Ball Volleyball. A beach ball is larger but lighter and is

TABLE 30.1 Suggested Volleyball Program

Developmental Level II	Developmental Level III
Skills	
Underhand serve	Forearm passing
Simple returns	Overhand serve
	Setting
	Hitting–attacking*
	Blocking*
Knowledge	
Simple rules	Basic game rules
Rotation	Game strategy
Activities	
Beach Ball Volleyball	Pass and Dig
Informal Volleyball	Mini-Volleyball
Shower Service Ball	Rotation Mini-Volleyball
	Regulation Volleyball
	Three-and-Over Volleyball
	Rotation Volleyball
	Four-Square Volleyball
	Wheelchair Volleyball
Skill Tests	
Simplified serving	Serving for accuracy
	Wall volleying

*Skilled players only.

handled more easily than a volleyball, and it allows a level of success not possible with a smaller and heavier ball. Students can use beach balls to practice simple returns and underhand serves. The games of Informal Volleyball and Shower Service Ball are played with a beach ball or a volleyball trainer ball, which moves slowly and is easy to handle.

Developmental Level III

Students can use beach balls and foam balls (figure 30.1) at Developmental Level III, but volleyball trainer balls can be used if students' maturity dictates. Trainer balls move slowly, afford an opportunity for successful play, and do not hurt children. Students should exhibit basic technique for handling high and low passes. Only the most skilled students can learn the overhand serve, set, attack, and blocking. Instruction focuses on the underhand serve and passing. An introduction to elementary strategy is part of the instructional approach.

FIGURE 30.1　Different balls for volleyball.

Pearson Education

Volleyball Skills

Serving

The serve is used to start play. The underhand serve is easiest for elementary school children to learn even though the overhand (floater) serve is the most effective. Few students will master the overhand serve. These instructional cues focus on correct performance of the serve:

1. Use opposition. Place the foot opposite of the serving hand forward.
2. Transfer the weight to the forward foot.
3. Keep the eyes on the ball.
4. Decide before the serve where to place it.
5. Follow through; do not punch at the ball.

Underhand Serve

Directions are for a right-handed serve. Stand facing the net with the left foot slightly forward and the weight on the right (rear) foot. Hold the ball in the left hand with the left arm across and a little in front of the body. Line up the ball with a straightforward swing of the right hand. Keep the left-hand fingers spread and rest the ball on the pads of these fingers. On the serving motion, step forward with the left foot, transferring the weight to the front foot, and at the same time bring the right arm back in a preparatory motion. The right hand now swings forward and contacts the ball just below its center. The ball can be hit with an open hand or with the fist (facing forward or sideways). An effective follow-through with the arm ensures a smooth serve (figure 30.2). Children should explore the best way to strike the ball—with the flat of the hand or the fist—and use the method that works best.

FIGURE 30.2　Underhand serve.

Overhand Serve

Present this serve as an option for students who have mastered the underhand serve. For the right-handed serve, stand with the left foot in front and the left side of the body turned somewhat toward the net. Weight is on both feet. The server must master two difficult skills: tossing the ball and contacting the ball. Hold the ball in the left hand directly in front of the face and toss the ball straight up so that it comes down in front of the right shoulder. As the ball is tossed, the weight shifts to the back foot. The height of the toss is a matter of choice but from 3 to 5 feet (90 to 150 cm) is suggested. As the ball drops, the server's striking arm comes forward, contacting the ball a foot or so (30 cm) above the shoulder. Shift the weight to the forward foot with a short step forward. Contact the ball with an open palm or with the fist. An effective serve is one that has no spin—a floater.

Passing

In a formal game of volleyball, players typically use the forearm pass to receive the serve and pass the ball to a teammate for a set. The set is then used to pass the ball in preparation for an attack. At the elementary level, setting and attacking are rare, so players use both types of passes to send the ball to teammates and hit the ball over the net. When teaching these skills, use beach balls and trainer volleyballs so that players have time to move

30

into the volleyball's path instead of reaching. Proper footwork is critical to success in volleyball; using proper balls helps ensure that students learn correctly.

Forearm Pass

To prepare for the pass, the player moves rapidly to the spot where the ball is descending. Body position is important. Lean forward and keep the back straight, forming a 90-degree angle between the thighs and the back. Bend the legs and bend to a partially crouched position with the feet shoulder-width apart (figure 30.3). The hands are relaxed, and the type of clasp is a matter of choice: (1) keeping the thumbs parallel and together, make a partial fist with the fingers of one hand and cup the fist with the fingers of the other hand; (2) cup both hands and turn them out a little, so that the thumbs are apart. In either case, turn the wrists downward and lock the elbow joints somewhat to form a "table." Hold the forearms at the proper angle to rebound the ball by slightly moving the shoulders, making contact with the fists or forearms between the knees while crouching. Here are cues for the forearm pass:

1. Move into the path of the ball.
2. Bend the knees.
3. Make a table with arms flat and shoulders stiff.
4. Guide the ball with your shoulders.
5. Contact ball with the forearms.

FIGURE 30.3 Forearm pass position.

Set

Elementary students often use the setting motion to return the ball to the other team. This skill is sometimes called an overhead pass. As players become more proficient, they use this skill to set up other teammates (thus, "the set"). To execute the set, move underneath the ball and control it with the fingertips. Move the feet to an easy, comfortable position with the knees bent. Cup the fingers so that the thumbs and forefingers are close together and the other fingers are spread. The hands are held forehead high, with elbows out and level with the floor. The player, when in receiving position, looks ready to shout upward through her cupped hands (figure 30.4).

FIGURE 30.4 Completing a set.

The player contacts the ball above eye level and propels it with the force of spread fingers, not with the palms. At the moment of contact, she straightens her legs and the hands and arms follow through. The object is to raise the ball with a soft, easy pass to a position 1 or 2 feet (30 to 60 cm) above the net and about 1 foot (30 cm) away from it. The set is generally the second pass in a series of three. Here are teaching cues for the set:

1. Move to the ball.
2. Hands up and cupped with fingers spread.
3. Shoulders square to target and ready to shout.
4. Push with finger pads through the ball.

Advanced Volleyball Skills

Attacking

The attack is the most effective play in volleyball; when properly done, it is extremely difficult to return. Its success depends a great deal on a teammate's ability to set properly. At the elementary school level, players should attack by jumping high in the air and striking the ball above the net, driving it into the opponent's court. Experienced players may back up for a short run, but they must jump straight up to avoid touching the net and to keep the striking hand from going over the net. Here are instructional cues for the attack:

1. Approach.
2. Knees bent, arms back, head up.
3. Jump with arms up.
4. Contact ball in front of body.
5. Follow through with hand to same-side hip.

Blocking

Blocking involves one or more defensive (receiving) team members, who form a screen of arms and hands near the net to block an attack. At the elementary school level, blocking is rarely used. To block a ball, a player jumps high with arms outstretched overhead, palms facing the net, and fingers spread. The jump must be timed with the attacker's jump, and the blocker must avoid touching the net. The blocker does not strike the ball; instead, it rebounds from his or her stiffened hands and arms.

Instructional Procedures

1. Most volleyball-type games begin with a serve, so a successful serve is critical. Regular volleyball rules call for one chance to serve the ball over the net without touching the net. Three modifications can ensure more successful serving: (1) serve from the center of the playing area instead of the back line; (2) allow another serve if the first is not good; and (3) allow an assist by a team member to get the ball over the net.

2. To save time, instruct players to roll the ball back to the server. Other players should let the ball roll to its destination without interception.

3. Effective instruction is possible only when players can rebound the balls from the hands and arms without pain. A heavy or underinflated ball takes much of the enjoyment out of the game. Beach balls and trainers are excellent for beginning players.

4. Focus the predominant instructional pattern on individual or partner work. For individual work, each child needs a ball.

5. Using the fist to hit balls on normal returns results in poor control and interrupts play. Players should use both hands when returning the ball. Make a rule that hitting with the fist will result in a loss of a point if the practice persists.

6. Introduce a rotation plan early, and use it in lead-up games. Figure 30.5 shows two rotation plans.

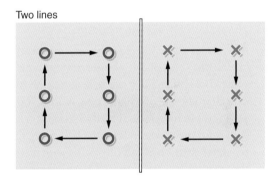

Two lines

Three lines

FIGURE 30.5 Rotation plans.

Organizing for Instruction

Practice sessions can be categorized as individual play, partner work, or group work. Teachers can preface these tasks with "Can you . . ." or "Let's see if you can . . ." A skill to learn early is tossing to oneself to start a practice routine. This occurs when the practice directions call for a pass from a student to herself or to another student.

Individual Play

1. For wall rebounding, the player stands 6 feet (2 m) away from a wall. The player throws the ball against the wall and passes it to the wall. The player then catches and begins again. The player should make two passes against the wall before making a catch. A further extension is for the player to pass the ball against the wall as many times as possible without making a mistake.

2. From a spot 6 feet (2 m) in front of the wall, the player throws the ball against the wall and alternates an overhand pass with a forearm pass. The player then catches the ball.

3. In another wall-rebounding exercise, the player throws the ball to one side (right or left) and then moves to the side to pass the ball to the wall. The player then catches the rebound.

4. The player passes the ball directly overhead and catches it. The player should try making two passes before catching the ball. Later, he or she can alternate an overhand pass with a forearm pass and catch the ball. A further extension of the drill is for the player to keep the ball going five or six times with one kind of pass or with alternate passes. This basic drill should be mastered before proceeding to others.

5. The player passes the ball 10 feet (3 m) high and 10 feet forward, moves rapidly under the ball, and catches it. Later, the player can try making additional passes without the catch.

6. The player passes the ball 15 feet (5 m) overhead, makes a full turn, and passes the ball again. The player should try other stunts as well, such as touching the floor, making a half turn, clapping the hands at two different spots, and others. Allow choice in selecting the stunt.

7. Two lines 3 feet (1 m) apart are needed. The player stands in front of one line, makes a backward pass overhead, moves to the other line, and repeats the procedure.

8. The player passes 3 feet (1 m) or so to one side, moves under the ball, and passes it back to the original spot. The next pass should be to the other side.

9. The player passes the ball directly overhead. On the return, he or she jumps as high as possible to make a second pass. The player makes as many passes as possible.

10. The player stands with one foot in a hoop and passes the ball overhead and tries to keep passing while his or her foot stays in the hoop. The player can then try it with both feet in the hoop.

11. The player stands about 15 feet (5 m) away from a basketball hoop, either in front or to the side. He or she passes toward the hoop, trying to make a basket. The player scores 3 points for making the basket, 2 points for not making a basket but hitting the rim, and 1 point for hitting the backboard only. A further challenge is for the player to pass to himself first and then pass toward the hoop.

Partner Work (Passing)

1. Players are about 10 feet (3 m) apart. Player A tosses the ball (controlled toss) to player B, who passes the ball back to A, who catches the ball. This continues for several exchanges, and then player B becomes the thrower. Another option is for player B to make a pass straight overhead, catch the ball, and then toss to player A. Yet another variation is to have one player toss the ball slightly to the side. Player B then passes to player A. Player A can then toss the ball so that player B must use a forearm return.

2. Two players are about 15 feet (5 m) apart. Player A passes to himself or herself first and then passes to player B, who catches the ball and repeats the pattern. Player B can then return the ball to player A.

3. Players A and B try to keep the ball in the air continuously.

4. Players are about 15 feet (5 m) apart. Player A stands still and passes in such a way that player B must move from side to side. An option is to have player B move forward and backward.

5. Players are about 10 feet (3 m) apart. Both have hoops and try to keep one foot in the hoop while passing. Then they try keeping both feet in the hoop.

6. Two players pass back and forth, contacting the ball while it is off the ground.

7. Players are about 15 feet (5 m) apart. Player B is seated. Player A tries to pass to player B. A second method is for both players to stand. Player A passes to player B and then sits down quickly. Player B tries to pass the ball back to player A, who catches it while seated.

8. Player A passes to player B and does a complete turnaround. Player B passes back to player A and also does a full turn. Other stunts can be used.

9. Player A stands near a basketball hoop, with player B in the lane. Player A passes to player B in the lane; player B tries a pass to the basket. They score 3 points for a basket, 2 points for a miss that hits the rim, and 1 point for hitting the backboard only. Any pass from player A that lands outside the center lane is void, and another chance is given.

10. Partners stand on opposite sides of a volleyball net. The object is to keep the ball in the air. The drill can include up to six players.

Partner Work (Serving and Passing)

1. Partners are about 20 feet (6 m) apart. Partner A serves to partner B, who catches the ball and returns the serve to partner A.

2. Partner A serves to partner B, who makes a pass back to partner A. Then they switch so that partner B serves.

3. *Service one-step.* Partners begin about 10 feet (3 m) apart. Partner A serves to partner B, who returns the serve, with partner A catching. If no error occurs and if neither receiver moved the feet to catch, both players take one step back. This process is repeated each time no error or foot movement by the receivers occurs. If an error or some foot movement occurs, the players start over at the original distance of 10 feet (3 m).

4. A player stands at the top of the key on a basketball court. The object is to serve the ball into the basket. Scoring can be as in other basket-making drills: 3 points for a basket, 2 points for hitting the rim, and 1 point for hitting the backboard but not the rim. The partner retrieves the ball.

Group Work

1. A leader stands in front of up to four other players, who are arranged in a semicircle. The leader tosses to each player in sequence around the circle, and they return the ball. After a round or two, another player comes forward to replace the leader.

2. For blocking, six players are positioned alongside the net, each with a ball. The players take turns on the other side of the net, practicing blocking skills. Each attacker tosses the ball to himself for attacking. A defensive player moves along the line to block a total of six attacks consecutively. The next step is to have two players move along the line to practice blocking by pairs.

3. Players can practice setting and spiking according to the drill shown in figure 30.6. A back player tosses the ball to the setting player, who passes the ball properly for an attack. The entire group or just the attackers can rotate.

4. Two groups of children stand on opposite sides of a net. They need from 8 to 10 balls to make this practice worthwhile. Players serve from behind the endline and recover balls coming from the other team. The action should be informal and continuous.

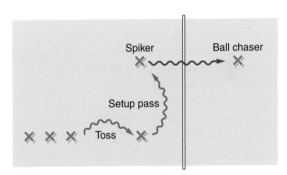

FIGURE 30.6 Setting and spiking drill.

Basic Volleyball Rules

Officially, six players make up a team; but any number from six to nine is suitable in the elementary school program. To begin, captains toss a coin for the order of choices. The winner can choose to serve or to select a court. The opposing captain takes the option not chosen by the winner of the toss. After finishing a game, the

30

teams change courts and the losing side serves first.

To be in proper serving position, a player may stand anywhere behind the endline and must keep both feet behind the line during the serve. The server covers the right back position. A point is scored with each serve (rally scoring). The server retains the serve, scoring consecutive points, until his or her team loses a point; then the other team serves. Members of each team take turns serving, according to the rotation plan.

Official rules allow a player only one serve to get the ball completely over the net and into the opponent's court. If the ball touches the net and goes into the correct court, it is considered a good serve and play continues. The lines bounding the court are inbounds; that is, balls landing on the lines are counted as good. Any ball that touches or is touched by a player is considered to be inbounds, even if the player who touched the ball was clearly outside the boundaries at the time. The ball must be returned over the net by the third volley—that is, the team has a maximum of three volleys to make a good return.

These major violations result in a point for the other team and loss of serve if the violating team is serving:

1. Touching the net during play
2. Not clearly batting the ball—sometimes called *palming* or *carrying the ball*
3. Reaching over the net during play
4. Stepping over the centerline (though contact with the line is not a violation)

A ball going into the net may be recovered and played if no player touches the net. The first team to reach a score of 25 points wins the game if the team is at least 2 points ahead. If not, play continues until one team secures a 2-point lead. Only players in the front line may attack, but all players may block. No player may volley the ball twice in succession.

Volleyball Activities

Developmental Level II

Beach Ball Volleyball

Playing area: volleyball court

Players: teams of six to nine students each

Supplies: a beach ball 12 to 16 inches (30 to 40 cm) in diameter

Skills: most passing skills, modified serving

Each team's players are in two lines on their own side of the net. As in regulation volleyball, the player on the right side of the back line serves. To ensure successful serves, have servers stand as close to the net as possible while staying in the right rear position on the court. Successful serving is an important part of an enjoyable game. Scoring is as in regulation volleyball. Play continues until the ball touches the floor.

A team loses a point to the other team when it fails to return the ball over the net by the third volley or when it returns the ball over the net but the ball hits the floor out-of-bounds without being touched by the opposing team. The server keeps serving as long as his or her team scores. Rotation is as in regulation volleyball.

Variations:

1. In a simplified version of Beach Ball Volleyball, the ball is put into play by one player in the front line who throws the ball into the air and then passes it over the net. Play continues until the ball touches the floor, but the ball may be volleyed any number of times before crossing the net. When either team scores 5 points, the front and back lines of both teams change. When the score reaches 10 for the leading team, the lines change back. The game is won at 15 points.

2. Any player in the back line may catch the ball as it first comes from the opposing team and may immediately make a little toss to a teammate. The player who catches the ball and bats it cannot send it across the net before a teammate has touched it.

Informal Volleyball

Playing area: volleyball court, 6-foot (180 cm) net

Players: teams of six to eight students each

Supplies: a trainer volleyball

Skills: passing

This game is similar to regulation volleyball, but players do not serve. Each play begins with a student on one side tossing to himself or herself and passing the ball high over the net. Points are scored for every play; there is no "side-out." When a point is scored, the nearest player takes the ball and immediately puts it into play. Otherwise, basic volleyball rules govern the game. When a team has scored 5 points, the front and back lines exchange places. Action is fast, and the scoring makes this game move rapidly.

Shower Service Ball

Playing area: volleyball court

Players: teams of 6 to 12 students each

Supplies: four to six trainer volleyballs

Skills: serving, catching

Mark the serving area by drawing a line parallel to the net through the middle of each court. Players are scattered in no particular formation (figure 30.7). The game involves the skills of serving and catching. To start the game, each team gets two or three volleyballs that are handled by players in the serving area.

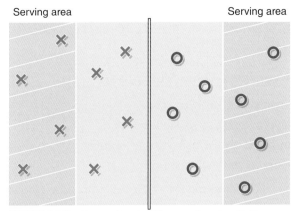

Serving area   Serving area

FIGURE 30.7   Formation for Shower Service Ball.

Balls may be served at any time and in any order by a server, who must be in the back half of the court. Any ball served across the net is to be caught by any player near the ball. The person catching or retrieving the ball moves quickly to the serving area and serves. Teams score 1 point whenever a served ball hits the floor in the other court or is dropped by a receiver. Two scorers are needed, one for each side. As children improve, have them make all serves from behind the baseline.

Developmental Level III

Pass and Dig

Playing area: playground or gymnasium

Players: teams of five to eight students each

Supplies: a trainer volleyball for each team

Skills: overhand and forearm passes

Each team forms a small circle of up to eight players. The object is to see which team can make the most passes in a specified time, or which team can keep the ball in the air while making the most consecutive passes without error.

On the signal "Go," a player starts the game with a volley. The following rules are in force:

1. Balls are passed back and forth with no specific order of turns, except that the ball cannot be returned to the last player who passed it.

2. A player may not pass a ball twice in succession.

3. Any ball touching the ground does not count and ends the turn.

TEACHING TIP

Make players take responsibility for calling illegal returns on themselves and thus interrupting the consecutive pass count. Be sure that the teams have equally good volleyballs so that one team does not have an advantage. Instruct teams to count the passes aloud to report their progress.

Mini-Volleyball

Playing area: gymnasium or badminton court

Players: teams of three students each

Supplies: a volleyball or trainer volleyball

Skills: most volleyball skills

Mini-Volleyball is a modified activity designed to provide successful volleyball experiences for children between ages 9 and 12. The playing area is 15 feet (5 m) wide and 40 feet (12 m) long. Many gyms are marked for badminton courts that are 20 by 44 feet (6.1 by 13.4 m) with a spiking line 6.5 feet (2 m) from the center. This court is an acceptable substitute.

Here are the modified rules for Mini-Volleyball:

1. Teams consist of three players. Two substitutions may be made per game.

2. Player positions for the serve call for two front-line players and one back-line player. After the ball is served, the back-line player cannot attack the ball from the attack area or hit the ball into the attack area unless the ball is below net height.

3. Net height is 6 feet, 10 inches (208 cm).

4. Players rotate positions when they receive the ball for serving. The right front-line player becomes the back-line player, and the left front-line player becomes the right front-line player.

30

5. The winner is the first team to score 15 points with a 2-point advantage over the opponent. A team wins the match when it wins two out of three games.

6. The back-line player cannot attack and thus serves a useful function by allowing the front players to receive the serves while moving to the net to set up for the attackers.

Variation: Modify the game to suit your students' needs.

Rotation Mini-Volleyball

Playing area: basketball or volleyball court
Players: teams of three students each
Supplies: a volleyball or trainer volleyball
Skills: all volleyball skills

Three games, involving 18 active players, can be played at the same time crosswise, on a regular basketball court. The remaining children, organized in teams of three, wait on the sideline. The teams are designated in a particular order. Whenever a team is guilty of a side-out, it leaves the game and the next team in line moves in. Each team keeps its own running score. If, during a single side-in, 10 points are scored against a team, that team leaves the game. Teams in this arrangement move from one court to another and play different opponents. The one or two extra players left over from team selection by threes can be substitutes; rotate them into play on a regular basis.

Regulation Volleyball

Playing area: volleyball court
Players: teams of six students each
Supplies: a volleyball or trainer volleyball
Skills: all volleyball skills

Regulation volleyball can be played with one possible rule change: In early experiences, give the server a second chance if the first attempt fails to go over the net and into play. Apply this rule only to the first serve. Some instructors like to shorten the serving distance during the introductory phases of the game. The serving needs to be done well enough to keep the game moving. Team play should be emphasized. Encourage backcourt players to pass to frontcourt players rather than merely batt the ball back and forth across the net.

A referee should supervise the game. The referee generally makes three calls:

1. *Side-out.* The serving team fails to serve the ball successfully to the other court, fails to return of a volley legally, or violates a rule.

2. *Point.* Either team fails to make a legal return or violates a rule.

3. *Double foul.* Both teams make fouls on the same play, in which case the point is replayed. No score or side-out results.

Variations: The receiver in the backcourt is allowed to catch the serve, toss it, and propel it to a teammate. The catch is limited to the serve, and the pass must go to a teammate, not over the net. This variation solves the problem of children in the backcourt being unable to handle the serve if the served ball is spinning, curving, or arriving so fast that it is difficult to control.

Three-and-Over Volleyball

Playing area: volleyball court
Players: teams of six students each
Supplies: a volleyball or trainer volleyball
Skills: all volleyball skills

The game Three-and-Over Volleyball emphasizes the basic offensive strategy of volleyball. The game follows regular volleyball rules, except that players must pass the ball three times before it goes over the net. The team loses the serve or the point if they do not pass the ball three times.

Rotation Volleyball

Playing area: volleyball court
Players: variable
Supplies: a volleyball or trainer volleyball
Skills: all volleyball skills

If four teams are playing in two contests at the same time, set up a rotation plan during any one class period. Divide the available class time roughly into three parts, less the time allotted for logistics. Each team plays against the other three teams on a timed basis. After a specified period, whichever team is ahead wins the game. A team may win, lose, or tie during any period, and the score is determined at the end of the period. The best win–loss record wins the overall contest.

Four-Square Volleyball

Playing area: volleyball court
Players: teams of two to four students each

Supplies: a volleyball or trainer volleyball

Skills: all volleyball skills

Place a second net at right angles to the first net, dividing the playing area into four equal courts. The courts are numbered as in figure 30.8. Four teams are playing, and an extra team can be waiting to rotate to court number 4. The object is to force one of the teams to make an error. Whenever a team makes an error, it moves down to court 4 or off the courts if a team is waiting. A team errs by not returning the ball to another court within the prescribed three volleys or by sending the ball out-of-bounds.

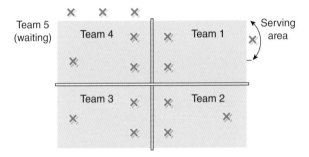

FIGURE 30.8 Four-Square Volleyball courts.

A team 1 player always puts the ball in play with a serve from any point behind the team's endline. Players must rotate for each serve. The serve is made into court 3 or 4. Play proceeds as in regular volleyball, but the ball may be volleyed into any of the other three courts. No score is kept. The object is for team 1 to retain its position.

The game seems to work best with five or more teams. With four teams, the team occupying court 4 is not penalized for an error, because it is already in the lowest spot.

Wheelchair Volleyball

Children in wheelchairs can participate successfully in some phases of volleyball. For example, a child who uses a wheelchair can compete one-on-one with another student when courts are laid out as shown in figure 30.9. The size difference of the playing areas equalizes the mobility factor. Set the net about 6 feet (2 m) in height and use a beach ball. The able child serves from behind the back line, and the child in a wheelchair serves with the wheels on the back line. Adjust the rules as necessary.

Volleyball Skill Tests

Serving and volleying are the skills to be tested in volleyball. Serving is tested in two ways: (1) with a simple serve and (2) with an accuracy score.

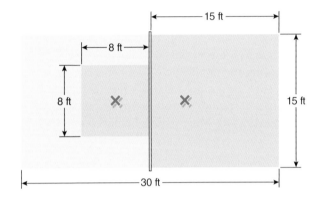

FIGURE 30.9 Court for Wheelchair Volleyball.

Simplified Serving

In the simplified serving test, the child to be tested stands in normal serving position behind the endline on the right side. The student receives 10 trials in which to serve. The score is the number of successful serves out of 10 trials. The serve must clear the net without touching and must land in the opponent's court. A ball touching a boundary line is counted as good.

Serving for Accuracy

To test serving for accuracy, draw a line parallel to the net through the middle of one of the courts. Further divide each half into three equal areas by lines drawn parallel to the sidelines. This makes six areas that correspond to the positions of the members of a volleyball team. Number the areas from 1 to 6 (figure 30.10).

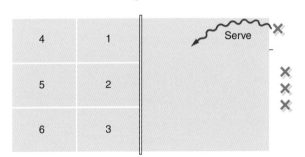

FIGURE 30.10 Court layout for service testing.

Each child is allowed one attempt to serve the ball into each of the six areas in turn. Players score 2 points for serving into the designated court area and 1 point for missing the designated area but landing in an adjacent area. No points are scored otherwise.

30

Wall Volleying

For the wall-volleying test, the player stands behind a restraining line 4 feet (120 cm) away from a wall. A line representing the net height of the net is drawn on the wall parallel to the floor and 6.5 feet (2 m) up. Each player has 30 seconds to make as many volleys as possible above the line while staying behind the restraining line. Each testing station has a counter who records the total successive volleys. The child makes a short toss to himself or herself for the first volley. If time permits, give players more than one 30-second period and use the best count as the score. A mat can mark the restraining line. Stepping onto the mat makes that volley illegal.

LEARNING AIDS

WEBSITES

American Volleyball Coaches Association, www.avca.org
United States Youth Volleyball League, www.usyvl.org

Volleyball Skills and Drills

www.volleyballadvisors.com
www.jes-volleyball.com/volleyball/plays.html

SUGGESTED READINGS

American Sport Education Program. (2015). *Coaching youth volleyball* (4th ed.). Ebook. Champaign, IL: Human Kinetics. https://us.humankinetics.com/products/coaching-youth-volleyball-4th-edition-pdf

American Volleyball Coaches Association. (2002). *The volleyball coaching bible, volume I.* Champaign, IL: Human Kinetics.

American Volleyball Coaches Association. (2014). *The volleyball coaching bible, volume II.* Champaign, IL: Human Kinetics.

American Volleyball Coaches Association. (2006). *Volleyball skills & drills.* Champaign, IL: Human Kinetics.

Dearing, J. *Volleyball fundamentals.* (2019). Champaign, IL: Human Kinetics.

Hebert, M. (2014). *Thinking volleyball.* Champaign, IL: Human Kinetics.

Mood, D.P., Musker, F.F., & Rink, J.E. (2012). *Sports and recreational activities* (15th ed.). Boston, MA: McGraw-Hill.

Schmidt, B. (2016). *Volleyball: Steps to success.* Champaign, IL: Human Kinetics.

Waite, P. (2009). *Aggressive volleyball.* Ebook. https://us.humankinetics.com/products/aggressive-volleyball-pdf

GLOSSARY

A

absorbing force Lessening the force of a projectile by bending the arms while catching it.

accent Certain notes or beats in a rhythmic pattern that receive more force than others.

act of God Defense that places the cause of injury on forces beyond the control of the teacher or the school; the defense is made that it was impossible to predict an unsafe condition, but through an act of God, the injury occurred.

act of omission See *nonfeasance*.

active listener One who convinces the speaker that he or she is interested in what the speaker is saying; much of this is done through nonverbal behavior, such as eye contact, nodding the head in agreement, facial expressions, and moving toward the speaker.

active sports This type of activity is typically more vigorous than lifestyle physical activity; sports often involve vigorous bursts of activity with brief rest periods; examples include basketball, tennis, soccer, and hiking.

active supervision Supervision that involves moving among students and offering them personalized feedback.

activity reinforcers Reinforcement that uses types of activities that children enjoy.

aerobic activities Activities performed at a pace for which the body can supply adequate oxygen to meet the demands of the activity.

aerobic capacity The maximum amount of oxygen that the body is able to use to produce work.

affective domain Deals with feelings, attitudes, and values; the major categories of learning in this area are receiving, responding, valuing, organizing, and characterizing.

agility The ability of the body to change position rapidly and accurately while moving in space.

anecdotal record sheet A record sheet that contains student names and has room for comments about student behavior that can be used to assess student progress.

anticipatory set Prefocuses on the skill and cognitive objectives of the lesson.

arousal Level of excitement stress produces; level of arousal can have a positive or negative impact on motor performance.

assessment The collection of information about student performance; traditionally directed at functions of compliance (i.e., participation, attendance, effort) and not on components that reflect student learning.

asymmetrical movements Different movements using similar body parts on opposite sides of the body.

attractive nuisance The legal concept of an *attractive nuisance* implies that some piece of equipment or apparatus, usually left unsupervised, was so attractive to children that they could not be expected to avoid it. When an injury occurs, even though students may have been using the apparatus incorrectly, teachers and school administration are often held liable because the attractive nuisance should have been removed from the area when unsupervised.

B

balance The body's ability to maintain a state of equilibrium while remaining stationary or moving.

ballistic stretching Strong bouncing movements; formerly was the most common method of stretching used, but this has been discouraged for many years because it was thought to increase delayed onset muscle soreness.

baseline and goal-setting technique Approach that requires each individual to identify her or his average daily activity (baseline) level to serve as a reference point for setting a personal goal.

basic urges An innate desire to do or accomplish something.

baton passing The passing of batons during a relay race.

batting Swinging at a ball that is pitched to you.

beat The underlying rhythm of the music; some musicians refer to the beat as the pulse of the music.

behavior contract A written statement specifying certain student behaviors that must occur to earn certain rewards or privileges; it is agreed upon and signed by the student and teacher.

behavior games Strategy for changing class behavior in the areas of management, motivation, and discipline; the shaping technique is useful in changing whole-class behavior.

blocked practice Practice in which all the trials of one task are completed before moving on to the next task.

body awareness Awareness of what the body can perform.

body composition The proportion of body fat to lean body mass; it is an integral part of health-related fitness.

body management skills Skills required for control of the body in a variety of situations; body management skills necessitate an integration of agility, coordination, strength, balance, and flexibility.

breach of duty Failing to conform to the required duty; after it is established that a duty was required, it must be proved that such duty was not performed.

C

cageball A large canvas-covered ball that is 24 inches (60 cm) or more in diameter.

cardiovascular endurance The ability of the heart, the blood vessels, and the respiratory system to deliver oxygen efficiently over an extended period.

cardiovascular fitness Fitness that includes aspects of physiological function that promote cardiovascular endurance; activities are aerobic in nature.

centering Involves transferring the football, on a signal, to the quarterback.

closure Brought on by the closing activity; stressing and reinforcing skills learned, revisiting performance techniques, and checking cognitive concepts.

cognitive domain Includes six major areas: knowledge, comprehension, application, analysis, synthesis, and evaluation; the focus of the cognitive domain for physical education is knowing rules, health information, safety procedures, and so on, and being able to understand and apply such knowledge.

comparative negligence Under the doctrine of comparative negligence, the injured party can recover only if found to be less negligent than the defendant (the teacher). Where statutes apply, the amount of recovery is generally reduced in proportion to the injured

party's participation in the circumstances leading to the injury.

competition Characterized by opponents working against each other as each tries to reach a goal or reward.

conceptual framework A series of statements that characterize the desired curriculum; directs the selection of activities and reflects beliefs about education and the learner.

conflict resolution Cooperative approach to solving problems; can help students build positive feelings and learn to solve conflicts in a peaceful manner with no apparent losers.

contrasting movements Movements that differ in their qualities, such as smooth and jerky.

contributory negligence Improper behavior by the injured party that causes the accident; harm that resulted from the injured party's contribution. This responsibility is directly related to the maturity, ability, and experience of the child.

cooperation Involves two or more children working together to achieve a common goal.

cooperative learning A style that focuses on the importance of people working together to accomplish common goals.

coordination The ability of the body to perform smoothly and successfully more than one motor task at the same time.

corrective feedback Feedback offered with the intent of correcting a problem.

criterion-referenced health standards Standards that represent a level of fitness that offers some degree of protection against diseases resulting from sedentary living; represent good health instead of traditional percentile rankings.

D

deadweight Fat; has a negative effect on motor performance because it reduces relative strength.

demonstration mat One mat that is placed in a central position and is used exclusively for demonstrations.

Developmental Levels I–III Levels used to group activities and units of instruction because they allow greater variation of skill development among students.

direct style The most teacher-controlled approach to teaching; the teacher provides instruction to either the entire class or small groups and guides the pace and direction of the class.

dramatization Acting out an idea with music or rhythmic accompaniment.

dribbling Moving the ball with a series of taps or pushes to cover ground and still retain control.

due process guidelines Guidelines required so that parents and children are informed of their rights and have the opportunity to challenge educational decisions they believe are unfair or incorrect.

duration recording Used to evaluate practice time; a student or fellow teacher observes the lesson and times when students are involved in practicing skills.

duty Responsibility or obligation.

E

ectomorph Identified as being extremely thin, with a minimum of muscle development, and characterized as "skinny"; may be less able in activities requiring strength and power, but able to perform well in aerobic endurance activities such as jogging, cross country running, and track and field.

endomorph Characterized as soft and round, with an excessively protruding abdomen; may perform poorly in many areas, including aerobic and anaerobic skill-oriented activities.

endurance training Exercises that increase one's endurance; examples include distance running, bicycling, and swimming.

equipment Items that is more or less fixed in nature, has a relatively long lifespan, needs periodic safety checks, and requires planned purchasing.

exploration style, or free exploration The most child-centered style of learning; guidance by the teacher is limited to the selection of the instructional materials to be used and designation of the area to be explored.

expulsion The act of removing a student from the class or school setting, usually as a punishment.

extinction Method of reinforcement wherein the teacher ignores performance that does not meet the predetermined criterion.

extrinsic reward Rewards offered to encourage performance; examples include trophies, published league standings, ribbons, and excessive parental involvement.

F

face-off Used at the start of the hockey game, after a goal, or when the ball is stopped from further play by opposing players.

fast-twitch (FT) fibers Fast-contracting fibers in skeletal muscle tissue that are capable of bursts of intense activity but subject to rapid fatigue. These fibers are well suited to activities demanding short-term speed and power (for example, pull-ups, standing long jump, and shuttle run).

feedback Any kind of information about a movement performance; affects what is to be learned, what should be avoided, and how the performance can be modified.

fielding Catching balls when they're hit out to the infield or outfield.

FitnessGram Test used to measure health-related physical fitness. The focus of the FitnessGram is on teaching students about the importance of activity for good health.

flexibility The range of movement through which a joint or sequence of joints can move.

flexibility exercises Exercises done specifically to build the part of physical fitness called flexibility.

folk dance A traditional dance of a particular culture.

follow through The final phase of any skill performance. In most cases, the follow through occurs after maximum force has been generated.

force The effort or tension generated in movement.

forearm pass Underhand pass in volleyball.

foreseeability The ability to foresee potentially harmful situations; courts expect trained professionals to predict and anticipate the danger of a harmful act or situation and to take appropriate measures to prevent it from occurring.

foreseeable dangers Dangers that school district personnel predict or anticipate happening (so that they can prevent such problems from occurring).

formation jumping Rope jumping in which four to six ropes with turners are placed in various patterns.

fundamental motor skills Locomotor and nonlocomotor skills that form the foundation for nearly all physical activities.

fundamental skills Basic or functional skills; requisite for children to function fully in the environment. Fundamental skills are divided into three categories: locomotor, nonlocomotor, and manipulative skills.

G

galloping A movement similar to sliding but progressing in a forward direction. One foot leads, and the other is brought rapidly forward to it. The body moves upward more than it does than in sliding.

game skills Games allow children to apply newly learned skills in a meaningful way; social objectives include development of interpersonal skills, acceptance of rule parameters, and better understanding of oneself in a competitive and cooperative situation.

general supervision Refers to broad coverage, when students are not under direct control of a. teacher or a designated person (for example, playground duty). A plan of supervision should be made, designating the areas to be covered and including where and how the supervisor should rotate.

gross motor movements Often referred to as large-muscle movements. Most often used to identify locomotor (skipping, walking, and so on) and nonlocomotor movements (twisting, turning, and so on).

guided discovery Used when there is a predetermined choice or result that the teacher wants students to discover.

gymnastics skills Help develop flexibility, agility, balance, strength, and body control; basic gymnastics skills include body rolling, balance skills, inverted balances, and tumbling.

H

heading In soccer, a special kind of volleying in which the direction of flight of the ball is changed through an impact with the head.

health-related fitness Can be integrated into regular everyday activities that are often characterized as lifetime activities; people who are generally unwilling to exercise at high intensities should aim for health-related fitness.

healthy activity zone (HAZ) A suggested way to promote physical activity using pedometer step counts.

healthy fitness zone (HFZ) Category that Fitness-Gram uses to classify fitness performance; students are encouraged to score in the HFZ.

Healthy People 2020 Document that addresses major health goals: (1) increasing the years of healthy life; and (2) eliminating health disparities; includes enabling goals concerned with promoting healthy behaviors, protecting health, achieving access to quality health care, and strengthening community prevention.

hidden curriculum Implied messages sent to students through how the lesson is organized, what types of activities are presented, how teachers view students who are less successful, and how children with disabilities are treated.

hop-step-and-jump An event that begins with a run similar to that for the running long jump. The takeoff is with one foot, and the jumper must land on the same foot to complete the hop. The jumper then takes a step followed by a jump. The event finishes like the long jump, with a landing on both feet.

hopping Propelling the body up and down on the same foot.

horizontal articulation See *scope*.

human wellness An area in which physical education can have a lifelong effect on students; wellness instruction teaches the principles of fitness, the importance of daily physical activity, and the benefits of physical fitness.

I

IDEA Individuals with Disabilities Education Act; Public Law 105-17 has the objective of providing handicapped people with the least restrictive environment in the school setting. Physical education services must be made available to every child with a disability receiving a free appropriate public education.

IEP Individualized Educational Program; a specific learning program for each disabled student as mandated by PL 94-142.

individualized style Individualized curriculum that uses a variety of teaching strategies designed to allow students to progress at an individual rate; each student's needs are diagnosed, and a program is prescribed to address those needs.

indoor facilities Indoor space designated for play; gymnasium.

institutional evaluation Program that involves examining the fitness levels of students to see if the institution (school) is reaching its desired objectives.

instructional cues Keywords that quickly and efficiently communicate proper technique and performance of skills and movement tasks.

instructional feedback given to students so that meaningful goals for improvement can be established.

instructional time The amount of instruction offered to students.

intensity The intensity of music can be loud, soft, light, or heavy. Mood is related to intensity but carries the concept deeper into human feelings.

interrupted flow Motion that stops at the end of one movement or part of a movement before beginning another.

intrinsic motivation Willingness to do something for the sake of doing it.

introductory activities Activities used for starting a lesson that require little instruction and immediately immerse students in large-muscle movements.

J

jump shot For a jump shot, the shooter executes a vertical jump, leaving the floor slightly. The supporting (nonshooting) hand remains in contact with the ball until the top of the jump is reached. The shooting hand then takes over with fingertip control, and the ball rolls off the center three fingers. The hand and wrist follow through.

jumping box Boxes of varying heights; 8 inches (20 cm) and 16 inches (40 cm) are suggested.

K

knowledge of performance Feedback that is verbal, extrinsic in nature, and occurs after the performance; relates to the process of the skill performance and refers to specific components.

knowledge of results Extrinsic feedback given after a skill has been performed; usually verbal information about performance.

L

large apparatus Climbing ropes, benches, balance beams, and jumping boxes; large-apparatus activities offer an opportunity to learn body management skills while free of ground support.

lead-up activities See *lead-up games.*

lead-up games Games developed for the express purpose of limiting the number of skills needed for successful participation.

leaping An elongated step designed to cover distance or move over a low obstacle.

least restrictive environment Refers to the idea that not all people can do all of the same activities in the same environment; used to help determine the best placement arrangement of students with disabilities.

liability The responsibility to perform a duty to a particular group; an obligation to perform in a particular way that is required by law and enforced by court action.

lifestyle physical activities Activities that people can do as part of their regular everyday work or daily routine; examples include yard work and delivering the mail.

locomotor movements Movements performed in which the body travels through space.

locomotor skills Skills used to move the body from one place to another or to project the body upward, as in jumping and hopping. These skills also include walking, running, skipping, leaping, sliding, and galloping.

M

mainstreaming The practice of placing children with disabilities into classes with able youngsters.

magic ropes Flexible ropes, similar to large rubber bands, that stretch between 30 and 40 feet (10 and 12 m).

malfeasance Act that occurs when a teacher does something improper by committing an act that is unlawful and wrongful, with no legal basis (often referred to as an act of commission).

management time Episodes that occur when students are moved into various formations, when equipment is gathered or put away, and when directions are given relative to these areas.

manipulative skills Skills in which a child handles an object with the hands, feet, or other body parts.

mastery learning An instructional strategy that takes a general program outcome and breaks it into smaller parts, providing a progression of skills.

measure A group of beats made by the regular occurrence of a heavy accent.

mental practice Involves practicing a motor skill in a quiet, relaxed environment—the experience involves thinking about the activity and its related sounds, color, and other sensations; used in combination with regular practice, not in place of it.

mesomorph Characterized as having a predominance of muscle and bone and often labeled "muscled"; in general, children who possess a mesomorphic body type perform best in activities requiring strength, speed, and agility.

METS Resting metabolic rate; used to quantify activity.

misfeasance Occurs when a teacher follows proper procedures but does not perform according to the required standard of conduct; based on performance of the proper action but not up to the required standard. It is usually the subpar performance of an act that might have been otherwise lawfully done.

mismatched opponents The mismatching of students on the bases of size and ability; just because the competitors are the same gender and choose to participate does not absolve the instructor of liability if an injury occurs.

modeling Teachers exhibiting behaviors they expect of students.

movement concepts The classification and vocabulary of movement.

movement education Instruction and training in skills and concepts associated with fitness and physical education.

movement themes Movements that are categorized in the major classifications of space awareness, body awareness, qualities of movement, and relationships.

multicultural education Creates an educational environment in which students from a variety of backgrounds and experience come together to experience educational equality.

muscular endurance The ability to exert force over an extended period; endurance postpones the onset of fatigue so that activity can be performed for lengthy periods.

muscular strength The ability of muscles to exert force.

MyPlate The food guidance system released by the USDA in 2011; it has accompanying tips, lesson plans, and coloring sheets designed to explain healthful eating to children.

N

NASPE National Association for Sport and Physical Education.

negative feedback Feedback that focuses on negative aspects of performance; should be avoided.

negligence Defined by the courts as conduct that falls below a standard of care established to protect others from unreasonable risk or harm; several types of negligence can be categorized.

nonfeasance Based on lack of action in carrying out a duty; this is usually an *act of omission* (i.e., the teacher knew the proper procedures but failed to follow them).

nonlocomotor movements Movements performed without the body traveling through space.

nonlocomotor skills Skills performed in place, without appreciable spatial movement. They include bending and stretching, pushing and pulling, balancing, rolling, curling, twisting, turning, and bouncing.

nonverbal behavior Another way to deliver feedback; nonverbal feedback is effective because it is easily interpreted by students and often perceived as more meaningful than words.

nonverbal feedback Feedback that is given nonverbally.

Norwegian start On the command "On your mark," the runner takes a position at the starting line with the right foot forward. On "Get set," the left hand is placed on the right knee and the right hand is carried back for a thrust. On "Go," the right hand comes forward, coupled with a drive by the right foot.

O

objectives Instructional goals designed and listed for the purpose of accomplishing standards.

opposition Refers to throwing or kicking skills most often. For example, proper form implies stepping forward with the left foot when throwing with the right hand.

outdoor apparatus Outdoor equipment that help users develop various components of fitness; abstract in nature and can be manipulated and changed to suit the needs of users.

outdoor facilities Outdoor area designated for play; the outdoor areas should include field space for games, a track, hard-surfaced areas, apparatus areas, play courts, age-group-specific play areas, covered play space, and a jogging trail.

P

PACER Aerobic fitness test that can be administered indoors and does not require running to exhaustion; as a cardiovascular fitness measure, the PACER is as accurate as the mile run and produces much less emotional stress for participants.

part practice Method that breaks down a skill into a series of parts and then combines the parts into the whole skill.

partial mainstreaming Students participate in selected physical education experiences but do not attend on a full-time basis because they can be successful in only a few of the offerings; their developmental needs are usually met in special classes.

partner resistance activities Partner activities in which each partner pulls against the other with a tug-of-war rope.

partner tug-of-war ropes A rope that is about 6 feet (2 m) long with a loop on each end.

passing Advancing the ball to a teammate.

pattern A regular and intelligible form or sequence discernible in certain actions or situations.

pedometers Small devices that measure the quantity of physical activity; they are fastened to a belt or waistband.

perceived competence How people feel about their ability level; becomes more specific as students mature.

personal wellness Developing a personal lifestyle that is balanced in all phases with *moderation* the keyword.

phrase A natural grouping of measures; phrases of music are put together into rhythmic patterns.

physical activity Bodily movement that is produced by the contraction of skeletal muscle and that substantially increases energy expenditure; it is a process-oriented outcome related to behavior and lifestyles.

Physical Activity Pyramid A prescription model for good health that helps students understand how much and what type of activity they need.

physical education Education through movement; it is an instructional program that gives attention to all learning domains: psychomotor, cognitive, and affective.

physical education specialist Teachers certified in physical education.

physical fitness A set of attributes that people have or achieve relating to their ability to perform physical activity; it is a product outcome with an emphasis on achieving a higher state of being.

pitching The act of throwing a softball to the catcher.

placheck recording Placheck (planned activity check) recording is a technique used to observe group behavior at different times during a lesson; used to monitor behavior that is yes or no in nature.

PL 94-142 Public Law 94-142 states that all youngsters have the right to a free and public education and must be educated in the least restrictive educational environment possible. Children with disabilities cannot be assigned to segregated classes or schools unless a separate environment is determined by due process to be in the child's best interest.

point-of-decision prompts Signs placed in areas around the school where students and faculty will be making choices regarding healthy behaviors.

posture Refers to the habitual or assumed alignment and balance of the body segments while the body is standing, walking, sitting, or lying.

power The ability to transfer energy explosively into force.

Premack principle Principle that states a highly desirable activity can be used to motivate students to learn an activity they enjoy to a lesser degree.

problem solving Teaching style that involves input, reflection, choice, and response; the problem is structured so that no single answer is prescribed.

process of learning outcomes Relates to the performance of movement patterns and skills with emphasis on correct technique; the form used to execute the movement is the point of assessment rather than the outcome of the skill performed.

product outcomes Focus on performance in terms of measurable increments of what learners accomplish.

progression Sequential presentation of skills.

proximate cause Defense that attempts to prove that the accident was not caused by the negligence of the teacher.

psychomotor domain This domain is the primary focus of instruction for physical educators; the seven levels in psychomotor domain taxonomy are movement vocabulary, movement of body parts, locomotor movements, moving implements and objects, patterns of movement, moving with others, and movement problem solving.

punting Kicking in football.

Q

qualities of movement How the body moves.

R

random practice Method whereby the order of multiple task presentations is mixed and no task is practiced twice in succession.

recreational activities Activities that involve playing games or sports for fun.

reinforcement Positive behavior given when students perform acceptable behavior.

relationship The position of the performer to a piece of apparatus or to other performers.

relative strength Strength in relation to body size.

reprimanding Approach used to decrease unacceptable behavior.

resistance training The term is used here to denote the use of barbells, dumbbells, rubber bands, or machines as resistance.

response latency The amount of time it takes for students to respond when commands or signals are given.

responsible behavior Implies behaving in a manner that doesn't negatively affect others; includes behaving in an acceptable manner and assuming responsibility for the consequences of one's actions.

return activities Activities that require children to perform a movement task (jumping, hopping, skipping, animal walks, and so on) after they have performed on an apparatus; this approach reduces the time children stand in line waiting for another turn after completion of their task on the apparatus.

reverse mainstreaming Able students are brought into a special physical education class to promote intergroup peer relationships.

rhythmic activities Activities performed to a rhythmic beat.

rhythmic gymnastics Routines done to music by a performer using a particular type of manipulative equipment.

rhythmic movement skills Skills involving motion with a regular and predictable pattern; can be attained through a rhythmic program that includes dance, rope jumping, and rhythmic gymnastics.

S

scope The yearly content of the curriculum; also referred to as the *horizontal articulation* of the curriculum.

screening A process that involves all students in a school setting and is part of the "child find" process; screening tests may be administered without parental permission and are used to make initial identification of students who may need special services.

self-concept A person's perception of self.

self-control Level 1 of responsible behavior; the student does not participate in the day's activity or show much mastery or improvement; these students control their behavior enough so they do not interfere with other students' right to learn or the teacher's right to teach.

self-responsibility Level 3 of responsible behavior; students take responsibility for their choices and for linking these choices to their own identities; they are able to work without direct supervision, eventually taking responsibility for their intentions and actions.

semicircular formation Students are positioned in a semicircular arrangement; this formation directs attention toward the teacher, who stands in the center.

sequence Defines the skills and activities to be covered on a year-to-year basis; also known as *vertical articulation*.

shaping technique Using extinction and reinforcement to build new acceptable behavior.

single-standard goal Approach that is based on a single standard with the assumption that it is possible to set one goal that fits all types of youngsters regardless of age, gender, or health.

skill refinement Teaching how to perform or refine skills properly; not synonymous with performance improvement.

skill-related fitness Activities that help improve performance in motor tasks related to sport and athletics; for people who can and want to perform at a high level because it requires training and exercising at high intensities.

skipping A series of step-hops done with alternating feet.

sliding A one-count movement done to the side, with the leading foot stepping to the side and the other foot following quickly; facilitates performance in endurance-oriented activities.

slow-twitch (ST) fibers Slow-contracting fibers in skeletal muscle tissue that have a rich supply of blood and related energy mechanisms; this attribute results in a slowly contracting, fatigue-resistant muscle fiber that is well suited to endurance-type (aerobic) activities.

small apparatus Magic ropes, individual mats, tug-of-war ropes, gym scooters; small-apparatus activities help develop body control in space and on the ground.

social reinforcers Praise, physical contact, and facial expressions to acknowledge acceptable behavior.

social skills Ability to interact with others.

somatotype Classification of body physique.

space awareness Awareness of where the body can move.

specialized motor skills Specialized skills used in various sports and other areas of physical education, including apparatus activities, tumbling, dance, and specific games; many of these skills have critical points of technique, and teaching emphasizes correct performance.

specific feedback Feedback that identifies the student by name and reinforces an actual behavior; it also might be accompanied with a valuing statement.

specific supervision Supervision that requires that the instructor be with a certain group of students (a class).

speed The ability of the body to perform movement in a short time; usually associated with running forward, speed is essential for the successful performance of most sports and general locomotor movement skills.

spiking Jumping high in the air and striking the volleyball above the net, driving it into the opponent's court.

sport skills Skills learned in a context of application, using an approach of teaching skills, drills, and lead-up activities.

spotting A safety precaution that involves assisting a performer by helping support the body weight and preventing a hazardous fall.

squad formation Mats are placed in a line, with squads lined up behind the mats. Each child takes a turn and then goes to the end of the squad line; the others move up. An alternative method is for each child to perform and then return to a seated position.

static stretching Involves increasing the stretch to the point of discomfort, backing off slightly to where the position can be held comfortably, and maintaining the stretch for an extended time.

strength training Weight training.

striking Hitting an object with an implement, such as a bat or a hand.

supplies Nondurable items that have a limited period of use.

sustained flow Smoothly linking different movements or parts of a movement.

symmetrical movements Identical movements using similar body parts on opposite sides of the body.

T

tackling A move by a soccer player to take possession

of the ball away from an opponent who is dribbling.

teacher movement Moving into position to observe skill performance; enhances teacher's ability to improve student learning.

tempo The speed of the music; can be constant or show a gradual increase (acceleration) or decrease (deceleration)

The Child Nutrition and WIC Reauthorization Act of 2004 This act highlights the importance of developing solutions that increase the physical activity of children, provide nutrition education, and ultimately teach youth healthy eating and activity habits that last a lifetime.

time on task The amount of time students spend practicing skills that result in accomplishment of program objectives; also known as practice time or ALT-PE (Academic Learning Time in Physical Education).

time-out Equitable technique for dealing with unacceptable behavior that occurs randomly on an individual basis; it moves youngsters out of the class setting and places them into a predesignated area when they misbehave so that they have time to reconsider and redirect their misbehavior.

Title IX Title IX of the Educational Amendments Act of 1972 rules out separation of sexes and calls for all offerings to be coeducational.

token enforcers Some type of token used as a reinforcer.

tort In education, a tort is concerned with the teacher–student relationship and is a legal wrong that results in direct or indirect injury to another individual or to property. *Black's Law Dictionary* defines a tort as a private or civil wrong or injury, other than breach of contract, for which the court will provide a remedy in the form of an action for damages.

trainability Ability of an individual to receive more benefit from training (regular physical activity) than others.

trapping Method of ball control.

trekking poles Poles used to assist in walking.

twisting The rotation of a selected body part around its own long axis.

U

U-shaped formation The mats are placed in the shape of a large U. This formation offers an excellent view for the teacher, and children are able to see what their classmates are doing.

V

validity The extent to which a measurement is well-founded and corresponds accurately to the real world.

value orientation A set of personal and professional beliefs that provides a basis for determining curricular decisions.

vertical articulation See *sequence*.

W

waiver forms Forms that explain the risks involved in voluntary participation and discuss briefly the types of injuries that have occurred in the past during practice and competition; participants in extracurricular activities should be required to sign a responsibility waiver form.

wand A sticklike piece of equipment about 3/4-inch (19 mm) thick and between 36 and 42 inches (90 and 105 cm) long.

whole practice Method that refers to the process of learning the entire skill or activity in one dose.

GENERAL INDEX

Note: The italicized *f* and *t* following page numbers refer to figures and tables, respectively.

A

AAP (American Academy of Pediatrics) 37, 39
Abdominal strength 275
Academic learning time in physical education (ALT-PE) 118
Academic performance 7, 45-46
Accelerometers 176
Accent, in music 416
Accident reports 232, 233*f*
Accountability outcomes 175-176, 181-182
Action-oriented cues 102-103
Active and Healthy School Program 54
Active listening 114
Active living, determinants of 11
Active monitoring 101-102
Active supervision 101-102, 122, 123*f*
Activity breaks 8, 49, 54
Activity calendars 57, 57*f*, 93
Activity reinforcers 143-144
Activity zones 55
Act-of-God defense 224
Acts of omission 223, 227
Adapted physical education 191-193, 197-202, 198*f*, 199-201*t*
Administrators
    facility and equipment responsibilities 232
    instructional responsibilities 227
    liability of 230
    supervision by 225-226
Adventure, urge for 72
AED (automated external defibrillator) training 231
Aerobic activities 12, 46, 48
Aerobic capacity 28-29, 275
Affective development 71, 100, 160, 161*f*
After-school programs 56, 236
Aggressive communication 127-128
Agility 40, 276
ALT-PE (academic learning time in physical education) 118
American Academy of Pediatrics (AAP) 37, 39
American Psychological Association 141
Anecdotal notes 160, 162
Anticipatory sets 100-101
Approach and delivery, in bowling 598
Approval, urge for 71-72
Apps 167, 244
Arabesque position 471, 471*f*
Arousal 31, 33
Assertive communication 127-128
Assessment 155-187. *See also* Assessment instruments
    of affective domain 160, 161*f*
    of children with disabilities 192-193
    of cognitive domain 158, 161*f*
    of CSPAPs 61-62
    of curriculum 79, 81, 156
    defined 156
    diagnostic 156

    of fitness. *See* Fitness testing
    formative 156-158
    of instructional effectiveness 115-123
    peer assessment 163-164, 165*f*, 166*f*
    of performance 157
    of physical activity 167-176
    of physical education programs 182, 184-185, 184-187*f*
    process-oriented vs. product-oriented 157
    of program accountability 175-176, 181-182
    of psychomotor domain 158, 159*f*
    purpose of 156
    self-assessment 116, 162-164, 163*f*, 164*f*
    summative 157, 158
    team evaluations 193
    technology in 160, 164, 167-176
    written 164-165, 166*f*
Assessment instruments
    accelerometers 176
    administration procedures 193
    anecdotal notes 160, 162
    bike racks 165, 167, 167*f*
    Brockport Physical Fitness Test 192
    checklist rubrics 159*f*, 160
    Children's Attraction to Physical Activity 182, 183*f*
    for children with disabilities 192-193
    exit slips 164-165, 166*f*
    FitnessGram 39, 171, 192, 274-275, 282, 282*f*
    grading 177-179
    heart rate monitors 176
    in lesson plans 85
    PECAT 78-81, 80*f*
    pedometers 167-176
    PE Metrics 162
    routines for distribution of 165
    selection of 192-193
    SOFIT 176
    student logs 162
    student progress reports 179-181, 180*f*
    teacher questioning 160, 161*f*
Assumption-of-risk defense 224
Attacking, in volleyball 699
Attitude position 471, 471*f*
Attractiveness, urge for 72
Attractive nuisance 232
Autism spectrum disorders 199*t*
Automated external defibrillator (AED) training 231

B

Backhand, in tennis 584-585, 584*f*
Backhand throw, in disc activities 594-595
Backhand underhand clear, in badminton 592
Back-support position 470, 470*f*
Badminton 590-594
    activities for 593-594
    backhand underhand clear 592
    drills 592-593
    equipment for 590, 590*f*

ACTIVITIES INDEX

Health Activities

Hockey